Newsmakers

ISSN 0899-0417

Newsmakers

The People Behind Today's Headlines

Peter M. Gareffa
Editor

Michael L. LaBlanc
Associate Editor

1989
Cumulation

Includes Indexes to
1985 through 1989

Gale Research Inc.
DETROIT • NEW YORK • FORT LAUDERDALE • LONDON

STAFF

Peter M. Gareffa, *Editor*

Michael L. LaBlanc, *Associate Editor*

David Collins, *Assistant Editor*

Stephen Advokat, Amy C. Bodwin, Ingeborg Boyens, Carolyn Chafetz, Victoria France Charabati, Harvey Dickson, Nancy H. Evans, Joan Goldsworthy, Gary Graff, Kelly King Howes, Tom Hundley, Anne Janette Johnson, Kyle Kevorkian, Virginia Curtin Knight, Mark Kram, Joe LaPointe, Cathleen Collins Lee, Jeanne M. Lesinski, Anita Pyzik Lienert, Paul Lienert, Frances C. Locher, Glen Macnow, Greg Mazurkiewicz, Donna Olendorf, Daniela Pozzaglia, Donna Raphael, Steve Raphael, Sharon Rose, Jon Saari, Susan Salter, Warren Strugatch, Diane Telgen, and Denise Wiloch, *Contributing Editors*

Linda Metzger, *Senior Editor, Newsmakers*

Jeanne Gough, *Permissions and Production Manager*
Patricia A. Seefelt, *Permissions Supervisor (Pictures)*
Margaret A. Chamberlain, *Permissions Associate*
Pamela A. Hayes and Lillian Quickley, *Permissions Assistants*

Mary Beth Trimper, *Production Manager*
Marilyn Jackman, *Production Assistant*
Arthur Chartow, *Art Director*
C. J. Jonik, *Keyliner*

Laura Bryant, *Production Supervisor*
Louise Gagné, *Internal Production Associate*
Sharana M.Wier, *Internal Production Assistant*

Cover Photos: Barbara Bush and Eddie Murphy (both AP/Wide World Photos)

835 Penobscot Bldg.
Detroit, MI 48226-4094

ISBN 0-8103-5303-2 (this volume)
ISBN 0-8103-2208-0 (complete 1989 set)
ISSN 0899-0417

Computerized photocomposition by
Atlis Publishing Services, Inc.
Beltsville, Maryland

Contents

Obituaries

Introduction

What's New About *Newsmakers*

Newsmakers (formerly *Contemporary Newsmakers*) has a new title and an attractive new cover. But the real news is inside *Newsmakers*, clearly the best source of biographical information on the people making today's headlines. You've told us what you want, and we've listened. And as a result, here's what's new:

NEW page design is pleasing to the eye and also makes it easier to locate the specific information you need.

NEW inclusion policy helps insure coverage of *all* the newsmakers you want to know about—people in business, education, technology, politics, law, international affairs, religion, entertainment, labor, sports, medicine, and other fields. Look first to *Newsmakers* for up-to-date biographical information on notable personalities in the news today.

NEW separate Obituaries section provides concise profiles of recently deceased newsmakers and groups them together for convenient access.

NEW price and publication schedule are good news for your budget. Now *Newsmakers* offers three paperback issues, each containing approximately 50 entries, and a hardcover cumulation, containing approximately 200 entries (those from the preceding three paperback issues—updated where necessary—*plus* an additional 50 entries), *all for $74 per year*!

Popular Features Continue

All the informative features you've come to rely on are still included in *Newsmakers* entries:

- **Clearly labeled data sections**—The *Newsmakers* format, which includes paragraphs headed Addresses, Career, Member, Awards, and Discography, still makes it easy to locate the information you need at a glance.

- **Informative Sidelights**—These unique essays provide the kind of in-depth analysis you're looking for.

- **Enlightening photographs**—Most entries include portraits of the listees, and many also offer additional "action photos" specially selected to enhance your knowledge of the subject.

- **Exclusive interviews**—Selected entries contain first-person interviews with the newsmakers, offering you fresh insight into the subjects' thoughts and feelings.

- **Sources for additional information**—This invaluable feature provides a list of books, magazines, and newspapers where you can find out even more about *Newsmakers* listees.

Indexes Provide Easy Access

Familiar and indispensable: the *Newsmakers* indexes! You can still easily locate entries in a variety of ways through our four versatile, comprehensive indexes, all of which cumulate information from both *Contemporary Newsmakers* and the new *Newsmakers* series:

- **Cumulative Newsmaker Index**—Listee names, along with birth and death dates, when available, are arranged alphabetically followed by the year and issue number in which their entries appear.

- **Cumulative Nationality Index**—Names of newsmakers are arranged alphabetically under their respective nationalities.

- **Cumulative Occupation Index**—Biographee names are listed alphabetically under broad occupational categories.

- **Cumulative Subject Index**—Includes key subjects, topical issues, company names, products, organizations, etc., that are discussed in *Newsmakers.* Under each subject heading are listed names of newsmakers associated with that topic. So the unique Cumulative Subject Index provides access to the information in *Newsmakers* even when readers are unable to connect a name with a particular topic. This index also invites browsing, allowing *Newsmakers* users to discover topics they may wish to explore further.

Suggestions Are Appreciated

The editors welcome your comments and suggestions. Many of the changes evident in the new *Newsmakers* are, in fact, the result of readers' suggestions, and we will continue to shape the series to best meet the needs of the greatest number of users. Send comments or suggestions to:

The Editor
Newsmakers
Gale Research Inc.
835 Penobscot Bldg.
Detroit, MI 48226-4094

Or, call toll-free at 1-800-521-0707.

Newsmakers

Giovanni Agnelli

Italian automaker

Born March 12, 1921, in Turin, Italy; son of Eduardo and Princess Virginia Bourbon (del Monte) Agnelli; married Princess Marella Caracciolo di Castagneto, 1953; children: one son, one daughter. *Education:* University of Turin, Dr. Jur., 1943.

Addresses: *Home*—26 Corso Matteotti, Turin, Italy, 10121. *Office*—Fiat SpA, 10 Corso Marconi, Turin, Italy, 10100.

Career

Fabbrica Italiana Automobili Torino SpA (Fiat), Turin, Italy, vice-president, 1945–49, vice-chairman of board of directors, 1949–66, managing director, 1963–66, chairman of board of directors and chief executive officer, 1966—. President of RIV (ball-bearing company; since 1965 known as RIV-SKF), Villar Perosa, Italy, beginning 1945; chairman of Instituto Finanziario Industriale (IFI; family-owned holding company), 1959—. Mayor of Villar Perosa, 1945—. Major stockholder of Societa Assicuratrice Industriale SpA (SAI; automobile insurance company). President of Giovanni Agnelli Foundation and of nursing school of International Red Cross. Vice-chairman of International Vocational Training Center in Turin.

Member of board of Mediobanca, 1962—, Credito Italiano, 1967—, Eurafrance (Paris), 1972—, Assonime, and Unione Industriale di Torino. Member of international advisory committee of Chase Manhattan Bank (New York), European advisory council of United Technologies Corp., 1983—, International

AP/Wide World Photos

Industrial Conference (San Francisco), executive committee of Trilateral Commission (Paris), and advisory board of Bildeberg Meetings (The Hague). Member of board of Italian Stock Companies and of Atlantic Community Development Group for Latin America. Member of steering committee and vice-president of economic understandings committee of Italian Chamber of Commerce. *Military service:* Italian army, 1941–43; served with cavalry unit on Russian front and later with armored-car unit in North Africa; became lieutenant; awarded cross for military valor; after Italy declared war on Germany, served as liaison officer with Italian Legnano Group, 1943–45.

Member: Italian Manufacturers Association (member of board), Societa Filarmonica, Whist Club of Rome, Hunt Club, Florence Club.

Sidelights

Giovanni "Gianni" Agnelli, chairman and chief executive officer of Fiat, is the richest man in Italy. Italian sociologist Aris Accornero asserts: "He is a precious symbol of the old capitalist order, but he is not a man of the past. He is a modern entrepreneur, an international man." Considered "one of the world's toughest and most astute businessmen," as Peter Fuhrman of *Forbes* magazine notes, Agnelli "will want to be remembered for the second half" of his period as chairman "rather than the first," declares the *Economist*.

In 1966 Agnelli inherited the chairman's job at the company his grandfather Giovanni Agnelli started in 1899. (The younger Agnelli was called Gianni to distinguish him from his grandfather, and the name is still in use today.) Groomed from an early age to play an important role in the family business, Agnelli acquainted himself with the American automobile industry in 1939, but after World War II, Agnelli immersed himself for a while in auto racing and jet setting. (An auto accident in 1952 gave him a permanent limp.)

When Agnelli became chairman, he reorganized Fiat into divisions based on the General Motors model to decentralize the cumbersome management process, but from 1969 to 1980 the auto company nearly collapsed. Trade unions struck and won large pay increases, which nearly wiped out profits, and Fiat started losing money when OPEC quadrupled the price of oil in the mid-seventies. At that point Agnelli diversified Fiat away from cars and into public transportation. Without developing new models, Fiat cars began looking very dated, and by the end of the seventies the auto company controlled less than 50 percent of its home market.

Agnelli also tried to accommodate Fiat's unions, a move the *Economist* dubbed the chairman's "second big mistake." Red Brigades terrorized Fiat managers, killing four and wounding 27, but Agnelli correctly sensed that the public was fed up with the terrorism. In 1979 Fiat fired 61 workers suspected of participating in the terrorist acts and laid off 23,000 workers. By the time 40,000 Fiat workers demanded the right to return to work, the unions no longer had power over Fiat.

As the *Economist* declares, this was the beginning of Fiat's "spectacular revival to its position as the most successful car company in Europe." Steven Greenhouse of the *New York Times* reports that in 1988 "the Fiat Group caught up with Volkswagen AG to tie for first place in car sales in Europe, while the company's new mid-size Tipo model has just won the continent's most coveted automotive award: 1988 European Car of the Year." Fiat's recovery has been amazing, but Greenhouse points out that "analysts say Fiat is hardly invincible." Recent economic changes have brought Agnelli new challenges, notably the unification of the European Community into a barrier-free market by the end of 1992. Investment analyst Gianpaolo Trasi declares: "It's vital for Fiat to spread outside Italy.... They have to overpass the Alps and make sure they can compete in an open, unprotected market."

To secure Fiat's position Agnelli has acquired Alfa-Romeo and Ferrari and has expanded into other areas, including financial services, aerospace, and telecommunications (the Fiat empire now represents 5 percent of Italy's gross national product), though Fiat does "not yet possess the critical mass necessary to compete internationally" in aerospace and defense. Agnelli also believes in "the need for alliances with American, Japanese and European companies," as the *New York Times* notes.

Nevertheless Agnelli is "an outspoken supporter of removing Europe's internal trade barriers," Greenhouse reports. "Only by growing, he asserts, can European companies finance the big investments in research and development needed to compete in the 21st century."

Agnelli has also insured that Fiat will be protected from hostile takeovers by persuading family members to place most of their shares in the family holding company, IFI, giving the Angellis firm control of the family business. Agnelli declares, "I want Fiat to have a long life."

Writings

Agnelli has contributed articles on economics and industrial affairs to publications in Italy and elsewhere.

Sources

Business Week, October 6, 1986; May 13, 1967; August 15, 1988.
Economist, August 30, 1986; October 4, 1986.
Forbes, November 14, 1988.
Fortune, August, 1971; October 12, 1987.
Newsweek, December 23, 1968.
New York Times, November 17, 1968; September 24, 1986; March 17, 1988; February 5, 1989.
Time, January 17, 1969.
Wall Street Journal, May 5, 1987.

—Sketch by Frances C. Locher

Roger Ailes

Media consultant

Full name, Roger Eugene Ailes; born May 15, 1940, in Warren, Ohio; son of Robert Eugene (a factory maintenance foreman) and Donna Marie (Cunningham) Ailes; first wife's name, Marge (divorced); married 1977; wife's name, Norma. *Education:* Ohio University, B.F.A., 1962.

Addresses: *Office*—Ailes Communications, Inc., 456 West 43rd St., New York, N.Y. 10036.

Career

While in college, worked as a disc jockey on campus radio station; KYW-TV, Cleveland, Ohio, 1962–65, began as prop boy, worked as assistant director, associate director, director, and producer; Westinghouse Broadcasting Corp., Philadelphia, Pa., producer of syndicated program "The Mike Douglas Show," 1965–67, executive producer, 1967–68; media consultant for Richard M. Nixon's 1968 presidential campaign; Ailes Communications, Inc., New York City, founder, president, 1969—; communications consultant to numerous political and business leaders, including Presidents Ronald Reagan and George Bush. Producer of plays, including "Mother Earth," 1972, and "Hot-L Baltimore," 1973; producer and director of television specials, including "The Last Frontier," 1974, "Fellini: Wizards, Clowns and Honest Liars," 1977, and "Television and the Presidency," 1984; executive vice-president, Television News, Inc. (syndicated news service), 1975–76; executive director of television program "Tomorrow Coast to Coast," 1981.

AP/Wide World Photos

Member: Directors Guild of America, Radio/TV News Directors Association, American Federation of Television and Radio Artists (AFTRA).

Awards: Award for Shakespeare production, *Fine Arts* magazine, 1964; Emmy Awards, 1967 and 1968, for work on "The Mike Douglas Show," and 1984, for "Television and the Presidency"; Emmy Award nomination, 1977, for "Fellini: Wizards, Clowns and Honest Liars"; Liberty Bell Award, Advertising Alliance of Philadelphia, 1971; commendation for contributions to communications, Ohio University, 1972; four Obie Awards, 1973, for "Hot-L Baltimore."

Sidelights

Media consultant and political adviser Roger Ailes is a master of television, teaching his clients how to present themselves to best advantage on the electronic medium. He established his reputation by producing a series of carefully staged TV programs for Richard Nixon's 1968 presidential campaign, the first to use television extensively as a campaign tactic. Most recently he was chief media strategist for George Bush's 1988 run for the presidency. Ailes is a balding, portly, sometimes caustic taskmaster who is not afraid to chop down those of presidential timbre to make his point. "There you go with that f—ing hand again. You look like a f—ing *pansy,*" Ailes once screamed at Bush during a coaching session, according to Margaret Garrard Warner of *Newsweek.* Reported Warner: "Bush, chastened but apparently appreciative, repeats his lines without a trace of hand waving, and the bald man smiles. The client is making progress."

"My intuition told me that the future was in television."

Born May 15, 1940, Ailes was raised in the factory town of Warren, Ohio. His father was a maintenance foreman at the Packard Electric plant, which produced wiring for General Motors cars. During his childhood, Ailes had to be hospitalized often for a chronic illness. Because of his condition, the neighborhood bullies frequently picked on him. When he was nine years old, he endured a severe beating, and his father decided to teach him how to fight and be fearless. Ailes told Warner that his father proclaimed: "The worst thing that can happen to you is you can die. If you're not afraid of that, you don't have to be afraid of anything." He took his father's words to heart and became so fearless that, at 13, he risked his life to save a couple of campers whose canoe had capsized. Later, in his working life, Ailes gained a reputation for being tough and combative.

After high school, Ailes enrolled at Ohio University. He needed a part-time job to help finance his education, so when he found an opening at the university's radio station, he auditioned and was hired. He became an early morning disc jockey, cohosting a show called "The Yawn Patrol." In his book *You Are the Message: Secrets of the Master Communicators,* Ailes wrote: "Although I enjoyed being on the air, I was more excited by the scripting, the deadlines, the creativity, and the enthusiasm of the other students.... For the next four years I was consumed by broadcasting."

He graduated with a bachelor of fine arts degree in 1962 and received two job offers. One was a sports announcer position at a Columbus radio station. The other was as a prop boy at Cleveland television station KYW. Although the radio job payed more, Ailes decided on TV. As he explained in his book, "My intuition told me that the future was in television."

KYW was at that time starting a talk show—"The Mike Douglas Show"—which they wanted to syndicate nationally. Ailes worked on the new show and, through hard work, he soon was promoted to assistant director. His duties included writing cue cards and picking up guests at the airport. He was now meeting and working with major stars, such as Bob Hope, Liberace, and Jack Benny. In 1965, Ailes was made producer of the show. The station president told him that he got the job, Ailes reported, because of his creativity and self-confidence. But another important factor was that two years earlier he had the courage to stand up to, and actually get in a fight with, another producer who regularly harassed and belittled the staff. Later in 1965, the show moved to Philadelphia.

"The Mike Douglas Show" became a popular program and, under Ailes's tenure as producer and later as executive producer, it quickly became even more popular. When Ailes took over, the show was seen in 32 cities. By the time he left, it reached 180 cities and was the most widely viewed nationally syndicated talk show of its day. In 1967 and 1968, Ailes won Emmy Awards for the program.

It was through a guest he met on "The Mike Douglas Show" that Ailes first became involved in political consulting. In the fall of 1967, Republican presidential candidate Richard Nixon appeared on the show. Talking with Ailes before he went on, Richard Stengel of *Time* reported, Nixon remarked, "It's a shame a man has to use gimmicks like this to get elected." Ailes replied, "Television is not a gimmick, and if you think it is, you'll lose again." Nixon warmed up to Ailes and his ideas and later persuaded him to join his campaign as a media adviser.

As described in Joe McGinniss's best-selling book *The Selling of the President, 1968,* Ailes's primary job in the campaign was to produce a series of 10 one-hour television programs, at various sites across the country, showcasing Richard Nixon. The regional shows would have him answering questions from local citizens' panels. Reported McGinniss, the shows "would be live to provide suspense; there would be a studio audience to cheer Nixon's answers and make it seem that enthusiasm for his candidacy was all but uncontrollable; and there would be an effort to achieve a conversational tone that would penetrate Nixon's stuffiness." At just 28 years of age, Ailes was suddenly playing a pivotal role in a presidential campaign.

The TV shows were well-planned to project the proper image. The panelists were hand-picked by Ailes and the campaign staff to provide a "balanced" group—at least one black, one woman, and so on. The studio audience was provided by the local Republican organization and also included an appropriate number of blacks. For maximum impact, Ailes designed what he called the "man in the arena" concept. For each show, Nixon would stand alone on stage, without even a podium, with the panelists sitting in a semicircle around him. The audience would sit in bleachers behind the panelists. Commenting on the arrangement, McGinniss wrote: "All the subliminal effects sank in. Nixon stood alone, ringed by forces which, if not hostile, were at least—to the viewer—unpredictable. There was a rush of sympathy; a desire—a need, even—to root. Richard Nixon was suddenly human: facing a new and dangerous situation, alone, armed only with his wits. In image terms, he had won before he began."

Television was now taking command of the election process. McGinniss reported that Ailes had commented to an associate, "This is an electronic election. The first there's ever been. TV has the power now." And the power of TV helped Richard Nixon to capture the presidency. After Nixon was in office, Ailes was brought in on occasion to produce various televised presidential announcements, including Nixon's announcement of the withdrawal of troops from Vietnam.

In 1969, Ailes established his own television production and communications consulting company in New York City, Ailes Communications, Inc. One of his firm's first clients was the Republican National Committee, which retained him to advise candidates who asked for media assistance. In addition to politicians, the company also took on business leaders as clients to provide media and general communications consulting.

Before long, TV producer Ailes branched out into the theater. In 1972, he debuted as a producer on Broadway with a rock musical called "Mother Earth." Unfortunately, the show closed after only 12 performances. His second attempt at theater, however, producing the Off-Broadway play "Hot-L Baltimore," was a great success. The play won four Obie Awards in 1973, including best new play Off-Broadway, and it ran from 1973 until 1976.

Ailes also produced and directed some television specials, including "The Last Frontier" in 1974 and "Fellini: Wizards, Clowns and Honest Liars," which earned an Emmy nomination in 1977. From 1975 to 1976, Ailes was executive vice-president of Television News, Inc., a syndicated news service that quickly disappeared. In 1978, he became a consultant to WCBS-TV in New York City. And in 1981, he served as executive director of "Tomorrow Coast to Coast," an NBC late-night show starring Tom Snyder and Rona Barrett.

In 1984, Ailes played another important role in a presidential campaign. Initially, he did some minor consulting work for Ronald Reagan's reelection campaign staff, called the "Tuesday Team." However, after Reagan's poor performance in his first debate with Democratic candidate Walter Mondale, Ailes was called in to correct the problems and avoid a second disastrous defeat. As Ailes recounted in his book, the president had looked "tired and confused" to viewers. "What the American people wanted from the president, I felt, was some reassurance that he wasn't too old for the job . . . . Clearly, they hadn't received that reassurance in the first debate." Ailes viewed one of the team's practice sessions and saw them put Reagan through a rigorous mock debate that was leaving him out of sorts. So Ailes had the mock debates cancelled and asked for access to the president between then and the second Mondale debate. "I felt pretty sure that if I could get him back to being *himself* again, he'd be okay."

When Ailes met with Reagan, he advised the president to concentrate more on ideas than facts. "You didn't get elected on details. You got elected on themes," he said. "Every time a question is asked, relate it to one of your themes." He then had the president go through a "pepper drill," firing questions at him and asking him to respond based on his experience. The plan was to help Reagan get his rhythm and confidence back.

Ailes was concerned about the age issue, and just before the debate he realized that it had never been brought up with Reagan. So he asked point-blank, "Mr. President, what are you going to do when they say you're too old for the job?" Reagan thought for a while, then remembered an old line he'd used before. The president repeated the line and Ailes told him to say that and nothing more. As Ailes expected, someone did ask the age question during the debate. Reagan answered: "I want you to know that I will not make age an issue of this campaign. I am not going to exploit for political purposes my opponent's youth and inexperience." Everyone laughed at the line; even Mondale smiled. Ailes remarked: "As far as I was concerned, the debate was over. The news media had their lead quote for the next day . . . . The public had the reassurance they were looking for." Reagan had bounced back, and he went on to win the election handily.

Also in 1984, Ailes achieved one of his most spectacular political victories. In the U.S. Senate race in Kentucky, Republican Mitch McConnell was behind the Democratic incumbent, Dee Huddleston, by 44 points in the polls. The situation looked hopeless. Ailes then produced a commercial of a hound dog chasing a Huddleston look-alike through the Kentucky hills while a voice-over talked about the incumbent running from his poor voting record. Suddenly, McConnell's candidacy took off, and despite being in a heavily Democratic state, he won the election. Ailes also reaffirmed his pugnacious image that year. "In a fight with two leather-jacket types in a Houston hotel lobby in 1984," said Stengel, "he broke one man's wrist and tossed the other man into the lobby fountain." In addition, Ailes produced another TV special, "Television and the Presidency," which won him a 1984 Emmy.

"My job is to present the best reality. We ignore the bad points and present the good."

Although he has had a number of successes, Ailes has not always been victorious in the political arena. In 1982, for example, he had to absorb two major defeats. In Senator Harrison Schmitt's New Mexico reelection campaign, Ailes permitted the senator's staff to prepare a couple of ads charging that his Democratic challenger was soft on crime. The ads were shown to be misleading, creating sympathy for the challenger. Schmitt then became the only incumbent Republican senator to lose in 1982. Ailes also worked on Lewis Lehrman's campaign for governor of New York. Even though Lehrman spent six times more money than Democrat Mario Cuomo, he still lost the election. Poor ad placement, which Ailes did not control, was given as one reason for the defeat. Since then, Ailes has supervised all media buying himself. Because of his aggressive style, Ailes has been called "a master of attack, of negative politics" by *Newsweek* and the "dark prince of political advertising" by *Time.* When he was called on to mastermind the 1988 presidential campaign of George Bush, Ailes put his attacking approach on full national display. Right from the start, he coached Bush to go on the offensive. In an October 1987 debate among Republican candidates, Ailes had Bush refer to former Delaware governor Pete du Pont as "Pierre," his given name, to remind viewers of his upper-class background. It was also, Ailes told *U.S. News & World Report,* "a signal. It said 'Don't keep screwing around with George Bush.'" In January of 1988, Ailes prepared Bush for a live interview with Dan Rather of CBS News. To head off persistent questioning on the Iran issue, reported Stengel, Bush was told to say: "It's not fair to judge my whole career by a rehash on Iran. How would you like it if I judged your career by those seven minutes when you walked off the set in New York?" Rather "looked thunderstruck," noted Fred Barnes of the *New Republic,* and Bush clearly "won" the confrontation.

After a poor showing in the Iowa caucuses, Ailes created a new TV ad for the important New Hampshire primary. Called the "Senator Straddle" ad, it claimed that Senator Robert Dole, Bush's chief Republican opponent, had flip-flopped on issues, including taxes and arms control. The ad helped give Bush a big primary win and stalled Dole's campaign.

In the fall, when Bush squared off against the Democratic presidential candidate, Governor Michael Dukakis of Massachusetts, Ailes went right for the jugular. His most controversial TV ad of the campaign focused on the Massachusetts prison furlough program, which freed convicted murderer Willie Horton who was later arrested for a rape and stabbing. Discussing the preparations for the ad, Ailes told *Time,* "The only question is whether we depict Willie Horton with a knife in his hand or without it." As Lee Atwater, Bush's campaign manager, said to Stengel, Ailes "has two speeds. Attack and destroy." The constant assaults put Dukakis on the defensive, and he quickly fell behind—and stayed behind—in the polls. The Bush campaign rolled to a comfortable victory.

For those who worry about the power and influence of media consultants, Ailes assures that they cannot remake their clients, only polish them. "My job is to present the best reality," he said to *U.S. News & World Report.* "We ignore the bad points and present the good." In his book, Ailes noted that he was once accused by a journalism student of "doing something immoral" by teaching people how to handle the media. He responded to the student that the thing that disturbed him most about the accusation was "you are here in journalism school learning how to ask the questions, yet you would deny a person the right to learn how to answer those questions. Remember, this is America. What's fair for one is fair for the other."

Ailes will continue to provide his communications consulting services to politicians and businesspeople. And he'll continue to counsel them to prepare carefully for their dealings with the media because "it's a natural adversarial relationship. The reporter is a professional. Don't get into the ring if you're a rank amateur."

Writings

You Are the Message: Secrets of the Master Communicators (with Jon Kraushar), Dow Jones-Irwin, 1988.

Sources

Books

McGinnis, Joe, *The Selling of the President, 1968,* Trident Press, 1969.

Periodicals

New Republic, June 16, 1986; February 22, 1988.
Newsweek, September 26, 1988; October 17, 1988.
New York Times, May 8, 1988.
Time, August 22, 1988.
U.S. News & World Report, February 8, 1988.
Wall Street Journal, April 29, 1988; October 28, 1988.
Washington Post, July 31, 1988; September 24, 1988: October 12, 1988; October 28, 1988.

—Sidelights by Greg Mazurkiewicz

Alvin Ailey

AP/Wide World Photos

Choreographer, director, dancer, and actor

Born January 5, 1931, in Rogers, Tex.; son of Alvin (a laborer) and Lula E. (Cliff) Ailey. *Education:* Attended University of California, Los Angeles (UCLA), Los Angeles City College, and San Francisco State University; studied modern dance with Lester Horton, Martha Graham, Hanya Holm, and Charles Weidman; studied ballet with Karel Shook; studied composition with Doris Humphrey; studied acting in New York City with Stella Adler and Milton Katselas.

Addresses: *Home*—New York, N.Y. *Office*—c/o The Alvin Ailey American Dance Theatre, 1515 Broadway, New York, N.Y. 10036.

Career

Made professional debut with Lester Horton Dance Company, Los Angeles, Calif., 1949; dancer, 1949—, principal stage appearances include *The Carefree Tree*, 1956, *Sing Man Sing*, 1956, and *Show Boat*, 1957; dance creator and choreographer, 1958—, principal works include *Blues Suite*, 1958, *Revelations*, 1960, *Knoxville: Summer of 1915*, 1961, *Masekela Language*, 1961, *Gymnopédies*, 1970, *Myth*, 1971, *Choral Dances*, 1971, *Cry*, 1971, *Archipelago*, 1971, *Mary Lou's Mass*, 1971, *The Lark Ascending*, 1972, *Love's Song*, 1972, *Hidden Rites*, 1973, *The Mooche*, 1975, *Night Creature*, 1975, *Pas de "Duke,"* 1976, *Memoria*, 1979, *Phases*, 1980, *The River*, 1981, and *Landscape*, 1981; director of Alvin Ailey American Dance Theatre, 1959—; choreographer of dance productions, including *Carmen Jones*, *Dark of the Moon*, and *African Holiday*; has staged operas, including *Four Saints in Three Acts*, Mini-Metropolitan Opera, New York City, *Anthony and Cleopatra*, Metropolitan Opera, New York City, and Bernstein's *Mass*, Kennedy Center for the Performing Arts, New York City; staged ballet *Lord Byron;* actor in theatrical productions, including "Call Me By My Rightful Name," "Tiger, Tiger, Burning Bright," "Ding Dong Bell," and "Talking to You"; has presented productions on television, including "Memories and Visions," 1973, and "Ailey Celebrates Ellington," 1974 and 1976.

Awards: Recipient of numerous awards, including first prize at Paris International Dance Festival, 1970; *Dance* Magazine Award, 1975; Spingarn Medal from National Association for the Advancement of Colored People (NAACP), 1976; Mayor's Award (New York City) of Arts and Culture, 1977; proclamation in New York City of Alvin Ailey American Dance Theatre Twentieth Anniversary Day, 1979; Samuel H. Scripps American Dance Festival Award for lifetime contributions to American modern dance, 1987. Holds hororary degrees in fine arts from numerous colleges and universities, including Princeton University, Bard College, Adelphi University, and Cedar Crest College.

Sidelights

Perhaps the most significant force in modern dance today, Alvin Ailey has drawn together elements of classical ballet, folk dance, modern dance, and the Broadway chorus line into an art form that has been widely imitated, yet remains distinctly his own. Celebrated as a choreographer, it has been as mentor to his own troupe of dancers that he has introduced modern dance to mass audiences across the world.

The Alvin Ailey American Dance Theatre, now entering its fourth decade, has expanded enormously since it began with eight dancers dedicated to the black folk arts. Today it consists of a main company with 30 dancers, a repertory of over 150 works, a junior troupe spotlighting young dancers, and a school training over 1000 students. Having toured the world many times over, the Ailey company has provided Ailey with the vehicle to introduce hundreds of new pieces, many of which have become repertory standards. The choreographer has been given a raft of honorary degrees and has garnered dozens of citations, ranging from the Capezio Award (1979) to the Kennedy Center Honor for Lifetime Achievement in the Arts (1988).

An athletic teenager, Ailey approached modern dance as an kind of gymnastics. He doubted he had talent for it and several times during his youth abandoned dance altogether, only to return with enthusiasm renewed. As a black dancer he found limited opportunities, at times supporting himself in supper clubs and theatrical venues. He did not disdain such work as "commercial," as some dancers do, but rather, enjoyed the experience.

Ailey's work is rooted in the black experience. His signature piece, *Revelations,* was performed to a jazz score by Duke Ellington and took the dance world by storm in 1959. "The black pieces that come from blues, spirituals and gospels are part of what I am," he told Ellen Cohen in the *New York Times Magazine* in 1973. "They are as honest and truthful as we can make them. I'm interested in putting something on stage that would have a very wide appeal without being condescending; that will reach an audience and make it part of the dance; that will get everyone into the theatre. What do they mean when they say it's Broadway? If it's art and entertainment—thank God, that's what we want it to be."

Happily, *Revelations* was not "written in the air," as is so much modern choreography, but has been entrenched in the Ailey repertory and is often interpreted by other companies as well. After *Revelations* came major works performed to jazz, blues, gospel, and field songs. By the early 1960s the Ailey company was a fixture on the highly competitive New York dance scene. In *The Private World of Ballet,* John Gruen observed that Ailey's work "is marked by the free use of disparate elements of the dance vocabulary. At its best, the Ailey group generates an uncommon exhilaration, achieved by a tumultuous and almost tactile rhythmic pulse. Ailey's own best works are charged with a dazzling and uninhibited movement and life."

Ailey has changed the dance world as much by his leadership as by his choreography. He performs some four dozen works every year and is generous in the opportunities he portions out to other choreographers. Audiences at Ailey programs can expect to see several Ailey works in revival; pieces created by the troupe's own dancers, past and present; dances created by Ailey students; and works by other modern choreographers. In the self-promoting world of modern dance this generosity is rare. By commissioning hundreds of new works over the years, the Alvin Ailey Dance Theatre has provided the financial backing and exposure necessary for young dance makers to survive.

Alvin Ailey was born in Rogers, Texas, a small town 50 miles south of Waco, on January 5, 1931. His father left the family when Ailey was three. He told Cohn: "I have deep memories of the situation . . . sharecropping, picking cotton, people being lynched, all the black men having been to prison, segregated schools, movie theatres where I had to sit in the balcony. I don't remember my people being bitter or it being discussed at home. It was simply the way it was." The church played a dominant role. Ailey attended Sunday school, belonged to the Baptist Young People's Union, and went to Holy Roller meetings at night. He recalls throwing rocks at cottonmouth snakes and Saturday night barbeques at the local roadhouse.

"What I remember of my childhood is that we lived around with relatives," he told Gruen. "There was poverty. Those were the Depression years. I went to elementary school in Navasota, Texas, a tacky little town. The school was across the railroad tracks. One of my earliest memories is climbing under the trains to get to school, and of course, it was a black school.

"There were certain parts of town one didn't go to—certain things one didn't do. The first dance I ever choreographed came out of these early experiences. I call them Blood Memories. I remember the Saturday night place where everybody went, doing the country dances. There were folk singers and guitar players and it all turned me on terribly. And there was the whole experience with the Baptist Church—the Baptisms and the gospel shouts—the itinerant folk singers, like Sonnyboy Williamson. So that early black experience colored everything that I did."

When Ailey was 12, he and his mother moved to Los Angeles, where she worked for Lockheed. She also cleaned homes but kept this fact from her son. In Los Angeles, he was exposed to the sophistication of 1940s Hollywood: Gene Kelly and Fred Astaire in particular became exemplars. Playing football and joining the gymnastics team in high school, the boy discovered a different sort of athleticism: tap dancing as taught by a neighbor, Loretta Butler, on her shellacked living room floor dance studio.

A high school friend who was studying classical ballet introduced Ailey to the black dance world of Los Angeles, the most vibrant such community in the country after Harlem. The dominant figure on the Los Angeles scene was Lester Horton. Horton, who found inspiration in Japanese, American Indian, and other dance forms, ran a school in Hollywood where black artists, intellectuals, and entertainers congregated. Ailey was enthralled and signed up as a student.

But doubt soon eroded his enthusiasm, and after one month he dropped out, then went to UCLA to study romance languages. He explained to Gruen, "I didn't really see myself as a dancer. I mean, what would I dance? It was 1949. A man didn't just become a dancer. Especially a black man. I mean, you could be a [Katherine] Dunham dancer, or you could be a tap dancer—you know, show business, big swing." Horton, though, reached out to the young man, offered him a scholarship, and brought him back to the fold.

Horton, himself a former set designer and stage manager, believed dancers should master every function associated with a production. Ailey, accordingly, found himself mopping the stage, changing the gels, working in the costume shop, and painting scenery. Now living on his own, he took work as a waiter to pay the rent. "I was happy," he reminisced to Gruen. "Lester let us know that we were all beautiful. There were Japanese and Mexicans and blacks, whites, greens and pinks. And it was great. I was very happy being in the milieu of the dancers. I was 18."

But a year later he again dropped out and moved up north to attend college in San Francisco. He supported himself loading baggage for Greyhound. Eventually he began dancing in a nightclub, a "marvelous experience" he would call it years later. The show toured Los Angeles, and Ailey met up with Horton once again. Horton was delving even further from the mainstream, choreographing works inspired by the painter Paul Klee, the novelist Garcia Lorca, and composers, including Ellington and Igor Stravinsky.

In 1953 Ailey once again dropped his college studies and declared himself a dance student, teaching dance to children when not dancing himself. That winter Horton suffered a fatal heart attack, and Ailey tried to assume his mantle. Facing a season at the prestigious Jacob's Pillow festival the next summer, Ailey choreographed two pieces in the only style he knew: Horton's. One work was a tribute to his master, *According to St. Francis*, and the other was based on themes by Tennessee Williams, *Mourning Morning*. The works went over badly; the festival manager wrote a scathing letter denouncing the pieces as "kitchen sink ballets" without form.

"I'm interested in putting something on stage that would have a very wide appeal without being condescending; that will reach an audience and make it part of the dance."

The dismal showing discouraged the faltering troupe, which dissolved a few months later. The next call Ailey got was from Broadway producer Herbert Ross, and the dancer hurried to New York to join the cast of "House of Flowers," the musical adaptation of Truman Capote's book. It was a troubled endeavor: the legendary George Balanchine had just been dismissed as choreographer, the director and the performers were not speaking, and audiences were meager. Nevertheless, the show lasted five months, providing Ailey with a foothold into New York. He took full advantage, broadening his education at every turn. He studied dance with Martha Graham, ballet with Karel Shook, composition with Doris Humphrey, and acting with Stella Adler.

In 1957 he worked the musical "Jamaica," starring Lena Horne, and continued to dance in various small companies. In March 1958 he and a friend, Ernest Parham, gathered 35 dancers and gave eight concerts at the 92nd St. YMHA. Audiences were treated to the premier of *Blues Suite*, some Latin dances, and a solo

Ailey tribute to Lester Horton. The *New York Times* praised the performance, and Ailey began planning a second concert for 1959, again to be held at the Y.

In 1959 Ailey formed his own company, a troupe of eight black dancers dedicated to black music and culture. The company took residence at the Clark Center for the Performing Arts, at Eighth Avenue and 51st St. There they remained until 1969, when they moved to a new venue in Brooklyn. The move was ill advised. An impressario was attempting to duplicate the Lincoln Center success in Brooklyn, but that borough lacked Manhattan's sophistication. Feeling out of place, Ailey stayed three uncomfortable years.

By that time Ailey had retired as a dancer—his chronic weight problem did not prolong his career—but his troupe was furthering its reputation as the country's most renowned modern dance assemblage. In Judith Jamison, Ailey had the first full-fledged star soloist of modern dance. And, in several young white dancers, Ailey now had an integrated company. Ailey rejected the argument that black dance should be only for blacks. "Whites and Orientals in 'Revelations' are historically inaccurate," he told Cohn. "But it works anyway. It's like saying only French people should do Racine or Moliere."

During the 1970s the company's popularity continued to grow, the result of a series of world tours sponsored by the U.S. State Department that performed in 44 countries on six continents. Other arts subsidies helped underwrite the enormous cost of running an ambitious dance company. Nevertheless, Ailey coped with a constant financial crunch. Often he would take a commission to choreograph a dance, then use the money to pay old phone bills.

In 1980 the choreographer suffered a serious personal setback: a mental breakdown that hospitalized him for several weeks. He attributed his problems to midlife crisis, the death of close friend Joyce Trisler, and financial pressures. But Ailey returned to work with a new philosophy. He explained to *Newsday*'s Janice Berman: "Give up something. Do less. Concentrate on what's really important."

Throughout the 1980s Ailey's reputation has grown as a patriarch of modern dance. Cohn described her impression of the man in the early 1970s: "Even slumped back in his chair, Ailey is imposing, an aristocratic figure, peering out at the world from narrow eyes in a massive proudly held head. Voluble, a gifted raconteur and mimic, his rich, musical voice slides in and out of accents with ease. He laughs often and with great gusto, delighting in show business anecdotes."

Sources

Books

Earl Blackwell's Celebrity Register, Times Publishing Group, 1986.

Gruen, John, *The Private World of Ballet*, Viking, 1975.

Rogosin, Elinor, *The Dance Makers: Conversations With American Choreographers*, Walker & Company, 1980.

Periodicals

Ballet News, November, 1983.

Dance Magazine, December, 1983; October, 1978.

Newsday, December 4, 1988.

New York Times Magazine, February 12, 1973.

—Sidelights by Daniela Pozzaglia

Garth Ancier

AP/Wide World Photos

Television network executive

Born September 3, 1957, in Perth Amboy, N.J. *Education:* Princeton University, B.A. in political science, 1979.

Addresses: *Home*—North Hollywood, Calif. *Office*—c/o Fox Broadcasting Co., Los Angeles, Calif.

Career

WBUD-AM and WBJH-FM (radio stations), Trenton, N.J., reporter, 1972; chairman and chief executive officer, "Focus on Youth" Radio Network, beginning 1974; NBC-TV, Entertainment Division, associate in comedy development, 1979–80, assistant to the president and manager of East Coast development, 1980–81, vice-president of comedy programming, 1981–86; Fox Broadcasting Co., Los Angeles, Calif., senior vice-president of program development, 1986—.

Sidelights

Garth Ancier is senior vice-president of program development at Fox Broadcasting Company, the first new television network to appear in over thirty years. Ancier has been in broadcasting nearly all his life. At 29 he was a seasoned network professional with a clear understanding of an executive's role in television entertainment. "[My job] is to be emotionally supportive," he explained to Robert Goldberg in *Cosmopolitan.* "To give objective overall notes when necessary. To recognize talented people and get them to work for you—and then to get out of the way."

Ancier began his broadcast career at the age of 12, working as an intern at a PBS station. Two years later he was employed as a reporter for NBC-radio affiliates WBUD and WBJH. When he was 16 he founded, produced, and hosted "Focus on Youth," a radio interview show. Ancier continued the program while he was student at Princeton University, expanding it into a nationally syndicated talk show that aired on over 200 stations. After earning a degree in political science, Ancier was hired by NBC-TV's programming director, Brandon Tartikoff. Within two years he rose to the rank of vice-president of comedy programming and helped to develop the network's biggest sitcoms, including "The Cosby Show," "Cheers," and "Family Ties." Ancier left NBC in 1986 to join the fledgling Fox Broadcasting Company as senior vice-president of program development.

Fox is the brainchild of former ABC executive Barry Diller and Australian media mogul Rupert Murdoch [see index for *Newsmakers* entry]. The latter purchased 20th Century-Fox, one of Hollywood's most successful studios, in 1985. A year later he bought six Metromedia television stations—at a cost of $2 billion—and set about acquiring other independent VHF and UHF stations that were looking for an affordable alternative to expensive syndicated programs. By the summer of 1986 Murdoch and Diller had 79 stations lined up; that fall they premiered "The Late Show with Joan Rivers." Fox was instantly billed the "fourth network," although its executives prefer to call it "a satellite-delivered national program service," as Ancier told David Crook of the *Los Angeles Times.* Regardless, as Crook noted, Fox is "the first serious challenger to the Big Three video hegemony in more than three decades."

Challenge is the main reason Ancier left the "Big Three," according to *Newsweek's* Penelope Wang and Susan Katz. "The networks are becoming dinosaurs," Ancier told them. "I want to redefine what's possible." Among his first acts as a Fox executive were to sign a small but prestigious group of writers and to recruit well-known producers to aid in program development. So far, Fox has created its share of flops, such as the Joan Rivers' talk show and "Mr. President," starring George C. Scott. It has also produced some notable successes, including the drama "21 Jump Street," the comedy "Married... With Children," and the award-winning comedy-variety "Tracey Ullman Show."

Ancier believes that television programming is best learned by watching and analyzing existing shows, with an eye to what works, what doesn't, and why. His advice to those considering a career in the television industry? "Start young," Ancier told Goldberg, adding: "Of course, I started younger than humans should be allowed to start working, but I'd advise starting at least during college, interning at local stations.... [If] your instincts are good and you work hard and you're an honest person who does a good job, you're going to advance quite fast."

Sources

Cosmopolitan, August, 1987.
Los Angeles Times, April 5, 1987.
Newsweek, September 1, 1986.
People, January 8, 1979.

—Sketch by Denise Wiloch

Yasser Arafat

Reuters/Bettmann Newsphotos

Palestinian leader

Given name sometimes spelled Yasir; full name, Mohammed Yasser Arafat; born August 24, 1929, in Cairo, Egypt (some sources say Jerusalem); son of Abder Rauf (a merchant) and Zahwa Arafat. *Education:* Degree in civil engineering from Fuad I University (now Cairo University).

Addresses: *Office*—c/o Palestine Liberation Organization, Tunis, Tunisia.

Career

Joined Union of Palestinian Students in Cairo, Egypt, 1944, member of executive committee, 1950, president, 1952–56; worked as a gunrunner in the late 1940s, helping smuggle arms from Egypt into Palestine; studied guerrilla tactics, recruited and trained Palestinian students, and served as guerrilla leader in the early 1950s; jailed in Egypt, 1954, after discovery of a plot to assassinate President Nasser; worked as a civil engineer in Kuwait, 1957–65; co-founder, 1957, of Al Fatah (a guerrilla organization that came under the Palestine Liberation Organization umbrella in 1964); began military action against Israel, 1964; following defeat of combined Arab armies in "Six Day War," 1967, increased guerrilla activities against Israel from bases in Jordan and Lebanon; named executive chairman of Palestine Liberation Organization (PLO), 1969; PLO evicted from Jordan, c. 1971, and increased worldwide terrorist activities; forced out of Lebanon by Israeli invasion, 1982, and relocated in Tunis, Tunisia.

Awards: Joliot-Curie Gold Medal, World Peace Council, 1975.

Sidelights

If for nothing else, history will remember Yasser Arafat as one of the twentieth century's great political survivors. His longevity—political and physical—has defied all odds. Dozens of times, his career as chairman of the Palestine Liberation Organization has been prematurely eulogized, yet each time he has somehow climbed back to the political forefront and forced the world to take note of the stubborn nationalist aspirations of the Palestinian people. Over the course of more than twenty years as chairman of the PLO, he has made many powerful enemies, any of whom would be happy to put a violent end to his tenure, but time and again he has slipped the assassin's gunsight.

Living his life as marked man, Arafat has settled into a rather unconventional lifestyle. He rarely sleeps in the same bed twice. His most productive working hours are late at night, and journalists are rarely granted interviews before midnight. According to biographer Alan Hart, Arafat never sits down in a room until he has calculated the most difficult line of fire for a potential assassin. Hart says there have been more than 50 attempts on Arafat's life.

Unappealing physically and a poor orator, he hardly fits the mold of a charismatic, nationalist leader. But his total dedication to the Palestinian cause, the fact that he has never been touched by the corruption that permeates much of the PLO's bureaucracy, and his jaunty optimism during the darkest hours are traits that have cemented his position as symbol of the Palestinian resistance. Westerners know him by his trademark kaffiyeh and three-day stubble—a rather sinister image—but to Palestinians he is a fatherly figure who likes to fuss over small children. They call him, simply, "the Old Man."

Ambiguity is the Arafat hallmark. It is the personality trait that has defined his political style; the glue that has enabled him to cobble together a working coalition of radical Marxists and Muslim fundamentalists, drawing room intellectuals and gun-toting guerillas—all under the nomadic roof of his PLO. It is the same ambiguity that so frustrates Western political leaders who have often found that his words and deeds only occasionally align.

The ambiguity begins with the slippery particulars of his birth. By some accounts, he was born in Jerusalem; others have claimed Gaza as his birthplace. According to the most authoritative sources, Mohammed Yasser Arafat was born in Cairo on August 24, 1929, the sixth of seven children from his father's first marriage. His mother, Zahwa, was from the Abu Saud family of Jerusalem, one of the city's most respected and distinguished lineages. His father, Abder Rauf Arafat, was from Gaza. He was also a distant relative to Haj Amin Husseini, the Grand Mufti of Jerusalem after World War I and an early nationalist leader. Abder was a modestly successful merchant who moved the family to Cairo to pursue his business interests. Arafat was four when his mother died and his father shipped him off to live with relatives in Jerusalem. He returned to Cairo four years later when his father remarried. Although Arafat has confided few details of his childhood to anyone, he has acknowledged that it was not a happy one.

Living in Cairo during the turbulent years between the two World Wars, his political awakening came at an early age. Before he was 17, he had established himself as a proficient gunrunner, acquiring arms and ammunition in Egypt and smuggling them into Palestine for the anticipated struggle against the British occupation and the Jewish nationalists. When Britain withdrew from Palestine in May 1948 and Israel proclaimed its independence, Arafat was already in Gaza fighting alongside other young Palestinian nationalists. The Egyptian army, however, disarmed the Palestinians, and Arafat returned to Cairo where he watched from the sidelines as the Israelis secured their homeland by humiliating half a dozen invading Arab armies.

A disheartened Arafat resumed his engineering studies in the Egyptian capital but devoted most of his energies to recruiting and training Palestinian students for paramilitary operations against the Jewish state. His political platform—and also the cover for the training activities—was Union of Palestinian Students, a group he headed for four years. He also established close ties to Egyptian President Gamal Abdel Nasser's Free Officers group, which was then plotting to overthrow King Farouk. It was during this time that he made the acquaintance of two other young Palestinians who would later help him establish Al Fatah and serve as lifelong confidents and political allies—Khalil Wazir, who took the *nom de guerre* Abu Jihad, and Salah Khalaf, better known as Abu Iyad.

In 1954, after a plot to assassinate President Nasser was uncovered, Arafat was among the scores of political activists rounded up and thrown into jail. He was released a few weeks later. But it would not be the last time he clashed with the ruling powers of an Arab state or saw the inside of an Arab jail.

Arafat completed his studies in civil engineering in 1956 and planned to continue his political activities in Cairo, but Egyptian authorities made it clear that he was no longer welcome there. He took a job offer in Kuwait, and within weeks of moving there he was busy with the Palestinian cause. In the fall of 1957, he and Wazir reunited in Kuwait and founded the first of Al Fatah's underground cells.

Fatah was destined to become the largest and most influential of guerilla organizations under the PLO umbrella, but it was not until 1959 that Arafat and Wazir even gave a name to their organization. Fatah is the reverse acronym for Harakat al-Tahrir Al-Watani al-Filastini—the Movement for the National Liberation of Palestine. According to biographer Hart, Arafat's stated goal for Fatah was the armed struggle for the liberation of Palestine; as a practical matter, Arafat merely hoped to keep the pot boiling on the Palestinian issue until the Arab armies regrouped and rearmed for the annihilation of Israel, an event Arafat assumed was inevitable. Fatah's only real weapon at this time was a magazine, *Our Palestine,* which spread the gospel to the Palestinian diaspora and helped draw new members to the nascent organization.

Outside of his political work, Arafat was apparently quite successful financially as an engineer and contractor with the government of Kuwait. He has told several interviewers that he easily could have been a millionaire and savored the privileged life-in-exile enjoyed by many enterprising Palestinian businessmen. Instead, he poured virtually all his earnings into his political cause. He made other personal sacrifices as well. Although he has never disclosed details, he told Hart that he once fell in love with a woman but chose to remain unmarried in order to devote all of his energies to the cause. "I am a normal man," Arafat told Hart. "I would like to have a wife and children, but I did not think it was fair that any woman should be asked to share the troubles I knew I would be facing in my long struggle. It was not fair at all."

The late 1950s and early 1960s were a time of endless political bickering and maneuvering within the Arab world and also within the disparate factions of the Palestinian nationalist movement. Arafat's Fatah was not immune. By this time, Fatah had gone public, but it mainly functioned as a noisy debating society for the theory and tactics of national liberation. It was in this crucible that Arafat refined the political skills that would eventually enable him to emerge as the undisputed leader of the Palestinian movement.

Nineteen sixty-four was an important year for Arafat and the Palestinian nationalists: Nasser cleared the way for the founding of the Palestine Liberation Organization, a maneuver that he hoped would enable him to control the growing Palestinian nationalist movement. Nasser's great fear was that the Palestinians would drag him into a war with Israel that he knew he could not win. Ahmad Shuqairi, a well-known but largely discredited nationalist leader, became the PLO's first chairman, largely because of his willingness to do Nasser's bidding. Arafat, meanwhile, was gearing up Fatah for guerilla strikes into Israel, a course that put him squarely at odds with Nasser and the newly-founded PLO. Fatah undertook its first military operations in 1964, but none were successful. It was not until 1965, with Syria's sponsorship, that Arafat was able to launch a string of successful hit-and-run strikes against Israel. These attacks scarcely dented the Jewish state's military armor but did much to boost Palestinian morale and Arafat's credibility.

In June 1967, Arafat finally got the Arab-Israeli War he had longed for—but not with the result he had anticipated. Israel defeated the Arabs in six days, conquering and occupying the last two pieces of the Palestinian homeland, the West Bank and Gaza. The PLO had only a token role in the fighting. The Six-Day War's lesson for Arafat was that he could not rely upon the Arab regimes to deliver Palestine. If the Palestinians were to regain their homeland, it would be through their own efforts.

From inside the occupied territories and from outside, the peripatetic Arafat organized cells of Fatah fighters. The ragtag guerillas, however, were no match for well-armed Israelis, and the blood seemed to flow in one direction only. The exception was the 1969 battle at Karameh, a village on the Jordanian border where Arafat and his men achieved a minor military victory and major morale boost when they killed 28 Israeli soldiers in close combat.

Despite the lack of progress on the ground, Fatah emerged as the dominant organization in the PLO, and in 1969 Arafat replaced Shuqairi as PLO chairman. At this time, Fatah was using Jordan as staging ground for cross-border raids into Israel. The Israelis retaliated against Jordan, putting heavy pressure on King Hussein to get rid of the PLO, which by this time had set up an elaborate infrastructure within Jordan that was beginning to threaten the stability of the King's rule. Thus began Black September—King Hussein's war against the PLO. The fighting began in September 1970; it was halted briefly by a truce and then resumed in July 1971 with the successful eviction of the Palestinian guerillas.

With this setback, Fatah and the PLO felt their backs against the wall. The terror card seemed the only option. A bloody string of hijackings and bombings that culminated with the murder of 11 Israeli athletes at the Munich Olympics—and which only in recent years seems to have finally run its course—became the PLO's calling card and made Yasser Arafat one of the world's most feared and despised men. Among Palestinians, though, he was a hero—he had made the world take note of their plight.

In October 1973, Egypt's Anwar Sadat launched a new war against Israel, and while it hardly could be called a resounding military success, it helped restore Arab self-esteem and began reshaping the political landscape. For Arafat and the PLO, its full implications would not be understood until a decade later. A year after the war, Arab leaders gathered in Rabat, Morocco, and proclaimed the PLO "the sole legitimate representative of the Palestinian people," a move which effectively gave Arafat the status of a head of state, at least in Arab eyes. Two weeks later, he made his dramatic appearance before the U.N. General Assembly. "I have come bearing an olive branch and a gun," he told the world. "Do not let the olive branch fall from my hand." A sidearm holster—empty, according to aides—revealed itself during the speech.

But Arafat was pushed aside by people and events he could not control. U.S. Secretary of State Henry Kissinger effectively blackballed the PLO from any peace talks during the Nixon Administration, and when Jimmy Carter brought Sadat and Israeli Prime Minister Menachem Begin together at Camp David in 1979, the PLO leader was again on the outside looking in as the fate of the Palestinian people was discussed.

Although the Camp David Accords were supposed to bring "autonomy" to the residents of Gaza and the West Bank, the Palestinians never embraced this concept of limited self-rule, and the Israelis never implemented it. Instead, Israel turned its attentions to rooting out the growing PLO presence in Lebanon. Sporadic fighting eventually culminated in Israel's June 1982 invasion of Lebanon and seige of Beirut.

During three months of heavy fighting, Arafat was fortunate to escape with his life. As he told Hart: "If you mean how many times should I have been killed because of the accuracy of the Israeli attacks, I can say twelve. Yes, I had twelve lives from these Israeli bombs." Israel eventually succeeded in driving the PLO out of Beirut, but for Arafat and the PLO fighters it was a triumphant retreat—they had stood up to the Israelis longer than any other Arab Army. And for Israel, it was a costly and impermanent victory. World opinion began to shift against them, and soon enough the PLO was back in Lebanon.

But Arafat, exiled to the PLO's new home in Tunis, was unable to take advantage of the opportunity. Instead he had to cope with a bloody revolt within his own ranks. A Syrian-backed faction of the PLO battled Arafat loyalists for turf in Lebanon. There was open criticism of Arafat's leadership even from loyalists, and many analysts predicted that the PLO would soon self-destruct. So low had Arafat's political stock fallen that at the 1987 Arab Summit in Baghdad, the question of Palestine was not even on the agenda. That changed abruptly in December 1987 when the Palestinian uprising began in the occupied territories. Although the PLO can claim little credit for the uprising, Arafat is still the undisputed symbol of the Palestinian nationalist movement, and he adroitly used the headlines generated by the uprising to maneuver himself and the PLO back to center stage.

While young boys armed with rocks battled Israeli soldiers, Arafat embarked on a sequence of diplomatic maneuvers that ultimately persuaded the United States to open a dialogue with the PLO. Along the way, he shaped a "moderate front" within his own organization, renounced terrorism, issued a "declaration of independence," recognized the state of Israel, and called for a two-state solution to the question of Palestine. Although a genuine solution still seems a long way off, Palestinians have never been more optimistic about their fate.

In a recent conversation with a group of Americans in Tunis, Arafat was asked about his place in history: "I hope my people will say I found a home for them; a place in which to live and be buried," Arafat replied. "Imagine the difficulty I faced finding a burial place for the Palestinian representing Kuwait at the United Nations. It took 11 days to find a suitable location. In the end I found a graveyard in one of the churches on the green line between East and West Beirut. We buried him while under fire."

Sources

Books

Cobban, Helena, *The Palestinian Liberation Organization: People, Power and Politics*, Cambridge University Press, 1984.

Hart, Alan, *Arafat: Terrorist or Peacemaker*, Sidgwick & Jackson, 1984.

Kelman, Herbert C., *Understanding Arafat*, International Center for Peace in the Middle East, 1983.

Periodicals

Chicago Tribune, November 16, 1988; December 14, 1988.

Economist, July 2, 1983; May 12, 1984.

Middle East International, December 2, 1988; January 6, 1989.

Nation, March 16, 1985.

New Republic, December 12, 1984; October 28, 1985; June 24, 1988.

New Statesman, August 3, 1984.

Newsweek, December 3, 1984; October 21, 1985; December 16, 1988.

New York Times, December 15, 1988; December 16, 1988; December 18, 1988.

Progressive, February, 1985.

Time, January 25, 1988; April 25, 1988; November 7, 1988; December 26, 1988.

—Sidelights by Tom Hundley

Oscar Arias Sanchez

President of Costa Rica

Born September 13, 1941, in Heredia, Costa Rica; son of Juan Rafael (a coffee grower and banker) and Lilian (maiden name, Sanchez) Arias Trejos; married Margarita Penon Gongora (a biochemist); children: Sylvia Eugenia, Oscar Felipe. *Education:* University of Costa Rica, Licenciatura en Ambas, 1967; University of Essex, Ph.D. in political science; also attended Harvard University and Boston University, 1959–60, and the London School of Economics and Political Science.

Addresses: *Home*—Casa Presidencial, San Jose, Costa Rica. *Office*—Oficina de Presidente de la Republica, San Jose, Costa Rica.

Career

University of Costa Rica, professor of political science, 1969–72; Republic of Costa Rica, minister of planning, 1972–77, member of legislative assembly, 1978–82, president, 1986—. Member of economic council of the President of Costa Rica, 1972–77, general secretary of National Liberation Party, 1979–84. Central Bank of Costa Rica, vice-president of board of directors, 1970–72, director, 1972–77; member of board of directors, Technical Institute of Costa Rica, 1974–77, and International University Exchange Fund, 1976.

Awards, Honors: Premio Nacional de Ensayo, 1970, for *Grupos de Presion en Costa Rica;* Nobel Peace Prize, 1987.

AP/Wide World Photos

Sidelights

Oscar Arias Sanchez is unique among Central American political leaders for his insistence on a peaceful solution to the region's problems and his resistance to the influence of either U.S. or Marxist leaders. The Costa Rican president's independent stance has not always endeared him to other world leaders, but it has brought him great popularity in his own country, which is currently the only true democracy in Central America. His work for a diplomatic resolution to Central American strife also earned him the 1987 Nobel Peace Prize.

Political ambitions stirred Arias early in life. He once joked that he first became aware of his desire to become president while still in his mother's womb. He was born into one of Costa Rica's most influential and wealthy coffee-growing families; the men on both sides of his family held prominent government posts. He was an asthmatic child who became a voracious reader during his periods of illness. After receiving his early education in Costa Rica, he went to the United States to study medicine at Boston University. While there, however, he became fascinated by the televised debates between Richard Nixon and John F. Kennedy that preceded the 1960 U.S. presidential elections. He corresponded with

Kennedy and later met with him on Cape Cod. The American politician became Arias's role model; twenty-five years after their meeting, he echoed Kennedy in his own presidential campaign when he referred to himself as the "leader of a new generation."

Dropping his medical aspirations, Arias returned to his native country to study law and economic science at the University of Costa Rica. He became involved with the Partido de Liberaciono Nacional (PLN) and favorably impressed the party's leaders with an essay on the confrontation between totalitarianism and freedom during the Soviet blockade of West Berlin in 1948–49. In 1964 he and the PLN's elder statesman, Jose Figueres Ferrer, began organizing groups to study national affairs, and in 1965–66, he worked for PLN candidate Daniel Oduber's unsuccessful presidential campaign. After graduating from the University of Costa Rica, Arias won a British government grant to study at the University of Essex and the London School of Economics and Political Science.

His three years in England left "a large imprint" on his political thinking, Arias told *Newsweek*. "I learned to look at things from a different perspective than that of a superpower." He came to admire British reserve and understatement and developed an antimilitaristic philosophy. As James LeMoyne explained in the *New York Times Magazine:* "One of [Arias's] most strongly held political beliefs [is] that war is the crudest form of political action, a brutal surgery to be avoided except in the most critical cases. The military cure, in his eyes, is as bad as almost any disease it purports to treat." His feelings on this subject were undoubtedly also influenced by Jose Figueres Ferrer, who had abolished Costa Rica's military in 1948 in order to help his country establish a strong civilian government. Returning to Costa Rica in 1969, Arias took a professorship in the University of Costa Rica's school of political science and began working on his doctoral dissertation for the University of Essex. His subject was the socioeconomic origins of Costa Rica's political leadership. He also wrote a book on pressure groups in his country, *Grupos de Presion en Costa Rica,* which won the Premio Nacional de Ensayo in 1971.

The opportunity to take a more active role in his country's politics came in 1970, when Jose Figueres Ferrer, returning to the presidency after twelve years, invited Arias to be a part of his economic council. In 1972, the president appointed Arias to his cabinet as minister of national planning and political economy, a position he retained when Daniel Oduber took over as president in 1974. Arias excelled in this role, implementing complex programs that stimulated employment, technological development, and economic growth. In 1978 he was elected by the people of Heredia, his home town, as their representative in the national legislative assembly. There he worked toward refining the electoral process and reforming the national constitution. He resigned from the assembly in 1981 to devote himself to the winning presidential campaign of PLN candidate Luis Alberto Monge.

In 1984 Arias gave up his position as secretary general of the PLN to seek his party's nomination for the 1986 presidential election. Luis Alberto Monge had been one of Costa Rica's most popular presidents, but was unable to run for a second term due to constitutional restrictions. Arias stepped into the void left by Alberto Monge's absence against the wishes of some of the PLN's elder statesmen, initially provoking damaging rifts in the party. Faced with defeat by a rival party, however, PLN leaders rallied behind Arias late in the campaign. "Oscar didn't have charisma," stated Arias's brother-in-law, Agustin Penon, in *Newsweek,* "yet everybody followed him anyway."

Arias's chief rival in the elections was Rafael Angel Calderon Fournier, the candidate of the right-leaning Partido Unidad Social Cristiana (PUSC). At first, the two men appeared equally matched. Both parties' platforms centered on recovery from the economic crisis Costa Rica was enduring (caused in part by its extensive welfare system and an influx of refugees from other Central American states) and a continuation of existing foreign policy: official neutrality, friendliness toward the United States, and hostility to Costa Rica's neighbor to the north, Nicaragua. At one point in the campaign, Calderon suggested that if Nicaragua invaded Honduras, he would send Costa Ricans to fight. Arias won popular support by denouncing Calderon as a threat to Costa Rica's neutrality and stability. As the "peace candidate," he pulled ahead of Calderon and won the presidency with 52.3 percent of the vote.

The election put a new slant on Central American affairs, pitting the anti-militaristic Arias against the Sandinista president of Nicaragua, Daniel Ortega Saavedra, described by LeMoyne as "a Cuban-influenced revolutionary who believes that true political change can only be brought about by a Marxist-oriented ruling party." Between them stood the leaders of El Salvador, Honduras, and Guatemala, who, "as the leaders of quasi-democratic states, bring the pragmatic views of weak civilian politicians who are daily forced to broker deals with power-hungry army officers." The United States had traditionally taken advantage of Costa Rica's differences with Nicaragua. The C.I.A. controlled much of Costa Rica's small intelligence service, and bands of U.S.-backed Contras were based on the Costa Rican border. Despite his opposition to the Sandinista regime, Arias had little sympathy for the Contras, and he vowed to end his country's support of them. American officials, whose country supplies millions of dollars in aid to Costa Rica, took his statements lightly. According to LeMoyne, "American money talked in the little country.... It must have seemed clear that the new President would soon settle down to the serious business of learning how to fit in with Washington's plans, just as his predecessors had done."

"Costa Rica is the most democratic country in the hemisphere and we are friends of the United States, but we want a relationship of mutual respect."

Within months, however, Arias had shut down all of Costa Rica's Contra bases. Lying to Arias about their activities, the American ambassador and the C.I.A. station chief continued to use the secret Costa Rican airstrip built under the orders of Lt. Col. Oliver North to supply the Contras. Discovering the truth, Arias used his allies in the U.S. Congress and the American press to have the ambassador and the C.I.A. station chief expelled from his country. "It was an almost unheard-of gesture in a backward region where American client states do not dismiss Washington envoys," noted LeMoyne. Arias further displeased U.S. officials by denying visas to two top Contra leaders. Such actions made it clear that Arias was determined to reclaim Costa Rica's national sovereignity, even if it meant straining relations with his country's closest and most powerful ally. He considered the airstrip incident unfortunate, but is quoted in the *New York Times Magazine* as saying that "there was no other way since, regrettably, the American Ambassador went behind my back after pledging to me that the airstrip would not be used.... Costa Rica is the most democratic country in the hemisphere and we are friends of the United States, but we want a relationship of mutual respect." One of his advisors elaborated: "We know where we stand with Cuba and the other Marxist states: we disagree deeply but we try to get along. With the United States, we share a great deal—but if we don't stake out our position clearly from the start, [the U.S. steps] on us."

Contra supporters in the United States were further annoyed when Arias arranged a peace summit between himself and the presidents of Honduras, El Salvador, Nicaragua, and Guatemala. Despite White House attempts to stymie the meeting, the five men gathered in Guatemala City in August 1987. "I told them 24 million people in Central America want and deserve peace," Arias told Garry Clifford of *People*. Negotiations went on until the early morning hours, when an accord agreeable to all was reached. The plan called for an end to outside aid for guerrilla troops, a cease-fire, continued peace talks, the promotion of democratic freedoms, and a ban on the use of one country's territory as a base for attacks on another. The Reagan Administration was particularly threatened by the peace plan's omission of the Nicaraguan Contras. Many Administration members felt that without Contra pressure, the United States would eventually be forced to personally invade Nicaragua in order to end the Sandanista regime. But Arias believes that the Contras could never really win a war with the Sandinistas. Continued support for them, in his view, will only result in increased Marxist aid to the Sandanistas and escalated fighting. LeMoyne explained, "Arias fears such a long, destructive war will bury Central America in turmoil at the very time its fragile, elected governments most need help in rebuilding their broken economies, and in gradually wresting power from affluent elites and domineering military officers." Arias expressed his feelings bluntly in a meeting with Reagan, when, according to *People*, he told the U.S. president, "You think the contras are part of the solution.... I think they are part of the problem."

Arias's diplomatic efforts received a ringing endorsement in October 1987 when he was awarded the Nobel Peace Prize. The Nobel Committee commended him for an "outstanding contribution to the possible return of stability and peace to a region long torn by strife and civil war," according to Jill Smolowe in *Time*. Committee chairman Egil Aarvik stated that there were political motivations in awarding Arias the prize, for which he had not been considered a serious contender. "We hope that the award will help to speed up the process of peace in Central America," Smolowe quoted him as saying. Many top Washington officials were unhappy with the award, knowing that it would interfere with efforts to win Congressional approval for more aid to the Contras. According to Smolowe, Arias, who accepted the Peace Prize on behalf of all Central

America, dismissed his U.S. critics: "There will always be people with small spirits."

Oscar Arias's critics accuse him of vanity and an obsession with his image. According to Nancy Cooper in *Newsweek,* "Arias can happily spend hours leafing through scrapbooks of his newspaper clippings and mementos, and he enjoyed watching his own television spots during the elections." His ambassador to the United States, Guido Fernandez, concurs that Arias is vain, but maintains in *People* that the characteristic is "not a sin.... He is self-confident, always believing that things will go right for him, but when he has a setback, he tries again." Arias is also characterized as unusually fair-minded, accessible to his countrymen, and as a man with great pride, integrity, and determination.

Although successful implementation of his peace plan has proved elusive, he has continued to work for a political rather than a military end to the strife in Central America. According to LeMoyne, Arias "[sees] the peace effort as a positive exercise in nation-building. No outside power, he believes, can give the Central American countries what they most need—the sense that they are responsible for their actions and must create their own futures." LeMoyne concluded: "Even if the Central Americans falter, Arias says, he sees their effort to negotiate peace as a necessary step toward creating a sense of shared public life in Central America, essential political achievements that have tragically eluded their narrow isthmus for 400 years."

Writings

Grupos de Presion en Costa Rica, 1970.
Quien Gobierna en Costa Rica, 1976.
Democracia, Independencia y Sociedad Latino-America, 1977.
Los Caminos para El Desarollo de Costa Rica, 1977.
Nuevos Rumbos para el Desarollo Constarricense, 1980.

Contributor of chapters to books and articles to magazines and journals.

Sources

Boston Globe, April 8, 1989.
Christian Science Monitor, May 8, 1986.
Commonweal, May 9, 1986.
Detroit Free Press, October 14, 1987.
Nation, December 20, 1986.
Newsweek, October 26, 1987; January 11, 1988.
New York Review of Books, March 17, 1988.
New York Times, February 4, 1986; September 23, 1987; August 10, 1988; September 18, 1988.
Newsweek, October 26, 1987; January 11, 1988.
New York Times Magazine, January 10, 1988.
People, November 9, 1987.
Time, October 26, 1987.

—Sketch by Joan Goldsworthy

Lee Atwater

UPI/Bettmann Newsphotos

Chairman of Republican National Committee

Full name, Harvey Leroy Atwater; born February 27, 1951, in Atlanta, Ga.; son of Harvey Dillard (an insurance claims adjuster) and Alma (a teacher; maiden name, Page) Atwater; married Sally Dunbar, June 24, 1978; children: Sarah Lee, Ashley Page. *Education:* Newberry College, B.A. in history, 1973; University of South Carolina, M.A. in journalism, 1977, doctoral candidate. *Religion:* Methodist.

Addresses: *Home*—Washington, D.C. *Office*—Republican National Committee, 310 First St. S.E., Washington, D.C. 20003.

Career

In high school, managed a classmate's campaign for student body president, and played guitar in a blues band; summer intern in the office of Senator J. Strom Thurmond (R-S.C.), Washington, D.C., 1971; manager of mayoral campaign of William Edens, Forest Acres, S.C., 1972; executive director of National College Republicans, 1972–73; founder of Baker & Associates (political consulting firm), Columbia, S.C., 1974; manager of campaign of Carroll Campbell for lieutenant governor of South Carolina, 1974; manager of several local political campaigns, 1974–78; field director for Thurmond's campaign for reelection to the U.S. Senate, 1978; manager or consultant on several campaigns, 1978–80; Southeastern regional director for Ronald Reagan's presidential campaign, 1980; special assistant to the president for political affairs, Washington, D.C., 1980–84; deputy campaign manager for Reagan's reelection campaign, 1984; partner in Black, Manafort & Stone (political consulting firm), Washington, D.C., 1984–86; chairman of George Bush's political action committee, 1986; manager of Bush's presidential campaign, 1987–88; chairman of Republican National Committee, Washington, D.C., 1989—.

Sidelights

Lee Atwater is anything but a stereotypical blueblood Republican. The 37-year-old South Carolinian looks like Tom Sawyer, plays guitar like B.B. King, and has as his heroes Machiavelli and Stonewall Jackson. He carries a jar of tabasco sauce wherever he goes, collects B-movies, and cusses regularly in front of those he figures might be shocked. In 1988, however, Atwater emerged as campaign manager for George Bush, directing a $330 million, 2,000-employee operation. And after Bush was elected to the White House, Atwater was rewarded with the post of chairman of the Republican National Committee, making him the man responsible for future positioning and financing of the party. He brings to the job a commitment to lead the GOP to majority status in the battles for control of Congress and state legislatures, and a record of striking success in more than 30 local, state, and national contests. Along the way, Atwater has earned a reputation as a specialist in negative campaigning, with a particular talent for driving wedges in the Democratic coalition. The *Columbus Dispatch* termed him "the prince of political pit bulls."

Experts give Atwater much of the credit for Bush's successful 1988 campaign. It was his scheme that guaranteed the Republican nomination for Bush in record time and his plan that helped the vice-president win 40 states in November. But some question Atwater's tactics. Bush's two key Republican opponents in 1988—Pat Robertson and Bob Dole—accused him of harassment and dirty tricks. Democratic nominee Michael Dukakis [see index for *Newsmakers* entry] tried to ignore Atwater's attacks but was clearly hurt by them.

As manager of Bush's campaign, Atwater vowed to make a household name of convict Willie Horton, who had raped a woman while on a furlough from a Massachusetts prison. And with the help of network television and millions of campaign dollars, he did just that, convincing a lot of people that Michael Dukakis might release thousands of criminals like Horton onto the streets of middle-class America. It was Atwater who decided to use the Pledge of Allegiance as a campaign issue against Dukakis and Atwater, Democrats believe, who started rumors that Dukakis had seen a psychiatrist earlier in his life.

To those who suggest that Atwater brings down the level of political campaigning, he told the *Columbia State-Record:* "I just laugh it off. I'm always in a position where people are shooting at me. I don't know whether it helps or it hurts. I just do what I do." Indeed, Atwater admits, he was somewhat of a troublemaker from the start. As a teen, he told the *Philadelphia Inquirer,* "I was king of the hell-raisers."

Atwater grew up in small-town South Carolina, where he made his mark in high school with music and comedy. He played guitar in his own blues band, Little Harvey and the Upsetter's Review. When popular acts like Percy Sledge and Sam and Dave would pass through town, Atwater's band would often play back-up. "My goal," he told the *Washington Post,* "was to be a musician, a blues man, the next Lee Dorsey." He also put out a high school newsletter called "Big At's Comedy Ratings," a list of the Top-10 funniest kids in school. "It got to the point where people actually competed to get into the comedy ratings," high school classmate Warren Tompkins told the *State-Record.* "He told me it was where he first learned the power of the press. But Lee was the class clown in that he could always be counted on to keep people laughing." Atwater's first political venture came when he convinced classmate David Yon (whom he dubbed Dewey P. Yon) to run as a write-in candidate for president of their South Carolina high school on a platform of free beer and guaranteed good grades. Yon won, but the principal overturned the results and ordered another vote.

Atwater got more serious about politics at Newberry College, which he attended only after his parents insisted he get a degree before becoming a rock star. After his sophomore year, Atwater was hired as a summer intern in U.S. Senator Strom Thurmond's office in Washington, and there he found his calling. At 19, he was elected president of the Newberry College Republicans. He later became state president and regional director and ran the winning campaign for the national College Republicans' president. "I got into Republican politics because I was always an anti-Establishment type of person, and the Establishment was run by the Democrats," Atwater told the *Boston Globe.* "I was a conservative libertarian, so the Republican Party had more natural appeal to me."

In 1973, he went to Washington as executive director for the College Republicans. There he met Bush, who was then chairman of the Republican National Committee. "I was 22," Atwater told the *Globe.* "He took an interest in me personally. I developed a loyalty to him and friendship with him way back then." One of Bush's first acts of friendship was to help Atwater get a date with his future wife, Sally, who worked for Thurmond. To impress her, Atwater took her to meet Bush. It didn't work. Afterward, Bush, who was going out of town, suggested Atwater borrow his boat and take Sally and some friends out for the weekend. Today, Lee and Sally Atwater have two daughters.

In 1974, a 23-year-old Atwater ran Republican Carroll Campbell's bid for lieutenant governor of South Carolina. Campbell lost, but Atwater was undeterred. He started over, building a winning record in state politics. "He was good on gaining intelligence as to what's happening in the other fellow's political camp and offsetting or rebutting that," Thurmond told the *State-Record.* "He just outmaneuvers the opposition."

Opponents see it differently. In 1980, a Democrat named Thomas Turnipseed was running for Congress in South Carolina against a candidate managed by Atwater. When Turnipseed attacked the accuracy of a Republican campaign poll, Atwater responded by reminding voters that Turnipseed had received electric-shock treatment when he was a teenager. "I'm not going to respond to that guy," Atwater said at the time. "In college, I understand they hooked him up to jumper cables." Atwater later told the *Philadelphia Inquirer* that he is ashamed of the crack, but Turnipseed remains bitter. "What's funny about teenage depression and teenage suicide?" he told the *Philadelphia Inquirer.*

In 1978, Atwater worked as field director for Thurmond's re-election. During that campaign he learned a new maneuver—using an obscure publication as a source of a dubious quote about an opponent—to bury Thurmond's opponent, Democrat Pug Ravenel. He found a quote in a New York-based weekly shopping guide in which Ravenel told a Manhattan audience that he would represent New York in the Senate as well as South Carolina. By the time Atwater got through with it, Ravenel was being denounced on television ads for promising to be a "third senator" from New York. "I go through trade publications and small newspapers looking for things that a guy said that he wouldn't say back home so I can nail a guy," Atwater explained to the *Philadelphia Inquirer.*

"I got into Republican politics because I was always an anti-establishment type of person, and the Establishment was run by the Democrats."

In 1980, Atwater was Southeastern campaign director for Ronald Reagan's presidential campaign—which pitted him against his old friend Bush. He was credited with unleashing a series of radio commercials attacking Bush on gun control. During Reagan's first term, Atwater was on the White House political staff. And in 1984, he was the deputy manager of Reagan's re-election campaign. Preparing for that campaign, he told the *Charlotte Observer* that, "the perfect GOP candidate for the South has a touch of populism. And the most effective tactic for winning populist votes is negative advertising."

After Reagan won re-election, Atwater became a partner in the lobbying firm of Black, Manafort & Stone. As a Washington-based political consultant, his income reached a reported $400,000-plus, and he engineered GOP congressional victories across the South. He briefly became head of Bush's political action committee in 1986 before becoming his campaign manager.

In that role, Atwater infuriated opponents of both parties. When news broke in 1988 that televangelist Jimmy Swaggart visited a prostitute, GOP presidential hopeful Pat Robertson told the *State-Record* that Atwater "had something to do with it," setting the whole thing up in an effort to discredit Robertson. "I wouldn't tolerate someone like that. I'd fire him in a minute," Robertson told the *State-Record.* Likewise, Atwater angered Bush's toughest party opponent, Kansas Senator Bob Dole. After Dole portrayed himself as a poor country boy running against the upper-class, Yale-educated Bush, Atwater challenged Dole and his wife, Elizabeth, to make public their income tax returns, knowing that the Doles in 1986 had earned nearly $600,000. Dole was incensed, telling ABC News, "Here's the Bush campaign, maybe not the vice-president himself, but Lee Atwater and others, out distributing things that they think might reflect on Elizabeth Dole."

Atwater's toughest salvos, however, were saved for Bush's eventual Democratic opponent. Michael Dukakis, Atwater told the *Los Angeles Times,* was "a bona fide, double-dipped, Frost Belt, George McGovern-style liberal, trying to snuggle up to the Republican philosophy and Republican values.... We'd be crazy to let him get away with it. He's a Northern-fried Jimmy Carter," lacking foreign policy experience. Atwater seized on Dukakis's veto of a bill requiring recitation of the Pledge of Allegiance in Massachusetts schools, as well as the state prison furlough program that allowed convicts to have weekend passes. He portrayed Dukakis as a gun foe, who believed only police and the military should own guns. And he painted him as too left-wing for America because he was a member of the American Civil Liberties Union. Democrats, of course, objected to the strategy. "Much of it was unfair, inaccurate, a disservice to the process," Dukakis adviser Richard Moe told the *Charlotte Observer.* "The defense ad they ran, they claimed [Dukakis] was against weapons systems that he was for. There was a lot of distortion." But Atwater told the *Observer,* "I prefer to call it comparative advertising."

Atwater was also behind other, less controversial, strategic moves. One was the decision to team Bush with governors in key states. The thinking was that governors have built-in organizations and the sharpest understanding of the local political chemistry and would be flattered if asked to be full partners. In addition, Atwater was instrumental in the decision to persevere in the first-in-the-nation Michigan caucuses in January, even though most experts said it would be futile to tangle with Pat Robertson's church army in this complicated, low-turnout event. Atwater insisted it could be won, and it was. He later encouraged Bush to concede South Dakota and Minnesota to Dole after New Hampshire to concentrate on campaigning in the South, which proved decisive.

After Bush's election, Atwater was quickly rewarded with the post of chairman of the Republican National Committee. "I can't think of another person in this country who brings such a breadth of political talent to this job," Bush told the *Charlotte Observer*. "He's a friend; I'm proud of his accomplishments." As party chairman, Atwater's responsibilities include helping Republicans win more state and local races and serving as a peacemaker among party factions and a spokesman with a strong public relations role. His first priority, Atwater said, will be recruiting more blacks and Hispanics into the party. "We have entered into a post-civil rights era," he told the *Washington Post*. "Civil rights are not the driving force.... On family issues, values issues, blacks may realize they are closer to the Republican Party than they think."

Still, Atwater faced immediate criticism when he first sought to recruit blacks. Indeed, his January 1989 appointment to the board of trustees of predominantly black Howard University drew so much student opposition that he was forced to resign in March. After students took over campus buildings, Atwater said he didn't want anyone hurt in his name. "I extended the olive branch, and it was broken, broken in my face," Atwater told the *Lexington Herald-Leader*. "But I'm going to turn the cheek and try again. The party needs to broaden its base."

Sources

Boston Globe, November 22, 1987; November 20, 1988.

Business Week, June 6, 1988.

Charlotte Observer, January 31, 1988; November 18, 1988; November 19, 1988; February 26, 1989; March 11, 1989.

Chicago Tribune, November 18, 1988.

Columbia State-Record, August 1, 1988; October 17, 1988; March 12, 1989.

Columbus Dispatch, November 27, 1988.

Esquire, December, 1986.

Fortune, February 17, 1986.

Lexington Herald-Leader, March 10, 1989.

Los Angeles Times, April 29, 1988.

National Review, January 27, 1989.

New Republic, July 27, 1987.

Newsday, June 2, 1988; January 18, 1989; February 3, 1989.

Philadelphia Inquirer, October 9, 1988.

U.S. News & World Report, June 6, 1988; January 23, 1989.

Washington Post, January 20, 1989; March 5, 1989.

—Sidelights by Glen Macnow

Dan Aykroyd

AP/Wide World Photos

Actor and writer

Full name, Daniel Edward Aykroyd; born July 1, 1952, in Ottawa, Ontario, Canada; came to United States, 1975; son of Samuel Cuthbert Peter Hugh (an assistant deputy minister of transport) and Lorraine (Gougeon) Aykroyd; married Maureen Lewis, May 10, 1974 (divorced); married Donna Dixon (an actress), 1984; children: (first marriage) Mark, Lloyd, Oscar. *Education:* Attended Carleton University. *Religion:* Roman Catholic.

Addresses: *Home*—Martha's Vineyard, Mass. *Agent*—Givertz Brillstein Co., 9200 Sunset Blvd., Suite 428, Los Angeles, Calif., 90069.

Career

Worked in a variety of odd jobs in Canada, including warehouseman, railroad brakeman, mailman, and road surveyor; manager at Club 505, an after-hours bar in Toronto, Ontario; performed with Second City comedy troupe in Toronto; performer and writer for television programs, including "Saturday Night Live," 1975–79, "Coming Up Rosie," and "All You Need Is Cash"; actor in motion pictures, including "Mr. Mike's Mondo Video," 1979, "1941," 1979, "The Blues Brothers," 1980, "Neighbors," 1981, "Doctor Detroit," 1983, "Trading Places," 1983, "Twilight Zone," 1983, "Ghostbusters," 1984, "Indiana Jones and the Temple of Doom," 1984, "Spies Like Us," 1985, "Dragnet," 1987, "The Couch Trip," 1988, "The Great Outdoors," 1988, "My Stepmother Is an Alien," 1988, and "Ghostbusters 2," 1989; recording artist.

Member: Writers Guild of America, American Federation of Television and Radio Artists.

Awards: Emmy Award, 1976, 1977.

Sidelights

Dan Aykroyd was arguably the best writer on the staff of "Saturday Night Live" when the NBC program was, in the words of *Esquire* writer David Michaelis, "at the center of the hip-comedy universe ... [with] the kind of electrifying aura that momentarily surrounds a hit Broadway play, a victorious political campaign, a World Series championship team." During his 1975–79 stint with the show, Aykroyd gave audiences inspired impersonations of real-life subjects ranging from Julia Child to Jimmy Carter and created such memorable characters as the extraterrestrial Beldar Conehead, sleazy entrepreneur Irwin Mainway, and the wild and crazy Czechoslovakian Jorge Festrunk. Aykroyd expanded on his television success by co-writing and performing in popular films, including "The Blues Brothers," "Trading Places," and "Ghostbusters."

Growing up in a strict Catholic family in Quebec and Ontario, Aykroyd had a penchant for minor delinquency that eventually led to his expulsion from the

St. Pius X Minor Preparatory Seminary. At home, "there was a lot of corporal punishment... many belt whippings," Aykroyd told *Rolling Stone.* He added that he "deserved it," however, and characterized his relationship with his father as "strong." And in spite of his self-described tendency to be a "hellion," he acquired a strong sense of industry from his father that carries over into his work today; he is often described as an unusually meticulous writer and performer.

Aykroyd's interest in crime and punishment led him to study criminology and deviant pathology at Carleton University in Ottawa. At the same time, he began a personal exploration of the city's underworld. Soon his friends included the likes of merchant seaman David Benoit—whom Aykroyd described to *Rolling Stone*'s Timothy White as "the guy who put my life on a different path.... He turned me on to music [and] let me smoke my first joint"—Ray the Green Beret, with whom Benoit and Aykroyd cruised the streets in a stolen Cadillac, and "a crazy French Canadian" called George the Thief. "I still see these people and probably will associate with them for the rest of my life," stated Aykroyd. His fascination with both sides of the law later led his associates at "Saturday Night Live" to joke that Aykroyd's greatest fantasy was to commit a crime and then arrest himself.

That same attraction to what Michaelis calls "the gritty, all-night, low-rent romance of blue-collar squalor" prompted Aykroyd to take over the management of "the best bootleg booze joint that there ever was in Canada, the Club 505 in Toronto," where he eventually met "Saturday Night Live's" creator, Lorne Michaels. It was about this time that he auditioned for a place with Toronto's Second City comedy troupe. His five-minute audition featured five characters and was a resounding success. His work with regional dialects and characters soon became well-known, attracting the attention of one of the hottest members of Chicago's Second City troupe, John Belushi.

The two young stars met in 1973 when Belushi came to Toronto to recruit talent for the "National Lampoon Radio Hour." "It was kind of like love at first sight," Aykroyd remembered in *Esquire.* We just connected immediately and knew that we were kindred spirits.... Our humor fit perfectly together.... I'm not a homo and neither was John, but when I saw him come into a room, I got the jump you get when you see a beautiful girl. It was that kind of feeling, that adrenaline, that pit-of-the-stomach rush. Being with him was electric, really electric."

According to Michaelis, this "romantic sensibility" shared by the two men "became the invisible bond of a highly visible, multimedia comedy team," that would "create folklore wrought from comedy."

Belushi and Aykroyd got their chance to work together the following year, when writer-producer Lorne Michaels asked them to audition for his new live, late-night comedy series, "Saturday Night Live." Aykroyd was initially skeptical about the project's chances for success. Live television hadn't been done since the 1950s, and it seemed unlikely that the sort of comedy Aykroyd enjoyed would be allowed on network television. With his career developing nicely, he had no wish to become involved with a failure. Belushi convinced him to audition, however. He assured his friend that he had already put Michaels in his place, telling him that television was garbage and warning him that they would have no part of the canned-laughter type of comedy found on prime-time television. Meeting with the pair in his office, Michaels felt both excited and apprehensive about working with them. They seemed likely to cause trouble, yet their screen tests showed remarkable talent. Aykroyd displayed a visionary imagination and a spontaneous, bizarrely original gift for impersonation. Michaels took a chance and signed them both.

Aykroyd held on to his doubts for the first few months after "Saturday Night" debuted in October, 1975. He commuted between NBC's studios and the set of a movie he was working on in Canada, sleeping on a foam slab in Belushi's apartment when he was in New York because he was unwilling to get a place of his own until he was sure the show was a hit. By December, however, even the conservative *New York Times* had called it "the hottest, hippest, most daring comedy show on television," and ratings were climbing higher every week. Over the next two seasons, "Saturday Night Live" won a regular viewing audience of about 17 million, and *People* magazine hailed Aykroyd as "the show's most brilliant writer-actor."

Reported White: "Aykroyd's night gallery of alter egos [was] voluminous, including such difficult subjects as Elliot Ness, Orson Welles/Citizen Kane, Julia Child, Clark Gable, both Scotty and Bones from *Star Trek*, plus such regional and/or dialect characters as curt southern state troopers, randy midwestern rubes, proud Aberdeen Scotch guards, mincing French waiters, and snobbish British theater critics—not to mention creations like Beldar Conehead, sleazy cable-TV personality E. Buzz Miller, and his Jorge Festrunk to Steve Martin's brother Yortuk in the 'Czech Brother' routines." Furthermore, noted Michaelis, Aykroyd "was seamless" in his varied roles. "In mid-sentence he could shift from one regional (or galactic) dialect to another with perfect pitch and fidelity.... When he stepped into a character, he zipped up the front and vanished."

Perhaps his most subtle work was seen in his parodies of real-life personalities, however. White praised Aykroyd's Jimmy Carter sendup, which "captures the president's ineptitude-masking fascination for folksy banality and quasi hipness with an unctuous schoolboy drawl and a Cheshire cat grin"; his "devastating" Richard Nixon, which featured "each nervous facet of this broken-down Cro-magnon crook sharpened to a cutting edge, from Dick's apelike shoulder roll and phlebitic shuffle, to his chomping, jowl-quivering monotone and his mail-chute smile"; and his "stunning" Tom Snyder, which "captures the desperation of Snyder's pursed-lip cigarette puffing, and the empty headed 'by gosh' and reference to 'the boys' that the perpetually ill-prepared *Tomorrow* host employs to buy time." White concluded: "Aykroyd's ability to mirror and then expand on any character he chooses... borders on the soul-snatching power of obeah. Thanks to Dan Aykroyd, we know things about Nixon, Carter and Snyder that they themselves could not have shown us."

In 1979, with their reputations firmly established, both Aykroyd and Belushi decided to leave the pressures of a weekly show behind to concentrate on other projects. Renting a suite of offices on Fifth Avenue in Manhattan, they formed Phantom-Black Rhino Enterprises (named after a bizarre dream of Aykroyd's in which he found and gentled a rhino that had Belushi's face) in order to develop projects for themselves. Their first co-starring film, "1941," had been an expensive flop, but Universal Pictures was still willing to invest more than $30 million in their next venture, "The Blues Brothers."

"The Blues Brothers" sprang from Aykroyd's love of blues music, which he passed on to Belushi. The two indulged their unfulfilled fantasies of being musicians by donning black suits, ties, hats, and sunglasses and becoming Jake and Elwood Blues. They had first used the act to warm up "Saturday Night Live's" studio audience, then to open for Steve Martin at the Universal Amphitheatre in Los Angeles, where they nearly stole the show. Belushi, as Jake, took the stage in a series of cartwheels, while Aykroyd, as Elwood, entered more sedately, with a briefcase containing his blues harmonica handcuffed to his wrist. Then they proceeded to sing and play their favorite music. Eventually, Belushi and Aykroyd parlayed the act into a 25-city concert tour and a double-platinum LP, *Briefcase Full of Blues.* "In comedy-variety terms, the act trumped both an ordinary music number and an ordinary comic sketch," noted Michaelis. "It drew laughter in three dimensions. Viewers were mesmerized: Belushi singing the blues? Aykroyd on harp?"

Belushi convinced Aykroyd to base his first film script on a story about the Blues Brothers. Drawing on their own brotherly relationship as well as "all his knowledge of criminology, Catholic education, recidivism, police procedures, and general human dereliction," Aykroyd created a rich past for Jake and Elwood. The finished film featured performance by the likes of Ray Charles, Aretha Franklin, Cab Calloway, and James Brown. Several critics found the movie demeaning to these great performers, but James Brown dismissed their objections in *People:* "The film was made with a lot of love and gave us all another chance....I hate to admit it, but these young people never heard of me. They come to the movies to see Belushi and Aykroyd, and they see James Brown and Aretha Franklin. If they like us, maybe they'll come hear us play."

Aykroyd managed to maintain his equilibrium as his fame increased, but Belushi's lifestyle was increasingly out of control. "He was running with real bad people," Aykroyd told Michaelis, "and I knew that he had to just relax and... get away from whatever substances were being pushed." In March, 1982, he tried to convince his friend to join him for a week on maneuvers on a navy ship as a way of cleaning him out, but Belushi refused. "If I had it to do over again," Aykroyd was quoted in *Esquire,* "I would have taken two or three of my friends and handcuffed him and put him in an institution just to turn him around." Later that week, as Aykroyd was working in Black Rhino's New York office, his agent called from Los Angeles to say that Belushi was dead from an overdose of heroin and cocaine. Aykroyd took charge of the funeral, held on Martha's Vineyard, where the two men had both purchased homes. Riding his motorcycle, wearing a Chicago policeman's jacket and a Confederate flag as a scarf, he led the cortege to the graveyard.

At the time of Belushi's death, Aykroyd was working on a script that would have featured the two of them as paranormal technicians. Eventually the film was made with Aykroyd, Bill Murray, and Harold Ramis as a trio of "Ghostbusters" who save Sigourney Weaver, and the rest of New York City, from demonic possession. Richard Schickel had high praise for the film, writing in *Time* that it delivered "political as well as paranormal satire.... Praise is due to everyone connected with *Ghostbusters* for thinking on a grandly comic scale and delivering the goofy goods, neatly timed and perfectly packaged." "Ghostbusters" eventually became the most successful comedy in movie history, earning more than $200 million dollars.

In 1987, Aykroyd indulged his law-and-order fascination to great effect in a movie version of the television show "Dragnet," co-starring Tom Hanks [see index for *Newsmakers* entry]. "With his tongue planted firmly in his cheek with obvious affection, Dan Aykroyd gives the performance of his career as the namesake nephew and '80s clone of detective sergeant Joe Friday," wrote Gene Siskel in the *Chicago Tribune.* Aykroyd told Siskel that his version of "Dragnet," in which the modern-day Friday and his partner defeat a Satanic cult, was a tribute to police as well as a comedy. Police, he said, "uphold the right and the good under God's name. I would hope people today who look to the media and to religion and to politicians for moral order would realize that the ultimate right and wrong are decided daily by a good cop. Sure there are bad cops and bad laws, but I'm talking about good cops and good, basic, Ten Commandments laws in God's name. Men of the cloth sermonize about those laws, but who upholds the law? The cop, God's real crusader."

Writings

Writer of comedy sketches for television series "Saturday Night Live," 1975–79. Co-author of screenplays, including "The Blues Brothers," 1980, "Neighbors," 1981, "Ghostbusters," 1984, "Spies Like Us," 1985, and "Ghostbusters 2," 1989.

Discography

Briefcase Full of Blues (with John Belushi), Atlantic, 1978.
The Blues Brothers (soundtrack; with Belushi), Atlantic, 1980.
Made in America (with Belushi), Atlantic, 1980.
The Best of the Blues Brothers (with Belushi), Atlantic, 1981.

Sources

Books

Michaelis, David, *Best of Friends,* Morrow, 1983.

Periodicals

Chicago Tribune, June 14, 1987.
Esquire, December, 1982.
People, December 24, 1979; August 4, 1980; July 19, 1982; December 19, 1988.
Playboy, June, 1982.
Rolling Stone, February 22, 1979.
Time, June 11, 1984.

—*Sketch by Joan Goldsworthy*

Roseanne Barr

AP/Wide World Photos

Comedian and actress

Born c. 1953, in Salt Lake City, Utah; daughter of Jerry (a salesman) and Helen Barr; married Bill Pentland, 1973; children: Jessica, Jennifer, Jake.

Addresses: *Home*—Encino, Calif. *Office*—American Broadcasting Companies, Inc., 1330 Avenue of the Americas, New York, N.Y. 10019.

Career

Held a variety of jobs, including window dresser and waitress; began performing in comedy clubs in 1981; has appeared on "The Tonight Show" and on several television specials; star of comedy series "Roseanne," ABC-TV, 1988—.

Awards: Recipient of cable-television's ACE awards for best female in a comedy and for best HBO special.

Sidelights

A self-described "domestic goddess," Roseanne Barr is best known for her nasal, laconic delivery of stinging barbs aimed at helpless husbands and demanding children. Her comedy has been called New Wave, feminist, and revolutionary; yet her subject matter—marriage, kids, housework—is conventional. Critics have found her both "dangerous" and irresistable. "Barr is a bear, a beast, a national treasure," wrote Michael McWilliams of the *Detroit News*. She is also the star of the comedy series "Roseanne," the most eagerly awaited new show of the 1988–89 television season.

Born and raised in Salt Lake City, Utah, Barr, who is Jewish, was one of the few non-Mormons at her school. At Christmas, her teachers would ask "our little Jewish girl" to sing about the dreidel (a toy brought out at Hanukkah). "So I would sing the dreidel song, and then explain why I didn't believe in Jesus," she told Gioia Diliberto of *People*. The rest of the time, she recalled to Stu Schreiberg in *USA Weekend*, "I'd sit in the back of classrooms and had very few friends." At the age of 16, Barr was hit by a car and knocked unconscious. She came out of a coma several days later and experienced "a grotesque personality change," quoted the *New York Times'* Joy Horowitz. Barr was hospitalized for nearly a year. Upon recovering, she left high school and moved to Colorado. There she met and married a local postal clerk, had three children, and worked at a variety of low-paying jobs. For entertainment, she frequently went to comedy clubs, most of which were dominated by male comics doing what Barr considered sexist material. She decided it was time to even the score.

In 1981 she delivered a five-minute monologue at a Denver club. Soon after, she was playing clubs throughout the West and Midwest. Her career took off after performing at the Comedy Store in Los Angeles. From there she appeared on network and cable television specials and was a frequent guest on "The Tonight Show." Her routines include jabs at men—married and single—motherhood, and housekeeping. "Listen to her bag the bachelor ethos," wrote *Vogue*'s Tracy Young. "'Get a relationship and face the *real* danger. Look at a mortgage for thirty years, you skydiving *wimps*.'" About her husband, who asks if there are any Cheetos left in the house, Barr comments, "Like he couldn't go over and lift up the sofa cushions himself." Young continued: "If husbands take a beating from Barr, kids don't fare much better.... [She] reads the instructions on a bottle of aspirin as, 'Take two and keep away from children.'"

In 1988, amid much publicity and fanfare, ABC-TV introduced "Roseanne," a half-hour situation comedy starring Barr as a married mother of three who works in a plastics factory. With few exceptions, "Roseanne" (which is produced by the creators of "The Cosby Show") was proclaimed a hit. McWilliams called it a "grungy-funny sitcom" and a "standup *tour-de-force* with plot and dialogue." Some critics have compared it to "The Honeymooners," with Barr playing Ralph Kramden to her television-husband's composite portrayal of Alice and Norton. Unlike other television wives and mothers, as Horowitz noted, "Roseanne is flawed." Though she loves "her romantic sop of a husband," she never hesitates to point out his faults. In one episode, according to the critic, Barr tells him: "I put in eight hours a day at the factory, and then I come home and put in another eight hours.... And you don't do NOTHIN'!" Schreiberg called "Roseanne" the "flip side of *The Cosby Show*." Horowitz agreed: "A beatific Clair Huxtable comes home from the law firm with briefcase in hand to a picture-perfect house. Roseanne, looking haggard in her sweatshirt and blue jeans, returns home... lugging an armload of groceries to a pigsty of a kitchen."

Barr, who serves as a creative consultant on the show, believes that family sitcoms virtually ignore the real world. "Nothing in reality is ever addressed on sitcoms," she explained to Schreiberg. "'Will Junior go out with the smart girl or the good-looking girl?' I want to deal with being broke, with the implied violence of American family life." Moreover, Barr is critical of television executives who perceive audiences outside of New York or Los Angeles to be narrow minded and socially isolated. "I grew up with people in the Midwest and, in fact, they're as hip as anyone else," she told Horowitz. "I want to do real revolutionary TV.... I want to do a show that reflects how people really live. Telling the truth at any point in time is really revolutionary. I want this show to tell the horrible truth rather than parody the truth. When you tell the truth you don't insult the audience's intelligence."

Sources

Detroit News, October 18, 1988.
New York Times, October 16, 1988.
Newsweek, October 31, 1988.
People, April 28, 1986.
USA Weekend, September 23–25, 1988.
Vogue, April, 1987.

—Sketch by Denise Wiloch

Sandra Bernhard

Comedian, actress, singer

Born c.1955 in Flint, Mich.; daughter of Jerry (a proctologist) and Jeanette (an artist) Bernhard. *Education:* Graduated from high school in Scottsdale, Ariz.

Addresses: *Office*—10100 Santa Monica Blvd., #1600, Los Angeles, Calif. 90067.

Career

After high school, worked for eight months on a kibbutz in Israel; worked as a manicurist-pedicurist in Beverly Hills, Calif., while doing stand-up comedy in area nightclubs, 1974–78; full-time comedian, 1978—; appeared in films "The King of Comedy," 1983, "Follow That Bird," 1985, "Track 29," 1988; appeared off-Broadway in the one-woman show "Without You I'm Nothing," 1988; special appearance on New York cable television's "The Robin Byrd Show," 1988; numerous guest appearances on "Late Night with David Letterman."

Sidelights

Sandra Bernhard has a reputation," observes Bill Zehme in *Rolling Stone*. "It precedes and pursues her. She is what they once called a caution. She is known to be a lissome guerilla, a terrorist flirt, the ultravixen of comedy whose sense of abandon is decidedly rock & roll." This is the typically muddled reaction of one writer to Sandra Bernhard. Indeed, perhaps the finest tribute to her is that she is so hard to pin down. She falls into a category all her own.

AP/Wide World Photos

New Republic's Robert Brustein describes her as "wonderfully foulmouthed, totally unbuttoned.... Bernhard is unashamedly Jewish, with the aggressive confidence of Lenny Bruce." Tall, lean, and mean looking with her long legs and gapped-tooth, Mick Jagger mouth, Bernhard is the prototypical bad-girl, with just enough sexiness to captivate men as she inspires women with her free-wheeling nastiness. She has taken Hollywood by storm, not through the traditional female channels of beauty and charm, but by sheer will-power and wit. She is the true working girl's star.

Bernhard assaulted Hollywood from the bottom. Born in Flint, Michigan, and raised in Arizona, she skipped college and took a job in Beverly Hills as a manicurist to the stars. A natural clown who entertained friends with clever impersonations, she was pressed into trying her act in Los Angeles comedy clubs. "I was 19 with a big mouth and a flair for being funny, so I started getting up in little clubs all over town," she told the *New York Times*. "The women I looked up to were performers like Lily Tomlin and Bette Midler, who took chances, were very emotional and had strong points of view." Bernhard was first "discovered" by Paul Mooney, the comedy writer who has assisted Richard Pryor and Eddie Murphy. "I found her fascinating," Mooney told *Rolling Stone.* "But I knew what hell Hollywood was gonna put her through.... They were all threatened by her face, her sexuality."

Mooney's words have been prophetically true, unfortunately. Despite her excellent performance in Martin Scorsese's "The King of Comedy," Bernhard has since received few offers for film roles. In "The King of Comedy," she won raves and a National Society of Film Critics Award for her portrayal of Masha, a sexual menace and rich neurotic who helps Robert DeNiro kidnap a Johnny Carson-like talk-show host, played by Jerry Lewis. Since then she has played small roles in the Muppet caper "Follow That Bird" and "Track 29," in which she plays a nurse in a geriatric hospital. "I can imagine they all have their sane-sounding reasons for not putting Sandra Bernhard in more films," writes David Thomson in *Film Comment.* "I daresay they say she is ugly and alarming, that her nervousness is communicated to the audience and keeps them awake, that she moves and thinks like someone on a day out from the Institution."

But rather than lamenting her quirky looks and softening her abrasive disposition, Bernhard has found a way to turn both into a plus. Her eclectic, one-woman show at the off-Broadway Orpheum Theater was a six-month smash that combined Bernhard's comic improvisations with a little rock & roll and a healthy satire that won her audience over. Bernhard describes the show, which she co-wrote with director John Boskovich, as one in which "rock & roll meets the theater with elements of performance art, cabaret and stand-up comedy," she told the *New York Times.* "The underlying statement is intentionally narcissistic, for my show deals with pop culture and how we're all self obsessed and looking in the mirror. It involves alot of confessional things and ideas about the way pop culture throws images at you so fast they become impossible to digest and interpret."

In the show, mockedly titled "Without You I'm Nothing," Bernhard caustically turns the audience back on itself, literally shining a flashlight onto unsuspecting members of the house and exposing their character to the world. As her imagination wanders, she assumes different roles, often singing her part with the help of a four-piece rock band. She imagines reading tarot cards with singer Stevie Nicks or assumes the identity of a bouncy, blond WASP who has a crush on her big brother Chip. "They are not characters so much as ironic fantasy voices that flit subtly through the performance, baring their respective souls and intermingling with Sandra's own voice," says *Rolling Stone*'s Bill Zehme. "There's a whole range of kinds of women I like to be," Bernhard says. "I like to create scenarios and exciting romantic myths."

What seems odd is that Bernhard herself is becoming one of those women. A genuine star, she is now an icon of the pop culture she has always maligned. In fact, a favorite target of her old stand-up act was singer Madonna; eventually the two met and became fast friends. "I spoofed her, and I will continue to spoof her," Bernhard told *Rolling Stone.* "But there's part of me that looks at her and goes, 'God, she's really done it.' She knows exactly what she wants. Nothing throws her off." The two made a much publicized visit to David Letterman's talk show. Wearing identical outfits of cut-off shorts and white t-shirts, they gave Letterman a double-dose of his own wise-guy medicine and stole the show. Bernhard has been a frequent foil for Letterman, appearing on Late Night more than twenty times. "There are very few guests who take Dave to that limit," says "Late Night" producer Robert Morton in *Rolling Stone.* "He's challenged by what she does. It's a harder game for him to play. It's a struggle."

Discography

I'm Your Woman, Mercury, 1985.

Writings

Confessions of a Pretty Lady, Harper & Row, 1988.

Sources

Chicago Tribune, October 30, 1988.
New Republic, October 31, 1988.
New York Times, March 31, 1988.
People, March 7, 1983.
Rolling Stone, November 3, 1988.

—Sketch by David Collins

Benazir Bhutto

AP/Wide World Photos

Prime minister of Pakistan

Born June 21, 1953, in Karachi, Pakistan; daughter of Zulfikar Al (a politician) and Nusrat (Ispahani) Bhutto; married Asif Ali Zardari (a businessman), December, 1987; children: one. *Education:* Radcliffe College, B.A. in government, 1973; Lady Margaret Hall, Oxford University, degree (with honors), 1976.

Addresses: *Home*—Larkana, Pakistan. *Office*—Office of the Prime Minister, Islamabad, Pakistan.

Career

Following graduation from Oxford University, returned to Pakistan, hoping to enter foreign service in the government headed by her father, who was prime minister; after her father was deposed in a military coup, she was arrested and placed under house arrest several times, 1977–84, by the military regime headed by General Mohammed Zia ul-Haq, which executed her father in 1979; allowed to travel to London, England, 1984, for medical treatment; returned to Pakistan, 1985, for her brother's funeral and was again placed under house arrest for several months before being allowed to leave the country; moved back to Pakistan after the cessation of martial law, 1986, and received a hero's welcome from thousands of supporters; elected co-chairwoman, with her mother, of Pakistan People's Party (the political party founded by her father), 1986; arrested again, 1986, and detained for one month; after Zia's death in a plane crash, free elections were held in 1988, and Bhutto was elected prime minister of Pakistan.

Sidelights

When Benazir Bhutto, then 35, and her Pakistan People's Party won the post of prime minister in late 1988, she became the first female leader of a Muslim country in centuries. Living with Bhutto became problematical for the nation's conservative clergy. Before the election, Islamic scholar Mohammed Amin Minhas exhorted believers, "A nation that elects to be governed by a woman will not prosper," according to the *Los Angeles Times.* But when the nation elected to do just that, Minhas went back to the Koran, the Islamic holy book, decided he was wrong, and said, "Allah has given us this woman as our leader and Miss Benazir has acknowledged that this new power she possesses is, indeed, Allah's gift." The *Times* wrote, "The nation is attempting to explain to itself how it broke new ground, choosing a female leader for an Islamic land where women are rarely seen, let alone heard or revered." The answer may be that Bhutto was elected not because she is a woman, but because she is a Bhutto. Ruling Pakistan is a family tradition. Her martyred father, the country's first and only elected leader, died at the hands of the general who overthrew him. Benazir Bhutto, tutored on the fineries of Pakistani politics in her father's jail cell, would defy that general until his death in an unexplained plane crash months before a national election that would have pitted him against the daughter.

Still, Pakistanis seemed to need to explain Bhutto, who is known by her childhood nickname, Pinkie, to friends. A Pakistani businessman told the *Los Angeles Times:* "She is respected for her defiance of authority. She is no ordinary woman. In fact, she is seen as more a man than a woman—more a man even than a man, because she has defied the authority of army generals and a dictator, and she has won. For us, she is like an Islamic 'Rambo.'" Novelist Salman Rushdie dubbed her "Virgin Ironpants" in his novel *Shame.* Now that she has fully become her father's political heir, critics are watching to see if her deeds can match the idolatry of her supporters. The *New York Times* wrote: "Benazir has captured the imagination of her people, almost as a religious idol. Her promises are grand and sweeping: freedom, prosperity, education. The way to fulfill these promises is left deliberately vague."

In Pakistan, politics can even swirl around maternal intrigue. The man who sentenced Bhutto's father to death, General Mohammed Zia ul-Haq, while still alive, called elections in mid-1988 only when it became clear that Bhutto would be late in her pregnancy during the final stages of the expected campaign. She once told *Ms.* magazine, "I have to make sure that the children come at a time when it is not politically unfavorable." But in her autobiography, Bhutto wrote, "I didn't know whether Zia's announcement was influenced by my condition, but it did follow the [newspaper] confirmation that I was expecting."

The campaign, when it did come following Zia's death, resembled nothing American. According to *Newsweek,* crowds estimated at 100,000 waited for Bhutto when she arrived 12 hours late for a rally in Faisalabad, and chanted, "Lead us forever." She led a 1,000-mile whistle stop train trip that had supporters shimmying up signal poles and flocking overpasses to get a glimpse of her. Bhutto often rode on the tops of trucks, spotlighted during nighttime parades—unmistakable in bright red glasses, her dark hair half-covered with a bright dupatta, or scarf.

And the rhetoric and dirty tricks of a Pakistani election campaign makes its American counterpart look like a PTA meeting. The *Los Angeles Times* reported: "The Islamic scholars and Mullahs . . . that opposed Bhutto and her party warned on election eve that a vote for the People's Party would 'damn the nation forever to the hell of Western corruption.' And opposition campaign workers handed out posters of Bhutto's face pasted on the bikini-clad body of a pinup girl." Even her chief opponent, Mian Nawaz Sharif of the Islamic Democratic Alliance, claimed "his party's triumph . . . would be the defeat of agents of India and Israel: 'Islamic order and social justice will win the battle against those who want to make Pakistan a secular state,'" according to the *New York Times.* The paper also wrote that Sharif, on a rural campaign swing, "tried to exploit equally primitive, but darker emotions . . . . 'The Bhutto ladies,' he said, referring to Benazir and her mother, Nusrat, 'danced with foreign men in London and Paris. I'd like to see them live here, in this village, with you and me.'"

At the nation's 33,328 polling places, Bhutto's PPP captured 92 of the parliament's 237 seats, with which she was able to build a ruling coalition with lesser parties. The election, mostly, was uneventful. According to *Time* magazine, a Pakistani editor wrote: "Peace has not broken down. Violence has remained well within the limits of subcontinental activity." Roughly 75 percent of the country is illiterate, which meant many voters had to cast their ballots by symbol rather than name—an arrow for Bhutto and the PPP, a bicycle for the Democratic Alliance. When Bhutto was officially appointed prime minister by the nation's president several weeks later, it marked the first time power was transferred peacefully in Pakistan's 41 years.

Pakistan, as a nation, has existed only since 1947 when it was carved from part of India. Throughout its brief history, Islam has been the uniting force of a country otherwise split into tribal, language, and divergent regional histories. The military ruled almost exclusively until 1971 when Zulfikar Ali Bhutto won a popular vote.

The Bhutto family came from the feudal southern province of Sindh, where they were wealthy landowners. Benazir's father, Berkeley-educated, sent her to Radcliffe at the age of 16, where she studied international relations. There, she dressed in sweat pants to play squash but refused to wear dresses or dance, and she kept to Islamic dietary laws in the dining room, according to *Vanity Fair* magazine. "I let my hair grow long and straight and was flattered when my friends . . . told me I looked like Joan Baez," she wrote in her autobiography. She traveled to Washington to march in a protest against the American war in Vietnam and wore a "Bring the Boys Home Now" button, she wrote in her book. She followed her father to Oxford where she became president of the Union Society debating club. According to the *Chicago Tribune,* the elder Bhutto imagined his daughter returning to Pakistan as foreign minister. But while at Oxford, General Zia, emboldened by what were widely perceived as rigged elections staged by the elder Bhutto in 1987, engineered a successful coup.

Zulkifar Ali Bhutto was jailed under brutal conditions, eventually wasting away to 80 pounds before he was executed in 1979. When she returned to Pakistan in 1977, Benazir Bhutto was also imprisoned and later kept under house arrest. Her hearing was damaged permanently after a six-month sentence in the searing heat of a Pakistani desert prison. She was held for months in solitary confinement (Zia was afraid that, free, she could topple his government) before finally being allowed to go into exile in Britain. She returned to Pakistan in 1986, a year after Zia lifted martial law that had been in place since his coup.

Even supporters of Bhutto have worried how her extreme devotion to her father will affect her stewardship over Pakistan. After the election, *Newsweek* wrote: "For a long time [Zulfikar Ali Bhutto's] daughter-protegee seemed to be bent on revenge. Lately she has talked instead of reconciliation." And the *Chicago Tribune* noted, "Prime Minister [Zulfikar Ali] Bhutto had run a corrupt, autocratic government, jailing dozens of opponents and demanding blind obedience from his ministers and other subordinates." Her autobiography, *Daughter of Destiny,* scoffs at the allegations of rigged elections. The *New York Times* said her "most intense, almost blind devotion centered on her father, who involved her in politics from an early age. Prime Minister Bhutto was a controversial figure, politically and personally, but Ms. Bhutto will brook no criticism of him." Benazir Bhutto, according to the *Times,* frequently tells the story of how her father, in his prison cell, took her hand and said, "My daughter, should anything happen to me, you will continue my mission."

But not only the father and daughter suffered. Her brother, Shah Nawaz, died of poisoning in Paris, a murder Benazir Bhutto believes was committed by rightist elements who had also plotted against the father. And her mother, Nusrat, also spent long stretches in detention, contracting tuberculosis in the crowded, unsanitary conditions. Much of Benazir Bhutto's time in prison was spent in solitary confinement. In her autobiography, she wrote of 1981: "Flaking cement. Iron bars. And silence. Utter silence. I am back in total isolation, the cells around me in the locked ward all emptied. I strain for the sound of a human voice. There is only silence."

Benazir Bhutto's final march to the office of prime minister began in 1986. On her return from exile, an estimated one to three million Pakistanis greeted her arrival at Lahore airport. Bhutto rode on top of a truck to a park where she gave her first homecoming speech. The drive, which would normally take 15 minutes, took 10 hours because of the huge crowd. Zia jailed her briefly, but by May 1988, he dissolved Parliament and called for elections. Government opponents were already fretting over the possibility of rigged elections, but Zia and 30 others, including the American ambassador to Pakistan, died in an unexplained plane crash on August 17, 1988. Without Zia to control the de facto military government, Bhutto and the PPP swept to victory three months later.

Her first state visit to Washington, in June of 1989, got rave reviews from most observers. But *Newsweek* reported: "Bhutto's visit comes at a particularly delicate time in U.S.-Pakistan relations. With the 10-year-old Afghan civil war moving to an end, Pakistani officials worry that the United States no longer needs a close ally in Islamabad [the Pakistani capital] to aid the Afghan rebels. Pakistan is the third largest recipient of U.S. aid, behind Israel and Egypt, and Bhutto's government desperately needs the aid to continue." By most accounts, she appeared to calm the fears of American officials, preserving, at least for the short run, the critical foreign aid. Bhutto appeared less excited about building nuclear weapons than many conservative politicians in the country. During her visit she pledged to pursue only peaceful uses of nuclear energy. Not all American observers took that entirely at face value. Her economics are capitalist. To erase Third World debt she prescribes decentralization, deregulation, and investment incentives. But *U.S. News & World Report* wrote that her exact economic plan will be largely dictated by the International Monetary Fund, which was ready with a $900 million loan by late 1988, provided Pakistan implement deficit cutting and tax reform.

At home, her first challenge—both politically and personally—will be getting along with the military, which still eats 60 percent of the nation's budget. The *Chicago Tribune* reported, "The military is the nation's only tightly run organization, analysts say, and its leaders have made no secret of their contempt for politicians whom they consider opportunistic and corrupt." And also at home, Bhutto declared war on the nation's illegal drug trade—both because of the internal social damage it caused and because U.S. officials have complained that tons of heroin from Pakistan end up on American streets each year.

Zulfikar Ali Bhutto urged his daughter—and other Pakistani women—to "throw off their veils and become productive members of Pakistani society," wrote the *Los Angeles Times*. Still, more than a decade later, many of those women were turned away at the polls because their husbands refused to give them the government identification card necessary to vote. "The main point is," said Pakistani author and women's activist Farida Shaheed, "you don't get political power in this country by representing women. You get power by representing men." Bhutto defies Western standards of women's liberation. Her arranged marriage to Asif Ali Zardari, another rich Sindhi, who came with his own polo team, surprised many in the west. But the arranged marriage, *Ms.* magazine reported, "may shield her from criticism by Islamic fundamentalists who attack her for advocating modern, Westernized ideals about the role of women." And Bhutto told an old Radcliffe friend writing for *Life* magazine: "My mother tells me that love will come. But Asif and I will have a marriage based on something stronger than love."

Bhutto, like Indira Gandhi or Corazon Aquino [see index for *Newsmakers* entry], inherited a dynastic mantle of leadership from a male relative: Gandhi from her father and Aquino from her slain husband. The *New York Times* wrote, "Ms. Bhutto believes herself to be the avenger of a martyred leader." The distinction is important to a society that sees her as something more than a woman. The *New York Times* wrote: "The worship of Benazir Bhutto is less a sign of liberalism or female emancipation than of Pakistan's essentially Indian heritage. The Great Mother, who can be both horribly destructive and divinely benevolent, is one of the foundations of Indian religious worship."

Writings

Daughter of Destiny (autobiography), Simon & Schuster, 1989.

Sources

Chicago Tribune, November 13, 1988; November 14, 1988; November 20, 1988.
Los Angeles Times, December 4, 1988.
Life, February, 1988.
Ms., March, 1988.
Newsweek, November 14, 1988; November 28, 1988; December 12, 1988; June 19, 1989.
New York Times, April 11, 1986; September 21, 1986; December 2, 1988; December 4, 1988.
New York Times Magazine, January 15, 1989.
Time, November 21, 1988; November 28, 1988; June 19, 1989.
U.S. News & World Report, November 28, 1988.
Vanity Fair, May, 1986; March, 1988.
Washington Post, December 2, 1988.

—Sidelights by Harvey Dickson

Steven Bochco

AP/Wide World Photos

Television producer

Born December 16, 1943, in New York, N.Y.; son of Rudolph (a concert violinist) and Mimi (an artist) Bochco; married second wife, Barbara Bosson, c. 1969; children: (second marriage) Melissa, Jesse. *Education:* Attended New York University; Carnegie Tech (now Carnegie-Mellon University), B.A., 1966.

Addresses: *Home*—Pacific Palisades, Calif. *Office*—Twentieth Century-Fox, 10201 West Pico Blvd., Los Angeles, Calif. 90064.

Career

Universal Studios, Los Angeles, Calif., script writer, 1966–78; MTM Enterprises, Studio City, Calif., writer-producer, 1978–85; Twentieth Century-Fox, Los Angeles, Calif., writer-producer, 1985—. Story editor for television series "Columbo"; co-creator of television series "Hill Street Blues" and "L.A. Law."

Awards: Emmy Award nomination, 1971, for an episode of "Columbo"; eight Emmy Awards, 1981–85, for "Hill Street Blues"; two George Foster Peabody Awards and three Image Awards from the National Association for the Advancement of Colored People, all for "Hill Street Blues"; four Golden Globe Awards; six People's Choice Awards; two Writer's Guild awards; Edgar Allan Poe Award; Emmy Award nomination, 1988, for "L.A. Law."

Sidelights:

Writer-producer Steven Bochco is the architect of a revolution in prime time network television programming. Bochco's tough and explicit dramas—most notably "Hill Street Blues" and "L.A. Law"—challenge the standards and even the very aims of television by exploring complex, realistic adult situations fraught with violence, moral ambiguity, and sex. *Time* correspondent Richard Zoglin noted that Bochco seeks the viewer who is dissatisfied with regular prime time fare, so he therefore "creates shows for people who don't watch TV. No producer of the 1980s has been more influential." If awards are a measure of influence, Bochco's stature cannot be questioned. He has received every major citation bestowed by the television industry, including eight Emmy Awards, four Golden Globe Awards, and two prestigious George Foster Peabody prizes. Moreover, he is consistently acclaimed by critics and his peers in production for showing that "there's an audience for excellence," to quote colleague David Milch in *Time.* "Hollywood's brightest and most innovative producer of television drama" is occasionally an abrasive and driven individual, according to *New York Times* contributor Robert Lindsey. Having been in the entertainment business almost twenty-five years, Bochco retains few illusions about his work or his high goals. "I look at myself as swimming upstream," he told the *New York Times.* "I want to do stuff that challenges folks and entertains folks, and I'm willing to take the risk that some people will not like what I do.... I've succeeded in spite of this business, not because of it."

Many talented artists consider television work beneath their dignity. Bochco revels in the medium. "I love the idea of communicating ideas to, and entertaining, a mass audience," he said in an *American Film* interview. "And I love the idea of doing it with, hopefully, some grace and style and wit and complexity." Therein lies television's greatest challenge, however—it demands 22 hour-long shows per season at reasonable cost and on a brutally short timetable. In a commentary for *U.S. News & World Report,* Bochco admitted that television's staggering demands far outstrip its creative community's ability to meet them. "The pressure becomes paralyzing," he said. "You settle for things that you normally wouldn't accept. Given these demands, there is a lot more on television that's good than people give the industry credit for."

Like most producers, Bochco surrounds himself with teams of writers and a support staff to help him meet the hectic pace. Just as his best-known shows use an ensemble cast, the stories themselves—and even the characters—are created by a committee. As David Freeman noted in *Esquire,* "the goal, of course, is for the collective whole to be greater than the sum of its parts." Still, Bochco has final say over every script, and he is most often personally responsible for the placement of scenes in the program's final cut. More importantly, Bochco himself undertakes the most harrowing aspects of television production, including conceiving new show ideas, demanding ample budgets, and defending his more graphic scenes and language against censorship by the network's "standards and practices" division. Bochco's aggressive maneuvers within the corporate environment—his stubborn refusal to abrogate power over his shows—have earned him enemies as well as admirers. "Steve's a difficult guy," former employer Grant Tinker told the *New York Times.* "I think he's somewhat free-form and somewhat erratic in his work habits, but he's very, very, talented. He is very competitive in a way that he probably wouldn't admit. He wants to do better than the other guys, and he won't let up."

Bochco was born in New York City on December 16, 1943. He grew up in Manhattan, the son of a concert violinist who always struggled to make ends meet. Bochco himself was attracted to music, and he attended the New York City High School of Music and Art, graduating with average grades. He told *Rolling Stone* that when he was a high school senior, his adviser informed him that he was "not college material." Nevertheless he applied, and having earned a scholarship from an aptitude test, enrolled at New York University. The following year he transferred to Carnegie Tech (now Carnegie-Mellon University) in Pittsburgh, where he majored in writing. "The penny finally dropped," he said. "I got in as a playwright. I'd always written stuff. And even in high school, teachers had told me I was talented, encouraged me. Now, all of a sudden, I was surrounded by people with whom I shared common interests." Indeed, Bochco's friends at Carnegie included Charles Haid and Bruce Weitz, who he would later cast as policemen on "Hill Street Blues," and Michael Tucker, who would eventually become a regular on "L.A. Law." Also while at Carnegie, Bochco met Barbara Bosson, his future wife and cast member of "Hill Street Blues" and "Hooperman." Bochco was married to someone else at that time, but his romance with Bosson was kindled some years later when they became reacquainted in Los Angeles.

Bochco is the first to admit that he got television work without the classic struggle. After a summer internship at Universal Studios, he was offered a full-time job upon graduation from Carnegie. "I didn't wait for my grades, my diploma, anything," he remembered in *Rolling Stone.* "Michael Tucker and I piled into my car and drove fifty-two hours from Pittsburgh to L.A. We were going to make our fortunes. It was wonderful." In Hollywood Bochco found himself taking unsold TV pilots and old episodes of "Chrysler Theatre" and padding them with extra material that was then filmed and spliced into the original show. He earned $15,000 his first year.

In 1970 he was appointed story editor for "Columbo," one of Universal's most promising series. Ironically, the first episode of "Columbo" that he wrote was directed by another ambitious youngster, Steven Spielberg. Both men were still in their mid-twenties. "Columbo" turned into a very popular show, with its wise-cracking, trenchcoat-clad detective who snooped among the rich and famous. Bochco received his first Emmy nomination in 1971 for his writing achievement on the program. "Because of 'Columbo's' success," he told *American Film,* "I gained a degree of professional recognition in the business that I hadn't had before." Gradually Bochco became known as a specialist in police shows; among others, he wrote for "Name of the Game," "Griff," "Delvecchio," and "McMillan and Wife."

Despite his success, Bochco grew dissatisfied with the way his work was abused by Universal's producers. He told *American Film:* "I was so disturbed, as I guess many writers are, at seeing the terrible disparity between what was in my head and what they were putting on the screen, that I thought: I've got to be able to do something about this. And I never had an impulse to be a director, ever, so I thought: Well, at least if I produced the thing, I'd have some significant input. I started producing the next year." In 1978 Bochco joined MTM enterprises, the production company then headed by Grant Tinker and Mary Tyler Moore. MTM had proven a fertile ground for innovative television, producing such programs as "The Mary Tyler Moore Show," "Rhoda," and "Lou Grant."

After a few failed attempts at launching shows, Bochco was approached by NBC executives in 1980 and asked to do another police drama. He and his partner Michael Kozoll were less than enthusiastic about the request. Only one aspect of the project intrigued Bochco and Kozoll: NBC, then the least popular network and in dire straits, offered an unprecedented degree of creative autonomy. The writers were given *carte blanche* to bring a fresh approach to the cops-and-robbers genre, and they did it by enlarging the number—and the psychological dimensions—of the characters. The pilot episode of "Hill Street Blues" uncovered both the personal and professional lives of some fictitious inner-city policemen, and the unusual carrying-over of plots from one week to the next followed thereafter. Bochco told *American Film:* "As we began to develop these characters, we knew that we couldn't tell conventional stories and also meet the needs of eight fully fleshed-out characters. So we began to think of it more in terms of a tapestry.... So the show kept getting denser and denser, with more and more information packed into the frame."

"Hill Street Blues" was a mid-season replacement in 1981. Had NBC been a stronger programming contender that year, the series may not have survived; it languished low in the all-important Nielsen ratings throughout its first season. NBC executives decided—unusually—to give the show a chance to attract an audience. Praise from critics and eight Emmy nominations in its debut season sparked interest in "Hill Street Blues," especially among young, urban, and relatively affluent viewers. In a *Harper's* magazine article, Bochco observed that this small audience nevertheless "represented a potent force in terms of buying power, and was thus very desirable to advertisers." "Hill Street Blues" eventually gained ground in the ratings—although it never reached the top ten in popularity—and ran for five years, garnering a record twenty-six Emmy Awards.

Often uncompromisingly violent, "Hill Street" portrayed the day-to-day events in a ghetto district police precinct, with open explorations of drug abuse, alcoholism, racism, child abuse, and marital infidelity. Todd Gitlin notes in *Inside Prime Time* that "Hill Street Blues" "was as good as series television has gotten.... *Hill Street* demonstrated that the instinct for craftsmanship does not automatically disqualify a show from noticeable, if not epoch-making, popularity. Intelligent writing, it seemed, had its appeals; so did some unusually good acting, the serial form, ensemble work, an interesting texture. Complexity of plot and atmosphere did not intimidate ten or fifteen million American households." In short, the success of "Hill Street Blues" proved that quite a few viewers wanted quality adult drama.

"I'm not afraid of failing, but I am afraid of doing bad work."

Any elation Bochco may have felt about his newfound power was quashed two years later. His first show after "Hill Street Blues"—a drama about a baseball team entitled "Bay City Blues"—lasted only four episodes. Then Bochco began to have difficulties with "Hill Street Blues," which he continued to produce. The program consistently ran over budget, and Bochco refused to compromise his standards in order to curb costs. In 1985 Bochco was fired by MTM—officially because of his "profligacy" and unofficially because of his strident personality. No unemployment checks were issued to Steven Bochco, however. He had a $15 million commitment from NBC to develop one or more new shows, so Twentieth Century-Fox gladly welcomed him into its ranks.

By that time Bochco had settled on producing a show about a law firm, and he was doubly determined to prove himself capable of creating quality work at reasonable expense. A series about lawyers, filmed mostly indoors and in Los Angeles, provided the right blend of story possibility and black-ink accounting. "This is the most litigious society, I think, in the history of mankind," he noted in the *New York*

Times. "Fifty per cent of the people in America get divorced. I can only guess at the percentage of the people who get sued or sue somebody else. It becomes an organized way of dealing with our hostilities."

"L.A. Law" had its debut in 1986, and it was an immediate hit. Similar in format to "Hill Street Blues," it offers a pastiche of the daily workings of the fictitious McKenzie, Brackman law firm, where partners and associates try to live by their consciences and make money, not necessarily in that order. According to Robert Lindsey in the *New York Times,* the attorneys "are nearly all unpleasant, portrayed, with few exceptions, as unprincipled hired guns who, uninterested in truth and justice, go for the jugular to win a case and make a buck." Conversely, Zoglin finds the characters "upright, principled, sensitive and dedicated. There are few hints that ethical compromises, or even a healthy professional detachment, might be part of the terrain." Such varied critical responses serve as evidence of the show's depth; its cast grapples with modern problems like AIDS, euthanasia, and employment of the disabled. Lindsey admits that the series "has little of the cartoon quality that tends to characterize prime-time soap operas like 'Dallas' or 'Dynasty,' though it revels in a similar villainy. Rather, the presumption seems to be that, yes, this is what life in the legal profession is like, and such a blunt vision has rarely been accomodated in prime-time programming."

For Bochco the show has been both a triumph and a tribulation. He has proven—to MTM and the industry in general—that he can bring a series in at budget, but a conflict with co-producer Terry Louise Fisher sparked a costly lawsuit against Bochco and Twentieth Century-Fox that has been settled out of court. Bochco intends to keep producing "L.A. Law" himself while he embarks on a lengthy project of program development for ABC. His ability to conceive a show and then turn it over to others for the daily production routine is demonstrated by "Hooperman," a comedy-drama of his creation that first aired in 1988.

His hectic schedule notwithstanding, Bochco manages to be home for dinner with his family most evenings. He lives in Pacific Palisades with Bosson and their two teenaged children, Melissa and Jesse. Home life is one antidote to the enormous pressure Bochco feels in his professional endeavors. The producer who has set new standards for network television told the *New York Times* that the drive for success "comes from inside." He added: "I'm not afraid of failing, but I am afraid of doing bad work. It's not so much that I want to top myself. It's how do I maintain the standard?"

Sources

Books

Contemporary Literary Criticism, Volume 35, Gale, 1985.

Gitlin, Todd, *Inside Prime Time,* Pantheon Books, 1983.

Periodicals

American Film, July, 1988.
Esquire, January, 1985; June, 1988.
Harper's, March, 1985.
New York Times, April 27, 1982; August 24, 1986.
People, September 28, 1981.
Rolling Stone, April 21, 1988.
Time, May 2, 1988.
U.S. News & World Report, June 20, 1983.

—Sketch by Anne Janette Johnson

Wade Boggs

AP/Wide World Photos

Professional baseball player

Full name, Wade Anthony Boggs; born June 15, 1958, in Omaha, Neb.; son of Win (a military officer) and Susan Boggs; married; wife's name, Debbie; children: Meagann, Brett. *Education:* Graduated from high school in Tampa, Fla.

Addresses: *Office*—Boston Red Sox, Fenway Park, 4 Yawkey Way, Boston, Mass. 02215.

Career

Baseball player in minor leagues, 1977–82, and in major leagues with Boston Red Sox, 1982–.

Awards: Winner of American League batting title, 1983, 1985, 1986, 1987, and 1988.

Sidelights

Most major league baseball players of Wade Boggs's stature are seen as local heroes and national icons. Boggs, the most consistent hitter since the end of the Second World War, has become a star of the scandal sheets as well as the baseball diamond in Boston, where he plays third base for the Red Sox. In the wake of a twelve million dollar palimony suit arising from a four-year extramarital affair, Boggs has been nicknamed "baseball's Lee Marvin" and has seen his accomplishments on the field almost eclipsed by his activities behind closed doors. According to Dan Shaughnessy of the *Boston Globe,* however, the "scandal and embarrassment haven't left open wounds. It is as if the man feels nothing." Shaughnessy is referring to Boggs's ability to keep his batting average well above .300 even as court appearances loom and his ex-lover, Margo Adams, gives details of their relationship to national magazines. "A hitter has to concentrate," Shaughnessy observed, "and Boggs is the ultimate hitter. He has inordinate powers of concentration." This single-minded concentration has been demonstrated over the course of his major league career, during which Boggs has become only the fifth player in history to bat at least .350 four years straight.

Often compared to baseball greats such as Ty Cobb, Lou Gehrig, and Pete Rose, Boggs has broken some of his sport's oldest standing records. He has won the American League batting title five times in six seasons, is the only player ever to have 200 hits six years in a row, and has the fourth-highest batting average in the history of the game. His name does not immediately come to mind as an all-time great—like Mickey Mantle or Gehrig—simply because most of his hits are singles and doubles, and he hits early in the lineup with fewer teammates on base.

Some fans and members of the Boston media have characterized Boggs as egotistical, a man striving for personal glory rather than the good of the team. Boggs answered this charge in the *Boston Globe.* "Naturally it's a game of winning and losing," he said. "It's a team game made up of 24 individuals. Everybody wants to do well. If you didn't, what fun would it be to get a hit or accomplish something? Once you get out there, it's one on one. There's no guy to set a pick for you. No guy to throw a block for you. No guy to shoot the puck over to you. When you get a hit, you've won. And the team wins, because you've contributed to a winning effort." Despite his personal problems, Boggs is determined to continue the record-breaking offensive play that has characterized his six-year career in the American League.

Boggs takes some good-spirited ribbing for his superstitious adherence to a strict daily regimen, based on exact timing for meals, warmups, and batting practice. In *People* magazine, Boggs admitted that his quiet obsession with precision dates to his childhood. His father, a career military officer, demanded a regimented lifestyle both at work and at home. "Some kids wouldn't have liked growing up in a military household, but it was the greatest thing that happened to me," Boggs told *Sports Illustrated.* "Dinner was always at 5:30, and if you weren't home at 5:30, you didn't eat. So you learned to always know where the clocks were in you friends' houses, and to this day I always notice clocks. I woke up at precisely the same time every day for 18 years. If I woke up, say, 30 minutes late, I was out of sync all day. From the time I was small, my pet peeve was being rushed, so I left for school at exactly the same time every day."

Boggs also remembers that his father's high standards made him aspire to excellence from a very young age. "When I was 6, I knew I wanted to be a baseball player," he told *People,* "and from the time I was 12 or 13, it became my obsession." Boggs's mother told *People* that her son was naturally gifted from earliest youth: "It seemed like he was born to hit just like some kids are born to play the piano." Still, Boggs practiced diligently, selected his bats with scrupulous care, and once even cancelled a Saturday night date in order to study Ted Williams's *The Science of Hitting.* Dedicated to sports though he was, Boggs managed to earn honor roll grades at his Tampa, Florida, high school, and he was offered a scholarship to the University of South Carolina. He turned down the scholarship—and college in general—in order to play professional baseball.

In his last two years of high-school ball, Boggs batted .520 and .485 with a wooden bat (aluminum bats, which cause hits to carry further, are more popular with high school and college players). Boggs fully expected to be drafted high, even though his running and fielding needed work. He was "crushed," he told *Sports Illustrated,* when he was picked in the seventh round by the Red Sox. He decided to sign, however, feeling that "the other scouts were wrong" about his ability. Accepting a $7500 bonus, he headed to Elmira, New York, for the first of six seasons in the minor leagues.

"When I was 6, I knew I wanted to be a baseball player, and from the time I was 12 or 13, it became my obsession."

His first year was his worst—he hit .263 with only six extra-base hits and made sixteen errors at third. In the off-season, he married his high school sweetheart, and according to *Sports Illustrated* writer Peter Gammons, he "hasn't seen the downside of .306 since." Slowly Boggs climbed through the minors, batting .311 in A, .325 in AA, and .306 in AAA. Needless to say, he was crushed again in 1980 when the Red Sox sent him back to the minors and traded with California for third baseman Carney Lansford. Boggs told Pete Axthelm of *Newsweek* that he didn't become impatient during his long tenure in the minors, because he decided that wherever he might play he would "give a 100 percent effort." On the other hand, Margo Adams has suggested in some of her interviews that Boggs feels cheated by the long years he spent waiting for a chance at the big leagues.

Boggs was finally placed on the permanent Red Sox roster in 1982. To quote *Sports Illustrated* correspondent John Garrity, the young player proceeded to accomplish "one of the most prodigious starts in history." In his first 200 big league games, Boggs batted .361, and soon he was close to the top of the American League in several offensive categories, including average, hits, runs, on-base percentage, and runs produced. An intensive program to improve his fielding and running improved both somewhat, but Boggs was still haunted by numerous errors. He also lacked game-winning RBIs and home runs, both standard measures of major league excellence. *Boston Globe* columnist Bob Ryan is quoted in *Sports Illustrated* as having said in 1983: "There is no evidence to suggest [Boggs] is a man you want to send up there in the late innings with men in scoring position." As if in retaliation for the criticism, Boggs went on a late-season streak that saw him batting .360 with runners on second and third, and he had three ninth-inning game-winning hits in an eight-game stretch. Walt Hriniak, then Red Sox hitting coach, quipped to *Sports Illustrated:* "For him to swing for home runs now would be a mistake. They'll come with maturity. Even if Wade stays the same, who *cares* if he hits home runs?"

Indeed, although Boggs has never become a home run hitter, he is a significant threat nonetheless, a patient performer who often hits cleanly after taking two strikes. Boggs described his view of hitting in *People:* "The main question ... is who's in control, the pitcher or the batter. From the moment the game begins, I watch the pitcher's every move. Even when he starts warming up, I watch to see what he's trying to work on, whether he's getting his breaking ball over. I can tell by looking in his eyes or from his whole body language how he's feeling that day, and then I prepare myself. Once I'm in the box, I settle in for as long as it takes to get a hit. I'm a firm believer that the more pitches you see the better your chances. I never let myself get up there and simply swing away .... I'm determined to stay in there until I get the pitch *I* want .... The trick is to hold out, to take the first strike and even the second, waiting for the pitcher to make a mistake—which he is bound to do, sooner or later .... My goal is to hit the ball as hard and as consistently as I can. Too many players lose it all when they reach for the home run."

Axthelm offered his own assessment of Boggs's talent: "Boggs tempts outsiders to label him as a natural. But natural ability is as illusory as luck. Wade is not particularly fast or strong and his defense at third base is modest at best. He has put a lot of careful thought and hard work into making hitting look so easy." Ironically, Axthelm concluded of the Red Sox star: "Pure of mind and pure of left-handed batting stroke, Boggs is as refreshing and innocent as a warm day at Fenway Park."

"Pure of mind" and "innocent" are hardly terms Axthelm might use to describe Boggs today. While he

In a game against the Texas Rangers, Wade Boggs dives for a sharply hit ball. He got up in time to make the play. AP/Wide World Photos.

compiled his impressive statistics on the field and won Bostonian hearts, Boggs was quietly leading a double life marked by infidelity and childish antics. He met Margo Adams in a bar in Anaheim, California, early in the 1984 season. Adams, a mortgage banker, accepted a date with Boggs and shortly thereafter traveled to Kansas City to be with him again. Soon she was flying in to meet him whenever the Red Sox played on the road. Adams claims that she and Boggs had a verbal agreement that he would compensate her for wages lost during these trips. Boggs and Adams continued their affair until 1988. After the breakup, Adams sought a financial settlement and opted for the courts when Boggs did not cooperate. The story broke in the spring of 1988, and while Debbie Boggs stood by her husband, other Red Sox players, Boston fans, and the Red Sox management were not so sanguine. At least one fight erupted on the Boston team bus when other Red Sox players were threatened with subpoenas. And trade rumors involving Boggs began to circulate liberally. Boggs finally apologized to his teammates in a private meeting, and he proceeded to have yet another .360 season at the plate. *Boston Globe* reporter Larry Whiteside commented: "Like the eye of a hurricane, [Boggs] remains calm while others call him egotistical and selfish. That is simply his manner, and Boggs has no idea of changing it."

If Boggs is able to triumph over the bad publicity, it may be because of the strange superstitious rules and regimens he follows like clockwork every day. Gammons calls Boggs's pre-game strategy a "cocoon" that is "woven daily from the delicate threads of nutrition, habit, discipline and superstition. When the minutiae are completed and he has eaten his chicken, left his [home], taken his ground balls, meditated, concluded his methodical batting practice, run his wind sprints and approached his position with Greenwich Mean Time precision, then—and only then—is Wade Boggs prepared to do what he does quite unlike anyone else. Hit." Boggs eats a steady diet of chicken because it is his "lucky" food. He draws a Hebrew character in the batter's box with his toe before each at-bat. He runs his wind sprints at exactly 7:17 each evening before a night game, and he segregates his bats so they don't "pick up bad habits." Boggs claims that these rituals are the secret of his success. "In my cocoon, I can eliminate distraction and variables and shut out the entire world except for me and the pitcher," he told *Sports Illustrated.* When asked for his reaction to the Margo Adams lawsuit in the *Boston Globe,* Boggs said simply: "It's very easy to block it out. I go between the white lines and forget about it."

Certainly Boggs's concentration is helped by the fact that his wife, Debbie, has forgiven him and intends to continue their marriage. Boggs expressed his relief at this happy outcome in a March 1989 interview with Barbara Walters. Facing what may be lengthy litigation and further sparks of scandal as Adams continues to tell tales, Boggs has decided to concentrate on one of the constants in his life: baseball. "Playing baseball is all I ever wanted to do," he told the *Boston Globe.* "I never wanted to do anything else. It's all fun. The day baseball doesn't become fun is the day that Wade Boggs goes home and goes fishing or something. It's over. Naturally with all this malarkey, . . . it has been hectic. But it's still fun."

Writings

Boggs!, Contemporary Books, 1986.

Sources

Boston Globe, July 28, 1988; September 23, 1988; October 5, 1988.
Newsweek, August 22, 1983.
Penthouse, April, 1989; May, 1989.
People, June 16, 1986.
Sport, July, 1986; November, 1987.
Sports Illustrated, August 8, 1983; August 12, 1985; April 14, 1986.

—Sidelights by Mark Kram

Alan Bond

AP/Wide World Photos

Entrepreneur and racing syndicate executive

Born April 22, 1938, in London, England; married Eileen Hughes, 1955; children: John, Craig, Susan, Jodie.

Addresses: 89 Watkins Rd., Dalkeith, Western Australia 6009, Australia.

Career

Former sign painter; later, a real estate developer; chairman of the board, Bond Corp., Perth, Australia. Executive of yacht-racing syndicates, including the syndicate that owns *Australia II,* winner of the 1983 America's Cup.

Sidelights

Considered one of Australia's foremost entrepreneurs, Alan Bond heads a financial empire with holdings that range from breweries and television stations to gold mines and a South American telephone company. Bond is often described as aggressive and impulsive. "He makes decisions quickly and then works out what they involve," noted the *Economist.* Outside the business world, he is best known as the chairman of the syndicate that ran *Australia II,* the first challenger to defeat the United States in the history of the America's Cup.

Born in London, England, Bond moved with his parents to Australia when he was 13. He dropped out of school one year later and took a job painting signs, most of which pertained to real estate. He also took night classes in accounting. While still a teenager, he borrowed for a deposit on some land, which he later sold for 1,000 percent profit. Bond then formed his own real estate concern. By the time he was 21, he was a millionaire.

He diversified in later years, eventually creating the Bond Corporation, a holding company with interests in mining, land development, transportation, energy, and communications. "Bond has specialised in raiding old established corporations that have grown sleepy or complacent," wrote the *Economist.* Breweries have been a frequent takeover target; Bond owns several—including Swan, Castlemaine Tooheys, Pittsburgh Brewing, and G. Heileman—in Australia and the United States. He has borrowed heavily to expand his empire, a fact that contributed to his corporation's lowered stock rating in the early 1980s. But Bond thrives on risks and challenges. This was made clear in 1983, when he backed *Australia II.*

It was his fourth try for the America's Cup. Bond's quest began in 1970, when he boarded, uninvited, an American yacht built for that year's race. He was run off by a crew member. Angered by the man's rudeness, and fascinated by the boat's design, Bond vowed to someday win the Cup. In 1974, he entered *Southern Cross,* which lost 4–0. In 1977 and 1980, he entered *Australia,* which lost 4–0 and 4–1, respectively. Finally, "Bond did what had been thought to be impossible," the *New York Times* noted. He introduced a winning challenger. Described as "an unusual 12-Meter with a winged keel," *Australia II* took the Cup from the American defender, *Liberty,* 4–3. In 1987, Bond tried—but failed—to defend the prize. The United States reclaimed the Cup with Dennis Conner's *Stars and Stripes.*

Nevertheless, as *Fortune* reported, Bond's earlier victory "made him a national hero, the most famous businessman in Australia." It also made him one of the richest. By 1988, he was the "biggest single private employer" in the city of Perth, according to the *Economist.* "If we have the determination to win the Cup, people figure we have the management to succeed with the company," Bond told *Fortune.* "[The Cup] took us five years, and it showed that nothing is impossible."

Sources

Economist, January 4, 1986; March 7, 1987; November 7, 1987; June 11, 1988.

Fortune, October 27, 1986; December 21, 1987.

New York Times, September 27, 1983; January 5, 1987.

Sports Illustrated, November 10, 1986.

—Sketch by Denise Wiloch

Lisa Bonet

AP/Wide World Photos

Actress

Born November 16, 1967, in San Francisco, Calif.; daughter of Arlene Bonet (a teacher); married Lenny "Romeo" Kravitz (a musician), 1987; children: one.

Addresses: *Home*—New York, N.Y.

Career

Member of cast of television series "The Cosby Show," 1984–; star of "A Different World," beginning 1987. Has appeared in film "Angel Heart" and on television series "St. Elsewhere."

Sidelights

In 1984, NBC introduced what would become one of the most successful series in television history—"The Cosby Show." The situation comedy revolves around the Huxtables, an upper-middle-class black family headed by a doctor (played by Bill Cosby) and his lawyer wife. The show's huge popularity made stars of its cast members, including a young actress named Lisa Bonet. Bonet was still a teenager when she signed to play Denise Huxtable, the family's second-eldest daughter. A relative newcomer to show business, Bonet has made a number of surprising—and sometimes controversial—career decisions.

Born in San Francisco, Bonet is the offspring of an interracial marriage that ended shortly after she was born. She was raised by her mother, a white teacher, and has not seen her father, who is part black and part Cherokee Indian, since she was a toddler. As a child, Bonet felt abandoned and confused; her racial background was a source of constant anxiety. "I had absolutely no idea where I belonged in life," she told Lynn Norment in *Ebony*. "The Black kids would call me 'Oreo,' and I just didn't feel totally at home and accepted with all those, you know, White rich people." Her sense of being an outsider began to fade when she entered high school and enrolled in acting classes. She worked in commercials and eventually landed a part in an episode of "St. Elsewhere." A short time later, she was cast in "Cosby."

Bonet is comfortable with her role and believes that it reflects much of her own personality. "I like playing Denise," she remarked to Dan Yakir of *USA Weekend*. "She's definitely not a geek. I admire her." Three years after "Cosby" debuted, Bonet was spun off into her own comedy series, "A Different World." This show follows Denise Huxtable as she leaves home to enter Hillman College, a fictional, largely black, school. "The show allows us to develop the themes of maturity and responsibility," producer Tom Werner noted to Andy Meisler of the *New York Times*. "This show would be exciting even if Denise Huxtable wasn't in it." In fact, Bonet was temporarily written out of the series when her pregnancy was announced.

Bonet's departure from "A Different World" fueled rumors of a rift between the actress and Bill Cosby. These stories began to surface in 1987, when her first film, "Angel Heart," was released. In this occult thriller, Bonet plays a voodoo priestess who becomes involved with a private detective. There is an explicit sex scene, which earned the movie an X rating. Director Alan Parker later deleted ten seconds from the footage, and the film's rating was reduced to an R.

"Angel Heart" met with mixed reviews and much publicity. Some observers believed that Bonet was making a deliberate attempt to break away from her "Cosby" image. This was reinforced when she posed nude for *Interview* and *Rolling Stone* magazines. According to Norment, Bill Cosby is philosophical about Bonet's choices: "As a young woman, it is very, very difficult to live and have the kind of freedom she has. Things move quickly. I think Lisa has matured . . . and I think she has her head in place in terms of protecting Lisa."

Sources

Boxoffice, May, 1987.
Ebony, December, 1987.
Interview, April, 1987.
Maclean's, March 16, 1987.
New York Times, April 26, 1987.
Newsweek, March 16, 1987.
People, March 16, 1987.
Time, September 1, 1986; May 9, 1988.
TV Guide, January 21, 1989.
USA Weekend, March 6–8, 1987.

—Sketch by Denise Wiloch

Brian Bosworth

AP/Wide World Photos

Professional football player

Born 1965, in Irving, Tex.; son of Foster and Kathy Bosworth. *Education:* University of Oklahoma, B.B.A., 1987.

Addresses: *Office*—Seattle Seahawks, 11220 Northeast 53rd St., Kirkland, Wash. 98033.

Career

Football player with Seattle Seahawks, 1987—.

Awards: All-American, 1984, 1985, and 1986; two-time winner of Butkus Award as nation's best college linebacker; Academic All-American; named to All-Big Eight Conference team, three years; UPI and AP Big-Eight Defensive Player of the Year, two years; Big Eight Conference Player of the Year, 1986.

Sidelights

While Brian Bosworth may not be the top linebacker in the National Football League, he is, nevertheless, one of the NFL's most recognizable personalities. By virtue of self-generated hype—which has included a paint-streaked Mohawk haircut and endless streams of tough-talk—Bosworth has become The Boz, a "superstar" who is either adored or despised, but always watched. *Los Angeles Times* sports writer Richard Hoffer referred to the horrific Boz as "248 pounds of upper-body strength... acquainted with karate, and [with] as fierce a visage as anything this side of the Neanderthal age." Having taken "the lunacy of being a linebacker" into a new and strange territory in the competitive arena of Big Eight collegiate football, Bosworth was lavished with a 10-year, $11 million contract with the Seattle Seahawks. His performance there has sparked less enthusiasm than his antics, but the consensus appears to be that the athlete with the "hairy spike of spite" will eventually leave his mark on the NFL. As Hoffer wrote, "He's got it all; the size, the speed and most of all, the reckless abandon that would indicate psychotic behavior anywhere but on the football field."

While Bosworth stories have exhausted reams of paper, little has ever been said of his childhood other than the fact that he was born and raised in Irving, Texas, to Foster and Kathy Bosworth. *Sports Illustrated* writer Rick Reilly offered some insight into those formative years in a 1986 profile of the eccentric player. According to Reilly, Bosworth plays "to please his father, who entered him into full-contact football... at age six and has driven him relentlessly since." Bosworth told Reilly that his father beat him and "expected a lot" from him. His mother added: "I felt Brian was playing as good as any nine or 10 year old, but it was never good enough. I guess Brian has his daddy's voice in his head now." If Bosworth resented the pressure from his father, he learned to channel his aggression toward the opposing players on the field; he remains on good terms with his family, and they are proud of his accomplishments.

On the other hand, if Bosworth himself can be believed—and that is a big "if"—his sisters must still harbor him ill will, "I love to tee people off," he told Reilly. "I always hope what I do bothers people. I used to beat my sisters with whips. They always say I was the most obnoxious kid they'd ever met." That "obnoxious kid" developed into a star high school linebacker who was inundated with college scholarship offers. In his senior year of high school he committed to Southern Methodist University but withdrew when overzealous alumni offered him cars, furnished apartments, and a new wardrobe. Instead he chose the University of Oklahoma, whose Sooners are a perennial football powerhouse.

"I should hurt a lot more people than I do....I'd like to hurt someone on every play."

Bosworth arrived on the Oklahoma campus with the force of a roaring prairie twister, and he kept Oklahoma in the headlines for three years. He led the Sooners in tackles with 131 as a sophomore and that season also won the prestigious Butkus Award. Observers drew comparisons between Bosworth and ex-Chicago Bears linebacker Dick Butkus, as well as others. Reilly went so far as to write: "Sideline to sideline, [Bosworth] may be the best in Big Eight history." His was also a candidate for the Heisman Trophy, an honor that has never been extended to a defensive player. The attention did not accent his playing ability, however. It dwelt on his meanness, his vulgar and offensive remarks, and his outlandish hair, which was emblazoned with a crimson 44, his jersey number. For example, in 1986, The Boz told Reilly: "I should hurt a lot more people than I do.... I'd like to hurt someone on every play.... I get more out of knocking the [expletive] out of somebody when they're just totally dumbfounded as to what hit them, than I do out of anything else.... I'm not talking about tearing up somebody's knee or sending anyone to the hospital, I'm talking about knocking the [expletive] out of them enough to where they have to go to the sidelines and count fingers or they don't want to carry the ball on the next play." Bosworth also bragged about humiliating his tackled opponents by spitting on them and twisting their helmets as he'd rise to return to play. Reilly noted, "For Boz, a man isn't really Bozzed until you hear 'a scream' and then see a motionless victim."

This sort of brutality is not unusual for a linebacker; indeed, it is expected of him. What separated Bosworth from the average college linebacker was his sheer dedication to physicality—and relish for it—off the field as well as on. He summarily refused to associate with members of visiting teams, and when forced to, could not be trusted not to start a fight. "Nothing personal," he told Reilly. "But who wants to be friends with guys you're fixing to kick the hell out of?" Bosworth also delighted in taunting opponents with insults. He said of rival Texas during his freshman year, "I hate Texas... and I hate that burnt orange color. It reminds me of people's vomit." Coach Barry Switzer allowed Bosworth to air his peculiar wit until, in a *Sports Illustrated* cover piece, The Boz boasted of hiding loose screws in the doors and engines of new cars while working at the General Motors plant in Oklahoma City. While Bosworth chuckled at the thought of car engines clattering with inexplicable noises, Switzer issued a public apology to the plant manager and the assembly line crew at GM. Hardly chastened by the incident, Bosworth continued. "I use the media," he told Reilly, "for controversy, as an attention-getter. That's what sells newspapers. That's what sells football teams. That's what sells tickets and brings revenue. It's a chain reaction. I'm doing exactly what the system has asked of me, but I'm not afraid to use the system."

The media was not the only system Bosworth used to his advantage. Upon being banned from the 1987 Orange Bowl for steroid use, he decided to forego his last year of college eligibility and turn professional. However, the list of teams he did not want to play for was far longer than the list of teams he preferred. He therefore bypassed the April 28, 1987, draft in favor of a supplemental draft held in late June. Between the two draft dates, Bosworth—who graduated early from Oklahoma with a B-plus average—wrote letters to each NFL team, telling them whether or not he would play for them and what it would cost to sign him. His teams of choice—the Los Angeles Raiders, the Chicago Bears, the Tampa Bay Buccaneers, the New York Jets, and the New York Giants—all rejected him; but after protracted negotiations that caused him to miss four weeks of training camp, he signed with the Seahawks. The decade-long contract, worth more than $1 million per year, was inked before he had played a single down as a professional. Seattle fans were delighted. According to Bill Sullivan of the *San Jose Mercury News*, "The courtship of Brian Bosworth was the biggest story to hit [Seattle] since the Worlds Fair some 25 years ago.... Soon enough, getting Bosworth to grace a Seahawks contract with his signature became something of a civic cause in this normally low-key community." True to form, Bosworth arrived on the scene—after honoring several lucrative endorsements, including a poster with a Playboy playmate—with the usual tough talk. In the period prior to the Seattle season opener against the Denver Broncos, reported the *Washington Post*, The Boz said, "I can't wait to get my hands on John Elway's boyish face." Denver won, 40–17.

Experts claim that Bosworth should not be judged on his rookie season. The fact that it was shortened by a strike, according to Seattle defensive coordinator Tom Catlin, was a "gigantic step backward" for Bosworth. Secondly, Bosworth was given a new position and thrust into a decidedly complex defense. Bosworth told the *Sacramento Bee*: "I was drafted to play one position—inside on the strong side—and they threw me on the other side, which is totally foreign to me.... The sophistication of this defense... is one of the most complicated in the game. My responsibilities are endless, which has also put pressure on me." Thirdly, Bosworth was not allowed to use his college number—44—in the NFL because it would violate a league rule. (Linebackers must wear numbers higher than 50.) This seemingly trivial matter was monumental to Bosworth; he wears a "44" earring and is president of 44 Boz, Inc., a marketing company. Bosworth vowed to take the NFL to court over the ruling, and his crusade affected his early professional play.

The number controversy was only one of the many distractions The Boz faced as he made his debut in professional football. Others included appearing on television talk shows, a guest role on the series "First and Ten," and work in numerous commercial spots. "Bosworth claims he is not distracted," observed Art Thiel in the *Seattle Post-Intelligencer*, "but how does he know? He's never played without distractions. He

During his rookie season with the Seattle Seahawks, Brian Bosworth (top) tackles Kenneth Davis of the Green Bay Packers, holding him to a one-yard gain. AP/Wide World Photos.

is not yet good enough to swashbuckle as if he were a Raider of yore or a Bear of today.... It's obvious that Bosworth is not the Seahawks' best linebacker. He may not even be the best rookie linebacker."

The problems Bosworth has had could stem from the demands of the persona he created, The Boz. In the *Seattle Post Intelligencer,* Bosworth described his colorful alter ego as a character he has "got to feed." Some observers believe that this character could ultimately ruin Bosworth, that while his tough talk was intimidating at the college level, it serves a fuel to his opponents in the pros. "Everybody in the league's out to take a shot at him," Catlin told the *Sacramento Bee,* "but he's brought that upon himself." He has also brought upon himself a level of notoriety in Seattle and elsewhere that severely restricts his movements and impinges on his privacy—once again the infamous Mohawk acts as a neon sign advertising his presence. Art Thiel summerized the quandry in which Bosworth finds himself: "After watching the Seahawk rookie in the opening scenes of what figures to be a decade or so of his football theater, a disquieting impression lingers. It doesn't come from hairstyles or jewelry. On the contrary, his pursuit of creative individualism in the personality barrio of the NFL is commendable. And anyone who's ever made a nickel from entrepreneurship should never begrudge Bosworth's right to sell himself. His vulnerability is not in the area of theory; it's in execution. Bosworth is plunging recklessly into a self-indulgent public phoniness that will alienate those from whom he seeks commercial approval, and, more importantly, those who work beside him." Thiel concluded that The Boz is merely "a contrivance whose chief asset is novelty. Once it fades, the only thing that can sustain the anti-hero posturing as a merchandising vehicle is relentless on-field excellence." Whether Bosworth can achieve that excellence—and sustain it—remains to be seen.

Writings

The Boz: Confessions of a Modern Anti-Hero (with Rick Reilly), Doubleday, 1988.

Sources

Boston Globe, April 5, 1987.
Interview, November, 1987.
Los Angeles Times, September 1, 1986; October 24, 1987.
Newsweek, January 5, 1987.
People, November 24, 1986.
Rolling Stone, August 25, 1988.
Sacramento Bee, December 15, 1987.
San Jose Mercury News, September 4, 1987.
Seattle Post Intelligencer, November 18, 1987.
Sport, January 1988.
Sporting News, May 25, 1987; June 23, 1987.
Sports Illustrated, September 3, 1986; January 5, 1987.
Washington Post, December 13, 1987.

—*Sidelights by Mark Kram*

Edward A. Brennan

UPI/Bettmann Newsphotos

Retail company executive

Born January 16, 1934, in Chicago, Ill.; son of Edward (a buyer) and Margaret (Bourget) Brennan; married Lois Lyon, June 11, 1955; children: Edward, Cynthia, Sharon, Donald, John, Linda. *Education:* Marquette University, B.A., 1955.

Addresses: *Office*—Sears, Roebuck & Co., Sears Tower, Chicago, Ill. 60684.

Career

Sears, Roebuck & Co., Chicago, Ill., 1956—, began as salesman, executive vice-president of southern territory, 1978–80, president and chief operating officer for merchandising, 1980–81, Sears merchandising group, chairman and chief executive officer, 1981–84, president and chief operating officer, 1984–86, chairman and chief executive officer, 1986—; also serves as director of Sears, Roebuck & Co. and Sears-Roebuck Foundation. Trustee, Atlanta University, Marquette University, and DePaul University. Member, Chicago Urban League, beginning 1980.

Sidelights

In 1984, Edward A. Brennan became president and chief operating officer of Sears, Roebuck & Company, the nation's largest retail chain. At the time of his appointment, Sears faced severe economic problems. Profits had dropped by 25 percent, and the company's efforts to offer a range of financial services in its stores were failing. Under Brennan's management, however, Sears has regained its leadership position.

Brennan's predecessor, Edward R. Telling, had launched Sears' campaign to establish itself as a supplier of financial services. Telling had acquired banking, stock brokerage, and real estate companies and installed financial offices in 300 Sears department stores. As Monci Jo Williams of *Fortune* reported, Sears aspired to become "the premier purveyor of stocks, insurance and loans to the great American public." By the time Brennan assumed the presidency, the firm was in trouble. Dean Witter, the stock brokerage wing, faced heavy losses; while Allstate Insurance and the real estate company, Coldwell Banker, were at a virtual standstill. It was expected that Brennan would turn things around. As Williams remarked, "Brennan has a reputation as a fixer, an operating man with an eye for trouble spots and a knack for cleaning them up."

This reputation was earned during a career that began in 1956, when Brennan joined Sears as a salesman (his father had worked with Sears as a buyer, as had two of his uncles and his brother). Brennan worked his way up to head of the company's southern territory, then on to president of the Sears merchandising group. *Esquire*'s Donald R. Katz called Brennan "one of the most gifted natural merchants to come along in years." Because of his ability to rescue failing stores in the Sears chain, Brennan was chosen to lead the corporation at a time when, as Katz explained, "Sears was dying."

To improve the company's performance and to rebuild morale, Brennan staged a series of meetings with employees throughout the United States. He also pushed for renewed cooperation between the firm's many branches. Moreover, in 1985 Sears introduced the Discover card, a national credit card similar to Visa or Mastercard. Through these and other efforts, Brennan has helped to reestablish Sears' leadership in the retail industry. Corporate profit has doubled, and the company's stock price has quadrupled. "When Sears does well," wrote *Time*'s John S. DeMott, "the ripples spread throughout the economy." And Katz added that "Sears, Roebuck has been reconstituted during the 1980s as a powerful, futuristic business machine."

Sources

Business Week, August 27, 1984.
Esquire, October, 1987.
Fortune, October 14, 1985.
Time, August 20, 1984.
Wall Street Journal, May 10, 1985.

—Sketch by Denise Wiloch

Gordon Bunshaft

AP/Wide World Photos

Architect

Born May 9, 1909, in Buffalo, N.Y.; son of David and Yetta Bunshaft; married Nina Elizabeth Wayler, December 2, 1943. *Education:* Massachusetts Institute of Technology, B.A., 1933, M.A., 1935.

Addresses: *Home*—New York, N.Y.

Career

Skidmore, Owings & Merrill, New York, N.Y., chief designer, 1937–42, partner, 1949–79. Member, President's Commission on Fine Arts, 1963–72. Trustee and member of international council, Museum of Modern Art; former trustee, Carnegie Mellon University. *Military service:* U.S. Army, Corps of Engineers, 1942–46.

Member: American Academy and Institute of Arts and Letters, American Institute of Architects (fellow), National Academy of Design (academician), Municipal Art Society of New York.

Awards: American Academy and Institute of Arts and Letters, Brunner Award, 1955, Gold Medal, 1984; American Institute of Architects, Honor Award, 1958, New York chapter's Medal of Honor, 1961; University of Buffalo, D.F.A., 1962, Chancellor's Medal, 1969; Pritzker Prize, 1988.

Sidelights

During the 1950s and 1960s, Gordon Bunshaft designed skyscrapers and office buildings that epitomized modern corporate architecture. He introduced what *Time*'s Kurt Anderson described as "humane, impeccable steel-frame-and-glass-skin office towers." Bunshaft's style—sleek, functional, and powerful—greatly influenced his contemporaries, but he fell out of favor in the postmodernist era of later decades. Nevertheless, in 1988, he received the Pritzker Prize, architecture's most coveted award.

The son of Russian-Jewish immigrants, Bunshaft studied architecture at the Massachusetts Institute of Technology. Shortly after earning his master's degree, he won a Rotch Traveling Fellowship, which he used to tour Europe and North Africa. He returned to the United States in 1937 and entered the New York offices of Skidmore, Owings & Merrill, an architecture firm. Some of his earliest designs were for the 1939 World's Fair. He left the firm in 1942 and served in the U.S. Army Corps of Engineers until 1946.

Bunshaft rejoined Skidmore following the war and was made a partner in 1949. He was then assigned his first major project, Manhattan's Lever House. Completed in 1952, Lever House is 24 stories of blue-green glass. Clean-lined and tight-skinned, it is "appropriately scaled, perfectly proportioned, graceful, tough, quiet, confident," wrote Anderson. Bunshaft's design, in essence, applied Europe's International Style (a 1920s architecture based on functionalism) to America's burgeoning corporate structure. As Wolf Von Eckardt of *Time* noted, "Lever House was at mid-century the proud proclamation of a new era." Still considered his finest work, it became the model for modern American skyscrapers. Bunshaft went on to design what Anderson called "several of the most thoughtful, deeply elegant office buildings of the '50s and early '60s." These include the Manufacturer's Hanover Trust building, the PepsiCo building, and the headquarters of the Chase Manhattan Bank. Located in New York, these structures are refined applications of the Lever House style.

In the 1970s, architecture moved away from postwar American modernism. Bunshaft stayed in the modernist school, "but his style evolved into a somewhat aggressively heavy, sculptural approach," explained Paul Goldberger of the *New York Times.* His later buildings, such as the Lyndon Baines Johnson Library and the Hirshhorn Museum and Sculpture Garden, are frequently described as inordinately massive and monumental. Towards the end of his career, Anderson wrote, Bunshaft "seemed to grow defeatist about minimalism and the possibilities of subtle invention, seduced instead by sheer size and pomposity." The architect's last project, the National Commercial Bank in Jeddah, Saudi Arabia, "is so abstract that it is impossible to judge its actual size except upon close examination," Goldberger reported. The triangular-shaped building stands 27 stories tall and features travertine marble walls with recessed windows. It has no discernible front or back. Goldberger found it scaleless, adding, "the National Commercial Bank is so stark, so completely at odds with anything around it, that it barely even reads as a building."

Bunshaft retired in 1979. Still a confirmed modernist, he is philosophical about current trends in his field. "The architecture today would have nothing to do with what I like doing," he told Anderson. "It's a different world—and I prefer mine." In 1988, Bunshaft received architecture's most prestigious award, the Pritzker Prize, in honor of his early, pioneering designs. In his acceptance speech, Bunshaft offered his view of architecture's future. "Young architects are turning away from postmodernism, and I think they're going to turn toward precision even more than modernism did. It'll make Lever House look like a sentimental old lady."

Sources

New York Times, January 30, 1983; May 24, 1988; May 29, 1988.

Time, February 21, 1983; May 30, 1988.

—Sketch by Denise Wiloch

Barbara Bush

AP/Wide World Photos

First lady of the United States

Full name, Barbara Pierce Bush; born June 8, 1925, in Rye, N.Y.; daughter of Marvin (a publishing company executive) and Pauline (Robinson) Pierce; married George Herbert Walker Bush (president of the United States), January 6, 1945; children: George Walker, Robin (deceased), John Ellis, Neil Mallon, Marvin Pierce, Dorothy Walker LeBlond. *Education:* Attended Smith College, 1943–44. *Politics:* Republican. *Religion:* Episcopalian.

Addresses: *Home and office*—The White House, 1600 Pennsylvania Ave., Washington, D.C. 20500.

Career

First lady of the United States, 1989—. Advocate for improved literacy among Americans; honorary chairperson, Barbara Bush Foundation for Family Literacy, National Advisory Council of Literary Volunteers of America, and National School Volunteers Program; member of board of directors, Reading Is Fundamental and Business Council for Effective Literacy; sponsor, Laubach Literacy International. Honorary chairperson, Leukemia Society of America, Hispanic American Family of the Year Program, and National Organ Donor Awareness Week, 1982–86; member of advisory council, Sloan-Kettering Cancer Center; honorary member of board of directors, Children's Oncology Services of Metropolitan Washington, the Washington Home, and the Kingsbury Center; trustee, Morehouse School of Medicine.

Member: Ladies of the Senate (president, 1981), Smithsonian Associates (member of women's committee), Texas Federation of Republican Women (life member), Magic Circle Republican Women's Club (Houston).

Awards: National Outstanding Mother of the Year Award, 1984; Woman of the Year Award, USO, 1986; Distinguished Leadership Award, United Negro College Fund, 1986; Distinguished American Woman Award, College of Mt. St. Joseph, 1987; named Outstanding Leader in the Literacy Movement, 1988; honorary degrees from Stritch College, 1981, Mt. Vernon College, 1981, Hood College, 1983, and Howard University, 1987.

Sidelights

Soon after beginning her reign as the nation's 38th first lady, Barbara Pierce Bush made a small change in the private quarters of the White House. She converted the room that had served as a beauty salon for Nancy Reagan into a delivery room for Millie, the Bushes' pregnant springer spaniel. As an aide to Mrs. Bush told the *New York Daily News:* "She had no need for a beauty salon. It's the only area without a rug, perfect for a litter of puppies." A few days after the room was made over, six puppies were born, with Bush serving as midwife. The salon-turned-puppy-nursery story illustrates a dramatic difference in personal style between Bush and her predecessor. While Nancy Reagan took pride in cultivating a look of elegance, bringing a kind of designer mentality to the role of first lady, Barbara Bush is practical, homey, and down-to-earth. She leaves her hair white, lets her wrinkles show, takes a size-14 dress, and wears fake pearls. If the Hollywood chic of Mrs. Reagan put a distance between the first lady and the American masses, the grandmotherly mien of Mrs. Bush has closed the gap, allowing her to establish a vital connection with the public.

For an Administration that stresses the American family, Barbara Bush is a particularly fitting first lady. In 1945 she married George Bush and began a family, dropping out of college in her sophomore year. Since then she has lived a life of devotion—not only to her five children and 11 grandchildren, but to a way of life. Her husband's wide-ranging public career demanded that she shoulder most of the parenting duties herself, and over the years, it has led them to put down roots in 17 cities and 29 homes.

Since entering the national spotlight, Bush has been determined to channel her visibility toward bettering society. Having made a career during her younger years in community volunteerism—what the president calls his "thousand points of light" concept—she now works to bring others to the mission. Homeless shelters, AIDS hospitals, and Head Start projects are a few of the types of facilities she visits in an effort to draw media attention to the need for local help. Lending her name to a string of social, health, and educational organizations, she also works to attract more private-sector funding of volunteer programs, agreeing with her husband that the federal government should not bear the brunt of the costs.

Over the past several decades it has become traditional for a first lady to devote herself to a specific cause. Jacqueline Kennedy and Pat Nixon each chose White House restoration, while Rosalynn Carter concerned herself with mental health and Nancy Reagan crusaded against drug abuse. By now, the pet cause of Barbara Bush is well-known: to raise the national level of literacy. During her husband's vice-presidency she participated in over 500 literacy events throughout the country, and as first lady she has intensified the effort. Her newly established Barbara Bush Foundation for Family Literacy, a private, Washington-based organization, has been soliciting grants from the public and private sectors. Rather than create new literacy programs, the foundation has been distributing the funds among existing ones, hoping to help curb the high dropout rates that afflict many of them. Bush is honorary chairwoman—a necessarily passive role, since, as the *Los Angeles Times* observed, "it might be considered unseemly for the first lady to be putting the arm on people for money." Meanwhile, she is a sponsor of Laubach Literacy International and a board member of the Business Council for Effective Literacy, which encourages business support for the cause. All of the proceeds from her 1984 book, *C. Fred's Story* (Doubleday), a collection of anecdotes about the Bushes' late cocker spaniel, went to major literacy organizations.

Underlying Bush's literacy campaign are startling statistics. Experts in the field estimate that some 23 million adult Americans are illiterate, lacking basic skills beyond a fourth-grade level, while 35 million are semi-illiterate, lacking skills beyond the eighth-grade level. Yet for her, the urgency of the problem is not so much in these figures as it is in the myriad of other problems that she considers to be caused by illiteracy. "Literacy fits in with so many other things," she told the *Chicago Tribune.* "If more people could read, fewer people would have AIDS. There would be less homelessness. I'm absolutely convinced of that."

The Bush Foundation is attacking the problem from an "intergenerational" approach, attempting to break the illiteracy cycle from generation to generation. Accordingly, it is awarding grants only to those programs that involve not only children but also their parents and grandparents. "In 10 years of traveling," Bush told the *New York Times,* "visiting literary programs, libraries, kindergarten groups, day-care centers, single-parent classes for high school dropouts, public housing projects, food banks—you name it, I've visited it—it has become very apparent to me that we must attack the problem of a more literate America through the family. We all know that adults with reading problems tend to raise children with reading problems. And when I talk about family literacy, I am talking about families of all kinds: the big and bouncing kind, the single parent, extended families, divorced, homeless and migrant."

Bush believes that the problem isn't simply a matter of parents who can't read. According to her, it's parents who can't parent. "There's not an awful lot we can do about that except try to train parents," she told the *Chicago Tribune.* "Missouri, for instance, has a parenting program where they talk to mothers literally in clinics before they have the babies and teach them how to parent. I think our school systems have been at fault some. I think we have been at fault enormously. We expect our teachers to be mother and father and church and teach our children morals . . . . I think a lot of our problems are because people don't listen to our children. It's not always easy. They're not always so brilliant that you want to spend hours with them."

Bush talks about parental devotion from personal experience: As a young mother she grappled tirelessly with her son Neil's dyslexia. "She expended more time and effort to help him overcome severe reading difficulty," the *Chicago Tribune* noted, "than many mothers spend on parenting, period." The experience not only inspired her to take up the cause of literacy but also sparked her interest in the related field of learning disabilities. In the 1989 issue of *Their World,* published by the National Center for Learning Disabilities, she wrote an introductory letter. "George Bush and I know the frustration of living with an undiagnosed or untreated learning problem, and we know the great joy and relief that comes when help is finally found," the letter begins. "I foresee the day when no American—neither child nor adult—will ever need to be limited in learning."

On the wide range of political, social, and ethical issues that confront the nation, Bush has firm opinions of her own. More than once this has led her outside the bounds of first-lady protocol, requiring her, as she told the *Philadelphia Inquirer,* to learn to "curb my mouth." Now when she's asked to comment on a controversial issue, she uses a stock answer: "Let me tell you how George Bush feels." "As the wife of an elected official," she explained to the *Diplomatic Digest,* "I feel exactly as the Vice President does to the President. You owe that person, that elected official, your support on the outside. What you say behind closed doors, that's fine. You can voice your own opinion there, but I'm not an elected official." With a smile, she added, "When I *am,* I expect George Bush to support me!"

Most nights, 1600 Pennsylvania Avenue has company—usually a family member, or perhaps one of the many friends the Bushes have cultivated over years of public life. It's usually not until the dinner hour that the couple has time to themselves. By now they have established a routine: eat by candlelight, work for a while, walk the dog. When she is alone in her spare time, Mrs. Bush enjoys needlepointing—the chintz sitting room displays a rug that she worked on for years—and, not surprisingly, reading. Her literary taste ranges from Louisa May Alcott to Tom Wolfe. She also likes to simply take in the grandeur of her 29th home. "It's so much more beautiful than I thought," she told the *Christian Science Monitor.* "Today I had lunch off of [Woodrow] Wilson's plates; sometimes I have lunch off of Lincoln's plates."

Barbara Bush already knows how she would like to be remembered after leaving the White House. "I hope people will say, 'She cared; she worked hard for lots of causes,'" she told the *Christian Science Monitor.* Many people write to her, she added, wishing to help with the various social concerns she has espoused. Her response: "If you'll just go out and help the neighbor who needs help, you'll be on my program."

Writings

C. Fred's Story, Doubleday, 1984.

Sources

Books

Bush, George, *Looking Forward: An Autobiography* (with Victor Gold), Doubleday, 1987.

Periodicals

Chicago Tribune, February 19, 1989.
Christian Science Monitor, February 16, 1989.
Diplomatic Digest, January, 1989.
Los Angeles Times, March 8, 1989.
Maclean's, January 23, 1989.
Newsday, February 14, 1989.
Newsweek, January 16, 1989.
New York Daily News, March 16, 1989.
New York Times, March 7, 1989.
Philadelphia Inquirer, February 14, 1989.
Time, January 23, 1989.
Washington Post, March 11, 1989.

—Sidelights by Kyle Kevorkian

Jerry Buss

UPI/Bettmann Newsphotos

Real estate developer and sports team owner

Full name, Jerry Hatten Buss; born January 27, 1933, in Salt Lake City, Utah; son of accountants; married Joann Mueller (divorced); children: John, Jim, Jeanie, Janie. *Education:* University of Wyoming, B.S.; University of Southern California, Ph.D., 1957.

Addresses: *Office*—Los Angeles Lakers, P.O. Box 10, The Forum, Inglewood, Calif. 90306.

Career

Member of faculty, chemistry department, University of Southern California, Los Angeles; worked for Arthur D. Little (a business consulting firm), Boston, Mass.; member of missile division, McDonnell Douglas Corp., Los Angeles; Mariana-Buss Associates (real estate firm), Santa Monica, Calif., partner, beginning 1959; owner, Los Angeles Strings (tennis team) 1974–78, Los Angeles Lakers (basketball team), 1979—, Los Angeles Kings (hockey team), 1979–88, and the Forum (sports-entertainment arena), 1979—. Part-owner, Prime Ticket (cable channel).

Sidelights

Jerry Buss is considered one of the most innovative businessmen in the field of sports. He is also one of the wealthiest. Buss owns several teams, including the Los Angeles Lakers of the National Basketball Association. He also owns the Forum, the 17,505-seat arena where his teams play. According to most estimates, Buss presides over the most profitable sports empire in the United States.

Born in Salt Lake City, Utah, Buss was raised in a small Wyoming mining town. He studied chemistry at the University of Wyoming and the University of Southern California (USC), where he earned his Ph.D. Initially, Buss wanted to be a college professor, and he joined the faculty of USC following his graduation. A short time later, he decided he needed a change and moved to Boston to work for Arthur D. Little, a consulting firm. Finding the weather unsuitable, he returned to Los Angeles and entered the aerospace industry. He worked in the missile division of McDonnell Douglas and, later, at a space laboratory. In 1958, he and a fellow employee, Frank Mariani, went into real estate. The next year, they bought a small apartment house in West Los Angeles. By the late 1970s, Mariani-Buss Associates owned 4,000 apartment units, three hotels, two office buildings, and 1,000 one-family homes.

Buss had also purchased his first sports franchise, the Los Angeles Strings of World Team Tennis. He rented the Forum for tournaments and met its owner, Jack Kent Cooke. The tennis league folded in 1978, and Buss, who had long wanted to own a major sports franchise, asked Cooke if he wanted to sell. Cooke, who had just been through a long and costly divorce, was ready. In 1979, they concluded one of the largest and most complex transactions in sports history. Buss and his partners paid $67.5 million for the Forum and two major league teams, the Los Angeles Lakers and the Los Angeles Kings.

"I don't just want winners," Buss told Sue Ellen Jares of *People.* "I want champions. Usually that means spending money, and I'm prepared to do that." As proof, Buss signed basketball star Earvin "Magic" Johnson [see index for *Newsmakers* entry] to a $25 million contract; and he agreed to pay hockey great Marcel Dionne $600,000 a year to play for the Kings. Moreover, "to add Hollywood glitz, Buss invites movie stars galore, even giving actor Jack Nicholson a free courtside ticket to every game and dubbing him 'First Fan,'" wrote Ronald Grover in *Business Week.* Buss's strategy has been hugely successful. The Lakers draw record crowds, and top ticket prices have jumped from $15 in 1979 to $150 in 1987. Buss has more than doubled the value of his sports empire. Though he eventually sold the Kings hockey club, he has added tennis and indoor soccer teams to his holdings. And the Forum, when it is not being used by one of these teams, is the site of rock concerts, rodeos, track meets, and boxing matches. Recently, Buss became part-owner of Prime Ticket, a regional cable channel that broadcasts Forum events. "Jerry has discovered the winning formula," Bruce McNall, one of Buss's partners, told Grover. "He has the whole operation working in sync with itself."

Sources

Business Week, March 16, 1987.
Forbes, July 1, 1985.
Los Angeles Times, February 14, 1985.
New York Times, May 30, 1979.
People, February 11, 1986.
Sports Illustrated, June 18, 1979.

—Sketch by Denise Wiloch

Mangosuthu Gatsha Buthelezi

Reuters/Bettmann Newsphotos

Chief minister of Kwazulu, South Africa

Surname pronounced boo-ta-*lay*-zee; full name, Mangosuthu Gatsha Ashpenaz Nathan Buthelezi; born August 27, 1928, in Mahlabatini, Natal, South Africa; son of Mathole (a Zulu tribal chief) and Constance Magogo Zulu (a Zulu princess) Buthelezi; married Irene Audrey Mzila, 1952; children: three sons; four daughters. *Education:* Attended Adams College and Fort Hare University; University of Natal, B.A. in history and Bantu administration.

Addresses: Private Bag X01, Ulundi 3838, Kwazulu, South Africa.

Career

While in college, took part in civil-rights activities promoted by the African National Congress (ANC); following graduation, worked for South African Department of Native Affairs for two years; became chief of the Buthelezi tribe, 1953; served as prime minister and advisor on national Zulu matters to King Cyprian, 1953–68; head of Masho Nangashoni Regional Authority, beginning 1968, and Zulu Territorial Authority, beginning 1970; chief minister of Kwazulu state, beginning 1972; revived Inkatha political and cultural movement, 1975, and serves as its head.

Awards: George Meany Human Rights Award, AFL-CIO, 1982; honorary LL.D., Capetown University and Zululand University.

Sidelights

As chief minister of the six-million member Zulu homeland in South Africa, Mangosuthu Gatsha Buthelezi has been received by more European and American heads of state than any other current South African leader. Books have been written about his rise to prominence as leader of the Zulus and international spokesman for millions of black South Africans. He is a controversial figure in South Africa and abroad because he leads the largest single population group, cooperates with the white minority government, and speaks out against sanctions and violence. He is denounced by liberation groups who accuse him of being a puppet of the government, while white South African politicians applaud him as the hope for the future of the country.

Buthelezi claims close ties with the early African National Congress (ANC), when it's ideals embraced nonviolence as a means of reforming the apartheid system. He now distances himself from the ANC in exile, which calls for violence against the state. He travels the world speaking against violence and sanctions, which he says hurt black South Africans. His stand on nonviolence is especially provocative because Inkatha, a political and cultural group that he established and leads, is particularly violent toward its rivals, the Congress of South African Trade Unions (COSATU) and the United Democratic Front (UDF).

Buthelezi rose from the ranks of chief of the small Buthelezi tribe to his present position as chief minister of the Kwazulu Legislative Assembly. As chief minister of the Zulus and leader of Inkatha, he is one of the major players who will have to be reckoned with by black and white alike in any sincere attempt to accommodate black political and economic aspirations.

Although he agrees with the white government on the harmfulness of sanctions and advocates nonviolence, he sets an independent course by opposing the government on several fronts. He refuses to make Kwazulu a so-called "independent homeland," like Transkei or any of the other three nominally independent states. He successfully opposed the government's attempt to transfer an area of Kwazulu and KaNgwane to Swaziland. And he is adamantly opposed to the new constitution and the tri-cameral system introduced in 1983 because it "enshrines racist principles as cornerstones of the State."

Buthelezi's family has been prominent in Zulu society since the 1870s. His great-grandfather was prime minister to King Cetshwayo and his successor King Dinuzulu. His father was Chief Mathole and his mother, Princess Constance Magogo Zulu, was the sister of Zulu King Solomon (the grandfather of the present King Zwelithini Goodwill).

Buthelezi was born Mangosuthu Gatsha Ashpenaz Nathan Buthelezi on August 27, 1928, in Mahlabatini, Natal Province, South Africa. He spent his early years in a traditional manner, working as a herdboy and attending local schools. In 1948 he went to university at Fort Hare, the university for blacks in the eastern Cape Province. He studied for a B.A. degree in Bantu administration and history under Professor Z. K. Matthews, an important figure in the ANC. Whether or not Buthelezi was a member of the ANC Youth League at this time is debated. His more admiring biographers claim he was a member, while ANC members say that he was not. The question is relevant because Buthelezi claims to be carrying on the traditions of ANC leaders like Albert Luthuli and Nelson Mandela. Whether a member or not, Buthelezi was expelled from the university for taking part in an ANC Youth League-led boycott of the visit to Fort Hare by South African Governor General G. Brand van Zyl in 1950. He was permitted to graduate from Fort Hare but he had to take his exams at another university.

Following graduation, Buthelezi accepted a job with the Department of Native Affairs. The South African authorities had warned him that he had to "wipe out" the Fort Hare episode if he wanted to become a tribal chief. He worked for Native Affairs for two years.

When his father died, Buthelezi claimed he was the successor to the chief. His elder brother Mceleli disputed his claim, saying that the South African minister of native affairs was imposing Gatsha on the tribe. Mceleli took his challenge to the South African Supreme Court, which denied him the chieftainship several years later. The Buthelezi chieftaincy was significant because the king traditionally chose his prime ministers from the Buthelezi tribe, one of nearly 300 such tribal groups. The tribal authorities installed Buthelezi as acting chief in 1953, and four years later the South African authorities recognized him as the official chief.

As acting chief of his own tribe and later as elected leader of all the Zululand chiefs, Buthelezi encouraged the chiefs to accept the Bantu Authorities Act of 1951, which they finally did in 1968. Many chiefs and ANC members were strongly opposed to this legislation because it gave limited self-government to various language groups under the authority of a chief whose position was dependent on the goodwill of the white authorities. Buthelezi is regarded by many blacks as a "sellout" because he acted as the voice of the whites and persuaded the chiefs to accept the system.

With acceptance of the act, the government began to consolidate control under one leader. By 1971 the government had compressed the 188 tribal authorities (out of 282 tribes) and 22 regional authorities into a single administrative unit called the Kwazulu Legislative Assembly. The consolidation into one massive unit based on language and traditional structures provided Buthelezi with a platform for national and international attention.

Buthelezi gained prominence in the early 1970s, a time when most liberation groups had been banned and voices opposed to the government had been silenced. As chief minister of Kwazulu and leader of then about four million people, Buthelezi filled the leadership vacuum for several years. He traveled to Europe and the United States, meeting with presidents and prime ministers. Buthelezi tried to win acceptance from both ends of the political spectrum. On one hand he claimed kinship with the early ANC and defied the government by refusing to make Kwazulu an independent homeland. On the other hand he advocated nonviolence and supported the government's position on sanctions and disinvestment.

Most opposition groups refuse to recognize Buthelezi as a legitimate leader of the blacks. The South African Students Organization (SASO), the Black People's Congress and later the rejuvenated black trade unions accused him and other homeland leaders of being manufactured commodities stamped "Made in Pretoria."

In 1975 Buthelezi revived a 1920s Zulu cultural organization called Inkatha Ya Kwazulu. According to Buthelezi the revived Inkatha (now renamed Inkatha Yenululeke ye Sizwe, or Freedom of the Nation) is not a political party but a national cultural liberation movement. So much does Buthelezi want to be seen as identifying with the early aspirations of the ANC that he adopted the green and gold colors of the ANC for Inkatha. Membership grew rapidly in the first few years. By the 1980s Inkatha claimed 1.5 million members, making it the largest black political organization in the history of the country.

In the early years, Inkatha was not perceived as a rival to the ANC; nearly half of all its members were also ANC supporters. As time passed, though, differences on several crucial issues split the groups. As Inkatha grew, Buthelezi became more assertive and began to criticize in public members of the ANC. ANC leader-in-exile Oliver Tambo met with Buthelezi in London in 1979 to try to smooth over their differences and include Inkatha in a national consensus. When Inkatha forces ruthlessly crushed a school boycott in KwaMashua in 1980 any tentative accord that existed between ANC and Inkatha was severed.

During the early 1980s in South Africa, black trade unions emerged as a powerful voice, showing people that they could resist the system if they acted together. Community groups organized boycotts against rent and bus fare increases and protested against community structures erected by white authorities. People also began resisting harrassment by Inkatha, which was already well established in the black townships around Durban and Pietmaritzburg in Natal. In 1983 the United Democratic Front (UDF), a national coalition of labor, social, and political groups, had just been formed. Buthelezi came to see actions by the UDF or COSATU (Congress of South African Trade Unions), the recently formed umbrella group for labor unions, as being an extension of the ANC. He said in an interview with the *Citizen* newspaper that "Since the day the UDF was formed, the UDF had declared war on Inkatha." During the upheavals of the mid-1980s, when black demands were not met, blacks staged transportation boycotts, consumer boycotts, and work slowdowns. Inkatha found itself against these mass actions and in the camp with the South African authorities and police force. Inkatha had become part of the problem.

In the midst of the political turmoil in Kwazulu townships, Inkatha began a recruitment drive for paid up members. Persuasion was often by force. To guard against the Inkatha recruiters, UDF and COSATU people set up defense teams comprised of young boys armed with pangas, knives, spears, and sticks. Many of these young soldier-children fled the townships in fear of their lives from revenge by Inkatha fighters. The violence escalated. Between September 1984 and December 1988 1,414 people died in political conflict in Natal.

Prior to the outbreak of violence, in 1982, Buthelezi appointed a committee of special interest groups in Natal to explore ways that would lead toward power sharing between whites and blacks. The commissions' recommendations were rejected by the government and by the liberal black community. Still, Buthelezi's reputation among South African whites and the international community continued to grow. In 1982 the AFL-CIO awarded Buthelezi and the late Dr. Neil Agget the George Meany Human Rights Award. In May 1986 *Time* magazine reported that a recent poll of South African Afrikaaner businessmen showed 83 percent picked Buthelezi as a good leader compared to 67 percent for the State President P. W. Botha. Buthelezi is popular with whites because he is a capitalist, committed (he says) to nonviolence, and favors compromise to solve the country's problems.

Riding high on the goodwill of the whites, in June 1986 he opened an Indaba (meeting) of whites and blacks to create a multiracial government in Natal. The awful violence in Natal, though, has undermined Buthelezi's reputation. And imposition of a state of emergency by the South African government in 1986 quashed any opportunity for a reaction to the Indaba at the grass-roots level. In late 1987 Archbishop and Nobel Peace Prize winner Desmond Tutu called for peace in the townships. Buthelezi reacted angrily, saying in an article in the *Citizen* that Bishop Tutu's call for the cessation of violence was made "as though he himself is whiter than snow and comes to his pedestal untainted with the forces that are doing their damndest to perpetuate violence."

In September 1988 Inkatha and COSATU signed a joint agreement to end the violence. They established a Complaints Adjudication Board to hear complaints of violence from either side. The violence in the townships continues but at a much lower rate. In January 1989 Buthelezi met with acting State President Chris Heunis. They indicated that their representatives were prepared to continue talks on power sharing. Buthelezi denies that his willingness to talk with the white authorities is reneging on his promise not to negotiate with the government until certain conditions are met, namely the release of ANC leader Nelson Mandela. Whenever and however any political accommodation is reached in South Africa, as long as Buthelezi is leader of the Zulus, he will be a major player in implementing that accord.

Sources

Books

Mare, Gerhard, and Georgina Hamilton, *An Appetite for Power*, Ravan Press, 1987.

Mzala, *Gatsha Buthelezi: Chief With a Double Agenda*, Zed Press, 1988.

Smith, Jack Shepherd, *Buthelezi: The Biography*, Hans Strydom Publishers, 1988.

Periodicals

Citizen, January 3, 1988.
Economist, November 7, 1987; February 6, 1988.
Los Angeles Times, August 11, 1986.
National Review, January 30, 1987.
New Republic, December 22, 1986.
New Statesman, March 28, 1986.
Newsweek, August 19, 1985.
New York Times, November 3, 1980; November 30, 1986; December 2, 1986; November 4, 1987; December 7, 1987; October 22, 1988.
Sowetan, January 11, 1988.
Star, March 3, 1989.
Time, August 5, 1985.
U.S. News & World Report, December 2, 1985.

—Sidelights by Virginia Curtin Knight

Belinda Carlisle

AP/Wide World Photos

Singer

Born August 17, 1958, in Hollywood, Calif.; married Morgan Mason (in public relations), April 12, 1986. *Education:* Graduated from high school in California, 1976.

Career

Singer with group the Go-Go's, 1978–85; solo artist, 1985—. Has modeled for Almay cosmetics. Appeared in a stage production of "Grease" at a California regional playhouse, 1983, and in film "Swing Shift," 1984.

Awards: Grammy Award nomination for best pop vocal performance, female, 1988, for "Heaven Is a Place on Earth."

Sidelights

Belinda Carlisle first gained fame as the lead singer for the Go-Go's, a hugely popular all-female group. The band's wholesome, fun image and lighthearted songs, such as "We Got the Beat" and "Head Over Heels," attracted legions of fans. But by 1985, the act had gone stale. The group split up, and Carlisle embarked on a successful solo career. "The Go-Go's was pretty much me when I was younger," she explained to Todd Gold of *People*. "But as I got older, I got kind of tired of being cute, bubbly and effervescent all day. I just didn't feel like being bouncy anymore."

Carlisle was raised in California's San Fernando Valley, the oldest of seven children. After graduating from high school in 1976, she began frequenting Hollywood's New Wave and punk clubs, where she met Charlotte Caffey, Jane Wiedlin, Gina Schock, and Kathy Valentine. They formed the Go-Go's "for laughs," Carlisle told Gold. "I had never been in any other band. That was my first time singing." Eventually, they acquired a manager and were booked to tour England. During the tour, they recorded "We Got the Beat." The single sold 50,000 copies in the United States. In 1981, the group signed with I.R.S. Records, and later that same year, they released *Beauty and the Beat*. The debut album sold over two million copies and topped the charts for six weeks. Their next effort, *Vacation*, was less successful; *Talk Show*, released in 1984, flopped.

Wiedlin announced that she was leaving the quintet. Carlisle and Caffey soon followed. The Go-Go's officially disbanded in May of 1985, and Carlisle decided to pursue a solo career. She also decided to straighten out her personal life. While the Go-Go's enjoyed what Steve Pond of *Rolling Stone* called a "cotton candy image," several members of the group had serious drinking and drug problems. Carlisle was one of them. She joined Alcoholic Anonymous, went on a diet, and began to work out regularly. She also saw a vocal coach three times a week. In 1986, Carlisle married Morgan Mason, the son of actor

James Mason, and she released her first solo album, *Belinda*.

"*Belinda* is a collection of love songs," *Creem*'s J. Kordosh wrote. Its tracks include "Mad About You," "I Need a Disguise," "Shot in the Dark," and "I Feel the Magic." Former Go-Go's Caffey and Wiedlin helped with the album, which many critics found reminiscent of the band's early work. "If you liked the Go-Go's, you'll get a kick out of *Belinda*," Jon Young noted in *Creem*. "Carlisle remains an optimistic bundle of energy, never less than charming." A *People* reviewer wrote: "She sounds as peppy and wholesomely sexy on her own as she did with the band.... Producer Mike Lloyd helped Carlisle maintain another of the Go-Go's qualities, the ability to evoke the sound of early rock without seeming to parody it." *Belinda* was well-received by audiences as well as critics. Carlisle's solo career gained momentum in 1988, when her hit single "Heaven Is a Place on Earth" was nominated for a Grammy Award.

Discography

With the Go-Go's

Beauty and the Beat, I.R.S., 1981.
Vacation, I.R.S., 1982.
Talk Show, I.R.S., 1984.

Solo

Belinda, I.R.S., 1986.
Heaven On Earth, MCA, 1988.

Sources

Creem, October, 1986.
Los Angeles Times, May 13, 1985.
People, October 26, 1981; June 16, 1986; June 23, 1986.
Rolling Stone, July 5, 1984; August 28, 1986.

—*Sketch by Denise Wiloch*

Lauro F. Cavazos

AP/Wide World Photos

U.S. secretary of education

Full name, Lauro Fred Cavazos, Jr.; born January 4, 1927, at King Ranch, Tex.; son of Lauro Fred (a ranch foreman) and Tomasa (Quintanilla) Cavazos; married Peggy Ann Murdock (a registered nurse), December 28, 1954; children: Lauro, Sarita, Ricardo, Alicia, Victoria, Roberto, Rachel, Veronica, Tomas, Daniel. *Education:* Attended Texas A & I University; Texas Tech University, B.A. in zoology, 1949, M.A. in cytology, 1951; Iowa State University, Ph.D. in physiology, 1954. *Politics:* Democrat. *Religion:* Roman Catholic.

Addresses: *Office*—U.S. Department of Education, 400 Maryland Ave. S.W., Washington, D.C. 20202.

Career

Texas Tech University, Lubbock, teaching assistant, 1949–51; Medical College of Virginia, instructor, then assistant professor, 1956–60, associate professor of anatomy, 1960–64; Tufts University, School of Medicine, Medford, Mass., professor of anatomy, 1964–80, chairman of department, 1964–72, associate dean, 1972–73, acting dean, 1973–75, dean, 1975–80; Texas Tech University, professor of anatomy, professor of biological science, and head of Health Sciences Center, beginning 1980, president until 1988; U.S. secretary of education, Washington, D.C., 1988—.

Member of special and scientific staff, New England Medical Center Hospital, 1974–80; member of advisory committee fellows program, National Board of Medical Examiners, 1978; National Library of Medicine, project site visitor, 1978, member of biomedical library review committee, 1981–85; consultant to council on medical education, Texas Medical Association, beginning 1980. Member of board of directors and campaign chairman, Texas Tech University United Way, 1980; member of Texas Governor's Task Force on Higher Education and Texas Governor's Higher Education Management Effectiveness Council, 1980–82; trustee, Southwest Research Institute, beginning 1982; chairman, Lubbock Boy Scout Campaign, 1981, Southwest Athletic Council president, beginning 1987. *Military service:* U.S. Army, 1945–46.

Member: American Association of Anatomists, Endocrine Society, Histochem Society, American Association for the Advancement of Science, Association of American Medical Colleges, Pan American Association of Anatomy, Philosophical Society of Texas, Lubbock Chamber of Commerce, Tufts Medical Alumni Association (honorary member), Sigma Xi.

Awards: Named Distinguished Graduate, Texas Tech University, 1977; Alumni Achievement Award, Iowa State University, 1979; Outstanding Leadership Award, presented by President Ronald Reagan, 1984; the Lauro F. Cavazos Award was established by

Texas Tech University, 1987; named to Hispanic Hall of Fame, 1987.

Sidelights

The first Hispanic cabinet member was selected because of his ethnicity, Washington scuttlebut had it, and given a token appointment in the waning days of the Reagan administration. But when Lauro F. Cavazos was confirmed in September 1988 as secretary of education, the former Texas university president let it be known he hadn't come to Washington to sit idly at a desk. "These months give me the opportunity to say some things I've been saying in Texas for years: that America must awaken itself to the serious problems it faces due to the decline in education of some of its citizens," he told Robert Marquand of the *Christian Science Monitor.* "Education is perhaps our most serious deficit."

Announcing the appointment of a Hispanic cabinet member in the heat of the Bush-Dukakis campaign gave rise to the suspicion that Cavazos owed his new job to Bush's campaign efforts. White House sources leaked the fact that the "A" list for the job had been limited at Bush's insistence to Hispanic candidates. The growing demographic strength of Hispanics throughout the country, especially in key electoral states like California, Texas, and New York, had made this minority a key constituency in the campaign. Yet Cavazos himself is non-partisan—is in fact a registered Democrat—and yet he will stay on for the Bush Administration.

"I see this [appointment] as a window of opportunity," he told Martin Tolchin of the *New York Times* the day he took office. "I'm trying to raise the awareness of citizens of this nation concerning the problems of lack of education. We hear so much about positioning America to compete. How can we achieve what we want to achieve if our citizens are not educated to their fullest potential?"

Barely unpacking his bags in Washington, the new cabinet member set out on a speaking tour of the southwest, where his pro-education, Don't-Drop-Out message did double duty for the surging Bush campaign. In an interview with Julie Miller of *Education Week,* Cavazos acknowledged that political priorities had colored his appointment but insisted he was more than merely a campaign ploy for the Republican ticket. Cavazos, a registered Democrat who voted in the 1988 party primary, told Miller: "If I can support [Bush], I'm going to support him. But keep in mind, I've really been out there pushing education issues."

As the new secretary of education, Cavazos brought to the office not only a new agenda but a markedly different personal style than his predecessor, William J. Bennett. Less strident than Bennett, who gained the reputation as the Administration's pit bull on education issues, Cavazos favors bilingual education, dropout prevention programs, and greater minority entry into higher education. Where Bennett had used the cabinet post as a bully pulpit to decry academic "elitism", "wasteful" university spending patterns, and "deadbeat" student borrowers, Cavazos delivers paens to the value of education and sees himself as a consensus-builder. Where Bennett loudly blamed rising tuition costs on university budget mismanagement, Cavazos cites high tuitions as a necessary cost of academic excellence. Like Bennett, however, the Texan emphasizes local solutions, not Federal directives, for educational problems. Both secretaries believe that encouraging parental involvement in education is necessary to improve the nation's schools.

Taking office during the Bush-Dukakis campaign, Cavazos publicly dissassociated himself from the outgoing secretary's controversial initiative on student borrowing: Bennett had sought to penalize institutions with student loan default rates higher than 20 percent. Cavazos put the Bennett proposal on the shelf and announced he would work out a better solution with the Congress and university interests. Insiders suggested that this management-by-consensus approach was characteristic of the new education boss.

But it is Cavazos's advocacy of bilingual education, a policy Bennett called a failure, that represents the clearest policy reversal. Cavazos, who grew up in a bilingual family, asserts that students should be taught English as quickly as possible; for him the question is, How soon is possible. He told *Education Week* that "it's so important to be able to command a number of different languages, and for an educator to say 'forget about the other one' is just absolutely not worth commenting on."

Cavazos's staunch support for bilingualism has its roots in personal history. He was born January 4, 1927, at Texas's legendary King Ranch, to the ranch's cattle foreman and his wife, and found that language was an issue early in his life. "On the ranch we all spoke Spanish," he recalled to the *New York Times'* Martin Tolchin. "That was the language of the ranch. I grew up speaking Spanish to my mother, and English to my father." Through second grade he attended the ranch's two-room Hispanic elementary school. When the family moved off the ranch to nearby Kingsville, Texas, the boy enrolled at the town's elementary school where he became its first Hispanic pupil. "Put yourself in the place of a young person who arrives the first day of school," he urged Tolchin. "Even if you understand the language, it's traumatic."

Cavazos cites his father for instilling in all three brothers a hunger for education. Each left the ranch to attend what was then Texas Technical College: brother Bobby was an outstanding running back on the football team and today owns his own ranch; and Dick became a four-star Army general, the first Hispanic to obtain that rank. Young Lauro, upon graduating from high school, decided college was not for him and enlisted in the Army. Upon his discharge he met his father at the Corpus Christi bus depot and stated that his plan was to become a commercial fisherman. Years later he remembered that moment with Martin Tolchin and could recall the words with which his father overruled him: "Well, son, tomorrow we'll go see the registrar at Texas A&I."

Cavazos later transferred to Texas Tech, and completed a bachelor's degree in zoology, then a master's in cytology, the study of cells. During graduate work he met his wife, Peggy, a registered nurse. He continued on for a Ph.D. in physiology at Iowa State University, then taught at the Medical College of Virginia and at Tufts University School of Medicine. At Tufts he was appointed medical school dean in 1975, then left in 1980 when Texas Tech offered him a professorship and several administrative positions. As Texas Tech president Cavazos was both the first Hispanic to serve in that office as well as the first alumnus. His other responsibilities included heading the institution's Health Sciences Center and teaching anatomy.

Early on in his administration he got a call from the White House, Cavazos says, sounding him out for the job of education secretary. Having just started his new job, he indicated he was not yet interested. Instead he plunged himself into the responsibilities of his new post and was successful on many fronts. Julie Miller of *Education Week* wrote, "He is credited with improving Texas Tech's fundraising efforts, increasing minority enrollment, enhancing the university's image with a successful public relations campaign, and beefing up its research programs, particularly in the health-sciences center."

In 1984 he launched a controversial initiative regarding tenure policy. He proposed that tenured professors make up not more than 60 percent of the faculty and suggested periodic reviews of tenured staff. The faculty reacted with predictable outrage, and an 80 percent majority handed him a vote of no-confidence. The American Association of University Professors found that his actions were "detrimental to the principles of academic government." His attempt to erode labor's position at the school earned him renewed attention from the White House; President Reagan presented him with an Outstanding Leadership Award that year. Despite laurels from the president, the dispute dragged on for two years until Cavazos retreated and negotiated a modified tenure policy, which included five-year performance reviews of tenured professors.

On the day Cavazos was nominated for his Cabinet position, the *Washington Post* published a profile that cited the cloud that came over the college's football team during his tenure. In the aftermath of a scandal in which the team was charged with violating recruitment procedures, the team was put on a one-year probation by the NCAA.

> *"We hear so much about positioning America to compete. How can we achieve what we want to achieve if our citizens are not educated to their fullest potential?"*

Other initiatives produced better feelings. Cavazos helped bring Texas Tech professors into West Texas public schools, and made numerous appearances himself. In 1987 he chaired a task force on dropouts for the Lubbock, Texas, school district. E.C. Leslie, superintendent of the Lubbock schools, told *Education Week* that the Texas Tech president visited local schools regularly, "talking about staying in school, speaking at our events, walking into my office suggesting ways we can work together." He also participated in task forces, committees, and panels dealing with such issues as undocumented Mexican workers, the Texas-South Australia Sesquicentennial Celebration, and the selection panel for NASA's journalist-in-space project.

The Cavazos tenure was notable for emphasizing minority enrollment, although Cavazos himself acknowledges the results fell short of the goals. Largely through making personal appearances, Cavazos says, he helped produce an increase in Hispanic enrollment to 6.3 percent in 1987, up from 3.6 percent when he took office in 1980. During this time black enrollment rose to 2.4 percent from 1.8 percent. Yet he called these gains "a failure" in an interview given to Robert Marquand, staff writer for the *Christian Science Monitor.* Texas Tech, like all Texas state colleges and universities, was named in a lawsuit filed by the League of United Latin American Citizens that alleged inadequate recruitment efforts were made towards Hispanic students.

According to the new Cabinet member, the problem for minority students is that they lack role models in their communities who could inspire them to remain in school and graduate. "Many dropouts see no examples in their lives where education has made a difference," he told *Education Week*'s Julie Miller. "You have to instill that attitude [of caring] in parents and teachers, and make sure that students understand the consequences of dropping out. When a person is 16 years old it's hard for them to focus on what life will be like when they're 30."

As secretary Cavazos continues his busy calendar of public appearances, trying to encourage students to stay in school and to transfer to parents his own respect for education. "Our family structure has changed a lot," he told Martin Tolchin. "People don't seem to value education the way they used to. People do not raise the expectations of their children and say, 'Yes, son or daughter, you can complete your high school education. You can go on to get a college degree.'"

Married to Peggy Ann, an operating room nurse, Cavazos has 10 children ranging in age from early twenties to early thirties—seven of whom were graduated from Texas Tech. Journalists who interviewed his colleagues at the university obtained a portrait of a man who is more technocrat than ideologue. One administrator described him to Lisa Belkin of the *New York Times* with the words "persuasive," "dependable," "a delegator," and "consensus builder," adding that "colorful is not a word that applies." In the profile that emerged, the administrator offered a rare glimpse into the private man: Cavazos is a guy who likes to relax by cutting and polishing precious stones in his spare time. The final products he gives to his wife as gifts.

Writings

Contributor of articles to professional journals and chapters to a number of books. Member of editorial boards, *Anatomy Review,* 1970–73, *Medical College of Virginia Quarterly,* beginning 1964, *Tufts Health Science Review,* beginning 1972, and *Journal of Medical Education,* 1980–85.

Sources

Christian Science Monitor, October 21, 1988.
Education Week, September 7, 1988; November 9, 1988.
New York Times, August 11, 1988; October 20, 1988.
Washington Post, August 10, 1988; August 11, 1988.

—Sidelights by Daniela Pozzaglia

John Chaney

College basketball coach

Born January 21, 1932, in Jacksonville, Fla.; stepson of Sylvester Chaney (a shipyard worker); married; wife's name, Jeanne; children: Darryl, John Jr., Pamela. *Education:* Bethune-Cookman College, B.S., 1955; Antioch College, M.S., 1974.

Addresses: *Home*—Mt. Airy, Pa. *Office*—Basketball Office, McGonigle Hall, Temple University, Philadelphia, Pa. 19122.

Career

Professional basketball player with Harlem Globetrotters, 1956, and in Eastern League, 1957–66; Sayre Junior High School, Philadelphia, Pa., basketball coach and health and physical education teacher, 1961–66; Gratz High School, Philadelphia, head basketball coach, 1966–72; Cheyney State College, Cheyney, Pa., head basketball coach and assistant professor of health and physical education, 1972–82; Temple University, Philadelphia, Pa., head basketball coach, 1982—.

Awards: Named Coach of the Year by Pennsylvania State Athletic Conference and by National Collegiate Athletic Association, 1978; named Atlantic Conference Coach of the Year, 1985, 1986, 1987, and 1988; named Coach of the Year by Associated Press, U.S. Basketball Writers Association, and Kodak, 1987, and by Associated Press, United Press International, and U.S. Basketball Writers Association, 1988.

AP/Wide World Photos

Sidelights

Temple University basketball coach John Chaney is fierce and he is gentle, demanding and forgiving, outspoken and private. But in one thing he has been constant—he is almost always successful. Chaney emerged as one of college basketball's premier coaches in the mid 1980s, lifting a down-and-out program to the top of the sport. In his first six years at Temple, he compiled a 154–38 record, highlighted by three straight trips to the NCAA tournament for the first time in the school's history. He has been named coach of the year by most of the organizations following basketball. But even more than his success on the court, Chaney has become known as a model coach off the court. He has pushed his recruits—mostly low-income, inner-city kids—to earn their degrees. And he has become the nation's most outspoken opponent to Proposition 48, the NCAA bylaw that bars athletes with low college board scores from playing their freshman year. Chaney regards the rule as counterproductive and discriminatory toward blacks.

Chaney's attitudes are deeply rooted in his own upbringing, which was one of poverty and prejudice. For him, basketball was the great equalizer and the best way to escape the harsh inner-city. Chaney was born into the projects of Jacksonville, Fla., in 1932. When World War II came, his stepfather, Sylvester Chaney, moved the family north to Philadelphia, where he found work in the Chester Shipyards. Young John chipped in by working as a busboy and waiter. The Chaneys lived over a garage, and friends used to joke that it was colder inside their home than outside. What toys Chaney had were homemade. But five blocks away was Philly's Barrett schoolyard, where young John used to play basketball against other kids for nickels, working on his shooting and ball handling. Wealth and poverty meant little on the playground. "I came from a very poor background," Chaney told the *Boston Globe.* "The only thing I wanted to do was leave home and play in the schoolyard. Then I'd take 'em all on." The toughest opposition came from Chaney's stepfather. "John wanted to play ball. His father wanted him to work," Chaney's childhood friend, Leon Whitley, told the *Philadelphia Daily News.* "His mother let him play. If it was up to John's father, he would have picked up a towel and started washing cars."

Chaney, a hard-nosed 6-foot-4 forward, went on to attend Philadelphia's Ben Franklin High. He had wanted to go to Southern High, which had a stronger basketball program, but doing so would have meant crossing three street gang boundaries. "My pop would give me just enough money to catch the subway one way," he told the *Philadelphia Daily News.* "And a nickel for lunch. They'd sell penny bags of broken cookies. I'd buy five bags. Fill my pockets. Ignored the lunchroom milk. Drank a lot of water." Despite the poor diet, he excelled as a player. Longtime Philadelphia basketball expert Sonny Hill recalled to the *Daily News* how slick a ball handler young Chaney was: "They talk about a game he played at [suburban] Narbeth. A guy tries to steal the ball off him, winds up breaking his ankle. John was truly a great basketball player. Had the same things going for him you see as a coach. That fiery tenacity. Do whatever had to be done."

Real life was a little tougher. Three days after winning the 1951 Markward Award as the best player in Philadelphia's public school league, Chaney learned he was expected to wear a suit to the awards banquet. His family could barely afford to buy him shoes, never mind a suit. So he borrowed an outdated, oversized zoot suit from his stepfather. "A zoot suit," he told the *Daily News.* "Big shoulders, wide lapels, narrow cuffs. A big, old flapjack tie. I hid in the men's room when it was time to get the [all-star team] picture taken."

Chaney had wanted to attend and play basketball at Philadelphia's Temple University but was never offered a full scholarship. His high school grades were not good and, besides, very few blacks got scholarship offers in those days. And his parents could not afford to pay his tuition. So he accepted an offer from Bethune-Cookman College in Daytona Beach, Fla., where he ended up becoming a National Association of Intercollegiate Athletics All-American and MVP in the NAIA's 1953 playoffs. At Bethune-Cookman, Chaney began to understand the importance of academics and also came face-to-face with the realities of Southern racism. And too, he got his first taste of coaching in 1953 when the team's regular coach, Rudolph "Bunky" Matthews, turned up too drunk to guide the club one night. Chaney quickly found a style that suited him. "I did a lot of screaming," he told the *Philadelphia Inquirer.*

After college, a professional career in the National Basketball Association should have followed. But once again, race was the barrier. "John had the talent to play in the NBA," former Temple and NBA player Guy Rodgers, told the *Philadelphia Inquirer.* "But there was an [unwritten] quota about how many blacks could be on a team. A lot of people don't want to admit that. John was truly one of the great ball handlers no one's ever seen." Instead, Chaney had a seven-month stint at something that seems odd for a major-college coach: He played for the Harlem Globetrotters. It is not a time he remembers fondly, and he says he was unaware when he signed a contract that the team was just a show-act. "I just wanted to play basketball, and it wasn't serious basketball," he told the *Los Angeles Times.* "I could do the dipsy-doo when someone said to, but I was serious. When I shot the ball, it was for real. I was very unhappy."

Afterward, he spent ten years playing in the Eastern League, a semi-professional league, where he was six times an all-star, and the MVP in 1959–60. He also doubled as a coach for two seasons. That led to his next job, coaching at Sayre Junior High in Philadelphia, where he built a 68–9 record. Then he went to Gratz High, turning a team that finished 1–17 the season before, into a 17–1 team. By the time Chaney left, he had compiled an 84–6 record.

Chaney moved on in 1972 to Cheyney State College outside of Philadelphia. In ten years at the school, his teams were 225–59, and won the National Collegiate Athletic Association Division II championship in 1978; that same year, he was named Coach of the Year by the NCAA. Four times he was named coach of the year in the Pennsylvania State Athletic

Conference. And in 1978, the NCAA chose him to coach the Division II and III All-America team that won an international tournament in Mexico. At the small-college level, Chaney coached a program that had no athletic scholarships, no televised games, no full-time assistant coaches, no high school all-Americans, no games played in luxurious arenas, and no rich alumni pumping money into the program. But he thrived on it. He would drive 35 miles to the gym early each morning with doughnuts and juice for his players. He would work 16-hour days. He was a tenured assistant professor of health and physical education, but the administration refused to grant him a full professorship. So, when Temple came knocking, he answered the door.

Chaney arrived at Temple in September 1982 after university president Peter Liacouras fired popular coach Don Casey. Casey had run up an impressive 151–94 record over nine seasons, but Liacouras was unhappy with how few players were graduating from the university and how few native Philadelphians were playing for the school. It was an ugly transition, rife with rumors that Casey, who was white, had been fired just so that Liacouras could bring in a black coach. The critics grew louder during Chaney's first season at Temple, when the Owls went 14–15—giving Chaney the only losing season of his coaching career. But things quickly turned around. In the next four seasons, Temple went 25–6, 26–5, 25–6 and 32–4, advancing to the second round of the NCAA tournament each time. In the 1987–88 season, Chaney's club spent several weeks ranked as the top college team in the nation. The Owls advanced to the NCAA's "Sweet Sixteen" before losing to Duke and finishing the season 32–2. It left Chaney's career record at Temple at 154–38. His career winning percentage of .802 ranks him third among active Division I coaches.

What makes Chaney's success even more impressive is that Temple, an urban school with no campus to speak of, is not the kind of university that typically attracts top-notch high school athletes. Chaney has built a program with players who, like him, have had to struggle. "I've never had the luxury of going out and recruiting the blue-chip players," he told the *Boston Globe.* "It doesn't change for a metropolitan school. There's no green grass here, no beautiful trees. Even if we won the NCAAs we'd still be fighting tooth and nail."

What John Chaney sells players is a value system based on toughness, discipline, and preparation. "Winning," Chaney frequently says, "is an attitude." As he explained to the *Philadelphia Inquirer:* "It's just an attitude I developed as a result of being around people who had to make do with a little, or who had to make something from nothing. I've never been able to turn the electric switch to make the lights come on. I always have to rub two sticks together." And, he told the *Boston Globe:* "You ought to be motivated by fear, especially if you come from a tough ghetto life. I tell my guys, 'You should approach everything with apprehension.' It is a necessary safeguard. You've got to decide early on, 'I don't want this. I don't want to be in a rat-infested house. I don't want to be in a neighborhood with drugs and stabbings and dissidence. I don't want it and I'm going to motor in the other direction.' Then you must have great aspirations. You've got to decide, 'I want to be this or I want to be that.' Do that, and now you are motoring 90 miles per hour."

> *"I only know one way to come at you, and that's to be coming at you angry."*

One method Chaney uses to instill the work ethic in his players is holding daily team practices at 5:30 A.M. The morning practices are held in part, he says, to allow the players the normal time to be students. And, he argues, it is an exercise in discipline and the order of things. "I wanted to find out when the winners worked," he told the *Philadelphia Inquirer,* "and then I wanted us to get up earlier than they did.... It helps, late in a game, to know the commitment we have made, to remember the kind of work we have put in, the sacrifice, the dedication." The tight discipline extends to the Temple Owls' style of play. In his efforts to get to the essentials of things, Chaney has boiled basketball down to one supreme statistic—turnovers. Other coaches stress defense, the fast break. Chaney puts his stock in a statistic that is often an afterthought for others. Temple's players do not celebrate big plays with a flurry of high-fives. They rarely stuff the basketball and always refrain from showmanship. "I've never liked high-fiving," Chaney told the *Boston Globe.* "In basketball, you can't rely on emotion to get it done for you.... I've seen too many guys high-fiving, pointing fingers at other players to thank them for a good pass, and somebody is running by them for a layup."

Chaney's own emotions are less reined in. He stalks the sideline, volatile, snarling—barking, he calls it—

tie loosened, arms flailing, veins straining in his neck, screaming at his players, haranguing the referees, sometimes even challenging other coaches. "With me, I only know one way to come at you, and that's to be coming at you angry," he told the *Philadelphia Daily News*. "Other coaches, they might go for the pat on the back, the reassuring smile, at that time. I can't do that."

In recent years, Chaney has become an outspoken opponent to Proposition 48, which, simply stated, is an NCAA guideline requiring a high school student-athlete to achieve a 2.0 grade-point average in high school and a minimum score of 700 in the Scholastic Aptitude Test (SAT) or 15 in the American College Test (ACT). Without one or the other, the student-athlete can enroll in a college but cannot participate in a varsity sport until he achieves a 2.0 grade-point average. "No one should legislate against opportunity," Chaney told the *Philadelphia Daily News*. "Why should the NCAA play God? What they're saying is that college is for the elite. Opportunity is what this country is all about.... Proposition 48 heads us back toward the Stone Age." Chaney admits he may be fighting windmills on this issue, that he may not be able to convince Proposition 48 proponents, but, he told the *Los Angeles Times*, "Don Quixote fought windmills. He thought he was damn successful, too. I fight 'em, too. I don't know if I'm winning, but I'm fighting."

That approach, and Chaney's coaching success have brought the inevitable accolades for his contribution as a black role model. But the coach wants no part of it. "I do not think about being a black coach," Chaney told the *Boston Globe*. "I'm not trying to set an example for anyone. I don't want to be anyone's role model. I don't like the idea." Instead, he regards himself as a man who believes in simple things, who clings to the basics. "I'm A-B-C, 1-2-3," Chaney told the *Los Angeles Times*. "I don't often make it to Z."

Sources

Boston Globe, March 6, 1988.
Los Angeles Times, February 9, 1988; March 17, 1988; March 23, 1988; March 27, 1988; April 2, 1988.
New York Times, March 14, 1988.
Philadelphia Daily News, November 21, 1985; January 29, 1987; March 26, 1987; December 3, 1987; February 22, 1988.
Philadelphia Inquirer, August 18, 1982; March 4, 1984; November 20, 1986; March 17, 1988.
Philadelphia Magazine, December, 1987.
Sporting News, February 2, 1987; March 28, 1988.
Sports Illustrated, February 1, 1988.
Washington Post, February 17, 1987; February 12, 1988.

—*Sketch by Glen Macnow*

Tracy Chapman

AP/Wide World Photos

Singer, songwriter, and musician

Born 1964, in Cleveland, Ohio; parents divorced when she was four years old; raised by her mother. *Education:* Tufts University, B.A. in anthropology, 1986.

Addresses: *Home*—Boston, Mass. *Office*—c/o Elektra Records, 75 Rockefeller Plaza, New York, N.Y. 10019.

Career

As a young child, played ukulele, organ, and clarinet; began playing guitar and singing original songs at the age of ten; during high school, performed at school functions and at local coffee houses in Connecticut; while in college, performed at church services, on street corners, and in coffee houses in Boston and Cambridge, Mass.; after graduating from Tufts University, signed a recording contract and began performing at clubs, festivals, and in concert; has toured throughout the United States and around the world.

Awards: Grammy Awards for Best New Artist, for Best Female Pop Vocal Performance, and for Best Contemporary Folk Performance, all 1989.

Sidelights

In an era when the label folksinger-songwriter does little to guarantee success, Tracy Chapman has seen her dreams come true. When Chapman takes the stage sporting dreadlocks, blue jeans, and a turtleneck sweater, accompanied only by her acoustic guitar, listeners lean forward to hear her husky contralto pour forth poignant reflections on contemporary urban life. As Steve Pond of *Rolling Stone* noted, Chapman's "is the sound of a smart black woman growing up in the city with her eyes wide open."

Though she is a relative newcomer to the folk music circuit, Chapman has always made music an important part of her life. Chapman's parents divorced when she was four years old, and she grew up with her mother and older sister in a largely black middle-class neighborhood in Cleveland, Ohio. At an early age she learned to sing, play the clarinet and organ, and compose simple songs that she sang with her sister, Aneta. While still in grade school Chapman began to teach herself how to play the guitar. She told *Washington Post* writer Richard Harrington: "I've been singing ever since I was a child. My mother has a beautiful voice, as does my sister. At that point I wasn't really listening to that much music at all, except what my parents were listening to, or my sister. I think I just picked up a guitar because my mother had played it at some point—started teaching myself things and writing my own songs."

Wanting to make a better life for herself than those she witnessed around her, Chapman worked hard to earn A Better Chance (ABC) minority placement scholarship to the Wooster School, a small, progressive, private high school in Danbury, Connecticut. There she was thoroughly immersed in an atmosphere of social and political consciousness. She also met other guitar players who introduced her to a variety of popular music, including the early protest works of Bob Dylan. Chapman's teachers recognized her talent and gave her ample opportunities to perform. In a gesture of support, the school chaplain took up a collection among the faculty and students and bought the young singer a new guitar to replace her battered one.

Despite the strong support for her musical talent, Chapman did not seriously consider music as a career. When she enrolled at Tufts University, near Boston, she aspired to become a veterinarian. However, a short while later she changed her major to anthropology with an emphasis on West African cultures, the field in which she eventually earned her bachelor's degree.

"I don't just think of what I do as folk music, which I define as music rooted in an Anglo-European tradition, but as music that also reflects Afro-American black music."

While in college, Chapman continued to perform her own compositions in coffee houses, on street corners, and at folk-oriented church services. She was offered a recording contract with an independent label but turned it down, not wanting to interrupt her education. Chapman's decision proved to be fortuitous. One of her classmates, Brian Koppelman, approached her after hearing her play to suggest that his father might be able to help her singing career. The father in question was none other than Charles Koppelman, the K in SBK, one of the world's largest music publishing and production companies. At Brian's suggestion, Charles Koppelman came to hear Chapman perform, and he later told *Newsweek:* "Her songs were wonderful melodies with important lyrics. That was enough. But when I saw her in front of an audience! When she smiled, everyone smiled. When she was serious, you could hear a pin drop."

Chapman had considered working toward a master's degree in ethnomusicology, the study of chiefly non-European music, especially in relation to the cultural that produces it. But after graduating in 1986, she signed a management agreement with SBK, to be represented by Elliott Roberts, who also manages singers Joni Mitchell and Neil Young. A demonstration tape recorded by Chapman at the SBK studios eventually led to a recording contract with Elektra Records.

After settling on producer David Kershenbaum and hiring a backup band, Chapman was ready to record. Because she is a prolific songwriter, there was no lack of music from which to select the pieces that make up her self-titled debut album. *Tracy Chapman* breaks all the rules of popular music marketing. The melodies wander and are oddly phrased, and many of the songs explore serious subjects—racism, domestic violence, the failed American dream, material and emotional self-determination—and do not fit the format of commercial radio. The background instrumentals are limited, focusing attention on Chapman's percussive use of the acoustic guitar, and one selection is even sung a cappella. In seeming defiance to trends, Chapman's album rose to the number one position on *Billboard's* best-seller chart without discernible airplay and has become a favorite of critics as well. The cut "Fast Car" has received the most airplay and engendered a music video, which alternates segments of Chapman singing in her usual concert attire and still photographs of gritty real-life scenes.

For just this sort of blunt realism, reviewers describe *Tracy Chapman* as downbeat, particularly the cuts "Talkin' 'bout a Revolution" and "Why?" Yet Chapman remains ever hopeful. As she told the *New York Times:* "On a certain level, I think something positive is going to happen, though I don't think it's necessarily going to be an actual revolution. Even though I'm a cynic, there's still a part of me that believes people will get to a certain point where they can't stand the way things are and have to change the way they think."

The power of Chapman's songs to motivate change lies in their psychological realism, their universal poignancy. With an eye for detail, Chapman uses just enough specifics to suggest events or situations known to listeners regardless of where they live. She chronicles in song the human condition. When asked about her songwriting ability, Chapman told *Musician* writer Kristine McKenna: "I don't have structured writing habits. I've written hundreds of songs and have enough material for three albums so I don't see writing as a problem. I play my guitar every day and always have fragments of ideas floating around my head, but I never force a song into being. My songs aren't autobiographical, but they usually combine a variety of things I've seen, heard or read about. Occasionally it will be something that happened to me, but I'll combine that with other things."

Chapman has frequently been compared to folksingers Joan Armatrading, Joni Mitchell, and Phoebe Snow. Some reviewers see her as "a bridge between the folk music revial of the eighties and the socially conscious folk movement of the sixties," a bridge girded by the efforts of another female folksinger—Suzanne Vega. [See index for *Newsmakers* entry.] Chapman balks at being labeled, whether the label is folksinger or black woman artist. As she told a *Chicago Tribune* writer: "I don't just think of what I do as folk music, which I define as music rooted in an Anglo-European tradition, but as music that also reflects Afro-American black music. Personally, it wasn't a matter of being drawn to a particular music; in a sense, the instrument you play defines what you play."

Chapman's performance schedule is no doubt influenced by her social conscience: the Sisterfire festival in Washington, D.C.; Amnesty International's worldwide Human Rights Now! tour; and a march to commemorate Dr. Martin Luther King. Chapman takes to the stage with more ease than she wears her celebrity status, however. Even as a young dreamer, Chapman never expected to sign with a major label, and when she did she didn't foresee the popularity of *Tracy Chapman,* album and person. She admitted to McKenna: "The idea of being famous doesn't appeal to me because I hate parties and it seems like it might be one big party. I value my privacy and I'm not used to dealing with lots of people. The prospect of wealth is scary too. When you're poor your first responsibility is to yourself, but when you have money you have to think about other people—and other people are definitely thinking about you!"

Discography

Tracy Chapman (includes "Fast Car," "Baby Can I Hold You," "Talkin' 'bout a Revolution," "She's Got Her Ticket," "Behind the Wall," "For My Lover," "If Not Now . . . ," "Why?" "Across the Lines," "Mountains o' Things," and "For You"), Elektra, 1988.

Sources

Chicago Tribune, August 14, 1988.
Detroit News, September 4, 1988.
Musician, June 1988.
Newsweek, June 20, 1988.
New York Times, September 4, 1988.
Rolling Stone, June 2, 1988; June 30, 1988.
Time, August 15, 1988.

—Sidelights by Jeanne M. Lesinski

Praveen Chaudhari

Photograph by Mario Ruiz

Physicist and electronics company executive

Born November 30, 1937, in Ludhiana, India; married in 1964; children: two. *Education:* Indian Institute of Technology (Kharagpur, India), B.Tech., 1961; Massachusetts Institute of Technology, S.M., 1963, Sc.D. in metallurgy, 1966.

Addresses: *Office*—Thomas J. Watson Research Center, IBM Corp., P.O. Box 218, Yorktown Heights, N.Y. 10598.

Career

Massachusetts Institute of Technology, Cambridge, research assistant in physical metallurgy, 1961–65, research associate in metallurgy, 1965–66; International Business Machines Corp. (IBM), Yorktown Heights, N.Y., member of research staff, 1966–80, director of physical science department, 1980—, vice-president for science, 1982—. Member of research staff of Danish Atomic Energy Commission (Denmark), 1964.

Member: American Physical Society.

Sidelights

The electronics industry has changed our lives ever since the transistor was invented in 1948. The transistor is the most familiar piece of equipment made from what scientists call semiconducting materials, and, since that invention in the late 1940s, many changes have occurred to it to make the transistor work harder and faster.

Making it smaller has allowed equipment made from transistors to shrink, so computers have become small enough—and cheap enough—to be used in the home. IBM vice-president Praveen Chaudhari notes the influence this has had in the marketplace. "The worldwide sales of the electronics industry will be approximately a trillion dollars by the end of the century," Chaudhari wrote in the *Scientific American.* "Estimates place its current sales above $200 billion, which is roughly equal to the gross national product of India and is larger than the G.N.P. of every country in the world except the top dozen or so." But to sustain such spectacular growth, Chaudhari says the electronics industry will have "to continue to make its products indispensable to society." Moreover "that task requires progress to be kept up simultaneously on several fronts," especially materials science.

It is on just that very front that an exciting revolution has been taking place, and Chaudhari's IBM team has had a tremendous breakthrough. The world has been focusing on materials that carry electricity at low temperatures without losing current. Called superconductors, these materials are superior to the semiconductors used so widely in the electronics industry. As semiconductor chips were made smaller, they worked faster, but that in turn introduced problems such as electromigration (unwanted movement of the material the chip is made from) or leaking of electrons through insulation made too thin as the size of the chip was reduced. But superconductors allow electricity to flow "somewhat like bullets fired from a high-powered rifle," as Chaudhari explains. And that speed doesn't produce heat, which is both wasteful and destructive.

All kinds of practical uses for materials with such properties have occurred to scientists—from ultrafast computers and hyperefficient power plants to new medical scanners and clean, safe, plentiful nuclear energy. But so far the metals that have superconductive properties have had to be chilled with costly liquid helium to minus 459 degrees Fahrenheit, and they don't carry that much current.

Then in May, 1987, Chaudhari's IBM team created a ceramic crystal conductor thinner than a human hair that could transmit current "a hundred times greater than anyone had demonstrated before," as Anthony Ramirez notes in *Fortune* magazine. The material doesn't need to be cooled so much either, so it can be chilled with cheap liquid nitrogen, which—as Ramirez points out—"is so user friendly that it can be carried around in a Styrofoam cup."

Chaudhari and his IBM team have largely solved the current-carrying problem, but there are other barriers, mainly the fact that the ceramic materials are brittle and hard to form into useful shapes. At the moment the superconductors aren't seen as substitutes for the silicon or other semiconducting materials used in chips, "but they could replace the metals that connect chips together. Superconducting circuits communicate with each other faster . . . because they use less energy and generate less heat, so they can be crammed together more tightly than silicon-based circuits," explains the *Fortune* reporter. "Higher-performance computers would result, and supercomputers that now occupy space the size of offices could be shrunk to the size of shoe boxes."

Will superconducting supercomputers arrive soon? Chaudhari is cautious. "'Those two supers in a row sound appealing, I know,' he says, but major difficulties remain with both cost and design." Nevertheless superconductors have released a worldwide scientific and commercial free-for-all, and scientists like Praveen Chaudhari are rushing to be at the forefront of this new frontier.

Sources

Fortune, June 22, 1987.
Newsweek, May 25, 1987.
Scientific American, October, 1986.

—*Sketch by Frances C. Locher*

John Cleese

AP/Wide World Photos

Actor, writer, and producer

Full name, John Marwood Cleese; born October 27, 1939, in Weston-super-Mare, Somerset, England; son of Reginald (in insurance sales) and Muriel (an acrobat; maiden name, Cross) Cleese; married Connie Booth (an actress and writer), February 20, 1968 (divorced, 1978); married Barbara Trentham (a director, actress, and artist), February 15, 1981 (divorced, 1988); children: (first marriage) Cynthia; (second marriage) Camilla. *Education:* Cambridge University, M.A., 1963.

Addresses: *Office*—8 Clarendon Rd., London W11 3AA, England.

Career

After graduating from high school, taught English, history, and geography to elementary school children; began writing and performing comedy revues in college; worked for two weeks as a writer for *Newsweek* magazine and, also briefly, as an articles clerk for a London law firm; appeared on stage in "Footlights Review," 1963, and "Half a Sixpence," 1965; writer and performer for BBC television series "The Frost Report" and "At Last the 1948 Show," 1966–67; co-founder (with Graham Chapman, Terry Gilliam, Eric Idle, Terry Jones, and Michael Palin) of Monty Python comedy troupe, 1969; performer and writer for television series "Monty Python's Flying Circus," 1969–73; star of series "Fawlty Towers," 1975–79.

Feature films include "Interlude," 1968, "The Rise and Rise of Michael Rimmer," 1970, "The Magic Christian," 1970, "The Statue," 1971, "And Now for Something Completely Different," 1972, "Monty Python and the Holy Grail," 1975, "Monty Python's Life of Brian," 1979, "The Secret Policeman's Ball," 1979, "Time Bandits," 1981, "The Great Muppet Caper," 1981, "The Secret Policeman's Other Ball," 1982, "Monty Python Live at the Hollywood Bowl," 1982, "Monty Python's The Meaning of Life," 1983, "Yellowbeard," 1983, "Privates on Parade," 1984, "Silverado," 1985, "Clockwise," 1986, and "A Fish Called Wanda," 1988.

Also appeared in BBC production of "Taming of the Shrew," 1980. Founder of Video Arts Ltd., 1972; creator of commercial advertisements for various companies, and of more than 50 business training films, including "Meetings, Bloody Meetings," "The Secretary and Her Boss," "The Balance Sheet Barrier," and "Time Management Delegation."

Awards: Honorary LL.D. from St. Andrew's University, 1971; Queen's Award for Exports, 1982, for a commercial series created for American radio broadcast; co-winner of Golden Palm from Cannes Film Festival, 1983, for "Monty Python's The Meaning of Life."

Sidelights

Some people know him as the Minister of Silly Walks from the BBC television series "Monty Python's Flying Circus." To others he is Basil Fawlty, the shrill and officious hotel proprietor from "Fawlty Towers." More recently, he was the upper-crust barrister in his own feature film production, "A Fish Called Wanda." Throughout his career, British comic actor John Cleese has played authority figures whose best-laid plans turn into major disasters. "The key to Cleese's appeal," wrote *Washington Post* television critic Tom Shales, is "the anticipation that this enormous, tautly wound rubber band will snap. Watching someone who looks to be the Upper Class Incarnate skid into lunacy is simply great fun." But John Cleese is much more than that. The tall (six-foot-five) actor is also the world's largest producer of corporate training films. And he was the co-author of a strong-selling book on family psychology. "I'm just a guy who never intended or expected to go into show business," Cleese told the *Chicago Tribune*. "Even now, my family keeps waiting for me to quit all the lunacy and go back to practicing the law." To Cleese's parents, the law always seemed an admirable profession. So, while they had little money, the lower-middle income family struggled to send their only child to esteemed prep schools. "I met my first twit in prep school," he told the *Philadelphia Inquirer*. "I got an early start."

Born one month after World War II started, Cleese grew up in a small, provincial English town; and, he told the *Chicago Tribune*, comedy provided, "a useful social tool for a child who was very solitary, although never lonely. I wasn't a good mixer, and my unusual height didn't help either. I was 6'5" by the time I was 14. Thank God it stopped the same year. Anyway, I made the other kids laugh, that made me popular, and I felt more accepted." As a child, he told the *Tribune*, his favorite comedians were, "Jack Benny, Phil Silvers, George Burns, Danny Kaye. In fact, all my favorites were American apart from Chaplin and Stan Laurel."

After high school, Cleese briefly taught English, history, and geography to 11-year-olds before entering Cambridge University, where he studied law. He also joined Footlights, the university comedy club, and became one of its star performers and writers. After graduation he had a two-week career writing for *Newsweek* (he was fired) and then was hired as an articles clerk for a prestigious London law firm. He continued to perform at Cambridge during his spare time. "I was going to be a lawyer," he told the *Wichita Eagle-Beacon*, "but then I appeared in a show, the Cambridge Footlights, which is like the Hasty Pudding at Harvard. The next thing I knew there were two very nice people from the BBC who said, 'Would you like to come and have a job with us?' They were offering me 2½ times as much as I would get as a lawyer, and I never wanted to be a lawyer, anyway. I was able to tell my parents it was the BBC and I would get a pension, so it was all right with them. If I had announced I was going to be an actor, I'm sure they would have stopped me. I would hope so, because it would certainly have been a dumb thing to do." So in 1966, at age 26, Cleese began writing jokes for the BBC. He wrote and performed for David Frost's show, "The Frost Report," and appeared in the musical comedy "Half a Sixpence," which played in London and New York.

He also met five other young comics who shared his peculiar madness. They banded together for the debut of "Monty Python's Flying Circus" in September 1969. The BBC bought the show without even asking for a pilot. "We were a very happy family when we started in '69," Cleese told the *Philadelphia Inquirer*. "We were such a disparate group. We used to write different types of sketches—Terry Gilliam's animations were quite different from anything anyone else was doing. Eric [Idle] wrote very intricate verbal stuff. Terry Jones and Michael Palin tended to write more visually. And all these were quite different from the Cleese and [Graham] Chapman sketches, which tended to be more structured and perhaps more logical, but usually had to do with people bumping into each other rather hard . . . abusing each other."

Monty Python (a name chosen to sound like a ruthless show business agent) exercised a brand of humor that gave new flavor to bad taste. Its quick-witted skits about dead parrots, cannibalism, transvestite lumber jacks, and other lighthearted topics transformed the group into BBC television stars virtually overnight. And the half-hour shows immediately attracted a cult following when they made their way onto public television in America. Cleese, with his great height and patrician bearing, often played the stuffiest of Tory wets or an inspired lunatic with the physical presence of a deranged stork. His roles included the Permanent Undersecretary in the Ministry of Silly Walks and the Upper Class Twit of the Year. The troupe's popularity led to Python records and Python books. Monty Python then collaborated on four films. The first, "And Now for Something Completely Different" (1972), was a compilation of the best of the television shows. The team's spoof on Arthurian romances, "Monty Python and the Holy Grail," was released in 1975, followed by a parody of the life of Christ called "The Life of Brian" in 1979 and "The Meaning of Life" in 1983. The films were all commercial—if not critical—successes. In all likelihood, Cleese says, the Pythons will have no future group projects. Creative differences caused the eventual breakup, as each member wanted to pursue his own avenue of comedy.

For Cleese, that proved to be "Fawlty Towers," a hilarious comedy he and then-wife Connie Booth wrote and starred in for the BBC in 1975. Cleese portrayed innkeeper Basil Fawlty, a character forever poised on the verge of raging fits over trivial matters. Cleese described Basil to the New Yorker as "a man of ranting protocol who overrides pleasure .... Your average professional neurotic." The series was a marginal hit in Great Britain, but—like Monty Python—a cult smash in the United States, where its dozen episodes still play on PBS. *Washington Post* television critic Tom Shales described Basil Fawlty as "an insufferable and unforgivable cad one both suffers and forgives, because while most of us are frequently or occasionally at war with the world, for Basil hostilities never cease .... Cleese is particularly magnificent when enraged; he explodes like Daffy Duck in a cartoon. The only thing that keeps him from going terminally to pieces is his awareness of what joy this would bring to his enemies."

"I'd rather scream with laughter at the end of the day than be touched by a film. And that's because it's much rarer to scream with laughter than it is to be touched."

As spontaneous as the hysterics appeared, Cleese said each moment was deliberately calculated. "You wouldn't believe the technical detail to which I worked on those shows," Cleese told *Newsday.* "During the course of a week, I would decide that during someone else's speech, I should look at him three times. And that the first look would be done one way, and the second another, and the third yet another. It was that technical. And you keep doing it until it feels right in your gut."

"Fawlty Towers" ended soon after Cleese's marriage to Booth broke up. He spent the next several years expanding his visibility—appearing in commercials endorsing Canadian peanut butter, British toffee, American credit cards, Norwegian mayonnaise, Danish shoes, and Japanese televisions. And, since 1972, Cleese and two partners have run their own business, Video Arts Ltd., which makes management training films. The London-based company grossed $14.5 million in 1987—making it the largest firm of its kind in the world—and has produced more than 80 training films that use dry, often surreal wit to make serious points. "I was after a fast buck," Cleese told *Forbes.* "But I made a disastrous miscalculation. I got interested." Today, Video Arts' clients include the Inland Revenue (England's IRS), the Turkish Navy, the Soviet National Health Service, and about 6,000 American companies. And, since 1987, shortened versions of the films have become a highlight of the show "Business This Morning," which is syndicated in about 100 American markets.

The business films rely on Cleese's humor to rise above the boredom of most training videos. Typically, Cleese stars as a befuddled executive trying to avoid the pitfalls of his business. In one, he was a befuddled CEO, struggling to run a weekly meeting of bored underlings and making every mistake known to the board room. "Humor is so effective in changing people's behavior," Cleese told the *Chicago Tribune.* "It has such an enormously strong, persuasive force—much more so, I believe, than the ordinary verbal statement. If you do comedy, you're involving the audience at a gut level, and that's the level at which you can change them."

Cleese's comedy work extends to writing. In 1983 he joined with his psychiatrist, Dr. Robin Skynner, to write a somewhat humorous therapy book entitled *Families and How to Survive Them.* An *Akron Beacon Journal* review said: "The book covers everything from how people fall in and out of love to what creates slow learners. The style is that of a leisurely and rather spontaneous dialogue." The two men met in 1973, when Cleese decided to explore psychotherapy for two reasons: He was having difficulties in his first marriage and had spent two years with low-grade flu symptoms, which his physician suggested might be psychosomatic. After three years in Skynner's therapy group, Cleese described his time there to the *New Yorker* as "the single thing that has freed me most to enjoy life more. Any problems I now experience are much milder and more manageable—almost an echo of their former selves."

Cleese appeared in films of mixed success in the 1980s. The most significant included "Privates on Parade" (1984), a war satire in which Cleese played the fussy and depressed Major Flack, head of the

British Army Song and Dance Unit; and Lawrence Kasden's "Silverado" (1985), in which he portrayed an English sheriff in the American West, spouting lines like, "What's all this, then?" His first starring role came in Michael Frayn's "Clockwise" (1986), in which he played an obsessively punctual British headmaster who, on the most important day of his life, misses the train and finds things going rapidly downhill. Cleese's reviews for "Clockwise" were excellent. The *Philadelphia Inquirer* wrote: "Cleese stars to perfection.... He always is a joy to watch, especially when he screams a determinedly self-assured 'Right!' in reaction to everything that goes wrong." A *Houston Post* writer stated: "As he branches out on his own in television and movies, Cleese, the most talented member of the Monty Python troupe, is fast establishing himself as a consummate comedian. He possesses a strongly defined screen personality that can turn the most banal predicament into hilarity, and he shows ever-growing command and confidence as a comic actor."

In 1988, Cleese put his comic skills to their greatest test in "A Fish Called Wanda," which he wrote, starred in, and produced. The film, a sleeper hit of the year, was, on the surface, a madcap comedy about a double-crossing gang of diamond thieves, co-starring Jamie Lee Curtis, Kevin Kline, and former Python Michael Palin. Under the surface, it was a story of clashing cultures—the British stuffiness versus the American spontaneity and vulgarity. Cleese cast himself as Archie Leach (Cary Grant's real name), a stuffy London barrister seduced into crime and romance. "It took me a long time—several years—to write 'Wanda,'" Cleese told the *Chicago Tribune*, "and stumble slowly, though not unhappily, through all the ideas and material before I could solve the puzzle and bring all the elements together so that they logically follow, one from another, in the most concentrated way possible." Overall, the film received excellent reviews. The *Tribune* called it "a tour-de-force of comic invention and timing, and one of the funniest films to come along in recent years." *Newsweek* wrote, "After years of creating wacky caricatures, Cleese gives a funny, touching performance that's more than skin deep."

His behind-the-camera involvement in Wanda convinced Cleese that his career might now follow the same path as a filmmaker he admires very much, Woody Allen. "It's much more interesting to try to write a 105-minute film than it is to do a 10-minute sketch or even an episode of 'Fawlty Towers,'" he told the *Philadelphia Inquirer*. "I think I've really gone the same route as Woody Allen. He went from things like 'Take the Money and Run,' which is really a series of sketches, to really three-dimensional movies like 'Manhattan' and 'Hannah and Her Sisters.' Maybe I'll end up like that, but I'd rather scream with laughter at the end of the day than be touched by a film. And that's because it's much rarer to scream with laughter than it is to be touched." And although Woody Allen complains that comedy is like sitting at the children's table, Cleese sees it as surpassingly important. He told the *Washington Post*, "I always say that if comedy is good enough for Shakespeare and Mozart, it's good enough for me."

Discography

The Frost Report on Britain (contributor with Tim Brooke-Taylor, David Frost, and others), Starline, 1966.
Monty Python's Flying Circus, BBC Records, 1969.
Another Monty Python Record, Charisma, 1970.
Monty Python's Previous Record, Charisma, 1972.
Monty Python's Matching Tie and Handkerchief, Charisma, 1974.
Monty Python Live at Drury Lane, Charisma, 1974.
The Album of the Soundtrack of the Trailer of the Film Monty Python and the Holy Grail, Arista, 1975.
Monty Python Live at City Center, Arista, 1976.
Monty Python's Instant Record Collection, Charisma, 1977.
Monty Python's Life of Brian, Warner Bros., 1979.
Fawlty Towers (with first wife, Connie Booth), BBC Records, 1981.
Monty Python's Contractual Obligation Album, Arista, 1980.
Fawlty Towers/Second Sitting (with Booth), BBC Records, 1981.
Fawlty Towers/At Your Service (with Booth), BBC Records, 1982.
Monty Python's The Meaning of Life, CBS Records, 1983.

Writings

The Strange Case of the End of Civilisation As We Know It (with Jack Hobbs and Joe McGrath), Star Books, 1970.
Monty Python's Big Red Book (contributor), edited by Eric Idle, Methuen, 1972.
The Brand New Monty Python Book (contributor), edited by Idle, Methuen, 1973.
Monty Python and the Holy Grail (contributor), Methuen, 1977, also published as *Monty Python's Second Film: A First Draft*, Methuen, 1977.
Fawlty Towers (with first wife, Connie Booth), Futura, Volume 1, 1977, Volume 2, 1979.
Monty Python's Life of Brian (of Nazareth) [and] *Montypythonscrapbook* (contributor), Grosset, 1979.

The Complete Works of Shakespeare and Monty Python (contributor; contains *Monty Python's Big Red Book* and *The Brand New Monty Python Papperbok*), Eyre Methuen, 1981.

Families and How to Survive Them (with Robin Skynner), Oxford University Press, 1983.

Sources

Books

Wilmut, Roger, *From Fringe to Flying Circus*, Methuen, 1980.

Hewison, Robert, *Monty Python: The Case Against*, Methuen, 1981.

Contemporary Literary Criticism, Volume 21, Gale, 1982.

Hewison, *Footlights!*, Methuen, 1983.

Perry, George, *The Life of Python*, Pavilion Books, 1983.

Contemporary Authors, Volume 116, Gale, 1986.

Periodicals

Akron Beacon Journal, January 6, 1985.

Boston Globe, June 5, 1982; July 10, 1985.

Chicago Tribune, September 21, 1979; April 1, 1983; November 2, 1986; July 24, 1988; July 29, 1988; August 4, 1988; August 17, 1988.

Forbes, May 26, 1988.

Houston Post, November 20, 1986.

Los Angeles Times, March 31, 1983; October 25, 1987; July 15, 1988.

Newsday, March 5, 1987; July 13, 1988.

Newsweek, September 3, 1979; July 12, 1982; April 4, 1983; August 8, 1988.

New Yorker, August 26, 1972; May 5, 1975; May 12, 1975; August 27, 1979; May 2, 1988.

New York Times, April 28, 1975; April 16, 1976; August 17, 1979; March 31, 1983.

New York Times Magazine, April 18, 1976.

People, August 22, 1982; September 26, 1983; August 15, 1988.

Philadelphia Inquirer, June 15, 1984; January 14, 1987; July 31, 1988.

San Jose Mercury News, December 28, 1986.

Time, May 26, 1975; September 17, 1979; March 28, 1983; October 20, 1986.

Times (London), June 10, 1983; September 28, 1983.

Washington Post, July 16, 1983; September 4, 1983; July 31, 1988.

Wichita Eagle-Beacon, December 10, 1986.

—Sidelights by Glen Macnow

Francis Ford Coppola

AP/Wide World Photos

Film director, producer, and writer

Born April 7, 1939, in Detroit, Mich.; son of Carmine (a flutist, composer, and conductor) and Italia (an actress; maiden name, Pennino) Coppola; married Eleanor Neil (an artist); children: Roman, Sofia, Gian-Carlo (deceased). *Education:* Hofstra University, B.A. in theater arts, 1958; University of California, Los Angeles, M.A. in cinema studies, 1966.

Addresses: *Home*—Napa Valley, Calif.; San Francisco, Calif.; Los Angeles, Calif.; New York, N.Y.; and Belize. *Office*—c/o Zoetrope Studios, 916 Kearny St., San Francisco, Calif. 94133.

Career

While attending graduate school, worked as an assistant to director Roger Corman, serving as writer, dialogue director, sound man, and associate producer; made debut as a director in 1963 with "Dementia 13"; screenwriter for Seven Arts Studios; co-founder, with George Lucas, and president of American Zoetrope production company, San Francisco, Calif., 1969; founder of Zoetrope Studios, San Francisco and Los Angeles, Calif., 1980.

Films include "Tonight for Sure," 1961; "Dementia 13" (writer and director), 1963; "Battle Beyond the Sun" (writer), 1963; "This Property Is Condemned" (writer), 1966; "Is Paris Burning?" (co-writer), 1966; "You're a Big Boy Now" (writer and director), 1967; "Reflections in a Golden Eye" (writer), 1967; "Finian's Rainbow" (director), 1968; "The Rain People" (writer and director), 1969; "Patton" (writer), 1970; "TXH 1138" (producer), 1971; "The Godfather" (co-writer, director, and producer), 1972; "American Graffiti" (producer), 1973; "The Godfather II" (co-writer, director, and producer), 1974; "The Conversation" (writer, director, and producer), 1974; "The Great Gatsby" (writer), 1974; "Apocalypse Now" (writer, director, and producer), 1979; "The Black Stallion" (executive producer), 1979; "Hammett" (executive producer), 1982; "One from the Heart" (co-writer, director, and producer), 1982; "The Escape Artist" (co-writer, director, and producer), 1982; "The Black Stallion Returns" (executive producer), 1983; "Rumble Fish" (co-writer, director, and producer), 1983; "The Outsiders" (co-writer, director, and producer), 1983; "The Cotton Club" (co-writer and director), 1984; "Peggy Sue Got Married" (director), 1986; "Gardens of Stone" (director and co-producer), 1987; "Tucker: A Man and His Dream" (director), 1988; "New York Stories" (writer and director of one of three segments), 1989. Director of play "Private Lives" and opera "The Visit of the Old Lady," both 1972; also director of television film "The People" and of short film "Rip Van Winkle" for "Fairy Tale Theater."

Member: Directors Guild of America, Academy of Motion Picture Arts and Sciences.

Awards: Samuel Goldwyn Award, 1962, for screenplay of "Dementia 13"; San Sebastian International Film Festival award, 1970, for "The Rain People"; co-winner of Academy Award for best screenplay, 1970, for "Patton"; Academy Awards for best film and best screenplay adapted from another medium, and nomination for best director, all 1972, for "The Godfather"; named best director by Directors Guild of America, 1972 and 1974; Golden Palm Award from Cannes Film Festival and Academy Award nominations for best director and best screenplay, all 1974, for "The Conversation"; Academy Awards for best film and best director and co-winner of Academy Award for best screenplay adapted from another medium, all 1974, for "The Godfather II"; honorary D.F., Hofstra University, 1977; FIPRESCI Award and co-winner of Golden Palm Award from Cannes Film Festival, and Academy Award nominations for best film, best director, and best screenplay adapted from another medium, all 1979, for "Apocalypse Now."

Sidelights

For all its jaunty charm, Francis Ford Coppola's "Tucker: A Man and His Dream" exposes the dark underside of the American Dream. The film chronicles the real-life story of Preston Tucker, a 1940s entrepreneur who tried to crack the auto industry with an innovative car he designed. In the end, even though he manages to manufacture 51 of his automobiles—and although his ideas would be exploited by future engineers—his company goes bankrupt, and he comes to be viewed as a con artist. It's the classic story of the individual versus the establishment: No matter how exceptional the individual, the status quo must be maintained, and so the establishment must triumph.

Though the conclusion of Coppola's own story has yet to be written, in certain ways his career has come to mirror Tucker's. Like Tucker's singlehanded challenge of the "Big Three" automakers, Coppola has always swum against Hollywood's commercial mainstream. Along the way he has pursued neither fame nor money (though each has come to him in sizable portions) but rather the chance to test his offbeat ideas and extend cinematic borders. As a whole, his films encompass a daringly broad range in subject and presentation, leaving viewers hard-pressed to categorize him. Since his "Godfather" hits of the 1970s—two of the most celebrated and profitable movies of all time—he has travelled far afield from Mafia territory, into the Vietnam war ("Apocalypse Now"), 1960s Oklahoma ("The Outsiders"), and jazz-age Harlem ("The Cotton Club"). Rather than content, though, it's form that distinguishes his *oeuvre:* With each film, he has tried—often unsuccessfully—to tell the story in a new way. This search for stylistic novelty is apparent even in "Godfather II," which could have been just as popular had he simply stuck to the approach of the original film. In his book *Hollywood Auteur,* Jeffrey Chown observed, "Although Coppola with 'Godfather II' is sometimes blamed for initiating the sequel craze of the last decade, no other sequel stands in such contrast to its predecessor as does 'Godfather II' to 'The Godfather.'"

In a 1982 interview with the *Christian Science Monitor,* Coppola lamented the lack of diversity in current film. "The corporations and the exhibitors, and even the critical press, want films to be more and more uniform, more of a product," he said. "It's a system of overlapping, vested interests which protect the way things are—because the way things are, they're on top. How can we compete with that?" While that reality may underlie the mediocrity of some of his films, it has never kept him from returning to his overriding impulse to challenge the system. As the director Tom Luddy once remarked to *Time* about his former employer, "He's a risk taker who likes to gamble everything on his art." And as Chown further noted, more specifically: "A decision to make a somber, operatic gangster film, or a surreal, hallucinatory war film"—alluding to "The Godfather" and "Apocalypse Now," respectively—"is a challenge to the industry's conventions, and the success of a good many of those gambles is the basis of Coppola's reputation."

By far the riskiest gamble of Coppola's career has been Zoetrope Studios, a company he created in 1980 as an alternative to the Hollywood system. In another parallel to Tucker's career, the enterprise failed. Not only was Coppola faced with paying off a $50 million debt, but in the process, he was forced to abandon many of his unconventional (*i.e.,* unprofitable) ideas. In 1988, when the debt cleared, he divorced himself from Hollywood and embarked upon a new phase in his career.

Raised mainly in Queens, New York, Coppola has traced the roots of his career to 1947, when, at the age of eight, he was struck with polio. To pass the bed-ridden hours, he fantasized about American inventors—it was then that he learned of Tucker—as well as read, played with puppets, and toyed with mechanical gadgets. In time, these hobbies would fuse into a singular film career combining entrepreneurship and technological innovation with the literary and theatrical. In the short-term, his confinement led him to write his own stories, and, at the encouragement of his older brother August, who later became a novelist, to read works by Camus, Joyce, Gide, and Sartre.

Coppola entered Hofstra University intending to become a playwright. After seeing Sergei Eisenstein's epic "Ten Days That Shook the World," however, he switched his allegiance to film and enrolled in the graduate film department at the University of California at Los Angeles. By virtue of his screenwriting talent, he went from UCLA to a writing and directing stint at a low-budget film factory run by Roger Corman; from there he went to Seven Arts studios as a top screenwriter. While he was with Seven Arts, Coppola would stay up late working on a personal project, the screenplay to what would become his first film for a major studio. The film, "You're a Big Boy Now," was released in 1967 to rave reviews, inspiring critics to speculate that a major new directorial career had been launched. Three years later, he won the first of his Oscars as co-screenwriter of the movie "Patton."

The first of a generation of celebrity directors trained at film schools, the young Coppola was outspoken, if idealistic, about beating the Hollywood system. "You can't just shake your fist at the establishment and put them down for not giving you a chance," he once insisted, as related in Fred Baker's *Movie People.* "You have to beat them down and take money from them .... You have to practice what might be called a 'creative compromise.'" It was by following this principle that he succeeded in maneuvering "You're a Big Boy Now" from screenplay to celluloid. As he explained to Rex Reed in the *New York Times:* "In this world of motion pictures, very few can resist getting in on something if it looks like it's going. And that's how I did *Big Boy* .... We said we were already making it, that it was almost too late to get in. So Warner Brothers/Seven Arts said, 'Well, we might as well make this movie.'"

With the phenomenal success of "The Godfather," Coppola acquired the clout to pursue his taste for the unconventional. His two subsequent films, each released in 1974, abandoned literal storytelling—in "The Conversation," for a reality that seemed to blend with fantasy; in "The Godfather II," for a plot created through a complex interweaving of two smaller plots. Critics applauded these narrative departures, and Coppola, confident from his "Godfather" fame, began to pursue bolder innovations in making "Apocalypse Now." Yet with that film, critical opinion began to turn. Many began to question and even condemn his brand of experimentation, accusing him of self-indulgence.

Originally, Coppola intended "Apocalypse Now" to be a quickie-action movie for $12 million. During production, though, he came to see it in epic terms, a film that could become his magnum opus. The production parameters swelled accordingly, stopping at the expense of $31 million and 16 months of shooting on location in the Philippines. (In an attempt to maintain control over the project, Coppola himself put up $16 million—a remarkable degree of risk for a director of his stature.) Numerous writers have noted that in its tendency toward excess, the production came to mirror U.S. involvement in the war.

"The corporations and the exhibitors, and even the critical press, want films to be more and more uniform, more of a product. It's a system of overlapping vested interests."

Yet to Coppola, that connection is what gives the film its potency. "The way we made it was very much like the way the Americans were in Vietnam," he told G. Roy Levin in *Millimeter.* "We were in the jungle, there were too many of us, we had access to too much money, too much equipment; and little by little, we went insane. I think you can see it in the film. As it goes up the river, you can see the photography going a little crazy, and the directors and actors going a little crazy." Later, in an interview with the *Saturday Review,* he indicated that the situation arose at least partially by design: "I wanted the film to *be* the war. I wanted you to have a direct experience with the film, as though you were having a direct experience with the war."

Like "Apocalypse Now," "One from the Heart," his 1982 romantic melodrama, sported a lavish production budget. Its set was one of the most expensive in Hollywood history, a $6 million recreation of Las Vegas that necessitated 125,000 light bulbs, 10 miles of neon, and a paved intersection. The movie was a flop—all the more reason for the accusals of self-indulgence—but Coppola defended his set. "I wanted to take a fable-like story and treat it almost the way Disney would approach a story in his animated films," he told *Saturday Review.* "Treat it with very expressive sets and lighting and music that heighten the story. If we had made the movie in Las Vegas, it would have been just another relationship movie set on a real location.... I wanted to do something people hadn't seen before." Echoing the aim he stated for "Apocalypse Now," he added: "The city is a metaphor for the state of love itself. I want the film to *be* the emotions of these people."

This philosophy—that a film should *be* what it's about—has dictated the style of many of his movies, giving rise to the voyeuristic camera shots of "The Conversation," which is about a surveillance expert, or the theatrical set for "One From the Heart," which explores the deceptive surface quality of romance. In a broader sense, the philosophy relates to Coppola's desire for his actors to *become,* rather than portray, their characters. Known as an actor's director, he has often guided them toward that goal after-hours. During the making of "The Godfather," he arranged a now-famous dinner at an Italian restaurant: The cast came in character and improvised, and the rapport that developed between the younger actors and Marlon Brando, the film's star, sparked a crucial chemistry. With "The Outsiders," a film about teens divided by social class, he extended the division off the set, assigning the actors playing "socs" (short for "socialites") to plush accommodations and the greaser actors to more common quarters, and encouraging members of each group to mingle only among themselves.

Throughout his career Coppola has mourned the demise of the old Hollywood studios, a personal, artist-oriented system that existed prior to World War II. With its collapse, the balance of power shifted to agents, lawyers, accountants, and businesspeople. "The enormous Hollywood machine is all but gone," Coppola told the *Christian Science Monitor* in a 1982 interview. "The craftsmen and artisans are replaced by a kind of cynical professional who goes from job to job. Each film is packaged. Everyone is in business for himself, and the ensemble tradition of the old studios has vanished. And with that erosion of our capabilities is an erosion of the kinds of film we can make."

Early on, Coppola realized that to exercise creative control over his work, he would have to become autonomous. In 1969 he and George Lucas formed American Zoetrope, a San Francisco-based production company that was backed financially by Warner Brothers. Not long afterwards, however, Warners withdrew its funding due to its dislike of Lucas' "THX 1138," leaving Coppola with a half-million-dollar debt. (Profits from "The Godfather" enabled him to pay it off.) Yet despite the shortness of its reign, American Zoetrope helped Coppola to accomplish at least one of his goals—to find and nurture talent, in the tradition of the old Hollywood studios. George Lucas, who would go on to create the "Star Wars" trilogy, first gained fame through American Zoetrope, where his "American Graffiti" was produced. Through other American Zoetrope productions, Coppola launched the careers of many celebrity actors, while enabling dozens of film editors, art directors, and technicians to hone their crafts. He also sponsored work by such experimental directors as Wim Wenders, Jean-Luc Godard, and Hans-Jurgen Syberberg.

In 1980 Coppola made a second attempt at autonomy. For a bargain price of $6.7 million, he bought the ten-acre Hollywood General Studios, renamed it Zoetrope Studios, and went to work transforming it into the studio of his dreams. As with its previous incarnation, he modeled the new Zoetrope after the studios of the thirties, creating an environment that might allow him and other independent-minded directors to pursue projects that were too costly or eccentric for the major studios. Yet according to his plan, Zoetrope would be more than a throwback to better times. Featuring rooms of electronic editing and processing gear, it would also herald a high-tech future for film, in which both the time and cost of production would be drastically reduced. That technology, in combination with a repertory company, celebrity artists-in-residence, and a distribution deal with Orion Pictures, got Zoetrope off to a promising start.

Unfortunately, failure to meet key production deadlines sent the studio into spiralling financial troubles; by the beginning of 1981, the payroll could not be met. Yet the staff stuck it out, agreeing to work for deferred wages and donning "I Believe in Francis C." buttons. Their boss, meanwhile, threw himself into "One From the Heart," the film on which the fate of the company rested. As it turned out, "Heart" was the final undoing of Zoetrope, grossing less than ten percent of its cost. Coppola, in debt for $50 million, sold Zoetrope at an auction in 1984, under a payback agreement that allowed him to keep it as a production company.

The 1980s for Coppola were characterized mostly by frustration. Beginning in 1982 he was forced to play the role of a cinematic hired gun, directing a string of other people's movies in an effort to climb out from his mountainous debt. Of these, only one became a box-office hit—the 1986 "Peggy Sue Got Married."

Meanwhile, his reputation as a director at best stood still. As Jeffrey Chown observed: "Both 'Gardens of Stone' and 'Peggy Sue Got Married' suggest Coppola was in a holding period, waiting for his financial troubles to abate so that he would again initiate his own projects and exert the care and consideration more characteristic of his earlier productions." The same can be said of his 1984 "The Cotton Club," a film he took over in pre-production that turned into a $47 million flop. His segment of the 1989 "New York Stories," a trilogy of short films made in collaboration with Martin Scorsese and Woody Allen, brought more mediocrity (albeit without the excuse of financial pressures). His professional problems, however, were far eclipsed by a personal tragedy: During the shooting of "Gardens of Stone," his 22-year-old son and assistant, Gian-Carlo, was killed in a boating accident.

Coppola is painfully aware of the years spent sidetracked from his own aesthetic. "I've been 'promising' all my life," he told the *New York Times Magazine.* "First, I was a 'promising writer'; then I was a 'promising director.' Well, maybe at 50, I'll fulfill the promise." He has been reluctant to discuss new projects specifically, but his overall aim is to create movies that present novel formats—such as his concept, as yet unrealized, of a cinematic "novel"—and to produce them cost-efficiently, with the latest technology. And, wealthy enough to finance his ventures himself, he is resolved to remain independent from Hollywood. "I need to be a solo guy, like I was when I had polio," he said. "I'm going to experiment with my own ideas—experiment without the fear that failure will finish me off."

Sources

Books

Baker, Fred, and Ross Fireston, *Movie People*, Douglas, 1972.

Jacobs, Diane, *Hollywood Renaissance*, Delta, 1977.

Johnson, Robert, *Francis Ford Coppola*, Twayne, 1977.

Coppola, Eleanor, *Notes*, Simon & Schuster, 1979.

Monaco, James, *American Film Now*, Oxford University Press, 1979.

Pye, Michael, and Lynda Myles, *The Movie Brats*, Holt, 1979.

Kolker, Robert, *A Cinema of Loneliness*, Oxford University Press, 1980.

Thomson, David, *Overexposures: The Crisis in American Filmmaking*, Morrow, 1981.

Loeb, Anthony, *Filmmakers in Conversation*, Columbia College (Chicago), 1982.

Schatz, Thomas, *Old Hollywood/New Hollywood*, UMI Research Press, 1983.

Zuker, Joel, *Francis Ford Coppola: A Guide to the References and Resources*, G.K. Hall, 1984.

Chaillet, Jean-Paul, *Francis Ford Coppola*, [New York], 1985.

Chown, Jeffrey, *Hollywood Auteur: Francis Coppola*, Praeger, 1988.

Periodicals

American Film, November, 1975; May, 1979; October, 1981.

Atlantic, August, 1976.

Chicago Tribune, December 16, 1984.

Christian Science Monitor, February 18, 1982.

Film Comment, March–April, 1985.

Film Journal, September 21, 1981.

Life, August, 1981.

Maclean's, October 24, 1983.

Millimeter, October, 1979.

Newsweek, February 20, 1967; April 4, 1983.

New York Times, August 7, 1966.

New York Times Magazine, May 28, 1978.

Rolling Stone, November 1, 1979; March 18, 1982.

Saturday Review, July, 1981.

Sight and Sound, spring, 1982.

Time, February 23, 1981.

Washington Post, August 29, 1982.

—Sidelights by Kyle Kevorkian

Kevin Costner

AP/Wide World Photos

Actor

Born January 18, 1955, in Compton, Calif.; married Cindy Silva, 1975; children: Annie, Lily, Joey. *Education:* California State University at Fullerton, B.S. in marketing, 1978.

Addresses: *Home*—Mammoth, Pasadena, and Santa Barbara, Calif.

Career

Appeared in theater productions at the South Coast Actor's Co-op, 1978–80; after graduating from college, worked briefly as a marketing representative; worked as a stage manager at Raleigh Studios, Hollywood, Calif., 1980–83; appeared in feature films "Shadows Run Black," 1981, "Sizzle Beach, U.S.A.," "Night Shift," 1982, "Stacy's Knights," 1983, "Table for Five," 1983, "The Big Chill," 1983, "Fandango," 1984, "Silverado," 1985, "American Flyers," 1985, "The Untouchables," 1987, "No Way Out," 1987, "Bull Durham," 1988, and "Field of Dreams," 1989; appeared in PBS television film "Testament."

Member: Delta Chi

Sidelights

Strong, silent and sexy, actor Kevin Costner emerged as one of Hollywood's most sought-after actors in the late 1980s. After his success playing the lead in "The Untouchables," "No Way Out," and "Bull Durham," Costner was described as a throwback to actors of an earlier era. "The heir to the legacy of Gary Cooper and Henry Fonda," wrote the *New York Times.* "Hollywood's new romantic leading man," wrote *Time* magazine. "The new James Stewart," wrote the *Chicago Tribune*'s Gene Siskel. "An Eagle scout with umpteen merit badges." Costner himself is bemused by all the comparisons. Although Cooper and Stewart are his acting heroes, he does not see himself as a star. "You want to see a movie star, go talk to Sean Connery or Robert De Niro or Gene Hackman," he told the *Los Angeles Times.* "I'm not a movie star. I'm an actor."

The decision to be an actor came relatively late to Costner. He grew up planning to become a professional athlete. Later, he went to college with the idea of becoming a businessman. Only after trying out for a few community theater productions did Costner realize his true ambition. "I was trying to sort out what acting meant to me," he told the *New York Times.* "I come from a pretty practical background, so I kept asking myself, 'Is this just a way of getting out of being something?' I didn't know if I was running from my own shadow. But there was something very real going on. With acting, I was on fire."

Costner grew up in middle-class Southern California. His family moved frequently, making him the perennial new kid who attended four high schools. "I was always on the outside," he told *Time*. "I didn't feel 'there' until the end of the year, and then we'd move again." Although he was just five-foot-two in high school (he is now six-foot-one), Costner found his niche in sports, lettering in football, basketball, and baseball. He sang in the church choir, participated in musicals, and wrote poetry. He later majored in marketing at California State University at Fullerton, but spent his first three years, he admitted, basically drinking beer and partying. While at school, he met his future wife, Cindy Silva, a former Disneyland Snow White.

In his senior year, Costner decided that pushing other people's products wasn't for him. He auditioned for college plays, landed a few roles, and changed his perspective. "I always knew I was performance-oriented, I just never listened to who I was," Costner told the *New York Daily News*. "This was the first time I made a real decision about anything. And I thank God it happened." The tug between acting and a business career lasted until after he graduated from college and took a job in marketing. He lasted 30 days before telling off the company's biggest account and quitting the job. Then he discovered the South Coast Actor's Co-Op and began appearing in community theater productions such as "Waiting for Lefty" and "A View From the Bridge."

Costner was not an overnight sensation. He appeared in a soft-core porno flick, "Sizzle Beach," and then spent years learning the ropes while being rejected for parts. When he was rebuffed by casting directors, he told the Fort Lauderdale *News and Sun-Sentinel*, "I'd walk out of their offices with my fingers in my ears so I wouldn't have to hear someone who didn't know as much as I did telling me what to do." Costner had a three-year shift as stage manager of the Raleigh Studios, where he would wait for everyone to go home so he could experiment with the equipment. He worked at another studio sweeping trash. "I made a promise to myself that I wasn't going to be a bartender and I wasn't going to sell shoes while seeking acting jobs," he told the *News and Sun-Sentinel*. "I was going to work close to the industry, where the action was. If I was going to push trash, it was going to be movie trash."

His movie debut in "Frances" was supposed to be a significant part. In the end, however, all but one line got cut out. He then had bit parts in "Night Shift" and "Table for Five" before delivering an impressive performance, as a young father whose baby daughter dies, in the PBS movie "Testament." Costner won his first leading role in the 1984 film "Fandango," playing a fraternity hell-raiser in crumpled tuxedo and shades. But his big break was expected to come later that year, when he was cast as the suicidal Alex in Lawrence Kasdan's "The Big Chill." Indeed, Costner turned down the lead in John Badham's "War Games" (Matthew Broderick ended up playing the part) to appear in Kasdan's movie. In the end, however, all of Costner's scenes were cut from "The Big Chill." He appeared only as a corpse in the opening scene. "It doesn't matter [that the part was cut]," he told the Atlanta *Constitution*. "I knew I was with the right circle of people. I had a pretty healthy idea of why I was in acting, and it wasn't for the reviews or the fact that I was in a $100 million hit. It bothered me a little bit because when the film was going around, you had this feeling, 'Hey, I was there—really I was there! But now it's in my soul, and I know why it happened to me."

Kasdan made amends by casting Costner as the rip-roaring gunslinger Jake in the so-called Yuppie western "Silverado." It was not a big role, but Costner nearly stole the show from stars Kevin Kline and Scott Glenn. He says he took great joy in the role and improvised a good deal. "I played that role for every boy or girl who ever wanted to get on a horse and play cowboys," he told the *Washington Post*. The performance opened new doors for Costner. But while he appeared as a bicycle racer in the box office flop "American Flyers" in 1985, he gained more notoriety turning down several roles in promising films. Costner said he did not want to be involved in movies that reminded him of those he had seen before during his career. He turned down the leads in "Big," "Jagged Edge," "Midnight Run," and "Mississippi Burning." "I'd like the kind of movies I do to be benchmarks for their genre," he told the *New York Daily News*. "That's my goal for the next 10 years. What's the point of doing something if it's not original? I have a very strong point of view about films. I don't think there is a point I can't make in movies." That kind of attitude is rare in Hollywood. Producer Anson Mount told the Atlanta *Constitution* that Costner "is a man with some values. He's a man who doesn't act like a movie star. We haven't seen that around these parts since Gary Cooper. He's a real guy."

Cooper, Spencer Tracy, and Henry Fonda remain Costner's on-screen heroes. "Those early movie stars taught me what it was like to be a man," he told the *New York Times*. "They taught me the kind of man I'd really like to be. You learn a lot from watching heroes act. Henry Fonda once said, 'I've played enough great men in my life that I felt like I learned something from them.'" In his next role, Costner got to play one of the strong, silent heroes that Fonda and Cooper made famous. In "The Untouchables," a stylish 1987 remake of Robert Stack's old television series, Costner was cast as supercop Eliot Ness. This Ness was a teetotaler who saved babies in runaway carriages with one hand and tossed gangsters from buildings with the other. And Costner played Ness as a tender father who gives his daughter an Eskimo bedtime kiss.

He received mixed reviews for the role. Some critics commended his restrained performance while others faulted him for a hollow, colorless portrayal of the famed Chicago fed. "I knew going in what people's problems would be with my character," Costner told the *Los Angeles Times.* "The reason I did 'Untouchables' was that I thought the movie had a chance to be a fresh, original movie. The notion that a traditional American hero doesn't have all the answers and asks for help confuses us. We'd rather have Rambo who kills a hundred people for us and does all our thinking for us. It bothers us to watch a movie where the guy who is supposed to be in charge doesn't know what's going on. It wasn't the most charismatic role, and that's unusual for a lead in a movie."

"I'd like the kind of movies I do to be benchmarks for their genre....What's the point of doing something if it's not original?"

"The Untouchables" established Costner as a solid leading man, a role he called "just a description," in the Atlanta *Constitution.* "I realize that just my physical features are going to dictate that I'm the guy in the middle going down the movie. So, I'm the lead. It's not as if they're looking for me to play the Elephant Man. I'm going to play kind of a circle of characters that aren't going to be too far removed from each other." In his next movie, the 1987 political thriller "No Way Out," Costner played a Soviet double agent. It was his first romantic lead. Wrote *Los Angeles Times* critic Sheila Benson: "'No Way Out's' greatest prize is Costner, a leading man at last: fiercely good, intelligent, appreciatively sensual in a performance balanced perfectly between action and introspection."

Costner's steamy love scenes with actress Sean Young in "No Way Out" had women in the audience looking at him in a different light. "My sex symbol status is not an easy thing for my wife to look at objectively," Costner told the *Houston Post.* "We hadn't orchestrated a sex symbol kind of thing. I'm not surprised I get paired with women, although for a long time I resisted it. But I don't want to hide from it now. My physical specifications dictate that I'm going to play that kind of role." His character of Commander Tom Farrell in "No Way Out" was "an easier guy to relate to than Eliot Ness," Costner told the *Philadelphia Daily News.* "Eliot was a harder role for me because I knew the problems that would come after the movie and people's interpretation of that role. Tom Farrell was a more complicated role for me to play because of the things he hid as a character in terms of his personal life. Always during a scene, I usually had mountains of notes to make sure I was concealing those things at all times."

Taking notes to develop his character is one of Costner's techniques. Another is to develop his character through dreams. "I dream all the time when I'm working," he told the *Chicago Tribune.* "It's not a technique or anything. It's just that I know actors are always thinking at the end of the day what they might have done in a given scene. And to my mind if you can think of it after you've been shooting, you can also think of it before. It's all concentration. I can't control what I dream about, but instead of thinking about what's going to be served for lunch tomorrow, I try to think about certain things pertaining to the day's scenes."

Costner's next film gave him his third consecutive box office hit. "Bull Durham," co-starring Susan Sarandon, featured Costner as Crash Davis, a minor-league catcher nearing the end of his career. The *Washington Post* described the 1988 movie as, "limber, funny and as in-touch with the pleasures of the flesh as it is with the pleasures of the game." And, wrote the *Post,* "for once, Costner has a role that he can sink into, that fits his skills, and he shows enormous authority and charm. Physically, it's a marvelous incarnation: He swings well (from both sides of the plate) and even has a good home run trot. He's totally in his jock character's body, and with this one performance, he emerges as a true star presence." Costner said his own strong background in athletics helped make "Bull Durham" a success. "I think a problem in sports movies in certain instances is that the people portraying the athletes don't really look like athletes," he told the Atlanta *Constitution.* "I knew I would be able to fulfill that obligation."

His next film, 1989's "Field of Dreams," was also about baseball—the tale of a young farmer obsessed by the legend of Chicago White Sox centerfielder Shoeless Joe Jackson, based on W.P. Kinsella's novel *Shoeless Joe.* Wrote the *Boston Globe*'s Jay Carr: "The movie succeeds. One reason is that it isn't afraid to take a few big swings. Another is Costner, in every facial expression and every flicker of body language. This one moves with a measured tread into a realm of enchantment and renewal, its warm energies anchored by Costner's rootedness and convincing ability to project in a dozen subtle ways the reactions of a man who loves his wife and kids deeply." Costner told the *Chicago Tribune:* "I think movies that can be great always run the risk of being bad movies. This is a very Capra-esque film, which means it can be schmaltzy or, if you pull it off right, it will endure. It could be our generation's 'It's a Wonderful Life.'"

"In retrospect, everything I've done looks like good career moves," Costner told the *New York Daily News.* "But the moves I make are simply about what I like in movies. My agenda is nothing but the movie. When I'm acting I leave a window open for creativity, but I still like to be very open about what I'm thinking about. I try to get so in control that then I get out of control when I act."

Sources

Boston Globe, April 21, 1989.
Charlotte Observer, April 29, 1988.
Chicago Tribune, April 16, 1989.
Constitution (Atlanta), June 24, 1988.
Houston Post, June 12, 1988.
Los Angeles Times, August 19, 1987; April 21, 1989.
Morning Call (Allentown, Pa.), August 16, 1987; June 17, 1988.
New York Daily News, April 20, 1989.
New York Times, April 23, 1989.
News and Sun-Sentinel (Fort Lauderdale, Fla.), June 12, 1987.
Orlando Sentinel, August 21, 1987.
Philadelphia Daily News, August 18, 1987.
People, December 26, 1988.
Rolling Stone, July 14, 1988.
Time, September 7, 1987; April 24, 1989.
Washington Post, August 14, 1987; June 15, 1988.

—Sidelights by Glen Macnow

Charles E. Curran

AP/Wide World Photos

Roman Catholic priest, educator, and author

Born March 30, 1934, in Rochester, N.Y. *Education:* St. Bernard's Seminary, Rochester, N.Y., B.A.; Gregorian University, Rome, Italy, S.T.B., 1957, S.T.L., 1959, S.T.D., 1961; Academia Alfonsiana, Rome, S.T.D., 1961.

Addresses: *Office*—University of Southern California, Los Angeles, Calif. 90007.

Career

Ordained Roman Catholic priest, 1958; St Bernard's Seminary, Rochester, N.Y., professor of moral theology 1961–65; Catholic University of America, Washington, D.C., assistant professor, 1965–67, associate professor, 1967–71, professor of moral theology, beginning 1971; University of Southern California, Los Angeles, professor of theology. Senior research scholar, Kennedy Center for Bioethics, Georgetown University, 1972; visiting professor, Cornell University, 1987–88.

Member: American Society of Christian Ethics (president, 1971–72), American Theological Society, Catholic Theological Society of America (vice-president, 1968–69; president, 1969–70), College Theology Society.

Sidelights

A Catholic priest, Charles E. Curran has long been in conflict with his church. His problems began in the 1960s, when he adopted a liberated approach to moral theology, the subject he taught at the Catholic University of America. In his lectures, as well as in his numerous books, Curran has questioned the Vatican's stance on birth control, premarital sex, divorce, and homosexuality. He has been disciplined twice for his dissenting views—once by the university; the second time by the Vatican itself.

Ordained in 1958, Curran first considered joining the priesthood at the age of 12. He received his secondary education at St. Andrew's Minor Seminary in Rochester, New York, and continued his studies at St. Bernard's Seminary. He went on to earn postgraduate degrees from Rome's Gregorian University and the Academia Alfonsiana. He joined the faculty of St. Bernard's in 1961. In addition to his teaching duties, the priest counseled families, many of whom were distressed by the church's views on sexuality and divorce. "It was in talking to them that all of a sudden I really began to question the whole thing," Curran told the *Washington Post*'s Lois Romano. He left St. Bernard's in 1965 to become an assistant professor at the Catholic University of America's School of Religious Studies.

Two years later, following the publication of his first book, *Christian Morality Today,* the university decided not to renew Curran's contract. No official reason was cited; unofficially, however, the school's board of trustees expressed disapproval of Curran's liberal statements on birth control. The faculty and students protested his dismissal with a boycott of classes, closing the university for three days. Curran was reinstated and promoted to associate professor. In 1968 he was again at the center of controversy. That summer, he led approximately 600 American Catholic theologians in open dissent from *Humanae Vitae*, a papal encyclical condemning all forms of artificial birth control.

Curran continued to disagree with the church's position on this and other moral issues. In books, speeches, and lectures, he called on the church to rethink its tenets on divorce and remarriage; he argued that, in some cases, abortion should be permitted, but only up to three weeks after conception; and he voiced support for homosexuals seeking permanent relationships. In essence, he urged the church to tolerate diversity and accept change.

Rome was largely silent until the 1978 election of Pope John Paul II. A conservative, he showed little tolerance for progressive-minded clergy. In 1979, the church announced that it would investigate the complaints against Curran. Seven years later, the Vatican ruled that Curran had deviated from official teachings on contraception, abortion, nonmarital sex, and divorce. In so doing, wrote Joseph Cardinal Ratzinger, prefect of the office that conducted the investigation, Curran had violated the conditions under which a professor could be called a Catholic theologian. Curran was dismissed from the university, the first time an American priest had been so punished by the Vatican. Curran responded by calling for the formation of a special faculty committee to investigate Rome's decision. Meanwhile, he accepted a post as a visiting professor at Cornell University. In 1988, the faculty committee ruled "that a competent, tenured professor may not be dismissed even though the Vatican objects to what he is teaching," reported Marjorie Hyer of the *Washington Post*. Catholic University of America agreed to reinstate the priest, but in a "new assignment." "I've made my point, established my principle," Curran told Hyer. "If I find [the new assignment] isn't stimulating enough, I will feel free to move on."

He did, indeed, move on—to teach theology at the University of Southern California. In March of 1989, a District of Columbia Superior Court disagreed with the faculty committee ruling and declared that Catholic University had the right to dismiss Curran in accordance with the Vatican's wishes. Curran decided not to appeal the court ruling. As he explained to *Time*, "I'm a free man now, and better for it."

Writings

Christian Morality Today, Fides, 1966.
A New Look at Christian Morality, Fides, 1968.
Contemporary Problems in Moral Theology, Fides, 1970.
Catholic Moral Theology in Dialogue, Fides, 1972.
The Crisis in Priestly Ministry, Fides, 1972.
Politics, Medicine and Christian Ethics, Fortress, 1973.
New Perspectives in Moral Theology, Fides, 1974.
Ongoing Revision: Studies in Moral Theology, Fides, 1975.
Themes in Fundamental Moral Theology, University of Notre Dame Press, 1977.
Issues in Sexual and Medical Ethics, University of Notre Dame Press, 1978.
Transaction and Tradition in Moral Theology, University of Notre Dame Press, 1979.
Moral Theology: A Continuing Journey, University of Notre Dame Press, 1982.
American Catholic Social Ethics, University of Notre Dame Press, 1982.
Critical Concerns in Moral Theology, University of Notre Dame Press, 1984.

Has also edited numerous books on moral theology, ethics, and dissent within the Catholic church; contributor to books and journals.

Sources

Christian Century, August 27, 1969.
New York Times, March 24, 1987.
Newsweek, September 1, 1986.
People, April 7, 1986.
Time, March 24, 1986; March 13, 1989.
Washington Post, September 4, 1986; April 17, 1988.

—*Sketch by Denise Wiloch*

Dalai Lama

AP/Wide World Photos

Buddhist religious leader

Born June 6, 1935, in Taktser, Tibet; son of Chokyong Tsering and Sonam Isomo. *Education:* Educated privately by Buddhist monks.

Addresses: *Home*—Dharamsala, India.

Career

Enthroned as fourteenth Dalai Lama of Tibet, 1940; exiled, 1959; since exile, has travelled widely in Asia, Europe, and the United States. Author of numerous works on Buddhist theology.

Awards: Albert Schweitzer Humanitarian Award, 1987; Nobel Peace Prize, 1989.

Sidelights

On February 22, 1940, an historic ceremomy took place in the city of Lhasa in Tibet. In this ceremony a four-year-old boy was enthroned as the nation's new leader, the Dalai Lama, a position of both political and religious significance. Since the 17th century, Tibet has been ruled by a Buddhist theocracy headed by a Dalai Lama who holds absolute authority. Each such ruler is believed to be a reincarnation of the Dalai Lama who preceded him; and he is looked upon by his followers as a bodhisattra, one who has reached a state of spiritual perfection and now devotes himself to aiding humanity.

The current Dalai Lama is the fourteenth in the line. Born to Chokyong Tsering and Sonam Isomo, a Tibetan peasant couple, he was named Lhamo, and was the fourth of their five children. Upon the death of the thirteenth Dalai Lama in 1933, the Buddhist monks began to search for the child in whom their ruler had been reincarnated. A number of omens, holy visions, and portents led the monks to the village of Taktser, where they found young Lhamo. After testing the boy to see if he recognized objects belonging to the previous Dalai Lama, tests which he consistently passed, the monks declared Lhamo to be the new Dalai Lama. He was taken to the capital city of Lhasa and installed in the 1,000-room Potala Palace, where he was tutored in religion, mathematics, geography, and other subjects.

In 1950, at the age of 15, the Dalai Lama was confronted with one of the most devastating events in his nation's history. In October of that year the Red Chinese army invaded and occupied Tibet. The Dalai Lama was thrust into the role of political mediator, attempting to end the brutality of the conquering soldiers. His efforts met with little success, however. The Chinese routinely tortured and murdered Buddhist priests and demolished centuries-old monastaries. By 1959 the situation had become intolerable, and the Tibetans staged an abortive revolt against the occupation forces. During the bloody suppression of the revolt, some 80,000 Tibetans died.

Fearing for the life of their spiritual leader, the Dalai Lama's followers urged him to flee the country. After travelling some 300 miles along remote and treacherous mountain roads, the Dalai Lama, his family, and 100 supporters arrived in India, where they were immediately granted political asylum. Since 1960 he has lived in Dharamsala, India, where he has served as spiritual leader to his people and has worked to alert the world to his nation's plight. Since the Chinese conquest of Tibet in 1950, over one million Tibetans have been killed. Many others have been forced into exile. Actor Richard Gere and Robert A.F. Thurman, writing in *Rolling Stone,* quoted the Dalai Lama: "We are not Chinese, never have been and never will be . . . . We are a peaceful people. We want our freedom of religion. We want Tibet to be a zone of peace. We want no more human-rights abuses."

Despite the Dalai Lama's efforts to bring peace to his homeland, it continues to be plagued by turmoil. In 1987, a few days prior to the 37th anniversary of the Chinese invasion, a crowd of 2,000 Tibetans attacked a police station in Lhasa, setting the building on fire. The ensuing battle left 14 people dead. The Chinese authorities cracked down on public protest, arresting over 600 Tibetans and reportedly beating scores of monks who attempted to stage a peaceful demonstration. Foreign newsmen were forced out of the country, and the entire region was sealed off to outside observers. In March of 1988 new rioting broke out at a temple in Lhasa. Up to 16 monks were killed by police.

As part of his crusade to secure peace and freedom in Tibet, the Dalai Lama visited the United States in 1987. He spoke before the U.S. Senate, asking for American help on behalf of his people. But as relations between the United States and China were normalized in 1972, the American government cannot recognize the Dalai Lama as the legitimate leader of Tibet. Throughout his travels, the Dalai Lama has called for civil disobedience in Tibet and a withdrawal of Chinese forces from the region. "If they would show some good faith," he remarked to Gere and Thurman, "we'd still like to get along with them."

Sources

Books

Dalai Lama, *My Land and My People* (autobiography), McGraw-Hill, 1962.

Periodicals

Los Angeles Times, April 3, 1959.
New York, September 3, 1979.
New York Times, April 2, 1959; April 3, 1959.
Newsweek, October 19, 1987; March 21, 1988.
People, September 10, 1979.
Reader's Digest, February, 1970.
Rolling Stone, September 20, 1979; December 3, 1987.
Time, September 17, 1979; October 19, 1979.
Washington Post, April 3, 1959; September 10, 1979.

—Sketch by Denise Wiloch

Jeff Daniels

AP/Wide World Photos

Actor

Born 1955 in Georgia; married Kathleen Treado, July 13, 1979; children: Ben. *Education:* attended Central Michigan University.

Addresses: *Home*—New York, N.Y.; and Chelsea, Mich. *Agent*—Hildy Gottlieb, International Creative Management, Inc., 40 West 57th St., New York, N.Y. 10019.

Career

Trained for the stage as apprentice with the Circle Repertory Company, New York City; stage credits include "The Farm," 1976, "My Life," "Brontosaurus," and "Feedlot," all 1977, "Lulu," "Slugger," and "The Fifth of July," all 1978, "Johnny Got His Gun," "Three Sisters," 1982, and "The Golden Age," 1984; film credits include "Ragtime," 1981, "Terms of Endearment," 1983, "The Purple Rose of Cairo" and "Marie," 1985, "Something Wild," and "Heartburn," 1986, "Radio Days," 1987, "The House on Carroll Street," and "Sweet Hearts Dance," 1988, and "Checking Out," 1989; television film credits include "A Rumor of War," CBS, 1980, "An Invasion of Privacy," ABC, 1983, "The Fifth of July," PBS, and "The Caine Mutiny Court Martial," CBS, 1988.

Awards: Obie Award, 1982, for one-man performance in "Johnny Got His Gun."

Sidelights

Jeff Daniels, also known as the Mr. Blasé of the acting world, achieves this image—and, undoubtedly, much of his appeal—by understating the characters he plays. "I was taught the whole idea was to hide it, not to show the seams," he told *People.* "But you can get in trouble. You can be boring." Boring is hardly the word to describe an actor who is without peer in bringing the average Joe to life and making him as memorable as the most glamorous type. "Daniels has a knack for playing despicable characters that audiences can't resist," observed the *Washington Post.* And, according to *People,* Woody Allen, who directed Daniels in the 1985 sleeper "The Purple Rose of Cairo," pegged him as "the guy everybody has been looking for—the guy who can do light comedy." Sometimes compared to movie idols William Powell and Robert Montgomery, Jeff Daniels has managed to charm Hollywood and movie audiences alike.

Yet least impressed by the rage he has caused is Daniels himself. The sandy-haired, blue-eyed actor remains as down-to-earth offscreen as he appears in front of the camera. "Back home in Michigan," he explained to *People,* "you didn't want to be in films, you wanted to be in movies." Though a native

Georgian, Daniels moved during his boyhood to the small town of Chelsea, Michigan (fifty miles west of Detroit), where he worked summers in his father's lumberyard until he realized that his heart wasn't in the lumber business. He began acting and dropped out of Central Michigan University during his junior year when director Marshall Mason sensed his potential and offered him an apprenticeship at New York City's Circle Repertory Theater. The year was 1975, and the young Daniels appeared to be getting his big break.

That break didn't actually come, however, until eight years later when Daniels became known to movie patrons as Flap Horton, Debra Winger's faithless, though not entirely loathsome, husband in the tear-jerking box-office smash "Terms of Endearment." Daniels, in the meantime, lived in an Upper West Side apartment and amassed a respectable list of credits doing off-Broadway theater. Plays he appeared in at the Circle Repertory Theater include "The Farm," "Brontosaurus," and "Lulu," as well as "The Fifth of July," for which he received critical favor as the hero's gay lover opposite Christopher Reeve. But these glimmers of limelight were overshadowed by years of struggle and fruitless hard work. Referring to a rundown coffee shop in his Manhattan neighborhood, Daniels told *People,* "I used to come in here every morning and read the paper and wonder why I wasn't working."

What tempered this rough period for Daniels were his two enduring loves—baseball and family. His most prized possession, a wallet autographed by Yankee Lou Piniella, was acquired when Daniels ran into his baseball idol back home in Michigan. Unlike acting, this is one topic Daniels talks about openly, his speech punctuated by enthusiastic "Good Lords!" Not merely a spectator of the sport, he played in Broadway's softball league, telling *People,* "I played first base, thank you. Some say I was the best first baseman in the league. It becomes your life. It should be a hobby. It's a sickness." His love for the game even infiltrated Daniels's wedding plans to Kathleen Treado, whom he had known in Chelsea. The couple got married on Friday, July 13, 1979, because Daniels wore the number thirteen on his jersey and had batted .361 that season. He and Kathleen have since started their family.

For Daniels, the early eighties were interspersed with uplifting successes and bitter disappointments. He experimented with new media by doing two television-series pilots and making his film debut in 1981 as a policeman in "Ragtime." His one-man performance in "Johnny Got His Gun" at the Circle Repertory Theater earned Daniels a prestigious Obie Award in 1982. Still, the young actor did not feel as if he had a foothold in the profession. Always "first runner-up," he lost out to John Lithgow for the part of transsexual Roberta Muldoon in "The World According to Garp" and to Peter Weller for the role of Diane Keaton's lover in "Shoot the Moon." While Daniels claimed that Keaton thought him too young for the part, it seems that his trademark of cool unenthusiasm might have, at times, worked against him. According to the *Washington Post,* casting director Juliet Taylor said of Daniels, "I was very high on him for a certain part. After the screen test, there was an interview. He sort of threw in the towel. He acted like he didn't care. I think it hurt him in that case."

But the term "uncaring" misrepresents this actor, who has been taught "not to show the seams," for beneath his facade of nonchalance, Daniels teems with ambition. He admits to being extremely competitive, to the point of not speaking to other actors in the same room while waiting for a screen test. Much of this drive, however, is borne of a survival instinct. Knowing that his rent payment depended on it, Daniels waited anxiously on the set of "Terms of Endearment" for the crossfire between Debra Winger and Shirley MacLaine to die down so that filming could resume. To prepare for their roles in the film, he and Winger wrote letters to one another as Flap and Emma, and Daniels's performance as the charming but feckless Flap received positive reviews. "Subtler, easier to overlook, but no less dead on is Jeff Daniels's Flap," commented *Newsweek.* "[he] gives a near definitive portrayal of the young, fairly hip academic who comes out of the '60s and moves from bush-league college to college, the eternal heartthrob of the English department." But perhaps the best gauge of Daniels's effectiveness in the part of Flap came in the form of a patron herself. One evening Daniels went to see "Terms" and inadvertently sat in front of a woman who talked loudly at the screen. She called Flap "a dip—" and an "irresponsible bastard," but broke down toward the end of the movie, Daniels remembered. He told *People,* "She's one of the biggest criers. The lights came up and I said, 'Did you enjoy the movie?' She looks at me and puff! She'll never talk in a movie again."

This incident foreshadowed the unusual cinematic trick Daniels used in his next film, "The Purple Rose of Cairo." In the dual role of Gil Shepherd, an egotistical Depression-era actor, and Tom Baxter, the gallant leading man Shepherd plays, Daniels walks off the screen and into the arms of Cecilia, the drab, diehard matinee patron played by Mia Farrow. Although Michael Keaton was initially cast as the male lead, he and director Woody Allen parted company two weeks after shooting began when Allen decided that Keaton was too contemporary for the role. Big names like Kevin Kline, Eric Roberts, and Dennis Quaid vied for the lead, but Daniels outdistanced them all. What was it about this oft-overlooked actor that captured Woody Allen's imagination and made him take the gamble? At first Allen didn't seem impressed, and Daniels understands why. "In a funny way, I tried to talk him out of it," he told the *Washington Post*. "I couldn't believe I was doing it. I was hearing myself. 'I'm blowing it. I know I'm blowing it. It's too big a job, anyway.'" But, after putting Daniels in 1930s garb, witnessing the magic between him and Mia Farrow in two key scenes, and taking a night to think about it, Allen knew he had his man. He was quoted in *People* as saying, "It was as though I dreamed this guy up. He never once asked me, 'What is this character about?'" Jeff Daniels was no longer "first runner-up," but "the guy everybody has been looking for," indeed.

Other directors since Woody Allen have cast Daniels in leading roles, a choice that has proven auspicious time and again. Such was the case with Jonathan Demme, director of the 1986 offbeat comedy/thriller "Something Wild," who, according to *Maclean's*, "keeps the initial comedy so light and even-tempered that the abrupt switch to terror comes like a frontal assault.... The laughter becomes the kind that catches in the throat and chokes." With comic dexterity, Daniels portrays Charlie Driggs, a staid Wall Street executive who derives sneaky pleasure from sidling out of a New York diner without paying. Observed by the aptly cast Melanie Griffith [see index for *Newsmakers* entry] as Lulu, a bohemian temptress with a Louise Brooks hairstyle, "closet rebel" Charlie accepts a lift from her back to his firm. Instead, he finds himself whizzing through the Holland Tunnel to New Jersey, and, for this pleasant but vacuous-looking businessman, there is no turning back.

Maclean's commended the actors in "Something Wild" for bringing "an eager freshness to their performances," noting that "Daniels, like a young Cary Grant, has a droll, open face and elastic features.... [He and Griffith] play off each other like gin and tonic—and the effect is just as bracing." As the light romp turns to horror, Daniels takes on the challenge of bringing off almost imperceptible changes in Charlie's character as he transforms from a stuffed shirt to a drunk and liberated party boy and, finally, to a hero who saves himself and Lulu from her crazed ex-husband. Crossing the line between comedy and drama, Daniels manages to make a grave impact in what the *New Yorker* called "a party movie with both a dark and light side."

Back from his brief foray on the "wild side," Daniels began to focus on more dramatic roles. In 1985 he starred with Sissy Spacek in "Marie," a story about Marie Ragghianti, the pardon and parole board chairperson who called into question a statewide clemency-for-cash scandal. No longer the quintessential good guy, Daniels played the role of legal counsel to governor Ray Blanton, Ragghianti's opposition. The *Washington Post* reported that Peter Maas, on whose book the film was based, felt that Daniels had "probably the most difficult part in the film. He's got to make you like him. And he does. It's amazing." Other movies Daniels has done include "Sweet Hearts Dance," which received mixed reviews, and "The House on Carroll Street," a thriller in the Hitchcockian vein, co-starring Kelly McGillis. In this story about a plot to smuggle Nazis into the U.S. in the early fifties, Daniels "brings good-natured charm to the role of the unsolicited detective," remarked *Maclean's*. More recent projects such as a television special called "The Caine Mutiny Court Martial" and "Checking Out," a medical comedy, are on Daniels's list of accomplishments.

Despite all the fascinating turns his life has taken during the eighties, Mr. Blasé still insists on understating. "I won't let the business make me crazy," he told the *Washington Post*, clasping his hands behind his neck. "I won't let it age me prematurely. If that means being laid-back, that's what it's going to have to be. The trick for me is not to take it that seriously."

Sources

Maclean's, November 10, 1986; March 21, 1988.
Newsweek, November 21, 1983.
New York, May 9, 1988.
New Yorker, November 17, 1986.
New York Times, September 23, 1988.
People, April 8, 1985; November 17, 1986.
Washington Post, April 16, 1985.
Wall Street Journal, November 6, 1986.

—Sidelights by Carolyn Chafetz

Tony Danza

AP/Wide World Photos

Actor

Born April 21, 1951, in Brooklyn, N.Y.; son of Italian immigrants; married; first wife's name, Rhonda (divorced); married Tracy Robinson (an interior designer), 1986; children: (first marriage) Marc Anthony, Gina; (second marriage) Katherine. *Education:* Graduate of University of Dubuque.

Addresses: *Office*—American Broadcasting Companies, Inc., 1330 Avenue of the Americas, New York, N.Y. 10019.

Career

Worked at various jobs, including bartending and moving furniture; amateur and professional boxer; actor, 1978—; regular member of cast, "Taxi," ABC-TV and NBC-TV, 1978–83; star of "Who's the Boss?," ABC-TV, 1984—. Has appeared in television movies "Murder Can Hurt You" and "Singles Bars, Single Women"; feature films include "The Hollywood Knights" and "Going Ape!"

Sidelights

Tony Danza is the star of the successful ABC-TV comedy series "Who's the Boss?" He first gained national attention as boxer-cab driver Tony Banta on the sitcom "Taxi." For Danza, unlike many performers, the road to fame was far from rocky. At 27, he was a mediocre fighter on the New York circuit; one year later, he was playing a mediocre fighter on a hit television series.

Danza learned to fight on the streets of his native Brooklyn. After high school, he won a wrestling scholarship to the University of Dubuque, where he earned a degree in history. Upon graduating, he returned to Brooklyn and entered the Golden Gloves amateur boxing competition. He later turned professional and compiled a 10–3 record as a middleweight. During this time, Danza was spotted by a television producer, who persuaded the fighter to test for a series pilot based on the movie "Rocky." The pilot never sold; but the experience prompted Danza to try for a part in "The Warriors," a film about gang warfare. He got the part, only to turn it down in favor of a more lucrative and long-term offer.

While auditioning for "The Warriors," Danza met James Brooks, a television director who was casting a new comedy called "Taxi." Brooks was looking for an Irish heavyweight to play the role of a cab driver who aspired to boxing greatness but was none too lucky in the ring. The character was eventually rewritten as an Italian middleweight, and Tony Banta was born. "Taxi" ran for five years and became one of television's "most respected comedy series," wrote Steve Pond of *Us*. It also made Danza a star.

When "Taxi" was cancelled, the actor's luck took a turn for the worse. His father died; soon after, Danza lost roles in two major films. Moreover, in 1984 he got into a brawl with a guard at a New York restaurant. Danza was convicted of assault and sentenced to 250 hours of community service. "It was probably the worst thing that ever happened to me," he told Pond, "but it turned out to be one of the most rewarding things of my entire life." Danza served as an activities director at Harlem's Jewish Home and Hospital for the aged.

That same year, 1984, he embarked on a new series, "Who's the Boss?" Danza plays Tony Micelli, a single father and ex-baseball player who is employed as a housekeeper by a female advertising executive. The show is one of ABC's most popular comedies. Danza is pleased by this latest success and gives a large share of the credit to the show's writers. He also credits his previous series experience. "'Taxi' . . . was a great kickoff for my career," he told Jack Hawn of the *Los Angeles Times*. "What's amazing is how much I've retained. I learned from the best. If I had retained this much from college . . . , I'd be teaching school someplace."

Sources

Los Angeles Times, September 19, 1985.
Ms., November, 1984.
People, May 14, 1979; April 21, 1986; July 14, 1986.
Us, August 26, 1985.

—*Sketch by Denise Wiloch*

Daniel Day-Lewis

Actor

Born April 29, 1957, in London, England; son of Cecil (a poet) and Jill (an actress; maiden name, Balcon) Day-Lewis. *Education:* Studied at Bristol Old Vic Theatre School.

Addresses: *Home*—London, England.

Career

Actor; films include "Sunday, Bloody Sunday," 1971, "Gandhi," 1982, "My Beautiful Laundrette," 1985, "A Room with a View," 1986, "The Unbearable Lightness of Being," 1988, and "Stars and Bars," 1988; has acted with Bristol Old Vic Repertory Company and with Royal Shakespeare Company; made London stage debut in "Another Country," 1981.

Awards: Named best supporting actor, New York Film Critics, for "A Room with a View."

Sidelights

Actor Daniel Day-Lewis has been compared to Laurence Olivier, Montgomery Clift, and Cary Grant. He has played such diverse characters as a moody, homosexual street punk in "My Beautiful Laundrette" and a prudish Victorian in "A Room with a View." His versatility and range have propelled him to the forefront of young English actors. "I'm in danger," he told David Hutchings of *People*, "of being typecast as a chameleon."

Day-Lewis is the son of the late Cecil Day-Lewis, Britain's poet laureate, and actress Jill Balcon, whose father produced Alfred Hitchcock's early films. Day-Lewis began acting at the Bedales Progressive School. This led to roles with the National Youth Theatre and to his first film, "Sunday, Bloody Sunday," in 1971. He studied drama at the Bristol Old Vic Theatre School, then joined the Bristol Old Vic and Royal Shakespeare companies. Day-Lewis made his stage debut in "Another Country" in London's West End. He later toured in Royal Shakespeare productions of "Romeo and Juliet" and "A Midsummer Night's Dream." He also appeared in the 1982 film "Gandhi" and in 1984's "The Bounty."

In 1985, Day-Lewis was cast as Johnny, a gay, tough London punk, in "My Beautiful Laundrette." The next year, he played Cecil Vyse, a repressed upper-class Victorian, in "A Room with a View." The actor's performances in these films were widely praised, and he was soon offered leading roles. He starred in 1988's "The Unbearable Lightness of Being," portraying a womanizing Czech neurosurgeon. In "Stars and Bars," he was Henderson Dores, a bewildered English art dealer. Critics, noting the variety of these roles, lauded Day-Lewis's talent and range. In a *Newsweek* review of "A Room with a View," Jack Kroll commented: "The metamorphosis of Daniel Day-Lewis from the punk street kid in 'My Beautiful Laundrette' into Cecil Vyse is astonishing. [He] makes a figure both appalling and poignant out of Cecil." *Interview*'s Christina de Liagre described Day-Lewis's film work as a series of "virtuoso screen performances," adding that he "has the uncanny ability to transform himself beyond recognition."

After "Stars and Bars," Day-Lewis decided to "do everyone a favor and just stop for a while," He told Graham Fuller in *American Film.* He plans to divide his time between the stage and films. When asked if he preferred film or stage work, he replied: "I've always rather believed that one shouldn't try to differentiate between film acting and stage acting: There's good acting and bad acting, whether you're fifty yards away from the audience, or whether the camera is stuck up your right nostril. If someone can get away with something on the stage but not in front of a camera, it just means that they're better at hiding the fact that they're not doing their job very well."

Sources

American Film, January-February, 1988.
Film Comment, February, 1988.
Interview, April, 1988.
New Statesman, November 15, 1985.
Newsweek, March 10, 1986.
New Yorker, February 8, 1988.
People, February 22, 1988.

—Sketch by Denise Wiloch

Laura Dean

© *Johan Elbers 1980*

Choreographer, composer

Born December 3, 1945, in Staten Island, N.Y.; daughter of Arthur Douglas and Esther Dorothy (Sweedler) Dean. *Education:* Graduated with honors from High School for the Performing Arts, New York City; attended Boston University for two months.

Addresses: *Office*—Dean Dance and Music Foundation, Inc., 15 W. 17th St., New York, N.Y. 10011.

Career

Member of Paul Sanasardo Dance Troupe, c. 1964; member of Paul Taylor Dance Troupe, 1965–66; Laura Dean and Dance Company, founder and choreographer, 1971–75; Laura Dean Dancers and Musicians, founder, choreographer, and composer, 1976—. Dances include *Stamping Dance,* 1971, *Circle Dance,* 1972, *Jumping Dance,* 1973, *Walking Dance,* 1973, *Spinning Dance,* 1974, *Drumming* (music by Steve Reich), 1975, *Song,* 1976, *Dance,* 1976, *Spiral,* 1977, *Tympani,* 1980, *Night* (for Joffrey Ballet), 1980, *Sky Light,* 1982, *Transformer* (music by Anthony Davis), *Impact* (music by Reich), 1985, *Patterns of Change* (music by Philip Glass), 1985, *Force Field* (music by Reich), 1986, *Magnetic,* 1986, *Equator,* 1988, *Space* (music by Reich), 1988.

Member: National Endowment for the Arts Dance and Inter-Arts Panel.

Awards: Creative Artist Public Service fellow, 1976; Guggenheim fellow, 1977, 1982; grantee, National Endowment for the Arts, 1977–85, grantee, Jerome Foundation, 1978–80; grantee of Mobil Foundation, 1979–85; grantee of Rockefeller Foundation, 1980; grantee of Chemical Bank, 1980–84; grantee of Consolidated Edison, 1983; recognized by New York City Commission on the Status of Women, 1985.

Sidelights

Choreographer and composer Laura Dean has achieved prominence as a major contributor to minimalist post-modern dance, in which patterns are set and developed in a complex manner with few changes of tempo or dynamics. Like choreographers Trisha Brown and Lucinda Childs, who with Dean form the female minimalist triumvarite, Dean spurns virtuosity and psychological and dramatic subject matter to focus on form—elementary steps and simple geometric patterns. Unlike most choreographers, Dean often composes the music for her dances as well, creating an integrated whole true to her artistic vision. During early performances of Dean's works, uncomprehending and disappointed spectators frequently walked out, and she has had a long road to acceptance. After years on the periphery of the modern dance establishment, by the 1980s Dean and her company, the Laura Dean Dancers and Musicians, had received recognition from audiences and institutions alike.

Dean was born into a mathematical family—her father was an architect, her mother a mathematician—and mathematics, particularly geometry, has played an important role in her life. A quiet child, Dean was obsessed with counting, and she had already become obsessed with movement after a tragic accident at age eighteen months. One of Dean's legs and the right side of her pelvis were crushed under the wheels of a milk truck at her parents' Staten Island, New York, home. The toddler had gone outside unnoticed to wave good-bye to the milkman. Though doctors doubted she would ever walk again, after eight months in traction Dean relearned to walk.

"I hated, absolutely hated, school. You couldn't move. If you did, you got into trouble. I wasn't hyperactive. I just needed to move."

Dean's parents introduced their daughter to dance when she was six and a half years old by enrolling her in Manhattan's Third Street Settlement Music School. Dean fondly remembers how dance came alive for her there under the guidance of the choreographer and former star of the José Limon Dance Company, Lucas Hoving, whom Dean credits with her decision to become a dancer. At age eleven, Dean became interested in ballet after seeing a performance of Tchaikovsky's *The Nutcracker* by the New York City Ballet and developing a crush on the lead dancer. In order to meet him, Dean insisted on taking ballet lessons at the American School of Ballet, which she did for two years.

Despite her youthful enthusiasm for dance, Dean maintains that as a child she never aspired to become a dancer or choreographer. "I didn't know what I wanted. But I was always a physically aware child. I was aware on the bus that my feet didn't touch the floor. I hated, absolutely hated, school. You couldn't move. If you did, you got into trouble. I wasn't hyperactive. I just needed to move," she told *Horizon* writer Ellen Jacobs. Even after graduating with honors from the New York High School for the Performing Arts, where she studied ballet, modern dance, and piano—and eventually majored in modern dance—Dean was uncertain of her career goals. She entered Boston University as a theater major but returned to her parents' home after only two months.

Dean came into contact with many styles of dance before she was able to define her own idiom. She danced briefly with the Paul Sanasardo troupe and in 1965 joined the Paul Taylor Dance Company, remaining for almost a year before she left in frustration over her minor roles. Dean also became aware of the works of Meredith Monk and Kenneth King, who both use aspects of theater in their dances, and spent two years studying with Merce Cunningham, who is widely considered the progenitor of post-modern dance. Cunningham had been a young star in the early days of Martha Graham's dance company, which was instrumental in forging modern dance. Cunningham rebelled against the psychological, expressionist choreography that plays an important part in modern dance and created instead dance that emphasizes pure movement and energy. Dean soaked up these varied styles but had yet to determine her goals or remake dance according to her own vision.

In 1968, believing that the world would soon end, Dean traveled to various parts of Mexico and the United States. Her odyssey finally led to San Francisco, where she set up a modest studio. After trying unsuccessfully to determine the style of dance that best suited her, Dean decided to divest herself of all her former habits. To this end she sat as still as possible for eight hours a day, which she told Jennifer Dunning of the *New York Times*, "had to be one of the most painful things I've done in my life. I had never consciously stopped and sat still. The tears wouldn't stop." After several weeks, Dean could no longer tolerate such inaction and began walking back and forth, then circling, and finally spinning. In this spinning Dean experienced a physical and emotional joy that lead her to make spinning a hallmark of her work.

After deconstructing dance, Dean re-created it from its foundations. She returned to New York and began to experiment. Her early works, *Stamping Dance, Circle Dance,* and *Jumping Dance,* focus on a single movement, which is repeated throughout the dance. Dean's use of simple structures, repetition, and gender-neutral costumes inspired commentators to label her work minimalist; yet Dean insists that she is only minimalist in her use of repetition, that her dance vocabulary is rich and has expanded as her idiom has evolved.

In many of what Dean terms "deanmusicdances," the dancers perform in unisex roles and costumes. They all occupy the stage throughout the work and make little eye contact with the audience or each other. The dance's structure depends strongly on geometry, knowledge Dean uses instinctively as she failed that subject in high school. From above, the dances look like fluctuating patterns of simple shapes; however, from the audience's perspective they are hypnotizing tapestries of motion. Spins play an integral part of Dean's dances, and often-repeated patterns may end abruptly and a new pattern begin. Frequently a particular pattern is repeated for lengthy periods, giving rise to comparisons with American Indian dances and Muslim dervishes—highly repetitive dances using spinning that often entrance the dancers—but Dean denies any intentional religious influence. "The reason I embrace it [spinning] so much is that it's such a kinesthetic, physical sensation, which I think dancing should be," she told *Valley News* writer Jeannie Scheinin. "If you lose that, you lose a sense of gravity. I enjoy working with it, and I love the way it looks. So it has theatrical appeal to me."

Dean Described herself to Gary Parks of *Dance* as "a strange creature, called a choreographer/composer, that works in an extremely different way than a choreographer works." When beginning a piece for which she will both compose and choreograph, Dean works like a painter starting with a blank canvas. The music and dance build from one another as the piece evolves. Choreographers usually have the rhythms and emotional content of a dance established for them by the music they select. While Dean's skill as a composer allows her artistic freedom that other choreographers do not enjoy, she has collaborated with a number of composers, including Steve Reich (*Drumming, Force Field, Impact,* and *Space*), Anthony Davis (*Transformer*), and Philip Glass (*Patterns of Change*).

In 1976 Dean founded the Laura Dean Dancers and Musicians, a troupe of eleven dancers (seven women and four men) and four musicians. As there are generally no entrances or exits and little eye contact between dancers, Dean's style of dance requires dancers with stamina who are able to count well. In choosing her dancers Dean looks for these abilities as well as for personalities that will mesh on long tours. Dean also employs musicians because she believes in using live music in performances and rehearsals, a rarity for a medium-sized dance company.

As Dean's work received greater public recognition, the company left its New York base to tour throughout the United States and abroad. Acclaim has come in other forms as well. Dean has received grants from many sources, including the National Endowment for the Arts (NEA) and the Rockefeller Foundation, and such prestigious producers as Harvey Lichtenstein of the Brooklyn Academy of Music and Charles Reinhart of the American Dance Festival have commissioned works. She has been honored by the government in being chosen to attend a national arts reception at the White House and travel to China as part of a cultural exchange, and her *Dance* was included in a Public Broadcasting Service series, "Dance in America." Dean is happy to see her works draw larger and larger audiences; yet she does not believe that dance is suited to television because it loses it sense of gravity and expressiveness when viewed on small television screens.

> *"The message for me is: love this life because it's the only one you're going to get and have a deep respect for it, because it's all made out of energy."*

When Robert Joffrey commissioned three pieces for his self-named New York ballet company (*Night, Fire,* and *Force Field*), Dean married post-modern dance to ballet. She used her knowledge of ballet to combine balletic vocabulary with her own. Working with a larger troupe foreign to her gestures and the rigors of continual on-stage presence and counting gave Dean both new challenges and opportunities. Some commentators have noted that from her work with ballet has come dance that is more theatrical and emotive—she has used some patterning, point work, and more expressive upper body movement—which they view as a concession to the dance establishment.

When an unfavorable climate for the humanities and mismanagement of the company almost bankrupted it, Dean stopped dancing to become the troupe's administrator. While she admits that her new role is difficult—she has struggled to keep the troupe viable—it has given her the opportunity to focus to a greater extent on composing, choreographing, and promoting dance. Dean sits on several NEA panels and is a member of other arts organizations, such as the Mid-America Arts Alliance and Dance/USA.

Critics have noted similarities between Dean's dances and those of many cultures, though Dean does not acknowledge any direct influences. She does, however, cite physicist Albert Einstein, some of whose works she has read in books for non-scientists, as a spiritual mentor. For example, in *Equator* Dean experimented with circular formations inspired by Einstein's investigations of the behavior of other planets' equators. When asked by Scheinin what message if any her work conveys, Dean again referred to Einstein, "The message for me is: love this life because it's the only one you're going to get and have a deep respect for it, because it's all made out of energy. Einstein taught me something really beautiful: energy is matter and matter is energy and it's a beautiful universe.... I want my dances to instill a kinesthetic feeling as well as a sense of gravity. You've got to go down to come up!"

Sources

Atlanta Journal, September 11, 1988; September 13, 1988.
Boston Herald, April 14, 1988.
Dance, April, 1987.
Horizon, January, 1981.
Interview, September, 1981.
New York Times, December 30, 1982; October 27, 1985; March 2, 1986; August 23, 1987.
Newsweek, December 7, 1981.
Saturday Review, March, 1982.
Staten Island Advance, May 8, 1988.
Times Union, July 3, 1988.
Valley News, May 27, 1988.

—Sidelights by Jeanne M. Lesinski

Edward J. DeBartolo, Jr.

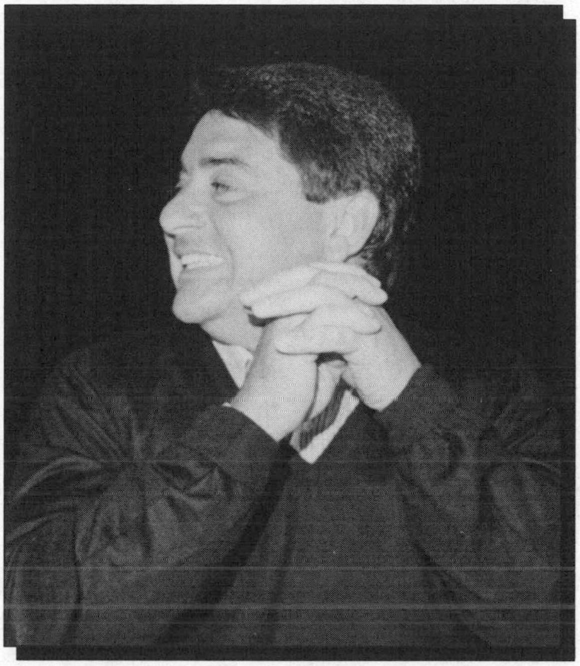

AP/Wide World Photos

Real estate developer and professional football team owner

Born November 6, 1946, in Youngstown, Ohio; son of Edward J. (a real estate developer) and Marie Patricia (Montani) DeBartolo; married Cynthia Ruth Papalia, November 27, 1968; children: Lisa Marie, Tiffanie Lynne, Nicole Anne. *Education:* University of Notre Dame, bachelor's degree in business, 1968. *Religion:* Roman Catholic.

Addresses: *Home*—Youngstown, Ohio; and Santa Clara, Calif. *Office*—DeBartolo Corp., 7620 Market St., Youngstown, Ohio 44512; and San Francisco 49ers, 711 Nevada St., Redwood City, Calif. 94061.

Career

DeBartolo Corp. (family real-estate development business), Youngstown, Ohio, various positions, 1960–72, vice-president, 1972–75, executive vice-president, 1975—, chief administrative officer, 1979—; owner, San Francisco 49ers football team, 1977—.

Trustee, Youngstown State University, 1974–77; local chairman, American Cancer Society fund drive, 1975—, and City of Hope, 1977; member of national advisory council, St. Jude Children's Research Hospital, 1978—, local chairman, 1979–80; member of National Cambodia Crisis Committee, 1980—. *Military service:* U.S. Army, 1969.

Awards: Man of the Year Award, St. Jude Children's Research Hospital, 1979, and Boys Town of Italy (San Francisco), 1985; citation of merit, Salvation Army, 1982.

Sidelights

Edward J. DeBartolo, Jr., is the owner of the Super Bowl champion San Francisco 49ers, a team that has had unparalleled success in the 1980s. DeBartolo, the franchise's sole owner, bought the 49ers in 1977 for $17 million. Now, with three Super Bowl championships since 1981, the club is worth $90 million—and DeBartolo does not intend to sell. The executive vice-president and chief administrative officer of the DeBartolo Corporation, the nation's largest developer of retail shopping space, DeBartolo presides over a billion-dollar enterprise that was launched by his father, Edward J. DeBartolo, Sr. Now owner of one-third of the company, DeBartolo will eventually inherit most of the business, still privately owned with his father and his sister, Marie DeBartolo York. Together the DeBartolos have built more than 70 million square feet of new shopping malls and shopping centers, as well as office towers and hotels, in the nation's suburbs. The corporation is better known, however, for its holdings in the sports business—the 49ers, the Pittsburgh Penguins, and numerous lucrative race tracks, including the state-of-the-art Remington Park in Oklahoma City, Oklahoma.

According to Eddie Donnally in the *Dallas Morning News,* the younger DeBartolo is far different from his taciturn and no-nonsense father. Donnally adds, though, that there is evidence "that when 'The Prince' ascends the throne, he will be well prepared. It is also likely that he will take a more active role than his father in running the family's sports franchises." That last observation is based on DeBartolo's reputation as a "hands-on" manager of the 49ers—a predisposition to run the football club that recently may have cost him the services of his coach, Bill Walsh. [See index for *Newsmakers* entry.]

"I did a lot of menial jobs. I worked on construction and got my share of scrapes. It wasn't always easy."

DeBartolo was just two years old when his father established his own company and began to speculate in real estate. The elder DeBartolo today is credited with great foresight, but in the early 1950s he must have looked silly to many developers of retail stores. DeBartolo took note that consumers were moving from the cities into the suburbs; he also watched with interest as highways were improved to move commuters from home to work in downtown areas. He realized that suburban homeowners could be easily convinced to shop near their neighborhoods, so he began to acquire land well outside the downtown districts of Ohio's biggest cities.

DeBartolo's first major project was Boardman Plaza, a strip shopping center in a nearly rural suburb of his native Youngstown. Martha Weinman Lear described what happened to the enterprise in a *New York Times Magazine* profile. DeBartolo, Lear wrote, "remembers standing on the brand-new sidewalk and overhearing one of the leading realtors from nearby Youngstown say to another: 'I'll give this place six months to fold.' It didn't, of course. The office buildings followed it out there, and the industries, and the medical facilities, and the apartment units, and the little strip is still out there thriving in the midst of a thriving suburb, while Youngstown, like so much of Downtown, U.S.A., looks like a lost gray soul. But that doesn't *necessarily* mean that Eddie [Sr.] made Boardman happen. He just guessed—one of those simple little throw-away, real-estate-genius guesses—which way the people were going, and was out there waiting when they arrived." Thus DeBartolo, Sr., became a pioneer and then a prolific builder of shopping malls, an entrepreneur, to quote Lear, who did "as much as anyone to extend a particular life-style, keep it vital and direct the traffic toward it."

By the time the younger DeBartolo was in his teens, the family business had grown to immense—and lucrative—proportions. The boy was not spoiled by an atmosphere of wealth and luxury, however. He told the *Dallas Morning News* that his childhood progressed in typical middle-class fashion, in a home outside Youngstown. "My mother would cook every day," he said, "and my dad, no matter how much he had to travel on business, would always try to be home for supper. We are a close-knit family, and I think I grew up in a normal household. And I think that has a lot to do with how you turn out. I think it's helped me a lot." DeBartolo grew up happy and well-adjusted, playing junior varsity football at his high school and earning sufficient grades to qualify for college at his father's alma mater, Notre Dame. When he graduated with a bachelor's degree in business in 1968, a position was waiting for him at the DeBartolo Corporation.

According to DeBartolo, he had to work his way up through the business ranks like any other ambitious youngster. "I did a lot of menial jobs," he told the *Dallas Morning News.* "I worked on construction and got my share of scrapes. It wasn't always easy." On the other hand, few construction workers become vice-presidents four years out of college and executive vice-presidents three years after that.

Fewer still have the assets, after less than ten years with a company, to buy a professional football team, even one with an abysmal record. DeBartolo's purchase of the 49ers was not a precedent in the family business; his father had already bought several race tracks and the Pittsburgh Penguins hockey team. The younger DeBartolo simply took a different attitude than his father. Where the older man used his sports enterprises as diversions from the favorite business of building malls, DeBartolo, Jr., set out to run the 49ers with the serious purpose of *winning*—and thereby increasing the team's worth.

At first DeBartolo's plan to resuscitate the 49ers must have seemed as foolhardy as his father's plan to build Boardman Plaza. In 1978 the team was 2–14, and four head coaches had come and gone in two seasons. The stands were nearly empty of spectators, and disorganization prevailed on the field and in the front office. DeBartolo instituted wholesale firings and then offered the head coaching job to Bill Walsh, a quiet but extremely knowledgeable tactician. DeBartolo also made Walsh the team's general manager, with the power to choose his own staff and personnel. Within three years Walsh had turned the 49ers around with the help of the brilliant play of quarterback Joe Montana. [See index for *Newsmakers* entry.] DeBartolo watched as the stands filled with fans, content to let Walsh run things. The 49ers won the Super Bowl in 1981 and, after a few setbacks, won it again in 1984. That same year DeBartolo promoted Walsh to president of the franchise.

The sailing has not always been smooth between Walsh and DeBartolo. Between 1985 and 1988, the 49ers made the playoffs every year, only to be knocked out by underdog teams in the first round. *Boston Globe* correspondent Ron Borges notes that by 1988, the retribution for this failure to advance "was swift and directed at one man: Bill Walsh.... DeBartolo didn't speak to Walsh for six weeks but talked loudly to anyone who would listen about Walsh's failings. Then DeBartolo stripped the winner of two Super Bowls in nine years of his title as team president." The move rankled Walsh, a man who had already considered retiring. Walsh decided that he could not leave the team on a low note and agreed to stay on as coach, perhaps until the 49ers won another Super Bowl. The team came through for Walsh in 1989, taking the championship in a dramatic game with the Cincinnati Bengals—and shortly thereafter Walsh announced that he would no longer serve as the 49ers' coach.

In a *San Jose Mercury News* interview, DeBartolo admitted that he has an "intense attitude, [a] killer instinct" where football is concerned, but he also said that he is trying to curb it. "I don't live and die anymore with what goes on," he said. "It was bad there for a while. It was very consuming. The peaks and valleys, the ups and downs, the roller-coaster rides from week to week. It would take me a day or two after the game to get back to normal. And the winning. Sometimes it was as tough to win as to lose. I didn't want this thing to consume me to a point

Edward J. DeBartolo, Jr. (right) congratulates coach Bill Walsh (left) and quarterback Joe Montana on the San Francisco 49ers' Super Bowl victory. AP/Wide World Photos.

where it affected my health and my family and friends, and I think I convinced myself that life is too short to let that happen. I think I'm a much more sedate person now and I have different priorities."

One welcome diversion from the 49ers is Remington Park, the race track the DeBartolo Corporation built in Oklahoma City. The $97 million facility opened in September of 1988 and quickly began to draw 10,000 spectators and a million dollars in bets per day. "Remington has taken the city by storm," wrote Steven Crist in the *New York Times*. "Tracks are often considered a necessary evil or a shady sideshow in [many] hometowns, but both residents and city officials here seem genuinely proud of Remington. The track has surpassed even the nearby National Cowboy Hall of Fame as the leading tourist attraction." One of the unique features of the Remington race course is the track itself, which is covered with Equitrack, a substance made by coating sand grains with a plastic polymer that is waterproof. Even on rainy days the track does not get sloppy; water runs through the grains and is drained away.

Both DeBartolos—father and son—are pleased with the success of their latest enterprise, especially since some observers thought the track too grandiose for a town the size of Oklahoma City. The younger DeBartolo is also trying to take a sportsman's interest in racing, as his father already has. "I must admit my interest in horse racing is purely business," he told the *Daily News* of Los Angeles. "I don't really know as much about it as I should. My father knows a lot more. He fully enjoys being at the track and the entire atmosphere surrounding it."

San Jose Mercury News columnist Mark Purdy described DeBartolo's approach to team ownership: "Eddie is no easy personality to capture in print. He is an amalgamation of various other famous sports owner/operators. There is a [George] Steinbrenner/Eddie, who can be just as angry and irrational as the Yankees' owner after a nasty defeat.... But there also is a Rooney/Eddie, who is inevitably sensitive and generous, taking after the late Steelers owner, Art Rooney. It is common knowledge that DeBartolo is a soft touch for charitable causes, and he seldom has been accused of stinginess in the 49ers' payroll department. Finally, there is a [Peter] O'Malley/Eddie, who knows dollars and sense as well as the [Los Angeles] Dodgers' ownership. This Eddie tends to intelligently ponder any major business decisions." Reporter Frank Cooney told the *Daily News* of Los Angeles that DeBartolo is a "spontaneous personality." Cooney added: "If he's happy, he'll be happy, and if he's sad, he'll let you know. He says what's on his mind. He's very close to the surface."

Despite his business interests on the West Coast, DeBartolo continues to live in an exclusive suburb of Youngstown. He married his high school sweetheart, Cynthia Papalia, and they have three daughters. Donnally concluded that Edward DeBartolo, Sr., "will leave large footprints" that his son will have to follow. But having shown himself capable of managing the 49ers, and other sensitive sports business deals, Edward, Jr., has proven that he, "at least, will march to the beat of a different drummer."

Sources

Barron's, May 4, 1987.
Boston Globe, January 1, 1989.
Business Week, October 19, 1987.
Chicago Tribune, October 9, 1988.
Daily News (Los Angeles), October 9, 1988.
Financial World, March 10, 1987.
Los Angeles Times, November 26, 1986.
New York Times, October 9, 1986.
New York Times Magazine, August 12, 1973.
San Jose Mercury News, March 22, 1987; December 4, 1988.
Sporting News, July 11, 1983; February 13, 1984.
Variety December 26, 1984.
Wall Street Journal, October 9, 1986; November 26, 1986.

—Sidelights by Mark Kram

Harry Edwards

AP/Wide World Photos

Educator and sports consultant

Born November 22, 1942, in St. Louis, Mo.; son of Harry (a laborer) and Adelaide (Cruise) Edwards; married Sandra Y. Boze (a teacher), August 25, 1970; children: Tazamisha Heshima Imara, Fatima Malene Imara, Changa Demany Imara. *Education:* San Jose State College (now University), B.A., 1964; Cornell University, M.A., 1966, Ph.D., 1972.

Addresses: *Home*—40573 Dolores Place, Fremont, Calif. 94538. *Office*—Department of Sociology, University of California, Berkeley, Calif. 94720.

Career

Santa Clara County Economic Opportunity Commission (SCCEOC), Santa Clara, Calif., researcher, 1966–67; San Jose State College (now University), San Jose, Calif., instructor in sociology, 1966–68; University of Santa Clara, Santa Clara, Calif., instructor in sociology, 1967–68; University of California, Berkeley, assistant professor, 1970–77, associate professor of sociology, 1977–; Miller scholar in residence at University of Illinois, Urbana, fall, 1982; Gazette scholar in residence at University of Charleston, W.Va., 1984. Lecturer in the United States and Canada. Served as sports and social issues commentator for National Public Radio and numerous television programs, including "Sixty Minutes" (CBS-TV), "Nightly News" (NBC-TV), "Sports World" (NBC-TV), "Sportsbeat" (ABC-TV), "Nightline" (ABC-TV), "James Michener's World" (PBS-TV), and numerous local, regional and international television programs focusing on issues relating to sports and society. Serves as mentor/liason to players, consultant to San Francisco 49ers and Golden State Warriors; special consultant to Major League Baseball, 1987—.

Member: American Sociological Association, Association of Black Sociologists (executive committee member, 1982–84), Society for the Study of Social Problems, North American Society for the Sociology of Sport, Pacific Sociological Association, California Association of Black Faculty and Staff.

Awards: Woodrow Wilson fellow, 1964; Cornell University fellow, 1968; Russwurm Award from National Newspaper Publishers Association, 1968; named man of the year by *San Francisco Sun Reporter*, 1968; honorary doctorate from Columbia College, 1981.

Sidelights

Sports sociologist Harry Edwards is a well-paid executive consultant these days, respected as an academic innovator, and holds a national reputation as an expert on racial issues. But he insists he is fundamentally unchanged—in philosophy, in manner—from the radical black activist who revved up a black boycott effort at the 1968 Olympics. Rather, he insists, society has evolved to the point where now his views are considered mainstream.

An early exponent of analyzing human behavior as manifested in organized sports, Edwards in the 1960s emerged as a vehement critic of the sports industry, in particular condemning as racist its treatment of minorities. In the 1970s Edwards earned a degree in sociology and helped develop sports sociology as a recognized academic discipline. By the 1980s he was earning an income "well into the six figures" advising professional baseball and football executives on racial issues.

"This notion that blacks are going to use sports to rise up the socioeconomic scale is nonsense....Why we are dominating sports is because of racism and discrimination and a malignant kind of integration."

While explicit racial barriers in organized sports had tumbled long ago, implicit limitations on opportunities for minorities remain, in the opinion of many. Black and Hispanic athletes participate in professional sports out of proportion to their presence in the population, but coaching and management positions generally elude them. Sports and broadcasting figures began mentioning this on the air in the mid-1980s, and in 1987 Edwards was hired as a special consultant to Major League Baseball. Specifically, he was asked to develop a list of minority individuals with front-office potential and facilitate their hiring.

To Edwards, the doors closed to minority athletes merely reflect the status quo of a society founded on racist assumptions. Young non-white males are channeled into sports, while other professional opportunities are denied them. "There's this garbage that's been floating around since [turn of the century heavyweight champ] Jack Johnson, that blacks have benefitted more from their sports involvement than anybody else. This notion that blacks are going to use sports to rise up the socioeconomic scale is nonsense. You can double the number of blacks in sports and actually have an intensificiation of racism. Why we are dominating sports is because of racism and discrimination and a malignant kind of integration," he told David Chamberlain, in an article published in *Sport* magazine.

Imposing of stature—6 foot 8, 240 pounds, shaven head and grey goatee—and articulate of opinion, Edwards became a popular media figure in the 1980s. He appeared on scores of television news and interview shows, gave his opinions frequently to newspapers and magazine reporters, and maintained a public speaking schedule that had him behind the podium two or three times a week. As the issue of blacks in sports became a major media preoccupation, Edwards was sought out with increasing frequency. When NBC broadcast "Black Athletes: Fact and Fiction" in April 1989, Edwards emerged as the program's star, angrily dismissing the view that blacks have a "natural ability" for sports. "What's really being said," he told moderator Tom Brokaw, "is that blacks are closer to beasts and animals . . . than they are to the rest of humanity." Essentially, Edwards sees sports as a microcosm of society, albeit a particularly important one given its role as a socializing agent for society. While he supports affirmative action for sports, he does not think that simply putting more minority athletes on the playing fields is the answer. "It's not a question of what sports will look like, it's a question of what society is going to look like. Sports recapitulates society," he told Chamberlain.

While best known as a social critic and former sixties radical, Edwards sees himself primarily as an educator. He told *Newsday* writer Paul Daugherty, "Foremost I am a teacher. And sports, like education, is focused on the young. When you influence sports and education, you're influencing the future." Edwards' classroom style owes more to evangelical fire and brimstone than to Socratic dialogue. Chamberlain describes a classroom exchange where a student offers an opinion at odds with Edwards' views. The professor, "gesturing muscularly, eyes staring through glower-tinted glasses, short beard jutting, shaved dome gleaming," restates his opinion until the student recants. Unplacated, Edwards reiterates his opinion, insisting that the student recant once again to prove she truly understands. Despite—or perhaps because of—his pedagogy, his three classes are "among the most popular offered at Berkeley," Chamberlain reports.

Edwards has published several books including *Black Student* (1970), *Revolt of The Black Athlete* (1970), *Healing Intelligence* (1971) and *The Struggle That Must Be* (1980). The last, an autobiography, describes Edwards' early struggle for literacy. Recalling the frustration he felt as a college freshman unable to grasp his reading assignments, he recounts an afternoon sitting at the school library trying to fathom a history textbook. Angrily he "slammed the book shut and began to sob—full height by now and 240 pounds, sitting in the library crying into my hands out of pure frustration." It was "just by chance" that he came across a passage that said "Columbus discovered America . . . and he and his small band of weary men . . . encountered people they thought to be Indians." Edwards wondered, How could Columbus have 'discovered' a land already populated? His account continues: "I read more. And more. More rapidly now, gulping down sentences, paragraphs and then entire pages . . . and the more I read, the more I realized that there was a story, an argument implicit within every sentence, every paragraph and every chapter of the book . . . I had learned to read critically . . . That night I was the last student to leave the library."

Born November 22, 1944, Edwards grew up one of nine children in an unstable home environment. His mother left during Harry's adolescence. His father, an ex-convict, worked off and on in factories and frequently departed for drinking binges. An amateur boxer, the older Edwards tried to impress on his son the opportunities sports presented to the black male. Harry's sports were track and basketball, and the sports helped him get into Fresno City College, a two-year institution. A prominent St. Louis attorney, who subsidized the college educations of "young men of promise," helped Edwards financially.

Edwards was a B-plus student at Fresno State and earned a track and basketball scholarship to San Jose State. Increasingly, howevever, he was becoming aware of the racial subtext of the sports he played. "I saw white athletes get [summer] jobs that black starters didn't get," he recalled to Aldore Collier of *Ebony*. "I saw [white basketball players] get tours to places that black athletes didn't even know were being given." He was not hesitant to voice his opinions to a displeased university sports establishment. After setting a college record in the discus throw, his budding militancy resulted in his being kicked off the track team. He continued to play on the basketball squad, where his style of play was so physical and unrestrained that referees removed him early from 82 out of 86 varsity contests.

In the classroom he displayed more finesse. After obtaining an undergraduate degree in sociology from San Jose State, he went to Cornell on a Woodrow Wilson fellowship, earning a doctoral degree in 1972. In those years, the apex of black radical protest, he kept FBI agents busy compiling a thick dossier on his activities. Costumed in the black militant costume of the day—dashiki, beret, goatee, dark glasses—Edwards helped galvanize a black protest movement among athletes at the 1968 Olympics in Mexico City. After orchestrating a black-gloved victory salute from sprinters Tommie Smith and John Carlos, Edwards was dismissed from his job as a sociology instructor at San Jose State. Further, the notoriety from his boycott effort unleashed a flood of hate mail and death threats. His heated racial rhetoric made him more enemies: he spoke of the President of the United States as "Lynchin' Baines Johnson," of white people as "pigs," "honkies," and "blue eyed devils."

As the black power movement faded from the national scene during the Ford and Carter years, Edwards continued flailing away at the sports industry, establishing himself as a minority rights activist without portfolio. As various executives began to acknowledge the seriousness of sports' problems in race relations, it began to turn to its loudest critic for help. The San Francisco Forty-Niners, a football team, and the Golden State Warriors, a basketball team, both hired the sociologist as a "mentor/liason"—his terms—to counsel athletes. The clearest signal that the former outsider had become respectable was when the commissioner of Major League Baseball hired Edwards in June, 1987, as a minority affairs consultant. Baseball commissioner Peter Ueberroth, ironoically, had been a student coach at San Jose State at the time Edwards was kicked off the team. There was not much communication between the two back then. The future commissioner was "just another white boy running around in shorts," Edwards told Chamberlain.

Working now for Ueberroth, Edwards began his new job by developing a five-page employment questionnaire, which he mailed to all former black and Hispanic major league baseball players he could track down. The approach earned Edwards the ire of a number of veteran black baseball players, who observed that no one sends questionnaires to white candidates. Edwards was verbally attacked as being unqualified for lack of baseball experience, and inappropriate because of his sixties sensibility and history. Retired slugger Reggie Jackson told Mark Hyman of the *Baltimore Sun*, "He is a radical . . . who does not stand for what I stand for."

Soon after attending the 1989 World Series, seated alongside the commissioner, Edwards admitted he too was tired of waiting. "We are at a volatile point," he told a November 22, 1989, press conference, as reported by *Newsday*'s Steve Marcus. "There is very little satisfaction to be taken in the eyes of the public with this [lack of] progress." It was possible, he suggested, that such sixties-era protest tactics as the public boycott could be utilized to persuade sports executives to change their ways. He told the press conference that public ownership of most stadiums leased to professional teams could be leveraged to change hiring practices. "In the not too distant future, people are going to begin to move more and more towards protest rather than cooperative effort," he warned.

A return to the old Edwards? Not at all, contends the sociologist. "In every aspect—my sports, my social philosophy—I have not changed one whit since the sixties," he told Chamberlain. "I was convinced that I was right at that time, I'm convinced that I'm right now. Not only do I not make any apologies about it, I insist on it." The change, he declares, has been in society, not him. "Americans are growing sick of [racism]," he told Chamberlain. "There's so many people who are sick and tired of this garbage, want to get this shit off the road, that it's not even funny. They want to move it on, so that we can move on as a society. Even though I was saying the same thing in 1981 I would not have gotten the same reception. People couldn't figure out what was wrong. Now, the only debate is, How do we solve the problem? And there are a lot of people convinced that if anybody knows how to resolve the problem, it's Edwards."

Edwards and his wife, Sondra, an Oakland elementary school vice principal, are raising two teenage daughters and a pre-teen son. All are surnamed Imara—an African language word for "strength." As the sociologist explained to *Newsday*'s Paul Daugherty, "There are no Edwards children in my family. Edwards is a name off the plantation."

Writings

The Revolt of the Black Athlete, Free Press, 1969.
Black Students, Free Press, 1970.
Sociology of Sports, Dorsey, 1973.
The Struggle That Must Be: An Autobiography, Macmillan, 1980.
Playing to Win: A Short Guide to Sensible Black Sports Participation, Institute for the Study of Social Change, Berkeley, Calif., 1982.

Contributor of numerous articles to periodicals, including *New York Times, Los Angeles Times, Newsday, Black Scholar, Sports Illustrated,* and *Inside Sports.*

Sources

Baltimore Sun, November 8, 1987.
Ebony, October, 1987.
Newsday, July 24, 1987; November 23, 1989.
Sport, December, 1987.

—Sidelights by Warren Strugatch

Michael Eisner

Reuters/Bettmann Newsphotos

Entertainment company executive

Full name, Michael Dammann Eisner; born March 7, 1942, in Mt. Kisco, N.Y.; son of Lester (a lawyer) and Margaret (Dammann) Eisner; married Jane Breckenridge; children: Michael, Eric, Anders. *Education:* Denison University, B.A. 1964.

Addresses: *Home*—Bel Air, Calif. *Office*—The Walt Disney Co., 500 South Buena Vista St., Burbank, Calif. 91521.

Career

Federal Communications Commission (FCC), Washington, D.C., worked as logging clerk at National Broadcasting Company (NBC), in New York, N.Y., 1964; Columbia Broadcasting System (CBS), began career in programming department, 1964; American Broadcasting Companies (ABC), assistant to the national programming director, 1966–68, director of program development for the East Coast, 1968–71, vice-president for daytime programming, 1971–75, senior vice-president for prime-time production and development, 1976; Paramount Pictures Corp., president and chief operating officer, 1976–84; Walt Disney Company, chairman and chief executive officer, 1984–. Serves on the board of directors for Denison University, the California Institute of Arts, the American Film Institute, the American Hospital of Paris Foundation, the Public Awareness and Education Council of the Committee for Food and Shelter, Inc., the National Committee on United States-China Relations, and the Performing Arts Council of the Los Angeles Music Center.

Sidelights

Once synonymous with prosperous children's entertainment, the light had gone out of the Disney Company following the death of its founder, Walt Disney, in 1966. While other film companies were making such family-pleasers as "Star Wars" and "Raiders of the Lost Ark," Disney executives were reluctant to veer from the once popular but tired Disney format, and experimentation was kept to a minimum. Indeed, the last hit film Disney had in the 1960s was "The Love Bug" (1969), about a Volkswagen named Herbie.

During the 1970s, Disney's creative side eroded further as executives concentrated on real estate development. This infuriated Roy Disney [see index for *Newsmakers* entry], Walt Disney's nephew and the company's largest single shareholder with 3 percent. "I remember thinking that if that pattern went on much longer, the company would become a museum in honor of Walt," Disney told *Time* magazine. "Movies were the fountainhead of ideas, the impetus for all the rest. Without 'Fantasia' and 'Snow White,' Disneyland couldn't have been built."

Disney's profits and stock price went plunging in the 1970s. Fearing an outside takeover, Roy Disney resigned and mounted an effort to topple Disney's upper management. At the same time, Wall Street corporate raider Saul Steinberg began buying up Disney stock, preparing to take over the company. Disney executives paid Steinberg $32 million in greenmail to go away. But the move so weakened the company that Roy Disney was able to push his own management slate.

"Movies were the the fountainhead of ideas, the impetus for all the rest. Without 'Fantasia' and 'Snow White' Disneyland couldn't have been built."

Heading the team was Michael Eisner, the number-two man at Paramount Pictures for the previous eight years, who had shepherded that motion picture company through a series of hits, including "Grease," "Beverly Hills Cop" and three "Star Trek" movies. Unlike many of his contemporaries, Eisner had not been weaned on Disney. The son of a wealthy New York attorney and investor, Eisner seldom watched television or went to the movies. Indeed, his parents required him to dress in tie and jacket for Sunday dinner, and Eisner had to read for two hours before he could watch one hour of television.

As a student at Ohio's Denison University, Eisner briefly considered a medical career, but he graduated with a degree in English literature. His first exposure to Disney material came years later when he and his wife, Jane, and their newborn son, Michael, saw "Pinocchio" at the drive-in. "I'd never seen anything like it," Eisner told *Parade* magazine. "It was fabulous. Sitting there, watching this marvelous puppet... from that point on, I was obsessed by Disney."

When Eisner took over, the company was virtually comatose. Profits had fallen from $135 million in 1980 to $93 million by early 1984. In one year alone, Disney stock fell from a high of $85 a share to $45. One of Eisner's first moves was to lure some 20 top executives from Paramount, including Richard Frank and Jeffrey Katzenberg, who now run the company's filmed entertainment division. Gary Wilson was imported from the Marriot Corp. to be Disney's chief financial officer. "The secret is to hire someone about whom people say, 'Are you crazy?'" Eisner told *Parade*. "And you don't hire someone to do the same job he has done before. You hire him to do something new, so that people say, two years later, 'Where do we get a guy like that?'"

"To me, the familiar is boring, excessive violence is anti-social, and stupid is just stupid," Eisner told *Parade*. "In this business, the script is the base of the pyramid. I'd rather hire 10 good writers than one big-name star. And it's self-defeating to be obsessed with any one star or director. If you can't get Steven Spielberg—well, there's another Spielberg coming of age in Columbus, Ohio, or someplace."

Eisner's next move was to bolster the company's filmmaking division. Their first project, "Down and Out in Beverly Hills" (1986), cost $13 million, and grossed over $62 million at the box office. For "Down and Out," Eisner hired Bette Midler, Richard Dreyfuss, and Nick Nolte (Midler and Dreyfuss later returned for other Disney projects). That was the basis of the new Disney formula: find actors and actresses whose careers are in need of a push and sign them for multi-picture contracts.

Through its Touchstone film division, Disney was also able to make more mature films that would appeal to older audiences. And, under Eisner, Disney remains frugal with its budgets. The average Disney film in 1987 cost about $12 million, compared to Hollywood's $16.5 million average. And 22 of the 23 films made and released by Eisner at Disney as of early 1988 have made a profit, compared to the film industry average of about three of every 10. "Disney is still Disney, the one ingrained in the American memory," Robin Williams, who stars in Touchstone's "Good Morning, Vietnam," told *Time*. "But it's a different Disney, doing different things. Touchstone is from the same family, but it's a new child in town. This Minnie has nipples."

"To me, the familiar is boring, excessive violence is anti-social, and stupid is just stupid."

Movies aren't the only area in which Eisner has applied his Midas Touch. Under Walt Disney, the company coveted its classic animated films, re-releasing them every seven years or so to new audiences.

Eisner cherishes them also. But under Eisner, the "classics" have slowly been released on videocassette. Those films, and hundreds of other programs in the Disney archives, have helped boost Disney's home video division from $55 million in sales in 1983 to $175 million in 1987.

Behind "E.T.," Disney's "Cinderella" and "Lady and the Tramp" have become the second- and third-best selling videocassettes of all time, each selling more than three million copies. The Disney Channel is the fastest growing pay-television channel in the country, rising from some 750,000 subscribers to over 4 million from 1984 through 1988.

Yet despite these lucrative film, video, and cable divisions, Disney theme parks provide the company with the bulk of its revenue: 62 percent of sales and 70 percent of operating earnings during fiscal 1987. Under Eisner, attendance at the parks has increased more than 10 percent, despite a hefty increase in admission fees from $18 to $28 for one-day adult passes at Florida's Disney World and from $14 to $21.50 at California's Disneyland. Part of the reason for this increase is a multi-million dollar expansion of the parks, including a $17 million, 17-minute, 3-D feature called "Captain Eo," starring Michael Jackson. Even more eye-popping is a $32 million thrill-ride that opened in January 1987 called Star Tours, a hydraulically powered ride that jostles passengers around as they watch a 4.5-minute spaceflight film by "Star Wars" director George Lucas.

To capture even more of the money theme park goers bring with them, Disney has planned a $375 million, twin hotel complex outside the parks, and a joint venture with MGM for a $400 million television and film studio in Orlando will start offering tours in 1990. Disney's $750 million Tokyo Disneyland, which attracted 12 million people last year, provides the entertainment company with 10 percent royalties on admission and 5 percent on food and souvenirs. But a proposed Euro Disneyland in France, expected

Michael Eisner (center) and "Star Wars" creator George Lucas are joined by several Disney and "Star Wars" friends at the opening of the "Star Tours" attraction at Disneyland. AP/Wide World Photos.

to open in 1992, will provide the company with even more: a 16.7 percent piece of the pie.

For overseeing what many consider the biggest corporate turnaround since Lee Iacocca pulled Chrysler off the skids, Eisner is well-compensated. In 1987 he earned a bonus of nearly $6 million on top of his $750,000 salary. Factored in with his stocks and stock options, Eisner is estimated to be worth between $125 million and $150 million. Yet Eisner remains an average man in appearance.

His well-tailored suits are often rumpled, tie askew. As host of the Sunday night Disney movie, Eisner comes across as more of a "dad" than Fred MacMurray. Weekend mornings, he says, are spent at home with his family. "My family comes first and Disney second," Eisner told *Parade*. "When I have to choose between them, I'll always choose the family, whether it's a school play or a hockey game or whatever. I also want to keep them out of the spotlight, and they're happy to stay out of it. After all, the corporate world doesn't impress kids."

How long Disney can stay on top is unclear. Indeed, these might just be the Golden Years Eisner is entering now. But however long Disney will be hot, Eisner says his formula for success will remain the same. "My theory is, don't try to second-guess the audience," he told *Parade*. "It's like, in basketball, you don't throw the ball all the way down the court or shoot for three-pointers all night. The trick is simply to take quality shots from close-in. That's what we're doing here—taking quality shots, over and over again, and not worrying about the audience. If we make good pictures, they'll find us."

Sources

Business Month, December, 1987; December, 1988.
Business Week, March 9, 1987; February 1, 1988.
California Business, December, 1986.
Fortune, January 5, 1987.
Marketing & Media, September, 1986.
New York Times Magazine, December 29, 1985.
Parade, November 15, 1987.
Time, April 25, 1988.
U.S. News & World Report, December 22, 1986.

—Sidelights by Stephen Advokat

Arthur Erickson

Photograph by Mary Ann Donohue

Canadian architect

Full name, Arthur Charles Erickson; born June 14, 1924, in Vancouver, British Columbia, Canada; son of Oscar (an administration executive) and Myrtle (Chatterson) Erickson. *Education:* Attended University of British Columbia, 1942–43; McGill University, B.Arch. (with honors), 1950.

Addresses: *Home*—Vancouver, British Columbia, Canada. *Office*—Arthur Erickson Architects, Inc., 2412 Laurel St., Vancouver, British Columbia, Canada V5Z 3T2; and 80 Bloor St., Toronto, Ontario, Canada M5S 2VI; and 125 North Robertson, Los Angeles, Calif. 90048.

Career

University of Oregon, Eugene, assistant professor of architecture, 1955–56; University of British Columbia, Vancouver, instructor, 1956–58, assistant professor, 1958–60, associate professor of architecture, 1961; Erickson-Massey Architects, Vancouver, partner, 1963–72; Arthur Erickson Architects, Vancouver, Toronto, Ontario, and Los Angeles, Calif., principal, 1972—. Member of board of directors of Canadian Conference of the Arts, 1972; past member of Canadian Council on Urban Research; member of board of trustees of Institute for Research on Public Policy. *Military service:* Canadian Army, Intelligence Corps, 1943–45; served in India, Ceylon, and Malaya; became captain.

Member: Royal Architectural Institute of Canada (fellow), Royal Canadian Academy of Arts (fellow), Institute for Research on Public Policy, Community Planning Association of Canada, Heritage Canada, Urban Land Institute, American Institute of Architects (fellow), American Society of Interior Designers, American Society of Planning Officials, Architectural Institute of British Columbia (honorary member), Planning Institute of British Columbia, Ordre des Architects de Quebec, Ontario Association of Architects, Museum of Modern Art, University of British Columbia Museum of Anthropology, Vancouver Art Gallery (life member), University Club of Vancouver.

Awards: McLennan fellowship for study in Egypt, Syria, Turkey, Greece, Italy, France, Spain, England, and Scandinavia, 1950–53; Canada Council fellowship for study in Japan, Cambodia, and Indonesia, 1961–62; Molson Prize, Canada Council, 1967; award from Royal Bank of Canada, 1971; honorary D.Eng., Nova Scotia Technical College, 1971; Tau Sigma Delta Gold Medal, American Institute of Architects, 1973; honorary LL.D., Simon Fraser University, 1973, McGill University, 1975, and University of Manitoba, 1978; named officer, Order of Canada, 1973; Auguste Perret Award, International Union of Architects, 1974; Chicago Architecture Award, 1984; Gold Medal, French Academy of Architecture, 1984, and American Institute of Architects, 1986; honorary L.H.D., University of British Columbia, 1986; has received more than thirty awards for architectural designs from various organizations, including Prestressed Concrete Institute, American Society of Landscape Architects, Canadian Housing Design Council, and National Society of Interior Designers.

Sidelights

Canadian architect Arthur Erickson is no stranger to controversy. After years of designing dramatic and challenging buildings throughout the world, he knows his work inspires strong reactions. And Erickson's latest creation is no exception. The architect's eclectic design for Canada's new embassy in Washington, D.C., is evoking fulsome praise and harsh criticism on both sides of the border. This should come as no surprise. Erickson's unusual style is imprinted on buildings around the globe. He has applied his art to almost every kind of structure, including several universities (most notably Simon Fraser in his native British Columbia); the Canadian pavilion at Expo '70 in Osaka, Japan; Roy Thomson Hall in Toronto; the Bunker Hill complex in Los Angeles; a proposed cultural complex in Shanghai; and many private homes and office buildings.

These various works have elicited a wide range of responses. Respected American architect Philip Johnson [see index for *Newsmakers* entry] calls Erickson "by far the greatest architect in Canada and perhaps the greatest on this continent." Indeed, in 1986, Erickson won the prestigious American Institute of Architects Gold Medal. Previous winners have included Frank Lloyd Wright and Buckminster Fuller. Critics, however, complain he doesn't pay enough attention to details and leaves too much responsibility to subordinates. They even say some of his buildings, like Simon Fraser and the British Columbia Museum of Anthropology, tend to develop leaks.

Now, with his new embassy project, Erickson continues to court contention. He has combined neoclassical and modernist influences in a limestone edifice that some are calling "strong and confident" and others are dismissing as "an awkward pastiche." Erickson himself is proud of his newest work. "It shows we can stand up in Washington with the best," he told *Maclean's* magazine. "I hope it will elicit pride about our presence in the United States." The building incorporates an open box design six stories high supported by a neo-classical rotunda with 12 concrete pillars. There are many open spaces that are intended to give a sense of lightness and access. The director of the nearby National Gallery, J. Carter Brown, believes Erickson achieved his aim. Brown told *Maclean's*, "It is saying to the American people, 'Come in, walk through.'" But there are those who say the $90 million structure, six years in the making, is too extravagant. It covers 186,000 square feet of prime Washington real estate. One embassy employee told *Maclean's* magazine the building was so lavish "we could do staff weddings and charity events once or twice a year, but we don't want to be a hire-a-hall for funerals and bar mitzvahs." Vancouver architect Bing Thom, among others, agrees. "To my eye, this building is fussy. I think Arthur was trying too hard."

The controversy over Erickson's embassy began long before the doors officially opened. In 1982 Canadian Prime Minister Pierre Trudeau overruled a selection committee that had short-listed four other Canadian architects for the contract. He awarded the contract to Erickson, a long-time friend. Opposition members of Parliament were incensed. They likened the decision to Adolph Hitler's favouring of Nazi architect Albert Speer. But Erickson simply brushed aside the storm of protest. "This is one of the most serious projects Canada can undertake," he told the *Toronto Globe and Mail*, "A lot of this reaction is sour grapes and an attempt to tarnish Trudeau a bit more." Later, even the site of the embassy sparked controversy. Located on Pennsylvania Avenue about halfway between the White House and Capitol Hill, it is the first foreign embassy allowed on America's most powerful street. While Canadian diplomats are delighted, some Americans think the Canadian presence is an intrusion. As Michael Stanton wrote in Washington's *City Paper*, "Perhaps Canada is pressing to become the 51st state ahead of [the District of Columbia] and Puerto Rico."

Like many architects, Arthur Erickson's career blossomed relatively late in life. He seemed destined for a more parochial career as an academic until he won a competition to design British Columbia's new Simon Fraser University in 1963. His dramatic design won him immediate accolades. The British magazine *Interbuild* claimed the complex had "a distinctive and total intensity—which is revolutionary in content." On the other hand, visiting sculptor Henry Moore said the university's grandeur reminded him of the podium at Nuremburg Stadium.

Erickson had originally wanted to be an artist. Born in Vancouver in 1924, he inherited an interest in art from his father. He began painting at an early age and had his first exhibit when only fourteen. He was influenced by Lawren Harris, the Group of Seven painter who rendered cool, pure, almost architectural mountain landscapes. But Erickson's fledgling career was interrupted by the advent of World War II. He joined the Canadian Army's Intelligence Corps, learned Japanese, and was then posted to India and Malaya. During this period, he acquired an abiding interest in Eastern cultures and philosophy.

When Erickson returned to Canada after the war he contemplated joining the foreign service. But then he saw some photographs of Frank Lloyd Wright's famous desert home, Taliesin West. And as he later told the *New Yorker*'s Edith Iglauer, "When I saw those pictures, I said immediately, 'If you can do as imaginative and creative a thing as that in architecture, I want to be an architect.'" Erickson enrolled in the architecture program at McGill University in Montreal. Four years later he graduated at the top of his class. He was offered an opportunity to study with Frank Lloyd Wright for a year, but Erickson's insatiable appetite for travel won out. He accepted a McGill travelling scholarship, which took him to Europe and the Middle East for almost three years.

Upon returning to Vancouver, he had an unsuccessful experience working for several local architectural firms. He was fired twice because of impractical and costly designs. In 1955 he retreated into academia, teaching first at the University of Oregon, then a year later at the University of British Columbia. But in 1963, Erickson and partner Geoffrey Massey won the Simon Fraser design competition. The university was completed in two years. With its covered mall and its appreciation for the landscape, it echoed the style of a Greek temple. And it guaranteed Erickson's elevation to the top ranks of his profession. It wasn't long before he was being offered major assignments across Canada.

He followed up the Simon Fraser project with another university, at Lethbridge in the province of Alberta. This design, like everything he does, attempts to incorporate the surrounding landscape. The structure sits like a long, low ribbon of concrete amongst the rolling prairie just east of the Rockies. He has likened his design to that of an enormous ocean liner riding the waves of the grainfields. *Time* magazine called it "a tour de force of form, scale and siting . . . a massive piece of minimalist sculpture." A series of Expo pavilions followed, including the Canadian pavilion at Expo '70 in Osaka. His mirrored glass and wood design was judged best of Expo by the Architectural Institute of Japan. He also did a rare office tower, for MacMillan Bloedel in Vancouver, and a 12-story glass and copper addition to the Bank of Canada building in Ottawa. Erickson's structures all featured what was to become his trademark design: an incorporation of strong horizontal lines, unconventional angles, concrete, British Columbia redwood, skylights, flooded roofs or pools to catch reflections, and an intrinsic harmony with the landscape.

Erickson's really big projects were still to come. In 1972, the new British Columbia government wanted to scrap the previous administration's plans to build a monstrous black government office tower in the heart of Vancouver. It called on Arthur Erickson for an alternative. He designed a sprawling, people-sized complex that included the transformation of the 67-year-old courthouse into the Vancouver Art Gallery and the construction of a new glass-roofed law courts complex. The elegant three-block area now stands at the heart of a city whose dreary architecture had long failed to match up to its breathtaking surroundings. But this testimony to Erickson's vision was his last major project in his home province. The Social Credit government apparently blacklisted him from government and commercial contracts after his name was linked with the New Democratic Party in a newspaper advertisement (although Erickson insists that he doesn't belong to any political parties). Expo '86, for example, did not feature a single design by Erickson, despite his acknowledged experience in the field.

> *"Routine of any kind is bad for the health. If I'm too long in a place, I become stale, or it becomes stale, or we both do."*

Erickson regrouped by returning to his old love—travel. He began working outside of Canada; there were several projects in Saudia Arabia and Iraq. But this international approach proved to be risky, particularly for someone who had always been more interested in the art and science of building than the business of it. Erickson was unable to ensure that fees were paid in the light of rising political tensions in the Middle East, falling oil prices, and changes in government. The unpaid bills, combined with Erickson's reputation for running over budget, robbed his company of vital in-house resources. He was forced to lay off 50 of the 100 employees in his three-office firm.

Erickson was relieved of many of his financial worries through the formation of a financial cartel that came together to act as private backers for his ventures. In 1987, a newly solvent Erickson took on his most ambitious project to date, the Bunker Hill complex: a $1 billion restructuring of the core of Los Angeles. Bunker Hill is a huge commercial-cultural-residential development that will take years to complete. And in 1988, Erickson was awarded a $140 million contract in Shanghai to build what will be one of the world's largest cultural complexes, covering an area eight times that of a football field.

Now in his sixties, Erickson is just hitting his stride. He lists his main interests as architecture and travel, and he shows no sign of letting up on either vocation. He continues to work non-stop on up to a dozen projects at a time and is habitually late and overworked. Erickson maintains three homes and offices: in Vancouver, Los Angeles, and Toronto. He says he never spends more than three days in any one location. He likes planes and even says he finds jet-lag invigorating. "Routine of any kind is bad for the health," he told the *New Yorker*. "If I'm too long in a place, I become stale, or it becomes stale, or we both do." Most importantly, Erickson says he finds constant inspiration for his work from his travels. When one finds a hint of an Inca ruin, a Japanese temple or a Florentine piazza somewhere in one of his buildings, it can no doubt be traced to one of Erickson's foreign pilgramages.

Erickson is a Canadian enigma. He may be a world traveller and an architectural superstar, but he remains intensely private. He gives few interviews and speaks only rarely to the public. He seems to prefer to let his work do his talking for him. Whatever Erickson's private pursuits, his gifts to the public are all around us. His visionary designs often provoke thought, even anger. But he has never sacrificed human needs for mechanical concerns. After 30 years in the business, Erickson's designs are considered almost a new form of classical architecture. Even his critics, such as architect Trevor Boddy, acknowledge Arthur Erickson's special genius. As Boddy wrote in *Canadian Heritage* magazine, "even when he fails, he does so with style and panache."

Writings

The Architecture of Arthur Erickson, Tundra, 1975.
Towards a Quality of Life: The Role of Industrialization in the Architecture of Urban Planning of Developing Countries, Hamdami Foundation, 1976.
A Political Art (contributor), William H. New, editor, University of British Columbia Press, 1978.

Contributor to *Canadian Architect Yearbook* and *House Beautiful Building Manual*. Also contributor of more than 100 articles to professional journals, popular magazines, and newspapers in Canada, the United States, and abroad.

Sources

BC Business, October, 1988.
Business Quarterly, October, 1982.
Canadian Collector, July-August, 1984.
Canadian Heritage, October-November, 1984.
Canadian Interior, April, 1985.
Financial Post, January 31, 1981.
Maclean's, September 10, 1979; May 31, 1982; November 11, 1985; September 15, 1986.
New Yorker, June 4, 1979.
Progressive Architecture, October, 1984.
Saturday Night, March, 1989.
Toronto Globe and Mail, May 11, 1982; March 31, 1984; May 9, 1984; July 13, 1985; October 11, 1985; March 17, 1988.
Toronto Star, June 1, 1982.
Vancouver Sun, November 2, 1986.
Washingtonian, July, 1988.

—*Sidelights by Ingeborg Boyens*

Susan Estrich

UPI/Bettmann Newsphotos

Political campaign manager, lawyer

Born 1953, in Lynn, Mass.; daughter of an attorney and a medical receptionist; married Norman Kaplan (an executive producer for Disney Studios), November, 1986. *Education:* Graduated (magna cum laude) from Wellesley College, 1974; law degree from Harvard Law School, 1976.

Addresses: *Home*—Cambridge, Mass.; and Nichols Canyon, Calif. *Office*—Harvard University Law School, Cambridge, Mass. 02138.

Career

Worked as a law clerk for U.S. Court of Appeals Judge J. Skelly Wright, 1977; law clerk for U.S. Supreme Court Justice John Paul Stevens, 1978; served as special assistant to the chief counsel of the U.S. Senate Committee on the Judiciary, 1979–80; Harvard University Law School, Cambridge, Mass., professor of law, 1981—; Tuttle & Taylor (law firm), Los Angeles, Calif., attorney, 1986–87.

Worked in the presidential campaigns of Edward Kennedy, 1980, and Walter Mondale, 1984; served as executive director of the Democratic National Platform Committee, 1984; deputy campaign manager for the presidential campaign of Michael Dukakis, 1987, campaign manager, 1987–88.

Awards: Named first woman president of the *Harvard Law Review*, 1975.

Sidelights

Susan Estrich's life has been a series of distinctions. She was the first female editor of the *Harvard Law Review* and the youngest tenured Harvard professor in more than 50 years. In 1988 she was named as Democrat Michael Dukakis's campaign manager, the first woman to direct a major presidential campaign. "I've always rejected that notoriety of being the first female this or the first female that," Estrich told the *Boston Globe*. "I figure you should be recognized for your achievements, not for your gender." Even as a child, Estrich's mother recalled, Susan strived for excellence. "She was always an achiever," Helen Kaplan told the *Los Angeles Times*. "She always had to do the best she possibly could, and she always did. If everyone got A's, she had to get A-pluses."

Estrich grew up in the Boston suburb of Swampscott, one of three children born to a middle-class, small-town attorney father and a medical receptionist mother. She was best known in high school as an excellent baton twirler, but even then she had an interest in politics, walking door-to-door in her neighborhood for author Michael Harrington, who was running for Congress as an anti-war candidate. Estrich went on to Wellesley College, where she majored in political science, graduated magna cum laude, and earned a Phi Beta Kappa key. She went on to Harvard Law School, where she was the first woman president of the *Harvard Law Review*.

Two prestigious clerkships followed. When Estrich clerked for Supreme Court Justice John Paul Stevens in 1978, she was modestly famous for wearing blue jeans to work. She also spent a year as president of the Massachusetts chapter of the American Civil Liberties Union before moving on to become a special assistant to the chief counsel of the U.S. Senate Committee on the Judiciary, chaired by Massachusetts Senator Edward M. Kennedy.

"I've always rejected that notoriety of being the first female this or the first female that. I figure you should be recognized for your achievements, not for your gender."

Kennedy was impressed with her work. In 1980 Kennedy hired Estrich to help with his challenge to then-President Jimmy Carter. After doing field work for the campaign in several states, Estrich negotiated on Kennedy's behalf to liberalize the party platform. "She tied the platform committee in knots with left-of-center proposals designed to wrest dissatisfied delegates from the Carter camp," observed the *Washington Post*. *Boston Globe* political writer Thomas Oliphant wrote: "She spent hours exacting concessions across a bargaining table in a Washington hotel from Carter aides, whom she kept off-balance with carefully aimed streams of Marlboro smoke."

Attorney Stu Eizenstat, who headed up the Carter team negotiating with Kennedy forces over the platform, later recalled his initial amazement at dealing with the 27-year-old Estrich. "Our mandate was to try to reach compromises," Eizenstat told the *Los Angeles Times*. "[Estrich's] was to find as many areas of difference and confrontation as she could, to move as far to our left as possible . . . and, at the end of the day, we would just go off and bang table tops in frustration, because she won more points than we did . . . . I was utterly amazed that someone so young, with so relatively little experience in national affairs, had such command of the issues, could understand the nuances so well. She wasn't personally obstreperous—she simply made her case, she was tough but fair, but, by God, she stood her ground, she never gave an inch!"

Estrich returned to Harvard to teach in 1981, just four years after graduating. Four years later she became one of the first women to get tenure and one of the youngest tenured professors in the school's history. Estrich taught criminal law and a course on sex discrimination. The final piece of her application for tenure in 1985 was an article she wrote for the *Yale Law Journal* advocating changes in the way the criminal justice system deals with rape. The article's introduction opened with an account of Estrich's 1974 rape by an unknown assailant during her senior year at Wellesley College. She was attacked in an alley behind her apartment building in Boston as she was struggling out of a car carrying two bags of groceries. "Eleven years ago, a man held an ice pick to my throat and said, 'Push over, shut up, or I'll kill you.' I did what he said, but I couldn't stop crying. When he was finished, I jumped out of my car as he drove away."

The attack left her with a determination to reform the criminal justice system's treatment of rape cases. And the article eventually became the first chapter in her 1987 book, *Real Rape*, which documented the legal system's reluctance to prosecute simple rape. The book argued that all rape is "real rape," that when a woman says no and a man persists in having sex that it is rape and should be treated seriously by the criminal justice system. "When I got to law school, no one ever talked about rape," Estrich told the *Washington Post*. "We spent a lot of [class] time talking about larceny, and assault, but not rape. So when I started teaching in 1981, I said I was going to teach it." A *Boston Globe* review called Estrich's book "brave, simply focused and powerfully reasoned." Harvard Law colleague and constitutional expert Laurence Tribe wrote on the dust jacket that "No one will ever again be able to address the legal problems of rape without taking Susan Estrich's landmark work into account."

Meanwhile, Estrich stayed busy on the Democratic Party circuits, earning membership in the tight world of professionally-run campaigns. In 1984, Rep. Geraldine Ferraro appointed her executive director of the Democratic National Platform Committee, where she got high marks for the skill she showed in juggling the competing interests of three campaigns and 200 committee members. "I hired Susan because it takes anybody meeting Susan about half a minute to see that she's incredibly smart," Ferraro told the *Los Angeles Times*. "I'd heard about her role on [the

Kennedy team] so I told her, 'OK, I need this platform to go through with a minimum of angst.' I said, 'If you know how to create disruptions, then you must also know how to avoid them'—and she did."

When Walter Mondale became the Democratic nominee, and Ferraro his running mate, Estrich interrupted her tenure bid to become a senior policy adviser and travel with the campaign. Political consultant Bob Shrum, a former Kennedy aide, told the *Boston Globe* at the time that "Susan is incredibly well organized, and very tough-minded. Susan could write a speech, arbitrate a dispute, organize a precinct, deal with a ward heeler and conduct a seminar at Harvard and do it all in the same day."

During that campaign Estrich met Marty Kaplan, a Mondale speech writer who later would become an executive producer for Disney Studios in Los Angeles. They married in November 1986, and Estrich requested and received a two-year leave of absence from Harvard. She moved to Los Angeles to work for the prestigious firm of Tuttle & Taylor and live with her husband in a mansion formerly owned by Gloria Swanson.

But corporate law, she later told the *Los Angeles Times*, was "incredibly boring. And I didn't want to go into criminal law, because who wants to spend their lives defending rich villains?"

So after four months Estrich moved back East. She and Kaplan have since accepted a cross-country commuter marriage, seeing each other every few weeks.

Estrich expected to return full-time to Harvard. But John Sasso, Dukakis's original campaign manager and a long-time acquaintance, called on Estrich in early 1987, asking if she would work—without pay—on speeches and fund-raising for the candidate. Estrich, who had met Dukakis in 1981 and worked briefly on his gubernatorial transition team in 1983, agreed. Part-time volunteer work eventually became a full-time paid job as deputy campaign manager, necessitating another leave from Harvard. And while Sasso laid out the original blueprint for Dukakis's bid for the Democratic nomination, Estrich was crucial in refining the governor's message. For example, when Dukakis's wife, Kitty, decided to make public the diet-pill dependency she had for many years, Estrich orchestrated the strategy, writing speeches for Mrs. Dukakis and traveling with her on campaign swings.

Then, in September 1987, the Dukakis campaign was rocked by revelations that Sasso had sabotaged Sen. Joseph R. Biden, Jr.'s, Democratic presidential campaign by leaking tapes to the media exposing Biden's plagiarism of a speech. Sasso was forced to resign. Nine days later, following the suggestion of his closest friend, Paul Brountas, Dukakis tapped Estrich to replace Sasso. Brountas told the *Boston Globe* he felt that Estrich—among 200 names he considered as campaign manager—was the most likely person to be a rallying, rather than a disruptive, force.

To the outside world, Estrich's selection looked like an adventurous choice, since she would be the first woman to run a presidential campaign. But inside the Dukakis campaign the decision to elevate Estrich to the $70,000-a-year post was a signal that things would go on as before—and that the strategic decisions that Dukakis, Sasso, and Estrich had already made would stand. "She has the political, managerial and leadership skills to lead," Dukakis told the *Philadelphia Inquirer*. "She believes, as I do, this must be a strong affirmative campaign. That's what we're all about. That's what we do."

"I didn't want to go into criminal law, because who wants to spend their lives defending rich villains?"

Estrich let it be known from the start that she would be more than a figurehead manager. "I am in charge," she told the *Los Angeles Times*. "I run it. I manage it. I decide where we're going, what we're going to do, where we will spend money, how much and on what; I decide what we're gonna say, who should do what. I am in charge of deciding what, ultimately, we are going to do. I have the power." The power and the strategy succeeded in gaining Dukakis the Democratic nomination with few setbacks. Estrich received high marks for pushing early fundraisers to get over the Biden fiasco, for guiding the campaign through its one other major low point, the back-to-back primary-season losses in Illinois and Michigan, and for keeping Dukakis above the fray when the New York primary was overtaken by nasty campaigning between forces supporting the Rev. Jesse Jackson and Tennessee Sen. Albert Gore.

Dukakis cruised to victory within the party and held an early lead against Vice-President George Bush, his Republican opponent. But Bush, using the Pledge of Allegiance as a major campaign issue, put Dukakis on the defensive and quickly caught up in the polls. In September Dukakis brought back Sasso, naming him vice-chairman of the campaign, and putting him in charge of countering Bush and getting out the campaign message, leaving Estrich with most of the organizational and financial responsibilities of the campaign. Dukakis told the *Boston Globe* that Estrich had been "stretched a little thin.... She's got a lot of responsibilities." Estrich and Sasso, he said, will exercise "shared responsibility; they'll split it up."

What will happen with Estrich now that the furor of the 1988 campaign has ended remains to be seen. She told the *Los Angeles Times* in mid-1988 that she had already requested another year's leave of absence "to leave my options open." There was speculation that if Dukakis won she would have become the nation's first female attorney general. "Politics is what I do," she told the *Boston Globe*. "Social change has always interested me. Politics is where we frame the issues agenda for the country, where we select the people who shape the kind of world we live in." She added, "My father was a lawyer in solo practice. He helped people one to one. I want to do the same thing. On a larger basis."

Writings

Real Rape, Harvard University Press, 1987.

Sources

Boston Globe, April 29, 1984; May 15, 1987; June 2, 1987; October 9, 1987; December 1, 1987; March 2, 1988; May 9, 1988; May 11, 1988; September 7, 1988.

Charlotte Observer, July 20, 1988.

Chicago Tribune, November 29, 1987.

Los Angeles Times, July 22, 1988.

Newsday, June 2, 1988.

Philadelphia Inquirer, October 9, 1987; February 5, 1988; September 11, 1988.

Washington Post, February 24, 1987; October 16, 1987; June 12, 1988; September 11, 1988; September 14, 1988.

—Sketch by Glen Macnow

Janet Evans

AP/Wide World Photos

Olympic swimmer

Born August 28, 1971, in Fullerton, Calif.; daughter of Paul (a veterinarian) and Barbara Evans. *Education:* Attends El Dorado High School, Placentia, Calif.

Addresses: *Home*—Placentia, Calif.

Awards, honors: Winner of three gold medals (400-meter freestyle, 800-meter freestyle, and 400-meter individual medley) as member of U.S. women's Olympic swim team, 1988.

Sidelights

Outside the glistening new natatorium the spectators walked through Olympic Park, heading home beneath a bright, full moon that shone down from the heavens above like a big gold medal. This was late September, 1988, and the place was Seoul, South Korea. Inside the building of the swim races Janet Evans, a slightly-built, 17-year-old from southern California, was packing her bags with her swimsuits, preparing for the long flight home. A senior at El Dorado High School and a resident of Placentia in south suburban Los Angeles, Evans had just won her third gold medal in her third race in the Summer Games of the 24th Olympiad.

For a little more than a week, from the other side of the Earth, Evans had been one of America's most publicized people, appearing on national television, magazine covers, radio reports, and the front pages of daily newspapers. Now, she said, she was homesick. She wanted to go back to her boyfriend and her classmates and be "Just Janet" again. "What do you think it will be like back at school?" she asked Tom Millich, coach of the El Dorado Golden Hawks, who was there with the best swimmer on his team. "I hope it's not different." "No," Millich reassured her. "It won't be." That seemed to satisfy Evans, who had voiced concern that she was behind in her homework and that her friends would treat her differently. As Evans headed for the door she asked her mother for the three gold medals Mrs. Evans had been keeping safely in her purse. "Why?" Barbara Evans asked daughter Janet. "You'll just lose them! What do you need them for tonight?" "I won't lose them," Janet replied, an insistent tone in her voice. "I want to sleep with them under my pillow."

In one sense, the success of Janet Evans in the 1988 Olympics was a dream come true, the fulfillment of the fantasy of every young athlete. In reality, her first-place finishes were fashioned through more mundane stuff: practice, practice, and more practice, to obtain the maximum results from enormous natural talent. "I'm proud of myself for not giving in," Evans said of her training habits. "I didn't skip workouts. I couldn't have won a gold medal if I did that. Not to be boastful or anything like that, but you have to be proud of yourself if you win an Olympic gold medal. To know all the work paid off. I accomplished my goal." Throughout her high school years, Evans had awakened at 4:45 A.M. most days to train in the Independence Park Pool in Fullerton, near her home. She would swim as many as 10 miles a day, six days a week. The first of two workouts lasted from 5:15 A.M. until 7 A.M., when she would get ready for school.

"[Janet Evans is] the most energy-efficient machine in the water today, male or female. Janet uses less oxygen, or less energy, to swim at a fast pace than anybody I've ever seen."

After that it was back to work, as described by Phil Hersh of the *Chicago Tribune* in an article published shortly before the Summer Games: "At 1:45 P.M., Janet walks home and does homework until 2:30 or 3, depending on whether it is one of the three days she works on Nautilus machines or one of the days she goes straight to the pool. The afternoon workout lasts until 6 P.M. Evans does another 9,000 meters, or nearly six miles, in a variety of strokes. Then she comes home, eats dinner, does homework and is in bed by 8, or 8:15 at the latest, except on Saturday, when she stays out until 10 P.M. because she has no Sunday workout." Evans said the schedule suited her. "If you go to bed at 8," she explained, "it's not so bad getting up at 4:45." Such training habits may seem rigorous to average people, but they are not that unusual for some athletes, especially world-class athletes in individualistic sports as demanding as swim racing. Besides, she always had been an active child. Her parents said she walked at eight months, swam at 13 months, and, at the age of two, used a Hula Hoop for 20 minutes at a time.

What made Evans special at the Olympics, even for a gold medalist, was a combination of things. At 5-foot-4 and 101 pounds, Evans was considerably shorter and lighter than most other swim racers at Seoul. "Evans went from a tiny prodigy who could swim the width of the pool at 2 to a swimmer who seemed laughably small at 14," the *St. Louis Post-Dispatch* noted. "When the public address announcer introduced her at the 1985 U.S. Nationals, Olympic champion Tiffany Cohen chortled at the sight of what was a 5-1, 87-pound tadpole with a mouth full of braces. Evans later admitted, 'That made me so mad.' When she was warming up at the 1986 Goodwill Games in Moscow, the Soviet women pointed at Evans and guffawed."

Her style may be related directly to her size. That was the interpretation of Jill Lieber, who described it in the *Sports Illustrated* Olympic preview. "In the pool," Lieber wrote, "Janet compensated for her size by taking more strokes than her competitors—36 to travel 25 yards [short course] and 62 to go 50 meters [long course]; a top female distance swimmer typically takes about 50 strokes for 50 meters." Dr. John Troup, the director of sports medicine and science for U.S. Swimming, Inc., told *Sports Illustrated* that Evans is "the most energy-efficient machine in the water today, male or female. Janet uses less oxygen, or less energy, to swim at a fast pace than anybody I've ever seen," he said. "I'll stop short of saying Janet's a fish, but physiologically she's very similar. Both have muscles with a high anaerobic capacity, which means great endurance as well as big bursts of speed at the end of a swim." Nort Thornton, coach of Matt Biondi, told *Time* magazine: "You think Janet doesn't have the body? She's a heart and lung pump, an incredible aerobic machine. Her chest expansion is six inches, and that's two or three inches more than any other woman on the team."

With her Olympic medals and her world records, Evans stood tall above most of the world's elite swimmers. Although Kristen Otto of East Germany won six gold medals and Matt Biondi of the United States won five at Seoul, Evans was America's most successful female and the most popular swimmer among most media at the meet. Coming into the Summer Games she held world records in the 400, 800, and 1,500-meter freestyles. (The 1,500 isn't an Olympic event.) In the Olympic 400-meter freestyle, she clipped 1.61 seconds off her own world record and finished in four minutes, 3.85 seconds. Heike Friedrich of East Germany, who won the silver medal behind Evans, was stunned. "I must say," Friedrich said, "Evans is in another dimension. She is one swimmer in 25 years."

In the 400-meter individual medley—a race that requires four different strokes—Evans won the gold medal with a time of 4:37.76. Although the time was neither a world nor an Olympic record, it broke her previous American record of 4:38.58. In the 800-meter freestyle, Evans finished at 8:20.2, more than three seconds slower than her world record at that distance but still an Olympic record. Her three gold medals were three more than any other American woman took home from individual events.

Evans seemed to win with charm and confidence. Her smile was a bright, white explosion across her face. Details of her personal taste and style became known and publicized. She ate a diet of 5,000 calories a day, much of it from fast-food restaurants. Her favorite rock groups were U2, Depeche Mode, Erasure, and the Cure. She spoke in the loud, exuberant bursts. "I was talking to my friends about meeting me at the airport," she said before leaving Seoul. "And they said, 'When you get off the airplane, there's going to be all kinds of photographers' and I say 'No, there won't' and they say 'Yes, there will!' and I say 'No!' and they say 'Yes there will!' and I think, 'Oh, NO!'"

She seemed impressed, in a humble way, at her own success. "There are so many people out there in the world, and I have a world record. Why me?" she told Dave Dorr of the *St. Louis Post-Dispatch.* "It's kind of weird. I try not to think about it too much, but it still boggles my mind." Evans feels the only drawbacks to swimming are the necessity of short hair and the effects of chlorine in the pool water. "The chlorine makes my feet sore and dries all my skin and I hate that," she told Hersh of the *Chicago Tribune.* "My hair sometimes gets yucky. I always wanted long hair, but I could never have it. I can do everything I wanted to do as a kid after I quit."

Evans projects the worldly innocence of a child-woman, sheltered within the strict discipline of a sport but at the same time exposed to the world on a wider scale than most persons her age. Bud Greenspan, a producer of Olympic documentaries, targeted Evans as one of the major subjects for films he would put together in 1989. "We spent two evenings this week, two of the most gratifying evenings ever, with Barbara Evans and Paul Evans," he said in Seoul, referring to Janet's parents. "And Janet Evans still makes her bed and she gets on the air [network television] and she says to her best friends 'Don't forget to get the notes because I'm four weeks behind in my schoolwork.' And Barbara and Paul were hearing about agents and Paul says 'Really? Agents are going to be calling?' It was the sweetest thing that has happened at the Games."

One of Evans's coaches, Bud McAllister, noted that Evans had a self-centered side. "Her motto should be, 'I may be spoiled, but I get what I want,'" he told a group of reporters. And *Time* magazine reported that Evans was "teasingly called 'Princess' by the swim-team staff because of her occasionally imperious ways." But her attitude rarely struck people as overly haughty. Matt Biondi, the American swimmer who won five gold, one silver, and one bronze medal, had difficulty with his media attention and celebrity status. He marveled at the way Evans handled hers. "I told her that, if I was her age and I had to go through what she is going through as a senior in high school, I wouldn't be nearly as effective and composed as she is," Biondi said. "So I just wanted to tell her she is doing a great job and keep it up because the U.S. needs that kind of reputation."

Many observers expected Evans to give up her amateur swimming career and accept commercial endorsements after the Olympics. Evans said she wanted to remain an amateur and participate in high school and college meets. She hadn't ruled out the 1992 Olympics in Barcelona, Spain. She will be 21 then. "I think a college education is more important to me," she said when asked about commercial endorsements. "I don't think it will be a tough decision." The choice between the two options was described symbolically by the *Orange County Register,* as quoted in the *St. Louis Post-Dispatch:* "A fairy in a sparkling white gown must be sitting on Janet Evans' right shoulder these days, reminding her of the virtues of being 'Just Janet.' On the other shoulder

Janet Evans raises her arms in triumph after winning the gold medal in the women's 400-meter individual medley at the 1988 Summer Olympics. Reuters/Bettmann Newsphotos.

must be a glitzy starlet, surrounded by the most wonderful things money can buy. She need not say a word; the gadgets and the clothes and the image say it all: Look what you can have. Just say yes."

When Evans returned to home and school in the early autumn, her neighbors on Brower Street gave her a block party with barbecued food, banners, and balloons. It was the first time she had been home in almost two months. "None of us wanted her to come home to nothing after all she had been through," Sharon Holt, a neighbor, told Sarah Ballard in *Sports Illustrated.* "Janet is such a nice girl." The rest of the week was chronicled by Ballard, who concluded her story with this touching scene of an assembly at her high school. "Janet was up on stage at the west end of the gymnasium," Ballard recounted, "and the 1,450-member student body lined the bleachers on either side. As videotapes of each of her three races flickered on screens scattered around the gym, the audience cheered as if it were watching them for the first time. After each race, the school band played NBC's Olympic theme, and a spotlight shone on a gold banner bearing her name and the event. It wasn't Seoul, but the little girl with the big smile didn't seem to care. She didn't even mind being the center of attention again. She was Just Janet, but different."

Sources

Chicago Tribune, August 18, 1988; August 28, 1988; September 19, 1988; September 23, 1988.

Detroit Free Press, September 25, 1988; September 30, 1988.

Newsweek, October 3, 1988.

Sports Illustrated, "Olympic Preview" special issue, September 14, 1988; October 3, 1988; October 10, 1988.

St. Louis Post-Dispatch, August 7, 1988; September 21, 1988; September 23, 1988; October 16, 1988.

Time, October 3, 1988.

—Sidelights by Joe LaPointe

Ray Flynn

AP/Wide World Photos

Mayor of Boston, Mass.

Full name, Raymond Leo Flynn; born July 22, 1939, in Boston, Mass.; son of a longshoreman; married Catherine Coyne; children: Raymond L., Jr., Edward, Julie, Nancy, Catherine, Maureen. *Education:* Providence College, B.A., 1963; Harvard University, M.Ed., 1981.

Addresses: *Home*—Boston, Mass. *Office*—Office of the Mayor, Boston City Hall, 1 City Hall Plaza, Boston, Mass. 02201.

Career

Professional basketball player with Syracuse Nationals for one season; had a tryout with the Boston Celtics; basketball coach at Stonehill College, North Easton, Mass., for one year; worked as a probation officer; member of Massachusetts House of Representatives, representing South Boston, 1971–78; member of Boston City Council, 1978–83; mayor of Boston, 1983—. U.S. Conference of Mayors, chairman of Task Force on Joblessness and Hunger, co-chairman of Committee on Community Development, Housing, and Economic Development; vice-chairman of Democratic National Platform Committee, 1984; chairman of Boston Harbor Pollution Committee for three years.

Awards: John Boyle O'Reilly Award, New England and Irish American Labor Coalition; leadership awards from Rhode Island and Cape Cod chapters of NAACP; honorary D.D.A., Providence College; honorary LL.D., Suffolk University and Emmanuel College.

Sidelights

Hours after Boston mayor Raymond Leo Flynn made his reelection announcement in 1987, he was playing at a celebrity basketball game in South Boston when flames were spotted coming from a nearby building. Flynn ran up a flight of stairs, kicked in a door, and found 68-year-old Manuel Rose. Rose told the *Boston Herald* later: "I was watching television. Then I heard the front door crash in and all of a sudden Mayor Flynn is standing in my parlor. I said to him, 'What the hell are you doing here?'" Flynn dragged the handicapped man to safety—and was rewarded with headlines that dubbed him "Fire Hero Flynn." It's the kind of press that makes political opponents grind their teeth.

But an even bigger task for Flynn, who easily won his second term later that year, may be rescuing Boston from its second racial maelstrom in as many decades. By doing that, Flynn is challenging the prevailing wisdom of his native South Boston—a tough, all-white neighborhood. In the 1970s, South Boston came to symbolize racial strife for its sometimes violent reaction to federally-ordered school busing. Flynn, a city councilor then, opposed busing, but not vociferously enough for some from the neighborhood, who rewarded him by firebombing his car.

Now, as mayor in the 1980s, Flynn is presiding over the integration of public housing projects in South Boston, trying to avoid a second federal intervention that all concede would be disaster. If he does that, rushing into burning buildings will seem like a walk through the Boston Common, which Flynn, incidentally, has swept of drug pushers since first taking office in 1983.

Flynn has already come a long way from his days as a state representative and city councilor when he backed a thoroughly homegrown platform of someone from "Southie." Then, he opposed birth control for minors, prison reform, prohibitions against housing discrimination, the Equal Rights Amendment, and gay rights. Flynn, as mayor, has adapted to new urban problems by advocating, among other things, free sterile needles for drug addicts to stem the AIDS epidemic. This astounds people back in his old neighborhood. Melba Hamilton, president of a South Boston civic association, told the *Boston Globe:* "He confuses me. I don't know whether he's a liberal or a conservative." The *Boston Globe* wrote, "Flynn is among the most enigmatic of Boston politicians, to his friends a man who has shed his parochial roots to embrace and understand the concerns of a racially and ideologically diverse city, but to foes an opportunist who adroitly shifts positions for political benefits alone."

Even so, Flynn holds impeccable working class and neighborhood roots. His family came to the United States from Galway in Ireland. His father was a longshoreman on the rough-and-tumble Boston waterfront. Flynn remembers him coming home in the winter with icicles hanging from his eyelashes. His mother scrubbed floors in downtown office buildings—when she could find work at all. After Flynn's father contracted tuberculosis, the family lived on welfare for a time. Today, with his wife and six children, Flynn lives in a modest home off a South Boston side street.

Flynn's Everyman style made him a sentimental favorite of Boston voters. During Flynn's first mayoral campaign, a resident of the Allston section of Boston saw the then-city councilor at a neighborhood association meeting. "Everyone else showed up in pin-striped suits with red ties," Charles Doyle told the *New York Times.* "Then came Flynn, an ordinary guy from the neighborhoods. He slouched in his chair. Then, when he took out his Blistex and put it on the cold sore on his lip, you knew he was one of us." Flynn couldn't possibly be less "one of us" than the man he succeeded, Kevin White, who chose not to run in 1983 after an increasingly controversial 16 years in office. They were opposite in every way. White was dubbed "Mayor Deluxe" by a newspaper columnist for his upscale lifestyle, which included a chauffeured luxury car and bashes at the Parkman House, the mayor's semi-official residence on Beacon Hill. Flynn, at the time, was driving a nine-year-old station wagon with rusting floorboards.

At South Boston High School in the late 1950s, Flynn was a three-sport star. High school teammate Jim Crowe told the *Boston Herald:* "I always thought Ray would be a priest, he was so religious. Every game he'd wear a scrapular, a kind of cloth vest with a picture of the Blessed Mary under his uniform." Flynn went on to Providence College in Rhode Island, again starring in basketball while also making himself a decent student, an even more notable achievement at the time for a kid from Southie. In his senior year, Flynn, then team captain, was named Most Valuable Player at the 1963 National Invitational Tournament. He was drafted by the Philadelphia 76ers professional basketball team, decided to fulfill his military service first, and later missed the last cut at a Boston Celtics tryout. He played one season in the Eastern League with the Syracuse Nationals. He worked as a college basketball coach and then a probation officer before serving three terms in the state legislature beginning in 1970 as a representative from South Boston. In 1977, he won a seat on the city council.

At every stop, Flynn has been known for his hard work, whether it was attending neighborhood functions, drafting legislation, or churning out press releases, especially on weekends when he was assured good play in the Sunday papers and on television. As one-time mayoral rival Larry DiCara told the *Boston Herald,* "He never disappeared on you." Twice, though, Flynn has been hospitalized for exhaustion because of the grueling daily pace he sets for himself.

When the school busing issue erupted in Boston in 1974, thrusting the city into the unwanted glare of national attention, Flynn was still a mostly unknown legislator. But representing South Boston, where the fiercest resistance to U.S. District Court Judge Arthur Garrity's busing order raged, made Flynn a leading voice of the opposition. Flynn, who called Garrity's plan "forced integration," considered for a time running for mayor in 1975 on an anti-busing platform. The *Boston Herald* reported Flynn once saying, "We must end busing before busing puts an end to this city." Two of Flynn's children stayed home as part of a busing boycott.

But at the same time he earned a headline that read, "Flynn Urges Non-Violence," and he advised parents to "bury the buses under an avalanche of mail." Flynn added: "We must continue to resist and vigorously oppose this tyranny dressed in [federal] judicial robes. But we cannot allow our resistance to resort to rock or bottle-throwing or confrontations in our city streets." And once busing started, Flynn helped patrol the hallways of South Boston High to ensure the safety of black and white students. All that made his loyalties suspect to the hard core busing opponents in South Boston. And they would remember Flynn's original sin when South Boston public housing integration became an issue more than a decade later. At the other end of the spectrum, minority and liberal camps in Boston politics still see Flynn as having been an obstructionist to school integration in the 1970s. Boston survived busing, although thousands of white students fled to the suburbs. Flynn, too, survived—first a bitter Democratic primary fight for mayor in 1983 and then an easy general election victory a month later.

Flynn's popularity was at an all-time high by 1987 when he was running for reelection. Voters in all neighborhoods of the city—black and white—gave him high approval ratings. The *Boston Globe* wrote, "Flynn has solidified the perception among the city's voters that he is an honest, accessible man doing his best for the city's neighborhoods—*all* neighborhoods." Then, just days before the November election, Flynn announced he would support a federal request to integrate South Boston's all-white public housing projects. South Boston was back in the national spotlight. Again, Flynn had confounded the expectations of his own neighborhood. South Boston is surrounded on three sides by Boston Harbor and is cut off from the rest of the city—literally and figuratively—by the Southeast Expressway. Attitudes in South Boston have always been insular. Flynn argued that it was better to have the city draw up its own public housing integration plan than wait for the inevitable federal intervention. He told the *Boston Globe*, "If it falls into the hands of the federal court, we'll be in the same situation that we were in with busing." His appeal fell on mostly deaf ears. At a public forum to explain the housing policy in Southie, the *Boston Globe* reported that Flynn appeared unnerved by one woman's comment: "I wish I were talking to the Ray Flynn of 10 years ago."

Eventually, Flynn lost South Boston wards to his rival, a city councilor, but dominated elsewhere in the city for an easy victory. "It hurts," Flynn told the *Boston Globe*. "You know you're doing the right thing. It's a community that I love . . . and what I'm doing is in their best interest. It's hard for people to see that now, I suppose. I'm not trying to be a martyr."

Martyrdom is not just idle speculation when mixing racial issues and South Boston. During the busing crisis, Flynn's car was firebombed, he received death threats, and a barrel was tossed through the front door of his home. In 1979, Flynn rescued a black teenager from white, bottle-throwing thugs on the Boston Common. A simple, undisputed act of heroism? Hardly. According to the *Boston Globe*, South Boston High headmaster Jerome Winegar drove down Broadway, Southie's main street, using a loudspeaker to blare the message, "Do you want a guy like that representing your town? He's over there on the Common saving niggers."

Reactions like that, though, haven't dulled Flynn's appetite for heroic deeds, or, critics would charge, the good press he gets out of doing them. Two weeks after his fire rescue in 1987, Flynn helped Boston Police subdue a rifle-wielding man by pinning the suspect's pit bull terrier against a fence. In the winter, he rides snowplows with maintenance workers and shows up at decrepit inner city apartments to make emergency repairs to furnaces. Flynn was the subject of a *People* magazine story in 1984 that said, "There is in Ray Flynn a fervor, almost religious in nature, that sometimes makes him seem more a visionary than a politician." The same year, "60 Minutes" profiled him because, as segment producer Joel Bernstein told the *Boston Herald*, "Boston has a reputation for deep racial problems. Suddenly, here comes a guy out of a neighborhood where some of the most heated battles took place. And the first priority of his administration is to restore racial harmony. That's a national story."

Flynn's biggest critics suggest that he latched onto public housing integration in Southie for the coarsest of political reasons. Knowing he would lose South Boston during the 1987 reelection campaign because of historic reasons anyway, these critics theorize, Flynn took the housing stand to make himself more attractive to voters elsewhere in the city and state—with an eye to running for governor in 1990. That scenario became more plausible the closer Governor Michael Dukakis got to the Democratic nomination and then the White House during his own presidential campaign. Flynn's only two likely opponents were Lieutenant Governor Evelyn Murphy and U.S. Representative Joseph Kennedy III, son of the late Robert Kennedy. Flynn himself expresses no interest in any job but mayor. Staff aides, though, are less ready to write him out of the statewide scene. And

Flynn's growing national profile on urban issues fuels speculation. Already, Flynn has testified before Congress several times on homelessness and was mentioned by two candidates as a potential vice-presidential contender in 1988.

The *Boston Globe,* on the eve of Flynn's reelection campaign in 1987, reported: "The conventional wisdom has always underestimated Flynn. The rap on him throughout his career was that he couldn't take the next step. The pols said he couldn't get elected rep, that he couldn't come out of Southie and successfully run citywide for the council, that he couldn't get elected mayor, that as mayor he would be unable to govern, and, finally, that he would get laughed out of office after one term." No one is laughing. As the first black families moved into the South Boston projects during the hot summer days of 1988, no ugly racial incidents that plagued the city a decade earlier were reported.

Sources

Boston Globe, March 23, 1981; November 3, 1983; November 16, 1983; March 20, 1987; July 27, 1987; September 26, 1987; November 30, 1987; March 6, 1988; March 20, 1988.

Boston Herald, October 16, 1983; November 13, 1983; November 16, 1983; November 17, 1983; November 19, 1983; December 25, 1983; September 25, 1984; July 15, 1987; July 26, 1987.

Christian Science Monitor, January 13, 1986; January 7, 1988.

Newsweek, October 24, 1983; November 28, 1983.

New York Times, November 17, 1983; October 31, 1987.

People, November 14, 1983; October 1, 1984.

Time, October 24, 1983; November 28, 1983; August 10, 1987; April 4, 1988.

Washington Post, September 20, 1987.

—Sidelights by Harvey Dickson

Jodie Foster

Actress

Full name, Alicia Christian Foster; born November, 1962, in Los Angeles, Calif.; daughter of Lucius III (a real estate executive) and Evelyn (Almond) Foster. *Education:* Yale University, B.A. in literature, 1985.

Addresses: *Agent*—International Creative Management, 8899 Beverly Blvd., Los Angeles, Calif. 90048.

Career

Began appearing in television commercials at the age of three; made acting debut in an episode of "Mayberry, R.F.D.," 1969; numerous other television appearances include "My Three Sons," "The Courtship of Eddie's Father," "Gunsmoke," and "Bonanza"; regular member of cast of series "Bob and Carol and Ted and Alice," 1973, and "Paper Moon," 1974–75; made-for-television movies include "Rookie of the Year," 1973, "Smile, Jenny, You're Dead," 1974, "The Life of T.K. Dearing," 1975, and "Svengali," 1983. Feature films include "Napolean and Samantha," 1972, "Kansas City Bomber," 1972, "Menace on the Mountain," 1973, "One Little Indian," 1973, "Tom Sawyer," 1973, "Alice Doesn't Live Here Anymore," 1975, "Taxi Driver," 1976, "Bugsy Malone," 1976, "Echoes of a Summer," 1976, "The Little Girl Who Lives Down the Lane," 1977, "Freaky Friday," 1977, "Il Casotto," "Moi Fleur Bleue," "Candleshoe," 1978, "Carny," 1980, "Foxes," 1980, "The Hotel New Hampshire," 1984, "The Blood of Others," 1984, "Siesta," 1987, "Five Corners," 1987, "Stealing Home," 1988, "The Accused," 1988, and "Backtrack," 1989.

AP/Wide World Photos

Awards: Emmy Award, 1973, for "Rookie of the Year"; New York Film Critics Award, National Film Critics Award, Los Angeles Film Critics Award, and Academy Award nomination, all for best supporting actress, 1976, for "Taxi Driver"; British Academy Award for best actress and Italian Situation Comedy Award, 1976, for "Bugsy Malone."

Sidelights

Jodie Foster, by her own admission, is an anomaly among Hollywood actresses. Her intellectual interests set her apart from her peers as does her attitude toward the acting profession. Foster, furthermore, has successfully made the transition from child to adult actress—something equally rare in Hollywood—because her mother had a definite plan not to have Jodie perceived as a "child actor" who did "kiddie parts." But, even more unusual, Jodie Foster interrupted her career in 1980 to attend Yale University, where she majored in literature and excelled in a program with a rigorous curriculum. "Practical things didn't interest me. I really wanted to go into the ivory tower and study mind things," Foster told *Harper's Bazaar.*

Foster's freshman year at Yale was complicated when she learned that John Hinckley had attempted to assassinate President Ronald Reagan on March 30, 1981, as a symbol of his "love" for her. Hinckley had become obsessed with Foster after repeated viewings of Martin Scorsese's "Taxi Driver," a 1976 film starring Robert DeNiro as an urban psychopath who decides to assassinate a presidential candidate but ends up killing a pimp and his partners who employ Foster's character as a prostitute. Foster did not know Hinckley and has had to live with the confusion his actions have created in the public's mind.

"Practical things didn't interest me. I really wanted to go into the ivory tower and study mind things."

A brilliant student, Foster has always taken her pursuit of knowledge as seriously as her acting career. In 1988, she told the *Rocky Mountain News:* "I miss being in an intellectual community. It was like living in a monastery where the richest monks were the ones who had read the most." A self-taught "instinctual" actress who has never had an acting lesson, Foster is a product of the Hollywood system without being a part of it. With the active guidance of her mother-manager, Foster has fashioned a career known for its bold risks that put the young actress in a position of distinct advantage.

Foster has no desire to be a "star" or to live like one, and she disdains the Hollywood way of life. She makes in the "low six figures" per movie, which is low for an actress with her name recognition. "I've never done a megabudget movie. I never had a limo carting me home. Never wanted one," she told *Mademoiselle.* In fact, Foster regards acting as "pure blue collar labor" and describes the film industry as "the only place that I really, really feel at home." Foster thoroughly enjoys the camaraderie of film making and thrives on the intense intimacy that crew members feel for each other while working on a set.

Born in Los Angeles, California, in November 1962 and named Alicia Christian, Jodie Foster is the daughter of Lucius Foster III, a real estate executive, and Evelyn Almond Foster, known as Brandy. Jodie is the youngest child of four in a family that includes sisters Lucinda and Constance and brother Lucius IV. Her parents were divorced when Mrs. Foster was unknowingly three months pregnant with Jodie, who has only met her father a few times. Evelyn Foster, a resourceful woman, worked as a publicist for producer Arthur Jacobs and then managed the career of Jody's older brother, who appeared in commercials and on the CBS television series, "Mayberry, R.F.D.," and whose income first supported the family, eventually being supplanted by Jodie's.

Jodie's career was launched quite accidently when she was discovered at the age of three at a Coppertone audition to which her mother had taken her brother. The advertising representatives spotted Jodie in the studio and then called Evelyn Foster with an offer. Jodie made forty-five commericials while a child for products with national reputations, such as Crest toothpaste, before her mother decided that Jodie, at the age of eight, was ready for television and movies. She made her debut on an episode of "Mayberry, RFD."

A precocious child, Jodie talked at nine months, spoke in complete sentences at one year, and could read and understand scripts by the time she was five. Besides being cute and photogenic, Jodie Foster was obviously an intelligent child who possessed an uncanny ability to act before a camera. As she explained to *Life* magazine: "I had tremendous responsibility, financial and otherwise, for my family. I never perceived myself as a kid. I saw myself as a small human being walking around."

Evelyn Foster regarded Jodie's education, and not the child's acting career, as the first priority. She took Jodie out of the public school system at the beginning of the third grade because school officials wanted Jodie to skip a grade and study science, a decision made on the basis of test scores on the state's gifted program. Evelyn Foster wanted her daughter to study a foreign language and enrolled Jodie in the bilingual Lycee Francais where she graduated class valedictorian in 1980. (She used her speaking knowledge of French in Claude Chabrol's "The Blood of Others," a film based on the novel by Simone de Beauvoir.) Whenever young Jodie had to miss school because of acting commitments, her mother sought out the best teachers in California's educational program for child actors. "If there was stage-mothering, it was about her classes. If I couldn't get certain teachers for her, she didn't work," Evelyn Foster told Jesse Kornbluth of *Vanity Fair.* Jodie Foster is close to her mother and depends upon her guidance and companionship. The bond is so strong that Evelyn Foster often accompanies her daughter on location. "I need to be with someone who loves me and who I can come home to every night, and that might as well be Mom," Foster told Kornbluth, adding, "She's been through so much and has sacrificed so much for us, it's great to be able to give her what she loves and deserves."

Nineteen eighty-eight concluded a two-year period in which Foster appeared in five films. But it is clearly "The Accused," a Sherry Lansing and Stanley Jaffe production, that has brought her critical praise and renewed respect as an actress delivering a top-rate performance in an important role of social significance. Foster plays Sarah Tobias, a lower-class young woman who is brutally raped one night in the back room of a seedy bar on a pinball machine by three men while a crowd of male onlookers cheers the rapists on. (The film takes its premise from a real incident in which a group of men raped a woman in a tavern in New Bedford, Massachusetts, an event described by one critic as "one of America's ugliest public moments.") Sarah, a foul-mouthed, hard-living woman, is no innocent, having smoked marijuana and danced provocatively with one of the rapists prior to the attack, even letting him kiss her. The assistant district attorney, Katheryn Murphy (Kelly McGillis), decides to settle for a plea-bargained lesser charge, reckless endangerment, given Sarah's unreliability as a witness, which angers Sarah because she was not consulted. Sarah wants to redeem her self-esteem by having her day in court. The case does end up in court with McGillis charging three men who cheered the rapists on with criminal solicitation in a tricky and difficult legal move.

"The Accused" is Foster's first movie in which she plays an adult whose presence dominates the screen. Described as "a model of non-nonsense, tight-lipped movie making" by Janet Maslin in the *New York Times,* "The Accused" succeeds because of Foster's command of the character, culminating in the movie's brutal rape scene, which sets a new film standard for realism. The scene took five days to film, and its intensity disturbed everyone involved. "The only difference between this and actual rape is someone yelling 'Cut,'" said director Jonathan Kaplan, who feels "The Accused" benefitted from Foster's suggestions on improving the film's production. Writing in the *Times,* Maslin concluded: "There's never been much doubt that she's a good actress as well as a vixenish beauty. Now it's clear that she's an exceptionally fine, intelligent, vivid actress whose beauty is undiminished. Here she has the benefit of a very well written role. One day she will get a great one." David Ansen in *Newsweek* added: "Always good, even in less than great films, Jodie Foster is one of Hollywood's more undervalued assets. In 'The Accused,' she unleashes a performance of blunt but marvelously controlled fury: one from the gut."

In Tony Bill's "Five Corners," a movie reminiscient of the director's "My Bodyguard," with a first-rate script by John Patrick Shanley, Foster plays another victim, this time of an attempted rape by Heinz (John Turturro), a violent psychopath. Foster as Linda, a young woman who works in a pet shop, is in need of protection when Heinz is released from prison. Set in the Bronx in the fall of 1964, "Five Corners" is a period piece of urban violence and terror. The civil rights movement and its appeal to young Northern whites form a subtext. Linda seeks protection from Harry (Tom Robbins), who saved her the first time but is now a pacifist who wants to join the voter registration drive in Mississippi.

Foster first saw the script as an update of the King Kong myth, but Turturro's interpretation of Heinz changed the film into something much more menacing and disturbing. Asked by Nina Darnton of the *New York Post* why she would make a movie that parallels her own personal experience with John Hinckley, Foster replied: "It's odd, I never even thought of the script in terms of Hinckley until about three weeks into the shooting. I don't know why. Maybe I was blocking it. But even my mom didn't think of it. When I read the script it seemed funnier. I laughed at some of the scenes.... There's another thing. I can't stop playing a victim just because of Hinckley. Being a victim is unfortunately a big part of women's lives." In reviewing "The Accused" in the *Washington Post,* Rita Kempley described Foster's interpretation of the victim theme: "Foster creates the ultimate victim without ever becoming a wimp, mixing dignity with defenselessness."

Foster dislikes talking about John Hinckley, and she recognizes that any public statement she may make gives the incident a kind of permanent life that she clearly does not want to perpetuate, although reporters feel compelled to continue to question her. In 1981, in the aftermath of the assassination attempt, the media attention took on a life of its own that was difficult to handle, even for a young woman as poised and full of self-control as Foster. The Hinckley publicity unfortunately brought death threats from other disturbed individuals. Foster had hoped that her social experience at Yale would be such that she would not draw attention purely for her celebrity status. She had wanted to be accepted as a typical Yale student. The media and public attention shattered her illusion; she realized that from the first day on campus she had been the object of constant public observation.

In an article Foster wrote for the December 1982 issue of *Esquire,* she described the personal pain the bizarre Hinckley episode had caused her: "Obsession is pain and a longing for something that does not exist. John Hinckley's greatest crime was the confusion of love and obsession. The trivilization of love is something I will never forgive him."

In her busy two-year period, Foster also appeared in Mary Lambert's "Siesta," an artsy experimental film set in Spain starring Ellen Barkin, and in Steven Kampmann and Will Aldis's "Stealing Home," a Philadelphia WASP coming-of-age story starring Mark Harmon as a washed-up baseball player who first learned about life and love from Foster's Katie Chandler character. In "Siesta" Foster as Nancy is paired with Julian Sands as two cynical British travelers who become momentarily involved in Barkin's surreal predicament. "Miss Foster does devilishly well with the mannerisms and speech of a petulant post-deb," concluded Maslin in the *Times.* As Katie Chandler in "Stealing Home," wrote Maslin, "Miss Foster works hard to give her a thrillingly madcap and indelibly romantic side.... Miss Foster is asked to overstate greatly Katie's allure, but she does this with impressive bravado."

In the 1984 "Hotel New Hampshire" Foster meshed her interest in serious literature with film making. British director Tony Richardson, who previously brought Henry Fielding's "Tom Jones" to the screen, adapted John Irving's comic novel of the eccentric Barry family and their odd assortment of guests. These include Nastassia Kinski wearing a bear costume to hide her shyness, first at the Hotel New Hampshire, and then in Vienna. Foster is Franny, the oldest of five children, "who talks tough but is true blue underneath." Her brother, John (Rob Lowe), the film's narrator, is in love with her, and "By the film's life-affirming end, Franny and John have joyously consummated their relationship, thus to be able to get on with their lives." Canby in the *Times* wrote that "Miss Foster, one of our loveliest young actresses, shows more flair than she ever has before" and credited Richardson for ably handling the various family adventures.

"Foxes" and "Carny," both released in 1980, are realistic slice-of-life films that demanded different kinds of performance skills from Foster, which she deftly provided. "Foxes," the first film by British director Adrian Lyne, who would later establish himself as a film stylist with "Flashdance" and "Fatal Attraction," portrays the lives of four high school girls in the San Fernando Valley. Lyne has a good eye for the details of the daily drama of the girls as they encounter parents, teachers, and boys. The costumes, soundtrack (disco predominates), and camerawork help punctuate the performances of Foster (Jeanie), Marilyn Kagan (Madge), Kandice Stroh (Deidre), and Cherrie Currie (Annie). Maslin said that Jodie Foster's performance is enough to make "Foxes" worth seeing, and the four young actresses together "give the film its spunk, and each of them emerges as a striking figure in the large-scale set pieces, the best parts of the film. At a rock concert, they strut and sass. At the supermarket, their principal acquistion is the boy at the checkout counter."

In "Carny" Foster plays a restless, unhappy small town girl named Donna who is transformed into a hard-nosed carnival worker. "Carny," directed by Robert Kaylor, and also starring Gary Busey as Frankie, the carnival bozo, and Robbie Robertson of The Band as Patch, a slick trouble-shooter, captures the atmosphere of carnival life while telling the story of Donna's loss of innocence. Although "Carny" does not resolve its plot satisfactorily for Vincent Canby, he praised Foster's contribution to the film: "Of most interest... is the enchanting presence of Miss Foster, who is not only one of the great beauties of American movies but who also shows every sign of becoming one of our most versatile and talented motion-picture actresses. She has the very rare gift of being able to play fumbling, inarticulate characters without ever hiding the intelligence that must illuminate any performance."

The role that changed Jodie Foster's career and would later have a larger, more personal meaning for her was that of Iris, the twelve-year-old prostitute, in Martin Scorsese's "Taxi Driver," in which Robert DeNiro delivered a bravura performance as the psychotic Travis Bickle. The highly controversial film hit a cultural nerve at the time of its release explained, in part, by Canby's comment that DeNiro as Bickle "is a projection of all our nightmares of urban alienation, refined in a performance that is effective as much for what Mr. DeNiro does as for how he does it." Foster at first did not want the part. "I was the Disney kid. I thought, 'What would my friends say?' I could just hear their little snickerings. So I didn't want to do it," she explained to Judy Klemesrud of the *New York Times.* But it was her mother who decided the opportunity to act with Robert DeNiro in a Martin Scorsese film could not be passed up. Foster had appeared in Scorsese's "Alice Doesn't Live Here Anymore," and the director had picked Foster for "Taxi Driver" on the strength of her "Alice" performance. The role won Foster best supporting actress awards from the New York Film Critics, National Film Critics, Los Angeles Film

Critics, and the all-important Academy Award nomination. She said no special research went into the role except being aware of the society in which she lives. However, the Los Angeles Welfare Board had Foster undergo psychological tests and an interview with a pyschiatrist before approval would be granted for her to work on the film. A welfare worker was on the set each day, and Foster could not be present on the set when DeNiro was doing a scene in which he used foul language. "Actually, I think the only thing that could have had a bad effect on me was the blood in the shooting scene. It was really neat, though. It was red sugary stuff. And they used Styrofoam for bones. And a pump to make the blood gush out of a man's arm after his hand was shot off," Foster explained to Klemesrud, with the typical enthusiasm of a thirteen-year-old.

In 1988, Foster dismissed the issue of violence in films and told Darnton: "Some of the films that have had the greatest influence on me have been violent.... I still think 'Taxi Driver' is a major classic. You can't avoid playing life as it is." In a 1976 interview, when Klemesrud asked Foster her opinion of the meaning of "Taxi Driver," the young actress had replied: "I think the taxi driver represents those people who are left anonymous in the crowds, the loneliness. I guess there's part of him in everybody, that part that is waiting to go out and do something to be recognized, rather than sitting home in a nothing apartment and poverty." In a 1987 *Mademoiselle* article Foster reflected on the film's personal significance: "It was an intuitive performance, uninhibited. I know how strong it was. And it's still my favorite film."

British director Alan Parker's 1976 "Bugsy Malone," is an original satire of American gangster movies of the 1920s, in which all the actors are children and gangland shootouts come equipped with machine guns that squirt Reddi-Whip, deadly custard pies, and hoodlums who race around in peddle-driven vintage automobiles. Foster, as Tallulah, "comes across as a combination of Jean Harlow, Twiggy and Glenda Farrell," wrote Vincent Canby in the *New York Times.* "Bugsy Malone" has a first-rate musical score and choreography to augment Parker's daring conception, which is "also something of an achievement in the cinema of the G-rated bizarre."

In American International's 1977 "The Little Girl Who Lives Down the Lane" Foster, as the orphan Rynn, uses a vial of poison to keep the child-molesting Martin Sheen character away from her. Director Nicolas Gessner and screenwriter Laird Koenig depend more on atmosphere and a realistic performance from Jodie Foster than violence and gore to create the film's sense of terror and suspense. Jodie Foster refused to appear nude, saying the public does not want to see a fourteen-year-old naked on screen; Jodie's older sister Constance was used in her place.

In the 1976 Cine Artists "Echoes of a Summer," filmed in 1974, when she was twelve, Foster is cast as Deirdre, a child dying of an incurable heart disease whose parents, Eugene (Richard Harris) and Ruth (Lois Nettleton), have two different attitudes toward death. The mother wants a cure, the father wants the child's last year to be one of "dignity and grace." Jodie Foster, wrote Richard Eder, in the *New York Times,* "must sustain the movie's major role. Her composure, her toughness, her bleak eye that dissolves into a rare but total glee, carry her over bad and embarrassing lines and turn the good ones into arrows."

"Some of the films that have had the greatest influence on me have been violent....I still think 'Taxi Driver' is a major classic."

Foster went through a Walt Disney period that included "Menace on the Mountains" and "Napoleon and Samantha," the latter starring Johnny Whitaker and Foster as Whitaker's "saucy chum" in the title roles, and co-starring a pet lion. Off-camera the lion picked up the eight-year-old Jodie in his mouth, resulting in an injury that hospitalized the child. But she returned to the movie ten days later, even though her mother said she could quit if she wanted. Foster also appeared in MGM's "Kansas City Bomber" in 1972 as Raquel Welch's neglected daughter in a movie about women who compete in roller derbies. In Disney's "One Little Indian," Foster had a small part, and she shared the lead with Barbara Harris in "Freaky Friday," playing daughter Annabel who wishes she could change places with her mother, Ellen, who is wishing the same thing. The two get their wishes, but after one day of comic mishaps each is content to be herself. Foster's last Disney movie was "Candleshoe," in which she appeared as a Los Angeles street kid who is tricked by Leo McKern to pose as the heir of Helen Hayes in a comedy that has David Niven playing a smug British butler.

Following her acting start on "Mayberry, R.F.D.," Foster's television career included a number of guest appearances on television shows such as "Bonanza," "Gunsmoke," and "My Three Sons." A 1972 CBS pilot, "My Sister Hank," did not make the fall lineup, and two ABC shows were short-lived. "Bob and Carol and Ted and Alice," in which Foster played Elizabeth, the daughter of Bob and Carol Henderson (Robert Urich and Anne Archer), went off the air on November 7, 1973, after debuting on September 26. In the sitcom "Paper Moon," based on the 1973 Peter Bogdanovich Depression era film, Foster was cast as Addie Pray, the little urchin who believes the con artist Moze Pray (Chris Connelly) is her father. The series ran from September 12, 1974 until January 2, 1975. In the "ABC Afterschool Specials," Jodie Foster starred in "Rookie of the Year," which won an Emmy, in 1973, and in "The Life of T.K. Dearing" in 1975.

Jodie Foster is five feet four inches tall, weighs one hundred and ten pounds, has long straight blond hair, deep blue eyes, and a rich, soft voice that has been a distinctive personal trademark since childhood. She stays in shape by kick boxing four times a week with a trainer. Foster has kept her success in perspective and has lived modestly for someone at her level of the acting profession. She has a reputation of being polite and thoughtful with the press despite the rough treatment she received at the time of the Hinckly debacle. She admits to being outspoken with a definite point of view concerning films and her ideas in general, but her own self-awareness takes the sting out of her brashness. She reads constantly but has decided not to pursue graduate school because the academic study of literature did not appeal to her. Foster told Jesse Kornbluth that she would someday "like to direct a real film about real people. A very American film about relationships and disappointments."

Sources

American Film, October, 1988.
Chicago Tribune, February 14, 1988.
Dayton Daily News, October 14, 1988.
Esquire, December, 1982.
Harper's Bazaar, July, 1987.
Film Journal, September–October, 1988.
Life, September, 1987.
Mademoiselle, September, 1987.
Newsweek, October 24, 1988.
New York, October 31, 1988.
New Yorker, April 7, 1973.
New York Post, January 19, 1988.
New York Times, July 20, 1972; August 26, 1972; January 30, 1975, February 9, 1976; March 7, 1976; May 15, 1976; September 16, 1976; September 26, 1976; January 29, 1977; February 29, 1980; March 19, 1980; March 9, 1984; January 23, 1988; August 26, 1988; October 14, 1988; October 16, 1988.
Phoenix Gazette, March 18, 1988.
Rocky Mountain News, May 8, 1988.
Time, April 2, 1973.
Vanity Fair, September, 1988.
Variety, August 10, 1988.
Washington Post, October 14, 1988.

—Sidelights by Jon Saari

Barney Frank

AP/Wide World Photos

U.S. congressman from Massachusetts

Born March 31, 1940, in Bayonne, N.J.; son of Samuel (a truck stop owner) and Elsie (Golush) Frank. *Education:* Harvard University, A.B., 1962, J.D., 1977.

Addresses: *Office*—U.S. House of Representatives, Washington, D.C. 20515.

Career

Executive assistant to mayor of Boston, Mass., 1968–71; administrative assistant to member of U.S. Congress, 1971–72; member of the Massachusetts House of Representatives, 1972–80; U.S. Congressman, 1981—.

Sidelights

Barney Frank has been a member of the U.S. Congress since 1981. An avowed liberal Democrat, he represents Massachusetts' fourth district, which is made up of conservative, blue-collar neighborhoods, as well as wealthier, liberal suburbs. Normally a party loyalist, Frank has been known, on occasion, to support Republican candidates and causes. Considered a quick study with a ready quip, he is a favorite of the Washington press corps and popular among his constituents.

The second of four children of a New Jersey couple, Frank became politically active while a student at Harvard. In the 1960s, he worked in Mississippi during the civil rights movement; he also built up "an awesomely detailed knowledge of Massachusetts politics," wrote Suzanne Garment of the *Wall Street Journal*. By the time he reached his mid-twenties, he was "already the very image of a rotund, cigar-chewing, fast-talking, tough-thinking old pol." At Harvard, and through his involvement with various Democratic organizations, Frank made several important contacts among journalists and party figures.

In 1968, at age 27, he became executive assistant to Boston's mayor. For the next three years, he was considered "the city's second most powerful man," according to Emily Yoffe of the *New Republic*. He then ran for—and won—a seat in the Massachusetts legislature. During the eight years that followed, he pushed for civil service reform, affirmative action, and housing programs. He also proved to a be a strong advocate of gay and abortion rights. But Frank was able to compromise with and, in a few instances, support his Republican colleagues. "He was a prudent liberal," James Segel, a longtime friend, told Yoffe. "He understood if liberals are not careful about their programs, those programs will be open to attack. He was a surprisingly effective legislator for someone who was so far out on some issues."

Frank was elected to the U.S. House of Representatives in 1981, one of the few liberals voted into

Congress that year. Recognizing the nation's politically conservative mood, he told Garment that he was willing to work with the then-new Reagan Administration. "Clearly," he remarked, "the nature of our economic problems has changed, and they require different proposals." Frank noted that "some kinds of antitrust enforcements" could be relaxed, he called for "more business-oriented tax changes," and he said that some social issues, such as federal handgun controls, would have to be put on the back burner.

Voters have returned Frank to the House in succeeding elections, despite redistricting attempts and the disclosure of his homosexuality. In 1987, prompted by the AIDS scare and by the press's scrutiny of politicians' private lives, he revealed that he was gay. "I had no choice," he explained to the *New York Times'* Linda Greenhouse. "You deal with the facts handed to you .... Will I become a role model for thousands of young gay men who smoke cigars and talk too fast? I don't think so."

Sources

Christian Science Monitor, February 12, 1987.
New Republic, July 4 and 11, 1981, January 6 and 13, 1982.
New York Times, June 3, 1987.
Time, September 20, 1982.
Wall Street Journal, February 27, 1981.
Washington Post, October 17, 1982.

—Sketch by Denise Wiloch

Ira Glasser

Civil liberties organization executive

Full name, Ira Saul Glasser; born April 18, 1938, in Brooklyn, N.Y.; son of Sidney (a glazier) and Anne (Goldstein) Glasser; married Trude Maria Robinson (a schoolteacher), June 28, 1959; children: David, Andrew, Peter, Sally. *Education:* Queens College of the City University of New York, B.S. in mathematics (magna cum laude), 1959; Ohio State University, M.A. in mathematics, 1960; graduate study in sociology and philosophy at New School for Social Research.

Addresses: *Office*—American Civil Liberties Union, 132 West 43rd St., New York, N.Y. 10036.

Career

Queens College of the City University of New York, instructor in mathematics, 1960–63; Sarah Lawrence College, Bronxville, N.Y., lecturer in mathematics and science, 1962–65; *Current* magazine, New York City, associate editor, 1962–64, editor, 1964–67; New York Civil Liberties Union, associate director, 1967–70, executive director, 1970–78; American Civil Liberties Union, New York City, executive director, 1978—. Consultant, University of Illinois at Urbana-Champaign, 1964–65; chairman, Community Advisory Board and St. Vincents Hospital, both New York City, 1970–72; director, Asian American Legal Defense and Education Fund, New York City, 1974—.

Awards: Martin Luther King, Jr., Award, New York Association of Black School Superintendents, 1971; Gavel Award, American Bar Association, 1972.

UPI/Bettmann Newsphotos

Sidelights

When Ira Glasser became its national executive director on September 24, 1978, the American Civil Liberties Union was in the throes of its most serious crisis since the organization began its work in 1920. Since that time, the ACLU had defended numerous unpopular causes in its effort to uphold the principals of the Constitution and the Bill of Rights. In early 1977, for example, the ACLU defended 15 Marines punished by the military for being involved with the Ku Klux Klan. Eleven years earlier, Glasser, as associate director of the New York Civil Liberties Union, the state affiliate of the ACLU, worked unsuccessfully to defend Captain Howard B. Levy, a United States Army medical officer charged in December 1966 with opposing U.S. military involvement in Vietnam and refusing orders to train Special Forces medics that were to be assigned there. But the ACLU's main purpose, its *raison d'etre,* is to defend those people whose causes make them unpopular but whose very existence qualify them for full protection under the laws of the United States. It is a calling that virtually guarantees the ACLU will occasionally be involved in sometimes unsavory cases.

Its lawyers—more than 30 full-time staff attorneys and some 2,000 cooperating attorneys throughout the country—have been involved in numerous disparate causes: a defense of surrogate parenting; advocating the pro-choice side of the abortion issue; opposition to President Nixon's bombing of Cambodia and later endorsing his impeachment; opposing the death penalty; fighting censorship of school textbooks; trying to repeal state laws requiring schools to teach "creationism" rather than evolution; defense of former White House aide Oliver North, charged with conspiracy in the Iran-Contra affair; and defense of Lyn Nofziger, President Reagan's former White House political director who was convicted of illegal lobbying.

But in the spring of 1978 the organization adopted a case that shook the 250,000-member ACLU. It was in that year that a small group of American Nazis announced they would march through the streets of Skokie, Illinois, a small Chicago suburb that is the home of a significant number of Jewish survivors of the Holocaust. About 40 percent of the ACLU membership was Jewish, and many of them resigned in protest. Charles Morgan, Jr., head of the ACLU's Washington, D.C., branch, had resigned two years earlier. Melvin Wulf, ACLU legal director, resigned one year earlier over philosophical differences in the organization. And now the entire membership seemed in revolt. Membership fell to 185,000 by the middle of 1978, and dues and gifts fell by more than $500,000.

Despite this revolt, Glasser and other ACLU executives held to their belief that whatever personal differences they may harbor with their clients, the ACLU had to pick its cases on legal, ethical, and moral grounds. "Our fundamental civil rights often depend on defending some scuzzball you don't like," Glasser told the *New York Times*. "I do not for one minute believe that what the Nazis or the Ku Klux Klan say deserves protection because it contributes to some grand marketplace of ideas. But I do believe it's of fundamental importance to stop towns from writing ordinances banning offensive speech, because while today it might be the Nazis that are considered offensive, tomorrow it might be what I have to say, or what you have to say."

Glasser's interest in defending the unpopular stretches back to his childhood in East Flatbush, New York. An avid baseball fan, Glasser often found himself at Ebbets Field, cheering on the Brooklyn Dodgers. Back then, professional baseball was a white sport. But Jackie Robinson changed all that in 1947, when he signed with the Dodgers and forever broke the race barrier. Robinson helped integrate the sport, and for Glasser, it meant his first exposure to another race and culture outside the then-largely Jewish New York community. A picture of Robinson still hangs in Glasser's New York office.

The son of a family of glaziers who hoped he would enter their trade, Glasser chose a different path. At sixteen he worked summers at a private holiday camp for the disabled. After nine years there he became the camp director's executive assistant. It was at this camp, in 1956, that Glasser met Trude Robinson, a New York City public school teacher and another camp employee. They were married in 1959, the same year Glasser became the first member of his family to graduate from college, getting a B.S. degree in mathematics, magna cum laude, from Queens College in New York City. He received his M.A. degree in mathematics from Ohio State University in Columbus and studied sociology and philosophy at the graduate level at the New School for Social Research in New York.

But school costs money. To pay the way, Glasser worked part time teaching mathematics at Queens College from 1960 to 1962. From 1962 to 1964, he served as associate editor of *Current* magazine, a liberal monthly review of social issues. He also served as a faculty member from 1962 to 1965 in mathematics and science at Sarah Lawrence College in Bronxville, New York. The same year he was named editor of *Current,* 1964, Glasser became research associate with the School Science Curriculum Project at the University of Illinois Graduate School of Education. Three years later, he joined the staff of the New York Civil Liberties Union.

The court-martial of Capt. Levy was one of Glasser's first assignments. While not a lawyer, Glasser nonetheless worked closely on the case with Charles Morgan, Jr., Levy's chief defense counsel, right up to the Supreme Court. In 1970, when Aryeh Neier became executive director of the ACLU, Glasser was named to take his place as head of the NYCLU. Despite its abundance of attorneys, it's not unusual for the ACLU, or its state affiliates, to be headed by a non-lawyer. Indeed, it's encouraged. "I represent civilian control of the lawyers," Glasser told the *San Francisco Banner Daily Journal*. "We like to believe that you can't leave social justice and civil liberties to the lawyers any more than you can leave war to the generals."

During his tenure with the NYCLU, Glasser became known as a man who concentrated on civil liberties for groups often deprived of those rights, including prisoners, homosexuals, and mental health patients.

"I really had no interest in the law," Glasser told the *San Francisco Banner Daily Journal.* "My primary focus was in free speech, the separation of church and state and an abiding interest in racial discrimination issues. Those were the kinds of issues the ACLU handled, so that is what really propelled me toward the organization."

The early 1970s were prosperous days for the civil liberties organization. Social unrest stirred by such events as the Vietnam War and the Watergate scandal drew thousands of people to the ACLU. Its ranks swelled by more than 50,000 members in 1974 alone, bringing total membership to a record 275,000. But by the late 1970s, much of that fervor had waned. Membership started to decline, and by 1978 the KKK issue seemed capable of destroying the organization.

But under Glasser, the ACLU has experienced a renaissance of sorts. His first goal in 1978 as national executive director was to re-evaluate the organization, establishing a five-year recovery plan. "The place was a disaster," Glasser told the New Jersey *Bergen County Record.* "We had no money in the bank. Had it not been a public-interest group, it would've been in bankruptcy." Glasser embarked on a program of budget slashing, consolidation and a direct mail membership campaign to try and lure back disaffected members. The plan worked. Declining membership stabilized. Then, in 1979, good fortune struck. Nellie Searle, heir to the Chicago pharmaceutical fortune, bequeathed $1 million to the ACLU in her will, enabling the organization to come out of debt and resume some of the programs it was earlier forced to slash.

Under Glasser, the ACLU began a concerted campaign against what it saw, and still sees, as a trend in the United States toward government repression. "I think we are experiencing extensive assault on First Amendment rights, ranging from a fairly clear attempt to break down the wall of separation between church and state and have the government get into sponsoring religion," Glasser told the *San Diego Union.* "By prayer in the schools. By funding of religious organizations, particularly in the family planning area. By adopting the position that the government has an obligation to accommodate religion in some official way and permit state and local governments to sponsor religion . . . . I think there has been an incredible attempt to unravel civil rights enforcement. This government is hostile to civil rights laws, it refuses to enforce them, and comes in on the side of Voting Rights Acts cases, discrimination in employment cases, school desegregation cases, in a way that no other government, Republican or Democrat, has done for 25 years."

The disharmony between the Reagan Administration and the ACLU was perhaps never sharper than in the 1988 presidential campaign. Vice-President George Bush, early in the campaign, interjected the organization itself as a campaign issue, charging Democratic presidential candidate Michael Dukakis with being a "card carrying member of the ACLU," implying that somehow such membership meant Dukakis was outside the mainstream of American thought. However politically damaging, if damaging at all, those charges were is debatable. But as it had during the Watergate era, ACLU executives say the controversy helped galvanize new members to the civil liberties group.

Today, Glasser remains in charge of a 250,000-member organization with a $15 million annual budget that handles some 6,000 cases a year, more than any organization except the Justice Department. "We turn down probably 90 percent of requests for assistance," Glasser told the *National Catholic Register,* "often because of a lack of resources, sometimes because we don't think a case presents a civil liberties issue, and sometimes because we've already got a case that presents the same civil liberties issue."

How much longer Glasser will remain head of the ACLU is uncertain. In the past he has been criticized for alleged power plays, of force feeding his hand-picked choice for new director of the ACLU's Washington office, and of dissuading minority members from applying for the position (a charge he vehemently denies). But one thing remains perfectly clear. Glasser is very happy to be in the fray. As he told the *San Francisco Banner Daily Journal:* "If you wake up in the morning and you open the newspaper and find out that somebody got arrested because of their race or were denied their rights and say, 'Damn it, somebody ought to do something about that,' and it is your job to do it, that is pretty exciting."

Sources

Bergen County Record, February 20, 1983.
Fortune, September 30, 1985.
National Catholic Register, June 19, 1988.
Newsday, November 8, 1981.
New York Post, November 20, 1970.
New York Times, October 2, 1988.
San Diego Union, June 1, 1986.

—Sketch by Stephen Advokat

Sharon Gless

AP/Wide World Photos

Actress

Born May 31, 1944, in Los Angeles, Calif.; father was a sales executive in the garment industry. *Education:* Attended Gonzaga University.

Addresses: *Agent*—Creative Artists Agency, Inc., 1888 Century Park East, Suite 1400, Los Angeles, Calif. 90067.

Career

Worked for advertising agency; actress; feature films include "The Star Chamber," 1983; has appeared in several television movies, such as "All My Daughters," 1972, "Richie Brockelman," 1976, "The Islander," 1978, "Hardhat and Legs," 1980, "Revenge of the Stepford Wives," 1980, and "Letting Go," 1985; regular cast member of television series "Faraday and Company," 1973, "Switch," 1975–78, "Turnabout," 1979, and "House Calls," 1980–81; star of series "Cagney & Lacey," beginning 1982.

Awards: Emmy Award for best actress in a dramatic series, 1986, for "Cagney & Lacey"; also received three Emmy Award nominations.

Sidelights

Actress Sharon Gless is best known for her work on the television series "Cagney & Lacey." The twice-canceled, twice-revived show focused on the relationship between two New York City policewomen, Mary Beth Lacey, played by Tyne Daly, and Christine Cagney. Gless's portrayal of Cagney—a tough, ambitious, sometimes manipulative, and essentially humorless character—earned her an Emmy Award as best actress in a dramatic series.

A native of southern California, Gless grew up wanting to be an actress. Her family did not approve. Her grandfather (a lawyer whose clients included directors Howard Hughes and Cecil B. DeMille) told her: "'It's a filthy business. Stay out of it,'" Gless recalled to Nancy Mills of the *Los Angeles Times.* "I always did what people told me." She entered Gonzaga University, a Catholic school in Spokane, Washington but was expelled for smuggling beer into her dormitory. Gless returned to Los Angeles and went to work for an advertising agency. At 26, she decided to try acting and began taking classes. During a class production, she was spotted by a publicist from Universal. A short time later, she was signed to a seven-year contract.

Gless appeared in several television movies while she was with the studio. These include "All My Daughters," "My Darling Daughters' Anniversary," "Crash," "The Immigrants," "Hardhat and Legs," and "Revenge of the Stepford Wives." She also worked regularly in series television. Gless was cast as Robert Wagner's secretary on "Switch." When that show ended, she starred in "Turnabout" for one year; and, in 1981, she replaced Lynn Redgrave on

"House Calls." She joined "Cagney & Lacey" in 1982.

Gless was not the first actress to play Christine Cagney. Loretta Swit originated the role in a 1981 television movie. When "Cagney & Lacey" debuted as a series, Meg Foster played the part. The show got off to a rocky start; its ratings were poor, and it was canceled a few weeks after its premier. The show's producer, Barney Rosenzweig, "began hounding" the network, CBS, with research proving that the series had failed because of its time slot. CBS finally agreed to give "Cagney & Lacey" another chance but stipulated that "Meg Foster had to go," wrote Sue Reilly in *McCall's.* "They wanted someone with a lighter touch."

Gless stepped in as Cagney when the show began its second season. This time, the series met with popular and critical success. The following year, however, its ratings slumped, and the show was again canceled. Fans responded with a "save 'Cagney & Lacey'" campaign, flooding the network with letters of protest. Meanwhile, Daly and Gless both received Emmy nominations. CBS brought the series back, "the only time in TV history that a network has reinstated a show because of viewer protests," Reilly reported. "Cagney & Lacey" stayed on the air until the late 1980s.

Gless received four Emmy nominations for her portrayal of Cagney. She lost to her co-star, Daly, three times. Finally, in 1986, she won. According to most critics, such recognition was well-deserved. "Her real gift is that she . . . allows us to peer behind her street-smart, tough-guy facade and see the vulnerability that lurks there," Barbara Grizzuti Harrison wrote in *Parade.* "And she can play an essentially humorless person with great good humor." Gless—described by interviewers as witty, ebullient, and prankish—in fact prefers light comedy roles. "I am a comedian by nature," she told *People*'s Michael Ryan. "Comedy comes much more easily to me than draaaaamaa . . . . I like to just pull out my rubber chicken and throw it into the air."

Sources

Los Angeles Times, May 8, 1985.
McCall's, April, 1985.
Ms., January, 1987.
Parade, February 23, 1986.
People, February 11, 1985.

—Sketch by Denise Wiloch

Gary David Goldberg

Television writer and producer

Born June 25, 1944, in Brooklyn, N.Y.; son of George (a postman) and Anne (Prossman) Goldberg; married Diana Meehan; children: Shana Goldberg-Meehan. *Education:* Attended Brandeis University, 1962–64; San Diego State University, B.A., 1975.

Addresses: *Office*—4024 Radford St., Studio City, Calif. 90049.

Career

Writer for "Bob Newhart Show," CBS, 1976; story editor for "Tony Randall Show," CBS, 1977, became co-producer; co-producer for "Lou Grant," CBS, 1978–79; creator and producer, "Last Resort," CBS, 1979; creator, writer, and co-producer, "Family Ties," NBC, 1982–89, and "Day by Day," 1988—; also produced "The Bronx Zoo" for NBC and "Duet" for Fox Broadcasting Network. Founder and president of UBU Productions.

Member: Writers Guild of America West, Actors Equity, American Federation of Television and Radio Artists (AFTRA).

Awards: Writers Guild Award for outstanding episodic comedy television script, 1978; Peabody Award, 1979; recipient of several Emmy Awards, Academy of Television Arts and Sciences.

AP/Wide World Photos

Sidelights

One of Hollywood's most successful television writer/producers, Gary David Goldberg seems to be one show-business character who has bucked "the system" on his way to the top. The son of a Brooklyn, N.Y., postman and his wife, Goldberg didn't show much initial promise as an entertainment mogul; indeed, as Harry F. Waters and Janet Huck point out in a *Newsweek* profile, Goldberg's beginning income "was so minuscule that he wasn't required to file a tax return until 1978." He found his niche, though, in writing television scripts for several popular situation comedies of that time.

One of the secrets to Goldberg's success is his tendency to base his hit comedies on his own life. The writer, for instance, was a self-admitted hippie who "bummed around the world with a girlfriend, a pet Labrador and an inveterate hippie's disdain for the fast lane, especially Hollywood's," as Waters and Huck note. But when Goldberg did settle down, marry, produce a daughter and start his career, he found that his free-spirited past didn't necessarily hold fascination for his eighties-era offspring. From that funny conflict came Goldberg's greatest success, the sitcom "Family Ties," which presents ex-hippie parents, Elise and Michael Keaton, at odds with their children, particularly the ultra-conservative Alex.

"Family Ties" ran for eight seasons on NBC, winning several awards and serving as a springboard for further Goldberg projects. One of them, "Day by Day," which debuted in 1988, is based on another facet of its creator's past. Fifteen years earlier, as the *Newsweek* piece relates, "Goldberg and [his companion and future wife] Diana Meehan . . . founded their own day-care center after the birth of their daughter. In the NBC version, a workaholic couple, in order to spend more time with their own infant daughter, abandon their careers and, yes, open a day-care center." A *New York Times* review characterized this series as "cute with an edge."

Though not every Goldberg series is a hit—"The Bronx Zoo," a drama about an inner-city high school, never caught on with viewers—they all share the writer/producer's commitment to pro-social values. To that end, Goldberg has spent some of his spare time touring with Rep. Pat Schroeder's Great American Family organization, spicing his lectures to students with inside information about "Family Ties" and his other shows.

While Waters and Huck report that Goldberg has begun work on a feature film, they add that when it's finished, he "intends to take some time off for lots of contemplation." As Goldberg told them, "I need to find more things in my life to write about. Right now, all that's left is my bar mitzvah."

Sources

Newsweek, May 9, 1988.
New York Times, September 12, 1982; February 29, 1988.
Wall Street Journal, May 4, 1987.

—Sketch by Susan Salter

Louis Gossett, Jr.

AP/Wide World Photos

Actor

Born May 27, 1936, in Brooklyn, N.Y.; son of Louis and Helen (Wray) Gossett; married third wife, Cyndi James-Reese (an actress and singer), December, 1987; children: (second marriage) Satie (son); Sharron (son; adopted). *Education:* New York University, B.A., 1959.

Addresses: *Home*—Malibu Canyon, California.

Career

Made Broadway debut in "Take a Giant Step," 1953; full-time actor, 1959—; has performed in several plays, including "A Raisin in the Sun," 1959, and "Golden Boy," 1964; feature films include "A Raisin in the Sun," 1961, "The Landlord," 1970, "The Deep," 1977, "An Officer and a Gentleman," 1982, "Iron Eagle," 1986, and "Iron Eagle II," 1988; has appeared in numerous television movies, including "Roots," 1977, "Backstairs at the White House," 1979, "Don't Look Back," 1981, and "Sadat," 1983; star of television series "The Lazarus Syndrome," ABC, 1979, "The Powers of Matthew Star," NBC, beginning 1982, and "Gideon Oliver," ABC, 1989—. Singer in nightclubs during the 1960s; wrote "Handsome Johnny," an antiwar song performed by Richie Havens at Woodstock.

Member: Academy of Motion Picture Arts and Sciences, Actors Equity, Screen Actors Guild, American Federation of Television and Radio Artists (AFTRA), American Guild of Variety Artists, Negro Actor's Guild, American Federation of Musicians, Alpha Phi Alpha.

Awards: Donaldson Award, 1953, for best newcomer of the year, for "Take a Giant Step"; Emmy Award, 1977, for "Roots"; Emmy Award nomination, 1979, for "Backstairs at the White House"; Academy Award for best supporting actor, 1982, for "An Officer and a Gentleman"; Los Angeles Drama Critics Circle Award for play "Murderous Angels."

Sidelights

A versatile and highly skilled actor, Louis Gossett, Jr., has appeared on television, the stage, and in film. He has received two of the entertainment industry's top awards, the Emmy and the Oscar, and he has rarely been without work in his long career. But Gossett feels that race has determined, and limited, the quality and quantity of the roles he is offered. "Black actors will look at the trade papers and if the casting list doesn't say 'black sergeant,' they won't go out for the part," he told Lois Armstrong of *People.* "And if the script doesn't say 'black sergeant,' the producers and directors won't look for one." Gossett has tried, with some success, to change these attitudes.

A native of Brooklyn, New York, Gossett first tried acting at the age of 17, when an injury forced him to sit out his high school's basketball season. A teacher suggested that the temporarily sidelined athlete try for a part in a school play. Gossett won the role. His efforts so impressed the teacher that he urged Gossett to audition for the lead in the Broadway production of "Take a Giant Step." Gossett was chosen over several hundred other young actors. He received the 1953 Donaldson Award as best newcomer of the year for his performance. Gossett entered New York University on an athletic-drama scholarship a few years later. After graduating in 1959, he planned to play professional basketball. Instead, he found himself back on the stage in "A Raisin in the Sun."

Gossett worked steadily throughout the 1960s and 1970s, performing in "The Desk Set," "Golden Boy," "Murderous Angels" (for which he won the Los Angeles Drama Critics Circle Award), and other plays. In 1961, he made his film debut in the screen version of "A Raisin in the Sun." He began working in television and appeared in episodes of several series. He was cast in "The Landlord," his second movie, in 1970. "The Skin Game," with James Garner, followed, as did roles in "Travels with My Aunt," "The Laughing Policeman," and "The White Dawn." Despite this string of stage, television, and film credits, Gossett still waited for his big break.

It came in 1977 with the television mini-series "Roots." Gossett's portrayal of Fiddler, the elderly slave who befriends Kunta Kinte, earned him an Emmy Award. "All of a sudden I got public affirmation," he told David Sheff of *People.* "I was invited to appear at every party, and a higher quality of [script offers] started coming in." The actor garnered his second Emmy nomination in 1979 for his work in "Backstairs at the White House." Two years later, he starred in "Don't Look Back," the television biography of baseball pitcher Satchel Paige. He also made feature films, such as "The Deep" and "Private Benjamin," and he starred in two short-lived television series, "The Lazarus Syndrome" and "The Powers of Matthew Star."

In 1982, Gossett received a second career boost, the role of Sergeant Foley in the blockbuster movie "An Officer and a Gentleman." The part was originally written for a white actor, but Gossett and his agent convinced the film's director to make the character black. Foley is a tough, mean, and sometimes abusive drill instructor who becomes "a father figure to the young officer candidates" he trains, explained the *New York Times*'s Judy Klemesrud. "It is a complex, showy role." Pauline Kael of the *New Yorker* wrote: "It's a beautifully hammy austere performance—Gossett has the grace never to display Sergeant Foley's soft, warm heart." The film community was also impressed; Gossett won an Academy Award as best supporting actor. He went on to star in "Iron Eagle" and its sequel, "Iron Eagle II." In 1989, he returned to network television in the series "Gideon Oliver."

For Gossett, winning the Oscar proved to be a bittersweet experience. "I expected a landslide of parts, but none came," he recalled in a 1988 *Parade* interview with Tom Seligson. "I became very disappointed, blaming it on racism." He began to question his profession, which "set me on a path of self-pity." Gossett turned to alcohol and drugs for escape. He eventually sought help and entered a group-support program. "It has helped me to get rid of resentments and anger and figure out what's truly important," he told Seligson. "Sure Oscars and Emmys are important. But much more important is happiness inside of me and inside my home."

Sources

American Film, April, 1983.
New Yorker, August 23, 1982.
New York Times, July 25, 1982; November 12, 1988.
Parade, July 17, 1988.
People, October 22, 1979; October 4, 1982.

—Sketch by Denise Wiloch

Nancy Graves

Artist

Full name, Nancy Stevenson Graves; born December 23, 1940, in Pittsfield, Mass.; daughter of Walter L. (assistant director of a museum) and Mary B. (a secretary and volunteer worker) Graves; married Richard Serra (a sculptor), 1965 (divorced, 1970). *Education:* Vassar College, B.A. in English literature, 1961; Yale University, B.F.A. and M.F.A., 1964.

Addresses: *Home*—New York, N.Y. *Office*—c/o M. Knoedler & Co., Inc., 19 East 70th St., New York, N.Y. 10021.

Career

Painter and sculptor; Fulbright-Hayes fellow in France, 1965; lived and worked in Florence, Italy, 1966; has had numerous individual shows of her work throughout the world, 1968—; participant in many group shows, 1970—; resident, American Academy, Rome, Italy, 1979; work represented in numerous museums, galleries, and private collections, including Whitney Museum and Museum of Modern Art, New York City, Chicago Art Institute, Museum of Fine Arts, Houston, Neue Gallerie, Cologne, and National Gallery of Canada, Ottawa. Filmmaker; films include "200 Stills at 60 Frames," 1970, "Goulimine," 1970, "Izy Boukir," 1971, "Aves: Magnificant Frigate Bird, Great Flamingo," 1973, and "Reflections on the Moon," 1974. Designer of set and costumes for experimental dance *Lateral Pass*, 1983.

Awards: Creative Artist Public Service Grant, 1974; Bessie Award, 1986, for *Lateral Pass*.

AP/Wide World Photos

Sidelights

Nancy Graves is a prolific sculptor and painter whose works form part of permanent collections in such institutions as the Museum of Modern Art and the Whitney Museum of American Art, both in New York City, as well as many private collections. Graves's reputation rests primarily on her painted bronze sculptures, which are usually human scale or smaller. In subject matter, Graves crosses back and forth from abstraction to representation and frequently incorporates natural forms into her sculptures, some of which seem to imitate the growth process itself. In the introduction to the catalogue raisonné, *The Sculpture of Nancy Graves,* Robert Hughes characterizes Graves's sculpture as "wonderfully inclusive; formally rigorous, it spreads a wider fan of poetic association than does any sculptor's of her generation."

Graves, who was born on December 23, 1940, in Pittsfield, Massachusetts, was introduced to art early by her parents, Walter L. and Mary B. Graves, who made it their hobby. Nancy's father was the assistant to the director of the Berkshire Museum of Art and Natural History, a position that gave the young girl an inside look at the workings of a museum that housed exhibits dealing with a wide array of disciplines. An ambitious and intelligent child, Graves drew and painted with unchildlike exactness and by age twelve was determined to be an artist.

Upon graduating from high school, Graves attended Vassar College in Poughkeepsie, New York, where she majored in English while also studying drawing. When she won a scholarship to the Yale Summer School of Music and Art in Norfolk, Connecticut, she glimpsed what continuing her arts education could mean. Her work at the summer school earned her entrance in 1962 to Yale's prestigious School of Art and Architecture, from which she earned B.F.A. and M.F.A. degrees.

In 1964, Graves went to Paris on a Fulbright-Hayes fellowship in painting. There she met such other expatriot Americans as minimalist composer Philip Glass and folksinger Joan Mitchell. Although at this time, Graves painted in the Fauvist style of André Derain and Henri Matisse and had become interested in Constantin Brancusi's abstract sculptures, she was searching for her own artistic vocabulary.

In 1965 Graves married Richard Serra, whom she would divorce five years later. The couple moved to Florence, where, still frustrated by her inability to discover her own idiom, Graves happened upon the work of eighteenth-century anatomist Clemente Susini in a local museum. She was fascinated by his life-size wax cross-sectional models of human beings and animals. Although Graves had previously had little desire to sculpt, her interest was kindled: she learned about carpentry, collected animal skins, and began to tackle the problems posed by working in three dimensions. After collaborating with Serra on a series of sculptural assemblages incorporating small stuffed animals and animals juxtaposed with found objects, Graves began anatomical studies of the camel, which included making several films about them.

In what has in retrospect been called Graves's neoprimitive period, the sculptor produced a series of life-size Bactrian (two-humped) camels of polyurethane, latex, wood, steel, plaster, and painted skins that could produce a natural appearance. The first was made in Florence and destroyed by Graves before she returned to New York in 1966. In her first solo show at New York's Graham Gallery, Graves presented the public with three more camels and in a second show a year later, another grouping of camels. In an era of conceptualism, art in which the artist's creative intent is more important than the process or the product, the critics were baffled. Graves's interest in camels lead her to investigate the fields of osteology, paleontology, anthropology, and archeology, which she has researched quite thoroughly from an artist's standpoint. Graves's studies of fossils were in truth studies of space, armature, weight, and gravity, and they suggested to her that she need not reproduce an entire creature. Her next works, all from 1970, featured bones. The scattered sculpted bones of *Fossils* suggest an archaeological dig, in *Inside-Outside* Graves placed bones inside pieces of skin, and *Variability of Similar Forms* depicts a group of life-sized Pleistocene camel leg bones, animated yet austere. For this work, Graves sculpted thirty-six individual leg bones in various positions, each almost the height of human, arranged upright in an irregular pattern on a wooden base. Other works of this period, *Variability and Repetition of Variable Forms* and *Shaman* were inspired by the totems of North American Indians.

From 1972 to 1976 Graves focused on painting, in part as a response to the burden of needing so many assistants to aid in the production and assembly of her sculptures. She created etchings, lithographs, and monotypes at Tyler Graphics in Bedford Village, New York. In her Camouflage Series of 1972 she used a pointillist technique to suggest the natural camouflage of sea animals, and in the Ocean Floor Series she used a dense pattern of almost connecting dots to produce a topography such as that found in bathymetric and marine topographic maps.

In 1977, German candy tycoon and art patron Peter Ludwig commissioned Graves's first bronze piece: *Ceridwen, out of Fossils* for the Museum Ludwig, in Cologne, West Germany. "Ceridwen" is the medieval Welsh name for death, and as in the earlier work *Fossils,* Graves places Pleistocene-period camel bones in a fashion suggestive of an archaeological dig. When Graves needed to locate a foundry to caste this piece, she remembered having been introduced to Richard Polich, owner of the Tallix Foundry in Peekskill, New York, by fine-art printer Kenneth Tyler. Graves had *Ceridwen* cast at Tallix using the lost-wax process in which a rubber mold is made of an object. Then a wax replica is made by pouring wax into the mold, and a ceramic mold is then made over the wax replica. When the ceramic mold is heated, the wax runs out leaving the final mold into which the molten metal is poured.

With the help of the Tallix artisans, Graves developed a seldom used process—direct casting, which allows minute details often obscured in the lost-wax process to remain visible. In direct casting, a ceramic shell is made to encase an object and the object itself is burned away in the furnace. Then molten metal is poured into the remaining hollow shell. Another characteristic of Graves's work from this point forward was also a result of her association with Tallix—color. Graves uses a wide variety of patinas specifically created for her by Toni Putnam at Tallix. *Quipu,* made of directly cast ropes vertically positioned, was Graves's first piece to use the new casting and patinating techniques. It was with this work that Graves first made color a seminal part of her work, and in many of her subsequent pieces Graves would use the trompe *l'oeil* aspect of *Quipu,* meaning here an illusion of weightlessness created by her use of color.

While a resident at the American Academy in Rome in 1979, Graves made prints that incorporate etching, aquatint, and drypoint. At this time she became particularly interested in archeological maps, an interest that is reflected sculpturally in *Bathymet-Topograph, Archaeoloci, Archaeolem, Trace,* and *Fayum,* among others. In these works Graves incorporated lacy objects that reflect the convoluted texture of detailed maps.

Since 1980 Graves has made over 200 bronze sculptures using directly cast objects. She collects a wide variety of forms to add to her inventory of cast parts: plants, fish, and paper or wooden objects whose shapes intrigue the artist. Until the twentieth century, sculpture had traditionally depicted the human figure, and even after the conceptualists and minimalists of the 1960s freed sculpture from the demand that it represent the human figure, sculptors avoided using botanical themes. Graves dares to make visual in her works her deep communion with the natural world, as well as a sense of humor. Commentators have remarked on the influences of such sculptors as Pablo Picasso, Alexander Calder, and David Smith, who create tension through shape and color and build forms from components that only slightly touch.

Graves lives in an enormous loft in SoHo, New York City, and commutes about twice a week to the Tallix Foundry, where she maintains an adjunct studio. Graves usually works on several pieces in various stages at any one time and is improvisational in her approach to sculpting. Early in her career, Graves would bring sketches of a proposed sculpture to the foundry, though later she decided to work improvisationally. The sculptor selects from her inventory cast objects that inspire a piece and welds them together using as few welds as possible. Then she brushes chemicals onto the surface heated by a gas torch to create unusually brilliant patinas that camouflage the original identity of the parts. Graves has also experimented with baked-on enamels, and for outdoor constructions, such as *Trace,* she employed polyurethane paint, which has become her preferred method of patination for all her sculptures.

Graves crosses back and forth from abstraction to representation and frequently incorporates natural forms into her sculptures.

Perhaps Linda L. Cathcart, director of the Contemporary Arts Museum in Houston, Texas, best described the essence of Graves's sculpture when she wrote in the catalogue essay, "Nancy Graves: Sculpture for the Eye and Mind": "There is no reason to believe that Graves is near to concluding her sculptural investigations. The possible inventory of forms for her art is endless. She does not fight her materials; rather, she builds with them and allows the process itself to suggest new avenues. Each of her sculptures functions as an energetic abstraction, never remaining merely literal and never giving way to dead weight. She has the ability to amplify forms and to achieve for each individual one many possible readings."

Graves draws inspiration from many sources. She is an avid and eclectic reader and has enjoyed many opportunities to travel. In the seventies she lived in Europe and visited India, Nepal, and Kashmir, and in the early eighties she traveled to Egypt, Peru, China, Australia and the Dominican Republic. Graves's paintings and sculpture have also informed each other: the map-like characteristics of her paintings in the 1970s later appeared in her sculptures, and a painterly use of color is evident in her three-dimensional works. Conversely, the paintings have sometimes become multidimensional, with sculptural projections protruding from them.

Graves has often been criticized for being so willing to experiment with various media: sculpture, painting, prints, filmmaking, and set and costume design. In 1983 Graves began a collaboration with choreographer of experimental dance Trisha Brown on the costumes and set for *Lateral Pass,* which was performed by the Judson Dance Theater in Minneapolis and New York in 1985 and earned Graves a New York Dance and Performance Bessie Award in 1986.

Because of Graves's work habits, and the complexity of the four scrims she designed, Brown had to wait until the set was constructed before she could choreograph the piece. The scrims of vertically hung styrofoam boulders (pink or green) and bent silver rods and ultraviolet tubing ascend and descend in a maze of color and motion, while dancers in pastel and white leotards appear and disappear. Brown, an energetic person herself, once described Graves as "a verb," always in motion.

Sources

Books

Nancy Graves: A Survey, 1969–1980, 1980.
Nancy Graves: Sculptures/Drawings/Films, 1969–71 (catalog), Neue Gallerie in Alten Kurhaus, 1971.
The Sculpture of Nancy Graves: A Catalogue Raisonné, Fort Worth Art Museum, 1987.

Periodicals

Art in America, June, 1988.
Art News, February, 1986.
Artscanada, May, 1973.
Arts Magazine, February, 1986.
New York, January 13, 1986.
New York Times, January 26, 1979; January 31, 1986; December 19, 1986; March 29, 1987; December 18, 1987.
New York Times Magazine, December 6, 1987.
Town & Country, September, 1988.
Vogue, June, 1980.
Wall Street Journal, April 17, 1987.

—*Sidelights by Jeanne M. Lesinski*

Wayne Gretzky

AP/Wide World Photos

Professional hockey player

Born January 26, 1961, in Brantford, Ontario, Canada; son of Walter (a telephone company technician) and Phyllis Gretzky; married Janet Jones (an actress) July 16, 1988; children: Paulina. *Education:* Attended high school in Sault Sainte Marie, Ontario.

Addresses: *Office*—Los Angeles Kings, P.O. Box 17013, Englewood, Calif. 90308.

Career

Professional hockey player in now-defunct World Hockey Association, with Indiana Racers, 1978, and Edmonton Oilers, 1978–79, and in National Hockey League with Edmonton Oilers, 1979–88, and Los Angeles Kings, 1988—.

Awards: Named World Hockey Association Rookie of the Year, 1979; Lady Byng Memorial Trophy for gentlemanly play, 1980; Hart Trophy as Most Valuable Player in National Hockey League, 1980–87; member of NHL All-Star team, 1980–89; named Sportsman of the Year by *Sports Illustrated* magazine, 1982; Art Ross Trophy, NHL, 1986; winner of numerous other awards; holds more than 50 NHL records.

Sidelights

In the summer of 1988, shortly before the wedding of Wayne Gretzky and his trade from one team to another, a *Chicago Tribune* reporter wrote about this extraordinary hockey star who then was the property of the Stanley Cup champion Edmonton Oilers. The article assessed Gretzky's tremendous popularity in his native Canada and his national hero status there: "He embodies most every attribute that's respected in this polite, conservative land, where it is considered exceedingly bad form to flaunt one's success. And—this is important—he's still here [in Canada]. Canadians long ago grew resigned to watching many of their best and brightest writers, actors, scientists, musicians and sports stars migrate southward to mine the celebrity riches of America. Gretzky is a proud exception. Not only has he elected to stay in Canada, he's made it clear that he's happy in Edmonton." Less than a month later, after his wedding to American actress Janet Jones, Gretzky was traded—with his consent—to a team south of the Canada-United States border.

The trade stunned Canadians. "Woe, Canada," said the headline in *Sports Illustrated,* a play on the title of the national anthem "O, Canada!" Gretzky didn't just move to the United States. He went so far south that he ended up near the Mexican border. He went to the Los Angeles Kings, deep in the heart of Hollywood, where he would live and raise a family with a woman who once had been featured in a photo spread in *Playboy* magazine. Even in the States, where hockey is, at best, fourth among the major team sports in fan popularity, the news media treated the trade as one of the major sports stories of the year, comparing it to the 1920 deal in which baseball player Babe Ruth moved from the Boston Red Sox to the New York Yankees. "The Wayne Gretzky trade saved a team and bolstered an entire league," stated *Sports Inc.*, an American magazine. "It was, in fact, the most important trade in sports history."

Why was it so important? What makes Gretzky different and better than the hundreds of other men who play professional ice hockey for a living in the United States and in Canada? As an historical figure, why will he rank so high in the record of organized sports in the twentieth century? What makes him so special? "He can stickhandle. He is a pinpoint passer. He has an almost extra-sensory idea of where the puck will go, or the spot into which a teammate might be breaking," wrote Peter Gzowski in the Canadian magazine *Saturday Night*. "He personifies everything hockey stands for in our lives.... He is tearing the league apart. As Gordie Howe put it at the last Charlie Conacher Awards banquet, 'The NHL needs someone to hang its hat on, and Gretzky looks like a hat-tree.'" Such words may have seemed like fitting praise in 1989, after Gretzky had set dozens of scoring records in a decade of work in the National Hockey League. But in fact, these words were written in 1980, after Gretzky's first NHL season.

It might be said that Gretzky is one of those rare athletes who proved to be better than promised in the rave advance notices. There were plenty of them. From his teen years, Gretzky was featured in newspapers, magazines, radio and television as something special, as a child prodigy. "16-year-old dazzles Junior A loop and packs the arenas," said the headline on a 1977 story in the *Toronto Globe and Mail*. He hardly dazzles as an imposing physical specimen. The Los Angeles media guide lists him at 6 feet tall and 170 pounds. He is slightly lighter than most hockey players and a bit taller. He has pale blue eyes and dark blond hair. Gretzky, a left-handed shooter who plays the center position on the three-man forward line, skates with his body bent forward at the waist, the shirt-tail of his jersey tucked inside his right hip pad, a characteristic quirk. He has a thin face that makes his helmet seem too large for his head. He wears number 99, the highest number in hockey, because the number 9—worn by his idol, Howe—wasn't available when Gretzky joined a junior team as a teenager. He isn't exceptionally fast or strong in a sport in which speed and strength are considered primary qualities. Another aspect of North American hockey, rough play and fighting, is almost never a part of Gretzky's game.

"He's smart," Hockey Hall of Famer Howe said of Gretzky in the *Detroit Free Press*. "He stays clear of the fracases. He leans back with the hit, and he has the way of rolling off a real hard body check." Instead of charging and colliding, Gretzky drifts and glides, rarely wasting energy, seeming to see the ice better than others, anticipating the flow of action the way a master chess player plans several moves in advance. Although he usually scores more goals than most players, it is his assists—the passes that create scoring opportunities for others—that make Gretzky especially valuable to a team.

Almost as soon as he joined the league in 1978 after one year in the now-defunct World Hockey Association, players, fans, team officials and reporters began comparing Gretzky's abilities and feats to those of Howe, Maurice Richard, Bobby Hull, Bobby Orr, and a handful of others in the pantheon of hockey legends. As the years went by, his statistics proved to be equal to or greater than those of the players who had come before. After nine NHL seasons, Gretzky held 49 NHL records. Along with leading the Oilers to four Stanley Cup championships in the five years from 1984 through 1988, he ranked third on the all-time list in career scoring, behind only Howe and Marcel Dionne. (Total scoring is computed as one point for a goal and one point for an assist). Howe, in 1,767 regular-season games played, amassed 1,850 points. Gretzky had 1,669 points in only 696 games prior to the 1988–89 season.

It can be tedious and mundane to define Gretzky by mere numbers, but many of them seem to jump off the pages of the record books. For instance: Gretzky led the league with 92 goals in 1981–82; he led the league with 163 assists in 1985–86. For most hockey players, a good season would feature 30 goals and/or 75 assists. A great season would feature 50 goals and/or 100 assists. While it is fair to point out that recent decades have seen an increase in scoring, it also is true that Gretzky's numbers far surpassed those of his contemporaries. For instance: When he led league with 92 goals and 120 assists for 212 points in 1981–82, the second-place finishers in each category notched totals of 64, 93 and 147. Another measure of his status among his peers is his awards. He won the Hart trophy as Most Valuable Player in the league in every year between 1980 and 1987. He didn't win it in 1988, after he missed 16 games due to a knee injury. He still led the league with 109 assists and won the Conn Smythe trophy as the most valuable player in the Stanley Cup playoffs, the postseason tournament that determines the league's annual champion.

Aside from the praise he receives for his performance on ice, Gretzky draws accolades for his conduct out of uniform. He rarely turns down a request for an interview or an autograph. Many stories written about his personality use words like "humble" and "polite." But there also is noted an aloof, almost mechanical quality about the way he recites pat answers to questions he has heard many times before. "It's impossible to know what he feels about anything," said Montreal writer-author Mordecai Richler in *USA Weekend*. "He's very bland. You get all the Rotary Club replies." One of his former Edmonton teammates, defenseman Kevin Lowe, noted this quality and more when interviewed on a video tape documentary called "The Boys on the Bus," a chronicle of the Edmonton team of the mid-1980s. "He is probably the greatest player that ever played," Lowe said of Gretzky. "He is a pretty amazing person.... He's an ambassador to the game, and he is very similar to any diplomat. Very similar to the president or the prime minister. He rarely lets his guard down. Do you ever hear what Brian Mulroney or President Reagan does away from his office? You never hear about that, just like you never hear what Gretzky does. He doesn't allow the general public to see that side of him because he is so conscious of his public image, which is fabulous. But he is so conscious of that image that he rarely ever lets his guard down. He hates to be alone in public and I can understand that. He thinks someone with a knife might come up to him in a crowd because his name is right up there. They call him 'The Greatest' like they called Muhammad Ali the greatest. Those are major concerns when your name is that recognizable."

Gretzky, in the same documentary, explained why he never goes out alone. "You just can't put yourself in that position of being vulnerable," he said. "I just always make sure I am with somebody when I am out of my apartment. There's always that one person who doesn't like Wayne Gretzky.... I really prefer

Wayne Gretzky (left) and Los Angeles Kings owner Bruce McNall display Gretzky's new Kings jersey shortly after the announcement of his trade from Edmonton to Los Angeles in August 1988. UPI/Bettmann Newsphotos.

not to argue with people and I prefer to walk away.... always nice to have someone else with you to tell them kindly to please leave."

Some of his most revealing comments came in an interview with Rich Sadowski of the *Los Angeles Herald Examiner.* Gretzky recalled how pressure in his small hometown of Brantford, Ontario, forced him to move to Toronto and board with a different family when he was 14. His home town had only 65,000 people and Gretzky was too much a celebrity to live a normal life. "I know it's the only thing in my life I regret so far," Gretzky said. "My brother Brent was three when I left home.... It was just to try and escape all the unnecessary pressures specific parents lay on kids. It's not kids against each other. It's the parents. It's not all of them. It's just takes one or two. But the older in life I get, the more bitter I am about [having to move]. I hate it more now than I did three years ago. The fact I moved away at 14.... I wish I could go all the way back again. I wouldn't have to do it. I'd be happy to be able to go back and grow up with my family. We just got to the point where it became uncomfortable to be stared at. More than anything, it came to the point where we enjoyed staying home. More than anything, you always felt like you were on display."

Oddly, this transition was echoed in the summer of his 28th year, when he moved from the small, Western Canadian city of Edmonton to the Southern California metropolis of Los Angeles. "L.A. is a great sports city, but hockey isn't as visible as basketball, baseball and football," Gretzky said in an interview for *Newsmakers.* "It gives me the opportunity to kind of get away." Gretzky's wife gave birth to their first child, a daughter, Paulina, on December 19, 1988. Before the birth, Gretzky had said that if the baby was a boy, he would be under intense scrutiny in Canada, where it would be expected that the boy would play hockey. "Let's face it, the child would be under a microscope living in Canada," he told *People* magazine. In L.A., he's just another child in the crowd."

Gretzky, of Russian and Polish descent, is the oldest of five children of Walter and Phyllis Gretzky. His brother Keith is a minor-league professional hockey player. His father, a telephone company technician, bought son Wayne a pair of skates before he was three years old and began to lead him in complicated skating drills on a backyard rink that was made smooth and fast with water sprayed from a garden sprinkler. Gretzky occasionally objects, in polite but pointed words, to the often-spoken theory that his skills are from natural instinct and not hard work and practice. "I've practiced so long, so many times, that nothing can happen that I haven't seen before," he told the *Washington Post.* "It's not so much anticipation as experience. A lot of people think what I do is instinct, but it isn't. Nobody would ever say a doctor had learned his profession by instinct. Well, I've spent almost as much time studying hockey as a med student puts into studying medicine."

This may be true, but many Canadian boys—as well as kids from other countries—work as long and as hard at hockey as Gretzky did. But few have the skills that get them signed, at the age of 17, to a major professional contract before they finish high school. This happened to Gretzky, when businessman Nelson Skalbania hired him to play for the Indianapolis Racers of the WHA. When that team's business forecast turned bleak early in Gretzky's rookie season, his contract was sold to Peter Pocklington, the owner of the Edmonton team of the WHA. Although the WHA ceased operation after Gretzky's rookie season, Edmonton was one of four teams accepted into the established NHL. Pocklington signed Gretzky to a 21-year contract for what was reported to be a total of $5 million. "The entire hockey playing world is still reeling from the extravagance, the preposterousness, the sheer gold-studded bravado of it all," the *Toronto Sunday Sun* said at the time.

It turned out to be a good investment for Pocklington, who became so friendly with Gretzky that he would sit with him on team airplane flights to try to calm Gretzky's nerves. (One of Gretzky's few public weaknesses was his terrible anxiety during air travel. This receded, Gretzky said, when he began traveling with his new team, Los Angeles). After the Oilers won their fourth Stanley Cup in five years in the spring of 1988, Gretzky began to hear rumors that Pocklington was trying to trade his contract to another team, even as Edmonton and much of Canada prepared to witness his wedding to Jones, who is from St. Louis, Missouri. The Canadian press compared it to the royal wedding in England between Prince Charles and Princess Diana in 1981. When Gretzky was traded, some Canadians compared his departure to the abdication of England's Edward VIII, who renounced his throne to marry a commoner in 1936.

In return for Gretzky, Mike Krushelnyski and Marty McSorley, Pocklington's team received Jimmy Carson, Martin Gelinas, and the Kings first-round draft choices for the years 1989, 1991, and 1993. Bruce McNall, the owner of the Kings, also paid Pocklington $15 million. The press dubbed it "A King's ransom." Gretzky wept at his press conference when he said good-by to Edmonton. Shortly thereafter, Pocklington told *People* that Gretzky had "an ego the size of Manhattan" and that Gretzky had been faking the tears. The statements angered Gretzky. "I'm sure it will inspire me," Gretzky said in the *Calgary Sun*. "Don't get mad, get even."

Also getting even, in a different way, was McNall, the owner of the Kings. Originally, he had predicted it would take about five years for the increased revenue generated by Gretzky to equal the sums paid to obtain him. By December of 1988, McNall revised that prediction. "The money has been double, it's been phenomeonal," McNall told *Newsmakers*. "We thought it would take a long time to recover Wayne's salary and so forth. But TV, merchandizing and fan support has been phenomenal. Very profitable. Very, very profitable. We thought it might take five years. Now, we think within a year, a year and a half for sure." Gretzky himself earned an estimated $1.5 million per year in salary and bonuses and another $1 million or more in endorsement fees.

All the dollars are predicated, of course, on Gretzky's continuing ability to play at a high skill level. By the middle of the 1988–89 season, he had helped transform the Kings from one of the NHL's perennial weak links to one of its top teams. McSorley, traded with Gretzky from Edmonton, said his teammate was taking a different approach with a new team. "I think he is [different] in the sense that he feels very responsible for how the team develops," McSorley said in a *Newsmakers* interview. "In Edmonton, the team had a lot of maturity. Wayne is a little more vocal in L.A. He realizes how much of an impact he makes at this stage as everyone is coming together. They look for Wayne for a lot of leadership. Our defensemen activate tremendously through his influence. Our goal scorers play responsibly in their own end through his influence. He is so concerned, he doesn't score as many points as he might because he is concerned with everyone else's development." Is Gretzky a man with a mission? McSorley was asked. "He's always on a mission," McSorley replied. "He gets three points, he wants four. He always, always pushes himself."

A few problems were evident in Gretzky's adjustment to his new team. His new coach, Robbie Ftorek, wasn't giving him as much ice time as Gretzky was accustomed to getting—as much as 30 minutes of a 60-minute game. After a brief benching during a game, the two exchanged harsh words, according to several published reports. "He's just a piece of the puzzle," the coach said in the *Hartford Courant*. "A bigger piece, the biggest piece, to be sure. But just a piece of the puzzle." Others thought Gretzky's skills seemed to be diminishing slightly. Some rated Mario Lemieux [see index for *Newsmakers* entry] of Pittsburgh—the Hart trophy winner the previous year—as hockey's new best player. Gretzky, who set up Lemieux for the winning goal over the Soviet Union for the championship of the Canada Cup tournament in 1987, merely continued to play at an extraordinary level while resisting comparisons to other individuals. As he told his teammates during dinner in the Oilers video documentary, hockey "is not a challenge to me. It's fun. I love it. I say I want that puck and you guys get your own puck.'"

Sources

Calgary Sun, October 17, 1988.
Chicago Tribune, March 29, 1981; July 15, 1988; August 22, 1988; October 7, 1988.
Detroit Free Press, March 28, 1981; January 17, 1982.
Edmonton Journal, October 19, 1988.
Edmonton Sunday Sun, January 7, 1979.
Hartford Courant, November 6, 1988; November 20, 1988.
Los Angeles Herald Examiner, September 17, 1988.
Los Angeles Kings Media Guide, 1988–89, 1988.
Los Angeles Times, September 18, 1988.
Maclean's, January 9, 1978; December 28, 1987.
Newsweek, January 18, 1982; August 22, 1988.
New York Times, March 7, 1982; May 16, 1988.
Playboy, August 29, 1988.
Saturday Night, November, 1980.
Sporting News, January 7, 1978; February 16, 1980; November 1, 1980; August 22, 1988.
Sports, December, 1988.
Sports Illustrated, February 20, 1978; December 11, 1978; March 9, 1981; April 20, 1981; October 12, 1981.
Sports Inc., October 3, 1988.
Time, April 27, 1981; January 4, 1982; August 22, 1988.
Toronto Globe and Mail, October 12, 1977; January 26, 1979; February 25, 1979; June 6, 1980; October 17, 1988.
USA Weekend, October 14–16, 1988.
Vancouver Province, September 26, 1979.
Washington Post, January 1, 1982; February 9, 1982.

—Sidelights by Joe LaPointe

Melanie Griffith

Actress

Born August 9, 1957, in New York, N.Y.; daughter of Peter Griffith (an advertising executive and real estate developer) and Tippi Hedren (an actress); married Don Johnson (an actor), 1976 (divorced, 1977); married Steven Bauer (an actor), 1983 (divorced); remarried Johnson, June 26, 1989; children: (with Bauer) Alexander. *Education:* Left high school at age sixteen; studied acting with Stella Adler.

Addresses: *Home*—Miami, Fla.; and Aspen, Colo.

Career

As a young child, appeared in several commercial advertisements; began acting at age sixteen; feature films include "Night Moves," 1975, "The Drowning Pool," 1975, "Smile," 1975, "Roar," "One on One," 1977, "Joyride," 1977, "Underground Aces," 1980, "Fear City," 1985, "Body Double," 1984, "Something Wild," 1986, "Working Girl," 1988, "Stormy Monday," 1988, and "The Milagro Beanfield War," 1988; regular member of cast of television series "Carter Country," 1978–79; other television appearances include "Steel Cowboy," "She's in the Army Now," "Golden Gate," and guest roles in several series, including "Alfred Hitchcock Presents" and "Miami Vice."

Awards: Golden Globe Award and Academy Award nomination for best actress, both 1989, for "Working Girl."

UPI/Bettmann Newsphotos

Sidelights

Melanie Griffith is on the verge of becoming a major Hollywood star and has set out to change both her career and her public image. Guy Trebrey in *Premiere* described Griffith's movie career as one in which she has played "beautiful-but-dumb nymphets. . . . The pear tattooed on her left buttock may be the feature her fans know best." But, wrote Trebrey, the actress "has seemingly reinvented herself: [she has] wised up." Clearly, Griffith now is in an enviable position, having emerged as a formidable screen presence who should be in competition for major screen roles for years to come. Already a cult favorite for her roles in films like Brian de Palma's "Body Double" and Jonathan Demme's "Something Wild," Griffith hit a bigger audience in Mike Nichols's "Working Girl," in which she stole the movie from the top billed Sigourney Weaver and Harrison Ford.

Critics like to compare Griffith to blond starlets of the past—Jean Harlow, Jean Arthur, Judy Holliday, and Marilyn Monroe. Pauline Kael, reviewing "Something Wild," wrote that Griffith's performance "suggests Kim Novak and, a bit later, Ginger Rogers, but Griffith's tarty, funky humor is hers alone." Griffith, like the legends before her, projects a definable

American eroticism tinged with innocence. "She has," wrote Kael, "the damnedest voice; it sounds frazzled and banal—a basic mid-American girl voice—but she gets infinite variations into its flatness. She can make it lyrically flat. That voice keeps you purring with contentment. It can be as blandly American as Jean Seberg's voice when she spoke French, and Griffith has a bland American prettiness, too."

The daughter of model turned actress Tippi Hedren and real-estate developer Peter Griffith, Melanie Griffith was born in New York City on August 9, 1957. Griffith moved to Los Angeles when her parents divorced, and there she lived a Hollywood childhood, appearing in Ivory Soap commercials. British director Alfred Hitchcock was obsessed with Tippi Hedren's icy blond eroticism, casting her in "The Birds" and "Marnie." When Griffith was six, the perverse Hitchcock gave her a present—a six-inch doll bearing Hedren's likeness encased in a wooden casket. The mother reported that her daughter never played with the doll. When Hedren married television director and producer Noel Marshall, they raised Melanie and Marshall's children on a ranch stocked with lions, tigers, leopards, llamas, and pumas, applying the same philosophy to the children as they did to the animals. "We give them living room. We only want them to be themselves and play and have a wonderful time," Marshall told *Newsweek.*

Griffith met actor Don Johnson who appeared with Hedren in "The Harrad Experiment" and, at fourteen, she became his lover. She later married him in 1976, but the marriage lasted less than a year. A high-school dropout who left home by the time she was sixteen, Griffith lived a free-spirit existence, indulging in alcohol and drugs as a teenager and then later in her twenties. "Yeah, well, it was sex that took me out of the house," she explained to Guy Trebay in Premiere. "I wanted to be a woman. Simple as that. I lived a certain kind of life, and I

Melanie Griffith and Don Johnson at the 1989 Academy Awards show, on which they presented the award for best supporting actress. Reuters/Bettmann Newsphotos.

don't live that life now. You grow up. You get tired of coming in stoned."

Griffith landed her first acting job in the film "Night Moves" by accident. As she told Myra Forsberg of the *New York Times:* "I thought it was a modeling job call. I had done commercials when I was little, but I didn't really want to act at all. Of course, I had watched my mother on the set, but I was too shy. And then I went into 'Night Moves' and I got hooked." *Newsweek's* Paul Zimmerman wrote that in the film Griffith seemed "disturbingly real as a wanton teen-ager," and Vincent Canby of the *New York Times* described "Night Moves" as "an elegant connundrum, a private-eye film that has its full share of duplicity, violence, and bizarre revelation." Also released in 1975, were Stuart Rosenberg's "The Drowning Pool" in which Griffith had a small role, and Michael Ritchie's "Smile," a satire of teenage beauty pageants in which Griffith had another small part playing a contestant described in the script as "hot, sweet, and dumb." Even at this stage of her career, Griffith was unhappy with the sexpot stereotype; as she explained to *Newsweek,* "Maybe it's because I was introduced to sex so early."

Despite Griffith's initial movie success in 1975, opportunities became slim for her. In 1977, she had small roles in the films "One on One," starring Robbie Benson and Annette O'Toole, and "Joyride," but she was not able to take her career beyond the first wave of success. She then played Tracy in ABC's "Carter Country," a situation comedy set in the South, during its second and final season in 1978–79. A low point was Robert Butler's "Underground Aces" in 1980, which directly borrowed from "Car Wash" in a story about the antics of hotel parking garage attendants.

At the urging of Steven Bauer—her second husband whom she married in 1983 and has divorced after giving birth to a son, Alexander, in 1985—Griffith moved to New York in 1980 to study acting with Stella Adler. She had realized she would never become the actress she wanted to be if she relied on instinct alone. She had tried to study with Adler when she was eighteen but found it too difficult. The second time proved successful, with Griffith also saying that she benefitted from the experience of living in New York City with little money.

Griffith's big break came when Brian de Palma cast her as Holly Body in "Body Double." Bauer had appeared in de Palma's "Scarface," and de Palma wanted Griffith to introduce him to her friend Jamie Lee Curtis, whom he wanted for the role of the porn star. Curtis was not available, but Griffith decided to pursue it. (She had to beat out real-life porn star Annette Havens for the role.) Griffith applied her lessons with Adler to her work in "Body Double," and the resulting critical plaudits gave her career new life. Vincent Canby in the *New York Times* described her as "a pretty, model-thin, absolutely up-front porn actress who has some of the comic candor of a contemporary Billie Dawn in a punk hairdo." She is, continued Canby, "the movie's real focal point" and "gives a perfectly controlled comic performance that successfully neutralizes all questions relating to plausibility." Jack Kroll in *Newsweek* wrote: "Melanie Griffith turns the porno actress into a vibrant delight. She has to strip, do a sinuous autoerotic dance, make love to herself and make wisecracks—all of which she does with the voice of a young Judy Holliday and the comic flair of a young Goldie Hawn . . . . Griffith makes the porno actress the warmest, most human character in the movie."

After seeing "Body Double," director Jonathan Demme offered Griffith the female lead in "Something Wild." The actress was excited about her first starring role and was flattered that she did not have to audition. As Audrey, a small-town Pennsylvania woman who reinvents herself as a Soho femme fatale named Lulu, Griffith is irresistible in her kinky sexuality and attraction to danger. She picks up a straightlaced yuppie executive named Charlie Driggs (Jeff Daniels) because she spots a trace of rebelliousness in him. Charlie is easily seduced by Lulu-Audrey who takes him to her high-school reunion after a series of sexual escapades and wild adventures that scare and fascinate the middle-class Charlie. At the reunion, they meet Audrey's husband, Ray, a psychopath who was just released from prison, and the film takes another turn—one that is unexpected and violent.

"Something Wild" was praised by the *New Yorker*'s Pauline Kael who was "struck by how authentically wild it is . . . . It's about crossing over—about getting high on anarchic, larcenous behavior and then being confronted with ruthless, sadistic criminality . . . . It breaks conventions and turns into a scary slapstick thriller." *Newsweek*'s David Ansen seconded this opinion, writing that Demme "finds new nuances in old formulas and wonderfully quirky textures as he journeys down some unfamiliar American back roads. Griffith's hard-drinking Lulu is more than just another fantasy free spirit. With her weather-beaten beauty, her little girl-voice, she's a poignant, schizoid creature, as melancholy as she is wild."

Griffith followed "Something Wild" with the female lead in an independently produced science fiction-action movie called "Cherry 2000" in which she played a "kind of Mad Maxine." The movie, she told Trebay, was "a disaster. It hasn't been released here, and I hope it never is."

In British director Mike Figgis's neo-film noir "Stormy Monday," a 1988 release set in contemporary Newcastle, Griffith plays Kate, an American from Minnesota controlled by Cosmo (Tommy Lee Jones), a shady American businessman who uses her as a sexual prize in his development deals. Rich in mood and style, "Stormy Monday" works because of Figgis's direction, which allows the four principle actors the freedom to be believable yet faithful to noir conventions. "The stellar Miss Griffith, with her sexy, singular blend of kittenishness and strength, is entirely at home here, making an irrevocably strong impression," wrote Janet Maslin in the *New York Times.* Figgis told Myra Forsberg: "Before Melanie came into the project, the character was much more cool and passive. Once she signed on, it was evident that the film became more about her. Before, the potential was always there for Kate to become a victim—to be a stereotype. But Melanie wouldn't let that happen."

In Mike Nichols's "Working Girl," Griffith plays Tess McGill, a Staten Island secretary who works for a Wall Street brokerage firm and ends up making the big deal. Here Griffith parallels her own personal transformation from a sex object to an intelligent, talented actress ready to compete and hold her own with the very best. "Working Girl" is about a woman who at thirty uses a single-mindedness of purpose to improve her career while retaining her humanity. One concern Nichols had with the script by Kevin Wade was that Tess's need to succeed might alienate the audience, but Griffith's Tess has a human warmth and gentleness that softens her determination. The film has a fable-like Cinderella quality with Tess, who has earned a degree at night school and takes voice lessons to overcome her accent, realizing that she must make her own success if she is going to get ahead. She learns that her boss, Katharine Parker (Sigourney Weaver), a cultivated Ivy League snob who has broken her leg on a ski trip, stole Tess's idea on a possible merger and acquisition strategy. Tess cuts her hair and uses Katharine's clothes and connections to pass herself off as an executive, initiating a merger deal and in the process stealing Katharine's business colleague and possible future husband, Jack Trainer (Harrison Ford).

"Working Girl" takes liberties with reality but succeeds as a modern update of 1930s screwball comedy with traces of a social message. Griffith combines Tess's feminine qualities with her business acumen in a winning performance that endears her to audiences. "Working Girl," wrote Janet Maslin in the *New York Times,* "derives a lot of its charm from the performance of Melanie Griffith, the baby-voiced bombshell who gives Tess an unbeatable mixture of street smarts, business sense and sex appeal." Terry Lawson, a film reviewer for the Cox Newspapers, added: "Even [Griffith's] fans will be surprised at the confidence she exudes in a showcase part. A great deal of the portrayal's power resides in her unique voice, which is able to convey the innate inadequacy invested in her social class with the equally innate desire to escape the box society has erected for her."

Griffith again became romantically involved with Don Johnson in the mid-1980's. She appeared in a 1987 episode of his "Miami Vice" television series, and he proposed to her on December 17, 1988, when she guest hosted "Saturday Night Live." They were remarried on June 26, 1989, at their ranch near Aspen, Colorado, and are expecting their first child.

Sources

American Film, March, 1988.
Cosmopolitan, July, 1987.
Dayton Daily News, December 21, 1988; December 25, 1988.
Interview, November, 1988.
Newsweek, August 4, 1975; November 10, 1986; October 24, 1988; January 2, 1989.
New Yorker, November 17, 1986.
New York Times, June 12, 1975; June 26, 1975; October 9, 1975; October 26, 1984; November 7, 1986; April 17, 1988; April 22, 1988; December 16, 1988; December 18, 1988.
People, May 9, 1988; February 27, 1989.
Premiere, December, 1988.
Rolling Stone, January 26, 1989.
Time, November 10, 1986; December 19, 1986; December 19, 1988.
Variety, December 14–20, 1988.
Vogue, October, 1986.

—Sidelights by Jon Saari

Florence Griffith Joyner

AP/Wide World Photos

Runner

Full name, Florence Delorez Griffith Joyner; born c. 1960, in Los Angeles, Calif.; daughter of Robert (an electronics technician) and Florence (a seamstress) Griffith; married Al Joyner (an athlete and coach), October 10, 1987. *Education:* Attended California State University—Northridge and University of California, Los Angeles.

Addresses: *Home*—Los Angeles, Calif.

Career

Began to compete in Sugar Ray Robinson Foundation track meets at the age of seven; set high school records in sprints and in the long jump; in college, won two National Collegiate Athletic Association (NCAA) titles; worked as a customer service representative for Union Bank and in an employee relations position for Anheuser-Busch; has also worked as a hair-dresser and nail stylist; competed in 1984 Summer Olympics in Los Angeles and in 1988 Summer Olympics in Seoul, South Korea. Set world record in 100-meter dash during 1988 Olympic trials; set world record in 200-meter race and Olympic record in 100-meter dash during 1988 Summer Olympics.

Awards: At 1984 Summer Olympics, won silver medal in 200-meter race; at 1988 Summer Olympics, won gold medals in 100-meter dash and 200-meter race, shared gold medal in 400-meter relay, and shared silver medal in 1600-meter relay.

Sidelights

The woman on the magazine cover is wearing shiny, red, high-heeled shoes over sheer, black hose stretched tightly over large, muscular calves and thighs. About halfway up the thighs is the hem of a red mini-dress that clings around her midsection. Just above the waistline, a strategically located hole in the dress reveals light brown skin, slightly more pale than that of her bare, muscular left arm, which bears a large bracelet on the wrist. The long, slender fingers of her left hand show two rings and long, shiny, red nails. The hand rests on the shoulder of a man in a blue, pin-striped suit. Her right arm is wrapped around his waist. The woman, with a string of white pearls hanging from her left ear lobe and long, brown, softly-curled hair cascading down her nearly bare shoulders, is gazing upward, as if entranced, at the face of the man, whose eyes face the camera. Her red-painted lips are parted in a frozen smile. Although this pose makes her appear to be comfortably subordinate to the man, she is, in fact, the star of this show. His name is Al Joyner, a track and field athlete of notable success and also a coach. Her name is Florence Griffith Joyner, the "greatest woman sprinter the world has ever seen," according to the *Washington Post.*

Griffith Joyner is the holder of two world records and was the winner of three gold medals and one silver medal at the Summer Olympics in Seoul, South Korea, in September of 1988. She announced her retirement in February of 1989 to pursue other commercial and entertainment careers. This magazine cover was *Ebony,* and this married couple was featured in an article entitled "Black Love: Ten most exciting couples." It was on the news stands for Valentine's Day, another pictorial manifestation of the continuing love affair between "Flojo," as she is known, and national magazines in the United States.

A few months before, *Sports Illustrated* showed her on its July 25, 1988, cover in more familiar surroundings: crossing the finish line, arms held high and extended as if in a "V" for victory, index fingers thrust upward as if to say "Number One." Next to her picture were the words: "Fastest Woman in the World." Again, her attire was remarkable. Instead of wearing a traditional track suit, Griffith Joyner was pictured wearing a blue top above white bikini bottoms over most unusual tights. The right leg was completely covered in blue fabric; the left leg was completely bare, except for the shoe on her foot. Magazine covers like her; she likes them. "I used to wonder what it would feel like to be on the cover of a magazine like Vogue or Essence," Griffith Joyner told the *New York Times.* "Now, when I see myself on those covers, it's a different feeling. It makes me happy."

"Happy" would be an appropriate word to describe Florence Griffith Joyner in early 1989. Her records spoke for themselves: During the Olympic trials in July of 1988, she shattered the world 100-meter record with a time of 10.49 seconds, .27 seconds better than the previous record held by Evelyn Ashford. During the Olympic games in Seoul that September, she won the gold medal in the 200-meter race with a world-record time of 21.34. About 90 minutes earlier, her time of 21:56 had broken the previous world record of 21.71, held by East Germany's Marita Koch. Although she didn't set any records in the 100-meter finals, she settled for a gold medal in 10:54. It wasn't an Olympic record because wind-measuring devices determined that the breeze behind her was over the allowable limit. But her 10.62 in the quarter-finals stands as the Olympic record. She shared a gold medal with three United States teammates in the 400-meter relay, won over East Germany and the Soviet Union in a time of 41.98. She shared a silver medal with three other teammates in the 1,600-meter relay, won by the Soviet Union in a world and Olympic record time of 3:15.18.

When it came to capitalizing on the winning of precious medals, others spoke for her. "She's great-looking, wears colorful costumes and is a personality," Evangeline M. Hayes, director of talent at J. Walter Thompson advertising in New York, told the *New York Times.* In the same article, Daisy Sinclair, vice president and head of casting for a New York advertising agency, said: "She happens to be a character of sorts. That's where the appeal is." During the Olympics, the rules forced her to wear more conventional track suits. But she remained distinctive for her long nails, painted in a variety of patterns, including one with polka dots and another with the world "GOLD" in gold on a blue background. "Florence Griffith Joyner, the body in Seoul, always plays fair," *Los Angeles Times columnist* Mike Downey wrote in the *Sporting News.* "It's just that if you leave your lane, those three-inch fingernails might claw you. Joyner is the only runner in the world nobody wants to hand a baton to—for reasons of personal safety."

Although few American Olympians were in demand for commercial endorsements after the 1988 Games, it seemed as if Griffith Joyner would be the exception. In February of 1989, the *New York Times* published a story that suggested that Griffith Joyner would make more money by turning down offers to run in races and accepting more lucrative offers for endorsing products and from the entertainment industry. Her agent, Gordon Baskin, was quoted as saying she would appear in only about five outdoor meets in 1989; that was less than a month before Griffith Joyner announced her retirement from track.

"Baskin has negotiated or is negotiating about 10 major deals that could generate as much as $3 million for her by the end of the year," said a *New York Times* story by Michael Janofsky. "They include contracts with Coca-Cola to do advertisements, commercials and personal appearances; IBM to head an in-house incentive program, Mitsubishi to promote video products, M.C.A. Corporation to develop a Flojo doll and a film studio that has given her a script to consider." The article also said Baskin had spoken to producer Norman Lear about a TV series around a fictional character Griffith Joyner had developed for children's stories: a 7-year-old boy named Barry Bam Bam. "I would say she is the first black female American athlete to be able to come into something like this," Baskin told the *Times.* Advertising executives have nicknamed her "Cash Flo."

Her personality seemed to explode on the national scene during her triumphant season of 1988. But as is the case with many "overnight sensations," she had worked many years to become a success. And she was part of a unique family in American track, a dynamic duo of sorts—or perhaps a quartet. Her sister-in-law, Jackie Joyner-Kersee, won two gold medals in Seoul, the first with a world record in the heptathlon, the second in the long jump. Florence is married to Jackie's brother; Jackie's husband is Florence's former coach.

Griffith Joyner, from a family of 11 children, was raised in housing projects in Los Angeles. Her father, Robert, was an electronics technician. Her mother, Florence, a seamstress. "We learned something from how we grew up," Griffith Joyner told the *Sporting News*. "It has never been easy, and we knew it wouldn't be handed to us, unless we went after it." According to the same article, Griffith Joyner trained three times a day and used weights.

Long before her one-legged track suits, Griffith Joyner had shown other eccentricities. In kindergarten, she would braid her hair with one braid sticking straight up. As a child, she wore her pet boa constrictor like a necklace. She read a lot and wrote poetry. At the age of 7, she began to compete in foot races at the Sugar Ray Robinson Youth Foundation. She graduated from Jordan High in Los Angeles in 1978 with school records in the sprints and the long jump. She attended Cal State—Northridge and worked as a bank teller. A young track coach named Bobby Kersee (he later married Jackie Joyner) helped Griffith apply for financial aid. According to a *Sports Illustrated* profile, Griffith Joyner reluctantly followed Kersee to UCLA when he took an assistant coaching job there in 1980. "I had a 3.25 grade point average in business [at Cal State—Northridge], but UCLA didn't even offer my major," she told *Sports Illustrated*. "I had to switch to psychology. But my running was starting up, and I knew that Bobby was the best coach for me. So—it kind of hurts to say this—I chose athletics over academics."

In 1982, she ran the 200 meters in 22.39 for the NCAA championship. She was showing potential in

Florence Griffith Joyner (left) celebrates after winning the gold medal in the women's 100-meter dash at the Summer Olympics in Seoul, South Korea, 1988. AP/Wide World Photos.

the 400. In the 1984 Olympics at Los Angeles, she finished second to teammate Valerie Brisco-Hooks in the 200 meter race. After that, she cut back on training and competition. She worked as a bank secretary and as a hair-dresser and nail stylist, developing elaborate styles of braiding hair and painting long nails. She broke off a wedding engagement with hurdler Greg Foster and then became close to Al Joyner, who had won the gold medal in the triple jump at the Summer Games in 1984. (They had met in the 1980 Olympic trials). By this time, Al Joyner's sister, Jackie, had married Kersee. On October 10, 1987, Florence Griffith married Al Joyner in Las Vegas, and they appeared on the television show "The Newlywed Game."

Nine months later, after setting the world record in the 100, Griffith announced that her husband would replace Bob Kersee as her coach. "The problems were multifold, Griffith Joyner said," according to a *Detroit Free Press* article. "She compared training with Kersee to 'Los Angeles International Airport on the track, everybody lined up to take off.' She said she had been using Kersee-designed workouts, but she trained with Bobby only two or three times a week." Although their relationships have evolved, both couples remained close friends, according to several articles written about them during the Olympics. A minor controversy kept them united when Griffith Joyner and Joyner-Kersee had to defend their reputations against rumors that they had used anabolic steroids.

The discovery of steroids—drugs that help build muscles—had caused the disqualification of Canadian sprinter Ben Johnson and the forfeiture of his gold medal in the 100-meter dash. Johnson failed a urine test. Both women passed their urine tests and resented suggestions that their muscle and ability had been enhanced by factors aside from vigorous training. Griffith Joyner is five feet, six and one-half inches tall and weighs 130 pounds; many pictures of her running seem to show large, well-developed muscles. "I know what the rumors are about me and they are not true," Griffith Joyner told the Washington Post. "I have never used drugs. I will never use drugs and I don't need to use drugs. They can come and test me every week of the year." Brazilian runner Joaquim Cruz had fueled the debate when, according to the *Detroit Free Press,* he said in a television interview: "Florence in 1984 was an extremely feminine person. But today she looks more like a man than a woman." In the same article, Al Joyner was quoted as responding, "If Cruz says my wife looks like a man, evidently he hasn't seen my wife."

Sources

Detroit Free Press, September 4, 1988; September 30, 1988.

Ebony, February, 1989.

Ms., October, 1988.

Newsweek, August 1, 1988; September 19, 1988.

New York Times, July 18, 1988; September 30, 1988; October 27, 1988; February 1, 1989.

People, August 29, 1988.

Sports Illustrated, July 25, 1988; special Summer Olympics preview issue, September, 1988; September 14, 1988; October 3, 1988; October 10, 1988; December 19, 1988; December 26, 1988.

Sporting News, October 10, 1988; October 17, 1988; February 23, 1989.

Time, September 19, 1988.

Washington Post, September 30, 1988.

—Sidelights by Joe LaPointe

Gene Hackman

AP/Wide World Photos

Actor

Full name, Eugene Alden Hackman; born January 30, 1931 (some sources say 1930), in San Bernadino, Calif; son of Eugene Ezra Hackman (a newspaper press operator); married Fay Maltese, January 1, 1956 (divorced); children: Christopher, Elizabeth, Leslie. *Education:* Studied journalism at University of Illinois; attended radio performance school and took art courses at Art Students League, New York City; studied acting at Pasadena Playhouse.

Addresses: *Home*—Santa Fe, N.M. *Office*—c/o Barry Haldeman, Haldeman & Peckerman, 9595 Wilshire Blvd., Suite 700, Beverly Hills, Calif. 90212.

Career

Worked at various jobs in New York City, 1956–58, including doorman, truck driver, and shoe salesman; appeared Off-Broadway in "Chaparral," 1958; other stage appearances include "The Saintliness of Margery Kempe," 1959, "Children from Their Games," 1963, "A Rainy Day in Newark," 1963, "Any Wednesday," 1964, "Poor Richard," 1964, and "The Natural Look," 1967. Television appearances include several roles on "U.S. Steel Hour," 1959–62, guest appearances on "The Defenders," 1961 and 1963, "Trials of O'Brien," 1966, "Hawk," 1966, "The F.B.I.," 1967, "The Invaders," 1967, "Iron Horse," 1967, "I Spy," 1968, and "Rowan and Martin's Laugh In,"; also made-for-television movie "Shadow on the Land."

Feature films include "Mad Dog Coll," 1961, "Lilith," 1964, "A Covenant with Death," 1966, "Hawaii," 1966, "Bonnie and Clyde," 1967, "Banning," 1967, "First to Fight," 1967, "The Split," 1968, "Riot!," 1969, "The Gypsy Moths," 1969, "Marooned," 1969, "Downhill Racer," 1969, "Doctors' Wives," 1971, "The French Connection," 1971, "Cisco Pike," 1971, "The Poseiden Adventure," 1972, "Prime Cut," 1972, "Scarecrow," 1973, "The Conversation," 1974, "Young Frankenstein," 1974, "Zandy's Bride," 1974, "The French Connection II," 1975, "Bite the Bullet," 1975, "Night Moves," 1975, "Lucky Lady," 1975, "A Bridge Too Far," 1977, "The Hunting Party," 1977, "The Domino Principle," 1977, "March or Die," 1977, "Superman," 1978, "Superman II," 1981, "All Night Long," 1981, "Reds," 1981, "Eureka," 1983, "Under Fire," 1983, "Two of a Kind," 1983, "Uncommon Valor," 1983, "Misunderstood," 1984, "Target," 1985, "Twice in a Lifetime," 1985, "Power," 1986, "Hoosiers," 1986, "No Way Out," 1987, "Superman IV," 1987, "Kid Gloves," 1988, "Mississippi Burning," 1988, "Full Moon in Blue Water," 1988, "Bat 21," 1988, "Split Decision," 1988, and "Another Woman," 1988.

Member: Actors' Equity Association, Screen Actors Guild, American Federation of Television and Radio

Artists, Academy of Motion Picture Arts and Sciences.

Awards: Clarence Derwent Award for most promising new actor, 1963; Academy Award nomination for best supporting actor, 1968, for "Bonnie and Clyde"; Academy Award for best actor, National Association of Theatre Owners Star of the Year Award, New York Film Critics Award, Golden Globe Award, and British Academy Award, all 1971, for "The French Connection"; British Academy Award, 1972, for "The Poseidon Adventure"; Cannes Film Festival Award, 1973, for "Scarecrow"; New York Film Critics Award nomination for best actor, 1975, for "The Conversation"; has received several other Academy Award nominations for best actor and best supporting actor.

Sidelights

Gene Hackman is no matinee idol. His hairline is receding, he is gray and slightly paunchy, and his features seem pulled from a longshoreman's pub. Hackman is, nevertheless, one of Hollywood's busiest stars, a hardworking actor who has appeared in well over fifty films since 1964. "Hackman may not always be the favored choice among studio executives concerned with box-office draw," wrote Nina J. Easton in the *Los Angeles Times.* "But he is a clear favorite among critics, directors and fellow actors. Even when he makes bad movies—and critics . . . say he has made plenty of those—Hackman invariably receives praise for his performance . . . . He is known as an 'actor's actor.'"

Hackman has never flinched from the sort of character roles shunned by some leading men. He is willing to portray an American "everyman," blue-collar, sometimes uneducated, and decidedly ordinary. "Why the high demand for a Gene Hackman?" asked *Newsday* reporter Mike McGrady. "The qualities he brings to a movie, or an interview, are as rare in Hollywood as calluses. He seems unaffected. He also seems decent, well-meaning, responsible, tough and earnest. He brings two invaluable qualities to any movie: likability and believability." Hackman, who was nominated for an Academy Award for his 1988 film "Mississippi Burning," is no stranger to prestigious awards. He won his first Oscar in 1971 for "The French Connection" and has been nominated as best actor and best supporting actor several other times. A *Time* commentator concluded that Hackman's success proves "what all actors yearn to believe: a nice, hard-working guy can still get ahead in the movies on his merits."

Eugene Alden Hackman was born in 1931 in California. While he was still young his parents moved back to Danville, Illinois, where his father and grandfather were both local journalists. In a *Los Angeles Times* interview, Hackman admitted that his childhood was not a happy one. He endured beatings and other punishments from his father and escaped when he could into a fantasy world fueled by the deeds of matinee movie heroes. "If you have some kind of disturbed childhood," he said, "you go into [acting] to exorcise that, to point out who you are . . . . When I'm given a role that has a lot of darkness in it, it appeals to me. I soak right into that." Hackman's father deserted the family when the boy was thirteen, and just three years later Hackman himself lied about his age and enlisted in the Marines. He missed World War II by several years, but he did serve in China, Hawaii and Japan, eventually becoming a disc jockey and newscaster for his unit's radio station.

Several times Hackman was promoted in the Marines, then demoted again for insubordination. Easton described him as a "surly, angry young man who never released steam from the volcano burning inside." After his 1952 discharge from the service, Hackman journeyed to New York City, where he worked at a succession of odd jobs. According to a *Time* reporter, Hackman was working as a doorman at a Howard Johnson's restaurant in Times Square when, one night, his former Marine captain walked by. "Their eyes met in awkward recognition," the reporter wrote. "The captain looked him up and down and sneered: 'Hackman, you're a sorry son of a bitch.'" That rude encounter galvanized Hackman into action. Although he had never considered a career on the stage, he joined The Premise, an Off-Broadway troupe, "simply to get some meaning into his life," to quote the *Time* correspondent.

While still in his twenties, Hackman went to California and joined the Pasadena Playhouse, where he met another young performer, Dustin Hoffman. Ironically, both men were asked to leave the group after a short time; McGrady noted that they were voted "least likely to succeed" because they "lacked promise." On their own again, Hackman and Hoffman returned to New York, where they became friends with a third struggling actor, Robert Duvall. Each one of them fought desperately against bankruptcy—Hackman by that time had a wife and three children to support.

Hackman's earliest roles were in Off-Broadway plays, most of which closed after short runs. In his Broadway debut at the Morosco Theatre he appeared as Charles Widgin Rochambeau in Irwin Shaw's

"Children from Their Games." The play folded after four performances, but Hackman earned the Clarence Derwent Award as the most promising new actor of the 1963 season. The next year he found more success with "Any Wednesday," in which he portrayed Cass Henderson, a proper businessman who falls in love with a free-spirited woman. Hackman also took roles in television dramas, including the "U.S. Steel Hour," "The Defenders," "CBS Playhouse," "I Spy," and "The F.B.I." His first notable film appearance came in 1964, when he took a small part in "Lilith," the story of life in a mental institution. That project brought him to the attention of Warren Beatty, who was casting the movie "Bonnie and Clyde." A virtual unknown, Hackman was given the role of Buck Barrow, Clyde's affable, bumbling brother. "Bonnie and Clyde" was released in 1967 and took in a staggering $22 million box office gross. Many critics singled out Hackman as the film's strongest performer, and he was nominated for an Oscar as best supporting actor.

Hackman was never again out of work after "Bonnie and Clyde" introduced him to Hollywood's producers. He quickly gained a reputation as an actor who was willing to work hard and fast on any film—if the price was right. A *Time* reporter noted that Hackman tended to grab any role, unselectively, and therefore "bogged down in a mire of forgettable films." Easton elaborated: "During the 1970s Hackman turned down major roles in 'Ordinary People' and 'Apocalypse Now' because the compensation wasn't high enough. But he accepted roles in such forgettable films as 'Lucky Lady' (for which he received more than $1.35 million) and 'March or Die.' . . . Associates say Hackman is prolific because of his love of the work; they also cite financial reasons." Hackman himself has been unapologetic about his willingness to take work of less than top calibre. "You have to recognize that there's a monster out there called unemployment," he told *Time* in 1972. However prolific he became, though, Hackman continued to attract critical attention, and good roles came to him along with the bad. In 1970 he earned his second best supporting actor nomination for the drama "I Never Sang for My Father," which cast him as an unhappy, put-upon son opposite a cranky Melvin Douglas.

The part that solidified his fame came in 1972—that of Popeye Doyle, the tough New York detective in "The French Connection." Hackman was the fourth choice for Popeye Doyle, behind such unlikely candidates as Jackie Gleason, Peter Boyle, and Jimmy Breslin. Even when he did receive the role he had great difficulty making the character forceful enough. "I have a tendency to underplay," he told *Newsweek*, "but Popeye was not a guy I could do that with. Then, one day, I heard his voice. . . . That voice I heard belonged to the drill sergeant. I had known that voice from five years I spent in the Marines. It helped." Indeed, finding the voice helped so much that Hackman won an Academy Award for his work as Popeye.

"When I'm given a role that has a lot of darkness in it, it appeals to me. I soak right into that."

He could have rested on his laurels at that point, but the memories of financial struggle were still with him, so he continued making movies at his regular hectic pace. He was very disappointed when two films, "Scarecrow" and "The Conversation," did poor business at the box office and failed to win any nominations for him. He told the *Los Angeles Times* that the role of the tormented surveillance expert in "The Conversation" was his favorite among all he had done. "He appealed to a lot of things in me," Hackman said, "a sort of malaise I have in me, a sort of darkness, a suspiciousness and paranoia." After those two movies performed poorly, Hackman decided to go completely mainstream; he willingly accepted work in such blockbusters as "The Poseidon Adventure," "Superman," and "Superman II," appearing in the latter two as arch-villain Lex Luthor.

Hard as it is to imagine, given the difference between Hackman and such muscle-bound film idols as Sylvester Stallone and Arnold Schwarzenegger, Hackman was among the first actors to star in a pure action-adventure film about Vietnam, "Uncommon Valor." In that film, Hackman led a band of soldier-of-fortune commandos into the jungle to liberate some American prisoners held there. In 1985 Hackman made another action film, "Target," in which he and Matt Dillon played a father and son caught in a web of international espionage. More recently Hackman told *Newsday* that he does not plan to appear in any more action movies. "I'm much less interested in adventure films. I don't have the need to play in them anymore," he said. "I don't have the need anymore to play movie actor. I'm really interested in just doing the acting. . . . There are roles that are movie-star roles and other roles that are pure acting roles. I don't need the movie-star roles."

Apparently Hackman does need to keep working, however. He has not slowed his pace, often appearing in as many as four films per year. Another Hackman favorite is "Hoosiers," a low-key movie released in 1986. In that film Hackman portrayed an ostracized college coach who gains new self-respect by leading a small-town basketball team to the state championships. "I liked that character," Hackman told *Newsday*. "He had a lot of different colors to him. He wasn't a real winner, right from the beginning. There was some kind of redemption involved."

"Mississippi Burning" returned Hackman to a character similar to Popeye Doyle—a weathered F.B.I. agent used to using muscle and tough talk to extract information. Although Hackman admits that he likes to play more sophisticated roles—"characters with, well, a little class"—he is comfortable as well with the more surly, more ordinary parts that often earn him his highest acclaim. "That's all pretty valid, you know. The blue-collar stuff," he told *Newsday*. "I'm fairly accessible to people." Hackman may have been referring to his accessibility offscreen, but most critics agree that his onscreen appeal lies in just that quality—the way viewers can identify with his vulnerability. A *Time* reporter stated that Hackman "has become one of the most gifted of character actors, a sublime technician for whom no inward emotion is too big to be fixed firmly in the smallest outward detail." Orion Films executive vice-president Mike Medavoy told the *Los Angeles Times* that Hackman has "an ease, a naturalness on screen.... He's an everyman. He brings a sense of reality to a film."

In what little spare time he has, Hackman lives quietly in Santa Fe, New Mexico. He likes to draw and paint and to spend time with his three children (he is recently divorced). Hackman is famous for *not* taking vacations; with the exception of a short period between 1977 and 1980, he has worked constantly. "I'm still learning," he told *Newsday*. "Maybe not so much technique anymore. But I'm learning how to use myself, how to make the best of my time. Much of the time early on [was] spent in self-conscious behavior, kind of destructive. I'm trying now to find a way I can be as artistic as I can in my work. And still be able to get along with everyone around. It's very, very hard." Commenting on his craft in *Newsweek*, Hackman concluded: "It isn't the life-style I care so much about. It's that moment when you do a scene and things are right. It's when something happens, maybe a word or a look from another actor. Maybe it's a way of saying something in a way no one else has ever said it before."

Sources

Film Comment, December, 1988.
Los Angeles Times, December 12, 1988.
Newsday, February 22, 1987.
Newsweek, May 1, 1972.
Time, April 24, 1972; January 9, 1989.

—Sidelights by Mark Kram

Jessica Hahn

AP/Wide World Photos

Media personality

Born in 1960 in Massapequa, Long Island, New York; daughter of Jessica Hahn; stepdaughter of Eddie Moylan. *Education:* Graduated from high school in Massapequa, N.Y.

Addresses: *Office*—c/o KOY-FM Radio, Phoenix, Ariz.

Career

Former church secretary in Long Island, N.Y.; became radio personality for KOY-FM Radio, Phoenix, Ariz.; also appeared in music video "Wild Thing," 1988.

Sidelights

"I was tired of being seen as some kind of slut or seducer," Jessica Hahn is quoted in a *Newsweek* article. The former church secretary was referring to the scandal surrounding her encounter with fundamentalist televangelist preacher Jim Bakker, best known as the founder of the PTL television network. The story, which broke in 1987, rocked the media. It portrayed a night in a Florida hotel room in 1980, when Hahn, at age 20 and "almost unimaginally naive, had been sexually abused . . . by Bakker and John Fletcher, another PTL minister, and [then] accepted a settlement of $265,000 for her silence," as a *People* article relates.

The furor over the disclosed information forced Bakker and his wife, Tammy, off the air and lost them control of PTL. Hahn, on the other hand, proceeded into the public eye with a surprising twist. While proclaiming her innocence ("I've been treated as less than human, as a thing, as a pawn," she told Paul Nowell in a wire story reprinted in the *Detroit Free Press*), Hahn emerged in the pages of *Playboy*, floating nude on a raft in a now-famous pictorial feature. She also granted that magazine a pair of extensive interviews in which she denied charges of blackmail. Instead, she insists she was a pawn in a power game run between Bakker and would-be PTL honcho Jerry Falwell.

As for the hush money, "I wasn't going to talk," Hahn tells *Playboy*. "Why would I talk? The PTL had no reason to shut me up. All they needed to do was to go back to where they started from and hush *their* people. All the people that Jim Bakker complained and cried to were the ones they needed to hush up, not Jessica Hahn."

Hahn eventually dropped out of the PTL scandal, while the Bakkers and Falwell continued to fight for leadership of the organization (Falwell finally did gain control, while the Bakkers vowed to start anew with their own television series.) In her new incarnation, Hahn aligned herself not only with *Playboy* (she was a frequent guest of publisher Hugh Hefner at the Playboy mansion, underwent cosmetic surgery, and posed for the magazine a second time), but also with a host of other cutting-edge figures, most notably the hostile, screaming comic Sam Kinison, whom Hahn briefly dated, and in whose music-video "Wild Thing" Hahn appears.

More recently, Hahn tried her hand as a radio disc jockey, working for a station in Phoenix, Arizona. On her debut she "read the horoscope and some Hollywood gossip in an enthusiastic, well-modulated voice and was on for a total of less than ten minutes," according to a *People* reporter. Nonetheless, fellow disc jockey Glenn Beck "pronounced her 'awesome.'"

When asked in the *Playboy* interview sessions what advice she would have for a young woman considering getting involved with a fundamentalist, evangelical ministry, Hahn offers: "Worship the way you want to, not the way the preachers tell you to. Have a relationship with God, not God's representatives. Realize that preachers are only a vessel, only a tool. And don't be misled, don't put your life in their hands, as I did."

Sources

Detroit Free Press, September 23, 1987.
Newsweek, October 12, 1987.
New York Times, June 13, 1987; October 21, 1987; January 4, 1988.
People, October 5, 1987; September 12, 1988.
Playboy, December, 1987.

—Sketch by Susan Salter

Tom Hanks

AP/Wide World Photos

Actor

Born July 9, 1956, in Concord, Calif.; son of an itinerant cook; married Samantha Lewes (an actress and producer), 1978 (divorced, 1985); married Rita Wilson (an actress), April, 1988; children: (first marriage) one son, one daughter. *Education:* Studied acting at California State University, Sacramento.

Addresses: *Home*—Brentwood, Calif. *Agent*—Mike Simpson, William Morris Agency, 151 El Camino Dr., Beverly Hills, Calif. 90212.

Career

Began acting in college productions; interned at Great Lakes Theater Festival, Cleveland, Ohio, 1976–78; worked as an actor in New York City, 1978–80; co-star of television series "Bosom Buddies," 1980–82. Feature films include "He Knows You're Alone," 1981, "Mazes and Monsters," 1982, "Splash," 1984, "Bachelor Party," 1984, "The Man With One Red Shoe," 1985, "Volunteers," 1985, "Nothing in Common," 1986, "The Money Pit," 1986, "Every Time We Say Goodbye," 1986, "Dragnet 1987," 1987, "Big," 1988, "Punchline," 1988, and "The 'Burbs," 1989.

Member: Actors' Equity Association, Screen Actors Guild, American Federation of Television and Radio Artists.

Sidelights

How has Tom Hanks been able to do it? How has the star of such mediocre films as "Volunteers," "The Money Pit," and "The Man With One Red Shoe" been able to not only survive but develop into one of Hollywood's most bankable stars? Here, after all, is a leading man who refers to himself as having "a goofy nose and geeky body," but who others have referred to as a modern day Cary Grant. Despite the negative reviews of some of his films, Hanks has usually risen above the criticism by turning in quality performances. His main attraction seems to be an ability to play a role most average people find comfortable to watch. And the looks that he finds "goofy" others find charming. "I don't think I'm ugly," Hanks told *Rolling Stone,* "but I do sometimes look in the mirror and say, 'What is with these lips?'"

Nevertheless, in many of his films, it's Hanks who gets the girl. In "Splash," Hanks falls in love with beautiful mermaid Darryl Hannah [see index for *Newsmakers* entry]; in "Volunteers," a gorgeous Smith College valedictorian (played by Rita Wilson, whom he later married) revels in glorious sex with him; in "Nothing in Common" he is torn between two beautiful women and has already dallied with a pretty stewardess barely before the credits have left the screen. "I think it's because there are a lot of writers who aren't very attractive but who are fairly funny and want to have sex a lot so they write about these guys who are not very attractive, but they're funny and do have sex a lot," Hanks told *New York* magazine, "so I guess I'm the chief beneficiary of that. It's not like I say, 'I'd like to do this movie... but I've got to have sex more often!'"

But as director Penny Marshall ("Big") told *Rolling Stone*, "He has that handsomeness that isn't too beautiful. It's approachable. I think he's adorable." Oddly enough, one of Hanks's endearing qualities is that he looks unextraordinary. "I guess I have that quality," Hanks told *New York*, "of being like everybody else." And to *Rolling Stone*, he added, "I guess I come off in movies as a guy who you wouldn't mind hanging around with."

But Hanks is being unnecessarily modest. Although he's honed an average-wise-guy persona into a Hollywood commodity, he is anything but average. "There is nothing normal about the guy," Peter Scolari, Hanks's co-star in the television sitcom "Bosom Buddies," told *Rolling Stone*. "He is an imaginative, eccentric individual. He's a very quirky, very unusual young man."

That wasn't obvious from the outset. As a child, Hanks experienced a nomadic, middle-class life with neither ambition nor talent much in evidence. He was born in Concord, California. By the time he was five, his parents had separated. They remarried several times before divorcing for good. His father later married an Asian woman with a large family. "Everybody in my family likes each other," Hanks told *Rolling Stone*. "But there were always about fifty people at the house. I didn't exactly feel like an outsider, but I was sort of outside of it." When his parents divorced, Hanks, his older brother Larry, and his sister went off with their father, an itinerant cook who rambled through various cities until settling in Oakland when Tom was eight. His younger brother stayed with his mother.

In school Hanks also was unremarkable. "I was a geek, a spaz," he told *Rolling Stone*. "I was horribly, painfully, terribly shy. At the same time, I was the guy who'd yell out funny captions during filmstrips. But I didn't get into trouble. I was always a real good kid and pretty responsible." Although he acted in a few school plays, the names of which he says he can't remember, acting never seemed a real possibility until Hanks transferred from a Bay Area junior college to California State University at Sacramento. "Acting classes looked like the best place for a guy who liked to make a lot of noise and be rather flamboyant," Hanks told *New York*. "I spent a lot of time going to plays. I wouldn't take dates with me. I'd just drive to a theater, buy myself a ticket, sit in the seat and read the program, and then get into the play completely. I spent a lot of time like that, seeing Brecht, Tennessee Williams, Ibsen and all that."

It was during these acting classes that Hanks met Vincent Dowling, head of the Great Lakes Theater Festival in Cleveland. At Dowling's suggestion, Hanks became an intern at the Festival, which stretched into a three year experience that covered everything from lighting to set design to stage managing. Such a commitment required that Hanks drop out of college. But by the end of the three years he had decided he wanted to become an actor. Part of the bug was due to the Cleveland Critics Circle Award, which he won as best actor for his performance as Proteus in "Two Gentlemen of Verona," one of the few times he played a villian.

"I don't think I'm ugly, but I do sometimes look in the mirror and say, 'What is with these lips?'"

In 1978 he moved to New York, where he married actress-producer Samantha Lewes. Seven years and a son and daughter later they were divorced, but Hanks still sees his children regularly. While in New York, Hanks acted for the Riverside Shakespeare Company. In addition, he made his film debut in a low-budget slasher movie and got a small part in a television movie entitled "Mazes & Monsters." He continued to audition around and finally landed an ABC pilot called "Bosom Buddies."

"It was flukesville," Hanks told *Newsweek*. Hanks flew to Los Angeles, where he was teamed with Peter Scolari as a pair of young ad men forced to dress as women so they could live in an inexpensive all-female hotel. The series ran for two seasons, and although the ratings were never strong, television critics gave the program high marks. "The first day I saw him on the set," the show's co-producer, Ian Praiser, told *Rolling Stone*, "I thought, 'Too bad he won't be in television for long.' I knew he'd be a movie star in two years." But if Praiser knew it, he wasn't able to convince Hanks. "The television show had come out of nowhere," Hanks's best friend, Tom Lizzio, told *Rolling Stone*. "Then out of nowhere it got canceled. He figured he'd be back to pulling ropes and hanging lights in a theater."

But it was "Bosom Buddies" that drew director Ron Howard ("Willow") to contact Hanks. Howard was working on "Splash," a fantasy/adventure about a mermaid who falls in love with a human. At first, Howard considered Hanks for the role of the lover's wise cracking brother, a role which eventually went to John Candy [see index for *Newsmakers* entry]. Hanks instead got the lead and an incredible career boost from "Splash," which went on to become a box-office blockbuster, grossing more than $100 million.

Hanks's next three films were weak. But with his role in "Nothing in Common"—about a young man alienated from his parents who must re-establish a relationship with his father, played by Jackie Gleason—Hanks had begun to establish credentials of not only a comic actor, but as someone who could carry a serious role. "It changed my desires about working in movies," Hanks told *Rolling Stone.* "Part of it was the nature of the material, what we were trying to say. But besides that, it focused on people's relationships. The story was about a guy and his father, unlike, say, 'The Money Pit,' where the story is really about a guy and his house."

Hanks's next two films—"Big" and "Punchline"—have also been successful, not only at the box office but within the industry for establishing Hanks as a major Hollywood talent. "It's not easy being successful in this town," his friend Scolari told *Rolling Stone,* "particularly for a man of conscious. You get fed a steady diet of adulation. You get fed things that aren't necessarily bad or poisonous or toxic in any way. But they're not really on your meal plan. You have to stop and say, 'Wait a minute—I didn't order this.' You have to take your life by the horns. You have responsibilities that have nothing to do with being an actor. Tom Hanks has dealt with his success. I have never known him to be happier."

Despite his successes, Hanks has the fear that it is all elusive; that somehow it will not last. In 1987 alone, for example, Hanks made three films—"Dragnet," "Punchline" and "Big"—an effort that left him so weak he caught pneumonia and had to spend a month recuperating. "I don't view myself as particularly successful," he told *Rolling Stone.* "I think of myself as lucky. I still work from the same set of insecurities as I always did. You know, do people really like me, and when will it all end?"

Inordinately defensive about keeping his private life private, Hanks does not let reporters into his Brentwood home and refuses to discuss his personal life except in the most general terms. It's not only with reporters. Hanks admits he has a tough time divulging bits of his personal life to anyone. "Volunteers" director Nicholas Meyer told *Newsweek:* "If you come on a set every morning and you say to the other person, 'How are you?' and he says 'Swinging,' there's no place for the conversation to go. He used to utterly confound me. He was always very professional; there was nothing you could fault; he would do anything you'd ask him, but he wasn't prepared to reveal himself as a human being."

Hanks doesn't disagree. "I think that for the most part I'm a somewhat shy and retiring guy," he explained to *Newsweek.* "I don't wear an awful lot of my emotions on my sleeve and I don't have any overriding passions that force me into other people's lives, so I probably pull back when anybody tries to do that to me. I think part of it might be because when I was growing up, we moved around an awful lot, so we didn't have an awful lot of friends around us that we knew really well. We were always taking off. I don't think it's part of my mental makeup to completely open myself up to people I know."

"There is nothing normal about the guy. He is an imaginative, eccentric individual."
—Peter Scolari

But close vested isn't necessarily nasty. It's merely private. Hanks is generally known as one of the nicer talents around Hollywood. But when he is not shooting, he is private. "Did you ever watch the TV show, 'Then Came Bronson?'" he asked *Rolling Stone,* explaining his loner ways. "Michael Parks as Jim Bronson—now that guy I honestly wanted to emulate. I wanted to be a friendly guy on a motorcycle who gave everybody a fair shake and yet always rode out of town at the end of the hour."

And as privacy is not nastiness, neither has Hanks turned popularity into arrogance. "I have other friends in that stratosphere and they're just not quite with us folk," Scolari told *Newsweek.* "Hanks has his head on his shoulders. He's always been a bit of a square. Two beers and you have to peel him off the ceiling. I see that as square; he hasn't developed adult sophistication." When his movie "Big" hit stride, director Joe Dante said he never saw a whit of change in Hanks's personality. "I remember he had to go to a 'Big' party during the shoot and he didn't look comfortable about it," Dante told *Newsweek.* "He wanted to get back to work."

"Punchline" director David Seltzer agrees. "I've seen so many actors lose access to that wonderful personal thing when they become arrogant," he told *Newsweek*. "Tom is humble, and I think humility is the key to an actor's success in film—you just see it right on their faces when they've become arrogant or self-important." But so as not to think Hanks's next role will be that of a saint, or a biography of Pope John Paul, Scolari offers this final view for *Newsweek:* "Oh, did I mention that he strangles kittens? One a day."

Sources

Boxoffice, September, 1986.
Chicago Tribune, July 27, 1986; May 29, 1988.
Cosmopolitan, July, 1985; March, 1987.
Esquire, March, 1987.
Film Comment, August, 1985.
Harper's Bazaar, December, 1985.
Ladies Home Journal, April, 1987.
Life, April, 1987.
Maclean's, March 19, 1984.
Mademoiselle, November, 1986.
Newsweek, August 26, 1985; August 18, 1986; July 13, 1987; September 26, 1988.
New York, March 12, 1984; July 28, 1986.
New Yorker, November 19, 1984, September 8, 1986.
New York Times, April 26, 1987.
People, April 9, 1984; August 26, 1985; August 11, 1986; August 29, 1988.
Playboy, October, 1984.
Rolling Stone, September 25, 1986; June 30, 1988.
Seventeen, August, 1985.
Teen, March, 1984.
Time, September 9, 1985; June 6, 1988.
Vogue, August, 1985.

—Sketch by Stephen Advokat

Barbara Harris

Episcopal bishop

Full name, Barbara Clementine Harris; born 1930, in Philadelphia, Pa.; married 1960 (divorced, 1965). *Education:* Graduated from Charles Morris Price School of Advertising and Journalism; attended Metropolitan Collegiate Center, 1976, and Villanova University, 1977–79; spent three months in informal residence at Episcopal Divinity School, 1979.

Addresses: *Home*—Boston, Mass. *Office*—Episcopal Diocese of Massachusetts, 138 Tremont St., Boston, Mass. 02111.

Career

Joseph V. Baker & Associates (public relations firm), Philadelphia, Pa., member of staff, c. 1948-58, president, 1958-68; Sun Oil Co., became head of community relations department; active in leadership of Church of the Advocate, North Philadelphia, Pa., serving on the vestry, working with prisoners, and participating in a campaign to open the church to female clergy; ordained deacon of Episcopal Church, 1979, and priest, 1980; served as priest at St. Augustine of Hippo Church, Philadelphia, and chaplain of Philadelphia County Prison, 1980–84; served as executive director of Episcopal Church Publishing Co. and writer, editor, and publisher of church journal *The Witness,* until 1988; and interim rector of Church of the Advocate until 1988; suffragan (assistant) bishop of Episcopal Diocese of Massachusetts, Boston, 1988, and bishop after consecration in 1989.

UPI/Bettmann Newsphotos

Sidelights

Barbara Harris is black, divorced, female, and lacking in seminary training and a college education. Her background is in business and radical politics. She is known as a powerful preacher and an opinionated writer, and her church is a frequent subject of her caustic wit. Therefore, when the Episcopal Church consecrated the Philadelphian as its first female bishop in February 1989, it was seen by many as a controversial and unwelcome move. There was even talk of a church schism.

The consecration marked the approval by the church's national body of a vote taken the previous September, when Harris was elected suffragan (assistant) bishop of the Episcopal Diocese of Massachusetts. The next day she preached a sermon in a predominantly white Boston church, then a short time later preached again in another neighborhood church, this one predominantly black. The following weekend she returned to preach in her home parish in North Philadelphia. "A fresh wind is indeed blowing," she told her old congregation, in a sermon quoted widely in media reports. "We have seen in this year alone some things thought to be impossible just a short time ago. To some the changes are refreshing breezes. For others, they are as fearsome as a hurricane."

The Anglican church, which is tied to the Church of England, claims some 70 million members worldwide, including 2.5 million Episcopalians in the United States. The U.S. Episcopal Church is one of the seven Anglican churches that ordain women; 20 others do not. The consecration of Barbara Harris brought generally negative pronouncements from Christian clerics worldwide, reflecting the Anglican church status as linking the various denominations of Christianity, especially Roman Catholicism. A strong denouncement came almost immediately from the Vatican.

"To some the changes are refreshing breezes. For others, they are as fearsome as a hurricane."

The consecration completed a heated campaign on Harris's behalf that culminated in the Cathedral Church of St. Paul in Boston on September 24, 1988. Wrote Matthew R. Lawrence in the *Christian Century,* "After years of discussion and debate, months of networking and organizing, eight grueling ballots and near defeat, a barrier was broken that was for centuries considered inviolable." The close election, consisting of separate balloting among laity and clerics, came a couple of months after an international Anglican meeting in England produced a compromise that affirmed, but did not endorse, the right of national bodies to name their own bishops.

There were many voices raised against Harris's selection, some claiming that this particular woman should not be the first female bishop. Her lack of conventional training and academic background, her lack of full-time rectorship experience, and her left-wing politics were cited by those who opposed her selection. The experience seemed to bear out what she had prophetically written two years earlier in *The Witness,* the independent church magazine she published: that a woman in the Episcopal hierarchy would need "a high tolerance for indecisiveness, an inordinate amount of patience with unimaginative leadership, . . . and an appetite for ambiguity."

That very appetite for ambiguity seemed to describe her own attitude following the election. Discussing the process with *Newsday* religion writer Geraldine Baum, Harris attempted to distance herself from the historic event. "I didn't ask to be a bishop. It's a little late to say 'no' now. I was asked if I would allow my name to go into process and after some prayerful consideration I decided it was the right thing to do. It's different from really wanting the position and running for it. I feel called."

In the glare of the sudden media attention, the new bishop seemed to be making a conscious effort to defuse the objections that had dogged her since September. She refused most media interviews and sought to convey a more conventional image for herself in her roles as a cleric and as a female. Photographed meeting other women rectors—there are now over 1200—at Christ Church in Boston's Hyde Park, she chatted and smiled over coffee and cake. She suggested to Geraldine Baum that she was not always "in deep theological debate" at such gatherings but liked to talk "about curling irons." In several interviews, she asserted that she would not become "an international Anglican gadfly" on women's issues, nor foist her views on conservative Massachusetts congregations.

The new posture represented a significant turnabout for Harris. The third-generation Episcopalian became active in the church in the 1960s, joining a small inner-city parish associated with the black power movement of the day. Although she lacked a college education, the young woman was offered a post with a public relations company and was soon moving professionally in corporate circles. She bought a house in an outlying suburb but remained visible and vocal within her original parish. She became involved as writer, editor, and eventually publisher of *The Witness,* a 70-year-old independent church leftist journal, which provided a pulpit for her views. Often she spoke critically of her church. According to *Time* magazine, she labeled the Episcopal Church a "male-dominated racist church", castigated "factious fathers" who fear "mitered mammas," called one conservative church caucus "demonic," and fumed over Reagan administration policies.

In 1974 Harris's involvement with the church's activist wing began in earnest. In July of that year she carried a cross at the head of a group of parish women, leading them into the Church of the Advocate to witness several retired bishops illicitly ordain 11 women as priests. The church eventually legalized the female priests.

Meanwhile, Barbara Harris had begun her own preparations to enter the clergy. In 1980 she left her corporate job for full-time church involvement. She did not serve as full-time rector of her own church, but achieved a national sectarian influence through her columns in *The Witness.* She took strong positions on such issues as apartheid and equality for women. Her regular column was entitled "A Luta Continua" (the struggle continues), a slogan favored by the Marxist revolutionaries in Angola.

After the election in Boston, sectarian voices spoke out against her not only from Episcopalian dioceses in this country, but from Anglican communities in Europe, Asia, and the Far East. The head of the Church of England "snubbed her," according to a *Christian Century* report. Death threats began arriving in her mail. There was a possibility that the church could split apart over the controversy. Harris told Geraldine Baum of *Newsday:* "If schism occurs, it must be remembered that there is fault on both sides. We recognize that it is a problem for some people, theologically . . . and emotionally. We must always . . . help them to understand what this means in the life of the church and to move towards some reconciliation."

In *Time* magazine, Richard N. Ostling wrote: "During eight years in the priesthood, she has developed a reputation as a bright, articulate activist. [As] the church's 29th black bishop, [Barbara Harris] is the convener of a coalition of minority and social-action caucuses that seeks to prod the Episcopal Church into what Harris calls 'an increased advocacy role and some real risk taking.' A prime risk that she favors: acceptance of practicing homosexual clergy." In an interview with Peter Steinfels of the *New York Times,* she said that although the church had not been "as inclusive of gay and lesbian people as it might have been, we are bound to working within [its] structures."

Barbara Harris was born in 1930 to a middle-class family in the Germantown section of Philadelphia, where her family took an active part in St. Barnabas Church. At age 18, upon graduation from high school, she was hired by Joseph V. Baker & Associates, a Philadelphia public relations concern. Baker's specialty was representing white corporations to black communities, and his executives traveled a good deal through the south. Baker allowed Harris more and more responsibility, eventually giving her the title of president. She was hired away by Sun Oil Co., rising to head the community relations department of that firm.

She remained active in the congregation of her old church, which by this time had moved into a formerly all-white church, St. Luke's, as the racial mix in the community became more black. Dissatisfied by the parish's conservative politics, she decided to leave St. Luke's and joined the Church of the Advocate in North Philadelphia. The Reverend Charles Poindexter, pastor of St. Luke's, recalled in an interview with *Newsday* that Barbara Harris "felt my congregation was too conservative for her. We didn't go to marches in Selma. We were black Anglo-Catholics who supported the civil rights movement, but in our own way." Along with other parishioners of the Church of the Advocate, Barbara Harris did participate in the Selma march, led by the Reverend Martin Luther King, Jr.

Under the rectorship of the Reverend Paul Washington, the parish was emerging as an epicenter of the black protest movement in Philadelphia. It sponsored buses to the civil rights protests down south. It hosted a 1968 Black Panther convention, attracting 10,000 members of that radical movement. According to *Newsday*'s Geraldine Baum, "There were often Muslims speaking in the pulpit, and the services on Sunday were anything but high-church." Barbara Harris served on the vestry, volunteered to work with prisoners, helped desegregate a Philadelphia orphanage, and joined a grassroots campaign aimed at opening the church to female clergy.

Harris expressed her desire to join the ministry with Washington, who advised a year of contemplation and prayer. She remained certain of her calling and the following year convinced the minister of her sincerity. Washington told Peter Steinfels that he strongly recommended Harris to the bishop for ordination. The minister described the aspiring clergyman to Steinfels as "extremely brilliant [with] a strong sense of justice and compassion for the poor."

"I've been asked how I moved from the business world into ministry, but I've had an active ministry all my life, a lay ministry."

Barbara Harris enrolled in an alternative theological education program, one tailored to her needs as an employed professional unable to attend classes full time. She attended the Metropolitan Collegiate Center in Philadelphia in 1976 and took several courses at Villanova University between 1977 and 1979. She also spent three months prior to ordination in informal residence at the Episcopal Divinity School in Cambridge. In an interview with James L. Franklin, writing in the *Christian Century,* she said, "I was able to put together the same number of credits as any seminarian by taking work where I could, at nights, on weekends and vacations."

After passing her exams, she was ordained a deacon in September 1979 and a priest in October 1980. She served as a priest in charge of St. Augustine of Hippo Church in Philadelphia and chaplain of Philadelphia County Prison from 1980 until 1984, when she became executive director of the Episcopal Church Publishing Company. She also served as interim rector at the Church of the Advocate.

Harris told Franklin, "I've been asked how I moved from the business world into ministry, but I've had an active ministry all my life, a lay ministry," referring to her work as a lay chaplain and counselor in county and state prisons. "I didn't have to leave [the corporate work] I was doing. For a while after ordination I continued some business pursuits as a consultant and then moved more fully into the position as executive director of the Episcopal Church Publishing Company and as a parish priest. My faith journey has been ongoing, if anything."

Divorced from her husband in 1965, after five years of marriage, Barbara Harris has no children. She has a brother and a sister. Her mother is alive; her father is deceased. Upon her consecration she took a furnished apartment in Boston but apparently intends to retain her ties to Philadelphia.

Sources

Christian Century, October 19, 1988; December 21–28, 1988.
Christianity Today, October 21, 1989.
Glamour, April, 1989.
Newsday, January 25, 1989; February 9, 1989.
New York Times, September 26, 1988; January 26, 1989; February 13, 1989.
Time, December 26, 1988.
The Witness, December, 1986.

—Sidelights by Daniela Pozzaglia

Jim Henson

AP/Wide World Photos

Television and film producer, director, and puppeteer

Full name, James Maury Henson; born September 24, 1936, in Greenville, Miss.; son of Paul Ransom (a government agricultural researcher) and Elizabeth Marcella (Brown) Henson; married Jane Anne Nebel (an investor and part-time consultant in Henson Associates, Inc.), May 28, 1959; children: Lisa Marie, Cheryl Lee, Brian David, John Paul, Heather Beth. *Education:* University of Maryland, B.A., 1960.

Addresses: *Office*—Henson Associates, Inc., 117 E. 69th St., New York, N.Y. 10021.

Career

Creator, the Muppets, 1954; producer, "Sam and Friends," Washington, D.C., 1955–61; puppeteer, Rowlf on "The Jimmy Dean Show," New York, N.Y., 1963–66; producer, "Sesame Street," 1969—; producer, "The Muppet Show," 1976–81; producer, "The Muppet Movie," 1979; director, "The Great Muppet Caper," 1981; co-director, "The Dark Crystal," 1981; creator, "Fraggle Rock" (HBO series), 1983—; executive producer, "The Muppet Babies" (CBS series), 1984—; producer, "The Muppets Take Manhattan," 1984; puppeteer, "Follow That Bird," 1985; director, "Labyrinth," 1986; president, Henson Associates, Inc., New York City.

Also made numerous television guest appearances, creator of numerous television commercials.

Awards: Winner of eighteen Emmy Awards, 1958, 1974, 1976–78, 1981–82, 1985–88; seven Grammy Awards, 1973, 1978–80, 1986–87; four George Foster Peabody Awards, 1970, 1978–79, 1987; and five ACE Awards (from the National Cable Television Association), 1979, 1983–84, 1986–87; Saturn Award for best fantasy film, "The Muppet Movie," 1979; "The Dark Crystal" was honored as best film of the year, 1983, at the Madrid Film Festival; earned Film Advisory Board Award of Excellence for "Fraggle Rock," 1984; recipient of March of Dimes Jack Benny Award, 1982; inducted into TV Academy Hall of Fame, 1987.

Sidelights

The soft-spoken television puppeteer who originated the Muppets over 30 years ago is often referred to these days as the new Walt Disney. As the creative force and managerial brains behind a coterie of lovable puppet-creatures adored by children—and adults—around the world, Jim Henson is still going strong, introducing new characters and advancing the role of computers and remote-control technology in the centuries-old art of puppeteering.

As a high school student in Washington, D.C., Henson was fascinated by the new medium of television, and wanted to get involved in it. A shy boy who avoided the limelight, he took naturally to puppetry, where he could perform out of sight. Learning as he worked, he devised his first character, Kermit the Frog, in order to audition for a local television spot. Recognizing the importance of television's close-up photography, he developed a style of conveying a puppet's emotions convincingly through hand-movements.

Henson's style suited the new, intimate medium of television perfectly. *Time* magazine writer John Skow observed in a 1979 feature story: "Kermit is not much more than a green felt sock that fits over a human hand, with a wide gash for a mouth and what look like glued-on halves of Ping-Pong balls for eyes. [But] the clenchings and wrigglings of the operator's fists can change the expression with considerable subtlety. Not simply smiles, but wistful smiles are possible."

After appearing on Steve Allen's "The Tonight Show" in 1957, the puppeteer knocked on network doors for more than a decade. He made a number of guest appearances, notably on "The Ed Sullivan Show," but did not get the series he sought. His big break came in 1969, when the Muppets got feature roles on the premier season of public television's "Sesame Street." "Sesame Street" revolutionized children's television, blending education with entertainment.

The Muppets snagged their first Emmy Award in 1974 for their "Sesame Street" hijinks, but Henson's goal was to break into commercial television. The following year a British producer staked the puppeteer to an independent distribution deal, and Henson's troupe of felt creatures began headlining "The Muppet Show." Henson and collaborators have accrued seventeen additional Emmy Awards, seven Grammys, and the Peabody and Humanitas Awards in the years that followed. He has been awarded enough plaques and certificates to wallpaper his office.

Henson attributes the Muppets' popularity both to the human puppeteers behind them and the intrinsic character of each Muppet. "An audience relates to the performer. But then there's also something about puppets that people relate to," he told Jack Slater of *Emmy* magazine. "Puppets are like teddy bears or dolls, something small that you can hug and feel safe about, as opposed to a person or a personality. It's slightly safer to have an emotional connection with a puppet. You're distancing yourself. Distancing is something you do with puppets. You're putting things in perspective."

In the twenty years since "Sesame Street" was introduced, millions upon millions of English-speaking children have received their pre-school education at the hands of Muppets: reciting the alphabet with Grover, learning opposites with Bert and Ernie, and learning to count with The Count, a toothless Dracula. The "Sesame Street" characters have been merchandized aggressively, and very successfully. The revenues have helped bankroll "Sesame Street" and other Children's Television Workshop programs. Revenues from "The Muppet Show," including licensing agreements and syndication deals, have gone directly to Henson Associates, financing the growth of the small puppet-making venture into a lucrative film industry property with offices in New York and London.

"Puppets are like teddy bears or dolls, something small that you can hug and feel safe about, as opposed to a person....It's slightly safer to have an emotional connection with a puppet."

Hardly a purist in his approach to children's programming, Henson has come in for his share of criticism. Many parents, generous in their praise for the puppeteer's track record in producing quality children's programming, nevertheless take him to task for his unabashed commercialism; Muppet characters peddle everything from lunchboxes to bedsheets. Henson blames the system itself: "Children's programming never has enough of a budget," he told *Emmy* magazine writer Jack Slater. "You can't get much commercial income from [quality children's shows]. Fortunately, we're able [to produce quality shows] by putting various sources of money together. A network doesn't pay us enough to do a good children's program. So we make a deal with both a network and another country and sell the stuff internationally."

The son of a government agricultural researcher, Jim Henson became interested in puppetry as an introverted adolescent. Puppetry not only provided a creative outlet out of sight of the audience; it offered a path into the intriguing new medium of television. As a high school senior, he learned of an audition for a local TV station seeking young puppeteers. He cut a puppet out of his mother's discarded spring coat, named it Kermit the Frog, and auditioned. He won a spot on "The Junior Morning Show." And when that show slipped off the airways, he got a call from local NBC affiliate WRC-TV and was offered a five-minute late-night slot. The spot, called "Sam and Friends," lasted from 1955 through 1961 and won the young puppeteer a local Emmy Award.

During the late 1950s Henson attended the University of Maryland and earned enough from TV to buy a Rolls-Royce and drive it to his college graduation. He was, however, uneasy about pursuing a career as TV puppeteer. After graduating, he travelled through Europe, where puppetry's traditions stretch back to the Middle Ages, and gained a deeper respect for the art. Upon his return stateside he resumed his TV career, and married Jane Nebel, an assistant on his WRC-TV show. She has remained active over the years in Henson Associates in a mostly administrative capacity but has given priority to raising the couple's five children, all of whom have worked in the company.

Throughout the late 1950s and early 1960s, the Muppets did guest appearances on a variety of programs, including "The Ed Sullivan Show" and "The Steve Allen Show." Henson lobbied hard for a network program, but network executives were reluctant to sign him for a series; the Muppets were seen as too sophisticated for children, but too childish for adults. Henson fought to change that viewpoint.

In 1975, British entertainment mogul Sir Lew Grade created a syndication network that again allowed Henson to bypass the networks. The timing was perfect, as the Federal Communications Commission had just created a new time slot, 7:30–8:00 P.M., earmarked for non-network, family-oriented programming. "The Muppet Show" ran from 1975 to 1981, and was by all accounts a phenomenal success. "When we did 'Sesame Street,' we got branded as a children's form, and it became very difficult to sell 'The Muppet Show,'" the illusionist complained to Alison Johns of *Millimeter* magazine. "But when ['The Muppet Show'] worked on the air, it opened people's minds to the fact that puppetry could be entertaining."

The series spawned a feature film, "The Muppet Movie," in 1979, which cost $8 million to make (and which had grossed over $44 million by March 1988). A long-term syndication agreement put all 120 episodes of the show into instant reruns in 146 U.S. markets, and broadcast rights were sold to 106 foreign countries as well. Henson Associates also sold licensing rights. Suddenly the Muppets were everywhere: on calendar covers and record albums, on toys, books, clothes, even telephones.

The success of "The Muppet Show" and the movie spin-off encouraged Henson to try his hand again at commercial filmmaking. In 1981 he produced "The Great Muppet Caper" and, three years later, "The Muppets Take Manhattan." In between he tried something quite different—the first live-action fantasy film starring computer-operated puppets. "The Dark Crystal" (1982) was a limited success, but Henson was not deterred. Four years later he released "Labyrinth," casting his puppets with live actors. These "puppets" were now sophisticated fantasy creations on the cutting edge of high technology, operated by remote-control electronics in conjunction with costumed human performers. The technology, dubbed animatronics, was impressive but failed to make the movies box office hits.

Henson, however, has continued to push ahead with his high-tech orientation. The use of electronic motors—including seven to control all facial features—allowed the Muppets to make the transition from television to feature movies. Its future, however, is probably with fantasy movie creatures who appeal to older audiences. Henson created and animated the popular Yoda character for the blockbuster George Lucas film "The Empire Strikes Back" and continues to work on contract for Lucas and other filmmakers.

"Basically, we started as puppeteers, and used very simple puppetry for many years," Henson reminisced to James Saynor of *Stills* magazine. "Kermit was the best example, because he's really just a glove puppet—a sock with a mouth. Now, your hand and your wrist is almost the most expressive part of your body. You can do wonderful things in terms of puppetry just by using your hands. Now to take all of this movement and put it into a mechanism that's radio-controlled is very, very difficult indeed. But we've done it."

Henson has not had a big hit since "The Muppet Show." In the 1980s he developed a new series called "Fraggle Rock," which aired on cable TV for four years before Henson hustled a deal with NBC, which now runs it as animation. Writing in *Channels,* Diana Loevy described it as a "kind of subterranean Our Gang with pro-social messages of working together and understanding others." Loewy suggested that the network exposure would quickly boost the show's popularity. "A bevy of the usual licensed products—dolls, puppets, lunch boxes and watches—is already appearing in stores," she reported.

Despite the popularity of old Muppet favorites like Kermit and Miss Piggy, Henson has been under pressure to create new faces for a new generation. In 1987 the puppeteer set up a research and development center called the Muppet Workshop, and he assigned 17 employees to create new characters and develop new puppetry styles and techniques. The emphasis so far has been on animatronics. Even more advanced work is done out of Henson's London office, which also handles international sales. *New York Times* writer Francis X. Clines described the operation as a "Frankenstein castle of technicians and engineers who make fake beings [for Henson projects] as well as for TV commercials and other studios' feature films."

In the late 1980s Henson remains an active force with "Sesame Street." As always, he directs the segments involving the Muppets and handles Kermit himself. He recently introduced a new character, Meryl Sheep. (There is often a satirical edge to Muppet humor; it is far from goody-goody.) "The Muppet Babies," a Saturday-morning CBS series featuring infant Muppets, began its fourth season in 1988. Muppet specials are holiday fixtures on the networks, and in 1987 NBC introduced a nine-part series called "The Storyteller." On the home video front, Henson has marketed a series of tapes for children and recently introduced a line of videos for business use. On these business videos, the Muppets satirize the maniacal tone of the typical sales meeting.

Henson has always been a strong advocate of what he calls "responsibility" in children's programing, and a critic of violence as a substitute for imagination. "I never get into fights or car chases, but I see hundreds of thousands of them on television," he complained to Jack Slater of *Emmy* magazine. "We've pushed it quite far in the wrong direction. There's just an overall lack of responsibility (among commercial television producers)."

Often described as a workaholic, juggling many projects at once, Henson is away from home at least six months a year. When he's not on the road, he's home in his Connecticut retreat or staying at his Manhattan *pied-a-terre;* in London he maintains an apartment in the Hampstead district. He is described as a calm man who practices transcendental meditation, reads a good deal, and lives fairly simply. While his five children were growing up he often found time to ski and play tennis with them and continues to enjoy those sports. *Time* writer John Skow described him as "a gaunt, bearded rather ascetic-looking craftsman," not particularly witty "without a puppet on his arm."

"I consider Jim an authentic American genius," declared Joan Ganz Cooney, president of Children's Television Workshop, to Diana Loevy, writing in *Channels* magazine. "I think he is some combination of Disney, Chaplin, Mae West, W.C. Fields, and the Marx Brothers. But he's always climbing a new Everest and those are expensive, high-risk ventures for him. I don't know if he will ever again have the kind of wild success "Sesame Street" plus "The Muppet Show" has created for him. [But] I would never count him out."

Sources

Channels, March, 1988.
Chicago Tribune, January 17, 1986.
Emmy, February, 1986.
Fine Tuning, December, 1986.
Millimeter, December, 1985.
NATPE Reporter, June, 1986.
New York Times, October 25, 1987.
Stills, January, 1986.
Time, December 25, 1978.

—Sidelights by Daniela Pozzaglia

Barbara Hershey

UPI/Bettmann Newsphotos

Actress

Name originally Barbara Herzstein; name changed to Barbara Seagull for a time during the early 1970s; born February 5, 1948, in Hollywood, Calif.; father was a bookie, author of a racing column, and operator of a clothing store; children: (with David Carradine) Tom (name originally Free). *Education:* Graduated from Hollywood High School.

Addresses: *Agent*—Creative Artists Agency, 1888 Century Park East, Suite 1400, Los Angeles, Calif. 90067.

Career

Actress. Feature films include "With Six You Get Eggroll," 1968, "Last Summer," 1969, "Heaven With a Gun," 1969, "The Liberation of L.B. Jones," 1970, "The Baby Maker," 1970, "The Pursuit of Happiness," 1971, "Dealing; or, the Berkeley-to-Boston Forty-Brick, Lost-Bag Blues," 1972, "Boxcar Bertha," 1972, "Angela-Love Comes Quietly," 1972, "The Crazy World of Julius Vrooder," 1974, "The Last Hard Men," 1976, "Diamonds," 1976, "A Choice of Weapons," 1976, "The Stuntman," 1980, "Americana," 1981, "The Entity," 1983, "The Right Stuff," 1983, "The Natural," 1984, "Hannah and Her Sisters," 1986, "Hoosiers," 1987, "Tin Men," 1987, "Shy People," 1988, "A World Apart," 1988, "The Last Temptation of Christ," 1988, and "Beaches," 1988. Regular cast member of television series "The Monroes," 1966–67, and "From Here to Eternity," 1979; appeared in made-for-television movies, including "Flood," 1976, "In the Glitter Palace," 1977, "Just a Little Inconvenience," 1977, "Sunshine Christmas," 1977, "Angel on My Shoulder," 1980, "My Wicked, Wicked Ways . . . The Legend of Errol Flynn," 1985, and "Passion Flower," 1986; other television appearances include guest roles on "Gidget," 1965, "The Invaders," 1967, "Daniel Boone," 1967, "High Chaparral," 1967, "CBS Playhouse," 1967, and "Kung Fu," 1973.

Awards: Named best actress at Cannes Film Festival, 1987, for "Shy People," and 1988, for "A World Apart."

Sidelights

Actress Barbara Hershey is the movie comeback story of the 1980s. Hershey did not just make a dramatic return, she made a phenomenal one and is now one of a few select actresses who are the premier film interpreters of their generation—women in their late thirties and early forties who can radically transform their personalities and body language to meet the challenges of the characters they portray on screen. Meryl Streep is at the head of this acting elite, but Hershey is now a close second with her excellent film portrayals. No actress in this decade has so convincingly reversed her fortunes; only Dennis Hopper with his Academy Award nomination for best supporting actor in "Hoosiers," his appearance as the burned out drug dealer in "River's Edge," and his return to directing in "Colors" comes close to rivaling Hershey's accomplishment.

The most obvious symbol of Hershey's success is her back-to-back best actress awards at the Cannes Film Festival, the only actress to accomplish this feat. In 1987, Hershey won her first Cannes award for her role of Ruth Sullivan, the hard-nosed Bayou matriarch, in Andrei Konchalovsky's "Shy People." She repeated the award the next year in Chris Menges's "A World Apart" as Diana Roth, based on the activism of South African journalist Ruth First, sharing the achievement with co-stars Jodhi May and Linda Mvusi.

Hershey won critical praise in rapid succession for her performances in "Hannah and her Sisters," "Hoosiers," and "Tin Men" before the Cannes success. Barbara Costikyan, writing in *Cosmopolitan,* concluded: "from these roles a pattern seems to be emerging as to the person Hershey plays best—the complicated, sensuous, ephemeral woman with conflicting emotions buzzing about her soul." She topped off her fame by playing a tattoo-wearing Mary Magdalene in Martin Scorsese's "The Last Temptation of Christ," the most controversial movie of 1988. Originally intended to be a modest art house project, "Last Temptation" gained a much larger audience when Christian fundamentalists in the United States organized nationwide protests of the movie's content as blasphemous.

All of Hershey's roles are marked by a physical and psychological transformation in which she becomes the character she is playing by research and attention to the smallest detail. Her movies may not be box-office hits, but they are distinguished by her seriousness as an actress to register performances that stand as film art—even those that are essentially commercial endeavors. Hershey's recent success was unexpected given her earlier reputation as an eccentric, a "flower child" who shocked the public by her outrageous behavior.

Her reputation was first as an ingenue and then as a Hollywood hippie and free spirit that was reinforced by the kind of movies she made. Hershey had not been perceived as a serious actress and it became difficult for her to find suitable roles in the late 1970s. She had the lead role in the 1983 movie "The Entity" in which she played Carla Moran, a woman who is raped and assaulted by a force no one can see. The screenplay was adapted from a Frank DeFelitta novel that was based on actual events that had happened to a Los Angeles woman in 1976. As a young widowed mother of three who just wanted to support her family, Hershey found herself up against a horrifying force.

Hershey made her screen debut as Brian Keith's daughter in the 1968 film "With Six You Get Eggroll," a Doris Day vehicle in which Day plays a middle-aged widow who gets involved with Keith in a movie with a plot no more ambitious than typical situation comedy fare. Hershey had appeared in the ABC-TV hour-long series "The Monroes" as Kathy Monroe during the 1966–67 season, a show that chronicled the struggle of five orphans who try to make a life for themselves on the Wyoming frontier. (In 1980 Hershey appeared as Karen Holmes, the lover of Sargeant Milt Warden, in the short-lived NBC series clone of James Jones's "From Here to Eternity," as she tried to re-establish her career.) But the acting experience that influenced Hershey the most and would determine her reputation a long time after she had outgrown the experience was "Last Summer."

In the 1969 film "Last Summer," Hershey plays Sandy, a teenager whose "beauty, wit and high I.Q. disguise a neurotic child who may actually be psychotic," wrote Vincent Canby in the *New York Times.* Sandy teams up with Peter (Richard Thomas) and Dan (Bruce Davison) for a summer of sun, fun, and sex on Fire Island; these three spoiled WASP rich kids live without parental supervision and all of the action first seems innocent until Sandy's cruelty reveals itself. The three nurse and tame an injured seagull, but when the bird turns on Sandy she calmly bashes its head against a rock. The three are joined by the unattractive Rhoda (Cathy Burns), a vulnerable younger girl. The two boys join together to rape Rhoda while Sandy looks on, giving her blessing to their crime, and the adult fates of these teenagers are presumably sealed. Critically faulted, "Last Summer" is important for other reasons.

Hershey has described an experience she had during the filming of "Last Summer" as having had a profound impact on her. In one scene she had to repeatedly throw a seagull into the air. "The trained bird was very special, I felt her spirit," she told the *New York Times.* "But we had to reshoot the scene over and over. I knew she was exhausted, and I told [director] Frank Perry that I couldn't throw her again; and he told me on the last throw she had broken her neck. At the moment I felt her soul enter me. I didn't tell anybody for a long time. I just realized, finally, that the only honest, moral thing would be to change my name."

She renamed herself Barbara Seagull, and when she and actor David Carradine had a child together, the boy was named Free (he has since been renamed Tom). Carradine's mystique added to her reputation; he is best known for the NBC television series "Kung Fu," a western in which he starred as a half-Chinese drifter in the American west who used his considerable marital arts talents to solve disputes. The series helped establish the popularity of the martial arts in the United States, and Carradine's own sense of individuality added to the public myth Hershey endured as "some sort of far-out flake," as Myra Forsberg observed, writing in the *New York Times* in 1986.

"In retrospect," Forsberg continued, "that reaction is somewhat puzzling for an era that prized liberalism, individualism and alternative lifestyles above all. And although Miss Hershey was part of an industry that frequently rewarded idosyncrasy and eccentricity in its members—seeing these as indisputable signs of creativity—she eventually found it hard to get major film work." About this period, Hershey told Forsberg: "I'm so bored by it. I hate it. I think it was just bad timing or something. It's such a specific little part of my life that has no more significance to me than many other parts. But to keep talking about it seems to perpetuate it and I really don't want to."

Hershey's selections of movie roles contributed to her countercultural persona. Following "Last Summer" Hershey played Tish Gray in James Bridges's "The Baby Maker," a story about a hip young woman who agrees to have a child for a wealthy couple for the sheer experience of it and for the money the couple will pay her. Tish agrees to give up smoking peyote and her hippie boyfriend, Tad Jacks (Scott Glenn); an unexpected romance develops between her and the father. "Tish and her lover," wrote Roger Greenspun in the *New York Times*, "who always smoke grass, play the drums or the guitar, live in leather, watch light shows, get busted, protest war and fascism—are for their part like demonstration hippies (West Coast, circa 1968) in a primer on the new life style," a description that fixed the Hershey myth in the public's consciousness.

In "The Pursuit of Happiness," a typical youth film of the period directed by Robert Mulligan (best known for the Academy Award winning "To Kill a Mockingbird"), Hershey is Jane Kauffman, a movement activist and college student who lives with William Popper (Michael Sarrazin), who prefers sailing boats in Central Park. Sarrazin is convicted of accidently killing a woman while driving in the rain to see his millionaire father. While in jail he escapes right before he would have been released, and flees to Mexico with Hershey's Jane Kauffman. Sarrazin as a existentially disaffected youth proved to be difficult to appreciate, judged Greenspan.

In "Dealing," subtitled "Or the Berkeley-to-Boston Forty-Brick Lost-Bag Blues," directed by Paul Williams, Hershey is Susan, a West Coast free spirit, who gets involved with Peter (Robert Lyons), an East Coast Harvard law student, who earns extra money as a marijuana courier. Peter falls in love with Susan on one of his missions—largely because she does not wear underwear and he wears long johns, a fact that supposedly symbolizes the differences between the cultures of the two coasts.

Wrote Paul Zimmerman in *Newsweek:* "As played by the beautiful Barbara Hershey, she [Susan] is the quintessence of liberated cool, not stirring a naked muscle when a colleague finds her on the floor of a recording studio draped about her instant boy friend." When Susan is busted for possession of two suitcases of marijuana, Peter cleverly sets a plot to blackmail the arresting detective who kept one suitcase. The plot, concluded Zimmerman, was marred by "the paranoid vision of its hero," which was unfortunately typical of the movie's milieu. *Film Journal* wrote: "Here Barbara Hershey gives her most winning performance to date, revealing a warmth and sly humor, a sense of the absurdity of things."

Hershey also appeared in two movies with strong social themes: William Wyler's "The Liberation of L.B. Jones" with a screenplay by Stirling Silliphant and Jesse Hill Ford, based on Ford's novel of the same title, and Martin Scorsese's "Boxcar Bertha," a low budget "Bonnie and Clye," based on the autobiography of Boxcar Bertha Thompson, which, wrote Howard Thompson in the *New York Times*, "stands curiously on its own." "Liberation" explored the collapse of race relations in a Tennessee town when the richest black man, Lord Byron Jones (played by Roscoe Lee Browne), divorces his pretty young wife for having an affair with a young redneck policeman. Hershey, as Nella Mundine, along with Lee Majors, "are the film's mouthpieces for moderation and liberalism," wrote Vincent Canby in the *New York Times.*

Scorsese cast Carradine as a heroic union organizer in love with Boxcar Bertha in the Great Depression period piece of the same name. Scorsese captured the "labor despair of the era" as well as the action of the train-robbing Carradine. "David Carradine is excellent in this role. Matching him, as the childlike boxcar itinerant, is Barbara Hershey," opined Thompson. (Hershey also costarred with Carradine in "Americana," a 1981 movie he directed about a Vietnam veteran who attempts to rebuild a merry-go-round in rural Kansas but meets with resistance from locals—the action obviously symbolizing post-Vietnam America.)

"Dazzling, original, inventive, playful, with an endearing nasty sense of humor," wrote *Film Journal* about "The Stunt Man," a Hollywood movie Pauline Kael called "a virtuoso piece of moviemaking" in the *New Yorker,* comparing it favorably to Truffaut's "Day for Night" and Fellini's "8 1/2." As Nina, Hershey is the female lead in a movie-within-a-movie that cast Peter O'Toole as a John Hustonesque director making an anti-war epic set in World War I. Steve Railsbach plays an ex-Vietnam veteran and fugitive from the law who finds refuge as a replacement for O'Toole's recently deceased stunt man. Based on a 1970 novel by Paul Brodeur, "The Stunt Man" is a movie of stylistic daring and dramatic playfulness.

The strange history of "The Stunt Man" kept it from the kind of success it merited. First announced as a film project in 1971, it was filmed in 1978, completed in 1979, but not released until 1980 after a successful run first in Seattle and then in Los Angeles. Melvin Simon Production Company financed the project largely because of the success of Rush's "Freebie and the Bean" in 1977. Judged "unreleasable" by Hollywood, it took a year after its completion to get the movie distributed. "The Stunt Man," despite its critical plaudits and warm regard among film buffs, was not the film that turned Barbara Hershey's career around.

Hershey had small but memorable roles as Chuck Yeager's wife in Philip Kaufman's patriotic epic of the Mercury astronauts, "The Right Stuff," and as Harriet Bird, the woman who shot Robert Redford's Roy Hobbs, in Barry Levinson's "The Natural." But it was the role of Lee in Woody Allen's "Hannah and her Sisters" that focused attention on Hershey as a serious actress. Considered by many critics to be Allen's best film, "Hannah" is certainly the best rendering of Allen's urban angst themes with superb ensemble performances that garnered Academy Awards for Michael Caine and Diane Weist. This multi-layered film with its Allen-rich situations mixes comedy and drama in equal amounts. "I've never done less acting in my life," Hershey told *Esquire* in describing her performance.

Hershey credits Allen for making it acceptable for Hollywood to hire her. "Woody made it all right to hire me again, to put me on that list they have," she said in *Esquire.* Hershey followed "Hannah" with a number of critically successful films. In "Tin Men," Barry Levinson's black comedy of feuding aluminum siding salesmen in Baltimore circa 1963, Hershey plays Nora, the discontented and ignored wife of Tilley (Danny DeVito), who has an affair with her husband's enemy, Bill Babowsky, called B.B. (Richard Dreyfuss). The film focuses on the Tin Men as a dying breed of con artists and hustlers who enjoy their own company. B.B. has never slept with the same woman two nights in a row, and when Nora moves in with him he starts to question his bachelor beliefs for the first time. Ed Kelleher in *Film Journal* wrote that Hershey's "evolution from drab, put-upon Mrs. Tilley to awakened romantic is as charming as it is adroitly realized." About Hershey's acting, Levinson told the *New York Times:* "It's technique without technique—someone just being. It's hard to describe acting when it's really right, and Barbara's really right."

In David Anspaugh's "Hoosiers," Hershey plays an unhappy, repressed, and angry schoolteacher who lives through her students in a tiny claustrophic Indiana village in which basketball is the center of life. She resents new basketball coach Norman Dale (Gene Hackman) but in time learns to love him as he fights against the insularity of the community that refuses to accept his unorthodox coaching methods, including hiring the town drunk (Dennis Hopper) as his assistant. A powerful period piece set in the recreated early 1950s, "Hoosiers" is a familiar, yet memorable, movie through the tension of its two leads. Hershey is "fine as a teacher trying to put a dispassionate face on a passionate nature," wrote *Time*'s Richard Schickel.

In "Shy People," the Andrei Konchalovsky film set in the Louisiana bayou, Hershey delivers the strangest, most bizarre performance of her career, a "performance of surprising dignity," noted Hal Boedeker of the Night-Ridder New Service in a *Cincinnati Enquirer* review. As Ruth Sullivan, Hershey keeps alive the authority and presence of a renegade dead husband by maintaining he is still alive; she rules over her sons with an iron fist and logic they fear to question. The film's conflict arises when a distant cousin, Diana Sullivan, played by Jil Clayburgh, a writer for *Cosmopolitan,* with her cocaine-sniffing spoiled daughter (Martha Plimpton), visits to write an article about her relatives. The presence of Diana and her provocatively sexual daughter brings the obvious contradictions of Ruth's matriarchy to the surface. Ruth keeps one son locked in a cage, scratches out the face in the family photos of another son who has left the homestead, and shoots a man for poaching. Ruth tells Diana that people should run hot or cold—"You city people, you're all warm like dishwater," capturing the film's core theme.

Much of the same intensity Hershey brought to "Shy People" is apparent in "A World Apart," set in apartheid South Africa circa 1963. Filmed in Zimbabwe, "A World Apart" is a realistic story of the effects of the arrest of Diana Roth on her thirteen-year-old daughter, Molly (Jodhi May), when Diana is the first white woman to be imprisoned under South Africa's 90-day Detention Act. The film is based on the real-life experiences of Ruth First, a journalist and political activist, and her daughter Shawn Slovo, the author of the screenplay. "Newcomer May is nothing short of a cinematic revelation in the demanding part of the troubled pre-adolescent who longs for her mother's solicitude," wrote Ed Kelleher in *Film Journal.* "Balancing May's remarkably unaffected performance is Hershey's superb evocation of Diana: brittle and distant at first, but gradually opening up to reveal a pained emotional core. Long regarded as an actress of exceptional range, Hershey is at the top of her form here, meeting with intelligence and insight every challenge."

Hershey's role as Mary Magdalene in "The Last Temptation of Christ" reunited her with Martin Scorsese, who had directed "Boxcar Bertha" (with obvious Christian symbolism, including a crucifixion scene). One of the most controversial films of the late 1980s, "Last Temptation" offended fundamentalist Christians, who mounted a concerted media campaign against the film. The campaign resulted in much national exposure, certainly more attention than the modest $6.5 million film would have received by itself. "Last Temptation," originally slated for art houses, became the center of a prolonged debate conducted through the media between the outraged fundamentalists and Scorsese.

"I guess it was the greatest experience of my life so far," Hershey explained to Associated Press writer Bob Thomas in the *Dayton Daily News.* "All I can say is that I know why we made the film: We made it not to thumb our noses at anybody or anybody's religion. Quite the opposite. We made it because we were moved by the book. It became a passion for Marty [Martin Scorsese]." "I find it ironic that the fundamentalists would object. I find it a very tender and moving version of the Christ story," Hershey said in answering critics of the film. Janet Maslin concurred in the *New York Times:* "Anyone who questions the sincerity or seriousness of what Mr. Scorsese has attempted need only see the film to lay those doubts to rest."

Hershey guards the facts of her private life. Born Barbara Herzstein in Hollywood in 1948, her father was, according to Costikyan in her *Cosmopolitan* profile, "a New York-born bookie, last name Herzstein, who wrote a racing column for a California paper and later ran a clothing store in Encino, California, with his wife, a Presbyterian from Arkansas." Hershey's family nicknamed her Sarah after Sarah Bernhardt because she wanted to be an actress. She reenacted her favorite movies for family members, and avidly watched "The Mickey Mouse Club." "I do not want anybody to know who or what I am," she told Costikyan. In keeping with this sentiment she will not discuss her hippie days or her six-year relationship with Carradine that ended in 1975. "I did a lot of growing up in public," she confessed to Costikyan. "We're all allowed to make our mistakes."

Sources

Cincinnati Enquirer, May 20, 1988.
Cosmopolitan, February, 1987.
Dayton Daily News, September 23, 1988; October 1, 1988.
Esquire, May, 1987.
Film Journal, June 24, 1969; March 18, 1970; September 30, 1970; March, 1971; February 3, 1972; February, 1986; January, 1988; July, 1988.
Newsweek, June 23, 1969; September 1, 1980; February 3, 1986; February 9, 1987; March 2, 1987; July 18, 1988.
New York Times, October 10, 1968; June 11, 1969; March 19, 1970; October 2, 1970; February 24, 1971; February 26, 1972; August 18, 1972; February 5, 1983; and October 21, 1983; May 11, 1984; February 2, 1986; July 1, 1988; August 12, 1988.
New Yorker, June 28, 1969; September 29, 1980; April 6, 1987.
Time, September 1, 1980; February 3, 1986; February 9, 1987; April 6, 1987.

—Sidelights by Jon Saari

Orel Hershiser

UPI/Bettmann Newsphotos

Professional baseball player

Full name, Orel Leonard Hershiser IV; born September 16, 1958, in Buffalo, N.Y.; son of Orel Leonard III (in the printing business) and Millie Hershiser; married Jamie Byars, February, 1981; children: Orel Leonard V, Jordan Douglas. *Education:* Attended Bowling Green State University for three years. *Religion:* Christian.

Addresses: *Home*—Los Angeles, Calif. *Office*—Los Angeles Dodgers, Dodger Stadium, 1000 Elysian Park Ave., Los Angeles, Calif. 90012.

Career

Professional baseball player in minor leagues in Clinton, Iowa, 1979, San Antonio, Tex., 1980–81, and Albuquerque, N.M., 1982–83, and in major leagues with Los Angeles Dodgers, 1984–.

Awards: Mulvey Award as best Los Angeles rookie, 1983; Cy Young Award as best pitcher in National League, 1988; named Most Valuable Player of 1988 World Series; named Sportsman of the Year by *Sports Illustrated* magazine, 1988.

Sidelights

The unassuming pitcher Orel Hershiser seems to be on his way to a Baseball Hall of Fame career. Hershiser's athletic performances and wholesome Christian values have captivated several nations of sports fans and have gained the pitcher entry to the White House on several occasions. *Sports Illustrated* contributor Steve Wulf noted that a great "to-do" is being made over Hershiser, a man who "was cut from his high school baseball team, who couldn't make the traveling squad of his college team, who almost quit in the minors, who never quite looked the part he was trying to play." Wulf added: "His really was a Cinderella story, and his triumph was a triumph for everybody who has been told 'No way.'"

No one would dispute the term "triumph" when applied to Hershiser's 1988 baseball season. He won the Cy Young Award with a phenomenal 23-8 record and 2.26 earned run average, became the World Series Most Valuable Player after shepherding the Los Angeles Dodgers through the playoffs and Series against superior teams, and was elected *Sports Illustrated's* Sportsman of the Year. In between honors, he dined with Margaret Thatcher and Ronald Reagan at a White House state dinner, took a red carpet tour of Disneyland, and landed enough commercial endorsements to more than double his seven-figure salary. All this acclaim and notoriety has been heaped on an athlete who, rare among his peers, accepts it with bewilderment and humility. To quote Maryann Hudson of the *Los Angeles Times,* "Perhaps the best thing about Orel Hershiser IV is that he can remember when he wasn't the best. He once was just a normal person and a very average pitcher."

Hershiser's name stems from his family's Hessian ancestry; his forebears were mercenaries hired to fight the American rebels during the Revolutionary War. Hershiser's Hessian ancestors stayed in America and settled near Buffalo. More recently, the Hershiser family has done a good bit of moving around. Hershiser's father, Orel III, was engaged in the printing business, locating at different times in Buffalo, Detroit, Toronto, and Cherry Hill, New Jersey. Young "O," as he is nicknamed by his family, was gifted with excellent hand-eye coordination from his toddling days. "He could play anything," his father told *Sports Illustrated,* "but it was baseball that he loved." Orel III elaborated in a *Newsday* interview: "He never played with trucks. He always played baseball with older kids. At 5, he was in the back yard playing whiffle ball."

Athletic ability was an asset for Orel IV as he moved from city to city. Playing organized sports helped him to break the ice in new places and gave him the confidence to interact with his peers. At nine he was a finalist in a national hit-run-throw competition sponsored by American Airlines; like most of the other major events in his life, he has preserved clippings about the competition in a scrapbook. Hershiser played Little League baseball in Southfield, Michigan, a Detroit suburb, and also found himself drawn to ice hockey. By the time he entered high school in Cherry Hill, a suburb of Philadelphia, he was adept at both sports.

Still, Hershiser's climb to prominence was "not one giant leap to glory," according to Wulf. The high school in Cherry Hill was large, and competition for spots on varsity teams was intense. Initially Hershiser got more recognition for his hockey skills. As a teen he played on the Junior Flyers squad, an interscholastic team sponsored by the Philadelphia professional hockey club. Hershiser's father told *Newsday* that his son "had a great slap shot, a great wrist shot. He loved ice hockey. He might have been a pretty good college player but he would never have been a good professional. He didn't have the demeanor."

Hershiser was a junior before he made the varsity baseball team, but then he turned in a better-than-average pitching record over the next two years. He was overlooked by the scouts, but he did get a combination hockey/baseball scholarship to Bowling Green State University. He chose Bowling Green primarily because he thought he would have a good chance of playing baseball regularly there, and he was bitterly disappointed when he was cut from the traveling squad as a freshman. After much soul-searching—he had contemplated joining his father's business—he decided to stay at Bowling Green, and he earned dean's list grades in his sophomore year. Wulf wrote: "In his sophomore year he also grew three inches, added about five miles an hour to his fastball and was finally good enough to crack the Falcons' traveling squad." With a junior year record of 6–2, he drew the attention of scouts for several clubs.

"People compare me to Clark Kent and Superman, but Clark Kent at least had a good body. I'm Jimmy Olsen."

Hershiser knew he would not be drafted by a professional team in an early round, so he decided that he would only sign with three clubs—the Yankees (closest to Buffalo, where he was born), the Phillies (closest to his friends in Cherry Hill), or the Dodgers. If none of those clubs wanted him, he would finish college and go into his father's business. The Dodgers chose Hershiser in the seventeenth round—hardly a fantastic vote of confidence—and sent him to a Class A team in Clinton, Iowa. Hershiser's first professional season, 1979, showed some promise. He went 4–0 and demonstrated a strong desire to learn all he could from the coaches in Clinton. That same year he also found Christianity, at the urging of teammate Butch Wickensheimer. Hershiser told *Sports Illustrated:* "At first, I thought, 'How can I be a Christian? I'm not straight enough.' I liked to have fun, I liked to be giddy. But in reading the Bible, I discovered that there was no contradiction there. You don't have to be boring to be a Christian. If anything, I felt freer after I found Christ, freer to express my emotions, freer to open up to people." The Dodgers thought enough of Hershiser to promote him, and he spent 1980 and 1981 with the Double A San Antonio team, working primarily as a reliever. There he met Jamie Byars, the daughter of an oil company executive, and they were married in February of 1981.

All did not go well for Hershiser in the Texas League. After an auspicious beginning in 1981, he watched his ERA soar to 4.72 during a disastrous road trip. Hershiser told the *Los Angeles Times* that he and his new wife "cried so much in the minor leagues together it was unbelievable. That's such an emotional trip down there. So tough. You're making bare minimum, living in places where you can't save a cent. And when you have a bad night or a bad week, it's like your dream is gone. When you're doing good it seems so close, but then the next day it can be gone again." After Hershiser gave up eight runs in less than four innings during a game in El Paso, he decided to quit. It took three people—the trainer, the manager, and the pitching coach—to talk him out of it, and he was still convinced they were "just trying to be polite." Hershiser stayed and improved measurably by the end of the year. He was promoted to Triple A Albuquerque in 1982. His frustration did not end in New Mexico, however. When spring training ended in 1983 he expected to be sent to Los Angeles. Instead he was placed back in Albuquerque, and according to Wulf, he "didn't exactly blow the Pacific Coast League away upon returning there." Luckily for him, Hershiser had a better season playing winter ball in the Dominican Republic. He was called to Los Angeles in 1984 as a long reliever. A key injury to pitcher Jerry Reuss gave Hershiser a place in the starting rotation on June 29. He has been there ever since.

"The key to Orel's success is his constant striving for perfection. Perfectionists are usually given a bad rap, but there's nothing wrong with trying to be better than you are."
—Sandy Koufax

Hershiser has rarely regarded his ascent to the big leagues as anything but a miracle. Thin and "nerdy," to use his own expression, he hardly fits the stereotype of the modern-day sports superstar. "Let's face it," he told *Sports Illustrated,* "I'm just a pale guy with glasses, long arms and a sunken chest. I look like I never lifted a weight. I look like I work in a flour factory. People compare me to Clark Kent and Superman, but Clark Kent at least had a good body. I'm Jimmy Olsen." Hershiser may lack imposing physical stature, but he has more than compensated for it by learning all he can about pitching and about each individual opponent he may face. He keeps statistics on most National League batters in a home computer, noting how they reacted to each pitch he threw them. These statistics are reviewed before game time in addition to the usual scouting reports, and where they vary, Hershiser trusts his own instincts. Wulf wrote: "If Hershiser gets [a three million dollar per year contract], it will be a tribute to his thirst for pitching knowledge, for that's what distinguishes him from most of his comrades in arms. Yes, he has a tremendous sinker, an above-average fastball and an outstanding curve, but other pitchers have 'stuff.' However, very few of them have hard disks on the opposition."

Hall of Fame pitcher Sandy Koufax, one of Hershiser's mentors, told *Sports Illustrated:* "The key to Orel's success is his constant striving for perfection. Perfectionists are usually given a bad rap, but there's nothing wrong with trying to be better than you are, the best that you can be. And Orel's going to have to get even better, not so much because the rest of the league will catch up to him, but because they're going to want to try that much harder to beat him." Batters may never find Hershiser an easy mark, though, given his native talent and his determination to out-think the opposition.

The 1988 baseball season was somewhat overshadowed by the Summer Olympics. When the Olympic smoke cleared, however, one name was on everyone's lips: Orel Hershiser. Midway through September, Hershiser was working at the peak of his form, compiling enough consecutive scoreless innings to threaten a longstanding record set by Hall of Fame great Don Drysdale. Hershiser simply had to pitch six straight shutouts—59 innings of scoreless ball—to break Drysdale's record. The feat seemed impossible, so Hershiser refused to think about it, especially when he was on the mound. By September 28, during a late-season game against the San Diego Padres, Hershiser was within reach of the goal. He had a shutout going into the ninth inning, enough to tie Drysdale's record, and he seemed satisfied with that. Manager Tommy Lasorda convinced him to try for the 59th inning, which was the tenth in an extra-innings game, and Hershiser managed a nail-biting three outs. "I had so much pressure on me," Hershiser told the *Philadelphia Inquirer.* "That is probably the most nervous I have ever been in my career." He also emphasized that he had other things in mind than a personal goal: "I was out there pitching for wins in a pennant race, not a streak."

Hershiser went on to pitch brilliantly in both the league championship series against the Mets and the World Series against the Oakland Athletics. His five-hit shutout in the seventh game gave his team the 1988 World Series crown. "As the very embodiment of the Dodgers' postseason Cinderella story," wrote

Wulf, Hershiser "pitched and occasionally hit L.A. to victory over the much better New York Mets and Oakland Athletics. Best of all, he carried himself with an amazing grace and amiability. He was stunning out there, but he also seemed a little stunned at what he was accomplishing, and his manner touched a responsive chord in a great many people."

Hershiser has found so many new fans principally because he has adhered to the ordinary, workday attitude that saw him through his years in school and in the minors. As he told the *Los Angeles Times:* "I grew up in middle class America.... I lived in a 4-bedroom home that was about 2,500 square feet.... I pumped gas for 3 years in high school to earn money and cleaned the garage on Saturdays." Now, he says, "when I do something, I want to do it to the fullest of my ability.... But that's just the way I was [raised]. You don't just sweep the garage, you clean the garage. You don't pick up your room, you clean your room."

Hershiser, who may become baseball's most highly paid player, lives in Los Angeles with his wife and two sons, Orel V and Jordan Douglas. He credits his wife—and his faith in Christ—for his success, noting that Jamie is everything from his "personal secretary" to his "best friend." On the mound Hershiser is a study in concentration and seriousness, but in off-hours he is described as relaxed and affable, "human, perhaps, but also very special," to quote *Newsday* reporter Joe Gergen. Asked what he thought might have contributed to his son's phenomenal success in baseball, Orel Hershiser III had no hesitation in his reply. Hershiser does so well, his father said, because "he was well brought up."

Sources

Los Angeles Times, September 22, 1988; October 24, 1988.
Newsday, October 17, 1988.
New York Times, October 16, 1988.
Philadelphia Inquirer, September 29, 1988.
Sports Illustrated, October 31, 1988; December 19, 1988.

—Sidelights by Mark Kram

Clifton Keith Hillegass

Courtesy of Cliff's Notes, Inc.

Publisher

Born April 18, 1918, in Rising City, Neb.; son of Pearl Clinton and Rosena (Dechert) Hillegass; married Catherine McDonald, 1937 (divorced); married Mary D. Patterson, April 17, 1968; children: James, Linda, Diane, Kimberly. *Education:* Midland College, B.S., 1937; graduate student, University of Nebraska, 1937–39.

Addresses: *Office*—Cliff's Notes, Inc., 1701 P Street, Lincoln, Neb. 68508.

Career

Employed by Nebraska Book Co., Lincoln, Neb., beginning 1939, became manager of wholesale division, 1946–64, consultant, 1964—; founder and president of Cliff's Notes, Inc., Lincoln, 1958–83, chairman of the board, 1983—.

Sidelights

Though the name Clifton Hillegass may not be as instantly recognized by high-school English students as names like Shakespeare, Hemingway, and Faulkner, chances are any one of those students has bought, read, and relished a Hillegass book. That's because Clifton Hillegass is the founder and guiding light behind Cliff's Notes (also known as Cliffs Notes and Cliff Notes), those seemingly ubiquitous literature study guides that have peppered classrooms and study sessions since 1958.

A self-made American success story, Hillegass was born to strict Lutheran parents in small-town Nebraska in 1918. "My parents told me if I wanted to go to college, I would have to pay for most of it myself," Hillegass told *Rolling Stone* interviewer Norman Atkins. "It seemed fair to me. So I spent a lot of my childhood concerned with how to make money." A lifelong bookworm, Hillegass began his career in the textbook division of the Nebraska Book Co., which gave him a firm grounding on what students were reading. In 1958 he encountered "Kismet in the form of Jack Cole—a Canadian publisher with a full line of study guides running from algebra to zoology," as Frank W. Martin relates in a *People* article. Hillegass, he adds, "smell[ed] a winner."

In partnership with Cole and with the help of Hillegass's first wife, Catherine, the fledgling publisher began producing literary guides in the Hillegass family basement in Lincoln, Nebraska. The Notes, behind their arresting yellow-and-black striped covers, offer character analyses, study tips, summaries, and sample test questions. Sales began briskly and then increased as the Notes' reputation caught on. Today, reports Atkins, "Cliffs annually ships out about 5 million Notes a year and rakes in more than $7 million in revenues and completely dominates the book-notes market." The reporter also offers some Notes trivia: "Did you know that the best-selling Note is *The Scarlet Letter,* followed closely by *Huckleberry Finn, Hamlet* and *Macbeth?*''

For almost as long as there have been Cliff's Notes, there has been controversy surrounding students' sometimes desperate dependence on them. Of course, many teachers would prefer that their students formulate their own summaries of literature. Hillegass has always maintained that his ''keys to the classics,'' as he calls them, are meant just as augmentation, not as a substitute for the actual book.

In Martin's article, Hillegass uncovers a bit of the mystique behind who actually writes Cliff's Notes. ''Someone involved in 20 years of teaching Shakespeare often has too specialized a knowledge. Eventually we found that the best *Notes* were written by graduate students.'' For a Note on Alice Walker's *The Color Purple,* Atkins reports, Hillegass accepted a manuscript by an 18-year-old Georgetown University sophomore.

Comparing Hillegass to another notable entrepreneur, the late founder of the McDonald's burger chain, Atkins remarks that the publisher ''became the Ray Kroc of study outlines, America's single greatest purveyor of fast food for thought.... Somewhere in that vast space between Ray Kroc and [famed educator] Horace Mann, Cliff will be remembered. If not the man, then surely the myth. For the expression *Cliffs Notes* has already become a part of our language.''

Sources

People, May 16, 1983.
Rolling Stone, March 26, 1987.

—*Sketch by Susan Salter*

Bruce Hornsby

AP/Wide World Photos

Singer, musician, songwriter

Born c. 1954; married. *Education:* Attended Berklee School of Music; graduate of University of Miami, 1977.

Career

Began playing in rock bands in the late 1970s; staff songwriter for 20th Century Fox in Los Angeles, Calif.; formed own band, Bruce Hornsby and the Range, c. 1980.

Awards: Grammy Award for best new artist, 1987.

Sidelights

Success long eluded rock performer Bruce Hornsby. While many in the recording industry considered his work promising, he was rejected by all the major labels. "I was going nowhere fast," he told Dennis Hunt of the *Los Angeles Times.* "I was writing these formula pop songs. It wasn't what I wanted to do." In 1985, Hornsby decided to follow his instincts. He and his brother, John, began writing music that blended jazz, country-folk, and New Age. The result, an album entitled *The Way It Is,* earned Hornsby and his four-man band, the Range, a Grammy Award.

A native of Williamsburg, Virginia, Hornsby grew up wanting to be a professional basketball player. While in high school, he discovered the piano. He later studied at the University of Miami School of Music, where he learned classical and jazz piano. After receiving his degree, he returned to Virginia and formed a rock cover band that played in bars and clubs throughout the South. In 1980, he moved to Los Angeles, where he worked as a staff composer for 20th Century Fox.

During this time, he recorded and distributed demo tapes. Some of the biggest names in the music industry took notice, and several record companies expressed interest. But Hornsby received no contract offers. He enlisted in Sheena Easton's road band for two years. In 1985, Hornsby recorded another demo. This time, he ignored the advice given him by industry insiders; he was tired of trying to write what other people thought was commercial. The tape consisted of four songs written by Hornsby and his brother, and it featured Hornsby, alone, singing and playing acoustic piano, bass, drums, and accordian. There was no electronic music. "I just wanted a tape to sound exactly like I heard the music in my head and not have to compromise with anybody about any of it," he explained to Pam Lambert of the *Wall Street Journal.* The tape led to a contract with RCA.

The debut album of Bruce Hornsby and the Range, *The Way It Is,* went platinum. Its title track, a song about racial prejudice, topped the *Billboard* chart. Another single, "Mandolin Rain," reached the top ten. Hornsby produced six of the album's songs, three others were produced by Huey Lewis, an early champion of Hornsby's work. The album's style, which Lambert described as "jazz-tinged folk-rock," and socially conscious material struck a chord with audiences and critics. Singer Lewis has called Hornsby's music "rural Southern highbrow." A *People* reviewer wrote: "With their small-town settings and common heros, Hornsby's are the sort of heartland tunes that just might knock a chip in the Springsteen-Mellencamp monopoly." At the 1987 Grammy Awards, Hornsby and his group were named best new artist.

Their second album, *Scenes from the Southside,* has also sold millions. Hornsby's music has been influenced by jazz pianist Keith Jarrett and singer George Jones; his lyrics are drawn from current events and social trends. Mostly, his work reflects his Southern roots. "I guess this sounds pompous, but we want to . . . create our own sort of microcosm of a place," he told *Rolling Stone.* "Kind of like Faulkner, I guess, had a county where all his things were set. If there's anything special about what we're doing, that's what it is."

Discography

The Way It Is, RCA, 1986.
Scenes from the Southside, RCA, 1988.

Sources

Christian Science Monitor, February 23, 1987.
Detroit Free Press, March 31, 1987.
Los Angeles Times, June 21, 1987.
Minneapolis Star and Tribune, March 13, 1987.
New York Times, September 19, 1988.
People, October 13, 1986; November 17, 1986.
Rolling Stone, February 12, 1987.
Stereo Review, December, 1986.
Wall Street Journal, February 19, 1987.

—Sketch by Denise Wiloch

Edward Horrigan, Jr.

Tobacco company executive

AP/Wide World Photos

Born September 23, 1929, in New York, N.Y.; son of Edward A. and Margaret V. (Kells) Horrigan; married Elizabeth R. Herperger, June 27, 1953; children: Ellen, Christopher, Gordon, Brian. *Education:* University of Connecticut, B.S., 1950; Harvard University, graduate of Advanced Management Program, 1965.

Addresses: *Home*—2815 Bartram Rd., Winston-Salem, N.C. 27106. *Office*—World Headquarters Bldg., RJR Nabisco, Inc., Reynolds Blvd., Winston-Salem, N.C. 27102.

Career

Procter & Gamble Co., New York City, sales manager, 1954–58; Ebonite Co., Boston, Mass., general manager, 1958–61; division vice-president, T.J. Lipton, Inc., 1961–73; Buckingham Corp., New York City, chairman and president, 1973–78; R.J. Reynolds Tobacco International, Inc., Winston-Salem, N.C., chairman and chief executive officer, 1978–80; R.J. Reynolds Tobacco Co., Winston-Salem, chairman, president, and chief executive officer, beginning 1980; R.J. Reynolds Industries, Inc., Winston-Salem, executive vice-president, 1981–84, president and chief operating officer, 1984–85; RJR Nabisco, Inc., Winston-Salem, vice-chairman, 1985—. *Military service:* U.S. Army, 1950–54, served as infantry officer; received Silver Star and Purple Heart.

Sidelights

For several years Edward Horrigan, Jr., has served as a top executive at R.J. Reynolds, a multibillion-dollar food, beverage, and tobacco company based in North Carolina. During the mid-1980s, Horrigan waged war against a powerful antismoking campaign. Through printed advertisements and in public appearances, he questioned the evidence of smoking's harmful effects on health. It was considered a bold, albeit risky, move by industry insiders. But Horrigan believed that his company stood to gain by tackling the anti-cigarette lobby.

Horrigan joined R.J. Reynolds Tobacco International in 1978. Two years later he was appointed chairman, president, and chief executive officer of R.J. Reynolds Tobacco Company. One of his first acts was to discontinue Reynolds' low-tar "natural" cigarette, Real. Despite a massive advertising campaign, the brand had failed. "There was no consumer need or desire for a so-called natural cigarette," Horrigan told *Forbes'* Jeff Blyskal. A short time later he introduced another low-tar product, Salem Ultra Lights, hoping to trade on the name of Reynolds' second most popular cigarette.

The company's need to successfully market a low-tar cigarette stemmed from medical research showing a direct link between smoking and heart and lung disease. The U.S. Surgeon General, health organizations (such as the American Cancer Society), and smaller groups opposed to smoking had long been engaged in a vigorous campaign to warn the public about the dangers of lighting up. Reacting to the mounting scientific evidence, as well as to pressure from lobby groups, states and the federal government imposed higher taxes on tobacco products; laws were enacted to restrict smoking in public buildings. The tobacco industry, though mindful of declining sales, largely ignored the opposition. R.J. Reynolds, however, decided to fight back.

In 1984 Horrigan unveiled a national advocacy campaign. In newspaper and magazine advertisements, and on television talk shows, Horrigan called for a "debate" on studies linking smoking and disease. While he shied from arguing the benefits of cigarettes, he presented the results of independent research which challenged the "causal relationship" between smoking and poor health. Horrigan did not want to "encourage smoking," wrote Kevin McManus in *Forbes,* "only to inform the public there's more than one side to the smoking issue."

Health authorities were quick to respond. In press releases and advertisements they attacked the Reynolds campaign. Why was Horrigan willing to expose the industry to fresh criticism? According to McManus, some observers noted that if the strategy "succeeds in quelling the health fears of only a fraction of those smokers who otherwise would have stopped smoking, Reynolds benefits." Or, as tobacco industry analyst Arthur Kirsch explained, "In a business as profitable as this . . . you can take the adverse press and everything else that goes along with selling cigarettes."

In 1985 R.J. Reynolds bought Nabisco Brands, Inc. Horrigan was named vice-chairman of the newly-formed RJR Nabisco, Inc., directing its foreign and domestic tobacco operations. In addition, Horrigan oversees corporate affairs and public and government relations.

Sources

Forbes, July 21, 1980; March 10, 1984.
Fortune, March 5, 1984.
New York Times, September 19, 1986.

—Sketch by Denise Wiloch

Bob Hoskins

AP/Wide World Photos

British actor

Born October 26, 1942, in Bury St. Edmonds, Suffolk, England; son of Robert (a bookkeeper) and Elsie (Hopkins) Hoskins; married Jane Livesey (divorced); married; wife's name, Linda (a former schoolteacher); children: (first marriage) Alex, Sarah; (second marriage) Rosa, Jack. *Education:* Studied accounting for three years.

Addresses: *Home*—London, England. *Agent*—Hope & Lyne, 5 Milner Place, London N1 1TN, England.

Career

Worked as a laborer, window cleaner, merchant seaman, circus fire-eater, and agricultural worker on a *kibbutz* in Israel; actor, 1968—. Stage appearances include "Romeo and Juliet," 1969, "The Country Wife," 1970, "The Baby Elephant," 1971, "Richard III," 1971, "King Lear," 1972, "Antony and Cleopatra," 1973, "Pygmalion," 1974, "As You Like It," 1974, "The Iceman Cometh," 1976, "England, England," 1977, and "Guys and Dolls," 1982. Feature films include "The National Health," 1974, "Royal Flash," 1975, "Inserts," 1976, "Zulu Dawn," 1980, "Pink Floyd's The Wall," 1982, "The Long Good Friday," 1982, "The Honorary Consul," 1983, "Lassiter," 1984, "The Cotton Club," 1984, "Brazil," 1985, "Sweet Liberty," 1986, "Mona Lisa," 1986, "A Prayer for the Dying," 1987, "The Lonely Passion of Judith Hearne," 1987, "Who Framed Roger Rabbit?" 1988, and "The Raggedy Rawney," 1988. Television films include "Her Majesty's Pleasure," 1972, "Softly, Softly," 1973, "On the Move," 1975, "Pennies from Heaven," 1977, "Sheppey," 1980, "Othello," 1981, "You Don't Have to Walk to Fly," 1982, "On the Road," "New Scotland Yard," "Three Piece Suit," "In the Looking Glass," "Mycenae and Men," "The Beggars Opera," and "Mussolini: The Decline and Fall of Il Duce."

Awards: Best Actor Award nominations, British Academy of Film and Television Arts, 1978, for "Pennies from Heaven," and 1982, for "The Long Good Friday"; *Evening Standard* Best Actor Award, 1982, for "The Long Good Friday"; Academy Award nomination, Best Actor Award from Cannes Film Festival, New York Drama Critics Circle Award, and Golden Globe Award, all 1986, for "Mona Lisa."

Sidelights

British actor Bob Hoskins is a performer of originality and resourcefulness who has emerged as an international screen star—much to his surprise. Hoskins is the first to admit that he lacks the good looks and social polish of typical movie stars; nonetheless, he has immense talent and has created a number of powerful, riveting screen interpretations that have made him a hot commercial property. Hoskins's lead role as private eye Harry Valiant in the megahit "Who Framed Roger Rabbit?" has cemented his star status. But it was his gripping portrayal of the ex-convict George in "Mona Lisa" that first brought him critical acclaim. Hoskins won a number of best actor awards for that performance, including the Golden Globe and Cannes Film Festival selections, as well as four from prestigious film critics associations. (Hoskins lost the Oscar to Paul Newman who won for "The Color of Money.") Although Hoskins may not live or look like a star, he has become one.

Commenting on his physical appearance, Hoskins told Michael Billington of the *New York Times,* "I'm 5 foot 6 inches and cubic. My own mum wouldn't call me pretty." *People* magazine described him as "a fireplug with eyebrows." Hoskins is balding with hair that looks glued to the side of his head. His physique is powerful but not muscular, and his short height exaggerates his physical density. "He has a wide, oblate face and a chunky dense presence of the sort associated with wrestlers or weight lifters. But like a lot of other small powerful men, he's surprisingly light and dainty on his feet," wrote William Boyd in the *New York Times Magazine.* Hoskins's physical appearance actually serves his acting quite well, giving his performances an unmistakable edge on screen. Hoskins admits to having "all the vices"; he smokes and eats what he likes without regard to the consequences. Clearly, he is not a leading man in the tradition of Sean Connery or Michael Caine. Boyd concluded: "Good looks and class—whether assumed or natural—were the criteria by which British leading men used to be chosen. Hoskins's fame and popularity show just how far those values have been inverted."

Hoskins was born in Suffolk but grew up in North London. Today he lives in the working-class borough of Islington, not far from his parents, with his second wife, a former schoolteacher, and their two young children. He takes great pride in his Cockney accent and background. "My accent is my identity. It's me," he told *People.* "And that's why I swear a lot, too. It's a kind of snobbery, a kind of pride, I like the way I am. It's a matter of integrity, you see, and of necessity. Whoever I play, whoever I become, I must 'ave a startin'-off point. I must be sure of who I am, so sure it doesn't worry me, before I become someone else." His acting, he believes, is tied to his roots. "This part of London is where I'm at 'ome . . . . I'm 'appiest among costermongers an' that. Nobody's impressed by me, 'ere. I'd feel nayked without relatives an' friends. An' I don't want to lose the street, because that's what I act from." Hoskins's Cockney accent is no impediment for his adept mastering of other dialects for his movie roles. In his Hollywood movies, he speaks with native American accuracy, as he has shown in "Who Killed Roger Rabbit?" "Sweet Liberty," and "The Cotton Club." His gangster and tough guys roles are always enhanced by his ability with accents.

Hoskins stumbled on an acting career quite accidently. He was in the bar of London's Unity Theatre one day in 1968 when he was mistaken for an actor waiting to audition. He read the lead and got the part. This fluke occurrence changed his life. Hoskins had dropped out of school at fifteen and done a number of jobs for the next ten years, including truckdriver, window cleaner, porter, even fire-eater. He had also studied to become a commercial artist and an accountant.

Hoskins paid his dues on the British regional theater circuit and got his big break when he stole a scene from John Gielgud in Charles Wood's "Veterans," a play about movie making, at London's Royal Court Theater in 1972. Producer Kenith Trodd was impressed by Hoskins's performance and recruited him to star as the sheet-music salesman in Dennis Potter's "Pennies from Heaven" for British television. In addition to television, Hoskins's theater credits include Sam Shepard's "True West" and the role of Nathan Detroit in "Guys and Dolls" for Britain's National Theater, and Iago in Shakespeare's "Othello" for BBC-TV.

Hoskins sets aside questions on the durability of his success in films. As he said to Boyd, "I'm a professional actor, that's all, and I've never been out of work." Acting is the center of his life. According to *People,* he defines acting as "my religion. A real performance is as much a shock to the system as a road accident. Every job that comes up, I love. It's bleedin' maavelous!" He credits Vanessa Redgrave, Helen Mirren, and Diana Rigg as actresses from whom he has learned the magic of acting as an art, which may be surprising given Hoskins's rough screen exterior. He also admires James Cagney, Humphrey Bogart, and Edward G. Robinson, and he sees himself in their mold—tough guys with the ability to show a depth of genuine emotion in films.

Hoskins's view of women and their traditional roles in society defines his aesthetic approach to acting. He explained to Billington: "For nearly 2,000 years women have had to play a secondary role to men, but women can express a private moment or hidden thought without saying a word. Acting is all about the revelations of those private, unshielded moments. If you want to find out how to express something, you watch the women, and that is what I have done all through my career. In acting you've got to use the feminine side of you. I don't mean the limp wrist but what are still considered the feminine qualities: vulnerability, affection, tenderness. I think a really dignified person is someone who allows all that to show and is not afraid to be themselves."

"Mona Lisa" proved to be a film that was ideal for Hoskins, exemplifying his acting talents as well as presenting a character close to his own streetwise background. The story is about a Cockney tough named George who serves a seven-year prison sentence for his boss, Mortwell (Michael Caine). Upon release George wants a job and is assigned to be a driver for Simone (Cathy Tyson), a beautiful young black call girl who works high-class hotels and has a rich clientele. George is a tough, vulgar man who is essentially an innocent. In preparing for the part, Hoskins went to the London Zoo and observed exotic caged birds. "To me that explained George, who's got a big soul trapped inside him. First of all he's been in prison. But he's also trapped inside his own ignorance," Hoskins told Billington. For George, Simone is both a "tart" and a "lady," and he falls in love with her. The beauty of "Mona Lisa" lies in the scenes between Hoskins and Tyson. They deliver superb, memorable performances in this moody romantic thriller.

Hoskins was the perfect choice for George who, wrote Canby, "talks tough and knows how to handle himself in the sleazy, violent world he inhabits. His masculinity is a serious business as well as his protection." Caine, as the evil crime boss, unscores the seamy side of "Mona Lisa." The film is built on contrasts and has a real-unreal tension. The pairing of Hoskins and Caine—they were also in Alan Alda's "Sweet Liberty" and the film version of Graham Greene's *The Honorary Consul,* retitled "Beyond the Limit"—is, wrote Pauline Kael in the *New Yorker,* an inspired casting decision: "They take paper conceptions and turn them into characters who are more alive than anybody else in their pictures."

"Who Framed Roger Rabbit?" the 1988 summer box office hit, is a technical marvel combining live action with animation to a degree never before realized in film. Executive producer Steven Spielberg got permission to use the great cartoon characters from Walt

Bob Hoskins tries to separate himself from his animated co-star in the 1988 film "Who Framed Roger Rabbit?" AP/Wide World Photos.

Disney Studios and Warner Brothers to tell a mock *film noir* story about Roger Rabbit, a cartoon star wrongly accused of the murder of Marvin Acme (Stubby Kaye), who was photographed by private eye Eddie Valiant (Hoskins) with Roger's voluptuous wife, Jessica. Hoskins as Valiant is an alcoholic private eye who hates the Toons, as they are called, because a Toon killed his brother, driving Valiant to drink and despair. The frameup is really a ploy by Judge Doom (Christopher Lloyd) who wants to destroy Toontown, making it possible for the construction of the new Los Angeles freeway system. The plot is similar to that of "Chinatown," and the 1947 setting gives the action its Raymond Chandler ambiance.

Directed by Robert Zemeckis, whose previous credit was "Back to the Future," another blockbuster hit, "Who Framed Roger Rabbit?" called upon over 300 animators and visual effects artists whose job was to integrate actors and cartoon characters. British animator Richard Williams directed these efforts, with the assistance of Walt Disney Studios and George Lucas's Industrial Light and Magic. "Roger" has over 80,000 drawings, accounting for its realistic animation effect, which took more than two years to complete.

For his part, Hoskins had the difficult job of working without being able to see the animated characters, who were drawn in later. Comedian Charles Fleischer, the voice of Roger, wore a rabbit costume out of camera range to help Hoskins visualize Roger and get the action correct. The triumph of the movie is in the appearance of cartoon characters coexisting in the same space with humans. The Toons also are faithful to their cartoon personalities. They live for the corny joke and sight gag; they are physically indestructible, and much of the humor is their ability to bounce back literally from any violent encounter. The contribution of "Who Framed Roger Rabbit?" as an innovative technical achievement is undisputable, even if the movie can be faulted for a flimsy plot and predictable ending.

Hoskins made his directing debut in "The Raggedy Rawney," a film about the effects of war on the innocent. He wrote the script from an idea he first heard from his grandmother. Hoskins stars as Darky, the leader of a gypsy-like band of refugees who are struggling to survive during a war fought at an unspecified time in an unnamed European country (it was filmed in Czechoslovakia). Hoskins's theme is "The enemy is war itself." With an excellent ensemble cast led by Hoskins, the film chronicles the brutality of war and the endearing humanity of the gypsies. "Theirs is the human spirit at its best, which is really the most compelling attribute of the film itself," wrote *Variety*. Hoskins's directing and screenwriting credit adds to his prestige as a major presence in the film industry.

In addition to the two lead roles in "Mona Lisa" and "Who Framed Roger Rabbit?" that have brought him critical acclaim and audience recognition, Hoskins has appeared in Francis Ford Coppola's "The Cotton Club," Alan Alda's "Sweet Liberty," Mike Hodges's "A Prayer for the Dying," and Jack Clayton's "The Lonely Passion of Judith Hearne." The common denominator in all of Hoskins's major performances is his intelligence as an actor. He transforms himself into the character he is playing, using both his mind and body to create a believable illusion. He finds pleasure in working with some of the best film actors today—such as Mickey Rourke and Alan Bates in "A Prayer for the Dying" and Maggie Smith in "The Lonely Passion of Judith Hearne."

Hoskins is at the top of his profession and has emerged as a British actor eagerly sought by American directors. When Brian De Palma was casting the role of Al Capone in "The Untouchables," his first choice was Robert De Niro but he asked Hoskins to be his second choice. Hoskins agreed, De Niro took the part, and De Palma gave Hoskins $200,000, a windfall for an actor who is honest, straightforward, and from all accounts untouched by the celebrity aspects of his profession.

Sources

American Film, September, 1987.
Columbus Dispatch, June 26, 1988.
Dayton Daily News, June 26, 1988.
New Republic, June 23, 1986.
Newsweek, June 16, 1986; September 14, 1987.
New Yorker, June 2, 1986; June 16, 1986; December 28, 1987.
New York Times, April 16, 1982; June 20, 1982; May 14, 1986; May 18, 1986; June 8, 1986; June 13, 1986.
New York Times Magazine, December 6, 1987.
People, September 10, 1985; May 14, 1986; June 16, 1986; December 22, 1986; February 1, 1988.
Time, September 14, 1987; February 1, 1988.
Variety, May 18, 1988.
Village Voice, January 5, 1988.

—*Sidelights by Jon Saari*

Godfrey Hounsfield

AP/Wide World Photos

Electrical engineer and inventor

Full name, Godfrey Newbold Hounsfield; born August 28, 1919, in Nottinghamshire, England; son of Thomas Hounsfield. *Education:* Earned radio communications qualification from City and Guilds College, London, England, c. 1939; diploma in electrical engineering from Faraday House Electrical Engineering College, London, 1951.

Addresses: *Office*—c/o EMI Central Research Laboratories, Trevor Rd., Hayes, Middlesex, England.

Career

EMI Ltd., Hayes, Middlesex, England, 1951—, headed design team that designed the EMIDEC 1100, the first large all-transistor computer in Great Britain, and later worked in area of memory storage, head of medical systems section of EMI's central research laboratories, 1972–76, senior staff scientist, 1977—.

Awards: Recipient of MacRobert Award, 1972; received Wilhelm-Exner Medal from Austrian Industrial Association, 1974; awarded Prince Philip Medal, 1975; Lasker Award, 1975; recipient of Duddell Bronze Medal, 1976; Golden Plate Award from American Academy of Achievement, 1976; Reginald Mitchell Gold Medal from Stoke-on-Trent Association of Engineers, 1976; recipient of Churchill Gold Medal, 1976; Gairdner Foundation Award, 1976; decorated commander of Order of British Empire, 1976, knight, 1981; co-recipient (with Alan Cormack) of Nobel Prize in Physiology or Medicine, 1979, for inventing and developing computerized axial tomography (CAT) scanner.

Sidelights

Soon after he received the 1979 Nobel Prize for Physiology or Medicine, Godfrey Hounsfield described himself as "not the sort of person to build model airplanes." Instead, the British electrical engineer was the sort of person to build a revolutionary gadget that astounded the medical world. It may seem glib to call the CAT (computerized axial tomography) scanner a "gadget"—the Nobel Committee stated in its citation that "No other method within x-ray diagnosis within such a short time has led to such remarkable advances in research and a multitude of applications." The CAT scan makes possible a two-dimensional, highly detailed peek inside the human body, often eliminating the need for exploratory surgery and painful diagnostic procedures. Still, Hounsfield's energetic, pragmatic approach to his miraculous invention suggests simultaneously the mind of an electronics genius and the skilled, greasy hands of an ace mechanic. Hounsfield probably wouldn't mind the term "gadget" at all.

Hounsfield was born in the English county of Nottinghamshire in 1919. As a child he not only avoided building model airplanes but had his own laboratory. "I played around with farm machinery," Hounsfield recounted in *Nature,* "and to prevent myself being bored I started to reason why things might work." That curiosity led to his constructing a record player out of spare parts when he was thirteen. In his later teens, Hounsfield built radio sets. Hounsfield had earned a radio communications qualification from City and Guilds College in London prior to the outbreak of World War II. From 1939 to 1945, he served in the Royal Air Force; after attending the RAF's Cranwell Radar School, he became a lecturer there. After the war was over, Hounsfield studied engineering at Faraday House Electrical Engineering College in London.

Immediately upon graduating in 1951, Hounsfield went to work for EMI Ltd., the British conglomerate which was to employ him throughout his career. Perhaps best known as a record producer (the Beatles recorded under the EMI label), EMI's holdings also included cinemas, dance halls and a medical electronics division. Hounsfield went to work at first on radar systems, later moving into computer design. He distinguished himself as an innovator at EMI. He served as Project Engineer on the first large computer developed in England, the EMIDEC 1100, and later worked in the area of memory storage.

While studying, in 1967, the capability of computers for pattern recognition, Hounsfield first got the idea that would eventually lead to the CAT scanner. While on one of his "rambles" through the English countryside, it occurred to Hounsfield that if a computer could recognize printed characters, it could assimilate the information derived from x-rays and reconstruct an accurate picture of the internal contents of a three-dimensional object—like a human head. If such an object was approached tomographically (in cross-sectional slices), it would be possible to systematically "scan" it with x-rays, record the changes in intensity of those x-rays as they passed through the object, and have a computer spit the data back out in picture form.

Hounsfield knew a great deal about computers, a little about radiology, and almost nothing about medicine. He couldn't be sure that the medical world would want a device for producing more accurate pictures of peoples' interiors. But he suspected that he could generate some interest. In fact, several other ramblers had traveled this very road even before Hounsfield. Dr. William Oldendorf had even produced a model, in the early 1960s, of a tomographic scanner. What the University of California neurologist and psychologist lacked was the technology needed to compute all of the information that a scan would generate. As recounted in the book *Breakthroughs* by P. Ranganath Nayak and John M. Ketteringham, Oldendorf lamented in a speech to the Institute of Radio Engineers that there was no alternative to unpleasant diagnostic tests like the angiography and the ventriculography. "Each time I perform one of these primitive procedures," said the doctor, "I wonder why no more pressing need is felt . . . to seek some technique that would yield direct information about brain structure without traumatizing it."

With his expertise in highly complex computer systems and his dedication to problem-solving, Hounsfield was ideally equipped to tackle the job before him. The authors of *Breakthroughs* note that as Hounsfield "was building a hypothesis on one side of his brain, he was building a gadget on the other." EMI was willing to listen to Hounsfield's idea, but the building of such a device as he proposed promised to be costly. Hounsfield applied to the British Department of Health and Social Services (DHSS), and received a grant for $15,000 with which to construct a prototype. He also received the help of two DHSS radiologists, James Ambrose and Louis Kreel.

Hounsfield's prototype had, as noted in *Breakthroughs,* "the aspect of a successful expedition to a flea market." He used a vacuum cleaner motor and an industrial lathe bed, into which was mounted a 10-inch plastic box filled with water and an odd assortment of metal fragments and other odds and ends. An x-ray "gun" was placed on one side of the box. It shot gamma rays through the box to a scintillation counter located on the other side. As the thin shafts of radiation came through the box, they were altered by what they encountered inside, and that change was read and stored by a computer. The scanning device was moved, one degree at a time, to give readings at a succession of angles or picture points. When the readings for the whole object being scanned had been compiled, the computer calculated all of the values and reassembled them on a monitor screen. This produced a picture of the object's interior, and the picture could then be photographed by an ordinary camera to produce a permanent record.

The first scans conducted by Hounsfield and his associates consisted of 28,800 readings—a process which took nine days (today's scanners can assimilate 115,000 picture points in less than a minute).

Hounsfield soon graduated from the box of water and metal fragments to scans of cow and preserved human brains and pig carcasses. The results were exciting. The scanner was producing very clear pictures that showed the varying densities of tissue in much more detail than could be seen on ordinary x-rays.

By 1971, DHSS was committed enough to Hounsfield's project to advance more money for its development. And DHSS promised to buy the first five scanners if EMI would build them. Accordingly, Hounsfield moved his operations to Atkinson Morley Hospital in Wimbledon, where in September of 1971 the first CAT scanner (designed to scan heads only) was installed. The first scan conducted on a human subject involved a woman with a brain tumor. Her doctors wanted to know more about the tumor—whether it was solid or cystic, necrotic or well-defined. The picture produced by the scanner was remarkably clear, showing a cystic tumor located in the left frontal lobe of the brain. Previously, this information could not have been obtained without exploratory surgery.

"The sciences are far more exciting than the arts, than fantasy."

It was obvious that Hounsfield and his cohorts were on to something very big. John Powell, EMI's new Group Technical Director for the electronics division, sensed that the CAT scanner could be a lucrative product for his company, and he was determined that it should succeed. In April 1972 he initiated an aggressive marketing campaign with the announcement, following a presentation to the British Radiological Society by Hounsfield and Ambrose, that EMI would begin to produce CAT scanners.

Powell believed that the CAT scanner—which promised to carry a high price tag—would have its best chance to thrive in the United States, where it was thought that physicians were more open to new, expensive technology because they could depend on private medical insurers to pay for it. In the summer of 1972 Hounsfield traveled to New York to present a series of neuroradiological lectures. Using the photos gathered through the months of testing at Atkinson Morley, Hounsfield wooed the American medical establishment. He recounted in *Breakthroughs,* "I sold a dozen machines . . . just for showing pictures."

Even more interest was generated in November of 1972, when Hounsfield presented EMI's first CAT scanner, the EMI CT 1000, to the Radiological Society of North America's annual meeting in Chicago. Hounsfield shared his year's worth of clinical experience with the assemblage, and the reaction was very enthusiastic. Despite the costliness of the machine, orders came in from all over the United States as well as other countries. With this, EMI began producing CAT scanners in earnest. By 1977, the company had built 1130 scanners, ranging in price from $300,000 to $1 million, comprising 20 percent of EMI's total profits for that year.

Meanwhile, Hounsfield had set to work on whole-body scanners, which EMI's Powell planned to produce in the United States. EMI was prepared to have the whole-body scanner ready for the marketplace by 1975, but during the late seventies problems arose. U.S. President Jimmy Carter's campaign to contain high medical costs, snags in the design of the whole-body scanner, and a severe downturn in the music industry resulting in a reduction in corporate profit all crippled EMI's efforts to succeed in the scanner segment of its operations. In 1980, after losing about $25 million, EMI completely withdrew from the medical electronics field, leaving the making of CAT scanners to several other companies.

Despite EMI's failure during the late 1970s to capitalize on Hounsfield's accomplishment, the man himself was thriving during the same period. He receive numerous awards and honors for his contribution to medical progress, and in 1979 came the most prestigious prize of all—the Nobel. Hounsfield shared the honor with Alan Cormack, a South Africa-born physics instructor at Tufts University. During the early 1960s, Cormack had, working independently, developed the mathematical calculations needed to determine the absorption rate of x-ray radiation by various tissues. By 1979 Cormack was involved in an entirely different field (nuclear and particle physics) and has said of his earlier research: "It was kind of a sideline. I was astonished to get the award." The 1979 prize was unusual not only in its recognition of applied rather than basic (theoretical) science, but because the two recipients had never met and had carried on their work entirely separately, and neither had ever earned a Ph.D. Hounsfield stated that he planned to use his share of the $190,000 prize money to build a laboratory in his home. Such a purpose was certainly in keeping with his conviction, reported in *Nature,* that "the sciences are far more exciting than the arts, than fantasy."

The world has benefitted from Hounsfield's passion for science—particularly those patients who would have had to undergo painful and invasive diagnostic procedures and exploratory surgery. Though critics contend that the CAT scanner's cost is too high and that it is too often used when less expensive techniques might suffice, the device has eliminated some of the terror and uncertainty that is so frequently a part of illness. Its creator emerged out of the mysterious realm of gamma rays and complex computers to produce, as the authors of *Breakthroughs* relate, "a *product,* a thing that worked."

Sources

Books

Nayak, P. Ranganath, and John M. Kettering, *Breakthroughs,* Rawson, 1986.

Periodicals

Nature, October 18, 1979.
Newsweek, October 22, 1979.
New York Times, October 12, 1979.
Physics Today, December, 1979.
Science, November 30, 1979.
Scientific American, December, 1979.
Time, October 18, 1979.

—Sidelights by Kelly King Howes

Holly Hunter

AP/Wide World Photos

Actress

Born March 20, 1958, in Conyers, Ga.; father a sporting goods manufacturer's representative and part-time farmer. *Education:* Carnegie Mellon University, B.A., 1980.

Addresses: *Home*—New York, N.Y. *Agent*—International Creative Management, 40 West 57th St., New York, N.Y. 10019.

Career

Began acting in high school drama club; spent two summers during high school in a summer stock troupe in upstate New York; stage appearances include "Battery," 1981, "Crimes of the Heart," 1981, "The Wake of Jamey Foster," 1982, "A Weekend Near Madison," 1983, "The Miss Firecracker Contest," 1984, "A Doll's House," 1985, and "A Lie of the Mind," 1988; feature films include "The Burning," 1981, "Swing Shift," 1984, "Raising Arizona," 1987, "Broadcast News," 1987, and "Miss Firecracker," 1989; television films include "Svengali," 1983, "An Uncommon Love," 1983, "With Intent to Kill," 1984, "A Gathering of Old Men," 1987, and "Roe vs. Wade," 1989; also appeared in pilot for television series "Fame."

Member: Actors Equity Association, Screen Actors Guild, American Federation of Television and Radio Artists (AFTRA).

Awards: Named best actress of 1987 by New York Film Critics Circle, Los Angeles Film Critics Association, and National Board of Review; Academy Award nomination and Golden Globe Award nomination for best actress, both 1988, for "Broadcast News"; Emmy Award for best actress in a miniseries, 1989, for "Roe vs. Wade."

Sidelights

Writer, producer, and director Jim Brooks had never heard of Holly Hunter before she auditioned for the part of Jane Craig in his film "Broadcast News." But not long into her first reading, Brooks was ready to hand her the role. He had to. A five-foot, two-inch dynamo who could focus all her energy on the task at hand, Hunter was the Jane Craig he had envisioned.

Jane Craig's character was reportedly fashioned after CBS senior producer Susan Zarinsky and others, and was first meant to be played by Debra Winger. However, Winger was pregnant when Brooks was ready to shoot the film. Other strong-willed, intelligent actresses were considered, including Mary Beth Hurt, Jessica Lange, and Sigourney Weaver. The problem was that these women were all too tall to play the part of the feisty network television producer envisioned by Brooks. He had two days to find a female protagonist, and he was running out of ideas. Aware of Brooks' plight, casting director Juliet Taylor suggested he invite a shoot-from-the-hip actress she'd seen, named Holly Hunter.

Hunter has said she wasn't nervous when she tried out for the part, because she was so sure she wouldn't get it. "I was lucky as s– to get that part," she said in *New York.* "I mean, I may never see another part that's this complex, this real, this human in all those weird vague ways that people are human." In *Newsweek,* David Ansen described the character of Jane Craig as "curt and abrasive under a deadline, warm and nurturing to her friends, by turns self-righteous and self-critical, sophisticated and earthy, Jane is a mercurial steamroller of a woman." And Hunter played her with panache. She was rewarded with an Academy Award nomination and by being named best actress of the year by the National Board of Review, the New York Film Critics Circle, and the Los Angeles Film Critics Association.

Like Craig, Hunter is a professional to the hilt. She researched the field of television production under the guidance of Susan Zarinsky at CBS. Then she put together a thick analysis of the job. Hunter is said to use graph paper to chart the emotional life of her characters as well.

In the beginning of "Broadcast News," Craig is on assignment in the midwest. It's early morning, and she's jogging. By the time she returns to the hotel, she's picked up a pile of newspapers: she doesn't want to miss anything. And she's so organized that she sets aside half an hour every day to release pressure from her job by crying her eyes out. She calls Aaron Altman (Albert Brooks), a reporter for the network and Craig's best friend. She and Altman share high standards in researching and delivering the news. They are both experienced, dedicated, and highly educated.

Then handsome, blond Tom Grunick—played by William Hurt—shows up. As it turns out, he is neither experienced in covering serious news (he was a sportscaster), nor highly educated. Yet it is Grunick who will be anchoring the news for the station. Craig and Altman are incensed. The superficial Grunick represents all they are against. But Grunick is interested in Craig and asks her if he can watch her in action. He witnesses an unforgettable performance when Craig skillfully improvises a segment on a war veteran—just before air time.

Later, during a staff party, a crisis occurs at an Air Force base in Sicily. Immediately the staff is galvanized to cover the event. Craig is named senior producer of the piece. Then the politically savvy Altman is passed up and the job of reporting the news is awarded to Grunick. A defiant Craig confronts the director privately at the party. He says, "It must be nice to always believe you're the smartest person in the room." "No, it's awful," is Craig's unexpected response.

Back at the station, the pressure is on. Craig must cue Grunick on what to cover next by feeding him data over an earpiece. The timing must be impeccable, so when another subordinate slackens off, Craig cracks the whip. Grunick takes direction from Craig with style and aplomb. Their combined energies pull the piece off magnificently. Afterward, Grunick tells Craig it was incredible having her inside his head during the performance. "It was like great sex!," he exclaims.

While Craig acts as a powerful force behind Grunick, she finds herself giving moral support to Altman. The reporter does get a crack at anchoring the news. There's no question he's capable of doing the job. There is a hitch, however. He gets so nervous during the broadcast that sweat seems to pour out of his body, down his face, through his shirt. He blows his one big break. It is during this especially vulnerable period that Altman realizes he's in love with Craig. But it's too late. She's already hung up on the attractive blond, despite her better judgment.

When Craig is about to meet Grunick at the airport to accompany him on an island vacation, she says good-bye to Altman. Altman lets slip that Grunick faked his poignant response in a segment he did on rape victims. Craig doesn't want to believe Altman but finds herself running through an unedited version of the tape. She discovers that Grunick was indeed moved to tears, but the camera didn't catch them. So he improvised later, recreating the tears. Craig becomes furious at what she considers a breech of journalistic moral code. She heads for the airport and tells Grunick she can't go with him; he's crossed some fine line. He answers that the line keeps changing, so it's hard to pinpoint it. Then he gets on the plane alone.

"Broadcast News" doesn't offer a pat ending. It shows the threesome meeting again seven years later. Altman comes in from the northwest, his little boy in tow. He works for a local station. Grunick has been promoted. He's about to accept a plum offer and is engaged to a blonde beauty. Craig is as dedicated to her career as ever. She has a boyfriend, but it's clear that the news still comes first for her.

Hunter plays a very different role in the comedy film "Raising Arizona." She is an unsophisticated policewoman named Edwina ("Ed"). Her husband H.I., played by Nicolas Cage, is a thief with a preference for robbing convenience stores. The couple discovers they can't have children of their own. So when locally known furniture salesman Nathan Arizona and his wife Florence are blessed with quintuplets, Ed talks her husband into stealing one of the babies. The Arizonas certainly have enough to go around, reasons Ed.

Ed and H.I. take Nathan Jr. back to their trailer. They want to raise him by the book, but it's not so easy. Problems crop up with neighbors, two escaped convicts (who happen to love children), and a fearsome, heavily armed biker. And the baby keeps getting left behind on the highway in his carseat. Hunter "gives an original comic performance, combining larceny and righteousness, covetousness and love," wrote David Denby in *New York.*

Hunter gained a great deal of stage experience before being cast in films. She's acted in several Beth Henley plays, including "The Wake of Jamie Foster" and "Crimes of the Heart." Both were on Broadway, and "Crimes of the Heart" came away with a Pulitzer Prize. Off-Broadway, Hunter starred in Henley's "The Miss Firecracker Contest." She played the redheaded Carnelle Scott, a high-spirited, former loose woman, whose nickname is "Miss Hot Tamale." She's from Yazoo City, Mississippi, and bent on trying out for the annual Fourth of July beauty contest. "Holly Hunter gives a fine, subtle performance as Carnelle, a role that demands both psychological and physical agility," wrote a *New Yorker* critic. Nine years of tap dancing and acrobatics in her childhood helped prepare Hunter for the physical demands. The psychological demands were even more challenging, Hunter has said. After 170 performances in the Manhattan Theater Club, the play moved on to the more spacious Westside Arts Theater. Hunter also stars in the film version of the play, called "Miss Firecracker." In it she gives "another flashy performance," commented a writer in *Playboy.*

Hunter now lives in Manhattan with photographer John Raffo. But she was born and raised on a 250-acre farm in Conyers, Georgia, outside of Atlanta. She was the youngest of seven children, with just one sister. Being the youngest didn't stop Hunter from bossing her parents and teachers around, she freely admits. She entertained herself by hanging out at the movie theatre. When that turned into a revivalist church, Hunter found the meetings even more interesting than the movies.

At school, Hunter joined the drama club. A judge at a state competition recognized her talent when she was sixteen. This led to summer stock in upstate New York for two years. After high school Hunter headed for Carnegie Mellon University in Pittsburgh. She channeled all her energies into acting, and dancing under Paul Draper. In 1980 Hunter got her degree, then moved to New York City.

She was cast right away in "The Burning," a horror film. The casting director, Joy Todd, had faith in Hunter and sent her on other auditions. Eventually Hunter read the part of a fifteen-year-old in "The Wake of Jamey Foster," and of singer Meg in "Crimes of the Heart" at the same time. "They were incredibly different readings, and both incredibly accurate," said Henley in *New York.* Hunter went away with both roles and was well-received in both.

After her success in "Broadcast News," Hunter's next challenge was a part in Sam Shepard's 1988 stage production entitled "A Lie of the Mind." "I'm very frightened," she told Harold Reynolds of Knight Ridder Newspapers before rehearsals began. She confessed that she had been scared when she filmed "Broadcast News," too. She added, "If I can keep doing roles that scare the hell out of me, I'll be in good shape."

Sources

Interview, April, 1987.
Ms., March, 1988.
Newsweek, December 28, 1988.
New York, March 16, 1987; December 14, 1987.
New Yorker, June 11, 1984; January 11, 1988.
New York Times, November 12, 1984.
People, February 1, 1988.
Playboy, June, 1989.
Rolling Stone, January 28, 1988.
Time, December 14, 1987; December 21, 1987.

—Sidelights by Victoria France Charabati

Anjelica Huston

AP/Wide World Photos

Actress

Born 1952 (some sources say 1951), in Los Angeles, Calif.; daughter of John (a screen director and actor) and Enrica (a ballet dancer; maiden name Soma) Huston. *Education:* Attended private schools in Ireland and England; studied acting with Peggy Feury.

Career

Film and stage actress, 1968–70; fashion model, 1971–73; film and television actress, 1976–. Films include "Sinful Davey," 1969, "A Walk with Love and Death," 1969, "The Last Tycoon," 1976, "Swashbuckler," 1976, "Ice Pirates," 1984, "A Rose for Emily," 1984, "Prizzi's Honor," 1985, "The Dead," 1987, "Gardens of Stone," 1987, "A Handful of Dust," 1988, and "The Witches," 1989. Television work includes episodes of "Laverne and Shirley" and miniseries "Lonesome Dove," 1989.

Member: Friars Club (New York, N.Y.).

Awards: Academy Award for best supporting actress, Los Angeles Film Critics Award, and New York Film Critics Award, all 1986, for "Prizzi's Honor."

Sidelights

For two decades Anjelica Huston languished in the shadow of her famous family and then her equally famous lover, Jack Nicholson. Since 1985, however, she has become a star on her own terms, a respected actress able to breathe vitality into an array of challenging character roles. The daughter of director John Huston—and granddaughter of Academy Award-winner Walter Huston—Anjelica underwent several particularly intense periods of self-doubt before finding both herself and her muse. To quote *Film Comment* interviewer Beverly Walker, "almost 20 years of study, struggle, and introspection would pass before she could stand in her own pink spotlight." Today Anjelica's work "is in high demand," according to James Kaplan in the *New York Times Magazine,* "yet she isn't quite, as they say, bankable. She seems quite pleased with this state of affairs. John Huston, after all, had commercial and artistic highs and lows, but is remembered as a great artist." The raven-haired Anjelica may be well on the way to similar artistic recognition; her first major role, as the manipulative Maerose Prizzi in "Prizzi's Honor" (1985), won her numerous awards, including the coveted Oscar for best supporting actress. More recently, critics have praised her performance as a pioneer woman in the television miniseries "Lonesome Dove." Director Nicholas Roeg offered a succinct description of her abilities in the *New York Times Magazine:* "Anjelica's work is so good because she's able to abandon herself and come out unscathed."

A childhood surrounded by the wealthy and famous is no guarantee against stress. In fact, it can present unusual complications of its own, not the least of which is the pressure to "measure up" to the standards of the famous parent. Anjelica Huston is not at all reticent about her formative years, when she both idolized and feared her father. John Huston was in his mid-forties when Angelica was born—she was the second child of his fourth wife, ballerina Enrica Soma. Huston had already compiled an impressive list of directing credits, including "The Maltese Falcon," "The Treasure of the Sierra Madre," and "Key Largo," and he was on the verge of winning another Academy Award for "The African Queen." This prestigious lifestyle was not lost on Anjelica, even though her father was often gone months at a time for location filming. In the *New York Times Magazine,* the actress recalled: "My father didn't like weakness. He couldn't abide it in others; he certainly couldn't tolerate it in himself. He didn't tolerate whining and bad behavior from children. He liked what was adult in children. If you were heard, you had to be very careful that you knew your stuff.... He had a cruel streak—made him interesting. He liked his fun. It was certainly sometimes at the expense of others.... But I think that if there were a sin there, it was that he was very much preoccupied with what he wanted to do, which didn't necessarily coincide with his having a wife, or having children." Still, Anjelica told the *Los Angeles Times Magazine,* when it came time for her father to leave on one of his extended trips, "we would cling to his legs as he was to be driven to the airport. A sense of magic would be gone from the house, and things would get a little dull again."

When Anjelica was still very small, her father bought a large estate, St. Clerans, in County Galway, Ireland. There Anjelica grew up in what she has called a "fairy-tale childhood," roaming the countryside, riding horses, and engaging in imaginative games with her brother, Tony. The two children liked to write and perform their own dramas for visiting adults, and Anjelica remembers performing antics for the likes of Jean-Paul Sartre, Carson McCullers, John Steinbeck, and Baron Philippe de Rothschild. "Oh, there was a lot of love and magic in St. Clerans!" she told *People* magazine. "I can't imagine why I ever chose to grow up." That choice to grow up was actually made for the youngster when she was eleven. Her parents separated, and her mother took her to live in London, where she attended an exclusive private school. Anjelica told the *Los Angeles Times Magazine* that life in the city "was very traumatic. I didn't feel particularly pretty at the time and clung to my makeup with some persistence. I was very, very skinny—the second-tallest girl in my class. I had knobby knees and this nose, which gave me some tribulation.... It was a difficult period. I was confused, wondering what was happening. My parents' separation wasn't explained to me. I have always been under the erroneous persuasion that if you don't ask, it won't harm you. I preferred to be mystified rather than depressed. I preferred to believe everything was all right, that my parents still loved each other, rather than hear they didn't."

Adolescence brought new conflicts between Anjelica and her father, culminating in a disastrous film they made together in 1968. Overlooking her lack of experience, Huston cast his daughter in the movie "A Walk with Love and Death," a love story about teenagers set in medieval France. *Los Angeles Times Magazine* contributor Mark Morrison, among others, noted that giving Anjelica the role "was a generous gesture on John's part, but the timing was wrong." The fifteen-year-old Anjelica did not like the part and took her father's direction resentfully. "The making of the movie was uncomfortable," she said. "I didn't communicate well with my father on the set or off the set. I had trouble with my lines. I thought I looked ugly. I felt terribly naked without my makeup." In the end, the project only served to heighten Anjelica's lack of self-esteem. According to Kaplan, critical reaction to the film "was less than ecstatic, and as its nepotistic centerpiece, Anjelica Huston took a lot of the heat." Her acting *and* her appearance were belittled, and the picture failed at the box office.

That blow was compounded by another of even greater severity. In 1969, when she was sixteen, Anjelica lost her mother to an automobile accident. Enrica Soma was only 39 when she was killed, and the sudden tragedy took Anjelica completely by surprise. "My mother's death was a complete overhaul of the world as I knew it," she told the *New York Times Magazine.* "I was in no way prepared for her to die.... It was like losing my best friend, my mother and my sister all in one. Nothing has happened to me before or since to equal the impact of that shock."

Devastated, Anjelica vowed to quit acting. The reviews of "A Walk with Love and Death," as well as a break with her father, contributed to the decision. "I was roundly criticized and made to feel very unattractive," she told the *New York Times Magazine.* "And I took these things to heart." In 1971 she turned to modeling at the insistence of photographer Richard Avedon, and shortly thereafter, to quote *People,* she became "the hottest thing on Kodachrome—in one issue *Vogue* devoted 30 pages to Avedon photographs of Anjelica in Ireland." Ironically, the young model still thought of herself as unattractive. "Day after day I shared a mirror with the world's most beautiful women and stared at eyes that were bigger than mine, noses that were smaller," she said in *People.* "I cried and cried because I thought I was ugly, but now when I see those photographs, I think I looked absolutely wonderful!" Anjelica was more than ready for a change in 1973, when she attended a party at the home of Jack Nicholson, then an up-and-coming film actor.

Nicholson recalled in *People* that when he first caught a glimpse of Anjelica Huston, he saw "cla-a-a-ss." For her part, Anjelica fell deeply in love with a man as charismatic—and flirtatious—as her father. Abandoning her modeling, she moved in with Nicholson and devoted herself exclusively to him for three years. Then both partners began to chafe under the restraints of the relationship. Nicholson's bouts of boredom were merely personal, but Anjelica's boredom had a professional aspect as well. She wanted to return to acting, but she refused to use "contacts" such as Nicholson to help her land roles. Eventually she enrolled in acting classes with Los Angeles teacher Peggy Feury. In *Film Comment* Anjelica remembered that Feury "did nothing but reinforce me and give me confidence. She calmed me down a lot, helped me be less demanding of myself, and she was extremely kind—which is what I needed most.... The conclusion I drew was that I had an instinct for good writing, and that I sought honesty in the parts I played. Rather than go to acting class to find out what I didn't know, I found out what I *did* know. Peggy changed my life. Everyone should have such a guardian angel."

Yet another near-tragedy solidified Anjelica's ambitions to return to performing. In 1982 she was involved in a head-on automobile collision with a drunk driver; her facial injuries required six hours of surgery to correct. She told the *New York Times* that the shock of the crash made her confront "the need not to waste my life." When she recovered, she took any work she could find. For a time this consisted of bit parts in television situation comedies and films, but in 1984 she was offered a starring role in a science fiction adventure, "Ice Pirates." Kaplan suggested that the film "was a harmless romp that would do nothing at the box office, but Anjelica Huston got to swagger and tough-talk her way through the movie, having fun and gaining confidence."

John Foreman, the producer of "Ice Pirates," was so impressed with Anjelica's performance in that film that he cast her first in his next project, "Prizzi's Honor." Only after Anjelica had agreed to play Maerose did Foreman hire her father to direct the movie and Nicholson to star in it. Most critics agree that "Prizzi's Honor" created a genuine demand for Anjelica Huston. She received almost unanimous praise for her portrayal of Maerose, a graceful Mafia princess with a deplorable Brooklyn accent and a penchant for orchestrating violence. "Maerose is a Borgia princess, a high-fashion Vampira who moves like a swooping bird and talks in a honking Brooklynese that comes out of the corner of her twisted mouth," wrote Pauline Kael in the *New Yorker.* "Anjelica Huston seems to have grown into her bold features: she's a flinty beauty here... [and] an inspired comedienne, especially when she parodies penitence and sidles into a room dolorously, her head hanging on her shoulder.... Maerose has more in her face than anyone else has; she has irony and the strangeness of what's hidden. She's like a bomb ticking away in the background of the movie."

"It doesn't really matter how big a part is, if it's got juice. I'd much prefer to be on the screen for 5 or 10 impactful moments... than to meander through a landscape in an epic fashion."

Anjelica won the Academy Award for her portrayal of Maerose, and her father had the distinction of having directed both his father and his daughter in Oscar-winning performances. Nicholson, too, was thrilled for his long-time lover, telling friends that he was more pleased with her victory than he would have been with another of his own.

Since "Prizzi's Honor" was filmed, Anjelica Huston has not lacked for substantive roles. She played Gretta Conroy in a film adaptation of James Joyce's story "The Dead" (her father's last directing effort before he died) and an antiwar activist during the Vietnam era in "Gardens of Stone." Asked whether she sees herself as a character actress or a leading lady, she told the *New York Times Magazine:* "I don't think about that. I think about parts that interest me. It doesn't really matter how big a part is, if it's got juice. I'd much prefer to be on the screen for 5 or 10 impactful moments... than to meander through a landscape in an epic fashion. I like ensemble acting—

it's bolstering. I'm more intrigued with playing characters than with playing people closer to myself."

When talk turns to her personal life, Anjelica is equally forthright. She is still involved with Nicholson, but now she owns her own home a few miles from his. They do not speak of marriage as a possibility but are nevertheless deeply committed to one another. "It's a real relationship," she said, "maybe not so far as a traditional idea of one is concerned, but it's extremely powerful. It changes—it's always changed. If you're dealing with two volatile people, you go through many changes a day. The relationship is a fact of my life. After a certain time you don't question those things.... He's a soulmate. It goes beyond commitment. It's not as if one has any choice in the matter."

After many years of fighting her image as a Huston and as Nicholson's lover, Anjelica has acquired a philosophical acceptance of her unique background. "I think Americans particularly, who don't have all that much history, are very pleased to have whatever history they have," she said. "And I think my family's name is strong in the theater and strong in movie history, and I think people like that. It makes me feel good. I feel very much backed by my ancestors." Still, she admitted in *Mademoiselle,* she has been buffeted somewhat by life—and has profited from the hard knocks. "When I look at myself I see the lines in my face, but I have a certain affection for them," she claimed. "You see, I've earned them."

Sources

Commonweal, May 22, 1987.
Esquire, September, 1987.
Film Comment, October, 1987.
Interview, September, 1985.
Los Angeles Times Magazine, June 21, 1987.
Mademoiselle, April, 1987.
Newsweek, June 17, 1985.
New Yorker, July 1, 1985; May 18, 1987.
New York Times, June 27, 1985; May 18, 1986.
New York Times Magazine, February 12, 1989.
People, July 8, 1985.
Vogue, September, 1985.

—Sketch by Anne Janette Johnson

Morton Janklow

AP/Wide World Photos

Attorney and literary agent

Full name, Morton Lloyd Janklow; born May 30, 1930, in New York, N.Y.; son of Maurice (an attorney) and Lillian (Levantin) Janklow; married second wife, Linda Mervyn LeRoy, November 27, 1960; children: Angela LeRoy, Lucas Warner. *Education:* Syracuse University, A.B., 1950; Columbia University, J.D., 1953.

Addresses: *Home*—New York, N.Y. *Office*—Janklow & Nesbit Associates, 598 Madison Ave., New York, N.Y. 10022.

Career

Admitted to Bar of State of New York, 1953, District of Columbia, 1959, and U.S. Supreme Court, 1959; Spear & Hill (law firm), New York City, attorney, 1960–67; Janklow & Traum (law firm), New York City, partner, beginning 1967; Morton Janklow Associates (literary agency), New York City, chairman and chief executive officer, 1977–88; Janklow & Nesbit Associates (literary agency), New York City, partner, 1988–.

Member of board of directors, Orbis Communications, Inc., New York City, and McCaffrey & McCall, Inc., New York City, 1962–87; chairman of executive committee, Harvey Group, Inc., New York City, 1968–71, and Cable Funding Corp., New York City, 1971–73; member of executive committee, Sloan Commission on Cable Communications, 1970–71; Andrew Wellington Cordier fellow, Columbia University School of International Affairs; visiting lecturer, Radcliffe College, Columbia University Law School, and New York University; member of business and financial advisory board, New York University Press and New York University School of Arts, 1977–; life member, Harlan Fiske Stone Fellowship, Columbia University Law School; founder, Morton L. Janklow Program for Advocacy in Arts, Columbia University Law School. Holds numerous positions in civic groups and charitable organizations. *Military service:* U.S. Army, 1953–55; served as an attorney.

Member: American Bar Association, Federal Communications Bar Association, American Judicature Society, Council on Foreign Relations, New York State Bar Association, New York County Lawyers Association, City of New York Bar Association.

Sidelights

Lillian Janklow saved every written record of her son's accomplishments as the future lawyer and deal-maker grew up in Queens. In 1988 Morton Janklow informed a *Manhattan, Inc.* staff writer: "One thing that struck her at the passing of President Roosevelt was the boxes of letters—now historic—that his mother had saved. So she started saving mine in case I ever became president." Janklow has not yet become president, but he has become a driving force in the world of blockbuster publishing, putting together scores of television and movie deals for such best-seller writers as Danielle Steele, Sidney Sheldon, and Jackie Collins. And he still preserves each document that emanates from his desk, assembling a leather-bound historical record of memos, letters, and contracts to benefit posterity. Morton Janklow sees to it that no one will ever underestimate his role in redefining the rules of the publishing industry.

Once a genteel profession, book publishing turned profit hungry in the 1970s, in part due to Janklow's involvement. Small, literary-oriented publishers were bought up by bigger publishers, themselves often properties of enormous media conglomerates. Independently owned bookstores, whose proprietors once took a personal interest in their inventories, gave way to national chains like B. Dalton and Waldenbooks. Books themselves came to be seen as merely one arm of a mega-deal, the other arms being television or movie rights and merchandising. Dealmakers like Janklow began to replace the traditional literary agent. "Mort's success is a combination of luck and genius," said author Michael Korda to Patricia Morrisroe of *New York* magazine. "He came out in a time of great change in the industry, and he was intelligent and quick enough to see it."

In the 1970s and 1980s, Janklow gained a reputation among authors for negotiating terms far more favorable than had been standard. Not only did he secure lucrative royalties for film and TV tie-ins, but he insisted on—and got—six figure advances. For writers, he became the slingshot to take on publishing's Goliaths. His biggest moment was putting together a record-breaking $3.2 million for Judith Krantz's *Princess Daisy,* a deal that reconfigured the relationship between writer and agent. Instead of the traditional 10 percent commission, Janklow charged 15 percent. Both the scale of the deal and the higher commission became industry norms, ushering in a new breed of agent: fast-talking, self-promoting, business-savvy, and above all financially successful.

"Mort brought publishing people into the space age," publishing executive Joni Evans told *New York*'s Morrisroe. Not everyone wanted to be in the space age, however. According to Hilary Mills, writing in *Seven Days,* Simon & Schuster president Richard Snyder reacted to the Krantz deal by firing off a telegram to Janklow snarling, "You have single-handedly destroyed publishing." Rival agent Andrew Wylie said to *Manhattan Inc.*'s Jennet Conant: "Mort sells the equivalent of heroin in books. One damages the body; his books damage the mind. He has dominated the downside of publishing."

Janklow is not altogether happy with his reputation. "It's a bit of a curse," he told Morrisroe. "I'd like to attract more literary figures, people like Norman Mailer, who is a friend, and Kurt Vonnegut, who is a friend." But he insists he does not solicit clients, a policy he attributes to his identity as a lawyer. "Lawyers never went after clients. They just waited for them to call. People either come here or they don't."

The first author to come to Janklow was an old college friend and former White House insider, William Safire. Safire's publisher, William Morrow, had tried to renege on a $250,000 contract, for a book on the Nixon presidency, for which it had paid Safire, then a special assistant to the president, an $83,000 advance. After Watergate, the publisher wanted out of the deal. Safire sued, with Janklow as his counsel. Janklow was able to sell the book to Doubleday, and the court ruled Safire could keep the Morrow advance. Since the decision, many publishers have included a clause in writer's contracts spelling out conditions of acceptability; Janklow calls this rider the Janklow clause.

Born May 1930 in New York City, Janklow grew up the precocious son of a lawyer whose practice was hobbled by the Depression. The oldest of two children, Janklow spent his early childhood in Hollis, Queens. His early memories include scrapes with anti-Semitic neighborhood bullies. "I got beat up a lot," he told Morrisroe. "I remember my father coming home one night and I was being pummeled by a bunch of kids. He stopped it, and then had me take them on one at a time. He stood there while I went at it with full force. It was a terrific self-confidence builder."

The family moved nearby to Laurelton when he was in fourth grade. The boy attended local public schools, then Far Rockaway High School, where he was editor of the school newspaper. He skipped several grades but does not recall the experience as making him shy among his peers. Rather, classmates remember him as a gregarious and self-confident youngster. Aspiring to an Ivy League education, he had to settle for Syracuse University, as few schools would accept a 16-year-old freshman. At Syracuse he studied public affairs, hopeful of entering government service. His interest in academics faded fast, however, replaced by the card table. Cards became Janklow's primary source of income until a streak of bad luck wiped him out. To repay his losses he spent eight months loading freight on railroad cars.

Playing cards, Janklow mastered the art of the poker face and learned to enjoy the rewards that come from taking risks. He spent enough time away from the card table, though, to obtain a bachelor of arts degree in 1950. He went on to Columbia to study law. "It was a huge move in every way," he told Morrisroe. "Syracuse was a typical middle class university. At Columbia, everyone was enormously accomplished. They were the Groton-St. Paul's-Princeton-Yale kind of people. I knew," he added, "that I was playing in a very different game." Receiving his law degree in 1953, he has remained an active Columbia alumnus. In 1982 he contributed $1 million to establish an arts advocacy program at the law school, which he named after himself.

"Publishing is becoming a very serious business. There is the growth of the idea that it is not unliterary to sell the product."

In 1953, the newly married young lawyer joined the Army, where he defended court-martial cases. He claims he won so many cases that the Army decided to relocate him; Janklow managed to make Paris the relocation spot. It was, apparently, a less demanding assignment than G.I.s usually receive. Janklow told *New York*'s Morrisroe that he lived in a chateau in the Loire Valley, spending his days hunting, playing tennis, and dining at various three-star restaurants.

His marriage, however, was a casualty of the experience. Another setback: upon returning to the States he learned he had a rare disease called coccidioidomycosis, picked up during basic training. He was told the disease was invariably fatal. Hospitalized in the Bronx, he submitted to an experimental drug program that left him with raging fevers, convulsions, and dramatic weight loss—but no sign of improvement. His weight dropped to a skeletal 106 pounds before the medication finally worked and he could be discharged.

Back on his feet, Janklow finalized his divorce and soon afterwards ran into a mysterious matchmaker he had first met a year earlier in France. The matchmaker, whom he describes enigmatically as the "woman in lavender," had promised to introduce him to a beautiful woman. Newly divorced, Janklow accepted the introduction and met Linda LeRoy, Smith College senior and daughter of Hollywood mogul Mervyn LeRoy. The two were soon wed.

In 1960 Janklow joined the law firm of Spear & Hill, handling corporate and securities cases. He found the work boring and daydreamed of entrepreneurial challenges. He perceived the fledgling cable TV industry as one with enormous potential for profit. He borrowed $10,000 and formed Trans-Video Corp. to receive a cable franchise for the San Diego market. He bid $101 and won. Six years later he sold his company to Cox Broadcasting and earned what he calls "f—k you money:" a big enough cash supply to allow him to pick and choose his clients.

In 1967 Janklow and Spear & Hill partner Jerry Traum left to form their own agency. Traum handled the operational details, leaving the outgoing Janklow to bring in the clients. Traum described his partner to Morrisroe: "Mort sets a beautiful table, but he's not interested in sitting through the meal, and he's certainly not interested in cleaning up." In 1969 Janklow's successful suit on behalf of William Safire brought in work from other disgruntled writers, some of them Safire's friends. Under Janklow's counsel a small cadre of authors began taking a more aggressive stance towards their publishers. Two were Bernard and Marvin Kalb, who resolved their rift with Norton, their publisher, when Janklow got their $20,000 advance refunded and resold their book to Little, Brown—for $250,000. Representing former Nixon insider John Ehrlichman, Janklow inserted an unusual clause into Ehrlichman's contract that guaranteed Ehrlichman additional royalties should the book generate a television production beyond two hours in length. This was the heydey of the network miniseries, and Ehrlichman's bestseller, *The Company*, became a 12-hour production. Ehrlichman got rich.

Janklow, though, was still regarded primarily as a lawyer. Most of his literary clients at this time were either political figures or political writers, often drawn from his social circles. An exception was Linda Goodman, the astrology writer, whose hardcover advance for *Love Signs* Janklow renegotiated from $35,000 to $350,000. The deal that marked a turning point for Janklow was the *Scruples* contract. As with most Janklow deals, it involved a client—Judith Krantz—who knew him socially. And it was a blockbuster. He even figured prominently in the story line, thinly disguised as Josh Hillman, husband of a Hollywood princess.

At the top of his game now, Janklow began emerging as a harsh critic of the publishing industry. He lambasted its executives as weak marketers, its practices as antiquated, other agents as inept, and authors as innocent victims in need of a guiding hand. "Publishing used to be a sort of mom-and-pop operation," he told *Manhattan Inc.*'s Jennet Conant. "It's going through a transitional phase. It's becoming more international. There are big changes in the retailing and distribution. The marketing side is vastly improved. Publishing is becoming a very serious business. There is the growth of the idea that it is not unliterary to sell the product."

In early 1988, Janklow shook up the publishing world once again by announcing he had formed a partnership with Lynn Nesbit, another superagent with an author list combining the prestigious with the lucrative: Tom Wolfe, Toni Morrison, John le Carre, Shirley MacLaine, and Nora Ephron. Industry scuttlebutt attributed Nesbit's decision to resentment over her standing at her former agency, International Creative Management Inc., a firm with a strong Hollywood presence. Nesbit enjoys a warm reputation among authors for her literary acumen, a factor Janklow recognizes. "Lynn is especially strong with literary support systems," he told *Publishers Weekly.* Trumpeting the formation of Janklow & Nesbit Associates, Janklow told Madalynne Reuter of *Publishers Weekly:* "Any time you can combine two people like us it's a good time [to start a business.] It's propitious to have two agents as strong as we are working together at a time when the number of publishers are declining and writers and agents have to face the enormous publishing entities that remain. I've known Lynn a long time; we're friends."

Janklow spins off many friendships into business deals and is one of the most visible members of the city's nocturnal social elite. The Janklows dine out most evenings, and the agent's favorite noon haunt is the Four Seasons, securing megadeals between entrees and desserts. He and his wife, Linda, lead a fast-track Manhattan social life whose details are organized by a full-time employee. Summers, the scene shifts to the Hamptons. The couple has two children: Angela, who began working for *Vanity Fair* as a reporter in 1988, and Lucas, a college student. Janklow is a fervent admirer and patron of modern art, particularly the works of Jean Dubuffet.

While his aggressive business methods have earned him many detractors, Janklow also lists many admirers who are more than quick to stand up for him. "To see Mort only as an agent who is interested in making millions of dollars is the superficial view," clucked historian David McCullough to *New York*'s Morrisroe. Added Korda: "Mort enjoys things 100%. And it's so refreshing. He enjoys being successful, and he's also happy when his friends do well. Success has really brought out the best in him."

Sources

Manhattan, Inc., December, 1988; January, 1989.
New York, February 2, 1987.
New York Times, December 5, 1988.
Publishers Weekly, December 16, 1988.
Seven Days, December 21, 1988.
Wall Street Journal, December 5, 1988.

—Sidelights by Warren Strugatch

Philip Johnson

Architect

Full name, Philip Cortelyou Johnson; born July 8, 1906, in Cleveland, Ohio; son of Homer M. (an attorney) and Louise (Pope) Johnson. *Education:* Harvard University, A.B. (cum laude) in philosophy, 1930, B.Arch., 1943.

Addresses: *Home*—New York, N.Y.; and New Canaan, Conn. *Office*—885 Third Ave., New York, N.Y. 10022.

Career

Museum of Modern Art, New York City, chairman of department of architecture, 1930–34, 1946–54, trustee, 1958—; architect, 1946—. Speaker and lecturer at numerous architectural forums and at colleges and universities. *Military service:* U.S. Army, Corps of Engineers, 1943–45.

Member: American Institute of Architects, Society of Architectural Historians, American Academy of Arts and Sciences.

Awards: Silver Medal of Honor, Architecture League, 1950; Award of Merit, American Institute of Architects, 1956; Bronze Medallion, City of New York, 1978; Gold Medal, American Institute of Architects, 1978; Pritzker Prize, 1979; certificate of achievement, President's Committee on the Arts and Humanities, 1983; Fellow Award, Rhode Island School of Design, 1983; Herbert Adams Medal, National Sculpture Society, 1984.

AP/Wide World Photos

Sidelights

When asked what he is most likely to be remembered for from his long and varied career, which has spanned over 50 years and led to the design of more than 100 buildings, architect Philip Johnson doesn't usually like to speculate. But he told *Esquire,* "I think the Glass House will endure, but it may be that I will be best remembered as a gadfly, an encourager of younger architects, and as an arbiter elegantiarum—the man who introduced the glass box and then, fifty years later, broke it." Philip Johnson, now in his eighties, has been one of the most unpredictable and influential architects of the twentieth century. He is widely seen as one of the principal forces behind the modernist movement, which dominated American architecture for decades. His "Glass House"—a house made entirely of glass, which he built for himself on an estate in Connecticut—and the Seagram Building, which he designed with Mies van der Rohe, are classic examples of modernist style. But in the seventies, when unadorned glass skyscrapers dotted the country, Johnson decided it was time for a change. As he told *Insight,* "It became obvious that glass boxes were too dull to look at, that's all."

Instead, Johnson threw his considerable influence behind what was becoming known as the postmodernist movement—an effort to reach back into the past for an eclectic assortment of architectural details. Johnson's AT&T building, built in the early eighties and topped with a controversial broken pediment reminiscent of a Chippendale secretary, is considered almost an icon of the postmodernist style. Never one to stay on course for long, Johnson has lately veered toward deconstructivism, a movement influenced by Russian modernist architecture from the twenties.

Throughout his career, Johnson has been noted not simply for what he builds, but for his power and influence in the architectural world. His support of younger architects, his urbane and often charming manner with clients, and his considerable political skills have made him a force to be reckoned with. Cesar Pelli, then dean of the Yale School of Architecture, said in *New York* magazine that Johnson "has the credibility to convince a corporate board of directors to spend huge sums for this one-of-a-kind work and the power within the architectural profession to defy, and, to some extent, change, critical opinion. It's formidable. And he knows it, too."

Because Johnson's career has take so many odd turns and flying leaps, he has always sparked a great deal of controversy. Some find his work derivative and accuse him of borrowing haphazardly from past architectural forms. "Ironically, for all of Philip Johnson's commercial success . . . and his status as the *de facto* dean of American architects, he has not won the critical approval that would be the logical result of his exalted position," wrote Martin Filler in *Interview.* "[The AT&T design] and most of his subsequent ones seem to many observers to be superficial and uninformed in their appropriation of historical styles, cynical and confused in their free-wheeling eclecticism from one project to the next, and symbolic of debased architectural attitudes mirroring a similar corruption of social values in the nation at large." Other observers have been kinder. "Mr. Johnson, who began his professional career as a historian, critic and curator of architecture, is not a great designer," stated the *New York Times.* "He is not the poet that James Sterling is or Arata Isozaki, or Robert Venturi. His sensibility is still that of the critic, looking constantly, evaluating, thinking, comparing. . . . What kind of buildings does this give us? Sometimes very fine ones, sometimes disappointing ones, on rare occasions some truly great ones."

For all the changes in his approach to architecture, a few things have remained constant in Philip Johnson's life. Always trim and elegantly dressed, he has never married. Every morning, he walks the five blocks from his one-bedroom apartment to his office at 885 Third Avenue, in "The Lipstick Building," which he designed. When he is in town, he lunches at the Four Seasons Restaurant in the Seagram Building, holding court with an assortment of clients and colleagues. On weekends, he retreats to the Glass House, where he does most of his actual design work.

Johnson traces the beginnings of his architectural career to a college trip to Europe. A philosophy major at Harvard who would take seven years to complete his degree due to bouts of depression, he was overwhelmed by the Parthenon. "Ephiphanies that move you to tears or leave you feeling exalted for weeks don't translate into words very well, but I had it twice, at Chartres and the Parthenon," Johnson said in *Esquire.* "Before that I had been rather straightforward, interested in philosophy and rationalism and intellectual things, but without a single devoted passion. After I saw the Parthenon, I had a call, as religious people might put it, and I've never changed." After graduating, Johnson pursued his interest in architecture through two visits to the Bauhaus, the center of the emerging modernist school in Germany. When he returned, his friend Alfred Barr, director of the newly formed Museum of Modern Art, named him head of its architecture department. Fortunately for the museum, which was struggling to be born in the middle of the Depression, Johnson didn't require a salary.

Born in Cleveland in 1906 to Homer Johnson, a successful attorney, and Louise (Pope) Johnson, young Philip had never lacked for much. And when he went off to Harvard, his father gave him some stock in an obscure company called ALCOA, which three years later had made him wealthier than his father. When he accepted the position at the Museum of Modern Art, Johnson was able to make a healthy donation to the museum and pay his secretary himself. He then proceeded to bring the avant-garde architecture he had found in Germany to the United States via what is widely regarded as the most influential architecture exhibition of the century. With Henry-Russell Hitchcock, a young art instructor at Wesleyan who had accompanied him to Germany, he wrote a guide to the show called *The International Style.* "So perfectly clear," said Johnson of the style in *Insight,* "so simple: the primary colors, the lack of overhanging roofs, the simplicity of cubic nature, the purity of surface, and lots of glass." When Bauhaus architects Mies, Gropius, and others fled Nazi Germany for the United States in the thirties, a design revolution was launched.

Having turned the architectural world on its ear, Johnson then made one of the abrupt jumps that was to characterize his life: he resigned from the museum and began dabbling in fascist politics. When he had visited Germany in 1934, he had been impressed by the economic improvements Hitler had made there. He supported Huey Long's presidential ambitions here and later served as a correspondent for Father Charles Coughlin, the right-wing radio commentator. When correspondent William Shirer called him "an American fascist" in his book, *Berlin Diary*, Johnson was snubbed by many who knew him. Saying in *Esquire* that at the time he hadn't grasped the extent of Nazi persecution of the Jews, Johnson expressed regrets: "I was a damned fool and I deserved what I got, but the next few years were the worst of my life."

By 1939, his political involvement had pretty much abated, and in 1940, at the age of 35, Johnson enrolled in architecture courses at Harvard. By 1946, after a few years in the Army, he was slowly setting up a private practice. One of his first projects was the Glass House, which Joseph Giovannini described in the *New York Times* as "symmetrical, serene, and entirely enclosed in glass." It is considered one of his best works. The house attracted widespread attention and became, for many years, the gathering place for an assortment of artists and architects, politicians and corporate leaders. In 1986, Johnson completed negotiations to turn the house and property over to the National Trust for Historic Preservation; he continues to live in the house and lease it from the trust.

In 1954, Johnson worked with Mies van der Rohe on the Seagram Building, a union of bronze, glass, and steel which is generally regarded as one of the finest examples of modernist design. Many of his other projects of the fifties and sixties were institutional—among them, the sculpture garden at the Museum of Modern Art and buildings at several Ivy League schools.

In 1967, Johnson made what he called in *Insight* a "quantum leap" and joined forces with architect John Burgee, twenty-eight years his junior. Burgee's organizational abilities enabled the firm to begin operating on a much grander scale. "Philip and I had the same objective—to build the best buildings in the world," Burgee told *Esquire*. "When he proposed the partnership, he said that I was young enough that he didn't have to be jealous of me. I had heard that he could be pretty stormy, and I told myself I'd give it a year and see how it worked out. The first time I made a suggestion, he said, 'That's the stupidest thing I ever heard,' and I said to myself, 'Uh, oh.' But the next time, he said, 'That's brilliant. Why didn't I think of that?'"

The first major project the new partners tackled was the Investors Diversified Services Center in Minneapolis. Built in 1973, it featured a smoke-blue facade and one of the first glass-covered galleries of shops and restaurants in the country. Next was Pennzoil Place in Houston, which they built with developer Gerald Hines. Its two thirty-six story glass towers have sloped tops set at right angles to each other so that the closest corners are only ten feet apart. Another Johnson-Burgee design from the seventies was the Crystal Cathedral, which they built for the Reverend Robert H. Schuller near Anaheim, California. It is built entirely of glass—ten thousand panes set in a network of steel.

Although these projects made no abrupt break with modernist principles, subtle changes were apparent. Johnson was beginning to be influenced by a new generation of architects who found the prevailing styles cold and unappealing. "Johnson had long before broken with the modernist tenet that form should follow function," wrote Craig Unger in *New York* magazine. "Johnson credits the 'kids' or 'the back room boys'—as he calls such architects as Venturi and Stern—with creating a new path in architecture, filling their buildings with eclectic historical and formal allusions and moving away from the dreary 'glass box.'"

Johnson admired the work of these young architects, and supported it by recommending them for commissions. But it was he who had the credibility to make a case for it in the corporate world. In 1979, he convinced AT&T's board of directors to back his postmodernist plans for their lavish New York headquarters. "Bernini persuaded the Pope to be his patron, and Johnson did the same with AT&T," architect Michael Graves told *New York* magazine. "On that level, Johnson is in a class by himself." Johnson decided that he wanted the headquarters to evoke the great granite buildings that characterized New York in the 1890s and 1920s. In order to give it a massive, solid feeling, he set the windows into granite as much as ten inches thick, using 13,000 tons in all. Some charge that this and other extravagant features made it, on a per-square-foot basis, one of the most expensive buildings ever built. But the feature that caused the most fuss and landed Johnson on the cover of *Time* was a graceful pediment with a hole in its center. "That broken pediment, as it is called, has caused more argument than any other empty space twenty feet or so in diameter in the history of architecture," Tom Buckley wrote in

Esquire. "Some critics have hailed it as spirited and imaginative, the crowning touch of another Johnson masterpiece.... Equally reputable critics damned the building, from its broken pediment on down, as a display of extravagance, arrogance and perversity."

In the mid-seventies, Johnson and Burgee had also begun collaborating with Houston developer Gerald D. Hines, a powerful combination that would "roll some people's ears back," as Hines commented in *Insight.* After working together successfully on Pennzoil Place, the team went on to complete several grand projects in the postmodernist vein. For Pittsburgh Plate Glass, they built a cut-glass complex evoking the Houses of Parliament in downtown Pittsburgh. And in Houston, they put up the Republic Bank Center, a pink granite tower reminiscent of Flemish Gothic architecture, which the *New York Times* calls "a highly electric and altogether splendid romantic composition, its profile truly lyrical against the Texas sky."

But the *Times* writer goes on to find many of Johnson's postmodernist designs glib and superficial. "So much of this recent work is facile, easy, quick. It seems to come from a single, fast idea, as if someone leaped up at a meeting and shouted, [I have it! Let's make the PPG building a glass version of the Houses of Parliament!' When it works, it is because Mr. Johnson and Mr. Burgee have not stopped there, but have gone back to the basics and been able to make their buildings succeed on more fundamental levels as well."

Johnson and Burgee have continued to build in the postmodernist style all over the country, from Crescent Court and Momentum Place in Dallas, to 580 California Street in San Francisco. But Johnson is also fascinated by a new tendency in the architectural world called deconstructivism, which he brought to the public eye through an exhibition at the Museum of Modern Art in 1988. That show presented the work of designers throughout the world—among them, Frank Gehry [see index for *Newsmakers* entry] and Bernard Tschumi—who are linked by their similarities to constructivism, the Russian modernism of the twenties. According to Cathleen McGuigan of *Newsweek,* these designers "shatter all the rules. They've kissed symmetry and classic geometry goodbye; in their weird, distorted designs, walls tilt crazily, beams twist and crisscross, angles are skewed." The influence of this unorthodox approach can be seen in Johnson's design for the Canadian Broadcasting Corporation Building in Toronto.

While some analysts praise Johnson's ability to embrace and popularize new design trends, others deplore it. "He has made it okay to do whatever the hell you want," said Nate McBride, a young architect and former architecture teacher at Yale, in *Insight.* "I don't think people my age take him seriously at all. I don't think we worry about whether he likes us or not or whether he knows we exist.... When he dies, it will be 'Ding, dong, the witch is dead,' and all the little munchkins will charge down the street going 'hurrah.'" But the *New York Times* concluded that, whatever the pros and cons of individual designs, Johnson's contribution to the field has been enormous. "As Mr. Johnson moves into his ninth decade,... his position in the history of American architecture seems more assured than ever. He is at once a dean of the profession and a gadfly to it, at once a stimulator of architecture and a supporter of it. He is not the greatest architect of our time—but he is our greatest architectural presence."

Seemingly unperturbed amid all the controversy and the complaints, Johnson continues to do what he loves best. "I hate vacations," he told *Esquire.* "If you can build buildings, why sit on the beach?" He told *Interview* that in his ninth decade he feels a sense of "freedom. A new sense of daring. You don't have to make anything. Where are you going? What are you trying to prove? What job do you want to get? Therefore a sense of freedom and being able to do things just for the hell of it and just for the benefit of the art of architecture is the most important feeling you can have."

Writings

The International Style: Architecture Since 1922 (with Henry-Russell Hitchcock), Norton, 1932.
Modern Architects (compiler), Museum of Modern Art, 1932.
Machine Art, Museum of Modern Art, 1934.
Mies van der Rohe, Museum of Modern Art, 1947, revised edition, 1953.

Sources

Architectural Digest, March, 1986.
Esquire, December, 1983.
Insight, February 23, 1987.
Interview, May, 1988.
Newsweek, November 19, 1984; July 11, 1986.
New York, November 15, 1982.
New Yorker, November 10, 1986.
New York Times, June 29, 1986; July 16, 1987.
Omni, October, 1984.
People, December 26, 1983.

—Sidelights by Cathleen Collins Lee

Charles M. Jordan

Courtesy of General Motors Corp.

Automotive design executive

Full name, Charles Morrell Jordan; born October 21, 1927, in Whittier, Calif.; son of Charles L. (a citrus grower) and Bernice May (Letts) Jordan; married Sally Irene Mericle, March 8, 1951; children: Debra, Mark, Melissa. *Education:* Massachusetts Institute of Technology, B.S. in mechanical engineering, 1949.

Addresses: *Home*—Bloomfield Hills, Mich. *Office*—General Motors Design Staff, General Motors Technical Center, Mound Rd. and Twelve Mile, Warren, Mich. 48090.

Career

General Motors Corp., Detroit, Mich., stylist, beginning 1949, chief designer in Cadillac Studio, 1957–61, group chief designer, 1961–62, executive in charge of automotive design, 1962–67, director of styling for Adam Opel AG in West Germany, 1967–70, executive in charge of Cadillac/Oldsmobile/Buick Studios, 1970–73, executive in charge of Chevrolet/Pontiac/Commercial Vehicle Studios, 1973–77, director of design, 1977–86, vice-president of General Motors Design Staff, 1986—.

Member: Society of Automotive Engineers, MIT Detroit Alumni Club, Ferrari Club of America, California Scholastic Federation (life member).

Awards: First National Award, Fisher Body Craftsman's Guild, 1947.

Sidelights

Chuck Jordan may be the world's most influential auto designer. As vice-president of the General Motors Design Staff, he is responsible for the styling of millions of new cars produced each year by GM and its affiliates around the globe. Another measure of Jordan's status: He is only the fourth person to head the automaker's far-flung design operations since the first GM Art & Colour Section was established back in 1927 by the legendary Harley Earl. Today, Jordan personally directs a staff of 1,200 at 35 studios from his headquarters at the GM Technical Center in Warren, Mich.

The son of a Whittier, Calif., citrus rancher, Jordan had a family that encouraged his childhood interest in drawing cars. During church services, his grandmother would give him a pencil and paper and let him sketch on top of a hymnal. He learned to drive pickup trucks in his father's orchards when he was 11 and bagged groceries in Richard Nixon's parents' store as a high-school student. Jordan's mother heard of the annual GM Fisher Body Craftsman's Guild model-car competition when he was 19 and a sophomore at the Massachusetts Institute of Technology. She urged him to enter. He spent 700 hours on the project, winning $4,000 and a trip to Detroit. "I'd always planned on working at Ford," Jordan told *Newsmakers*. "If I hadn't won that contest, that's where I'd be." His winning entry is now in the Henry Ford Museum in Dearborn.

"We're bringing excitement back into the business. The excitement was gone for awhile as far as the product was concerned."

After graduating from MIT in 1949 with a mechanical engineering degree, Jordan went to GM as a junior designer and worked for a time under Earl. One of his first creations was the Chevrolet Cameo pickup, for which Jordan still holds the design patents. Earl's successor, the late William Mitchell, once recalled that Jordan early in his career designed a Buick show car that "was one of the best we ever did.... It showed me he had flair." Recognizing Jordan's talent, Mitchell promoted his protege to head of the prestigious Cadillac Studio in 1957; Jordan was 30 years old. In 1962, Jordan was named executive in charge of automotive design, with responsibility for the exterior styling of all GM cars and trucks. That year, *Life* magazine named him one of the 100 most important young men and women in the nation.

After a stint in Europe at GM's West German affiliate, Adam Opel, Jordan continued his rise through the design ranks. He returned to Detroit in 1970 to run the Cadillac, Buick and Oldsmobile studios, then directed the Chevrolet, Pontiac and commercial-vehicle studios. Jordan hit a low point in an otherwise charmed career when his mentor, Mitchell, retired in 1977 and Irving Rybicki was chosen to succeed him as design vice-president. Jordan then served as director of design till Rybicki retired in 1986.

In 1989, his third year as GM design boss, Jordan was at the pinnacle of a 40-year career with the automaker—a long way from the days when Mitchell took him aside and told him his sport coats were too loud. The tall, silver-haired Jordan now favors elegant dove-gray suits and pastel shirts with matching silk pocket squares. Described by colleagues as flashy and irreverent, he worships Ferraris while acknowledging that Henry Ford I was a childhood hero. A personal highlight, he told *Newsmakers*, was visiting the late Enzo Ferrari at his headquarters in Maranello, Italy, which Jordan likened to "a devout Catholic going to see the Pope."

Today, Jordan insists, the "era of lookalike cars is over" at GM, citing such recent creations as the Chevy Beretta and Olds Cutlass Supreme and the next generation of Cadillacs that will hit the market in 1992. Asked about his priorities at GM Design Staff, Jordan told *Newsmakers:* "We're bringing excitement back into the business. The excitement was gone for awhile as far as the product was concerned. On my first day here, I assembled the entire staff. I stood in the middle of the group without a written text. I knew we had gotten bogged down and overly organized. This is not a business. These are a bunch of emotional people. I told them, 'It's time to let loose and go and do some design. Have fun.' We had been doing lookalike cars aimed at meeting federal fuel-economy laws and because our priorities were different. Now, we've got to be strong with design. We're focusing on divisional images. It adds up to stronger images and clear designs, but not cartoons. You won't see fat cars or flat cars; they won't be slabby or flabby."

"I can't think of any car I'd rather have than a Ferrari. I can say that because I don't think they'll fire me now."

Owning and driving Ferraris, as well as building scale-models of the famed Italian sports cars, appear to be his consuming passion. His personal collection ("my therapy") numbers more than 3,000 kits and models. He also has owned a string of life-size Ferraris, including a Berlinetta Boxer, a Testarossa and an F40. As Jordan told *Newsmakers:* "A Ferrari looks, sounds, smells and goes like a thoroughbred. I can't think of any car I'd rather have than a Ferrari. I can say that because I don't think they'll fire me now.... I'm fascinated by the shape of the car and by the Pininfarina heritage. [The car] is a wonderful illustration of good design that's timeless. A 1962 Ferrari looks as good today as it did in 1962." Jordan, who has likened himself to "an orchestra leader," hopes to imbue some of that passion and flair in his younger designers, and one of his targets is Cadillac. "I grew up in Cadillac, but I didn't drive them for years," he told *Newsmakers.* "They tended to be more old folks' cars. Now we've put some young people in this studio and brought excitement back in."

Describing design trends in a 1982 interview with the *Detroit Free Press,* Jordan observed: "We have to be careful as we make cars smaller and rounder that we don't make them fat and ugly.... In the pell-mell rush to build smaller, more fuel-efficient vehicles, some of us seem to have forgotten an important ingredient—simple attractiveness and excitement. The love affair with the automobile is alive and well. All it takes is an exciting car to kindle the flame." In a 1985 interview with the *Free Press,* he added: "We're never going to design a dumb, ordinary, vanilla piece of transportation. We don't believe in it. We believe everything ought to have some spirit to it, appropriate to the function or purpose of that car." Referring to his team of designers, Jordan later told *Newsmakers:* "We have a lot of talent, but we don't have magic.... We're not a bunch of intellects at Design Staff. We're car nuts. You've got to watch out for designers who talk too much. You can't design a car with words."

Sources

Automobile, December 1988.

Detroit Free Press, September 3, 1982; March 3, 1983; September 11, 1983; October 7, 1986; July 25, 1988; January 8, 1989.

—Sketch by Anita Pyzik Lienert

Norma Kamali

UPI/Bettmann Newsphotos

Fashion designer

Born June 27, 1945, in New York, N.Y.; daughter of Sam Mariategui (a candy-store owner) and Estelle Arraez; married Eddie Kamali (divorced). *Education:* Graduated from Fashion Institute of Technology, 1964.

Addresses: *Office*—OMO Norma Kamali, 11 West 56th St., New York, N.Y. 10019.

Career

Worked as a reservations booker for Northwest Orient airline; founder and owner of Kamali Ltd., New York City, 1967–78; founder and owner of OMO Norma Kamali, New York City, 1978—.

Awards: Coty Award for fashion design, 1981 and 1982; named Outstanding American Talent in Women's Fashion Design by Council of Fashion Designers of America, 1983.

Sidelights

Americans are getting out of their jeans," declared famed photographer Francesco Scavullo in a 1982 *People* article, "and into their Kamalis." He was referring to the fashions of Norma Kamali, the designer who took Seventh Avenue by storm starting in the late 1970s and who helped revolutionize an industry already in constant flux. While the image most people associate with Kamali is the "sweats" look that helped seal her reputation, the two-time Coty Award winner has actually dressed her followers in a wide variety of looks, from shiny maillot swimsuits to slinky evening gowns. "Her clothes are for confident people, not women who want to feel pretty or tailored," explained a Neiman-Marcus buyer to *Newsweek* writer Susan Cheever Cowley.

Born Norma Arraez, of Lebanese-Basque parents in New York City, Kamali describes her early years as the daughter of a candy-store owner and his wife as being "like *Happy Days.*" In a *Cosmopolitan* interview with Robert Goldberg, she said: "In all the neighborhoods there were settlement houses where the kids would put on plays and everyone would come. My mother made our costumes. I remember those elaborate costumes—a butterfly with layers and layers of color and wiring. It's so clear now, looking back, why I'm in the fashion business. I didn't really have a choice. I didn't have an instinct for anything else."

Kamali was graduated from the prestigious Fashion Institute of Technology as a fashion illustrator. Soon after, as she told Goldberg, she "found out the realities" of the business. "How many jobs for an illustrator are there? What do you do—wait till someone dies?" Instead, Kamali took advantage of a job as a reservations booker for Northwest Orient airlines to travel frequently to London, which, during the mid-1960s, drew attention for its devotion to radical fashions. "Oh, the sixties," Kamali recalled in the *Cosmopolitan* article. "The energy, the freedom, so many new things—there were no copies. I don't think that anything revolutionary has happened since then. All those people—and you never knew what planet, what time zone they were in."

Inspired by the forward-thinking fashions she brought back from England, Kamali decided to open her own boutique, a tiny nine-by-six studio in lower Manhattan. She and her husband, Eddie Kamali, ran the place together. She soon found, however, that the clothes she designed herself were as popular as the imports and, by 1970, she was selling her clothing exclusively. "I couldn't believe anyone would *pay* for them," she remarked to Goldberg.

But pay they did, in increasing numbers. Kamali's funky postmodern designs caught on initially with such celebrities as Bette Midler, Donna Summer, and Carly Simon. As her reputation among the avant-garde grew, Kamali, by this time divorced, "took the plunge," as Goldberg put it, and moved to a larger boutique on Madison Avenue. The designer's new haven, dubbed OMO (for "On My Own"), opened for business in 1978. "Three years later, she was famous—and all due to one idea," Goldberg continued, quoting Kamali: "I always wore a big sweatshirt over my swimsuits. So I thought it would be great if I had a line made of gray sweatshirt material—coats, dresses. I knew I had something. It just went boom. People were standing in line to get into my store."

Kamali had tapped into America's growing fitness craze and the subsequent need for "sweats" that could look as good on the street as they did in the gym. It wasn't the first time the designer had successfully flaunted convention—Kamali had made news earlier by cutting apart a cotton sleeping-bag and turning it into a coat—but her many adaptations of sweatshirt material, that thick, soft, go-anywhere cotton, helped make her name known beyond the garment district and turned OMO into a multimillion-dollar enterprise.

As Kamali sweats began to be seen everywhere—from flowing suits to flouncy, thigh-high "rah-rah" skirts—the designer branched out once again with a line of hosiery, shoes and accessories. "She's . . . done oversize men's shirts for women and shown them with white anklets and penny loafers, all-white holiday looks in a disposable fabric, divet coats and outfits in lycra and parachute fabrics," wrote Marge Colborn in a *Detroit News* article. "If you've seen an especially smashing jumpsuit with broad, padded shoulders on the street in the last few seasons, chances are it was designed by Ms. Kamali or is a knockoff of one designed by her."

Vogue editor Grace Mirabella told Georgia Harbison of *Time* that Kamali's clothes "have a little wit and a little dare." But they also have their drawbacks, according to Harbison: "The exaggerated silhouette and overgrown pants and tops are not for the timid. Moreover, while sweat material is not delicate, it must get special care so it will not shrink or droop." Such caveats did not deter a style-hungry public, especially when the majority of Kamali designs could be had for $80 and under. In the early days of OMO, "no store could keep Kamalis in supply long enough to satisfy her votaries," said Harbison. "In one day, New York's Saks Fifth Avenue sold out its entire stock. A few blocks away, Bloomingdale's was forced to close down its separate Kamali shop [one summer] because her clothes went so fast the manufacturer could not keep up with reorders."

Andre Leon Talley interviewed Kamali for *Vogue* and found "nothing aggressive, pushy, or strident" about the woman. "If she were a painting, instead of a designer, she would be a Manet: his portrait of the exotic magnetism of Jeanne Duval, Baudelaire's mistress; or indolent Odalesque—Olympia." Kamali herself might give pause to such a description. She sees herself as a street-level artist, as she revealed to Talley: "Fashion today is born in the streets, in my mind, and it must then be made or geared to the streets. It's a matter of honesty with myself, my work. I have to be and do what I understand. I understand the streets, that's my background. It would be bad, very mediocre at best, if I tried to be somebody who understands castles."

The clothier does, however, acknowledge a classical influence to her work. "One half of me is attracted to the European idea of design; Europeans treat design with the same kind of respect they give theatre or ballet or art," she stated in a *Vogue* interview with Kathleen Madden. America, she continued, "is a newer country, we have newer values, different kinds of values; and money in our society is success. The side of me who always wanted to be the artist would love to be an artist in that European kind of world. The other side of me, being an American and a capitalist, says, 'God, wouldn't it be great if I could be a woman making tons of money like all those guys?' "

The capitalist American in Kamali often manifests itself in her devotion to her work. To that end, the designer's work methods are unique, according to Harbison: "Unlike other designers who create from sketches, Kamali drapes a fabric over her own body to see how it falls. She then begins cutting and sewing with the fabric still on her. It is from this master sample that patterns are made. The curious system may well stem from her teen-age days, when she would stitch herself into tight pants, then extricate herself with a seam ripper."

At the New York headquarters of OMO, "clothes hang—like artwork—on free-standing poles," noted Madden. "A sewing machine buzzes upstairs. Kamali designs by need and by ideas, not 'seasons.' The boutique is her lab." And Kamali may well be the only world-famous clothing manufacturer who doubles as saleswoman in her own shop. Indeed, many customers dealing with the soft-spoken artist, whose long hair may likely be braided, are unaware that they're being advised by Norma Kamali herself. But as the designer tells it, that direct interplay with her customers helps account for her success. "In the shop, I know instantly if I'm doing right or wrong; I know what clothes are doing when they are on a body," she told Madden. "I know what people are buying—which is the most honest, straightforward comment on whether they like something or not; they don't buy things because you're a nice person. I find out what's doing, what's going on with women, what's going on in this city. People bring information in, and it's a wealth of information."

Kamali's imagination is sparked further by another kind of style, namely Hollywood of the glamorous 1930s. In Talley's article, Kamali cited the film choreographer Busby Berkley, known for his elaborate geometric movements, as an influence: "Very few things in our lives bring us entertainment. Busby Berkley is visually original to me. His sense of multiples, repeats of shapes, and creating shape with human bodies are graphically beautiful. The inspiration of that is somehow directly a part of my idea of creating multiple clothes for many types of women. Repeats that become individual when women put my clothes on.... To be serious all the time is not important in fashion."

The twin influences of New York street and Hollywood swank have manifested themselves in another way for Kamali. The designer has in the past eschewed the traditional seasonal fashion show in favor of producing fashion videos, an innovation that sets her apart from other manufacturers. At the same time, Kamali has distinguished herself by her personal absence from the Seventh Avenue publicity machine. In an age when designers make as many headlines as their clothes—the untimely deaths of Perry Ellis and Willie Smith, and the continuing romantic foibles of Calvin Klein are notable examples—Kamali is something of a comparitive recluse. "To quote Beth in *Little Women*," wrote Talley, "Kamali could say, 'I have an infirmity, I am shy.' That's what she's said for years. She avoids public appearances, turns down requests from magazines to be photographed." A self-confessed workaholic, the artist "lives by her shop; most everything she does is somehow work-directed," as Madden put it. Noted Kamali: "At this point, it's what's giving me the most joy. It's total dedication."

> *"Fashion today is born in the streets, in my mind, and it must be made or geared to the streets."*

Kamali did garner some public notice, though likely not the kind she'd prefer to read, in early 1987, when the designer was slapped with a record $10,000 fine for illegally employing homeworkers. The New York State Department of Labor invoked the 1935 sweatshop law, created in the notorious days when garment workers faced perilous conditions. But as *Wall Street Journal* reporter Joseph Perkins pointed out, not only are such conditions very rare today, but the ten Asian and Hispanic immigrant women Kamali employed "were at least as well off as most garment workers who belong to the [International Ladies Garment Workers Union]. Their average compensation was comparable, Miss Kamali said. What's more, they worked at home because it was more convenient for them. The flexible hours that the homework afforded them gave them more time to take care of their children, study or ease back into work after an illness."

Noting that "rather than contest the ban, the fashion designer made room for the 10 workers in her factory," Perkins went on to say that the charge of exploitation in this industry seemed a confusing issue: "Homework is perfectly legal in other industries, provided the work arrangements between employer and homeworker meet federal wage requirements such as minimum wage and overtime, and applicable local requirements.... In [Kamali's] case, the disruption of her homework operation prompted her to suspend her wholesale operation and cancel her spring line of clothes. Not only does this mean a loss of $15 million to $30 million in revenues for OMO,... it also means a substantial loss of jobs for garment workers."

This setback forced Kamali "to stop supplying clothes to any stores other than her two Manhattan shops," *Time* reported. It could prove a blow to the many consumers who have grown accustomed to new Kamali creations provided on a regular basis. As the designer told Goldberg, hers is a look "for the 1980s woman—more physical, less inhibited, with a better sense of humor. Clothes have to be comfortable, easy to care for, 'cause who has time to stand over an ironing board? They have to fit in new ways, because women today are taking care of their bodies. And above all, there's a sexuality that comes through, a new confidence."

"I don't want to be the biggest," Kamali told a *New York Times* writer. "I want to love what I'm doing. But I do know that I want to work for a long time. I like to keep changing and experiencing change. Since I'm in an age group that is changing, I can almost see how I'm going to be as a little old lady. It's going to be a new way to be old. I'm going to be outrageous. Personally, I'm so conservative now, I express myself only through my clothes. I'm not a flamboyant personality. But when I'm 80, I'd like to let it all hang out."

Norma Kamali, as Colborn sees her, "is clearly out to woo the baby-boom generation with [her] clothes. Many of the women who were born after World War II think these getups are new and, to them, they are. New and different and fun. And that's what fashion is all about, isn't it?"

Sources

Cosmopolitan, December, 1985.
Detroit News, August 3, 1986.
Newsweek, July 10, 1978.
New York Times, February 13, 1983.
People, December 27, 1982.
Time, October 5, 1981, March 9, 1987.
Vogue, June, 1982, November, 1984.
Wall Street Journal, March 6, 1987.

—Sidelights by Susan Salter

Elaine Kaufman

AP/Wide World Photos

Restaurateur

Born in New York, N.Y.; daughter of Russian immigrants who ran a dry-goods store in Queens, N.Y. *Education:* Graduated from high school in New York, N.Y.

Addresses: *Home*—New York, N.Y. *Office*—Elaine's, 1703 Second Ave., New York, N.Y.

Career

After graduating from high school, worked in the cosmetics departments of S.H. Kress and Woolworth's stores; worked for a time at a used book store; waitress at an espresso house in Greenwich Village, New York City, in the late 1950s; co-manager then co-owner of restaurant Portofino, New York City, in the early 1960s; founder and proprietor of restaurant Elaine's, New York City, 1963—.

Sidelights

For more than 25 years, a small, dimly lit eatery on Manhattan's Upper East Side has meant as much to New York's writing community as has any publishing house or literary agency. As a second home to a wide variety of authors, intellectuals, entertainers, and hopefuls, the restaurant called Elaine's has become a celebrated edifice in its own right. Mentioned in mediums as diverse as a Woody Allen film and a Billy Joel song, Elaine's is the kind of place where on any evening "ballet star Mikhail Baryshnikov and director Milos (*One Flew Over the Cuckoo's Nest*) Forman trade jokes in Russian, [while] Margaret Trudeau complains of a draft," according to *People* magazine's Christopher P. Andersen.

The proprietor and guiding force behind the restaurant is its owner, Elaine Kaufman, arguably one of the most influential businesswomen in New York, or at least one of the most feared by other influential people. "That winking mogul with the young beauty on his arm is secretly praying that Elaine will recognize him, that [maitre d'] Gianni will escort him to one of the best tables, and if not, at least to one of the decent ones with a view," noted Judith Thurman in an *Architectural Digest* piece. That's no small fear. For in the delicate hierarchy of Elaine's, seating placement is tantamount to personal worth, with Kaufman's favorites garnering the choice tables near the back. Indeed, seeing and being seen in this cafe takes precedence over lesser matters like the quality of the cuisine (it's considered satisfying if unremarkable, with pasta and veal dishes being house specialties).

"The public perception of Elaine's—to an extent justified—is that of a forbidding, cliquish preserve restricted to the favorites of the lady whose name it bears, and these outsiders wonder what qualifies those who dine at the favored tables," wrote A. E. Hotchner. Hotchner, part of a 1983 *New York* magazine cover story celebrating the twentieth anniversary of the eatery, went on to say, "The irony is that few of the illustrious who do frequent Elaine's unhallowed walls can explain why they are there."

Even Kaufman herself is at a loss to explain her success, except to acknowledge to Hotchner that she likes writers and doesn't mind if they spend more time than money at her tables. But her attraction to artistic souls predates her famous restaurant. It has its roots in Kaufman's Greenwich Village days, when she and her then-companion Alfredo Viazzi worked in various restaurants to help support their literary habits. Soon Kaufman realized that serving food "was the easiest thing in the world—it was like it was there waiting for me," as she told Lucy Saroyan in *Interview* magazine. "I mean, it seemed very natural, dealing with people, finding out what they like to eat, remembering it, and being able to take care of a few tables at the same time—all that kind of thing."

By 1963, Kaufman was convinced of her lifelong calling. "All I was after was a nice place that would attract neighborhood people, and I figured if I ran it right I could make a living," she remarked to Hotchner. "Right from the beginning I cared about the people who came in, cared about their enjoying themselves. I liked that, and I guess that's what gave [Elaine's its] atmosphere." In those days, the Upper East Side was not considered a prime location to open any business. Kaufman found the challenges stimulating. She reported to Saroyan: "We had to find a chef who would work this far uptown. Nobody even thought about this neighborhood, but it was the only area where we could find a space for $11,000. We had a very funny opening—we were still painting."

But soon the fledgling restaurant began playing host to what Kaufman, in the Saroyan article, described as a "collection of guys meeting every night, with or without their ladies," adding that she most enjoyed their "talk, the funny stuff that they were going through." The collection of guys included the likes of George Plimpton, Norman Mailer, Gay Talese, Dan Jenkins, and a host of other young writers looking for a haven. In fact, throughout the early years, Elaine's had a reputation as a writer's hangout, and their number increased as the restaurant's reputation grew. In Andersen's *People* article, Talese called Kaufman "probably the only restaurateur in New York who reads books. The most fragile egos in the world pass through her doors, and Elaine is Mother Shrink to us all."

Kaufman nurtured not only the appetites but also the talents of the group she calls "my boys." That appellation was not one she took lightly; In the words of Jules Feiffer, in the *New York* article, "Women were not welcomed at early Elaine's, except as decor. There were a few exceptions, but all in all it was understood that the proprietress was not crazy about the sex. Women would cry out in terror when told you had made reservations. It was a test of love. If a wife or date still spoke to you after a long evening in which you were celebrated and she was ignored, few ways remained to damage the relationship." In later years, though, Kaufman admitted to Andersen that with the help of a female analyst, she has lost much of her hostility toward those of her own gender.

Another Elaine's tradition rankles some patrons, and that is the highly arbitrary methods Kaufman uses to make tables available to her favorites. In fact, the owner has endured the label of snob but defended herself this way to Hotchner: "We honor reservations, and if you have booked a table, you get seated. But people who walk in off the street without reservations have to take their chances, like they do at other restaurants. As for certain tables' going to my regulars, listen, I like having steady customers—it's my neurosis about being separated. I don't like people who just pass through and eat a meal to take a look. I save my tables for my family, the ones I know and care about. I don't have any family of my own—who needs all those problems? I prefer my restaurant family because no matter if I have a rotten day, I know that comes night I'll be in my place and it'll revive me and I'll have a good time."

Though known primarily as a literary haven throughout the 1960s, the eatery's reputation began to suffer as a wider variety of celebrities and self-styled Beautiful People began infesting Elaine's. "By the mid-seventies Elaine's began to change and we began to change," as David Halberstam remembered in the *New York* article. "It was, if anything, far more successful (a tribute to Elaine's skills—sustaining success in America in something as fragile as a restaurant for so long seems a remarkable achievement), but it was more a celebrity hangout than a writers' club. Many of us who had gone there in our thirties were moving into our late forties. More and more Hollywood people were showing up. Soon Table Four [the table of Kaufman's favorite patrons] was quietly disbanded. We continued to show up, we were, in a way, still regulars, but now we came less regularly, and we arrived with other friends simply to eat dinner in a favored restaurant. But it was a wonderful party while it lasted."

The restaurant continues to attract notable diners who might not otherwise frequent such a public place. One Elaine's regular lends a presence that inspires awe even among the celebrities in attendance. Woody Allen, the reclusive screenwriter/director, is known to spend several nights each week at Elaine's, ensconced at a permanently reserved table at the back, near the kitchen and the men's room. In the *New York* article, Plimpton offered this advice: "At Elaine's, there is one famous house rule. At a place where table-hopping and squeezing in at a table to join even the vaguest of friends... is very much *de rigueur,* it is *not* done at Woody Allen's table. Even on the way to the Gents, nothing more than a side glance at the brooding figure of Woody Allen, mournfully glancing down at his chicken francese, which I am told is his favorite dish, is permissible. To interrupt his meal by leaning over and calling out 'Hiya, Woody, how's it going?' would be unheard of."

As famous as Elaine's the restaurant may be, relatively little is known of Elaine the person. Kaufman describes a happy childhood with her Russian immigrant parents in New York City. "My parents had a general store in Queens and not much money," she told Judith Thurman. "But even then living well—graciously—was a priority. That meant books, flowers—making an effort. I get that nesting instinct from my family." Kaufman now resides in a luxury penthouse on the East Side. Thurman noted: "On most nights, New York's best-known *salonnarde* gets home between 3 and 4 a.m. and does an hour of reading ('You have to do your homework—who's writing what?') before bed. The splendid lair she retires to has paisely-upholstered walls, a bamboo-and-cane bedroom suite, a fur spread."

Kaufman admits that running her restaurant consumes most of her time, but that she wouldn't have it any other way. "I like all aspects of it," she told Saroyan. "In the afternoon there are a lot of purveyors—wine merchants, food people—and I like all of that. I like caviar-tasting; I like cheese-tasting and wine-tasting. I don't find any of it a chore. All of those things are fun. The nuisance of this business is just when you have problems with personnel." Kaufman may in this case be referring to her former headwaiter, Nicola Spagnolo, who "defected," as Andersen put it in the *People* article, "and started a competing restaurant (Nicola's) six blocks away."

In the *New York* tribute, Frederick Morton not only claimed that Kaufman's establishment nurtured a generation of writing talent, but also suggested that patronizing Elaine's would have benefitted talents from the past. "Elaine would have taught humility to Nietzsche: All she'd have to do was point at Woody Allen, the [restaurant's] resident Superman.... Kafka would have refined his angst at Elaine's—especially after a Broadway opening night.... Elaine's would have expanded the horizons of Francois de Sade. The good marquis in his simplicity thought that the infliction of cruelty stimulated only sexual pleasure. But in this establishment, patrons stand in line for hours, waiting to be seated, being jostled by waiters, having wine spilled on them by hand-waving bar convivialists, being mistaken for Jack Oakie—all of which only heightens the joy on their faces when they are allowed to sit down at last to their chicken."

"Some people ask me why Elaine's popularity has endured," wrote Barbara Goldsmith in *New York.* "I put it down to the theory of proliferating personalities: All the people who used to be with someone else keep coming back with their new pals." In the same article, Irwin Shaw, one of the early regulars, said of Kaufman: "She is an institution who refuses to become institutionalized. No pity is ever expressed; she never says, 'Time, gentlemen, please.' She knows that the first night you are in town, from no matter what quarter of the globe you have come, you must pay the ceremonial visit to the uptown Queen of the Night."

To Hotchner, the appeal of both the woman and her restaurant lies in "the invisible atmosphere, the tantalizing spirit of the place, the ebb and flow of arrivers and departers, table-hoppers who plunk themselves down for a couple of minutes, the milling, amorphous bar people who lead a life of their own, the camarderous waiters who sometimes philosophize while reciting the menu, but more than anything Elaine herself, stopping by to deliver spicy bulletins, greeting and kissing her friends, scolding waiters,... Elaine, the source of the warm *gemutlich* ions that fill the room." And Plimpton had this recipe for success, as quoted by Glenn Collins in the *New York Times:* "You don't make it as long as Elaine has by serving good food. You serve good people."

Sources

Architectural Digest, November, 1988.
Interview, July, 1988.
New York, May 2, 1983.
New York Times, April 26, 1988.
People, April 10, 1978.

—Sketch by Susan Salter

Michael Keaton

AP/Wide World Photos

Actor

Name originally Michael Douglas; born September 9, 1951, in Pittsburgh, Pa.; son of a civil engineer; married Caroline McWilliams (an actress), 1982 (separated); children: Sean Willie. *Education:* Attended Kent State University for two years.

Addresses: *Agent*—Rogers & Cowan, Inc., 10000 Santa Monica Blvd., Los Angeles, Calif. 90067-7007.

Career

After two years of college, returned to Pittsburgh, Pa., and began performing as a standup comic in local comedy clubs while working at various jobs during the day; engineer at WQED-TV (educational television station) in Pittsburgh, 1972; moved to Los Angeles and held jobs bartending and parking cars while performing in comedy clubs; made guest appearance on television series "Maude," which led to parts on several other series, including "All's Fair," 1977, "Mary," 1978, "The Mary Tyler Moore Hour," 1979, "Working Stiffs," 1979, and "Report to Murphy," 1981. Feature films include "Night Shift," 1982, "Mr. Mom," 1983, "Johnny Dangerously," 1984, "Gung Ho," 1986, "Touch and Go," 1986, "The Squeeze," 1987, "Beetlejuice," 1988, "Clean and Sober," 1988, "The Dream Team," 1989, and "Batman," 1989.

Awards: Named best actor by National Society of Film Critics, 1988.

Sidelights

Long before the film "Batman" opened in thousands of theaters in the summer of 1989, the casting of Michael Keaton as the Caped Crusader had already sparked a firestorm of controversy. A legion of Batman fans—by some estimates more than 50,000—had written to Warner Bros. Studios complaining that Keaton was a terrible choice for the Bruce Wayne/Batman role. After all, Keaton was a jokester, a clown. He had made a name for himself as the high-strung, manic attendant in "Night Shift" who turned a morgue into a brothel. His later roles gave little indication that Keaton could bring anything but a buffoon approach to the Batman. In such films as "Gung Ho" and "Mr. Mom," Keaton had parlayed a wise-cracking persona into a major motion picture star. Then there was the down period, with such duds as "Johnny Dangerously," "Touch and Go" and the attrocious "The Squeeze" that sent his career into a seemingly irreversible tailspin.

Yet despite a comeback that included the highly successful offbeat comedy "Beetlejuice" and the critically acclaimed drama "Clean and Sober," Batman fans were aghast at the thought that some wiseguy would play their brooding, vigilante hero. After all, Keaton admitted he only occasionally watched the campy television series, never read the comics as a kid, knew virtually nothing about the super hero and didn't intend to research the role before shooting the movie.

Besides, it wasn't his idea to star in "Batman" in the first place. In fact, when director Tim Burton suggested the role he turned it down. "When Tim first came to me with the script, I read it out of politeness," Keaton told *Rolling Stone*. "All the while I'm thinking there's no way I'd do this. It just wasn't me. My name doesn't spring to *my* mind when somebody says, 'Batman.' But I read it and thought, 'This guy's fascinating!' I saw him as essentially depressed. I told that to Tim, thinking he wouldn't agree, but he said, 'That's exactly what I see.' The choice was to play Batman honestly. So I started thinking, 'What kind of person would wear these clothes?' The answer seemed pretty disturbing. This is a guy in *pain*."

For their part, Warner Bros. welcomed the controversy and the free publicity it generated. Burton, meanwhile, never waivered from his decision. "It's his [Keaton's] eyes," he told *Rolling Stone*. "Eyes are the windows into the soul. You can see in Michael's eyes that the guy has something going on. And Bruce Wayne is somebody who's definitely got too much going on in his mind. It's funny. Getting Michael wasn't my idea. One of the producers, Peter Gruber, I think, said to me, 'What about Michael Keaton?' I said. *'Whoaaa.'* I actually had to think about it. The more I did, the more it made sense. I met with some very good square-jawed actors, but I had real trouble seeing them put on the outfit. Physical presence didn't seem to be enough. I was looking for the unknown." It took Keaton a while to graduate from the unknown.

He grew up in Forest Grove, near Pittsburgh, Pa., the youngest of seven children. His father was a civil engineer whose education came through a correspondence course. At home Keaton fooled around entertaining his large family with jokes and Elvis impressions. In school he learned to make friends by being the class clown. "I was kind of a wild kid," he told the *Los Angeles Times*, "and I was the ring leader in the sense that I was funny and could make the guys laugh."

For two years he majored in speech at Kent State University before dropping out. Then he returned to Pittsburgh to drive an ice cream truck. He also sold silk-screened T-shirts while working on his first comedy skit about a folk singer who rushes to his gig and then realizes he's forgotten his guitar. In 1972, when he was 21, Keaton got a job as an engineer at WQED, Pittsburgh's public education station. It was about this time that he and a station co-worker began working up a routine in which Keaton would pretend to be the ventriloquist and his buddy would be the dummy. While at WQED, Keaton sometimes worked on "Mister Rogers' Neighborhood," running the trolley or Picture-Picture.

It wasn't long, however, before Keaton left the station for Los Angeles. He had $500 and the name of a producer who earlier worked at the television station with him. To get by, Keaton got a job as a singing bus boy. It lasted two nights. In the daytime he parked cars; at night he waited on tables and would perform at the local comedy club during open mike nights. His Hollywood contact, who had a job as a story editor on the "Maude" program, landed him a one-shot audition as a reporter on the show. Norman Lear liked him and wrote Keaton into the short-lived "All's Fair" show.

That was one of several television roles Keaton had during the next five years, each connected to the other by how unmemorable they were. He auditioned often for movie roles; didn't get many offers. And he was almost fired from his first real movie role, the manic morgue attendant in "Night Shift." Warner Bros. studio executives had doubts about Keaton's performance. But the critics loved it, praising him as much if not more than they did the movie's star, Henry Winkler.

For his second movie, "Mr. Mom," Keaton made $300,000, five times his salary for "Night Shift." After his third movie, "Johnny Dangerously," Twentieth Century Fox offered him a four-picture contract. Things couldn't have looked better. Even Woody Allen was on the phone, seeking him out for the lead in "The Purple Rose of Cairo." But things weren't as good as they looked. Allen was unsatisfied with Keaton's performance. After three days of shooting, Allen told him it wasn't working and fired him. It was around this time that Keaton also made several business decisions that later proved to be devastating. He had turned down a role in the highly successful "Splash" for the marginally popular "Johnny Dangerously." Worse still, he thumbed his nose at "Stakeout" for the horrible "The Squeeze," a movie so bad that the phones just stopped ringing. "Life is short in Hollywood," Keaton's partner and business manager Harry Colomby told the *Los Angeles Times*. "You're either in a buy position or you're in a sell position. A half year ago we were in a sell position."

That's about the time Keaton decided to take some risks. Before then, he had always played the good-hearted, sarcastic, wiseguy, the kind of character he called the "approachable Everyman." With "Beetlejuice" Keaton broke that mold. Like he did with "Batman," Keaton at first balked at "Beetlejuice." "I turned down the role because I didn't quite get it," he told *Rolling Stone.* "I went home and I thought, 'Okay, if I would do this role, how would I do it?' It turns out the character creates his own reality. I gave myself some sort of voice, some sort of look based on the words. Then I started thinking about my hair: I wanted my hair to stand out like I was wired and plugged in, and once I started gettin' that, I actually made myself laugh. And I thought, 'Well, this is a good sign, this is kind of funny.' The I got the attitude. And once I got the basic attitude, it really started to roll."

Most critics praised Keaton for his portrayal of a bio-exorcist demon. And they liked even more his turnabout in "Clean and Sober," in which Keaton plays Daryl Poynter, a successful real estate agent addicted to drugs. "These last two movies were choices that were real risky and absolutely right," Keaton told the *Los Angeles Times.* "At a time when I should have been playing it as safe as I possibly could, I said, 'These parts are just what I want to do.' What was my next movie going to be—another script that starts, 'He's young and handsome in an offbeat way?' Two of those make me bored."

Considering the outcry Batman fans raised just at the mention of Keaton playing their favorite hero, that film provided yet another set of risks. Suppose he could not pull off the schizophrenic elements that cause a wealthy playboy to don body armor and a cape at night to fight the underworld? Suppose up against an actor like Jack Nicholson, who had been tapped to play Batman's nemesis, The Joker, Keaton came off looking like a second fiddle? Suppose the comic book fans who lobbied Warner Bros. so hard against him were right? "Risk really works for me," Keaton told *USA Today.* "I like my back against the wall. I love it when people count me out. It's my favorite thing."

Judging from the box office returns in the summer of 1989, Keaton had little to worry about. In a summer of blockbuster movies ("Indiana Jones and the Last Crusade," "Ghostbusters II," "Star Trek V: The Final Frontier," "Lethal Weapon 2," "The Abyss"), "Batman" jumped out its first weekend to a commanding box office lead. Already, even before its first weekend was through, there was talk of a "Batman II" and "Batman III." Indeed, of all the second guessing and controversy that surrounded the casting of Michael Keaton as Batman, success may be his greatest risk of all.

"This is what will happen," he told *Rolling Stone,* perhaps only half in jest. "I'm gonna do four or five of these movies, and it's going to become my career. I'll have to keep expanding the bat suit, because I get fatter every year. I'll be bankrupt. I'll have a couple lawsuits going. I'll be out opening shopping malls, going from appearance to appearance in a cheesy van. I'll kind of turn into the King, into this bloated Elvis, smoking and drinking a lot. I'll invent a little metal attachment, like a stool, for my hip, where kids can sit, because my back can't take their weight. I can hear myself already—'Just climb right up there, li'l pardner. Is that yer mom over there? *Heh-heh-heh.* Go tell her ol' Batman would like to have a drink with her a little bit later.'"

Sources

American Film, July–August, 1983.
Boxoffice, May, 1986; November, 1986; February, 1987.
Chicago Tribune, March 9, 1986.
Detroit Free Press, June 18, 1989.
Los Angeles Times, March 30, 1986; August 9, 1988.
Maclean's, March 31, 1986.
Newsweek, August 29, 1988.
People, March 31, 1986.
Playboy, July, 1983.
Premiere, July, 1989.
Rolling Stone, June 2, 1988.
Time, March 31, 1986; June 19, 1989.
Us, May 5, 1986.
USA Today, August 10, 1988.
Video, November, 1988.
Vogue, June, 1989.

—Sketch by Stephen Advokat

Don King

AP/Wide World Photos

Boxing promoter

Full name, Donald King; born August 20, 1931, in Cleveland, Ohio; son of Clarence (a steelworker) and Hattie (a baker) King; married; wife's name, Henrietta; children: Eric, Carl, Deborah King Lee. *Education:* Attended Western Reserve University (now Case Western Reserve University), for one year.

Addresses: *Home*—Orwell, Ohio; and New York, N.Y. *Office*—Don King Productions, Inc., 32 East 69th St., New York, N.Y. 10021.

Career

While in elementary school, began delivering live chickens for a poultry retailer; sold peanuts and pies, baked by his mother, to gamblers at policy houses; boxed in Golden Gloves tournament, 1948; numbers runner in Cleveland, Ohio, 1950–67; after serving a term in prison, began promoting boxing matches; chairman and chief executive officer, Don King Productions, Inc.; owner and president, Don King Sports Entertainment Network; owner, King Training Camp. Has promoted more than 200 championship fights throughout the world; also promoted the Jacksons' 1984 "Victory" tour. Member of board, President's Council on Physical Fitness.

Member: Operation Push, Martin Luther King Center for Social Change, Trans-Africa, Anti-Apartheid Association.

Awards: Named Man of the Year by National Black Hall of Fame, 1975; Urban Justice Award, Antioch School of Law, 1976; Heritage Award, Edwin Gould Society for Children, 1976; named Man of the Year by NAACP; cited for outstanding support and service by U.S. Olympic Committee, 1980; George Herbert Walker Bush Award, President's Inaugural Commission, 1981; Award of the Year, National Black Caucus, 1981; named Promoter of the Year by North American Boxing Federation, 1983; cited for unselfish dedication and general contributions by Police Athletic League, 1983; named Promoter of the Year and awarded Humanitarian Award from World Boxing Council, 1984; Merit Award, Black Entertainment and Sports Lawyers Association, 1986; Freedom Award, Indiana Black Expo, 1986; Crack Buster of the Year Award, National Youth Movement, 1986; Dr. Martin Luther King Jr. Humanitarian Award, Jamaica America Society and U.S. Information Service, 1987; cited as a true champion of humanitarian causes by Indiana state branch of NAACP, 1987; Martin Luther King Humanitarian Award, Chicago chapter of Indiana Black Expo, 1987.

Sidelights

More than any fighter, Don King, the man with the electroshock hair and rapid-fire mouth, has dominated boxing in recent years. King has promoted more than 200 title fights—including at least 35 of the last 45 heavyweight championship bouts—earning more than $100 million in the process. King's grip on the market is such that for a four-year period in the early 1980s, every boxer who fought for the heavyweight title was managed or promoted by King and his son Carl. From Larry Holmes through Mike Tyson, each champ won his title from, and often lost it back to, another King fighter. King is known as much for his personality as his considerable power. With the retirement of Muhammad Ali, King became boxing's most visible figure, with his purplish prose and bombastic patriotism. Wrote columnist Bill Lyon of the *Philadelphia Inquirer*, "Don King and his light-socket hair have come to symbolize boxing, and all of the flamboyance and fraud, the occasional dignity and the frequent duplicity that entails."

It all came despite a persistent drizzle of suspicion of how King's success came about, despite constant lawsuits from his fighters and legal battles with the government, and despite King's background as a Cleveland numbers runner and conviction for manslaughter. King told *Playboy* that his shady image actually helped his career. "Society didn't want to get in on it," he said. "They looked at boxing and decided that it was infiltrated with racketeers. So because it's unorganized, it allowed a guy like me to come in."

King was born in a Cleveland ghetto in 1931, one of the six children of Hattie and Clarence King. His father, a steelworker, was killed in an explosion of molten metal on December 7, 1941. Hattie King used the insurance settlement to move her children to a nicer neighborhood. Soon, however, money became scarce. Hattie baked pies and sent her children out to sell them. In addition, King and his four brothers bought 100-pound sacks of peanuts which they roasted and sold in smaller bags. Into each bag they placed a "lucky number," making their product extremely popular with those playing the illegal lotteries. "Even at 20, I was very organized," King told *Playboy*. "I'd write down where I sold my bags and what the numbers were, and if a customer won on one of them, I'd track him down and get a tip."

While a high school student, King boxed in the Cleveland Golden Gloves tournament as a 108-pound flyweight nicknamed "The Kid." In the second round of a bout against an amateur from New York, King caught a right to the chin and was knocked out. "It felt like somebody had hit me with a lead pipe," King told *Playboy*. "I remember thinking, 'What am I doing here? There's got to be a better way.' After that, the Kid's career in fisticuffs was over, at least from the perspective of becoming a boxer."

After graduating high school, King was accepted at Kent State University. He worked all summer as a numbers runner to earn the $600 he needed for tuition but then misplaced a winning betting slip for $580 and had to personally come up with the money. At that point, he decided to go into the numbers racket full time, and by the time he was 30, he had become one of Cleveland's most successful lottery men. In 1967, King and an employee tussled over a $1,000 disagreement. The man's head hit the pavement, and eight days later he died. King was convicted of manslaughter and spent four years at the Marion Correctional Institution in Ohio. In 1983, he was granted a full pardon on the manslaughter conviction by Ohio Governor James Rhodes.

King used his time in prison to gain the education he felt he missed by not going to college. Wrote *Los Angeles Times* columnist Jim Murray: "King's cell mates were poets and authors, philosophers and playwrights. King didn't spend his time with yeggs and hit men, strong-arm robbers and boosters, he spent it with Homer and Shakespeare, Pushkin and Rostand." King himself told *Playboy:* "The Don King who went in [to prison] was armed with a pea shooter. The one who came out was armed with an atomic bomb of knowledge and understanding.... I had changed considerably."

Shortly after his release, as King told the *Los Angeles Times*, he received "a sign from God." King said he was sleeping when, "all of a sudden, there was this rumbling in my head, it was just like a volcanic eruption. My hair began to pop up. Ping! Ping! Ping! Ping! Each hair, each strand, pristine and beautiful, each standing up beautifully." King said he went to the barber shop the next morning but the scissors would not cut his hair, and the electric clippers produced sparks when they got near him. Since then, he said, he has not cut or combed his hair. "God had put this head on me like he did Samson and Delilah," King told the *Los Angeles Times*. "I thought, Whadda you know, I'm chosen by God. And as long as I remain godlike and took God's blessing He sent me from on high, I would continue to succeed, and, sure enough, God did for me what He did for Jonah, extricating him from the belly of the whale."

King's first foray into boxing came through three-time heavyweight champ Muhammad Ali. The two men met in 1974, shortly after King's prison release, when King recruited Ali to fight an exhibition in Cleveland to raise money for a struggling hospital. King convinced Ali and Herbert Mohammed, Ali's business manager, that Ali was morally obligated to do business with a black promoter. King had no background in the business, but, with Ali's blessing, he arranged for Ali to challenge titleholder George Foreman. King promised the fighters purses of $5 million each—twice the highest amount that had previously been paid to a fighter. And he convinced the government of Zaire to put up $10 million for the fight, arguing it would introduce that country to America and Western Europe. "The Rumble in the Jungle," as King dubbed the fight, was a stunning financial success for all concerned. Ali won back the title and vowed to stay with his new promoter.

King next promoted the spectacular "Thrilla in Manila," pitting Ali against Joe Frazier in 1975, which many regard as the best heavyweight title fight ever. And as Ali's talents dissipated, King emerged as the sport's largest personality. "I came into boxing because it is the last vestige of free enterprise," King told the *Washington Post.* "You can make money on your talent and hard work. I outcompete every promoter in the business.... I've had a hell of a life. I never cease to amaze myself. I say this humbly."

In 1977, the FBI investigated a series of bouts that King helped arrange for ABC, which turned out to involve phony records for fighters. The tournament was killed by the investigation, but no formal charges were brought against King or anyone else. "The government shouldn't be bothering with me," King told the *Washington Post,* "it should be supporting me. Man, I'm true testimony to the American dream, a role model from Appalachia to Harlem.... Look at me, black, born poor, been in jail and still a success. Look at what I've achieved. This tells that guy suffering from hopeless desolation that there is a chance."

When Larry Holmes succeeded Ali as heavyweight champion in the late 1970s, Holmes signed on with King, saying he preferred to do business with a fellow black. The promoter became a passage to the championship—fighters signed with King because only he could get them a shot at the belt. Holmes and King feuded over the years, but the boxer stayed loyal. Only after retiring did Holmes accuse King of skimming money from his purses. "Don said to me, 'Why give money to the white man? Don't you want to help your brother?'" Holmes told the *Philadelphia Inquirer.* "Well, I wanted to help my brother. But it turned out he [cheated] me. Don King doesn't care about black or white. He just cares about green." In 1988, Holmes sued King for more than $300,000, which he said King improperly took as a "consultant's fee" after Holmes's January fight against Tyson. He settled for $100,000. Settling lawsuits has been a longtime practice for King. He was sued, at various times, by more than a dozen fighters, trainers and competitors. Few of the cases ever went to trial; most ended with King paying the aggrieved party to drop the suit.

"I transcend earthly bounds. I never cease to amaze myself, because I haven't yet found my limits."

King's biggest legal hassles, however, came with the federal government. For three years in the early 1980s, the FBI investigated King and a few other boxing promoters on suspicion of coercion, extortion, and organized-crime links. No charges were filed. Current New York State Inspector General Joseph Spinelli, who headed that FBI investigation, said King made boxing his dominion by knowing how to prosper from the sport's incredible chaos. "There was no criminality," Spinelli told the *Philadelphia Inquirer,* "because there are no laws that govern this industry.... There are three different organizations, different rankings, three different champions, different rules, all kinds of divisions. It's just a mess, and Don King is smart enough to know how to exploit that mess." Asked his reaction to the investigation, King told the *Inquirer,* "Sweet are the uses of adversity, which like the toad, ugly and venomous, yet wears a precious jewel in his head. I found the jewel in adversity."

In 1984, the federal government arraigned King and his secretary, Constance Harper, in New York on a 23-count indictment involving charges of tax evasion of nearly $1 million. The charges could have sent King to prison for 46 years. One year later, a jury of 12 acquitted King but convicted Harper. King signed autographs for the jury afterward and told the *Philadelphia Daily News:* "Only in America could this happen. This is truly the land with liberty and justice for all."

And so it was back to business as usual for boxing's P.T. Barnum. King got involved in promoting Michael Jackson's 1984 Victory Tour, experimented with hosting a television talk show, and stayed on top of the boxing world. Since 1984, the jumble of heavyweight titleholders that included Mike Weaver, Michael Dokes, Gerrie Coetzee, Greg Page, Tony Tubbs, Tim Witherspoon, Pinklon Thomas, Bonecrusher Smith, and Trevor Berbick were all under exclusive promotional contracts with King. Some of those fighters said they were forced to sign contracts making King's son Carl their manager and giving Carl the rights to 50 percent of their purses. Don King never denied the allegations, telling *Playboy*, "A father wouldn't be worth his salt if he didn't help his son."

By mid-1988 it appeared that King's influence over boxing might be waning. Heavyweight champion Mike Tyson had fulfilled a contract allowing King to promote five of his fights. After knocking out Michael Spinks in the fifth fight, Tyson said he would stay away from King. But after feuding with his manager, Bill Cayton, and breaking up with his wife, Robin Givens, Tyson turned once again to King. The two men flew together to Venezuela for the World Boxing Association convention and then spent a week in solitude at King's 190-acre compound in suburban Cleveland. "All Don King cares about is Don King," Tyson's trainer, Kevin Rooney, told the *Philadelphia Inquirer*. "King is just using Mike. He doesn't care about fighters. Boxers come and go, but managers and promoters stick around for a long time."

To King, it was just more criticism to roll off his back. "All of my fighters should get down on their knees and thank me for what I've done for them," King told the *Philadelphia Inquirer*. And, asked his opinion of himself, King told *Playboy*: "I transcend earthly bounds. I never cease to amaze myself, because I haven't yet found my limits. I am quite ready to accept the limits of what I can do, but every time I feel that way—boom!—God touches me and I do something that's even more stupendous than whatever I've done up to then."

Avocational Interests: Golf.

Sources

Akron Beacon Journal, November 20, 1985.
Boston Globe, September 30, 1980.
Chicago Tribune, August 10, 1987.
Dallas Morning News, August 3, 1987.
Los Angeles Times, June 15, 1985; April 17, 1986.
Newsday, August 20, 1987; January 22, 1988.
New York Times, August 19, 1987; June 21, 1988.
Philadelphia Daily News, October 25, 1984; November 20, 1985.
Philadelphia Inquirer, January 18, 1984; December 14, 1984; November 23, 1986; June 26, 1988; October 19, 1988.
Playboy, May, 1988.
Rolling Stone, January 19, 1984.
Sports Illustrated, December 10, 1984; December 22, 1986; June 13, 1988.
Time, May 2, 1977.
Washington Post, December 21, 1984; December 26, 1984.

—Sketch by Glen Macnow

Frances Kissling

Photograph by Charlie Archambault

Pro-choice activist

Born June 15, 1943, in New York, N.Y.; daughter of Florence Rynkiewicz (a medical administrator) and Thomas Romanski; adopted daughter of Charles Kissling (a building contractor). *Education:* Attended St. John's University, New York, 1961–64; New School for Social Research, B.A., 1966. *Religion:* Roman Catholic.

Addresses: *Home*—2701 Connecticut Ave. NW, Washington, D.C. 20008. *Office*—Catholics for a Free Choice, 1436 U Street NW, Suite 301, Washington, D.C. 20009.

Career

Pro-choice activist. Held a variety of jobs during the late 1960s, including positions with Macmillan Publishing and American Association of Psychiatric Services for Children; director of ABC Clinics, New York City, 1970–74; consultant to international agency establishing abortion clinics in Italy, Austria, and Mexico, 1974–75; founder and executive director of National Abortion Federation, 1976–80; director of The Youth Project, Washington, D.C., 1980–81; Catholics for a Free Choice, Washington, D.C., president, 1982—.

Co-founder and treasurer of the Global Fund for Women; board member of International Women's Health Coalition; member of development committee of Women's Alliance for Theology, Ethics, and Ritual; member of District of Columbia Mayor's Panel on Teen Pregnancy Prevention. Lecturer and international consultant on reproductive health; has made numerous radio and television appearances, including CBS-TV's "Morning News," ABC-TV's "Nightline," and NBC-TV's "Today Show."

Member: American Public Health Association (member of standing committee on women's rights), Women-Church Convergence.

Awards: Named one of the eighty women to watch in the '80s by *Ms.* magazine.

Sidelights

The president of Catholics for a Free Choice (CFFC), Frances Kissling is widely regarded as one of the most controversial voices in the Catholic church. She believes that women have the right to safe, legal reproductive health care, including birth control and abortion, and she is not afraid to say so. Indeed, the trailblazing Kissling has spent much of her life fighting not only for the right of women to make their own decisions but for transformation in the very structure of the church itself.

The precocious Kissling first began challenging the boundaries of church authority as a youth. She grew up in a working-class neighborhood in Flushing, New York, attended Catholic schools, and aspired to be a nun. But as the daughter of a divorced and remarried Catholic, Kissling saw disparities between the way the church treated divorced Catholics and the way it treated its other members, and she began to question this injustice. More than once she asked priests why her mother couldn't receive the sacraments. And later, after her mother worked out a private agreement with the church so that she could receive the sacraments, Kissling perceived even greater hypocrisy.

Upon graduating from high school, Kissling headed for college. In an interview with Janet Wallach for the *Washington Post*, Kissling recalled that she posed so many questions in one theology class that the professor told her, "Sit on your hands. You just have *too* many questions." After one year she left school to enter a convent. Nuns, she felt, had always provided her with excellent role models, and she also believed that there was much to be learned from the intellectual model of Catholicism. Several months later, however, the postulant decided to leave the Sisters of Saint Joseph. She found that she disagreed with any number of the church's teachings, including those on birth control and sexuality, and considered it hypocritical to continue participating in the institutional church.

Temporarily leaving the church behind, Kissling became a social activist. She attended the New School for Social Research, protested the war in Vietnam, and joined in the feminist movement. She began living with a man and practicing birth control, both taboo in the eyes of the Catholic church, and in 1970 accepted a job running an abortion clinic. At that time New York was one of only two states where abortion was legal, and Kissling witnessed women arriving from all over the country to avail themselves of the clinic's services. "Most people I saw knew what they were doing," Kissling told Wallach. "It was a hard decision, but given their circumstances, it was the best decision they could make."

Although the activist left both her job and New York after abortion was legalized in 1973, it wasn't long before she returned to the state. This time, her mission was to help establish clinics overseas where women could receive safe abortions. One of the planned locations was Rome where, despite opposition from the pope and the Vatican, abortion was eventually legalized. Reflecting on her work there, Kissling explained to Wallach: "I felt that what we were doing was correct, that abortion goes on whether it's legal or illegal. The question was what kind of abortion is a woman going to get."

During the late seventies, Kissling's activism took another turn. In 1977 Congress passed the Hyde Amendment, a measure that eliminated federal funding for abortions except when a woman's life is in jeopardy. That October Rosie Jimenez, a Mexican-American mother in her late twenties, died from an illegal abortion. Although a government investigation indicated that Rosie had secured her abortion in Mexico rather than in her McAllen, Texas, hometown, reporter Ellen Frankfort distrusted the government's findings. Determined to uncover the truth, she traveled to Texas to inquire into Rosie's death herself. She was subsequently joined by Kissling, and the two together documented Rosie's as the first U. S. death by illegal abortion following the withdrawal of Medicaid funds for the procedure. They recounted their findings in a book titled *Rosie: The Investigation of a Wrongful Death.*

As the seventies drew to a close, Kissling found herself returning to the church. In a conversation with writer Connie Lauerman for the *Chicago Tribune,* she revealed that she "began seeing the limitations of a secular perspective on the world. Having gained a certain maturity and depth, I saw that now what I could do was combine that early religious training and background and the knowledge that I had gained in the world and put those together to work on some of the same issues in terms of women's equality and women's rights and a more open and respectful attitude toward people's sexuality and human reproduction."

Kissling feels that the changes inaugurated by Vatican II were instrumental in guiding her as well as others back to the Catholic church. It was only after the Second Vatican Council that the church really began to stress the social justice message of the gospel as the foundation of Catholic faith, only then that it committed itself to community organizing, poverty programs, antiwar and other campaigns. But when questioned by Annie Lally Milhaven in an interview for *The Inside Stories: Thirteen Valiant Women Challenging the Church*, Kissling also maintained: "When I say I came back to the church, I never came back on the old terms. It is true you can't go home again. I came back to the church as a social change agent; I came back to woman-church." She continued: "When I talk about coming back into *the* church, I'm not talking about coming back to Sunday mass, confession and all of those things that are the memories of my childhood. I'm talking about coming back to a new vision of church established in the late 1970s by women within the church. Women recapturing the church." According to Kissling, what's really called for is a revolution in the church, an effort to create a church that is "more sensitive to all powerless people."

In her own attempts to help transform the church, Kissling became president of Catholics for a Free Choice in 1982. A national, educational organization, CFFC advocates access to safe, legal reproductive health care for all women, including abortion, and encourages minimizing the need for abortions through family planning services and child and family support programs. One of the organization's goals is to bring the ethical discussion on reproductive rights into the public arena.

Speaking with Milhaven, Kissling commented: "I myself have just begun to understand this place that I and many others in the church are in. We want to be, but are not able to connect with, the church. I have made the conscious decision that I will speak about abortion. It's not just abstract talk about theology and ethics. Rather, I will speak about who I am; how my life experience and the ethic flowing from it is universal. Many people have the same experience. The development of a sexual ethic (never mind abortion) involves getting the institutional church to address reality." Part of the goal, she observed, is "to force the church to a point where pastoral reality becomes consistent with the objective, public, political message."

Both CFFC and Kissling have gained notoriety since she became its head, and now neither remains out of the public eye for long. In 1982 CFFC became the first pro-choice group to organize briefings on abortion and family planning for Congress. Although the strategy is now common practice among pro-choice organizations, that first meeting proved especially controversial. The attendant briefing book included a statement affirming the legality of abortion in a pluralistic society that was signed by Catholic congresswoman Geraldine Ferraro. Her stand on the issue incurred the ire of Cardinal John O'Connor as well as an uproar among Catholics when she ran as the Democratic Party's 1984 candidate for vice-president of the United States.

To support Ferraro, Kissling and others decided to make public the conflict over abortion in the Catholic church by running a full-page ad in the *New York Times.* Appearing in October, 1984, the ad contained a declaration of support for Ferraro that testified to a diversity of opinion on abortion among Catholics. It was signed by twenty-four nuns as well as more than seventy religious leaders, and it immediately provoked the wrath of the Vatican. Church leaders warned the nuns that they would have to recant or risk being dismissed, and efforts were made to disgrace the others. A year later, a second ad appeared featuring a declaration of support for those involved with the first ad as well as a statement attesting to the right to disagree with church teachings.

Although the official church has since tended to ignore CFFC, fearing that recognizing the organization will confer it with legitimacy, the Vatican's attention to the *New York Times* ad did help propel CFFC into a leading role in the reproductive rights debate. It now issues a variety of publications, including a guide to ethical decision making, a history of abortion in the Catholic church, and a bimonthly journal of pro-choice opinion titled *Conscience.* It also makes efforts to educate Congress as well as conduct seminars, workshops, and conferences. Early in 1989 the organization established an office in Uruguay as part of its international activities.

As president of CFFC, Kissling spends much of her time on the road, bringing her message to Catholics around the world. Central to her point of view is the belief that the real issue is not reproductive rights but control over women. Birth control, abortion, women's ordination—these issues, according to Kissling, are not spiritual struggles at all; rather, they are political struggles. As she articulated during a lecture in the Philippines, subsequently published in *Health Alert:* "Society after society, country after country, has battled deeply, profoundly and divisively on the question of whether or not it will allow women to make the decision of when, whether and under what circumstances we will bring children into this world. That indeed is the heart of the ethical questions that we face when we consider reproductive health care."

Today's Catholic church does not permit induced abortions under any circumstances, Catholics are told, because the fetus is a living person with a right to life. But as Kissling pointed out during a 1988 speaking tour in England, reported the *Independent:* "the Catholic Church has spent millions of dollars opposing abortion. So far they have not saved a single foetal life. If they were really concerned about abortion, as the most heinous crime, they would be better off spending that money on preventing unwanted pregnancy." Such an expenditure, however, would conflict with the church's position on birth control. It also reveals what the *Independent* quoted Kissling as calling a "misconceived" understanding of sexuality, one that "leaves no room for such values as love and companionship." Which returns her to the idea of control over women. Studies indicate that Catholic women have abortions at the same rate as the general population of childbearing women, and this concerns the bishops "because they have been unable to assert control over women through the Church. Having lost the battle they are now resorting to using the state to enforce control, not just over Catholic women, but over all women."

As recently as 1974, in its Declaration on Procured Abortion, the Vatican admitted that its position on fetal personhood had changed over time, that there had been and is today no unanimity on exactly when a fetus becomes a living human being. Indeed, the Catholic church has a long tradition of intellectual freedom, allowing that where doubt exists, there is freedom. And since there is room for uncertainty on the abortion issue, there must also be freedom. The Catholic church has a tradition, as well, of insisting that Catholics follow their conscience when it conflicts with church teachings. Thus "in Catholic theology," Kissling told her Philippine audience, "we begin to understand that we are agents, we are subjects of our own lives. We are not objects. And as moral agents, we must be free to act in accordance with our own circumstances."

Getting the church to trust women to make good decisions, to recognize their moral agency, is at the heart of the abortion debate, according to Kissling. As she summarized for Milhaven: "The basic question has got to be *who* shall decide? How shall we, as a society, make this decision? Do I want the state to decide? Do I want the doctors to decide? Or do I want a pregnant person to make this decision?"

Although affectionately called the "Cardinal" by her friends, Kissling also has more than her share of detractors, with critics typically attacking her Catholicism. While on a speaking tour in Michigan in 1988, for example, one woman accused Kissling of not being a real Catholic, arguing that her activism on the abortion issue automatically excluded her from participation in the church. And during that same tour, the *Detroit News* reported that an official church spokesman believed CFFC was masquerading as a Catholic organization in order to generate publicity for its true, "anti-Catholic" cause. Kissling, however, remains undaunted. Indeed, she acknowledges that there are no easy answers but stands firm in her belief that the church today can accommodate a pro-choice Catholic viewpoint. In her opinion, not only Catholics but all members of our society must begin to focus more on values than on rights, asking "What kind of society do we wish to live in? What sort of society affirms and values the well-being of all its members, including women? What kind of reproductive policy will that society adopt?"

Ms. magazine named Kissling one of the eighty women to watch in the 1980s. But with the eighties not yet at an end the outspoken Kissling, articulating values that bespeak her Catholic heritage, has already taken the debate into the next decade. "As we approach the 1990s," she concluded during an address in Albuquerque in the fall of 1988, "it is time for us to talk about the survival of this planet and about the kind of people we want to be—not the things we want to be allowed to do."

Writings

Rosie: The Investigation of a Wrongful Death (with Ellen Frankfort), Dial Press, 1979.

Contributor to periodicals, including *Journal of Feminist Studies in Religion, Washington Post,* and *Boston Globe.*

Sources

Books

The Inside Stories: Thirteen Valiant Women Challenging the Church, edited by Annie Lally Milhaven, Twenty-third Publications, 1987.

Periodicals

Ann Arbor News, April 7, 1988.
Boston Globe, August 17, 1984.
Chicago Tribune, September 28, 1986.
Conscience, January-February, 1989.
Detroit News, April 5, 1988.
Guardian (England), March 29, 1988.
Health Alert, March 15, 1988.
Independent (England), March 28, 1988.
Manila Bulletin, February 1, 1988.
Miami Herald, August 21, 1987.
Philippine Starweek, January 31–February 6, 1988.
U.S.A. Today, January 31, 1989.
Washington Post, August 21, 1985; August 24, 1986.

—Sketch by Nancy H. Evans

Beate Klarsfeld

AP/Wide World Photos

Nazi hunter

Born February 13, 1939, in Berlin, Germany; daughter of Kurt (a clerk) and Helene (Scholz) Kuenzel; married Serge Klarsfeld (an attorney), November 7, 1963; children: Arno David, Lida Myriam. *Education:* Attended schools in Germany. *Religion:* Lutheran.

Addresses: *Home*—Paris, France. *Office*—c/o Beate Klarsfeld Foundation, 515 Madison Ave., New York, N.Y. 10022.

Career

Typist in West Germany, 1957–60; secretary, French-West German Youth Service, Paris, France, 1963–68; activist against impunity of Nazi war criminals and for support of Jewish people and the nation of Israel, 1968—. Member of Central Committee, International League Against Racism and Antisemitism, Paris, 1971—.

Member: B'nai B'rith (Tel Aviv, Israel), Legion of Honor (France).

Awards: Medal Lambrakis from World Council of Peace, Berlin, 1969; Medal of Courage of the Revolt of the Ghetto from Israeli government, 1974; nominated for Nobel Peace Prize, 1977; Human Rights Award from Women's American Organization for Rehabilitation Through Training, 1983.

Sidelights

Beate Klarsfeld does not like the term "Nazi-hunter." Nevertheless, the description fits. The petite native of Germany has been one of the most tireless crusaders in the long and ongoing struggle to locate Nazi war criminals and bring them to justice. For more than twenty years Klarsfeld and her husband, Serge, have devoted themselves to the search for those members of the Third Reich—and its satellites in France and elsewhere—who organized and engineered the systematic murder of millions of Jews as part of Hitler's heinous "Final Solution." Using a sophisticated blend of media blitz, civil disobedience, and painstaking documentation, the Klarsfelds confront war criminals and force governments to prosecute them. Their efforts have led to imprisonment for more than a half dozen men who are collectively responsible for over 100,000 wartime civilian deaths. Beate Klarsfeld told the *Los Angeles Times:* "As a German and not a Jew, I think that the great tragedy of the Hitlerian experience cannot be accepted by Germans as a historic accident, after which we can draw a line of oblivion and non-responsibility." She expressed a similar sentiment in *U.S. News & World Report:* "My generation—symbolically the children of the Nazis—has a special duty to fight anti-Semitism and to help Jews who are being persecuted today." Klarsfeld has devoted all her time, talents, and energy to this task since 1968.

Beate Klarsfeld was born in Germany in 1939, the very year Hitler's armies invaded Poland. Her father was a soldier in the *Wehrmacht,* the army of the Third Reich. Klarsfeld was too young during the Second World War to be able to grasp the politics behind the conflict; she also grew up, like many German children, unaware of the staggering crimes against European Jewry perpetrated by the Nazis' SS force. Her family simply did not talk about the war when it was over. Klarsfeld told the *Los Angeles Times* that her parents were members of Germany's "silent majority." She said that from their point of view, "it is better not to speak about it [the Holocaust]." She added: "If that generation did not support Hitler, they were silent and allowed him to continue."

> *"My generation—symbolically the children of the Nazis—has a special duty to fight anti-Semitism and to help Jews who are being persecuted today."*

Klarsfeld herself might have spent her life in this state of silent denial had she not journeyed to Paris in 1960 as an *au pair* girl—an unpaid servant who receives the compensation of travel and lodging in exchange for help with housework and children. In Paris she met Serge Klarsfeld, a young Jewish graduate student whose father had been killed at Auschwitz. They were married in 1963, and from her husband's family Beate learned about the full extent of the wartime atrocities against the Jews. She told *Mother Jones* magazine: "Because Serge's father died at Auschwitz and because my father was in the *Wehrmacht,* we always felt we should make something special out of our marriage. We wanted to do something other than just run for money."

Together the Klarsfelds began to research the Holocaust in their spare time after work. In 1967 they were shocked by the election of Kurt Georg Kiesinger—known to have been a high-ranking official in the Nazi Foreign Ministry—to the Chancellorship of the Federal Republic of Germany. Beate began to write articles denouncing Kiesinger, at one point noting that the head of state represented "the respectability of evil." Her outspokenness cost her her secretarial job; some eight months after her articles began appearing in leftist periodicals, the French-West German Youth Service fired her. *New York Times* contributor Peter Hellman wrote of the Klarsfelds: "Just as their marriage had been one turning point, this was another." Beate described the milestone she and her husband faced in her own words: "We made up our minds then and there to fight. It was a decision reached in a moment and with scarcely a word spoken. But it was a total commitment. We would fight not to ease our conscience, but to win. Serge's career, our family life, our material security, all would take second place." Serge travelled to East Germany to research Kiesinger's war record, and Beate made dramatic plans to unseat the Chancellor—singlehandedly, if need be. She told the *New York Times* that she began to campaign against Kiesinger "like a mongrel on his cuff."

Serge was able to prove that Kiesinger, as a Nazi propaganda minister, was instrumental in promoting racial hatred against the Jews. Armed with extensive documentation, Beate began to visit Germany regularly, speaking out on the Chancellor's wartime activities. She found that she was not attracting enough attention, however, so she turned to acts of civil disobedience—a radical step for a shy and polite woman. First she attended a Kiesinger speech in the German parliament and disrupted the proceedings by shouting, "Nazi! Nazi!" from the visitor's gallery. Several weeks later she took an even more dramatic step. By virtue of some connivance she managed to confront Kiesinger on the podium in Berlin's Congress Hall. Once again shouting "Nazi! Nazi!" she slapped the Chancellor on the face. She was dragged away—and almost shot—by security guards. Kiesinger only doubled the publicity when he pressed charges against Beate. She used the ensuing court appearances to detail his Nazi past and helped to erode his image to such an extent that he lost the 1969 election to an anti-Nazi candidate. Reflecting on his wife's audacious gesture, Serge told *Mother Jones,* "That slap showed, symbolically, that German youth *despised* the actions of their parents' generation."

Inspired by the conviction that their acts had influenced political events, the Klarsfelds began to research the wherebouts of some Nazi criminals still at large. In 1971 France and Germany initiated a treaty allowing Germany to prosecute war criminals even if France had already convicted them—and vice versa. The Klarsfelds turned their attention to the former Nazi administrators of occupied France who had ordered the roundup of French Jews for deportation to concentration camps. They found several of these kingpins living openly in France and West Germany. Unlike Nazi-hunter Simon Wiesenthal, who has located war criminals and then notified national authorities in writing, the Klarsfelds confronted the ex-Nazis directly—often with a cameraman in tow. Sometimes they plastered homes with Nazi banners or led protesters dressed in concentration camp uniforms in public marches at the suspects' business addresses. Eventually—the process was slowed by a delay in the treaty ratification—they saw several war criminals brought to trial.

In addition to ending the political careers of Kiesinger and Parliament member Ernst Achenbach, they provided documentary evidence and identification for the convictions of Herbert Hagen, Kurt Lischka, Ernst Heinrichsohn, Ernst Ehlers, and Kurt Asche. All of these men shared a common legacy: they had by some means sent innocent Jews to sure death in the concentration camps. Beate described the men in *Mother Jones* as being particularly dangerous because they seemed so ordinary. "If they would be like Frankenstein, it would be easy [to hate them]," she said. "But they are normal people. They are handsome-looking, nicely-dressed. This is a problem. When you see Nazi criminals in the movies, they are portrayed with leather coats and cruel eyes. In person . . . they don't look that way."

Simultaneously, the Klarsfelds began to seek several notorious Nazis who had escaped to South America—Klaus Barbie, the Gestapo "Butcher of Lyons," and Dr. Josef Mengele, who performed brutal medical experiments on children at Auschwitz. They located Barbie living under an assumed name in La Paz, Bolivia. In 1972 Beate travelled to Bolivia with Itta Halaunbrenner, the mother of three of Barbie's victims. Klarsfeld and Halaunbrenner chained themselves to a bench outside Barbie's office, holding signs advertising his Nazi past. Quickly they were arrested and thrown out of the country; Bolivia's military government had no sympathy for their cause. Beate and Serge then contemplated radical measures for returning Barbie to France, including a complicated kidnapping plan. But a dozen years passed with no action. Finally, a new regime came into power in Bolivia, and it turned Barbie over to the French authorities for prosecution. He is quoted as having said that all his troubles began when "that woman Klarsfeld" came to La Paz. With Mengele the Klarsfelds had less luck. Frustrated by the German authorities' unwillingness to follow up on their leads, they were relieved to receive concrete proof that Mengele died in 1979. "It would have been better if he was brought to justice," Beate told *Mother Jones*. "But better he is dead than to continue to live his life with impunity. If it is true that he was living in modest circumstances in Brazil, constantly afraid of being captured, that is a small comfort for his victims. At least he was not living in luxury."

Nazi-hunting the way the Klarsfelds do it is a very dangerous activity. They may be the recipients of numerous medals and two prestigious Legion of Honor memberships, but their highly-publicized feats have made them the targets of neo-Nazi hatred. In 1979 their car was bombed at midnight on a Paris street; they have also received letter bombs and threatening phone calls. Nor have they ever taken the easy road professionally. When Kurt Lischka turned up in Cologne, Germany, and his extradition to France for trial was stymied by bureaucracy, the Klarsfelds tried to kidnap him and take him to France themselves. The attempt was earnest but inept; Lischka struggled and called for help from the police. Both Klarsfelds were arrested, and Beate spent more than a week in jail. In fact she has been arrested and jailed repeatedly since the day she slapped Chancellor Kiesinger. During a 1984 trip to Chile to agitate for the deportation of Walter Rauff, one of the designers of the lethal gas chambers used to kill Jews during the war, Beate was arrested twice. (The Chilean police joked that she was "being taken away for gassing.") Certainly Beate has not become accustomed to being arrested and imprisoned, but she does accept it as a perceived means to an end—more publicity for her position. "Our [two] children know it is their fate [for us to do this]," she told the *Los Angeles Times*. "In the beginning we did not know our destiny. . . . Even when I married my husband, we had no idea what would happen to us. But we will go on."

Beate and Serge Klarsfeld have pursued their goals at great personal and financial risk. Modest funding comes to them through donations to the Beate Klarsfeld Foundation, but they have never enjoyed financial security. What they have enjoyed is a sense of justice done, a feeble but palpable vindication for some of the Holocaust's victims. Hellman suggests that the couple is "strong on documentation—without that strength, their media events would be more splash than substance." That same scrupulous paperwork brings quick convictions when Nazi criminals are tried. Hellman wrote that a typical Klarsfeld-initiated case "is based not on emotional but easily challenged accounts of the victims but on unequivocable orders, memos and telegrams of the accused." Asked if their work is depressing, Serge told *Mother Jones*: "No, not at all. Both Beate and I are happy people. The work is a positive thing for us. As a child of the Holocaust, to work against it is a kind of duty and honor. I deeply believe that all those who died during the Holocaust believed that some would try to right this wrong after the war."

As a child not of the Holocaust but of Nazi Germany, Beate expresses her conviction differently. "It is my moral and historic responsibility to bring Nazi criminals to trial and to support the Jewish people and state," she said. "And to stop anti-Semitism . . . . I am building a bridge between the German and Jewish people." A *New York* magazine columnist offers the best summation of Beate Klarsfeld's work. The former Nobel Prize nominee, to quote the columnist, "was, and still is, a sword, while the rest of us push pens."

Writings

The German Girls in Paris, Voggenreiter Verlag, 1964.
Kiesinger: A Documentation (foreword by Heinrich Boell), Melzer Verlag, 1969.
Kiesinger ou le facism subtil (with Joseph Billing), [Paris], 1969.
Partout ou ils seront, Editions Jean-Claude Lattes, 1972, translation published as *Wherever They May Be,* Vanguard, 1975.

Also helped to compile a comprehensive list of the names of French victims of the Holocaust.

Sources

Books

Contemporary Authors, Volume 65–68, Gale, 1977.

Periodicals

Chicago Daily News, February 12, 1973.
Jewish Chronicle, March 12, 1972; July 12, 1974; January 24, 1975.
Los Angeles Times, October 20, 1983.
Le Monde, February 5, 1972; July 11, 1974.
Mother Jones, October, 1985.
National Jewish Monthly, November, 1975.
National Observer, November, 1975.
Newsweek, July 22, 1974.
New York, March 19, 1984; November 24, 1986.
New York Times, November 4, 1979.
Philadelphia Jewish Exponent, November 23, 1973; February 28, 1975; October 24, 1975.
Pioneer Women, October-November, 1975.
Sunday Times (London), March 5, 1972.
Time, March 10, 1973, July 22, 1974.
U.S. News & World Report, May 18, 1987.

—Sketch by Anne Janette Johnson

C. Everett Koop

AP/Wide World Photos

Former U.S. surgeon general

Full name, Charles Everett Koop; born October 14, 1916, in Brooklyn, N.Y.; son of John Everett and Helen (Apel) Koop; married Elizabeth Flanagan, September 19, 1938; children: Allen van Benschoten, Norman Apel, David Charles Everett (deceased), Elizabeth Thompson. *Education:* Dartmouth College, A.B., 1937; Cornell University, M.D., 1941; University of Pennsylvania, Sc.D. in medicine, 1947. *Religion:* Christian.

Addresses: *Home*—Bethesda, Md.

Career

Pennsylvania Hospital, Philadelphia, intern, 1941–42; Boston Children's Hospital, Boston, Mass., fellow in surgery, 1946; Children's Hospital of Philadelphia, surgeon-in-chief, beginning 1948; University of Pennsylvania School of Medicine, Philadelphia, began as instructor, assistant professor, 1949–52, associate professor, 1952–59, professor of pediatric surgery, beginning 1959, professor of pediatric surgery in Graduate School of Medicine, 1960–71, professor of pediatrics, beginning 1971; deputy assistant secretary for health, U.S. Department of Health and Human Services, 1981; member of U.S. Public Health Service commissioned corps, beginning 1981, surgeon general, 1982–89. Consultant to U.S. Navy, 1964—. Member of board of directors, Medical Assistance Programs, Inc., Wheaton, Ill., Evangelical Ministries, Inc., Philadelphia, Daystar Communications, Inc., Eugene, Ore., and Eastern Baptist Seminary and College, Philadelphia.

Member: International Society of Surgery, American Medical Association, American College of Surgeons (fellow), American Academy of Pediatrics (fellow), American Surgical Society, Society of University Surgeons, British Association of Pediatric Surgeons, Deutschen Gesselschaft fur Kinderchirugi, Societe Suisse de Chirugie Infantile, Societe Francaise de Chirugie Infantile.

Awards: Distinguished Service Medal, U.S. Public Health Service; William E. Ladd Gold Medal, American Academy of Pediatrics; Dennis Browne Gold Medal, British Association of Pediatric Surgeons; Copernicus Medal, Polish Surgical Society; decorated chevalier, Legion of Honor, France; medal from city of Marseilles, France. Honorary degrees include LL.D., Eastern Baptist College, 1960; M.D., University of Liverpool, 1968; L.H.D., Wheaton College, 1973; D.Sc., Gynedd Mercy College, 1978; Sc.D., Washington and Jefferson University and Marquette University.

Sidelights

With his stiff, gray beard and stern countenance, C. Everett Koop looks like an Old Testament prophet preaching gloom and doom. The surgeon general of the United States from 1982 to 1989, Koop became known for predicting doom for Americans who don't take care of themselves. Wearing the traditional white admiral's uniform with gold braids, epaulets, and ribbons in public appearances, he often warned Americans against the evils of smoking, once equating nicotine to heroin and cocaine addiction. Koop, who wears a hearing aid, also has preached against the fatty diets of many Americans, although he eats omelets, steaks, and potato chips, and drinks two dry martinis a day. His response to people who criticize his diet, as reported in *U.S. News & World Report:* "If you look and feel as well as I do . . . call me."

But Koop's most controversial statements came in 1986 when he advocated sex education for elementary school children and condoms for adults to counter the scourge of AIDS. Koop is an Evangelical Presbyterian, and his no-nonsense advice stunned his conservative allies and delighted his one-time liberal foes. Liberals had battled Koop's nomination in 1981 because they viewed him an extremist on a number of social issues, such as abortion. Congressman Henry A. Waxman (D-Calif.), chairman of the House Subcommittee on Health and the Environment, said during the early days of the Koop nomination battle in a widely reported remark: "Dr. Koop scares me. He is a man of tremendous intolerance." In April 1982, Koop told *Life* magazine: "I think I scare most people. I don't think people quite know what to do with me."

A *New York Times* editorial in May 1981 suggested that Koop was nominated for the surgeon general post by President Ronald Reagan because the two men shared the same anti-abortion views and not because of Koop's medical skills. But Koop, a pioneer in the field of pediatric surgery, is also a man of great compassion, and once confirmed as surgeon general by the Senate, he decided to use the job as a pulpit to help the weak and to be a strong advocate for the nation's health. Even though his controversial 1986 AIDS report angered conservatives, he told the *New York Times Magazine* in October 1988: "I'm a public health officer. I can't deliver a public health message to just those people whose behavior the conservatives approve of."

Nicknamed Chick by friends, as in chicken coop, Charles Everett Koop was born October 14, 1916 in Brooklyn, New York, to John Everett and Helen Apel Koop. A descendant of Dutch colonists, Koop grew up in Brooklyn's Flatbush section. As a 15-year-old boy, he masqueraded as a medical student and snuck into Columbia Presbyterian Hospital to watch abdominal surgery. He practiced surgery on neighborhood cats, anesthetizing them with ether and then stitching them up and setting them free.

He entered Dartmouth College in 1933 at age 16 and graduated in 1937 with a B.A. He then enrolled in Cornell Medical College and got his M.D. in 1941. He interned at Pennsylvania Hospital where he decided to enter the field of pediatrics. When he settled on pediatric surgery there were only a handful of pediatric surgeons in the nation, primarily because the field lacked prestige. Koop received graduate training at the University of Pennsylvania School of Medicine, Boston Children's Hospital, and the Graduate School of Medicine at the University of Pennsylvania. In 1947, the Graduate School of Medicine awarded Koop an Sc.D degree in medicine.

He was appointed surgeon-in-chief at Children's Hospital in Philadelphia in 1948, one of the few surgeons in the United States to devote his entire practice to children. He also served on the faculty of the University of Pennsylvania School of Medicine, and then began his ascension to the top of the university's medical schools. Koop was named assistant professor of surgery in 1949 and associate professor in 1952. He was appointed professor of pediatric surgery at the School of Medicine in 1959 and to the same position at the Graduate School of Medicine in 1960. In 1971 he was named professor of pediatrics.

When Koop began practicing pediatric surgery, infant mortality rates following surgical procedures were approaching 95 percent. Koop improved pre- and post-operative care and developed dozens of new surgical and diagnostic procedures, including correcting some birth defects considered uncorrectable. He once reconstructed the chest of a baby born with a heart outside its body, and in different operations he separated three different sets of Siamese twins. Koop established the nation's first neonatal intensive surgical care unit and a total-care pediatric facility at Philadelphia Children's Hospital. He helped make anesthesia safe for children and was instrumental in halting the x-raying of children's feet in shoe stores, a move aimed at ending exposure to radiation. A workaholic, Koop over the years developed migraine headaches, which he cured by more work, and a peptic ulcer, which he treated himself. *U.S. News & World Report* said Koop loves to talk and give advice.

On September 19, 1938, Koop married Elizabeth Flanagan, whom he met when he was at Cornell Medical College and she was a student at Vassar. They have two sons, Allen van Benschoten and Norman Apel, one daughter, Elizabeth, and five grandchildren. The couple raised an orphan girl and established an adoption agency in Philadelphia. Another son, David, was killed in 1968 while rock climbing. The tragedy led the Koops to write a book, *Sometimes Mountains Move.*

Koop also co-wrote a book with theologian Frances A. Schaeffer, called *Whatever Happened to the Human Race.* He toured the United States in 1979 and 1980 promoting the book's themes as part of a multimedia presentation. The book denounced abortion as symptomatic of the erosion of human values and said abortion could help create the political climate that led to the Nazi death camps of World War II. Koop also wrote an anti-abortion book in 1976, *The Right to Live; The Right to Die.*

As Koop neared retirement as a surgeon, President Reagan announced that he would name Koop surgeon general. He was slightly over the 64-year-old age limit set down by law. But that requirement was waived when Senator Jesse R. Helms (D-N.C.) sponsored an amendment to an unrelated budget bill that the Senate passed. The surgeon general is charged by law to promote and assure the highest level of health attainable for every individual and family in America and to develop cooperation in health projects with other nations. The surgeon general also advises the public on health matters, from smoking to diet.

Hearings on Koop's nomination began in the fall of 1981 before the Senate Labor and Human Resources Committee. Liberals saw Koop as a one-dimensional caricature, an extremist on abortion and the role of women in society. Koop called abortion euthanasia, and although he favored amniocentesis to determine the mother's Rh factor, he called amniocentesis a search-and-destroy mission when used as a pretext for abortion. The National Organization for Women, Planned Parenthood, and the American Public Health Association lined up against Koop. The American Public Health Association argued that Koop had little training or experience in public health, a requirement of the law.

Koop's supporters detailed his volunteer work in Third World nations as proof of his public health service. They also said he trained women in medicine long before it was popular. At the hearings, seven people who disagreed with Koop's views on abortion still testified in his behalf. Defending himself, Koop said he taught young women in an isolated Mexican tribe how to give medicine and vitamin supplements. He said he helped combat a dysentery epidemic in the Dominican Republic, and for his efforts received that nation's highest civilian award. He also said he promoted the development of training programs for doctors in underdeveloped nations and set up a medical school in Ghana. Koop was confirmed by the Senate by a vote of 68–24 on November 16, 1981. He was sworn in as surgeon general on January 21, 1982.

The first indication that Koop was his own man on public health issues came in February 1982. A pipe smoker until 1972, Koop issued a scathing indictment of cigarette smoking, calling it "the most important public health issue of our time." He said he would press for legislation to strengthen the health warning on cigarette packages, a move that a reluctant President Reagan ultimately endorsed. He wasn't through crusading on the hazards of cigarettes. In 1988 he issued a second report on smoking that equated nicotine with cocaine and heroin addiction. Koop espouses smoke-free workplaces and speaks out against tobacco exports to Third World nations.

"I think I scare most people. I don't think people quite know what to do with me."

During his tenure as surgeon general, Koop generally remained true to his conservative principles. He backed legislation, adopted in 1983, that prevents hospital personnel from denying food or medical treatment to severely handicapped infants. He favored the so-called squeal rule that would require health officials to tell parents if their children try to obtain contraceptives. And he expressed doubts about the effectiveness of living wills, in which an individual expresses the wish not to be kept alive by medical equipment if the individual is comatose.

But Koop made his biggest news in October 1986 when he issued a lengthy report on AIDS. His suggestions to stop the spread of the deadly disease were the most controversial. Telling the nation that "this silence [on how to deal with AIDS] must end," he recommended education for children and condoms for adults. He also backed abortion as a legal option for pregnant women with AIDS and rejected compulsory blood tests, favored by conservatives. He said, "We are fighting a disease, not a people." Koop consulted scores of people before writing the report and rewrote it 26 times.

Conservatives were appalled. Phyllis Schlafly, as reported in *U.S. News & World Report,* said Koop's AIDS report "looks like it was written by the Gay Task Force." Responded Koop, "You may hate the sin, but love the sinner." Koop told the *New York Times Magazine* his views hadn't changed, and he still believed that abstinence and monogamy were better shields against AIDS than condoms. But the conservatives were not through. Led by Schlafly, they initiated a movement to boycott a dinner in Koop's honor organized by the United Senior Americans in May 1987. People who boycotted the dinner included Senator Robert Dole (R-Kan.), former Buffalo Congressman Jack Kemp, and former Delaware Governor Pierre du Pont.

In July 1988, Koop issued a report on nutrition that called for Americans to cut out fat and sugar from their diets, while adding more fiber and complex carbohydrates. However, he didn't call for food labeling as liberals had hoped.

Koop also has clashed with advertising agency association executives and network broadcasters over alcoholic beverage advertising in the print and broadcast media. At a December 1988 workshop in Washington, D.C., Koop accepted eight recommendations to control advertising. However, Association of National Advertisers President DeWitt Helm, Jr., American Association of Advertising Agencies President John O'Toole, and National Association of Broadcasters President Eddie Fritts criticized the panel's recommendations because they said most of the panel members favored some kind of restrictions on alcohol advertising. Helm, O'Toole, and Fritts boycotted a panel Koop was conducting on drunken driving, because Koop accepted the eight anti-alcohol recommendations. As reported in *Advertising Age,* Koop called the protest of the three men "predictable" and doubted they would provide positive input "because the history of smoking and health makes that not very encouraging."

On May 4, 1989, C. Everett Koop informed President Bush that he would not serve out his second term as surgeon general, scheduled to end in November 1989. In a two-page letter, Koop gave no reason for the early resignation but simply stated that he would leave office in July 1989, taking 11 weeks of leave time, and then retire October 1. The *Detroit Free Press* reported that Koop resigned amid "growing pressure from former friends in the conservative movement angered by his efforts to stamp out smoking and his failure to oppose abortion at every turn." Upon hearing of Koop's resignation, Congressman Henry Waxman, who at one time had called Koop "a man of tremendous intolerance," stated: "One of the great surprises of the last eight years is how wrong I was. I take a great deal of pleasure in admitting how wrong I was. If they could find a clone of Koop, they ought to appoint him."

Writings

The Right to Live; the Right to Die, Tyndale House, 1976.
Sometimes Mountains Move (with wife, Elizabeth Koop), Tyndale House, 1979.
Whatever Happened to the Human Race? (with Frances A. Schaeffer), Revell, 1979.

Contributor of almost 200 articles on surgery, pediatrics, physiology, public health, and medical ethics to professional journals and popular periodicals. Founder, editor-in-chief, *Journal of Pediatric Surgery,* 1965–77.

Sources

Advertising Age, December 19, 1988.
Christianity Today, November 6, 1981.
Detroit Free Press, May 5, 1989.
Esquire, June, 1988.
Harper's, August, 1987.
Health, August, 1982.
Interview, April, 1985.
Life, April, 1982.
Newsweek, June 8, 1981.
New York Times Magazine, October 9, 1988.
People, April 21, 1986; March 16, 1987.
Saturday Evening Post, May-June, 1982.
Time, November 24, 1986; June 8, 1987.
U.S. News & World Report, May 25, 1987; May 30, 1988.
Washington Post, July 19, 1981; March 24, 1987; May 18, 1988.

—Sidelights by Steve Raphael

Ted Koppel

UPI/Bettmann Newsphotos

Broadcast journalist

Born February 8, 1940, in Lancashire, England; came to United States, 1953; naturalized U.S. citizen, 1963; son of an industrialist; married Grace Anne Dorney (an attorney), 1963; children: Andrea, Deirdre, Andrew, Tara. *Education:* B.A. from Syracuse University; Stanford University, M.A. in journalism, 1962.

Addresses: *Office*—c/o ABC News, 1717 De Sales Ave., N.W., Washington, D.C. 20036.

Career

WMCA (radio station), New York City, writer, news correspondent, 1963; American Broadcasting Companies, ABC News division, 1963—, worked as radio correspondent, 1963–73 (began as head of Miami Bureau, served as correspondent in Vietnam, 1967 and 1969–71, covered Richard Nixon's 1968 presidential campaign, served as Hong Kong Bureau chief), diplomatic correspondent, 1971–76 and 1977–79, anchor of Saturday television news broadcast, 1976–77, host of television news show "Nightline," 1980—. Worked as free-lance writer, 1976–77.

Awards: Winner of Overseas Press Club awards, 1971, 1974, and 1975; DuPont-Columbia award, 1979, for "ABC World News Tonight" series, "Second to None?"; Emmy award, 1981, for "Nightline" analysis of Ronald Reagan's 1980 presidential election victory; George Polk Award, 1982, for "best television reporting."

Sidelights

Just how much longer Ted Koppel will host "Nightline," the popular news program that has helped ABC News gain respectability and ratings, is unclear. Koppel has often talked of leaving the program and changing careers, perhaps opting for a role in government. Indeed, in 1975, Secretary of State Henry Kissinger offered Koppel a position as State Department spokesman, which he rejected for fear that he would never be able to return to journalism.

Instead, Koppel has spent the last nine years hosting/refereeing/orchestrating a national forum on "Nightline" with some of the most interesting, and controversial, people in the world. When an important news story breaks, millions of Americans have gotten into the habit of staying up a half hour later to sort it all out through "Nightline." Indeed, Koppel has sometimes been referred to as the most intelligent interviewer on television.

Yet, within the patchwork of incongruities that make up Ted Koppel, he does not see himself as growing intellectually from the show. "I look upon myself as being a much shallower person than I ever thought I was going to be, for the simple reason that on

'Nightline,' today it's Angola, tomorrow it's the economy, the day after that it's skin cancer," he told *Life* magazine.

"I was smarter, in a sense, when I was diplomatic correspondent. And even then my days would go from the Middle East to U.S.-Soviet relations to Central America. But at least then I had a field of expertise. There was one subject, foreign affairs, that I concentrated on every day. Now weeks may pass, months may pass, before we revisit a particular subject. So all I need to do is know enough about a subject to ask reasonably intelligent questions, and that does not require a great deal of background."

Koppel, considered by many one of television's most piercing interviewers, may also be one of its poorly briefed. He rarely prepares questions in advance. Nor does his small staff brief him about what to ask his guests, who have varied from such controversial international figures as PLO chief Yasir Arafat and Libyan leader Muammar Kaddafi to the PTL's Jim and Tammy Bakker to such unusual couplings as the Revs. Jesse Jackson and Jerry Falwell appearing together to debate the United States' position on South African apartheid.

Instead, he listens to the opening reports from any one of several ABC journalists assigned to lay the basis of the evening's telecast, then cuts to a commercial and while the rest of the nation sees some advertisement, Koppel jots down what he believes is the most arresting question to emerge from the preceding lead-in. "It's important to listen and, for me, not to have a bunch of prepared questions," Koppel told *New York* magazine. "I have a half hour in which to do a show, out of which maybe twelve or thirteen minutes is interviewing. If I come with three or four questions already in my head, the answer to the first question may be so extraordinary that it'd be foolish to use those other questions. Most of the time, if you give people a halfway-decent opening question, they end up telling you fairly interesting things."

Just what he might do instead of quarterbacking one of the most respected news programs on television isn't quite clear. Indeed, after nine years, it's a little difficult to imagine Koppel doing anything else.

"'Nightline' was tailor made for Ted," Richard Threlkeld, a "World News Tonight" correspondent who has substituted for Koppel, told *Esquire*. "It was designed around him like a suit." He has considered starting a communications company with his lawyer wife and confidante Grace Anne. And although he quickly turned down the State Department spokesman offer, he still considers entering public service in some high government office.

Tackling the Oval Office, however, is out of the question. Koppel was born in Lancashire, England, in 1940, the only child of wealthy German Jewish parents who left the country in 1938 during the rise of Nazism. His father, 44 at the time of Koppel's birth, ran a large rubber tire company that he eventually lost. "My father had been in prison at least once," Koppel told *New York* magazine. "He was taken prisoner because he was Jewish. He had some influential friends who said to him, 'The writing's on the wall; you'd better leave,' and helped him get out. That was 1938."

While an adolescent, Koppel was sent to a British boarding school, where he told *Newsweek* he learned to be self-sufficient and close-vested. "You cannot let people know what you think too clearly in a British boarding school," he told *Newsweek*. "Nothing is resented more than emotional outbursts. Nothing makes you more vulnerable than a perception of weakness among 10-, 11- and 12-year-old English schoolboys." He moved to New York with his family in 1953, where he enrolled in McBurney School, a private school.

The differences between America and England, where rationing from the war had only recently ended, were tremendous. Even as a youth, Koppel carried a seriousness about him. "My first memory, in terms of any kind of analysis of this country, was, I think, on the second or third day," he told *Life*. "I was sitting in the hotel room listening to a radio program that was interrupted by a commercial for an antacid called Brioschi. And there was a jingle that went, 'Eat too much, drink too much, try Brioschi, try Brioschi.' My mother walked in to find me crying on the edge of the bed, and she asked what was wrong. I said, 'I don't know what kind of country we've come to here. I can't believe people have to worry because they eat too much or drink too much. No one is forcing them.'"

After graduating from private school at age 16, Koppel enrolled in Syracuse University, where his interest in television, inspired by Edward R. Murrow, steered him toward a major in speech and hours of work in radio and drama. During his graduate studies in journalism at Stanford, in 1960, Koppel met his future wife, someone he was attracted to in part because he thought she was smarter than he was. Newly married, he quickly learned that trying to get a job in journalism in the New York area with no experience was not going to be easy.

"Essentially, I began as a copyboy at WMCA radio," Koppel told *New York* magazine. "One day, a friend told me that WABC radio was hiring seven on-air people to do this program called 'Flair Reports.' So I went over, and they said they had a radio program that was going to be three and a half minutes, and that there'd be seven of them a day. The pay was $375 a week. I was earning $90 at that point. They told me to go home and return with two scripts.... They called me back three days later and said, 'You're really very good, and we'd love to hire you, but you're too young. Radio news, however, will hire you as a writer for $175.' I said, 'No, I didn't apply for that job. I want to be on this program.' After I hung up, I really felt it. But two days later they called and said, 'It's radio and no one will know how old you are, so come on in.'"

At the time, he was the youngest correspondent on network television. But even without experience, Koppel excelled. "He had this incredible self-assurance for somebody 23 years old and was astounding with a live mike," CBS newsman Charles Osgood told *Newsweek.* From 1963 to 1973 Koppel covered the world, landing such assignments as Richard Nixon's 1968 presidential campaign and serving two stints in Vietnam, in 1967 and again from 1969 to 1971. He also became Hong Kong bureau chief.

Finally, in the hope of spending more time with his family, Koppel accepted a position covering the State Department. Coincidentally, Henry Kissinger was the Secretary of State at the time, one of the most traveled secretaries in the 20th century. During this period Koppel not only developed his friendship with Kissinger—a relationship other journalists have chided him for—but he honed his ability to question and discern nuances. "It was somewhat akin to playing tennis with Boris Becker every day for a year and then going back to the club and playing everyone else," Koppel told *Newsweek.* If he erred in his relationship with Kissinger, Koppel says it was getting too close to the former Secretary of State. Trouble was, he liked him.

"I admire his lucidity, the agility of his mind," Koppel told *Esquire.* "I still find I learn more in a half hour of talking foreign policy with him than I do in listening to the mostly muddled explanations of what our foreign policy is about from people who followed him. I also like him personally." But the danger in liking newsmakers is that you can be accused of treating them deferentially. "It doesn't do any good to say that sometimes I lean over backwards to be a little tougher on him, because that's wrong too," Koppel told *Life.* "I like him, I'm not about to surrender the friendship. But I've also made sure that I haven't gotten into that kind of relationship with anyone else."

In 1976, Koppel gave it all up to stay home. His wife had entered law school, and Koppel took a year off to be with their son and three daughters. It wasn't a total abstinence from news. Koppel did radio reports from his home, he flew to New York weekly to anchor ABC's Saturday evening news program and, with Marvin Kalb, co-wrote a spy novel titled *In the National Interest.* He returned to covering the State Department in 1977, and two years later American hostages were taken in Iran.

"All I need to do is know enough about a subject to ask reasonably intelligent questions, and that does not require a great deal of background."

That event launched "The Iran Crisis: America Held Hostage," the precursor of "Nightline." The show, which reported and dramatized the situation, not only boosted ABC's reputation and fortunes, but catapulted Koppel into a nightly must for many viewers. In March 1980, "Nightline" became a regular fixture at 11:30 P.M. Koppel wasn't ABC's first choice to moderate the program, however. Veteran newsman Frank Reynolds initially anchored the program while still doing "ABC World News Tonight." But Reynolds was tiring of 15-hour days. On November 29, the show's executive producer gave Reynolds the night off as a birthday present and Koppel filled in. When the 1980 political season took hold, Reynolds found he couldn't handle both responsibilities and Koppel took over permanently. Even then, it took a while for "Nightline" to catch on.

When it chronicled the American Hostage situation in Iran, the show was chided in the industry as a cheap attempt by ABC to gain news respectability at the expense of the hostages. But the program slowly began to show it could offer a depth that was lacking on regular nightly news broadcasts. The program's popularity is also attributed in part to its ability to quickly react to the news. "Remember when they [President Jimmy Carter's military foray] went to get the hostages out?" Koppel asked *New York* magazine.

"We had another program on that night. But when I got home, about 12:30, the phone was ringing and they said, 'The White House just announced this rescue attempt.' I came racing back, and by 2:30 A.M. we did another show for the West Coast. We've literally changed the show as it's been on air and as late as ten o'clock at night."

"Nightline" has also been willing to tackle topics other programs might consider boring or just not realize are part of the social consciousness. For example, "Nightline" addressed surrogate motherhood in 1985, before it had become a public issue. And Koppel has wanted for years to start a running feature every Friday night devoted to civil rights. If that happens, it would hardly be the first time "Nightline" has tackled unusual subject matter.

Koppel has taken his show past 3 A.M. (Eastern time) holding national town meetings on AIDS. He's had Ferdinand Marcos and Cory Aquino—in separate interviews—on the same program during the 1986 Philipine election. Shortly before his suicide attempt, Robert McFarlane appeared in 1987 to give his side of the Iran arms deal for the first time. And, in 1985, "Nightline" broadcast from South Africa, where Foreign Minister R.F. (Pik) Botha and Bishop Desmond Tutu spoke to Koppel and the world, together.

Koppel is well compensated for his ability to orchestrate journalistic coups, earning more than $1 million a year. But despite the heady salary, nine years of the same program seem to be taking their toll. Already, during the 1988 presidential season, ABC has relieved Koppel of some of his "Nightline" duties, affording reporter Jeff Greenfield an opportunity to do political analysis. And while he does not regret turning down the position as State Department spokesman 10 years ago, Koppel obviously does not see himself as remaining the host and referee for national and international debates indefinitely.

And there are influential people who believe he could do other things. "If I were to give him a job, it would be a substantive one," Kissinger told *Newsweek*. "Say, assistant secretary for Europe." And Correspondent Marvin Kalb, one of Koppel's closest friends, told the same magazine, "Ted could do better than that, and I would be surprised if he would not want to. He is a man of great talent and considerable ambition." Indeed, apparently smoothing the way for his own departure, Koppel started a separate production company in 1987.

When asked by *Life* magazine why he did that, the late night anchor replied: "Because I'm 48 years old, because I've seen many of my colleagues who were 58 and older who had lost their usefulness to the corporation. Even though people throw them a nice party, they have to leave under somewhat painful circumstances. Sometimes it's rather humiliating. The other reason is that I see the nature of the business potentially changing. The day may come when networks are not what they once were. I wanted to launch a lifeboat. If for some reason things change a lot, then maybe I'll do without the farewell party, go sit in my lifeboat and cruise into the sunset."

Writings

(Compiler) *The Wit and Wisdom of Adlai Stevenson*, Hawthorn, 1965.

(With Marvin L. Kalb) *In the National Interest* (novel), Simon & Schuster, 1977.

Sources

Channels, April, 1986.
Esquire, January, 1984; June, 1988.
Harper's, January, 1986.
New Republic, April 15, 1985.
Newsweek, June 15, 1987; June 20, 1988.
New York, August 13, 1984.
People, August 18, 1986.
Progressive, December, 1986.
Time, January 30, 1984.
Vogue, August, 1986.

—Sidelights by Stephen Advokat

Mark Kostabi

Photograph by Raffi Ekmekji

Artist

Born 1960 in Whittier, Calif.; son of Kaljo (a musical instrument craftsman) and Rita (a fundraiser) Kostabi. *Education:* Attended Fullerton College and the University of California at Fullerton.

Addresses: *Home*—New York, N.Y. *Office*—KostabiWorld, 361 West 36th St., #3A, New York, N.Y. 10018.

Career

Artist; first showed work at Piezo Electric, New York City; has shown in more than 450 group and 33 one-man shows throughout the world; opened own studio, KostabiWorld, in New York City, 1988; has appeared on numerous television programs, including "The Morton Downey, Jr. Show" and "A Current Affair."

Sidelights

As one of a number of young artists who emerged in the 1970s and 80s seeking to stretch the boundries of the late Andy Warhol's unabashedly commercial pop-art aesthetic ("Andy's Children" they are called in art circles), Mark Kostabi has surfaced in the 1980s as the richest, most famous, and most outrageous of them all. He is suddenly a commanding presence on the New York art scene, and the method he has used to gain this stature is probably his greatest masterpiece. Indeed, though most critics dismiss his work as, at best, mediocre, Kostabi has made his name with a relentless barrage of hype, a selling of himself so contrived that he even sneers at the collectors who pay up to $50,000 for one of his paintings. "Anyone who buys my paintings is a total fool," Kostabi acknowledges in *People.* "But the more I spit in their faces, the more they beg me to sell them another painting."

With hyperbole and fashion the potent forces that they are in modern society, Kostabi's crass self-promotion does not seem all that shocking, even in the world of art, where the image of the dedicated but starving artist is, since Warhol, a less romantic notion. What has caused a real uproar among art critics, and hence brought Kostabi even more of the publicity he craves, is the fact that he does not even execute many of the paintings that bear his name. Rather, the paintings are done by other artists who work for Kostabi at wages of $4.50 to $10.50 an hour, imitating Kostabi's style or working from Kostabi drawings or concepts. Dating back to the Renaissance, Kostabi points out, artists have traditionally hired assistants to do some of the minor tasks in the creation of large-scale works. But Kostabi boasts that he is the first to have his assistants do all the work. In addition, Kostabi in 1987 hired Diana Gentleman, a young sketch artist, to be his "full-time idea person," to literally think up new concepts for future Kostabi paintings (Gentleman eventually parted with Kostabi when she realized she was getting no credit for her ideas). Thus, many of the pictures that bear Kostabi's signature, and sell for thousands of dollars, were neither conceptualized nor painted by Kostabi himself. He produces, in a sense, factory art, and in the process he has created an uproar that would make Warhol himself envious.

Born to Estonian-immigrant parents in southern California, Kostabi was an outcast and self-described "weirdo" in high school, but a precocious talent for drawing led him to enroll in art classes at Cal-State Fullerton. Moving to Manhattan in 1981, Kostabi instantly established himself as a fixture on the burgeoning East Village art scene, not so much for his painting but for his constant presence at exhibits and galleries. "I was immediately a part of the scene," he told *People.* "I stayed up till 3 a.m. in clubs, just collecting business cards." Kostabi meanwhile continued to sketch and paint, honing his style to one he thought might appeal to a wider audience. He also made his works larger and asked a higher price for them. "His work was graphic and stripped down," wrote Anthony Haden-Guest in *Vanity Fair,* "as populist as Keith Haring's, but less insistently lovable, and it depicted featureless tubular humanoids, sometimes sporting conical hats or wielding domestic appurtenances, like plungers."

Taking a cue from the late Salvador Dali, Kostabi began to promote his work vigorously, asking ever higher prices and playing dealers off one another. In 1984 he had six one-man shows, with nine more the next year. In 1986 he held a successful show at Ronald Feldman Fine Arts, the respected SoHo gallery, where his paintings sold out at $10,000 to $20,000 each, and his pictures had been acquired (though not hung) by the Museum of Modern Art, the Metropolitan Museum, and the Guggenheim. But Kostabi had just begun. Realizing he would rather go to parties and gallery openings, increasing his exposure and thereby selling more paintings ("To me," he told *People,* "fame is love. And I need love"), Kostabi came up with the idea that others could do his painting for him. His ads in the *Village Voice* received hundreds of responses, and soon, with Gentleman supplying the ideas and as many as six artists cranking out Kostabi paintings at one time, Kostabi-World (Kostabi's answer to Warhol's Factory) was born.

Serious critical reactions to Kostabi's work have been far more sobering, ranging from a grudging respect (a few of his works "even arguably approach a quality of graphic invention," said Walter Robinson in *Art in America*) to outright contempt ("Kostabi's paintings are so bad," said an *Artforum* reviewer, "that they even subvert the good name of bad painting"). Most critics will concede, however, that Kostabi has touched a major nerve in the art world and society as a whole. "Mark has staked out a valid conceptual idea of art, dealing with status and the hypocrisy of the art world," said Brown University art professor Richard Fishman in *People.* "It's a natural outgrowth of the way we've evolved aesthetically," Whitney museum curator Patterson Sims told *New York* magazine. "What we worship is the product, not the process." Adds collector Michael McKenzie in *New York:* "It's a logical extension of the communications era. Painting is arcane. It's mandatory that he produce. And artists . . . who would put Mark down for paying people to generate ideas and execute his work are just *jealous.*"

What does the future hold for Kostabi? Expansion, of course. "Ultimately, I'll have a studio in every major city," he told *People.* "Or I could start a company town in the desert where there would be Mark Kostabi theaters, laundromats, restaurants." "The first question I always get asked," said Kostabi's principal dealer, Ronald Feldman, in *Vanity Fair,* "is how can you justify working with Mark Kostabi? But he's full of ideas. He's genuinely coming from some other place."

Sources

Art in America, November, 1984.
New York, September 7, 1987.
New York Times, September 12, 1986; June 24, 1988.
People, July 11, 1988.
Vanity Fair, June, 1989.

—Sidelights by David Collins

Mathilde Krim

AP/Wide World Photos

Geneticist and virologist

Name originally, Mathilde Galland; born July 9, 1926, in Como, Italy; emigrated to Switzerland, 1932; emigrated to Israel, 1953; came to United States, 1959; daughter of an agronomist; married David Danon (a medical student; divorced); married Arthur B. Krim (an attorney and movie studio executive), December 7, 1958; children: (first marriage) Daphna. *Education:* University of Geneva (Switzerland), B.S. in genetics, 1948, Ph.D. in biology, 1953.

Addresses: *Office*—American Foundation for AIDS Research, 40 West 57th St., New York, N.Y. 10019.

Career

As a graduate student in Geneva, Switzerland, worked in the laboratory of geneticist Jean Weigle and was probably the first person to see the DNA structure of chromosomes through an electron microscope; joined a group of Jewish activists at the university and began working for the Zionist cause, eventually joining the Irgun (the underground Zionist movement); spent several months in the south of France helping prepare arms for shipment to Zionists in Palestine; moved to Israel, 1953, and worked as a junior scientist and then research associate in cancer research at Weizmann Institute of Science in Rehovot; research associate, Cornell Medical Center, Ithaca, N.Y., 1959–62; Sloan-Kettering Institute for Cancer Research, 1962–86, research associate, beginning 1962, founder of Interferon Evaluation Program, 1975, head of interferon laboratory, 1981–85; organized international conference on interferon at Rockefeller University, 1975; founder of AIDS Medical Foundation, 1983, merged with National AIDS Research Foundation, 1985, and renamed American Foundation for AIDS Research, currently co-chairman; founder of molecular-virology laboratory and AIDS research facility, St. Luke's-Roosevelt Hospital Center, 1986; associate research scientist, College of Physicians and Surgeons, Columbia University, New York City; lecturer and fund-raiser for increased AIDS awareness and research.

Sidelights

Mathilde Krim's life encompasses what could be the lives of several distinct people—the young Zionist rebel, the Swiss geneticist, the wife of an American movie mogul, the cancer researcher, and, most recently, the outspoken crusader for increased AIDS education and research. A petite woman who speaks six languages and has a talent for translating scientific jargon into layman's terms, Krim is motivated by a tireless passion for humanitarian causes. As the founder in 1983 of the AIDS Medical Foundation, now known as the American Foundation for AIDS Research, Krim has marshalled the rich and famous in her fight against the deadly disease. Her weapons include public education, speaking out to win compassion for AIDS victims, and raising millions of dollars for promising research. "I didn't set out in advance to be The Human Bridge," Krim told Lindsy Van Gelder in *Ms.* magazine, "but I do have certain contacts, there is a vacuum. I felt it was my duty to fill it." Arthur Lubow wrote in *Savvy:* "What fuels Krim, in the end, is a limitless reservoir of compassion and her ability to identify with outsiders.... What sparks the fuel is her moral indignation at how little is being done when so much needs to be done."

Krim was born Mathilde Galland in 1926 in Como, Italy, one of four children. Her father was a Swiss agronomist and her mother was Czechoslovakian. When she was seven, she first heard the word "biologist," and learned that people could make a living studying the science of life. She decided to pursue a career in science.

Her family moved to Geneva, Switzerland, when she was eight to escape the depressed economy of prewar Italy. Eventually, she enrolled at the University of Geneva, where she was one of only two women in the basic science department. She earned a B.S. in genetics in 1948 and a Ph.D. in biology in 1953. As a graduate student, she studied genes using an electron microscope; to the best of her knowledge, Krim was the first person to actually see the DNA structure of chromosomes (in a frog's egg) through a microscope.

Her parents were great admirers of German culture. Krim told Van Gelder she could remember hearing talk about Jews being "dirty," or "not very honest." But shortly after the war, she was appalled by a newsreel about the liberation of the concentration camps. "I was shocked out of my wits," she told Van Gelder. "I went around crying for a week afterward. I decided right then that I just didn't want to belong in the world that had done things like this." Krim sought out a group of Jewish activists at the university, converted to Judaism, and joined the militant Zionist underground organization, Irgun. She cleaned guns and helped smuggle weapons across the French-Swiss border to be taken by boat to Palestine.

She married a fellow Zionist, David Danon, a medical student from Bulgaria. For this, her family disowned her. The couple had a daughter, Daphna, and moved to Israel in 1953, making a home first in Jaffa, then in part of a former British barracks in the desert. Krim got a job as a scientist at the Weizmann Institute of Science in Rehovot. Over time, the couple drifted apart and divorced. Several years later, Krim gave a tour of the Weizmann Institute to one of its trustees, Arthur B. Krim. A lawyer, Krim was then chairman of United Artists. He currently heads Orion Pictures. The two fell in love and married in 1958. Six months later, Krim reluctantly left Israel and joined her husband in his posh apartment in New York City.

For several months, Krim played the role of the socialite wife of a movie executive, meeting many of the famous celebrities she would later win over to her crusade against AIDS. But Krim soon grew bored with that lifestyle, and in 1959 she took a position as a research associate in the division of virus research at Cornell Medical Center in New York. Three years later, she took a similar position at Sloan-Kettering Institute for Cancer Research and began studying the role of viruses in cancer.

When Arthur Krim became active in the Democratic Party, eventually serving as finance chairman, Mathilde made valuable contacts among political leaders. In 1970, she was asked to compile an extensive report on the history of cancer research for Congress. While writing the report, Krim ran across references to a naturally-occurring virus-fighting agent called interferon. She became excited by the idea of using interferon in the fight against cancer. She believed that using a natural substance would be less brutal than the current methods of treatment—surgery, chemotherapy, and radiation therapy.

Krim lobbied for funding from the federal government and foundations for research into interferon. In 1975, she organized an international conference on interferon at Rockefeller University, funded by $12,000 from the National Cancer Institute. The meeting energized the field of interferon research, and as a result, the NCI agreed to increase its funding for basic research. "She more or less singlehandedly rescued the field from oblivion," Massachusetts General Hospital researcher Martin S. Hirsch told George Johnson in the *New York Times Magazine.*

Krim established the Interferon Evaluation Program at Sloan-Kettering in 1975 and was head of Sloan-Kettering's interferon laboratory from 1981 to 1985. Her efforts earned her the nickname "Interferon Queen." However, experiments with the drug proved disappointing, and the cost of the substance was prohibitive. Krim was discredited by many of her colleagues for her unceasing support for interferon. Critics said she had let her heart rule her head, breaking an unwritten rule of research. Arthur S. Levine, who headed an interferon study group for the NCI told Johnson, "There are many examples of fine scientists who, when challenged with the possibility of curing cancer, do not demonstrate the same rigor as they do with their own work." In 1980, researchers at the University of Zurich developed a way to artificially clone the gene for interferon, making the substance available in large quantities for research. Eventually, interferon was found to be effective in treating a rare form of leukemia.

Through her work with interferon, Krim met Dr. Joseph Sonnabend, who had set up a clinic in New York's Greenwich Village. In the early 1980s, he began to see a number of homosexual patients with Kaposi's sarcoma, a rare form of cancer. He further observed that these patients had an extremely low count of the T-4 white blood cells that regulate the immune system. Sonnabend was one of the first in this country to diagnose what would come to be called acquired immune deficiency syndrome or AIDS. It was found to be a viral infection acquired during sexual intercourse, through exchange of blood, or by the sharing of needles among intravenous drug users. By causing a collapse of the immune system, AIDS left its victims defenseless against cancers, pneumonia and other deadly infections. In 1983, researchers at the Institute Pasteur in Paris isolated the virus that causes AIDS. A year later, NIH scientists were able to develop a blood test to detect evidence of antibodies to the virus, called HIV.

As [Krim] learned more about AIDS, she grew infuriated that so many young people were dying, while so little money was being spent on research.

Krim initially became involved with efforts to use interferon to treat the sarcoma. As she learned more about AIDS, she grew infuriated that so many young people were dying, while so little money was being spent on research. In 1983, Krim founded the AIDS Medical Foundation to fund promising research. At first Krim found it difficult to raise money for AIDS research. As she told Johnson in the *New York Times Magazine:* "They felt that this was a disease that resulted from a sleazy life style, drugs or kinky sex—that certain people had learned their lesson and it served them right. That was the attitude, even on the part of respectable foundations that are supposed to be concerned about human welfare." But soon she was able to garner support through her social and political contacts. Two years later, the group merged with the National AIDS Research Foundation in Los Angeles to form the American Foundation for AIDS Research (AMFAR). The organization is co-chaired by Krim and Dr. Michael Gottlieb, a Los Angeles AIDS researcher, who treated Rock Hudson.

The list of celebrities that Krim has rallied to support the cause includes Elizabeth Taylor, Paul Newman, Joanne Woodward, Woody Allen, Joan Rivers, Phil Donahue, Rosalynn Carter, and Malcolm Forbes. AMFAR has raised more than $10 million and has awarded more than $5.3 million in funding innovative research projects. Through countless television and newspaper interviews, Krim began to spread the message that AIDS would not restrict itself to one group, that the general public must become aware of the dangers and protect themselves. She believed that if people thought AIDS was a threat to the general public, the government would be pressured to do more. As Lubow wrote in *Savvy,* "she repositioned AIDS from a gay-targeted to a general-interest disease" in the hope of changing the behavior of heterosexuals and averting a pandemic.

Krim was concerned about the sociological impact of AIDS, as well, "especially when I realized that the disease was spreading because it was mainly affecting a stigmatized group," she told Van Gelder in *Ms.* magazine. "Gay men should be the first people to ask to be treated for evidence of infection, but as a community, they've understandably resisted that step. The test has become a marker for gayness, not just exposure to AIDS." Krim spoke out strongly against mass screenings for the AIDS virus. She wrote in the *Humanist:* "A diagnosis of HIV infection constitutes psychologically devastating news. Secondly, the social stigma attached to such a diagnosis can, and often does, result in serious social and economic harm to individuals. Last, but not least, awareness of one's infected status cannot lead to useful medical intervention at this time, since none exists." Instead, she favors public education as the way to control the spread of AIDS and supports distributing sterile needles to intravenous drug users.

In 1986, the drug azidothymidine (AZT) came under study as a treatment to stop the spread of the AIDS virus. Its producer, the Burroughs Wellcome Co., set up a traditional "double blind" study, in which some AIDS patients would receive AZT and others would receive a placebo. Two hundred sixty patients with fully developed AIDS participated in the study to determine whether AZT was safe and effective. Krim voiced strong objections to the study, saying it was immoral to give any AIDS sufferers a placebo or restrict AZT to a few AIDS victims. "People who are on their last legs should get anything they want," she told Johnson in the *New York Times Magazine*. She testified before Congress, but the trials continued. In the end, AZT was found to be safe in prolonging life for AIDS patients and was approved for use by the Food and Drug Administration in 1987. But the search for a more effective treatment continues. Krim lobbied for larger research funding from National Institutes of Health and spoke out against the Reagan administration. In 1987, NIH issued $47 million for AIDS research and education.

Due in part to the visibility of her AIDS crusade, Krim fell out of favor at Sloan-Kettering and left the institute in 1986. She set up a molecular-virology laboratory and AIDS research facility at St. Luke's-Roosevelt Hospital Center. She is also an associate research scientist at the College of Physicians and Surgeons, Columbia University in New York. However, most of her work now is in the lecture hall, not the laboratory. She told Johnson: "I came to the conclusion that it's better if I stay on the outside and help people inside the labs. I'm not such a genius that somebody else cannot do what I was doing. And these would be people who cannot do what I can."

As the grim specter of AIDS settles on the country, the death rate is more than 200 a week. An estimated one to five million Americans may be infected with the AIDS virus. Krim told Van Gelder that she believes the way societies deal with AIDS will "measure to what extent they have the right to call themselves civilized."

Sources

Humanist, November–December, 1987.
Interview, February, 1987.
Ms., January, 1986.
New York, April 25, 1988.
New Yorker, September 1, 1986.
New York Times Magazine, February 14, 1988.
Savvy, May, 1988.

—Sidelights by Donna Raphael

Alexander S. Kroll

Fred R. Conrad/NYT Pictures

Advertising executive

Born November 23, 1938; son of a steel mill worker and a housewife; married Phyllis Benford; children: two sons, one daughter. *Education:* Attended Yale University; graduate of Rutgers University.

Addresses: *Office*—Young & Rubicam, Inc., 285 Madison Ave., New York, N.Y. 10017.

Career

Young & Rubicam, Inc., New York, N.Y., began in research department, copy writer, beginning 1965, senior vice-president and associate creative director, beginning 1969, executive vice-president and creative director, beginning 1970, president, Young & Rubicam U.S.A., beginning 1975, president and chief operating officer, beginning 1982, currently chairman and chief executive officer. Linebacker on New York Titans (later named Jets) football team. *Military service:* U.S. Army, two years.

Sidelights

Alexander S. Kroll is the chairman and chief executive officer of Young & Rubicam, Inc., the largest advertising agency in the United States. Its list of clients includes General Foods, Colgate-Palmolive, Pillsbury, and the Lincoln-Mercury division of Ford Motor Company. Kroll's rise to the top has been called meteoric and inevitable. A former pro linebacker, he believes in team playing, and he expects the best from those around him. "What I learned from both advertising and football is how really hard it is to win," he told Walecia Konrad of *Business Week.* "And how terrific it feels."

Kroll was raised in Leechburg, Pennsylvania, a small mill and mining town near Pittsburgh. He entered Yale University on a scholarship but left in his sophomore year. Following a two-year stint in the army, he enrolled in Rutgers University. He became captain of the football team and made All-American, then went on to play professionally with the New York Titans (later named the Jets). In the off-season, he interned at Young & Rubicam. This arrangement lasted for one year, ending with Kroll's decision to make advertising, not football, his career. He went to work in research but soon transferred to the copy department. Within four years, he was senior vice-president and associate creative director. By the mid-1970s he had been promoted to president of the company's domestic operations; some ten years later, he was named chairman and chief executive officer.

Observers attribute much of Kroll's success to hard work and long hours. He arrives at the office early to look over various reports, accounts, and memos. As others arrive, he begins a series of management meetings and creative sessions. Kroll is highly skilled at motivating his employees. "He just expects work to be right, and this attitude makes us all work harder for him," a company executive told *New York*'s Bernice Kanner. A former co-worker, however, had a different view: "He manages by intimidation, throwing his power around to get his way. In the end, he stimulates out of fear rather than inspiration." Though his leadership style may be open to debate, the results he gets are not. In 1987, billings at Young & Rubicam reached $4.9 billion; gross income, or sales, increased 17 percent to $735 million.

Young & Rubicam has been the country's leading ad agency since 1979. But the industry is changing. A recent "wave of megamergers" has created several new agencies "with tremendous marketplace clout and huge efficiencies of scale," Konrad explained. Young & Rubicam, a private company, has been unable to tap the public resources that fueled this expansion. Moreover, it is a research-oriented firm with a reputation for producing "well-executed, but conservative" commercials, according to Ellen Prescott of the *New York Times.* Its new rivals, on the other hand, pay less attention to studies of consumer trends and buying habits. Instead, they go for immediate consumer response, creating ads that are often striking, provocative, and outrageous. Another problem is Young & Rubicam's size. Like all large agencies, it offers a number of quality services, such as state-of-the-art research capabilities, worldwide networks, and greater media access. These services acquire "layers of bureaucracy" that "often slow down the creative process," wrote Konrad.

In 1987, Kroll positioned key members of the creative and management staffs closer to actual production. He reorganized Young & Rubicam's New York headquarters, dividing its 1300 employees into three groups. Each group is headed by its own general manager and creative director. He also altered research's approach to consumer studies. Kroll hopes this strategy will lead to more creative, effective advertising. He knows that if Young & Rubicam is to maintain its lead, it must adapt. "Advertising is not a business you can take for granted," he told Kanner. "It keeps you hungry. Take it for granted and you get hit in the chops."

Sources

Business Week, April 4, 1988.
New York, November 8, 1982.
New York Times, October 29, 1982; June 7, 1987.

—Sketch by Denise Wiloch

Julie Krone

Jockey

Born c. 1963; daughter of Don (a teacher) and Judy (a horse breeder and trainer) Krone.

Addresses: *Home*—Cherry Hill, N.J.; and Atlantic Beach, N.Y.

AP/Wide World Photos

Career

Apprentice jockey, 1980; began racing career at Tampa Bay Downs in Florida; currently races on East Coast tracks, including Monmouth Park and the Meadowlands in New Jersey, Pimlico in Maryland, and Aqueduct in New York.

Sidelights

In the sport of thoroughbred racing, Julie Krone is considered the best woman jockey to emerge in the past two decades. In 1987, she placed sixth among the nation's riders with 324 races won and over $4.5 million in purses. At 4 feet 10 inches and 100 pounds, Krone has fought long and hard for her success. Since 1980, she has battled sex discrimination, a drug-related suspension, a broken back, and a physical fight with a male colleague.

Krone grew up on a farm in Eau Claire, Michigan, and learned to ride from her mother, who bred and trained show horses. From the start, she was determined to be a jockey. Her mother taught her precision riding and urged her to compete on the county-fair circuit. At 16, during a spring vacation, Krone got a job walking horses at Churchill Downs. She became an apprentice jockey at Tampa Bay Downs in 1980, shortly after graduating from high school. Within a couple of years, she was racing at the larger, more prestigious tracks in Maryland, Delaware, and New Jersey.

Krone is frequently compared to the legendary Willie Shoemaker. "Both jockeys ride with finesse, communicating to the horse with sensitive hands, careful weight distribution, and a properly tuned voice," J.E. Vader explained in *Ms.* "They work *with* the horse, instead of trying to muscle it down the stretch." Krone is praised as an intelligent rider, able to make her mounts "run for her." She is also considered tough and fiercely competitive. "In a lot of people's minds, a girl jockey is cute and delicate," she told *Newsweek*'s Pete Axthelm. "With me, what you get is reckless and aggressive." These qualities have served her well. By the mid-1980s, Krone was one of the top five riders on the East Coast.

Krone has encountered her share of problems along the way. Male jockeys resented her, while owners and fans were reluctant to trust her abilities. Moreover, she suffered major setbacks early in her career. At the age of 17, she was caught smoking marijuana and received a 60-day riding suspension. In 1980, at Maryland's Pimlico Park, she took a spill that broke her back. Krone was out of racing for four months.

"When I came back I was probably more reckless and aggressive than ever," she noted to Jack Friedman of *People.* Then, in the summer of 1986, Krone faced another crisis. During a race at Monmouth, jockey Miguel Rujano slashed her with his riding whip. (Rujano later claimed that Krone had crowded him in the stretch.) After the race, Krone punched him. Rujano retaliated by pushing her into a swimming pool and holding her under water. Krone broke free and hit him over the head with a lawn chair. Both jockeys were fined $100; Rujano was also suspended for five days.

Krone has worked hard to put such incidents behind her and to build what she calls an "apple-pie image." As she noted to Axthelm: "That fight would never happen now.... Every year I get a little more intelligent. At least I hope so." Since the fight, she has become one of only three riders, male or female, in the history of Monmouth Park to win six races in one day. In 1987, she became the first woman to win four in one day in New York. A year later, she beat Patricia Cooksey's career record of 1,203 victories, earning the rank of top female jockey. Thus far, Krone shows no signs of slowing down. "You can't fake anything in racing," she told Axthelm. "Every race, you have to prove yourself again."

Sources

Ms., June, 1988.
New York Times, November 25, 1987.
Newsweek, December 28, 1987.
People, May 2, 1988.
Sports Illustrated, August 24, 1987; May 22, 1989.

—Sketch by Denise Wiloch

Leon Max Lederman

UPI/Bettmann Newsphotos

Physicist

Born July 15, 1922, in Bronx, N.Y.; son of Morris and Minna (Rosenberg) Lederman; married Florence Gordon, September 19, 1945; children: Rena S., Jesse A., Heidi R. *Education:* City College of New York, B.S. in chemistry, 1943; Columbia University, A.M. in physics, 1948, Ph.D., 1951.

Addresses: *Office*—Department of Physics, University of Chicago, Chicago, Ill. 60637.

Career

Columbia University, New York City, associate in physics, 1951, assistant professor, 1952–54, associate professor, 1954–58, professor of physics, 1958–73, Eugene Higgins Professor of Physics, beginning 1973, director of Nevis Laboratories, 1960–67, and beginning 1969; Fermi National Acceleration Laboratory, Batavia, Ill., director, 1979–89; University of Chicago, Chicago, Ill., professor of physics, 1989—. Guest scientist, Brookhaven National Laboratories, beginning 1955; member of high energy physics advisory panel, Atomic Energy Commission, 1966–70; consultant to national acceleration laboratory, European Organization for Nuclear Research (CERN), beginning 1970; member of advisory committee, National Science Foundation, 1970–72; member of President's Committee on the National Medal of Science, beginning 1979. *Military service:* U.S. Army, Signal Corps, 1943–46; became second lieutenant.

Member: American Association for the Advancement of Science (fellow), American Physics Society (fellow), National Academy of Science, Italian Physics Society.

Awards: Guggenheim fellow, 1958–59; Ford Foundation fellow, European Center for Nuclear Research, 1958–59; National Medal of Science, 1965; National Science Foundation fellow, 1967; Townsend Harris Medal, City University of New York, 1973; Elliott Cresson Medal, Franklyn Institute, 1976; Wolf Prize, 1983; Nobel Prize in Physics, 1988.

Sidelights

"This is the year for the geriatric Nobel Prize," said 66-year-old Leon Max Lederman in *Time.* "I'm so old I can remember when the Dead Sea was only sick." This physicist known for both his mastery of the one-liner and his dedication to science had himself just won the 1988 Nobel Prize for Physics. The groundbreaking experiment recognized by the Nobel Committee had taken place more than 20 years before, when Lederman was in charge of Columbia University's Nevis Physics Laboratory. By 1988, he had served for nine years as director of the Fermi National Accelerator Laboratory (Fermilab), located outside of Chicago, where he oversaw the work of resident and visiting scientists conducting laborious, often surprisingly answered inquiries into the nature of things.

The son of Russian immigrants, Lederman was born in the Bronx, New York City, in 1922. He majored in chemistry at City College of New York but eventually found that he liked physics more—so much so that he went on to earn a Ph.D. in the subject at Columbia University. Quoted in *Physics Today,* Lederman recalled that "Columbia in those days was a fabulous place.... The cross-fertilization between theory and experiment—often in Chinese restaurants on Broadway—was very close." After his graduation in 1951, Lederman went to work at Columbia, teaching and directing the Nevis Laboratory. During his association with the university, which lasted until 1979 when he became Fermilab's director, his work was frequently recognized both nationally and internationally. A recipient of several prestigious fellowships and a participant on such advisory panels as the Atomic Energy Commission (from 1966 to 1970), Lederman received the National Medal of Science from President Lyndon Johnson in 1965.

The collaborative experiment that was to result in a Nobel Prize for Lederman and his two associates, Melvin Schwartz and Jack Steinberger, was conducted at Brookhaven National Laboratory on Long Island between 1960 and 1962. The three scientists were interested in finding a way to use neutrinos as an aid in their study of the "weak" nuclear force that creates certain kinds of radioactivity. Neutrinos are highly abundant but elusive subatomic particles that have no electrical charge and no detectable mass; they don't respond to either of the two forces—the "strong" nuclear force or the electromagnetic force—that exist within atomic nuclei. Lederman, Schwartz, and Steinberger wanted to find a way to isolate neutrinos, which pass through matter constantly but rarely collide with other particles. It is collisions that make particle physicists happy—miniscule smash-ups that verify the existence of, and report information about, the particles that are colliding.

The group's solution was to use the particle accelerator at Brookhaven to create a beam of neutrinos. An accelerator is a huge device that propels streams of particles at very high voltage into a target; on impact the particles break up into even smaller pieces. A detector then records information about the collisions—about the resulting "debris." Lederman and his associates rigged the accelerator to shoot huge quantities of protons into a target made of beryllium metal. The impact, they knew, would smash apart the beryllium nuclei into protons, neutrons, and other particles. One of these other particles—the "pi" or "pion"—would immediately decay into one muon and one neutrino (a pair for each pi).

The scientists surmised that after the initial collision, the fragments would keep moving until they hit a 40-feet-thick steel barrier. The highly elusive neutrinos would be the only particles capable of penetrating the barrier, resulting in a neutrino beam that would emerge on the other side of it. The beam would then enter a 10-ton aluminum detection chamber, where whatever collisions occurred would be recorded.

During the eight-month experiment, about 100 trillion neutrinos were generated—and 56 collisions were detected. Though the number sounds meager, the results were sufficient to give Lederman and his associates new information about the subject. Their work paved the way for a deeper study into the weak nuclear force and its role in radioactive decay. But perhaps most importantly, the experiment revealed the existence of a previously unsuspected, second kind of neutrino. This discovery led to the development of the "standard model" of physics, which holds that "quarks" and "leptons" are the basic units that make up protons, neutrons, and other compound particles. This standard model has proved enduringly reliable: Bertram Schwartzschild noted in *Physics Today* that "the 1988 Nobel Prize can be regarded as recognition of the present ascendancy of the standard model and of an experiment and a method that contributed significantly to its beginnings."

Among Lederman's most significant accomplishments during the years before he went to Fermilab were his discoveries of the upsilon particle (which has the heaviest mass of any particle yet identified) and of the fifth quark (the term "quark" comes from an obscure reference in James Joyce's novel "Finnegan's Wake"). The Wolf Foundation, based in Israel, awarded its 1979 prize honoring "outstanding contributions on behalf of mankind" jointly to Lederman and to Professor Martin Perl of the Stanford Linear Accelerator Center. The foundation noted that "the discovery of a fifth quark and sixth lepton came as a complete surprise and a opened a new direction in particle physics."

The Fermi National Accelerator Laboratory—named for Enrico Fermi, the physicist whose work led to the development of the atomic bomb—is located in Batavia, Illinois. Lederman became its director after the 1979 departure of Fermilab's founding director and guiding spirit, Robert Wilson. During his ten years in this position, Lederman perpetuated the enthusiastic spirit of advocacy for science established by Wilson. Conducting himself in an informal, blue-jeaned managerial style, Lederman supervised a staff of 2100 and an annual budget of $150 million. He spent much of his energy not on the tasks of teaching and experimenting, which he claims to prefer to anything else, but to pleading Fermilab's case to the Department of Energy and to the politicians whose decisions could affect its present and its future.

"What we would like to do is to discover a law of nature that is so simple and elegant that it can be written as an equation that will fit on a t-shirt and yet be a 'theory of everything.'"

The Chicago Tribune's Dennis Brio described Fermilab as "a temple to the new physics" in which "the religion is the belief that humans can unlock the secrets of the universe through high-energy physics." Scientists come from all over the world to explore—with the aid of Fermilab's $240 million Tevatron accelerator—some very basic questions about the universe, the primary one being; of what is it made? "What we would like to do," said Lederman in the *Chicago Tribune,* "is to discover a law of nature that is so simple and elegant that it can be written as an equation that will fit on a t-shirt and yet be a 'theory of everything.' It will answer the questions the Greeks raised 2500 years ago."

The 4500-ton Tevatron is comprised of a 4-mile, underground ring that has superconducting magnets fixed along it. The temperature inside the ring is kept very low in order to reduce electrical resistance to such an extent that particle beams may be created and sent whizzing around the ring. The Tevatron—which can produce 50,000 information-revealing collisions per second while releasing less energy than a sneeze—allows scientists to re-create the conditions they believe existed less than a second after the "Big Bang" that created the universe. Thus experimenters get as close a look as is yet possible at the most fundamental particles and forces that make up matter. Lederman described both the difficulty and the satisfaction of this work in *The Chicago Tribune:* "Most of the magic moments of discovery—the times when you get goose bumps on goose bumps—occur when you're out in an experimental shed at 4 a.m., staying awake with gallons of coffee. There are four billion people living on this planet, and at the moment of discovery, you are the only one in the world to know this new bit of information."

Lederman lobbied ardently, during the latter part of his tenure, in favor of Fermilab as the ideal site for the proposed Superconducting Super Collider (SSC), the colossal accelerator that scientists believe will achieve American ascendancy over the prestigious CERN (European Organization for Nuclear Research) accelerator in Switzerland. Lederman argued that the Batavia facility was already equipped with many of the basic systems and operations needed to launch the SSC, and that if Fermilab was not utilized in this way it would be outdated in ten years—an eventuality Lederman saw as wasteful. The SSC would be ten years in the building, and came with a $6 billion price tag. It would create about 5000 jobs for the community that managed to land it. Of the original 43 being considered, Fermilab was one of seven chosen as strong contenders. But in November of 1988, the Department of Energy announced that the prize had been won by Texas: the SSC would be built 35 south miles of Dallas, near the town of Waxahatchie.

Congress will decide whether to fund the somewhat controversial SSC—which some critics believe is environmentally questionable and which others see as representing the encroachment of "big science" over small, independent research laboratories—in 1990. Even after Fermilab lost its bid to host the SSC, Lederman remained an outspoken advocate for the project, stating in the *New York Times Magazine* that "the Supercollider is the logical next step for our science. It will be the most sensitive probe ever to test our understanding of the nature of space and time."

In a 1985 editorial published in *Science,* Lederman bemoaned the cuts in spending for scientific research that were resulting from the Gramm-Rudman-Hollings Act. Asserting that scientists should join together in defending the value of their work (instead of fighting each other for what few spoils might be available), Lederman stated, "My own science, high energy physics, is as remote from applications as you can get; nevertheless, it too contributes to a conclusion that science has always, and will always, be the best possible investment, next to education, that this nation can make in its future."

Despite Lederman's suggestion that his beloved physics is remote from applications, he has in other instances pointed out that humankind does enjoy the fruits of this highly theoretical science in many practical ways. From everyday conveniences like electronic laser printers and compact discs to the amazing new tool of medical diagnosis, nuclear magnetic resonancing, the products of physics are all around us. At the Midwest Institute for Neutron Therapy (MINT), for instance, a method that uses neutron beams created in the Fermilab accelerator to attack tumors has been effective in treating several kinds of cancer. And to ensure the continuation of benefits to humanity wrought by science, Lederman oversaw Fermilab's sponsorship of educational programs designed to encourage talented young people to pursue scientific careers. One of these was a Saturday morning physics lab for gifted high school students—taught by Lederman himself.

Reporter Brio described Lederman as "a master teacher with a gift for popularizing the baffling realities of particle physics." It's not surprising, then, that Lederman returned to teaching in 1989—the tenth anniversary of his association with Fermilab. He said he would like to teach a course called "Quantum Mechanics for Poets" in his new position as a professor at the University of Chicago. A return to the realm of education seems appropriate for a man who, discussing with Brio the need for the SSC, said: "The doing of science, as well as the supporting of science, is an expression of faith in the future. It would have been possible to have told Newton and Faraday, Maxwell and Einstein that given the poverty and squalor around them, their research endeavors were unaffordable luxuries. To have done so would have prevented the science that led to the economic gains that were the major factor in relieving that poverty and squalor!"

Sources

Chicago Tribune Magazine, November 6, 1988.
ENR, January 26, 1989.
New Scientist, October 29, 1988.
New York Times, August 29, 1979; January 16, 1983; October 20, 1988.
New York Times Magazine, April 30, 1989.
Physics Today, January, 1989.
Science, May 30, 1986.
Science News, October 29, 1988.
Scientific American, December, 1988.
Time, October 31, 1988.
Washington Post, October 20, 1988.

—Sidelights by Kelly King Howes

Sugar Ray Leonard

AP/Wide World Photos

Professional boxer

Full name, Ray Charles Leonard; born May 17, 1956, in Wilmington, N.C.; son of Cicero and Getha Leonard; married Juanita Wilkinson, January 19, 1980; children: Ray Jr., Jarrel. *Education:* Graduated from high school in Palmer Park, Md.

Addresses: *Agent*—Mike Trainer, 4922 Fairmont Ave., Bethesda, Md. 20814.

Career

Amateur boxer, 1969–76; professional boxer, 1976—. Became World Boxing Council (WBC) welterweight champion, 1979; won junior middleweight championship, 1981; became undisputed welterweight champion, 1981; in retirement, 1982–84; retired again after one fight, 1984; in retirement, 1984–86; became middleweight champion, 1987; became WBC super middleweight champion and light heavyweight champion, 1988. Boxing commentator and analyst for television broadcasts.

Awards: As an amateur, won gold medals at Pan American Games, 1975, and Summer Olympic Games, 1976.

Sidelights

Sugar Ray Leonard has blazed a bright path across the boxing ranks since his professional debut in 1977. Handsome and glib outside the ring—and unusually crafty within it—Leonard has beaten a number of formidable opponents on his way to wealth and superstardom. Ironically, Leonard's is a career that might never have gotten started; he "retired" as early as 1976 and has claimed to be through with boxing no less than three times since then. His comebacks have been celebrated with a great deal of hoopla, attesting to Leonard's healthy ego, but they have also proven that the fighter possesses unusual degrees of stamina and determination. As Leonard's lifetime lawyer/manager Mike Trainer puts it, Sugar Ray "is the kind of guy who's always looking at the edge of the cliff, fascinated as to how close he can get to it. He hasn't gotten to the edge yet."

Sports Illustrated contributor William Nack calls Leonard "the man who truly has it all, the very embodiment of the American dream." Observers note that a number of Leonard's fans admire him more for his sideline work—color commentary on others' fights, product endorsements, speeches against drug abuse—than for his achievements in the ring. There is no question, however, that Leonard personally draws his identity from his continuing ability to box with the best. He is quoted in *Sports Illustrated* as having said that when a man wins a championship, he is "so proud. You want people to say, 'Hey, champ, way to go.' You can sit there and listen to it over and over again. But it's always good to hear a different person tell you—that's why you walk across the street to another hotel.... You want to fight the monsters. In doing that, your persona becomes greater. You become bigger. There are more lucrative contracts and phenomenal deals."

Leonard knows, too, that boxing is an unforgiving sport—any loss he sustains will inevitably erode his popularity and possibly endanger his health. Therefore, to quote Pat Putnam in *Sports Illustrated,* there is a significant difference between Leonard the man and Leonard the fighter. Putnam writes: "Fight fans... see the handsome, youthful face, the sweet smile and the gentle manner, and they're afraid for [Leonard] when he goes into combat. Hardly anyone seems to see the Leonard with the cold eyes, the cruel warrior ready to spring forward at the first call of the bugle, the first roll of the drums."

Ray Charles Leonard was born in Wilmington, North Carolina, on May 17, 1956. He is named not after a boxer but after jazz great Ray Charles, because his mother wanted him to be a singer. The fifth of seven children, Leonard grew up in Palmer Park, Maryland, a suburb of Washington, D.C. Palmer Park is hardly a ghetto, but it is not posh Georgetown, either. *Sports Illustrated* correspondent Rick Reilly calls the area "a poor, mixed neighborhood with more than enough trouble to go around." Somehow the shy Ray Leonard was able to avoid the trouble. He sang with his sisters in a church choir and behaved himself in school. In a *Washington Post* interview, Leonard's father called the fighter "a funny sort of kid" who "always hung back." He continued: "It used to worry me. All my other boys were always into something, but Ray... not until boxing."

Leonard discovered the sport when he was fourteen, and he threw all his energy into it. He was tutored by two volunteer boxing coaches, Dave Jacobs and Janks Morton, both of whom worked out of the Oakcrest Community Center in Palmer Park. Jacobs and Morton knew they had a potential contender in Leonard, so they demanded good discipline outside the ring as well as in it. Sure enough, Leonard compiled a 145-5 record as an amateur and won gold medals at the 1975 Pan American games and the 1976 Olympics. The handsome light-welterweight gained a degree of instant celebrity as one of the American Olympic medalists. His post-fight interviews, Reilly writes, "delighted the nation."

When Leonard won the gold medal at the Olympics in Montreal, he stunned viewers by announcing his retirement from boxing. "This is my last fight," he said after his difficult decision win over Andres Aldama of Cuba. "My decision is final. My journey is ended, my dream fulfilled." Leonard planned to return home to study at the University of Maryland, but he also planned on receiving some lucrative product endorsements that never materialized. The press revealed that Leonard had fathered a son out of wedlock (he eventually married the child's mother, Juanita Wilkinson), and advertisers balked at the negative publicity. At the same time, both of Leonard's parents fell seriously ill. Feeling that he had to help out with the family burdens, Leonard decided to go professional after all. Rather than turn his career over to a promoter, however, Leonard placed himself in the hands of attorney Trainer who, with the help of several investors, incorporated Leonard and signed all the shares in the enterprise over to the fighter himself. Trainer also signed Leonard to nonexclusive television contracts and brought in Angelo Dundee, Muhammad Ali's former trainer, to work with the young boxer. Every move Trainer made was designed to promote Leonard's best interests, and while boxing's regular promoters snarled, Leonard used his post-Olympics fame to great advantage. Calling himself "Sugar Ray" after the great Sugar Ray Robinson, Leonard began to compile a record of wins, mostly by technical knockout, over carefully-chosen opponents who could challenge but not overmatch him.

Leonard's ascent through the boxing ranks was hardly smooth sailing, despite the advance publicity he could count on. He often suffered severe pain in his hands for days after a fight, and Dundee's training regimen was fierce and unrelenting. By 1979—just two years after turning pro—Leonard challenged for his first title. In the first welterweight fight in history that paid its participants more than a million dollars apiece, Leonard beat Wilfredo Benitez by a fifteenth round TKO. Having won the World Boxing Council's welterweight championship, Leonard began to defend his crown. His second title defense brought him into the ring against Roberto Duran, a Panamanian brawler with far more stamina than finesse. Leonard lost in his first match with Duran, suffering a brutal beating in a toe-to-toe punchout. The now-famous rematch with Duran, held in New Orleans on November 26, 1980, revealed a more canny Leonard. Weaving and feinting, Leonard outboxed *and* humiliated Duran, who eventually quit voluntarily in the eighth round. His reputation mended, Leonard went on to win a fourteenth round TKO victory over then-undefeated Thomas Hearns to unify the welterweight title. After that, Ray Leonard's troubles began.

During a training bout in 1982, Leonard felt a sharp pain in his left eye. He had suffered a detached retina, a serious and potentially blinding injury. Surgery repaired the damage, but the doctors warned Leonard that fighting could aggravate the condition. Leonard decided to retire. "There isn't enough money in the world for me to risk my eyesight," he told *Sports Illustrated.* "You can't put a price tag on that." Leonard may have stepped out of the ring, but he still sought the limelight. He served as a color commentator at the major boxing matches on the Home Box Office network, and he could often be seen on the other major television networks as well. Inevitably his popularity eroded, though, and against the wishes of his wife and most of his fans, he decided to make a comeback. "To retire at 26, that was the biggest burden in my life," he told *Sports Illustrated.* "For . . . years, I dealt with that. Twenty-six years old and I was through with my career . . . . It burned inside. It ate at me every single day."

Leonard was haunted by one overriding ambition—to meet Marvin Hagler [see index for *Newsmakers* entry] in the ring. Hagler, a boxer several years Leonard's senior, had been considered almost invincible since he won the middleweight championship in 1980. He therefore served as a silent indictment of Leonard's premature retirement, or so Ray Leonard thought. In 1984 Leonard met unranked Kevin Howard after six weeks of lackluster training, hoping the match would warm him up for Hagler. Howard surprised everyone—especially his opponent—by knocking Leonard to the canvas in the fourth round. Leonard eventually won the fight in the ninth on a TKO, but the match revealed his many deficiencies. He quickly re-retired that same night. This time his retirement lasted just over two years. "The flame had gone down," Leonard told *Sports Illustrated,* "but the pilot light was always lit." In the autumn of 1986 Leonard returned to serious training, challenged Hagler to a match, and began boasting that he could defeat one of the most savage and resourceful champions in middleweight history.

Leonard and Hagler squared off in the spring of 1987. "By all logic," Nack writes, "in the face of all

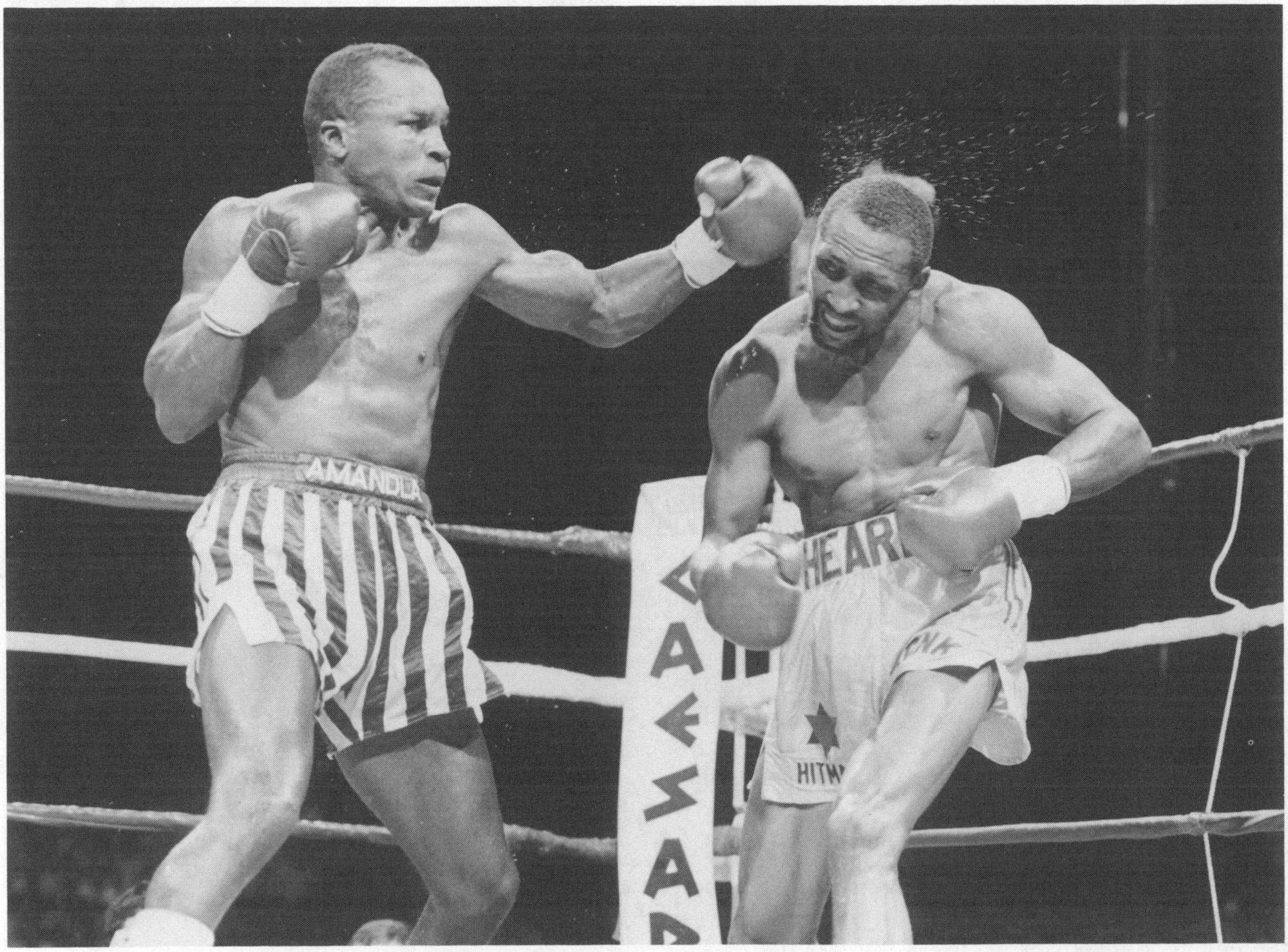

Sugar Ray Leonard (left) lands a blow to the head of Thomas Hearns in the tenth round of their fight in Las Vegas, June 1989. AP/Wide World Photos.

history, Leonard should never have been in that ring in the first place. Except for one sad, brief encounter with an unknown fighter in May 1984, he had not fought in five years and 50 days. And yet here he was, facing one of the most remorseless, murderous punchers in the . . . middleweight division, without a single tune-up to hone his boxing skills. What he was trying to do was unprecedented in the history of this consuming sport." Amazingly, Leonard won the twelve round fight, deftly avoiding the punches of an aging Hagler. Nack declares that the challenger scored an "upset of upsets," fought "magnificently," and displayed "great courage and resolve." *Washington Post* contributor William Gildea likewise contends that taking the title from Hagler "was Leonard's greatest Houdini act."

After the Hagler match, Leonard decided to improve his physique even further. He added bulk and muscle, worked on his stamina, and strengthened his hands by punching the big bag. On November 7, 1988, he added two more WBC titles to his list by defeating then-super middleweight and light heavyweight champion Donny Lalonde. Then, to the delight of promoters and boxing fans, he signed for a rematch with Thomas Hearns. The June 1989 fight was preceded by all the usual publicity, with each boxer predicting his own victory. At one press conference, Hearns even suggested that Leonard had used steroids to enhance his musculature. Leonard took the jibe in stride at the press conference, but afterwards he vehemently denied the suggestion, offering the counter opinion that Hearns had the proverbial "glass jaw." "I'm stronger," Leonard told the *Washington Post*. "Wiser. More economical. Just as determined, even greater determination. I thrive off it. I'm still ascending, still gaining altitude. I still have the desire, the self-discipline, the self-motivation." Determined though he may have been, Leonard was only able to fight Hearns to a draw—and Hearns knocked him down twice. The judges' decision was more popular with the two fighters than it was with the fans; a rematch seems inevitable.

The key to Leonard's success is quite simple: he is agile enough to avoid his opponents' most devastating punches while he is skilled enough to land savage punches of his own. He is renowned for frustrating and embarrassing his foes, using ring histrionics to throw them off their game plans. He is also cunning and coy, performing in a way calculated to win points from the judges. Observers describe Leonard as a finisher with the proverbial "killer instinct"—his knockout punch may not be the hardest in the game, but it meets its mark with uncanny precision. "The high points of Leonard's career certify him as genuinely remarkable," writes Gildea. "While the well-intentioned implore him to stop while he has secured fortune and history like a lock, to say nothing of his health, success drives him for still more."

Indeed, success—fame—is like an addictive drug to Leonard. Having earned more than $90 million dollars to date, he lives regally on the interest his money generates. The paycheck is secondary for Sugar Ray Leonard, however. "Something happens when I get into the ring," he told *Sports Illustrated*. "That's all the motivation I need. It's the competition. I love the competition. People say it's the money. The center stage. My ego. It's none of those things. It's the competition. And I love to win. I really love it."

Sources

Sports Illustrated, September 8, 1986; March 30, 1987; April 13, 1987; April 20, 1987; November 21, 1988.

Washington Post, August 26, 1977; May 28, 1989; May 29, 1989; June 11, 1989.

—Sketch by Mark Kram

David Letterman

AP/Wide World Photos

Comedian, talk-show host

Born April 12, 1947, in Indianapolis, Indiana; son of a florist and a church secretary; married Michelle Cook, 1969 (divorced, 1977). *Education:* Degree in radio and television broadcasting from Ball State University, 1970.

Addresses: *Home*—New Canaan, Conn. *Office*—c/o Press Relations, NBC-TV, 30 Rockefeller Center, New York, N.Y. 10020.

Career

Began as radio and television announcer in Indianapolis, Ind.; became TV weathercaster; worked as standup comic in clubs in Los Angeles, Calif., beginning 1975; television appearances at that time included "Rock Concert," "The Gong Show," "The Peeping Times," and "The Starland Vocal Band" (variety show); joined cast of variety series "Mary," starring Mary Tyler Moore, 1977; made first appearance on "The Tonight Show," 1978; became recurrent guest-host for the series, 1978–79; host of live morning talk-variety series "The David Letterman Show" for National Broadcasting Corp. (NBC-TV), 1980–81; host of talk-variety series "Late Night with David Letterman" for NBC-TV, 1982—.

Sidelights

When I think about television and show business, it grinds my stomach. I want to say to people, 'Don't you understand this is just bullshit, driven by egos, and that's all it is?' I mean, nothing makes me madder than to be sitting there, watching somebody who's just the winner of the genetic crapshoot, and there they are, big stuff on the air, a *star.*" This opinion comes not from a scholar or a critic, but from a figure who has in his own career conducted on-air elevator races, presided over "Stupid Pet Tricks," and thrown himself against a Velcro wall. David Letterman, speaking to *Rolling Stone* reporter Peter W. Kaplan, continued: "There's nothing I love more than getting hot over what's really bad."

Letterman has himself become a star by pointing out to a receptive America the wretched excess of Hollywood-style showbiz. The former TV weatherman and announcer has parlayed his success as a standup comic into two eponymous talk shows, the latter of which, "Late Night with David Letterman," has all but redefined a tired genre's conventions. "Consider this Great Moment in 'Late Night' history," offered *Newsweek*'s Bill Barol in a Letterman cover story. "The guest was Don King, who is probably as well known for his mile-high electrified Afro as for his career in boxing promotion. As King launched into his usual bombastic spiel, Letterman listened politely. But the first time King paused for breath Letterman leaned over and said: 'Let me ask you something. What's the deal with your hair?'

[That exchange] violated every single rule of talk-show politesse. And it got a big laugh besides."

"I'm not malicious. I don't want to get a laugh at the expense of others...Then again, if I see an opening, I go for it."

Though Johnny Carson has taken pains to point out that his own "Tonight Show" is a comedy program, not a talk show, Letterman appears more literal-minded about "Late Night." "I think it is a talk show," he told Tom Shales in an *Esquire* cover story. "It has exactly the structure of Merv and Johnny and all the others. I sit at a desk and guests come out." Other conventions of traditional talk-show structure prevail, including the obligatory bandleader/comic foil, personified by self-styled hipster musician Paul Shaffer [see index for *Newsmakers* entry] on "Late Night." Shaffer's nightly banter with Letterman is considered by some a highlight of the show.

The comic, often described in the press as boyish and gap-toothed, follows another tradition of TV hosts—he seems nonthreatening. As Shales put it, talk-show stars "have to be mellow boys next door—after all, you'll be spending many hours of your life with them. Letterman is the mellowest and most neighborly yet. He's a cutup, he's a caution, but you'd welcome him at a barbecue or church supper. He'd be good playing baseball with nuns .... He's the boyish padre serving up a big yummy heap of the opiate of the masses."

On the other hand, Letterman has cultivated such a strong reputation as an acerbic interviewer that some celebrities have resisted invitations to "Late Night" for fear of being publicly skewered. One such instance affected Letterman personally. "I've always been a big fan of [1960s talk-show phenom] Jack Paar's," he told *Time*'s Richard Zoglin, "and he had invited me to his home a couple of times. I had always found him to be really interesting and still very energetic and dynamic, and I had wanted to get him on the show. But the response was that he had been advised by friends not to go on our show because we would make fun of him. I was saddened by that."

Responding to Zoglin's charge that he has been perceived as "condescending, smug, even mean," Letterman acknowledged: "I suppose I am all of those things, but we never invite somebody on to demonstrate condescention—or condensation. If somebody comes on and is a bonehead and is loafing through an interview, I resent that, and maybe I will then go after them. But if you come on and are polite and well groomed and behave yourself, then you've got nothing to worry about. I'm stunned at the number of people in show business who come on and don't seem to get that what we want from them is a performance."

Nonetheless, Letterman's satiric edge "can be rough," wrote Glenn Collins in a *New York Times* article, especially on non-celebrity "civilians" who sometimes bear the brunt of "Late Night" jokes. The columnist cited the host's "unrehearsed phone calls to unsuspecting people or [his] on-camera forays to places like the General Electric building in Manhattan, where a hapless security official doing his job was made to look foolish preventing Mr. Letterman's entry. Some people have written the network to say they won't watch because of the show's cruelties." In his defense, Letterman offered Collins his opinion that his humor may border on cruelty, "but I'm not malicious. I don't want to get a laugh at the expense of others .... Then again, if I see an opening, I go for it."

Though on-air stunts and remote segments are as old as the talk-show itself, what distinguishes "Late Night" is its postmodern approach to the genre. "The talk show is ideal television because of its shriveled minimalism," explained Shales. "Two people talking to each other, the director cutting back and forth between them, really has enough movement and visual substance to occupy this small and imprecise electronic canvas .... [Big-budget film producer] David Wolper can put three thousand extras on that screen and not generate anything a whit more kinetic than David Letterman talking to [actress] Teri Garr and making her laugh."

In his own way, Letterman has helped define the 1980s attitude toward television. "Talk to [the comic] and his staff about the mass of TV, and the phrase 'it's only television' comes up again and again," noted Barol. "They're well aware that the sense of wonder that suffused the medium in the early days, when wild men like Steve Allen ruled, has given way to a snoozy familiarity. Among the 'Late Night' staff, it's literally true that familiarity has bred contempt. What they have done in response is energize the talk-show format by melting it down and recasting it in Letterman's own odd image."

Some of that image is based on a youthful ideal of what makes good comedy. As Collins wrote, many of the show's popular mainstays—"like crushing things as disparate as bowling balls and a six-pack in a hydraulic press—seem to work because they use the awesome power of the television medium to evoke a silly sense of wonder." As "Late Night" director Hal Gurnee added in that article, "It's every 14-year-old's dream of what he'd do if he had $100,000 and a big press to crush things. And everyone is tempted to drop things off a five-story building without worrying about the consequences." "His off-camera and sometimes on-camera apparel (floppy sweatshirt, baseball cap, high-top sneakers) matches his mental attitude: collegiate," according to James Wolcott in a *Vanity Fair* article. "And not just collegiate but undergraduate. Intellectually, [Letterman's] never left the dorm—he's still playing hall hockey with a rolled-up pair of socks."

Though Letterman keeps a low profile concerning his personal life (he has talked more of his beloved dogs, Stan and Bob, than he has about his early marriage, which ended in divorce, and his long liaison with former "Late Night" writer Merrill Markoe), he's faced some controversies that can only be called Lettermanesque. In one instance, the comedian was hit with a multimillion-dollar suit by a woman whose poodle, Benji, appeared on "Late Night" performing a Stupid Pet Trick. It seems Letterman was unimpressed by Benji's talent for walking around on his hind legs, and told a Boston television station that he was sure the owner had "performed some sort of unethical and intricate spinal surgery on the dog, and that's illegal and she'll end up doing time," as *American Film* critic Peter Exline quoted. The suit contended that Letterman's remarks caused the owner "to suffer contempt and scorn and have impaired her standing in the eyes of a considerable class of the community." The defendant's lawyers stated only that the woman should have known that Letterman was just kidding.

David Letterman (left) plays first base as his "Late Night" team takes on CBS "Evening News" in their annual softball game at Yankee Stadium. AP/Wide World Photos.

In another, more serious, incident, a 36-year-old woman repeatedly broke into Letterman's vacated Connecticut home. Identifying herself as Mrs. Letterman, the woman and her three-year-old son lived on the premises for days, even driving Letterman's Porsche. When the woman, who had a history of mental problems, was finally discovered and arrested, the comedian, "his heart as big as the gap between his teeth, declined to press charges," as a *People* reporter wrote. "This may have been a tactical error, though, because five days later [the woman] was back in the house .... This time Dave decided to prosecute."

Letterman's reticence to reveal his inner self stems from a larger sense of modesty noted by Barol in the *Newsweek* piece: "At a Bruce Springsteen concert [one summer], he was astounded to hear Springsteen mention 'Late Night,' and to hear 'a significant number of people in the audience not boo.'" "I like talking about things that happen in my life if I think I can make me the butt of the joke," Letterman told Zoglin. "But I'm not crazy about actually talking about real things in my life .... If something funny happens in the supermarket, I like trying to talk about that. Because I think—and this may be completely misguided—if I were at home watching a show, I'd like to hear about Johnny Carson's getting a flat tire. But I don't want to start explaining in great detail what makes me happy, what makes me sad, that kind of crap."

Whatever the formula, the comedian has successfully fended off the advancing horde of "Late Night"-style competitors that has flooded the airwaves in recent years. Letterman's talk-show contemporaries have included a cadre of newcomers armed with their own desks, couches, and bandleaders. So far Letterman has shared airtime with chatty comedians like Joan Rivers, David Brenner, Wil Shriner, Arsenio Hall, and game-show refugee Pat Sajak.

But none of these upstarts compares with the host most often named alongside Letterman—"Tonight Show" icon Johnny Carson. Indeed, Letterman was once considered Carson's heir apparent after a well-received tour of duty as a "Tonight Show" guest host (a job since taken permanently by Jay Leno). Comparing the two comics' styles, and theoretically putting Letterman in charge of "Tonight" when Carson finally retires, Shales found advantages and disadvantages to each: "Under Carson's narrow vision ['The Tonight Show'] rarely wanders from the incestuous confines of show business. Guests that young viewers might consider quaint, however, strike others as classy; Johnny still plays host to the occasional opera star, classical pianist, Chinese acrobat troupe, and jazz artist. One does suspect that when Letterman moves in and sets up shop, Itzhak Perlman and Wynton Marsalis will be out, and the lady who dresses up parrots as Cesar Romero will be in. Dave isn't nearly as funny with animals from the zoo as Johnny is; Dave makes fun of the trainer, whereas Johnny lets the animals make fun of him."

"There's no great satisfaction in succeeding in television," the comedian noted to Shales. "What good is it? CBS could come along with a new package of action shows and knock us right to hell. It's not much of an accomplishment, really. That's why we try to take it in stride." "And with that," concluded the columnist, "Dave retreats to his magical little kingdom of pet tricks and viewer mail and crushing things with a steamroller and yelling out the window with a megaphone .... *Late Night* is built on the ruins of television's thirty-year failure to become the cultural savior of the American people; that's the grave it dances on. David Letterman says, oh gosh, you might as well laugh."

Sources

Books

Latham, Caroline, *The David Letterman Story*, Franklin Watts, 1987.

Periodicals

American Film, June, 1987.
Chicago Tribune Magazine, January 6, 1980.
Esquire, November, 1986.
Newsweek, July 7, 1980; February 3, 1986.
New York Times, July 27, 1986.
People, February 4, 1980; March 21, 1988; June 13, 1988.
Rolling Stone, November 3, 1988.
Time, February 6, 1989.
U.S. News & World Report, June 23, 1986.
Vanity Fair, February, 1989.
Washington Post Magazine, April 21, 1980.

—Sketch by Susan Salter

Barry Levinson

Film director, screenwriter, and producer

Full name, Barry Michael Levinson; born June 2, 1932, in Baltimore, Md.; father was in the appliance business; married Valerie Curtin (a screenwriter and actress; divorced); married Diana Mona; children: (second marriage) Sam, Jack. *Education:* Attended American University, Washington, D.C., for seven years.

Addresses: *Office*—514 West End Ave., New York, N.Y. 10024; and Savan-Levinson-Parker, Inc., 59 East 54th St., New York, N.Y. 10022. *Agent*—Creative Artists Agency, 1888 Century Park E., Suite 1400, Los Angeles, Calif. 90067.

Career

While attending college, worked in his father's appliance store and sold encyclopedias door-to-door; floor director, WTOP-TV, Washington, D.C., 1963–67; actor and stand-up comic in Los Angeles, Calif., 1967–70; television comedy writer for "The Lohman and Barkley Show," "The Carol Burnett Show," and "The Tim Conway Show," 1970–75; film producer, 1970—; director and screenwriter, 1975—.

Producer of films, including "First Love" (with Maximilian Schell), 1970, "The Internecine Project," 1974, and "Who?" 1975; director of films, including "Diner," 1982, "The Natural," 1984, "Young Sherlock Holmes," 1985, "Tin Men," 1987, "Good Morning, Vietnam," 1988, and "Rain Man," 1988. Author of screenplays, including "The Internecine Project" (with Jonathan Lynn), 1974, "Silent Movie" (with Mel Brooks), 1976, "High Anxiety" (with Brooks and Rudy Deluca), 1978, "... And Justice for All" (with Valerie Curtin), 1979, "Inside Moves" (with Curtin), 1980, "Diner," 1982, "Best Friends" (with Curtin), 1982, "Unfaithfully Yours" (with Curtin), 1984, "The Natural," 1984, "Young Sherlock Holmes," 1985, and "Tin Men," 1987. Has also written, directed, or produced a number of television films, pilots, and specials.

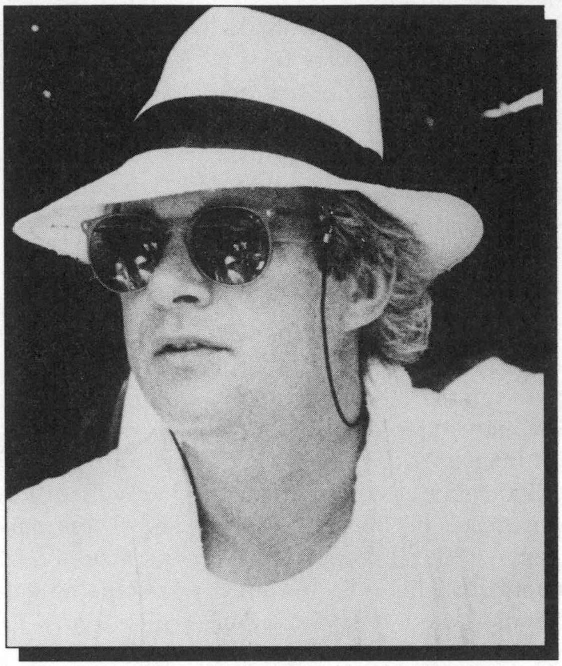

AP/Wide World Photos

Awards: Emmy Awards for best writing in a variety or music program, 1974 and 1975, for "The Carol Burnett Show"; Academy Award nominations for best original screenplay, 1979, for "... And Justice for All," and 1982, for "Diner"; Academy Award for best director, 1989, for "Rain Man."

Sidelights

Academy Award-winning director Barry Levinson has forged a somewhat unique career in the ranks of West Coast filmmakers. As a director and writer of screenplays, Levinson has concentrated on creating human characters in believable, almost aggressively nondramatic situations. Other filmmakers may revel in car crashes, flaming explosions, and explicit lovemaking scenes, but Levinson avoids such contrivances and builds intimate stories instead. Several of his movies—most notably "Good Morning, Vietnam," and "Rain Man," for which he won the Oscar, have been critical and commercial hits; these and other Levinson works display a "fascination with the ordinary," according to Alvin P. Sanoff in *U.S. News & World Report.* Sanoff suggests that Levinson has managed to thrive in Hollywood "in part because he brings films in on schedule and under budget in an industry where cost overruns are almost as frequent as in defense procurement, and partly because he has gained critical acclaim and drawn fans even from the hardened ranks of studio executives." Having been trained as a stand-up comedian and writer for such slapstick artists as Carol Burnett and Mel Brooks, Levinson imbues his own film work with humor, but, as he told the *Chicago Tribune,* he has a very serious aim. "What I respond to," he said, "is behavior, lack of communication, inability to express feelings and emotions." It is not surprising, therefore, that "Rain Man," the quintessential film about emotions gone awry, has been Levinson's most successful effort to date.

The port city of Baltimore has spawned several notables in the last two decades, including Barry Levinson. Like fellow Baltimoreans John Waters [see index for *Newsmakers* entry] and Anne Tyler, Levinson has exploited his colorful home town in his work—and he plans to make more films on location there. He was born and raised in a middle-class section of Baltimore, in a two-story frame house that he actually used during the filming of "Tin Men." Recalling his youth, Levinson told the *Chicago Tribune:* "When I was growing up there, Baltimore probably was one of the ten largest cities in the nation, but in a way it was still a town—a place of neighborhoods. And the people there are very colorful, extremely open and 'out there' about what they're up to—which is a quality I find intriguing."

As a boy Levinson was less interested in his schoolwork than he was in his friends and the local sports teams, especially the Orioles and the Colts. In his high school years he completed only the assignments that interested him, ignored the rest of the curriculum, and consequently earned near-failing grades. Handsome and affable, he was popular with his classmates, and he forged close friendships with a clique of fellows who liked to end long evenings by snacking together in a local diner. Levinson spent seven years attending American University in Washington, D.C. in a haphazard manner, sometimes missing terms to work in his father's appliance store, sometimes selling encyclopedias door-to-door. Finally, in his last years at American University, he became interested in television production and took an entry-level job at WTOP-TV in Washington.

At WTOP Levinson did everything from set construction to working hand puppets on "The Ranger Hal Show," a regional version of "Captain Kangaroo." His apprenticeship lasted from 1963 until 1967 when, on a whim, he journeyed to Los Angeles to study acting. He soon found formal acting classes rather pretentious, so he switched to stand-up comedy. His first partner was Craig T. Nelson, who has gone on to become a film star seen recently in the "Poltergeist" movies. Together, Levinson and Nelson perfected a number of silly skits, one of which featured stuffy attorneys carrying around live pigs and another of which depicted a bus stop meeting between Mickey Mouse and Walt Disney.

"More and more movies today revolve around the same thing—cops...There are fewer cops than salesmen...Are we so exotic? There is room for [films] about just people."

Eventually Levinson discovered that he could make more money writing comedy for others than he could performing himself. He became a regular contributor to "The Carol Burnett Show" and later to "The Tim Conway Show," earning two Emmy Awards for his sketches. Levinson moved to feature-length screenplays in 1975 when his friend Mel Brooks asked him to collaborate on several comedies. Brooks was at the height of his popularity at the time, and Levinson helped him script both "High Anxiety" and "Silent Movie," two Brooks hits of the late 1970s. Recalling those days in a *Gentleman's Quarterly* profile, Levinson said that he enjoyed writing the broad slapstick humor as much as he has enjoyed crafting the subtle humor of his later work. "I think it's unfortunate that, to some people, only sophisticated comedy has real merit," he maintained. "There's nothing wrong with broad comedy, if it's done well. Just because there are serious, underlying themes to some comedies does not mean they have more value than a clever piece of slapstick. But still, there is a certain satisfaction to something that's well written, whether it's funny or not. I take a lot of pleasure in the writing."

Even though he does not consider himself a "writer" *per se* anymore, Levinson has authored or co-authored a number of successful screenplays. After working with Brooks, he teamed with his first wife, actress Valerie Curtin, to script several comedies, including "Unfaithfully Yours," "Inside Moves," and "Best Friends," and a drama set in Baltimore entitled ". . . And Justice for All." The latter film, a story about corruption and inefficiency in the legal profession, earned Levinson an Oscar nomination for best original screenplay. ". . . And Justice for All" was also the first Levinson offering to be filmed in Baltimore; and it was successful enough at the box office to give its author some much-needed clout in Hollywood. Generally speaking, the Levinson-Curtin comedies were less well-received than their joint serious drama, with the exception of "Best Friends." That work, featuring Goldie Hawn and Burt Reynolds as lovers who also collaborate on screenplays, was a modest box-office hit. Levinson and Curtin dissolved their professional and personal relationship in the late 1970s.

It was Mel Brooks who suggested that Levinson write a movie about his youthful experiences in Baltimore during the late 1950s. In 1982 Levinson wrote and directed "Diner," an ensemble comedy about young men facing the adult world with little enthusiasm for what they find in it. "*Diner* dissects that moment in young adulthood when teenage preoccupations—the minor one-upmanships, mating dances and shared experiences of schools and sports—are no longer satisfying," wrote Michael Sragow in *Rolling Stone.* "Yet to Levinson's characters, the prospect of living without these tribal rites is terrifying." Levinson explained his premise for "Diner" in *Rolling Stone:* "The movie didn't come together for me until I realized that underlying most of my anecdotes was one idea: Boys play with boys until they're twelve or thirteen. Then they start talking about girls. Then they date, which is like stealing someone from another tribe and then returning to your tribe to talk about it. But after you're twenty-one or twenty-two, you're not supposed to go back to your own tribe!" Using two marriages as a backdrop, Levinson explored that moment of tribal dissolution in "Diner." He was careful, however, to avoid stretching the material into the realm of melodrama. He told *Rolling Stone,* "I thought, why can't I go ahead and make a movie that's really just about these characters at a certain moment in our culture?"

"Diner" was almost shelved before its release. Test-marketed in several midwestern cities, it failed to generate business, so MGM nearly decided not to give it wide exposure. Only the intervention of some influential New York film critics saved the work from obscurity. Never a blockbuster, "Diner" still turned a profit and earned its writer-director the respect of his peers. Levinson was subsequently invited to direct a big-budget picture, "The Natural," starring Robert Redford as a heroic, near-mythical baseball player. "The Natural" was well-received by critics and moviegoers alike, and Levinson has called it one of his favorite films. *Washington Post* contributor Rita Kempley contended that "The Natural" reveals Levinson's "flair for expressing other people's stories." In a related statement, Levinson told Kempley that he does not distinguish between his scripts and those written by others. "You have to be committed to the other person's work as your own, otherwise you're not being honest with the material," he said. "You've got to be kind of connected to it. I don't have much pride in ownership. I don't care if I wrote it or somebody else wrote it. It's the material."

Since 1987 Levinson "has suddenly become one of the hottest directors in Hollywood," to quote *Playboy* correspondent Dan Greenburg. Comedy-dramas such as "Tin Men," "Good Morning, Vietnam," and "Rain Man" have solidified Levinson's reputation to the extent that his future projects are almost certain to find financing. "Tin Men" is the second Baltimore-based film scripted and directed by Levinson. It concerns the feud of two flamboyant aluminum siding salesmen, played by Richard Dreyfuss and Danny DeVito [see index for *Newsmakers* entry]. "Good Morning, Vietnam" is a drama based on the career of Saigon disc jockey Adrian Cronauer, who tickled American servicemen with his anti-authoritarian banter. The movie starring Robin Williams [see index for *Newsmakers* entry] was one of the five biggest box office hits of 1988, grossing well in excess of $125 million. Both of these films have been eclipsed by "Rain Man," however. The winner of numerous Academy Awards—including Levinson's for best director and star Dustin Hoffman's for best actor—"Rain Man" chronicles the budding of brotherly love between a self-centered young businessman (Tom Cruise [see index for *Newsmakers* entry]) and an autistic savant with extraordinary mathematical abilities (Hoffman). Initially interested only in his brother's hefty inheritance, Cruise's character eventually comes to appreciate his sibling's plight—and to understand how his own personality was formed. *Chicago Tribune* critic Ann Kolson wrote of the film: "That 'Rain Man' succeeds on screen is as much a testament to the powers of its director, Barry Levinson, as to the strengths of its stars . . . . It may just be Levinson's finest work to date." Ironically, Levinson was the fourth director assigned to the movie, after

Martin Brest, Steven Spielberg, and Sidney Pollack all bowed out. What Levinson did was what he has done with each script under his control—he minimized the so-called "action" sequences and concentrated on a meaningful exploration of two interesting characters.

If Levinson's works can be said to have a common theme, it is certainly that of male bonding in all its various forms. Greenburg contends that Levinson "does seem to know how men talk to one another and behave with one another—the loving and competitive and distrustful and tender and cocky way that men act toward other men because they've been brought up to be successful and *macho* and not show their vulnerability—and he manages to make that behavior seem extremely natural when it gets translated to the screen." And Kempley wrote: "Buddies, like Baltimore and ball games, fill [Levinson's] screens.... His plots often hinge on the actions of peripheral female characters.... But mostly his movies evoke a mellowed masculinity, a mix of English Leather, sweat socks and whisker burn."

Levinson prefers to think of himself as a creator of movies about ordinary people in ordinary—or only slightly extraordinary—situations. As he put it in the *Washington Post:* "more and more movies today revolve around the same thing—cops.... And there's always a disclaimer: 'It's really about a relationship between two men who happen to be cops; it's a man struggling with conflicts of a family, but he's a cop... he's with the FBI; he was a CIA agent; he was an ex-cop when she met him.' There are fewer cops than salesmen. Why can't we have a woman who was on the run and she met a guy who used to work in a shoe store as opposed to ex-CIA? Are we so exotic? There is room for [films] about just people." The director concluded: "I'm not trying to make dull movies, but there's a lot of us who enjoy our lives." Sanoff observed that Levinson's "endless curiosity about the way people act" is sure to spark future screenplays, and he added that whatever vehicle the director chooses, "it will be about real people, and Levinson will do it his way, not the Hollywood way."

Sources

Chicago Tribune, March 15, 1987; December 30, 1988.
Gentleman's Quarterly, February, 1988.
Maclean's, January 9, 1989.
Newsweek, December 19, 1988.
New York, March 9, 1987; December 19, 1988.
People, January 18, 1988.
Playboy, March, 1989.
Rolling Stone, May 13, 1982.
Time, December 28, 1987.
U.S. News & World Report, January 9, 1989.
Washington Post, March 13, 1987.

—*Sidelights by Mark Kram*

Arthur Liman

AP/Wide World Photos

Attorney

Full name, Arthur Lawrence Liman; born November 5, 1932, in New York, N.Y.; son of Harry K. (a dressmaker) and Celia (a Latin teacher; maiden name, Feldman) Liman; married Ellen Fogelson (a writer, painter, and interior decorator), September 20, 1959; children: Lewis, Emily, Douglas. *Education:* Harvard University, A.B. in government, 1954; Yale University, LL.B. (magna cum laude), 1957.

Addresses: *Home*—New York, N.Y. *Office*—Paul, Weiss, Rifkind, Wharton & Garrison, 1285 Avenue of the Americas, New York, N.Y. 10019.

Career

Admitted to Bar of the State of New York, 1958; Paul, Weiss, Rifkind, Wharton & Garrison, New York City, attorney, 1957–61, 1963–, partner, 1966–; assistant to U.S. attorney for southern district of New York, 1961–63. Special assistant to U.S. attorney, 1965; chief counsel, New York State Special Commission on Attica, 1971–72; Legal Aid Society, New York City, 1975; member, New York State Executive Advisory Committee on Sentencing, 1977; member of advisory committee on civil rules, U.S. Judicial Conference, 1980—; chairman, governor's advisory commission on the administration of justice in New York, 1981—; chairman of New York City mayor's commission to investigate the medical examiner, 1985; chief counsel, special Senate committee investigating Iran-Contra affair, 1987. Member of board of directors, Continental Grain Co. and Equitable Life Assurance Society.

Member: American Bar Association, American Bar Foundation, American College of Trial Lawyers (fellow), New York State Bar Association, Bar Association of the City of New York (member of executive committee), Lawyers Committee on Civil Rights Under Law.

Sidelights

In recent years, attorney Arthur Liman's clients have included real estate tycoon John Zaccaro, corporate raider Carl Icahn, junk bond merchant Michael Milken and CBS executive William S. Paley. He represented Pennzoil in its successful multi-billion dollar litigation against Texaco. And, in 1987, Liman became a network television regular, jousting with witnesses like Oliver North and Richard Secord as the chief counsel of the Senate committee investigating the Iran-Contra affair. It is no surprise, therefore, that *Fortune* magazine termed Liman, "a courtroom giant, a master legal strategist, and a trusted corporate adviser . . . whom many colleagues regard as the greatest litigator of his generation." *Manhattan Inc.* magazine rated him one of New York City's 31 power brokers in 1988. And *American Lawyer* magazine said he earned $1.1 million in 1985.

Liman's blue chip clients—who pay him at the rate of $350 per hour—include Warner Communications, Weyerhaeuser, Continental Grain, Time Inc., and Lazard Freres. He is expert at corporate strategies, both initiating takeovers and defending against them. But it is Liman's high-profile clients who have kept him in the spotlight. And it is his work for various government committees that had many politicians considering him a shoo-in for attorney general in the next Democratic administration. "He's investigating Oliver North one day, and he could be negotiating a takeover deal tomorrow," Robert Fiske, a New York lawyer who has known Liman 20 years told the *Wichita Eagle-Beacon.* "He's extremely versatile. He handles an enormous variety of cases."

Liman was born in New York City in 1932, the son of a successful dress manufacturer. "I came from a bookish family where everyone had a college degree," he told the *New York Post.* Liman studied government at Harvard, graduating Magna Cum Laude and making Phi Beta Kappa. Appalled at the time by Senator Joseph McCarthy's misuse of power, he wrote his senior thesis on the constitutional limits of congressional investigations. He went on to Yale Law School, where he was known as an excellent poker player who always received excellent grades in class. He graduated first in the class of 1957.

Liman was recruited by several law firms but accepted a position at the New York firm of Paul, Weiss, Rifkind, Wharton & Garrison, a distinguished Democratic firm with a long tradition of public service. Senior partner Ernest Rubenstein, who recruited Liman, told *Fortune* that his hiring was, "one of my greatest contributions to the firm.... After he had been here for two weeks, no one doubted he would one day be a partner." At first, Liman says, he was the office "garbage pail," taking small cases that colleagues shunned. Liman once won a case against a bartender for diluting liquor but got just a $1 fine—the judge had a bartender father.

In 1959 he met writer and painter Ellen Fogelson at a cocktail party; four months later they married. "He was persuasive, decisive," Ellen Liman told *Fortune.* "I guess you could say he brought his courtroom skills to the courtship."

Liman cut his teeth on white-collar crime during a 2½-year stay at the U.S. attorney's office in Manhattan under Robert Morgenthau, starting in 1961. "I had never worked on a securities case because there really weren't any," Liman told the *Wichita Eagle-Beacon.* "We were breaking new ground." He then returned to Paul, Weiss, quickly gaining a reputation as one of New York's best inquisitors and a master at reading a jury. He was gaining another reputation also—as a brilliant, but absent-minded man. In a 1989 profile of Liman, *Esquire* magazine wrote: "At Paul, Weiss there is a delirious oral tradition of taking-a-shower-with-his-shoes-on, calling-his-secretary-and-saying-'Where am I?' stories about Liman, most of them apocryphal. But it is true that once when his secretary told him that someone he had wanted to reach by telephone was dead, he replied, 'Well, that's okay. Just leave word.'"

Liman first gained public notice when he was named chief counsel to the New York State Special Commission investigating the 1971 riot at Attica Prison, which left 39 dead. It was the first probe inside a prison, and Liman's team interviewed 3,000 witnesses, including every inmate. "I looked into the eyes of a lot of prisoners," he told the *New York Times.* "They are saying to the establishment, 'How can you understand us? How can we trust you?' There is little for them to identify with in my background. But we won them over." Liman's 470-page report was published in book form and went on to be nominated for a National Book Award. It was strongly critical of Governor Nelson Rockefeller and state prison officials for their response to the uprising.

Meanwhile, Liman's private practice flourished in the middle 1970s. He was the defense attorney for fugitive corporate embezzler Robert Vesco, who fled the United States in 1973. He supervised the 1975 New York State disbarment of former President Richard Nixon. And, representing New York City in 1979, he won a $72 million damage claim against Pullman, Inc., and Rockwell International for 754 defective subway cars. His closing argument in that case was described as brilliant. "I relax in the courtroom," Liman told *Esquire.* "It's a sanctuary from all the distractions of the day, the 100 phone calls, the dozens of problems. I can remember every word that every witness says, there isn't a gesture that I miss—there's a level of concentration that you almost can't attain anywhere else."

Liman continued his practice of alternating private work with public service. He headed a 19-member panel that studied New York State's criminal justice system. In 1982 the commission called for the creation of a central administration headed by a new cabinet-level administrator. Governor Mario Cuomo endorsed and acted on the recommendations. Likewise, Liman was appointed by New York City Mayor Edward Koch in 1985 to head a commission investigating charges that city medical examiner Dr. Elliott Gross had produced false autopsy reports on police-custody deaths. Liman, who was charged with determining criminal culpability, found evidence of serious mismanagement but concluded there had been no criminal wrongdoing or cover-up.

A sampling of Liman's private clients during the last few years demonstrates his versatility. On the corporate side, he represented Pennzoil against Texaco in 1985 and even delivered eight days of testimony on the witness stand that helped send Texaco into bankruptcy court. Time Inc. and Warner Communications are clients—the two, not coincidentally, announced a massive merger in 1989. In 1986, Liman negotiated a handshake between clients Laurence Tisch and William Paley that led to the ouster of CBS Chief Executive Officer Thomas Wyman.

Liman also has carved out a specialty in white-collar crime. In the 1980s—a decade permeated with Wall Street crime—he became known as New York's most prominent securities-fraud lawyer. He defended the likes of inside trader Dennis Levine, real estate tycoon John Zaccaro (husband of vice-presidential candidate Geraldine Ferraro), corporate raider Carl Icahn, and the founders of Studio 54. He was lead defense attorney in a major stock manipulation case against GAF Corp., winning a mistrial in 1989. And he represents Michael Milken, the Drexel Burnham Lambert junk-bond financier who was indicted in 1989 for fraud and racketeering.

Liman's reputation was solidly entrenched when, in January 1987, he was named chief counsel of the special Senate committee charged with investigating the Iran-Contra arms scandal. He spent three months pouring through mountains of government documents, seeking to understand the motives of men like Oliver North [see index for *Newsmakers* entry], John Poindexter, Richard Secord and Albert Hakim. "I'm not dealing with insider traders here," Liman told the *Washington Post.* "I'm dealing, with Col. North, with a person who didn't stay in government in order to make money. And that makes it in my mind, this phenomenon, much more dangerous and difficult to control. Because if you start with people who had good motivations—they wanted to serve their country—and things go as wrong as this, you have to say why and who's responsible?"

Liman's first national exposure in the case came in May 1987, when he cross-examined retired Air Force Major General Richard Secord. Wrote the *Washington Post:* "By the end of the day, Secord, who had begun his testimony cloaked in the flag, was somewhat less tightly wrapped." As committee chairman Senator Daniel Inouye (D-Hawaii) told the *Post:* "The great American hero was not as shiny as he once was made to appear, and in that sense Arthur did a superb job. Somebody had to do it. You can't question General Secord by saying 'Thank you very much and you've been very kind.'" That opinion was not universal. U.S. Representative Michael DeWine (R-Ohio) told the *Houston Post:* "I think his questions are loaded questions. Arthur Liman is now the spear carrier for the liberals who want to get the president of the United States." Inouye's office was flooded with negative mail, much of it anti-Semitic. Liman answered just one letter, a suggestion that he move to Moscow. "I said I wouldn't be comfortable there," he told the *Washington Post.* "I'm as American as the writer, and that the purpose of the hearings is to make sure that the United States never becomes a Kremlin. Period."

For many, the highlight of the Iran-Contra hearings came in July 1987 when Lieutenant Colonel Oliver North was questioned about his role in the scandal. In cross-examination, Liman faced off against Brendan Sullivan, North's feisty Washington attorney. "Despite his mild appearance, Sullivan is a tireless worker and tenacious courtroom fighter," wrote *Time* magazine. "Liman was expected to treat North as he had earlier witnesses, using a blend of relentless hammering and withering sarcasm. Instead he addressed the Marine calmly but sternly, pressing forward to expose the contradictions in North's answers. While some thought Liman may have been intimidated by North's popularity, others viewed the chief counsel's cross-examination as a cagey shift in strategy." Liman himself told the *Washington Post,* "If in order to get the same facts out of a witness you have to use honey, I use honey."

North's four days of testimony made for riveting television. The Marine lieutenant colonel burnished his hero image and tapped a well of sympathy across the country. "The television viewers saw my questioning as, 'Why is this lawyer bothering this man, why don't they canonize him?'" Liman told the *Fort Lauderdale News and Sun-Sentinel.* "I'm not surprised that he emerged as a sympathetic character.... I understood that Oliver North was an evangelical figure. He was persuasive. He believed in what he advocated. He was good-looking. And he was described to us as one of the most natural speakers that anyone had encountered. Because any effort to control his speeches would have appeared to be bullying, North had more of a pulpit than any of us expected."

The hearings ended after eight months in August 1987. Afterward Liman recalled the hearings as an exercise in unearthing evidence, rather than bringing anyone to justice. The philosophy of the mission, he told the *Wichita Eagle-Beacon,* was that "sunlight is the best disinfectant in a democracy. There are some events in American history where it's most important for the American people to understand how it happened and why it happened. If we weren't able to find out everything that happened, we were able to find out much and let the American people judge." In the end, Liman helped author a 690-page report of the House and Senate committees on the Iran-Contra affair. Liman summarized it in a piece he wrote for the *New York Times,* writing, "We can have a coherent, effective foreign policy only if [Congress and the president] work together with a high degree of trust. This trust is shattered when a president and his aides circumvent the law and do not level with Congress. But it is also impaired when Congress acts feebly and erratically." In a decade, Liman said, Americans will look at the facts of the Iran-Contra hearings in the summer of 1987 not in terms of the innocence or guilt of Oliver North, but in constitutional terms. "In due time they will appreciate the fact that the government of the United States has got to be a government of law, not men," Liman told the *Fort Lauderdale News and Sun-Sentinel.* "I think that in time the people of the United States will come to appreciate that."

When he escapes—which he rarely does—Liman enjoys playing tennis, boating and going to the theater. He is also an avid fisherman. "He used to say he'd buy a new rod every time he was frustrated," Ellen Liman told the *Washington Post.* "Maybe it's the challenge that appeals to him. When you're fishing you can't control everything like you can in the courtroom."

Liman figures to garner more national attention as attorney for junk bond trader Michael Milken. Beyond that, there is talk of his entry in politics. Liman himself has admitted being intrigued at the attorney general's post, telling *Newsday,* "An attorney general has got to have the capacity to say "no" to a president, just as I as a private lawyer say "no" to clients. The most valuable advice I've given to clients has really been when I've told them that they should not do something. The attorney general has not said "no" to the president. Senator Warren Rudman (D-Vermont) told the *Washington Post:* "I don't know what life holds for Arthur. Maybe someday there'll be a Democratic president. If there is, I hope Arthur Liman ends up in government."

Sources

Fort Lauderdale News and Sun-Sentinel, July 12, 1987.
Fortune, June 8, 1987.
Esquire, January 1989.
Houston Post, July 11, 1987.
Los Angeles Daily News, July 10, 1987; January 11, 1989.
Manhattan Inc., October, 1988.
Newsday, July 8, 1987; December 28, 1987; October 12, 1988.
Newsweek, July 20, 1987.
New York Times, September 13, 1972; March 20, 1988.
Rochester Times-Union, July 11, 1987; September 7, 1988.
Time, July 20, 1987.
Washington Post, July 7, 1987.
Wichita Eagle-Beacon, April 2, 1989.

—Sidelights by Glen Macnow

Andrew Lloyd Webber

AP/Wide World Photos

British composer

Born March 22, 1948, in London, England; son of William Southcombe (a composer and director of London College of Music) and Jean Hermione (a piano teacher; maiden name, Johnstone) Lloyd Webber; married Sarah Jane Tudor Hugill (a singer and musician), 1971 (divorced, 1983); married Sarah Brightman; children: (first marriage) Nicholas, Imogen. *Education:* Attended Magdalen College, Oxford University; also attended Royal College of Music.

Addresses: *Home*—London, England; and New York, N.Y. *Office*—20 Greek St., London W1V 5LF, England.

Career

As a young boy, began playing piano, French horn, and violin; at the age of eight, began staging musical theater productions in his home; at nine, composed and published a suite; while in college, composed his first full-length musical, "The Likes of Us," with lyrics by Timothy Rice. Composer of music for musical productions, including "Joseph and the Amazing Technicolor Dreamcoat," 1967, "Jesus Christ Superstar," 1970, "Jeeves," 1975, "Evita," 1976, "Tell Me on a Sunday," 1980, "Cats," 1981, "Song and Dance," 1982, "Starlight Express," 1984, "The Phantom of the Opera," 1986, and "Aspects of Love," 1988; composer of scores for films "Gumshoe," 1971, and "The Odessa File," 1974; also composer of "Variations" (based on *A-minor Caprice No.* 24 by Paganini), 1977, and a requiem mass, 1985. Producer of "Daisy Pulls It Off," 1987, "The Hired Man," 1984, and "Lend Me a Tenor," 1986.

Awards: Drama Desk Awards, 1971, 1980, and 1983; Tony Awards for best score, 1980, for "Evita," and 1983, for "Cats," and for best producer, 1983, for "Cats"; Plays & Players Award (London) for best new musical, 1986, for "The Phantom of the Opera"; Tony Award nominations for best composer, 1987, for "Starlight Express," and 1988, for "The Phantom of the Opera."

Sidelights

Andrew Lloyd Webber is the most successful British composer of musicals to date. His seven commercially popular musicals include "Jesus Christ Superstar," "Cats," "Evita," and "The Phantom of the Opera." He is the first composer ever to have three musicals play simultaneously on Broadway and London's equivalent, the West End.

Born in London, England, in 1948, Lloyd Webber was influenced by his musically talented family. His father, William Lloyd Webber, a composer and the director of the London College of Music, and his mother, Jean Johnstone, a piano teacher, steered his interests toward music. The young boy played the piano, French horn, and violin and staged productions of musicals in a toy theater in his home. The young Lloyd Webber idolized composer Richard Rodgers of the Rodgers and Hammerstein duo that created such classics of musical theater as "Oklahoma," "South Pacific," and "The King and I."

"What I would hate to happen would be to find that I was genuinely not...reaching people....Because in the end people respond to the music, and I obviously like to reach people through music."

Lloyd Webber attended Westminster School in London and then Magdalen College, Oxford, for a term before transferring to the Royal College of Music. While a student Lloyd Webber met Timothy Rice, and the two immediately recognized each other's potential. In a PBS television documentary Rice remembered thinking during their first encounter: "This guy's going to make it. It's a red hot certainty." Lloyd Webber's impression was similar: "Timothy had this extraordinary way with words and it was like something I had never heard or seen before in my studies of musicals. He would rhyme in a way that anybody else at that time would say 'How dare you!'" Lloyd Webber composed many pieces during his student days, including collaborating with Rice on the full-length musical "The Likes of Us," which has never been produced.

Their second joint venture—"Joseph and the Amazing Technicolor Dreamcoat"—proved more successful. Loosely based on the Old Testament story of Joseph and his brothers, this theatrical production was originally written as a 20-minute oratorio and combined country-western, calypso, French vaudeville, opera, and rock and roll styles of music. It attracted a following on college campuses and was first staged in the United States in 1970. In 1972 a television version aired and an album and score were produced. Over the years, changes in "Joseph" were made until in 1981 it appeared in its final version in New York.

With "Jesus Christ Superstar," Lloyd Webber and Rice returned to a biblical theme. This rock musical adapted from the Gospels was first released as a double-album in October 1970, because no one would agree to produce it on stage. The record piqued the public's interest, and though it was produced unsuccessfully in New York, after its staging in London's West End it gradually became a hit. It eventually sold over 5 million records worldwide and engendered a feature film directed by Norman Jewison. "Jesus Christ Superstar" also rekindled interest in "Joseph."

During the early 1970s Lloyd Webber generally focused his attention on various productions of "Jesus Christ Superstar," but he also composed the scores for the films—"Gumshoe" and "The Odessa File." During this time he also composed the musical "Jeeves," with lyrics by dramatist Alan Ayckbourn, which was short lived on the British stage. Based on the works of the reknowned humorist P. G. Wodehouse, "Jeeves" portrays the comical adventures of an English valet named Jeeves. Lloyd Webber maintains that some parts of this piece work very well, though the entire work is unsuccessful; thus, he says, he may someday revise it.

Lloyd Webber and Rice again collaborated on "Evita," a musical about the life of Eva Peron, wife of Argentinian dictator Juan Peron. After Peron's death Eva became the ruler of Argentina until she died of cancer a short while later. Rice became intrigued by the Eva Peron story after one day turning on his car radio and hearing a documentary about her. The story is told in flashbacks that begin at Eva Peron's funeral. As in his other works, Lloyd Webber employed a variety of musical forms, but in "Evita" he employed only sung dialogue and composed lush orchestration, thus using a more operatic style. Like "Jesus Christ Superstar," this musical's premier was preceeded by the release of a two-record album of the show's music, whetting the public's appetite. "Evita" was very popular in Britain when it opened in 1978 and in the United States a year later, and it earned Lloyd Webber a Tony Award. Lloyd Webber and Rice also co-authored a book on the subject: *Evita: The Legend of Eva Peron, 1919–1952,* which includes a short biography of Peron and the lyrics to the musical.

In 1981 another Lloyd Webber production opened in London—"Cats"—based on esoteric poet T. S. Eliot's *Old Possum's Book of Practical Cats.* In this work Lloyd Webber employed seven synthesizers, a full orchestra, and a large cast of singers and dancers in feline costumes. "Cats" was unsuccessful in London but quickly gained a following in the United States. Before its American debut in 1982, the ballad "Memory" was popularized with recordings by Barbra Streisand and Judy Collins, among others. Critical reaction followed the preset pattern: "Cats" was labeled excessive and banal. Jay Sharbutt of the *Los Angeles Times* quoted Cameron Mackintosh, the producer of "Cats," as saying, "Nobody wanted [Lloyd Webber] teaming up with [director] Trevor Nunn to do a very serious poet's off-duty poems."

"Song and Dance" is just what its title implies. The first act is a collection of songs for soprano originally entitled "Tell Me on a Sunday" and the second a dance ensemble piece set to Lloyd Webber's rock and roll variations based on Paganini's *A minor Caprices.* Lloyd Webber had for some time been interested in dance but had never composed specifically for dance until this time. "Song and Dance" ran for two years in London and was produced on Broadway in 1985 with Bernadette Peters in the role of Emma, an English hat designer who emmigrated to America to make her fortune. The twenty songs of the "Song" part of the work are thematically tied together by the love life of Emma.

Inspired by a child's love of trains, "Starlight Express" was a commercially popular visual and musical extravaganza about trains. A cast of more than twenty, all on roller skates, imitated locomotives racing along the tracks of a very complicated set. The plot, with lyrics by Richard Stilgoe, involves a race between trains powered by electricity, steam, and diesel and is narrated by a young boy. "Starlight Express" uses non-stop music in a variety of styles: rock, country, rap, blues, and gospel. It garnered mixed reviews from British critics when it was first staged in London under the direction of Trevor Nunn but became a popular success in Britain and the United States, where it appeared on Broadway with two additional songs. Lloyd Webber commented to Stephen Holden of the *New York Times:* "With *Starlight,* which was actually begun before *Cats,* Trevor and I are indulging a whole fantasy that is about fun and nothing else.... It's really only rock and roll."

Lloyd Webber's list of accomplishments grew in 1986 with the musical gothic melodrama "The Phantom of the Opera." Charles Hart and Stilgoe wrote the lyrics for this play, which is based on Gaston Leroux's 1911 novel of the same title about a disfigured mad man who falls in love with a singer at the Paris Opera. Lloyd Webber's first attempt at an old-fashioned romance was well received by the public. Tickets for "Phantom" were sold out months before performances in London and New York. It won the London critics' Plays & Players Award for best new musical in 1986 and in 1988 it won seven Tony Awards, including the award for best musical. Critical appraisals were mixed, ranging from raves to merely faint praise.

Frank Rich of the *New York Times* has been a longtime Lloyd Webber critic and not always a very kind one. In a television documentary on Lloyd Webber, "The Andrew Lloyd Webber Story," Rich assessed the composer's career: "I think Andrew Lloyd Webber has produced some very interesting shows and some not so interesting shows. Whether there's a straight progression from the uninteresting to the interesting is debateable. In some ways some of the earlier shows—or middle shows if you will—, *Jesus Christ Superstar* and *Evita,* are more interesting than some of what's come after, particularly in the case of *Starlight Express* and *Cats,* which are sort of amorphous pageants and don't have the sophisticated ambitions of *Jesus Christ Superstar* or *Evita.* In *The Phantom of the Opera* Lloyd Webber is again sort of taking another twist in this progression because he's returning to the kind of storytelling he did in the earlier shows. But throughout his career he's really been held hostage by his lyricists. If a composer is working with unsophisticated lyrics, he's in trouble. The most sophisticated lyricist, in my view of Lloyd Webber's career, has been Tim Rice, and while *Evita* may in some ways be a naive and simplistic historical view of the Perons, as show business lyric writing Rice's work is very clever, and I think Lloyd Webber responded with a more interesting score and a more varied score than usual."

When asked about the disparity between critical and popular reaction to his works Lloyd Webber told Joseph McLellan of the *Washington Post:* "I'm surprised that in this country there does seem to be a certain ... I really don't know how to describe it. It seems to me that either people genuinely don't like what I do, ... or there's something about the fact that it has been successful ... that worries people. On the other hand, recently there have been people who have been encouraging .... But it's very hard. I think everybody tends to feel that they've been knocked around more than they really have. In England, I think there's far more familiarity with me as a person, and there are critics who know what I'm up to, and they know some of the things that have happened in between that don't have quite as much commercial success, and there's more knowledge of the intention ... and the intention is serious."

In the final analysis, Lloyd Webber does not allow himself to be adversely affected by critics' sometimes harsh evaluations of his work. He values the audience response more than critical appraisals. As he told McLellan: "What I would hate to happen would be to find that I was genuinely not—repeat not—reaching people. I mean I find that the reaction of the audience to, for example, *The Phantom of the Opera* is to me very gratifying. Because in the end people respond to the music, and I obviously like to reach people through music. So in one sense I find that I don't really care, providing I know that the music I'm writing at any particular time is as good as I can do."

Lloyd Webber was uncertain when asked in the television interview about future projects: "I don't really know what I'll do next and I want to take stock of quite a lot of things at the moment. I realize, in fact, that there aren't any suites of *Cats, Evita,* or *Superstar.* They've never been done and I'd quite like to do them myself and get back to orchestrations again.... I'd quite like to go back over some of my older things and I think something will emerge soon."

Sources

"The Andrew Lloyd Webber Story" (television documentary), PBS, 1988.
Chicago Tribune, June 16, 1986.
Detroit Free Press, July 7, 1987.
Los Angeles Times, January 26, 1988; January 28, 1988; June 6, 1988, June 7, 1988.
Newsweek, September 30, 1985.
New York Times, September 27, 1983; September 8, 1985; September 30, 1985; July 9, 1986; February 23, 1987; March 1, 1987; March 16, 1987; November 24, 1987; January 18, 1988; January 20, 1988; January 27, 1988; January 28, 1988; May 10, 1988; May 11, 1988.
Time, September 30, 1985.
Times (London), September 27, 1983; January 18, 1988; January 28, 1988.
Times Literary Supplement, June 23, 1978.

—Sidelights by Jeanne M. Lesinski

Nancy Lopez

UPI/Bettmann Newsphotos

Professional golfer

Born January 6, 1957, in Torrance, Calif.; daughter of Domingo (an auto repair shop owner) and Marina (Griego) Lopez; married Tim Melton (a sportscaster), January, 1979 (divorced, 1982); married Ray Knight (a professional baseball player), October 25, 1982; children: (second marriage) Ashley, Erinn. *Education:* Attended University of Tulsa, 1976–78.

Addresses: *Agent*—Mark H. McCormack Agency, 1 Erieview Plaza, Cleveland, Ohio 44114.

Career

Began playing golf as a young child; won first New Mexico state tournament at age twelve; as a senior in high school, finished second in Women's Open; as a college student, won intercollegiate title before leaving school and turning professional after her sophomore year; professional golfer, 1978—.

Member: Ladies Professional Golf Association (LPGA).

Awards: Named Athlete for 1978 by Associated Press; named LPGA Player and Rookie of the Year, 1978, appointed to LPGA Hall of Fame, 1987.

Sidelights

Since becoming a professional golfer in 1978, Nancy Lopez has consistently ranked among the top women on the circuit. She is one of only five women in the sport to have earned more than $1 million in her career. In addition, she has won over 40 tournament victories and has been named to the Ladies Professional Golf Association (LPGA) Hall of Fame.

Lopez first became a golf enthusiast as a child when her parents took up the game for her mother's health. By the age of 11, she was a better golfer than either of her parents. Her father became convinced that Nancy was champion material and began to groom her for tournament play. The family scrimped on its own needs to finance her golfing. The family's dedication seemed justified by her performance on the golf course. At the age of 12, she won the first of three state women's tournaments. While still in high school, she finished second in the Women's Open. In 1972 and 1974, she won the U.S. Girls Junior title. And as a student at the University of Tulsa, she won the intercollegiate title before dropping out of school to turn professional.

During her first year on the professional circuit, Lopez broke several standing records. She began the year by winning the Bent Tree Classic at Sarasota, Florida, in February, then went on to win a record five tournaments in succession, including the prestigious LPGA title. (Lopez has since won a second LPGA title as well as a Nabisco Dinah Shore title.) By August of 1978 she had surpassed the highest earnings record, $150,000, set by Judy Rankin in 1976. Lopez went on to earn more than $200,000 by the end of the year. She also endorsed or made commercials for various golf products.

Since her initial appearance on the pro circuit, Lopez has always been ranked at the very top of her sport. In 1979, she won 8 of the 19 tournaments she entered, a feat Bruce Newman of *Sports Illustrated* called "one of the most dominating sports performances in half a century." Lopez had her best year in 1985, when she earned more money—over $400,000—than any other player on the circuit. She won five tournaments and set a record-high scoring average of 70.73 percent. In 1987 Lopez was named to the LPGA Hall of Fame, "which has the most difficult requirements for entry of any sports Hall of Fame in the nation," as Gordon S. White, Jr., noted in the *New York Times.* Thirty tournament victories, two of them major titles, are needed for Hall of Fame inclusion.

Through it all, Lopez has managed to balance the demands of a sports career with those of a wife and mother. In fact, she told Joseph Durso of the *New York Times:* "I like being a wife and mother more than I like professional golf." She and her husband, baseball player Ray Knight, share the necessary domestic duties between them. "We complement each other," Knight told Durso. "We help each other with the chores." And Knight occasionally caddies for his wife. Because of their respective status in golf and baseball, Lopez and Knight are "probably the most prominent married couple in sports," according to Durso. They are also among the happiest. Lopez told Jaime Diaz in *Sports Illustrated:* "I'm so happy with my life, that now when I play, there is no pressure. It's just all fun, and when it's fun, you perform better."

Writings

The Education of a Woman Golfer, Simon & Schuster, 1979.

Sources

New York Times, March 31, 1985; May 19, 1988.
People, April 25, 1983.
Sports Illustrated, August 5, 1985; August 4, 1986; February 9, 1987.

—Sketch by Denise Wiloch

Miriam Makeba

AP/Wide World Photos

Singer and activist

Born March 4, 1934, in Johannesburg, South Africa; married five times; husbands have included musician Hugh Masekela (divorced, 1968) and activist Stokely Carmichael (divorced, 1978); children: (first marriage) Bongi (daughter; deceased).

Addresses: *Home*—Guinea. *Office*—c/o Jazz Singer, 472 North Woodlawn St., Englewood, N.J. 07631.

Career

Singer; has appeared in concert in the United States, Europe, and Africa; recording artist. Delegate to the United Nations from Guinea, 1975. Appeared in documentary "Come Back to Africa," 1958. Author of autobiography *Makeba: My Story.*

Awards: Grammy Award, 1965.

Sidelights

Known as "Mother Africa" to her fans, singer Miriam Makeba is often called a survivor. She has battled cancer and endured the death of her only child. One of the first South Africans to receive international attention, she was eventually banned from her native land. She found refuge in the United States, until her marriage to a black activist. An outspoken critic of apartheid, Makeba continued to perform in Europe and the third world. Her career in America was revived in the late 1980s, with the release of a new record and the publication of her autobiography.

Born in Johannesburg, Makeba's first "run in" with the authorities occurred when she was just 18 days old. She was put in jail with her mother, who had been arrested for brewing homemade beer to support the family. Early on, Makeba was recognized as a gifted singer; she became a star while still a teenager. She was asked to perform in a 1958 documentary called "Come Back to Africa." She soon began receiving offers from other countries, including the United States, where she was invited to appear on "The Steve Allen Show." In London, she met Harry Belafonte and told him of her upcoming engagement on Allen's program. Belafonte offered to help. "When I came I had nothing," Makeba wrote in the *Chicago Tribune.* "He put things together for me. Musicians, clothes to wear on stage and someone to write down my songs, and the band that played during the Steve Allen show." Belafonte became her mentor, helping her career and encouraging her to speak out against apartheid. Makeba hit the American charts with the single "Pata Pata." Then, in 1960, her mother died. Makeba wanted to return home but found that the South African government had revoked her passport.

Living in exile, she divided her time between Europe and the United States. In 1968, she married Stokely Carmichael, a black activist. Her concerts were cancelled and her records boycotted in America and Great Britain. She settled in Guinea and served, in 1975, as a delegate to the United Nations. She continued to sing in Africa and Europe. Her repertoire included protest songs from her native country, as well as material from the Continent and the Near East. In the 1970s, Makeba helped found a maternity hospital in Guinea. In memory of her daughter, who died after giving birth, she still provides medical equipment and supplies.

In 1987, Makeba enjoyed a comeback in the States, when she performed with Paul Simon's *Graceland* tour. The tour was a huge success, and Makeba's appearance was widely acclaimed. The following year, she published her autobiography, *Makeba: My Story:* she also released her first American album in twenty years, *Sangoma,* which contains African tribal chants taught to the singer by her mother, a sangoma, or healer. Of her exile and the later boycott of her music, Makeba told the *New York Times*'s Stephen Holden: "I don't feel I should complain because there are so many people at home who are much worse off.... I know they are going through more pain than I. At least I don't have to dodge bullets. What keeps me strong is the hope of getting back home."

Sources

Chicago Tribune, March 20, 1988.
Ms., May, 1988.
Nation, March 12, 1988.
New York Times, January 27, 1988; March 13, 1988.

—Sketch by Denise Wiloch

Edward "Monk" Malloy

AP/Wide World Photos

Roman Catholic priest and educator

Full name, Edward Aloysius Malloy; born May 3, 1941, in Washington, D.C.; son of Edward Aloysius (a claim adjuster) and Elizabeth (Clark) Malloy. *Education:* University of Notre Dame, B.A. in English, 1963, M.A. in English, 1967, Th.M., 1969; Vanderbilt University, Ph.D. in Christian ethics, 1975.

Addresses: *Home*—141 Sorin Hall, University of Notre Dame, Notre Dame, Ind. 46556. *Office*—Office of the President, University of Notre Dame, Notre Dame, Ind. 46556.

Career

Ordained Roman Catholic priest, 1970; University of Notre Dame, Notre Dame, Ind., teaching assistant, 1969–70; Aquinas Junior College, Nashville, Tenn., instructor in theology, 1972–73; University of Notre Dame, instructor, 1974–75, assistant professor, 1975–81, associate professor, 1981–88, professor of theology, 1988—, associate provost, 1982–87, president, 1987—.

Consultant to Catholic Bishops of Indiana on defining the moment of death and the right to die, 1976–77; member of Institutional Review Committee, Memorial Hospital of South Bend, 1981—; member of Institutional Review Board, St. Joseph Medical Center, 1983—; member of board of regents, University of Portland (Ore.), 1985; member of Indiana Organ Transplantation Task Force, 1986—.

Member: Catholic Theological Society of America, Society of Christian Ethics, Business and Higher Education Forum.

Sidelights

He is tall, fair and graying. He lives in two book-filled rooms in a student dormitory steps away from Notre Dame's Golden Dome. A hand-written sign on his door says "Welcome," and students take him at his word; they stop by at all hours for conversation and perhaps a little counselling. Edward Aloysius Malloy, appointed president of Notre Dame in 1987, brings his own unique style to the leadership of a major university. Where his predecessor, Theodore M. Hesburgh, was forceful and charismatic, Malloy is low-key and approachable. Students, professors, and trustees alike all call him Monk, a nickname he was given in grade school. Once a member of the best high school basketball team in the country, Malloy continues to hone his famous jump shot at twice weekly basketball sessions—called Monk Hoops—with students. And every spring he plays Bookstore Basketball, a Notre Dame tradition involving 500 to 600 teams playing tough single-elimination ball. The name of his team: All the President's Men.

Malloy continues to play basketball, live in the dorm, and take freshmen out for pizza because he feels his most important role is to serve the needs of the students. "Living in the dorm allows me to be a pastor and not just a bureaucrat or fund raiser," he told the *Chicago Tribune Magazine.* "It's one of the distinctive things about Notre Dame.... It's really important that people know my primary identity is as a priest. I just think it's hard to argue that being president makes me some great muckety muck."

As a successor to the legendary Hesburgh, Malloy has a tough act to follow. In his 35-year tenure as president of Notre Dame, Hesburgh took a small Catholic school with a good football team and molded it into a respected university. He built more than 40 buildings on campus, doubled the student body, upgraded the faculty, increased the operating budget five-fold, and opened the doors of the university to women. In 1988, *U.S. News & World Report* rated Notre Dame the eighteenth best university in the country.

But Malloy, who began teaching theology at Notre Dame in 1974 and served as associate provost from 1982 until 1987, thinks there is room for improvement. He would like to place more emphasis on research and graduate work, increase the number of minority students, provide better child care for employees, and become more involved in the local community in South Bend.

Malloy's appointment, the result of a five-year search by the board of trustees, has been a popular one. "Monk just intuitively has a sense of self, a presence and a deep understanding of the university," said Donald R. Keough, president of Coca-Cola and chairman of the Notre Dame board of trustees, in the *Chicago Tribune Magazine.* "And it's frankly remarkable that a man could come in behind Fr. Hesburgh and in a relatively few months be known around the U.S. as the unquestioned leader of the place. He makes everyone in a room think he's speaking to them. You could put him in a room with corporate leaders, students, athletes, people from all walks of life and he'd make them feel comfortable."

If Malloy has an instinctive grasp of the spirit and workings of Notre Dame, it is because he himself has grown up, found his calling, and spent much of his adult life there. He first came to the university as a freshman on a basketball scholarship after being heavily recruited by 50 colleges. He had been a key player on an outstanding team from Archbishop Carroll High School in Washington, D.C., which won 55 straight games in the late fifties. But his basketball career fizzled when he reached Notre Dame. "I just didn't fit that well into the style of ball here," he told the *New York Times Magazine.* "They didn't need a slow player with a good jump shot.... I never had the kind of success I had hoped for as a basketball player at Notre Dame. And that was probably the best thing that ever happened to me. I looked around and saw there were other things."

Among the other things that captured Malloy's interest were opportunities to serve the poor in Central and South America. He spent three summers in Mexico and Peru with groups of students distributing food, assisting at a health clinic, and helping to build a parish center. In the summer of his junior year, he took a day trip from the central Mexican town where he was living into the mountains to visit the Basilica de Cristo Rey (Christ the King) and experienced a call to the priesthood. "The combination of being in another culture, feeling motivated to be in a helping profession, and really being moved by that place gave me a profound sense of certitude about what I wanted to do with my life," he told the *New York Times Magazine.*

"Living in the dorm allows me to be a pastor and not just a bureaucrat or fund raiser."

After graduating with a degree in English, Malloy entered Moreau Seminary on the Notre Dame campus. While studying for the priesthood, he earned master's degrees in English and in theology. After his ordination as a member of the Congregation of the Holy Cross, he enrolled in Vanderbilt University Divinity School and earned a Ph.D. in Christian ethics. In 1974, Malloy returned to Notre Dame and began teaching theology.

From the beginning, he wanted to be approachable and accessible. Rather than live in the priest's residence, he moved into two simple rooms at Sorin Hall, the university's oldest dorm. Painted yellow, they contain a couch, a television set, a cot, a rocking chair, several hundred books—and a white-noise machine Malloy uses to block out the rock music that is a standard feature of college dorms. He keeps student hours, up until 2:00 or 3:00 in the morning and waking at 9:00 or 9:30. The students seem to appreciate their unusual dorm-mate. "A person as intelligent as Monk you might think would be unapproachable," said Ken Dice, then a senior resident assistant at Sorin Hall, in the *Washington Post.* "Would you ask Einstein to help you with a physics problem, or e.e. cummings to diagram a sentence? Monk's not above it all—that's what makes him so special." In addition to teaching, playing basketball, and chatting with students, Malloy has found time to write scores of articles and two books exploring the ethical dimensions of many important issues—among them, biotechnology, drugs, capital punishment, law enforcement, homosexuality, and gambling.

Then, in 1982, Hesburgh announced he wanted to retire, and the search for his successor began. The university's board of trustees identified five candidates, Malloy among them. He was named associate provost and, along with the others, groomed for the post. The nature of the search was an unprecedented one for Notre Dame because it was the first conducted by the primarily lay board of trustees, to which Hesburgh had given control of the college in 1967. Hesburgh cites the transfer of power from the Congregation of the Holy Cross to the trustees and the admission of women to the university as his most significant accomplishments.

In these and other areas, Hesburgh's influence on the university was incalculable. "No person is all over one particular place like Hesburgh is at Notre Dame," one employee told the *New York Times.* "This university, its landscape, its physical plant and his ego are all meshed." Hesburgh not only transformed the university but brought it national and international attention by keeping a high profile himself. He served four popes, held fourteen presidential appointments, and travelled extensively. In fact, Hesburgh was off campus so much that, this joke, reported in the *New York Times,* began circulating: What's the difference between Father Hesburgh and God? God is everywhere. Hesburgh is everywhere but Notre Dame.

Finally, in 1986, the trustees named Monk Malloy Notre Dame's next president. Most on campus were enthusiastic, but some worried that Malloy would not be as willing to keep the university in the limelight through travel. Others wondered about his fundraising skills.

But, apparently unconcerned about how he compares with Hesburgh, Malloy has brought his own skills, interests, and collaborative leadership style to the job. "Father Ted is one of the great Catholics of the 20th Century and a great educational leader, but he built a strong institution that was ready for a transition," Malloy told the *Chicago Tribune Magazine.* "It's not dependent on his charisma and personality." Malloy does travel, but in small doses. He tries not to be away from the university more than three days at a time, explaining in the *New York Times Magazine,* "The student-life dimension is the soul of this university, and it's important for me to be a presence here."

At a time when many colleges and universities are struggling with high costs and lower enrollments, the university Malloy took over is in fine shape. In one recent year, it received 9,634 applications for 1,822 openings in the freshman class, despite annual tuition and room and board of $13,400. Eighty percent of the students accepted ranked in the top ten percent of their high school classes. And Notre Dame boasts alumni who are among the most generous contributors in higher education; in 1987, they donated $17 million to the university.

One of Malloy's major goals during his initial five-year term is to increase the number of minority students. In 1988, only three percent were black, and a slightly higher percentage were Hispanic. By 1992, Malloy would like minority representation in the freshman class to be at least 15 percent. Toward that end, he has increased financial aid from $8 million to $20 million dollars. Martin Rodgers, a black student who works part-time in the admissions office recruiting minority students, said in the *New York Times Magazine* that Malloy has helped foster an acceptance of diversity on campus. "Fr. Malloy's made a commitment with the task force, with financial aid, with counselling for minority students. But it's more than that—he's also raised the level of consciousness.... There's a spirit now that wasn't here when I was a freshman and sophomore. Instead of saying, 'You're different, and that's that,' we're starting to appreciate our differences."

Despite his fondness for basketball, Malloy doesn't plan to place increased emphasis on sports. He resists continuing pressure to expand Notre Dame's 59,000-seat stadium to the 90,000 to 100,000-seat capacity of other stadiums, saying the school has other priorities. And he takes pride in the fact that Notre Dame's athletic program has avoided the scandals and exploitation of athletes found at other schools. "We will lower our admission standards for an athlete," he told the *New York Times Magazine.* "But we still have to be convinced he can do the work here. If he has to go to summer school, ok. If he needs tutoring help, he'll get it. But we want him to graduate in four years like everyone else."

Like Hesburgh, Malloy is more concerned with the school's academic achievements than with its football record. Although Notre Dame offers a highly respected undergraduate education, Malloy would like to improve graduate programs and increase the level of research. In 1988, Notre Dame did only $20 million worth of research—compared with $100 million at the University of Chicago.

One possible obstacle to recruiting leading faculty and researchers is the fear among some that the Catholic Church will impose intellectual restraints. But Malloy, who as associate provost resisted Vatican proposals to do just that in 1985, asserts the university's right to intellectual freedom. "The European model of church control over institutions just doesn't prevail here," he told the *New York Times Magazine*. "People don't realize, for instance, that we get zero dollars from the Catholic Church. It isn't that we don't think we have any responsibility to the church at large or to the Vatican, we do. But if our tradition of academic freedom, a tenured faculty system and the right to adjudication in civil courts is not respected, then you could destroy the best vehicle for, as Ted used to say, the church to do its thinking."

Some worry, though, that with the increased emphasis on research and academic credentials, the Catholic nature of the university will be diluted. "Why do they [Catholic students] come here?" asked Francis J. Castellino, dean of Notre Dame's College of Science, in the *Chicago Sun-Times*. "Because we're a small place with a Catholic sense of values. If we lose that, there's no other reason to come here, with all the alternatives around us."

So far, Notre Dame has retained its own unique character. All undergraduates take two semesters of theology, and every residence hall has a chapel. One in seven students contribute their time to a worthy cause, such as working in a soup kitchen or visiting the elderly. And the university recently opened a shelter for the homeless in downtown South Bend. Drawing on his background as an ethicist, Malloy stresses teaching moral values that are important to Catholics and non-Catholics alike. "I would very much like Notre Dame to be a place where people go to prepare for their professions and the ethics of their professions," he said in the *Indianapolis News*. "I would like to see us do a better job of having people look at the ethical implications of their choices—whether they be choices they make as lawyers, doctors, journalists or scientists."

Notre Dame continues to be a place where future lawyers and scientists can hammer out some of those choices—not only in the classroom, but in two small dormitory rooms at Sorin Hall. There, leaning back in his chair at midnight or two in the morning, a quiet, unassuming man is relaxed and ready to talk.

Writings

Homosexuality and the Christian Way of Life, University Press of America, 1981.

The Ethics of Law Enforcement and Criminal Punishment, University Press of America, 1982.

Sources

Chicago Sun-Times, February 22, 1989.
Chicago Tribune Magazine, February 26, 1989.
Indianapolis News, March 5, 1987.
New York Times, November 15, 1986.
New York Times Magazine, June 12, 1988.
Sports Illustrated, April 13, 1987.
Washington Post, December 28, 1986.

—Sidelights by Cathleen Collins Lee

Howie Mandel

AP/Wide World Photos

Actor and comedian

Born 1955, in Toronto, Ontario, Canada; son of a lighting manufacturer and realtor; married; wife's name, Terry; children: Jackelyn. *Education:* Earned high school diploma through equivalency courses.

Addresses: *Home*—Los Angeles, Calif.

Career

In carpet business, c. 1975–79, beginning as door-to-door salesman and eventually owning two carpet stores; owner of a novelty business; actor and comedian, 1979—. Has appeared on television programs, including "Make Me Laugh," "The Shape of Things," "Laugh Trax," "The Tonight Show," and "The Merv Griffin Show"; regular member of cast of series "St. Elsewhere," 1982–87; star of cable television shows "Cinemax Comedy Experiment," 1985, and "The Watusi Tour," 1986. Feature films include "Funny Farm," "The Princess Who Never Laughed," 1985, "A Fine Mess," 1986, and "Bobo, the Dog Boy," 1987; contributor of voice-overs to films "Gremlins" and "Once Upon a Star," and cartoon show "Jim Henson's Muppet Babies and Monsters." Recorded comedy albums *Howie Mandel Fits Like a Glove* and *The Watusi Tour.*

Sidelights

Comedian Howie Mandel has risen to stardom by being tasteless, childish, and exuberantly silly. His humor, plumbed discreetly on the television show "St. Elsewhere" and more openly in his stand-up routines, evokes the days of early adolescence when barnyard noises, crude insults, and toys put to new uses caused moments of high hilarity. A *Variety* reviewer noted that Mandel's "lunatic, splay-footed stance and endless, restless pacing" bring to mind a prankster "who'll perform any practical joke for a laugh—even if he's the only one who is laughing." The performer's jokes may not suit every taste—the *Variety* writer called them "too filthy to repeat"—but younger audiences have embraced Mandel with great enthusiasm. "As a comic, . . . Mandel is a modern-day Jerry Lewis—a repository of strange noises and weird, aggressive humor," observed *Us* magazine contributor Michael Auerbach. "Unlike many of his more cerebral fellow comedians, his comedy seems adolescent. While the work of, say, Robin Williams is steeped in irony, Howie gets up on stage and grabs his crotch. But that uncultivated energy serves him well."

Still in his thirties, Mandel seems destined for a lucrative and high-profile Hollywood career. In addition to his dramatic role in "St. Elsewhere" and his popular comedy act, he has starred in several movies and has provided voices to cartoon and film characters, including Gizmo in "Gremlins." Mandel told *People* magazine that, despite his success, he still finds performing nerve-wracking. "I actually feel sick," he said, "but it's something you have to do. It's like people who pay a buck to go on a ride and get thrown 100 feet in the air. When they get off, they say, 'That was great!' Well, that's the same thrill I get."

Few Hollywood careers have been more fortuitous than that of Howie Mandel. He was born and raised thousands of miles from California, in Toronto, Canada. *People* correspondent Deirdre Donahue wrote: "As the cherished firstborn son of a Toronto lighting manufacturer and realtor, Howie had the best of everything middle-class: trips to Florida, Hebrew school, the works." Mandel admits that an "insatiable desire to be the center of attention" has stayed with him since childhood. Once he discovered that he could make people laugh, he began to put clowning before everything else, including his studies. He was expelled from three high schools because of pranks he engineered—he calls them "extravaganzas" that "took lots of work and planning"—and had to earn his diploma through equivalency courses. Mandel never intended to be a professional performer even though he entertained his mother and his girlfriend, Terry, incessantly. Instead he went to work selling carpeting and throw rugs, first from door to door and then from two stores he bought himself. By the time Mandel proposed to Terry, he had a twenty-four person staff and what appeared to be a promising future in carpet distribution. Then he went to Los Angeles on business and the direction of his life changed overnight.

While in Los Angeles, Mandel and his business partners visited the Comedy Store in Hollywood. It happened to be amateur night at the well-known nightclub, and with a bit of prompting from his friends, Mandel took the stage. He caused a sensation with the audience and caught the attention of producer George Foster, who booked him on the spot for fifteen segments of a syndicated television show, "Make Me Laugh." Mandel filmed the "Make Me Laugh" shows in three days and returned to Canada, figuring his moment in the spotlight was over. But several television executives courted him for situation comedies and singer Diana Ross called and asked him to open her Las Vegas show. Six weeks before his wedding, Mandel left the carpet business—and Toronto—for a whole new life. "Since then," noted Donahue, "Mandel's career hasn't slowed down for a minute, thanks to his talent and some luck."

Talent and luck may have launched Mandel, but the grueling pace he set for himself certainly accelerated his climb to fame. In 1985 Auerbach observed that Mandel's "real passion seems to be his work" as Mandel juggled live appearances in such far-flung cities as St. Louis and Cleveland with his Monday-through-Friday work on "St. Elsewhere" and his one-day-a-week voice work for "Jim Henson's Muppet Babies and Monsters" cartoon show.

The tight scheduling of projects began in 1981 when Mandel successfully auditioned for "St. Elsewhere." On that show, which ran for six seasons and is now in syndication, Mandel appeared as Wayne Fiscus, a young emergency room doctor whose professional grace under pressure is offset by daring sexual adventures and an array of social *faux pas*. "St. Elsewhere" commonly portrayed hospital routines realistically, even graphically, and Mandel had to learn medical terminology and life-saving procedures that doctors often use. Although his role in the show was serious, Mandel did offer some moments of comic relief in most episodes—indeed the juxtaposition of his gentle comedy with moments of intensity in the medical setting added dimension to the series. "St. Elsewhere" never achieved high Nielsen ratings, but the executives at NBC renewed it year after year because it attracted an audience of young, relatively affluent viewers that advertisers wanted desperately to reach. These same viewers became the core of Mandel's live audience when he took his comedy routine on the road.

Mandel began performing his stand-up act at the Comedy Store regularly even while he was filming "St. Elsewhere." From there he moved to the university circuit and to other, larger nightclubs. Now he headlines at the major theaters in Los Angeles, Las Vegas, New York, and Atlantic City, and his album, *The Watusi Tour,* is a best seller. A "typical" Howie Mandel show does not exist; the comic thrives on free association, improvisation, and audience response. He told *People* that on stage he feels "like a kid . . . with a playground for doing whatever I feel like." That "playground" contains a dizzying array of toys, hats, and masks, most of them bought at shopping malls. Mandel leaps around the stage, playing with his toys, insulting his fans, and making wry comments on the vagaries of modern life.

Only one element of his act remains the same from show to show, and it has become his trademark. Auerbach describes it as "the trick that made him famous," and details it thus: "He takes a surgical glove and places it over his head so that the rim covers his nose. Then, breathing in through his mouth and out through his nostrils, he inflates the glove so that the fingers stick out over his head like the Statue of Liberty's crown." Eventually the bloated glove pops off the top of Mandel's head with an appropriately dramatic noise. This trick served as the grand finale of Mandel's Home Box Office special, "The Watusi Tour" and is almost always incorporated into his act—though sometimes he goes through several gloves before the bit works.

Since concluding his work with "St. Elsewhere," Mandel has been working on feature films. His first starring movie role, in Blake Edward's "A Fine Mess," excited little critical or commercial enthusiasm; nor did his 1987 movie, "Bobo, the Dog Boy." Ironically, Mandel's biggest film success to date has been as the voice of the character Gizmo in Steven Spielberg's "Gremlins." Gizmo is a baby-voiced "mogwai," or gremlin, and the sounds Mandel made for the creature were ones he had been doing since his eleventh birthday. "It started when I was at a party," Mandel told *People.* "I began to choke on some cake. This weird voice came out instead, and it seemed, as I was gagging, to entertain all the kids." Mandel practiced the voice—without the cake—and when he was cast as Gizmo, his "blend of Donald Duck and a Heimlich emergency squeal" beat out hundreds of professional competitors.

Mandel has never restricted his antics to the stage alone. His parents, wife, friends, and co-workers often find themselves embroiled in carefully-devised pranks. Stephen Furst, one of Mandel's "St. Elsewhere" co-stars, told *Us:* "He's always playing practical jokes on me. Once, he put my house up for sale. Another time, he put a chemical on my wardrobe to make it seem as if I had body odor." Terry Mandel also admits that "life with Howie is scary" at times, although success has tempered a destructive element that was once part of her husband's humor. Still, the man who told *People* that his greatest fear "is growing up" has become a father. His daughter, Jackelyn, was born early in 1985. "Having a kid really changes your life," Mandel told *People.* "She's the most important thing in the world, now. Suddenly you have so much responsibility. The way she's going to be, the kind of human being she's going to be, and what she does in this world, all depends, I think, mostly on us."

Sobering though fatherhood may be, however, Mandel intends to prolong his own glorious childhood, offstage and on. In fact, he told *People,* his daughter provides the thrill of "an audience that's always willing to be there." His biggest fear, he said, "is how I'm going to react to her dates. But we've already discussed that. The way to ensure that she's always home early is to not potty-train her." In the ever-growing pantheon of Canadian comics winning raves in the United States, Howie Mandel is likely to remain outstanding. Whether he returns to serious drama or continues in stand-up comedy, his eternally juvenile spirit will offer rich amusement to his world-weary fans. As the *Variety* reviewer noted, Mandel can continue to expect "a resounding hand for daring to be a jerk."

Sources

Boxoffice, October, 1986; February, 1987.
Maclean's, June 9, 1986; August 18, 1986.
Newsweek, March 16, 1987.
New York Times, February 10, 1985; October 20, 1985; July 9, 1986.
People, September 5, 1983; June 4, 1984; July 30, 1984; August 13, 1984; March 11, 1985; June 2, 1986; June 16, 1986.
Us, December 16, 1985.
Variety, January 1, 1986.

—Sketch by Anne Janette Johnson

Winnie Mandela

Reuters/Bettmann Newsphotos

South African political activist

Full name, Nkosikazi Nobandle Nomzamo Winifred Mandela; born 1934, in Bizana, Pandoland, Transkei, South Africa; father, Columbine Mandikizela, was a history teacher and government official; mother was a domestic science teacher; married Nelson Mandela (an attorney and political activist), June, 1958; children: Zindziswa, Zenani Dlamini (both daughters). *Education:* Graduated from Jan Hofmeyer School of Social Work, 1955.

Addresses: *Home*—Soweto, Transvaal, South Africa.

Career

Medical social worker at Baragwanath Hospital, Soweto, Transvaal, South Africa, beginning 1955; member of Federation of South African Women and other women's political groups; joined Women's League of African National Congress (ANC), 1957, and became head of its local branch; participated in numerous demonstrations protesting South Africa's apartheid policy of racial segregation; since her husband's imprisonment in 1964, has acted as his spokesperson and carried on political activity on his behalf; arrested many times for political activities; named a banned person by South African authorities, 1962; held in solitary confinement, 1969–70; served a six-month sentence for violating banning orders, 1974.

Awards: Robert F. Kennedy Humanitarian Award, 1985; Third World Prize, 1985.

Sidelights

As the wife of imprisoned African National Congress (ANC) leader Nelson Mandela, Winnie Mandela has become a symbol for the political goals and ideals of the black people of South Africa. As such she is revered by the people and vilified by the government. South African Anglican Archbishop Desmond Tutu says that she "has made a major contribution to Nelson's image. They have become a symbolic couple with their incredible strength and refusal to be broken." Ever since 1958, Winnie Mandela has been detained, imprisoned, harassed, and threatened by the authorities. She has been held in detention for more than two years and under banning orders for almost 27 years. In South Africa a person may be banned arbitrarily with no avenue for appeal. Banning orders restrict her to a specified magisterial district; from being quoted in the South African press; from entering schools or universities, publishing houses or courts; from communicating with more than one other person at a time; from communicating with another banned person; and sometimes from leaving the premises at all. For more than eight of those 27 years, until 1985, Mandela was banished to a small Afrikaner town about 250 miles from Johannesburg. In 1985 her home and clinic in

Brandfort were firebombed. She returned to Johannesburg and moved into the home she and her husband had shared. Since then she has refused to be bound by government restrictions, speaking out defiantly against the white government.

In 1986 she spoke to a crowd of people assembled for a funeral—the first mass rally she had addressed in 25 years—and was quoted as saying, "together, hand in hand with our boxes of matches and our necklaces, we shall liberate our country." Necklacing refers to a brutal method of mob execution whereby a car tire is placed around the victim's neck, filled with gasoline, and ignited. This punishment has been meted out to people suspected of being collaborators or traitors to the black community. Later, Mandela denied she had called for violence and said that she had been quoted out of context.

Winnie Mandela first came to Johannesburg in 1953 at the age of 19 to continue her studies at the Jan Hofmeyer School of Social Work. Nothing in her upbringing prepared her for the life she would lead as Nelson Mandela's wife. She was born in rural Pondoland in 1934 and named Nomzamo Winifred Madikizela. Her mother, a domestic science teacher and religious fundamentalist, died when Winnie was nine years old. She left 9 children; the youngest was three months old. Her father, Columbine, was a history teacher and later Minister of Agriculture in the Transkei government. Winnie attended Bizana and Shawbury schools in the Transkei. She graduated from Jan Hofmeyer in 1955 and took a job at Baragwanath Hospital in Soweto. She was the first black medical social worker in South Africa.

In 1952, the year before Winnie moved to Johannesburg, Nelson Mandela and others in the ANC had led the nationwide Defiance Campaign against government apartheid regulations. Many people, especially in the urban areas, were politicized through the campaign. When Winnie went to Johannesburg she made many friends who were members of the ANC. One of her closest friends was Adelaide Tsukudu, the wife-to-be of Oliver Tambo, the ANC's current president in exile. In 1957 friends introduced her to Nelson Mandela, a member of the ANC executive committee and one of the accused in the treason trial, which was then going on. They had a brief and rather unorthodox courtship because of the time taken up by Nelson Mandela's court case and his law practice. Nevertheless, on June 14, 1958, Nelson Mandela received permission to go to the Transkei where he and Winnie were married.

That year also marked the beginning of Winnie Mandela's encounters with the security police. In September 1958, she and thousands of other women were arrested for demonstrating against the government for issuing passes to women. She was detained for two weeks and then released. At the time of her arrest, she was on the national executive committee of the Federation of South African Women and chairperson of its Orlando branch and on the national and provincial executive committees of the ANC's Women's League. She lost her job at the hospital because of her arrest—a real hardship because she was the wage earner in the family.

In 1960 police fired on a group of people protesting the pass laws in the small town of Sharpeville. With the ensuing nationwide and worldwide demonstrations, the government declared a state of emergency, detained thousands of people, and outlawed the ANC. Although he was already out on bail during the treason trial, Nelson Mandela and other defendants were detained for nearly five months.

In March 1961, after a trial that lasted four and a half years, the court found the defendants in the treason trial not guilty. The few months between March and December were the only time Nelson and Winnie and their two small girls would have any semblance of a family life. In December he went underground, addressing meetings throughout the country and abroad with the purpose of establishing a military wing of the ANC. In August 1962, he was picked up and charged with inciting Africans to strike in the 1961 work stoppage and with leaving the country illegally. While he was serving a five-year sentence on these charges, he was accused of sabotage, put on trial, and found guilty. In 1964 he was sentenced to life in prison.

In 1962 the government placed banning orders on Winnie Mandela. Because of these orders she had to get special permission to attend her husband's trial, which was held in Pretoria, outside her restricted area. The women of the men on trial wore their traditional dress to court because they believed it inspired people and evoked a sense of militancy. When the authorities banned the dress, in a gesture typical of her defiance, Winnie Mandela began wearing gold, green and black, the colors of the outlawed ANC.

After the trial, Winnie Mandela was alone, without an income and with two small children to care for. Although she had visitation rights, she was not to have any physical contact with her husband for the next 22 years. In an interview with Anne Benjamin for the book *Part of My Soul Went With Him,* she said of those times: "The difficult part was finding myself with a spotlight on me. I wasn't ready for that."

Winnie Mandela is a beautiful woman; she photographs well and is a striking symbol of defiance in her traditional dress. She drew a bright light to herself and became a symbol of the black cause for the international media. In the same interview she said: "I had to think so carefully what I said—as his representative. I don't mean careful because of my banning orders but because of the responsibility."

Banned in 1962, and with more stringent restrictions imposed on her in 1965, Mandela was forced to leave her job with the Child Welfare Society because she could not travel outside of Orlando in Soweto. Additional restrictions were placed on her and she remained banned, except for two weeks in 1970, until 1975. As she recalled for Anne Benjamin, years later she asked security branch head Johan Coetzee about her banning in 1962. She had delivered only one speech—to the Indian Youth Congress—and did not understand why she was banned. She said he replied: "There is a saying in Afrikaans that if you have a field with a lot of pumpkins and you see a pig next to those pumpkins, you don't have to be told that the pig is going to eat those pumpkins."

On several occasions between 1962 and 1975 Mandela was charged with violating her banning orders. In 1967 she was sentenced to 12 months' imprisonment for failing to give her name and address to security police in Cape Town (the authorities allowed her to visit her husband who was in prison on Robben Island in Cape Town). Her sentence was suspended, except for four days. In May 1969 she and 21 others were detained under the Suppression of Communism Act and accused of promoting the aims of the outlawed ANC. The charges were withdrawn in 1970 but she was immediately redetained on the same charges and placed in solitary confinement in Pretoria Central Prison under Section 6 of the Terrorism Act.

She served 17 months, 491 days, in detention—most of it in solitary confinement. She described her confinement to Anne Benjamin: "Those first few days are the worst in anyone's life—that uncertainty, that insecurity.... The whole thing is calculated to destroy you. You are not in touch with anybody. And in those days all I had in the cell was a sanitary bucket, a plastic bottle which could contain only about three glasses of water, and a mug.... The days and nights became so long I found I was talking to myself.... Your body becomes sore, because you are not used to sleeping on cement."

Because of her circumstances, Winnie Mandela had to send her daughters away from her, to school in Swaziland. Headmasters in private South African schools, after visits from the security forces, invariably found reasons to dismiss the Mandela girls.

On her release in September 1970, the government renewed her banning orders for five years, only two weeks after they expired. She was also restricted to her home in Orlando at night and on weekends and public holidays. In addition, she was now prohibited from having any visitors at all, except her two daughters. Between 1970 and 1973 she was accused several times of violating her banning orders. All of the convictions were set aside on appeal. In October 1974, though, she was sentenced to six months in Kroonstad Prison for meeting with a banned person. In 1975 her banning orders expired and were not renewed for 10 months. After 13 years of banning she tasted "freedom" for nearly a year.

During this time of freedom, she helped organize the Black Women's Federation. Later, after the 1976 Soweto riots, she helped establish the Black Parents' Association to assist people with medical and legal problems caused by police action during the uprising. Her freedom was brief, however, because in August, after the riots, she and thousands of others were picked up under the Internal Security Act and held until December 1976. On the 28th of December she received new banning orders. And in May of 1977 her banning orders were amended, banishing her from her Orlando home to Phatakahle, a black township of about 5,000 people on the outskirts of Brandfort, an Afrikaner town of 1,900 in the Orange Free State.

Winnie Mandela was confined to the Brandfort area for eight years. Because she was a figure of international standing, she received many foreign visitors at her isolated farm community. Through her contacts and training she helped the local black community establish a nursery school or creche, a soup kitchen for the school children, a mobile health unit, and self-help projects that ranged from growing vegetables to knitting clothes to sewing school uniforms. While in Brandfort, she was charged innumerable times with violating her banning orders—she could entertain no visitors in her home and could only be in the company of one person at a time. She was under 24-hour police surveillance. In 1982 she was served with her fifth banning order which was renewed in 1983.

In August 1985, her Brandfort house was firebombed. She accuses the government of responsibility for it. She defied her banning orders and returned to her home in Orlando. Faced with her refusal to return to Brandfort, the government amended her banning order to allow her to stay anywhere in South

Africa except in the Johannesburg and Roodeport magisterial districts. She defied the order, and the police tried several times to forcibly remove her, but she always returned. Eventually, in February 1986, the authorities provisionally withdrew their charges. Advised by her lawyers that her banning order was invalid, she had been speaking out in public gatherings, and in July 1986 her restrictions were officially lifted.

Winnie Mandela moved out of her Orlando home and into a large newly built house in an exclusive area of Soweto. She became a controversial figure in Soweto, and in 1988 other anti-apartheid groups took steps to distance themselves from Mandela. Much of the problem surrounded the so-called Mandela United Football Club, a group of young men who lived in Mandela's house and acted as her bodyguards. Many members of the club were implicated in robberies, assaults, and murders in the Soweto area, and the club was despised by neighbors of Mandela, who accused the young men of intimidation and extortion.

The most serious development came when two members of the club were charged by police in the killing of 14-year-old renegade Stompie Moeketsi, an extraordinary young leader whose 1,500-member "children's army" had opposed the tactics of oppressive groups like the football club for years. Mandela claimed that the charges were lies made up by the police, and that Stompie had died of beatings and sexual abuse incurred at the Methodist church he had been hiding out in.

Nevertheless, Mandela's bodyguards came under suspicion in two other murders, and South Africa's two largest organizations, the Congress of South African Trade Unions and the banned United Democratic Front, both made formal statements condemning Mandela and her entourage and distancing themselves from Mandela. Embarrassed, even the ANC stepped up its pressure to have the football club dismantled and, after discussions with her husband, Mandela announced that the bodyguards would be removed from her home. By that point, however, Mandela's once lofty reputation in the eyes of her people had been somewhat tarnished.

In mid-1988, Nelson Mandela was transferred to a private clinic from his jail cell at Pollsmoor Prison in Cape Town. He is reported to be ill with tuberculosis, and there is speculation that he may be released in the near future.

Sources

Books

Benson, Mary, *Nelson Mandela: The Man and the Movement*, Norton, 1986.

Mandela, Winnie, *Part of My Soul Went With Him*, edited by Anne Benjamin, Rowohlt Taschenbuch Verlag, 1984, English translation, Norton, 1985.

Periodicals

Chicago Tribune, October 16, 1983.

Christian Science Monitor, December 9, 1985.

Ebony, December, 1985.

Ms., November, 1985; January 1987.

Newsweek, December 16, 1985; December 30, 1985.

New York Times, August 18, 1985.

People, September 28, 1987.

Washington Post, August 26, 1985; September 23, 1985; December 24, 1985; May 12, 1985.

—Sidelights by Virginia Curtin Knight

Hamish Maxwell

AP/Wide World Photos

Holding company executive

Born 1926, in England; son of Sir Alexander Maxwell (a tobacco-leaf dealer); married; wife's name, Georgene. *Education:* Cambridge University, B.A. in history, 1949.

Addresses: *Home*—Brooklyn, N.Y. *Office*—Philip Morris Companies, Inc., 120 Park Ave., New York, N.Y. 10017.

Career

Thomas Cook Sons & Co. (travel agents), New York City, salesman, 1949–54; Philip Morris, Inc., New York City, salesman in Richmond, Va., 1954–69, vice-president, 1969–76, senior vice-president, 1976–78, executive vice-president, 1978–83, president and chief operating officer, 1983–84, chairman and chief executive officer, 1984–85; Philip Morris International, advertising director, 1961–63, vice-president of marketing, 1963–65, regional vice-president for Asia and Pacific region, 1965–73, executive vice-president for Canada, Asia, and Pacific regions, 1973–75, executive vice-president for Canada, Asia, Pacific, Europe, and Middle East regions, 1975–78, president and chief executive officer, 1978–84; Philip Morris Companies, Inc. (holding company for Philip Morris, Inc., and Philip Morris International), New York City, president and chief executive officer, 1983–84, chairman and chief executive officer, 1984—.

Sidelights

As chief executive of a corporation ranked tenth in size among American industrials by *Fortune* magazine, and one widely admired for its management quality, Hamish Maxwell has overseen the diversification of cigarette-maker Philip Morris into America's largest consumer packaged goods concern. During his tenure the company has made some of the most important takeovers of the decade, acquiring General Foods in 1985 and Kraft in 1988. What had been a $13.8 billion tobacco and beer concern became, in just four years, a $42 billion diversified food, beverage and tobacco conglomerate.

The dapper, British-born and Cambridge-educated executive is redefining the company in a world where its main product, the cigarette, is increasingly shunned as a health menace. Recognizing this, Maxwell has broadened the company's product line enormously while continuing to build foreign sales and solidifying popular support through sponsorship of art activities and civic causes. Maxwell, who invariably poses for photographs with lit cigarette in hand, has emerged as the most felicitous spokesman for smoker's rights. "Of course, we're concerned about smoking and health and public perception of the issue," he told *Fortune* magazine in January 1989.

"But I have no feelings of guilt, no trouble sleeping at night. There was a time when people thought drinking was much worse a sin than smoking. Both can be abused, but each gives pleasure and has social value."

"Of course, we're concerned about smoking and health and public perception of the issue. But I have no feelings of guilt, no trouble sleeping at night."

The company's fortunes even today remain closely entwined with those of its signature product, Marlboro cigarettes. Marlboro is today the biggest-selling cigarette in the world, and industry insiders give Maxwell much of the credit. Two decades ago, Maxwell used savvy marketing to expand Marlboro from its niche as an American women's cigarette into one smoked by men and women from Berlin to Tokyo. The Marlboro man's cowboy cool became that rare commodity in international business, the truly international brand symbol.

Despite its success in international marketing, Philip Morris's corporate strategy has been diversification. Maxwell, since he became chairman and chief executive officer in July 1984, has planned and implemented that strategy, in the process acquiring the manufacturers of such products as Miller beer, 7-Up, Jello, and Velveeta cheese. He has won widespread admiration for doing this without resorting to the much-maligned financing tool of the eighties, the leveraged buy-out, in which a company is bought and systemically dismantled to pay debt incurred by the deal. He has also smoothed the way for a good fit between Philip Morris and the companies he has bought, keeping the best managers and minimizing transitional strife. "Any acquisition requires a lot of work, after the fact, trying to make sure you get the full benefits of it," he explained to Fortune. "I'm inclined to think, after experience with smaller ones as well as General Foods, that the management task is somewhat less with bigger acquisitions than a series of smaller ones."

Management experts credit Maxwell with taking a sophisticated approach to handling the problems attendant in corporate expansion through acquisition. In May 1989, *Business Month* called Maxwell's recent deals "two of the the quickest, slickest mega-mergers on record. The ease with which these multi-billion dollar deals were accomplished is a credit to Philip Morris's management under Maxwell. He took over a company whose big-league marketing reputation had been tarnished by missteps in its soft-drink and beer divisions and moved decisively to restore confidence among investors, customers and employees."

Maxwell had only recently taken over the management reins at Philip Morris before he was knee-deep in engineering two of the biggest corporate acquisitions of the decade. The 1985 friendly buyout of General Foods for $5.7 billion established the tobacco concern as America's biggest consumer packaged goods concern. The 1988 hostile takeover of Kraft for $13 billion doubled the size of Philip Morris's food business and displaced Unilever N.V., a Dutch firm, as the world's largest consumer goods concern. Even before the Kraft deal, Philip Morris had become the nation's biggest advertiser, nudging aside Procter & Gamble.

"Philip Morris is . . . widely acknowledged to be one of the best-run corporations in America—lean, cocky . . . and immensely profitable."
—L.J. Davis

Although sales of Marlboro account for fully one quarter of all cigarette sales internationally, Maxwell has chosen to broaden the company's product line as a hedge against the shrinking U.S. cigarette market. "People may ultimately stop drinking or smoking, though I don't believe it, but you can bet your life they will keep eating," Maxwell told the *Wall Street Journal* as he prepared to close the Kraft deal in October 1988. "We can't bet our future on the success of, say, Jell-O. We need more than that. Very few food companies have just one enormous product like a Marlboro or even a Miller Lite."

Maxwell, who represents the fourth generation of his family to prosper in the tobacco industry, has gone about expanding Philip Morris using traditional financial strategies. The cash-rich company has found investment bankers virtually pushing their way through his door to lend capital. When the Kraft deal was imminent, Maxwell's financial staff was able to arrange $10 billion financing on 24-hours notice from a consortium of 64 banks, 21 of them European and seven Japanese. "For any company to raise more than $10 billion at a moment's notice is a fairly astonishing performance," stated L.J. Davis in a corporate profile published in the *New York Times Magazine.* "But Philip Morris is not just any company. It is widely-acknowledged to be one of the best-run corporations in America—lean, cocky (some would say arrogant) and immensely profitable."

Yet not every deal showed a Midas touch. General Foods was widely regarded as a lumbering behemoth, and even under Maxwell some opportunities have slipped by. Colin Leinster, a *Business Week* associate editor, describes General Foods' success under Philip Morris as "lackluster at best; other food companies are probably twice as profitable." There have been earlier gambles that failed. Maxwell, in one of his first major moves as chief executive, was forced to sell 7-Up; acquired in 1978, the soda subsidiary was sold in 1986 after it failed to keep up with Pepsi and Coke in restaurant and dispenser sales. More satisfying to Maxwell has been the performance of Miller beer. The brewery was seventh-ranked in sales in the U.S. when Philip Morris bought it in 1970, and Maxwell and others brought it to second rank behind industry leader Anheuser-Busch. Nevertheless, Miller's growth seems to have stalled, and a new $450 million brewery had to be shut down—a major embarrassment.

While Maxwell's corporate shopping expeditions have made him a headliner, it was his earlier accomplishments as a young corporate fast tracker that originally gained him a reputation as a go-getter. From 1968 on, he spearheaded the company's all-out international expansion, in effect globalizing the Marlboro man into a symbol without international boundaries. Much of Maxwell's attentions as chief executive have been on the world market, where the company's fortunes ultimately rest.

The dapper tobacco mogul was born into the business. The only son of a Sir Alexander Maxwell, a third-generation London tobacco-leaf dealer of Scottish nationality, Maxwell served in the Royal Air Force 1944 through 1947, and returned to study history at Cambridge. In 1949, intent on seeing the world, the recent graduate emigrated to the United States and took a job selling tours for Thomas Cook in New York City. The job proved a dead end in all respects but one: he met his future wife, Georgene, a receptionist at Cook. Prodded by his fiancee, who insisted he find a better job before the marriage, he approached Alfred Lyon, then head of Philip Morris. Family connections helped, he acknowledges, but did not spare him the mandatory from-the-ground-up process of corporate training. Philip Morris sent him to Richmond, Va., where he sold cigarettes.

The following year he transferred to the market research department at corporate headquarters in New York. In 1956 he joined the corporate advertising department and in 1961 transferred over to the international division and became advertising director. It was at Philip Morris International that he hit his full stride. He became a vice-president in two years, taking on full marketing responsibilities. In 1965 he was elected executive vice-president for Canadian, Asian and Pacific markets. Based in Australia through 1974, he laid the foundation for the company's presence in Asia, the fastest-growing tobacco market in the world. In 1975 he added Europe, the Mideast, and Africa to his bailiwick. He told *Business Week,* "The international business was Philip Morris's first and, to some extent, most successful diversification."

His international savvy has paid off many times over for his employer. In 1981, when archrival R.J. Reynolds (now RJR Nabisco) was on the verge of acquiring Rothmans, the British cigarette concern, Maxwell hopped a plane and spoiled the deal by smooth-talking a major shareholder into dissenting. A source told *Fortune* magazine's Alan Farnham that Maxwell "snatched the deal out of Reynolds's briefcase."

Hamish Maxwell was elected Chairman of the Board and chief executive officer by the Board of Directors of Philip Morris Companies Inc. on July 1, 1984. A director of the corporation since 1974, he had served as president and chief operating officer since December 1983. As chief executive, Maxwell's style could be characterized as aloof affability, or dour gregariousness. *Business Week*'s Amy Duncan described him as "a private man with a low-key style and a soothing voice." An account in *Fortune* found him "studious and dour." Philip Morris director Margaret B. Young elaborated in that profile that Maxwell "likes the kind of joke you have to think about—playful, ironic, something with a twist to it."

A strong believer in corporate philanthropy, Maxwell presides over a charitable donations budget of approximately $13 million. The company's giving record has emphasized the arts but has also showered its bounty on a variety of grassroots civic organizations. Recipients include the Brooklyn Academy of Music, the Metropolitan Museum, the American Crafts Museum, the Dance Theatre of Harlem, and the Whitney Museum. When the New York Public

Library needed money for basic custodial services, it got a million dollar grant earmarked for dusting. Checks go out to special interest and grassroots groups across the country, ranging from the Urban League to local volunteer ambulance squads. Critics point out a dark side to the company's role as cultural benefactor. Mike Synar, an Oklahoma congressman and a leader of Capitol Hill's anti-smoking forces, has complained that Philip Morris leverages its philanthropy by creating a pro-tobacco lobby among recipients of its largess, ranging from rodeo workers to local arts organizers.

Outside his corporate role, Maxwell remains a confirmed globe-hopper. Every other year he and his wife join three other couples on exotic vacations. There have been tours of India, safaris in Kenya, boating the Nile, canoeing down Idaho rivers, and sailing off the coast of Turkey. Maxwell the traveller is, by one account, much like Maxwell the manager: no crisis phases him. "I've seen him lose his clothes [at airport baggage belts] but never his aplomb," Dow Jones chairman Warren Phillips quipped to *Fortune*'s Alan Farnham.

Paid $1.3 million a year in salary and benefits, the executive is said to have kept the common touch: he shops for his own groceries, and puts his own products on the table at home, including Jell-O pudding pops, Miller beer, and Oscar Mayer bologna. "It's hard to emphasize how down-to-earth this guy is. He has a humanity that most CEOs lose," Philip Morris director Jane Evans told *Fortune*'s Alan Farnham. Maxwell and his wife, nicknamed GeeGee, live in Brooklyn Heights just outside Manhattan. They often attend arts events sponsored by Philip Morris.

Sources

Business Month, May, 1989.
Business Week, August 8, 1988; October 21, 1988; October 31, 1988.
Forbes, May 30, 1988.
Fortune, August 3, 1987; January 2, 1989; May 8, 1989.
New York Times, April 9, 1989.
Wall Street Journal, October 19, 1989.

—Sidelights by Warren Strugatch

Bobby McFerrin

AP/Wide World Photos

Singer, songwriter, and musician

Born March 11, 1950, in New York, N.Y.; son of Robert (an opera singer) and Sara (an opera singer and educator) McFerrin; married Debbie Lynn Green; children: Taylor, Jevon. *Education:* Attended Sacramento State University and Cerritos College.

Addresses: *Home*—San Francisco, Calif.

Career

Pianist with lounge bands and with the Ice Follies; singer, 1977—.

Awards: Two Grammy Awards, 1986, for "Another Night in Tunisia," on album *Vocalese* by Manhattan Transfer; Grammy Award, 1987, for Best Male Jazz Vocalist, for "'Round Midnight."

Sidelights

In Germany they call him *Stimmwunder* (wonder voice), in America Bobby McFerrin is considered the most innovative jazz vocalist to emerge in twenty years. Singing solo and a cappella, he uses his four-octave voice to "play" a variety of instruments—such as the guitar, the trumpet, and the drums. "I like to think of my voice as being my body," he told Micheal Bourne in *down beat.* "That's my equipment." A triple Grammy winner, McFerrin recently topped the popular-music charts with his single "Don't Worry, Be Happy."

The son of opera singers (his father was the first black man to perform regularly with the Metropolitan Opera), McFerrin was born in New York City. In 1958 his family moved to Los Angeles. McFerrin attended Sacramento State University and Cerritos College but dropped out to play piano for the Ice Follies. Over the next few years, he played keyboard with lounge acts and for dance troupes. In 1977 McFerrin decided, suddenly, to become a singer. "I was in a quiet moment when a simple thought just came into my head: 'Why don't you sing?' It was as simple as that, but it must have had some force behind it because I acted on it immediately," he explained to Bourne. He sang with various bands and was eventually discovered by singer Jon Hendricks. While on tour with Hendricks, McFerrin was again discovered—this time by comedian Bill Cosby.

Through Cosby, McFerrin was booked in Las Vegas and at the Playboy Jazz Festival in Los Angeles. He later performed at New York's Kool Jazz Festival and began touring or recording with such jazz greats as George Benson and Herbie Hancock. In 1982 he released his first album, *Bobby McFerrin.* His fans were disappointed. "He sang with some of his vocal pyrotechnics fully alight," *Horizon*'s Leslie Gourse wrote, "but he had loud electronic instrumental accompaniment that essentially was pop." McFerrin learned from his mistake; and his next effort, *The Voice,* was widely praised. Recorded live during a solo concert tour of Germany, the album is all a cappella and displays the singer's virtuosity. "McFerrin coaxes up a daffy assortment of vocal effects and characterizations on *The Voice*," Francis Davis noted in *Rolling Stone*. "His circular breathing technique enables him to sing while inhaling and exhaling, thus allowing him to be his own background choir on 'Blackbird' and 'T. J.' He slaps himself into a percussive frenzy on 'I Feel Good' and creates the sound of static between frequencies on 'I'm My Own Walkman.'"

McFerrin's later works have also been well received. Of *Spontaneous Inventions* Susan Katz of *Newsweek* wrote: "[It] shows off his ability to Ping-Pong between sweet falsetto melody and what sounds like a walking-bass accompaniment. . . . McFerrin delivers a cappella improvisations on everything from Bach to 'The Beverly Hillbillies' theme song." Similarly, his more recent album, *Simple Pleasures*, contains versions of old pop and rock tunes, such as "Good Lovin'," "Suzie Q," and "Sunshine of Your Love." *Interview*'s Glenn O'Brien found that "the way he does these near chestnuts makes them new and restores the power that made them parts of your memory banks in the first place." So far, the album has sold over one million copies; and one of its tracks, "Don't Worry, Be Happy," has become a hit single.

McFerrin has received three Grammy Awards, two for his work on "Another Night in Tunisia," recorded by Manhattan Transfer. His third, as Best Male Jazz Vocalist, was for "'Round Midnight," the title song of the 1986 movie. McFerrin has also recorded the theme for "The Cosby Show" and the soundtrack for "Just So," an animated series of specials that aired on cable television. He has appeared on "The Tonight Show" and "Sesame Street," and he provides the vocals for Levi's commercials. McFerrin tours extensively as well. During his concerts, he often improvises his material. Spontaneity is an important part of McFerrin's music. "I like being an improviser, expecting the unexpected," he told Bourne. "Even when something is rehearsed, I want it to be spontaneous."

Discography

Bobby McFerrin, Elektra Musician, 1982.
The Voice, Elektra Musician, 1984.
Spontaneous Inventions, Blue Note, 1986.
Simple Pleasures, EMI Manhattan Records, 1988.

Sources

Christian Science Monitor, April 17, 1987.
Down Beat, May, 1985.
Horizon, July/August, 1987.
Interview, August, 1988.
Newsweek, October 6, 1986.
New York Times, November 20, 1987.
People, September 21, 1987.
Rolling Stone, March 28, 1985.
Time, October 17, 1988.

—Sketch by Denise Wiloch

Kelly McGillis

UPI/Bettmann Newsphotos

Actress

Born 1957, in Newport, Calif.; daughter of a physician; married c. 1979 (divorced, c. 1982). *Education:* Left high school at age sixteen; studied acting at Pacific Conservatory of Performing Arts, 1975–78, and at Juilliard School, 1979–83.

Addresses: *Home*—Brooklyn, N.Y. *Office*—c/o Paramount Pictures Corp., 1 Gulf + Western Plaza, New York, N.Y. 10023.

Career

While studying acting, worked as a waitress and had a job at a plastics factory; feature films include "Reuben, Reuben," 1983, "Witness," 1985, "Top Gun," 1986, "Made in Heaven," 1987, "The House on Carroll Street," 1987, "Dreamers," 1988, "The Accused," 1988, and "The Winter People," 1989; stage roles include "Peccadillo," 1985, and "A Seagull," 1985-86; has appeared on television in several daytime serials and in a made-for-television movie.

Sidelights

"I'm not your classic beauty," actress Kelly McGillis told Paul Attanasio of the *Washington Post.* Yet she's been compared to a list of captivating film stars that includes Grace Kelly and Lauren Bacall. McGillis's friend Don Yesso pointed out other qualities in *People.* She's "strong-headed, smart and very special," he said. She has also developed a reputation as hard-working and extremely talented actress who is rapidly becoming one of Hollywood's hottest box-office attractions.

One of McGillis's most challenging roles to date is in "The Accused," in which she co-stars with Jodie Foster. The screenplay, written by Tom Toper and directed by Jonathan Kaplan, is about a young waitress named Sarah Tobias who is gang-raped in a bar while onlookers cheer on the three rapists rather than attempt to rescue the victim. McGillis plays Katherine Murphy, the assistant district attorney who prosecutes the case. Filmed in Vancouver, Washington (although set in Seattle), the story recalls an actual 1983 case in New Bedford, Massachusetts, in which a woman was raped by several men in a bar while people watched but didn't help. "The Accused" uses material from a mixture of other actual rape cases as well. The film is particularly controversial, pointed out Kathy Huffhines in the *Detroit Free Press,* because of the excruciatingly realistic rape scene at the end and its portrayal of the insensitivity of many of the male characters. Producers Sherry Lansing and Stanley Jaffe, who made "Fatal Attraction," wanted to convey three messages. The first was that no means no, despite provocation of *any* kind; the second was that rape is *not* sexy; and the third was that bystanders do have a responsibility toward the victim. Rape centers strongly supported the film, many acting as consultants.

In the beginning of the story, the rapists get off with the lesser charge of reckless endangerment. This is because there was a strong case against Sarah for having allegedly "provoked" her attackers. But Sarah convinces Katherine that she must reopen the case; that the men got off far too easily for such a heinous crime. Originally, McGillis was asked to play the part of Sarah. But in 1982 she had been brutalized and raped by two men in her Brooklyn apartment, and she felt the role of rape victim would dredge up too many memories. As she told *People,* "The pain doesn't ever go away."

The parts played by McGillis and Foster complement each other in "The Accused." McGillis as the self-controlled prosecuting attorney forms a stark contrast to Foster's vulnerable, less stable Sarah. Peter Travers noted in *People* that McGillis "brings ringing conviction to her role." But in *Maclean's,* Brian D. Johnson saw Katherine as a weak point of the film, the character being too "stiffly rendered." Off the screen, Foster and McGillis became friends. They went on a promotion tour together through six cities before "The Accused" opened at 800 cinemas. "She's very professional and that's the key to my heart," McGillis said of Foster in *Interview.* "I'm not into games and ego padding and neither is Jodie," she told Dan Yakir. "There was an immediate closeness between us."

While "The Accused" is an adult melodrama that explores a serious social issue, McGillis's previous movie, "Top Gun," is an action film geared toward teens. In the words of *Chicago Tribune* critic Gene Siskel, the latter is "a rousing, at times dazzling, extended music video that celebrates the guts and glory of becoming a Navy jet pilot." In this film, McGillis plays a civilian astrophysicist, Charlotte ("Charlie") Blackwood. When Charlie walks into a bar frequented by the cream of the Navy's crop of fighter pilots, "Maverick" tries to pick her up. Played by star Tom Cruise, Maverick starts crooning "You've Lost That Lovin' Feeling," and his cohorts join in. Then Charlie quips that it's a good thing Maverick doesn't depend on singing for his living. At this point, Maverick isn't aware that Charlie is a Top Gun instructor.

As might be expected, Maverick becomes one of Charlie's star pupils. He is an adventurous individualist who takes exhilarating (some say foolhardy) risks in the air. Teacher and student fall in love, but not until Charlie "engages Tom Cruise in solemn banter about thrust ratios," as David Denby put it in *New York.* Sharing her opinion of Cruise with *USA Weekend,* McGillis noted that not only is her "Top-Gun" co-star "intelligent, talented and understanding," he's also "a hunk." But she put an end to rumors that the two were having a romantic liaison off screen. McGillis did live with another actor from the film, however: Barry Tubb, who played one of Maverick's fellow fighter pilots.

Before doing "Top Gun," McGillis starred in the critically acclaimed thriller "Witness," which marked a turning point in her career. She had been supporting herself by waiting on tables when director Peter Weir spotted her. He offered McGillis the part of Amish widow Rachel Lapp but then had to wait with her co-star, Harrison Ford, until she was done with her shift. To better understand her character, McGillis immersed herself in Amish society. She stayed at the farm of a true Amish widow who had seven children. There she adopted the family routine by waking up at 4 A.M. to milk the cows and shovel manure. She stopped for breakfast at 7 A.M., then it was off again to clean the barn or plant rows of potatoes or perhaps plow the fields. The afternoons were for recuperating from the dramatic change from twentieth-century life to that of the more physically demanding eighteenth-century rural existence still preserved by the gentle Amish. McGillis took her research further by taping the local dialect, ostensibly while listening to cassettes on her Walkman. She also attended church services that were held in Amish homes, and she read her books by candlelight, because the Amish eschew the use of electricity. As McGillis told *Newsweek,* these people maintain "a wonderful, nonaggressive, nonagitating society."

In "Witness," Rachel and her young son, Samuel, are in a Philadelphia train station waiting to return to Lancaster County, Pennsylvania, after visiting a relative. Samuel, played by Lukas Haas, watches as a city policeman murders a fellow member of the force in the bathroom. Harrison Ford plays the part of John Book, himself a policeman who's life is threatened as he becomes aware of the complexity of the crime and the identity of the murderer. The screenplay "brings together the scuzzy, violent, urban world of narcotics, murder, and crooked cops and the pastoral, time-warped world of the Amish," explained Jack Kroll in *Newsweek.* Russian ballet dancer Alexander Godunov is creatively cast as an Amish farmer in love with Rachel. But it is the cop from Philadelphia whom Rachel cares for; and he for her. The two "court with their eyes—McGillis's work is highly controlled, conflict playing across her large, fine features," observed Pooley in *New York.*

The movie became a box-office hit. Critics generally acclaimed McGillis's Rachel. "Her incandescent performance alerted a wide audience to the wonders of Kelly McGillis," wrote Richard David Story in *USA Weekend*. And *Newsweek*'s Jack Kroll went on to say, "In her severe Amish dress she has the solidity and sensuality of a Frans Hals portrait."

McGillis was first discovered by Phil Epstein for his father Julius's screenplay "Reuben, Reuben." She was cast as Geneva, a vivacious undergraduate in a small New England town, where she encounters a fortyish, burned-out Scottish poet, played by Tom Conti, who has a penchant for women and booze. After years of writer's block, he feels ready to take up the pen again thanks to Geneva's spirit and zest.

Still a senior at Juilliard at the time, McGillis learned her part well. She is "entirely competent in the role, and her personal effect is like a shower of gold," wrote Stanley Kaufmann in *New Republic*. She studied in New York during the week, then flew to North Carolina to do the movie on weekends. *Newsweek* said, "Despite this tough schedule, McGillis made a potent impression in the film." Then, when "Reuben, Reuben" was over, McGillis went back to waitressing.

In-between "Top Gun" and "The Accused," McGillis had major roles in three other films. The first was "Made in Heaven," directed by Alan Rudolph, with Timothy Hutton as the male lead. In this fantasy, two souls fall in love while they're in heaven. The plot takes off when both are suddenly sent to Earth. In *Interview*, McGillis described working with Hutton: "He always kept me on my toes with the choices that he made—they could be very spontaneous and unusual, which is very hard for me."

The second film, "The House on Carroll Street," is a Peter Yates thriller set in the 1950s. Here McGillis plays a picture editor for *Life* magazine who lives in Greenwich Village. The woman finds out that Nazi war criminals are being handed new identities in the United States thanks to a corrupt senator. She becomes blacklisted for involvement in an ACLU-like organization; Jeff Daniels is an FBI agent who tails her. McGillis explained to *Interview:* "My character is very positive in that innocent kind of way people had in the 1950s. She has strong ideals and beliefs."

"Dreamers," directed by Peter Yates, is the third of these films. It's about a feminist Viennese doctor, McGillis's character, who travels to a pre-Israeli kibbutz with Eastern European Jews in the 1920s. The woman is a Zionist from an upper-class family. As a pioneer in forming the state of Israel, she works the land along with her idealistic friends, all the while undergoing a major transformation of her own. "I loved working with [McGillis]," Yates said in *Time*.

McGillis has worked in other productions as well. For example, she toured with Christopher Plummer in the Garson Kanin play "Peddacillo." She also appeared on stage in "A Seagull" at the Kennedy Center's American National Theater. And she narrated the sound-track recording of the television special "Santabear's First Christmas." In addition, she appeared in several daytime dramas and a made-for-television movie earlier in her career.

"So far, I'm very happy with my choices. I don't want a career where I do the same kind of movie and play the same kind of person all the time."

McGillis grew up in an upper-middle-class home in Newport, California, where her father was a doctor. She was tall even at thirteen (she's 5 feet 10 inches tall now), and because she looked older than her age, she found it natural to hang around with a more mature crowd. Before long she was skipping school and going to the beach, drinking, and experimenting with drugs. "I was crazy and very rebellious," she told an interviewer from *Playboy*. During her teens, McGillis also battled a weight problem. At one point she weighed 190 pounds. She candidly observed in *Playboy* that she'd gotten "really ugly and fat" and felt like a "terrible social outcast." But by the time she reached eighteen she had slimmed down dramatically. McGillis quit school and left home at the age of sixteen. She paid her bills by waitressing and working in a Styrofoam factory. And she attended the Pacific Conservatory of Performing Arts in Santa Monica, California, from 1975 to 1978. The following year she entered the prestigious Juilliard School in New York City, where she studied acting for four years.

This independence of spirit is evident in McGillis's choice of film roles. She has appeared in a wide variety of movies, playing a diverse assortment of characters, and has thus avoided the kind of typecasting that often negatively affects acting careers. As she told *Interview:* "So far, I'm very happy with my choices. I don't want a career where I do the same kind of movie and play the same kind of person all the time. Why should you put yourself in a position of doing, say, only socially relevant pictures? I just want to do as many different kinds of movies, plays, readings, and paintings as I can. I'm only here once and I want to have a hell of a good time."

Sources

America, November 12, 1988.
American Film, June, 1986.
Chicago Tribune, May 11, 1986.
Interview, October, 1987.
Maclean's, October 24, 1988.
New Republic, January 30, 1984; November 21, 1988.
Newsweek, February 11, 1985; March 11, 1985.
New York, May 19, 1986.
New Yorker, June 16, 1986.
New York Times, October 14, 1988; October 16, 1988.
People, December 6, 1984; October 24, 1988; November 14, 1988.
Playboy, November, 1987.
USA Weekend, May 23–25, 1986.

—Sidelights by Victoria France Charabati

David McTaggart

UPI/Bettmann Newsphotos

Environmental activist

Born c. 1932, in Vancouver, British Columbia, Canada; little has been reported about his private life; he comes from a prominent Vancouver family, was a Canadian badminton champion, and became interested in environmental issues as a young boy when he was able to observe whales from his family's summer home on a bay.

Addresses: *Home*—Stockholm, Sweden. *Office*—Greenpeace International, Temple House, 25-26 High Street, Lewes BN1 2LU, United Kingdom.

Career

Began working in construction business, 1950; founded his own construction company, 1954; construction and development company executive, 1954–68; member, Greenpeace, 1972—; chairman of the board, Greenpeace International, 1979—.

Sidelights

As part of a kind of global environmental police force, the tenacious, idealistic members of Greenpeace International have in recent years garnered growing worldwide support for their ambitious cause: the creation of a more peaceful and ecologically balanced earth. By practicing their unique brand of protest—something they refer to as "nonviolent direct action"—Greenpeace workers have focused the attentions of the world's environmentalists and, perhaps more importantly, the international press, on those individuals, businesses, and governments they have targeted as the principal environmental menaces throughout the world. With equal parts intelligence and daring, Greenpeace members have confronted huge commercial whaling ships in small, highly mobile boats and placed themselves between the whales and the ships' deadly harpoons; rendered the coats of baby harp seals unsalable by painting them green to prevent their slaughter; parachuted from smokestacks to protest acid rain; and plugged the drainpipes of countless factories releasing toxic wastes into lakes and streams.

As a charter member and principal guiding force of Greenpeace since 1973 and the group's first and only elected chairman since 1979, David McTaggart has patiently and masterfully paced Greenpeace's growth since its days as a small, loosely based group of Canadian environmentalists. As a child he had grown up reveling in the wilderness surrounding his native Vancouver and he had often watched whales. When he was 21 he founded his own construction firm, designing villages and ski lodges that lived in harmony with the environment. Later, as he rose to vice-president of a large development corporation, a gas explosion at a ski resort in his charge shattered McTaggart's career. "My stride had been broken," he told *Oceans* magazine. "I decided the hell with it. In the end, I got tired of the coldbloodedness of the business."

With what little cash he had left after the accident, McTaggart decided to live out a fantasy and bought a 38-foot ketch, the *Vega,* and set out to sea, wandering from port to port. In 1973 he saw a small item in a New Zealand newspaper about a group named Greenpeace, which was protesting French nuclear testing in the South Pacific. Partly for the adventure, McTaggart decided to lead the protest by sailing his yacht into the restricted test zone, which had been set up in international waters. When the *Vega* wandered within sight of the balloon that was to drop the bomb, the boat was rammed by a French minesweeper and removed from the area. The following year McTaggart returned to the same test site near the atoll Mururoa. This time French security forces boarded his yacht. "They beat me up," he told the *New York Times.* "I was blinded in one eye for a long time. I went back to Canada and sued the French government." At the same time publicity mounted over the French nuclear tests, which were finally discontinued when New Zealand began patrolling the waters. Soon, McTaggart was receiving donations from people all over the world. He set up a chain-letter system to organize his support and the formation of Greenpeace International had begun.

Under McTaggart's leadership, the organization has grown steadily into a network of chapters in 17 countries, with 250 paid staffers and 1.5 million contributing members. Greenpeace's operating budget for 1988 was approximately $14 million, with most of the money coming in $5 and $10 donations and rarely exceeding $1,000. Paid staff members, many of them highly educated and science oriented, work for half the pay they could earn outside the organization. While money is clearly not what Greenpeace workers are after, neither are they operating on a naive idealism commonly associated with other peace groups. "We want to draw attention to something," McTaggart told the *New York Times,* "and we know what our plan is years in advance. It's easy to say, 'I want to clean the whole world up,' but all our goals are just possible and can be got to."

While Greenpeace has become highly visible through its media-conscious publicity stunts and dramatic confrontations, the group has become more sophisticated in its intelligence gathering, taking advantage, particularly, of the of the United States Freedom of Information Act. "We use action," said McTaggart in the *New York Times,* "and once there's attention, we move into lobbying." Greenpeace lobbying efforts were instrumental in pressuring the International Whaling Commission to vote a moratorium on commercial whaling ("Man doesn't need to kill whales, period," McTaggart told *Oceans*), though Japan and Norway have ignored the deadline. Greenpeace has also helped to reduce the slaughter of harp seal pups by 90 percent and has established a permanent base in Antarctica, declared a "world park" by the group, to keep an eye on increased oil exploration there.

Greenpeace and McTaggart have been particularly annoying to the French government. After McTaggart's two famous run-ins with the French in the 1970s, Greenpeace provoked another international scandal in 1986 when their flagship, the *Rainbow Warrior,* was sunk by French secret service agents during a protest of underground nuclear tests at Mururoa. A photographer was killed in the incident, and the publicity forced Francois Mitterand's defense minister to resign. Perhaps more importantly, the affair served as a poignant illustration of the power that can be wielded by a small but committed group of individuals such as Greenpeace. Recalling his first confrontation with the French in 1972, McTaggart saw it as the seed to everything he has done since. "There was an image of a big nuclear bomb and a little wooden boat," he told the *New York Times.* "You can talk of Gandhi and all that. But if you can see this huge steel navy grinding along, a little piece of sand can get caught in the machinery and bring it to a halt. Our philosophy is to put yourself between the problem in a nonviolent way."

Sources

Macleans, September 16, 1985.
New York Times, September 2, 1984.
Oceans, June, 1987.

—Sketch by David Collins

George Michael

AP/Wide World Photos

Singer, composer, and producer

Name originally Georgios Kyriakou Panayiotou; born June 25, 1963, in London, England; son of Jack (a restaurant owner) and Lesley Panayiotou. *Education:* Left school at age sixteen to pursue a career in music.

Addresses: *Home*—London, England; and France. *Office*—c/o Columbia Records, 1801 Century Park W., Los Angeles, Calif. 90067.

Career

Member of group the Executive, 1979-80; worked at odd jobs while composing songs and working on music, 1980-82; member (with Andrew Ridgeley) of duo Wham!, 1982-86; solo performer, 1984—.

Awards: Grammy Award nomination (with Andrew Ridgeley) for best pop performance by a duo, 1985, for "Wake Me Up Before You Go-Go"; American Video Award (with Ridgeley) for best new video artists, 1985; Igor Novello Award for best songwriter, from British Academy of Songwriters, Composers, and Authors, 1985; Grammy Award (with Aretha Franklin) for best rhythm and blues performance by a duo, 1987, for single "I Knew You Were Waiting (For Me)"; MTV Music Award for best direction, 1988, for video of single "Faith"; Grammy Award for album of the year, 1988, for *Faith;* American Music Awards for best pop male vocalist, best soul/rhythm and blues vocalist, and best soul/rhythm and blues album, all 1989, for *Faith.*

Sidelights

Nineteen eighty-eight proved a banner year for British singer George Michael—sales of his critically acclaimed *Faith* album topped 20 million worldwide, the album generated a record six number-one singles, and the pop star played to sell-out crowds in stadiums all over the world. He topped this success in early 1989, winning a Grammy Award for Album of the Year by beating out such esteemed competition as Tracy Chapman and Bobby McFerrin. Michael rose to stardom through a calculated path that began with his partnership in the pop duo Wham! The group achieved fame and success with their light, upbeat music and tanned, carefree, pretty-boy image, exemplified in songs like their breakthrough hit "Wake Me Up Before You Go-Go."

After appearing on the British pop scene in 1983, Michael and his partner, long-time friend Andrew Ridgeley, suddenly found themselves the focus of intense media and popular attention. Under the spotlight as lead singer, Michael became, as he has frequently described it, "a sex symbol to thousands of virgins." But the rising pressures of fame and the deepening limitations of Wham!'s style led Michael to leave the group in order to prove himself as a musician and composer. With the serious songs of passion and commitment on his solo album, *Faith,* Michael has demonstrated that he is not just a sex symbol, he is a singing and song-writing force to be reckoned with in the pop world.

Being a sex symbol was the furthest thing from his mind, however, when Michael first met Wham! partner Ridgeley at the age of eleven in a London area school. Ridgeley was stylish, popular, and self-confident, while the then Georgios Panayiotou was shy, pudgy, and bespectacled. "His clothes were always perfect, he was really stylish, all the girls liked him," Michael said of Ridgeley in a *Rolling Stone* interview with Steve Pond. "And that was something that I always wanted to be, because I was such a mess to look at. The whole idea of being a physically attractive personality never really occurred to me until I met him." Despite their superficial differences, the two had a love of pop music in common and formed a fast friendship. Ridgeley recalled to Pond that "George was incredibly consumed by music, and I think it was my desire to entertain and his desire to write that really brought the whole thing together." "Andrew and I," Michael continued, "in a sense, totally changed each other. I suppose we spent all that time aspiring to be different parts of each other."

Michael and Ridgeley spent hours together getting involved in the latest British dance and music crazes, including "mod," "soul boy," and "ska." Although his father, a Greek-Cypriot immigrant, "wanted me to go into something very stable, like the legal profession," Michael was set on a musical career, he related to *Rolling Stone* reporter David Fricke. "By the time I was eight or nine, I knew what I wanted to do. And I basically argued with him about it for the next eight years." Michael and Ridgeley dropped out of school, and after dabbling briefly with a band called the Executive, made their first demo tape at age 17. Including the songs "Wham! Rap," from which they took their name, and "Careless Whisper," the tape earned them a contract with the CBS-distributed Innervision label. When their first album, *Fantastic,* appeared six months later, Wham! became an overnight sensation in Britain, generating four hit singles from the album. Their success gave Michael and Ridgeley leverage to renegotiate a new, more lucrative contract with CBS.

Wham!'s approach to success was calculated from the very beginning, for Michael and Ridgeley paired a stylish, happy-go-lucky image with slick, catchy pop tunes deliberately crafted to resemble the Motown hits of the sixties. "The time was right to strike home with Sixties escapism," Michael told Fricke. "Sixties presentation, Sixties attitude towards the songs. That's what made us big. Basically, we made everything look wonderful. Wham! was a Sixties pop group in the Eighties." The formula worked once again for the duo's second collection, 1984's *Make It Big,* which became a number-one album on the U.S. charts and spawned hits like "Wake Me Up Before You Go-Go" and "Careless Whisper." But along with the group's success came rumors of difficulties between the two members.

> *"I totally threw away my personal credibility for a year-and-a-half to make sure my music got into people's homes."*

The whispers of unrest were generated from the observation that Michael was doing most of the work on Wham!'s albums—singing, songwriting, and co-producing. Other hints came when "Careless Whisper" was released as a George Michael single—not a Wham! work—outside of the United States. Michael and Ridgeley insisted that the obvious imbalance in their roles was not causing problems. "We never lied to anybody about it," Michael told Fricke. "What people wouldn't accept was that Wham! was a vehicle, a successful image—two kids who strike it lucky.... It was working for both of us. It was no con." Wham! continued their collaboration, compiling a third album, *Music from the Edge of Heaven,* and embarking on a much publicized and precedent-setting tour of mainland China, the first Western group ever to do so. But in 1986, while Wham! was still at the top with two more hit singles and a sold-out performance at London's Wembley Stadium, Michael announced that he was leaving the group.

Increasing pressures from Wham!'s popularity and a soured relationship with a long-time girlfriend contributed to Michael's defection. As he told Pond, "The actual Wham! split was definitely provoked by my emotional distress around that period. It's hard to tell whether or not it would have happened at that time had it not been for that relationship failing. Maybe if I'd felt more secure," he continued, "I would have felt no need to shake things up. But at the time I just wanted to make a clean start." "I'm not very good at being a pop star in broad daylight," Michael recalled to Fricke. "When people started expecting it twenty-four hours a day, it became very stressful to me. That's when I'd say to Andrew, 'I can't see this going on forever.' And he never gave me the impression that I had any obligation to continue." In addition, Michael felt the need to break out of the lightweight, prettyboy image imposed by Wham!'s style.

Michael was now directing his own business affairs, for he had left the management firm of Napier-Bell & Summers when he learned of their plans to sell to a company with South African ties. Even though he had separated from Wham!, Michael realized he would have to work hard to combat the public's perception of him. The singer had already changed his physical image, allowing his hair to return to its original dark color and maintaining a two-day beard, but knew he still had a rough task ahead of him: "I totally threw away my personal credibility for a year-and-a-half to make sure my music got into people's homes," he told Jon Bowermaster in the *Chicago Tribune.* "It was a calculated risk and I knew I would have to fight my way back from it. I did it out of choice."

"People want to be able to hear something and like it instantly, and those are the type of songs I write....I don't have to make it sound like a pop record. It just comes naturally."

Nevertheless, Michael admits that "musically I don't think it held me back one bit.... It's one thing to have to fight for your credibility from a position of success. It's another to have to fight for both credibility *and* success from nowhere. So I don't find this a difficult position at all." As part of this effort to change his image and move to a sexier, funkier sound, Michael decided to record a duet with the Queen of Soul, Aretha Franklin. The ensuing collaboration, "I Knew You Were Waiting (For Me)," hit number one world-wide and earned Michael a Grammy Award in 1987, for best rhythm and blues performance by a duo. But Michael still needed to prove his worth throughout a whole album, and fans and critics alike awaited his first solo effort, *Faith.*

If Michael had wanted to overcome the Wham! image of lightweight, nonthreatening "sexual virginity," he couldn't have done better than the early release of the single "I Want Your Sex." Containing lyrics such as "Sex is natural, sex is good/ Not everybody does it/ But everybody should," the song immediately raised a storm of controversy over its content, even though Michael claimed that the song was about monogamous sex. British stations restricted it to nighttime play, and close to 30 percent of American radio stations banned the song entirely. Nevertheless, the record rocketed to number one, and set the stage for the release of the "new" George Michael's first solo album.

When *Faith* finally appeared in November of 1987, its eclectic mix of pop styles forced Michael-watchers to reassess him as a singer and songwriter. As he related to Bowermaster: "I knew this album would be a shock or a surprise to people in this country. The uptempo side of the new music is more overtly sexual, more black," an observation upheld by *Faith*'s position as the first album by a white solo artist to top *Billboard*'s black music charts—an achievement Michael called a "highlight" of his career. "The other side is based on the fact that my strongest songs are ballads," he added. "The album is more adult, more representative of my feelings than most of the Wham! material."

Many critics agreed with Michael's appraisal of *Faith;* the *New York Times*'s Stephen Holden commented that the album "demonstrates that Mr. Michael's stylistic range and skill at integrating invented new sounds into strong, well-shaped tunes is unequaled by any young pop craftsman with the possible exception of Prince. And while Mr. Michael's more conventional songs bespeak a chilly, premeditated commerciality, there are ample signs on 'Faith' that as a songwriter he has only begun exploring his own artistic potential." Mark Coleman similarly observed in his *Rolling Stone* review that "with this album, George finally proves once and for all that he's no mere genius chart hack.... One of Michael's secret weapons is his knowledge that the power and eloquence of soul music come from singing what you feel." The critic continued: "As *Faith* proves, he's got the equipment to render some relatively complex feelings." Michael was pleased with such vindications of his efforts. "I think it says something for the power of the music that I've managed to change the perception of what I do to the degree that I have in this short a time," he told Pond. "Because it's something that a lot of people though wasn't possible."

Michael also recognizes that it has been "a stroke of luck that what I like to do musically relates to an awful lot of people," as he remarked to Bowermaster.

And he explained to *People* writer Todd Gold: "People want to be able to hear something and like it instantly, and those are the type of songs I write.... All my life has been spent listening intensely to chart music. The structures that people feel comfortable with are the ones that come to mind. So when I'm writing, I don't have to make it sound like a pop record. It just comes naturally." It is this instinctive talent for finding the right melody that has led critics like Holden to name Michael "the most talented heir to the tradition of pop craft that embraces Paul McCartney, Elton John and the Bee Gees."

Michael also believes, as he told Pond, that he's "already regarded as one of the main pop writers for the Eighties." So what does a twenty-six-year-old writer, performer, and producer of hot hit records do for an encore? "I want to be regarded as [a main pop writer] through the Nineties and do something to carry on, something that's really memorable, so the music becomes historical. I think that my music deserves it." But Michael has other goals beyond his musical aspirations, goals perhaps more related to a young man's search for identity. "I still need challenges, apart from the main challenge of just writing better music," he revealed to Bowermaster. "Being successful has to be something you earn, and my challenge now is to have my music heard above people's perceptions of me. So this is a new beginning, this is a new me."

Discography

Solo

Faith, Columbia, 1987.

Also released single "I Knew You Were Waiting (For Me)," with Aretha Franklin, 1987.

With Wham!

Fantastic, Innervision, 1982.
Make It Big, Columbia, 1984.
Music from the Edge of Heaven, Columbia, 1985.

Sources

Books

Crocker, Chris, *Wham!*, Simon & Schuster, 1985.

Periodicals

Chicago Tribune, September 4, 1988.
New York Times, May 29, 1988.
New York Times Magazine, June 22, 1986.
People, September 23, 1985; March 10, 1986.
Rolling Stone, November 20, 1986; January 14, 1988; January 28, 1988.

—*Sketch by Diane Telgen*

Bette Midler

Reuters/Bettmann Newsphotos

Actress and singer

Born December 1, 1945, in Honolulu, Hawaii; daughter of Fred (a house painter) and Ruth Midler; married Martin von Haselberg (a commodities trader and performance artist), December 1984; children: Sophie. *Education:* Attended University of Hawaii.

Addresses: *Office*—c/o Kathy Acquavna, Atlantic Records, 75 Rockefeller Plaza, New York, N.Y. 10019. *Agent*—Rick Nicita, Creative Artists Agency, 1888 Century Park East, Suite 1400, Los Angeles, Calif. 90067.

Career

Actress in films, including "Hawaii," 1966, "The Rose," 1979, "Divine Madness," 1980, "Jinxed," 1982, "Down and Out in Beverly Hills," 1986, "Ruthless People," 1986, "Outrageous Fortune," 1987, "Big Business," 1988, and "Beaches," 1988; performer in stage shows, including "Fiddler on the Roof," 1966–69, "Salvation," 1970, "Tommy," 1971, and "Clams on the Half Shell Revue," 1973–74; singer and comedienne in nightclubs and concert halls, beginning at the Continental Baths in New York City, 1970; recording artist; television appearances include "The Tonight Show" and the NBC special "Bette Midler: Old Red Hair Is Back," 1978. Partner in All Girl Productions movie production company.

Awards: *After Dark* Ruby Award, 1973; Grammy Award for best new artist, 1973, and for best pop vocal performance by a female, 1980; Antoinette Perry Award, 1973; Emmy Award for outstanding special, 1978, for "Bette Midler: Old Red Hair Is Back"; Academy Award nomination for best actress, 1979, for "The Rose."

Sidelights

Bette Midler's show business career has been one of remarkable variety. Although she became famous in the early 1970s as "The Divine Miss M.," a powerful singer with a raunchy sense of humor, she has most recently acted as the savior of the ailing Walt Disney Studios, for whom she made a series of hugely successful family comedies. Between those two extremes, Midler endured a period of personal and professional difficulties that left her virtually unemployed. Considering her career as a whole, *Time*'s Richard Corliss asserts that Midler is "the most dynamic and poignant singer-actress of her time."

Midler was born in Honolulu, Hawaii, where her father painted houses for the U.S. Navy. Ruth Midler named her daughter after her favorite actress, Bette Davis, whose name she mistakenly believed was pronounced "bet." Bette and her three siblings grew up in rural Aiea, living in subsidized housing in the middle of sugarcane fields and feeling out of place as the only Jews in a community of Chinese, Japanese, Samoans, and Hawaiians. At an early age, Bette's alienation and loneliness translated itself into a powerful desire to perform. In the first grade, she won an award for her rendition of "Silent Night." "After that you couldn't stop me from singing," she recalled in *Time.* "I'd sing *Lullaby of Broadway* at the top of my lungs in the tin shower—it had really good reverb. People used to gather outside to call up requests or yell that I was lousy." Midler's father, a strict man who flushed the girls' makeup down the toilet and locked his eldest daughter out of the house if she missed her curfew, disapproved of Bette's ambitions, but his wife was encouraging. She sent her daughters to hula lessons and shared with them her great love of musicals.

Midler attended a stage show, "Carousel," for the first time when she was twelve years old. "I couldn't get over how beautiful it was," she remembered in *Time.* "I fell so in love with it. Everything else in my life receded once I discovered theatre, and my mother was all for my starting on this journey and going full-speed ahead." Her father remained skeptical even after his daughter became world-famous, however: "He never chose to see me perform—except on Johnny Carson," Midler admitted. "He said I looked like a loose woman."

After a year at the University of Hawaii, Midler quit school to dedicate herself to drama. Her first professional job came in 1965, when she played the bit part of a missionary's seasick wife in the film adaptation of James Michener's novel *Hawaii.* When the production company returned to Hollywood to complete the movie, Midler went with them. She hoarded her weekly salary until shooting was complete, then headed for New York City. There, she worked variously as a hat-check girl, typist, go-go girl, and sales clerk while expanding her theatrical range with work in children's theatre, revues in the Catskills, and experimental plays. In 1966 she landed a part in the chorus of "Fiddler on the Roof." Shortly thereafter she graduated to the part of Tzeitel, Tevye's eldest daughter, which she played for the next three years.

During her stint with "Fiddler," Midler met two men who profoundly influenced her career. One was Ben Gillespie, a fellow cast member, who introduced her to soul and r&b music. Midler referred to him as her "mentor" in a *Rolling Stone* interview with Nancy Collins, explaining: "He opened up the world for me.... He taught me about music and dance and drama and poetry and light and color and sound and movement.... I never lost the lessons he taught me." The other influential man in her life at this time was Tom Eyen, author of offbeat plays such as "Sarah B. Divine!" and "Who Killed My Bald Sister Sophie?" He began casting Midler in the dizzy bimbo leads of his productions and gave her a sense of camp. She cultivated a retro-chic look created from thrift-shop clothes from the 1930s and worked up a repertoire of songs from the past, which she performed at any club that would have her. The best known was the Improvisation, where aspiring stars often went to be discovered. Here Midler's unique blend of humor and song began to gel. She reminisced in *Time:* "In my velvet dress with my hair pulled back and my eyelashes waxed, I was convinced I was a torch singer. Because the Improv was a comedy club, you had to be a little bit funny, so I added chatter between songs. There I was, singing my ballads and crying the mascara off my eyes, and in the next breath I'd be telling whatever lame joke I'd just heard."

In 1969, Midler left "Fiddler on the Roof," only to find she was unable to get another Broadway job. For about a year, she devoted herself to psychoanalysis sessions, singing lessons, and acting lessons at the Berghof Studio. Her acting coach told her that the Continental Baths, a public bathhouse catering to gay men, was looking for weekend entertainment. Midler landed the $50-a-night job and began rehearsing with her pianist and arranger, Barry Manilow. Performing at the Baths forced her to expand her material and set her more firmly on the road to comedy, she stated in *Time:* "By the time I got to the Baths, I had 20 minutes of material but needed 50. So I had to wing it. The Baths was gay, gay, gay in a heartfelt way. The guys would check their clothes, get towels, and sit on the floor. They thought my show was *fab*-ulous. So eventually the big brassy broad beat the crap out of the little torch singer and took over." Her attention-getting outfits ranged from a simple ensemble of wedgies, a bath towel, and a flower for her hair to rhinestone girdles, glittery strapless tops, and sequinned gowns. Her repertoire came to include bawdy jokes, novelty songs, blues, and rock. "I was able to take chances on that stage that I could never have taken anywhere else," she wrote in her book *A View from a Broad.* "The more outrageous I was, the more they liked it. It loosened me up."

"The Divine Miss M.," as Midler now billed herself, was emerging as "one of the first—and few—distinctive personalities of the Seventies," according to *Rolling Stone* contributor Nancy Collins. Word quickly spread about this exciting new performer, and soon the Baths were flooded with people from all walks of life wanting to see the woman whose motto was "Flash with class and sleaze with ease." Offers came pouring in from big nightclubs, television, and record companies. Midler's career was given an additional boost from the shrewd business sense of Aaron Russo, who became her manager in 1971. Their eight-year alliance, which was both personal and professional, was stormy but productive. "Aaron began booking me in theatres," Midler noted in *Time*, "and lo and behold, I was a big success." Her material had to be toned down for mainstream audiences but retained its bite, and the first album sold over 100,000 copies in the month after its release. She showed her usual irreverence during her 1972 New Years Eve performance at the Lincoln Center, where she rose from the stage clad only in a diaper and a vinyl sash marked "1973."

Exhausted by the hectic pace of her initial success, Midler stopped working for several months, then came back strong with a record-breaking Broadway show, "Clams on the Half Shell Revue." Richard Corliss commented on the physicality of her style, which was evident in this show: "As chanteuse or bawd, . . . Midler has put her body to non-stop work. Harnessing the energy of some Rube Goldberg perpetual-motion machine, prancing on those fine filly legs like the winner of the strumpet's marathon, Bette uses her body as an inexhaustible source of sight gags." Of her singing, he stated, "Her phrasings were as witty as Streisand's, her dredgings of a tormented soul as profound as Aretha's, her range wider than all comers'." Midler's next challenge was a major film role. She and Russo selected "The Rose," a serious script about a self-destructive rock star modeled on Janis Jopin. "The picture did good business, I got fabulous reviews, I was nominated for an Oscar," Midler told Cathleen McGuigan in *Newsweek.* "But the fact is that *I never got another offer.* I died. I was devastated. I really felt I had been shut out." Marjorie Rosen speculated in *Ms.* that perhaps "no one could separate the real Bette from her boozy screen heroine, so convincing was her performance."

Other failures followed: "Divine Madness," a concert film that was panned by both critics and audiences, and "Jinxed," a black comedy notable mainly for the vicious power struggle that took place between Midler, her co-star Ken Wahl, and director Don Siegel. "*Jinxed* was the worst working experience of my life," Midler told Collins. "I wanted to make the best movie I could, but not everyone felt that way. And they resented me because I did." Siegel and Wahl put out the word that Midler was impossible to work with, and she entered a prolonged depression, turning to psychotherapy to restore her shattered self-confidence. She continued to make recordings and to do concert tours, but her career seemed hopelessly stalled.

"I couldn't face the world," Midler told *Time.* "I slept all day and cried all night. I was drinking to excess—I was miserable." Just as she reached her lowest ebb, however, Midler got a phone call from Martin von Haselberg, a commodities trader who occasionally went onstage as Harry Kipper, one-half of a bizarre performance-art duo known as the Kipper Kids. He and Midler had met briefly some time earlier, but in October 1984 they began an intense relationship that culminated two months later in an impromptu Las Vegas wedding ceremony, conducted by an Elvis impersonator. Von Haselberg helped Midler to revitalize her personal and professional lives. "He asked what I really wanted to do," she told *Time.* "Singing? Comedy? I realized I didn't care that much about singing anymore. Nobody else seemed to like it either. But I knew they liked it when I was funny."

"I realized I didn't care that much about singing anymore. Nobody else seemed to like it either. But I knew they liked it when I was funny."

It was about this time that Midler signed a contract with Touchstone Films, a new division of Walt Disney Studios. Disney hoped to find its way out of serious financial trouble by releasing films through Touchstone that were more sophisticated and adult-oriented than the studio's traditional fare. The decision to hire Midler was made in part because her career problems meant she could be hired relatively cheaply. She turned out four comedies in quick succession: "Down and Out in Beverly Hills," a comedy about the nouveau riche; "Ruthless People," in which she played a wealthy kidnap victim whose husband refuses to pay her ransom; "Outrageous Fortune," which teamed her shrill, vulgar character with a prim Shelley Long; and "Big Business," in which she and Lily Tomlin portrayed sets of identical twins separated at birth. The films proved very popular, all grossing over $60 million, and were largely responsible for Touchstone's becoming the most powerful studio in Hollywood. Corrigan notes that these roles "do not stretch Bette; they shrink her to farce-sized roles." Midler joked about the formulaic quality of the Touchstone comedies—"Was it *Outrageous Ruthless People in Beverly Hills?*"—but voiced no real complaints in *Time,* explaining: "I'm too happy that anybody noticed I had any talent at all." She concluded: "The whole package is a surprise: to be a box-office success hand in hand with Disney.... I mean, Walt Disney *never* would have hired me."

The star's fifth film for Touchstone, "Beaches," was a more serious look at two women from radically different backgrounds and their evolving friendship. Rosen reported in *Ms.* that "critics have panned *Beaches* for its unabashed sentimentality, [but] the picture—very much in the fashion of *Love Story* and *The Way We Were,* other soap operas about doomed love, transcends critical objections quite simply because of Bette. For the first time on-screen we're treated to the full force of her personality—the comedienne, the chanteuse, the romantic leading lady." Considering Midler's body of work for Touchstone, Rosen wrote: "Has Bette embraced stardom at the expense of those qualities that made her unique? Certainly, if you look at her Disney characters... she seems to have temporarily hung up her naughty alter ego. Yet witness the 'Otto Titsling' number in *Beaches,* a lewd ditty concerning the invention of the brassiere. Co-written by Bette... it is reassurance, after all, that Miss M. is still alive, even if a shadow of her former self." Corliss concurred: "Fettered Bette is better than no Bette at all."

Writings

A View from a Broad, Simon & Schuster, 1980.

The Saga of Baby Divine, Crown, 1983.

Discography

The Divine Miss M, 1972.
Bette Midler, 1973.
Broken Blossom, 1977.
Live at Last, 1977.
Thighs and Whispers, 1979.
New Depression, 1979.
Divine Madness, 1980.
No Frills, 1984.
Mud Will Be Flung Tonight, 1985.

Sources

After Dark, May 1971.
Detroit News, January 31, 1986.
Ms., March, 1989.
National Observer, March 2, 1973.
New Republic, August 2, 1975.
Newsday, July 9, 1970; August 6, 1972.
Newsweek, May 22, 1972; June 30, 1986; January 26, 1987.
New Yorker, June 27, 1988.
New York Sunday News, February 20, 1972.
New York Times, December 3, 1972; December 29, 1972; January 14, 1973.
People, November 14, 1983; February 3, 1986.
Rolling Stone, December 9, 1982.
Savvy, July, 1988.
Time, March 2, 1987.

—Sketch by Joan Goldsworthy

George J. Mitchell

Reuters/Bettmann Newsphotos

U.S. senator from Maine

Full name, George John Mitchell; born August 20, 1933, in Waterville, Me.; son of George J. (a janitor) and Mary (a textile worker; maiden name, Saad) Mitchell; married Sally Heath, 1959 (divorced); children: Andrea. *Education:* Bowdoin College, B.A., 1954; Georgetown University, LL.B., 1960. *Politics:* Democrat.

Addresses: *Office*—176 Russell Senate Office Bldg., Washington, D.C. 20510.

Career

Admitted to Bar of the State of Maine, 1960, and District of Columbia, 1960; trial attorney for U.S. Department of Justice, 1960–62; executive assistant to Senator Edmund Muskie (D-Me.), 1962–65, campaign aide, 1968, 1971–72; partner in law firm Jensen & Baird, Portland, Me., 1964–77; assistant attorney for Cumberland County, Me., 1971; U.S. attorney for Maine, 1977–79; U.S. district judge, Maine, 1979–80; U.S. senator from Maine, 1980—; senate majority leader, 1988—. Chairman of Maine Democratic Committee, 1966–68; national committeeman from Maine, 1968–77. *Military service:* U.S. Army, 1954–56; served as counterintelligence officer in Germany.

Sidelights

George J. Mitchell became one of the most powerful political figures in America late in 1988. The owlish but droll Mitchell, a traditional liberal and articulate debater, was elected by fellow Democrats to serve as majority leader of the U.S. Senate. The move gives Mitchell the platform to lead the attack on a range of issues he feels strongly about, particularly the environment.

Senate Democrats chose Mitchell to replace West Virginia's Robert Byrd as their leader because of his diligence, his willingness to take on tough assignments, his ability to work with people of differing points of view, and—perhaps most important of all—his talent as a speechmaker. He earned the admiration of his colleagues when as chairman of the Democratic Senate Campaign Committee he worked as a tough political infighter and helped sweep the Democrats back into majority control of the Senate in 1986. And he received national attention as a leading participant in the deliberations of the Iran-Contra committee in 1987. "George Mitchell is a class act—bright, tough and very partisan," Senate Republican whip Richard Cheney of Wyoming told the *Phoenix Gazette.* "He's going to be difficult for us to deal with."

For his part, Mitchell entered 1989 vowing to work hand-in-hand with incoming President George Bush. In his first major speech on the Senate floor, he echoed pleas for bipartisanship made by Bush in his inaugural address. And he advised senators not to seek old ideas to current problems. "We enter a new era," he said. "The New Deal and the Reagan reaction to it are over. We face new circumstances." Mitchell says his low-key approach has made him more effective. But while Mitchell's style has helped him gain esteem among colleagues, it also kept him one of the Senate's more anonymous members during his first eight years in office. "No one tells funny stories or colorful anecdotes about George J. Mitchell," wrote the *Boston Globe*'s Chris Black. "It is not his style to be quotable or controversial. In fact, characteristics attributed to [Mitchell] read like a chapter from a Boy Scout manual: Prepared, honest, compassionate, bright, conscientious, loyal, cautious, curious. They are also traits some critics say really add up to bland, stiff and colorless."

Unlike many of his Senate colleagues, Mitchell rose rapidly in politics without the help of wealth or family reputation. He was born in the textile town of Waterville, Me., the fourth of five children. His mother, a Lebanese immigrant, worked the night shift as a weaver in a woolen mill. His Irish father was raised in a Catholic orphanage in Boston until an elderly couple adopted him and brought him to Maine. He worked as a janitor. "My parents both in their lifetimes acquired a real reverence for this country, having seen the opportunities it presented to people like themselves," Mitchell told the *Boston Globe*. "My father had an absolute belief in the importance of education and the ability of one with education to do anything he or she wanted in America."

Mitchell's three older brothers became basketball legends in Maine, leading Waterville High to two consecutive New England championships. George, however, was no athletic star. Instead, he read and he read, starting with comic books and graduating to history texts. His father insisted that George read the newspaper every day to the rest of the family and also work on his public speaking. "George was always the bookworm," older brother John (Swisher) Mitchell told the *Boston Globe*. "My father insisted that he study a lot. The rest of us were shooting hoops, but George was always the scholastic type." Mitchell skipped a grade and finished high school at the age of 16. He then worked his way through Bowdoin College, graduating at the age of 20.

After a stint in the intelligence division of the U.S. Army in Germany, he moved to Washington to attend Georgetown University Law School at night while working as an insurance adjuster. In 1960, he joined the Justice Department as a trial lawyer in the antitrust division. "He worked for [then-Attorney General] Bobby Kennedy and I think he was really inspired by the Kennedy aura of the time," brother John Mitchell told the *Boston Globe*. "It was a time when young people wanted to do something to make a difference." Two years later, Mitchell learned of a vacancy on the Washington staff of U.S. Senator Edmund Muskie of Maine. Muskie knew the Mitchell name well because of the family's basketball feats. He hired the 27-year-old attorney and became his mentor. Soon, Mitchell became a top aide, researching bills and proposing ideas.

"We enter a new era. The New Deal and the Reagan reaction to it are over. We face new circumstances."

In 1964, Mitchell returned to Maine to establish a private law practice. But he took a leave from his law firm in 1968, 1971, and 1972 to be deputy campaign manager on Muskie's vice-presidential and presidential campaigns. Also in 1972, Mitchell ran for chairman of the Democratic National Committee, narrowly losing to Robert Strauss of Texas. Mitchell briefly served as Maine's Democratic chairman and ran for the governorship in 1974. He was leading in the polls until the day before the election, but an independent candidate, James B. Longley, was gaining on him. Muskie advised Mitchell to go on the attack, "but he didn't want to rock the boat, he was ahead in the polls. I thought he was too cautious," Muskie told the *Los Angeles Times*. In a stunning upset, Longley beat Mitchell.

The election of President Jimmy Carter in 1976 gave Mitchell new political life. With Muskie's backing, he was appointed in 1977 as U.S. attorney for Maine. During a two-year tenure, Mitchell successfully prosecuted child pornography peddlers, marijuana smugglers and antique thieves. In 1979, again through Muskie's urging, Carter named Mitchell to the newly created federal judgeship in Maine's first circuit. Just five months later, when Muskie resigned from the Senate to become secretary of state under Carter, Muskie recommended Mitchell to fill the Senate vacancy.

Initially, most of Maine's political observers expected Mitchell just to keep the Senate seat warm until a stronger candidate could be found. Entering the 1982 race, Mitchell was regarded as a prohibitive underdog against Republican Congressman David Emery—indeed, at one point, Emery held a 36-point lead in the polls. But Mitchell focused on environmental issues and the Reagan Administration's handling of natural resources. Emery made some foolish errors during the campaign, and Mitchell wound up garnering 61 percent of the vote to win a full term. He won a second full term in 1988 with a full 81 percent of the vote—the largest margin of any incumbent that year.

Evaluating Mitchell's success, Washington lawyer and former Muskie staffer Eliot Cutler told the *Boston Globe:* "In many respects, he is a later version of Ed Muskie without the temper. He doesn't have the charisma, the forceful personality. But in many other respects, in terms of the thoroughness, the priorities, he is very similar to Muskie." In his first nine years in the Senate, Mitchell compiled a largely liberal voting record and became a champion of the environment—especially in the battle against acid rain—and was an early and outspoken critic of the Reagan Administration environmental policies. As chairman of the Finance Committee's health panel, he was an advocate of a major long-term health-care plan. He tried without success to increase tax rates for the wealthiest taxpayers in the nation. On the Veterans Affairs Committee, Mitchell backed successful 1984 legislation to help Vietnam veterans cope with diseases believed to be caused by exposure to the herbicide Agent Orange.

Mitchell first began to gain prominence among fellow senators as chairman in 1986 of the Democratic Senatorial Campaign Committee. He steered thousands of dollars into Senate campaigns, helped 11 new Democratic senators get elected, and put the Democrats back in the majority for the first time since 1980. His reward: instant influence and clout on the Democratic side of the aisle and appointment as the Senate's deputy president pro tempore, a largely honorary post but an important mark of the high regard of Democratic senators.

Mitchell first reached a national audience during the Senate's 1987 Iran-Contra Committee hearings when he bucked a tide of sympathy for Lieutenant Colonel Oliver North [see index for *Newsmakers* entry]. After North appealed for congressional aid to the Contras "for the love of God and the love of country." Democrats turned to Mitchell to explain their side of the story. "Although He's regularly asked to do so," Mitchell admonished the young Marine, "God does not take sides in American politics. Please remember that it is possible for an American to disagree with you on aid to the Contras, and still love God, and still love this country, just as much as you do. In America, disagreement with the policies of the government is not evidence of lack of patriotism." In his address to North and the public watching on television, Mitchell invoked the memory of his immigrant mother and laborer father and the emotions he said he felt when, as a federal judge, he conferred citizenship on immigrants. He told North that when he asked new immigrants why they wished to live in the United States, many of them said the reason was that "in America, you can criticize the government without looking over your shoulder." That's what democracy is all about, the senator said, "the freedom to disagree with the government."

After the hearings, Mitchell co-authored a book with Senator William S. Cohen (R-Me.) about the Iran-Contra investigation entitled *Men of Zeal.* The book took a long look at, among other issues, then Vice-President Bush's role in the arms-for-hostages deal, concluding that, "The vice president endorsed the weapons sale to Iran either out of loyalty to the President or because he, too, was consumed by the passion to obtain the freedom of the hostages."

For Mitchell, the Iran-Contra hearings represented his debut on the national scene. Just one year later, Senate Democrats chose him to set that chamber's agenda during the 101st Congress. Mitchell defeated two more-senior colleagues—Senators Daniel Inouye of Hawaii and J. Bennett Johnston of Louisiana—to gain the majority leader post. He won despite common belief that Inouye was Senator Byrd's hand-picked successor and despite a campaign on Johnston's behalf by Senator Lloyd Bentsen, who had gained considerable power as a result of his vice-presidential candidacy. Johnston had promoted himself as the kind of Southern conservative the party needs to prosper.

Mitchell's voting record shows him to be a traditional liberal who, more often than not, votes with the majority of his party. Senator Edward Kennedy of Massachusetts told the *Los Angeles Times* that Mitchell's election was "a welcome signal that the liberal and progressive ideals of the Democratic Party have broad support among Senate Democrats from all parts of the country." For his part, Mitchell told the *San Jose Mercury News* that he planned to share his authority with colleagues, saying, "I do not intend to be a one-man band." And he said he was not interested in needless confrontation with President Bush, telling *Newsday,* "My view is that we should cooperate to the fullest extent possible, beginning with the budget and trade deficits." Senator Joseph

Biden [see index for *Newsmakers* entry], a Delaware Democrat, told *Newsday:* "He's not going to embarrass the opposition. George Mitchell is a consensus builder."

In January 1989, in his first speech to the Senate as its majority leader, Mitchell again vowed to work with President Bush and declared an end to both Democrat Franklin Roosevelt's New Deal policies and those of Republican Ronald Reagan. He signaled that bipartisan foreign policy, needed to respond to challenges put forth by Soviet leader Mikhail Gorbachev, will surface only if Bush pursues "meaningful consultation with Congress. Like other policies, bipartisanship begins with words. But it cannot be made real by words alone, or by good intentions. It requires deeds to match words, action to carry out intention. Bipartisanship draws from shared responsibility."

Writings

Men of Zeal (with William Cohen), Viking, 1988.

Sources

American Spectator, January, 1989.
Arizona Republic, November 30, 1988; January 26, 1989.
Boston Globe, May 16, 1980; November 30, 1988.
Business Week, November 7, 1988.
Chicago Tribune, December 22, 1988.
Economist, September 24, 1988; December 3, 1988.
Los Angeles Times, November 30, 1988.
Newsday, November 30, 1988.
Philadelphia Daily News, November 30, 1988.
Phoenix Gazette, January 2, 1989.
San Jose Mercury News, November 30, 1988.
Washington Post, September 9, 1988.

—*Sketch by Glen Macnow*

Marvin Mitchelson

UPI/Bettmann Newsphotos

Attorney

Full name, Marvin Morris Mitchelson; born May 7, 1928, in Detroit, Mich.; son of Herbert (a building contractor) and Sonia Mitchelson; married Marcella Ferri, December 19, 1961; children: Morgan. *Education:* University of California, Los Angeles, B.A., 1953; Southwestern University, J.D., 1956.

Addresses: *Home*—Hollywood, Calif. *Office*—1801 Century Park E., Los Angeles, Calif. 90067.

Career

Admitted to Bar of State of California, 1957, and U.S. Supreme Court, 1962; engaged in private practice of law in Beverly Hills, Calif., 1957–67, and Century City, Calif., 1967—. Has made numerous appearances as an expert on family law on national television, and has lectured to bar associations and law schools. Member of board of directors, Los Angeles Music Center Opera Association. *Military service:* U.S. Navy, 1946–47; served as medical corpsman.

Member: American Bar Association, American Trial Lawyers Association, Trial Lawyers of America, California Trial Lawyers Association, Century City Bar Association.

Sidelights

No trial attorney has generated more publicity—for his clients and himself—than Marvin Mitchelson, the flamboyant Los Angeles divorce lawyer. Mitchelson has been handling celebrity divorce cases since 1964, and his client list reads like a Who's Who of the Hollywood and jet-set glitterati. At one time or another, he has represented Sonny Bono, Carl Sagan, Joan Collins, Zsa Zsa Gabor, Tony Curtis, and Robin Givens; but his most famous case—the "palimony" suit brought against actor Lee Marvin by his live-in lover—made Mitchelson a national figure while striking a blow for women's rights. According to Ted Rohrlich in the *Los Angeles Times,* Mitchelson "is as well known for his dramatic flair and courtship of the media as for his legal victories." Indeed, the attorney's notoriety now rivals that of his movie star clients, and some of the publicity has been decidedly negative. In a *Los Angeles Times* profile, Ann Louise Bardach observed that those who know Mitchelson well "are surprised that his troubles didn't swallow him some time ago. Mitchelson, they say, has been crumbling before their eyes for a long, long time."

Mitchelson himself completely discounts any notion that his career is in jeopardy—even in the midst of allegations of misappropriation of funds, mismanagement of fees and overcharging, and even rape. "I think people who don't know me think less of me reputationwise," he told *Rolling Stone.* "But as soon as I get in their courtroom, I think they're surprised for the better. They think I'm not that good until they see me." Critics have been forced to admit that

Mitchelson has a courtroom manner that brings in victory after victory. Robert Ross, an associate since 1972, told the *Los Angeles Times* that Mitchelson has a less-than-encyclopedic knowledge of the law in terms of education and training, but that he succeeds anyway. "Marvin is not a book-wise lawyer, he's a street-wise one," Ross said. "No one can charm a jury like Marvin." Bardach wrote: "Mitchelson's methods and successes propelled him into the front ranks of divorce attorneys throughout the late '60s and '70s. His proximity to scandal, newsworthy clients, big-money settlements and his own antics also made him a media darling."

Bardach called Mitchelson's life story "the stuff of Hollywood fable: An ambitious young man from a poor family learns early on that he too can be rich and famous by riding the coattails of the rich and famous." Marvin Mitchelson was born in Detroit to Russian immigrant parents who arrived in America almost penniless. The youngest of three children, he was taken to California at the age of two—his parents moved there to be near a polio clinic treating their daughter. Mitchelson remembers his parents as extremely hard-working. "They knew what deprivation was," he told *Rolling Stone*. [My father] would buy a house, fix it up and sell it. They fought for every penny." When Mitchelson was eighteen his father died of a sudden heart attack. His mother somehow managed to make ends meet and support him through school at the University of California, Los Angeles, and then at Southwestern University School of Law. Mitchelson passed the California Bar examination on his second try and began a private practice in Los Angeles.

"I started out alone, and I had been kind of a mediocre student," Mitchelson told *Rolling Stone*. "I passed the bar, but I didn't have a Harvard degree, and I wasn't the highest in my class. I got a job as a process server, and the last paper I served was on Joan Collins. It was her first divorce.... Anyway, when I started out I had my own practice. I had this little office on Beverly Drive for $100 a month and I took every case I could get. I worked night and day. The first fee I ever got was from this waitress who asked if I'd help her on a case. She worked at this bar up the street on Sunset that I used to hang out in, and she'd been arrested on a bad-check charge. I said, 'Sure, I'll do it.' She writes me a check. I went all the way home and showed it to my mother. I said, 'Look, Mom, it's my first case.' She asked what kind of case it was and I told her. She said, 'You took a check on a bad-check case? Go back and get cash.' So I went all the way back, and the waitress gave me a hundred-dollar bill. I ran home and gave it to my mother." Mitchelson did not remain long in such modest circumstances. In 1963 he became involved with a controversial case, *People vs. Douglas*, that established the right to free legal representation for indigent people charged with crimes. The case made its way to the Supreme Court and helped to create the *Miranda* decision that substantially improved the rights of those charged with crimes. "Through all those strings of cases, I paved my way to Washington," Mitchelson told *Rolling Stone*. "It was a 'cause' case, and God, does it feel great to stand in front of the Supreme Court and argue a case."

In 1964 Mitchelson was offered the first of his celebrity divorce cases. He represented Pamela Mason, wife of British actor James Mason, in an adultery suit. Mrs. Mason was asking for one million dollars—a staggering settlement by the standards of that day. Mitchelson began playing hard ball with Mason's attorneys, issuing 43 subpoenas and threatening to disclose depositions describing Mason's private sexual encounters. Bardach wrote: "Terrified, the actor settled his divorce out of court for $2 million and put Marvin Mitchelson on the map." Mitchelson quickly became known as a tough bargainer who was not above leaking scandalous tidbits to the press when it served his client to do so. To quote Bardach, he "cultivated his image as a lovable bad boy, with the media's cooperation."

Mitchelson seemed the perfect attorney for Michelle Triola Marvin, who enlisted his services in the early 1970s. The young actress had given up her career to become the live-in mistress of Lee Marvin, and when he left her she sought financial support similar to alimony. Mitchelson spent seven years preparing the case. The trial itself lasted eleven weeks and won Martin's companion $104,000. And although the award was overturned on appeal, the case resulted in new laws in California and elsewhere, recognizing the right of unmarried partners to sue for "palimony"—a term Mitchelson himself coined.

Mitchelson told *Rolling Stone* why he took the Marvin case, even though he did not receive his usual fee for his services. "In living together, the court used to say that they were not going to recognize it because they were not married, they were having an illicit sexual affair, and there are laws for adultery in every state," he said. "Here's a situation where, theoretically, a woman could develop a whole business with the man, and twenty years later he could say, 'I don't want to be with you anymore,' even though he was a drunk and she turned his hot-dog stand into McDonald's or some other $100 million empire. He could say, 'Take a walk,' and she would have no access to the courts. They had the same duties, the same responsibilities. Why should one person be able to just take everything? That's why I wanted to change the law." Mitchelson said he took the case and challenged the law all the way to the Supreme Court. "I knew I'd go to the Supreme Court on this," he said, "and I was the only one who believed I could do it because the precedents were against me."

The limelight has been squarely fixed on Mitchelson throughout the 1980s. One of his most notorious trials was the Joan Collins-Peter Holm divorce. Mitchelson subpoenaed Romina Danielson, Holm's alleged mistress, as a witness against Holm, who was seeking a divorce settlement from Collins. On the stand Danielson testified that Holm called her his "passion flower," asked her to have his child, and told her he planned to divorce Collins and collar a mass of cash in the process. At a particularly emotional point in her testimony, Danielson appeared to faint on the stand, somehow exposing her breasts to the spectators. Mitchelson told *Rolling Stone:* "People [were] going mad. Reporters [were] running around. It was the most dramatic scene I have ever seen. People think I had her faint on cue but I didn't. I [kept] trying to put her up, and she's falling down. Forget cross-examination." In fact, Danielson's testimony was stricken because she could not sit for cross-examination. Mitchelson feels, however, that her story helped to win a certain victory for Collins. Holm did not receive the money he sought for himself.

It is perhaps inevitable that Mitchelson's own life would come under scrutiny as he continued to court attention from the media. As early as 1972 some clients began filing complaints about the attorney's management of fees and retainers; at least one woman, Forrest Lander, accused Mitchelson of spending all the money she had given him to set up a trust fund for her. Mitchelson has settled most of these sorts of disputes quietly, out of court. However, he has also had to face allegations that he used clients' money to buy cocaine, that he was addicted to Percodan, a prescription narcotic, and that he gambled excessively in Las Vegas and elsewhere. Mitchelson denies all these charges vehemently, and he is equally vehement in his denial of raping two women clients. Those clients both appeared in a segment of CBS-TV's "Sixty Minutes," during which they levelled their charges against Mitchelson. Both said they had been sexually assaulted in the bathroom adjoining Mitchelson's office. Other female clients also reported aggressive sexual advances from Mitchelson, but in no case has he been formally charged or brought to trial for his actions. Mitchelson defended himself in the *Los Angeles Times.* Claiming that he "didn't put a hand" on the two women who have accused him of rape, he added: "I'm the least aggressive sexual person I know. If a girl in high school didn't want to kiss me, I'd run away and probably never talk to her again because I was so embarrassed." Bardach contends, however, that Mitchelson's "friends and associates . . . describe him as an inveterate womanizer. [His former secretary] Linda Acaldo says he once told her that he thought of himself 'as Rhett Butler—that he takes what's his.'"

The wealth of negative publicity has had a rather predictable outcome for Mitchelson's career—he is losing business and is rumored to be in debt. "Mitchelson's assets have long been a topic of speculation and rumor," Bardach reported. "The attorney who once worked with him says Mitchelson lived in a vicious cycle of debt, that he was constantly 'robbing Peter to pay Paul.'" Still, Mitchelson is optimistic about his future and excited about his prospects. "I like publicity, though no one likes bad publicity," he told *Rolling Stone.* "I'm an actor, but it's acting for real. People's rights and lives are at stake . . . . Being a lawyer is part-time psychiatrist, part-time psychologist, part-time priest, part-time rabbi, part-time detective . . . . I know that I really care about helping people. I know that's my reward when I go to bed."

Writings

Made in Heaven, Settled in Court, J.P. Tarcher, 1976.
Living Together, Simon & Schuster, 1980.

Sources

Los Angeles Times, June 25, 1988; August 19, 1988; October 9, 1988.
Los Angeles Times Magazine, October 9, 1988.
New York, January 10, 1983.
New York Times, July 3, 1988.
People, April 24, 1978; December 24, 1979.
Playboy, January, 1985.
Rolling Stone, July 14, 1988.
Washington Post, October 20, 1982.

—Sidelights by Mark Kram

Robert Mondavi

AP/Wide World Photos

Wine company executive

Full name, Robert Gerald Mondavi; born June 18, 1913, in Virginia, Minn.; son of Cesare (a vintner) and Rosa (Grassi) Mondavi; married Marjorie Declusin, January 27, 1940 (divorced); married Margrit Biever, 1980; children: (first marriage) Robert, Timothy, Marcia. *Education:* Stanford University, B.A., 1936.

Addresses: *Home*—St. Helena, Calif. *Office*—Robert Mondavi Winery, P.O. Box 403, Oakville, Calif. 94558.

Career

Sunny St. Helena Wine Co., St. Helena, Calif., director, 1937–45; Charles Krug Winery, St. Helena, vice-president and general manager, 1943–67; Robert Mondavi Winery, Oakville, Calif., president, beginning 1967, currently chairman. Director, C. Mondavi & Sons, beginning 1943.

Member: Wine and Food Society of America, Napa Valley Wine Association, San Francisco Wine and Food Society, Press Club of San Francisco, Commonwealth Club, Olympic Club, Meadow Wood Country Club.

Sidelights

An award-winning vintner, Robert Mondavi has been called an icon and a patriarch. He is credited with raising an obscure wine producing region to world prominence. Through his innovative techniques, his willingness to share his methods, and his efforts to promote *all* California premium wines, Napa Valley has become a celebrated wine country.

Mondavi was born into the industry. A native of Minnesota, he was 9 when his family moved to California. His father shipped grapes to Italian wine makers in the eastern United States. Following Prohibition, he invested in the St. Helena Wine Company, a small bulk wine manufacturer in the Napa Valley. His sons, Robert and Peter, joined the business after graduating from college. In 1943, the family purchased the Charles Krug Winery and began to make fine wines. Robert was responsible for marketing and development, while Peter was put in charge of production. The brothers soon clashed over Robert's spending. Peter wanted to proceed with caution; Robert wanted to experiment and to move quickly into new markets. In 1965, their differences came to a head and Robert broke from the family business. He found two partners and raised enough money to start the Robert Mondavi Winery.

Up to the mid-1970s, California wines maintained a dubious reputation. Mondavi knew the reason. "We used the same process on every type of grape, so [the wines] did come out tasting very similar," he explained to *People*'s Tony Chiu. "But we had the natural elements here—the climate, the soil, the grape varieties." Baron Philippe de Rothschild, one of the world's greatest vintners, agreed. In 1978, he suggested a joint venture: Mondavi would run the operation in the Napa Valley; Rothschild would lend him his wine master. A deal was struck, and they harvested their first vintage in the fall of 1979.

Even before his partnership with the Baron, Mondavi had vastly improved the quality and stature of California wines. He helped to popularize oak-barrel aging, which "allowed American vintners to develop distinctively varied wines in the European mode," Chiu wrote. Shortly after launching his venture, Mondavi wines were among California's best. Within ten years, he was one of America's premier winegrowers. California wines became acceptable, then praiseworthy, among connoisseurs and collectors. This was due, in large part, to "Mondavi's openness to new ideas and winemaking techniques, and his generosity in sharing them with anybody who was wise enough to listen," reported Nika Hazelton of the *National Review*. Mondavi also campaigned vigorously on behalf of all fine California wines. As one longtime friend told the *New York Times*' Frank J. Prial: "Don't tell Bob you're having a little tasting at home.... He'll fly in and give a speech."

Mondavi is less involved in the business today. His children now oversee the day-to-day concerns of the company, which include several prize vineyards, a winery in Woodbridge, California, and the Robert Mondavi Winery. This last attracts some 300,000 tourists a year. Despite his accomplishments, Mondavi continues to look to the future. "This is only the beginning," he told Prial. "We've only begun to learn."

Sources

Books

Ray, Cyril, *Robert Mondavi of the Napa Valley*, Heinemann/Peter Davies, 1985.

Periodicals

National Review, November 6, 1987.
New York Times, July 15, 1979; January 2, 1985; June 29, 1988.
People, October 20, 1980.
Time, April 28, 1980.
Town & Country, December, 1983.

—*Sketch by Denise Wiloch*

Joe Montana

AP/Wide World Photos

Professional football player

Full name, Joseph C. Montana, Jr.; born June 11, 1956, in New Eagle, Pa.; son of Joseph C., Sr. (a finance company manager) and Theresa (a secretary) Montana; married Kim Monses, 1975 (divorced); married Cass Castillo (an airline stewardess), c. 1980 (divorced, 1983); married Jennifer Wallace (a model), 1984; children: (third marriage) Alexandra, Elizabeth. *Education:* Notre Dame University, B.S. in business administration and marketing, 1978.

Addresses: *Home*—Redwood City, Calif. *Office*—c/o San Francisco 49ers, 4949 Centennial Blvd., Santa Clara, Calif. 95054.

Career

Professional football player for San Francisco 49ers, 1979—. Commercial spokesperson for various products and services. Has made numerous guest appearances on television talk and variety shows, including "Saturday Night Live."

Awards: Selected most valuable player of Super Bowl XVI (1982) and Super Bowl XIX (1985); named to seven National Football League Pro Bowl teams.

Sidelights

There were less than three minutes to go in Super Bowl XXIII, and the San Francisco 49ers were on their own eight-yard line, three points behind the Cincinnati Bengals. "Some of my teammates were already starting to celebrate," Cincinnati wide receiver Cris Collinsworth told the *Boston Globe.* "I said, 'Have you taken a look at who's quarterbacking the 49ers?' And that's what it came down to. Joe Montana's the greatest quarterback who ever played the game. Joe Montana is not human."

Certainly Montana performed the superhuman in 1989's Super Bowl. With time running out, he led the greatest drive of Super Bowl history—pushing the 49ers 92 yards in 11 plays. He completed eight of nine passes, finishing with a 10-yard touchdown toss to John Taylor with just 34 seconds left. In the end, the 49ers won their third Super Bowl, 20-16, behind the quarterback appropriately known to teammates as "Joe Cool." Montana's view of himself? "I see myself as a man struggling in a business that's very competitive," he told the *Los Angeles Times.* Well, hardly. Montana is a player who has specialized in salvaging hopeless causes, who has beaten not only opponents but the clock, time and again, who can spot the tiniest seam in an apparently flawless defense. He is a perennial Pro Bowl star, twice the Super Bowl's most valuable player and, statistically, the second-highest-ranked quarterback ever to play in the National Football League.

Before joining the 49ers, Montana caught the nation's attention at Notre Dame when he led the Fighting Irish back from a 34-12 fourth-quarter deficit to a 35-34 victory over Houston as time ran out in the 1979 Cotton Bowl. And before that, he led Notre Dame to a national collegiate championship in 1977, once again bringing his team from behind in the closing minutes. "I don't want to call him a god but he's somewhere in between," Collinsworth told the *Boston Globe.* "I have never seen a guy, and I'm sure he did it in college, high school and youth football and now in professional football, that every single time he's had the chips down and people are counting him out, he's come back." Indeed, Montana's father—Joe, Sr.—insists that young Joe pulled out a last-minute victory in his first start as a junior at Ringgold High in Monongahela, Pennsylvania.

"Joe Montana's the greatest quarterback who ever played the game. Joe Montana is not human."
—Chris Collinsworth

Montana was born in the Western Pennsylvania area, which has come to be fertile territory for great NFL quarterbacks. His grandfather, "Hooks" Montana, played semipro football in the 1920s. His father quit a job that kept him on the road when Joe was young so that he could help nurture his son's obvious athletic abilities. "Joe never really had a choice," Theresa Montana, Joe's mother, told the *San Jose Mercury News.* "His father wanted him to play football and that was that." Young Joe was a star at the peewee football level (his father lied about his young age to get him in), and threw three perfect games in Little League baseball. He went on to star in several sports in high school, once high-jumping 6-foot-9. North Carolina State offered him a basketball scholarship, but Joe chose to play football under Notre Dame's famed Golden Dome.

Brian Boulac, an assistant football coach at Notre Dame during Montana's tenure, told the *Mercury News:* "When Joe first came here he was extremely quiet. He was always in the back of the picture. He never thrust himself forward like a Joe Theismann." Indeed, Montana ranked last among the three quarterbacks when he was first on the freshman roster. He did not practice hard. He was admittedly homesick. And at 18 he entered into a brief and disastrous marriage to hometown girlfriend Kim Monses.

Montana spent much of his sophomore year, 1975, coming off the bench. In 1976 he separated his shoulder and sat out the entire season. He did not start at Notre Dame until the fourth game of his junior season. By then, he had already become a legend in South Bend: In Montana's first six games—all as a substitute—he played a total of less than 40 minutes and brought the Irish back from 88 points behind. Only as a senior, however, did Montana emerge as a potential NFL player. His greatest college game was his last—the 1979 Cotton Bowl. Montana, playing with the flu and a badly scraped arm, led the great comeback over Houston, tossing the winning touchdown pass on the final play of the game.

The San Francisco 49ers drafted Montana in the third round of the 1979 draft. "I knew of his inconsistency," 49ers coach Bill Walsh told *Sports Illustrated.* "I also knew about his competitiveness. If he could be great for one game, why not two, why not repetition? He was willing to learn. That was easy to tell. I knew he would improve." The 49ers were horrid in Montana's first season, and Walsh was careful not to throw the rookie to the wolves. Montana threw just 23 passes all year. And in Montana's second season, 1980, Walsh broke him in slowly, playing him sparingly behind starter Steve DeBerg. Still, he completed an impressive 64.5 percent of his passes, leading the league. Montana's breakthrough finally came in the 14th game of that season. The 49ers trailed the New Orleans Saints 35-7 when Walsh called Montana into an apparently hopeless game. In less than a half, Montana marched the team on four touchdown drives totalling 331 yards, and engineered an overtime drive that led to a field goal and a 38-35 victory. It was, in terms of points, the greatest comeback in the history of the NFL.

Montana never looked back. The 49ers finished 1980 with just six wins against 10 losses, but in 1981, fully behind Montana, they soared, winning the National Football Conference Western Division championship. The inexperienced 49ers entered the playoffs as a prohibitive underdog, but beat the Minnesota Vikings and suddenly found themselves preparing to play the Dallas Cowboys for the right to go to Super Bowl XVI. San Francisco trailed most of that game, and at the end found themselves 86 yards from the Dallas end zone with just three minutes to play. Montana ran what became known later as "The Drive," finishing it off with a game-winning fastball to Dwight Clark. They went on to defeat Cincinnati in the Super Bowl—the first of three they would win during the 1980s. Montana was named MVP of that Super Bowl. Looking back at "The Drive," Clark told the *Los Angeles Times,* "That was probably the moment that made Joe Montana known to most sports fans. That was when people started realizing how great he was. But those of us who played with him every week already knew he was great. He was just waiting for a chance to show it."

Through the 1980s, Montana continued to show it on an annual basis. After the 1989 season, he ranked as the second-best quarterback in league history, using the NFL's complicated quarterback ratings. He is both the most accurate passer (in terms of completion percentage) and the one with the lowest percentage of interceptions who has ever played in the NFL. Montana brought the 49ers back to the Super Bowl in 1985, again winning the game's MVP award as the 49ers whipped the Miami Dolphins, 38-16. After that season, he negotiated a six-year, $6.6 million contract which made him, at that time, the highest-paid player in football.

This is a player who neither looks nor acts like an NFL quarterback. *Los Angeles Times* columnist Jim Murray once wrote that "Montana's physique runs more along the lines of a praying mantis saying a novena. Reed-thin, pale, almost gaunt, he looks like a shut-in." At 6-2 and 192 lbs., he is one of the league's smaller quarterbacks. He is quiet and fairly colorless, but still, wrote the *San Jose Mercury News* Kristin Huckshorn, "Joe Montana has become the most popular athlete in Bay Area sports history. An area that considers itself sophisticated and sublime has fallen in love with an intensity that suggests teen-age naivete."

Harry Edwards, the University of California's prominent sports sociologist, told the *Mercury News*, "Joe Montana probably has had as great an impact on people's ideas related to sports as any athlete who's come through the Bay Area." When Montana underwent back surgery in San Francisco, well-wishers sent more than 10,000 pieces of mail. More than 10,000 people jammed the hospital's special hot line telephone number to hear updates on his condition. And he also has had a national effect. A 1988 poll in *USA Today* concluded that Montana was the readers' favorite professional athlete, favorite NFL athlete, and the athlete they'd most like to meet.

In his 1988 autobiography, *Audibles: My Life in Football*, Montana said he isn't comfortable receiving attention. "Don't ever let anyone tell you being in the spotlight, under America's microscope, is fun," he wrote. He called himself "a regular guy who cherishes his peace of mind, the right to be left alone and enjoy life." His most trying time in the public eye came in 1983, when he went through an acrimonious and much-publicized divorce from his second wife, Cass. Soon after, he married Jennifer Wallace, a model he met while shooting a commercial for Schick razors.

In the first game of 1986, Montana sustained a rupture of the lowest disc of his spinal column. After it was determined that he might be facing permanent nerve damage, Montana had surgery, removing a major portion of the disc. At the time, physician Dr. Arthur White said there was a good possibility Montana might never play again and that he certainly would miss the rest of that season. "I have my schedule and the doctors have theirs," Montana told *Sports Illustrated*. "Naturally, I will push harder than they want." And there he was, two months later, starting against the St. Louis Cardinals. He threw for 270 yards and three touchdowns as the 49ers won, 43-17.

He came back in 1987, leading the NFL in passing and throwing a team-record 31 touchdowns. In one game, he set a league record by throwing 22 straight completions. Late in that season, 49ers coach Bill Walsh told the *San Jose Mercury News* that Montana could fairly be ranked among the NFL's all-time great quarterbacks—men like Johnny Unitas, Joe Namath, Roger Staubach, Y.A. Tittle, Terry Bradshaw, and Dan Fouts. "When it's all said and done, he will have to be ranked in the very elite of the great at his position," Walsh said. Montana's reaction? He told the *Mercury News*, "I sit back and think about it sometimes. I think back to when I was a kid, seeing Terry Bradshaw, Len Dawson, and Bart Starr, and what everyone said about them. Then you realize you're on the field, just like those guys, and people are saying those things about you. It's still hard for me to visualize it."

At age 32, Montana started the 1988 season hoping to take the 49ers to their third Super Bowl of the decade. But early in the season, Walsh said he wanted to give more playing time to Montana's younger and quicker backup, Steve Young. When Montana was hurt in practice, Young started two games, winning one. There were rumors that Montana might be traded and hints that he should consider retirement. "I've never doubted myself, but sometimes you wonder a little," Montana told the *Boston Globe*. "I wasn't surprised you have to reprove yourself. I was just a little surprised after the year I'd had in 1987. If I'd had a bad year, I might have understood. When those benchings start to happen, it's hard to take as many chances as you'd like. You're a little more tentative, and you tend to aim the ball a little bit and say, 'I hope it gets there because if it doesn't, I might not be here.'"

In the end, Montana was there, leading San Francisco back from a 6-5 record to a berth in the Super Bowl; a comeback from mediocrity that was fueled by his explosive postseason performances. He threw six touchdown passes in playoff wins over Minnesota and Chicago, completing 61 percent of his attempts for 466 yards. Older and wiser, Montana compared his championship seasons for the *Mercury News.* "This trip to the Super Bowl is more gratifying than the others because the road has been harder. In 1982, we were so young we didn't have a gauge. In 1985, we were so confident that nothing could have stopped us."

And there he was in 1989, running a no-huddle offense and calling audibles at the line of scrimmage as the 49ers played catch-up ball in the final two minutes. In the end, Montana's primary receiver, Jerry Rice, won the game's most valuable player award, but no one doubted Montana's greatness. He set Super Bowl records for most passing yards in a game (357), most career Super Bowl passes without an interception (93), and highest career completion percentage in the Super Bowl (65.6). "This game put Joe Montana in the Hall of Fame," 49ers owner Eddie DeBartolo, Jr., told the *Mercury News* after the game. "All that's left is the coronation." Montana's reaction? "I'm not ready for history yet," he told the *Los Angeles Daily News.*

Writings

Audibles: My Life In Football (autobiography; written with Bob Raissman), Morrow, 1988.

Sources

Boston Globe, January 20, 1989; January 21, 1989; January 23, 1989.

Discover, January, 1987.

Fort Lauderdale News & Sun-Sentinel, January 19, 1989.

Los Angeles Daily News, January 22, 1989.

Los Angeles Times, August 9, 1987; November 12, 1988; January 22, 1989.

Newsday, January 24, 1989.

San Jose Mercury News, July 18, 1985; October 13, 1986; November 9, 1986; January 19, 1989; January 23, 1989.

Sports Illustrated, December 21, 1981; January 25, 1982; September 4, 1985; November 17, 1986; August 15, 1988.

Time, January 25, 1982; January 21, 1985; November 29, 1986.

Washington Post, January 21, 1989.

—Sidelights by Glen Macnow

Akio Morita

AP/Wide World Photos

Electronics company executive

Born January 26, 1921, in Nagoya, Japan; son of Kyuzaemon (a sake manufacturer) and Shuko (Toda) Morita; married Yoshiko Kamei, May 13, 1950; children: Hideo, Masau, Naoko. *Education:* Osaka Imperial University, B.S., 1944.

Addresses: *Home*—5-6 Aobadai 2-chome Meguro-ku, Tokyo 153, Japan. *Office*—Sony Corporation of Tokyo, Box 5100, Tokyo 100-31, Japan; and Sony Corporation of America, 9 West 57th St., New York, N.Y. 10019.

Career

Sony Corporation of Tokyo, Tokyo, Japan, co-founder, 1946, executive vice-president, 1959–71, president, 1971–76, chairman and chief executive officer, 1976—; Sony Corporation of America, New York, N.Y., president, 1960–66, chairman of the board, 1966–72, chairman of finance committee, 1972–74, chairman of executive committee, 1974–77, 1981—.

Sidelights

Akio Morita, founder and chairman of the Sony Corporation, is a pioneer in Japan's postwar industrial development. Morita, nearing seventy, remains one of the technological innovators who has transformed the "Made in Japan" label from a synonym for cheap imitation to an indicator of high quality, sophisticated consumer goods. Having co-founded Sony in 1946 with an initial investment of about $500, Morita has overseen his company's growth into a multi-billion-dollar producer of everything from televisions to compact disks to rock and roll music.

Forbes contributor Michael Cieply wrote: "For . . . decades Sony has been the proudest of Japan's great multinational corporations. Starting from nothing, just after World War II, it has earned a name that stands for quality, innovation and growth. Global in its reach, Sony lists its shares on 23 stock exchanges in 12 nations. In its main line of business, consumer electronics, it has long since dwarfed the competing operations of such pioneering U.S. companies as Zenith and RCA and helped drive many others out of business." In *Business Week,* Larry Armstrong noted that the very name Sony "speaks volumes about the company. It comes not from a Japanese word that foreigners might find difficult to pronounce, but from *sonus,* the Latin word for sound, fine-tuned for Japanese tongues. The name symbolizes the company's origins in its pioneering tape recorders and transistor radios. It also has come to signify the international orientation among so many mightily successful Japanese companies. Some 70% of Sony's sales come from outside Japan." Sony's success is due in no small part to Morita's imagination and foresight—and to his dedication to staying two steps ahead of the competition in the development of new products.

"Sony Corp. has built its reputation by staying up-to-date in the consumer electronics business," wrote Amy Borrus in *Business Week.* "But the company might not be around today without help from a 300-year-old enterprise that is the single largest shareholder in Sony." Borrus refers to Morita & Company, the business of Akio Morita's family since the late 1600s. Located in Nagoya, Japan, Morita & Company is one of its nation's most prestigious brewers of *sake,* the traditional Japanese rice wine. The firm also produces *miso,* a fermented soybean paste used in soups and sauces, and soy sauce.

When Morita was born in 1921, his father, Kyuzaemon, was running the business and earning hefty profits, enough so that Akio and his three siblings enjoyed an affluent lifestyle. As the eldest son, Akio was expected to follow his father in the *sake* business when he came of age. Instead, the youngster found himself drawn to electronics—especially phonographs—from his teen years onwards. "When I was in high school," Morita told *American Film,* "a new phonograph came in from the United States—an RCA Victor electric. My father bought the first electronic phonograph for us. And that gave us fantastic sound which, in fact, impressed me so much, I started to wonder how or why such a sound came out. That's where my interest in electronics began. In high school, we had no chance to study electronic technology, so I bought many, many books about it. My grades began to suffer, as I spent all my time studying electronics." Morita added that he tried to assemble a radio, a phonograph, and even a tape recorder, failing only on the last project. He went off to college determined to succeed one day in producing a usable audio recorder.

Morita was able to persuade his father to allow the second son, Kazuaki, to run the family brewery. Akio was therefore allowed to attend Osaka Imperial University, where he earned a bachelor's degree in physics in 1944. After graduating he was commissioned a lieutenant in the Imperial Japanese Navy, but he never saw any active combat during the Second World War. Instead he was assigned to a Naval Research Center at Susaki, and there he met an engineer named Masaru Ibuka. At the time, Ibuka was running the Japan Precision Instrument Company, but he, too, was interested in developing a tape recorder. In 1946, Morita and Ibuka pooled their meager resources—including some funds supplied by the Morita family in return for stock—and formed Tokyo Tsushin Kogyo Kabushiki Kaisha (Tokyo Telecommunications Company). Housed in a former army barracks, the tiny fifty-employee firm began to manufacture vacuum-tube voltmeters, amplifiers, and sophisticated communications devices aimed at broadcasting and industry. The tape recorder they finally developed for the consumer market was simply too expensive, at $500, to attract much business. Still, the company sold enough units to schools and libraries to turn a modest profit, so the two entrepreneurs began to think of other consumer-oriented items to sell.

During his first trip to the United States in 1952, Ibuka encountered a promising new technology—transistors. Developed by Bell Laboratories in 1948, the long-lived, solid state electronic devices were at the time thought to be useful only in hearing aids. Ibuka decided to gamble that transistors could also be made to work in radios, and possibly even in televisions. While Ibuka took over the company's research, Morita began to handle the business transactions—a division of labor that proved fortuitous. Morita offered $25,000 for a patent to manufacture transistors in Japan but found himself in an uphill battle when his government failed to approve the transaction. Eventually, after ten months of patient explanation, Morita was able to buy the patent. Then Ibuka had to fit the technology to radios, requiring another three years of research. Finally, in 1955, they succeeded, and Morita left to peddle the product in America. His first marketing step was to change the name of his company to Sony. "We found a Latin word, *sonus*—that's 'sound'—and an English phrase, 'sonny boy,'" he told *American Film.* "We were a group of 'sonny boys' dealing with sound, so we made 'sonny boys' short and combined it with *sonus* to create Sony."

From the outset Morita saw America as the most likely market for Sony's products. "Our first transistor radio of 1955 was small and practical—not as small as some of our later efforts, but we were very proud of it," he remembered in his book *Made in Japan: Akio Morita and Sony.* "I saw the U.S. as a natural market; business was booming, employment was high, the people were progressive and eager for new things, and international travel was becoming easier." Morita's pitch was simple enough: a portable transistor radio could enable every member of a family to tune into his or her favorite music; it could be taken anywhere, and the price was modest.

His first taker, the mighty Bulova company, ordered an incredible 100,000 units—but insisted on having the name Bulova on them instead of Sony. After much soul-searching, Morita turned down the offer.

"We would not produce radios under another name," he said. "When I called again on the man from Bulova, he didn't seem to take me seriously at first. How could I turn down such an order? He was convinced I would accept. When I would not budge, he got short with me. 'Our company name is a famous brand name that has taken over 50 years to establish,' he said. 'Nobody has ever heard of your brand name. Why not take advantage of ours?' I understood what he was saying, but I had my own view. 'Fifty years ago,' I said, 'your brand name must have been just as unknown as our name is today. I am here with a new product, and I am now taking the first step for the next 50 years of my company. Fifty years from now, I promise you that our name will be just as famous as your company name is today.'"

"Our plan is to lead the public with new products rather than ask them what kind of products they want. The public does not know what is possible, but we do."

The prediction may have been brash, but it proved true—and in far less than fifty years. By 1959 Sony had pioneered the first pocket-sized transistor radio, the first two-band transistor radio, the first FM transistor radio, the first transistorized television, and a transistorized videotape recorder. Sony was also the first company to produce small-screen televisions that could be moved easily from room to room. The Sony name appeared prominently on all the units, although sometimes the "Made in Japan" stamp was nearly impossible to see.

In the early 1960s Morita spent fifteen months in Manhattan organizing the Sony Corporation of America and overseeing the sale of stock in the United States—a first for a Japanese company. He also hired the high-posture advertising agency of Doyle Dane Bernbach to convince consumers that Sony offered a quality product. By 1969, when Sony brought its Trinitron television to market, its sales were eclipsing those of such American giants as RCA and Zenith. It also had never lost its edge in portable radios, tape recorders, and other electronic equipment. One of its biggest successes has been the Walkman, a tiny stereo outfitted with headphones, first introduced in 1979. The Walkman was such a windfall for Sony because its technology proved difficult to duplicate—it was more than two years before other companies could make competing models, and by that time Sony had sold 20,000,000 units worldwide in 70 versions. Reflecting on the Trinitron, the Walkman, and other Sony "firsts," Morita said, "What I had in mind for my product line was an image of class and high quality, which really represented the products." The Sony reputation soared worldwide, especially in the United States.

Morita became president of Sony in 1971 and chief executive officer in 1976. His family still owns 9.4 percent of Sony stock—Borrus points out that the initial $500 investment is worth more than $430 million today. Still, Sony's rise to the corporate heights has not been without its setbacks. The first company to offer affordable videotape recorders, it stuck steadfastly to its Betamax format, even when the VHS format began to corner the market. As a result, Sony's massive videotape recorder sales of the late 1970s and early 1980s soon dwindled and eventually became a liability.

Other strategies of Morita's, while estimable, also helped to stagnate Sony's growth in the 1980s. First, Morita insisted on a research and development budget of almost 10 percent of sales. While some of Sony's new products, such as 3.5 inch floppy disks for computers and portable compact disk players have been profitable, other items, such as the hand-held 8mm video camera, have been costly flops. Morita also took an unusual stand on employment. He has built factories in the United States, Ireland, Belgium, and other markets where labor costs are high, rather than opting for countries where per capita wages are lower, and he still adheres to the lifetime contract employment in Japan that gives workers there unlimited job security. Unfortunately for Morita, his competitors—especially those in South Korea and other Asian countries—are improving item quality while controlling production costs with cheaper labor or robotics.

Armstrong suggested, however, that Sony will survive any slump and may even transcend the anti-Japanese sentiment that is beginning to appear in American consumers. "Where Sony has earned almost universal respect is in its effort to become a more global company," Armstrong wrote. "All told, 20% of Sony's manufacturing is overseas. It aims to increase that to 35% by 1990 .... Of all the problems besetting Sony, the two most frustrating are how to deal with copycat competitors and how to mute the impact of the rising yen on manufacturing costs. But Sony has shown it can rise to the challenge. Its experience with the Walkman is proof of that."

Under Morita Sony has continued to diversify. Late in 1987 the company purchased CBS Records for $2 billion, thus placing in Japanese hands the works of such artists as Bruce Springsteen, Duke Ellington, Bing Crosby, Michael Jackson, Barbra Streisand, Isaac Stern, and Miles Davis, to name only a few. While some observers bemoaned the overseas acquisition of such a quintessential American company, the president of CBS records, Walter Yetnikoff [see index for *Newsmakers* entry], applauded the deal, and almost all of CBS's famous names remained with the label. Industry observers agree that Sony's substantial portion of the compact disk player market will be greatly enhanced by its ownership of CBS Records.

In reference to Sony's goals, Morita told the *Los Angeles Times* that he will continue the mission he set for his company more than forty years ago—"to utilize the most advanced technology for the general public." Although he has been compared to any number of American industrial giants, Morita told the *Times* that he differs from American managers in that he prefers a long-term, slow ascent to success over the quick-fix, quick-return viewpoints of U.S. executives. The secret of Japan's industrial success, he said, "lies on the shelves and the showroom floor of stores all around the world: good quality products that people want and in such variety that any consumer whim can be satisfied. This is how Japanese goods managed to take so much of the U.S. market . . . . We did not 'invade' the American market as it is sometimes charged; we just sent our very best products to America."

In recent years Morita has spent as much time travelling as he has at Sony headquarters. Though not interested in retirement, he is phasing back his commitment to the corporation and enjoying himself more. Armstrong noted, however, that for all his outside activities, "Morita still makes sure he gets involved in the crucial decisions at Sony." *Fortune* magazine correspondent Irwin Ross described Morita as "outwardly all breezy self-assurance and optimism" but adds that "by his own account, he is a driven man with a huge appetite for success." That appetite must certainly have been satisfied by the history of Sony and by the bright future portended by its fusion of software and hardware goods. Morita explained his philosophy in *Fortune* magazine, a philosophy that mirrors his company's goals and highlights his own personal confidence. "Our plan," he said, "is to lead the public with new products rather than ask them what kind of products they want. The public does not know what is possible, but we do."

Writings

Made in Japan: Akio Morita and Sony (with Edwin M. Reingold and Mitsuko Shimomura), Dutton, 1987.

Sources

American Film, December, 1984.
Business Week, June 1, 1987.
Forbes, October 24, 1983; October 6, 1986.
Fortune, October 27, 1986.
Los Angeles Times, November 1, 1986.
New York Review of Books, March 12, 1987.
New York Times, September 10, 1967; September 27, 1970.
New York Times Magazine, September 18, 1988.
Rolling Stone, January 14, 1988.
Time, May 10, 1971; November 30, 1987.

—*Sketch by Anne Janette Johnson*

Charles Moritz

AP/Wide World Photos

Business information and services company executive

Full name, Charles Worthington Moritz; born August 22, 1936, in Washington, D.C.; son of Sidney and Ruth Whitman (Smith) Moritz; married Susan Prescott Tracy, June 14, 1958; children: Peter, Tracy, Margaret. *Education:* Yale University, B.A., 1958.

Addresses: *Home*—Darien, Conn. *Office*—Dun & Bradstreet Corp., 299 Park Ave., New York, N.Y. 10017.

Career

With R.H. Donnelley Corp., 1960—, began as account executive, served as vice-president and general manager of marketing, 1972–74, senior vice-president, 1974–76, director, 1975—; Dun & Bradstreet Corp., New York City, executive vice-president, 1976–79, vice-chairman and director, 1979—, president and chief operating officer, 1981—, chairman and chief executive officer 1985—.

Trustee, Seamen's Bank for Savings. *Military service:* U.S. Naval Reserve, 1958–60; became lieutenant junior grade.

Member: Direct Marketing Association (director, 1973–76), American Marketing Association, American Management Association, Sales Executives Club, Zeta Psi.

Sidelights

Founded in the mid-1800s, Dun & Bradstreet Corporation provides information and services to businesses in the United States and Europe. Consistently efficient and profitable, it has performed well in both good and bad economic times. The company's latest chairman and chief executive officer, Charles Moritz, intends to maintain this tradition.

Moritz has been with Dun & Bradstreet nearly all of his career. In 1960, after serving in the Navy for two years, he joined R.H. Donnelley, publisher of the Yellow Pages, as an account executive. Dun & Bradstreet bought the publisher the next year. As Moritz rose through the ranks at Donnelley, its parent company continued to acquire new businesses, including television stations, airline guides, and trade magazines. When Moritz was named president of Dun & Bradstreet in 1981, it had 20 divisions in operation.

Although acquisitions are a large part of Dun & Bradstreet's business, it is perhaps best known for its credit report services. Dun & Bradstreet tracks the credit history of some 10 million companies. In addition, Donnelley Marketing keeps updated addresses and other information on millions of American households. Ellen Benoit of *Financial World* likened the firm's data-gathering operations to "a giant beehive." The workforce collects "tiny pieces of information from clients and potential clients and feeds them to the queen bee, the D & B mainframe computers." The company then looks for ways to repackage its information for use by new customers.

Moritz wants to expand Dun & Bradstreet's products and services. His strategy includes investing assets gained from recent divestitures "into high-growth acquisitions in the U.S. and Europe," *Fortune*'s Stuart Gannes explained. During the mid-1980s, Moritz sold the company's television stations and most of its publishing interests. At the same time, he bought 33 new businesses, including A.C. Nielson, the world's largest market research firm, Thomas Cook Travel U.S.A., and McCormack & Dodge, a software developer. Dun & Bradstreet also opened a $40-million computer center in Great Britain. Large sums have been marked for internal development projects as well, such as information delivery systems and data recycling. "The more uses a single fact can be put to, the more efficient and profitable the business becomes," Benoit wrote. "The more D & B can learn about its clients' information needs, the more new products it can invent and sell."

According to most observers, Moritz has a hands-on approach to management. He visits branch offices, accompanies his sales representatives on customer calls, and holds monthly breakfast meetings with randomly chosen employees. He is dedicated to customer service. "I think the thing that probably has enabled us to steer a successful path through the minefield is the attention that we put on good old fundamentals and basics," he told Benoit. "And the key fundamental as far as I'm concerned is customer focus.... Without our customers nobody in this organization would have a job."

Sources

Business Week, October 13, 1986.
Financial World, April 21, 1987.
Fortune, August 19, 1985.

—Sketch by Denise Wiloch

Brian Mulroney

Reuters/Bettmann Newsphotos

Prime minister of Canada

Full name, Martin Brian Mulroney; born March 20, 1939, in Baie Comeau, Quebec, Canada; son of Benedict (an electrician) and Irene (O'Shea) Mulroney; married Mila Pivnicki, May 26, 1973; children: Caroline Ann, Benedict Martin, Robert Mark, Daniel Nicholas Dimitri. *Education:* St. Francis Xavier University, B.A.; Dalhousie University, postgraduate study; Laval University, LL.D. *Religion:* Roman Catholic.

Addresses: *Office*—Office of the Prime Minister, Langevin Block, Parliamentary Buildings, Ottawa, Ontario, Canada K1A 0A2; and Progressive Conservative Party, 178 Queen St., Ottawa, Ontario, Canada K1P 5E1.

Career

Ogilvy, Cope, Porteous, Montgomery, Renault, Clarke & Kirkpatrick (law firm), Montreal, Quebec, partner until 1976; Iron Ore Company of Canada, Montreal, vice-president of corporate affairs, 1976–77, president, 1977–83; leader of Progressive Conservative Party, 1983–84; member of Canadian Parliament, representing Manicouagan Riding, Quebec, beginning 1984; prime minister of Canada, 1984—. Co-chairman of an investigation into union violence and corruption in the Quebec construction industry, 1974; former national vice-president, Youth for Diefenbaker; appointed to Cliche Royal Commission, 1974; chairman, Centraide Campaign of Greater Montreal, 1977; member of Conference Board of Canada; member of board of governors, Concordia University.

Sidelights

Recent opinion polls have shown that Canadian voters neither like nor respect their prime minister. Yet Brian Mulroney became the first Conservative leader in nearly a century to win consecutive majority governments. This paradox is characteristic of a man some are predicting may become one of the most important politicians in Canada's history. No one claims for Mulroney the vision or the charisma of his predecessor, Pierre Elliott Trudeau. The Liberal prime minister was cosmopolitan, sexy, and intellectualy intimidating. Through sheer force of his personality, Trudeau convinced Quebeckers not to separate from Canada in the 1980 referendum. His impact on the nation was profound. But in the past four years Mulroney has quietly stepped out of Trudeau's shadow. Using mediation rather than confrontation, he has set into motion several major initiatives. He negotiated a far-reaching free trade agreement with the United States that he claims will ensure permanent prosperity for Canada. In addition, Mulroney reached an important constitutional agreement with Quebec that he insists will help keep Quebec in Confederation.

The paradox of Mulroney's personal unpopularity is difficult to understand. In many ways he is the ideal

Canadian politician. At 50, he is young and dynamic with an attractive family. He has a successful background in both law and business. And most importantly, he is a fluently bilingual native of Quebec. In a recent profile, the *Observer* of London suggested Mulroney's Irish love of exaggeration and embellishment is one of his main problems. "To Canadians, used to dour precision among their politicians, it can appear slick and untrustworthy." *Globe and Mail* columnist Jeffrey Simpson said simply, "It is Mulroney's singular misfortune on television to look phoney even when he's being natural." And when comparing how Mulroney and U.S. president Ronald Reagan handled the various scandals that beset them, Simpson said Mulroney is not a teflon leader but "a flypaper prime minister to whom everything opprobrious about the government stuck."

In his critical biography *Friends in High Places,* Claire Hoy stated that while one can admire Mulroney's accomplishments, "there is a quality about the man which most Canadians find disconcerting, an uneasiness one gets when dealing with the slick talking proprietor of a cut-rate used car lot." Trying to probe a little deeper, Hoy then went on to quote a Mulroney college friend: "[Brian's] full of a lot of energy, but he doesn't have any sense of direction, and after a while . . . you feel let down and disappointed. Later on it comes out as dishonesty, but I don't think that's his fundamental motive. I think he wants to govern well and do well, but I think more than anything else he wants to be loved."

And yet in 1987, just a year before his second electoral majority, opinion polls showed Canadians had no love for their leader at all. Mulroney and the Tories trailed both the New Democrats and Liberals by a wide margin. Time and again the political media pointed to the only obvious answer—the Canadian public was profoundly unsure just who Brian Mulroney was. In a profile in *Saturday Night* magazine, Jeffrey Simpson wrote: "Even [Mulroney's] closest friends and professional associates . . . struggle to define him. The contradictions and complications abound at every level. Here is a prime minister, widely believed to lack any set of core beliefs, who has undertaken two of the most dramatic policy changes since the Second World War: free trade with the United States and the Meech Lake constitutional accord."

Mulroney came into office promising a change from the Trudeau era. He said compromise and conciliation would be the hallmarks of his government. On that promise, he has delivered. He managed to keep his party, historically fractious, under control. And he negotiated quietly and successfully with the provinces on a number of issues. After the first round of Meech Lake talks, even Liberal and New Democrat premiers were congratulating Mulroney on his skill and fairness.

Mulroney's background helps explain how mediation became his defining political style. Born in Baie Comeau, a pulp and paper town on the St. Lawrence River's north shore, he was the son of Irish immigrants. His father worked as an electrician at the local mill. Mulroney, an Irish Catholic in a district made up of Protestants and Catholics, was connected by religion to the French and by language to the English. The Irish in Quebec have traditionally played the role of bridge between the two solitudes. It is a role that fit Mulroney perfectly. In his biography *Mulroney: The Making of the Prime Minister,* L. Ian MacDonald wrote that young Brian loved to sing and was equally adept at old Irish songs and French-Canadian ballads. One day, Colonel Robert McCormick, owner of the *Chicago Tribune* and the local paper mill, arrived in town. Mulroney was asked to sing for the famous American capitalist. Apparently he performed so well, he was rewarded with a fifty dollar bill. Mulroney's political foes claim he has been singing for the Americans ever since.

After high school, Mulroney was sent to St. Francis Xavier college in Nova Scotia. There he developed his interest in politics. He joined the Conservative party and began forming the lifelong friendships that were to become so important in his later career. Mulroney studied enough to graduate but seemed more interested in politics. Again, perhaps aware of his future goals, he developed into a champion debater. But it was when he entered the Laval law school in Quebec that Mulroney blossomed. Mixed in with his legal studies, he became a key Conservative organizer in Quebec. He acted as an unofficial advisor to Conservative prime minister John Diefenbaker. And the young Mulroney made friends with sons of both the English and French elite at Laval, many of whom would end up as advisers and ministers in his government twenty years later.

After Laval, Mulroney was hired by the biggest law firm in Montreal. Within a short time, he became one of the firm's most trusted labor lawyers. Although Mulroney later cited this part of his career as evidence of his working class connections, Claire Hoy in his biography revealed that Mulroney worked exclusively for management. Nonetheless, labor leaders insist that Mulroney was fair in his dealings with them during strike talks. Mulroney's first real exposure to the public spotlight occurred in 1974 when he co-chaired an investigation into union violence and corruption in the Quebec construction industry. The hearings were televised and Mulroney, speaking colloquial Baie Comeau French, was a hit with the francophone audience. And, being English, he acted as spokesman to the anglophone media. He was soon a household name in Quebec.

Not one to rest on his laurels, one short year later Mulroney thought he was ready to challenge for the leadership of the federal Conservatives. Many in the party, however, felt he was being presumptuous. He had never held any elected office, and he entered the race with an ostentatious, expensive campaign. Convention delegates rejected the slick lawyer from Montreal and elected Joe Clark instead. Smarting from his defeat, Mulroney accepted a position as president of the American-owned Iron Ore Company of Canada. This later provided fuel for his critics who would suggest he was a habitual frontman for U.S. interests. But Mulroney needed a high-profile job, and he needed corporate connections to help him for a second grab at political power.

In 1983, Mulroney was ready to take another run at the Tory leadership. This time he was cast in the role of plotter. The party was still being run by Joe Clark, who was generally perceived as weak and ineffectual. Mulroney led the forces that demanded a leadership review. When the bitter battle was over, Mulroney became the new leader. Mulroney was now in a position to take advantage of the accumulating unpopularity of the Liberal government under Pierre Trudeau. After sixteen years of almost uninterrupted power, the Liberals had lost their luster in the eyes of Canadian voters. In the 1984 general election Mulroney and the Tories swept into office with the biggest majority in Canadian history, winning 211 out of 282 seats.

The first two years of his mandate were difficult, due mainly to the inexperience of his new members of Parliament. Six of his ministers were forced to resign following indiscretions that ranged from conflict of interest to visiting an off-limits West German strip bar. The mistakes were seen as indictative of the new prime minister's bad judgement. As Brian Cole wrote in the *Winnipeg Free Press,* "Mulroney finds himself painted as the untrustworthy leader of an unmitigated public relations disaster."

Looking beyond the superficial political mistakes of his first administration, there is no doubt Mulroney oversaw a prosperous period in the nation's development. Canada's economic performance was among the best of the Western industrialized nations. His government moved to deregulate the energy and transportation industries, reform the tax system, loosen restrictions on foreign investment and, most significantly, forge a free trade agreement with the United States. Internationally, Canada became a full member of the Group of Seven economic club, helped found a new commonwealth of francophone nations, and was elected to the United Nations security council. And drawing on skills honed at the labor negotiating table, Mulroney initiated an unexpected constitutional accord at a meeting of premiers in May, 1987. During a marathon overnight session, Mulroney convinced all ten premiers to recognize Quebec as a distinct Francophone society. That recognition would finally make the province of Quebec a full partner in the Canadian constitution.

The paradox of Mulroney's personal unpopularity is difficult to understand. In many ways he is the ideal Canadian politician.

The Meech Lake accord assisted Mulroney in his primary political objective—the establishment of the Conservative party in Quebec. As the Tories have painfully learned over the years, carrying Quebec is the key to any federal campaign. The province's six million citizens tend to vote in a bloc, usually for the party that is favored to win. Mulroney used federal spending, patronage, cabinet appointments, and Meech Lake in an attempt to convince Quebeckers that the Conservatives could represent them as well as the Liberals had.

Mulroney tested his Quebec support with an election call in November, 1988. The election was dominated by a single issue, Mulroney's plan to allow free trade between Canada and the United States. Mulroney had been against the concept, right up to 1984. And his party had traditionally resisted free trade with the American giant to the south. But in 1988, the Tories were for it. Once again—when the election results were counted—it became clear Quebec believed Mulroney's claim that free trade was good for Canada. Even though the rest of the country was split on the issue, the Quebec vote was enough to win Mulroney a respectable majority.

Despite his win, Mulroney has not been viewed as the most likeable of Canada's leaders. But he has slowly earned the country's respect as a manager and negotiator. Most political observers are now coming to the conclusion that it took Mulroney much of his first term to grow into the role of prime minister. As he settles into his second four-year mandate, a veteran leader and confident in his majority, Canadians may finally give Mulroney what he seems to crave most—affection.

Sources

Books

Beruison, David Jay, *Sacred Trust?: Brian Mulroney and the Conservative Party,* Doubleday (Toronto), 1986.

Gratton, Michael, *So What Are the Boys Saying?,* McGraw Hill-Ryerson, 1987.

Hoy, Claire, *Friends in High Places,* Key Porter Books, 1987.

MacDonald, L. Ian, *Mulroney: The Making of the Prime Minister,* McClelland & Stewart, 1984.

Mulroney, Brian, *Where I Stand,* McClelland & Stewart, 1983.

Periodicals

Financial Post, November 23, 1985; September 5, 1988.

Globe and Mail (Toronto), June 20, 1983.

Maclean's, June 20, 1983; July 25, 1983; May 6, 1985; September 2, 1987; November 2, 1987; October 10, 1988.

Observer (London), November 27, 1988.

Winnipeg Free Press, August 30, 1986.

—Sidelights by Ingeborg Boyens

Eddie Murphy

AP/Wide World Photos

Actor and comedian

Full name, Edward Regan Murphy; born April 3, 1961, in Brooklyn, N.Y.; son of Charles (a police officer) and Lillian (a telephone operator) Murphy; stepson of Vernon Lynch (a foreman at an ice cream factory). *Education:* Attended Nassau Community College.

Addresses: *Home*—Englewood, N.J. *Agent*—Entertainment Management Associates Ltd., 232 East 63rd St., New York, N.Y. 10021.

Career

While in high school, began performing as a stand-up comedian at New York comedy clubs; later worked at numerous clubs on the East Coast; regular member of cast of television series "Saturday Night Live," 1980–84; actor in feature films, including "48 Hours," 1982, "Trading Places," 1983, "Best Defense," 1984, "Beverly Hills Cop," 1984, "The Golden Child," 1986, "Beverly Hills Cop II," 1987, "Raw" (concert film), 1987, and "Coming to America," 1988. Released comedy albums *Eddie Murphy,* 1982, *Eddie Murphy: Comedian,* 1983, and an album of songs, *How Could It Be,* 1984.

Awards: Emmy Award nomination for outstanding comedy performance and outstanding comedy writing, for "Saturday Night Live"; Grammy Award nomination for best comedy album, 1982, for *Eddie Murphy;* NAACP Image Award, 1983; Golden Globe Foreign Press Award, 1983, for "Trading Places"; Grammy Award for best comedy album, 1984, for *Eddie Murphy: Comedian;* Golden Globe Award nomination for best actor, Star of the Year Award, and People's Choice Award for favorite all-around male entertainer, all 1985, for "Beverly Hills Cop."

Sidelights

Eddie Murphy once told his 10th grade social studies teacher, reported *Rolling Stone,* "I'm going to be bigger than Bob Hope." And the enormously popular entertainer is well on his way toward turning that youthful boast into a statement of fact. He has starred on late-night television, toured before sell-out audiences, recorded a couple of best-selling comedy albums, and had leading roles in several blockbuster movies. *Newsweek* has called him "the hottest performer in the land" for whom "the sky seems to be the limit." And *Time* has named him "Hollywood's uncontested box-office champ."

Born on April 3, 1961, Murphy was raised in the Bushwick section of Brooklyn, New York. His father, Charles Murphy, was a New York City policeman and amateur comedian, and his mother, Lillian, a phone operator. When Eddie was three years old, his parents divorced. Later, when his mother was forced to spend an extended period in the hospital, he and his older brother Charles were taken care of by a woman whom Murphy recalled as "a kind of black Nazi." He told Richard Corliss of *Time:* "Those were baaaad days. Staying with her was probably the reason I became a comedian."

Murphy's father died when Eddie was eight, and a year later, his mother married Vernon Lynch, a foreman at a Breyer's ice cream factory and a part-time boxing instructor. Shortly thereafter the family moved to the black middle-class suburb of Roosevelt, Long Island. Growing up, Murphy spent a great deal of time in front of the TV, absorbing and soon doing impressions of cartoon characters such as Bugs Bunny and Tom and Jerry. "My mother says I never talked in my own voice—always cartoon characters," he related to Gene Lyons of *Newsweek.* "Dudley Do-Right, Bullwinkle. I used to do Sylvester the Cat ('thufferin' thuccotash') all the time." He also developed impressions of comics like Laurel and Hardy and Jerry Lewis. Film director John Landis later told Corliss that Murphy's unique point of view is rooted in his early TV perceptions: "I grew up hooked on TV, but Eddie is TV. His world experience comes from the tube."

Before long, Murphy began working up comedy routines after school, and developing his comedy skills became his passion. At Roosevelt Junior-Senior High School, he became an expert at "ranking," trading witty insults with his classmates. Murphy made his first stage appearance in 1976, at the age of 15, when he hosted a talent show at the Roosevelt Youth Center. He did an impersonation of soul singer Al Green, and the kids loved it. "Looking out at the audience, I knew that it was show biz for the rest of my life," he recalled to Corliss.

Murphy soon started performing stand-up comedy at local clubs. According to Lyons, he was "making between $25 and $50 a week appearing in 'Gong Shows' at Long Island nightclubs where he was still too young to buy a drink." He was a less than dedicated student, and schoolwork took a back seat to his evening club dates. "My focus was my comedy," he said to *Time.* "You could usually find me in the lunchroom trying out my routines on the kids to perform them in clubs later that night." His inattention to the books, however, caught up with him when he had to repeat the tenth grade. "As vain as I was," he told Corliss, "I don't have to tell you what that did to me. Well, I went to summer school, to night school, I doubled up on classes, and I graduated only a couple of months late." In his yearbook, Murphy declared his career plans: comedian.

He enrolled at Nassau Community College to please his mother, but he continued to appear at area clubs. Just a few months out of high school, he performed at the Comic Strip, a popular Manhattan club. One of the owners, Robert Wachs, noted to Lyons, "his material wasn't out of this world, but he had great presence." That first appearance led to club dates up and down the East Coast. Wachs and his partner, Richard Tienken, later became Murphy's managers. Murphy's childhood idols included Elvis Presley and comedian Richard Pryor. Like Pryor, his stand-up act is raunchy, filled with four-letter and twelve-letter words. Unlike his idols, however, Murphy believes in clean living. He doesn't smoke, drink, or use drugs.

When Murphy learned that the producers of NBC-TV's "Saturday Night Live" were looking for a black cast member for the 1980–81 season, he quickly auditioned—and auditioned again and again—six times. He finally was hired as a featured player, or as he told Richard Rein of *People,* "an extra." He appeared only occasionally and didn't win a spot as a regular until later in the season. Because that year's show was a flop, NBC cleaned house, and most of the cast was fired. The only performers retained were Murphy and Joe Piscopo. The next season Murphy emerged as a star. As Rein explained, "he did wickedly adept—and less than worshipful—impressions of Muhammad Ali, Bill Cosby, Stevie Wonder and Jerry Lewis." He also created some memorable new characters such as Mister Robinson, a ghetto version of TV's Mister Rogers, with comments like "Can you say 'scumbucket,' boys and girls?" and a grown-up version of the Little Rascals' Buckwheat. Other hilarious characters included an irreverent version of Gumby; Velvet Jones, a pimp and huckster selling books like "I Wanna Be a Ho," a guide for would-be prostitutes; and Tyrone Green, an illiterate convict-poet doing pieces like "Cill My Lanlord." The *New York Times* proclaimed that "Eddie Murphy has stolen the show."

In 1982, Murphy recorded an album of his stand-up material. It received a Grammy nomination and eventually went gold. Also in 1982, he landed his first movie role in the film "48 Hours." Director Walter Hill selected Murphy on the basis of some videotapes of "Saturday Night Live" that he had seen. Murphy played a fast-talking convict who is released from prison for two days to help a policeman, played by Nick Nolte, track down a pair of killers. Once again, Murphy "stole the show," according to *People. Newsweek* called it "a fast, furious and funny movie debut." Released in December, the film was an instant hit, grossing over $5 million in just its first week.

In mid-1983 Murphy's second movie, "Trading Places," was released. Co-starring Dan Aykroyd, this film likewise was a hit. Director Landis told *Time,* "Eddie is definitely a movie star now." Both "48 Hours" and "Trading Places" ended up among the top-ten grossing films of 1983. Murphy also launched a major concert tour that year. In addition, he recorded his second comedy album, *Eddie Murphy: Comedian.* This time he won a Grammy, and again the album went gold.

The next year Murphy left "Saturday Night Live" after his fourth season. His next movie, however, called "Best Defense" with co-star Dudley Moore was, stated Richard Grenier of *Commentary,* a "failure," causing some people to wonder if Murphy was "a mere novelty, possibly just a flash in the pan." But Murphy followed up with a blockbuster hit movie, "Beverly Hills Cop." It was his first solo starring role and, according to Grenier now writing in the *New York Times,* it broke box-office records: "'Beverly Hills Cop' has quite stunned Hollywood. Released in early December, it has grossed more than its next five competitors combined." (Interestingly, the role was first intended for Sylvester Stallone.) As a result of Murphy's astounding success, Paramount Pictures signed him—then just 23 years old—to a $25 million six-picture contract. Added Grenier, "No black actor has ever come anywhere near the position Eddie Murphy holds today. He is quite simply a historic figure." Trying to explain Murphy's tremendous appeal, Lyons wrote that "Murphy's most valuable gift as a performer is his saucy charm; he's not wicked, just naughty. He's a good little bad boy who can get away with murder when he smiles." "Beverly Hills Cop" eventually reached No. 9 among all-time box-office hits.

Murphy was not being universally praised, however. Grenier noted that the *Village Voice* made a "vitriolic attack" on Murphy for being an expression of "comedy for the 80's," one of "Reagan's court jesters." And due to his penchant for doing homosexual jokes, a militant gay group took out full-page ads in *Billboard* and *Rolling Stone* to denounce him as a "homophobe." Also in 1984, Murphy tried branching out into a new field, recording an album of R&B tunes called *How Could It Be?* Elvis Mitchell of *Interview* magazine remarked that Murphy's singing "sounded thin and forced," and Murphy agreed that "a lot of it turned out bad." Nevertheless, the album sold well anyway, and he had another gold record.

Murphy's next film, released in 1986, was "The Golden Child." A number of critics panned the movie. David Ehrenstein of *American Film* called it "a confused fantasy-adventure." David Handelman of *Rolling Stone* labeled it "abysmal." But, despite the critics, the movie did well at the box office. Janet Maslin of the *New York Times* commented that Paramount "has done a much better job of marketing 'The Golden Child' than making it." She added that it was probably just the popular Murphy's presence that brought people in.

Early in 1987, Murphy was beset by bad news. In March, Handleman reported, Murphy "made headlines when taken to court by his first manager, a small-time agent named King Broder." Fired in 1980, Broder wanted a cut of all Murphy's earnings since. Murphy settled out of court for about $700,000. Later that same month, an Atlantic City tax-shelter scam was uncovered into which Murphy had invested $240,000. And in April he was hit with a paternity suit.

In May of 1987 his next movie, "Beverly Hills Cop II," was released. Again, many critics downgraded

Eddie Murphy (center) becomes the 171st star to imbed his name and footprints in concrete at Mann's Chinese Theater in Hollywood. UPI/Bettmann Newsphotos.

the film. *USA Today* said it was "a robotic, hard-sell sequel by folks whose Malibu Beach house mortgage payment is due." Maslin said, "Lively as it is, 'Beverly Hills Cop II' can't help but suffer from the lack of any originality at all." Handleman exclaimed that Murphy "has ended up producing soulless, self-serving junk." Some critics, though, liked the reprise. Michael Buckley of *Films in Review* stated that "Murphy repeats his character's bravado, pushy ways and funny bits—and they work." The movie-going public also liked the reprise—a great deal. The *New York Times* reported that the film "proved itself a box-office blockbuster ... marking up the biggest single-day earnings in film history," $9.7 million. At a press conference for "Beverly Hills Cop II," Murphy also introduced what he called "The Black Pack," a group of rising young black comics including Robert Townsend, Arsenio Hall, Keenen Ivory Wayans, Paul Mooney, and Damon Williams.

His next movie, "Raw," was released in December of 1987. "This feature-length concert film," stated Maslin in a review, "is hilarious, putting Mr. Murphy on a par with Mr. [Richard] Pryor at his best." She continued, "Even the ushers were laughing." Audiences poured in to see the movie, and it became the biggest-grossing concert film ever.

After Murphy's rise to stardom, some blacks chided him for not supporting black causes. The truth, according to Walter Leavy of *Ebony*, is that all along Murphy was working quietly behind the scenes, donating to organizations like the Martin Luther King Jr. Center for Nonviolent Social Change. At the 1988 Academy Awards show, however, Murphy went public, calling the Academy to task for having awarded only three Oscars to black actors in its 60-year history.

In the summer of 1988 Murphy came out with a film that was a change of pace for him, "Coming to America." Here he was playing the lead in a lighthearted romantic comedy, a departure from the brash, swaggering characters of his previous films. Peter Travers of *People* liked the change: "This is Murphy's most heartfelt and hilarious performance. And his riskiest." Other critics knocked it. David Ansen of *Newsweek* said that "'Coming to America' may be more interesting as a career move than as a movie." Vincent Canby of the *New York Times* said that the film has a "screenplay that seems to have escaped its doctors before it was entirely well." The public continued to flock to see Murphy, however, and the movie ended up as the second biggest grossing hit of the year. "Coming to America," unfortunately, also brought additional legal problems for Murphy. *Washington Post* columnist Art Buchwald and writer Shelby Gregory, reported *People*, both claimed that Murphy stole their ideas for the film's screenplay. Buchwald said he did a story treatment which was optioned to Paramount for Murphy. Gregory said he did a screenplay that was given to Murphy. Gregory filed a $10 million lawsuit against Murphy and his co-screenwriters, and Buchwald was considering a suit.

Murphy's future plans include directing and a try at dramatic acting. He'll direct a comedy starring Arsenio Hall called "The Butterscotch Kid." And he also wants to co-star with James Earl Jones in a film version of the drama "Fences." In addition, Murphy signed a three-year contract with CBS for shows that he will produce, direct, or appear in.

"I live to make people happy," Murphy told James McBride of *People*, and his huge popularity attests that he's done exceptionally well in achieving this goal. In fact, the ability to leave his audiences happy in whatever he does may very well be the simple secret to his phenomenal success. As Corliss wrote, "More than any other entertainer in recent memory, Eddie Murphy just plain makes people feel good."

Sources

American Film, December, 1987; September, 1988.
Commentary, March, 1985.
Ebony, July, 1988.
Esquire, December, 1985.
Films in Review, August-September, 1987.
Interview, September, 1987.
Newsweek, January 7, 1985; July 4, 1988.
New York Times, March 10, 1985; February 15, 1987; May 20, 1987; May 28, 1987; December 19, 1987; June 29, 1988.
People, January 25, 1982; January 31, 1983; July 4, 1988; August 8, 1988.
Rolling Stone, July 7, 1983; July 2, 1987.
Time, July 11, 1983; January 7, 1985; July 4, 1988.

—Sidelights by Greg Mazurkiewicz

Ralph Nader

UPI/Bettmann Newsphotos

Attorney and consumer advocate

Born February 27, 1934, in Winsted, Conn.; son of Nadra (owner of a restaurant) and Rose (Bouziene) Nader. *Education:* Princeton University, B.A. in government and economics (magna cum laude), 1955; Harvard University, LL.B. (with distinction), 1958.

Addresses: *Home*—Washington, D.C. *Office*—P.O. Box 19367, Washington, D.C. 20026.

Career

Admitted to Bars of Connecticut, 1958, Massachusetts, 1959, and U.S. Supreme Court, 1959; research assistant to Harvard University law professor Harold J. Berman, 1958; attorney in private practice in Hartford, Conn., beginning 1959; traveled throughout the Soviet Union, Scandinavia, Africa, and South America as a freelance journalist in the early 1960s; University of Hartford, Hartford, Conn., lecturer in history and government, 1961–63; U.S. Department of Labor, Washington, D.C., consultant on automotive safety, 1964–65; Princeton University, Princeton, N.J., lecturer, 1967–68; consumer advocate; founder of Center for the Study of Responsive Law, Public Citizen Inc., National Insurance Consumer Organization, Public Interest Research Group, Aviation Consumer Action Project, Center for Auto Safety, Profiles for Auto Safety, Critical Mass Energy Project, Project for Corporate Responsibility, Health Research Group, Clean Water Action Project, Disability Rights Center, Center for Science in the Public Interest, and Pension Rights Center. *Military service:* U.S. Army, 1959.

Member: American Bar Association, American Academy of Arts and Sciences, Phi Beta Kappa.

Awards: Nieman Fellows Award, 1965–66; named one of ten Outstanding Young Men of the Year by U.S. Junior Chamber of Commerce, 1967; first annual Public Defender Award from *New Republic*, 1969.

Sidelights

Much of the credit for the consumer movement that took shape in the 1960s goes to Ralph Nader, self-appointed "people's lawyer" who rose to national prominence by exposing dangerous flaws in such products as automobiles, packaged meat, and synthetic fabrics. Through the late 1970s and 1980s he continued his consumer advocacy outside the glare of the media spotlight. Many of his skilled and dedicated young followers—nicknamed, inevitably, Nader's Raiders—entered government service or think tanks during the Carter administration, forming a network of permanent Washington insiders. In the wake of the Reagan administration, Nader enjoyed a major resurgence as two of his crusades came to fruition.

After years of declining influence, the ascetic "Everyman's lobbyist," as *Newsweek* once dubbed him, was at the forefront of two successful public interest campaigns: one, the movement to roll back car insurance rates in California, and, two, the grassroots drive that blocked the proposed 50 percent Congressional pay hike. In California, Nader helped win a state referendum that rolled back car insurance rates 20 percent and limited future rate increases. In the Congressional pay increase defeat, he helped mobilize public opinion against the raise.

People under thirty sometimes are unfamiliar with the name of the once widely admired young lawyer whose accomplishments include forcing a defective car off the market, bringing about federal regulations governing meat packaging, and prodding Washington to standardize safety regulations for factory worksites. His most significant accomplishment transcends specific issues: he helped launch consumer rights as a national issue. With no one paying his salary, working without an office staff, and living in a Washington boardinghouse, the olive-skinned young attorney in the wrinkled suit quickly seized the public imagination. "He has already proved himself to be one of the most shrewd, controversial and enigmatic players to mount the political stage in many a year," declared Washington political writer Patrick Anderson in a 1967 *New York Times* magazine profile.

Nader's agenda today essentially expands his longstanding concerns. On the national level he continues to push for mandatory wearing of auto seatbelts, a national health insurance plan, and a savings and loan bailout plan that would shift the tax burden to the rich. On the state level, he is lobbying for restrictions on the use of chlorinated fluorocarbons that deplete the ozone layer, legislation that would erode the barriers that protect corporations from being sued for wrongdoing, and for reforms in auto insurance/liability legislation.

In 1988 one indication of Nader's resurgence was the publication of an article in the prestigious *Harvard Business Review,* written by Nader and commissioned for a special Election Year 1988 issue. The article, words of advice to the next occupant of the White House, appeared alongside a score of similar articles with illustrious bylines. To those who equated the sixties advocate with unyielding contempt for U.S. business, the article offered some surprises, not the least of which was the author's heralding of Dow Chemical chief executive Paul Oreffice as a model of organizational leadership. Wrote Nader, "Our best corporations do provide some relevant principles that can be adapted toward making government more efficient, more responsive, more creative and more humane." He cited other corporate examples worthy of government emulation. Washington insiders recognized Nader's familiar contempt for bureaucratic lethargy and incompetence, as well as his dry, caustic humor. "If the U.S. government were a public corporation, Carl Icahn would have launched a hostile takeover years ago," he chided.

Respected for his apparent altruism and, seemingly, beholden to no one, Nader withdrew gradually from the public spotlight in the mid seventies with his reputation untarnished. When he emerged in California in 1987 and began urging voters to support Proposition 103, a bill that would rollback auto insurance rates, voters responded affirmatively—exit polls showed Nader's endorsement had swung their vote. His more recent forays into the spotlight have demonstrated he has updated his media skills, using such events as celebrity endorsements and calls to radio talk shows to influence public opinion. In 1988 he convinced such celebrities as Dustin Hoffman, Paul Newman, and Phil Donahue to publicly demonstrate the inflate-on-impact auto air bag. Manufacturers announced the device would be standard in some models.

"My job is to bring issues out in the open where they cannot be ignored."

Once again, the eccentric Harvard Law grad was in the spotlight. Calling a press conference to promote the details of his Savings and Loan bailout plan, Nader walked into a packed room. "Four years ago nobody would have paid any attention," he told *Business Week.* "It's not the ideas. It's persistence."

Nader emerged in the mid-sixties as an enigmatic young man who personified the ideals of the time. He had passed up a lucrative career in corporate law to further his vision of a more humane existence, a healthier environment, and empowerment of the individual over the corporation. The man himself shunned public attention, living frugally on public transportation, cheap restaurants, and public telephones. He gave few interviews, avoided the Washington social scene, dated no one, and seemed impassioned only over regulatory issues and Federal agency reports. A limited circle of intellectual journalists and Congressional aides knew a witty, sharp-tongued young man; the public knew only the one-dimensional opponent of engineering flaws. As writer Jack Newfield put it in *Life,* what developed around Nader was a cult of non-personality.

The young lawyer told *Time* in 1969: "My job is to bring issues out in the open where they cannot be ignored. There is a revolt against the aristocratic uses of technology and a demand for democratic uses. We have got to know what we are doing to ourselves. Life can be—and is being—eroded." Nader produced a flow of articles for influential magazines like the *New Republic,* thereby publicizing his crusades. He also wrote books, the most celebrated of which was 1965's *Unsafe At Any Speed,* depicting an auto industry unwilling to design and build cars capable of transporting passengers safely. The expose brought about the demise of the Corvair, the General Motors vehicle Nader charged was unable to negotiate turns at fast speeds. It changed engineering practices significantly.

"I don't like to think of myself as an idealist....I think of myself as being very practical because I want to be effective."

At his small office at the National Press Building—phone number unlisted—or in his room in a $20 per week boarding house, Nader read his way through reams of government transcripts, agency reports, panel testimony, and whatever government verbiage he could obtain. The reading helped him identify new issues and suggested new campaigns. He would assign topics to teams of young proteges—Nader's Raiders—who would fan out throughout Washington on fact-finding missions. He would add their completed reports to his reading list: five daily newspapers, ten weekly magazines and twenty monthly publications. A *Newsweek* reporter found Nader's residence a warren of "newspapers, yellowed Congressional records and legal journals, all of which he has read or clipped but none of which he has ever bothered to throw away."

Nader early mastered the Washington art of information distribution. Often he aired his findings at press conferences. Just as often, however, he turned his "case" over to others who might present it to better effect: often congressmen or journalists. In the sixties and seventies he worked closely with consumer-minded senators such as Washington's Warren Magnusin, Minnesota's Walter Mondale, and Wisconsin's Gaylord Nelson, and did plenty of legwork for *Washington Post* columnist Drew Pearson. "A reformer can't afford to have an ego," he told Patrick Anderson. "That's not modesty, just tactics."

Nader was born to a Lebanese immigrant couple, Nadra and Rose (Bouziane), the second of two brothers and three sisters. He grew up speaking Arabic as well as English, and has since learned Chinese, Russian, Spanish, and Portuguese. The family settled in Winsted, Conn., and converted a dilapated diner into a successful restaurant and bakery. Young Ralph attended Princeton University and graduated magna cum laude in 1955. Encouraged by his parents, he went on to Harvard Law School and graduated with distinction in 1958. He joined the Connecticut bar, then opened a practice in Hartford. He found time to teach history and government at the University of Hartford for several years in the early sixties, and later in the decade to teach at Princeton.

As a young attorney Nader took on a number of auto accident cases and in the process began to delve into highway mortality statistics. His concern prompted his own investigation into Detroit's engineering practices. He was invited to testify before a Congressional auto-safety committee. General Motors' response was to hire a private detective to tail Nader, hoping to find misdeeds—sexual or otherwise—that could be used to undermine him. The plan backfired, producing a personal apology from the chairman. Nader emerged from the confrontation, according to a *Newsweek* profile, as "a knight in shining armor, irrestibly appealing: a slender, boyish, vulnerable figure standing up to a giant industry."

Nader at this time was already in Washington in the employ of Daniel Patrick Moynihan, then Assistant Secretary of Labor (and today senator from New York). Moynihan shared his interest in auto safety and in 1964 had hired him as a consultant on auto safety issues. President Johnson cited the issue in his 1966 State of the Union message, and a tire safety bill gained Congressional support. The timing was perfect for a young idealist struggling against corporate Goliaths.

Nader, however, was never that idealist. In 1969 he rejected that image in an interview with political writer Jack Newfield. "I don't like to think of myself as an idealist," he protested. "If you define an idealist as someone who recedes from the real world because he wants his own world to be pure, then I'm not an idealist. I think of myself as being very practical because I want to be effective. One of the reasons I do what I do is that I feel very strongly the inadequacies of the traditional reformers. They don't do their homework. They get all involved with status, egotism and the rituals of publicity. Even the great old muckrakers like Upton Sinclair and Lincoln Steffens didn't follow through by politically mobilizing a concerned constituency."

Nader proceeded to do exactly that. He brought attention to health hazards in mining, inadequate gas pipeline safety standards, inequities suffered by the American Indian, and the dangers inherent in routine dental X-rays. He celebrated a major victory when Congress enacted the 1967 Wholesome Meat Act, which imposed Federal inspection standards on nearly all meat processed in this country. He later led the way for similar legislation covering fish processing.

In the early seventies, the bulk of Nader's agenda became law in the Nixon Administration, including bills that created the Occupational Safety and Health Administration, the Environmental Protection Agency, and the Consumer Product Safety Commission. Talk began of Nader running for President, talk he never encouraged and which came to nothing. Nevertheless he had left his fingerprints on Washington, as dozens of his proteges were recruited for administration posts when Jimmy Carter came to office in 1974.

The loss of key proteges slowed down Nader's movement somewhat, but during the Reagan administration he himself became almost invisible in Washington. The Reagan free-market philosophy took the teeth out of agencies that had previously guarded the public interest against special interests. Regulatory agencies were gutted by funding cuts and were often headed by appointees disdainful of public interest causes. These were years in the shadows for the consumer activist.

But he remained active, if unheralded, focusing his attention on nurturing the web of Washington based research institutes he had launched in the seventies. The model was his original base of operations, the Center for Responsive Law. A consortium of nonprofit groups, influenced directly or indirectly by Nader, it operated on a budget of $5 million by 1989, according to *Business Week.* The organizations include the Public Interest Research Group, the Center for Auto Safety, the Clean Water Action Project, the Disability Rights Center, the Pension Rights Center, and the Project for Corporate Responsibility. In 1983 he established the U.S. Public Interest Research Group, the umbrella for 26 state PIRGs.

The Reagan years were hard times for Nader personally as well. In 1986 his older brother Shafeek died of prostate cancer, plunging the lawyer into a deep depression. Nader developed a case of Bell's palsy that left the left side of his face paralyzed for several months. He emerged from that depression seemingly revitalized and intent on a more public role. He orchestrated a telephone linkup of 200 radio talk shows in which he railed against the proposed Congressional pay raise, and followed up by stumping the state in person for two weeks—a dramatic change in style.

But not, colleagues and associates say, a change in philosophy or agenda. Mark Green, a New York politico and Nader protege, told *Fortune* magazine's Thomas Stewart: "I don't know anyone who's changed less in a quarter of a century than Ralph. He has a belief system he sees the world through, and it's largely the same."

Writings

Unsafe At Any Speed: The Designed-in Dangers of the American Automobile, Grossman, 1965.
What to Do With Your Bad Car (co-author), Grossman, 1970.
Beware, Law-Arts, 1971.
Whistle Blowing: The Report of the Conference on Professional Responsibility (co-editor), Grossman, 1972.
The Consumer and Corporate Accountability (editor), Harcourt, 1973.
You and Your Pension (with Kate Blackwell), Viking, 1973.
Corporate Power in America (with Mark Green), Viking, 1973.
Action for a Change: A Student's Manual for Public Interest Organizing (with Donald Ross), Viking, 1973.
Working on the System: A Comprehensive Manual for Citizen Access to Federal Agencies, Basic Books, 1974.
The Commerce Committees (co-author), Viking, 1975.
The Environment Committees (co-author), Viking, 1975.
The Judiciary Committees (co-author), Viking, 1975.
The Revenue Committees (co-author), Viking, 1975.
The Money Committees (co-author), Viking, 1975.
Ruling Congress (co-author), Viking, 1975.
The Ralph Nader Congress Project, six volumes, Viking, 1975.
Government Regulation: What Kind of Reform?, American Enterprise Institute for Public Policy Research, 1976.

Taming the Giant Corporation (co-author), Norton, 1976.
Verdicts on Lawyers (co-editor), Crowell, 1976.
The White House, Viking, 1977.
The Menace of Atomic Energy (with John Abbotts), Norton, 1977.
The Lemon Book, Caroline House, 1980.
Who's Poisoning America? (co-editor), Regnery, 1981.
Eating Clean: Food Safety and the Chemical Harvest (co-editor), Center for Responsive Law, 1982.
The Big Boys: Styles of Corporate Power (with William Taylor), Pantheon, 1986.
More Action for Change: Students Serving the Public Interest (with Kelley Griffin), Dembner Books, 1987.
Being Beautiful (with Kathy Isaac), Center for Responsive Law, 1987.

Also author of introductions to several books. Contributor of articles to numerous periodicals, including *Saturday Review*, *Atlantic*, *Christian Science Monitor*, and *New Republic*. Contributing editor, *Ladies Home Journal*, beginning 1973.

Sources

Books

Acton, Jay, Ralph Nader: A Man and a Movement, Warner, 1972.
Buckhorn, R.F., Nader: The People's Lawyer, Prentice-Hall, 1972.
McCarry, Charles, Citizen Nader, Saturday Review Press, 1972.
Sanford, David, Me & Ralph: Is Nader Unsafe for America?, New Republic Book Co., 1976.

Periodicals

Business Week, January 25, 1969; February 15, 1988; March 6, 1989.
Chicago Tribune, January 4, 1985.
Esquire, December, 1983.
Fortune, May 22, 1989.
Harvard Business Review, November-December, 1988.
Life, October 3, 1969.
New Republic, December 9, 1985.
Newsday, March 9, 1986.
Newsweek, January 22, 1968.
New Yorker, October 15, 1973.
New York Times Magazine, October 29, 1967.
Time, December 15, 1967; December 12, 1969.
Washington Post, September 13, 1981.

—Sidelights by Daniela Pozzaglia

Martina Navratilova

AP/Wide World Photos

Professional tennis player

Born October 18, 1956, in Prague, Czechoslovakia; came to United States, 1975; naturalized citizen, July 21, 1981; daughter of Jana (an office worker) and stepdaughter of Mirek (an economic adviser and tennis coach) Navratil. *Education:* Attended school in Czechoslovakia.

Addresses: *Home*—Fort Worth, Tex.; and Aspen, Colo.

Career

Professional tennis player, 1974—. Ranked No. 1 female tennis player in the world, 1978, 1979, 1982, 1983, 1984, 1985, and 1986; winner of numerous competitions and tournaments, including singles championships at Wimbledon, 1978, 1979, 1982, 1983, 1984, 1985, 1986, and 1987, Australian Open, 1981, 1983, and 1985, French Open, 1982 and 1984, and U.S. Open, 1983, 1984, 1986, and 1987; doubles championships at French Open, 1975, 1983, 1984, 1985, 1986, and 1987, Wimbledon, 1976, 1979, 1981, 1982, 1983, 1984, and 1986, U.S. Open, 1977, 1978, 1983, 1984, 1986, and 1987, and Australian Open, 1980, 1982, 1983, 1984, 1985, and 1987. Has accumulated more than 1,000 career match victories; in 1984, earned more money ($2,173,556) than any other athlete in the world, except two boxers. Has done extensive work on behalf of underprivileged and abused children.

Member: Women's International Tennis Association (president, 1979–80, 1983; member of board of directors, executive committee, and ranking committee), Sierra Club.

Awards: Named Player of the Year by Women's International Tennis Association, 1978–79, 1982–86; named Female Athlete of the Year by Associated Press, 1983.

Sidelights

The clouds gathered, the sky darkened, and the summer rain fell on the grass, center court in the suburbs of London, England. This was early in the summer of 1988, late in the fortnight at Wimbledon, the most prestigious tennis tournament in the world. In progress: the championship match of the women's competition between Martina Navratilova and Steffi Graf. Navratilova, 31, was the defending champion. A native of Czechoslovakia who is now an American citizen, she was seeking her seventh straight English crown and ninth there in the past 11 years. On the other side of the net was Graf, 19, a West German who had lost the previous year's title match to Navratilova but seemed on her way to her first victory here.

When the rains came, each woman had won one set of the best-of-three finale. Navratilova had won the first, 7-5, but Graf had rebounded with an impressive 6-2 victory in the second set and had taken a 3-1 lead in the third. At one point, Graf had won nine straight games and had broken Navratilova's service five straight times. To borrow a cliche from another individualist sport, boxing, Graf had Navratilova on the ropes. "No one had treated Navratilova so rudely in years," wrote Paul Attner of the *Sporting News.* Would Navratilova, queen of this court through most of the 1980s, use the unplanned rest to gather her strength, adjust her strategy, prepare a dramatic comeback, and keep her title? With time on her hands, would Graf dwell on the enormity of her opportunity, lose her momentum, and squander what seemed in reach?

Perhaps it would happen in dreams, in fairy tales, or in movie scripts, but not on the lawn at Wimbledon in 1988. "In truth," wrote Curry Kirkpatrick of *Sports Illustrated,* "it was a reign stoppage." When they returned to the court, Graf quickly won the next three games to take the final set, 6-1, and leave with the silver plate that is presented to the champion by the Duchess of Kent. "It wound up being a sad scene for [Navratilova]," Graf said, "but a special one for me." Admitted Navratilova: "I got blown out. This is definitely the end of a chapter.... Pass the torch, I guess."

Although the defeat at Wimbledon meant the end of a chapter, it certainly didn't close the book on the career of Navratilova, one of the world's most successful, colorful, and controversial athletes of her generation. Top female players in the past have excelled well into their late thirties, and Navratilova intends to join that list. "Retirement is still a ways off," Navratilova wrote in her autobiography, *Martina,* co-authored by George Vecsey, in 1985. "People say I can play until I'm forty, and I don't see any reason why I can't.... Robert Haas used to claim that with all the work I was doing on myself, I could be winning Wimbledon at the age of forty. People scoffed, but that's really not unreasonable when you look at Billie Jean King, who reached the 1982 and 1983 semifinals at Wimbledon at age thirty-nine and forty. Barring an injury or lack of motivation, I can see myself doing it."

Certainly, she always has shown determination, motivation, and a willingness to shape her future for herself. Even if she hadn't been a tennis champion, Navratilova would have been an unusual and interesting person for at least two reasons. First, she is a political defector from Czechoslovakia, a communist country of the Soviet Eastern Bloc, who was outspoken about her desire to become a citizen of the United States; and second, she says she is a bisexual and has often discussed the sometimes taboo subject of lesbian love in interviews and in her autobiography.

Even in terms of tennis, she has been unique in that she has shown more willingness than others of her generation to seek technical, physical, and emotional coaching from other persons inside and outside her sport. While Navratilova isn't the first to do such things, some experts feel her dedication to coaching and training has influenced the approach of other tennis players for the next generation. "I'm not saying she's the first to do it," said Mary Carillo, a former player who is now a television commentator, in an interview for *Newsmakers.* "Margaret Court did it and Billie Jean King did it. But when Martina did it, everybody followed her lead. A lot of players now go to sports psychologists. Martina soared so far beyond everybody else, the only thing to do was to follow her lead. She did more than dominate the early 1980s. She set a whole new standard. She changed her diet and her fitness status. She made it scientific. She made it specific."

Navratilova was born on October 18, 1956, in Prague, Czechoslovakia and was raised in the suburb of Revnice by her mother and her stepfather. (Her real father committed suicide after the divorce.) As a lean, small child, Navratilova excelled in many sports, including hockey and skiing. She often competed against boys. "I'm not very psychologically oriented and I have no idea how I was affected by my real father's abandonment, the secrets and the suicide, or my feeling about being a misfit, a skinny little tomboy with short hair," she wrote in her autobiography. "In Czechoslovakia, nobody ever put me down for running around with boys, playing ice hockey and soccer. From what I've been told, people in the States used to think that if girls were good at sports, their sexuality would be affected."

As a teenager, Navratilova's tennis skills allowed her to tour foreign countries, including the United States. She felt stifled in Czechoslovakia and defected at the U.S. Open in 1975, shortly before her 19th birthday. At the time, she said it was strictly a matter of tennis. "Politics had nothing to do with my decision," she said in an Associated Press story. "It was strictly a tennis matter." In Prague, a reporter told her grandfather, who was quoted as replying, "Oh, the little idiot, why did she do that?" The defection was prompted in part, she said, by an incident early in 1975 when she was playing in a tournament at Amelia Island off the coast of Florida. She received a telegram from the officials of the Czech Sports

Federation demanding that she return home. "I was in the middle of the tournament," she said. "I had to call upon the U.S. Tennis Association to help get me permission to play. That was when I really decided that I should leave Czechoslovakia."

"Retirement is still a ways off. People say I can play until I'm forty, and I don't see any reason why I can't."

Life in a capitalist country brought wealth—and problems. "I didn't do it for the money, but it's nice to have," she told the *Detroit Free Press* more than two years after the defection. She began to buy cars and houses, often owning several of each at the same time. She currently maintains a home in Fort Worth, Tex., and a townhouse in Aspen, Colo. Among the problems were loneliness and a fondness for the fattening foods sold in fast-food restaurants in the United States. "I miss my family badly," she told Bud Collins of the *New York Times Magazine*. "I worried for awhile that there would be retaliation against them, but there wasn't much." Her weight grew to 167 pounds shortly after her defection. She is five feet, seven and one-half inches tall. A decade later, after undergoing her physical conditioning program, she was 145 pounds of lean muscle.

Her physique stood in contrast to that of many American female athletes of the past who tried to maintain the unlikely combination of round, soft, "feminine" curves and the athletic ability that comes with muscle tone and conditioning. Her appearance and personal behavior quickly led to public discussions of her sexual preference. "I never thought there was anything strange about being gay," she wrote in her book. "Even when I thought about it, I never panicked and thought, Oh, I'm strange, I'm weird, what do I do now?"

The book details many of Navratilova's relationships and living arrangements with women and how some soured and ended in bitterness. She tells of her professional relationship with Renee Richards, a female tennis player and coach who at one time was a man but had undergone a sex-change operation. Another one of her professional aides was Nancy Lieberman, a basketball player who Navratilova used for training and motivational purposes. At times, her many coaches and associates didn't get along. "Things got worse at Wimbledon when Renee was not invited to a surprise birthday party for Nancy, planned by some friends of Nancy's," Navratilova wrote in her book. "Renee thought it was Nancy's idea, but that was ridiculous. I knew the party was being planned, but I had other things on my mind."

The political side of her life story came to the fore in the summer of 1986, when she returned for the first time to Czechoslovakia. As an American citizen, she represented the United States in the Federation Cup in Prague. The return was a major media event as soon as she stepped off the plane. "Lights. Shouts. Rudeness. Pushing. Shoving," wrote Frank Deford in *Sports Illustrated*. "How Kafka must have chuckled in his nearby grave as Navratilova beat a retreat." As she played well and won, she became a favorite of the fans, if not of Czech tennis officials. "Every day the lady from Revnice was winning more hearts," Deford wrote. "Young men dashed on the court to give her roses. The crowds began to acclaim her, and she grew more responsive—first waving shyly, then

Martina Navratilova prepares to return a shot from South Africa's Karen Schimper during their third-round match at Wimbledon, 1988. AP/Wide World Photos.

giving the thumbs-up sign and, last, blowing kisses. Why, it almost seemed as if the Statue of Liberty had gone on tour, turning in her torch for a Yonex racket. Czech officials grew so enraged that on Friday they ordered the umpire not to introduce Navratilova by name. She became 'On my left the woman player from the United States.'''

Although her personal life is interesting, there are other persons who are defectors from Czechoslovakia and others who overcame obesity and others who are bisexual. What makes Navratilova a famous person is her ability to play tennis consistently with the best in the world. She holds the racket in her left hand and plays aggressively. "The pattern of attack is a vital factor in Martina's supremacy," Shirley Brasher wrote in *Weekend Magazine of Canada.* "She gives her opponents no time to find their own rhythm, no time to play at a safe speed. Instead, she rushes them and pushes them around the court, hitting out for the lines and blanketing the next with her reach, power and speed."

As the years went by and her victory totals grew, Navratilova became a favorite subject of sports writers who watched her grow from an emotional teen-ager to a more self-assured adult. "She has evolved in the eyes of many," John Ed Bradley wrote in the *Washington Post,* "into a strong-armed automaton with a mean top spin forehand... and a tough, insensitive attitude that has wiped clean the memory of her emotional loss to Tracy Austin in the 1981 U.S. Open. Has the world forgotten that she wept violently at center court after dropping the third-set tie breaker?" As her career peaked, late in 1986, Peter Alfano wrote in the *New York Times:* "For the fifth consecutive year, Ms. Navratilova will finish as the No. 1 player in the world in the computer rankings. Her hold is so strong that a rare defeat is celebrated like a holiday on the tour, her victorious opponent treated like a conquering hero. Then come the whispers: Is Martina slowing down?"

Two years later, the whispers were common conversation. Her computer ranking fell to No. 2 and held there for 1988. Going into competition in 1988, she had won 17 Grand Slam titles. (A Grand Slam event is one of the four major tournaments: Wimbledon, the U.S. Open, the French Open and the Australian Open.) Only three women had won more: Margaret Court (26), Helen Wills Moody (19), and Chris Evert (18). Prior to 1988, Navratilova had won at least one Grand Slam singles title in seven consecutive years. But the year 1988 was difficult for her with no Grand Slam titles. After being upset by Zina Garrison in the U.S. Open in suburban New York, Navratilova said, "If this year were a fish, I would throw it back."

Avocational Interests: Golf, basketball, skiing.

Writings

Martina (with George Vecsey), Knopf, 1985.

Sources

Associated Press, September 8, 1975.
Boston Globe, November 5, 1988.
Chicago Tribune, November 16, 1987.
Christian Science Monitor, August 25, 1986; September 8, 1986; September 9, 1986.
Detroit Free Press, February 19, 1975; August 12, 1985; July 6, 1986; June 28, 1987; July 5, 1987.
Los Angeles Times, September 15, 1985; September 22, 1985; July 27, 1986; August 25, 1986; September 7, 1986; September 8, 1986; November 24, 1986.
New York Times, December 7, 1975; August 25, 1986; September 8, 1986; September 10, 1986.
New York Times Magazine, June 19, 1977.
Orlando Sentinel, April 25, 1985.
People, September 22, 1986.
Sport, March, 1976.
Sporting News, July 11, 1988.
Sports Illustrated, February 24, 1975; April 4, 1983; September 19, 1983; May 26, 1986; August 4, 1986; September 12, 1986; July 11, 1988.
Tennis, December, 1974.
Time, July 11, 1983; July 16, 1984.
Washington Post, January 9, 1985; September 8, 1986.
Weekend Magazine of Canada, June, 1979.
Women's Sports, August, 1985.
Women's Sports Fitness, November, 1986.
World Tennis, May, 1975; March, 1983; October, 1983; December, 1983; May, 1985.

—Sidelights by Joe LaPointe

Jack Nicholson

AP/Wide World Photos

Actor, director, and screenwriter

Born April 22, 1937, in Neptune, N.J.; son of June Nicholson; grandson of John (a sign painter) and Ethel May (operator of a beauty parlor) Nicholson; married Sandra Knight (an actress), 1961 (divorced, 1966); children: Jennifer. *Education:* Graduated from high school in New Jersey; studied acting with Jeff Corey and several other drama teachers.

Addresses: *Home*—Los Angeles, Calif.; and Aspen, Colo. *Agent*—Artists Agency, 190 North Canon Dr., Beverly Hills, Calif. 90210.

Career

Office boy in cartoon department of MGM Studios, beginning 1957; member of Players Ring Theatre acting troupe in late 1950s; feature films include "The Cry Baby Killer," 1958, "Too Young to Love," 1959, "The Little Shop of Horrors," 1960, "The Wild Ride," 1960, "Studs Lonigan," 1960, "The Raven," 1963, "The Terror," 1964, "Ensign Pulver," 1964, "Back Door to Hell," 1964, "Ride the Whirlwind," 1966, "The Shooting," 1967, "The St. Valentine's Day Massacre," 1967, "Hell's Angels on Wheels," 1967, "Rebel Rousers," 1967, "Psych-Out," 1968, "Easy Rider," 1969, "On a Clear Day You Can See Forever," 1970, "Five Easy Pieces," 1970, "Carnal Knowledge," 1971, "King of Marvin Gardens," 1971, "A Safe Place," 1971, "The Last Detail," 1973, "Chinatown" 1974, "Tommy," 1975, "The Passenger," 1975, "The Fortune," 1975, "One Flew Over the Cuckoo's Nest," 1975, "The Missouri Breaks," 1976, "The Last Tycoon," 1977, "Goin' South," 1978, "The Shining," 1980, "The Postman Always Rings Twice," 1981, "Reds," 1981, "The Border," 1982, "Terms of Endearment," 1983, "Prizzi's Honor," 1985, "Heartburn," 1986, "Ironweed," 1987, and "The Witches of Eastwick," 1987. Producer of "Ride the Whirlwind," "The Shooting," and "Head"; director of "Goin' South"; producer and director of "Drive, He Said." Writer of films, including "Ride the Whirlwind," "Flight to Fury," "Head," "The Trip," and "Drive, He Said."

Awards: Academy Award nomination for best supporting actor, 1969, for "Easy Rider"; Academy Award nomination for best actor, 1970, for "Five Easy Pieces"; Academy Award nomination and Cannes Film Festival prize for best actor, 1973, for "The Last Detail"; Academy Award nomination and New York Film Critics Circle Award for best actor, 1974, for "Chinatown"; Academy Award, Golden Globe Award, and New York Film Critics Circle Award for best actor, all 1975, all for "One Flew Over the Cuckoo's Nest"; Academy Award nomination for best supporting actor, 1981, for "Reds"; Academy Award for best supporting actor, 1983, for "Terms of Endearment"; Academy Award nomination for best actor, 1985, for "Prizzi's Honor"; also has received awards from the National Society of Film Critics and the British Film Society.

Sidelights

In the last fifteen years the name Jack Nicholson has become synonymous with remarkable acting talent, maverick personality, and cinematic versatility. A consummate performer, Nicholson has made his reputation on a series of demanding roles—each uniquely eccentric—that explore man adrift in a hostile or indifferent world. *Film Comment* contributor Beverly Walker wrote that, time after time, Nicholson "has evoked empathy and identification with characters whose actions and attitudes are repellent or obstreperous.... Many of [his] films have pushed at the outer edges of what mainstream society can tolerate. This... is part of his mystique."

Nicholson's appeal has never been based on his physical appearance, so he has avoided the stereotyping that traps so many of Hollywood's leading men. As he has aged, so too have his characters; where once he played agitated younger men, he now exalts in the special dilemmas of mid-life. Ron Rosenbaum analyzed Nicholson's ongoing character development in the *New York Times Magazine:* "In part, it's been a matter of timing, a confluence of the content of Nicholson's roles with the concerns of the baby-boom generation, growing out of adolescence into adulthood. While Marlon Brando's and James Dean's naive rebelliousness could be models for teens in the silent generation of the 50's, Nicholson's characters embody the modulations those adolescent attitudes must undergo to survive the disillusion of adulthood." Walker maintains that any role Nicholson brings to the screen becomes recognizable—comfortably or uncomfortably—as an American everyman, someone "close to home." The critic stated: "Nicholson's brilliance is his obvious, intelligent gift for both embodying and commenting upon his character in one seamless evocation.... We intuitively sense something of the man himself in those squirming fictional men."

Nicholson told the *New York Times Magazine:* "I like to play people that haven't existed yet, a future something, a cusp character. I have that creative yearning. Much in the way Chagall flies figures into the air—once it becomes part of the conventional wisdom, it doesn't seem particularly adventurous or weird or wild." "Adventurous," "weird," and "wild" certainly describe many of Nicholson's memorable characters; but his approach to his craft is conventional, based on years of training and a predisposition to analysis and investigation. Rosenbaum characterized Nicholson as "one of those fanatic believers in the method and mystique of the craft of acting, an actor who, even during the dozen lean years in Hollywood when he was doing only B pictures, D pictures, biker epics and schlock, would nonetheless devotedly go from acting teacher to acting teacher seeking truth the way others of his generation would go from guru to guru or shrink to shrink.... If Nicholson's film persona tends toward world-weary disillusion and cool cynicism, Nicholson himself is still the kind of excitable acting-theory enthusiast who is capable of great earnestness on the subject."

Natural as he may appear on the screen, Nicholson brings careful preparation to each part. His overall estimation of acting is also based on intellectual discoveries. "You know," he told Rosenbaum, "they say it takes 20 years at a minimum to make an actor, a full actor, and that's the stage I'm talking about. After you've got some kind of idea of how your instrument is, after you have developed some kind of idea thematically of what you think you're about, after you've got some kind of ease with the craft, then possibly you might have some style." Nicholson himself might serve as the perfect embodiment of his twenty-year plan: a long apprenticeship and much self-searching contributed to the effortless, stylish performances he is able to give today.

Nicholson was born and raised in Neptune, New Jersey, under much less than ideal circumstances. The people he knew as his parents—John and Ethel May Nicholson—were, in fact, his grandparents; and the woman he regarded as an older sister was actually his mother, who had given birth to him out of wedlock. John Nicholson was a sign painter with a drinking problem; he left the family while Jack was still very young. Ethel May opened a beauty parlor in her home to support her three children, and Jack was left to his own devices in the blue collar community. According to Rick Reilly in *Sports Illustrated,* Nicholson "wore a DA, blue jeans and a motorcycle jacket—a greaser down to the tips of his chukka boots." Growing up in the 1950s, young Jack became a sports fanatic, playing basketball and football and working summers as a lifeguard at a Jersey shore beach. He was banned from organized high school sports after his sophomore year because he defaced an opposing team's locker room, but his enthusiasm for playing did not diminish. Barred from athletics, he channeled some of his energy into school plays; soon he was a regular performer in Manasquan High's theatrics. He also was a popular class clown who was voted both Class Pessimist and Class Optimist when he graduated in 1954.

Nicholson got high scores on his college entrance exams, but he decided to postpone college until he had done some traveling. In 1957 he visited his older sister in Los Angeles and took a job as office boy in the cartoon department at MGM. There he became the protege of producer Joe Pasternak, who persuaded him to join the Players Ring Theatre troupe. He did join the troupe and also began acting classes with director Jeff Corey, the first of many drama teachers he was to consult over the years. Through that class Nicholson met Roger Corman, a budding director whose B-movie thrillers have since earned a measure of critical respect. Corman cast Nicholson as the lead in one of his early films, "Cry Baby Killer," a standard picture about troubled adolescence. Nicholson thought the part would put him in contention with Brando and Dean, but the film did not generate that much interest. He went a year between roles and then was only able to land more work as a character actor in Corman's low-budget movies such as "The Raven" and "The Terror." Nicholson may have been frustrated by the lack of work, but he channeled his frustration into rigorous acting classes and the hedonistic abandon that characterized the early 1960s. "This was the era of the Beat Generation and West Coast jazz and staying up all night on Venice Beach," he told *Film Comment.* "That was as important as getting jobs, or so it seemed at the time. I don't reckon it has changed today.... At the beginning you're very idealistically inclined toward the art of the thing. Or you don't stick it because there's no money in it.... I say this by way of underlining that it was *then* and is *still* the art of acting that is the wellspring for me."

In addition to his acting classes, Nicholson learned all he could about filmmaking and screenwriting, feeling that the medium offered a creative outlet equal to painting or poetry. By 1965 he was sufficiently well known in the industry to wrangle a job producing Westerns. He shot two in which he also starred, "Ride the Whirlwind" and "The Shooting"; both were more cerebral than standard American fare. The films did little business in the United States but were cult hits in Europe, especially France. Nicholson continued to write and produce movies (he had written "Ride the Whirlwind"), getting some attention for a psychedelic fantasy called "Head" and even more notice for "The Trip," a story about a television executive who experiments with LSD.

The latter project brought him to the attention of Dennis Hopper and Peter Fonda, two experimental filmmakers who were casting a movie about motorcycling hippies, "Easy Rider." Nicholson got a part in the film by default when actor Rip Torn dropped out; he proceeded to make "Easy Rider" an unprecedented hit. In "Easy Rider" Nicholson plays George Hanson, a hard-drinking Southern lawyer who joins Hopper and Fonda for a stretch of their cross-country bike trip. Many critics praised Nicholson's monologues as the highlight of the movie, and he was nominated for his first Academy Award for the performance.

After "Easy Rider," work came much more frequently for Nicholson. A 1970 film, "Five Easy Pieces," brought him a second Academy Award nomination for his portrayal of a disillusioned concert pianist in rebellion against his artistic background. The next year he seemed to throw sensitivity to the wind when he played a ruthless male chauvinist in the controversial "Carnal Knowledge." *Cue* writer William Wolf notes of that role: "Jack Nicholson is more brilliant than he's ever been as the empty bastard of a guy who can be potent only with the ego-building, undemanding, totally sexual plaything." Nicholson earned a third Academy Award nomination in 1974 for "The Last Detail," a dark comedy about two sailors in desperate search of a fulfilling fling. In the Toronto *Globe & Mail,* Betty Lee wrote of Nicholson's character: "Bad-ass Buddusky is still a fascinating picture of a man questioning himself and his reason for being alive. Nicholson's brilliant reading of the Buddusky character makes the answer apparent. No man is an island."

If any roles can be said to have established Nicholson permanently as Hollywood's reigning artistic actor, they would have to be those in "Chinatown" and "One Flew Over the Cuckoo's Nest." In "Chinatown," Nicholson portrays J. J. Gittes, a private detective whose worldly ways do not prepare him for the corruption he finds in Depression-era Los Angeles. Hired on a case of marital infidelity, Gittes discovers far more sinister work afoot, and learns too late of his essential naivete. His character in "One Flew over the Cuckoo's Nest," Randle Patrick McMurphy, needs no introduction. Nicholson finally won an Academy Award for his role as an affable inmate of a mental hospital who finds himself pitted against a vicious nurse. Rosenbaum wrote: "What seems distinctive about Nicholson's Oscar-winning performance in 'Cuckoo's Nest,' what distinguishes his... McMurphy from [novelist] Ken Kesey's hero, is the suggestion of a dark side, a pathological impulse behind the drive for pure liberation, a self-absorbed quality that ignores the destruction that 'liberation' can bring upon more fragile souls."

Nicholson claims that he brought that impulsiveness to the role through his own analysis of the part. He told Rosenbaum: "The guy's a scamp who knows he's irresistible to women and in reality he expects Nurse Ratched to be seduced by him. This is his tragic flaw. This is why he ultimately fails . . . . It was one long, unsuccessful seduction which the guy was so pathologically sure of." McMurphy may not have seduced Nurse Ratched, but he certainly seduced audiences; "One Flew Over the Cuckoo's Nest" remains one of the most popular films released in the 1970s.

In the 1980s Nicholson has continued his fascination with "cusp" characters, from self-destructing writers in "The Shining" and "Reds" to over-the-hill heroes in "Terms of Endearment" and "Ironweed." (Rosenbaum feels that no other actor "has captured so well the dark side of the writer's disposition, the special bitterness of it.") Nicholson won another Oscar for "Terms of Endearment," in which he plays a paunchy, cynical ex-astronaut with a penchant for avoiding emotional attachments. Critics have praised Nicholson for taking a part that called for an overweight, middle-aged man—just the sort of casting many Hollywood leading men actively avoid.

Although he did not win an Academy Award for "Prizzi's Honor," a 1985 release, he does count that picture among his favorites, because his real-life lover, Angelica Huston, starred in it with him and turned in her own award-winning performance. Nicholson also relished his own role in "Prizzi's Honor," that of a mafia killer with few social graces and even fewer scruples. "I took a certain level of intelligence away from the character," Nicholson told Rosenbaum, adding that he affected facial tics to accent the character's lack of self-consciousness.

Nicholson also enjoyed the challenge of playing the devil himself in the acclaimed 1987 film "The Witches of Eastwick." Before he began filming, he told Rosenbaum: "I'm going to play the Devil, and I don't want to play him safely. I want people to think Jack Nicholson *is* the Devil. I want them to be *worried.*" Nicholson got his wish; "The Witches of Eastwick" did brisk business when it was released and enjoyed a significant measure of critical approval.

Jack Nicholson has been romantically involved with Angelica Huston, the daughter of director John Huston, for more than a dozen years. They maintain separate residences, however, and both feel this strengthens their relationship. In *People* magazine, Nicholson called Huston "a dark, coiled spring of a woman with long flowing lines [who has] got a mind and a literary sense of style, and you better believe she's got imaginative energies. She's absolutely unpredictable and she's very beautiful. What is it that holds me to her? It's love, I guess, and only love!" Not to be outdone, Huston offered her assessment of Nicholson: "Most actors are vain and egotistical, but Jack is very sensible, not easily swayed. He's at home with himself, and when you're with him, you feel as if you've come home. You feel he's *family.* Audiences feel this too. They feel he understands what *they're* feeling, and that's the essence of his power as a star. People who know him feel understood too. He has many, many friends and he wins their loyalty because he is so loyal. He takes care of his people."

Nicholson's other well-publicized passion is for the Los Angeles Lakers. He is a fixture at Lakers home games and often travels to road games as well, despite the jeers of opposing fans. *Sports Illustrated's* Reilly feels that Nicholson's affection for basketball is just part of his "successful project to have more fun than anybody on the planet."

Nicholson may be dedicated to having fun, but he is also an intensely earnest performer who admits to moments of depression, disillusion, and self-doubt. "I think of myself as a very fortunate person, about which I'm happy," he told *Rolling Stone* magazine. "But I'm deeply moody. It's been a long time since I went through a day that I just thought was splendid and I didn't have some deep self-loathing or depression or fear." Nicholson attributes part of this anxiety to middle age. Having reached fifty, with a grown daughter, he is constantly examining himself and his work. Asked by *Rolling Stone* about future projects, he said: "In all honesty, so what if I never made another movie again? I'm already fifty; nobody's gonna say I failed."

Avocational Interests: Skiing, basketball.

Sources

Cue, July 3, 1971.
Film Comment, May-June, 1985.
Globe and Mail (Toronto), May 30, 1967; February 23, 1974.
Life, September 18, 1970.
Newsday, June 21, 1974.
Newsweek, December 7, 1970.
New York Times, February 10, 1974.
New York Times Magazine, July 13, 1986.
People, July 8, 1985.
Rolling Stone, November 5-December 10, 1987.
Sports Illustrated, November 3, 1986.
Time, November 30, 1970; August 12, 1974.

—Sketch by Anne Janette Johnson

Roger Norrington

Conductor, musicologist

Full name, Roger Arthur Carver Norrington; born March 16, 1934, in Oxford, England; son of Arthur and Edith Joyce (Carver) Norrington; married Susan Elizabeth Maclean, May, 1964 (divorced, 1982); children: one son and one daughter. *Education:* Clare College, Cambridge University B.A.; attended Royal College of Music.

Career

Worked for Oxford University Press; singer, 1962–72; music director, Schütz Choir of London (also founder), 1962—, Kent Opera, 1966–84, London Baroque Players, 1975—, and London Classical Players, 1978—. Has been guest conductor with several orchestras in England, Europe, and the United States; performances have been broadcast on radio and television; has recorded numerous symphonies. Author of articles for music journals.

Awards, honors: Officer, Order of the British Empire, 1980; Cavaliere, Order al Merito della Repubblica Italiana, 1981.

Sidelights

Conductor Roger Norrington is at the vanguard of the historical-performance movement. Norrington and others of this school are credited with revitalizing the works of seventeenth-, eighteenth-, and nineteenth-century composers by using period instruments and early-music techniques. The movement, which began in the late 1970s, attempts to recreate what audiences of those early composers actually heard.

Historical-performance musicians have abandoned "the romanticized, overblown approaches" characteristic of modern orchestras, explained *Newsweek*'s Katrine Ames and Donna Foote. Instead, they favor scaled-down orchestras using "gut-stringed violins, wooden flutes, valveless horns, [and] leather-headed kettledrums," *Time*'s Michael Walsh reported. Moreover, they adhere to the performance practices of long ago, such as looser strings and lighter bowing. "We haven't created early music, we've discovered it," Norrington told Ames and Foote. "It's an amazing revelation, and it's not going to go away."

Norrington began his music career as a singer. A tenor, he founded the Schütz Choir of London in 1962 and also served as its music director. He went on to conduct the Kent Opera, the London Baroque Players, and the London Classical Players. In 1985, he staged the "Haydn Experience," a weekend-long series of concerts and lecture-demonstrations by Norrington and his musicians. Subsequent "experiences" have focused on the works of nineteenth-century composers Beethoven and Hector Berlioz.

Thus far, Norrington has met with popular and critical success. Audiences have been "enthusiastic" and "knowledgeable," according to Ames and Foote. John Rockwell of the *New York Times* found the "Beethoven Experience" to be "the most thoroughgoing examination yet of what Beethoven's symphonies sounded like at the time of their premieres."

He continued, "Most of what Mr. Norrington did was both intellectually and emotionally convincing." Walsh, in a review of the "Berlioz Experience" wrote: "When the music is played by a homogenized modern orchestra, its raw power is sanded away along with its rough edges.... But on early instruments, the flutes purr, the oboes squawk, the brass barks, and the strings alternately cajole and bite."

Norrington has had little formal music education. "Such independence may have solidified his common-sense approach," noted Lesley Valdes in the *Wall Street Journal.* Norrington believes that "many very great artists are too uncreative to think for themselves, too intimidated by tradition." He told Valdes that he "used to play that way too," adding: "I even sang in the chorus under [Otto] Klemperer, when he was chief conductor of the [London] Philharmonia, and I'd think because he was a great conductor, he had to be right. Now the Philharmonia are asking me to do Beethoven. And they're really shocked!"

Avocational interests: Reading, walking, sailing.

Sources

High Fidelity, June, 1988.
Newsweek, October 3, 1988.
New York Times, February 10, 1987, February 7, 1988, March 20, 1988.
Time, March 21, 1988.
Wall Street Journal, June 3, 1987.

—*Sketch by Denise Wiloch*

Yoko Ono

AP/Wide World Photos

Artist and singer

Born February 18, 1933, in Tokyo, Japan; came to United States, 1951; naturalized citizen; daughter of Eisuke (a banker) and Isoko (Yasuda) Ono; married Toshi Ichiyanagi (a composer), 1957 (divorced, 1964); married Anthony Cox (a filmmaker), 1964 (divorced, c.1968); married John Lennon (a singer, songwriter, and musician), March 20, 1969 (died, December 8, 1980); children: (second marriage) Kyoko; (third marriage) Sean. *Education:* Attended Gakushuin University, Tokyo, Japan; and Sarah Lawrence College, Bronxville, N.Y.

Addresses: *Home*—New York City. *Office*—c/o Polydor Records, 1930 Century Park E., Los Angeles, Calif. 90028.

Career

As a child, wrote poetry and plays and studied ballet, the Bible, Buddhist scripture, music, and English; in 1958, began to publicly display her art and stage performance "events" in New York City; returned to Japan for a prolonged visit in the early 1960s, where she appeared on television and staged a number of "events"; has exhibited art throughout the United States and around the world; wrote and directed films, including "Bottoms," 1966, and "Smile," 1968; after meeting and marrying John Lennon, engaged in a number of highly publicized demonstrations for world peace; began recording with Lennon, 1968, and solo albums, 1970; after Lennon's death in 1980, concentrated on music, on various charitable and peace-related enterprises, and on managing his estate; in 1989, the Whitney Museum of American Art in New York City staged a major exhibition of her art works.

Sidelights

When John Lennon died, Yoko Ono entered a widowhood of world legend. Her husband, whose fame as a Beatle was matched in his later years as a peace activist and solo rocker, was in a class of stardom barely one notch below deity. (Lennon himself, in fact, often drew parallels between his work and the life of Christ.) His "assassination," as his murder is often called, inevitably strengthened that image, confirming that his was a mission like those of Ghandi, Martin Luther King, and John F. Kennedy. And after December 8, 1980, Yoko Ono was the world's only human link to him.

On the basis of her artistry alone, Ono had sought public recognition throughout her life, mostly in vain. Now, under the harshest imaginable circumstances, the spotlight had come to her—along with an inheritance of at least $150 million. This twin legacy did little to improve her public image. As revered as Lennon was, Yoko, for a variety of reasons, has always been scorned and even hated. Since his death, she has been charged with living off his name and wealth. In reality, however, Yoko has always been a workaholic, and in the years following John's death she has been busier than ever. Throughout the couple's 13 years together, virtually all of their work was centered around the single mission of promoting world peace. In John's absence, Ono has continued to spread their message—in concert and on new love songs she has written and recorded, through media announcements and million-dollar donations to charity, and through other projects she has undertaken in her self-titled role as "keeper of the wishing well."

Ono's romance with Lennon brought her international recognition. Yet when they first met in 1966, she had already made a name for herself as an artist. Ten years earlier she had dropped out of Sarah Lawrence College, where she was studying poetry and music, to marry Toshi Ichiyanagi, a young avant-garde composer. More than anything, the marriage was Ono's ticket out of an oppressive family environment and into New York's underground art scene. That scene was defined by John Cage, a composer who had discarded pitches and harmonies for everyday sounds that he arranged using methods based on chance rather than standard musical notation. Ono found his ideas liberating, as did the young composer La Monte Young. Together the two organized a weekend performance series at Yoko's loft to give themselves and their peers a venue for their own ideas. Beginning in December 1960 and lasting six months, the "Chambers Street Series," as it was called, is now legendary. Not only was it the first collective forum for the avant-garde, but by integrating various arts within single works, it also marked the onset of a genre that came to be called mixed media. The idea was to break the barriers among the arts, and, in the tradition of Cage, to redefine what constituted "art" by using mundane, task-oriented activities as subject matter. Ono's 1962 piece, *Bicycle Piece for Orchestra,* for example, called for 100 bicyclists to pedal silently around the stage.

The Chambers Street Series paved the way for Fluxus, a loosely knit group of artists, dancers, musicians, filmmakers, and poets that emerged in the early 1960s. Borrowing from such disparate sources as Dadaism, TV commercials, Zen philosophy, and children's games, Fluxus sought to create a new art that would undermine the status quo. First, they rejected the creation of precious art objects that only the wealthy could afford, opting to work instead in intangible media. Second, by creating pieces that required no special artistic skill, they tried to remove elitism from within the art world and suggest that anyone can be an artist. Ono's book, *Grapefruit,* first published in 1964, is now regarded as a cornerstone of these philosophies. The book offers about 100 instructional "pieces," such as "Lighting Piece": "Light a match and watch it till it goes out," or "Kitchen Piece," which instructs the reader to hang a blank canvas on the wall and throw the day's leftovers onto it. Playing off the title conceptual art, used to describe the Fluxus approach in general, Yoko wryly called herself a "con" artist.

"Ono's emphasis was the idea," *ArtForum* wrote. "She challenged us to see the invisible." In 1961 at Carnegie Recital Hall she staged a "happening" entitled "A Grapefruit in the World of Park." Jerry Hopkins' biography *Yoko Ono* quotes her explanation of part of the event: "There was a point where two men were tied up together with lots of empty cans and bottles around them, and they had to move from one end of the stage to the other very quietly.... What I was trying to attain was a sound that almost doesn't come out. I wanted to deal with the sounds of people's fears." In her music as well Yoko sought to activate the listener's imagination. With Lennon in the late 1960s, she recorded two albums entitled *Unfinished Music.* "The unfinished part that's not in the record—what's in you, not what's in the record—is what's important," she told *Rolling Stone.* "The record is just there to stimulate what's in you."

Between 1960 and 1971 Ono created art objects that, like her films and performance pieces, stressed idea over substance. Early in 1989, New York's prestigious Whitney Museum of American Art mounted an exhibition of some of those works. Not content with simply a retrospective, Ono added to each object a new version cast in bronze—a move that marked her re-entrance, after nearly two decades, into the art world. The 1988 versions serve as comments on the original objects. Her 1961 *Painting to Hammer a Nail In,* a wooden panel with hammer and nails, becomes a physical impossibility in bronze. *Painting to Let the Evening Light Go Through* (1961), originally a clear plastic rectangle, is also rendered meaningless.

These twists of meaning are part of a larger theme contrasting the 1960s with the 1980s. Cast in bronze, her original works no longer highlight transience and imagination but rather material wealth. Yet Ono, who has always championed art-as-idea, is neither casting a disapproving glance at 1980s materialism nor selling out to it. Instead, she is viewing the business roots of today's art as a force that might offset the war industry. Art is "much better than guns selling," she told *Splash.* "The way to look at it is that this is the eighties and what is the most practical way of changing the world. It's not to march down the street and wave flags. There's a way of changing it through corporate decisions.... If you think in the sixties norm then it's distasteful. It's not now."

In a sense, Ono's current wealth brings her lifestyle full circle. She was born on February 18, 1933, into a family that was descended from *samarai* and Japanese royalty. Since her banker father worked mainly abroad and her mother busied herself with social engagements, Yoko was raised by servants. After World War II, she attended the exclusive Gakushuin University, where one of her classmates was then-prince Akihito, now the Japanese emperor. She moved to Scarsdale, New York, with her parents in 1951. (Her parents later returned to Japan.)

However comfortable, this world precluded Ono's artistic vision, and so she left it for Manhattan's poverty-striken underground. Throughout the 1960s, married first to Toshi Ichiyanagi and then to Tony Cox, a New York underground filmmaker, she lived the role of suffering artist, rewarded only occasionally by an enthusiastic review. Yet because of her wealthy background, her peers often discredited her commitment. "People just didn't believe she was serious about her art, figuring she could always go home to Mom and Dad," an old friend of hers said in Hopkins' biography.

Distrust of Ono's work spread from her peers to the international public in 1969, when she re-entered the upper class as Lennon's wife. Years later, she told *Playboy* she felt "castrated" by the assumption that through John she was seeking instant success. "Before that I was doing all right, thank you. My work might not have been selling much, I might have been poorer, whatever. But I had my human pride intact and I was doing all right. The most humiliating thing was to be looked at as a parasite."

Public opposition to Ono goes back to the early days of her relationship with John, when the media portrayed her as a force that was driving apart the Beatles. While that report was based upon some degree of truth—Paul McCartney and George Harrison were openly resentful of her constant presence at rehearsals and recording sessions—the larger cause of the breakup was John's growing restlessness with his role as a Beatle. As his allegiance shifted from the band to Yoko, his adoring public blamed her. The public, of course, took its cue from the media. In 1971 *McCall's* wrote, "Paul and George looked at Yoko as though she were the Dragon Lady with a dagger in her garter." Throughout the decade, the "Dragon Lady" label stuck, perpetuating an evil image of her that evaporated only with Lennon's death.

Meanwhile, Ono's budding music career did little to endear her to the public. On record and in concert performances with John, her eerily strident singing became another source of attack. "In the aftermath of the Beatles' breakup," *Rolling Stone* wrote in 1981, "she was an easy target, and her records probably stirred up more animosity and drew more critical barbs than the work of any other (nominally) popular artists. How many listeners knew, or cared, that Ono was combining vocal techniques derived from such disparate sources as Japan's traditional kabuki music and Alban Berg's operas? How many knew or cared that this fusion was a logical by-product of her upbringing, which combined traditional Japanese and modern Western elements, or that she had nurtured her art during a performing career of almost ten years' duration before John Lennon brought her to the attention of a wider public? Yoko Ono's records sounded like a woman screaming, and that, as far as most pop listeners were concerned, was that. 'It's easier for people to listen to mechanical sounds,' Ono commented recently, 'than to listen to a woman cry out.'"

Yet by the close of the seventies, her once-alienating shrieking and moaning was being popularized by punk and New Wave groups, most notably the B-52s and the Pretenders. At the same time, Ono had been modifying the context of her vocal signature, moving closer to a pop style that would mirror the populist spirit of her visual art. "I came to a point where I believed that the idea of avant-garde purity was just as stifling as just doing a rock beat over and over," she told *Rolling Stone*. "People were silent. I felt the lack of a sense of humor. John was doing this healthy beat music, and I got stimulated with that." The result was first heard on *Double Fantasy*, the album she recorded with John a few months before he died. For the first time in her recording career, she received almost consistently positive reviews, a few of which rated her contributions above Lennon's.

That *Double Fantasy* would improve her critical standing had been one of Lennon's hopes. As Hopkins relates in his biography of Ono, John made this clear to David Geffen, whose company released the album: "You and I have what we set out to have, but Yoko never got what she deserves. And that has to be our goal with this record." In a sense, he was trying to pay a long-term debt. From the time they met, he had been crediting Ono with fueling his own work—his song "Imagine," which became a rock classic, was inspired by her *Grapefruit*—and with raising the level of his artistry in general. "I'm the famous one, the one who's supposed to know everything, but she's my teacher," he told *Playboy* in 1980. "She's taught me everything I f—ing know." Indeed, Ono's influence on her legendary husband is both remarkable and undeniable. When English journalist Ray Coleman wrote a biography of Lennon, he appropriately divided the work into two volumes—before and after Yoko.

Throughout their marriage, they relied upon Lennon's leverage with the media to publicize their message of world peace. Yet for years before she met John, Yoko had been staging "events" in protest of war. His murder only led her to strengthen her commitment, as she expressed a month later in advertisements that ran in London and New York newspapers. "The only solace," she wrote, will be to show "that we [can] create a world of peace on earth for each other and for our children." In 1981 she began to design what four years later would become "Strawberry Fields," a section of New York's Central Park that, as a memorial to John's peace mission, is planted with trees sent by world leaders. In 1986 she released *Starpeace*, an album which, titled in response to President Reagan's "Star Wars" program, reflected her belief that the economy can prosper with a "peace industry." Interestingly enough, during her *Starpeace* tour she performed to her largest and most enthusiastic audience—15,000 in Budapest, Hungary—behind the Iron Curtain.

Ono still works and lives in Manhattan, in the Dakota apartment building that she moved to with Lennon in 1973. Since his death she does not leave her home unaccompanied. Yet despite the difficult adjustments she has had to make, she continues to communicate optimism through her art work. It was this quality, in fact, that caught Lennon's interest in 1966. In his words, the book *Imagine* recounts their now-legendary meeting at London's Indica Gallery, where Yoko was having an exhibition: "The first thing that was in the gallery . . . was a white stepladder . . . and a spyglass hanging down. In those days most art put everybody down—got people upset. I walked up this ladder and picked up the spyglass. In teeny little writing it just said 'Yes.' . . . . I thought, Okay, this is the first show I've been to that's said something warm to me." Twenty-three years later, Ono's exhibition at the Whitney museum carried the same message. On a plaque alongside one of her works, she wrote: "All my works are a form of wishing. Keep wishing while you participate."

Discography

Solo Albums

Yoko Ono/Plastic Ono Band, Apple, 1970.
Fly, Apple, 1971.
Approximately Infinite Universe, Apple, 1973.
Feeling The Space, Apple, 1973.
Season Of Glass, Geffen, 1981.
It's Alright, Polydor, 1982.
Every Man Has a Woman Who Loves Him (written by Ono, performed by other artists), PolyGram, 1984.
Starpeace, Polydor, 1986.

With John Lennon

Unfinished Music No. 1: Two Virgins, Apple, 1968.
Unfinished Music No. 2: Life with the Lions, Apple, 1969.
Wedding Album, Apple, 1969.
The Plastic Ono Band—Live Peace in Toronto, Apple, 1969.
Some Time in New York City, Apple, 1972.
Double Fantasy, Geffen, 1980.
Milk and Honey, Polydor, 1984.

Writings

Grapefruit, 1964, revised edition, Simon & Schuster, 1970.

Sources

Books

The Ballad of John and Yoko, Rolling Stone, 1982.
Hopkins, Jerry, *Yoko Ono*, Macmillan, 1986.
Pang, Mary, and Henry Edwards, *Loving John*, Warner Books, 1983.
Sheff, David, and G. Barry Golson, *The Playboy Interviews with John Lennon and Yoko Ono*, Playboy, 1981.
Solt, Andrew and Sam Egan, *Imagine*, Macmillan, 1988.

Periodicals

ArtForum, February, 1989.
Interview, January, 1985; February, 1989.
Life, November, 1985.
Mademoiselle, October, 1984.
McCall's, January, 1985.
Newsweek, December 16, 1985.
New York Times, February 5, 1989; February 10, 1989.
People, February 3, 1986.
Rolling Stone, December 5, 1985; November 5, 1987.
Splash, February, 1989.

—Sketch by Kyle Kevorkian

Brian Peckford

AP/Wide World Photos

Premier of Newfoundland

Full name, Alfred Brian Peckford; born August 27, 1942, in Whitbourne, Newfoundland, Canada; son of Ewart (a provincial police officer) and Allison (Young) Peckford; married Marina Dicks, 1969; children: two daughters. *Education:* Memorial University of Newfoundland, B.A.Ed.

Addresses: *Office*—Office of the Premier, 8th Floor, Confederation Bldg., St. John's, Newfoundland, Canada A1C 5T7.

Career

High school English teacher, 1962–72; member of Newfoundland Legislature, 1972–76; special assistant to the premier, 1973; minister, Department of Municipal Affairs and Housing, 1974; minister of energy, 1976–79; premier of Newfoundland, 1979—.

Sidelights

The announcement in July, 1988, of a massive oil field development off the east coast of Canada was the realization of a dream for Newfoundland premier Brian Peckford. For nearly ten years, the Hibernia oil project had served as a metaphor for Newfoundland's struggle to attain a measure of economic self-reliance. The decision to begin drilling signalled a coming-of-age for both Newfoundland and Peckford.

Peckford's entire career in politics has been devoted to a tireless, often militant battle with Canada's federal government over control of offshore resources. Peckford, a self-styled Newfoundland nationalist, argued for provincial jurisdiction of resources like Hibernia. He believed the residents of Canada's poorest province would regain their dignity only when they had control of their own destiny. "I will keep coming," Peckford told *Saturday Night*. "I am relentless. Wave after wave after wave, just like the ocean. I have a dream to realize and I think I can advance Newfoundland society to be something it might not have been had I not been this way."

A gifted orator, Peckford developed a political persona in which he played the champion who would stop Newfoundland's wealth from being siphoned off by outside interests. His brash, persistent style with politicians on the "outside" earned him the title of "Confederation's bad boy." His exploits put him on the cover of *Atlantic Insight* magazine, holding a beaker of oil. The cutline read, "He won't give it all away." Stephen Neary, a member of the Liberal Opposition in Newfoundland, told *Saturday Night*, "He's the most vocal and childish of all the premiers. Ordinarily, you'd see the fellows with the white nets coming for him."

But to the average Newfoundlander, Peckford was doing just fine. After years of being the butt of mainland jokes, Newfoundland residents saw in

Peckford a cause for renewed parochial pride. Even *This Magazine,* Canada's left-wing journal, heaped praise on the populist Conservative premier: "His power base is in the people at large, and this is reflected in his populist-provincialist rhetoric, and his 'man of the people' and 'fighter for the people' leadership style."

Before the Hibernia announcement, it almost seemed as if the pugnacious premier was fated for obscurity. After years of effort, Peckford finally signed an agreement with Ottawa in 1985 that gave Newfoundland a measure of control over offshore development. But it was a hollow victory. Faced with a volatile oil market, Mobil Oil of Canada refused to proceed with the multi-billion dollar development. The announcement, three years later, sparked by a commitment of federal government dollars, was Peckford's gift to Newfoundland.

Peckford's fierce nationalism is a product of his past. Unlike his predecessors, Peckford is not a member of Newfoundland's bourgeoisie. "He is perhaps the only premier to ever use the flap of a book of matches to pick his teeth after a meal in Ottawa's plush Canadian Grill," wrote Roy McGregor in *Saturday Night.* As one of six children of a provincial policeman, Peckford found himself living in a collection of small towns where his friends were the sons of outport fishermen. He says the worst year of his life was the one he spent on the mainland in Toronto when his father was sent off on a job improvement course. Peckford was said to be a serious boy who would turn off "Rin Tin Tin" in favor of the news. But he was already a scrapper, always prepared to come to the physical defence of his brother.

Peckford grew up along with Newfoundland. The former British colony had joined the Canadian confederation in 1949, deeply divided over whether the union with Canada would prove to be beneficial. The windswept island off Canada's eastern extremity, known as "The Rock," was almost totally dependent on the fishing industry. Newfoundland's "Father of Confederation" was Joey Smallwood. Smallwood used to speak of "Uncle Ottawa" and "two jobs for every Newfoundlander." But in twenty years as premier, Smallwood was unable to erase Newfoundland's history of unemployment, poverty and dependency. In fact, he aggravated the province's plight with a legacy of natural resource giveaways. The most persistent symbol of that legacy was the agreement Smallwood signed with the province of Quebec for the sale of Labrador's hydro electric power. Under the long-term deal, Quebec purchased power from Churchill Falls and exported it for a profit of $1 billion a year to the United States. Newfoundland garnered nothing from the arrangement—other than an irritating reminder of what it had given away.

Peckford attended university in St. John's and became a high school English teacher. He introduced himself to politics by writing angry letters to the editor of the St. John's *Evening Telegram.* Then, growing more and more restless with teaching, he decided to run for president of a local Liberal Party riding association. His efforts were foiled by a plot hatched by members of the party establishment who wanted a president they could count on to support Smallwood. Peckford was a witness later that year when Smallwood suffered the first challenge to his leadership. Some of the crowd at the 1969 Liberal Party leadership convention, who believed Smallwood ran the party with a dictatorial fist, rushed the stage chanting "Ho Ho Ho Chi Minh." John Crosbie was the favorite son of this crowd. But he didn't have the support to unseat Smallwood. A few months later he left to join the Conservative Party. Brian Peckford followed close behind.

Two years after his first attempt at politics, Peckford tried again. This time he stacked the meeting himself and walked away with the presidency of the Green Bay Conservative riding association. A few months later he became the riding's candidate. And in 1972 he earned a seat in the Newfoundland legislature with the new Conservative government of Frank Moores.

Moores appointed Peckford as his minister of energy in 1976. The portfolio had been well developed by his predecessor, but thanks to fortuitous timing, Peckford was able to present himself as the author of Newfoundland's first systematic effort to regain control of its offshore oil resource. Peckford introduced a sweeping range of regulations that would require oil companies to give Newfoundland preference for jobs, supplies, and services and to comply with the province's development regulations. In indignation, the oil companies suspended exploration and threatened to move their rigs to more friendly waters. Although Premier Moores was close to capitulating, Peckford and his supporters in the cabinet refused to soften the regulations. The oil companies returned, and Peckford was vindicated.

Armed with his new reputation as a Newfoundland nationalist, Peckford defeated nine other contenders for the leadership of the party in 1979 when Moores resigned. With their rallying cry "Never Again," Peckford's Conservatives swept into power. Ostracized by every ruling clique he had ever encountered,

Peckford shaped the new premier's office in his own image. His advisers were "outport boys" who shared his persistence. He determinedly eschewed the cocktail circuit: "Bullshit. I'll have no part of it," he told Roy McGregor. "I don't follow an elite circle, premier or no premier."

At first, according to *Atlantic Insight*, Peckford was just "a mildly intriguing regional curiosity." But he quickly became a national phenomenon when Standard Oil discovered oil under the ocean floor southeast of St. John's in an area known as Hibernia. Now Newfoundland's angry young premier had a cause worthy of his passion.

"I am relentless. Wave after wave after wave, just like the ocean. I have a dream to realize and I think I can advance Newfoundland society to be something it might not have been had I not been this way."

The federal government claimed it had control over resources off of Canada's coasts. Peckford insisted Newfoundland owned its resources before it joined Confederation and it continued to own them afterwards. And so he argued the province deserved three of every four tax dollars collected. He went on prime-time radio and television and promised to go to England, if necessary, to block the federal's government plans to assume jurisdiction over Hibernia. Although he continued his highly-charged rhetoric, he sent his officials to negotiate a compromise agreement with the federal government. The talks were close to a resolution but then, inexplicably, they broke off in early 1983. Peckford's political opponents accused him of scuttling the deal for political reasons. One month later, in the first high court test of Peckford's position, Newfoundland's Supreme Court ruled that Ottawa, not Newfoundland, owned the offshore resources.

The populist premier was suddenly under siege. And Peckford responded badly. *Atlantic Insight* reported that "the premier's office has become a kind of sandbagged bunker, a pinched and paranoid place from which Peckford fires salvos at anyone who opposes him or is believed to oppose him or may oppose him or has simply expressed a view he does not share." Peckford's former energy minister, Leo Barry, told the magazine that Peckford had turned public opinion in Canada against Newfoundland: "There was an image created that Newfoundland was going crazy with greed."

The news for Peckford simply got worse. In March, 1984, the Supreme Court of Canada also ruled that Canada owned the offshore resources. Peckford responded by declaring that he was willing to stake his political career on settling the offshore issue in Newfoundland's favor. His political patience paid off. In 1985 he was able to sign an agreement with the new Conservative government in Ottawa. But when Hibernia proved to be too expensive to develop, Peckford's opponents were able to claim the deal came too late. "Brian Peckford was left with a piece of paper representing a triumph that might not be celebrated until well into the next century," wrote Michael Harris in *Saturday Night.*

Peckford now appeared to be a patriot without a cause. It grew increasingly difficult for him to score with his fed-bashing routine. His expense sheets showed he had abandoned his much-vaunted outport lifestyle: there were $450,000 charges for renovations to his office; $45,000 for one year's worth of meals in his private dining room; $100,000 for a bodyguard. He strained in an effort to bring industrial development to Newfoundland. His government poured more than $11 million into Sprung Greenhouse, a high-tech venture that produced what critics called the world's most expensive cucumbers. As his new cause, Peckford then embraced the "cod wars," in which Canada and France were locked in a dispute about jurisdiction over waters around St. Pierre and Miquelon, small French-controlled islands off Newfoundland's south coast.

In 1987, Peckford's Tories suffered a stunning loss to the NDP in a provincial by-election. There were hints that the "King of the Rock" was considering abdication before he was dethroned. A miracle was needed. And it was delivered, with the announcement that an oil consortium had been persuaded to develop Hibernia with $2.6 billion in federal government aid. This was to be the largest development in Atlantic Canada's history. Peckford allowed his rhetoric to flow like it had in the old days: "The next generation of Newfoundlanders and Labradorians will be free once and for all, free from the agonizing choice to stay in poverty or to leave for prosperity, free from having to leave home, leave family and go off to live in another part of this world to earn a living."

In the final analysis, Brian Peckford has been able to tap into his dream of an oil-rich province. But he needs more than one oil project, no matter how big. Unemployment in Newfoundland still stands at more than 17 percent. Hydro power is still being shipped out of the province, and Quebec is still drawing the profits. And according to the *Globe and Mail,* it would take three fully developed Hibernias to change Newfoundland from a "have not" province to one that "has." But The Rock's image has changed. Thanks in part to Peckford's brand of nationalism, the jokes are no longer about the "Newfie" who studied all night for a urine test. With the development of Hibernia, Brian Peckford can rest assured that Newfoundland's future will now include a measure of pride and self-reliance.

Avocational Interests: Reading, swimming, sports.

Sources

Atlantic Insight, June, 1983.
Chatelaine, September, 1981.
Financial Post, January 12, 1985.
Globe and Mail (Toronto), May 14, 1984; November 21, 1987; February 1, 1988; February 18, 1988; April 29, 1988.
Maclean's, November 3, 1980; June 14, 1982; November 28, 1983; March 5, 1984.
Saturday Night, March, 1988.
This Magazine, February-March 1981.
Winnipeg Free Press, March 4, 1988.

—*Sidelights by Ingeborg Boyens*

William Pedersen

Courtesy of Kohn Pedersen Fox Associates, P.C.

Architect

Born c. 1938, in St. Paul, Minn.; married Elizabeth Essex; children: two. *Education:* Massachusetts Institute of Technology, master's degree in architecture, 1963.

Addresses: *Home*—New York, N.Y. *Office*—Kohn Pedersen Fox, 251 West 57th St., New York, N.Y. 10019.

Career

Worked for a number of well-known architects before starting his own firm in 1976; partner, Kohn Pedersen Fox, New York City, 1976—. Responsible for the design of more than 20 major buildings in the United States, England, and West Germany, including 333 Wacker Drive, Chicago, 135 East 57th Street, New York City, and Procter & Gamble world headquarters, Cincinnati.

Sidelights

William Pedersen's architectural forte is skyscrapers with classic character and style. In cities where tall buildings are a dime a dozen—New York and Chicago—Pedersen's designs are standouts. His New York-based firm, Kohn Pedersen Fox, has earned an international reputation with more than twenty major buildings in the United States, England, and West Germany to its credit.

Pedersen was raised in St. Paul, Minnesota and graduated from M.I.T. in 1963 with a master's degree in architecture. He worked for a number of architects, including the famous I.M. Pei, before forming a partnership with A. Eugene Kohn, an already successful salesman in 1976. Together with Sheldon Fox they developed a firm that has grown to 150 architects who are busily recreating urban landscapes across the country.

Even as a child, Pedersen had an eye for sleek design. He reportedly saved $20 for shiny new blades to attach to an old pair of ice skates, not because they'd improve his speed or skating style, but because he admired their smooth, curved lines. Pedersen repeated that skate blade design in several of his celebrated buildings including the ultra-modern 333 Wacker Drive in Chicago, which he designed in association with Perkins & Will. The 36-story, $60 million office building, Pedersen's first high-rise, was completed in 1983 and established KPF as a major presence in its field.

Pedersen combines contemporary and classical elements in his designs to achieve a style called postmodernism. His Procter & Gamble world headquarters, finished in 1985 in Cincinnati, is one example. The challenge was to create something new that would blend harmoniously with P&G's old headquarters next door. Pedersen designed an unusual six-story, L-shaped building dominated by twin, octagonal 17-story towers rising at the corner of the L. He tied the new headquarters to the old with a limestone facade and eye-catching pyramid-shaped roofs on the towers.

Pedersen claims classicism is concerned with scale, the relationship of a human being to a building, and the different parts of the building to itself. He believes today's corporate executives are more interested in architecture that complements the quality of their employee's lives. Included in the Procter & Gamble complex is a five-acre park with a fountain, walkways and benches designed to provide employees with an attractive and peaceful lunchtime setting. "The C.E.O., John Smale [see index for *Newsmakers* entry], wanted to give something back to the community," Pedersen told *Fortune*. "With Procter & Gamble we could have easily built the tallest building in town. Instead we designed a relatively small building with a large park, which provides a great amenity to the city."

With Procter & Gamble, Pedersen tamed the urban office building. With another project, 135 East 57th Street, he startled staid New Yorkers by creating, according to the *New York Times*, an "urban event." His 34-story tower for Madison Equities at the corner of 57th Street and Lexington Avenue successfully breaks accepted rules of urban design by taking a giant, curving step back from the corner and creating an unusual entrance plaza. In the resulting ice-cream-cone-shaped space, Pedersen placed a 30-foot high circle of classical columns, which emphasize and reflect the gray, granite-clad building's spirited classical style. The *New York Times* described the tower as, "a brilliant building, one of the best office towers of the last generation in New York.... The panache it has comes from Mr. Pedersen's fundamental idea, which will continue to look fresh into the next generation."

With business booming, Pedersen moved his family from a five-story Victorian brownstone in Brooklyn to an apartment on Central Park West. The spatial change was dramatic. As in many of his corporate projects, the move involved compromising the ideal with reality, sacrificing space, but not style. He undertook the interior renovation and design of the apartment with relish. Nearly all the rooms had to double-up on function in order to accommodate the Pedersen family and their elegant collection of French Empire and English Regency furniture. The entrance hall is also a gallery for their architectural drawing collection. The living room is also the library—its walls lined with glass-fronted shelves. The sitting room doubles as master bedroom and the dining room shares space with a grand piano. Shiny, parqueted floors, richly lacquered Honduras mahogany paneling, polished and precious antique furniture blend with brass, marble, and mirrored accents to create a darkly gleaming interior.

When Pedersen is not designing skyscrapers or collecting classy antiques, he finds time to practice classical music on his piano—a hobby he likens to architecture. "Designing a building is like interpreting a piece of music," he told *Fortune* magazine. "You have to think about how each detail of building, like each musical phrase, is begun, how it is ended, and the way it's sculpted."

Sources

Architectural Digest, November, 1988.
Fortune, June 22, 1987.
New York Times, October 9, 1988.

—Sketch by Sharon Rose

Ronald Perelman

Holding company executive

Full name, Ronald Owen Perelman; born 1943, in Greensboro, N.C.; son of Raymond Perelman (a sheet-metal manufacturer); married Faith Golding c. 1965 (divorced, 1984); married Claudia Cohen (an entertainment reporter), January 11, 1985; children: (first marriage) four. *Education:* University of Pennsylvania, B.A. in economics, 1964; Wharton School of Finance, M.B.A., 1966.

Addresses: *Office*—Revlon, Inc., 767 Fifth Ave., New York, N.Y. 10022; and MacAndrews & Forbes, Inc., 36 East 63rd St., New York, N.Y. 10021.

Career

Belmont Industries (family metal-fabricating firm), Philadelphia, Pa., member of staff, 1966–78; moved to New York City, 1978, and purchased his first company, a jewelry distributorship; since 1978, has been involved in acquisition and sale of numerous companies; MacAndrews & Forbes, Inc. (conglomerate), New York City, chairman, chief executive officer, and director, 1980—; Technicolor, Inc., Hollywood, Calif., chairman, 1983—; Revlon, Inc., New York City, chairman and chief executive officer, 1985—. Also chairman of several other companies, including Consolidated Cigar Co.; member of board of directors, Four Star International, Inc., and Compact Video, Inc.

AP/Wide World Photos

Sidelights

Corporate raiders with billion-dollar war chests and the affinity for deal-making are taking on an increasing presence in the news of the day, but few have moved up the takeover ladder as quickly and as aggressively as Ronald Perelman, chairman of Revlon, one of the world's best-known cosmetic firms. The cigar-smoking Perelman, who would prefer to remain unrecognized, inconspicuous, and generally forgotten about, has fought a losing battle in his efforts to remain out of the public spotlight. And buying Revlon in 1985 for $1.8 billion in cash quickly pushed him into the ranks of the nation's foremost takeover giants, with the likes of T. Boone Pickens and Carl Icahn. Headline-making was suddenly the province of a man who insists he is just "an operations guy." But despite his protestations of modesty, Perelman has earned a reputation as a hard-bargaining investor who is tenacious in his quest for new companies. The pillows in his office sum up the story. One reads, "Love me, love my cigar." The other, "No guts, no glory."

In recent years, Perelman, whose net worth is estimated by *Fortune* magazine at $300 million, has made three nearly simultaneous bids to acquire giant companies: Transworld, a hotel chain and food vendor; food processor CPC International; and Gillette, the razor and toiletries company. His strategy is to buy a company and then keep only those parts of the operation that are particularly attractive to him. His practice of stripping off operations and streamlining what he considers to be overdiversified companies has won him the title of the Wall Street Stripper. In slimming down companies, he gets back much of what he spent to acquire it, and he is left with a leaner, more profitable business that he is interested in running. Perelman's critics say he is a greenmailer because of the money he pockets from making passes at companies; for example, he reaped a $94 million profit from his unsuccessful 1986 bid for CPC International, according to *Fortune*. Perelman maintains, however, that he is interested in companies to purchase them, and not to make money on their stock. One high-ranking executive who was involved in a deal with Perelman described him in *New York* magazine as "an opportunist...in the nicest sense." In 1984, Perelman purchased Consolidated Cigar for $124 million from Gulf + Western. And Martin Davis, chairman of Gulf + Western, told *New York* that Perelman is "astute enough to know what will work and what won't."

Perelman's management finesse first began to take shape when he was growing up in Philadelphia as the first of two sons in an upper-class family. His father, Raymond Perelman, owns Belmont Industries, a metal-fabricating firm. As early as elementary school, the younger Perelman had his first brushes with business while sitting in on board meetings of his father's company. He attended the Haverford School outside of Philadelphia and then enrolled in the University of Pennsylvania, where he received a B.A. in economics. He later received an MBA from the Wharton School of Finance. For 12 years, he apprenticed with his father's business, learning the art of buying, selling, and running companies. For example, *Fortune* magazine reported, Perelman sold a galvanizing firm and a shoe manufacturer, then purchased a small, financially troubled bank that he brought back to life and resold. Perelman's father told *Fortune* magazine that his son provided input in many of the elder's corporate purchasing decisions. "When Ronnie was a boy, whenever I was thinking of making an acquisition, we would drive out to look at the company and discuss the pluses and minuses together," the elder Perelman recalled.

Ronald Perelman left the family business in 1978, and that same year took the advice of a business broker and purchased for $2 million about 40 percent of a jewelry retailer and distributor. The company, Cohen-Hatfield Industries, proved to be the project on which Perelman would cut his teeth. He sold off most of the company's assets, retaining the reliable and profitable wholesale watch distribution business. By selling off the assets that were not performing as Perelman wanted, he was able to use the company as a shell to purchase other companies. In two years, he used Cohen-Hatfield to purchase MacAndrews & Forbes, a troubled company that supplied licorice extract and chocolate. By finding new sources of licorice in areas more stable than world licorice suppliers Iran and Afghanistan, Perelman was able to turn a faltering company into a profitable business. Then MacAndrews—once the object of an acquisition—was in turn able to provide the cash flow Perelman needed to finance other buys, such as the $105 million purchase in 1983 of Technicolor—the company that gives vivid color to many Hollywood films. At the time, nobody wanted to buy Technicolor, although it had been on the market for years. But with typical style, Perelman sold off five divisions of the company and has turned Technicolor into a winner. He also purchased Consolidated Cigar and a videocassette duplicator named Video Corporation of America.

Perelman's run at Revlon began through his 1985 purchase of a controlling interest in Pantry Pride, a Florida-based chain of supermarkets. He purchased the supermarket chain for $60 million, but at the time, Perelman was not trying to buy Revlon, *New York* magazine reported. Pantry Pride, however, wanted to buy Revlon. The beauty company, once the nation's leading maker of cosmetics under founder Charles Revson, had faded over the years in the face of stiff competition from other beauty companies and waning enthusiasm from department stores, who had lost a good deal of interest in stocking the product line. Said one industry consultant in 1987 in *Fortune:* "Revlon was the No. 1 cosmetic in any store no matter how you measured it. Now it's not even a good No. 3 in the mass-market outlets like drugstores, and it's getting slaughtered in department stores."

Supermarket chain Pantry Pride provided the cash that Perelman needed to purchase Revlon. By selling off the grocery chain's assets, Perelman was able to gather together much of the $1.8 billion he needed to buy Revlon's outstanding shares. But it was not an easy purchase. A takeover fight ensued, during which Perelman announced that he would keep Revlon's cosmetic business but rid the company of other divisions, including those that sold such products as Tums and hospital diagnostic aids, *New York* magazine reported. To fight Perelman, Revlon announced that its management would take the company private and give chairman Michel Bergerac continued control. But after considerable court battles that went all the way to the Delaware Supreme Court, Perelman won his bid for the cosmetics firm. His next challenge was to turn it around.

After 20 months of owning Revlon, Perelman took the company private in July 1987, vowing to return it to its former prominence on the department store beauty aisles. The company faces weighty competition from high-priced brands such as Estee Lauder as well as drugstore brands like Cover Girl. Both Noxell and Maybelline lead Revlon at drug and discount stores. Department stores, whose cosmetics buyers had discontinued buying Revlon products, once relegated the center aisles to other brands, leaving Revlon behind. But through Perelman's efforts, department stores are giving the brand a second chance. After becoming chairman of Revlon in 1986, Perelman went knocking on the doors of department store heads, trying to persuade them to give Revlon the exposure it once had. Since those visits, the number of department stores carrying Revlon products rose by 1,000 in one year, *Fortune* reported. In Bloomingdale's prestigious Manhattan store, Revlon now can be found in the main aisle. Bloomingdale's chairman Marvin Traub told *Fortune:* "Revlon is becoming a strong competitor in department stores."

Perelman's makeover of Revlon doesn't stop at department stores. He spent $500 million to purchase Max Factor and the cosmetics and fragrance lines of Yves Saint Laurent. He also directed that Revlon lipsticks and nail enamels be reformulated and discarded old packaging in favor of upscale bottles and boxes targeted at the well-heeled department store shopper. To gloss up the company's image, Perelman hired famed beauty photographer Richard Avedon. The photographer heated up magazine pages with print ads of seductive women and the tag line, "The world's most unforgettable women wear Revlon."

Most of all, Perelman wants the Revlon name to once again be synonymous with the beauty business—an area he feels it strayed much too far away from. On his third day at Revlon, he discovered a bronze head of founder Revson gathering dust in a closet and quickly restored it to a prominent post in Revlon's New York City offices. "Charles Revson not only founded this company, he founded the beauty industry." Perelman told *Fortune.* "He had to have been a fantastic individual, and he deserves recognition. Prior management tried to hide his involvement." Perelman added in *New York* magazine that he has established a pattern for acquiring companies that he intends to follow. "I think we've defined a strategy of seeking out companies with certain basic common characteristics," Perelman said. "They're all basic cash-flow generators, where the cash flow is free from fad, fashion or styles. We won't look at fashion companies. We won't look at retailing chains like Macy's. We won't look at anything that's high-tech oriented or fad-oriented."

Perelman's personal life has been nearly as colorful as his acquisitions. His first marriage to Faith Golding—a member of a wealthy New York City real estate family—fell apart after she learned Perelman was having an affair with a local florist. Golding sued for divorce on grounds of adultery and hired private detectives to trail the couple. Details of the detectives' observations were listed in an affadavit in the divorce filing, including secret breakfasts between Perelman and the florist. *New York* magazine reported that Golding discovered the affair when the bill for an expensive Bulgari bracelet arrived at their home—a bracelet that was not for Golding. After a messy divorce, Perelman's relationship with the florist ended.

In January 1984, he met entertainment reporter and former gossip columnist Claudia Cohen. One year to the day after they were introduced, Perelman and Cohen were married, and the two held a reception several months later at the trendy Palladium nightclub in Manhattan. Entertainment was by the Pointer Sisters, and scores of prominent guests including Elizabeth Taylor attended the event. But despite all the glitz that has surrounded him, Perelman insists he is a private person. He is a member of the Orthodox Fifth Avenue Synagogue, and in keeping with strict Jewish tradition, does not work on Saturday. While Perelman is tight-mouthed about his plans for the future, many speculate that another multimillion dollar acquisition will soon catch his eye. Perelman, 46, replied in *Fortune:* "I'm still a young man. We'll see."

Sources

Business Week, April 18, 1986; December 1, 1986; October 12, 1987.

Forbes, January 27, 1986.

Fortune, January 5, 1987; September 14, 1987; September 28, 1987.

New York, November 18, 1985.

—Sidelights by Amy C. Bodwin

Carrie Saxon Perry

Mayor of Hartford, Conn.

Born c. 1932; daughter of Mabel Saxon; divorced; children: James. *Education:* Graduate of Howard University; attended law school.

Addresses: *Home*—Hartford, Conn. *Office*—Office of the Mayor, 550 Main St., Hartford, Conn. 06103.

Career

Social worker in the early 1960s; later held a variety of jobs with social services; worked as campaign manager; member, Connecticut House of Representatives, 1980–87; mayor of Hartford, Conn., 1988—.

Awards: Named Woman of the Year by YMCA; Outstanding Community Service Award, Black People's Union, University of Hartford.

Sidelights

In 1987, Carrie Saxon Perry was elected mayor of Hartford, Connecticut, the first black woman to hold that office in a major Northeastern city. Considered "the insurance capital" of America, Hartford is the state's second largest city. It is also one of the poorest, although Connecticut has an unemployment rate of only three percent and ranks highest in the country in per capita income.

A Hartford native, Perry studied political science at Howard University. She later attended law school there, but left to marry and return to Hartford. She became a social worker in the early 1960s and

AP/Wide World Photos

worked in the social services field before entering politics as a campaign manager. In 1976, she made an unsuccessful bid for a seat in the Connecticut House of Representatives. She ran again in 1980 and won. Over the next several years, she was a proponent of enterprise zones and job training programs. At the beginning of her fourth term, Perry announced that she would enter Hartford's mayoral race.

Running on "people issues," she focused her campaign on the gap between the city's thriving downtown area and its decaying neighborhoods. "Downtown continues to prosper while our neighborhoods don't flourish," she told the *Washington Post*. Hartford's development boom has been fueled by rapid growth in its insurance and banking industries. Meanwhile, Perry continued, "some of our neighborhoods look like war-torn areas—filled with vacant apartments and housing that needs rehabbing." She defeated her Republican opponent by some 16 percentage points. Shortly after the election, Perry formed task forces to study methods of reducing crime and unemployment. She also stressed the need for job training, "especially among the hardcore jobless, at-risk young people, teen parents, and phased-out older workers," Luix Overbea of the *Christian Science Monitor* explained. Moreover, she wants to "bring young people back into the mainstream." Some of her reforms "include more foot patrolmen, formation of a crime commission, [and] an educational task force on dropouts."

Perry may encounter a few roadblocks along the way. Hartford has a strong city council and city manager. The mayor, who earns $17,500 a year, is considered a figurehead. But Perry is optimistic. "The office is a terrific forum for ideas," she told Marilyn Marshall in *Ebony*. "And I have the authority and the responsibility to be the major spokesperson for the city."

Sources

Christian Science Monitor, February 11, 1988.
Ebony, April, 1988.
New York Times, November 4, 1987.
Washington Post, November 5, 1987.

—Sketch by Denise Wiloch

Richard Hooper Pough

AP/Wide World Photos

Conservationist

Surname pronounced Poe; born April 19, 1904, in Brooklyn, N.Y.; son of Francis Harvey (a chemist) and Alice (Beckler) Pough; married Moira Flannery, December 3, 1937; children: Edward, Tristram. *Education:* Attended Washington University (St. Louis, Mo.), 1921–24; Massachusetts Institute of Technology, B.S., 1926; Harvard University, postgraduate studies, 1926–27.

Addresses: *Home*—Martha's Vineyard, Mass.

Career

Chemist and engineer at Southern Acid & Sulphur Co., Port Austin, Tex., and at Fulton Iron Works, St. Louis, Mo., 1927–31; MacCallum Stores, Philadelphia, Pa., proprietor, 1932–36; National Audubon Society, member of staff, 1936–48; American Museum of Natural History, New York, N.Y., chairman of department of conservation and general ecology, 1948–56; president, National Area Council, Inc., 1957–84, and Goodhill Foundation. President, Nature Conservancy. Member of board of directors, Chevron Conservation Awards and Feinstone Environmental Awards; member of advisory council, Trust for Public Lands; honorary trustee, National Science Youth Foundation and Sapelo Island Research Foundation.

Awards: Federated Garden Clubs of Connecticut medal, 1958; Frances Hutchinson Medal, Garden Club of America, 1961; conservation award, American Motors Corp., 1962; Horace M. Albright Medal, American Scenic and Historic Preservation Society, 1963; National Audubon Society medal, 1981; recipient of silver medal from Federated Garden Clubs of New York State and distinguished service medal from Brooklyn Botanical Garden; named Man of the Year, Pelham Men's Club; L.L.D., Haverford College, 1970.

Sidelights

Since the mid-1930s Richard Hooper Pough has been one of the nation's most active conservationists. As the "founder and early president of the Nature Conservancy [and] president or trustee of countless other conservation organizations," according to Frank Graham, Jr., of *Audubon,* Pough has played an influential role in several environmental battles. He is also considered a tireless advocate of land preservation, urging conservation organizations to buy wilderness areas in order to protect their natural beauty. Literally thousands of acres have been saved due to Pough's efforts.

Pough first became professionally involved in conservation in 1936, when he joined the staff of the National Audubon Society. A long-time bird watcher, he had come to the Society after taking part in the creation of the Hawk Mountain Sanctuary in Pennsylvania. The mountain, a popular nesting site for hawks, was also well known to hunters who used the birds for target practice. To stop the slaughter, Pough and conservationist Rosalie Edge arranged to buy the mountain, turning it into a sanctuary for birds. The project brought Pough into contact with Audubon Society president John Baker, who offered Pough a position with the organization.

For the next twelve years Pough worked on the problem of "persecuted species" and played a major role in a number of efforts to preserve endangered birds. One such effort involved the house finch, a bird native to the American West and protected under federal law as an endangered species. In 1940 Pough discovered that the birds were being sold illegally in New York pet shops. He reported the stores to the authorities, prompting some of the shops to release the birds rather than face charges. Ironically, soon after their release the once-endangered house finch became a common sight along the East Coast; the birds are now found from Canada to the Gulf Coast. In addition to his field work, Pough wrote the *Audubon Land Bird Guide*, which describes the various species common to the eastern United States and details their nesting and feeding habits. He subsequently published the *Audubon Water Bird Guide* and the *Audubon Western Bird Guide*. "Some experienced birders," Graham reported, "believe that they are the best bird guides ever published."

In 1948 Pough joined the American Museum of Natural History as chairman of its Department of Conservation and General Ecology. In the next eight years he instituted the museum's Hall of Forests exhibit and led its efforts to preserve natural wildlife areas. At Pough's suggestion the museum purchased Great Gull Island off the coast of Connecticut, transforming it into one of the country's foremost tern research centers. During this time Pough also served as president of the Nature Conservancy, which lends money to local conservation groups wishing to purchase land for preservation. Its efforts have created, as Graham explained, "the largest privately owned sanctuary system in the United States."

Perhaps Pough's most important conservation work was with the now defunct Natural Area Council and the Goodhill Foundation. The former served as an umbrella organization for scores of smaller conservation groups, including the Open Space Institute and the America the Beautiful Fund. These smaller groups focused on particular projects or on regional preservation work. As president of the Goodhill Foundation, founded by Katharine Ordway, Pough oversaw the distribution of funds allocated to buy and preserve ecologically valuable land.

Now in his eighties, Pough has begun to curtail his activities. In 1984 the Goodhill Foundation was dissolved; that same year Pough closed the Natural Area Council. He devotes most of his time to his own four acres of land on Martha's Vineyard, a parcel he has kept in its natural, forested state for over 25 years. Commented fellow conservationist Charles Little to Graham, "Dick Pough practically invented the land preservation business in this country."

Writings

Audubon Land Bird Guide: Small Land Birds of Eastern and Central North America from Southern Texas to Central Greenland, Doubleday, 1949.
Audubon Water Bird Guide: Water, Game, and Large Land Birds, Doubleday, 1951.
Audubon Guides: All the Birds of Eastern and Central North America, Doubleday, 1953.
Audubon Western Bird Guide, Doubleday, 1957.

Sources

Audubon, November, 1984.
National Parks and Conservation, January, 1981.

—Sketch by Denise Wiloch

Dennis Quaid

Actor

Born April 9, 1954, in Houston, Tex.; son of William Rudy (an electrician) and Juanita (a real estate agent) Quaid; married Pamela J. Soles (an actress), November 24, 1978 (divorced, 1983). *Education:* Attended University of Houston, 1972–75.

Addresses: *Home*—North Hollywood, Calif.

Career

Became interested in acting in college; decided to pursue an acting career after visiting his brother, Randy Quaid, on the set of "The Missouri Breaks" in 1975; feature films include "September 30, 1955," 1978, "Breaking Away," 1979, "Tough Enough," 1980, "The Long Riders," 1980, "Caveman," 1981, "All Night Long," 1981, "The Night the Lights Went Out in Georgia," 1981, "Jaws 3-D," 1983, "The Right Stuff," 1983, "Dreamscape," 1984, "Enemy Mine," 1986, "Innerspace," 1987, "The Big Easy," 1987, "Suspect," 1987, "D.O.A.," 1988, "Everybody's All-American," 1988, "Great Balls of Fire," 1989; appeared with brother, Randy, in Off-Broadway production of "True West," 1984; also appeared in television films "Bill," 1981, and "Bill on His Own," 1983. Singer, musician, and songwriter; formed band the Eclectics and began recording, 1989.

Sidelights

Dennis Quaid is an actor who always seems to be on the verge of becoming Hollywood's next film sensation. As David Ansen of *Newsweek* wrote,

AP/Wide World Photos

Quaid has received "spectacular reviews, steady work, repeated prophecies that he was on the brink of major stardom . . . and bad luck. Oddly, every would-be blockbuster that was supposed to make Quaid a household word somehow never got off the block." His recent film successes, though, have made him a recognizable star. And he may yet experience the blockbuster that will propel him to super-stardom.

Quaid's trademark is his sly, appealing grin. Katherine Dieckmann of *Rolling Stone* stated that when Quaid "flashes that grin" he is transformed into "a major-league charmer, an irresistable seducer. Like [Jack] Nicholson's eyebrows, it says 'Oh, yeah? Think I can't do it? Just watch me!'" And *People* magazine called it "devilish, sassy, too fun-loving [such was its redeeming quality] to ever be truly offensive."

Quaid was born April 9, 1954, in Houston, Texas. His father was an electrician and his mother a real estate agent. He grew up in a modest home in a Houston suburb with his brother, Randy, three-and-a-half years his senior. According to Michael Norman of the *New York Times Magazine,* the brothers shared a room and "lived a 'Beaver Cleaver' childhood: BB guns, baseball games, nifty cars and shopping centers." Their parents helped instill in them "the essentials for an actor's life: pluck, the habit of hard work and the inspiration that can come from a missed opportunity." Quaid's mother and father separated when he was 14 and soon divorced. "It was tough on me when they split up," he told Kevin Sessums of *Interview* magazine. "It's tough on all kids when that happens. But you get through it."

Randy Quaid would later become an actor and achieve fame before his brother. While Dennis was still in school, Randy was appearing in such films as "The Last Picture Show," "What's Up Doc," "Paper Moon," and "The Last Detail" (which earned him Academy Award and Golden Globe nominations for his acting). Dennis was a student at the University of Houston from 1972 until 1975, when he quit in the middle of his junior year. "I signed up for psychology classes at 8 in the morning, and I was usually asleep in my seat by 8:15," he said to Gene Siskel of the *Chicago Tribune.* "I owe the little formal education I got to my drama teacher." So Dennis decided to move to Los Angeles and try making it as an actor himself. He got his first up-close look at moviemaking by visiting his brother on the set of "The Missouri Breaks" in 1975. He met stars Marlon Brando and Jack Nicholson, and it was during that trip, he told Dieckmann, "when I became completely enamored of making movies." Despite having a brother who was already established, he did not immediately gain an acting job. Noted *People,* "Quaid spent a year eating sardines and peanut-butter sandwiches before getting work."

Quaid's film debut was in a supporting role in a low-budget movie called "September 30, 1955," released in 1978. Later in 1978, he married actress P.J. Soles. In 1979, he was in the hit bicycle-racing movie "Breaking Away," playing one of the three teenage buddies of the lead character. All four received critical praise. Charles Michener of *Newsweek* said the ensemble gave "superbly unstudied performances." Richard Schickel of *Time* said the roles were "well played by the young actors."

In 1980, Quaid appeared with his brother in "The Long Riders," a western that depicted the exploits of the outlaw James and Younger brothers. Several sets of real brothers played the film characters: James and Stacy Keach; David, Keith, and Robert Carradine; the Quaids; and Christopher and Nicholas Guest. The movie garnered good reviews and, once again, the actors were uniformly praised. "All of them turn in finely controlled performances," proclaimed Schickel. And the *New Yorker* stated, "The picture is notable for its actors' strong performances."

After these early successes, Quaid then starred in a string of less than first-rate movies, including "Caveman," "All Night Long," "The Night the Lights Went Out in Georgia," and "Jaws 3-D." Quaid later admitted that he was accepting what Norman called "dreadful roles in dreadful films" just to make money to help build his dream house. "It got to the point," Quaid explained to Ansen, where he took on work "not for me but for the house." Dissatisfied, he ended up selling the house, divorcing his wife (in 1983), and determining that he would only take roles he believed in. "Then if it doesn't work out [commercially], well, I can still feel good about it."

He landed one of the astronaut roles in the 1983 film "The Right Stuff," and it looked like Quaid's career was about to take off. The film received critical raves and many people expected it to become a box-office smash. *Newsweek* stated, "If there's a scene-stealing role it's Dennis Quaid's Gordo Cooper—a man so untroubled, and so uncomplex, that he could fall asleep in the space capsule just before his historic flight." *Time* also singled him out for capturing "the innocent braggadocio and sublime (but not misplaced) self-confidence of Gordon Cooper." Unfortunately, the movie flopped at the box office, and Quaid's career did not get the anticipated boost.

In 1984, Quaid suffered further disappointment. According to David Seeley of *Playboy,* the movie "Urban Cowboy" was written for Quaid, and he read for the part with Debra Winger, the actress who co-starred in the film. Then, suddenly, "John Travolta wanted the role, which meant $33,000,000 in advance film rentals," and Quaid was "out on the street." He then took a trip to New Delhi to get away from it all, and his agent frantically had to call him back. "They want you for 'An Officer and a Gentleman!'" he was told. But by the time he arrived at the airport, Richard Gere was signing a contract.

Quaid then headed to New York to co-star with his brother in Sam Shepard's Off-Broadway play "True West." Quaid had something of a complex about Randy, wrote Dieckmann, which stemmed from "the insecurity that comes with following in someone's footsteps." Performing together in the play, which explored a volatile relationship between two brothers, resolved the issue. "We just about killed each other a couple of times offstage," he said to Dieckmann. "One night we got into this insane kicking, hitting, screaming match. I went into my room, punched a hole in the wall . . . . I hated his guts. Then I took a shower, but I forgot the hair dryer was in his room. And it's January in New York City. So I go over and we start talking. Real quiet. About what we hate in each other, love in each other, admire and envy. And we wound up . . . having the time of our lives."

After two more films that did not do well at the box office, including the science-fiction flop "Enemy Mine," Quaid starred with Martin Short [see index for *Newsmakers* entry] in a comedy called Innerspace. Released in 1987, the film, "which insiders confidently predicted would go through the roof," reported Ansen, "barely made it off the floor." Later in 1987, however, Quaid's luck finally turned around. "The Big Easy," a romantic thriller with Ellen Barkin [see index for *Newsmakers* entry] quietly became a hit. Lawrence O'Toole of *Maclean's* hailed "the superb performances of Quaid and Barkin. His New Orleans accent, with its soft consonants and lazy cadences, is almost perfect. But beyond technical prowess, Quaid has a depth of feeling rare in current actors." With their romantic chemistry, added O'Toole, "Quaid and Barkin burn a hole in the screen." *Newsweek* concurred, stating that their screen romance "may be the most indelible sexual encounter of the year." Quaid finally started to gain the recognition that had long eluded him. He also got a chance to show off his musical talents. A song he composed was used in the film.

In yet another 1987 movie, Quaid and Cher starred in a courtroom drama and romance called "Suspect." This film did not fare as well as "The Big Easy," but its stars both received good reviews. Ansen said of Cher and Quaid, "Her pugnacious, earthy charm and his playful self-confidence delightfully divert the audience from the script's glaring contrivances." Scott Rose of *Films in Review* remarked that despite "misguided direction" and a "suffocating script" the stars manage "to rise above the occasion."

Quaid has acquired a reputation in Hollywood for thoroughly researching his roles. For "The Right Stuff," he told Sessums, he spent about 15 hours with Gordon Cooper "over a period of weeks and picked his brain." For "The Big Easy," noted *Rolling Stone*, he "hung around with locals" to perfect his New Orleans accent and with "cops to get an idea of the violent encounters common to police rounds." For "Suspect," "he spent a month . . . researching the judicial system."

Early in 1988, Quaid starred in "D.O.A.," a remake of a 1949 thriller. Schickel called the film "engaging" and said that Quaid's hero was "charming even unto death." Later that year, Quaid appeared in "Everybody's All-American," a role that brought him widespread praise. David Denby of *New York* magazine proclaimed, "Dennis Quaid gives a terrifically moving performance as a star athlete, a great running back from Louisiana who responds to the common fate of growing old as if he had contracted a crippling disease." Richard Corliss of *Time* stated that "Quaid creates a genuine pathetic hero, first exuding charm, then marketing it." Brian D. Johnson of *Maclean's* said that he "turns in an admirable performance." And John Ed Bradley of *Esquire* called it "the best performance of his career." Quaid told Siskel that "Everybody's All-American" was his most demanding role to date because he had to age from a 20-year-old football star to a fleshy 45-year-old has-been. "It's easy to play young or old," he said, "but how do you play 45? It's not easily defined."

Next, Quaid took on the role of rock-and-roll piano legend Jerry Lee Lewis in the biographical film "Great Balls of Fire." Quaid again carefully researched his character. Robert Palmer of *American Film* reported that he went to see Lewis play in L.A. and later went on the road with him. He also studied film and video footage of Lewis's early performances. Since Quaid is an aspiring musician, he wanted to perform the songs in the movie himself. "At first," he explained to Palmer, "I wanted to do my own singing. Jerry was dead set against it." Quaid then recorded his own version of the song "Great Balls of Fire" and played it for Lewis, who liked it. "At that point, we decided that he'd do half the songs and I'd do half. Then as I heard Jerry cutting his tracks, I came to my senses . . . . He's a real virtuoso, you know . . . . And in the end, he recorded new versions of 'Great Balls of Fire' and 'Whole Lotta Shakin' that are, I think, better than the originals."

Visiting the set during the shooting of the film, Palmer noted that Quaid was successfully capturing the persona of Lewis, nicknamed the Killer. "He's got the cocky walk, the posture, the wild-eyed look down cold." Bradley wrote that "Roland James and James Van Eaton, former band members of Jerry Lee's, remark how spooky it's getting watching Quaid fall into character: more and more each day he looks and behaves like the Killer."

The movie was released in June of 1989 and a number of critics saw it as a whitewash of Lewis's controversial life. Caryn James of the *New York Times* stated the "film is a compressed, cleaned-up version of the Jerry Lee Lewis story." Kathy Huffhines of the *Detroit Free Press* said "Quaid was clearly coached to avoid anything disturbing," and because of that "the movie's diluted picture of a funny, nice guy isn't entirely his fault." And Mike Clark of *USA Today* called it a "junk-food chronicle." But James added that the movie does recreate "the soul-shaking, brain-rattling fun of rock-and-roll" and though it "may skimp on the truth, it is loaded with terrific music and outrageous fun."

Those critics who have interviewed Quaid note that he is a high-energy person who, as Norman wrote, "cannot seem to stay still. He stands, he sits, he fidgets." Siskel said, "During a conversation, he dashes enthusiastically about his hotel room, singing songs, showing pictures, and modeling clothing—all this after three-dozen short TV interviews and a photo shoot for the cover of Italian Vogue."

With his success, Sessums related, Quaid does "try to give something back." He is involved in a medical relief effort for the children of Honduras, and while he was in Memphis filming "Great Balls of Fire," he took time to visit a cancer ward at St. Jude Children's Hospital. "You've got to do stuff like that," he said to Sessums. "I've been blessed. What's all this money for? What purpose can you find for all this media recognition? Sometimes you can draw attention to things you believe in."

Recently, Quaid has been attempting to launch a musical career, in addition to his acting career, with a band he formed called the Eclectics. He sings, plays piano and guitar, and composes for the group. Quaid told Sessums that they are negotiating a record deal and expect to start recording sometime during the summer of '89. When asked by Huffhines about a pan of the group in the *Los Angeles Times,* Quaid said, "Well, they're out to get me, you know what I mean? We got, like, 10 great reviews and then we get this review in the *LA Times* and it gets in *People* magazine and then it's all over the place.... The music'll speak for itself." And, Quaid emphasized to Norman, "The music is not a diversion. I'm not giving up being an actor. I want to be both. I just want it all and I want it now. I'm just like everybody else."

Sources

American Film, June, 1989.
Chicago Tribune, November 6, 1988.
Detroit Free Press, June 25, 1989; June 30, 1989.
Esquire, March, 1989.
Films in Review, February, 1988.
Interview, June, 1989.
Maclean's, August 24, 1987; November 16, 1987; November 21, 1988.
Newsweek, April 17, 1978; July 23, 1979; October 3, 1983; September 7, 1987; October 26, 1987; November 14, 1988.
New York, November 14, 1988.
New Yorker, May 19, 1980.
New York Times, June 30, 1989.
New York Times Magazine, November 6, 1988.
People, December 28, 1987.
Playboy, December, 1987.
Rolling Stone, September 24, 1987.
Time, July 30, 1979; June 16, 1980; October 3, 1983; August 24, 1987; March 21, 1988; November 7, 1988.
USA Today, June 30, 1989.

—Sidelights by Greg Mazurkiewicz

Dan Quayle

AP/Wide World Photos

Vice-president of the United States

Full name, James Danforth Quayle; born February 4, 1947, in Indianapolis, Ind.; son of James C. (in newspaper publishing business) and Corinne (Pulliam) Quayle; married Marilyn Tucker (an attorney), November 18, 1972; children: Tucker Danforth, Benjamin Eugene, Mary Corinne. *Education:* DePauw University, B.S. in political science, 1969; Indiana University, J.D., 1974. *Politics:* Republican.

Addresses: *Legal residence*—Huntington, Ind. *Office*—The White House, 1600 Pennsylvania Ave., Washington, D.C. 20501.

Career

Worked as a reporter and pressman for the *Huntington* (Indiana) *Herald-Press* while an undergraduate, 1965–69, associate publisher and corporate vice-president, 1974—; Office of the Attorney General of the State of Indiana, named chief investigator of the state's consumer protection division while still a law student, 1970–71; served as administrative assistant to Indiana Governor Edgar D. Whitcomb, 1971–73; named director of Indiana Inheritance Tax Division, 1973–74; admitted to the Bar of Indiana, 1974; partner (with wife) in law firm Quayle & Quayle, 1974–76; member of U.S. Congress as Republican representative from 4th Dist. of Indiana, 1977–81, and as U.S. senator from Indiana, 1981–89; vice-president of the United States, 1989—. Taught business law at Huntington College, 1975. Columnist and contributor of articles to periodicals, including *American Psychologist, Business and Health, New York Times,* and *Washington Post.*

Member: Rotary Club, Hooiser State Press Club, Chamber of Commerce, Huntington, Indiana, Huntington Bar Association.

Awards: Named "One of Ten Outstanding Young Men in America" by U.S. Jaycees, 1982; named "Taxpayers' Best Friend" by National Taxpayers Union; received Golden Bulldog award from Watchdogs of the Treasury; named "Guardian of Small Business" by National Federation of Independent Business; recipient of National Security Leadership award from the Coalition for Peace Through Strength, 1985.

Sidelights

In choosing Dan Quayle as his running mate, George Bush selected a handsome, affable young Midwesterner from a background of privilege. The junior senator from Indiana arrived in Washington in 1980 and began compiling a conservative voting record that earned him the admiration of the party's right wing. At the Republican convention in New Orleans in August 1988, waves of enthusiasm greeted Bush's choice of a "fresh face"; much was made of Quayle's supposed resemblance to Robert Redford. But support wavered as the media began to dig into the candidate's background. Reports surfaced that Quayle had used family connections to avoid active military service during the Vietnam War, that he had attended a Congressional retreat in the company of a lobbyist who posed nude for magazines, and that he had gotten into law school despite a sub-par undergraduate grade history.

The sudden flurry of charges threatened to bring down Quayle, and with him the Republican ticket. The campaign of election rival Michael S. Dukakis depicted Quayle as an immature, brainless pretty boy—a kind of male bimbo—whose selection cast Bush's judgment in a bad light. Polls showed even staunch Bush supporters quavering on the "heartbeat issue": Could Quayle, if necessary, handle the responsibilities of President?

As negative media coverage swelled, Bush repeated his confidence in his running mate, albeit in general terms. Soon thereafter he refused comment on the issue, and the two men campaigned together only twice. Quayle was sent to campaign primarily before small town audiences in the Midwest, and media coverage was skirted. Campaign advisors bit their fingernails at the prospect of Quayle embarrassing himself in televised debates with his more experienced Democratic opponent, Lloyd Bentsen.

Indeed, the low point came at a televised debate between Bentsen and Quayle when Quayle, seeking to establish his maturity, began comparing his experience to that of President John F. Kennedy. "Senator, I served with Jack Kennedy," Bentsen interrupted, in a much-celebrated jibe. "I knew Jack Kennedy. Jack Kennedy was a friend of mine. Senator, you're no Jack Kennedy."

The Democrats, however, failed to capitalize on the "Quayle factor" and lost in November. Quayle had been made to seem acceptable to the voters, but apparently the Bush inner circle itself remained unconvinced. Bush delivered his Election Day victory speech with his running mate several steps behind him, and did not urge him forward for the traditional clasped-hands salute. Several days later the name James Danforth Quayle was conspicuously omitted from the guest list when British Prime Minister Margaret Thatcher dined at the White House.

After the election the new vice-president admitted he had been unprepared for the rigors of a national campaign. The intense criticism had spilled over onto his family, "something I wish hadn't happened," he complained to *New York Times* reporter B. Drummond Ayres, Jr., on election day. Reflecting on the campaign, he told Ayres that he should have broken free of the "controlled environment" imposed by his "handlers", or aides. But he stopped short of blaming the campaign staff, which had carefully scripted the Senator's every appearance after the National Guard fiasco. "Believe me, it takes a while to understand what the ground rules are of a national campaign, having not run in one before."

He found out quickly enough, when journalists revealed he had avoided possible Vietnam service in 1969 by using connections to obtain a coveted post in the state's National Guard. Quayle had been an enthusiastic supporter of American intervention in that war, but turned to family connections—his grandfather, Eugene C. Pulliam, is the state's premier newspaper publisher—to secure entrance into the Guard. His explanations seemed fumbling and defensive, as quoted by the *Wall Street Journal*'s James Perry: "Well, growing up in Huntington, Indiana, the first thing you think about is education . . . , raising a family. I was fortunate enough to be able to go on to law school, meet my wife, be blessed by three beautiful children. I did not know in 1969 that I would be in this room, I confess."

Next came the Paula Parkinson mini-scandal. Parkinson, employed as a lobbyist by the insurance industry, did much of her lobbying horizontally. By her own count she had affairs with "less than" one dozen Republican Congressmen. On the heels of the National Guard stories it was reported that Quayle joined three fellow Congressmen and Ms. Parkinson on a golfing weekend back in 1980. All four later voted against a bill her employers had opposed; no improprieties were proven. Quayle insisted that his only recreation that weekend had been playing golf. His "handlers" helped defuse the charges by arranging for the candidate to face the anticipated battery of television cameras while carrying out the family's garbage to the curb. His prepared comment likened the Parkinson charges to trash he was hauling, and the joke seemed to satisfy television audiences.

Quayle's reputation as an intellectual "lightweight" proved more difficult to alleviate. Investigations into his academic career found he had flunked the comprehensive political science examination required to graduate from DePauw University, but was allowed to take another test and passed it. Quayle's grades were in the C range, apparently inadequate to gain admission to Indiana Law School—yet the next semester he began attending night classes there. A private conference with the admissions dean had done the trick.

The silver spoon story of Dan Quayle's life has been: Don't worry, call home. "For Dan Quayle, the family name and family fortune . . . have stayed with him and shaped him from the outset, guiding him up the sturdy rungs of a ladder to remarkable success," wrote Wayne King of the *New York Times.* "As Mr. Quayle himself put it [the day Bush announced his selection] 'I never had to worry about where I was going to go.'"

Born in Indianapolis into the family of Eugene Pulliam, Quayle was the beneficiary of the enormous power and wealth his grandfather had amassed. The Pulliam publishing empire spreads out over Indiana and Arizona and is estimated to be worth a billion dollars. Politically, it carries enormous weight in Republican circles as a conservative standard bearer. Quayle has said that his grandfather was the key factor in Barry Goldwater's 1964 Presidential bid.

"What the position of vice-president lends itself to is national security. That's my area of expertise and where I've spent a lot of time."

James C. and Corinne Pulliam Quayle, in 1955, transplanted their household to Phoenix, where James managed the Pulliam newspapers. In the Arizona sunlight young Danny worked on his golf swing and developed an enduring devotion to conservative causes. The family involved itself in right-wing activities in Phoenix, and James Quayle remains proud of his membership in the John Birch society during those years.

In 1963 the family moved back to Indiana, where James Quayle became publisher of the *Huntington Herald-Press.* Dan Quayle passed his junior and senior years at Huntington High School, and played varsity baseball and golf. He dated a classmate, Carla Rice (now Knoop), who remembers him as intensely political—and so devoted to his grandfather that he broke dates with her when the old man needed a golf partner. Their romance continued through one year of college, when Dan attended DePauw University in Greencastle, and Carla attended Ball State, in Muncie. They broke up after their freshman year.

"As an undergraduate at DePauw, a small, private school attended and heavily endowed by his father, his uncle and his grandfather, young Dan Quayle felt no more the weight of the world than the five-iron that often rested on his shoulder, those who knew him recall," wrote Wayne King in the *New York Times.* "While not flaunting his wealth and family position, he seemed quite content to be swaddled in their warmth, classmates remember."

He was never one of the "brainos," his father's word for DePauw students. Instead, he displayed what one political science professor called "an ostentatious indifference" to academics. He came into his own on the golf course and in the frat house, where he was a popular member of the Delta Kappa Epsilon fraternity (as was George Bush at Yale, two decades earlier). Quayle was soon elected vice-president, but ran for frat president and lost. It was the only election in which he's ever come in second.

Then the Vietnam War intervened. Six weeks before he was to graduate, he lost his student draft deferment. He passed his physical and faced the likelihood of induction. So he turned to his family. A phone call was made by a former National Guard major, who worked for Pulliam, to an old friend, a former Guard commander. A vacancy was found in headquarters. The slot was kept vacant until Quayle applied. "I did what any normal person would do at that age," he told the *New York Times.* "You call home. You call home to mother and father, and say, 'I'd like to get in the National Guard.'"

It was not the only time family clout helped. His mediocre academic record at DePauw, which included one grade of D in political science, failed to pass admissions requirements at the night Law School program at Indiana University at Indianapolis. Quayle would not take no for an answer, though, and paid a visit to the admissions dean. He apparently managed to convince him that his background and motivation made him qualified, despite grades below admission requirements.

Attending law school at night and fulfilling his National Guard requirements on weekends, Quayle began looking for a salaried job, and approached his father for help. The editor of Pulliams's *Indianapolis News* landed an interview for the young law student with the Attorney General's office. Quayle got the job, apparently a low-level one, but soon was named chief investigator of the consumer protection division. He left in 1971 for a job in the administration of Indiana Governor Edgar D. Whitcomb.

Quayle continued to pursue his law studies, doing better scholastically than he did as an undergrad. He also began dating a classmate, Marilyn Tucker. In 1974 both graduated, passed the state bar exam, and were married. They choose not to work for an established law firm, as most young lawyers do, but instead opened their own firm, Quayle & Quayle. Office space was provided above the *Herald-Press.* Family contacts helped get the practice off the ground. The 27-year-old was also named on the newspaper masthead as associate publisher, though employees rarely saw him involved in the business.

A year into his law practice Quayle was asked by a county political leader, Orvas E. Beers, if he would run for Congress. After phoning his father Quayle agreed, and ran a campaign attacking the Democratic incumbent, J. Edward Roush, as too liberal on social issues and weak on defense. He won as an underdog and in 1978 was reelected easily. Two years later he surprised the state political establishment by challenging incumbent Birch Bayh, an Indiana institution, for his Senate seat. Quayle won an upset victory amid the Reagan tidal wave, and in 1986 won again, this time with a state record 61 percent majority.

Quayle came to Congress with a reputation as a likable fellow with no particular leadership ability. By most accounts he worked hard to overcome that image, and emerged as a reliable point man for the Reagan administration on conservative issues. Serving on the Senate Budget Committee he faithfully championed the conservative agenda. On the Senate Armed Services Committee he has worked tirelessly on behalf of the Strategic Defense Initiative, commonly called Star Wars, a key Reagan program. As a senior member of the Labor and Human Resources Committee, he has voted against abortion and school busing, while supporting prayer in school. He earned bipartisan respect in 1983 when he teamed with Senator Ted Kennedy to author the Job Training Partnership Act.

Still, the senator was a surprise choice to nearly everyone at the Republican convention. When he took the podium he delivered a short and not particularly memorable acceptance speech. "Let's go get'em," he shouted. Then: "We are obviously honored. We're obviously a bit humbled. But George Bush's America believes and has the commitment to the American family that's so important to all of us. George Bush's America understands the problems that confront us and can lead us to the future and the 21st century."

The explanation that Bush advisors gave for the selection, at first, was that Quayle would appeal to young voters, being of their generation, and to women, being so good-looking. That reasoning was soon modified as it became clear that women would not vote automatically for the best-looking candidate, nor young voters vote automatically for a Baby Boomer. Quayle was repositioned as a military and national security expert. "What the position of vice-president lends itself to is national security," he told a *Newsday* reporter. "That's my area of expertise and where I've spent a lot of time. National security meetings, formulating strategies and discussing foreign policy: I really look forward to that."

Sources

Newsday, August 17, 1988; August 20, 1988; August 21, 1988; November 10, 1988.

New York Times, August 17, 1988; August 18, 1988; August 19, 1988; August 23, 1988; August 24, 1988; August 26, 1988; October 6, 1988; November 5, 1988; November 10, 1988; November 17, 1988; November 19, 1988.

Wall Street Journal, August 18, 1988; August 19, 1988; August 23, 1988.

Washington Post, August 17, 1988; August 18, 1988; August 19, 1988; August 20, 1988; August 21, 1988.

—Sidelights by Warren Strugatch

Jean-Pierre Rampal

Flutist

Full name, Jean-Pierre Louis Rampal; born January 7, 1922, in Marseilles, France; son of Joseph (a flutist and professor of music) and Andrée (Roggero) Rampal; married Francoise-Anne Bacqueyrisse (a harpist), June 6, 1947; children: Isabelle Rampal Dufour, Jean-Jacques. *Education:* University of Marseilles, degree in science, 1941, studied medicine for three years; studied flute at National Conservatory, Paris, France.

Addresses: *Home*—Paris, France. *Agent*—M.L. Falcone, 155 West 68th St., Suite 1114, New York, N.Y. 10023.

Career

Flutist with Paris Opera orchestra, 1945–58, principal flutist, 1958–64; has performed in concert throughout the world. Conductor of numerous orchestras; professor at National Conservatory, Paris, and at Paris Conservatory; editor, International Music Co., New York City, beginning 1958. Has appeared on television programs, including "The Tonight Show," "Dick Cavett," "60 Minutes," and "The Muppet Show."

Member: French Musicological Society, Association of Music and Musicians (president, beginning 1974).

Awards: Grand Prix du Disque, eight times, 1954–78; Oscar du Premier Virtuose Francais, 1956; decorated officier Legion d'Honneur, 1966, officier de l'Ordre des Arts es Lettres, 1971, and commandeur de l'Ordre National du Merite; Prix Edison, 1969; Prix Leonie Sonning, 1978; Prix du President de la Republique, 1978; Prix de l'Academie Charles Cros, 1978.

Photo by Larry Couzens. Courtesy of Colbert Artists Mgt. Inc.

Sidelights

Called the master of his instrument, Jean-Pierre Rampal is the first flutist to attract audiences worldwide on the scale done by virtuoso pianists and violinists. Rampal's legendary technical ability and breath control, full-bodied tone, and charismatic personality regularly draw large audiences. Rampal has popularized the flute to an even greater degree than during the instrument's Golden Age—the Baroque—and in so doing created what has popularly been called a "flute boom."

Rampal was born in 1922 in Marseilles, France, to Andrée Roggero and Joseph Rampal, a flute professor at the music conservatory in Marseilles. Though born into a musical family, Rampal did not begin to play the flute until he was almost 13 years old, when he started learning from his father. Even then he was not serious in his training, though he took first prize for his work in flute at the Marseilles Conservatory. Instead, he aspired to become a surgeon. With that goal in mind, when he graduated from the local Lycée Thiers with a degree in letters and philosophy in 1939, he enrolled at the University of Marseilles, where he earned a pre-medical degree. After completing three years of medical school studies, Rampal's plans were thwarted by World War II and the German Occupation forces' orders that Rampal's military unit be sent to a German forced labor camp. Rampal deserted and fled to the Marseilles underground; at the end of the war he went to Paris, where he enrolled in the National Conservatory.

"I decided to be a flute player," he told Elizabeth F. von Bergen of *The Instrumentalist*. "Up until I was 21 I had thought my future was to be a surgeon, no doubt about it. But then I changed my mind.... Suddenly I just knew that I would be unable to do anything but music. That's all. Without reason. I was excited but also upset, because I didn't want to disappoint my parents by leaving medical studies. Finally I did it." Several months after he entered the conservatory Rampal graduated with honors and began his performance career with the Paris Opera orchestra, with which he became principal flutist. Rampal also soon became a mainstay on the French national radio and gradually developed a following for his solo performances.

The flute is generally considered to be one of the oldest of all musical instruments. During the Baroque period, essentially 1600 to 1750, it became very popular and was featured in orchestral solos and small ensemble pieces. In the nineteenth century, however, the flute seemed to disappear into the orchestra as a soft-spoken member of the ensemble, giving way to the heavy sonorities of the Romantic period. Yet due in large measure to Rampal, in the twentieth century the flute has come into its own again as a solo instrument.

Many people find the sound of the flute attractive, and Rampal attributes this appeal to its naturalness. "I think it really has something to do simply with the flute and the way it reaches audiences," he explained to Howard Reich of the *Chicago Tribune*. "For me, the flute is really the sound of humanity, the sound of man flowing, completely free from his body almost without an intermediary.... Playing the flute is not as direct as singing, but it's nearly the same." Its popularity among music students stems also from its ability to be easily played at a beginning level. To become a masterful player, however, as Rampal would assure anyone, requires the skill and dedication necessary to perform any other instrument. Other advantages of the flute are numerous: It is relatively inexpensive; it does not require extensive tuning, and it is easily portable.

Looking back to his early career, Rampal explained the sudden resurgence of the flute in the 1940s to *New York Times* writer David Wright: "With all this bad mess we had in Europe during the war, people were looking for something quieter, more structured, more well balanced than Romantic music. This is why Baroque music was so successful after the war."

As a seasoned performer, Rampal maintains a rigorous concert schedule of performances throughout the world. He made his American debut in 1958, and in his many years as a soloist, he has appeared with every major orchestra in the United States. Rampal possesses great natural affinity for the flute. His rich tone and enormous technical ability have received raves worldwide. He credits the teaching of his father and his fourteen karat gold flute for the warmth of his sonority. Rampal is a master at producing varied tone color, and even the most difficult allegro passages seem to flow effortlessly from under his fingers.

Rampal performs a wide array of music, from works of the Baroque era to Japanese pieces and jazz. He carefully gauges the attention span of his audience at a particular location before planning his programs. He often begins with Baroque works and then moves on to those of the early twentieth century. Rampal has appreciably enlarged the repertoire of flute literature by reviving little-known older works, transcribing pieces originally written for other instruments for the flute, and inspiring works by such renowned twentieth-century composers as Pierre Boulez, Jean Françaix, André Jolivet, Francis Poulenc, and Aaron Copland, as well as contemporary composers like David Diamond and Ezra Laderman.

Critics have objected to some of Rampal's transcriptions and his forays into jazz, but Rampal takes none of it to heart. "I never follow what is fashionable," he explained to Reich. "In France there is now a revival of interest in music by Erik Satie. They say he is a genius and so on. But I have never seen any genius in this music, and I still don't. I'm very faithful to my ideas and proud of my tastes." Unlike many performers, Rampal enjoys the luxury of playing only the works he prefers, and the flutist has a marked dislike for much late twentieth-century music, particularly aleatoric works, music in which an element of chance is introduced by the performer along the set guidelines of the composer.

Purists of the Baroque have also criticized Rampal for not performing works of that era on the Baroque flute, a keyless precursor of the modern flute. In response, Rampal told Mark Schulgold of the *Los Angeles Times:* "Why should we avoid the improvements on the instrument? It's too frustrating to play the Baroque flute. People back then were always complaining. Why do you think Quantz spent 20 years in his shop to invent one key? And then these critics want us to take that key off when we play pre-Quantz music!"

With so many concerts to his credit, one would think Rampal must never be nervous before a performance, and he does not outwardly appear so. Yet, "It's always scary to start a concert, and there is always something in the work that you're scared about," he confided to Bergen. "It's an excitement to be on the stage and it makes you a little more nervous than usual, which is good. It would be no good to go on the stage as routinely as you go to have lunch. So I guess I'm scared like everybody. But it's not a big scare. I am not in a panic, you know. It's terrible if you panic; then it's better to change and to be an accountant or something else other than a virtuoso." On stage Rampal is a poised performer. When he makes an error, which happens even for a virtuoso, he does not allow it to shatter his attention.

While on tour, Rampal often conducts master classes, and when not touring he teaches at the National Conservatory in Paris. Rampal believes that technical ability is the base of musical ability, and when a student is technically capable, the musicality will come naturally. Yet Rampal is annoyed by the highly technical scientific studies of such performance practices as vibrato and multiple tonguing. Rampal's ability seems to defy the general counsel of flute teachers the world over. His embouchure is off center and he holds his flute slanted downward—two bad habits from his student days that he has never attempted to correct. Rampal freely admits that he was never a self-disciplined student, though he maintains that students need to maintain regular practice regimens to achieve the technical ability. Rampal prefers to practice in concentrated bursts whenever he feels it is necessary.

Rampal began recording very early in his career, and he lays claim to an impressive discography of over 100 records on 18 labels, including CBS Masterworks, London, RCA, and Musical Heritage Society. These recordings include the standard classical repertoire for the flute; adaptations for flute ensembles of duos, trios, quartets and woodwind quintets; English folk songs, Japanese flute classics; East Indian compositions; and jazz. Rampal was awarded the French Grand Prix du Disque eight times for his bestselling recordings, and his record of Claude Bolling's *Suite for Flute and Jazz Piano Trio, No. 1* has been on the *Billboard* charts for over ten years, a first for any classical musician, and only the second time any record has been so classed.

Rampal has also been heard via another mass medium—television. He is a regular on French television and has appeared on several American talk shows, and even on "The Muppet Show," where he played the Pied Piper. Rampal enjoys his celebrity status. "I never dislike the signing of autographs," he told Melinda Bargreen of the *Seattle Times/Seattle Post-Intelligencer.* "When they stop asking for autographs, that is when one is in trouble."

Recently Rampal has taken up the baton to guest conduct many North American orchestras, including those of San Francisco, Houston, and Montreal. Reviews of his conducting have generally been positive, yet Rampal admitted to Reich that conducting will never replace his flute performances: "Orchestras invite me to guest-conduct occasionally, and I do, but it is not really for me .... I am still happy to play the flute."

A true *bon vivant,* Rampal enjoys the social activities that are an integral part of touring. He has developed a sensitive palate during his world travels and will happily talk about his favorite dishes. He has even written about Japanese cuisine in a forward to *The Book of Sushi* published by Kodansha International. Rampal's pace has slowed somewhat in the past few years. He told Bergen: "I am taking more time to relax now, but I still am touring. A little travel, a little rest in the afternoons, a nice concert, some good food afterwards: This is the life I like."

Discography

Antonio Vivaldi, *Flute Concertos.*
Vivaldi, *Complete Flute Concertos, Volume I, Opus 10, Nos. 1–6.*
Vivaldi, *Complete Flute Concertos, Volume II, Nos. 7–11.*
Vivaldi, *Complete Flute Concertos, Volume III, Nos. 12–18.*
Wolfgang Amadeus Mozart, *Quartets for Flute and Strings.*
Music for Flute, Violin and Viola.
Claude Bolling, *Suite for Flute and Jazz Piano.*
Bach family, *Trios and Quartets.*
Favorite Encores.
Greatest Hits.
Sakura, *Japanese Melodies for Flute and Harp.*
Vivaldi, *Concerto in D Minor for Violin and Strings* [and] Georg Philipp Telemann, *Suite in A Minor.*
Greatest Hits, Volume II.
Mozart, *Symphonies Number 36, "Linz," and 38, "Prague."*
Japanese Folk Melodies.

Johann Sebastian Bach, *Complete Flute Sonatas.*
George Frideric Handel, *Flute Sonatas.*
Bach/Telemann, *Flute Concertos.*
Mozart, *Flute and Harpsichord Sonatas.*
Telemann, *Twelve Fantasies for Flute.*
Music for Flute and Harp.
Francis Poulenc/Sergei Prokofiev, *Flute Sonatas* [and] Claude Debussy, *Syrinx.*
Aram Khachaturian, *Concerto for Flute and Orchestra.*
Vivaldi, *Diverse Concertos.*
César Franck/Gabriel Pierné, *Flute Sonatas.*
Mauro Giuliani, *Sonata for Flute and Guitar.*
Bolling, *Picnic Suite for Flute, Guitar and Jazz Piano.*
Mozart, *Concertos for Flute and Harp, for Oboe and Orchestra.*
Carl Philipp Emanuel Bach/Johann Sebastian Bach/Telemann, *Trio Sonatas.*
Giuseppe Tartini, *Flute Concertos.*
Franz Schubert, *Sonata in A Minor, "Arpeggione"* [and] Ignaz Moscheles, *Sonata Concertante.*
Franz Joseph Haydn, *Guitar Concerto in F Major* [and] Ferdinando Carulli, *Guitar Concerto in A Major.*
Pastorales de Noel.
Antonin Dvorak/Jindrich Feld/Bohuslav Martinu, *From Prague With Love.*
Yamanakabushi, *Japanese Melodies, Volume III.*
Haydn, *"London" Trios Nos. 1-4.*
Bolling, *Suite for Chamber Orchestra and Jazz Piano Trio.*
Johann Sebastian Bach and sons, *Trio Sonatas.*
Rampal Plays Scott Joplin.
Weber, *Flute Sonatas.*
Bach, *Three Flute Concertos.*
Vivaldi, *Six Concertos.*
A Baroque Festival.
Sakura, *Sakura: Rampal Plays Favorite Melodies of Japan.*
Rampal Plays Mozart.
Fascinatin' Rampal.
Bach, *Sonatas for Flute and Harpsichord.*
Mozart, *The Complete Flute Quartets.*
Haydn, *Concertos for Flute and Oboe.*
A Night at the Opera: The Magic Flute.
Bolling, *Suite for Flute and Jazz Piano Trio No. 1.*
Mozart, *Flute Sonatas.*
Flute at the Court of Frederick the Great.
Carulli, *Concerto in G Major for Flute, Guitar and Orchestra.*
Flute and Harp Duets.
Mozart, *Symphonia Concertante in E Flat* [and] *Concerto for Flute and Harp.*

Sources

Buffalo News, February 8, 1987; February 14, 1987.
Chicago Tribune, January 24, 1988; March 16, 1988.
Detroit Free Press, February 2, 1987.
Gazette (Montreal), March 22, 1988.
Instrumentalist, January, 1984.
Los Angeles Times, August 28, 1985; February 8, 1986; March 21, 1987; February 26, 1988.
Montreal Daily News, March 22, 1988.
New York Times, April 3, 1988.
New York Times Magazine, February 22, 1976.
Newsweek, January 1, 1968.
Quarter Notes, September 1981.
Seattle Times/Seattle Post-Intelligencer, February 15, 1987.
Star-Ledger (Newark), January 16, 1988.
Washington Post, April 24, 1986; February 23, 1987.

—Sidelights by Jeanne M. Lesinski

Simon Rattle

AP/Wide World Photos

Conductor

Born January 19, 1955, in Liverpool, England; son of Denis (a teacher and import company executive) and Pauline Rattle; married Elise Ross (a singer), 1980; children: Sasha. *Education:* Studied piano and conducting at Royal College of Music, 1971–74.

Addresses: *Home*—London, England; and Birmingham, England. *Agent*—Harold Holt Ltd., 31 Sinclair Rd., London W14, England.

Career

Showed musical aptitude as a very young child and studied piano and percussion in Liverpool, England; percussionist with Merseyside Youth Orchestra, Liverpool, 1966–71; solo pianist in Liverpool, beginning 1967; occasional percussionist with Royal Liverpool Philharmonic, beginning 1970; made conducting debut, 1970, at a charity concert in Liverpool with an orchestra he had organized; conductor with Bournemouth Symphony Orchestra, 1975–76; guest conductor with London Symphony Orchestra, Scottish National Orchestra, and Northern Sinfonia, 1975–77; associate conductor with Liverpool Philharmonic and BBC Scottish Orchestra, Glasgow, beginning 1977; principal conductor and artistic adviser, City of Birmingham Symphony Orchestra, 1980—. Principal guest conductor, Los Angeles Philharmonic, 1981—, and Rotterdam Philharmonic Orchestra, 1980–81; principal conductor, London Choral Society, 1981–84; artistic director, Southbank Summer Music Festival, 1981–84; regular conductor with Glyndebourne Festival Opera.

Awards: First Prize, John Player International Conducting Competition, 1974; Grammy Award for best classical recording, 1978; named commander, Order of the British Empire, 1987.

Sidelights

One of the leading conductors of his generation, Simon Rattle is known for his powerful interpretations of contemporary music, graceful style on the podium, and determination to establish the City of Birmingham (England) Symphony Orchestra into a world-class orchestra. Rattle has risen to the top of his profession in a very short time and has to the surprise of many turned down numerous offers of prestigious musical posts to devote his efforts to the Birmingham Symphony. In 1987, Queen Elizabeth II honored his contribution to the world of British music by making him a commander of the British Empire.

On January 19, 1955, in Liverpool, a northern port city in England, Rattle was born into a musical family. As amateurs, both Pauline and Denis Rattle played the piano well. In fact Denis Rattle had played piano in a jazz ensemble as a student at Oxford University and considered becoming a professional musician before settling on a business career.

At an early age Rattle became interested in classical music and jazz. He listened to radio broadcasts of symphony concerts from London and read books on music far beyond his age level. The young Rattle soon learned to play percussion and piano, and he tried to organize concerts with family members. At age eleven Rattle became the youngest member of the Merseyside Youth Orchestra in Liverpool as a percussionist. At this time Rattle's musical goals were unfocused, but after hearing a performance of Gustav Mahler's *Symphony No. 2* by the Liverpool Philharmonic in 1966, his desire to become a conductor crystallized. He continued his piano studies and showed such an affinity for the Mozart piano concerti that at age twelve he began a successful solo performance career in Liverpool. Then in 1970 he was first formally employed as a percussionist by the Royal Liverpool Philharmonic Orchestra for a performance of Roberto Gerhard's *Symphony No. 3.*

The young Rattle often lingered around the backstage of the Liverpool Philharmonic, learning as much as he could about conducting and interpretation and in the process becoming particularly interested in works by twentieth-century composers.

In 1970 Rattle made his conducting debut with a charity-sponsored concert of Franz Schubert's *Symphony No. 8* and Ralph Vaughan Williams's *Fantasia on a Theme by Tallis.* That year Rattle also played percussion for the National Youth Orchestra. Due to his association with this orchestra, he discovered the works of contemporary French composer and conductor Pierre Boulez and even met with the composer himself when he tried, and failed, to bring together the ensemble needed to perform Boulez's *Le Marteau sans Maître.*

Despite his parents' wish that he attend a university, in 1971 Rattle enrolled on a scholarship at the Royal Academy of Music in London, where he studied conducting. At the Royal Academy he came into contact with John Carewe—a highly respected conductor of modern music—who profoundly influenced him. Yet because Rattle often found the curriculum of the Royal Academy too stifling, he forged ahead on his own, organizing and rehearsing ensembles for unauthorized performances, much to the consternation of school officials. One such concert, Mahler's *Symphony No. 2,* was discussed widely in the media and caught the attention of Martin Campbell-White of Harold Holt Limited, a well-known London music agent, who offered Rattle a management contract to begin after his 1974 graduation.

On May 29, 1974, with an interpretation of Richard Strauss's tone poem *Don Juan,* Rattle became the youngest winner ever of the prestigious John Player International Conducting Competition held in Portsmouth, England. Though in retrospect Rattle considered his interpretation very immature, this single performance opened doors wide: he was given a two-year contract to conduct the Bournemouth Symphony Orchestra, a large monetary award, and guest appearances with the London Symphony Orchestra, the Scottish National Orchestra, and the Northern Sinfonia.

Upon reflection, Rattle sees his stint with the Bournemouth Orchestra as a testing ground for his own capabilities, a time when he learned where the gaps in his education lay and suffered serious doubt about the choice of a conducting career. "I remember standing in front of the . . . orchestra for my first rehearsal and wondering what on earth I was going to do. We did about eighty concerts in two years and I think even they, and they're very nice people, would agree that seventy of them were bad," he told *London Times* music critic Nicholas Kenyon. "I very seriously nearly gave up several times. You don't realize as a student what professional standards are." Rattle later declined an offer to conduct the London Philharmonic when the renowned conductor Dietrich Fischer-Dieskau canceled, maintaining that he lacked the necessary experience. He did not pass up the opportunity to work with the Glyndebourne Opera, however, and earned the reputation of a promising young operatic conductor.

In 1977, Rattle was appointed associate conductor of both the Liverpool Philharmonic and BBC Scottish Orchestra in Glasgow, Scotland, positions that allowed him, as an apprentice, to expand his repertoire. With the BBC Orchestra Rattle made his first recordings: a series of nineteen television documentaries, in which he conducted and discussed works by contemporary composers. These recordings made outside the commercial sphere allowed Rattle to polish his recording technique, and other recording contracts and guest conducting appearances, including his American debut with the London Schools Symphony Orchestra on tour, rapidly followed. By 1979, Rattle had firmly established his reputation as a capable interpreter of twentieth-century music. He appeared regularly as a guest conductor with London's major orchestras and internationally renowned soloists, and his 1978 recording on the EMI label of Serge Prokofiev's *Piano Concerto No. 1* and Maurice

Ravel's *Piano Concerto in D for the Left Hand* with soloist André Gavrilov and the London Symphony Orchestra was awarded a Grammy.

In 1980 Rattle accepted the directorship of the City of Birmingham Symphony Orchestra. The ensemble's former conductor, Louis Fremaux, had resigned several years earlier, and no replacement had yet been hired. Rattle set out to make this lesser-known orchestra in central England one of the premier orchestras in that country. With this goal in mind he has greatly limited his guest conducting activities, an unusual decision for a young conductor in an age of jet-set traveling conductors. Rattle explained to a writer for the *New Yorker:* "Guest conducting is hard on the nerves—it's like being married to a different person every couple of weeks. It can be a great experience, but it can also be harmful to the repertoire, because as a guest one has to be terribly careful to do only works that can be prepared in a given rehearsal time. Almost all the great orchestras of the past have been built by individuals working away for many years, and it's this tradition that appeals to me. It [the conductor's imprint on the orchestra] lingers on long after the conductor has left."

"I remember standing in front of the...orchestra for my first rehearsal and wondering what on earth I was going to do."

Despite his devotion to his home orchestra, Rattle has not declined all guest conducting invitations. He has regularly appeared with the Los Angeles Symphony and graced the podium of orchestras in San Francisco, Cleveland, and Boston as well. For the 1980–1981 season, Rattle accepted the post of principal guest conductor of the Rotterdam Philharmonic, while taking a sabbatical to study English literature. As a postgraduate student he studied the works of John Donne, Andrew Marvell, James Joyce, and T.S. Eliot with the recommendation that fellow musicians do likewise to clean their ears and sharpen their senses. When asked by Herbert Kupferberg of *Stereo Review* what advice he would give to aspiring young conductors, Rattle stressed the nonmusical: "I would tell young people of all persuasions to listen to everything, all styles of music, all styles of interpreters. I would say, read as much as you can—all kinds of books. Race to your nearest art gallery. Immerse yourself in every aspect of the world of the arts, and the life around you, so that you actually have something to bring to music when your time comes. In the end, playing the right notes is the least important part."

Rattle's rise as a conductor parallels the burgeoning success of the City of Birmingham Symphony. He is known for programs that feature the unusual and contemporary—for example, Toru Takemitsu's *Riverrun for Piano and Orchestra*—and he has had opportunities to premier new works. A podium manner devoid of wild personal idiosyncracies that might distract the audience's attention from the music, and rhythmic clarity, are hallmarks of Rattle's style. The Birmingham Symphony has risen in stature from a little-known orchestra to one that has toured with great success in Europe, Japan, and the United States, and made critically acclaimed recordings. The orchestra enjoys an amazing 98 percent subscription rate, the envy of many organizations, and in 1991 the symphony is slated to move into a state-of-the-art concert hall in the Birmingham's new convention center.

Rattle is surrounded by controversy because he dares to do things at his own pace and in his own manner. When asked by Kenyon if his limiting his activity to working closely with only a couple of orchestras was swimming against the tide in the twentieth century, Rattle replied: "Completely against the tide, yes. But it seems to me that unless conductors start doing that again orchestras aren't going to play as well as they can. It's very sad to see great orchestras playing at 40 percent or 50 percent of their capacity because they don't have a close relationship with the conductor. In Birmingham what's so noticeable is that they play at a fantastically high percentage of capacity all the time, and that makes the work so rewarding. I do believe there's an advantage in fidelity." Prior to performances, Rattle extensively rehearses pieces with the orchestra and does not record pieces with the Birmingham Symphony until after they have been widely performed.

Since his conducting debut, Rattle has made more than twenty-five recordings of mostly twentieth-century works: Igor Stravinsky's *Pulcinella,* Benjamin Britten's *War Requiem,* George Gershwin's *Porgy and Bess,* Oliver Messiaen's *Turangalîla Symphony,* Dmitri Shostakovich's *Symphony No. 13* and Leos Janáček's *Glagolitic Mass.* He has also recorded Mahler's *Symphony No. 10* [unfinished] and *Das Klagende Lied,* and a cycle symphonies by Jan Sibelius, a composer for which Rattle has a particular affinity. Much of Rattle's reputation outside Great Britain rests on his discography because his small number of guest performances and tours have thus far limited the number of concert-hall listeners to appreciate his art.

Rattle spends at least six months each year in Birmingham and also has a home in London. Like many in the limelight, he values his family life and his privacy. Rattle is married to American soprano Elise Ross and has a young son Sasha. Rattle's wide-ranging interests include playing squash, watching old movies, and collecting vintage records.

Rattle has been offered musical directorships of the Los Angeles Philharmonic and the Glyndebourne Opera, and guest conducting opportunities at the Metropolitan Opera, the Vienna State Opera, and the Berlin Philharmonic. And to the chagrin of all he has declined them, preferring instead what he terms a "conducting monogamy." When his contract with the City of Birmingham Symphony comes up for renewal in 1991, Rattle will certainly have ample opportunities from which to select the next direction of his already auspicious career.

Discography

Serge Prokofiev, *Piano Concerto No. 1* [and] Maurice Ravel, *Piano Concerto in D for the Left Hand,* EMI, 1978.
Igor Stravinsky, *Pulsinella.*
Benjamin Britten, *War Requiem.*
George Gershwin, *Porgy and Bess.*
Oliver Messiaen, *Turangalila Symphony.*
Dmitri Shostakovich, *Symphony No. 13.*
Leos Janacek, *Glagolitic Mass.*
Gustav Mahler, *Symphony No. 10 (Unfinished).*
Mahler, *Das Klagende Lied*
Has made a total of twenty-five recordings, mostly of works by twentieth-century composers.

Sources

New Yorker, February 8, 1988.
New York Times, January 13, 1985, March 27, 1988, April 15, 1988.
Newsweek, February 11, 1985.
People, April 8, 1985.
Stereo Review, May 1988.

—Sidelights by Jeanne M. Lesinski

Vanessa Redgrave

AP/Wide World Photos

Actress

Born January 30, 1937, in London, England; daughter of Michael Redgrave (an actor and director) and Rachel Kempson (an actress); married Tony Richardson (a director), April, 1962 (divorced, 1967); children: (with Richardson) Natasha, Joely; (with Franco Nero) Carlo. *Education:* Attended Central School of Speech and Drama, London.

Addresses: *Home*—London, England. *Agent*—Marina Martin Management, Ltd., 7 Windmill St., London W1P 1HF, England.

Career

Began appearing onstage in Stratford-on-Avon and London, England, 1958; plays include "Major Barbara," "A Midsummer Night's Dream," "Coriolanus," "Look on Tempests" (London debut), "The Tiger and the Horse," "Lady from the Sea," "The Taming of the Shrew," "The Seagull," "The Prime of Miss Jean Brodie," "Cato Street," "Threepenny Opera," "Twelfth Night," "Design for Living," "Lady from the Sea," "The Aspern Papers," and "Orpheus Descending." Made feature film debut in "Morgan!—A Suitable Case for Treatment," 1965; subsequent films include "Sailor from Gibralter," 1965, "La Musica," 1965, "Blow Up," 1967, "A Man for All Seasons," 1967, "Camelot," 1967, "Isadora," 1968, "Charge of the Light Brigade," 1968, "The Sea Gull," 1968, "A Quiet Place in the Country," 1968, "Dropout," 1969, "The Trojan Women," 1970, "The Devils," 1970, "Mary Queen of Scots," 1971, "The Holiday," 1971, "Murder on the Orient Express," 1974, "Winter Rates," 1974, "The Seven Percent Solution," 1975, "Julia," 1976, "Agatha," 1978, "Yanks," 1979, "Bear Island," 1979, "The Bostonians," 1984, "Wetherby," 1985, and "Steaming," 1986. Television films broadcast in America include "Playing for Time," 1980, "My Body, My Child," 1981, "Three Sovereigns for Sarah," 1985, "Second Serve," 1986, and the miniseries "Peter the Great," 1986. Also producer and narrator of documentary film "The Palestinians," 1977.

Awards: Evening Standard Drama Award, 1961, 1979, 1985; Variety Club of Great Britain Award for best actress, 1961, 1966; British Guild of TV Producers and Directors Award, 1966; Cannes Film Festival Award for best actress, 1966, for "Morgan!—A Suitable Case for Treatment"; Golden Globe Award, 1978; Academy Award for best supporting actress, 1978, for "Julia"; Emmy Award for best actress, 1981, for "Playing for Time." Recipient of Order of the British Empire, 1967.

Sidelights

Few modern actors provoke as much emotional reaction as Britain's Vanessa Redgrave does. Whether her critics are praising her performances or decrying her politics, Redgrave often ends up making headlines. But then, Redgrave was virtually born in the spotlight. On the night of her birth, in prewar London, her father, the Shakespearian actor Sir Michael Redgrave, was playing Laertes to Sir Laurence Olivier's Hamlet. At the end of the play, Olivier informed the audience, "Tonight a lovely new actress has been born. Laertes has a daughter." Growing up in a theatrical family (her mother, Rachel Kempson, is also an acclaimed actress), Redgrave studied ballet to complement her above-average height, and played "endless old ladies," as she once put it, in summer stock theatres.

After a season of Shakespeare at Stratford-on-Avon, the 23-year-old Redgrave made her London debut in "Look on Tempests," in a role that "placed her instantly in the front rank of our younger actresses," as Eric Shorter said in *Plays & Players*. From there Redgrave played in a number of acclaimed theatrical productions and in 1966 parlayed her success into a movie debut in "Morgan!—A Suitable Case for Treatment." In that role, as the upper-class wife of a left-wing fanatic, Redgrave won best actress honors at the Cannes Film Festival.

At the same time she was establishing her acting career, Redgrave began going public with her political sensibilities. Redgrave's Marxist leanings led to her affiliation with the Committee of 100 and the Campaign for Nuclear Disarmament. Eventually the actress turned her attention to the Palestine Liberation Organization (PLO), a group with a global reputation for terrorist activities. In addition, she has stood for Parliament twice, representing the Workers Revolutionary Party, and lost both times (Redgrave's brother, Corin, also has tried to gain election and also has failed).

Perhaps the most controversial merging of Redgrave's professional and political personae occurred at the Academy Awards telecast in the spring of 1978. Accepting the best supporting actress award for her role in "Julia," she made a speech denigrating Israeli policy and ignited the audience by referring to the "Zionist hoodlums" protesting her appearance outside the theater. As Redgrave spoke, a group from the Jewish Defense League burned an effigy to express its opinion of her. The "Zionist hoodlum" remark led to on-air reaction, most notably from best screenplay winner Paddy Chayefsky, who remarked, "A simple thank-you would have sufficed." Later, Redgrave told Fred Hauptfuhrer that "an actor has a public responsibility to speak the truth," although, Hauptfuhrer reported, a year earlier the actress had gone on the record as saying, "It makes nonsense of both to mix movies with politics." That same year, Redgrave produced and narrated a pro-PLO documentary called "The Palestinians."

Another Redgrave controversy surfaced two years later, when the actress was signed to play the role of Holocaust survivor Fania Fenelon in the CBS television movie "Playing for Time." The announcement of Redgrave's casting brought comments from a variety of spokesmen—few of them supportive. "Rabbi Marvin Hier said it's like 'selecting J. Edgar Hoover to portray Martin Luther King,'" wrote *Newsweek*'s Jack Kroll in a cover story about the film. Kroll also quoted Sammy Davis Jr.: "It would be like my playing the head of the Ku Klux Klan." The protest over a PLO supporter playing a Jewish heroine resulted in some advertisers pulling out their commercials, though, as Kroll elaborated, "It's likely that this demand will only add millions to the audience that will see what may well be the finest performance ever given on a television screen."

The true story of Fenelon's ordeal as an inmate at the Auschwitz death camp, "Playing for Time" "is something not even Dante could have envisioned," described Kroll. "Fenelon, a well-known French cabaret singer who had been a member of the Resistance until she was shipped off to Auschwitz, owed her survival to the ingenious perversity of the Nazis, who formed an orchestra among the female inmates of the camp. Fenelon was put into this orchestra, whose job was to provide music for the butchers who needed cultural refreshment during their work of murdering 4 million prisoners, mostly Jews, in the gas chambers and crematoriums of the vast extermination camp."

As the *Newsweek* piece continued, the controversy over advertiser wariness "has brought back some of the issues that were rampant during the blacklist days of the McCarthy period in the '50s. Tremendous pressure has been put on potential sponsors by some Jewish groups, and the Simon Wiesenthal Center lists many major advertisers who plan to stay away from the program. Undoubtedly, some of their resistance reflects a fear that the show's subject matter will turn viewers off. But the main reason for the protest, says the Wiesenthal Center, is that 'CBS has chosen to tell Fania's story by using an actress who has used the arena of the arts to inject her politics of hatred.'"

For her part, Fania Fenelon, 61 years old when the film was made in 1980, told Kroll that she found Redgrave to be "a very great actress . . . . I don't want to have her blacklisted. I fought blacklisting through the McCarthy period. But casting her is for me a moral wrong because she is a fanatic. Fanatics frighten me very much, whether they be Israeli,

Palestinian or Iranian. Vanessa actually said that Israel must be wiped off the map of the world. I just don't see how a woman who is so much my opposite can play me."

Ironically, Redgrave's interpretation of Fenelon proved an enormous success. Her virtuoso performance "only deepens the mystery," in Kroll's words. "How does the actress co-exist with the Vanessa who belongs to the Trotskyite Workers Revolutionary Party and trumpets its line about 'Zionist imperialism and racialist terror'?" Playwright Arthur Miller, who wrote the script for "Playing for Time," told the *Newsweek* correspondent that while he was initially upset at Redgrave's casting, "I decided to keep my mouth shut and let the results justify themselves. Well, I never saw an artist better prepared. She'd take something on page 60 and connect it to something on page 8, things I'd forgotten in the year and a half I'd been writing it. She had a complete view of [the story] like a piece of architecture. I thought the play could be a tremendous statement. She's amplified that statement. But it's hard to reconcile Vanessa the sensitive, vulnerable artist with Vanessa the strident doctrinaire Trotskyite. It's like there's a membrane down the middle of her brain."

"It's hard to reconcile Vanessa the sensitive, vulnerable artist with Vanessa the strident doctrinaire Trotskyite."
—Arthur Miller

The actress won an Emmy for playing Fania Fenelon and continued to work steadily following the controversies. Neither her politics nor her unusual height (in a memorable scene from the film "Agatha," Redgrave bends down to bestow a kiss on co-star Dustin Hoffman) has prevented the Briton from sampling a variety of characters. Among the more unorthodox of her dramatic projects is another television movie, "Second Serve." In it she again portrays a real-life character, the transsexual tennis player Renee Richards. Speaking to *New York Times* correspondent Michael Billington about her propensity for taking on television films even though she is primarily known as a film and theater actress, Redgrave states: "I don't share the snobbish attitude that exists toward TV as a medium. I think that is peculiar to Britain. From my own experience I know that American television handles a lot of major stories."

Richards's story, major in some medical and sociological ways, is one of a "Yale tennis champion, naval officer, husband and father who underwent transsexual surgery, became a tennis pro, coached Martina Navratilova and now has a busy public and private practice as a Manhattan eye-surgeon," as Billington related. Redgrave told the interviewer that she decided to take on the film because the facts "threw light on a lot more problems than that of Renee Richards herself and raised the whole question of sexual stereotyping." That the actress had to begin the role as a man, shaving off her hair and adopting masculine mannerisms had taught her many things, Redgrave continued to Billington. "One is the way male and female are so incredibly interwoven in all of us," she said. "In Renee Richards's case, the two were so closely entwined that she felt as a man she had to be very macho and assertive.... ["Second Serve"] certainly makes you think about our social conditioning."

Controversy again followed Redgrave when, in 1982, the actress, hired to narrate six performances of "Oedipus Rex" for the Boston Symphony Orchestra, was abruptly fired when protest arose over her pro-PLO politics. "The [Boston Symphony Orchestra organization] later claimed that it canceled on Redgrave in response to threats of disruption, although in fact the decision to fire her preceded the one communication that might have been construed as a serious threat: a phone call from a member of the Jewish Defense League who allegedly said there would be 'bloodshed and violence' should Redgrave appear at Symphony Hall," according to Marjorie Heins in a *Nation* article. The actress filed suit against the Boston Symphony Orchestra, citing breach of contract and violation of the Massachusetts Civil Rights Act. In November of 1984, a Federal jury ruled that the Symphony organization had indeed committed a breach of contract and awarded Redgrave her contract salary plus $100,000 in damages. By February of 1985 a Federal District Court judge threw out the damages award, ruling that the orchestra had not violated Redgrave's civil rights.

"Redgrave appealed these rulings, but as her appeal inched its way through the courts, it became apparent that [the judge in this case] was not alone in his ambivalence about her claims," reported Heins, who went on to compare this incident to the McCarthy-era political blacklisting of suspected Communists in the entertainment industry during the 1950s. "Both the actress's claims and the orchestra's defense—fear of performance disruption or economic loss—echoed arguments made at that time by studios defending their firing and blacklisting of hundreds of writers and performers, and indeed by universities, governments and industries that purged employees who had suspect political associations or opinions or who failed to clear themselves before legislative committees. "The issue of blacklist proponents' right of free speech is troubling but may not be critical," Heins concluded. "The message of the Redgrave case . . . was that the blacklist that engulfed entertainment, academia and industry in the 1950s was precipitated not just by intolerant screamers but by employers who acquiesced when faced by their vitriolic noise."

Despite the personal choices that have brought her professional conflict, Redgrave still works steadily and has even seen the continuance of her family's theatrical dynasty when her daughters by ex-husband Tony Richardson, Natasha and Joely, themselves became actresses. Billington referred to the Redgrave lineage when he assessed Vanessa this way: "From her actor-father, . . . she has inherited a Stanislavski-based quest for truth and a blazing emotional intensity; from her actress-mother, . . . a look of slightly sorrowful beauty. What distinguishes her further is her ability to portray tough-minded, independent women rather than passive heroines."

In a *New York Times* interview, Benedict Nightengale saw in Redgrave an artist who's "always enjoyed the challenge of, as she puts it, 'compelling the attention of 700 people with 700 problems and preoccupations who are probably wishing they'd come to the theatre another night.' But what really excites and fulfills her is the communion across the footlights." Quoting Redgrave: "What's so special about the stage is that in the space of two and a half hours, the actors, the author and the audience are all three creating something that will not ever happen again in quite that way. When the conditions are right, when the play is really good, when the actors are really listening to each other and to the audience, you get this wonderful, contradictory feeling that it's all occurring for the very first time."

Sources

American Film, May, 1985.
Life, July 1, 1966.
Los Angeles Times, March 19, 1985.
Ms., October, 1985.
Nation, December 12, 1987.
Newsweek, May 23, 1966; September 29, 1980.
New York Times, May 11, 1986; September 20, 1987; April 7, 1988.
People, April 24, 1978.
Plays & Players, April, 1964.
Time, May 27, 1966; August 19, 1985.

—Sketch by Susan Salter

Hal Riney

© 1984 Ed Kashi/Gamma-Liaison

Advertising executive

Full name, Hal Patrick Riney; born July 17, 1932, in Seattle, Wash.; son of Hal Patrick (a writer, salesman, actor, and cartoonist) and Inez Marie (a schoolteacher) Riney; married third wife, Elizabeth Kennedy (a casting director), 1982; children: (first marriage) Matthew Jonathan; (second marriage) two stepsons, one stepdaughter; (third marriage) one child. *Education:* University of Washington, B.A., 1954.

Addresses: *Home*—San Francisco, Calif. *Office*—Hal Riney & Partners, 735 Battery St., San Francisco, Calif. 94111.

Career

While in school, worked at a variety of jobs, including positions at a food store, a newspaper, and a logging camp; BBDO, Inc. (advertising agency), San Francisco, Calif., 1956–72, began as mailroom worker, became vice-president and creative director; Botsford Ketchum (advertising agency), San Francisco, executive vice-president and creative director, 1972–76; Ogilvy & Mather (advertising agency), San Francisco, senior vice-president, managing diretor, and creative director, 1976–81, executive vice-president, 1981–86, member of board of directors; Hal Riney & Partners (advertising agency), San Francisco, chairman and chief executive officer, 1986–. *Military service:* U.S. Army, two years; served as press officer.

Member: American Association of Advertising Agencies, San Francisco Advertising Club, San Francisco Society for Communicating Arts, Sierra Club, Federation of Fly Fishermen, Oregon Fly Fishers.

Awards: Recipient of fourteen Clio Awards, nine Addy Awards, and three Lions d'Or from Cannes Film Festival; Academy Award nomination for best documentary film, 1971; Grand Prix in advertising from Cannes Film Festival.

Sidelights

His commercials often contain few words of copy. Some are understated and wryly humorous, while others are quietly matter-of-fact. No glitz, no hard sell, no this-is-the-best-thing-since-sliced-bread-and-you-have-to-buy-it approaches here. Yet the commercials created by San Francisco ad man Hal Riney draw powerful emotions from 30 to 60 seconds of music and film. And, they work.

Take, for example, Riney's ads for E. & J. Gallo Winery's Bartles & Jaymes Premium Wine Cooler. Gallo, late in entering the burgeoning wine cooler field, called on Riney to make a name for its coolers. In late 1985, a TV spot appeared with two hayseed characters, named Frank Bartles and Ed Jaymes, sitting on a porch. The ad, a laid-back explanation of why and how the two characters created their wine cooler, even closed by thanking the viewer for their support of the product. Within a year of rolling out the coolers nationwide, Frank and Ed propelled the wine cooler to the top-selling spot among more than 40 wine cooler brands that had crowded onto supermarket shelves. And suddenly, people began hearing about Hal Riney.

Pegged by the *Chicago Tribune* as a "laid-back California rebel that has the Madison Avenue boys on the run," Riney defies being fit into a mold. A relentless perfectionist who writes his ads either by hand or on a treasured old Underwood typewriter, Riney uses feelings to sell his clients' products. His ads often use a beautiful setting, causing those on the creative side of the advertising industry to wax poetic about Riney's work.

A man with a passion for the outdoors and the simplicity it affords, Riney uses back-home, everyday types of folks for the characters in his commercials. His ads have been called some of the most watchable, best-written ads on television, and some say his work reflects Riney's personal background. Longtime Riney friend Dick Maugg, the northern California contractor who also happens to play Ed Jaymes on the Bartles & Jaymes commercials, described Riney as "warm, humorous, ordinary people." Said Maugg in the *Chicago Tribune:* "He doesn't hire movie stars. Just ordinary people like himself. He still thinks of himself as a little guy from Longview, Wash., who's worked hard. And, he's worked so damn hard."

Born in 1932, during the Depression, Hal Patrick Riney grew up in a broken home. His parents divorced when he was in kindergarten, and with his mother and sisters, Riney moved from Burbank to Washington state. The younger Riney idolized Hal Riney Sr., even though his father—a writer, cartoonist, salesman, actor, and newspaper man—left home when Riney was six. Riney keeps a picture of his father near his typewriter and proudly told the *Chicago Tribune* that he is "a junior" of the man in the picture. Riney's mother, a former schoolteacher, now lives with Riney's sister in Europe.

In the third grade, Riney began delivering newspapers. He has held a variety of jobs ever since: working at a Safeway food store during high school, at a newspaper and at a logging camp while attending the University of Washington. Riney majored in art and minored in journalism and advertising in college. Following a two-year stint as an Army press officer in Italy, Riney in 1956 began what was to become a long career in advertising. He started in the mail room of ad agency BBDO in San Francisco, at a rate of $250 a month.

Rising swiftly through the advertising ranks, Riney became vice-president and creative director at BBDO and began winning top ad industry awards. By 1972, he was the executive vice-president and creative director at the Botsford Ketchum agency in San Francisco, and in 1976 he started up Ogilvy & Mather's San Francisco office. Riney's shop, Hal Riney & Partners, operated as a subsidiary of the Ogilvy Group until August 1986, when Riney bought out Ogilvy's interest and spun off as an independent agency.

"I've had few products to work with that were demonstrably superior.... Most purchase decisions are made for emotional—not rational—reasons."

While Riney's ads may work magic, many say that Riney himself is complex, scornful, and mistrustful of others. "He's deeply contemptuous of others and he's very good at camouflaging his darker side," a former Riney copywriter told the *Chicago Tribune.* "You are dealing with two people: himself and this persona he's created over the years, the wry, twinkly, country fella. At some point the persona sort of replaces the real guy."

Other staffers have complained that Riney takes credit for their ideas, and some say he has even been cruel. But despite their complaints, whatever it is Riney exudes draws staffers back to him. Although they may have a love-hate relationship with Riney, some staffers who have quit have returned several times. And many say that Riney is not unreasonable—rather, he only expects of others what he expects of himself. Never mind that what Riney expects of Riney is perfection.

One Los Angeles director who has worked on the majority of Riney's television commercials told the *Chicago Tribune* that, "It's almost illogical, the lengths he goes to. We built an entire Western street for two seconds of film once because he couldn't find anything that looked authentically 1882 Oregon to him. But because he worked so hard, because he went the last step of the final mile, the people in the ad really became those people, those cowboys of a hundred years ago. It's as if we're all miners and he's already found one rich vein, but he thinks that if he pushes just a little bit harder, there's a mother lode still there. And that's what makes Riney ads magic."

Riney's obsession with detail is well-known among those who have worked with him. And there are many stories and "remember when" tales that paint Riney to be either tyrannical, or merely fiercely quality-conscious. Once, after his secretary had purchased some wine glasses for an internal agency wine-tasting for Gallo, Riney sent the glasses back, saying they were too thick. Yet for all his demands, the Riney that few see is insecure. In a letter several years ago to *Advertising Age* editor-at-large Joe Winski, Riney said: "I'm still curious about—and unsure of—my abilities. Compulsively, inevitably, eternally insecure. I don't mind that anymore. Insecurity, uncertainty, the demand for others' approval, is what makes many people better at what they do. In this business, there are two things pulling on you all the time. Success and the exact opposite."

"I suspect the advertising business isn't the greatest platform from which to wield the lever that moves the world; nevertheless, it has some small influence."

He may have self-doubts, but Riney has firmly established himself as a master of television commercials. The initial Bartles & Jaymes ads, besides propelling the cooler to a top-selling slot, were believable to viewers. They were so believable that several viewers, after watching the ads, sent money to Ed Jaymes to help him pay off the second mortgage that the advertising copy described was necessary to fund Ed and Frank's backyard wine cooler endeavor. Beautifully-orchestrated ads for Gallo wines contain little copy, just the words "Only the best. From Ernest and Julio Gallo." Yet they are remembered for the warmth and nostalgic feelings they evoke—unusual emotions from a television ad. In a similar vein, an ad that Riney wrote for a California bank was so successful that the bank was forced to cancel the ad. Why? Because the ad, targeted at young couples just beginning their life together, brought in too many such couples. And they had too little money to make their business worthwhile for the bank.

Part of the 1984 Reagan campaign's official advertising agency, Riney produced commercials that packaged the president in an optimistic and patriotic, yet soft light. The ads, showing smiling children, factory workers, and newlyweds, did not contain political arguments or controversial issues. Just Riney's voice, as in many of his commercials, ending the ad with a quiet-spoken thought. "It's morning again in America," the ad said. "Why would we ever want to return to where we were, less than four short years ago." While the ad was well-received by viewers, it did not sit well with some advertising agency executives who worried about using the same tactics to sell a president as are used to sell wine. But Riney was unruffled. "In political advertising you can get away with innuendo and just plain falsehoods that you'd never get away with in advertising garbage bags or soap," he told *Fortune* magazine.

And, of selling products in general, whether presidents or wine, he said in *New York* magazine: "Often I don't have a damned thing of importance to say about a product. I've had few products to work with that were demonstrably superior. I've seldom worked with products or services that are new. Most purchase decisions are made for emotional—not rational—reasons."

In late May 1988, Hal Riney & Partners won an account that may provide them with one of their biggest challenges yet. In a surprise move, General Motors Corp. named the agency to handle the account for Saturn Corp., the GM unit that is launching the first new-car brand for GM since 1919. Saturn cars will be GM's direct challenge to the imports, and the choice of Riney's agency is expected to challenge importers' advertising as well. Riney will have two years to come up with a campaign that he told *Advertising Age* may emphasize "pride and personality"—which he believes are as important as the actual product and its price in convincing consumers to purchase a car. "I don't think anyone can sell a car without involving people's emotions somewhat," Riney told *Advertising Age.* "We're going to try to talk to people in other ways than the standard things that agencies do." The account, considered extremely lucrative, has been estimated to reach at least $100 million, pushing Riney's medium-sized agency into a full-service operation. But the Saturn account was to be just the beginning of a hot summer for Riney's firm.

In July, the Stroh Brewery Co. named Riney's agency to handle advertising for its Stroh's, Stroh Light, and Signature brands. The account, an estimated $20 million in Stroh advertising, may involve a lot of

Riney's personal touch. Much of Riney's early fame came from commercials he created for brewer Blitz-Weinhard. Said an executive at the advertising agency that lost the Stroh account: "When a company is in trouble, they turn to Merlin the Magician. The truth is," he told *Advertising Age,* "some people just like to say, 'My agency is Hal Riney & Partners.'"

In the end, Riney wants to create more than "just" advertising. In his 1982 letter to *Ad Age's* Winski, he said: "I suspect the advertising business isn't the greatest platform from which to wield the lever that moves the world; nevertheless it has some small influence. That, no doubt, is why I admire the work of those of us who try to find a way to charm, entertain, touch or inspire—in addition to doing our obviously fundamental job of conveying a selling message."

Sources

Advertising Age, May 30, 1988; July 11, 1988; October 24, 1988.
Chicago Tribune, February 15, 1987.
Esquire, June, 1988.
Fortune, August 6, 1984; January 5, 1987.
New York, December 22, 1986.
New York Times Magazine, December 14, 1986.
San Francisco Magazine, January, 1987.

—Sidelights by Amy C. Bodwin

Geraldo Rivera

AP/Wide World Photos

Broadcast journalist and talk-show host

Given name is pronounced Her-*all*-doe; born July 4, 1943, in New York, N.Y.; son of Cruz and Lilly (Friedman) Rivera; married first wife, Linda (divorced after one year); married Edith Vonnegut (divorced); married Sheri Raymond (divorced); married C.C. Dyer (a television producer), 1987; children: (third marriage) Gabriel Miguel. *Education:* Attended University of Arizona, Brooklyn Law School, University of Pennsylvania Law School, and Columbia University School of Journalism.

Addresses: *Home*—New York, N.Y.; and Cape Cod, Mass. *Office*—The Investigative News Group, 311 West 43rd St., New York, N.Y. 10036.

Career

Worked as a salesman and merchant seaman before attending college; after earning law degree, worked for a time as an attorney; television news reporter for WABC-TV, New York City, 1970–74; host of late-night program "Good Night, America," 1974–77; reporter and producer for television news program "20/20," 1978–85; host of television specials, including "The Mystery of Al Capone's Vault," "American Vice: The Doping of a Nation," and "Murder: Live from Death Row," 1986–; host of syndicated talk show "Geraldo," 1987—; founder and owner of The Investigative News Group production company, New York City, 1985—.

Awards: George Foster Peabody Award for distinguished achievement in broadcast journalism; ten Emmy Awards (three national and seven local) for broadcast journalism; two Robert F. Kennedy Awards; two Columbia-DuPont Awards; three honorary doctorates; has received more than 150 additional awards for achievements in broadcast journalism.

Sidelights

Back in the 1960s, Geraldo Rivera never dreamed he'd have a television career, let alone become one of the most controversial TV journalists in history. Then a self-described "radical lawyer," he switched to news reporting through a chance incident. "I was representing a lot of activist groups," he told *Playgirl*, "and my clients had seized a church in Spanish Harlem. For three days I was the spokesman, and the news came around every day. I was on the "Today Show" three days in a row. And then the guy at ABC said, 'Sign that boy.'" Often a ticket into the acting or modelling professions, getting "discovered" is not a typical way to launch a reporting career. Yet Rivera is no typical journalist. With the start in 1987 of his hour-long syndicated talk show "Geraldo," he has become as much a celebrity as any of his prime-time colleagues. He brings some two decades of reporting experience to the show and is usually on top of the news. He was the first to obtain national interviews with Theresa Jackson, the Florida mother convicted of causing her daughter's suicide, with the advisers of Tawana Brawley, who made headlines by claiming to have been brutalized by racists, and others with prominent news stories. Yet Rivera's aim is not only to inform; it's also to reassure. By reacting emotionally—sometimes tearfully—to the issues he presents and espousing traditional values, he seems to have won over mainstream America. "Geraldo" airs daily in 150 cities, representing over 90 percent of the nation, and Rivera's occasional documentary specials tend to garner record ratings.

During Rivera's 15 years at ABC, many of the nearly 2000 stories he filed were on-site reports. Whether from war-torn Afghanistan or the crime-ridden streets of Guatemala, his world-wide coverage has helped him portray himself as a fearless, aggressive reporter. These days he travels less, since "Geraldo" is taped before a studio audience in New York. But he has sustained his bravado image by continuing to involve himself personally in his subject—in his words, by "getting down and dirty." "Take the last 12 months," he told *Playgirl* in September, 1988. "I've been threatened by the mob.... I've had an AIDS-infected needle stuck at me by junkies in a shooting gallery. I've put my ass on the line probably a half a dozen times in the last year. And I bet if you went through the core of network newspeople, you wouldn't find that."

An early example of what he has christened "Geraldo journalism" dates back to 1983, when he was reporting for ABC. On assignment in Tripoli, Rivera did more than document the destruction that has marked the Israeli-Palestinian conflict. He and his crew were in the safety of a car when an explosion wounded a young Palestinian soldier. Geraldo made a dash for the teen, pulling him out of the line of fire, then wrapped his wounded leg and lifted him into a nearby ambulance. ABC's "World News Tonight" used the rescue sequence but cut Rivera out of it—an incident that began souring his relationship with the network and in 1985 led to his termination. Though initially bitter, Geraldo soon found that being let go was perhaps the best thing that could have happened to his career. In April 1986 he made his first TV reappearance as the host of a special called "The Mystery of Al Capone's Vault." Although the show was somewhat of an embarrassment for Rivera—the vault, opened on live TV, contained nothing but a few dusty bottles—it proved to be the most watched syndicated special ever. More importantly for Geraldo, its ratings placed him in high demand among the major syndicators. The offer he accepted was with Tribune Entertainment, who signed him to host a series of prime-time syndicated specials, as well as two pilots for what would become "Geraldo."

As documentary host, Rivera at last found the freedom to create action as well as document it—to practice the passionate brand of journalism he had always advocated. For his 1986 special "American Vice: The Doping of a Nation," he assembled a real-life cast of junkies, addicts, and undercover police—and then added himself to the group, posing, in sunglasses and bandana, as a drug buyer. (Like "Capone," "American Vice" was both blooper and boon for Rivera. The live "drug busts" targeted three innocents, yet the show ranked eighth in the history of syndicated TV.)

Perhaps the most dramatic illustration of his "down and dirty" approach is the "Geraldo" segment titled "Young Hatemongers," which aired in November, 1988. In effect, riskiness was written all over his guest list: Three white supremacists were pitted against a rabbi and a black activist. Midway through the show, verbal abuse from the racists' side escalated into an on-the-air brawl in which about 50 audience members participated. Rivera, whose nose was broken when he was hit with a chair, was among them. As the *New York Daily News* reported, he "hit the deck, scuffled with several members of the audience, and emerged from the brawl with blood running down the right side of his face." Defending his involvement, Rivera told the *Daily News*, "These racist thugs have to know that we're not backing down."

Immersing himself in the action of his subject is only one ingredient in Geraldo journalism. Equally important is his verbal commentary, in which he departs sharply from the media's tradition of objectivity. He has strong feelings about what's lacking among today's major-network reporters. "The world's calamities are recorded by them, but not felt," he wrote in *Esquire*. "They rely on the memorized language of objectivity to disguise their own subjective yearnings." In contrast, Rivera seldom lets the subject speak for itself; he feels compelled to offer his own views. On the air, he has referred to criminals as "vicious, cowardly thugs." During his "Hatemongers" show, he compared his racist guests to cockroaches. And in his April, 1988, special "Murder: Live from Death Row," he had these words for Charles Manson: "You're a mass-murderin' dog, Charlie."

Rivera's style has been blasted by critics and other journalists for the subjective liberties he takes as well as the attention he draws to himself in his reports. According to *Newsweek*, former NBC News president Reuven Frank has said that "Geraldo should be arrested for exposing himself." Yet for Rivera, subjectivity means caring—and that, he maintains, takes courage. "*Soul* is the missing ingredient in television journalism," he wrote in a *TV Guide* article titled "Why TV News Needs More Passion." He continued: "Coolness has become synonymous with objectivity, aloofness with professionalism. [Network news] is seldom courageous or involved and almost never passionate." As for whether a newscaster should star in his report, he feels there is nothing unprofessional about it. "When I get into . . . that exotic, foreign situation," he told *Playgirl*, "I become a translator of that scene. It's almost like their friend is there."

> *"Sometimes the reporter has to become involved in helping society change the thing he is complaining about."*

Geraldo's desire to correct social injustice as well as report it goes back to the early days of his media career. In 1972, while at WABC-TV in New York, he sneaked a camera into the Willowbrook State School for the Mentally Retarded. According to *Newsweek*, his report—in which he cried and said that the place "smelled of filth, it smelled of disease and it smelled of death"—triggered better care for the hospital's residents. Writing in *Esquire* several years later, he spelled out his mission: "Sometimes the reporter has to become involved in helping society change the thing he is complaining about."

One of the issues that bothers his critics concerns overstepping one's professional bounds: Is a journalist qualified to also be a social worker? Rivera might argue that he's an investigative reporter, one who digs beneath the surface facts to learn an event's own history as well as its place in society. Yet his commentary is usually simplistic, reducing an issue to good guys and bad guys. In *TV Guide* he describes a rap session he held with some New York Hispanics on the representation of their people on television. On the street after leaving the group, he encountered a young Hispanic cocaine dealer. "Realizing this dealer . . . has a better chance of getting on TV than the good people I've spent the evening with," he wrote, "I just say, 'Get lost, creep.'" In October, 1988, Rivera presented a horror-filled special on Satanism. Though the content alone was shocking to media observers, many were equally disturbed by the host's interpretation—one that was deemed unlikely, bordering on ridiculous. As the *New York Times* noted: "Mr. Rivera tied together under the rubric of Satanist ritual such events as the killing of Lisa Steinberg, . . . the largely discredited McMartin preschool child molestation case in California, the murders committed by the Charles Manson clan, and dozens of other violent incidents."

Shortly after getting fired from ABC, Rivera revealed his painful awareness of his outsider status among TV news reporters. "Guys like Peter Jennings, Ted Koppel, Sam Donaldson, John McWethy, Brit Hume, and dozens of lesser-known, mostly Washington-based reporters from ABC and the other networks were the fraternity guys," he wrote in *Esquire*. "A long-haired, ethnic, former radical lawyer and local newsman from New York, I was the goddamned independent, scorned and excluded except by the viewing audience." When he began "Geraldo," Rivera no longer had to worry about establishing himself among the "fraternity" crowd; he was now a success on his own. And among his peers on daytime talk-show television—Phil Donahue, Oprah Winfrey, Sally Jessy Raphael, and other hosts—he has been singled out for the newsy edge he brings to his subjects. Rivera may have left the world of news reporting in anger, but he has not disowned it. From Ted Koppel, who hosts ABC's news program "Nightline," he took two important aspects of "Geraldo"—the use of a pre-taped video field piece to introduce a topic, and the use of satellite TV for guests who can't come to the studio.

Yet if these features lend Rivera a newsy image, they do not prevent critics from bemoaning his subject matter. His special "Murder: Live from Death Row," prompted *People* to rate it "the single most disgusting and abhorrent event in television." As usual, the stab was for the host's sensationalistic focus: "Rivera played a tape of a man being shot to death—not a reenactment but the real thing. He showed picture after picture of dead and bloody bodies . . . . He talked, via satellite, with convicted killers on death rows and asked them to describe their crimes in lurid detail; even the killers had too much discretion to comply." The reviewer went on to question whether Geraldo should be considered a journalist: "He does things even a tabloid reporter on the UFO beat wouldn't do, like showing that real-life death scene or devoting entire hours of his daily talk show to topics like three-way sex and voodoo. Thus he lowers the standards and the credibility of all TV journalism while pandering to the most base and brainless emotions of his audience."

Critics say the result of such pandering—by Rivera and several others who host human-interest documentary shows—has been a growing trend in what they call "tabloid" or "trash TV." Their theory is that cable and home video offer viewers more tantalizing fare than what's on regular television, leading shows like "Geraldo" to compete through shock value. Nevertheless, Rivera's audience is growing. His Satanism special—in which Devil worshippers discussed bloody orgies and ritualistic child abuse—incensed the critics but earned the highest rating ever for a two hour documentary shown on network TV. "I have every ratings record there is on documentaries," Rivera told *Newsweek,* "and nothing but scathing reviews. When you get 50 million viewers . . . that's not a fringe audience, that's the *people.* So are these handful of critics . . . right and all those 50 million people wrong?" While admitting that soap opera themes tend to dominate "Geraldo," he says his treatment of such topics raises them above mere entertainment. "Instead of doing every titillating angle on [a] male exotic dancer's story," he explained in a press release, "we would do a series on how social sex has changed as a result of AIDS, herpes, marriage, mores, and yuppie exhaustion. It's still about human sexuality, but it's also about conveying useful information."

In the 1989 season, Rivera plans to launch a weekly syndicated show called "The Investigators." The program will present investigative reports on major current issues by local newspeople, with Rivera most likely acting as chief correspondent. He also has plans, though on the back burner, to improve news coverage for Spanish-Americans through a bilingual newsmagazine show. As for "Geraldo," he remains as committed as ever. "I think my show's really gonna take off," he told *Playgirl.* "I think I'm gonna have that effect on the psyche, on the social consciousness of the country." Alluding to his substantial audience, he added, "When you get into those kinds of numbers, you really have a chance to affect national dialogue."

Avocational Interests: Sailing.

Writings

Willowbrook: A Report on How It Is and Why It Doesn't Have to Be That Way, Random House, 1972.

Puerto Rico: Island of Contrast, Parents Magazine Press, 1973.

Miguel Robles: So Far (with Edith Vonnegut), Harcourt, 1973.

A Special Kind of Courage, Simon & Schuster, 1976.

Contributor of articles to a number of periodicals, including *Esquire, Yachting,* and *TV Guide.*

Sources

Barron's, October 21, 1985.
Channels, June, 1987; May, 1988.
Esquire, April, 1986.
Newsweek, November 14, 1988.
New York Daily News, November 4, 1988.
New York Post, November 5, 1988.
New York Times, October 27, 1988.
People, December 7, 1987; May 2, 1988; September 19, 1988.
Playgirl, September, 1988.
Time, December 22, 1986.
TV Guide, April 18, 1987; March 26, 1988.
Vogue, May, 1988.

—Sidelights by Kyle Kevorkian

Anita Roddick

AP/Wide World Photos

Cosmetics entrepreneur

Name originally Anita Perilli; born c. 1943, in West Sussex, England; daughter of Italian immigrants who ran a cafe; married Gordon Roddick (a businessman), c. 1971; children: Justine, Samantha. *Education:* Graduated from Bath College of Education, 1962.

Addresses: *Home*—Sussex Downs, England; London, England; and Scotland. *Office*—The Body Shops International, Littlehampton, West Sussex, England.

Career

While in school, worked summers in her family's cafe; after graduating from college, taught school in Southampton, England, for a short time; worked briefly at the clip desk in the Paris office of the *New York Herald Tribune;* studied women's rights in Third-World countries for the United Nations Labor Organization; ran a cafe in Littlehampton, England; founder and managing director, The Body Shops International (natural cosmetics franchise company), Littlehampton, 1976, currently operating more than 300 stores in 34 countries.

Awards: Named British businesswoman of the year, 1985; named officer, Order of the British Empire.

Sidelights

Never mind beauty. The Body Shops' Anita Roddick is successful selling cosmetics with a cause. She's as concerned with her impact on Third World economy as on first-world complexions. And visitors to her fragrant boutiques are as impressed with her all-natural line of products as they are with her social projects.

No miracle cures, no instant make-overs, no glamorous models or empty promises—Roddick pledges only to cleanse, polish, and protect her customers' skin and hair. She's grabbed a healthy corner of Britain's cosmetics market with such things as Elderflower Eye Gel, pineapple facials, banana conditioners, and herbal shampoos. Prominent members of England's Royal Family are devoted customers. In the thirteen years since she opened her first tiny shop in Brighton, she's expanded to more than 300 Body Shops in over 34 countries. "The others are all talking about 'beauty.' We've eliminated that word," Roddick told *Stores* magazine. "We want to align ourselves with the health industry. For the cosmetics industry to survive into the next century, it has to go the route of health."

But the thing that really makes The Body Shop different is Roddick's commitment to social causes. Each franchise must agree to support some local community or environmental project. Anita sets the example by using only biodegradable packaging, ingredients on which no animal testing has been done, paying her Third-World suppliers top prices, and backing such organizations as Greenpeace, Friends of the Earth, and The Boy's Town Trust in India.

Daughter of first-generation Italian immigrants, Anita Perilli was raised in West Sussex and graduated from the Bath College of Education in 1962. She taught school in Southampton, worked on the clip desk in the Paris office of *The New York Herald Tribune,* then spent a year traveling to and studying women's rights in third world countries for the United Nations' International Labor Organization.

After returning to England, she met and married poet Gordon Roddick. In 1976, they were supporting daughters Justine and Samantha by running a small, Littlehampton cafe. One day Gordon announced he'd like to take a couple of years off to ride a horse from Buenos Aires to New York—a feat accomplished once in the 1930s by a Swiss adventurer. Anita so admired her husband's pluck, she agreed to sell their restaurant to finance the trip. Then, confronted with the reality of caring for herself and the girls, she decided to open a small shop and peddle some of the back-to-nature cosmetic knowledge she had gleaned during earlier travels.

Roddick borrowed $8,000 from a bank, contacted an herbalist found in the Yellow Pages to help with her unusual list of ingredients, painted the walls and shelves of her backstreet store emerald green, and started the business with fifteen products in plain bottles with neatly printed labels. Then, as now, she kept prices down by eliminating advertising from her budget—a well-placed interview promoting her social causes served quite as well. The odds against her success in the fast-paced, competitive cosmetics industry were staggering, but within six months her simple products proved so popular that she opened a second store. A year later, husband Gordon's horse met with an untimely demise in a fall down a ravine in the Andes, and he returned to run the financial end of the business.

Lacking capital for further expansion, the Roddicks offered franchise options to other eager entrepreneurs. In 1984, The Body Shop went public, and shares rose more than 50 percent on the first day. Body Shops all sport green interiors, suggestion boxes, cheerful background music, and soft-sell techniques. Posters, pamphlets, and flyers keep customers informed about the latest social causes; monthly newsletters, videos, and workshops are effective internal communicators between shops. Testers are available for customers to try before they buy, and in Britain, at least, bottles and jars can be returned for a discounted refill.

"There's very little difference actually between an entrepreneur and a crazy person," Roddick told *Life.* "I have the ability to convince people, and they follow. I don't think you should ever go to bloody school. It's instinct, enormous instinct. And being there at the right time.... Where are those great people who made a lot of money by making honest products and telling no lies and being part of the community and good citizens?.... I mean that the business is not just the profit and loss sheet. The bottom line should stay—at the bottom. Basically it comes down to being a little bit gentler and taking on human qualities."

Roddick's pleasant philosophy has earned her sufficient publicity and customers for continued expansion. HRH the Princess of Wales attended the opening of The Body Shop International's multimillion dollar headquarters in West Sussex in 1986. With 50,000 square feet of factory and warehouse space it should accommodate the company's planned growth by adding the "Colourings" line of makeup and "Mostly Men" skin and hair care products. Beginning in 1988, The Body Shop opened in several locations in the United States.

Sources

Business Week, May 23, 1988.
Life, November, 1988.
Management Today, June, 1987.
Ms., September, 1988.
People, October 10, 1988.
Stores, September 1987.

—*Sketch by Sharon Rose*

Steven Rosenberg

Reuters/Bettmann Newsphotos

Physician, cancer researcher

Full name, Steven Aaron Rosenberg; born August 2, 1940, in New York, N.Y.; son of Abraham (owner of a luncheonette) and Harriet (Wendroff) Rosenberg; married Alice Ruth O'Connell (a nurse), September 15, 1968; children: Beth, Rachel, Naomi. *Education:* Johns Hopkins University, B.A., 1960, M.D., 1963; Harvard University, Ph.D. in biophysics, 1968.

Addresses: *Office*—National Cancer Institute, National Institutes of Health, Building 31, 900 Rockville Pike, Bethesda, Md. 20205.

Career

Peter Bent Brigham Hospital, Boston, Mass., surgical resident, 1963–64, 1968–69, and 1972–74; Harvard University Medical School, Cambridge, Mass., resident fellow in immunology, 1969–70; served as an officer with the United States Public Health Service, 1970–72; National Cancer Institute, Bethesda, Md., clinical associate in the immunology branch, 1972–74, chief of surgery, 1974—. Associate editor of the *Journal of the National Cancer Institute,* 1974—; member of the U.S.-U.S.S.R. Immunotherapy Program, 1974—; member of the U.S.-Japan Cooperative Immunotherapy Program, 1975—; clinical associate professor of surgery at George Washington University Medical Center, 1976—; served as professor of surgery at the Uniformed Services University of Health Sciences.

Member: American Association for Cancer Research, American Association of Immunologists, Society of Surgical Oncology, Society of University Surgeons, Transplantation Society, Halstead Society, Phi Beta Kappa, Alpha Omega Alpha.

Awards: Meritorious service medal for cancer research, 1981, from U.S. Public Health Service; co-recipient of the Armand Hammer Cancer Prize, 1985.

Sidelights

Steven Rosenberg is a commander in the war against one of mankind's most feared enemies—cancer. As chief of surgery at the National Cancer Institute (NCI) in Bethesda, Maryland, Rosenberg is one of the key developers of a new class of cancer-fighting weapons that harness the body's immune system. Along the way, he has earned the praise of his colleagues as a scientist and surgeon. John Cameron, chief of surgery at Johns Hopkins Medical School told *U.S. News and World Report,* "The excitement he has for medicine, for research and for surgery is readily picked up by those around him. He is a very stimulating individual."

Rosenberg first came into the public eye in July 1985 as part of the surgical team that removed a two-foot piece of cancerous bowel from President Ronald

Reagan. During the post-surgery news conference Rosenberg faced the nation with the simple words, "The President has cancer." In direct, understandable language, he explained what that meant. He told the country that the tumor was removed and the President required no further treatment. Afterwards, he was praised by reporters for his candor and straightforward explanation of the President's condition.

Cancer strikes one in five Americans. Every year it kills more than four million people worldwide, 450,000 of them Americans. And, despite decades of research at the nation's top medical centers, the battle against the disease has produced more than its share of false hopes. In recent years many researchers have come to believe that cancer may actually be as many as 100 different diseases, each requiring a different treatment. Traditional treatment includes surgery, chemotherapy and radiation therapy. But Rosenberg's technique adds a new dimension to the fight. It bolsters the body's own immune system by activating natural killer cells that destroy tumor cells.

Rosenberg was born in the Bronx, the youngest of three children. His parents, Jewish immigrants from Poland, owned a neighborhood luncheonette. As a high school student at the Bronx High School of Science, Rosenberg read the medical textbooks of his older brother, Jerry, who was then in medical school. "I cannot remember a time when I didn't want to be a doctor," Steven Rosenberg told *People* magazine. Steven earned his medical degree from Johns Hopkins University and a doctorate in biophysics from Harvard University. He then spent his residency at Peter Bent Brigham Hospital in Boston. There he dated the head nurse, Alice O'Connell, and married her in 1968. Today they have three daughters.

After Boston, Rosenberg worked as a research fellow at Harvard before joining NCI in 1970 as a clinical associate in immunology. He became chief of surgery four years later, at age 33. Today he oversees an 80-member surgery department in addition to a 25-member immunotherapy team. In addition to his work at NCI, Rosenberg teaches at George Washington University, Johns Hopkins, and the Uniformed Services University of the Health Sciences in Bethesda, which trains military personnel in medicine. In his spare moments, he pursues an interest in astonomy and is an amateur magician who does tricks for co-workers and friends.

From his early years in medical school, Rosenberg had been intrigued with the idea of rallying the body's immune system to attack malignant cells. The NCI provided him the access to its vast laboratory facilities to support his studies. He focused his research on interleukin-2 (IL-2), one of the complex substances produced by the white blood cells called lymphokines. These substances, including gamma interferon, tumor necrosis factor, and colony-stimulating factor, are formed by white blood cells in response to a threat by a foreign substance.

Rosenberg's early experiments involved injecting IL-2 directly into laboratory animals with tumors. He found no significant response. However, in 1980, Rosenberg tried a new approach, which he called "adoptive immunotherapy." He treated white blood cells with IL-2 outside the body and then reinjected these treated cells into the body. The technique shrunk tumors in mice. His research team began human trials in 1984 at the National Institutes of Health's Clinical Center in Bethesda, Maryland. The first 25 patients had a variety of cancers, including lung, bladder, skin, and kidney cancer, which had not responded to conventional treatment.

During the experimental procedure patients underwent apheresis, a process in which about 10 percent of the white blood cells are filtered and separated from the other components in the blood. These cells were then incubated in a bath of IL-2, where they multiplied and became powerful antitumor cells called lymphokine-activated killer (LAK) cells. The LAK cells were then reinjected into the patients. Rosenberg found that 11 out of the 25 patients responded to the treatment, with shrinkage of their tumors by 50 percent or more, after nine months of treatment. Additionally, the treatment eradicated cancer cells that had spread throughout the body, but unlike chemotherapy, it did not harm healthy cells.

However, there were drawbacks. The treatment was both expensive and time-consuming. Estimated costs vary between $30,000 and $100,000. Patients must be treated in an intensive care ward for up to five weeks. In addition, the treatment produces side effects, such as severe fluid retention, respiratory problems, sudden changes in blood pressure, and fever. Rosenberg and other research teams are working with mixtures of other lymphokines to reduce the side effects. Rosenberg told *MacLean's:* "Solving the problems is going to take a lot of hard work. We have a lot of ideas of ways to overcome some of them, but I think we are talking years before this treatment will be widely applicable."

In December 1985 Rosenberg reported his findings in the *New England Journal of Medicine*. The report was greated with optimism mixed with caution in the medical community. Former NCI director Vincent T. DeVita [see index for *Newsmakers* entry] told *News-*

week it was "the most interesting and exciting biological therapy we've seen so far." Frank J. Rauscher, Jr., senior vice-president for research for the American Cancer Society and former director of the NCI told *Newsweek:* "The major significance of what Steve Rosenberg and his people have done is to present yet another means of treating the whole body." One Washington cancer researcher who asked not to be identified, told *MacLean's:* "Of course, everyone is being very cautious. They have to be. But many of us believe that this could be it. The big one."

But some called Rosenberg's treatment impractical. Roland Mertelsmann, a hematologist at New York's Memorial Sloan-Kettering Cancer Center, told *Fortune:* "It would be hard to picture Rosenberg's work as a generalized treatment for cancer because of the complexity, skill and cost involved in that system." A year later, the *Journal of the American Medical Association* published a letter from Charles G. Moertel, of the Mayo Clinic, that criticized Rosenberg for inappropriately describing his results as a breakthrough. Moertel questioned the effectiveness of the treatment and emphasized the severe side effects.

In April, 1987, Rosenberg issued a new report in the *New England Journal of Medicine* that confirmed the success of his earlier experiments. Out of a new group of 157 patients who were treated with their own white cells bathed with IL-2, 20 percent had a 50 percent or more shrinkage of their tumors. Nine patients went into remission. In an editorial in the same issue of the *New England Journal,* John Durant of the Fox Chase Cancer Center in Philadelphia wrote, "Perhaps we are at the end of the beginning of the search for successful immunotherapy for cancer." Rosenberg and his colleagues have taken the process one step further by successfully isolating the white blood cells found within tumors in mice. When these cells, called tumor-infiltration lymphocytes, were mixed with IL-2 and reinjected to the animal, they destroyed tumor cells left untouched by the previous IL-2 method. Human studies using tumor-infiltration lymphocytes on patients with advanced cancer began in 1988. In this procedure, researchers surgically remove a piece of tumor from a patient and isolate the tumor-infiltrating lymphocytes within the tumor. These cells are cultured with IL-2 and reinfused into the patient. Results indicate that tumors regress 50 percent or more in about half the patients.

To further study how and why the process works in some patients and not in others, Rosenberg proposed to conduct the first experiment in which a genetically altered cell would be inserted into human beings. Along with W. French Anderson, of the National Heart Institute, Rosenberg's proposed experiment would tag some of the tumor-infiltrating lymphocytes with a marker gene through genetic engineering. Then the marked cells—along with the unaltered cells—would be reinfused in the patient. By tracking the marked cells, researchers could read how the tumor-infiltrating lymphocytes are distributed throughout the body and whether there are certain types of tumor-infiltrating lymphocytes that attack the tumors.

Rosenberg told *Business Week:* "This is not *the* cure for cancer. One of the real tragedies of this is that someone dies of cancer in this country every minute. This could be a big step, but it's so complex, we can only treat a few people at a time." IL-2 is only one of a family of lymphokines under study that shows promise in fighting tumors. Others include gamma interferon, tumor necrosis factor, and colony-stimulating factor. Some researchers feel these substances will eventually be harnessed to treat a variety of diseases, such as rheumatoid arthritis, multiple sclerosis, allergies, and AIDS.

A number of biotechnology companies, such as Cetus Corp., Genentech [see index for *Newsmakers* entry on Herbert Wayne Boyer], Biogen [see index for *Newsmakers* entry on Walter Gilbert], and Immunex, are mass-producing IL-2 and other lymphokines through recombinant DNA technology. These substances are being used in research and will be available if and when the experimental therapies are approved for general use. Rosenberg told *Time* that the technique "is an experimental treatment in the infancy of its development. It is a first step in a new direction of cancer therapy. It can work. The challenge is to improve it."

Sources

Business Week, December 23, 1985.
Fortune, November 25, 1985.
MacLean's, December 16, 1985.
Newsweek, December 16, 1985; September 22, 1986; December 22, 1986; April 20, 1987.
People, December 23, 1985.
Science, July 22, 1988.
Time, July 29, 1985; December 16, 1985; April 20, 1987.
U.S. News & World Report, July 29, 1985.

—Sidelights by Donna Raphael

Robert Runcie

Reuters/Bettmann Newsphotos

Archbishop of Canterbury

Full name, Robert Alexander Kennedy Runcie; born October 2, 1921, in Liverpool, England; son of Robert Dalziel (an electrical engineer) and Anne (a hairdresser) Runcie; married Angela Rosalind Turner (a pianist), September 5, 1957; children: James, Rebecca. *Education:* Brasenose College, Oxford University, B.A. in literature and humanities (with first class honors) and M.A., both 1948; studied theology at Westcott House, Cambridge University.

Addresses: *Home*—Old Palace, Canterbury, England; and St. Albans, England. *Office*—Lambeth Palace, London SE1 7JU, England.

Career

Ordained deacon of Church of England, 1950, and priest, 1951; curate in Gosforth, England, 1950–52; Westcott House (theology school), Cambridge University, chaplain, 1953–54, vice-principal, 1954–56; Trinity Hall, Cambridge University, fellow, dean, and assistant tutor, 1956–60; vicar in Cuddesdon, England, 1960–69; bishop in St. Albans, England, 1970–80; Archbishop of Canterbury, 1980—.

Principal of Cuddesdon Theological College, 1960–69; Teape Lecturer at St. Stephen's College, Delhi, India, 1962; select preacher at Cambridge University, 1957, 1975, and Oxford University, 1959, 1973. Canon and prebendary of Lincoln, 1969; chairman of central religious advisory committee, Church of England, 1973–80; Anglican chairman of Anglican-Orthodox Joint Doctrinal Commission, 1973–80. Chairman of British Broadcasting Corp. and Independent Broadcasting Authority central religious advisory committee, 1973–79; Freeman of the city of St. Albans, 1979, city of London, 1981, and city of Canterbury, 1984. *Military service:* British Army, Scots Guard, 1939–45; served as tank officer; became lieutenant; received Military Cross.

Awards: Honorary fellow of Trinity Hall, Cambridge, 1975, and Brasenose College, Oxford, 1979; privy councillor, 1980; honorary bencher at Gray's Inn, 1980; honorary D.D., Oxford University, 1980, Cambridge University and University of the South, both 1981, University of Durham, 1982, and Trinity College, University of Toronto, 1986; fellow of King's College, London, 1981; honorary D.Litt., University of Keele, 1981, and University of Liverpool, 1983; honorary D.C.L., University of Kent at Canterbury, 1982, and University of the West Indies, 1984.

Sidelights

In January 1980, self-proclaimed "radical Catholic" Robert Alexander Kennedy Runcie assumed the Anglican Church's most revered ecclesiastic position as Archbishop of Canterbury and Primate of All England. A long-time pig breeder and soccer fan, Runcie tempers the seriousness of the primacy by having, as described by Rushmore M. Kidder in the *Christian Science Monitor,* a "chatty disposition, a philosophical turn of mind, and a tolerance so genial that his maid reportedly calls him 'Bish.'" As successor to the retired F. Donald Coggan, Runcie became the first archbishop chosen by the Crown Appointments Commission. This sixteen-member committee, established in 1977, canvassed both clergy and lay people prior to recommending Runcie's nomination to Queen Elizabeth II by way of Prime Minister Margaret Thatcher. Differing from the old method, in which the prime minister and consultants within the secular government made the choice without input from the clerical realm, this break from convention seems fitting for an archbishop who advocates a fresh approach to ethical and other issues. According to *People,* Runcie set the tone for his new position by stating: "I think the church is looked to with not much expectation, because it seems wedded to outmoded ideas and is rather dated in social ways. Breaking through that barrier is the major challenge."

Born on October 2, 1921 in Liverpool, England, Runcie entered a family in which unconventionalism was the precedent. His mother, Anne, had worked as a hairdresser on Cunard liners before her marriage. His father, Robert Dalziel Runcie, was an electrical engineer and a disenchanted Presbyterian Scot who found the rituals of the Anglican Church self-important and remote. Despite his father's questionable faith, Runcie was baptized an Anglican at ten months and later enrolled in a Methodist Sunday school that he quit after only a few lessons. Eventually, he accompanied a friend to confirmation lessons and was confirmed in the Church of England at age fourteen.

After graduating from the Coronation Road council school in Liverpool and the Merchant Taylors' School in nearby Crosby, Runcie entered Brasenose College at Oxford University on a scholarship in 1938. The onset of World War II interrupted his schooling, and he went immediately to Sandhurst, the British military academy, for training. As a tank commander in the Scots Guards, Runcie saved a fellow soldier from a burning tank in the Rhineland and won the Military Cross for bravery under fire in 1945. He returned to Oxford after the war, earning a B.A. degree in literature and the humanities, with first-class honors, and an Oxon M.A. degree. His religious vocation had grown during this period, primarily through the inspiration of an older sister who studied social work, and, in 1950, while reading for holy orders at Cambridge University, he became a deacon. The next year, upon completion of his theologic studies, Runcie was ordained a priest.

Much of Runcie's personal appeal stems from an ability to impart his knowledge and Christian devotion to others without appearing "holier-than-thou." In the *Guardian,* writer Baden Hickman predicted that Runcie would be "one of the most uninhibited and refreshing as well as scholarly Primates of the Church of England," while *Newsweek* noted that Runcie was "chosen for his relative youth, his flair for communication, his expertise in Eastern Orthodoxy, and his reputation as a reconciler of diverse factions." Yet Runcie did not come to the primacy without years of hard work and little limelight behind him. He returned to Cambridge University as chaplain in 1952, becoming a vice-principal there two years later and teaching church history at Trinity Hall. In 1960 Runcie was appointed principal of Cuddesdon College, a theological school near Oxford. His ecumenism, or effort to develop closer ties between the Anglican Church and other Christian denominations, manifested itself during this period. At Cuddesdon, Runcie guided an Anglican mission that eventually led to full communion with the Church of South India. Apparently, enrichment of many Christian communities has been a long-time goal of Runcie's, evidenced by a belief he expressed to *People:* "Our aim should be to make people more fully human than perfectly religious."

Runcie's family life parallels the closeness and mutual respect he advocates between the Church of England and other Christian communities. In 1957 he married Angela Rosalind Turner, an accomplished classical pianist, with whom he had two children, James and Rebecca. Runcie, who reportedly serves his wife tea in bed every morning, confided in an interview with *People* that "she is a real strength to me. She can see flannel [pretentious nonsense] for what it is." Mrs. Runcie, who goes by Rosalind, differs considerably in style from predecessors Joan Ramsey, acclaimed as a gifted hostess, and Jean Coggan, a devout Christian who zealously shared in her husband's work. Accused by the press of having greater interest in giving charity concerts than in accompanying Runcie on his religious excursions, Rosalind Runcie admittedly leads an autonomous lifestyle. She has her own career teaching music, a separate set of friends, and a love for their house in St. Albans that she expressed a wish to remain in until she is, according to the *Christian Century,* "carried out in a coffin." Evidently, neither Mrs. Runcie's pursuit of her own interests nor her preference for the St. Albans house over Lambeth Palace bothers Runcie. A proud testimony to his wife's spirited candor, he told *People:* "If she thinks one of my speeches is going on too long, she'll kick me under the table."

In February 1970 Runcie was consecrated Bishop of St. Albans, a diocese comprising Bedfordshire and Hertfordshire. This position qualified him for a seat in the House of Lords, and he later became chairman of the Central Religious Advisory Committee, the Anglican liaison with the BBC. When Archbishop Coggan announced his retirement in June 1979, the newly formed Crown Appointments Commission set out to find his successor. Although Runcie stood well to her left politically, Prime Minister Margaret Thatcher [see index for *Newsmakers* entry] was reportedly pleased with the commission's nomination, and, on September 7, 1979, she formally announced his appointment to Canterbury. In the enthronement ceremony that ensued the following March, Runcie walked to Canterbury Cathedral, knocked three times on the door of the church where Thomas à Becket was killed, and was enthroned as the Archbishop of Canterbury and the Primate of All England on the marble chair of St. Augustine, the first to assume the primacy in 597. Runcie's memorable sermon warned the church against misusing its power and expanded his message to include those of other religions. He envisioned a world in which infinite learning could take place if, together, people untangled the complexities of modern society.

Dubbed "the man for the season" by *London Times* religious affairs correspondent Clifford Longley, Runcie has expressed a diversity of views on current issues. He has publicly opposed former Archbishop Coggan's endorsement of exorcism, calling it a throwback to the Middle Ages. While believing that abortion is irreconcilable with Christian doctrine, he does not necessarily support the legislation that made it illegal. But Runcie's most active stance regards the topic of divorce and remarriage. The archbishop espouses marriage as a lifelong commitment; however, he also believes that Christian jurisdiction should demonstrate forgiveness by permitting divorced Anglicans to remarry in the church under certain circumstances. As it stands, the Anglican church blesses second marriages, but requires that they be contracted in civil ceremonies. The General Synod, a powerful religious council, finally slackened its ecclesiastic reins by allowing the matter to be turned over to the diocese for further discussion. According to *People,* Runcie remains hopeful that such a change will not devalue the institution of matrimony, noting that "many people who wish to marry for a second time are far more serious than those who arrived at church for their first marriage."

Runcie's most notable work, however, is ecumenical in nature. As the Anglican chairman of the Anglican-Orthodox Joint Doctrinal Commission, he met with leaders of Orthodox churches in the Soviet Union, Greece, and other countries to discuss doctrinal obstacles to unification. His willingess to compromise was best exemplified when Runcie asked his own communion to eliminate a clause from the Creed that had contributed significantly to the division of the universal church during the Middle Ages. Yet Runcie's ecumenical vision is most clearly focused on Rome, with an eye toward repairing the religious schism that evolved so dramatically during the marital woes of King Henry VIII. When Runcie and Pope John Paul II discovered that their paths would inadvertently cross in May 1980, they arranged to meet in the home of the Roman Catholic archbishop of Accra, Ghana. It was reported that in a joint statement following their visit, the two leaders agreed that Christian energies should not be spent revitalizing old rivalries and that in order for Christ to be seen and heard effectively, the efforts and resources of all communions must be shared.

"Our aim should be to make people more fully human than perfectly religious."

Prior to Pope John Paul II's historic visit to Britain in 1982, there was optimism that rapid progress toward reunification would be made. This hope proved premature, however, and little headway was seen until 1986, when a signal to resume negotiations came from Rome. In March, the Anglican-Roman Catholic International Commission, set up expressly to explore reunification, received a letter from the Pope's top ecumenical advisor, Jan Cardinal Willebrands, asserting the Vatican's newfound willingness to recognize Anglican clergy. As part of the arrangement, however, Willebrands requested a formal Anglican statement on all essential doctrines regarding the nature of the Eucharist and the role of the priesthood in celebrating it. While Runcie has no reservations about providing what *Time* called "the strongest possible stimulus toward Roman Catholic recognition of Anglican orders," he is concerned with still another issue that threatens to halt reunification indefinitely—the ordination of women.

In sharp contrast to Runcie's otherwise liberal views is his opposition to ordaining women as priests. At a synod debate at Westminster Abbey in 1984, he announced his negativism, *Time* reported, on the basis that "Scripture and church tradition are highly discouraging to the idea." Runcie's position, an even softer version of the Vatican's adamant refusal to accept female priests, faces dissent within his own communion. Deaconness Diana McClatchey could not be soothed by Runcie's confessed admiration for the female priests he had met in the United States, Canada, and New Zealand. According to *Time*, she argued that as long as the church "retains the atmosphere of an exclusive men's club on ladies' night . . . a generation of young women will [be unable to] find a place for themselves in the Christian tradition." Hers was the voice heard at the synod debate; the proposal for female priests passed with ease, although it now faces more rigorous and widespread scrutiny in other Anglican communities. The implications for Runcie's dream—to reunite the Anglican and Roman Catholic churches—seem dreary. For the Vatican's assertion that the all-male priesthood conforms to God's plan for his church allows no leeway for female priests, and, in fact, ensures that while one liberal reform moves forward, the long-cherished goal of reunification has been most certainly set back.

But not even this cloud has succeeded in dimming the archbishop's spirit. In 1980 he officiated at the wedding of Prince Charles and Lady Diana Spencer, and his homily at the ceremony was quoted worldwide. He is a connoisseur of wine, drinks ale on occasion, and plays tennis for recreation. One of his primary concerns when he moved to the archbishop's residence, Lambeth Palace, was that he would not find time to care for his pedigreed Berkshire pigs. If there is one thing this "radical Catholic" does not lack, it's character. "When I speak," *Newsweek* reported him saying, "I will not be a platitude machine."

Writings

Cathedral and City: St. Albans Ancient and Modern (editor), Humanities, 1977.
Windows Onto God, 1983.
Seasons of the Spirit, 1983.

Sources

Christian Century, December 17, 1986; January 20, 1988.
Christian Science Monitor, June 9, 1980.
Christianity Today, October 5, 1979.
Guardian, September 16, 1979.
Los Angeles Times, September 8, 1979.
Maclean's, October 22, 1984.
Newsweek, September 17, 1979; December 21, 1987.
People, February 25, 1980.
Time, November 26, 1984; March 17, 1986.
Toronto Globe and Mail, March 26, 1980.
Washington Post, January 28, 1987.

—*Sidelights by Carolyn Chafetz*

Nolan Ryan

Professional baseball player

Born January 31, 1947, in Refugio, Tex.; son of Lynn Nolan (an oil company executive) and Martha (Hancock) Ryan; married Ruth Elsie Holdruff, June 26, 1967; children: Reid, Reese, Wendy. *Education:* Attended Alvin (Tex.) Junior College, 1966–69.

Addresses: *Office*—Texas Rangers, Arlington Stadium, Arlington, Tex. 76010.

Career

Professional baseball player with New York Mets, 1966–71, California Angels, 1972–79, Houston Astros, 1980–88, and Texas Rangers, 1989—. *Military service:* U.S. Army, 1967.

Sidelights

When Nolan Ryan walks to the mound, a reputation for distinguished pitching goes with him. Ryan, 42, is one of the oldest players in major league baseball; many of the batters he faces were mere preschoolers when he signed his first professional contract. This fact is particularly astounding in view of Ryan's personal strong suit as a player—he is renowned for his fastball, a pitch notorious for ruining far younger arms. "In baseball terms," writes *Newsday* columnist Joe Gergen, "Nolan Ryan is a relic. He also is a treasure. Others... have pitched for more years, started more games and amassed more victories. But no other pitcher in baseball history has carried his special gift

AP/Wide World Photos

with such distinction into a third decade. Twenty-three years after his major-league debut, Ryan remains what he was, a premier power pitcher. At 42, he has conceded little, if anything." Ryan holds more than forty major league records, including most no-hitters (five), most one-hitters (ten), and most strikeouts (nearly 5,000). *Los Angeles Times* correspondent Denne H. Freeman notes that as the oldest player ever to don a uniform for the Texas Rangers, the sturdy Ryan "not only has a bionic arm but he's got a brain to match."

Around the major leagues, Ryan is known as "the Texas gentleman." A native of the Lone Star State, Ryan speaks with a slight drawl and likes to spend his off-season on horseback, herding cattle. He still makes his home in Alvin (population 16,515), the Texas town where he and his wife, Ruth, grew up. *Sports Illustrated* contributor Ron Fimrite observes that baseball "has taken Nolan Ryan to both coasts, but it has never taken him out of Alvin. It's what he's all about." The youngest of six children of Lynn Nolan Ryan and his wife, Martha, Ryan grew up in the quintessential small town, making the best of what little amusements were offered. He told *Sports Illustrated* that he and his buddies enjoyed throwing rocks at water moccasins on the long summer afternoons when school was out. Ryan was also an avid ballplayer from his Little League years onwards. He remembered, however, that he was "successful but not superior to other kids" as a youngster; his talent developed much later. Ryan attended Alvin High School, where he played both basketball and baseball. At six-foot-two he seemed a natural for basketball, and he admits it was his favorite sport. Still, he pitched for the Alvin baseball team, developing a fastball that could go "through a wall," to quote his high school coach, Jim Watson.

The teenaged Ryan's pitches might have been fast enough to go through a wall, but they were rarely accurate enough to be called strikes. He managed to strike out fifteen or sixteen hitters in each seven-inning game, though, because his velocity was so frightening. "He didn't have any idea where the ball was going," coach Watson recalled in *Sports Illustrated,* "but he didn't have to exactly thread the needle back then. Those kids were so scared, they'd swing at anything just to get out of there." Ryan's exploits drew the attention of New York Mets coach Red Murff, who watched the young pitcher develop through his junior and senior years. When Ryan graduated, the Mets drafted him in the fourteenth round. Such a low pick was hardly a vote of confidence, and Ryan was tempted to turn down the $20,000 offer in favor of college. His father persuaded him to sign, however, so in 1966 Nolan Ryan joined the Mets organization in the minor leagues.

Raw though his talent remained, Ryan made the Mets late in 1966. The following year he had to pitch around his obligation to military service—he was a member of a Texas Army Reserve unit—and he was unable to develop any consistency. His repertoire was still almost exclusively fastballs, and control remained a problem. Furthermore, Ryan the Texas farm boy felt inferior to his teammate Tom Seaver, a cool Californian who had obviously mastered the fundamentals of pitching. To make matters worse, the Mets organization openly favored Seaver and expressed grave reservations about Ryan's future in the big leagues. In 1969, the "Miracle Mets" went to the World Series, where they were considered decided underdogs to the Baltimore Orioles. Ryan's contribution to the 1969 Mets World Series crown consisted of a win in the pennant-clinching League Championship game against Atlanta and a save in game three of the five-game World Series triumph. Ryan remembered the against-the-odds victory with relish in *Sports Illustrated.* "Things were happening so fast," he said. "We were suddenly the toast of the town, ticker-tape parades, the whole thing. You almost got to the point where you were taking all this for granted."

The euphoria was short-lived for Ryan. He and his wife began to suffer under the metropolitan New York lifestyle, so different from their rural upbringing. He also felt that, in an effort to repeat the 1969 victory, the Mets created a pressurized atmosphere that was particularly damaging to him. In 1971 Ryan quietly suggested that he be traded. The Mets were glad to oblige, sending him to the California Angels in an off-season, four-player deal. Fimrite notes: "The trade was a bonanza for Ryan and the Angels.... On a struggling, building team that couldn't climb higher than fourth in the standings, he won 62 games during his first three years... and struck out a mind-boggling 1,079 hitters. The fireball legend was building." Indeed, in those early days of radar guns that could track pitch speed, Ryan was clocked several times at 100 and even 102 miles per hour. And under the tutelage of the Angels' pitching coach, Tom Morgan, Ryan "finally made the gargantuan leap from thrower to pitcher," according to Paul Domowitch in the *Philadelphia Daily News.* Domowitch continues: "Morgan refined Ryan's mechanics, helped him develop a breaking pitch and changeup he could throw often enough for strikes, and Ryan went on a six-year tear that saw him average more than 18 wins a season, lead the American League in strikeouts five times and throw four no-hitters."

Unfortunately, even as the "Ryan Express" legend grew, a counter claim began to challenge the pitcher's reputation. Beginning in 1975—after three seasons of nineteen or more wins—Ryan spent a number of years flirting with a .500 record. His earned run average was among the lowest in the game, but he seemed to be dogged by inconsistency and his own team's poor run production. This disconcerting statistic followed Ryan to the Houston Astros when he moved to that club in 1980; it is the primary reason why Ryan has never contended for the Cy Young Award. *Washington Post* columnist Thomas Boswell calls the pitcher "untouchable one day. Then a certainty to allow a three- or four-run inning in his next start." Such uncharitable observations have not been Boswell's alone; despite all his records, Ryan may face opposition when he becomes eligible for induction into the Hall of Fame. In *Newsday,* Marty Noble describes the debate over Ryan's record as "one of the stickier baseball issues in recent years." To Noble's way of thinking, however, Ryan deserves a place in the Hall. "Ryan's career record (274–253 at the beginning of 1989) is no factor," writes Noble. "His strikeout total, the glut of records he has established, his five no-hitters and the remarkable appeal of this Texas gentleman are more than enough to warrant his induction. People still pay to watch Ryan pitch. He has been an attraction for the better part of two decades. And... he still gives a crowd what it has paid to see. Clearly, Ryan is the best ever at what he does—striking out batters."

When Ryan went to the Astros in 1980, he figured his career was just about over. Few power pitchers can maintain fastball velocities of better than ninety miles per hour after the age of thirty. "I just assumed that if I lasted 10 years that would be a successful career for the style of pitcher I was," Ryan told the *Philadelphia Daily News.* He is, in fact, rather surprised himself at the length of his stay in professional baseball. "I don't know why I've been able to maintain my velocity this long," he said. "I think people think I do something different than anybody else has done. But it's not true. I don't have a secret potion. I can't say that my conditioning program is that much different than Tom Seaver's or Steve Carlton's was. It probably has more to do with genetics than anything else. Believe me, I'm as surprised as everybody else." Over the years Ryan's fastball has slowed a bit, but few batters can judge the difference between 100 miles per hour and 95, a speed he can still reach with some regularity. Additionally, he has widened his arsenal, adding a curveball to his list of offspeed pitches. Twice since 1987 he has flirted with a sixth no-hitter, both times giving up singles in the ninth inning.

As an Astro, Ryan was able to move his family back to his home town—Alvin is less than fifty miles from Houston—and he also began to earn an impressive salary ($1.1 million in 1988). Ryan has admitted that he considered retirement two times, first in 1986, when elbow problems seemed to warrant surgery, and again in 1989, when the Astros dropped his salary below the one million mark. In the 1986 case, Ryan suffered pain each time he tried to pitch and was told that he would continue to decline without an operation. He refused the surgery and was rewarded with a natural off-season recovery. The proposed salary cut by the Astros was more distressing; Ryan felt that the club management was manipulating him because he liked being close to home. Ryan turned free agent, and a bidding war began between his former team, the Angels, and the Texas Rangers. The Rangers won—Alvin, Texas's favorite son preferred to stay in his home state, and the team's $1.8 million salary offer was flattering indeed. In 1989 Ryan donned his new Rangers uniform and began to chase two remaining milestones, his 5,000th strikeout and his 300th win. Both could conceivably come soon if he is able to continue to pitch.

Ryan makes no predictions about his future in major league baseball. "I enjoy working out and being in shape and I like the one-on-one competition with the hitter," he told the *Los Angeles Times.* "I enjoy it more than ever because I don't have that much longer to go." Ryan is gradually being lured away from baseball by his off-season pursuits. The father of three teenagers, he owns a small ranch in Alvin and a larger working beef ranch south of Houston. He enjoys riding with the hired cowboys during roundups of the Texas-bred cattle, and he claims to be looking forward to the day when he can work with abandon—fearless of injuries to his arms or hands—on his ranches.

In the meantime, Ryan continues to ply his trade in a profession dominated by men young enough to be his sons. *Washington Post* correspondent Richard Justice contends that each time Ryan pitches "there's the anticipation that something magical will happen, that fans will see something they may never see again." Even the doubting Thomas Boswell has ultimately been convinced of Ryan's worth. "Nolan Ryan is something more fascinating than a star," Boswell concludes. "He's a star who is star-crossed by the very nature of his spectacular talent. Most baseball fans have been smart enough to grasp that from the start and root for him. Now, one more will."

Writings

Nolan Ryan: Strike-Out King (with Steve Jacobson), Putnam, 1975.

Nolan Ryan: The Other Game (with Bill Libby), Word Books, 1977.

Pitching and Hitting (with Joe Torre), Prentice-Hall, 1977.

Throwing Heat: The Autobiography of Nolan Ryan (with Harvey Frommer), Doubleday, 1988.

Sources

Los Angeles Times, March 4, 1989; April 2, 1989; April 9, 1989; May 2, 1989.

Newsday, April 16, 1989.

Philadelphia Daily News, June 8, 1989.

Sports Illustrated, September 29, 1986; May 1, 1989.

Washington Post, April 28, 1989; May 2, 1989.

—Sidelights by Mark Kram

Joe Satriani

© Deborah Feingold/Outline Press

Guitarist and songwriter

Born c. 1957 in Carle Place, New York; married; wife's name, Rubina. *Education:* Attended Five Towns College.

Addresses: *Home*—Berkeley, Calif. *Office*—c/o Relativity Records, 187–07 Henderson Ave., Hollis, N.Y. 11423.

Career

Began teaching himself guitar and playing local clubs on Long Island, N.Y., at the age of 14; at age 17 began teaching guitar; played with pop-rock trio the Squares in Berkeley, Calif., 1979–84; recorded and toured with the Greg Kihn Band, 1985; lead guitarist for Mick Jagger's world tour, 1988; solo performer. Studio work includes collaborating with drummers Tony Williams and Danny Gottlieb, writing commissioned pieces for PBS, Dole Pineapple, and Otari, singing back-up vocals for Crowded House, co-producing Possessed's EP *Eyes of Horror,* and contributing to the soundtrack for the 1989 film "Say Anything."

Awards: Named best overall guitarist and best new talent, and cited for best guitar album in *Guitar Player Magazine* reader's poll, 1988.

Sidelights

In 1988, Joe Satriani blasted into public consciousness with an entrance that was as unexpected as it was grand. For the past 15 years he had inhabited the crowded world of lesser-known rock guitarists, honing his virtuosity away from the celebrity limelight. But with his second album, *Surfing with the Alien,* he rose from the multitudes to a place where Jimi Hendrix, Eric Clapton, Eddie Van Halen, and other guitar greats once stood. In fact, by the end of the year Satriani had already cut some deep marks into the history of rock guitar. *Surfing* shot to number 29 on the charts, becoming the first rock guitar instrumental LP to enter the Top 40 since Jeff Beck's 1980 *There And Back.* (Remarkably, it remained at that spot for 77 weeks.) In the 19th annual readers poll of *Guitar Player Magazine,* he won the categories of best overall guitarist, best new talent, and best guitar album—the only guitarist other than Beck (in 1976) and Stevie Ray Vaughan (1983) to score a triple victory in the poll's history. To the critics, the meaning of all of this was clear: The rock guitar messiah of the '90s had arrived.

At 32, Satriani is indeed a guitar hero. "He has amazing chops," declared Jas Obrecht in *Guitar Player,* "unorthodox approaches to whammy and one- and two-handed techniques, and a talent for melodies that venture beyond the common." What gives wings to his music is a desire to transcend everyday life. His mission, as he told *Guitar Player* in a tongue-in-cheek nod to the TV series "Star Trek," is "to boldly go where no man has gone before. To seek peace and harmony." His songs on *Surfing,* though wordless, explore the realms of science fiction—one of his favorite authors is Kurt Vonnegut, Jr.—and the supernatural. "Echo," for instance, "deals with the reincarnation of lost loved ones," as he explains in the liner notes; in other songs on the album, he seeks to evoke dreams, "the journey of our spirits through time," and the site of Jesus's execution. On the whole, his songs are aptly described by both the title of his previous album—*Not of This Earth*—and the name of his music publishing company, Strange, Beautiful Music.

As a child, Satriani grew up in a musical environment. Each of his four older siblings played instruments; he himself took up piano and then drums. It was a Hendrix solo, though, that ignited his passion for guitar. He was 11 at the time, he told the *Los Angeles Times,* and "Purple Haze" came on the radio. "It's still vivid when I think about it sometimes," he recalled, referring to the guitar solo, "like it happened this morning or something. His music was overwhelming. I felt it deep inside. He was talking to me. It opened up a new world for me. I had tunnel vision all of a sudden. I could only focus on the radio. It was like there was this tuning fork in my body waiting for someone to come along and play the right note and make me vibrate." The full impact of that experience hit him about three years later, on the day that Hendrix died. "My life, my purpose was different," he told the *Los Angeles Times.* "After I heard about his death, I went home and played my Hendrix records. Then I *had* to play." Abandoning his drums and quitting the school football team, he turned instead to a Hagstrom III solid-body guitar. His parents, recognizing the seriousness of his new interest, supported and encouraged him. "My father taught me discipline," he told *Pulse!* "If he knew I didn't practice one day, he'd wake me up in the middle of the night and march me downstairs in my pajamas to sit there and practice."

It wasn't long before Satriani was playing local gigs on Long Island. At home, during marathon practice sessions, he would play along with records, absorbing styles and techniques from Hendrix, Beck, Led Zeppelin, the Beatles, the Who, the Stones, and Johnny Winter. Though he never took guitar lessons, high school studies in music theory enabled him, at the age of 17, to take on a few students—one of whom was his classmate and future guitar great Steve Vai. His background in music theory carried a second bonus: "When I got to Five Towns College to study music," he told *Guitar Player,* "there was absolutely no point in my being there." Dropping out and confused about what musical direction to take, he tried a variety of things: lessons with jazz pianist Lennie Tristano for a couple of months; a cross-country tour with a several-piece dance band called Justice; a brief stay, mostly spent practicing, in Los Angeles; and then, desiring a complete change of pace, six months in Japan. His time in Japan, he told *Rolling Stone,* refreshed his attitude and boosted his playing: "I lived in a tiny little house way up in the mountains in Kyoto. It was great for my playing because I only played by myself and it was just Japanese nature all around me. It was starting all over, and there were no distractions, no one telling me that what I was playing wasn't relevant."

Returning to the States in 1977, Satriani settled in Berkeley and set up shop teaching guitar—a part-time job that helped pay the bills and soon established him as the whiz who had coached Vai and Metallica's Kirk Hammett. Beginning in 1979, he put in five years with the Squares, a pop-rock group whose style—an unlikely cross between the Everly Brothers and Van Halen—impressed critics but failed to win them a record contract. In 1984 he struck out on his own, recording and producing a self-titled EP that showcased his experimental side. "For the few people who heard the EP," wrote *Guitar Player,* "the much-needed clarification 'every sound on this record was made on an electric guitar' was hard to believe, especially after hearing the sound effects of 'Talk To Me' and the popping bass in 'Dreaming Number Eleven.'"

Not of This Earth was born of the same adventuresome spirit. Satriani financed the project with a credit card—"I couldn't get anyone to lend me a *dime,*" he told *BAM Magazine*—and, in his strong, melody-based style, unleashed more of his unique guitarisms. "His writing, arranging, and production kept the guitar centerstage," *Guitar Player* noted, "with tones ranging from dentist drills and record-scratch rubs to crunch metal and the squeaky clean." He also outdid himself in the recording process. "The guitars were recorded in a different way, just to be different," he told the *Los Angeles Times.* "Why compromise and go for something commercial? I figured people would hate it and no one would buy it, so why not make the kind of record I wanted?" At the urging of Vai, who is still close with his former teacher, Relativity Records gave the record a listen. An independent label that had Metallica and Megadeth as young bands, Relativity has had experience in selling new artists; in Satriani they saw both artistry and accessibility. Their vision proved correct: *Not of This Earth,* which they released in 1986, sold 30,000 copies—no small feat for an all-instrumental LP. While most mainstream listeners unknowingly passed the album by, musicians were flipping over it, hailing its maker, according to the *Los Angeles Times,* as "the new king of the two-handed tap technique." But as Joe wrote in the album's liner notes, the best was yet to come: His next effort would "turn heads" and "drop jaws."

He was right, of course. With over 360,000 copies sold, his 1987 *Surfing with the Alien* represented a quantum leap over his previous work. Initial momentum for the album sprang from a few radio stations that were adventurous enough to feature a little-known instrumentalist. Then came the big break. Mick Jagger had scheduled a tour of Japan for the spring of 1988, and he needed a lead guitarist. Again through Vai's recommendation, Satriani got an audition. "Mick wanted someone fresh and new," Satriani told the *Los Angeles Times.* On the other hand, he added, "A lot of the younger guitarists don't know [the] music—but I did. I grew up playing the Stones and Hendrix and old blues." Needless to say, he got the gig—a role that cast him alongside Beck, who had played lead on Jagger's solo LP *Primitive Cool.* In Japan Satriani was mobbed for autographs; upon returning to the States three weeks later, the media were upon him. *Surfing* began a swift ascent up the charts, eventually surpassing Jagger's *Primitive Cool.* Meanwhile, he toured almost constantly throughout the year, alternating between Jagger's band and his own.

Having recorded his third LP in the spring of 1989, Satriani plans to hit the road. For him, the rigors of touring actually help to improve his playing. "Having a constant outlet for your ideas just increases your ability to play better," he told *Guitar Player,* "and finding acceptance in the musical community gives you more confidence.... I remember when there was so much music I wanted people to hear, and they didn't hear it. They only heard me at my musical job, doing these other things, and this had a negative effect on my playing. That's why I dropped out of playing in traditional-type bands and decided to go into doing instrumentals." Yet at that time, going solo brought its own share of disappointment: The world simply was not ready for what Joe Satriani had to offer. "People would tell me, 'You gotta use a vocalist or nobody will want to listen to it,'" he told *Pulse!* "Or they would say, 'It's not fusion, it's not metal—what is it?' But I never got so frustrated that I put it on the shelf. I just kept working on it. And I thought, 'One of these days people will like it, they'll be ready for it.' I just really believed all along that it would eventually happen."

Yet while Satriani hoped for public acceptance of his music, he never set out to achieve fame. "I've never been a career-minded, guitar-solo kind of guy," he told *Rolling Stone.* Ironically, he is now a premier "guitar-solo kind of guy"—and remarkably, his outlook as a musician has not much changed. Unlike the many rock guitarists who are motivated by stardom, his concern is still simply to grow as an artist. And as he told *Guitar Player,* that means forging ahead on his own path: "I try to do what people say they won't do. Whatever is considered standard operating procedure, I generally try to go the other way, just to see what happens—usually with good results. I take chances a lot. A year or two goes by, and I look back at what we've worked on, and I like it because it's so outrageous and strange."

Discography

Solo albums

Joe Satriani, Rubina Records (EP), 1984.
Not of This World, Relativity, 1986.
Surfing with the Alien, Relativity, 1987.
Dreaming #11 (EP), Relativity, 1988.

Other

Rock & Roll & Love (with the Greg Kihn Band), EMI.
Aquamarine (with Danny Gottlieb), Atlantic Jazz.
Say Anything (soundtrack), 1989.

Sources

Cash Box, May 7, 1988.
Guitar Player, February, 1988; January, 1989.
Guitar World, December, 1987.
Los Angeles Times, April 24, 1988.
Pulse!, March, 1988.
Rolling Stone, April 21, 1988.
USA Today, May 6–8, 1988.

—Sketch by Kyle Kevorkian

Roger Schank

Evelyn Floret/PEOPLE Weekly/©1984 Time Inc.

Educator and computer company executive

Full name, Roger Carl Schank; born March 12, 1946, in New York, N.Y.; son of Maxwell and Margaret (Rosenberg) Schank; married Diane Levine, March 22, 1970; children: Hana, Joshua. *Education:* Carnegie-Mellon University, B.S., 1966; University of Texas, M.A., 1967, Ph.D., 1969.

Addresses: *Office*—Yale University, Computer Science, 10 Hillhouse Ave., New Haven, Conn. 06520.

Career

Stanford University, Stanford, Calif., assistant professor of linguistics and computer science, 1968–73; Institute of Semantics and Cognition, Castagnola, Switzerland, research fellow, 1973–74; Yale University, New Haven, Conn., associate professor of computer science, 1974–76, professor of computer science and psychology, 1976—, chairman of department of computer science, 1980—; Cognitive Systems, Inc., New Haven, chairman of board, 1979—; president, CompuTeach, Inc., New Haven. Author of books, including *Conceptual Information Processing,* 1975, *Dynamic Memory,* 1982, and *Cognitive Computer,* 1984; editor, *Cognitive Science Journal.*

Member: Cognitive Science Society (founder).

Awards: Honorary masters degree, Yale University, 1976.

Sidelights

Considered one of the nation's most creative computer scientists, Roger Schank has devoted his career to simplifying computer use. He wants to build an intelligent machine and eliminate the need for access codes and "computerese." A Yale professor of computer science and psychology, and the director of the university's artificial intelligence program, Schank also heads two software companies. He advises consumers to postpone buying a personal computer, stating that those now on the market are too complicated and time consuming to be of real value. "If you can't use today's computers without pain, then just wait," he told Lynn Schnurnberger of *People.* "We can look forward to computers that will respond to questions typed in plain English with answers displayed in plain English."

Raised in Brooklyn, Schank was an average student in high school and college. He became "an academic achiever" in graduate school, "where he could work only on things that interested him," according to Alex Kozlov in *Discover.* He was introduced to computers as a freshman at Carnegie-Mellon University. Schank was unimpressed, finding them "the dumbest damn things in the world." He later took note of the machines "because of the possibilities," he recalled to Kozlov, "not because I liked them as they were."

An innovator in the field of artificial intelligence, Schank is also a student of the mind. He has long tried to determine how the human brain works; specifically, its memory functions, how it learns, conceptualizes, and understands language, an interest he has applied to computers. "To gain access to [information] on a computer today you have to know the right access codes and the right query language," he explained to Schnurnberger. "You don't want to bother with access codes." With artificial intelligence technology, the user will be able to operate in, and the computer respond with, everyday English. Schank has studied how people understand the language and is trying to divide the process "into a set of step-by-step instructions for understanding English that can be fed into a machine."

Schank is a businessman as well as an academician. He has founded two software firms, Cognitive Systems, Inc., and Computeach, Inc. Believing that artificial intelligence has practical applications, he formed the companies to "satisfy my vision of what artificial intelligence can be on the nonacademic side," he told Kozlov. "I always felt that at some point there was no reason to build intelligent computer programs if you weren't going to get them out to the people." The bottom line, Schank noted to Schnurnberger, is that computers should be as easy to use as a television set. "You don't have to pore over instruction manuals or know what goes on inside your TV to get it to work."

Sources

Discover, July, 1988.
New York Times, June 9, 1985.
People, December 17, 1984.
Psychology Today, April, 1983.

—Sketch by Denise Wiloch

Charles Schwab

UPI/Bettmann Newsphotos

Brokerage company executive

Born c. 1937, in Woodland, Calif.; married; second wife's name, Helen O'Neill; children: five. *Education:* Stanford University, M.B.A.

Addresses: *Office*—Charles Schwab & Co., 101 Montgomery St., San Francisco, Calif. 94104.

Career

Worked for an investment advisory company; managed a mutual fund in Marin County, Calif.; Charles Schwab & Co., San Francisco, Calif., founder and president, 1971–.

Sidelights

Charles Schwab is probably the most recognizable stockbroker in the United States. He also owns its largest discount brokerage, Charles Schwab & Co. In the early 1980s, he sold his business to BankAmerica Corporation for 2.2 million shares of BankAmerica stock. He thought he had made the deal of his life—until the stock began to plunge. Schwab lost a fortune but managed, eventually, to regain control of the company he had founded. Today, he faces stiff competition. Discount brokers abound, and Schwab's prices are comparatively high. He hopes to survive by expanding and diversifying his services.

Charles Schwab & Co. began in a two-room office with a handful of employees and about 2,000 clients. It remained a small, struggling brokerage until 1975, when the Securities and Exchange Commission (SEC) deregulated the industry. The SEC abolished fixed rates on broker's fees, which enabled investors to negotiate commissions. Schwab offered his clients huge discounts on financial services. He opened branch offices across the country and launched a highly effective advertising campaign that featured Schwab himself as spokesman. "We'd interview customers and they'd talk about 'Chuck' or 'Charlie,'" a Schwab executive told *Fortune*'s Gary Hector. "It gave them a human being to relate to." In a short time, Schwab became the largest discount broker in America, with 600 employees and over 200,000 clients. As his business grew, he added cash management accounts and insurance programs to his line of services.

Schwab's success so impressed BankAmerica that it offered to buy his company for $57 million worth of bank stock. Schwab accepted and became the bank's biggest individual shareholder. He was appointed to the board of directors, and he was named chairman and chief executive officer of Schwab & Co. The deal began to sour almost immediately. While Schwab's group enjoyed healthy profits, BankAmerica suffered losses. As the bank's stock plummeted, Schwab urged his fellow board members to cut overhead and reorganize. He was ignored. In 1985, he began to unload his shares; a year later he resigned from the board of directors. Finally, in 1987, he bought his company back in a $280-million leveraged buyout.

According to John Heins of *Forbes,* Schwab "wants to be a big player in the investment business." With 1.6 million customers and a 21 percent profit margin, he is still the nation's largest discount broker. But he plans to expand by taking his company public and by venturing into foreign markets. He would also like to introduce real estate investment trusts, home equity loans, and gold certificates to his line of services. He believes diversification is the key to his firm's survival. As Heins noted: "The discount business has gotten cutthroat, with the invasion of hundreds of independent firms, banks, savings and loans and mutual fund companies, all competing on price. [Their advertisements] don't simply compare commissions with full-service brokers, but with other discounters like Schwab—which generally has the highest rates among discounters."

Writings

How to Be Your Own Stockbroker, Dell, 1986.

Sources

Business Week, August 17, 1987.
Forbes, June 15, 1987.
Fortune, January 20, 1986; August 31, 1987.
New York Times, April 28, 1985.
Time, February 15, 1982; August 25, 1986; February 9, 1987.
Wall Street Journal, August 14, 1986.

—Sketch by Denise Wiloch

Martin Scorsese

AP/Wide World Photos

Film director and screenwriter

Born November 17, 1942, in Flushing, N.Y.; son of Charles (in the garment business) and Catherine (Cappa) Scorsese; married Larraine Marie Brennan, May 15, 1965 (divorced); married Julia Cameron (a writer; divorced); married Isabella Rosellini (a model), September 29, 1979 (divorced); married Barbara DeFina (a film production worker), February, 1985; children: (first marriage) Catherine Terese; (second marriage) Domenica Elizabeth. *Education:* New York University, B.S. in film communications, 1964, M.A. in film communications, 1966.

Addresses: *Home*—New York, N.Y. *Office*—c/o Jay Julien & Associates, 1501 Broadway, New York, N.Y. 10036.

Career

New York University, New York City, faculty assistant and instructor in film department, 1963–66, instructor in film, 1968–70; director and editor in British and American television, 1966–68; news editor, CBS-TV, 1968; director of Movies in the Park series, sponsored by Lincoln Center Film Society, New York City, 1970; associate producer of "Medicine Ball Caravan," 1970; supervising editor and assistant director, "Woodstock," 1970; films made as a student include "What's a Girl Like You Doing in a Nice Place Like This?" 1963, "It's Not Just You, Murray," 1964, "Bring On the Dancing Girls," 1965, "I Call First," 1967, "The Big Shave," 1968, and "Who's That Knocking at My Door?" 1968; director of feature films, including "Boxcar Bertha," 1972, "Mean Streets," 1973, "Alice Doesn't Live Here Anymore," 1974, "Italianamerican," 1975, "Taxi Driver," 1976, "New York, New York," 1977, "The Last Waltz," 1978, "American Boy: A Profile of Stephen Prince," 1978, "Raging Bull," 1981, "The King of Comedy," 1982, "After Hours," 1985, "The Color of Money," 1986, and "The Last Temptation of Christ," 1988. Actor in films, including "Cannonball," 1976, "Taxi Driver," 1976, and "Triple Play," 1981.

Awards: Edward L. Kingsley Foundation award, 1963 and 1964; Rosenthal Foundation award, 1964; Society of Cinematologists award, 1964; Screen Producers Guild award, 1965, for "It's Not Just You, Murray"; first prize, Brown University Film Festival, 1965; Palm d'or for best film, Cannes Film Festival, 1976, for "Taxi Driver"; Academy Award nominations for best director, 1976, for "Taxi Driver," and 1981, for "Raging Bull"; named best director, Cannes Film Festival, 1986.

Sidelights

Since he first began making films in the early 1970s, Martin Scorsese has been the talented outsider able to ignore, or at least sidestep, Hollywood's rigid formulas. The director of a string of commercial and critical successes including "Taxi Driver" and "Raging Bull," Scorsese has managed to remain true to his artistic vision. His films refer to familiar genres—the Hollywood musical, the stage-door romance, the romantic comedy—but distort the definitions in ways that Joseph Galmis of *Newsday* called "a disquieting mixture of pain and humor."

One of America's most provocative as well as successful filmmakers, Scorsese scored high on both accounts in 1988 when "The Last Temptation of Christ" reached American theaters amidst wide-spread picketing by religious fundamentalists, prompting Scorsese to hire a bodyguard. In an interview with Joseph Gelmis of *Newsday,* the film-maker defended his movie. "The last temptation, for Jesus, is the temptation to live an ordinary life," he said. "To get married, to make love to your wife and have children with your wife .... I know that Jesus' sexuality upsets a lot of people. [But] some directors might have gone even further than I did."

Controversy has followed Scorsese before. His most explicitly violent film, "Taxi Driver," reportedly mesmerized John Hinckley, Jr., who later attempted to assassinate President Ronald Reagan. "Violence has always been a pretty scary thing for me, but I'm fascinated by it, especially by the aimlessness of it," he told Guy Flatley of the *New York Times.* "It's always erupting when you don't expect it, particularly in a city like New York. You're sitting in a restaurant eating, and suddenly a car crashes through the window and you're dead."

Scorsese's breakthrough into the elite circles of America's leading filmmakers came with the success of "Mean Streets" (1973), a story set in the sleazy world of Italian-American toughs and pool hall loungers. In a change of pace Scorsese followed with "Alice Doesn't Live Here Anymore" (1974), a more conventional film that helped unleash a flood of women's liberation films. "Alice" also did well at the box office, enabling Scorsese to remain independent of Hollywood's studio system.

Scorsese's films have been characteristically personal and, frequently, autobiographical. Little Italy, the Lower Manhattan neighborhood where Scorsese grew up, features prominently in several early films. Stories from his neighborhood, stories his father told, and stories from his own life are woven into his plots. He told movie journalist Mary Pat Kelly, for her book *Martin Scorsese: The First Decade:* "I just had no compunction about drawing on my personal life because I never really thought the films were going to be seen anyway. I didn't think 'Mean Streets' was going to get sold. So I said, 'Screw it, I'll put it all on film.'"

As an undergraduate at New York University, Scorsese set his first attempts at filmmaking in Little Italy, a short walk from campus. He often used the family apartment for filming. His second student project, "It's Not Just You, Murray!" (1964), a 15-minute 35-mm comedy blending Fellini with a 1940s gangster movie, was set in his old neighborhood. "Murray" won the Screen Producer's Guild award as the year's best student film. Scorsese managed to get his other student films screened at prestigious film festivals and reviewed by well-known critics.

The director's aim, in these early shorts as well as in later professional efforts, was in part to depict on film the ethnic ambience of the streets and the homes of working-class New York. He was himself a product of this environment, having grown up in a Roman Catholic home steeped in Italian tradition. The boy was actually born in Flushing, a city neighborhood of quiet working-class streets, to which Charles and Catherine Scorsese had moved from Little Italy. Martin was baptized in St. Leo's Church in nearby Corona. Soon finding themselves financially strapped, the family moved back to their old neighborhood in Little Italy. There Martin attended Old St. Patrick's School. He graduated in June 1956 and entered Cathedral College that fall, intending to become a priest. A year later he transfered to Cardinal Hayes High School in the Bronx, where he graduated with honors in June 1960.

In a 1976 interview, Scorsese described his lonely, sickly childhood to Guy Flatley of the *New York Times:* "My parents worked, and I came home from school at 3 and sat at the kitchen table making up stories on my drawing board, or watching TV or escaping to the movies, not being able to be physical on the same level as the other kids, not being able to play ball or to fight. So I went off in the other direction, as chronicler of the group, trying to be a nice guy to have around."

He enrolled at New York University as an English major in 1960, but soon switched to film, graduating in June 1964. Scorsese returned to NYU as a graduate film student in 1966, got his master's a year later, then relocated to Europe where he made television commercials. Several films he made as a graduate student were screened at various film festivals, including his anti-Vietnam War short, "The Big Shave," (1968).

A year later Scorsese was back in New York, teaching film at his alma mater. He remained peripherally active as a filmmaker, and participated in the making of the rock documentary "Woodstock." He was already becoming known to New York's film community and in September 1970 was hired to put together a Movies in the Park series sponsored by the Lincoln Center Film Society. That fall he returned to Europe to represent American independent filmmakers at the International Incontri del Cinema at Sorrento, Italy.

The next year Scorsese moved to Hollywood, where he worked as an editor and met Roger Corman, a successful producer of Grade B material. Corman staked Scorsese's first film, "Boxcar Bertha" (1972), a Bonnie and Clyde-type crowd pleaser that included a memorable crucifixion scene. The project became a trial run for Scorsese's "Mean Streets," which he had been planning in his mind since childhood. He took the same cast and began filming his violent opus about his old neighborhood.

Pauline Kael, then a critic for the *New Yorker,* wrote that "Mean Streets" is about American life here and now, and it doesn't look like an American movie, or feel like one. Because what Scorsese has done with the experience of growing up in New York's Little Italy has a thicker-textured rot and violence than we have ever had in an American movie, and a riper sense of evil." She added, "The zinger in the movie—and it's this, I think, that begins to come together in one's head when the picture is over—is the way it goes at the psychological connections between Italian Catholicism and crime, between sin and crime." *New York Times* critic Vincent Canby declared that the movie "deserves attention as one of the finer American films of the season."

Scorsese moved in a very different direction with his next release. A mainstream movie with an upbeat finish, "Alice Doesn't Live Here Anymore" (1974), helped solidify Scorsese's reputation as a bankable director. "There are times when the movie teeters on the edge of commercial cuteness," declared *Time* critic Richard Schickel, citing the cheery romantic ending. Guy Flatley of the *New York Times* suggested "Alice" might be "an act of atonement" for the "shamefully uncommercial 'Mean Streets'." Generally, though, the film was well received.

Scorsese returned to Little Italy to film "Italianamerican" (1975), a very personal counterpart to "Mean Streets." Filmed in the Scorsese's Elizabeth Street apartment, and starring the director's parents, the documentary revels in the chaotic, emotional spontaneity of the Scorsese household and, by implication, of Italian-American life in general. Charles Scorsese reminisces about his role in unionizing the garment center in the 1930s and notes the disappearance of neighborhood bars as many Irish people move out. Catherine Scorsese's recipe for tomato sauce, appearing after the credits, earned a standing ovation from the New York Film Festival preview audience. "He had me up at four in the morning cooking pasta for that film," she told Mary Pat Kelly. "Marty involved me in all those films." Mrs. Scorsese continues to get walk-in roles in many of her son's films. Her husband, though, decided he doesn't like his face on film.

Scorsese's next release, "Taxi Driver," marked a return to violence in his filmmaking. It also began a vital collaboration with actor Robert De Niro. In "Taxi Driver" De Niro portrays an alientated Vietnam War veteran who drives a cab in a hellishly spasmodic New York, an insomniac world of faceless savagery. "By drawing us into his vortex [Scorsese] makes us understand the psychic discharge of the quiet boys who go berserk," wrote Pauline Kael. "No other film has ever dramatized urban indifference so powerfully; at first, here, it's horrifyingly funny, and then just horrifying."

Scorsese's most explicitly violent film, "Taxi Driver," reportedly mesmerized John Hinckley, Jr., who later attempted to assassinate President Ronald Reagan.

Scorsese released an altogether different film the following year. "New York, New York" (1977) again starred De Niro, this time as a 1940s jazz saxophonist whose innovative performances are spurned by a public that prefers familiar dance tunes. Co-starring Liza Minelli, "New York, New York" was a setback for Scorsese, drawing smaller audiences and leaving most critics cold.

Something of a comeback was scored with "The Last Waltz" (1978), a documentary about the farewell performance of the rock group The Band, released in 1978. That same year he released another documentary, "American Boy: A Profile of Stephen Prince," which was conceived during the filming of "Taxi Driver." He told Mary Pat Kelly that this project "came out of the same impulses" as "Taxi Driver," and is "the better film." But few critics agreed.

Scorsese returned in 1980 with another shift of artistic gears, releasing "Raging Bull," starring DeNiro as boxer Jake La Motta. La Motta's career had gone from championship to disgrace, which he recounted in a 1970 autobiography. The actor read the book and told Scorsese he wanted to play La Motta in a movie. Scorsese, who had never been to a boxing match, balked. But DeNiro brought the skepticl Scorsese to several fights, and as the director later explained to Thomas Weiner, writing in *American Film,* he gradually began to see LaMotta's story as one of personal redemption, "of a guy attaining something and losing everything, and then redeeming himself."

Scorsese elaborated to Mary Pat Kelly that La Motta was "on a higher spiritual level, in a way, as a fighter. He works on an almost primitive level, almost an animal level. And therefore he must think in a different way, he must be aware of certain things spiritually that we aren't, because our minds are too cluttered with intellectual ideas, and too much emotionalism. And because he's on that animalistic level, he may be closer to pure spirit."

In 1982 Scorsese released "The King of Comedy," which featured Jerry Lewis as a Johnny Carson-like talk show host who is abducted by a celebrity-crazed creep played by De Niro. His next film came three years later. "After Hours," was a return to a New York setting, this time the funky-chic streets of SoHo. Made during a time when Scorsese was newly single and moving into this artsy vicinity, "After Hours" is the story of an unassuming young man whose plans for a romantic date with a new acquaintance disintegrate into a surreal, violent chaos. Scorsese's 1986 film, "The Color of Money," starred Paul Newman and Hollywood heartthrob Tom Cruise in a sequel to "The Hustler," the movie a young Newman made about pool hustler Eddie Felson. All three of these films were commercially successful, and garnered generally good reviews.

With the release in 1988 of "The Last Temptation of Christ," Scorsese and his backers found themselves at the center of a roaring national controversy. Religious fundamentalists organized boycotts of theaters showing the film. But the publicity seemed to generate even bigger box office receipts, and "Temptation" became the summer's seventh-biggest film. For the most part, however, critics were not complimentary. Joseph Sobran, writing in the *National Review,* noted that "Scorsese and [scriptwriter Paul] Schrader have tried to freshen the old story with a relentlessly anti-ritualistic approach. But the only thing standing between this movie and total incoherence is our knowledge of the general structure and our assumption that the salvation story underlies it, in spite of all the new twists .... Scorsese has made a little film about a little man—only the little man, we're casually told, happens to be named Jesus." James M. Wall, in a *Christian Century* review, wrote that the film "doesn't deserve the publicity that fundamentalist Christian preachers have given it. For anyone who cherishes the Scriptures as passionate presentations of God at work in history, this film is dead at its core." And *New Republic* critic Stanley Kauffmann, while expressing the opinion that "some of it is excellent: the confrontation with Pilate, the Via Dolorosa, the Crucifixion itself, among other passages," nevertheless found that "the whole film labors under the burden of its dialogue. In this screenplay ... some of the most famous utterances in history are rendered in a new, unprepossessing vulgate, and some of the other dialogue is painfully flat."

Interviewers generally focus on two Scorsese trademarks: his staccato, rapid-fire New York voice and his intense, bearded face. Visitors to his three-floor Tribeca loft invariably remark on his enormous video library containing hundreds of movies on cassette; several films seem always to be playing at once in various rooms. Scorsese is married to his fourth wife, Barbara DeFina, one of the producers of "The Color of Money." As an incurable movie buff, for Scorsese the cinema is not just work but his passion. His spare hours are spent absorbing vintage films or working on behalf of the campaign to preserve aging color movies. Scorsese appears often at film forums around New York City doing what he likes best after filming, talking.

Sources

Books

Jacobs, Diane, *Hollywood Renaissance,* Barnes, 1977.

Kelly, Mary Pat, *Martin Scorsese: The First Decade,* Redgrave Publishing, 1980.

Kolker, Robert Phillip, *A Cinema of Loneliness: Penn, Kubrick, Coppola, Scorsese, Altman,* Oxford University Press, 1980.

Periodicals

American Film, November, 1980; November, 1982; November, 1986.

Christian Century, May 12, 1976; August 17–24, 1988.

Christian Science Monitor, February 19, 1976; May 1, 1978.

Film Comment, December, 1973; January, 1981.

Film Quarterly, spring, 1975.

Horizon, January, 1981.
Interview, January, 1987.
National Review, September 16, 1988.
New Republic, October 27, 1973; December 6, 1980; September 12, 1988.
Newsday, August 11, 1988.
Newsweek, May 16, 1977; February 21, 1983.
New York, September 23, 1985; September 15, 1986.
New Yorker, October 8, 1973; February 9, 1976; July 4, 1977; December 8, 1980; March 7, 1983.
New York Times, September 9, 1969; September 15, 1970; July 18, 1972; December 16, 1973; March 30, 1975; June 23, 1977; February 18, 1983; February 20, 1983; August 8, 1988.
New York Times Magazine, February 8, 1976.
Rolling Stone, November 8, 1973; June 16, 1977; June 1, 1978.
Time, February 3, 1975.

—Sidelights by Warren Strugatch

John Sculley

UPI/Bettmann Newsphotos

Computer company executive

Born April 6, 1939, in New York, N.Y.; son of John and Margaret (Blackburn) Sculley; married Carol Lee ("Leezy") Adams, March 7, 1978; children: Margaret Ann, John Blackburn, Laura Lee. *Education:* Attended Rhode Island School of Design, 1960; Brown University, B.Arch., 1961; University of Pennsylvania, Wharton School of Finance, M.B.A., 1963.

Addresses: *Office*—Apple Computer Inc., 20525 Mariana Ave., Cupertino, Calif. 95014.

Career

Marschalk Co., New York, N.Y., assistant account executive, 1963–64, account executive, 1964–65, account supervisor, 1965–67; Pepsi-Cola Co., Purchase, N.Y., director of marketing, 1967–69, vice-president of marketing, 1970–71, senior vice-president of marketing, 1971–74, president of Pepsico Foods, 1974–77, president and chief executive officer of Pepsi-Cola Co., 1977–83; Apple Computer Inc., Cupertino, Calif., president and chief executive officer, 1983—, chairman, 1986—.

Member of board of directors of Comsat Corp. and Keep America Beautiful. Chairman of Wharton Graduates executive board; member of board of overseers of Wharton School, University of Pennsylvania. Member of art advisory committee of Brown University, 1980. Member of U.S. Chamber of Commerce.

Member: Wharton Business School of New York (member of board of directors), Indian Harbor Athletic Club (New York), Camden Yacht Club (Maine), Coral Beach Club (Bermuda).

Sidelights

The self-acknowledged creator of the Pepsi generation, John Sculley totally shocked his colleagues when he quit Pepsi to work at Apple Computer. "They thought I had absolutely lost my mind," Sculley recalls. He was phenomenally successful while at Pepsi figuring out how to get more product into homes, because he discovered through marketing research that there was no upper limit on the amount of soft drinks people would consume. His 1983 move from "high fizz" to "high tech," as he calls his move from Pepsi to Apple, may seem more like a change of planets than a change of careers, but—for someone who fell in love with marketing during college—it was a dream come true.

Sculley was studying architecture during his undergraduate years at Brown University. He got a summer job at an industrial design company just when the American Dental Association gave its seal of approval to Crest, and Sculley helped add that seal to the toothpaste package. His firsthand look at how successful a marketing scheme that was eventually led him to study marketing at the University of Pennsylvania's Wharton School of Finance, where he earned his M.B.A. When companies shifted away from letting agencies do their marketing, Sculley abandoned his agency job and hired on at Pepsi-Cola, and he was the first M.B.A. they had ever hired. Eventually Pepsi wanted him to come up with a better-shaped bottle, but, as Sculley told *Playboy*'s interviewer Danny Goodman, "I thought about this for a while and said, 'I think we're trying to solve the wrong problem. Why are we trying to make a better bottle? . . . What we should be doing is figuring out how to get more product into homes.'" The Pepsi Challenge he issued made Pepsi the top-selling soft drink in the country.

He admits he had a ball running Pepsi's international operation, but Apple has turned out to be "one of the greatest adventures anyone could possibly have." Though some of Sculley's peers told him the computer was just a fad that would go the way of the C.B. radio and the Hula-Hoop, Sculley himself—who had been a radio and electronics hobbyist as a kid—knew better. Apple co-founder Steve Jobs lured Sculley to Apple with the legendary query, "Do you want to spend the rest of your life selling sugared water or do you want a chance to change the world?" By the time Sculley had been Apple president and chief executive officer for two years, he'd helped successfully launch the Macintosh line and ousted Jobs of all operating authority when he realized Jobs—a tremendous technologist—was not a good manager.

Sculley has made Apple Computer a successful $4 billion company, as a mid-1989 *Fortune* magazine attests, and he predicts Apple will be a $10 billion-a-year business in the 1990s. He has had to reorganize the company three times in six years to respond to the rapid changes typical in high technology, and critics have noted the upheaval. "An era is ending," *Fortune*'s Brian O'Reilly observes. "With its computers came a sassy California mystique that enveloped customers and employees alike." O'Reilly claims Sculley is "transforming Apple into an outfit that plays as well in Peoria as it does in Pasadena." But Apple senior vice-president Kevin Sullivan argues: "As we move from countercultural to mainstream, all that California stuff doesn't mean as much . . . . My 81-year-old mother shouldn't have to like surfing before she can consider using a Macintosh." Sculley sees the computer as the tool of the coming information economy, ideal for business and education. And Sculley, ever the marketing man, means to move more product into that large potential market.

Writings

Odyssey: Pepsi to Apple; A Journey of Adventure, Ideas, and the Future (with John A. Byrne), Harper, 1987.

Sources

Business Week, January 23, 1989.

Fortune, September 14, 1987; November 9, 1987; August 1, 1988; March 27, 1989; May 8, 1989.

Playboy, September, 1987.

—Sketch by Frances C. Locher

Ally Sheedy

AP/Wide World Photos

Actress and writer

Full name, Alexandra Elizabeth Sheedy; born June 13, 1962; daughter of John (an advertising executive) and Charlotte (a literary agent; maiden name, Baum) Sheedy. *Education:* Attended University of Southern California.

Addresses: *Home*—Los Angeles, Calif.

Career

Began modeling and appearing in commercials at age 15; has had roles on "Hill Street Blues" and other television shows. Films include: "Bad Boys" and "WarGames," both 1983; "Oxford Blues," 1984; "The Breakfast Club," "St. Elmo's Fire," and "Twice in a Lifetime," all 1985; "Short Circuit" and "Blue City," both 1986; "Maid to Order," 1987.

Sidelights

One of the most popular actresses of the 1980s, Ally Sheedy has had major roles in a string of box-office successes. She is considered a talented and appealing performer; critics praise her clean good looks and find her a lively yet sensitive screen presence. For the most part, however, her presence has been confined to youth-oriented films. Now in her mid-twenties, Sheedy is looking for more adult roles.

Born in New York City, Sheedy is the daughter of an advertising executive and a literary agent. At 12, she published a children's book, *She Was Nice to Mice,* which sold over 120,000 copies; she also contributed articles to the *New York Times, Seventeen, Ms.,* and the *Village Voice.* At 15, she became a model and appeared in ads for Burger King and Clearasil. Two years later, Sheedy moved to Los Angeles, where she worked as a waitress and acted in McDonald's and Pizza Hut commercials. She also enrolled at the University of Southern California to study dance. While still a student, she landed her first movie role, playing Sean Penn's lover in "Bad Boys."

A succession of hit movies followed. From 1983 to 1987, she was featured in "Wargames," "The Breakfast Club," "St. Elmo's Fire," "Short Circuit," "Maid to Order," and other films. Her co-stars have included Rob Lowe, Judd Nelson, Molly Ringwald, and Emilio Estevez—Hollywood's "brat pack," which was described by *Time's* John Skow as "a group of kinda talented, kinda famous young actors." It wasn't long before the media dubbed Sheedy a "pack" member. The actress resents this label. "It's so unfair," she told Margy Rocklin in *Ms.* "The term 'brat pack' is so condescending."

In her films, Sheedy is usually cast as a girlfriend, sister, or daughter—a "pretty post-high schooler," as Skow noted. The limited scope of such roles angers Sheedy. "A guy can be in murder movies, sports movies, or military movies," she remarked to Rochlin. "A woman can be a girlfriend. Period." Most critics agree that she is capable of handling a wider range of roles. Richard Gehr of *Film Comment* found that, so far, none of her movies "has done justice to the potential potency discernible beneath [her] wholesome surface." And *American Film*'s Jeffrey Lantos wrote: "The fact is, most of her films have been aimed at the Clearasil crowd. Adults don't know who she is."

Recently, Sheedy bought the rights to *I'm with the Band*, Pamela Des Barres' autobiographical account of life as a rock groupie. The film version will "focus on the relationship of the groupies and what their lives were like," the actress explained to Stephen Fried in *Rolling Stone*. "I see it as sort of an ensemble piece for women." She is also set to star, with Sean Penn, in the Los Angeles production of the play "Hurlyburly." One of Sheedy's goals is "to play characters," she told *USA Weekend*'s Jeff Silverman. "Give me a character to play."

Writings

She Was Nice to Mice (children's book), McGraw, 1975.

Sources

American Film, November, 1985.
Film Comment, April, 1985.
Moviegoer, November, 1985.
Ms., May, 1986.
New York Times, June 22, 1986.
Newsweek, May 11, 1987.
People, June 20, 1983.
Rolling Stone, September 26, 1985; October 20, 1988.
Time, May 26, 1986.
USA Weekend, April 25–27, 1986.

—Sketch by Denise Wiloch

Daniel P. Sheehan

Lawyer, head of public interest group

AP/Wide World Photos

Born 1945, in Warrensburg, N.Y.; married; wife's name, Sara Nelson. *Education:* Attended Northeastern University, Harvard University, Harvard Divinity School, and Harvard Episcopal Theological Seminary; Harvard Law School, J.D., 1970. *Politics:* Liberal. *Religion:* Roman Catholic.

Addresses: *Office*—The Christic Institute, 1324 N. Capitol St. N.W., Washington, D.C. 20002.

Career

Worked as lawyer at Cahill, Gordon & Reindel, New York, N.Y., the American Civil Liberties Union, and Jesuits' Office of Social Ministry, Washington, D.C.; founder and chief counsel of the Christic Institute, 1980—.

Sidelights

Attorney Daniel P. Sheehan, founder and chief counsel of the Christic Institute, has been described as a "missionary" zealously pursuing a "quest" with monumental implications for American politics. Since 1980 Sheehan's Christic Institute—a nonprofit liberal organization—has been engaged in charting an alleged conspiracy among an elite "Secret Team" that thwarts federal authority by acting independently on its own deadly agenda. *Interview* magazine contributor Eric Alterman explains that Sheehan "has been arguing that a group of 29 men, many of whom are ex-U.S. intelligence officers, have been overseeing a secret war of covert assassination, drug smuggling, gunrunning, and general terrorism with the assistance of U.S. officials who approve of their anticommunist orientation." The recent Iran/*contra* scandal, in Sheehan's view, is only the latest in a long series of illegal activities involving essentially the same people and stretching back to the Cuban Revolution of 1958–59.

According to James Traub in *Mother Jones* magazine, Sheehan feels that the so-called Secret Team "has, for 25 years, supplied weapons as well as its unique assassination services to destroy Communist and Socialist movements in Cuba, Southeast Asia, Iran and the Middle East, and, latterly, Nicaragua. The Secret Team is the nightmare of the American Left come to life." Exposing this conspiracy, and exacting justice against the participants, has become Sheehan's personal and professional crusade. By virtue of his tireless public speaking, his lawsuits, and his numerous mailings, Sheehan has attracted a concerned following. "Polling organizations haven't yet bothered to count," Traub wrote, "but it's clear that tens of thousands of Americans now believe Danny Sheehan."

The Christic Institute takes its name from the "Christic force," a concept pioneered by the late

Jesuit priest Pierre Teilhard de Chardin. The force is a "harmony that bonds all things together and overpowers manmade destructive forces," according to *New York Times* correspondent Keith Schneider. The sixty-plus employees of the institute—all of them salaried at $15,000 or less per annum—accept the religious overtones of their decidedly secular work. Their aim is to take on social-issue cases that could ultimately affect public policy, hence the "Christic" force applied against wrongdoing.

Traub stated: "Think of Christic, then, as one of those early outposts of Christianity, say in Smyrna, when the gospel was beginning to advance. The shabby digs are suffused with a sense of destiny and high purpose—of 'unfinished business,' as assistant general counsel Lanny Sinkin put it. The founders and principals emerged from the '60s with their purity intact. They sincerely believe that the world is finally coming around. They are men and women of faith, in humanity if not necessarily in God." Traub likened the leader of this group, Sheehan, to a charismatic preacher. In Traub's words, Sheehan speaks not of the crimes of twenty-nine men, "but of the world of evil that spawned them, and of the possibility of renewal through a great commitment."

Daniel Sheehan has been a maverick most of his life, but his youth and young manhood were quite conventional. He was born and raised in Warrensburg, New York, and was an excellent student who wanted to be an astronaut. Upon graduation from high school he applied for the United States Air Force Academy, but he was passed over in favor of a less-qualified, but more politically-connected, competitor. Instead Sheehan attended Northeastern University, where he signed up for Green Beret training under ROTC. When the training became graphic, with demonstrations of killing techniques and descriptions of their consequences, Sheehan walked out on the program.

But soon after, Sheehan was drafted. Traub wrote: "Sheehan told his draft board to go to hell, and when his [student] deferment was revoked he threatened to tell the world what his Green Beret trainers had told him—that he would be killing noncombatants in Vietnam. The draft board relented." Thus Sheehan was allowed to finish law school at Harvard in the late 1960s, and his consciousness was raised concerning liberal and radical causes. Ironically, his first professional position was with a prestigious Wall Street law firm, Cahill, Gordon & Reindel, where he served as a junior associate.

The first major case Sheehan worked on at Cahill, Gordon was the celebrated "Pentagon Papers" litigation in which the federal government sued the *New York Times* for publishing sensitive government documents. Traub suggested that Sheehan has subsequently exaggerated his role in the groundbreaking case, but the reporter does admit that as one of a team of twelve, Sheehan's research was indispensible to the winning verdict. However much he helped with that particular case, Sheehan was eventually fired from the firm because he devoted too much of his time to *pro bono* public interest cases.

He was not sidelined long. The American Civil Liberties Union called him to help represent the Native American defendants in the Wounded Knee case—they had seized a government building in protest over unfair treatment under America's laws. That case earmarked Sheehan as a "liberal" attorney who would champion social and economic underdogs, and he was soon working for the Jesuit Office of Social Ministry in Washington and other left-of-center organizations.

Late in the 1970s Sheehan made news with two important lawsuits, both of which he won. In the first he was hired by the National Organization of Women to represent the family of Karen Silkwood, an employee of the Kerr-McGee corporation who died mysteriously after having been contaminated by radioactive materials on the job. According to Traub, in this case Sheehan "began to perfect his unorthodox methods, mounting a costly investigation with professional gumshoes, trading information with reporters, paddling through layers of secrecy." Sheehan's thoroughness led Kerr-McGee to propose a generous $1.3 million out-of-court settlement; he has since concluded that Silkwood was killed because she had stumbled on a secret conspiracy to steal nuclear fuel (the evidence of the conspiracy is as yet inconclusive).

Sheehan then took the lawsuit of five demonstrators who were killed while protesting a Greensborough, North Carolina Ku Klux Klan rally. Even though the Klan defendants had been found not guilty in state and federal trials, Sheehan was still able to exact $405,000 in damages from the city of Greensborough, the police, and the Klan, for the families of the slain protesters. With his fees from the Silkwood and Greensborough cases, Sheehan founded the Christic Institute in 1980. He and his wife Sara Nelson have been running it ever since, drawing financing from private donations, grants from liberal foundations, and awards from other nonprofit organizations such as some churches, the National Organization for Women, and Americans for Democratic Action.

In March of 1984 Sheehan travelled to Brownsville, Texas, to take the defense of a group of Catholic-Americans who had helped illegal aliens from El Salvador find harbor in America. Through this inauspicious case Sheehan began to uncover a sophisticated plan to funnel arms to the *contra* rebels fighting Nicaragua's Sandinista regime. The arming of the *contras* had to be done clandestinely because the 1984 Boland Amendment gave Congress the final say over legal shipments of weapons to Nicaragua, and Congress had severely curtailed such shipments.

Sheehan discovered that significant amounts of weaponry—and manpower in the form of soldiers of fortune and hired assassins— were being sent to Nicaragua

Sheehan discovered that significant amounts of weaponry—and manpower in the form of soldiers of fortune and hired assassins—were being sent to Nicaragua by way of a ranch in Costa Rica owned by an American, John Hull. Traub wrote: "Sheehan had the crime for a civil suit; now he needed a victim." He did not have to wait long. On May 30, 1984, *contra* leader Eden Pastora—who openly disagreed with other *contra* generals—was bombed during a press conference in La Penca, Nicaragua. An American journalist was injured by the blast; his wife launched an investigation of the incident that ultimately linked the terrorist bombers to John Hull. Hull sued the two journalists for libel, and Sheehan's Christic Institute was called in to defend them. Sheehan won the libel suit and got the journalist couple to agree to be plaintiffs in a suit for damages against those responsible for sending weapons into Nicaragua in violation of federal law. The legislation under which they sued is the Federal Racketeering Statute, a law that allows an entire criminal enterprise to be sued for one overt act.

Of course, Sheehan had to prove that a criminal enterprise—independent of the government—was indeed afoot. He took numerous depositions, interviewed drug smugglers, reporters, and ranking CIA and FBI officials, and subsequently published a three hundred page affidavit outlining thirty years of covert activity in Cuba, Laos, Iran, Chile, and Nicaragua, beginning with an alleged "secret assassination unit" formed by Richard Nixon in 1960. Sheehan's investigation centers on two former CIA agents, Theodore Shackley and Tom Clines, who he accuses of terrorist activities funded by drug money with the intended goal of curtailing communism worldwide. Sheehan's original affidavit was later narrowed to a forty-five page statement that he has disseminated widely to supporters of the Christic Institute.

The statement itself—and Sheehan's passionate speeches on the "Secret Team" conspiracy—have drawn as much skepticism as belief from listeners. Ken Silverstein summarized the difficulties of Sheehan's position in *Interview:* "Despite some dubious assertions, the portion of Christic's investigation dealing with the immediate circumstances of the [La Penca] bombing carries weight. It's when Sheehan and his associates start to spin their worldwide web of intrigue that questions arise. One central problem stems from Christic's apparent desire to avoid charging any agency of the U.S. government, and particularly the CIA, with complicity in the plot.... The practical consequence of confining the accusation to... individuals is that Christic's case will not be contested by the U.S. Justice Department, with its limitless financial resources, but this expedient—if such it was—has not helped the persuasiveness of the case."

Nation essayist David Corn put it another way. "With its advocacy of the Secret Team theory, the Christic Institute has painted itself into a corner," Corn contended. "If all these ventures are the handiwork of a few rogues, there is no reason to worry about the national security system at large. What's the remedy for a few bad apples? Better screening of personnel." Traub stated that many Capitol Hill investigators believe Sheehan's entire case to be a "gorgeous tapestry woven of rumor and half-truth and wish-fulfillment."

Sheehan's case was dismissed one week prior to trial in June 1988. Federal Judge James Lawrence King ruled that the Christic Institute had failed to prove the conspiracy theory. Claiming that the judge's decision was an election-year ploy to deflect any bad press for George Bush, Sheehan vowed to appeal. Traub noted that such setbacks hardly daunt an ardent activist like Sheehan. "He's spent a lifetime standing up for unpopular truths;" Traub wrote, "opposition only proves to him how right he is."

The energetic attorney is convincing others of his rightness, too. "The institute's effort to interpret cardinal events of the past thirty years has undoubtedly influenced the way in which some Americans view the world," Corn concluded. "It deserves credit for trying to help people make sense of all these episodes, and for recognizing the Iran/*contra* scandal and its significance early on. It has kept the investigative fires burning, sought to hold individuals accountable for their roles in the affair and probed issues overlooked by the Congressional investigating committees [including the *contra* drug connection and the La Penca bombing]. Depositions taken by its lawyers... have yielded important new information. These are no small accomplishments."

Corn went on to call Sheehan's Christic Institute "the investigator of last resort, the last hope of bringing the guilty to justice." In *Interview*, Sheehan summarized his own actions. "I'm simply saying that the Constitution is in major danger here," he claimed. "There is a certain structure in place, which Congress knows is in place. These guys are not dumb. They know this thing exists, but they don't want to talk about it.... I've set forth the information on the basis of a good faith belief as to what is true, and I have dared to say what nobody wanted to say."

Sources

Christian Science Monitor, June 24, 1988.
Interview, April, 1988.
Mother Jones, February/March, 1988.
Nation, July 2–9, 1988.
New York Times, July 20, 1987.
Time, July 4, 1988.

—Sketch by Anne Janette Johnson

Michelle Shocked

© 1989 James McGoon

Singer, songwriter, and activist

Name originally Michelle Johnston; name changed, 1984; born c. 1963; raised in Maryland, Massachusetts, West Germany, and Texas; daughter of Bill Johnston (described variously as an English teacher and/or part-time carny ride operator) and a mother Shocked refuses to identify; stepfather was in the military. *Education:* Attended University of Texas, briefly.

Addresses: *Home*—London, England. *Office*—c/o PolyGram Records, 450 Park Ave., New York, N.Y. 10022.

Career

Became interested in music at age sixteen when she went to live with her father in Texas, and he introduced her to blues and country music; after periods of being committed to two mental institutions by her mother, went on the road in the United States and Europe, singing and participating in peace protests; signed a recording contract, 1986; has toured throughout the United States.

Sidelights

The newest angry, young woman to burst onto the music scene is Michelle Shocked (nee Johnston). She chose her stagy surname to reflect outrage over a troubled past and uses her music to deliver stinging social commentary and recount dreamy Texas memories. Her songs seem headed for the top of the charts, but Shocked isn't sure she wants to follow suit.

Thin and pale with close-cropped hair often hidden under a British sailor's cap, Shocked is defiantly reluctant to answer personal questions. A sassy Texan who's achieved more professional success in Europe than her homeland, she's a difficult talent to categorize. Her music has been described as country, punk, protest, folk, blues, rock and pop.

She's the daughter of Bill Johnston, who has been described as a former teacher, part-time carny ride operator, and sixties-style hippie, and a mother whose name Shocked won't reveal but cynically describes as a "Tammy-Bakker-type." When her parents divorced in 1963, Michelle lived with her converted-Mormon mother and career-Army stepfather, who moved them from Maryland to Massachusetts, West Germany, then Texas. In 1979, at sixteen, she quit school and left home to live with her father in Dallas. Johnston encouraged her musical talent, convinced her to buy a second-hand guitar, and took her to local blues and country music festivals.

Shocked enrolled at the University of Texas but didn't stick with classes for long. She began a period of restless wanderings, which took her from the homes of relatives and friends to student housing coops, then on to San Francisco and involvement with local hardcore bands and a squatters' movement. Shocked calls this her period of homelessness, when she aligned herself with a number of causes from save-the-whales to anti-nuclear activities. Evictions drove her back to Texas where her mother, alarmed over Michelle's wild lifestyle, had Shocked hospitalized in mental institutions. "They kept me till the insurance ran out," Shocked told *People* magazine. "I guess you can't be crazy without insurance."

In 1984, she continued her political involvement and was arrested twice during public protests—once at the Republican Convention, then again in a protest against a defense contractor. For the next two years, she bounced from California to New York to Europe. "I was never gonna come back. If I could actually survive in a foreign country with no money, taking care of myself, I couldn't be crazy," she explained to *Musician.* Things didn't work out as she planned. She was raped while wandering through Italy and retreated back to Texas.

It was there, while performing at the Kerrville Folk Festival in 1986, that Shocked was accidentally discovered by English producer Pete Lawrence. He taped her performance on his Sony Walkman, complete with background crickets chirping, then released the crude recording as *The Texas Campfire Tapes* and watched it soar to the top of British independent charts. A surprised Shocked moved to London and was received with open arms.

PolyGram offered her a $130,000 advance on a second album, but Shocked would only accept $50,000. "When it comes to it," she explained to *Musician,* "I have to confess I'm not that committed to the medium of making albums. It's a nice means, but it's not the end as far as I'm concerned. If it gets people to the live shows where I can spit my two cents worth of politics, it's done the job . . . . I knew if I was going to keep the album as simple as I wanted, it was never gonna take that much money."

A dramatic photo of a raging Shocked being restrained and arrested by riot police, which appeared in the *San Francisco Examiner,* serves as the cover of her second album, *Short Sharp Shocked.* PolyGram is hoping that, plus a 30-city tour, will make Shocked a star in the United States. Meanwhile, Shocked is content to return to the houseboat on the Thames she now calls home.

Discography

The Texas Campfire Tapes, Cooking Vinyl, 1987.
Short Sharp Shocked, PolyGram, 1988.

Sources

Musician, June, 1988.
Newsweek, October 3, 1988.
New York Times, September 4, 1988.
People, November 7, 1988.
Rolling Stone, November 3, 1988; October 6, 1988.
Stereo Review, March, 1989.

—Sketch by Sharon Rose

Joe Slovo

AP/Wide World Photos

South African attorney and political activist

Born 1926, in Lithuania; emigrated to South Africa, 1935; son of a van driver and Matilda Slovo; married Ruth First (a writer and academic), 1949 (died, 1982); children: three daughters. *Education:* University of Witwatersrand, law degree (with honors). *Politics:* Communist.

Career

Left school after sixth grade to work as a warehouse assistant in a chemical plant; while attending law school after World War II, became active in Springbok Legion (a radical ex-servicemen's league) and in Young Communist League; joined Communist Party of South Africa before it was outlawed in 1950; began working as an attorney and civil rights activist in the 1950s, defending a number of political activists; continued to work on behalf of the underground Communist Party; banned, along with his wife, under Suppression of Communism Act in 1950 and 1954; worked with Congress of Democrats and helped write Freedom Charter, 1955; arrested for treason, acted as his own defense, and got charges dropped, 1958; arrested again in 1960 and held without trial for five months; helped organize military wing of African National Congress (ANC), 1962, and served as chief of staff, 1962–87, and on its Revolutionary Council, beginning 1969; in exile since 1963, first in Tanzania, then in Mozambique, Zambia, and elsewhere; whereabouts a secret; constantly on the move from one safe place to another; has continued to organize militant opposition to South African government while in exile; became first white member of ANC National Executive Council, 1985; became general secretary of South African Communist Party, 1987. *Military service:* South African Army; served in World War II.

Sidelights

Joe Slovo is a white South African who has devoted his life to overturning that country's white minority government and its system of apartheid. A lawyer and political activist, Slovo became involved in a number of anti-government activities through the years. He was a founding member of the South African Communist Party in 1953 and in 1987 became its general secretary. Slovo helped organize the military wing of the African National Congress (ANC) and was its chief of staff for 25 years. In exile since 1963, Slovo has planned and coordinated for the ANC acts of sabotage and guerrilla warfare against the South African government. In 1985 he was appointed to the National Executive Council of the ANC, the first white to become a member of the ruling council.

Slovo has recently come to the attention of the western media partly because of the 1988 film "A

World Apart," written by his daughter Shawn Slovo about her parents. Her mother, Ruth First, was a journalist and political activist who was detained and tortured by the South African authorities in the early 1960s. She was assassinated in 1982 in Maputo, Mozambique.

In the past, Slovo avoided interviews and publicity. Ironically, because of his reticence, stories have circulated about him, and his reputation has grown to mythic proportions. The South African authorities have contributed to the mystique by branding him "Public Enemy Number 1," the mastermind behind the ANC. As part of "a process of demythologising Joe Slovo," Slovo granted his first interview with a western news organization in 1985. In a later interview with the *Wall Street Journal,* Slovo said that "Botha and Botha [at the time South Africa's President and Foreign Minister] have done for me what Saatchi and Saatchi [a well-known public relations firm] have done for Mrs. Thatcher."

In April 1987 Slovo resigned his post of chief of staff of Umkhonto we Sizwe (the ANC military wing) to become general secretary of the South African Communist Party. He told an interviewer with the Harare *Herald,* "Since my election to the highest post of the Communist Party . . . , it became difficult for me to carry both burdens." When he was asked by the *Wall Street Journal* about the liberation of South Africa taking so long he joked: "I said in 1969 it would take five years, and I haven't changed my position. Actually, I'm not too pessimistic. You never know what will happen. If you had asked Lenin this question when he was drinking coffee in Zurich at the beginning of 1917, he probably would have said: 'Oh, it will be a protracted struggle.'"

The Slovo family came to South Africa from Lithuania in 1935 when Joe Slovo was nine years old. His father was employed as a van driver but was unable to support the family. Slovo quit school and went to work in a chemical wholesale plant as a warehouse assistant. He joined the National Union of Distributive Workers and was elected shop steward. During World War II, Slovo enlisted in the South African Army and was stationed in Italy.

On return to South Africa, he took advantage of a demobilization grant and enrolled in the law school of Witwatersrand University in Johannesburg. He graduated four years later with distinction. While at the university, he was active in a radical ex-servicemen's league, the Springbok Legion, and was a member of the Young Communist League. He joined the Communist Party of South Africa and was a member until it was outlawed in 1950. Slovo later helped reconstitute the party as the South African Communist Party. The SACP was banned in 1960.

In 1949 Slovo married Ruth First, the daughter of a wealthy furniture manufacturer. Both her parents were founding members of the Communist Party of South Africa and her father, Julius, was treasurer. Between the 1920s and 1940s, close ties were formed between the Communist Party and the ANC. The party had played an important role in organizing black labor unions, and many African nationalists were in the leadership of the party. Conversely, many Communist Party members were also members of the ANC.

In 1948 the Nationalist Party won control of the government. From then on, South Africans would experience a more and more repressive government intent on depriving blacks of the few rights they had. The first major piece of legislation passed by the Nationalists was the 1950 Suppression of Communism Act.

Slovo and First were among the 600 people who were restricted in 1950 under the new act. As a barrister, Slovo had undertaken the defense of many political activists and had himself continued working in the underground party. He was banned again in 1954 and restricted from attending all gatherings in South Africa. At this time he was working with the Congress of Democrats, representing them on the national consultative committee of the Congress Alliance. The Alliance was drafting the revolutionary Freedom Charter, and Slovo secretly continued his work on it despite the banning order. The charter was presented to the Congress of the People in Kliptown, Soweto, on June 25, 1955. Because of his banning orders, Slovo had to watch the proceedings through binoculars from a rooftop 500 yards away.

Shortly after the congress meeting, the government picked up 156 people on treason charges. Slovo was one of the accused. Already under banning orders, he had to get special permission to attend his own trial in Pretoria. He acted as his own defense, and the charges against him were dropped in 1958. All of those who were brought to trial were eventually acquitted. In 1960, 1600 people were arrested, and all the organizations involved in the campaign against the restrictive pass laws were banned. These included the South African Communist Party and the ANC. Slovo was picked up and detained without trial for five months.

ANC leaders had reluctantly come to the conclusion that nonviolent protest was not going to persuade the authorities to do away with the system of apartheid.

The government's response to peaceful protest had been to increase the level of repression. In 1961, under Nelson Mandela's direction and with the consent of the ANC leadership, a small group of ANC members formed a military wing of the ANC. They planned Umkhonto We Size (the Spear of the Nation) at Liliesleaf Farm, a hideaway in the Johannesburg suburb of Rivonia. Slovo was a member of this elite group.

Umkhonto's manifesto read in part: "The people's patience is not endless. The time comes in the life of any nation where there remain only two choices: submit or fight. That time has come to South Africa. We shall not submit and we have no choice but to hit back by all means within our power in defence of our people, our future and our freedom." Of the four different types of violence open to them—guerrilla warfare, terrorism, sabotage, and open revolution—the group decided on sabotage, because it would limit the violence and yet hit at the economic life of the country. Strict instructions were given to avoid injuring or killing people. During the next 18 months Umkhonto carried out 150 acts of sabotage.

Stories have circulated about him, and his reputation has grown to mythic proportions.

In July 1963, the police raided the farm house and rounded up most of the ANC leaders, including Govan Mbeki and Walter Sisulu. Slovo escaped arrest because he was out of the country at the time. A month after the arrests at Rivonia, Ruth First was picked up and detained without trial for four months. On her release, she left the country with her three daughters.

With its leaders jailed or in exile, the internal structures of the ANC collapsed. The task of those in exile was to rebuild the party. Slovo made his way to Dar es Salaam, Tanzania, where the ANC set up its headquarters. Life in exile was bleak. Mary Benson, an ANC supporter, described the Tanzania office in her book as "really desperate. Just a couple of tatty rooms. Maybe one typewriter." As chief of staff of Umkhonto (or MK) Slovo set about rebuilding the smashed underground network. He brought Soviet bloc support to the ANC for weapons and training, and he set up training camps in Tanzania.

Throughout the 1960s the ANC was in decline, crippled by repression at home, where people feared even to talk about the organization, and displaced in the early 1970s by the popularity of the Black Consciousness movement. Isolated and frustrated by its inability to effect change, the ANC reexamined its policies at an important meeting in Morogoro in 1969. Its new program, as outlined in its publication "Strategy and Tactics," called for a shift from sabotage to full-scale guerrilla warfare. The NEC named Slovo to the newly created Revolutionary Council, which was instructed to bring the struggle inside South Africa by strengthening the internal underground.

In the 1970s in South Africa, African workers reasserted themselves in a series of nationwide strikes. They formed black labor unions, and, although they had no legal status, the unions became arenas for organization and politicization. Events elsewhere on the continent in the early 1970s also furthered the ANC's aims. In 1974 the military took power in Portugal and withdrew from Portugal's African colonies. Independent black governments in the former colonies of Mozambique and Angola gave the ANC greater access to its underground networks and made it easier to infiltrate arms and trained cadres. In 1977 Slovo moved to Maputo, Mozambique, where he set up an operational center.

In 1976 Soweto erupted. In the aftermath of the riots, an estimated 12,000 young people left the country with nearly two-thirds of them joining the ANC in exile. After Soweto, the ANC gained in self-confidence as it became visible again throughout the country. Many former cadres of the ANC who had seemingly dropped out of politics reemerged as key personnel. Support for the ANC grew as it became more effective militarily. In the early 1980s Umkhonto targeted key economic and military targets. In July 1980 it set off limpet mines at the SASOL plant, a heavily guarded government plant where coal is converted to oil. In August 1981 the Voortrekkerhoogte barracks was bombed. In December 1982 the Koeberg nuclear power station near Cape Town was sabotaged. And in May 1983 a car bomb was detonated outside the South African Air Force headquarters in Pretoria, killing 19 people.

In a 1985 interview with the *Washington Post*, Slovo confirmed publicly for the first time that as chief of staff of the military wing, he was involved in planning the various bombings of government buildings and strategic installations. Twenty-four people were killed in these attacks.

With ANC bases now much closer to its borders, South Africa acted quickly to preempt ANC strikes. In 1981 South African commando units disguised as Mozambican soldiers crossed the border into Mozambique and attacked three ANC houses, killing 13 people. Mozambican authorities believe they were actually after Joe Slovo and that the one white they killed had been mistaken for Slovo. In newly independent Zimbabwe, Joe Gqabi, the ANC representative to Zimbabwe, was assassinated in 1981. In 1982 Slovo's wife was killed in her office. The level of violence on both sides escalated.

Two years after Slovo's wife was assassinated, a daily Johannesburg newspaper, the *Star*, ran an article saying that diplomats familiar with South Africa said that Slovo "was ruthless enough to have arranged the August 17, 1982, killing of his by then estranged wife." Slovo sued the publisher of the *Star*, Argus Printing and Publishing Co., in a London court. In 1986 the court awarded Slovo damages of $50,000 plus costs. Although he was vindicated, he received no monetary compensation because the South African company refused to comply with an English court.

In September 1984 violence erupted once again in Soweto when residents refused to pay rent increases imposed by the local councils. Council members were perceived as sell-outs because they were in office at the behest of the white authorities. Between September 1984 and December 1986 over 2,200 people died in sporadic rioting. The police conceded that at this time the ANC had unprecedented freedom of movement. Training of ANC supporters inside the country increased and grass-roots level organizations spread throughout the townships.

Anxious to remove ANC bases from Mozambique, South Africa pressured the Mozambique government to sign the Nkomati Accord of 1984 and expell all members of the ANC—especially Slovo. He left Mozambique and rejoined the ANC leadership at their headquarters in Lusaka, Zambia. The ANC was unprepared for Mozambique's hasty decision, and they departed from Mozambique without adequate preparations. Four years later, the ANC would be forced out of Angola by an agreement between Angola, South Africa, and the Cubans. Zambia and Tanzania are now their main areas of operations.

In 1985 the ANC regrouped. At a consultative conference in Kabwe, Zambia, the ANC revised its policy in regard to violence and civilian targets. By adopting the concept of a "people's war" it expanded the acceptable number of people involved in military action. It also included those civilians involved in implementing apartheid as legitimate targets and accepted the possibility of unintentionally injuring or killing innocent civilians in attacks on hard targets. And for the first time in the history of the movement, non-Africans were invited to sit on the National Executive Council; Slovo was the first of these.

In response to the worsening violence, in 1986 the government declared a state of emergency, detained thousands of activists, broke up underground groups in Cape Town, Johannesburg, and Pretoria, arrested 80 foreign-trained guerrillas and killed another 26. Despite the crackdown, the ANC says 400 trained guerrillas were infiltrated into the country in 1988 and joined a similar number of fighters trained inside.

The level of planned violence in South Africa escalated in 1988. Bombings occurred at public places like hamburger chain restaurants, outside a rugby game as the crowd was leaving, art galleries, and shopping malls. Chris Hani, who succeeded Joe Slovo as chief of staff of Umkhonto, is quoted by the *New African* as saying that apartheid "guarantees a happy life for [whites], a sweet life. Part of our campaign is to prevent that sweet life."

As ANC's strength grew it received acknowledgment of its leading role in the liberation movement from a variety of quarters. In 1985 representatives from the Anglo American Corporation met in Zambia with the ANC. U.S. Secretary of State George Schultz met with Tambo in New York in 1987. ANC representatives have met with Afrikaner businessmen, politicians, lawyers, and sports officials, all in defiance of the government.

From its early years in exile, the ANC has received all of its military assistance from the Soviet Union and Eastern bloc countries. Non-military aid has been provided by Sweden, Norway, Denmark, and Finland. U.N. organizations and anti-apartheid groups in Europe and the United States also provide funds. In an interview with the *Washington Post*, Slovo said that the Soviet Union has given the ANC "enormous support throughout our history but has never tried to take control of the movement. It has never in my experience happened that we were told in the ANC what to do or say by Moscow." Slovo's high position in both organizations has lent credence to South African charges that the ANC is under the thumb of the Communist party. As a spokesman for the party, Slovo says the "party has held a precious and unique position" within the ANC. "We have jealously safeguarded the independence of the organization and avoided behaving in any kind of manipulative way."

Slovo has been in the front lines of the liberation struggle most of his life. In the process, he lost his wife, his home, and his professional life to the struggle. He endured the early years of exile and helped build up the organization from the ashes of the 1960s to its status today as the acknowledged representative of the vast majority of South Africa's people. In the *Washington Post*, Slovo was asked if he thinks he will return as a free man to black-ruled South Africa. Unhesitatingly, he replied, "Absolutely yes."

Sources

Books

Benson, Mary, *The Struggle for a Birthright*, Penguin (London), 1966.

Tambo, Adelaide, compiler, *Preparing for Power: Oliver Tambo Speaks*, George Braziller, 1988.

Periodicals

Guardian (Manchester), February 10, 1985.
Herald (Harare), April 4, 1987.
Independent, November 4, 1988.
Leadership, Vol. 7, 1988.
New African (London), October, 1988.
Newsweek, June 30, 1980.
Star (Johannesburg), May 2, 1987.
Time, November 6, 1980; March 2, 1987.
Washington Post, February 1, 1985; July 14, 1985; July 19, 1985; February 24, 1987.
Wall Street Journal, April 18, 1988; April 22, 1988.
Weekly Mail (Johannesburg), May 4, 1988; June 16, 1988.

—Sidelights by Virginia Curtin Knight

Phil Spector

Sygma/Tony Korody

Record producer and songwriter

Born December 25, 1940, in Bronx, N.Y.; mother's name, Bertha; married Veronica Bennett (a singer), 1968 (divorced, 1974); children: Gary and Louis (twins), Donte, Nicole and Phillip (twins). *Education:* Attended University of California at Los Angeles.

Addresses: *Office*—Phil Spector Records International, P.O. Box 69529, Los Angeles, Calif. 90069.

Career

Member of musical groups Teddy Bears, 1958–59, and Spectors Three; producer with Atlantic Records, 1960–61; founder, Philles Records, 1962; currently president of Phil Spector Records International. Has produced records and albums for numerous artists, including Gene Pitney, Connie Francis, the Crystals, the Ronnettes, the Righteous Brothers, the Beatles, Ike and Tina Turner, John Lennon, George Harrison, Yoko Ono, Cher, and the Ramones. Composer of songs, including "To Know Him Is to Love Him," "Oh Why," and "I Really Do"; also composed, with others, "Spanish Harlem," "Da Doo Ron Ron," "Then He Kissed Me," "Be My Baby," "Chapel of Love," "You've Lost That Loving Feeling," "River Deep—Mountain High," and numerous other songs. Producer of television documentary "A Giant Stands 5 Ft. 7 In." and of movie "The Big T.N.T. Show." Appeared in films "The T.A.M.I. Show" and "Easy Rider."

Sidelights

Considered a rock-and-roll legend, Phil Spector is credited with revolutionizing the recording industry. From 1962 to 1965 he produced a number of rock classics and made stars of such groups as the Crystals, the Ronnettes, and the Righteous Brothers. His influence declined, however, with the "British invasion" of the mid-1960s. Ironically, the vanguard of that invasion—the Beatles—later helped to revive his career. Today, the reclusive and somewhat volatile Spector serves as president of his own record label.

Born in the Bronx, Spector moved to Los Angeles with his family when he was 12. He became interested in music (particularly rhythm and blues) while in high school and was influenced by the work of Jerry Leiber and Mike Stoller, who had produced a number of hits for Elvis Presley, the Coasters, and other performers. Spector eventually met the producers and became something of a regular at their studio. Spector wrote his first song, "To Know Him Is to Love Him," in 1958. He recruited a local high school student to sing the female lead, sang the background harmonies himself, and named the group the Teddy Bears. "To Know Him," which sold over one million records, was the Teddy Bears' only hit. In 1959 Spector recorded two singles under the name Spectors Three. Both records failed to make the charts.

Three years later Spector founded Philles Records and began producing what *Time*'s Jay Cocks called "some of rock's greatest records." Spector-produced hits include "He's a Rebel," "Da Doo Ron Ron," "Then He Kissed Me," "Be My Baby," "You've Lost That Loving Feeling," and "River Deep—Mountain High." During this time he perfected his trademark "wall of sound," which was described by Cocks as "vaulting arrangements and majestic delirium." In *Out of His Head: The Sound of Phil Spector,* Richard Williams noted that the producer used his singers "as tools, manipulating their every musical move with infinite care." It was, he continued, "'spontaneous' excitement through precise preplanning."

As British rock came into prominence in the mid-1960s, the Spector era drew to a close. Though semiretired, in 1970 he produced several tracks on the Beatles' *Let It Be* album; he worked with John Lennon on *Imagine* and with George Harrison on *All Things Must Pass.* He also produced *A Concert for Bangladesh,* as well as records by Cher, Dion, Leonard Cohen, Nilsson, and the Ramones.

Spector has been variously described as a mad genius, an eccentric, and a recluse. "In a recording studio, he throws tantrums as easily as other producers turn dials," wrote Cocks. "His excesses of style and manner are legend, and some call him mad." In a review of a documentary on Spector, the *New Statesman*'s Mary Harron commented: "He had one perfect moment in the early 60s, and never recovered. And maybe that was all he could have because, as Sonny Bono said, 'everything he did was perfect, but it was always that one wall of sound.' But what a sound."

Discography

"To Know Him Is to Love Him," Dore, 1958.
The Teddy Bears Sing!, Imperial, c. 1958.
"I Really Do," Trey, c. 1959.
"My Heart Stood Still," Trey, c. 1959.

Sources

Books

Williams, Richard, *Out of His Head: The Sound of Phil Spector,* Outerbridge & Lazard, Inc., 1972.

Periodicals

High Fidelity, June, 1977.
Interview, March, 1980.
Los Angeles Times, April 1, 1983; November 4, 1983.
New Statesman, August 19, 1983.
Newsweek, April 22, 1985.
New York, July 18, 1977.
New York Times, March 15, 1984.
Time, March 10, 1980.

—Sketch by Denise Wiloch

Penelope Spheeris

Film director

Born c. 1945; daughter of a carnival strongman and a ticket taker; children: Anna Schoeller. *Education:* Graduate of University of California, Los Angeles.

Addresses: *Home*—Los Angeles, Calif.

Career

Worked briefly as an actress; later worked as a film editor; founder of music video production company, Rock 'n' Reel, 1974; produced series of short films for "Saturday Night Live"; producer of film "Real Life"; film director, 1980—. Films include "The Decline of Western Civilization I: The Punk Years," 1980, "Suburbia," 1984, "The Boys Next Door," 1986, "The Decline of Western Civilization II: The Metal Years," 1988, and "Dudes," 1988.

Sidelights

Penelope Spheeris is the director of several films that deal with America's disaffected youth. She has chronicled the punk and heavy-metal movements; and she has addressed the issue of random violence committed by seemingly normal, middle-class teenagers. Her work is graphic and often disturbing. Young men and women are depicted as apathetic, materialistic, and violent. "If I make films that are on the heavy side," Spheeris commented to *People*'s Fred Bernstein, "it's because that's what I've been dealt . . . . I was born into a collection of freaks."

© 1988 Jim McHugh/Visages

Spheeris's childhood was both unusual and tragic. Her father, a circus strongman, was shot and killed when she was seven. Her mother, a ticket taker, later married and divorced several times. She also became an alcoholic. Spheeris was abused as a child but says she bears no grudge. "My mother had been abused herself," she told Bernstein. "She had it rough. But she always told me, even when I was bleeding, that she loved me." Spheeris was shuffled from household to household, and school to school. Somehow, she made it to college.

After earning a degree in film from the University of California at Los Angeles, Spheeris tried acting. She then became a film editor. During this time, she was asked to film a rock band for a record company. Her employer jokingly suggested that she form her own organization and call it Rock 'n' Reel. Spheeris liked the idea and, in 1974, founded one of the first music-video companies. As the business prospered, Spheeris grew bored. She then approached her friend Lorne Michaels of "Saturday Night Live" for a job. He set her to work producing short films for Albert Brooks, who then contributed to the show. Brooks later asked her to produce his first movie, "Real Life." In 1980, shortly after the film's release, Spheeris discovered punk music. She became something of a regular at Hollywood's The Masque. "It was this dungeonlike club, and it just turned my life around," she recalled to Peter Occhiogrosso in *American Film.* "I couldn't believe people looked and acted this way, so I cut off my hair and threw myself into it." This experience led to "The Decline of Western Civilization I," Spheeris's directorial debut.

A controversial documentary, "Decline I" focuses on the nihilism and violence of the punk movement. It also served as the blueprint for Spheeris's later films, all of which treat "teenage disaffection in its most extreme modern forms," Janet Maslin of the *New York Times* wrote. "Suburbia" concerns runaways who take up residence in an abandoned house. In "The Boys Next Door," two teenage outcasts go to Los Angeles for a weekend. Their trip turns into an unplanned murder spree. The *New York Times*'s Vincent Canby called it "a very well made, disorienting movie about inarticulated despair and utter hopelessness."

In 1988, Spheeris directed "The Decline of Western Civilization II." Considered her best work to date, "Decline II" documents Los Angeles's heavy-metal clubs, where musicians and their followers are motivated by money, sex, and drugs. Tim Appelo of *Savvy* declared it "the definitive heavy-metal film." Maslin found both "Decline" movies "illuminating": "They say a great deal about how self-destructive adolescent behavior reflects the society that shapes it. And they show how a witty and perceptive film maker can take any subject and make it her own."

Sources

American Film, December, 1984; April, 1985.
New York Times, March 14, 1986; June 26, 1988.
People, July 4, 1988.
Savvy, September, 1988.

—*Sketch by Denise Wiloch*

John Sununu

White House chief of staff

Full name, John Henry Sununu; born July 2, 1939, in Havana, Cuba; son of a motion picture distributor; married Nancy Hayes, 1958; children: Catherine, Elizabeth, Christina, John, Michael, James, Christopher, Peter. *Education:* Massachusetts Institute of Technology, B.S., 1961, M.S., 1962, Ph.D., 1966. *Religion:* Roman Catholic.

Addresses: *Home*—Salem, N.H. *Office*—The White House, 1500 Pennsylvania Ave., Washington, D.C. 20500.

Career

Astro Dynamics, founder and chief engineer, 1960–65; JHS Engineering Co. and Thermal Research, Inc., Salem, N.H., president, 1965–82; Tufts University, Medford, Mass., associate professor of mechanical engineering, 1966–82, associate dean of College of Engineering, 1968–73; member of New Hampshire House of Representatives, 1973–74; governor of New Hampshire, 1983–89; White House chief of staff, 1989—. Member of New Hampshire Governor's Energy Council, 1973–78, Governor's Committee on New Hampshire's Future, 1977–78, and Governor's Advisory Committee on Science and Technology, 1977–78. Chairman of George Bush's 1988 presidential campaign in New Hampshire; head of Bush's platform committee; one of five national campaign co-chairmen.

Member: National Governors' Association (vice-chairman, 1986), New England Governors' Association (chairman, 1984–85), Coalition of Northeastern Governors (chairman, 1985–86), Alliance for Acid Rain Control (vice-chairman).

UPI/Bettmann Newsphotos

Sidelights

When President-elect George Bush named his White House chief of staff in November 1988, he chose not the traditional Washington insider, or even someone regarded as a great conciliator. Instead, Bush chose New Hampshire Governor John Sununu—a strong-willed, blunt-speaking New Englander. The chief of staff has the responsibility of running the White House staff, dispensing information, and controlling access to the president. It is the ultimate consultant's challenge, and Sununu, a politician by trade but a consultant at heart, was an interesting choice. He has a history of troubleshooting, on state government and on Bush's once-sputtering presidential campaign. Still, the chief of staff's job is an ambitious undertaking for a governor from a small state, an MIT-trained mechanical engineer with no experience in Washington.

But Sununu has never lacked confidence in his abilities. He was born of a Lebanese-American father and Lebanese-Greek mother in 1939 in Havana, where his father was working as a distributor of

French motion pictures. The word "sununu" is Arabic for a small bird. The family moved to an exclusive section of Queens, New York, when John was a baby. Young John attended the La Salle Military Academy, a Catholic high school on Long Island, and received so many medals at his graduation that the administrator on the podium presented him with a silver bowl to put them in. Sununu married Nancy Hayes of Cape Cod, Massachusetts, at 19, when both were students in the Boston area.

In 1960, shortly before graduating from MIT, Sununu was hired by Leonard Katz, an engineer and inventor, to help set up an electronics company, Astro Dynamics Inc. He worked there for five years, eventually becoming chief engineer. He helped produce and design heat sinks for semi-conductors and worked on a brushless DC electric motor that was used in the U.S. space program. "He was indefatigable," Katz told the *Boston Globe* in 1982. "He was always there. I keep on telling him he is too bright to go into politics." In 1966, Sununu joined the faculty at Tufts University as an associate professor of mechanical engineering. Two years later, at the age of 29, he became associate dean of the engineering college. At the same time he started and ran two engineering consulting firms.

While still at Tufts in 1969, Sununu moved his growing family (there are now eight children) to New Hampshire, citing the clean environment, the better business climate, and the low taxes. "I had visited here a number of times and it attracted me," Sununu told the *Boston Globe*. "It seemed like a more conservative state." He soon got involved in local politics, beginning with the Salem Planning Board. In 1972 he won a seat in the 400-member New Hampshire House of Representatives. During his two-year term, however, Sununu was asked by the U.S. Agency for International Development to go to the African nation of Ghana to help form an industrial development plan. That caused him to miss more than 60 percent of the roll-call votes.

In 1974, Sununu filed for the state Senate, but was kept off the ballot because he failed to meet the seven-year residency requirement. Two years later, he ran for the state Senate again but lost to incumbent Democrat Del Dowling. He lost other races in 1978 and 1980, and most New Hampshire observers believed Sununu's political career was over. In 1981, he was a finalist to head the Department of Energy under President Reagan. U.S. Senator Warren B. Rudman, who beat Sununu in the 1980 Republican primary, now speaks well of his former opponent. "I think anybody who gets to know John well is attracted by his competence, his no-nonsense approach to things and that he works enormously hard," Rudman told the *Washington Post*.

In 1982, Sununu decided to give politics one more try. He challenged Governor Hugh Gallen, a seemingly popular Democrat with four solid years in office and the best-financed campaign in the state's history. Sununu was able to focus the campaign on his own opposition to taxes and his opponent's alleged mismanagement. In a surprise, he beat Gallen, taking 52 percent of the vote. Sununu won re-election in 1984, with 67 percent of the vote, and again in 1986, with a slightly less impressive 54 percent.

When he became governor, Sununu found himself facing a deficit that exceeded $40 million. He brought in teams of private industry experts to canvass the state government. He dismantled budgets, focusing on sometimes minute matters. Temporary surcharges were added. Departments were streamlined and services computerized. In Sununu's six years as governor, the deficit was erased and a $26-million rainy day fund was established. In addition, Sununu cut taxes while boosting government services. He helped upgrade prisons and mental health facilities. He revamped the state budget process. He set aside million of dollars to protect wildlands. Personal income rose in New Hampshire, while unemployment dropped.

He was less successful in his zealous support for the fully built but idle $5.7-billion Seabrook Nuclear Power Plant, which was unpopular with people around New England. As an engineer, Sununu once appeared in a nuclear industry ad declaring that changes triggered by the 1979 accident at Three Mile Island had made nuclear power safer. As a governor, he wanted the power plant opened. His chief foe on the issue was Massachusetts Governor Michael Dukakis, who effectively blocked licensing of the nuclear reactor by refusing to cooperate in an emergency planning program. "I honestly believe that John Sununu hates Michael Dukakis," Joe Grandmaison, the New Hampshire Democratic chairman, told the *Los Angeles Times*. "And the fact that he has put so much time and effort into [criticizing Dukakis], that he obviously receives such a tremendous psychological and emotional high from this, I think, is from Seabrook."

In his nearly six years as New Hampshire governor, Sununu developed a reputation as a demanding and tough executive with a quick mind and a penchant for taking controversial stands and sticking by them. He displayed little tolerance for aides or outsiders who had not prepared themselves. "When someone did something that he disapproved of, he would summon them in and dress them down," Grandmaison told the *Boston Globe*. "What emerges is professorial. You are certainly talked down to." Sununu worked long hours and expected his staff to do the same. And he demanded that staffers share his ideology and his vision. He had difficulty delegating authority. That style sometimes created problems and led detractors to brand him arrogant and abrasive. State legislators sued him several times to block contracts he had worked out at private meetings. Even in a Republican-dominated state, he often battled with a GOP legislature and appeared to go out of his way to exert his power.

During the 1988 New Hampshire presidential primary, Sununu's critics—including some in his own party—produced a button with a picture of Sununu's face and the words, "Will Rogers Never Met This Man." "He believes that the way to win battles is to be the aggressor," Thomas Rath, a friend of Sununu, told the *Los Angeles Times*. "He is one for preemptive strategies. And I think that he overwhelms you at times with his combativeness." And Peter Goelz, a former aide to Gallen, told the *Los Angeles Times:* "He is an arrogant, cocky know-it-all. The problem is that he's also very smart."

Indeed, few doubt Sununu's intellectual prowess or his analytical abilities. New Hampshire political lore is filled with stories of his ability, for example, to conduct a meeting and simultaneously find the one mathematical error in the $10 million, 150-page proposal before him. His abilities were clearly tested in 1988, when he served as chairman of Bush's campaign in New Hampshire. The campaign had limped into New Hampshire, wounded by a humiliating third-place finish in Iowa eight days earlier. Sununu urged a confrontational style with expensive media attacks on chief opponent, Senator Bob Dole. It worked. Bush left New Hampshire with a reinvigorated, winning campaign and a big debt of gratitude to Sununu. After that primary, Sununu boldly placed on his blue station wagon the very license plates that a previous New Hampshire governor, Sherman Adams, had on his car when he was the powerful chief of staff to President Dwight D. Eisenhower. He did not deny rumors of his eventual interest in the job.

Sununu stayed with the Bush campaign, serving as the head of Bush's platform committee and one of five national co-chairmen. His largest role, however, was traversing the country as Bush's surrogate to attack Dukakis. "It's my job," Sununu told the *Boston Globe*, "to show that the Duke has no clothes. It is my job to make sure that the difference between mainstream America's conservative approach and Michael Dukakis' liberal approach is understood." Sununu was effective in the role of Bush's pit bull. The *Boston Globe*, Dukakis's hometown paper, referred to him as "Jarrin' John Sununu, the right wing's favorite technocrat, Mr. Nuclear Power himself, a brilliant, irascible, overbearing and under-appreciated (in his own mind, for sure) New Hampshire governor whose contempt for Dukakis propelled him into George Bush's inner circle."

As New Hampshire governor, Sununu developed a reputation as a demanding and tough executive with a quick mind and a penchant for taking controversial stands and sticking by them.

On election night, the first line of Bush's victory speech was, "Thank you, New Hampshire." It was evident that Sununu, if he so desired, had a job in the new administration. Publicly, Sununu said he needed a job in private industry. With eight children and a $40,000 tuition bill, he told the *Washington Post*, he needed "to find a real job . . . . I would rather die an old engineer than an old politician." Privately, according to reports, he was more forthright, telling the president-elect which jobs were beneath his ambitions. "I have said it before," Sununu told the *Boston Globe*. "The only way I would go to Washington is if I could make a difference in something significant. There are just one or two jobs . . . and even those I would have to think awfully hard."

On November 17, 1988, Sununu got one of those jobs when Bush named him White House chief of staff for the incoming administration. Bush called Sununu, "a take-charge kind of guy; he's very active, very energetic, and I am very, you know, close to him personally." The president-elect went on to tell the Chicago Tribune, "John Sununu has the background and experience necessary to work not only with his former colleagues in the nation's statehouses, but also to build a constructive relationship with the U.S. Congress." The chief of staff oversees the more than 300 employes on the president's staff. More importantly, he controls access and the flow of information to the president. He is customarily the first key player to see the president each morning and the last to see him in the evening. The personality of the chief of staff—be he H.R. Haldeman, Hamilton Jordan, Donald Regan, or Howard Baker—often becomes the personality of the entire White House.

Sununu's appointment was praised by conservative leaders, while Democrats braced themselves for a tough, no-nonsense adversary. Admirers predicted that he would prove adept at juggling the many demands of the job and at dealing with problems quickly and decisively. Critics questioned whether he would be able to take a back seat to Bush and compromise with the Democrats who control the House and Senate. "Intellect is his Achilles' heel," Ned Helms, former director of New Hampshire's Department of Health and Human Services, told the *Los Angeles Times.* "His intellectual capacity has made him what he is. But at times his intellectual arrogance keeps him from getting beyond that. The first time he talks to [House Speaker] Jim Wright the way he's talked to some Democratic leaders in this state, he's going to be in big trouble." Wrote the *Boston Globe:* "Sununu makes Don Regan look like Mr. Rogers. We're talking tough! Where the Reagan administration preferred to leave its political enemies out in the cold, Sununu is the type to turn loose the dogs, holler for the floodlights, and flip the safety off the machine guns.... One month after his arrival, the Congress will be scratching its collective noggin: where did Bush get this guy?"

For his part, Sununu told the *Washington Post,* "I'm a pussycat," and predicted he would have little trouble handling the job. But even before heading to Washington, he hinted that he might set a limit on his term under Bush and was thinking of running for the U.S. Senate in 1990 or 1992. "I am not going down to Washington to be there forever," he told the *Boston Globe.* "I want to do this job for the vice-president, the president-elect, as long as he needs me to do this job.... We are keeping our home in New Hampshire and I intend to come back to New Hampshire."

Sources

Boston Globe, October 3, 1983; May 31, 1987; May 22, 1988; July 3, 1988; November 17, 1988; November 18, 1988; November 19, 1988; December 8, 1988.
Chicago Tribune, November 18, 1988.
Los Angeles Times, November 18, 1988; December 6, 1988.
Newsday, November 17, 1988; December 12, 1988.
Philadelphia Inquirer, November 17, 1988; November 28, 1988.
Time, January 27, 1986.
Washington Post, November 16, 1988; November 17, 1988.

—Sketch by Glen Macnow

Helen Suzman

AP/Wide World Photos

South African politician

Born November 7, 1917, Germiston, in Transvaal, South Africa; daughter of Samuel (in real estate) and Frieda Gavronsky; married Moses Meyer Suzman (a physician), 1937; children: two daughters. *Education:* University of Witwatersrand, B.Com.

Addresses: *Home*—49 Melville Rd., Hyde Park, Sandton, 2199 Transvaal, South Africa. *Office*—House of Assembly, Room 281, P.O. Box 15, Cape Town 8000, South Africa.

Career

University of Witwatersrand, Johannesburg, South Africa, lecturer in economic history, 1945–53; member of South African Parliament, 1953—; member of United Party, 1953–61, and Progressive Federal Party, 1961—.

Awards: Nominated for Nobel Peace Prize, three times; United Nations Award of Human Rights, 1978; New York Medal of Merit, 1980, International League for Human Rights Award, 1983; American Liberties Medallion, 1984; Moses Mendelssohn Award, Berlin Senate, 1988; honorary doctorates include Oxford University, 1973, Harvard University, 1976, Columbia University, 1977, Brandeis University, 1981, Denison University, 1982, and Jewish Theological Seminary, 1986.

Sidelights

For more than 35 years, Helen Suzman has waged a lonely but vehement battle against apartheid in her native republic of South Africa. Since her 1953 election to Parliament, Suzman has persevered in her crusade against the government-imposed system of racial segregation with little success and with the constant hostility of her peers in the whites-only House of Assembly. It is a campaign that has, paradoxically, earned her respect and admiration on the international scene but persecution and notoriety within her homeland.

On the surface, there is little to explain her determination against such great odds. As the well-to-do wife of a respected physician living in an affluent suburb of Johannesburg, she could easily spend her time on the golf course or at the bridge table, indulging in two of her favorite hobbies. Instead, she represents the upper-middle-class voting district of Houghton as the leading liberal member of her Progressive Federal Party. Greatly outnumbered within the House of Assembly, she is frequently the target of insults and injustice, obscene phone calls and death threats as she continues her well-publicized fight against a government that safeguards the liberty of a few at the expense of many.

Suzman was the daughter of Samuel and Frieda Gavronsky, Jewish Lithuanians who emigrated to South Africa in the early part of the century. Samuel settled in the Transvaal region of South Africa and prospered first at a butchering business then branched into real estate. Helen was born in 1917; her mother died two weeks later of postnatal complications. According to his daughter, Samuel was a sociable man, not rigidly religious, nor overly concerned with the issues of religious or racial persecution. In his household, Helen's only contact with blacks was with their servants. Years later, when she embarked on her liberal career, she reminded Samuel that blacks in South Africa were restricted in much the same way that Jews had been in the old country, but by then his property holdings were substantial, and he was unimpressed with his daughter's views. His opinion of her political career varied from amazed disbelief when she began, to concerned disapproval when she threatened to quit. Samuel loved his adopted country until he died in 1965. Helen credits him as the source of her impressive energy.

Suzman attended the Catholic Parktown Convent in Johannesburg for her early education. In 1934, at the age of 16, she enrolled at the University of Witwatersrand in Johannesburg to earn a Bachelor of Commerce degree. In 1937, she interrupted her education to marry Doctor Moses Meyer Suzman, an internist specializing in heart, blood, and nervous diseases. During World War II, Suzman completed her degree, gave birth to two daughters and worked for the Governor-General's War Fund and as a statistician for the War Supplies Board. Dr. Suzman served a Medical Corps commission at an Army hospital in Egypt and other distant posts.

In 1945, Suzman began an eight-year stint as a tutor and lecturer in economic history at the University of Witwatersrand. It was during this time that she became interested in politics and involved with the South African Institute of Race Relations. When then Prime Minister Smuts created the Commission of Inquiry into Laws Applying to Urban Blacks, Suzman was asked by the Institute to examine laws that limited the places blacks could live and work for the Commission. It was this study that awakened her social conscience and led her to become politically active. Smuts agreed with the Commission's recommendation to legalize the position of blacks in urban areas, and, along with his United Party, was promptly ousted from power. The more conservative Nationalist Party took control in 1948 and retains a majority in the House of Assembly to this day.

As the Nationalists enacted even more racially restrictive laws—the Group Areas Act, the Separate Amenities Act, the Job Reservation Act, the Prohibition of Mixed Marriages Act, the Immorality Act, the Ninety-Day Detention Act, and the Race Classification Act—Suzman organized a United Party branch among the Witwatersrand faculty and students. In 1952, Party leaders of Houghton, a relatively liberal voting district several miles north of Johannesburg whose homes commonly include tennis courts, swimming pools, and burglar alarm systems, invited Suzman to compete for the honor of representing them in the House of Assembly. At the urging of her husband, the petite professor won the nomination and was unopposed in the 1953 election for a five-year term. She has been a particularly annoying thorn in the side of the reigning party ever since.

The House of Assembly, South Africa's main law-making body, meets for about half of each year in Cape Town where Suzman maintains a small apartment. With more than 35 years of service, she is its senior front-bencher, a distinction that has earned her some measure of power, a good deal of notoriety, but little political clout. Her views are still very much in the minority, and aside from a few victories over the years, she can point to few personal political accomplishments. Yet her list of international awards and honorary degrees is impressive. She has been nominated for the Nobel Peace Prize three times.

During the fifties, Suzman observed the rise of the African National Congress and its declaration of a Freedom Charter, as well as the increasing popularity of Hendrik Verwoerd, inspiration for many of the restrictions that are now known as apartheid. Social conflict contributed to political unrest, and in 1961 the United Party split into rival factions with Suzman joining its more liberal members to form what is now known as the Progressive Federal Party. That same year, Prime Minister Verwoerd converted the Union of South Africa into a republic, withdrew from the British Commonwealth, and called for a general election. When the returns were counted, Suzman was the only member of her new party to retain a seat in Parliament. For the next thirteen years she was the solitary but sharply vocal member of the Progressive Party in the House of Assembly. For the following six years she was the only female in the 165-member House. Suzman remembered those years for the *New Yorker* as both her "heyday" and her "period of trial."

She was the darling of the English-language press and took full advantage of her forum. At five-feet-three, Suzman is hardly a commanding figure, yet she skillfully earns headlines by dressing in bright colors, employing a fearlessly razor-sharp tongue, and occasionally calling for "divisions" (a stand-up-and-be-counted procedure), which sometimes lands her alone on one side of the room while every other member crowds to the opposite side. If she cannot significantly affect legislation, she makes sure that its unjust application is properly reported in the public press. This is not as easy as it may seem, since the government bans the reporting of news that it deems "subversive." Suzman circumvents this ban by pestering her adversaries publicly in the House with repeated questions on sensitive topics. Parliamentary proceedings are exempt from the news ban.

"Parliament is the only place where laws can be repealed and the government can be held to account and information can be extracted," she told the *New Yorker.* "I've built up a body of statistics by asking questions—numbers of people detained, for instance, those prosecuted, those hanged. The press has found this valuable, and I've found the press valuable. I've been accused by the Nats [Nationalists] of getting more coverage than I've any right to. I say to them, 'You say something worth reporting and you'll get publicity, too.' When one Nat M.P. accused me of giving South Africa a bad image by the questions I asked in Parliament, I said to him, 'It's not my questions that give the country a bad image. It's your replies.'" Suzman has her principles and clings tenaciously to them. She listed them for the *Detroit Free Press:* "No discrimination on the statute books. Equal opportunities in education, training, jobs. Individual rights to be protected by a bill of rights. Equal franchise for everybody, irrespective of race, color, creed, whatever. That's it."

Stubborn adherence to these principles has earned her no small amount of abuse in Parliament. She's been called blind, unbalanced, subversive, a simpleton, an agent for revolution, and holier-than-thou. She's been rudely told to "Sit down," "Shut up," and "Go back to Moscow." But she gives as well as she gets. *Hansards,* the South African equivalent of the *Congressional Record,* quotes her using such adjectives as dense, dumb, desperate, disastrous, disgraceful, disgusting, distressing, malicious, and miserable when describing her fellow members of Parliament. "Dastardly" is a term she reserved for former Prime Minister P. W. Botha. In 1966, he publicly accused her of somehow being responsible for the assassination of then-Prime Minister Verwoerd. A reluctant apology from him did nothing to soften her outrage, and she has not spoken to him outside the House since. Several years ago, Botha suggested her presence at a peaceful anti-apartheid demonstration was bordering on the illegal. Suzman addressed Parliament and Botha himself in response: "The honorable prime minister has been trying to bully me for twenty-eight years, and he has not succeeded yet. I am not frightened of you. I never have been and I never will be. I think nothing of you."

Suzman's political specialty is law and order—detentions without trial, human rights, prisons, and prisoners. She is a frequent visitor of prisons and has intervened on behalf of prisoners' rights repeatedly over the years, righting some small wrongs, easing fears, and generally sounding the alert over inhumane conditions. She has met several times with Nelson R. Mandela, the African National Congress leader who has served 25 years of a life sentence in prison. Suzman sees Mandela as a key figure who could help end the injustices of apartheid nonviolently and makes no secret of her friendship with his activist wife, Winnie. In her end-of-session remarks to Parliament in 1979, the *New Yorker* reported that Suzman warned, "Increasing numbers of young blacks are going to become despairing. More and more of them will resort to change by violence, not because they want violence but because they see no other way to change the circumstances of their lives, which are filled with frustration and lack of opportunity."

Suzman is often invited to black funerals. One of South Africa's emergency regulations prohibits outdoor gatherings without permission, excluding sports events and funerals. Black funerals, especially one for an activist who has died at the hands of the government, may draw a crowd of fifty thousand and often include political speeches, freedom songs, and violent confrontations with police. Suzman's presence is accepted by the black population and is felt to have an inhibiting influence on police. Increasingly, however, she is finding herself rejected by both sides of the apartheid issue. White conservatives reject her as a radical. Radical blacks believe she isn't nearly radical enough. "I'm realistic enough to understand that things have moved beyond an old-time liberal like myself," she told *Vogue* magazine. "And I'm not about to change. I couldn't become a radical.... I'm the sort of person who likes to have reasonable solutions, and I think possibly things have gone beyond that."

An unreasonable solution, she believes, is the imposition by Western countries of economic sanctions on South Africa. It is an idea gaining momentum in the United States and is one of Suzman's worst fears. She wrote a rational, impassioned, and widely-quoted article for the *New York Times Magazine* in 1986 explaining her opposition to such measures. "Those who believe that a quick fix is likely to follow the imposition of sanctions, and that the Pretoria regime will collapse within a short time thereafter, are sadly misinformed," she wrote. "Far more likely is a retreat into a siege economy, more oppression and more violence. There will be a long, drawn-out confrontation between a well-armed military force shoring up the Government and a popular movement backed by the masses and using Irish Republican Army-type tactics in urban and rural areas. The latter strategy has already been put into effect."

A number of American companies have withdrawn from trade with the beleaguered country, taking with them, Suzman feels, any influence they could have had to help bring about change peacefully. "The moral outrage and desire for punitive action is something I understand very well," she warned, "but the reality that will come as a result of a grievously afflicted economy will not be seen by those living thousands of miles away. That reality, compounded by decades of unequal employment opportunities and oppression, is bleak beyond belief."

Her background in economics has led Suzman to believe that the most practical way to abolish apartheid and to achieve a nonracial democratic society in South Africa is through a healthy and expanding economy. She explained in her *New York Times Magazine* article: "The process of integrating blacks as skilled workers into such an economy would be expedited. Their economic muscle would then, through increased trade-union action, be a potent force not only in the workplace but also in the sociopolitical sphere." Suzman favors strike action and consumer boycotts by blacks as tools for change.

Many liberal white South Africans, and Suzman insists their ranks are increasing, feel the sting of world criticism sorely and are shocked and saddened to see many of their young people leaving the country. "I scarcely know a family that hasn't lost a child to emigration," Suzman told the *New Yorker*. Her own daughters now live abroad with their families, in London and Boston. Only occasionally pessimistic, Suzman continues to campaign for her principles, and points with pride to any examples of progress which occur within her native land. Her long-time friend and former member of Parliament, Harry Oppenheimer, wrote a tribute upon her 35th year in Parliament, which was published in the *New York Times:* "Today, every South African who travels abroad, even if he is not prepared to condemn his country is at least forced to apologize for her. This is no little matter for us who want to be able to feel proud of our country. But here again, as in so much else, we can look to Helen Suzman and draw comfort. Here is one South African known around the world, a great international figure, for whom none of us has to apologize. Here is the living proof that the struggle for a just society in South Africa is not a lost cause."

In 1987, Suzman was persuaded to run for her seat in Parliament "one more time" and was re-elected. "If things didn't keep happening within my own party," she told the *Detroit Free Press,* "I can assure you I would . . . get the hell out of it, and enjoy the last few years of my active life doing other things." Retirement plans include more time for travel, golf, bridge, and the writing of her memoirs.

Avocational Interests: Golf, swimming, fishing, bridge.

Sources

Christian Science Monitor, August 12, 1986; October 22, 1986.
Detroit Free Press, October 26, 1987.
New Yorker, April 20, 1987.
New York Times, August 7, 1986; May 11, 1988; September 4, 1988.
New York Times Magazine, August 3, 1986.
Reader's Digest, March, 1987.
Time, November 7, 1988.
Vogue, March, 1988.

—Sidelights by Sharon Rose

Margaret Thatcher

UPI/Bettmann Newsphotos

Prime minister of Great Britain

Full name, Margaret Hilda Roberts Thatcher; born October 13, 1925, in Grantham, Lincolnshire, England; daughter of Alfred (a grocer, local politician, and lay minister) and Beatrice Roberts; married Denis Thatcher (a businessman), December, 1951; children: Mark and Carol (twins). *Education:* Oxford University, B.Sc., 1947, M.A.; studied law in the early 1950s. *Politics:* Conservative. *Religion:* Methodist.

Addresses: *Home* and *office*—10 Downing St., London SW 1, England.

Career

Worked as a research chemist for two industrial firms near London, England, 1947–51; worked briefly as personal assistant to the director of the Joint Iron Council; ran unsuccessfully as Tory candidate for Parliament, 1950 and 1951; called to the bar, 1954; barrister, specializing in tax and patent law, 1954–61; member of Parliament (House of Commons) representing town of Finchley, beginning 1959; joint Parliamentary secretary to Ministry of Pensions and National Insurance, 1961–64; held a number of positions while Tories were in opposition, 1965–70, including "shadow" minister of power and "shadow" minister of education and science; secretary of state for education and science, 1970–74; named privy councillor and co-chairman of Women's National Commission, 1970; named opposition spokesperson for the environment, 1974; leader of Conservative Party, 1975—; opposition leader, 1975–79; prime minister and first lord of the treasury, 1979—.

Sidelights

As a girl, Margaret Hilda Thatcher lived over her father's grocery store in Grantham, England. Five decades later she was still living over the shop. Starting in 1979, though, the shop was No. 10 Downing Street in London, the residence of the prime minister and equivalent of the American White House. Even before Ronald Reagan left office in 1989, she was "the elder statesperson of the Western world," the first British prime minister in 160 years to win three consecutive terms and the longest serving English leader since Lord Liverpool, who governed 15 years in the early 19th century. As prime minister, Thatcher has neared her main political objective: "destroy socialism." The *Los Angeles Times* described "her apparent belief that socialism is oppressive and incompatible with the British character." That Britain's socialism was little more than an advanced model of the American welfare state didn't matter. Political commentator Anthony Bevins observed, "She's never seen an institution she doesn't want to bash with her handbag." Now, in her third term, Thatcher's crusade goes on. The *Los Angeles* Times added: "Thatcher's impatience is undiminished. Head thrust forward, purse in hand, she marches on, pursuing her crusade to put the 'great' back into Great Britain."

Thatcher became the 50th prime minister—a lineage going back more than 250 years—just five years after Conservative Party backbenchers (a term signifying Britain's minority party at any time) elected her their leader in a revolt against Edward Heath. Heath was blamed for losing to Labour the previous year when he called an election ostensibly "on the issue of who ruled Britain—the Government or the coal miners, who were on strike," according to the *New Yorker*. Ironically, it was Heath who led Thatcher, then a member of the House of Commons, into national politics, first making her his spokeswoman for energy policy while the party was out of power in 1967. When Heath and the Conservatives recaptured the House in 1970, she joined his cabinet as secretary of state for education and science.

In each of her three national elections, Thatcher capitalized successfully on external events. By early 1979, the Labour Party had governed for five years. The country was in a shambles. Chronic strikes crippled the nation. Hospitals and schools closed, fuel wasn't delivered, trash collection ceased. Even gravediggers were on strike. Nature also seemed to conspire against Britain, dumping more than a foot of snow in the worst Arctic storms of two decades. The English called it "The Winter of Their Discontent." Thatcher, according to biographer Allan Mayer, trumpeted, "The government has failed the nation. It has lost credibility and it is time for it to go." She easily won a three-way election.

Four years later "Mrs. Thatcher's War"—the Falkland Islands conflict with Argentina—seemed exactly the kind of quixotic cause (John Newshouse wrote in the *New Yorker*, "Thanks to her, the Falkland Islands, a worthless and costly appendage, remain British.") that rallied Britons not yet fully convinced of Thatcherism to give her another term. Then in 1987, already defending proposals to clear all American nuclear weapons out of Britain, Labour Party candidate Neil Kinnock told a television interviewer that the country's best defense against the Soviets was to use "all the resources you have got to make any occupation [of Britain] totally untenable," according to *Time* magazine. Within hours, the magazine reported, Thatcher was accusing Kinnock of raising "the white flag of surrender." She won 43 percent of the vote and a 101-seat majority in the 650-member House of Commons.

If Ronald Reagan was the Great Communicator, Thatcher became known as the Great Dismantler. Her Winter of Discontent victory in 1979 gave her a mandate to begin scrapping Britain's socialist infrastructure. The first fight was against the unions. Unlike their weak American cousins, British unions evolved into a direct rival for institutional power with the government. Newhouse wrote in the *New Yorker*, "By the spring of 1979, when she arrived in office, the unions were thought to be a more potent force than government." Thatcher didn't care. Laws were passed curtailing the powers of the unions to strike and picket. The steelworkers fell in 1980; the coal miners in 1985, after a traumatic one-year struggle; and the teachers in 1986. Some attributed Thatcher's triumphs simply to the unions losing influence in a weakened economy. Still, The Chicago Tribune reported that 30 million working days were lost to strikes in 1979, compared to barely one million by 1987.

Next came Thatcher's sale of state-owned industries, nearly 40 percent of them. Among the concerns peddled to private buyers: British Gas, British Airways, Jaguar, British Telecom, and Rolls Royce. The divestitures added $29 billion to the national treasury. It also turned many ordinary Britons, who entered the stock market for the first time, into little capitalists. Stock ownership has tripled since 1979. More importantly, at least politically, Thatcher's Tory government began selling apartments in municipally controlled buildings to the tenants. Not only does that reduce the size of the government apparatus still further, but the residents of the apartments are usually solid Labour voters who are being given, so the theory goes, their first taste of capitalism and liking it. And, since the old system allowed many local Labour Parties to control the leasing and thus the tenants' lives, it removes one more layer separating the people from Thatcher.

The most tangible result of all those programs was the taming of inflation. By Thatcher's third term, the inflation rate had dropped from 18 to four percent. Real wages had risen 17 percent. But there has also been a human cost: unemployment. Manufacturing in Britain collapsed. London and most of southern England remained unaffected, a sort of haven for British Yuppies. In the industrial north, still Labour country, unemployment in inner cities stands in the double figures. Some young people there have never held a job. Newhouse wrote in the *New Yorker* that the region "by and large, is in bad shape." Nationwide there were 3.1 million jobless by 1987 representing more than 11 percent of the workforce. *U.S. News & World Report* estimated more than 2 million jobs lost to foreign markets from steel, shipbuilding, coal mining, and auto production.

Jane Kramer wrote in the *New Yorker:* "Mrs. Thatcher rarely talks to [constituents] about the punishing monetary strategies of her administration, which are keeping three and a half million people out of work [by 1983] for the sake of stable prices at the supermarket . . . . It is a human problem and involves a certain unwillingness to comprehend that working people are not a raw material, like oil or iron, that can be put away for five years and taken out again when markets change." In the same magazine three years later, John Newhouse stated: "Her policies are blamed for Britain's having become a net importer of manufactured goods—for the first time since the days of Henry VIII . . . . The average Briton, the International Monetary Fund says, is poorer today than the average Italian."

That mix of inefficient, outmoded, and strike-prone industries with rampant unemployment was dubbed the "British Disease." The malaise has seen a concurrent drop in social services. The once-vaunted National Health Service is critically ill. Some patients hoping for elective surgery (Time magazine estimates 700,000 country-wide) have showed up at their government-scheduled appointments—a year early. Thatcher announced plans to revamp the massive bureaucracy in early 1989, but critics accuse her "of trying to make the system more closely resemble health care in the United States, which is perceived by many Britons as a formula for high-cost inequitable treatment," according to the *New York Times.*

Thatcher and Reagan, during their separate tenures, had more than just the traditional "special relationship" between the United States and Britain. The *New Yorker* wrote that "she feels very comfortable in America, and is said by people around her to prefer it to other places outside Britain." Their careers as Western leaders, besides the fact of having served during the same era, bear striking similarities. Both are unashamed free enterprise advocates, and like Reagan, Thatcher has been able to portray herself as an outsider even as she controls the government. One associate told the *Chicago Tribune:* "She will say, 'Do you know what the government's done now?' She sees it as them, not us."

On closer inspection, though, differences between the two leaders surface. The *New Republic* reported: "In fact, the only thing they share is conservatism. She's a detail person, lacking in charisma, warmth, and even self-confidence . . . . She refuses to put jokes into speeches, claiming this is unbecoming to a prime minister." Even on economics, their approach is different. Thatcher has yet to significantly lower taxes. In her household model of national economics, Thatcher would never cut out a tax until the rest of the budget was balanced. The basic tax rate on income fell just two points to 25 percent during her first eight years in office.

And Thatcher, with no formal grounding, evolved into a formidable expert in foreign affairs. She developed a surprisingly strong relationship with Soviet leader Mikhail Gorbachev, after meeting in 1984 in London—four years before Reagan managed a successful summit with the Soviet leader. Part of her appeal to Gorbachev, several observers noted, may have been his recognition of the unique access—Thatcher would call it influence—she had with Reagan. For example, in 1984 she rushed to Washington when it appeared Reagan might abandon the Anti-Ballistic Missile Treaty because it could slow work on his Star Wars system, according to the *Los Angeles Times.* After a presentation over lunch, she got the commitment she was looking for.

Thatcher isn't the first woman to lead a modern country—witness Israel's Golda Meir or India's Indira Gandhi. She is, though, the first to lead a major Western power. Thatcherism, though, has never made room for explicit feminism. A woman who knows Thatcher told the *New Yorker* in 1986: "She is no feminist. When Justice Sandra Day O'Connor visited her recently and said how much the women of America admired her, Mrs. T. turned all gloomy. It wasn't what she wanted to hear." In his biography of Thatcher, Allan Mayer wrote simply, "In Margaret Thatcher's view, her sex is an irrelevancy, and she is annoyed by people who make too much of a fuss over it."

Britain's first woman Prime Minister has also resulted in the first First Husband: Denis Thatcher, a retired businessman and every bit the clubby British insider that his wife is not. Her mother was a housewife, her father a lay Methodist minister, grocer, and successful local politician in the Lincolnshire region 100 miles north of London. Before entering local politics in the 1950s, Thatcher worked as a research chemist and later as a tax lawyer. The couple has two children, twins, Carol and Mark, born in 1953. Carol stops at No. 10 Downing for dinner on occasion. And the *Los Angeles Times* reported that when callers to Carol's late-night radio talk show dried up, Thatcher phoned in to keep the program rolling. When she is accused of being all-iron, supporters point to the obvious concern she showed for Mark when he became lost for six days in the vast Sahara Desert during the 1982 Paris-to-Dakar automobile rally. And there was her despair over the Falkland casualties, of which she says now: "We lost 255 of our best young men. I felt every one." Critics won't admit to seeing that side of her. One told the *Chicago Tribune*, "She's terrified of compassion."

Aides and colleagues describe Thatcher as a workaholic, who only accepts a portion of her $84,000 yearly salary. She gets by on three to four hours of sleep a night and still insists on fixing breakfasts and dinners (shepherd's pie or coronation chicken) for Denis Thatcher and herself. She has been known to interrupt a late-afternoon briefing to run out to buy bacon for the next morning's breakfast. Her day starts, according to the New Yorker, "at 6 a.m., when she is awakened by a brief radio news report, followed by another program called 'Farming Today,' from which she picks up bits of information to turn into questions for unfortunate aides who don't listen to the program and, in any case, know very little about agriculture."

English polls have doggedly shown that Britons don't particularly like Thatcher. She inspires terror and maybe respect rather than fondness. One former Cabinet minister told the *Chicago Tribune*: "I like her, but we had some terrible rows. There were times I got so mad at her, I wanted to hit her." She is a self-described "conviction politician," asking the *New Yorker*, "Do you think you would ever have heard of Christianity if the Apostles had gone out and said, 'I believe in consensus?'" She makes choices, not compromises. Ray Hattersley, deputy leader of the Labor Party, told the *Tribune* that Thatcher has "the certainty of the second-rate. While I do not respect her as a human being, that is a very substantial piece of armor. The thought that she might not be right has never crossed Mrs. Thatcher's mind. It is a strength in a politician."

Thatcher has always been the kind of leader to inspire imaginative nicknames, starting with "Mrs. Thatcher, milk snatcher" when as Education Secretary in 1970 she proposed that schoolchildren pay for their own milk. A sampling of others: "Attila the Hen," "Aunt Maggie," "Sweetie" from her husband, "Mrs. T." from aides, "The Westminster Ripper," the "Plutonium Blonde," and perhaps the most lasting, ironically from a Soviet newspaper, "The Iron Lady." In the rowdy House of Commons sessions, cries of "Ditch the bitch" often erupted from the Labor benches before she became Prime Minister. One former official of her government told the *New Yorker*: "Many say maybe she's what we deserve. The nanny tradition dies hard."

The agenda for her third term is more of the same. More sales of public housing to tenants. More choices for parents in the schools for their children. And more tinkering with the National Health Service. Whether the Thatcher revolution will survive without Thatcher is still open to question. Even one Tory party official told the *New Yorker*: "The next leader will make a course correction of 10 to 15 degrees back to where we were. He will have to. At best, he'll be a lesser version of her." No one is being groomed as a likely successor. Days after winning her third term, Thatcher told *Time*: "I have no wish to retire for a very long time. I am still bursting with energy." And to the *Los Angeles Times* she added: "I hope to go on and on. There is so much still to do."

Sources

Books

Mayer, Allan J., *Madam Prime Minister*, Newsweek Books, 1979.

Wapshott, Nicholas, and George Brock, *Thatcher*, Macdonald, 1983.

Periodicals

Business Week, January 17, 1983; May 25, 1987; March 28, 1988.

Chicago Tribune, April 19, 1987; May 17, 1987; May 18, 1987.

Christian Science Monitor, December 29, 1959; December 31, 1971.

Forbes, February 27, 1984.

Fortune, May 9, 1988.

Guardian (Manchester), November 2, 1971.

Harper's, December, 1979.

Los Angeles Times, May 26, 1987.

Maclean's, May 23, 1984; June 20, 1983; October 10, 1983.

National Review, July 22, 1983; November 25, 1983.

New Republic, June 22, 1987.

Newsweek, May 14, 1979; May 16, 1983; May 30, 1983; June 20, 1983; June 22, 1987.

New Yorker, September 5, 1983; February 10, 1986.

New York Times, September 18, 1975; June 10, 1983; June 2, 1987; February 1, 1989.

New York Times Magazine, June 1, 1975.

Observer (London), February 16, 1975.

Parade, July 13, 1986.

People, December 24, 1979; December 27, 1982.

Reader's Digest, April, 1982; October, 1983; November 1987.

Time, January 24, 1983; June 20, 1983; October 24, 1983; January 2, 1984; February 13, 1984; June 22, 1987.

Times (London), June 1, 1987.

U.S. News & World Report, May 23, 1983; May 30, 1983; June 20, 1983; March 19, 1984; April 6, 1987; June 22, 1987.

Washington Post, October 10, 1987.

—*Sidelights by Harvey Dickson*

Isiah Thomas

UPI/Bettmann Newsphotos

Professional basketball player

Full name, Isiah Lord Thomas III; born April 30, 1961, in Chicago, Ill.; son of Isiah Lord II (a plant foreman and janitor) and Mary (a civil service employee) Thomas; married Lynn Kendall, 1985; children: Joshua Isiah. *Education:* Indiana University, bachelor's degree, 1987.

Addresses: *Home*—Bloomfield Hills, Mich. *Office*—Detroit Pistons, The Palace of Auburn Hills, 3777 Lapeer Rd., Auburn Hills, Mich. 48057.

Career

Professional basketball player with Detroit Pistons, 1981—. Member of U.S. Olympic basketball team, 1980; vice-president of National Basketball Association Players Association, 1986—.

Awards: Named to NBA All-Star Team, 1982–1988; named All-Star Game Most Valuable Player, 1984 and 1986.

Sidelights

I'm in love with basketball," Isiah Thomas once told *Sports Illustrated.* "It's my release. It's my outlet. If I get mad, I go shoot. It's my freedom. It's my security. It's my drug; it's my high. It's my nowhere. When I'm playing, I'm nowhere. Nothing else exists. Nothing else matters." Since entering the National Basketball Association in 1981, Isiah Thomas's love for the game—and his special talent—has been apparent. His disarming smile and warm personality have made him one of the league's most popular players, while his skills have made him "the most perfect point guard in the game today," as former Milwaukee Bucks coach Don Nelson said to *Sports Illustrated.* Thomas averaged an impressive 20.5 points per game over his first seven seasons, broke the league record for assists, and has been credited with pushing a shaky Detroit Pistons franchise to the top of the NBA in both record and attendance. "I'm just lucky I've had the opportunity," Thomas told *Jet* magazine. "I'm living the dream I had since I was a little boy. How many kids, especially kids who grew up as poor as I did, ever live to see their dreams come true?"

Isiah Lord Thomas III grew up in the heart of Chicago's West Side ghetto, the youngest of seven boys and two girls born to Mary and Isiah Thomas II. "He was well behaved, but spoiled," Mary Thomas told *Sports Illustrated.* "He's still like that, spoiled rotten—by me and his brothers. They try to put the blame on me, and I can't say I didn't treat him special. He was the baby. He got special attention." Father Isiah II was a plant supervisor who pushed his children to read, barred them from watching anything but educational television, and lectured them to stick together and protect one another. When Isiah III was an infant, his father lost his job as a supervisor at International Harvester and could find work only as a janitor—at a much reduced rate of pay. Eventually, he and Mary Thomas separated.

Mary was the family disciplinarian who required her children to be home by the time the street lights came on. Born a Baptist, she turned the family toward Catholicism before Isiah was born and thus came under the wing of the local church, Our Lady of Sorrows, and its schools. Fearlessly protective of her family, there was little that Mary Thomas would not do to shield her children from the gangs that prowled the West Side streets. Once, when Isiah was six, a dozen members of a menacing street gang known as the Vice Lords knocked on the family's front door looking for recruits among the seven Thomas boys. Mary Thomas chased them away with a shotgun, and they never returned. For the next few years, the Thomas children had the run of the neighborhood, free of molestation by the gangs.

That allowed Isiah to spend his time playing basketball at tiny Gladys Park, next to Chicago's Eisenhower Expressway. "Go anywhere on the West Side and say, 'Meet me at the court,' and they'd know what you were talking about," Thomas told *Sports Illustrated.* "That's where I really learned to play. There were some basketball players there. You could always get a game there. Any time of day, any time of night. Me and my brothers used to go over there with snow shovels in the winter so we could play."

Isiah Thomas goes up for a basket as his good friend Earvin "Magic" Johnson of the Los Angeles Lakers looks on. UPI/Bettmann Newsphotos.

When Isiah was 12, the street gangs began moving in more ferociously, so Mary Thomas moved her family five miles west to Menard Avenue. "Those were probably the worst times as a kid," Thomas recalled in Sports Illustrated. "We very rarely had heat. We had an oil furnace but no money to buy oil. In the winter, it was always cold, and you had to sleep all the time with your clothes on. Everything broke down in the house once we bought it. The staircase was falling down. The plumbing didn't work. I mean everything was a disaster." Isiah slept in the closet between his brothers' and sisters' rooms, or on the ironing board in the hall. The family lived on food donated to the church. Isiah took to stealing classmates' lunches. He was thrown out of one school for slapping a girl across the face.

His idol at the time was brother Larry, who was nine years older. Larry had become a heroin dealer and pimp, and Isiah saw it as a way out of poverty. "I'd go in and try on Larry's clothes. I'd walk like him, talk like him," Thomas told *Sports Illustrated.* "The street was the game. The con, shooting dice, making a living, hustling. I knew how to hustle at an early age." When Larry discovered his youngest brother emulating him, he sat Isiah down, lectured him on the ways of the street, and told him that he was the last family hope to make it big in professional sports. The first three with real athletic talent had already failed. The oldest, Lord Henry, had turned to heroin and become an addict. The second, Gregory, struggled with alcohol. And Larry, a college star, suffered an ankle injury during a professional tryout.

Isiah, the youngest, was regarded as the most talented brother. When he was three, he was performing in halftime shows at his brothers' basketball games. After his early schoolboy games, his brothers would critique his performance and work to improve him, sometimes until 2 A.M. He was the one, the brothers decided, who would lead the family out of poverty. The brothers took their mission to St. Joseph High School, a Christian Brothers school in a white Chicago suburb. They convinced the school's basketball coach, Gene Pingatore, to give Isiah financial aid so he could enroll. Isiah commuted three hours each day, taking three buses each way and arriving home long after dark. He struggled with grades initially and had to have his undisciplined playing style toned down, but by his junior year, playing with more restraint, he led St. Joseph to a second-place finish in the state high school championship tournament. And in his final year he was one of the most coveted prospects in the nation.

Rick Majerus, who was then an assistant coach at Marquette University, was one of dozens who recruited Thomas. "What I remember most was his authenticity," Majerus told the *Los Angeles Times.* "He was a really genuine person. The neighborhood was extraordinarily tough. I used to say they addressed the arrest warrants to 'Occupant.' Everybody was under arrest. There was garbage strewn everywhere, a typical ghetto.... You'd go in there and here was this young guy who's got this big smile. He was unbelievably optimistic for someone who had gone through all the misfortune that had occurred in his family. He was very focused."

Thomas's family wanted him to stay home and attend DePaul, but he chose to go to Indiana. He made All-Big Ten his freshman year, and was everyone's All-American as a sophomore, the year he took Indiana to the NCAA title. But his relationship with volatile Indiana coach Bob Knight was filled with conflict and turmoil. In 1981, on the advice of his friend Magic Johnson, he decided to leave Indiana and apply for the NBA draft. He was selected second, behind Mark Aguirre, by the Detroit Pistons, at the time one of the NBA's sad-sack organizations. The Pistons had won only 37 of their 164 games the previous two seasons. Though he was only 19 years old, Thomas was burdened with rescuing the NBA's longest losing team. A *Detroit News* headline hailed him as "Isiah The Savior." Pistons season ticket sales jumped 50 percent. The Pistons gave him a four-year, $1.6 million contract and began talking about a trip to the NBA Finals. Asked at the time about the high expectations, Thomas told the *Boston Globe:* "It doesn't bother me. I can't play basketball or live the way they want me to. So I have to set my own goals and objectives."

By all accounts, his rookie season was a success. The Pistons improved from 21 wins to 39. Thomas won a starting place on the All-Star team. He scored an average of 17 points a game and led his team in assists and steals. "Sparkle, glitter, pizzazz—those words come to mind when I think of Isiah Thomas," Philadelphia 76ers general manager Pat Williams told the *Boston Globe.* "Incandescence and joie de vivre come to mind, too. There is just a certain joy he radiates on the court."

Thomas improved his second season, averaging nearly 23 points and eight assists a game, but the Pistons won just 37 of 82 games. Indeed, through his first four years, Thomas consistently outplayed his teammates. He was the first player in league history to be voted to the All-Star team his first five seasons, and in 1984 and again in 1986 his performances in the All-Star game were so spectacular that he was named the contest's Most Valuable Player. During the 1984 playoffs, Thomas scored a remarkable 16 points in 94 seconds to singlehandedly send a game into overtime. In the 1984–85 season he set what was then a league record for assists. Soon after that, the Pistons tore up his contract and signed him to a 10-year, $12 million deal that was intended to keep him on the team for the rest of his career.

But as the Pistons failed to become a serious contender, Thomas grew depressed over that career. Late in 1985, as his team lost 15 of 16 games, Thomas briefly considered retiring or asking the Pistons to trade him. The turnaround came when Detroit hired Chuck Daly to coach the team. Daly slowed down the Pistons' offense and forced Thomas to play within the system. "I knew what a talent he was," Daly told the *Los Angeles Times.* "He's such a competitor. He wanted to win so bad it obscured his judgment at times. He'll go one on five. He thinks he can score on them, and he does a lot of times."

"How many kids, especially kids who grew up as poor as I did, ever live to see their dreams come true?"

Under Daly, and led by Thomas, the Pistons improved each season. In the 1987 playoffs, they came within seconds of eliminating the defending champions, the Boston Celtics. But in what should have been Thomas's finest moment, he earned the label of a choker. With Detroit leading by a point, and five seconds left in Game 5 of the Eastern Conference finals, Celtics star Larry Bird stole Thomas' inbound pass and set up a layup that cost the Pistons the game and, as it turned out, the series. Five days later, after Detroit's loss in Game 7, Thomas's dubious judgment earned him an even more damning label—that of a racist and a whiner. He suggested that Bird was overrated and stated that if Bird were black, he'd be "just another good guy."

The backlash among media and fans was immediate. Thomas apologized to Bird at a press conference, but he had seriously damaged his image. Bob Ryan, the respected *Boston Globe* writer, called Thomas a "megalomaniac" and suggested he "find himself a shrink to help Isiah relieve himself of the demon that lurks within." Wrote *Newsday*, "It would be hard to imagine an athlete confronting defeat with less class and dignity than Isiah displayed." The remarks particularly stung Thomas because, since coming to Detroit, he had tried hard to become not just a solid basketball player but a solid citizen. He threw himself into community service work, making anti-drug commercials and speeches. He worked with Detroit Mayor Coleman Young in 1986 to organize a "No Crime Day," an idea he conceived and promoted. Although there were certainly crimes committed on that day, Thomas told *Sports Illustrated:* "We accomplished the things we really wanted to. There were masses of people who organized themselves in block clubs and neighborhoods and communities to try to prevent crime. That's what we really wanted to do—raise people's consciousness."

Thomas viewed the 1987–88 season as an opportunity to rebuild his image. He had a typically solid season, averaging close to 20 points a game. The Pistons won 54 regular season games and breezed past the Washington Bullets, Chicago Bulls, and Celtics to reach the NBA Finals for the first time in franchise history. Before the first game against the defending champions, the Los Angeles Lakers, Thomas told the *Los Angeles Times:* "I'm not on a mission or anything. This is really for peace of mind. Seven years I've waited for a chance to win the championship. I want to get this disease out of my body." Thomas's play in the series was spectacular. He injured his back in Game 2 and severely sprained his ankle in Game 6. Still, he averaged 19.7 points per game during the seven-game series, including a phenomenal performance in Game 6, in which he scored 43 points—including a record 25 points in one quarter. In the end, it wasn't enough. The Lakers won the series, four games to three. But Thomas's effort was regarded as heroic. "He was out of this world," wrote *Los Angeles Times* columnist Mike Downey. "He was I.T., the extra-terrestrial. He was making shots off the wrong foot, off the glass, off the wall."

So Thomas entered his eighth season still seeking a championship. But he remains recognized as one of the game's truly great players. Daly, his coach, compared watching Thomas to watching Julius Erving a decade ago. "I used to sit out there and look around at the crowd and say, 'I hope these people know what they're seeing,'" Daly told the *Philadelphia Inquirer.* "'I hope they know they will never see this again.' I'm doing that again, watching Isiah: I hope these people understand that they will never see that move again." Thomas himself told the *Chicago Tribune:* "When people talk about great guards today, they compare them to Bob Cousy and Nate Archibald. But when I'm retired, I'd like for people to be comparing them to Isiah."

Sources

Boston Globe, November 1, 1981; April 26, 1985; June 7, 1987.
Chicago Tribune, February 8, 1987.
Detroit Free Press, April 25, 1987; April 28, 1987.
Detroit News, October 11, 1981.
Los Angeles Daily News, June 19, 1988.
Los Angeles Herald Examiner, June 6, 1987.
Los Angeles Times, February 10, 1986; June 7, 1988; June 11, 1988; June 20, 1988.
Newsday, June 2, 1987; May 30, 1988.
Philadelphia Daily News, June 15, 1988.
Philadelphia Inquirer, June 7, 1988.
Sports Illustrated, January 19, 1987; May 18, 1987.

—Sketch by Glen Macnow

Tiffany

AP/Wide World Photos

Pop singer

Full name, Tiffany Renee Darwish; born October 2, 1972, in Norwalk, Calif.; daughter of Jim Darwish (a pilot) and Janie Christine Williams. *Education:* Attended high school in Norwalk, Calif.; studies with a tutor while on tour.

Addresses: *Home*—La Mirada, Calif. *Office*—c/o MCA Records, 70 Universal City Plaza, Third Floor, Universal City, Calif. 91607; and c/o Winterland Fan Asylum, 13659 Victory Blvd., Van Nuys, Calif. 91401.

Career

Began singing publicly at age nine with country-western bands in Norwalk, Calif.; signed a contract with MCA Records, 1987, and recorded her first album; has performed in concert throughout North America, Europe, and Japan; has appeared on television programs, including "The Tonight Show" and "Entertainment Tonight."

Sidelights

I don't want anyone to think I'm controlled," Tiffany Darwish declared. "I'm not. I'm the only one who can tell you when I can and can't work, what I will and will not do. There's not some drill sergeant ordering me around." Speaking to the *Detroit Free Press* via a cellular phone in a limousine that was taking her to the Los Angeles International Airport, the 17-year old pop singer sighed. She was once again on The Topic, the dreaded line of questioning that dogged her throughout 1988. The question—Who's in charge of Tiffany?

It was a valid concern. In 1987, seemingly out of nowhere, the young singer had popped into shopping malls, singing to the accompaniment of backing tapes to shoppers clutching bags from the Gap and Sibley's Shoes. The stench of prefab contrivance was heavy in the air. This'll never work, said the critics. But because of that mall tour, Tiffany's debut album sold more than five million copies and became the first No. 1 record by a teenager since Stevie Wonder did the same at age 13 in 1963. She also had three Top 10 singles, including remakes of Tommy James's "I Think We're Alone Now" and the Beatles' "I Saw Her Standing There," songs Tiffany claims she wasn't familiar with until she recorded them.

But the media world doesn't give teen stars a whole lot of respect. Visions of David Cassidy, Donny Osmond, Leif Garrett, Shaun Cassidy, and all those Phil Spector-produced singers come to mind. They were young, modestly talented performers who were jerked, pulled, and hyped towards success by calculating businessmen. Tiffany certainly has the svengali quotient in manager George Tobin. A onetime Motown Records staffer, he found Tiffany, at age 12, singing with a country band in Southern California.

He once told *Rolling Stone* that "Tiffany is signed to me, 100 percent to *me*." And he told *Life* magazine that "She *is* the girl next door. I've done nothing to change her. My role is to make sure nothing does."

That sounded like a frightening amount of control. And things got scarier in early 1988, when Tiffany filed for emancipation from her mother's custody. "My mother was not making smart career moves," Tiffany told *Rolling Stone*. But there were many who felt this move was engineered by Tobin. A compromise was reached by the California courts: Tiffany controlled the finances, and her mom was still her legal guardian, though the star—who would get lump-sum payments of her previous earnings when she turns 18, 21, and 25—continued to live with her paternal grandmother in Norwalk, Calif. "I like the way it's done," she told the *Orange County Register*, "because it keeps me working now."

But as her first full-scale tour of arenas and auditoriums began in the summer of 1988, Tiffany was staying away from the subject. "Later on," she told the *Detroit Free Press*, "I'll come out with the whole thing. Right now, it's not the time to comment." She added, acknowledging the great deal of concern about her welfare: "I'm fine. I'm not working too hard. I work at my own pace. George says to me, 'This is what we can do. Do you want to do this?' No one can force me to do anything.... And I promise—I won't get mentally sick or physically sick. Neither is good, especially if you're trying to hold on to a long career."

Tiffany's career was actually well under way before she started having hit records. Her parents—Jim, a small-aircraft pilot, and Janie Darwish—divorced when Tiffany was two. It was her stepfather, Dan Williams, who set up her first performance at age nine: a handful of songs with a band at a local barbeque. Within three years, she was singing with country bands around the Los Angeles area. "I wanted to get something started from that time on," she told the *Detroit Free Press*. "I've been working for my career from that age. It's not like I've just begun."

Things got rolling for her in 1981, when Tiffany agreed to sing on a demo tape by a local songwriter. The session took place in Tobin's North Hollywood studio, where he was producing a Smokey Robinson album. One of his assistants suggested that Tobin give a listen to the girl singing in the next room, and he was hooked. "I was enthralled by her voice," Tobin told *Rolling Stone*. "It was like taffy—you could pull it anywhere. In under 10 minutes, I decided to sign her. I had a dream of where she could go.... I got really obsessed with her. I just kept thinking that I had to do something with her."

Tobin kept in close contact, helping Tiffany and her mother look for a manager so that he could begin producing records for her. In 1986, Tobin got tired of searching; he decided to manage Tiffany himself and signed a seven-album exclusive production and management contract that gave him complete control of any records, videos, and performances by Tiffany during that period. "I learned a lot working at Motown," Tobin explained to *Rolling Stone* when asked about the possibility of excessive control.

The stench of prefab contrivance was heavy in the air. This'll never work, said the critics.

The quarrels between Tobin and Tiffany's mother started early, according to the *Rolling Stone* feature. Mom wanted Tiffany to be a straight country singer; Tobin had his eye on the more lucrative pop market. "Her mother did think covering a Beatles song was sacrilegious, so we just never sent those tapes home," Tobin said. "But her mother doesn't get involved. The family has decided that I manage the act." The Tobin-Tiffany deal also meant that record companies would sign a contract with George Tobin Productions, which would, in effect, lease them the Tiffany material. The only problem was that, early on, no one was biting. "Teen acts had burned so many record companies in the past that they were afraid," Brad Schmidt, Tobin's partner, told the *Detroit Free Press*. "They were all saying that they didn't know how to promote her."

So Tobin played hardball. He took Tiffany to the hotel room of Arista Records chief Clive Davis so that she could perform live for him. He barged in on countless executives and badgered others with phone calls. The persistence paid off; MCA signed a $150,000 deal for Tiffany's first album in early 1987. "The main reason I went with MCA is because their offices are one mile from my office," Tobin told *Rolling Stone*. "If I want to get something done, I can drive down there and block their cars on their driveway with my car, which I have done, and not let them out until it's settled."

It took a while to settle Tiffany into a niche into the marketplace, however. While she went about the business of being a teenager—going to malls, talking on the phone, and watching TV, according to a *Life* magazine profile—Tobin and MCA mulled over marketing plans while her album sat in record stores, unable to interest buyers or radio programmers. MCA's own promotion department, in fact, told Tobin that Tiffany's record didn't have the hit song necessary to garner attention. "To market a 14 or 15-year-old to the record industry was a tough sell," Larry Solters, MCA's vice president of artist development told *Advertising Age.* "Do we ignore how old she is? Do we convey the image of 15 or make her look older? At first we didn't know what to do." There was even a photo session in which Tiffany was made up to look older; Tobin has made several attempts to buy back those photos.

The "Beautiful You" shopping mall tour idea was a bolt from the blue for Solters and Tobin. It came from simple deduction. Who's likely to buy an album by a teenager? they asked. Other teenagers. Where do you find teenagers? At shopping malls! It was a novel idea for the music industry, but not for the marketing world. Manufacturers like the Campbell Soup Co., Clairol, and General Foods had staged successful promotions in which they gave away free samples. So MCA was going to give away a free sample of Tiffany. "It was the first time a record company tried it," Phil Rosenthal of the Miami-based Shopping Center Network, which set up the tour, told *Advertising Age.* "They've been in the marketing Dark Ages, but it took someone more aggressive and creative to give it a try. Now we're negotiating with other record companies and a couple of movie companies."

Tiffany wasn't an immediate smash in the malls, however. The tour, which started in July 1987, drew tiny crowds at first, and, as Tiffany told *Rolling Stone,* "people were laughing and giving me weird reactions." That was O.K., because it was odd for her, too. "I was singing to backing tracks," she told the *Detroit Free Press,* "and when the guitar solo came on, I was left filling in that time. When you have a live band, people can look at the guitar player, but in that situation, all people had to look at was me." But as the tour went on, the crowds got bigger, and scores of teenagers began calling their favorite radio stations and requesting Tiffany music. By the time the tour hit Salt Lake City in September 1987, an overflow crowd of more than 4,000 packed the stagefront.

Tiffany's album soared up the charts after that, as did her single. "I Think We're Alone Now" knocked Michael Jackson out of the No. 1 spot. Tours of Europe and Japan boosted album sales there; in Japan, she even starred in a TV commercial for an M&Ms-like candy. In America, her story was splashed across the pages of everything from *People* to *Sixteen.*

Her success also opened the doors of record companies to other teen artists. Following in her wake were: Debbie Gibson, an accomplished 17-year-old from Long Island who composed most of her own material; Glenn Medeiros, a 17-year-old from Hawaii who had a Top 20 hit with "Never Gonna Change My Love for You"; 14-year-old Shanice Wilson; and Tracie Spencer, the 12-year-old winner of the TV talent contest "Star Search." "Kids buy kids," co-manager Schmidt told the *Detroit Free Press.* "The record companies are starting to be open to the possibility of there being a youth market out there. They're trying to find the best of the talent out there that will accommodate that." Added Tom Arndt, associate editor of *Tiger Beat,* a teen-oriented magazine, "A lot of kids are surprised to hear that Tiffany and Debbie Gibson are as young as they are."

Tiffany, meanwhile, tried to keep the perils of success at bay. She toured with a tutor—27-year-old Craig Yamek, who doubled as the drummer in her band—to keep up with her studies. She told *Life* that her friends still "don't care if they come over and I'm lying in bed." And, she contended, she was still able to hang out, just like in the pre-star days. "I went to Knot's Berry Farm the other day," she told the *Detroit Free Press.* "Not a lot of people recognized me. Most seemed to be thinking, 'That looks like Tiffany, but why would she be here by herself, with just friends, no bodyguards or anything?' Even if they do ask for autographs, they've always been nice people."

Approaching the end of 1988, Tiffany and Tobin were already mulling over her next album. Tobin had recorded 48 songs for the first record, but they kept working up new music, including a remake of the Young Rascals' "I Ain't Gonna Eat Out My Heart Anymore," another of those oldies that was new to Tiffany. A new record could come out at any time, but as co-manager Schmidt told the *Free Press,* "this one is so hot, we're just waiting for it to cool down." So Tiffany passed the time by touring and singing to her young fans. And she told all the adults not to worry, that she was perfectly happy with the way things were going. "This is my dream," she told *Advertising Age.* "I've never thought of anything else, and now that it's happening, it's almost too overwhelming, but it's great." And, she told the *Orange County Register,* "I've learned to enjoy my success now. It's not always going to be like this, so I'm making the best of it."

Discography

Tiffany (includes "I Think We're Alone Now," "Could've Been," and "I Saw Him Standing There"), MCA, 1987.

Sources

Advertising Age, June 6, 1988.
Detroit Free Press, December 4, 1987; July 29, 1988.
Life, May, 1988.
Los Angeles Herald Examiner, July 1, 1988.
Los Angeles Times, June 12, 1988.
Orange County Register, July 1, 1988.
People, June 27, 1988.
Rolling Stone, April 21, 1988.

—*Sidelights by Gary Graff*

Donald Trump

UPI/Bettmann Newsphotos

Real estate developer

Full name, Donald John Trump; born 1946, in New York, N.Y.; son of Fred C. (a real estate developer) and Mary (MacLeod) Trump; married Ivana Winkelmayr (an interior designer, business executive, and former fashion model), 1977; children: Donald, Ivanka, Eric. *Education:* Attended Fordham University for two years; University of Pennsylvania, Wharton School of Finance, B.A. in economics, 1968.

Addresses: *Home*—New York, N.Y.; Greenwich, Conn.; and Palm Beach, Fla. *Office*—The Trump Organization, 730 Fifth Ave., New York, N.Y. 10020.

Career

The Trump Organization, New York City, began working in various jobs while attending school, currently president; owner of subsidiary companies, including Trump Enterprises, Inc., The Trump Corp., Trump Development Co., Wembly Realty, Inc., Park South Co., and Land Corp. of California.

Sidelights

In a decade when the business wheeler-dealer replaced the rock star, movie idol, and sports legend in the public imagination, Donald Trump became a true hero of the eighties. To say he is a real estate tycoon is the epitome of understatement. Donald Trump is, in fact, a mega-developer, a major shaper of the New York City landscape, a landlord to the high and mighty, a gambling impressario in Atlantic City, a corporate raider whose mere interest in a company sets off tremors on Wall Street. But even more than that, Donald Trump is a deal-maker in a very public way, a handsome young man whose triumphs at the conference table are widely chronicled by the media and followed by an attentive public, many of whom seem startstuck in his presence.

In a narrative introducing an excerpt from his best-selling book, *The Art of The Deal*, *New York* magazine declared, "Donald Trump is one of the most remarkable figures of the roaring eighties—a true creature of the age. More than a New York real estate developer and deal-maker, Trump has become the personification of hustle and chutzpah, flogging Mayor Koch one day, raiding Holiday Inns or United Airlines the next, pronouncing on the Persian Gulf on the back page of the *Times* the day after that."

A self-made billionaire by age 40, Donald Trump can claim the title of America's ultimate yuppie, the number one impressario of self-promotion in a city that thrives on egotism. Aside from buying and selling the landmark hotels and luxury condominiums, the office towers and gambling palaces, what Donald Trump really markets is his image of success. Megasuccess. More than making deals, Donald

Trump seems to exist to publicize his deals, reveling in the high life he leads. No matter how busy his day, he always seems to find time to take calls from reporters, answer questions from television news people, and write diaries recounting his deals. Spoofing this aspect of the Trump persona, TV personality David Letterman once showed up in the lobby of Trump Tower, unannounced, with his camera crew and, as props, an out-of-town couple visiting New York. Trump agreed immediately to an interview, and as they made small talk Letterman joked that Trump seemed to have nothing to do. Trump laughed and agreed with him.

Of course, that's hardly the case. In addition to managing his interests in real estate and casino gambling—and, increasingly, stock market speculating—the developer has also been active in the New York political arena, having taken out full-page advertisements in several major dailies in 1987, asserting his political views on national issues. "I'm not running for President," he told *Newsweek* in 1987. "But if I did, I'd win."

At present, Trump is busy enough marketing his image of top-of-the-line luxury to everyone who can afford his prices. (Apartments at Trump Tower go for as much as $10 million.) Among the contractors who build his projects, he is known as a hands-on, detail-oriented boss who makes every decision, no matter how small. In a 1985 interview he explained his philosophy to the *New York Times'* William E. Geist: "You sell them a fantasy. Spend whatever it takes to build the best. Then, let people know about it. In New York, there is no limit to how much money people will spend for the very best, not second best, the very best."

To many, New Yorkers and out-of-town tourists alike, the Trump image is personified by three luxury midtown buildings that bear the developer's name: the Trump Tower, Trump Plaza, and Trump Parc. He also owns a 50 percent share in the country's largest gambling casino, the former Hilton Casino which he bought in 1985 and renamed Trump's Casino & Hotel. For a while he owned a football team, the New Jersey Generals, of the now-defunct United States Football League.

Then there's the private Trump, who flies in his 727 jet to spend weekends at Mar-a-Lago, his 118-room Palm Beach mansion, one of three homes; who soars over midtown traffic in one of three private helicopters; who seems so obsessed by money that he can't utter a sentence that lacks dollar figures. He explained in *The Art of the Deal:* "I don't do it for the money. I've got enough, much more than I'll ever need. I do it to do it. Deals are my art form. Other people paint beautifully on canvas or write wonderful poetry. I like making deals, preferably big deals. That's how I get my kicks."

Real estate deal-making is part of the Trump family tradition. Donald's father, Fred C. Trump, an entrepreneurial developer of Swedish descent, built and sold middle-class housing in Brooklyn and Queens, two residential boroughs of New York City. The business prospered, and the Trumps moved their young family—three boys and two girls—into a 23-room mansion in Queens. Donald took an early interest in his father's work, tagging along to visit construction sites around the city. He attended military school and began working for his father part-time at age 16. The family business at the time was worth an estimated $40 million.

After graduating from military school, Donald attended Fordham University, then went on to complete his undergraduate education at the University of Pennsylvania's prestigious Wharton School of Finance. When he got bored with classes, he bought and sold parcels of Philadelphia real estate. He graduated in 1968 and returned home to the family business. At 28, he left Queens behind and moved out on his own. Setting himself up in Manhattan, he began scouting midtown for opportunities. Land was relatively cheap at the time; the city's financial status was beginning to worsen, and developers were shying away from projects. By 1975 New York City was staring bankruptcy in the face. When the crumbling Commodore Hotel came on the market, Trump studied the situation and decided the hotel's prime location in midtown—next door to Grand Central Station—was reason enough to buy. Against his father's advice, he bought the old hotel, then gutted it and rebuilt it as a chrome-and-glass showplace. By 1982, when the hotel was re-opened as the Grand Hyatt, New York was well on its way back to fiscal health.

Trump's second big deal was a $1 million land investment in Atlantic City, which he made prior to gambling's legalization there in 1976. He bought the land quietly, a few parcels at a time. For each purchase, he was represented by a different employee. "If the seller was Italian, we sent an Italian," he told William Geist of the *New York Times.* By the early 1980s the investment was worth an estimated $22 million. With construction underway on his casino hotel, he sold a half-interest in the property to Harrah's, the casino management company, for $50 million, also receiving Harrah's insurance against loss for many years into the future.

But it has been in New York that he has most attracted public attention. Building on his father's lifelong connections in city government and local Democratic clubhouses, Donald Trump quickly mastered the art of obtaining zoning variances and tax abatements, without which his castles would have been built in the sky. He also learned how to make deals without putting his own money at risk. The 68-floor Trump Tower, for example, was built with $200 million provided by Equitable Life Assurance Society. Reported *Business Week*'s Terry Thompson, "With a 10-year tax-abatement and no debt on the property, Trump and Equitable take in about $14 million a year each by renting retail and office space at some of the highest rates in New York."

It wasn't Trump Tower's financing, though, that seized the public imagination—it was the style, bold and brassy, that Trump gave it. The shimmering glass skyscraper on Fifth Avenue almost instantly became one of the city's most popular tourist attractions. There is the million-dollar waterfall in the lobby, the pink marble floors, the upstairs tenants like Johnny Carson, Stephen Spielberg, and Sophia Loren, the main-floor merchants like Calvin Klein, the doormen who, outfitted in red military tunics, gold braid, and black bearskin hats, stand at attention beside *revolving* doors. There are two-foot high bronze "T"s in the lobby, and nearby are a pianist and violinist who wear tuxedoes and play duets. Describing the building's spirit of excess in a *New York* magazine profile, gossip columnist Liz Smith trumpeted: "I like his style. Because he isn't a phony and a fake. How can we really fault him? For isn't he the perfect synthesis of competition—striving, elbowing, wheeling, dealing, showing off, getting, and flaunting it?"

But the developer's biggest plan yet—the 92-acre riverfront project he calls Television City—rests on the drawing board, stymied by city hall, political opponents, business rivals, and environmental groups. The centerpiece calls for a 150-story tower, planned as the world's tallest building, rising above

Donald Trump poses with one of his three Sikorsky helicopters, which carry passengers between New York City and Atlantic City, N.J. AP/Wide World Photos.

11 other skyscrapers, each 45 stories high. The project, long the subject of controversy, received a severe setback in 1987 when NBC, whom Trump sought to lure as his chief tenant, announced it would renew its lease and remain in Rockefeller Center.

Characteristically, Trump's response was to plunge ahead with more deals. As if he had suddenly discovered the stock market, he began investing some of the profits he seemed to make so effortlessly in real estate. The novice investor bought large chunks of three different companies—Allegis (formerly United Airlines), Holiday Corp. (owner of Holiday Inns) and Bally's—and watched as Wall Street rumors sent the price of the stock skyrocketing. Each time he sold his holdings and, in total, realized a profit in excess of $122 million.

Unlike most business tycoons, Trump clearly prefers the goldfish bowl to the seclusion of a penthouse citadel. While he professes a dislike for public appearances, he frequents such high-profile restaurants as the "21" Club, enjoys walking the floor at his casino, and is often photographed at society galas or charity events. New Yorkers treat him like a celebrity, and his face is one of the best-known in town. Blanche Sprague, who manages condo sales at Trump Tower, told William Geist of the *New York Times,* "When I walk down the street with Donald, people come up and just touch him, hoping that his good fortune will rub off."

Trump has been married since 1977 to the former Ivana Winkelmayr, a Czechoslovak Olympic skier who became a Montreal fashion model. The couple met at a reception for Olympic athletes. A licensed interior designer, Ivana Trump took charge of designing the new Trump casino and then became its chief executive officer. Today she supervises more than 3,500 employees in Atlantic City. The couple has three children.

Six foot two and sandy-haired, Trump has an athletic build he maintains by keeping to a healthy diet. Published profiles generally describe him as handsome and boyish. Wrote William Geist, "His smile is an impudent-looking curl of the lips that makes his portrait appear less like the head of a billion-dollar corporation in his office than Elvis Presley in Viva Las Vegas." He doesn't have many close friends and told *Newsweek* his only "real friends" are his family members. He spends little time on hobbies (although he is capable at golf and tennis), and soon after purchasing his Palm Beach retreat he was investing in local real estate in order to keep busy on weekends.

Outside of business matters, Trump is most concerned with the issue of nuclear disarmament. He has visited the Soviet Union, based in part on his expressed convictions, and has let it be known he would like to negotiate with Moscow as a representative of the United States. He believes that private enterprise could speed disarmament faster than the Washington bureaucracy, civil servants being a longstanding object of his derision. "There's a vast difference between somebody who's been consistently successful [in private business] and somebody who's been working for a relatively small amount of money in governmental service for many years," he told Ron Rosenbaum of *Manhattan Inc.* "In many cases because the private sector, who have seen these people indirectly, didn't choose to hire these people, any of them, because it didn't find them to be particularly capable. But then, years and years later they get slightly promoted, promoted, promoted. The private sector has passed them by and all of a sudden these people are negotiating the lives of you and your children, your families."

Writings

Trump: The Art of the Deal (with Tony Schwartz), Random House, 1987.

Sources

Business Week, July 22, 1985; July 20, 1987.
Fortune, October 12, 1987.
Manhattan Inc., November, 1985.
New Republic, February 1, 1988.
Newsweek, September 28, 1987.
New York, November 17, 1980; November 24, 1986; November 16, 1987; April 25, 1988.
New York Daily News Magazine, August 10, 1980.
New York Times, November 1, 1976; August 26, 1980; August 7, 1983; December 7, 1987; January 18, 1988
New York Times Magazine, April 8, 1984.
People, December 7, 1987.
Sports Illustrated, February 13, 1984.
Time, April 16, 1984.
Town & Country, September, 1983.
Wall Street Journal, January 14, 1982.
Washington Post, November 22, 1987; December 2, 1987.

—Sidelights by Warren Strugatch

Ted Turner

UPI/Bettmann Newsphotos

Broadcasting and sports entrepreneur

Full name, Robert Edward Turner III; born November 19, 1938, in Cincinnati, Ohio; son of Robert Edward, Jr. (in billboard business) and Florence (Rooney) Turner; married Judy Nye (divorced, 1962); married Jane Smith, June 2, 1964; children: (first marriage) Laura Lee, Robert Edward IV; (second marriage) Rhett, Beauregard, Sarah Jean. *Education:* Attended Brown University.

Addresses: *Home*—Residences include Atlanta, Ga.; Buchanan, Ga.; Georgetown, S.C.; Jacksonboro, S.C.; and Tallahassee, Fla. *Office*—Turner Broadcasting System, Inc., 1050 Techwood Dr. N.W., Atlanta, Ga. 30318.

Career

Turner Advertising Co., worked summers while in school, branch manager in Macon, Ga., 1960–63; Turner Broadcasting System, Inc. (originally Turner Communications Group), Atlanta, Ga., president and chief operating officer, 1963—. President of Atlanta Braves baseball team, 1976—; chairman of Atlanta Hawks basketball team, 1977—. Yachtsman; began racing sailboats as a young boy; three-time winner of U.S. 5.5 Meter championship; Y-Flyer national champion, 1963; Flying Dutchman North American champion, 1965; winner of Southern Ocean Racing Conference, 1966, 1970; competed in 1974 America's Cup trials; winner of America's Cup race, 1977. *Military service:* Served in U.S. Coast Guard.

Awards: Martini & Rossi Trophy for Outstanding Yachtsman of the Year, 1970; named U.S. Yachtsman of the Year, 1970, 1973, and 1977.

Sidelights

Ted Turner has been called variously a genius, a flake, a fruitcake, a maniac, and a visionary. When he succeeded in establishing his independent Atlanta station as a national "superstation" in the late 1970s, followed by the start-up of an unprecedented, 24-hour news network, skeptical broadcast analysts conceded that the brash, cigar-chomping Turner was a pioneer in an industry woefully short of new ideas. His Midas touch grew somewhat tarnished in the mid-eighties, when a series of bad deals landed the cocky Southerner in enormous debt. But proceeding at full speed despite the debt, Turner began laying the groundwork for a new cable network that would, he promised, compete with CBS, NBC, and ABC in the areas of program quality, audience share, and advertising revenues. In the fall of 1988, the new network opened its broadcast schedule with "Gone With The Wind," the epic melodrama of Southern tragedy and rebirth that Turner has claimed as his own emblem.

The "Mouth of the South" established his reputation in the late 1970s as a gambler whose risks always seemed to pay off, confounding industry veterans and the TV-watching public. In 1970 Turner bought a small, independent Atlanta television station and made it the flagship of the nascent Turner Broadcasting System. Using new technology to access an orbiting telecommunications satellite, WTBS seized a coast-to-coast audience. In 1980 Turner used profits from WTBS to launch a 24-hour cable news network that secured a niche for itself with alacrity.

Never one for false modesty, Turner flaunted his track record in proving the industry wrong, making few friends in conventional broadcasting circles. Many anticipated his decline with eagerness. In the mid-1980s their wait seemed to be over. Turner made two big errors: a preposterous attempt at a hostile takeover of CBS that cost him $20 million; and the $1.6 billion acquisition of the MGM film library. Both deals put him under enormous debt, forcing most of his attention on just raising capital. Turner nevertheless had another surprise in store, and in the fall of 1988 launched yet another network. Potentially his most ambitious project yet, Turner Network Television (TNT) was intended to go beyond cable's traditionally narrow audience and compete for mass numbers with broadcasting's Big Three.

Like the plot of "Gone With The Wind," Turner's life has been an epic melodrama on a grand scale. Ed Turner, his father, was a Mississippi cotton plantation owner who, ruined by the Depression, was forced to become a salesman. Ed Turner met his future wife while staying in a Cincinnati hotel owned by her family. The couple married and had two children, Ted and his sister, Mary Jane, who eventually died of Lupus. Ted was sent to boarding school at an early age, and his father joined the Navy.

When the family was reunited after World War II, Ted began attending Cincinnati public schools. He was transferred to military preparatory schools near Atlanta when his father moved there to start an outdoor advertising business. The boy was enrolled at the Georgia Military Academy and the McCallie School in Chattanooga, Tennessee. Years later faculty members recalled "Terrible Teddy" as showing both leadership qualities and certain eccentricities, including a taste for taxidermy.

Summers, the boy worked for his father. Years later an adult Ted Turner recalled earning $50 a week as a teenager, half of which his father deducted for room and board. The choice of which college to attend caused friction: Ted picked the U.S. Naval Academy at Annapolis; his father urged a business major at Brown University in Providence, Rhode Island. The boy agreed to Brown but once there registered for mostly liberal arts courses, particularly the classics. His extra-curricular activities included debate, yachting, and girls. The latter resulted in his getting suspended from Brown after being found with a bunch of pals in a women's college late one night. His father handed down his own disciplinary action: A six-month tour of active duty in the Coast Guard. Upon its completion, young Turner returned to Brown, where his nocturnal activities soon resulted in a second, and final, suspension.

Like the plot of "Gone With the Wind," Turner's life has been an epic melodrama on a grand scale.

Returning home, the youth was given a managerial job with the company's office in Macon, Georgia. It was a growing firm, and Ted quickly became enamoured of the risk-taking entrepreneurial spirit. In 1960 his father put together a deal to buy out his competitor, the largest firm in the business. The acquisition resulted in enormous debt. Facing impending bankruptcy, the senior Turner hastily began selling off pieces of the company. His son urged him to try to make it work, but the older man was despondent. In 1963 Ed Turner took a gun into the bedroom of his South Carolina plantation and killed himself. The company fell into his son's hands where it quickly thrived. Just 24 and inexperienced in management, Turner put the company on solid footing, continuing to expand and diversify.

In 1970 Turner bought Channel 17 in Atlanta, seeing it as a springboard to greater things in a broadcasting environment where network control was disappearing. In 1975 he testified before the Federal Communications Commission in Washington, prodding that agency to relax restrictions limiting the growth of independent stations. Later that year, Turner began using the first orbiting telecommunications satellite, owned by RCA, to broadcast the WTBS signal nationwide. The station suddenly doubled its audience to two million households, and Turner declared it the nation's first "superstation." By 1986 WTBS was reaching 36 million U.S. homes.

There was, however, the programming dilemma. The enormous cost of creating new programming forced

Turner to take the traditional route followed by most independent stations: He bought syndicated reruns from the networks, leased old films, and budgeted enough to produce a limited schedule of original programming. He realized his success left him vulnerable to being shut out of the syndication market. In 1976, to keep himself in programming, he bought two Atlanta sports franchises and made their schedules a WTBS mainstay. Neither the baseball Braves nor the basketball Hawks, perennial cellar-dwellars, improved appreciably under his ownership. As a sports owner, however, Turner makes the most of his position. Several years ago, during a particularly disastrous season, he fired the Braves' field manager, donned a uniform himself and began calling the shots from the dugout. The baseball establishment reprimanded him, but Turner clearly enjoyed his day in the dugout.

His true interest, however, remained broadcasting. WTBS was generating sufficient cash for Turner to launch another new venture in 1980, a 24-hour news network. Turner's announcement of his plan drew hoots from the industry: TV news traditionally drew losses, not profits, and few thought a journalistic novice like Turner could do what the networks could not. Turner hired non-union staff, acquired state-of-the-art technology, and within several years the Cable News Network (CNN) had established its credibility, both journalistic and financial. CNN disspelled any lingering doubts of its viability when its correspondents, alone among broadcast journalists, managed to provide immediate, on-site coverage of the Challenger shuttle disaster in 1986.

In the mid-1980s, however, Turner's Midas touch seemed suddenly to vanish. Concerned as always over his access to programming material, Turner steered his company on an unbelievable course: attempting a hostile take-over of mammoth CBS. The ploy failed, at a cost of $20 million, and gave the New York broadcasting establishment good cause to laugh at a man they always considered an out-of-town rube.

On the heels of the CBS debacle, Turner was contacted by a man many believe to be the shrewdest deal-maker in America: Kirk Kerkorian. Kerkorian, a casino owner whose properties also included MGM/UA Entertainment, sold Turner on the value of owning his own library of films to assure proprietary broadcast material. Lured by the prospect of

Ted Turner (left) poses with athletes Jackie Joyner-Kersee and Edwin Moses at the 1988 announcement of the extension of the Goodwill Games into 1994 and 1998. AP/Wide World Photos.

owning 3650 films ranging from "Gone With The Wind" to "2001: a Space Odyssey," Turner paid Kerkorian's $1.6 billion asking price. Kirkorian had, simply, taken Turner to the cleaners. Wall Street analysts estimated he had overpaid by perhaps half a billion dollars.

To finance the deal Turner had to sell back to Kerkorian nearly everything he had just bought, except for the films and the glass cases loaded with Oscar trophies. (A follow-up deal brought the total to 3,301 films, including 265 Academy Award winners.) Burdened by a staggering debt load, Turner had to restructure his company. He was forced to issue new shares of stock and sell additional equity in Turner Broadcasting to meet operational costs. His ownership of the company fell from 81 percent to 51 percent. He now needed a consensus to manage his business. Debtor agreements determined how he would spend his own hard cash. Yet the face he presented to the world was that of a riverboat gambler holding an ace. "I'm elated," he told *Broadcasting* magazine. "But I'm also apprehensive, I guess. We owe a lot of money right now, and that would give any intelligent person cause for concern. We're concerned, but not worried. We intend to deal with the debt in a judicious and intelligent manner."

The next fiasco was the 1986 Goodwill Games, held in Moscow in July. The games brought together U.S. and Soviet athletes in an Olympic-style competition, staged by Turner Broadcasting for its broadcast and syndication. Turner had center stage to himself in Moscow, and he had a ball. The games set Turner back by $10 to $15 million, a loss he wrote off as a contribution to world peace. "By our bringing the U.S. athletes to Moscow, I believe we . . . did a lot to start a thaw in U.S.-Soviet relations," he told *Broadcasting* magazine.

The cause of world peace has preoccupied Turner for several years. Turner cites the inspiration of Jacques Cousteau, oceanographer and television personality, whose expeditions Turner helps underwrite. Converted to the cause of world peace, Turner formed the Better World Society, an international organization dedicated to ending the arms race, advancing environmentalism, and leveling the population growth. His deadline to meet those goals is the year 2000. He points out that the eradication of world hunger would help business. "In the long term you can't have a world where the people are starving," he declared to *Broadcasting*. "And there's no reason for it, not with the tools we have available to us today. And its bad for the developing world because we're in the business of commerce, and you can't sell somebody something if he's starving to death."

Beleagued as he was by the MGM debt load, Turner managed to find time in 1988 to launch a new network intended to rival the Big Three. He praised the timeliness of his move to interviewers. "The power is shifting all over the place in this business," he told *Broadcasting*. "The future is up for grabs, and it depends on who makes the right moves. Cable is poised to storm the citadel, and we hope to be part of making the charge. That's what we want to do, and we need TNT to do it." The new Turner Network Television debuted in October, 1988.

Turner's policy of colorizing old black-and-white prints, ostensibly to give the films greater mass appeal, has antagonized very vocal segments of the filmmaking industry. Anti-colorists contends Turner has no right to alter completed films that are, in effect, public property. Woody Allen, Martin Scorsese, and Steven Spielberg have testified before Congress to try and prevent Turner's continued colorization of the MGM library. Turner responds to their charges at characteristic top volume: "I knew [colorization] would make these movies worth ten times as much," he told Gwenda Blair of *Business Monthly*. "Doesn't this just blow your mind? You'd never know that [colorized film] wasn't shot yesterday. The whole thing about colorization destroying films is just stupid. Women put on makeup every day, and no one bitches about that!"

Outside of his broadcast activities Turner is also known for his lavish leisure style. As a yachtsman, he races frequently, and in 1977, at the helm of *Courageous*, he won the America's Cup. He owns three 5,000-acre plantations, a large island off the coast of South Carolina, a beach house in Big Sur, and a 10,000-acre ranch in Montana. The father of five, he has been married twice, and recently left his wife of 24 years for a younger woman. "Turner displays a considerable lack of discretion in his associations with other women," sniffed Stratford Sherman of *Fortune*. Wrote Gwenda Blair in *Business Monthly:* "For nearly two decades, the man who looks like Clark Gable and sounds like Huey Long has been an unpredictable joker in the cable industry—and in the American psyche. He built a communications empire by taking enormous risks, always flouting the conventional wisdom. Then he gambled it all once too often and came perilously close to losing. That last gamble, some say, cost him his nerve and with it his place in the high-stakes game. Don't bet on it: he's just been gathering strength for a new attack."

Writings

The Racing Edge (with Gary Jobson), Simon & Schuster, 1979.

Sources

Books

Contemporary Authors, Volume 120, Gale, 1987.
Fields, Robert Ashley, *Take Me Out to the Crowd: Ted Turner and the Atlanta Braves,* Strode, 1977.
Vaughan, Roger, *The Good Gesture: Ted Turner, Mariner, and the America's Cup,* Little, Brown, 1975.
Vaughan, Roger, *Ted Turner: The Man Behind the Mouth,* Sail Books, 1978.
Williams, Christian, *Lead, Follow, or Get Out of the Way: The Story of Ted Turner, Sportsman, Entrepreneur, and Media Magnate,* Time Books, 1981.

Periodicals

Broadcasting, March 31, 1986; July 14, 1986; August 17, 1987; December 14, 1987; February 29, 1988; August 1, 1988.
Business Monthly, July–August, 1988.
Business Week, November 22, 1978; January 11, 1982; June 14, 1982; May 12, 1986.
Esquire, October 10, 1978; February, 1983.
Financial World, April 5, 1988.
Forbes, August 31, 1981.
Fortune, July 7, 1986; January 5, 1987; February 16, 1987.
Newsweek, June 7, 1976; July 11, 1977; September 12, 1977; September 19, 1977; January 1, 1979; June 16, 1980; June 28, 1982; July 15, 1985; August 19, 1985.
New York Times, March 26, 1972; September 19, 1977.
Parade, June 29, 1986.
People, December 28, 1981.
Playboy, August, 1978; August, 1983.
Preview, October, 1988.
Sports Illustrated, July 19, 1976; March 21, 1977; May 23, 1977; August 21, 1978; June 30, 1978; June 23, 1986.
Time, April 26, 1976; August 8, 1977; September 19, 1977; January 1, 1979; August 6, 1979; June 9, 1980; August 18, 1980; August 9, 1982.

—Sidelights by Warren Strugatch

Mitsuko Uchida

Christian Steiner/Philips Classics.

Pianist

Name pronounced *Mits*-ko Oo-*Chee*-da; born c. 1949, in Tokyo, Japan; daughter of diplomat father. *Education:* Began studying piano at age six; attended Vienna Academy of Music, beginning 1961; later studied privately with Stefan Askenase and Wilhelm Kempff.

Addresses: *Home*—London, England. *Office*—c/o Philips Classics, 810 Seventh Avenue, New York, N.Y. 10019.

Career

Began playing piano at age six; moved with family to Vienna, Austria, at age 12 and studied there, privately and at the Academy of Music, for ten years; at 22, ended formal training in piano and moved to London; performed complete Mozart piano sonatas in London and Tokyo, 1982; made New York debut at the Mostly Mozart Festival, summer, 1985; performed complete Mozart piano concertos with the English Chamber Orchestra in London and Tokyo, 1985–86; continues to record and perform throughout the world.

Awards: First prize in Vienna Beethoven Piano Competition, 1969; second prize in Warsaw Chopin Competition, 1970; second prize in Leeds International Competition, 1975; Japanese Suntory Music Award for her "outstanding contribution to international music in Japan," 1987.

Sidelights

Mitsuko Uchida introduced herself to the world through the music of Wolfgang Amadeus Mozart. First were the 20 piano sonatas; in 1982 she performed them in a five-night program for London audiences, repeating the event later that year in Tokyo. Her vibrant, earthy performances won her an instant following among the public and left the critics in somewhat of a daze. Who was this pianist who played with such conviction and originality? Why hadn't they heard of her before? During the 1985–86 season she brought out a second helping: the 21 piano concertos. She premiered the set in London with the English Chamber Orchestra, playing while conducting from the piano bench. When she repeated the set in Tokyo, this time she was mobbed by the public like a rock star.

While many pianists perform Mozart regularly and several specialize in his works, few have undertaken such a large chunk of his *oeuvre* at one time. For Mitsuko Uchido, however, it was all or nothing. For ten years she scrutinized the deceptively jovial face of Mozart's music, hoping to glimpse the mystical, mystifying spirit that lies hidden within. She studied the composer from a historical perspective, reading several books on his life. She philosophized about how his life might have influenced his art. She thought about his character in terms of psychoanalysis. In the end, she threw all these notions aside and simply played the music—a music that, over the course of her exploration, had become wholly her own.

"To me, Mozart's world is the Twilight Zone," the pianist told *Keyboard* magazine. "It is the most human and the most introverted world that I know. He hides so much. He doesn't make things happen demonstratively. You have to look for it, or it will pass. You think it is beautiful, and you can dwell on the beauty, then the whole thing passes over you. But once you get involved and start seeing things, you realize how very quickly he functions. You have to catch him, or he has slipped away already. You think there is sunshine. Then, the moment you realize that, it's already too late; he turns the other way."

Although Mozart seems to pervade Western culture, the intensity of Uchida's fascination with him has inspired music lovers to take a new look. "She is that rare find," wrote *Digital Audio*, "a pianist who has the key to Mozart's soul: passion veiled by elegance, sublime inspiration made more precious by the sweet constraints of form." Her recordings for Philips of the piano sonatas made several critics' "Ten Best" lists for 1988; her recordings of the concertos, with conductor Jeffrey Tate and the ECO, have been earning high marks as well. That cycle is slated for completion in 1991, to coincide with the 200th anniversary of Mozart's death.

During the late 1980s, Uchida has pursued her passions for other composers—Beethoven, Chopin, Debussy, Bartok, Schoenberg, and Britten, among others. Yet while she has left "the vacuum of Mozart," as she refers to her decade-long study, she is far from abandoning his music. In fact, her interest in Mozart remains one of the strongest threads connecting the various stages of her career.

Born in Tokyo, Uchida began piano lessons at the age of six. "Already as a small child I remember vividly listening to Mozart again and again," she told the *Detroit Free Press*. "When I was five or six I was always playing Mozart." When she was 12, her father moved his family to Vienna, where he was a member of the Japanese diplomatic mission. Vienna offered an ideal environment for a budding Mozartian—it was there, after all, that the composer spent the last ten years of his life and composed his greatest works. Throughout her teens, Mitsuko dug deeply into the Mozart piano *oeuvre*, first at the Vienna Academy of Music and later in private studies.

Uchida's student years were a "ghastly agony," as she confessed to *Keyboard*. "I always need to understand what it is I am playing and why it is so," she elaborated, "and why I feel in a particular way." This inquisitiveness was left unsatisfied during her childhood. "There is a tradition in Japanese society that one is not to question," she told the *New York Times*. "It is so difficult for people to grow into individual musicians under those circumstances." Yet attention to the individual was perhaps the least of what she found missing from the Japanese teaching approach. A society in which music was taught more to build social *savoir-faire* than to foster musicality, Japan had little to offer of the Western musical tradition. "Children are taught Western music, but the cultural background, the cultural necessity for Western music is not there," she observed. "It becomes part of the social scheme, which is very strong; the outline is very clear. For middle-class families, having their kid play the piano is a part of sending him to school, just as girls learn flower arrangement or the tea ceremony.... Since there is no tradition, it becomes very technical, very mechanical."

"To me, Mozart's world is the Twilight Zone. It is the most human and the most introverted world that I know."

In Vienna, of course, her thirst for Western musical culture could easily be quenched. During her teens, as her main language switched from Japanese to German, she became firmly rooted in the Viennese school of piano-playing. Yet once again she felt more stifled than inspired by her teachers. "God, it is rigid!" she told the *New York Times*, referring to the society. "Full of fixed ideas. There are masses of do's and don'ts, and 'music should be played this way,' especially for what they consider to be a Viennese composer. So I had to get out of that as well." Ending her formal studies at the age of 22, she moved to London, where English became her third and final "first" language. Today, London remains her adopted city. "I'd rather be in London than anywhere else," she told the London publication *Time Out*. "You're free to be what you want. People don't bother about your religious or political convictions or whether you wear red stockings every day."

Uchida's artistry is a product of her own design. During her twenties she placed first in Vienna's Beethoven Competition and second in both the Warsaw Chopin Competition and Britain's Leeds International. None of them, however, did much to boost her career. As a result she has had to build it herself, which she has done at her own pace. Undaunted by the bias her profession holds toward young virtuosi, she has always focused on the music rather than the need to succeed. "I was lucky enough to always have enough work to keep me going," she told *Ovation.* "My life has been built very slowly and securely. If the career goes ahead of you, there will be one day when you fall off of it."

This philosophy—that the music is more important than the public image—is implicit in her conservative approach to concertizing. One year, she told the *New York Times,* she played 70 concerts. "It was excessively hard for me. If you stick to two piano concertos plus one recital program, you can play 100 concerts. But I like to play different things. The repertory is so vast." "I believe it is not necessary from a career point of view to play that many concerts," she told *Keyboard.* "I play 50—at the maximum, 60. Plus recordings. That is already a lot .... Many musicians are over-exposed. When you are over-worked, you dry up. Playing a concert is giving. You give a piece of your flesh, as it were, and you need time to recuperate. I need it. So I firmly believe in keeping my own time."

To minimize distractions when she is at home practicing, Uchida has decorated her home sparingly and in neutral colors. "Sound has color," she told *Keyboard,* "so I don't want to have too many other colors around." When she is not on the road, she both guards and relishes her time at home. "I have all the things I need there—my piano, my music, my records, my books—so I just won't be left alone! I don't want to go out in my spare time. I want to sit at home and listen to music, and play the damn piano! I love it so much! I am frustrated when I haven't got enough time for the music. Everything else has such a remote, secondary role."

It seems to be no coincidence that Uchida has reached an artistic peak. "I am happier now than when I was a child, than when I was 20, than I was in every other period," she disclosed to *Keyboard.* As a young pianist, she explained, "There were so many things I didn't understand about why things were as they were, in life as well as in music. But one was never really to ask, and I didn't have the habit of asking. So all these *whys* accumulated in me." Time passed and answers began to present themselves. Rather than a source of conflict, her inquisitiveness became vital nourishment for her music. "I think getting older and knowing more ought to mean that you get simpler," she told *Gramophone.* "Knowledge must not clutter; by knowing more one ought to be able to shed unnecessary things. Experience doesn't mean that you heap more upon what you already have—it must not. I hope that my Mozart, for example, has become simpler than in the first recordings of it that I made."

Selected discography

Wolfgang Amadeus Mozart, *Concertos Nos. 20 and 21,* Philips, 1988.
Mozart, *Concertos Nos. 22 and 23,* 1988.
Mozart, *Concertos Nos. 26 and 27,* Philips, 1988.
Frederic Chopin, *Piano Sonatas Nos. 2 and 3,* Philips, 1988.
Mozart, *The Complete Piano Sonatas,* Philips, 1989.
Mozart, *Concertos Nos. 13 and 14,* Philips, 1989.

Sources

Detroit Free Press, November 28, 1984.
Digital Audio, May, 1988.
Gramophone, July, 1984; February, 1989.
Keyboard, April, 1989.
New York Times, February 23, 1988; October 16, 1988.
Ovation, October, 1988.

—*Sketch by Kyle Kevorkian*

P. Roy Vagelos

Pharmaceuticals company executive

Full name, Pindaros Roy Vagelos; born October 8, 1929, in Westfield, N.J.; son of Greek immigrants who operated a diner; married 1955; children: four. *Education:* University of Pennsylvania, A.B., 1950; Columbia University, M.D., 1954.

Addresses: *Office*—Merck & Co., Rahway, N.J. 07065.

Career

Massachusetts General Hospital, Boston, intern, 1954–55, assistant resident, 1955–56; National Institutes of Health, National Heart Institute, Bethesda, Md., senior assistant surgeon in Cellular Physiology Laboratory, 1956–59, surgeon, 1959–61, acting chief of enzymes section, 1959–60, senior surgeon in Biochemistry Laboratory, 1961–62, senior surgeon and research chemist, 1963–64, head of comparative biochemistry section, 1964–66; Pasteur Institute, Paris, France, senior surgeon, 1962–63; Washington University, School of Medicine, St. Louis, Mo., chairman of department of biological chemistry, 1966–75, director of Division of Biological and Medical Science, 1973–75; Merck & Co., Rahway, N.J., senior vice-president of research, Merck, Sharp & Dohme Research Laboratories Division, 1975–76, president, 1976–84, executive vice-president, Merck & Co., 1984, president and chief executive officer, 1985—. Sloan visiting professor of chemistry, Harvard University, 1973; member of board of trustees, Rockefeller University, 1976—, and Danforth Foundation, 1978—; member of national research advisory board, Cleveland Clinic Foundation, 1984—.

UPI/Bettmann Newsphotos

Member: National Academy of Science, National Institute of Medicine, American Association for the Advancement of Science, American Society of Biological Chemistry.

Awards: Enzyme Chemistry Award, American Chemical Society, 1967; grants from National Institutes of Health and National Science Foundation; honorary D.Sc. from Washington University, 1980, Brown University, 1982, and University of Medicine and Dentistry of New Jersey, 1984.

Sidelights

Some people call Roy Vagelos the country's leading medicine man. But the simple title of one who cures disease belies the man of power who has also been named by Wall Street analysts as the corporate executive with the highest credibility in the pharmaceutical industry. Vagelos is credited with guiding what has become one of the most innovative companies in the drug industry, and leading news media describe his more than $5 billion firm in such terms as "the miracle company" and "superstar." Yet the man behind the world's top prescription drug company is also said to be persuasive without being abrasive, and closely in touch with his employees—

he always leaves his office door open for any of his 32,000 workers to drop in. But the down-to-earth attitude does not mean that Vagelos is lax or content to rest on his laurels. He is described as a demanding corporate chief who is completely dedicated to his work and expects the highest standards of both himself and his employees. "When the phone rings on a Sunday morning, you know it's Vagelos," said a Merck president in *Time* magazine. In *Fortune*, which in 1988 named Merck one of America's most admired corporations, Vagelos said: "I think Merck is a very competitive company, and I push our people to be competitive. We would like to be No. 1 forever. While other people are talking about the drugs they are making, we're in there with a second one. I like that. It's understanding that the most important thing you can contribute as a human being is improving the lives of millions of people."

"The most important thing you can contribute as a human being is improving the lives of millions of people."

It has been more than 40 years since Vagelos, as a boy, first learned of the intriguing medicines made at the Merck laboratories in his hometown of Rahway, N.J. The giant firm, whose history can be traced back to a 17th-century German apothecary, proved a source of fascination to the young man. The son of Greek immigrants, Vagelos spent much of his free time as a boy working after school in his family's luncheonette just six blocks from the Merck factories. It was there that he became intrigued by conversations he overheard among research scientists from Merck who dropped into the diner for a bite to eat. "They seemed to be leading a very exciting life," Vagelos told *Time* magazine. Taking technical courses in high school, Vagelos earned a reputation as a serious student. He attended the University of Pennsylvania and the medical school at Columbia University and went on to receive further training at Massachusetts General Hospital and the National Institutes of Health. He was named to head up Washington University's biological chemistry department, and it was there that he received a phone call from a Merck official whose laboratory he had once interned in, asking Vagelos to join Merck Labs as a senior vice-president of research. Vagelos told *Time* he was eager for the chance to head the research laboratories: "I had been in basic research and biomedical science for 20 years. I had taught medical students, but I hadn't really put it all together to make something of it."

At Merck, Vagelos found himself among many of the wonder drugs he had heard about in his youth. When he was young, he had eavesdropped on conversations about penicillin and vitamin B-12. But the company had not stood still since that time. Four years after Vagelos joined Merck Labs, the company adopted his suggestions for new lab techniques to build upon Merck's 1956 discovery of an acid necessary for the chemical reactions that produce cholesterol. Vagelos suggested a process to inhibit the production of the acid and block one step of cholesterol formation. Vagelos had earlier recruited a former fellow faculty member from Washington University, and the two men had extensive experience working with the fatty substances responsible for clogging arteries and causing strokes and heart attacks. The creation of Mevacor, an anticholesterol drug, was possible through the coordination of a large team of Merck scientists who devoted their budgets to work on the project. "It's like running a battle in which you have different forces lined up," Vagelos told *Business Week*. "You call on an infantry, a cavalry, an air force. That's the great strength of Merck."

The team of researchers grew from an initial 20 people to 100, and during Mevacor's final development Merck devoted as much as 25 percent of its total research and development resources to the project. Time was precious. Not only was it important to beat other drug companies to market with a drug to lower cholesterol, but Merck had to produce a product markedly superior to its competitors' offerings. Once a drug passes safety trials, it must win approval from the U.S. Food and Drug Administration—a process that can take more than 30 months. Merck, however, has the best record in the drug industry for winning new drug application approval, due in part to the company's practice of keeping the FDA informed of development and test results and performing exhaustive trials of its proposed drug. Merck spent eight years testing the safety of its anticholesterol drug, looking for adverse reactions in animals and humans. In 1980, the company encountered a setback when it learned that a similar compound being tested by a rival drug company caused cancer in dogs. Merck developed backup compounds for its own drug and delayed chemical testing for nearly four years. Its competitor later announced that the rumors of cancer caused by its drug were false. In November 1986, Merck was finally ready to seek FDA approval.

The company loaded up a van with 104 400-page volumes and sent them to the FDA. It was the result of years of painstaking work—some 120 people were on a Merck team to prepare documents for the FDA, attending to such minute details as the required size of margins on typed pages. Some Merck staff kept in constant contact with FDA officials during the testing of the drug, and all staffers had strict responsibilities and deadlines. A Merck official responsible for meeting the requirements of regulatory bodies said in *Business Week* of FDA officials: "We want to make them part of the development process. We inform them immediately of all issues. If they are ever surprised, they will be more skeptical." Merck's diligence paid off—just three months after filing its application the drug company won a date for a meeting with FDA officials to publicly present the drug and the research to back up its findings. In August 1987, Merck won final FDA approval for its anticholesterol drug after just nine months of review.

Waiting in the wings was a Merck marketing team ready to sell the drug to physicians, who often shy away from prescribing newly approved drugs. In a field where salespeople are known for making inflated claims of a drug's capabilities, Merck's Vagelos insists that his staff of some 5,000 salespeople adhere only to claims that they can back up with scientific findings. With Mevacor, Merck believed, the dangers of high cholesterol levels were a selling point in themselves. In 1987, thirteen of Merck's more than 100 prescription drugs produced sales of $100 million. Some of the drugs like Mevacor are relatively new, and are expected to continue to ring up sales in the top-selling range of prescription drugs. Merck's other wonder drugs include Vasotec, which lowers blood pressure; Noroxin, an antibiotic; Indocin, an anti-inflammatory drug; Timoptic, which fights glaucoma; and Pepcid, for peptic ulcers.

Roy Vagelos believes there are plenty of diseases left to invent new drugs for. And he's not one to sit back, even if his company is considered one of America's most admired corporations. The company holds the largest share of the drug market in the United States, Canada, and Australia, but Vagelos would like for it to be at the top of every market in the world. The company is testing a drug that would shrink the prostate gland without creating side effects, and some analysts believe it may be the company's next top-seller. Continuing to steadily develop such drugs is vital to the company's financial health, Vagelos believes. "The trick is to take advantage of the fact that we have numerous new products doing well to lay the foundation for long-term growth of the corporation. Pharmaceuticals is a very fragmented market, and a company that can put everything together for a series of years should be able to gather up a much larger and more significant share of the market," Vagelos said in *Fortune*. The company is also developing over-the-counter drugs aimed at the consumer market.

In addition to searching out new drugs, Vagelos is not complacent in the hiring of new staff. He continually hunts out talented research scientists and often makes surprise visits to corporate divisions, asking managers for progress reports on recruitment. Vagelos's personal life mirrors his corporate style of running a clean, tight operation: he runs five miles a day, plays tennis, and is one of the country's most admired executives. He expects only the best of himself and puts successes behind him to look ahead to the future. "I tend to discount immediately what we have accomplished," Vagelos told *Time*. "Once you know you have a drug or it is coming along, you really want to get on with the next thing. After all, what's more exciting than trying to do something that's never been done before?"

Sources

Business Week, October 19, 1987.
Financial World, April 5, 1988.
Forbes, August 15, 1983; January 11, 1988.
Fortune, January 18, 1988.
New York, February 22, 1988.
New York Times, April 24, 1985; December 28, 1987; June 28, 1988.
Time, February 22, 1988.
Wall Street Journal, November 4, 1988.

—Sidelights by Amy C. Bodwin

Grover Washington, Jr.

AP/Wide World Photos

Jazz saxophonist

Born December 12, 1943, in Buffalo, New York; father was a saxophonist, mother was a singer in a choir; married, 1967; wife's name, Christine; children: Grover III, Shana. *Education:* Attended Wurlitzer School of Music and Temple University School of Music.

Addresses: *Office*—c/o Lloyd Z. Remick, 700 Three Penn Center, Philadelphia, Pa. 19102; and 1515 Market St., Suite 700, Philadelphia, Pa. 19102. *Agent*—ABC, 1995 Broadway, New York, N.Y. 10023.

Career

Saxophonist in musical group the Four Clefs, 1960–63; played with Keith McAllister, 1963–65; following induction into the U.S. Army became member of 19th Army Band, 1965–67, during this time he also appeared, off-duty, with numerous musicians and musical groups in the Philadelphia-New York City area, including Billy Cobham; played with Don Gardner's Sonotones, 1967–68; worked for a record distributor, Philadelphia, 1969–70; with Charles Earland's band, 1971; recording artist, featured and solo performer, 1971—. President of G.W. Jr. Music, Inc. (music publishing company) and of G-Man Productions, Inc. (production company). *Military service:* U.S. Army, 1965–67; served as member of 19th Army band.

Awards: Grammy Award for "best jazz fusion performance, vocal or instrumental," 1981, for album *Winelight;* winner of 1983 "outstanding achievement in the arts" award at the Pitt Jazz Seminar, University of Pittsburgh; holder of one platinum and six gold record albums.

Sidelights

Robert Palmer of *Rolling Stone* called Grover Washington, Jr., "the most popular saxophonist working in a jazz-fusion idiom." And because of Washington's great success some critics have downgraded his music, calling it bland, too commercial, and not real jazz. However, Washington is an obviously talented musician who always surrounds himself with other top-notch musicians and who has had the good fortune to string together a long procession of hit albums. As Albert De Genova wrote in *down beat,* "Grover Washington Jr. has found his niche, and though some are offended by his commercial ventures, no one can deny his musical abilities (or those of the musicians behind him). He creates mood music, soothing and pastoral, tinged with urban funk, done with taste and quality."

Washington was born in Buffalo, New York, on December 12, 1943. He came from a musical family; his father played tenor saxophone, his mother sang in a choir, one brother was an organist in church choirs, and his youngest brother, Darryl, became a drummer (who would later also join the professional ranks). Washington soon took up the saxophone like his father. "I started playing at around age ten," he told Julie Coryell and Laura Friedman writing in *Jazz-Rock Fusion: The People, The Music,* "and my first love was really classical music." He took lessons at the Wurlitzer School of Music and studied a variety of instruments. "My early lessons were on the saxophone, then it was the piano, the drum and percussion family, and the bass guitar." Asked how he found the time for all these instruments, he said, "It was basically what I wanted to do at a very early age, so I had the time. I could really get into all of them on the basic level." Washington also loved basketball as a child but quickly realized that music would be his future. "I stopped growing at 5′ 8-1/2″," he told *People.*

"My music is for the everyday person—people music. There's no pretense. It's honest. It transmits feelings and moods. That's about all you can hope to achieve."

Washington played in his high school band and for two years was a member of the all-city high school band as a baritone saxophonist. He also studied chord progressions with Elvin Shepherd. At the age of 16, Washington finished high school and left Buffalo to become a professional musician, joining the Four Clefs. Based in Columbus, Ohio, the band was on the road much of the time. The Four Clefs split up in 1963 and Washington joined organist Keith McAllister's band. Two years later, in 1965, Washington was drafted into the U.S. Army. Stationed at Fort Dix, New Jersey, he was headed for Vietnam until, according to Joy Wansley of *People,* "he talked his way into the base band." Besides the 19th Army Band, he also played in Philadelphia during his free time, working with a variety of organ trios and rock groups. In addition, he played in New York City with jazz drummer Billy Cobham.

It was at one of his off-post gigs that Washington met his future wife, Christine, who was then an editorial assistant. Christine told *People,* "We met on a Saturday and he moved in on Thursday." They were married in 1967. Washington was discharged from the service that same year. Washington and his new wife then moved to Philadelphia. From 1967 to 1968 he played with Don Gardner's Sonotones. In 1969 he took his first full-time job out of the musical arena, working for a local record distributor. "I was totally immersed in jazz at the time," he told Coryell and Friedman, "and this taught me another side of music. I got to check out people like Jimi Hendrix, Jethro Tull, and John Mayall." In 1971, he returned to music, playing with Charles Earland's band. He also began recording as a sideman with various musicians such as Joe Jones, Leon Spencer, and Johnny Hammond.

His first big musical break came quite by accident. Commercially-minded record producer Creed Taylor had put together a set of pop-funk tunes for alto saxophonist Hank Crawford. On the eve of the recording date, Crawford was arrested "on a two-year-old driving charge," Washington told *Rolling Stone.* Taylor then called in the little-known Washington as a last-minute replacement and had him play the alto parts. The album, *Inner City Blues,* was released in 1971 under Washington's name. It became a hit—an album, said Palmer writing in the *New York Times,* "that sold hundreds of thousands of copies and did much to break down barriers between jazz and pop." As Washington admitted to Wansley, "My big break was blind luck."

He continued to record as a sideman with Randy Weston, Don Sebesky, Bob James, and others, as well as record his own albums. In 1972 he released *All the King's Horses,* followed by *Soul Box* in 1973. It was his next album, *Mister Magic,* released in 1974, that established Washington as a major jazz star. It was the first of several of his albums to reach number one on the jazz charts and go gold. Succeeding best-sellers included *Feels So Good, Live at the Bijou,* and *Reed Seed.*

Washington developed what is called a jazz-pop or jazz-rock fusion musical style. It consists of jazz improvising over a pop or rock beat. Although he came from a jazz background, influenced by such artists as John Coltrane, Joe Henderson, and Oliver Nelson, Washington's wife later got him interested in pop music. "I encouraged him to listen to more pop," Christine told *Rolling Stone.* "His intent was to play jazz, but he started listening to both, and at one point he told me he just wanted to play what he felt, without giving it a label." Recognizing that Washington is unrestrained by labels and tradition, Joachim Berendt wrote in *The Jazz Book: From New Orleans to Rock and Free Jazz* that he plays contemporary music "not worrying about styles and schools." A versatile musician, Washington plays tenor, alto, soprano, and baritone saxophones, plus clarinet, electric bass, and piano. He also composes some of his own material.

The popularity of Washington's brand of jazz-pop music helped make jazz-pop music a success. Keyboardist Bob James told Wansley, "Grover was one of the main people to make this crossover movement happen. We had people intrigued by jazz, but a lot of it was so complex they didn't relate to it. Grover maintained a very high level of musicianship and yet his playing was very melodic and direct."

Critics had mixed reactions to Washington's music, some praise and some pans. The "commercialism" of his music was what usually earned the pans. In a review of his 1979 album *Skylarkin'*, Frank-John Hadley of *down beat* said that "were commercial jazz saxophonists exalted to monarchic positions, Grover Washington Jr. would be the sovereign." Hadley added that Washington's "credo might read: Let my music reach out and spread love. Alas, his past recordings . . . have been as superficial, contrived and dishonest as a Harlequin romance." The *Skylarkin'* album, on the other hand, received high marks from Hadley because of the emotion of Washington's playing. "Now and then his phrases are predictable, tremeloes as cliches, but there's enough unrehearsed excitement and compassion in his playing to permanently exile the affected waxings of any dozen commercial jazz pretenders."

Respected critic Ron Welburn noted in *Radio Free Jazz* that "Grover is perhaps the strongest young fusion reedman in the tradition of Hal Singer, Gatortail Jackson, and Junior Walker. That which is predictable about his music can be excused because of the power and . . . sincerity of his projections." Although some writers considered his music "fuzak," Palmer, in *Rolling Stone*, stated: "Powerful live performances make it clear that, whatever his commercial proclivities, Washington knows his soprano, alto, tenor and baritone saxophones thoroughly. On soprano and alto especially, his sound is attractively personal; he combines liquid grace with an understated residue of R&B grit."

Even some fellow jazz musicians knocked Washington's music. Wansley reported that bassist Percy Heath accused Washington of "bastardizing" jazz. But he defended himself against the barbs: "My music is for the everyday person—people music. There's no pretense. It's honest. It transmits feelings and moods. That's about all you can hope to achieve."

In 1980, Washington released his most successful album ever—*Winelight*. And from that album came a smash hit single—"Just the Two of Us," with vocalist Bill Withers. Both the album and the single had wide appeal. As *People* noted, the two recordings were "simultaneously among the top five sellers on five record charts: Soul Singles and LPs, Pop Singles and LPs and Jazz LPs." The popular jazz saxophonist achieved even broader popularity. The album eventually went platinum and the single went gold. Remarked the *New York Times*, "[Washington's] commercial success is unusual for a contemporary jazz instrumentalist."

Ever since he moved to Philadelphia, Washington had been a big fan of the Philadelphia 76ers professional basketball team. His love for the 76ers, and particularly their star player, went public with the *Winelight* album. One of the tracks on the record is called "Let It Flow ("For Dr. J")," dedicated to the team's Julius "Dr. J" Erving. Around the same time, Washington approached the team and began playing the national anthem occasionally before games. "Why not?" he said to Lisa Twyman of *Sports Illustrated*. "I was at the games anyway."

Also in 1980, Washington applied for a doctoral program in music composition at Temple University. He explained to Wansley that he "was told he had to audition. 'The next day,' he smiles, 'I came back with a stack of my albums and told them to listen and let me know if they thought I could play.' He was admitted."

Washington's following albums carried on his familiar mellow sound and the critics continued their mixed reactions. In a 1982 review of his recording *Come Morning*, De Genova said: "Commercial? Yes. Trite? No. Appropriately titled, this album sets a 'cool summer morning, grass still wet with dew, lover laying next to you' mood." He added that "Grover's sincerity and his natural, almost whimsical saxophone interpretations make his refreshingly lyrical phrasing a pleasure to listen to." However, De Genova maintained, "Some may call this music vinyl Valium, and depending on personal taste, the album may become monotonous. Similarities in mood, texture, and tonality often make some of the tunes seem to blend together."

In addition to producing some of his own albums, Washington has also worked as a producer for the group Pieces of a Dream. In a review of their 1982 recording *We Are One*, Robert Henschen of *down beat* proclaimed, "With Grover Washington in a producer's role, you know the final mix is going to have a light, enjoyable touch. It does." Washington also had a featured solo on one of the songs and his playing, Henschen said, was "as sweet as ever."

Reviewing Washington's 1983 album, *The Best Is Yet to Come, People* suggested that he definitely is capable of better. This album "is more pop than jazz, taking wing only in occasional bursts from Washington that break out of a staid set of arrangements." Better things did happen to him when he attended the annual Pitt Jazz Seminar at the University of Pittsburgh and was presented with the year's Outstanding Achievement in the Arts award.

In 1984 Washington released the album *Inside Moves*. Robert Hiltbrand of *People* remarked that "Grover's jazz is accessible to listeners of all musical tastes. Turn him loose on choice material, as on *Inside Moves*, and his fluid and graceful style is incomparable." Describing some of the cuts, Hiltbrand said, "'Dawn Song' moves from soft and dreamy to sharp and funky. The title cut undergoes a similar change, with Washington blending alto, tenor and baritone saxes over the sweet opening and then pulling out all the stops on top of a bass-percussive riff that is reminiscent of the pioneer fusion ensemble Weather Report."

The next year saw Washington collaborate on an album with jazz guitarist Kenny Burrell. A review by Ralph Novak of *People* stated that "Even those people who find Washington's popular solo-saxophone albums too bland and unchallenging don't question his sense of melody and tone. This LP lets him unleash those talents with a passionate vengeance." Burrell and Washington mesh well together, according to Novak. "There are few more enjoyable moments in jazz than when two imaginative soloists mix and match with each other's moods, and this album is full of such moments."

Washington will undoubtedly continue to create his smooth, melodic saxophone sounds for years to come. And if he follows the advice of Hadley, he will also "continue his present policy, the policy of circulating warmth."

Discography

Inner City Blues, Kudu, 1971.
All the King's Horses, Kudu, 1972.
Soul Box, Kudu, 1973.
Mister Magic, Kudu, 1974.
Feels So Good, Kudu, 1975.
Secret Place, Kudu, 1976.
Soul Box, Volume 2, Kudu, 1976.
Live At the Bijou, Kudu, 1978.
Reed Seed, Motown, 1978.
Paradise, Elektra, 1979.
Skylarkin', Motown, 1979.
Winelight, Elektra, 1980.
Baddest, Motown, 1981.
Come Morning, Elektra, 1981.
The Best Is Yet to Come, Elektra, 1982.
Inside Moves, Elektra, 1984.
Anthology Of, Elektra, 1985.
Strawberry Moon, Columbia, 1987.
Then and Now, Columbia, 1988.
Greatest Performances, Motown.
Anthology, Motown.
At His Best, Motown.

Has also recorded as a sideman or featured artist with numerous musicians, including Eric Gale, Bob James, Ralph MacDonald, Don Sebesky, Randy Weston, and Bill Withers.

Also producer of and occasional guest performer on albums by musical group Pieces of a Dream, including *We Are One*, 1982; has also produced Jean Carne.

Sources

Books

Berendt, Joachim, *The Jazz Book: From New Orleans to Rock and Free Jazz*, translation by Dan Morgenstern, Barbara Bredigkeit, and Helmut Bredigkeit, Lawrence Hill & Co., 1975.
Coryell, Julie, and Laura Friedman, *Jazz-Rock Fusion: The People, The Music*, Dell, 1978.
Feather, Leonard, and Ira Gitler, *The Encyclopedia of Jazz in the Seventies*, Horizon Press, 1976.
Pareles, Jon, and Patricia Romanowski, *The Rolling Stone Encyclopedia of Rock & Roll*, Rolling Stone Press, 1983.

Periodicals

down beat, October, 1980; June, 1982; December, 1982; February, 1983.
New York Times, April 24, 1981.
People, May 18, 1981; February 7, 1983; October 29, 1984; April 22, 1985.
Rolling Stone, October 18, 1979.
Sports Illustrated, July 11, 1983.

—Sidelights by Greg Mazurkiewicz

Faye Wattleton

Registered nurse; association executive

Full name, Alyce Faye Wattleton; born July 8, 1943, in St. Louis, Mo.; daughter of George Edward and Ozie (Garrett) Wattleton; children: Felicia Megan. *Education:* Ohio State University, B.S. in nursing, 1964; Columbia University, M.S. in nursing, 1967. *Politics:* Democrat. *Religion:* Church of God.

Addresses: *Office*—Planned Parenthood Federation of America, Inc., 810 Seventh Ave., New York, N.Y. 10019

Career

Miami Valley Hospital School of Nursing, Dayton, Ohio, instructor in nursing, 1964–66; Dayton Public Health Nursing Association, assistant director, 1967–70; Planned Parenthood Association of Miami Valley, Dayton, executive director, 1970–78; Planned Parenthood Federation of America, Inc., New York, N.Y., president, 1978—. Member of advisory council of the Peace Corps, 1980—; member of advisory committee of the Women's Leadership Conference on National Security.

Member: American Public Health Association, American College of Nurse-Midwives, National Academy of Sciences, National Urban Coalition, National Urban League, Ohio State University Alumni Association (member of board of directors).

Awards: Awarded Ohio State University citation for outstanding achievement, 1979; received annual award of the New Jersey chapter of the American Civil Liberties Union, 1980.

Courtesy of Faye Wattleton

Sidelights

For the past ten years, Faye Wattleton has served as president of the Planned Parenthood Federation of America, the nation's oldest and largest voluntary family planning service. When she was appointed to that post in 1978 at age 34, she was the first woman, the first black, and the youngest executive ever to serve in that capacity. She entered the job with a battle cry. Aware of the value of a high public profile, the former nurse from Ohio vowed to lead the Federation in its first active campaign for reproductive rights and to transform the traditionally low-keyed organization into a visible force. Specifically, she targeted three areas of concentration: abortion funding for the poor, advances in contraceptive development, and development of a national strategy to reduce teen pregnancy. Though Wattleton could not have known it at the time, gains in these areas were the very ones that would be jeopordized by the Reagan administration in the 1980s.

Rather than yielding to conservative pressure, Wattleton turned Reagan's attempts to reverse reproductive rights and slash federal programs into a strategic approach, using opposition as a platform for her work. "If people perceive something is under attack they are more likely to support it," she explained in a

February 1985 issue of *Savvy* magazine. Under her direction, the 72-year-old Federation has successfully lobbied for increased sex education in schools, continued federal funding of family planning programs, the rights of teens to obtain contraceptives without notification of their parents, and women's continued right to abortions.

Despite some setbacks at the state level—both Michigan and Colorado recently voted to rescind public funding of abortions for the poor—Wattleton is convinced that the battle for reproductive rights is being won. And she is not unduly concerned about abortion being outlawed through a reversal of the *Roe* v. *Wade* Supreme Court decision that guarantees a woman's constitutional right to terminate a pregnancy—even though the possibility has been hotly debated in the press. Planned Parenthood and its affiliates provide medical, educational, and counseling services to over three million people, and she believes these figures reflect public support. "Our strength lies in the fact that we are supported by the majority of Americans," she told *Newsmakers*. "And our motivation lies in our obligation to make sure their voices are heard and acknowledged by those who set public policy in this country." Rather than predicting setbacks, Wattleton looks forward to possible gains under the Bush administration.

Newsmakers Interview

Newsmakers interviewed Faye Wattleton by telephone at her New York City office on November 18, 1988.

Newsmakers: *In 1978, when you first became president of Planned Parenthood, you announced that the traditionally low-keyed organization was going to become more aggressive in the battle for abortion rights. How well has your campaign succeeded?*

Wattleton: I don't know that I would describe it as a campaign. It was a statement of what I felt the organization's obligations were and are. And I think the record shows that we have become more aggressive. When I made that statement in 1978, I don't think that I had any real idea of what was ahead in terms of the Reagan administration's right-wing policies on reproductive rights in general and abortion rights in particular. It was almost prophetic that I made such a statement because it became even more necessary after the Reagan election than it was at that time.

Newsmakers: *What accounts for the public success tht some pro-life groups have achieved in defeating public funding of abortions for the poor?*

Wattleton: Anti-abortion groups—I'm reluctant to call them pro-life because that suggests that people who believe in abortions are against life—but anti-abortion groups have seized upon any element of sensitivity to try to make gains on their agenda to outlaw abortion and make it illegal. With respect to funding for low-income women for abortions, we hit upon two elements. One, people believe that even though the government should not interfere in the right of a woman to have a safe abortion, they don't necessarily believe that the government should pay for it. And then we fall into the problem of an overall discomfort with welfare programs in general. These funding issues have really centered around whether welfare financing should pay for abortions, and so we have additional elements to deal with. And we were not, at least in the last election, successful in maintaining those programs in two major states.

Newsmakers: *And is Michigan one of them?*

Wattleton: Michigan and Colorado were the two. Arkansas was a third state that had a referendum, but it had no practical effect because Arkansas does not fund abortions.

Newsmakers: *Will Planned Parenthood solicit private funds to pay for abortions that are not funded through public agencies?*

Wattleton: We have always tried to support poor women and to aid them in obtaining abortions if they did not have the resources to do so, and we will certainly continue to do what we can. But I think it's important to recognize that it is not possible to replace a government program with private financing. We're speaking first of all of the money being cut off at the federal level in 1978–79 and then, in major states where there are large populations of poor women, continuing to fund abortions on a state basis. State funding does continue in many states across the country, but we are saddened by the loss in Michigan, because Michigan does have so many low-income women who would be elegible for Medicaid and who, I'm certain, will experience unintended pregnancies and now will take the very few resources they have to seek a safe abortion or resort to unsafe means to terminate the pregnancy. So we don't seek to replicate—nor is it possible for us to replace—government financing of programs, but we will certainly do everything possible to help low-income women obtain safe abortions.

I think it's unfortunate and really reflects the mean-spirited nature of the anti-abortion movement that it is willing to sacrifice poor women in this debate as a means of making gains. Abortion is legal in this country and is not something that should be denied women, but anti-abortion advocates suggest that if they can't deny it to every woman, they will at least deny it to low-income women.

Newsmakers: *Earlier you said that really, there was no question that people believe that it is a right for a woman to have an abortion, but among some constituents, there is a belief that the real issue isn't the funding of abortion but abortion itself...*

Wattleton: I think that is true among some constituents. I did not suggest that there was 100 percent support for legal abortion in this country. What I said was that there was a broad concensus, not a unanimous concensus.

Newsmakers: *What do you think are the chances that the* Roe v. Wade *Supreme Court decision could be overturned?*

Wattleton: Very remote. There is a good chance that *Roe* v. *Wade* will be restricted. I think sometimes we forget that when *Roe* v. *Wade* was handed down in 1973, it was by no means received with celebration by the pro-choice community. But what has happened over the years, in subsequent Supreme Court decisions, is that *Roe* v. *Wade* has been broadened. In *Roe* v. *Wade,* the decision formulated the pregnancy in three trimesters. And it was in the first trimester that the woman could not have her decision to terminate a pregnancy interferred with—it was between a woman and her physician; in the second trimester, the state might regulate the circumstances under which an abortion would be permitted; and in the third trimester the state could take a direct intervention in preventing the abortion, but never in cases where the woman's health or well being was threatened.

In subsequent cases, the Supreme Court has basically said that in the second trimester there is very little that the state can do. It struck down the ordinances which imposed a waiting period and certain restrictions and said those were burdensome and unnecessary and interfered unduly in a woman's right to seek and obtain an abortion.

So I think there is a good chance that this court as it is presently constituted could roll back some of those subsequent decisions on questions of waiting periods and questions of regulations, making it more difficult for women to obtain abortions, but not impossible. When we talk about the reversal of *Roe* v. *Wade,* let's hope that this Supreme Court is not so highly politicized that it believes that women should be criminalized for interrupting an unintended pregnancy.

Newsmakers: *There's some concern about the reversal of* Roe v. Wade *because of the likelihood that any new Supreme Court appointees will be conservatives...*

Wattleton: The leading candidate for retirement right now is Byron White and he is strongly in the right-wing camp. I guess I am not one of those people who prognosticates about doom and gloom on the Supreme Court. I think there's no question that this court has shifted to a more conservative posture, but I don't believe that automatically means that *Roe* v. *Wade* is going to be reversed. Yes, there is a good possibility that it may be modified, but reversed—no.

Newsmakers: *Do you sense a new conservatism among Americans or is it simply that anti-abortion forces have remained vigilant while pro-choice advocates have become complacent, taking for granted earlier gains?*

Wattleton: I don't think any of that is true.

> *"Our strength lies in the fact that we are supported by the majority of Americans."*

Newsmakers: *You don't sense a new conservatism among Americans?*

Wattleton: There is no evidence that Americans believe these issues should be any different than they are now. In fact, there is a lot of evidence that Americans have not changed since *Roe* v. *Wade* was handed down, that Americans' positions are basically frozen: we don't like abortion, we don't particularly like having to talk about it, but we don't want the government interfering.

The media has given a tremendous amount of attention of late to a few noisy people who are engaged in demonstrations and sit-ins. A few years ago these same people were burning down our clinics. So we're not talking about anything that is new—picketing and harrassment have been going on for years. One of the things that has been rather peculiar is that the media has not covered it before now. But it is certainly not any newly awakening movement of demonstrations and violence. The movement was even more violent a few years ago. It had been very persistent, but I think we have been extremely persistent in our efforts to counter their attacks. For instance, we think one of the reasons Planned Parenthood has not been the focus of the so-called "Operation Rescue" activities is because we are so well prepared for this type of activity. They like to hit clinics that are not so fully prepared to confront them and to prevent their efforts from succeeding.

Newsmakers: *What became very clear to voters in Michigan during the November election was that the people who wanted to repeal abortion funding had an enormous campaign—they had billboards, they had television ads, they were very organized and focused and very, very visible.*

Wattleton: Well, they outspent the pro-choice side two-to-one.

Newsmakers: *And the pro-choice advocates were basically women on street corners handing out brochures. So in terms of what the average citizen encountered, the anti-abortion forces were much more visible.*

Wattleton: They were more visible but I think it's important to make the distinction between whether pro-choice forces were complacent. I don't think there was complacency. I think there was a difficult time in raising funds and putting together the kind of organization that the anti-abortion movement had, with the efforts of the Catholic Church behind them, and—in the year of a Presidential campagin—the media director of the Bush campaign being responsible for a lot of the media coordination and the development of their ads. And we were simply outspent significantly. I mean, we don't have the benefit of the Sunday morning pulpit on these issues, so it is tougher. It is more difficult.

But even at that I think we should point out that Michigan and Colorado are exceptions. We have lost three [counting Arkansas] this year, after having won 21, so we have won 21 of the 24 initiatives that have been on the ballot the past seven or eight years. I don't think this is any significant trend away from being on the winning side. I think we just have to go back and do a better job of organizing and try to raise more resources to fight these campaigns.

Newsmakers: *What do you foresee happening to reproductive rights during the Bush administration?*

Wattleton: I don't think there's anything that can happen any worse than what happened during the Reagan administration. It was the most violent administration against reproductive rights in history. The worst that could happen is that we'll have a continuation of the same. The best that we can expect is that there will be some moderation. We're not talking about an administration, in the case of the Reagan administration, that was just anti-abortion, it was also anti-family planning. It tried to destroy the family planning program. It tried to restrict international family planning. It was a disaster.

I go around to towns all over the country and I make this speech and, of course, Republicans get very upset and very nervous. I say to them, I really wish there were one thing good that happened in the Reagan administration on family planning. There wasn't a single thing done that was helpful to family planning. Every year the Reagan administration went to Congress and said, end this program. We're not just talking about legal abortion. Every year it said, we don't feel that the Federal government should finance services to prevent unintended pregnancy. It was a great curiosity. I can't believe the Bush administration will be any worse, and let's just hope there is some moderating influence and that we can end these four years saying, while we may not have agreed on all things, at least Mr. Bush did try to advance family planning or did try to make sex education more widely available.

Newsmakers: *What specific plans do you have to insure that your ideas are communicated to him?*

Wattleton: We have written and developed policies for the administration and have published them in a transition paper that we will use to communicate with the transition team and with the incoming cabinet members and key appointees. We do have policy proposals that we think will get us back on track.

Newsmakers: *Given the current political climate, what do you think the term "pro-family" means?*

Wattleton: I think pro-family means those concerns that contemporary families—that is families surviving in contemporary America—must face and address. We live in a very mobile, changing society with many pressures and new challenges that may not have been the kind of issues that families had to confront a generation ago. So the concerns of government need to be with those programs that will strengthen families. And certainly when you think about reproductive rights and family planning, the availability of family planning services helps families to get off to a good start.

Newsmakers: *Over the years anti-abortion forces have often gone to extremes to publicize their stance, including bombing abortion clinics and harrassing clients and* *staff members. How do you counteract these incidents and why do you think the issue has become so ugly?*

Wattleton: I think the issue has become so ugly because they have been so unsuccessful. They have not been able to persuade the courts, the Congress, the state legislatures, the American people that their view is the one that should be adopted as a matter of national policy. We do everything possible to protect our clients, our people, our facilities. We have aggressively pursued trespassers and other vandals and arsonists and criminals in courts and we will continue to do so, but whether we're going to stoop to their level to engage in violent demonstrations and breaking the peace and intimidating women who may be experiencing very difficult situations in their lives is just unthinkable.

Newsmakers: *Is this what you were alluding to earlier when you said that many Planned Parenthood clinics are left alone because you are so well prepared to deal with the situation?*

Wattleton: We're not only well prepared legally, but we are also well prepared physically. Back in the early and mid-seventies we developed a program to instruct our affiliates on the proper security to maintain in their facilities to prevent acts of violence and destruction from succeeding. It's difficult to go through the elaborate security measures that are now in place in most of our affiliates; it's just easier to attack those facilities that are less well-prepared.

Newsmakers: *In 1978, when you took office, you said that one of your primary goals was to place reproductive biology research and contraceptive development at the highest level on the nation's research agenda. Why haven't there been any recent advances in the area of birth control? Why isn't the "morning after" pill, which is on the market in France, available in the United States today?*

Wattleton: The conditions that have created a lack of satisfactory advancement in birth control are multiple, and they are formidable. Perhaps the most serious of them is the litigious climate around product liability, with contraceptive products at the very top of the list. The result is that most pharmaceutical companies have moved out of the development of contraceptive agents, believing that there are more lucrative markets that are less fraught with economic peril.

Newsmakers: *So it's a question of there not being enough money in it to attract private enterprise?*

Wattleton: Exactly. And now we have the additional element of the controversy that has been created by anti-choice forces who don't want to see these drugs developed and come to market. The most recent example is the "morning after" pill that you refer to where the company, Roussel-Uclaf, in France, withdrew the drug briefly from the market and replaced it after a few days when the French government directed them to do so. What we see is that these drugs will not come to market without a tremendous amount of controversy. And corporations in America do not like to get involved in products that are going to be controversial.

This is going to be a tough battle. I think it will probably be the last really major battle over abortion rights, because the anti-abortion forces recognize that, if this drug comes to market in this country, abortion will truly become a matter of privacy. And they won't be able to picket every woman's home on Main St., USA, and they won't be able to picket every pharmacy in the country. And their battle to interfere in the lives of women will be lost.

> *"We had to repay our guilt for exploiting sex so explicitly in our society by preserving a shroud of ignorance."*

Newsmakers: *Pro-choice groups generally feel that education is the key in combatting such problems as teen pregnancy and sexually transmitted diseases. What is your evaluation of sex education programs in American schools?*

Wattleton: Well, we have very few of them in American schools so there isn't really much to evaluate. We are making progress in that area. There are now 17 states that require sexuality education, and that's a very recent phenomenon. Just a few years ago I went around the country and there were only three states and the District of Columbia that required sex education.

Newsmakers: *What do you feel is the best way to introduce topics such as contraception and AIDS into these programs?*

Wattleton: Sex education should be available from kindergarten through twelfth grade. We think, in fact, sex education should start in the home before children reach school age. That will happen with varying degrees of success and in an inconsistent fashion. So just as we send our children to school to learn about their world, we don't think their sexual lives should be excluded. We think that subjects such as birth control and AIDS should be talked about before adolescence, so that when adolescents confront these issues they are well prepared ahead of time. And we don't believe that birth control and information about AIDS should be taught in isolation. Our children should have a solid background of understanding about their sexuality and about their sexual health before we have to talk to them about some of the problems and some of the complex situations that they must confront as adults.

We're basically an illiterate society sexually. We're not well educated. We're not much better educated than our parents, and even though sex is merchandised and exploited, there is very little sexuality education available in American schools. It is almost as though we had to repay our guilt for exploiting sex so explicitly in our society by preserving a shroud of ignorance.

Newsmakers: *Are there other countries that have model programs of sex education that we might turn to?*

Wattleton: There are a number of European countries who have programs that are much better than ours, particularly the Netherlands and Sweden. Both are known for the outstanding quality of their sex education efforts. And that has not always been the case. Those countries decided a number of years ago that the condition of teenage pregnancy was unacceptable and they were going to make a commitment to education and to wider and easy availability of birth control. For their efforts they have significantly reduced the rate of unintended pregnancy both among the adolescent and the adult population.

Newsmakers: *What is your reaction to the recent papal announcement that condom use, because it interferred with conception, could not be endorsed in the fight against AIDS?*

Wattleton: I think that not very many people pay attention to papal pronouncements.

Newsmakes: *Including the Catholic population?*

Wattleton: Especially the Catholic population. If you look at Catholics as a group, Catholics live their lives in the moral context of their environment and not on the basis of pronouncements from the Vatican.

Newsmakers: *In closing, what do you think have been your biggest gains in your ten years as president of Planned Parenthood?*

Wattleton: My greatest satisfaction is in leading an organization that has had such an enormous influence on the future of humankind. It's interesting that we're doing this interview right now because I'm about to take a four-month sabbatical after ten years of doing this, and I take this break with a great deal of satisfaction that we have preserved reproductive rights in this country. We have expanded services to people. We have raised the consciousness about the need for better education around sexuality and have seen significant gains in that area. And we have survived and thrived in one of the most hostile periods in American life for reproductive rights for Americans. And I'm very proud to have been a part of that fight.

Sources

Interview, April, 1987.
Jet, March 18, 1985.
Money, November, 1985.
New York Times, February 3, 1978; March 11, 1978.
New York Times Magazine, March 30, 1980.
People, May 24, 1982.
Savvy, February, 1985.
Time, February 7, 1983.

—Sidelights and interview by Donna Olendorf

Bill White

AP/Wide World Photos

Baseball executive

Full name, William DeKova White; born January 28, 1934, in Lakewood, Fla.; son of a steelworker; divorced; children: five. *Education:* Attended Hiram (Ohio) College, 1952–53.

Addresses: *Home*—Bucks County, Pa. *Office*—National League of Professional Baseball Clubs, 350 Park Ave., New York, N.Y. 10022.

Career

Baseball player in minor leagues, 1953–56, and in major leagues with New York Giants, 1956, San Francisco Giants, 1958, St. Louis Cardinals, 1959–65, 1969, and Philadelphia Phillies, 1966–68; sportscaster for WPVI, Philadelphia, 1967–68; broadcaster and baseball analyst for WPIX-TV, New York City, 1970–88; president of National League of Professional Baseball Clubs, New York City, 1989—. *Military service:* 1956–58.

Awards: Named to National League All-Star team six times; winner of seven Gold Gloves for fielding excellence.

Sidelights

By his own account, nothing in baseball ever came easy for Bill White. He was not a great natural hitter, but he made himself good enough to bat .300 or better four times, drive in 100 or more runs four times, hit 20 or more home runs seven times, and leave his name scattered through baseball's record book. "I would see guys like [Willie] Mays and [Roberto] Clemente who just naturally knew how to play," White told the *Philadelphia Daily News.* "It didn't come that easily to me. I had to bust my butt to stay out there." Indeed, White made himself into a powerful hitter, a seven-time Gold Glove first baseman, a six-time National League All-Star and, when his playing days were over, one of the country's most respected baseball broadcasters. He accomplished it all through hard work.

In 1989, the owners of the 12 National League baseball clubs chose William DeKova White—a man of determination and conviction—to become the 13th president in the league's 113-year history. In some ways, White was a surprising choice; for instance, he had no prior administrative or business experience. In one way, it was a novel move: he was the first black man to become the head of any major professional sports league.

But in many ways, Bill White had been a leader from the start. In 1961, even though his status with the St. Louis Cardinals was not secure, White spoke up about the miserable spring training segregation that persisted in Florida. He reminded officials of the Anheuser-Busch company, which owned the Cardinals, that black people, too, drink beer. The Cardinals, embarrassed, quickly made changes. "You won't see Bill marching," former teammate Bob Gibson told *Newsday*. "He does things quietly. He thinks that sometimes that's the best way to get something accomplished. That's the fashion in which he's used to doing things."

"I'm aware of how far the game has come from the segregated conditions I encountered when I first broke in. I will obviously try to encourage continued advancements. But you do the job no matter what your color is."

White was born in Florida in 1934 and grew up in Warren, Ohio, hoping to become a doctor. He graduated second in his high school class and attended Hiram College on an academic—not athletic—scholarship. For a diversion, he played first base for the school's baseball team. A New York Giants scout spotted White in a game and signed him to a $2,500 bonus. Years later, White told the *Washington Post* that he signed the contract and quit Hiram's pre-med program because, "I needed money. I promised my mother I'd go back, which I never did. I just needed to add a little bit to help my people send me to college and did better at baseball than I thought."

At age 19, White was sent to the minor league team in Danville, Virginia. In 1953, he was the only black player in the Carolina League. In those days, black players stayed in separate hotels. "I always had to find my own way to the ballpark and from the ballpark," he told the *Philadelphia Inquirer*. "And I had to put up with the crap from the fans, which had never happened to me before. I was called names I had never heard. They were allowed to call me anything they wanted, but I couldn't do anything back, you see."

White took out his anger on opposing pitchers, hitting .298 with 20 homers and 84 RBIs in Danville. His next stop was Sioux City, Iowa, in the Western League. He recalled to the *Philadelphia Inquirer* an incident in Wichita, Kansas, where he was thrown out of a restaurant while a white diner, covered with dirt and grease, was allowed to eat. "As far as letting them break me, I couldn't and wouldn't do that," he told the *Inquirer*. "But this one time I did get disturbed out of frustration. I mean, to sit there, halfway decently dressed, and to see some guy I would consider an animal—I wouldn't let him come in, he was so dirty—be allowed to eat in peace simply because of his color, while I couldn't eat .... I think that's the only time in my life I cried."

White broke into the majors in 1956 with the New York Giants—hitting a home run in his first at-bat. He played in 138 games his rookie season, batting .256 with an impressive 22 home runs. His career was then interrupted by a two-year stint in the military. He played the last few weeks of the 1958 season with the Giants (who had since moved to San Francisco), before being traded to the St. Louis Cardinals.

White, who considered himself a power hitter, flourished with the Cardinals after accepting the advice of hitting coach Harry Walker—go up the middle, hit for average, don't worry about the homers. He hit for the cycle during one game in 1960, hit three consecutive homers in a game in 1961, and, in a truly astonishing feat, totaled 14 hits in two days in 1961 while playing back-to-back doubleheaders, matching a record set by Ty Cobb in 1912. *St. Louis Post-Dispatch* sports writer Bob Broeg, who watched White through his years with the Cardinals, described him as, "not blessed with extraordinary talent, certainly not agile, and so muscular that his swing, at first, was stiff and deliberate. He ran in such careful, plodding strides that Gibson, his close friend, used to tease him with the nickname 'Robot.' Then, day by day, he molded himself into an outstanding player with a desire he carried like a weapon. He was so consumed by his pursuit to excel that for years he scrawled in magic-marker on the outside of his mitt a personal reminder. It said, 'RELAX.'"

On social issues, White never really did relax. Once, after winning an award from an all-white St. Louis civic club, he refused to go to the banquet. When the Cardinals sent a representative to accept on his behalf, he ordered the plaque sent back. "Bill doesn't just do things," former teammate Gibson told *Newsday*. "He does his own thing." In 1964, White had committed to speak at a grade school long before the Cardinals came from nowhere to win the World Series on the very same day he was scheduled to appear. The school had lined up another speaker, but White—insisting that a commitment was a commitment—skipped the champagne party his teammates were holding and showed up to speak to the children.

White's best seasons were 1962 (when he hit .324), 1963 (when he hit .304 with 27 homers) and 1964 (when he hit .303 with 21 homers). On October 27, 1965, he was traded to Philadelphia with shortstop Dick Groat and catcher Bob Uecker for catcher Pat Corrales, pitcher Art Mahaffey, and outfielder Alex Johnson. *Philadelphia Daily News* baseball writer Bill Conlin wrote of White: "The first thing you noticed interviewing Bill White was that he spoke in complete sentences, rare in a baseball locker room. But more than that, those sentences often ended in question marks." White had a solid 1966 season with the Phillies, hitting 22 home runs and driving in 103 runs. During the next off-season, however, he severed an Achilles' tendon during a handball match, and then aggravated it trying to come back too soon. He hung on with the Phillies for two more seasons and then returned to the Cardinals in 1969 as a pinch-hitter before retiring. He finished his 13-year career with a .286 batting average, 202 homers, and 870 RBIs. He was remembered mostly as a player who always gave his best effort. "He had a burning desire to succeed," former Cardinal teammate Dal Maxvill told *Newsday*, "but he always kept it under the surface."

After he retired, White was asked by the Cardinals to manage their minor-league team in Tulsa, Oklahoma, for $12,500, plus the honor of being America's first black manager. White turned them down. In 1975, New York Yankees owner George Steinbrenner offered White the job of club general manager. "I wasn't ready then," White told the *Washington Post*. "As far as managing, I had no interest. I didn't want to do anything that depended on 24 other guys doing their jobs."

Instead, he went into broadcasting, spending 18 years as broadcaster of New York Yankees games on WPIX-TV, as well as calling some games for the CBS Radio Network. At first, White admits, his home-run calls sounded about as exciting as a mid-inning plug for season tickets. But he worked at this career—much like he worked as a player—taking tapes home, listening to them for hours, critiquing himself. As a broadcaster, he was known to speak his mind. A National Leaguer at heart, White frequently criticized

As Bill White (left) prepares to throw out his first ceremonial pitch as National League president to start the 1989 season, New York Mets owner Fred Wilpon points out scuff marks on the ball. AP/Wide World Photos.

the "American League style of play" and knocked the designated hitter rule. His arguments were always well-reasoned, never inflammatory. "He can be a very serious guy," his long-time broadcast partner, Phil Rizzuto, told *Newsday.* "When he tackles something, he sets his mind that he's going to get the job done. We'd be on a plane going somewhere and he'd take out the *New York Times* crossword puzzle and he'd stay at it until he finished it. And then he'd hand it to me and say, 'Here, check it.' He had to get it right." By 1989, however, White was ready for a new career. "I had nice security with the Yankees and a relaxed pattern to my life," he told the *Los Angeles Times,* "but how many ways can you say, 'There's a ground ball to short'? I was simply ready for something more meaningful."

National League owners were looking for a new president to replace A. Bartlett Giamatti [see index for *Newsmakers* entry], who was to become the commissioner of major league baseball. A five-man search committee worked for several months but was initially unable to find a candidate suitable to the majority of owners. Eventually, the committee hired a Chicago-based executive search firm, which came up with two candidates—White and Simon Gourdine, the director of labor relations for New York's Metropolitan Transit Authority. White told the *Washington Post* that when he was first approached about the job, his initial thought was: "Are they serious? I'd been told many times that Bill White was being considered, but I was never approached. My first reaction was, 'Are these people serious about this?'"

Both White and Gourdine are black, which was more than a coincidence. Outgoing commissioner Peter Ueberroth had been pushing the sport's owners to hire blacks for executive positions for several years. Baseball was embarrassed in 1987 when Los Angeles Dodgers executive Al Campanis, in an appearance on ABC's "Nightline," said blacks may lack the "necessities" to hold important front-office jobs. Campanis was fired for his remarks, but, in the firestorm that followed, baseball began an affirmative action plan for its front offices. On February 3, 1989, White signed a four-year contract to become the first black to head a major professional sports league. "It's a very important day for baseball," Ueberroth told the *Washington Post.* "It's another step along the way and hopefully some more doors are being opened."

White himself downplayed the significance of race. "I'm aware of my social responsibility," he told the *Los Angeles Times.* "I'm aware of how far the game has come from the segregated conditions I encountered when I first broke in. I will obviously try to encourage continued advancements. But you do the job no matter what your color is." Broadcast mate Phil Rizzuto, however, emphasized that White was keenly aware of his barrier-breaking significance. "He felt this was important for baseball, for himself and for blacks in general," Rizzuto told the *San Jose Mercury News.* Others compared White's hiring with Jackie Robinson's breaking of baseball's color barrier more than 40 years earlier. But White did not see himself having that impact. "When Jackie got the chance," he told the *Philadelphia Daily News,* "it caused progress for the whole country. It gave lots of people more hope. This job involves dealing with umpires, with league matters, with financing. It deals with expansion, with social problems such as drugs, the hiring of minorities."

Indeed, the job of National League president is quite often largely symbolic and involves such mundane duties of working out details of the league schedule and helping with umpiring assignments. But the job does not end there. There is the ever-volatile issue of labor negotiations, expansion and, perhaps most important, discipline for those on the field. The league president is often the first and final authority on what punitive measures will be taken. Under Giamatti, the position gained teeth. Giamatti did not hesitate to hand out stiff fines and long suspensions in an effort to curb on-field fighting. *Chicago Tribune* columnist Bob Verdi wrote: "A league president can make of the position what he wants. He can autograph baseballs, or he can leave his signature on the office. There is precedent for being a mannequin, but there is also room to stretch out and be felt. One can't envision any scenario whereby White will be invisible, and not because he's black, but because he cares. Expect White to come out strongly in favor of firm yet fair, without wavering. He might even be able to cut through a lot of politics and posturing, because he's made it through worse."

White initially said he planned to work to improve labor-management relations, as well as the deteriorating relationship between players and umpires. But, he admitted to the *Washington Post,* "I still need to learn this job." And, he said he had been thinking about the pressures of the new job and the loss of freedom it would entail. "I had a lot of security with the Yankees," he told the *San Jose Mercury News.* "I lead a very nice life now. I only work 90 days broadcasting. I can go fishing, drive my truck, cut the grass and wear overalls. I can't do that with this job. It's a 24-hours-a-day job. Things happen on the [West] Coast and you've got to be with it even if it's late at night. It's going to be hard to leave that comfort of broadcasting. I don't think overalls would go over too big on this job."

Sources

Chicago Tribune, February 6, 1989.
Los Angeles Times, February 4, 1989.
Newsday, February 3, 1989; February 5, 1989; February 6, 1989.
New York Times, February 3, 1989; February 4, 1989; February 5, 1989; February 8, 1989.
Philadelphia Daily News, February 1, 1989; February 9, 1989.
Philadelphia Inquirer, February 5, 1989.
St. Louis Post-Dispatch, February 3, 1989; February 9, 1989.
San Jose Mercury News, February 3, 1989.
Sports Illustrated, February 13, 1989.
Time, February 13, 1989.
Washington Post, February 4, 1989.

—*Sketch by Glen Macnow*

Christopher Whittle

AP/Wide World Photos

Publisher, information entrepreneur

Born August 23, 1947, in Etowah, Tenn.; son of Herbert (a physician) and Rita Whittle. *Education:* Graduated from University of Tennessee; attended Columbia University Law School for four months.

Addresses: *Home*—Knoxville, Tenn.; New York, N.Y.; and Vermont. *Office*—Whittle Communications, 505 Market St., Knoxville, Tenn. 37902.

Career

As a young man, worked as a newspaper stringer, pumped gas, waited tables, and played saxophone in a dance band; while in college, co-founded Collegiate Enterprises, Inc. (publishing company), Knoxville, Tenn.; student intern to Tennessee Senator Howard Baker; worked as a laborer in a Louisiana oil town for a month; campaign aide to Connecticut gubernatorial candidate Wally Barnes; national sales manager, 13–30 Corp., Knoxville; founder and head of Whittle Communications, Knoxville.

Sidelights

The idea, says Christopher Whittle, came to him "out of the blue" during a meeting with an advertiser some 15 years ago. Then the neophyte publisher of *Nutshell*, a campus magazine aimed at college freshmen, Whittle was trying to convince the Nissan advertising buyer of the value of reaching the student market. Nissan was reluctant, and Whittle brainstormed an offer: We'll eliminate the competing advertisements so yours will stand out. "The essence of entrepreneurship," he told Candace McRae of the *Daily Beacon*, "is that you break the rules."

Over the years Whittle has refined and expanded the way he breaks the rules of publishing. Essentially his strategy is this: Deliver a target audience to the advertiser, eliminate such distractions as the "clutter" of other advertisements, and build circulation through free distribution. Whittle's ventures grew throughout the eighties, including *Special Reports*, a series of magazines mailed to doctors' waiting rooms; Channel One, an experimental effort to commercialize classroom television; and advertiser-sponsored hardcover book publishing. His critics charge that by emphasizing the advertiser over the reader or viewer, Whittle lowers the quality of his product.

The controversial publisher with the trademark bow-tie came to national attention in the 1970s as co-publisher of *Esquire* magazine. *Esquire* had a long history as an ambitious literary publication, but it was losing an estimated $100,000 a week by the time it was sold to Whittle and his associates. In partnership with former college chum Phillip Moffitt, Whittle revitalized *Esquire*, repositioning it as a glossy magazine for upscale young professionals. The *Esquire* turnaround established the whiz-kid reputations of both young men. A split developed, however, and Whittle sold his interest to Moffitt in 1986 and returned to his hometown, Knoxville, Tennessee, to start his own company.

Certain that advertisers would respond to more efficient ways of reaching consumers, Whittle developed what he called "wall media," posters that combined eye-catching graphics with short, punchy editorial items. Advertising completed the mix and provided the profit. The posters made money. Displayed in laundromats, college dormitories, and other well-trafficked locales, they offered what one journalist labeled, somewhat sarcastically, "eye-grazing for the 80s." Whittle expanded the idea into single-advertiser publications given away to demographically desirable audiences; business executives for a magazine sponsored by Xerox Corp., for example. Free distribution assured the advertiser of a large audience.

The introduction of *Special Reports*—rather bland, doctor's waiting room fare on topics such as sports and health—stirred up a hornet's nest due to a controversial subscription clause that required physicians to drop all but two other magazine subscriptions. Those who complied received a free handsome oak magazine rack, along with the free subscriptions to six reports. Fearing the loss of multiple readers with each unrenewed doctor's subscription, other publishers roared in anger. One of the loudest roars came from Time, Inc.

Some of the wailing ceased in 1988 when Time, Inc. switched positions and announced it was acquiring a 50 percent share in Whittle Communications for $185 million, leaving Whittle with 11 percent ownership. The new partnership, Whittle told Jessie Bond of the *Knoxville Journal,* would enable him to tap Time, Inc.'s considerable expertise in broadcasting and hardcover publishing. This he did quickly, announcing two major innovations over the next six months.

The first was Channel One, a highly controversial experiment in commercial sponsorship of classroom television. In six pilot schools, Whittle installed $50,000 worth of color monitors, VCRs, and satellite equipment, and began transmitting teen-oriented information programming. The programming included commercials for Snickers candy bars, Gilette razors, and other products. Whittle was accused of commercializing the education process and was rebuffed by, among others, the national PTA and the American Federation of Teachers. Critics contended that students would be "forced" to watch commercials, implying school endorsement for those products. Action for Children's Television president Peggy Charren told *Village Voice* staff writer Leslie Savan, "We can't let them sell our children to advertisers while they sit in school. They're learning the commercials because they're sandwiched between material they're going to be tested on."

The programming and presentation came under national scrutiny. A *Wall Street Journal* headline wondered if Whittle's offer of free use of equipment was striking a "Faustian bargain with the schools." Many took issue with Channel One's flashy style, which borrowed directly from rock videos in graphics and pace. "Its news stories are narrated by young, attractive stylishly groomed anchors who look as if they don't quite understand themselves what they are talking about," sneered Michael Newman, writing in the *New Republic.* "The lead stories last about 20 seconds and are subdivided into lots of fleeting visual fragments." In the *Wall Street Journal,* Robert Goldberg mocked this "Cuisinart approach to news, as if only little morsels were appetizing," an approach that "trivialized" the subject matter.

The argument drew Whittle more heat than he expected. "We didn't anticipate the emotional aspect of it," he told N.R. Kleinfield of the *New York Times.* "The debate got personal against me, and that hurt. One of the things that's been thrown out is motivation. Is this just a capitalistic venture? Is money all I'm interested in? I'm not. First I'm interested in providing a real service and second in making a profit. I haven't apologized for the second, and I don't feel I have to."

Whittle's next project brought commercial sponsorship to another medium, this time book publishing. In April 1989 Whittle startled the industry by launching a line of hardcover nonfiction books that would carry advertising and be distributed free to selected "opinion leaders." A roster of well known authors was signed up, including John Kenneth Galbraith and David Halberstam. "Without having even a completed manuscript, much less a finished book, Whittle Communications is forcing conventional publishers to rethink some of their ways of doing business," observed Edwin McDowell in the *New York Times.*

Whittle got his start in publishing during his senior year at the University of Tennessee, working on a student venture called Collegiate Enterprises, Inc. The junior entrepreneurs decided a magazine guide to Knoxville's restaurants and other diversions would appeal to incoming freshmen and launched an entertainment guide called *Knoxville in a Nutshell.* Six thousand copies were printed and distributed free to freshmen, with advertising providing revenue. The idea worked, and eventually similar guides were introduced to 115 other campuses.

Upon graduation, Whittle enrolled at Columbia University Law School in New York, got distracted by the diversions of Greenwich Village, and dropped out after four months. In accordance with the spirit of the times, he took up the life of a laborer in a Louisiana oil town. Soon enough the romance wore thin, he explained to Tom Williams of the *Knoxville Journal.* "After a month of this, I got a call from a friend who said, 'How'd you like to run a political campaign?' I said, 'I'll be on the next plane.'"

He arrived in Connecticut to help with the ill-fated gubernatorial campaign of a Republican, Wally Barnes. Politics was nothing new to Whittle, who had been a student intern to Tennessee Senator Howard Baker and student body president at the University of Tennessee. "In a funny way, [the Barnes campaign] was my first experience with targeted marketing," he told Williams. Barnes's staff tried to create an "anti-establishment coalition" but failed to survive the primaries. At loose ends, Whittle took a year off to travel the world.

Upon his return to Knoxville, he resumed his involvement with *Nutshell.* The company had renamed itself 13–30 Corp., in deference to its target age group. The name change hadn't helped its financial problems: debts totaled nearly $1 million when Whittle returned to become national sales manager. It was during these troubled times that he came up with his single-sponsor publication concept to retain the Nissan account. The company began to make money. Nissan kept on advertising, and additional consumer goods producers signed on. A remarkable turnaround was underway. By 1979, 13–30 Corp. was able to acquire *Esquire* magazine. Publishing *Esquire* gave Whittle national exposure. "*Esquire* actually served me very well," he told *Newsday*'s Colford. "It forced 13–30 to perform brilliantly because we had to have the money. When we separated the two companies, it kinda made me take it to a new and larger level."

Acknowledging that he is no journalist or editor, Whittle takes pride in being a conceptualist, able to think up solutions to whatever problems arise. He is also acknowledged as an ace salesman, which pleases him, too. *Manhattan Inc.* staff writer James Kaplan branded him "just one of the best salespeople on the planet." In his profile, Kaplan quoted Steve Florio, president of the *New Yorker* magazine: Whittle's "great strength is selling advertising, not magazines. He's never won any awards for journalism."

Whittle is seen by many conventional publishers—and, increasingly, broadcasters—as a threat because of his insistence that traditional advertising no longer serves the needs of the advertiser. His products, which aim primarily at meeting advertisers' needs, benefit from the growing, widespread dissatisfaction among advertisers with conventional media. "My own view is that an enormous amount of [television] advertising could be turned off and there'd be absolutely no effect realized, because I don't think it works the way it once did," Whittle asserted in an episode of "Adam Smith's Moneyworld" in which he was profiled. Elaborating to *Newsday*'s Paul Colford, he said, "People are watching less [network television] every year. Even when they do watch, more and more of them don't watch commercials. And even when they watch commercials, more and more of them don't remember them." Whittle's future projects are expected to involve television in a big way, and in the spring of 1989 he began dropping hints of a new project in the works.

"First I'm interested in providing a real service and second in making a profit. I haven't apologized for the second, and I don't feel I have to."

Christopher Whittle was born August 23, 1947 in Etowah, Tennessee, a small town some 50 miles south of Knoxville, one of three children of Herbert Whittle, a family physician, and his wife Rita. In an interview with Tom Williams of the *Knoxville Journal,* the publisher reminisced: "I was never an academic whiz. I wasn't an athlete. I was a small kid. I was an organizer and an entrepreneur," carrying three newspaper routes and writing news stories as a stringer. Other jobs included pumping gas, waiting on tables, and playing saxophone in a dance band.

Despite the increasing success of his company, Whittle opted to live in a sagging two-room Knoxville log cabin he bought and renovated in 1971 for more than 15 years. "I can see the roots of many projects right there in that cabin," he told *Knoxville Journal* reporter Karen Martin. His tastes are not uniformly rural, however; in addition to owning a weekend retreat in Vermont, he also maintains a home in Manhattan's hyper-luxurious Dakota building. Interviewers often describe his manner as at once intense and mischievous, and his personality as "classic entrepreneur," one who thinks in big ideas rather than small details and motivates others by enthusiasm, optimism, and sheer energy. A bachelor, Whittle says he is too busy to find time for a close relationship or marriage. His hobbies include art collecting, especially works from the late eighteenth and early nineteenth century. He is actively involved in civic and business activities in Knoxville and in March 1989 contributed $5.2 million to his alma mater, the largest donation in University of Tennessee history.

Whittle's typical workday starts before seven and continues until ten, six days a week, including a working dinner. "It is grueling," he told Tom Williams. "Some days it's a lot of fun, and I laugh a lot. Particularly when we're creating. Other days, I'm completely stressed out. But I enjoy it." Musing on the psychological underpinnings of his success, the publisher told Williams, "I have this theory that most successful people are compensating for some perceived weakness of their own. Part of that was being a small kid in a world where athletics was king. You say to yourself, I can't excel there, so where else can I excel?"

Sources

"Adam Smith's Moneyworld," April 7, 1989.
Daily Beacon (University of Tennessee), October 6, 1986.
Knoxville Journal, October 4, 1986; October 26, 1986; April 22, 1987; May 9, 1988.
Knoxville News-Sentinel, October 22, 1988; March 31, 1989.
New Republic, April 10, 1989.
Newsday, October 21, 1988.
New York Times, March 19, 1989; April 18, 1989; April 24, 1989.
Wall Street Journal, March 13, 1989.

—Sidelights by Daniela Pozzaglia

S. Brian Willson

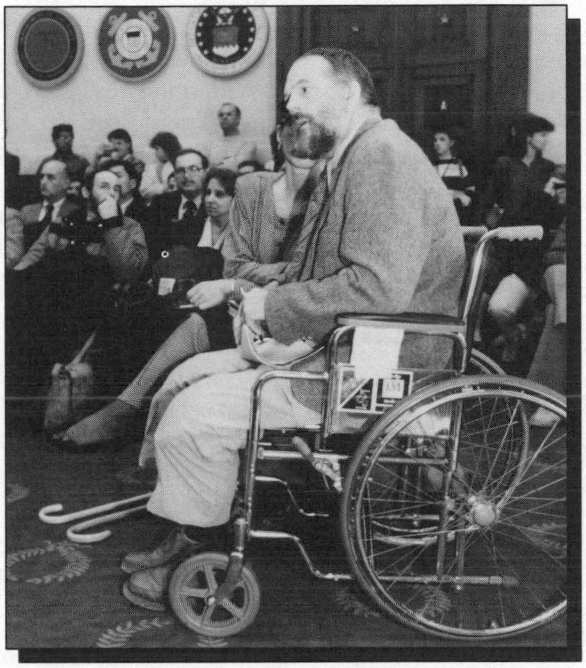

UPI/Bettmann Newsphotos

Anti-war activist

Born c. 1942; married Holley Rauen, 1987; children: Gabriel (stepson).

Addresses: *Home*—San Rafael, Calif.

Career

Has worked as dairy farmer, yogurt-drink manufacturer, public defender, and legislative assistant; founder of a veteran's counseling center in Greenfield, Mass.; anti-war activist, 1984—. *Military service:* U.S. Air Force; served as intelligence officer in Vietnam, 1966–70; became captain.

Sidelights

During the Vietnam War, S. Brian Willson served as an intelligence officer in the U.S. Air Force. Two decades later, he headed the Veterans Peace Action Team, an organization formed in protest of the United States' involvement in Central America. Chiefly, Willson opposes government aid to the Nicaraguan contras, a rebel group fighting to overthrow that country's Sandinista regime. Willson's efforts, which have included fasts and walks through Nicaraguan war zones, were fitfully reported by the news media. But in 1988, he made national headlines. During a demonstration that year, Willson was struck and critically injured by a munitions train.

A native of upstate New York, Willson held a variety of jobs following his service in Vietnam. He worked as a dairy farmer, a yogurt-drink manufacturer, a public defender, and a legislative aide. He also started a counseling center for veterans. In 1981, he became critical of America's intervention in Nicaragua. Three years later, he decided to devote all his time to nonviolent anti-war activities. Willson and three other veterans drew a measure of national attention in 1986, when they fasted on the steps of the Capitol to protest contra aid. The men received hundreds of letters of support and were visited by then-House Speaker "Tip" O'Neill. They "were prepared to starve to death," Joel Brinkley of the *New York Times* wrote. But when death actually threatened two of the vets, they ended the fast.

In 1987, Willson was the center of intense attention and debate. Leading a group of about 25 protestors, he sat in the path of a munitions train leaving a Naval Weapons Station in Concord, California. Willson was convinced that the train was carrying arms bound for Central America. As he concluded a last-minute press conference, arranged by his supporters, he was hit by the train and dragged some 20 feet. Willson lost both of his legs and suffered a fractured skull. The other demonstrators jumped clear of the train.

As Willson recuperated, the charges and countercharges flew. The Navy stated that the train was traveling at only five miles per hour; that the civilian crew had braked when they realized that not all of the people would leave the track in time; and that the group had been warned that a train could not stop in a short distance. Willson's lawyer said that the Navy's investigation amounted to a "cover-up," and that the train's crew had been "deliberately ordered" to accelerate as it approached the protestors. In 1988, the crew filed suit against Willson. They charged that he and the other demonstrators had used their bodies to block a moving train "with conscious and deliberated disregard to the rights, feelings and consequences to plaintiffs," reported Katherine Bishop of the *New York Times*. The collision and Willson's injuries "caused the crew to suffer humiliation, mental anguish and embarrassment."

A short time later, Willson sued the crew and the Navy. According to Montgomery Brower in *People*, the Navy's own investigation had disclosed that the "trainmen saw the protesters when they were still 120 feet away, yet the train was going 16 mph in a 5 mph zone." In addition, the civilian engineer testified that "he had been ordered not to halt the train outside the base."

Willson recovered from his injuries and was fitted with artificial limbs. He maintains that he has no animosity toward the crew, and that he is not bitter about the experience. "I haven't felt anger or grief over the loss of my legs," he told Brower. "Nonviolence doesn't shield you from suffering. The thing is that suffering is part of the truth."

Sources

Commonweal, October 24, 1986.
Los Angeles Times, September 12, 1987.
Nation, October 3, 1987.
New York Times, October 17, 1986; September 2, 1987; September 13, 1987; January 24, 1988.
People, February 15, 1988.
Time, September 14, 1987.

—Sketch by Denise Wiloch

Stephen M. Wolf

AP/Wide World Photos

Airline executive

Born August 7, 1941, in Oakland, Calif. *Education:* San Francisco State University, B.S., 1965.

Addresses: *Office*—United Airlines, P.O. Box 66100, Chicago, Ill. 60666.

Career

American Airlines, Los Angeles, Calif., worked in various positions, 1965–79, vice-president of Western Division, 1979–81; Pan American World Airlines, New York City, senior vice-president of marketing, 1981–82; Continental Airlines, Houston, Tex., president and chief operating officer, 1982–83; Republic Airlines, Minneapolis, Minn., president, 1984–86, chief executive officer, 1985–86; Tiger International, Los Angeles, president, chief executive officer, and chairman, 1986–87; United Airlines, Chicago, Ill., president and chief executive officer, 1987—; Allegis Corp., Chicago, president, chief executive officer, and chairman, 1987—. Member of board of directors, Payless Cashways, Inc.

Sidelights

Called the consummate turnaround artist, Stephen M. Wolf has revived two financially troubled airlines, Republic and Flying Tiger. Though his critics find his methods somewhat brutal, few would argue that Wolf gets results. "A skilled labor negotiator and masterful strategist," according to Carol Jouzaitis of the *Chicago Tribune,* he is also obsessive about details. Wolf has been known to personally monitor telephone traffic and ticket lines and to report less-than-clean terminal restrooms. In 1987, he brought his skills to bear on United Airlines, which suffered a waning market share, slow growth, high operating costs, and slight profit margins.

A veteran of the airline industry, Wolf has worked for American, Pan Am, and Continental. He joined Republic when it was on the verge of bankruptcy. Under Wolf, it became highly profitable and was sold to Northwest Airlines. Flying Tiger, a freight carrier, was also struggling when Wolf signed on as president. From 1980 to 1986, it lost $233 million. Wolf instituted drastic salary cuts, and he closely monitored work practices. Within two years, the cargo line enjoyed record profits. "The guy took half my paycheck and yet I have incredible respect for him," Frank Maguire, president of Tiger's pilot union, told Jouzaitis.

United, unlike Republic and Tiger, was financially sound when Wolf took over the reins. However, it had lost its place as the nation's top-ranked passenger line. In reaction to the stiff competition created by deregulation, United had diversified; its competitors had invested in company operations. American, which rose to first place, and Delta Air Lines expanded their fleets. United, under Wolf's predecessor, Richard J. Ferris, assembled a travel conglomerate that included the Hertz car-rental operation and two hotel chains. "Where the industry turned right, we turned left," Wolf explained to Agis Salpukas of the *New York Times.* Moreover, United's pilots, angered by Ferris's diversification strategy, made a bid to buy the airline.

Wolf set out to restructure United and to improve relations with its employees. He sold Hertz and the hotels, getting back to the "core business" of air travel, as he noted to Jouzaitis. Next, he held meetings with employee representatives to explain his strategy and to respond to their concerns. In the first eight months of 1988, operating earnings rose sharply, which eased the company's debt and helped to generate over $1 billion in cash. Wolf says that if United continues to profit at this level, he will consider expanding, domestically and internationally. Industry analysts approve. David G. Sylvester of Kidder, Peabody & Company told Salpukas: "It's a prudent move to say, 'We have to put our own house in order before we're going to grow it and try to take market share from other people.'"

Sources

Business Week, September 1, 1986; May 30, 1988.
Chicago Tribune, May 22, 1988.
Forbes, February 11, 1985; February 24, 1986; May 4, 1987.
Fortune, January 18, 1988.
Los Angeles Times, December 10, 1987.
New York Times, January 8, 1989.
Wall Street Journal, December 10, 1987.

—Sketch by Denise Wiloch

Kenichi Yamamoto

UPI/Bettmann Newsphotos

Auto executive

Born September 16, 1922, in Hiroshima, Japan; married; children: one son, one daughter. *Education:* Imperial University (now Tokyo University), B.S.M.E., 1944.

Addresses: *Office:* Mazda Motor Corp., 3-1 Shinchi, Fucho-cho, Aki-gun, Hiroshima 730-91, Japan.

Career

During World War II, briefly supervised production of fighter planes for Japanese Navy; Mazda Motor Corp. (formerly Toyo Kogyo Co.), Hiroshima, Japan, 1946—, began as assembly worker, then worked as engine designer, manager of design department in Technology Division, 1956–59, deputy manager of Engine and Vehicle Design Division, 1959–63, manager of Rotary Engine Research and Development Division, 1963–78, member of board of directors, 1971—, managing director and general manager of research and development, 1978–80, general manager of advanced technology, 1980–82, senior managing director of advanced technology and research and development, 1982–84, president, 1984–87, chairman, 1987—.

Awards: Director's Award, Japan Science and Technology Agency, 1969; Director's Award, Japan Society of Mechanical Engineers, 1970; Medal of Honor with purple ribbon from prime minister of Japan, 1971; named Man of the Year by *Automotive Industries* magazine, 1986.

Sidelights

Widely known as the "foster father" of the rotary engine, Kenichi Yamamoto began his pioneering work in 1963 on development of the engine originally designed in Germany in the late 1950s by Dr. Felix Wankel. *Automotive Industries* magazine, in a 1980 article, observed: "Although Felix Wankel invented it, Yamamoto is certainly responsible for making [the rotary engine] a viable powerplant for production cars." In a subsequent article the magazine described Yamamoto as "one of a rare breed of visionary executives," while *Road & Track* magazine called him "the rotary wizard."

A 1944 mechanical engineering graduate of Imperial University (Now Tokyo University, Japan's top school), Yamamoto briefly supervised production of fighter planes for the Japanese Navy. After World War II, he returned to his hometown of Hiroshima, which had been devastated by the atomic bomb, and went to work in 1946 for Toyo Kogyo Co., the forerunner of Mazda, first as an assembly worker building truck transmissions, then as an engine designer. In 1950, he designed the company's first overhead-valve engine, an air-cooled two-cylinder unit, for its three-wheeled trucks, and was named manager of the Technical Division's design department in 1956. As deputy manager of the Engine and Vehicle Design Division in 1959, he helped develop the company's first production passenger car, the tiny R360, a two-cylinder coupe.

Yamamoto's association with the Wankel engine began in 1963, when he was became manager of the newly formed Rotary Engine Research and Development Division. Over the next 15 years, his development of the rotary engine and its subsequent application in production cars would be described by *Road & Track* as "one of the most fascinating chapters in automotive history."

In a 1984 interview, Yamamoto told *Car and Driver* magazine, "I felt a genuine surprise when I first saw a running prototype of the rotary engine in 1961. It was so compact and turning so smoothly. Like any engineer, I was impressed by the novelty, because there was so little variation in internal-combustion engines at the time. I felt a passionate desire to challenge and perfect the rotary engine.... In the beginning, we experienced lots of difficulties. Some were technical, others were not.... I had to not only spur [the younger engineers], but I also had to keep their morale high and give them hope. Fortunately, management had decided the new technology was indispensable. The challenge was difficult, and I was forced to work more than the young people in my division to stay ahead. In fact, I made a point of placing a notebook beside my pillow at night so that when any new ideas dawned on me, I could write it down.... If the engineers saw an enthusiastic leader, they responded with greater passion. I challenged each one to come up with at least one new idea every day, and I promised that I would do likewise."

Under Yamamoto's direction, Mazda produced the world's first two-rotor Wankel engine in 1967, and by the early 1970s, the rotary was being installed in more than half of Mazda's vehicles, including three-fourths of the cars and trucks it sold in North America.

But the fuel crunch of 1973, and the rotary's reputation as a gas guzzler, caused Mazda's U.S. sales to plummet. By the late 1970s, the rotary engine was being sold in this country only in the RX7 sports car, which was introduced in 1978. General Motors, in the meantime, had abandoned its plans to produce rotary engines in the United States, leaving Mazda as the only major automaker in the world building rotary-powered vehicles. The crisis, which sent the company to the edge of bankruptcy, convinced Yamamoto, by then a managing director of the company and head of all R&D activities, that a major redesign of the engine to make it more reliable and efficient was necessary; an improved second-generation version was introduced in 1982. Continued development has made the engine more refined, with fuel economy and performance comparable to conventional piston engines. New variants of the rotary engine developed under Yamamoto's guidance include three-rotor and supercharged models. Production of the Mazda rotary engine since its introduction has reached nearly 2 million units.

In a 1988 interview with *Road & Track*, Yamamoto recalled the effects of the fuel crisis on the rotary and why Mazda decided to continue its development: "There were 350,000 Americans who had bought our rotary-engine products prior to the [crisis]. Those people recognized the rotary's virtues and helped rear our child. Withdrawal of the rotary from the American market would have been an outright betrayal of that faith. Our re-entry vehicle was . . . the first-generation RX7, specifically conceived, designed and developed as a sports car for the rotary.... Mazda and the rotary are inseparable; it's the image of the company." He added: "At the birth of the rotary, we had Daimler-Benz, Mazda, Toyota, NSU, GM, practically a who's-who in the world's automotive industry, all in the early Wankel family of licensees. At the beginning, all intended to make Dr. Wankel's dream a day-to-day prime mover. For us at Mazda, it was a destiny."

The author of a technical book on the engineering of the rotary engine, Yamamoto has received numerous honors for his developmental work on the Wankel. He was given the Director's Award from Japan's Science and Technology Agency in 1969 and a similar award the following year from the Japan Society of Mechanical Engineers. In 1971, he was awarded the Medal of Honor with purple ribbon by Japan's prime minister, and in 1986 he was named Man of the Year by *Automotive Industries* magazine—the first non-American so honored. The same year, an all-new edition of the rotary-powered RX7 was named Import Car of the Year by *Motor Trend* magazine.

Yamamoto was named senior managing director of advanced technology and research and development in 1982 and elevated to president in 1984. He assumed the chairmanship of Mazda in 1987, some 41 years after he had joined the company. Under his leadership, Mazda redesigned its entire line of vehicles for the United States and, in 1985, broke ground for a new $450-million assembly plant in Flat Rock, Michigan. Yamamoto, in an interview in *Business Week*, observed: "The key [to Mazda's success] is to find something consumers hadn't thought of. Toyota and Nissan are designing cars by computer. The segment we're focusing on is modernistic styling with good handling—making driving fun.

In his official Mazda biography, Yamamoto is quoted as saying: "Being at the leading edge of technical discovery and innovation is crucial—but not enough. Maintaining high quality affects brand reputation, warranty costs, customer loyalty and the like—yet quality, too, is not enough. Both technological leadership and superior products are interwoven with Mazda's identity. In the end, however, it will be our ability to enrich [customers'] lives with their products, to even touch their hearts, that will be the measure of our success."

In a 1986 company publication called *Reliability and Innovation,* Yamamoto further described Mazda's approach to engineering, called *kansei:* "This unique concept involves a totally integrated development process aimed at producing vehicles to suit specific, carefully differentiated groups of users. Mazda automobiles offer much more than a means of travel; they offer a mode of personal expression. All our research and development, manufacturing and commercial activities worldwide are dedicated to this end. It's a philosophy which, by its nature, demands the closest cooperation with our customers, employees, business partners and all the local communities where Mazda has a presence."

Sources

Automotive Industries, December, 1980, February, 1986.
AutoWeek, October 14, 1985.
Business Week, January 25, 1982.
Car and Driver, March, 1984.
Forbes, December 15, 1986.
People, February 18, 1985.
Road & Track, March, 1978, July, 1979, September, 1979, March, 1985, August, 1988.

—Sketch by Paul Lienert and Anita Pyzik Lienert

Zhao Ziyang

Reuters/Bettmann Newsphotos

Chinese government official

Born November, 1919 (some sources say 1918 or 1921), in Huaxian County, Hunan Province, China; son of a grain merchant and landlord; married Liang Baiqi; children: four sons, one daughter. *Education:* Attended secondary schools in Kaifeng and Wuhan, China.

Addresses: *Home*—Zhongnanhai, People's Republic of China. *Office*—State Council, Beijing, People's Republic of China.

Career

Joined Communist Youth League, 1932, and Communist Party, 1938; during the war against Japan, 1937–45, and later in the civil war between the communists and the Nationalist Party, served as a local government official in communist-held areas of central China; sent to Guandong Province to oversee agricultural reform, 1949; South China sub-bureau of Chinese Communist Party, secretary-general, 1950–54, third secretary, 1954–55; Guandong Communist Party, third deputy secretary, 1955–62, secretary, 1962–65, first secretary, 1965–67; Guandong military district of People's Liberation Army, commissar, 1964; Central-South Bureau, Chinese Communist Party, secretary, 1965–67; Nei Monggol Revolutionary Committee, Inner Mongolia, vice-chairman, 1971; Chinese Communist Party, Nei Monggol, secretary, 1971; Guandong Revolutionary Committee, vice-chairman, 1972, chairman, 1974; Chinese Communist Party, Guandong, secretary, 1972, first secretary, 1974; member of Tenth Central Committee, Chinese Communist Party, 1973, alternate member of Eleventh Central Committee, 1977–79, member of politburo of Twelfth Central Committee, 1982; Chinese Communist Party, Sichuan, first secretary, 1975–80; Sichuan Revolutionary Committee, chairman, 1975–80; Fifth National Chinese People's Political Consultive Conference, executive chairman, 1978; Chengdu military district of People's Liberation Army, first political commissar, 1976–80; member of Standing Committee of Politburo, beginning 1980; premier of State Council, beginning 1980; deputy premier, then premier, 1980–87; minister of State Commission for Economic Reconstruction, beginning 1982; general secretary of Chinese Communist Party, 1987—.

Sidelights

In late 1987, *Newsweek*'s Dorinda Elliott quoted Chinese Communist Party chief Zhao Ziyang as having said, "It is more interesting to swim amid the wind and waves." It seems appropriate that, nearing the end of another challenging year in his career, the weathered and resilient Zhao might make such a statement. For during his long swim toward prominence in Chinese politics, he has often found himself pushing against the current. After a promising start as a Communist Party official, Zhao fell victim to the

Cultural Revolution of the 1960s, along with many like-minded, reform-oriented officials who were persecuted for their "capitalist" tendencies. But Zhao resurfaced, and his tremendous success in revitalizing the economy of Sichuan Province brought him to the attention of Deng Xiaoping, China's top leader. Deng ensured Zhao's rise to the position of Prime Minister, and eventually to his current role as General Secretary of the Chinese Communist Party. The man whom Christopher Wren described in the *New York Times* as "the forerunner of a younger generation of Chinese officials willing to bend the constraints of traditional Marxist ideology to make things work," keeps trying to make things work. To do so he must balance the long-entrenched conservative forces that would maintain in China a strongly Marxist society with the demands for reform that have played such an important role in the country's recent history.

Zhao was born in 1919 in the central Chinese province of Hunan. His father was a grain merchant and landlord who could afford to send his son to school in Kaifeng and Wuhan. When he was thirteen years old, Zhao became a member of the outlawed Communist Youth League, and six years later he joined the Communist Party.

In 1949, the civil war between the communists and the Kuomintang (the Chinese Nationalist Party led by Chiang Kai-Shek) ended with a victory for the communists and the establishment of the People's Republic of China. Zhao, who had spent the war years as a local party official in an area of central China held by the Communists, was sent to the important coastal provice of Guangdong (the large, bustling city of Canton is located there). In Guangdong Zhao earned respect for his expertise in agricultural reform, and in 1965 he was named first secretary of the Guangdong Province Communist Party.

Despite his success in Guangdong—and perhaps because of it—Zhao was not to be spared the scourges of the Cultural Revolution. During the late 1950s, China's leader, Mao Zse-Dong, had attempted to boost his country's troubled economy with the "Great Leap Forward," an agricultural program that centred on "people's communes." When the program failed, several leaders—most notably Liu Shaoqi and Deng Xiaoping—began to advocate such measures as increasing the size of the farmers' plots and rewarding individual enterprise. But the more rigid Maoists then in power felt that these reforms ran counter to communist ideals, and in the mid-1960s the "capitalist roaders" were severely censored.

Like others who had taken an unacceptably pragmatic approach to China's economic development, Zhao was paraded through his province in a dunce cap by the Red Guards, which were comprised of soldiers, workers, and students who went around doing the dirty work of the Cultural Revolution. Zhao was called a "counterrevolutionary" and "stinking remnant of the landlord class," forced to make a public statement of self-criticism, and dismissed from his post.

Though it made a dramatic and frightening statement at the time, the Cultural Revolution eventually lost public support. With the rise to power of a more moderate prime minister, Zhou En Lai, in the early 1970s, many of the purged officials found themselves "rehabilitated," as did Zhao. After serving briefly in Inner Mongolia, he was made a party functionary back in Guangdong, in 1972. Before long he had resumed his duties as first secretary of the province's Communist Party.

In late 1975, Zhao was appointed to the position of first secretary of the Communist Party of Sichuan Province. During the years since the birth of the People's Republic, Sichuan—formerly the most populous and wealthiest area of China—had experienced frequent political turmoil, and the province was in serious economic trouble. Zhao set about restoring the faltering local economy using the same techniques championed by Liu and Deng in the early 1960s. Factories were allowed to determine their own prices, and to keep some of the profits for investment purposes; 15 percent of all arable land was made available for private enterprise; tax incentives were instated; and peasant markets were introduced.

These measures emphasized pragmatism rather than rigid ideology, and they worked. Within three years, industrial production in Sichuan Province was up 81 percent, and agricultural output had increased by 25 percent. Zhao's success in Sichuan Province was much heralded, and the steps taken there were to be used as a model during the next decade of China's history. As reported in *Newsweek*, Sichuan's peasants took as their slogan, "For gain to soothe your hunger pangs, seek Zhao Ziyang."

But it wasn't just the grateful peasants who were seeking Zhao Ziyang. Deng Xiaoping was now at China's helm, having come to power after the 1975 death of Mao. Always a pragmatic leader himself, Deng admired Zhao's abilities. Zhao was called to Beijing in early 1980 and named deputy prime minister, in charge of the daily operations of the government. Five months later, Deng maneuvered Zhao into one of the most powerful posts in China's ruling hierarchy—that of prime minister. Deng and Zhao would now set out to transform China into (according to Zhao, as reported in the *New York Times*) "a modernized, highly democratic and civilized state" by the year 2000. To do so would require a loosening of the bindings of Marxism, and new "enthusiasm for the enterprises.... We must not bind ourselves as silkworms do within cocoons."

So Zhao began applying on a broader scale those principles that had worked so well in Sichuan Province. Almost 7000 state-owned enterprises were allowed self-management—they could set goals as they saw fit, sell their products, and keep a share of the profits. Although the program had to be scaled down somewhat in 1981, the wheels of change had been set in motion all over China.

> *"Zhao enjoys the reputation of being a capable, pragmatic administrator who is not outspoken on the question of political reform."*

In late 1982, Zhao announced the implementation of a five-year plan that would carry China through 1985 at a growth rate of 4 to 5 percent. Such capitalist devices as taxes and interest rates would be utilized to stimulate the economy and also boost government revenues. Even more market-oriented measures were introduced in 1984, with the clear intent of loosening government's tight grip on industry.

An important part of the new program was (and continues to be) foreign investment. After diplomatic ties with the United States were reestablished in 1979, China's leaders had made it clear that exchanges between the two countries in trade, science, and culture would be welcomed. Through the early and mid-1980s, the diplomatic relationship between the two countries was characterized by a tone of conciliation (though occasionally disturbed by such troublesome matters as the United States' sale of arms to Taiwan).

Zhao's trip to the United States in January, 1984, was marked by good feelings all around. In the years from 1972 to 1983, bilateral trade had risen from $95.9 million to $4.3 billion. American tourists were flocking to China at the rate of 150,000 per year (up from 10,000 in 1978). Three hundred joint research projects were underway. Thus Reagan and Zhao were meeting at a time when relations between the two countries seemed the complete reverse of those of the confrontational 1960s. As reported in *Time,* Zhao said at a White House ceremony, "I come as a friendly envoy of the Chinese people for the purpose of seeking increased mutual understanding." Displaying some of his celebrated charm, Reagan (quoted in *Newsweek*), greeted his guest with an ancient Chinese saying: "Is it not delightful to have friends come from afar?"

During the January 1984 visit, Zhao and Reagan signed an agreement on industrial cooperation and renewed a 1979 accord encouraging exchanges in science and technology. When Reagan paid a visit to Beijing in April of the same year, the two leaders completed a nuclear power agreement and a pact to encourage assistance from American businesses in developing China's industrial base.

The shift away from a strict Marxist orientation engineered by Deng and Zhao has not always been a smooth one. In late 1986 and early 1987, for instance, students demanding increased intellectual latitude rioted in several Chinese cities. The question of where to draw the line when loosening formerly tight controls became a central issue. Communist Party chief Hu Yaobang—like Zhao a Deng protegee—was caught in the crossfire when he did not act decisively enough to quell the disturbances. Accused of being too liberal on the issue of intellectual freedom, Hu was ousted from office.

Hu's misfortune was to Zhao's advantage, since he was next in line for this second most powerful office in China. Zhao was made acting general secretary of the Chinese Communist Party, a role which would be formalized at the 13th Party Congress in November of 1987. As noted by Marie Gottschalk in the *Nation,* "Unlike Hu, Zhao enjoys the reputation of being a capable, pragmatic administrator who is not outspoken on the question of political reform." Although Zhao did not have a strong foothold in China's "old boy" network and lacked clout with the military, he did have the advantage of widespread support from the Chinese public for the economic reforms he had championed.

As the 13th Party Congress approached, Zhao was faced with many challenges. However popular his economic program might be, it was not without its problems. Manufacturing costs were rising, as were prices, and there were incidences of such maladies as hoarding, black marketeering, and bribe-taking. China's students and intellectuals continued to feel that reform should spread to the realm of thought as well as that of money. And there were those in the Party who believed that Zhao was moving too far, too quickly.

Nevertheless, the 13th Party Congress proved a fortuitous occasion for Zhao. He was elected general secretary of the Chinese Communist Party by the 175-member Central Committee and was named vice-chairman of the Military Commission. The Congress was especially significant for its major reordering of the powerful Politburo Standing Committee, which had been dominated by elderly conservatives. Of the five members, only Zhao was reappointed. The average age of the members dropped from 77 to 63; the Committee was now dominated by younger men with more reform-oriented outlooks. The new members included former Vice-Premiers Li Peng, Qiao Shi and Yao Yilin, and former Party Secretariat member Hu Qili. The 83-year-old Deng retired from all of his posts except the powerful one as Chairman of the Central Military Commission. He would, however, remain firmly at China's helm.

Zhao wants to see China eventually rival Taiwan, South Korea, and Hong Kong as an active force in the world trading system.

In his speech to the Congress, Zhao's tone was cautiously optimistic. As reported in *Time,* he said that the Party should "accelerate and deepen" those changes already underway but should do so slowly. He described China as being in the "primary stage of socialism," so that through the year 2050 the country's primary focus should be on production rather than class struggle. Such problems as the 10 percent inflation rate (which Western observers calculated as closer to 20 percent) might only be solvable by capitalist methods, and if so those methods would have to be tolerated. Zhao also criticized China's bloated bureaucracy, and proposed that committees, commissions, and agencies be reduced and that a civil service system be established.

One of the most important questions remaining as the 13th Party Congress drew to a close was who would replace Zhao as premier. Most observers felt that Li Peng, an engineer and energy expert trained in the Soviet Union, was a likely choice. Li, the foster son of the last premier Zhou En Lai, now enjoyed the backing of Chen Yun, a member of China's "old guard" who had often been critical of Deng's policies. Despite the strong possibility of future clashes, Zhao named Li Peng acting prime minister on November 24, 1987.

Li's position as premier was formally confirmed at the National People's Congress (China's parliamentary body) in March of 1988. This session was heralded as a groundbreaking event, since for the first time a wide variety of differing opinions were allowed to be expressed openly. Participants spoke out on a number of controversial issues, and—also a first—none of China's top leaders gained unanimous support.

As 1988 progressed, the blending of market-oriented reforms with state structures remained problematic. Zhao continued his efforts to encourage foreign investment and individual initiative. But poor management and shoddy workmanship, seen as by-products of China's policy of guaranteed job security, were formidable obstacles. Still, in places like Sha Zui village in Guangdong Province, industrious Chinese entrepeneurs have proved themselves willing and able to help increase China's productivity. Residents of Sha Zui pooled funds to set up a manufacturing operation, which now brings in $400,000 per year—a figure far beyond the dreams of most Chinese workers.

Zhao wants to see China eventually rival Taiwan, South Korea, and Hong Kong as an active force in the world trading system, but the always-present conservative element worries that things are changing too fast. In a speech to the National People's Congress, Li Peng, as reported in *Business Week,* said "In the economic sphere there is still a tendency to be too impatient for quick results."

And indeed, by September of 1988 observers were pointing to economic "overheating" as factories began closing for lack of supplies, and food shortages and hoarding became more prevalent. The inflation rate rose to 20 percent, forcing the government to rethink the decentralization of control. At an emergency meeting, the Central Committee agreed to "improve the economic environment and straighten out the economic order" by putting a hold on reforms. A young Chinese economist, quoted in *Newsweek,* noted that "Zhao has lost a lot of points in recent months. He based his power on his [price reform] plan, and his plan is not working."

Despite the loss of face Zhao may have suffered as his ambitious plans for propelling China into the future have run into trouble, the outlook is not necessarily dismal. As a Western diplomat observed in a *Newsday* wire service article, "This is a very complex, very bold undertaking, going from one system to another, and bringing a billion people along." Most observers agree that Zhao Ziyang, dressed in the dapper Western suit that marks him as a forward-looking, pragmatic person, will remain at the forefront of that difficult undertaking. He has proven himself a strong swimmer as he negotiates the turbulent waters of China's recent history.

Sources

Business Week, November 16, 1987; April 11, 1988.
Economist, February 28, 1987; November 28, 1987.
Far Eastern Economic Review, March 19, 1987; March 24, 1988.
Honolulu Star-Bulletin & Advertiser, November 20, 1988.
Nation, May 23, 1987.
New Republic, April 4, 1988.
Newsweek, January 23, 1984; November 2, 1987; November 16, 1987; October 10, 1988.
New York Times, January 10, 1984; November 3, 1987; December 5, 1987.
Time, January 16, 1984; January 23, 1984; November 9, 1987; October 10, 1988.
U.S. News & World Report, April 18, 1988.
World Press Review, January, 1988.

—Sidelights by Kelly King Howes

Obituaries

Edward Abbey

Born January 29, 1927, in Home, Pa.; died of a circulatory disorder, March 14, 1989, in Oracle, Ariz. American writer and environmentalist. Described by Edwin Way Teale in the *New York Times* as "a voice crying in the wilderness, *for* the wilderness," Abbey was a combative writer and naturalist whose dozen works of fiction and nonfiction exposed the enemies of the American wild and fueled the sentiments of radical environmentalist groups. In bitter, cynical, racing prose style, he decried the advance of developers, cattle ranchers, giant corporations and tourists upon the dwindling American West, an area of the country he dreamed of returning to its natural, unspoiled beauty. He particularly detested tourists, who flocked to the national parks in mobile homes, turned on their televisions and blow dryers, and spewed noise and litter. "No more cars in national parks," Abbey wrote in Desert Solitaire (1968). "Let the people walk. Or ride horses, bicycles, mules, wild pigs—anything—but keep the automobiles and motorcycles and all their motorized relatives out. . . . A civilization which destroys what little remains of the wild, the spare, the original, is cutting itself off from its origins."

Born in Pennsylvania, Abbey received graduate and postgraduate degrees from the University of New Mexico in the 1950s, during which time he wrote and supported himself by working as a park ranger and firefighter. His writings made him a popular cult figure in the West, particularly among environmental groups like Earth First!, who adopted Abbey's philosophies to support their often illegal sabotage activities. Such a group is depicted in Abbey's 1975 novel *The Monkey Wrench Gang,* about a group that plots to destroy the Glen Canyon Dam in Arizona. The book sold more than 500,000 copies. At the time of his death Abbey was working on a sequel to *The Monkey Wrench Gang;* the novel, tentatively titled *Hay Duke Lives,* was expected to be published in 1990. Other Abbey titles included *The Journey Home* (1977) and *Abbey's Road* (1979). Two of his books were made into films: *The Brave Cowboy* (1956) was made into the 1962 film "Lonely Are the Brave," starring Kirk Douglas: and *Fire on the Mountain* (1962) was put on film in 1981. **Sources:** *Chicago Tribune,* March 15, 1989; *New York Times,* March 15, 1989.

Charles Addams

Full name, Charles Samuel Addams; born Jan. 7, 1912, in Westfield, N.J.: died of a heart attack, September 29, 1988, in New York, N.Y. Cartoonist. Described by friends as a quiet, gentle man, Addams was also the ghoulish wit who delighted readers of the *New Yorker* magazine for five decades with his devilishly macabre cartoons. Many of his drawings depict the fiendish Addams family, a collection of ugly oddballs who occupy a haunted Victorian-style home and terrorize neighbors; the idea spawned an ABC television comedy, "The Addams Family," which ran for two years in the 1960s and later became widely syndicated. Addams's drawings are considered brilliant examples of a cartoonist's mastery—many achieve their full effect without requiring a caption, and others are so deliberately subtle that they take a moment to figure out. In one Addams classic, the driver of an empty bus notices that the stop buzzer has been pulled—as he approaches a forbidding graveyard.

Even while growing up in comfortable Westfield, N.J., Addams later admitted, he had a strange fascination with skeletons, graveyards, and coffins. He particularly enjoyed scheming to scare the wits out of his grandmother, who lived in his parents' home. Addams began drawing cartoons while in high school. After brief stays at Colgate University and the University of Pennsylvania, he attended the Grand Central School of Art in New York in 1931–32. In the 1930s he began to establish himself as a freelance illustrator, selling drawings to *Collier's* and other magazines. His first major cartoon appeared in the *New Yorker* in 1940; in it, a man looks on quizzically as a woman skis past, her tracks passing strangely by either side of a large tree.

Addams quickly became a *New Yorker* institution, his name as synonomous with the tradition of that magazine as those of James Thurber, S.J. Perelman, and E.B. White. His cartoons and illustrations have been collected in 12 books, and he left behind several unpublished cartoons and cover illustrations, which the New Yorker plans to use in future issues.

Addams claimed that many of his best ideas came to him in the long hours he spent people-watching; he had a gift for putting a bizarre twist on everyday characters and occurrences. *New York Times* art critic John Russell applauded Addams's solid artistic technique, calling it "the calculated ordinariness that lures us into the trap." In his personal life, Addams was a sociable fellow who collected fine automobiles and enjoyed the company of celebrities and beautiful women. He played to his reputation by decorating his apartment with gloomy artifacts, including an antique embalming table. In 1980 Addams and his third wife, Marilyn Matthews Miller, were married in a pet cemetary. The bride, of course, wore black. **Sources:** *New Yorker,* October 17, 1988; *New York Times,* September 30, 1988; *People,* October 17, 1988.

Henry Armstrong

Real name, Henry Jackson; born December 12, 1912, in Columbus, Miss.; died of heart failure, October 22, 1988, in Los Angeles, Calif. Former boxing champion. Armstrong, a Depression-era fighter known for his relentless, hard-charging style, captivated the boxing world in 1938 when he became the first man to simultaneously command three world titles. Known to his fans as Homicide Hank, Perpetual Motion, and Hurricane Henry, Armstrong bombarded opponents with flurries of punches at close range, a style which, over a span of 174 professional fights, forced him to absorb many punches himself and later contributed to the health problems which ended his life. When his boxing career had ended, a gentler Armstrong emerged. He became a Baptist minister, a published author, and a proponent of charitable foundations for disadvantaged youths. "I guess I proved something, but what?" Armstrong said of his boxing exploits, as quoted in the *Detroit Free Press.* "You see, being a fighter wasn't what I really wanted."

Growing up in St. Louis, Armstrong worked as a railroad hand and shined shoes. After high school he rode freight trains to California, where he began boxing, winning 58 of 62 amateur bouts. He began fighting professionally in 1931 under the ring name Honey Mellody. He became known as Henry Armstrong in 1935, and by 1937 his success in the ring carried him to the attention of the big boxing promoters in New York, where he began a string of 46 consecutive victories, including 27 straight knockouts. During one incredible 11-month period he won and held three world championships. On October 29, 1937, fighting at 126 pounds (featherweight), Armstrong won his first world title by knocking out Pete Sarron in the sixth round. He bypassed the lightweight division to become the welterweight (147-pound) champion by defeating Barney Ross by decision in a fifteen-round fight that forced Ross into retirement on May 31, 1938. The following August 17, Armstrong dropped down to the lightweight (135-pound) division to capture Lou Ambers's world title with a fifteen-round decision before 19,216 spectators at Madison Square Garden. Armstrong eventually lost all three titles before retiring in 1945 with a total of 145 professional victories. His career earnings exceeded $1 million.

By the time he left boxing for good, Armstrong, known for his expensive tastes and love of a good time, was broke. He turned himself around in the 1950s, when he was ordained a Baptist minister in Los Angeles. He spent his time preaching and raising money for the Henry Armstrong Youth Foundation, which he founded to combat juvenile delinquency. He also published two books, *Twenty Years of Poems, Moods, and Meditations* and *Gloves, Glory and God* (his autobiography), the proceeds of which went to his charities. In his later years, suffering from a string of maladies, Armstrong and his wife, Gussie, lived on a monthly Social Security check of $800. He had been inducted, along with Jack Dempsey and Joe Louis, into the Boxing Hall of Fame when it opened in 1954. **Sources:** *Detroit Free Press,* October 25, 1988; *Los Angeles Times,* October 24, 1988; *New York Times,* October 25, 1988.

Lucille Ball

Full name, Lucille Desiree Ball; born August 6, 1911, in Celoron, N.Y.; died of heart disease, April 26, 1989, in Los Angeles, Calif. American actress. Known throughout the world as the irrepressible "Lucy," for the character she played in television comedies for 20 years, Ball was a bit-part character actress in Hollywood who became a comedy queen and savvy producer, revolutionizing the television industry and winning several Emmy Awards in the process. At the time of her death "I Love Lucy," the

1950s sit-com which she produced and starred in with then-husband Desi Arnaz, was still being shown in syndicated reruns in 80 countries, making her face one of the most recognizable and beloved in all the world. "I Love Lucy" was for six years the most popular program on television, watched by nearly 40 million viewers each week and never finishing lower than third in the ratings. After the show went off the air and her marriage to Arnaz dissolved, Ball revived the Lucy character in "The Lucy Show" and "Here's Lucy," comedies that enjoyed long success and saw Lucy cope with widowhood, her growing children, and the working life—problems women across America were encountering for themselves. "I love Lucy," Ball said of her trademark character in the *Los Angeles Times*. "She always had a domineering figure over her.... Lucy was always knocking somebody's top hat off."

As an actress, Ball also had to tackle the authorities to get what she wanted. An admirer of vaudeville shows and silent films as a girl, she went to Manhattan at age 15 to study acting, only to be labeled a "no talent" by her instructor. Undaunted, Ball tried modeling and ended up getting national exposure as the Chesterfield Cigarette Girl in 1933, which won her a job in Hollywood as a chorus girl in the film "Roman Scandals." Over the next several years she appeared in small roles in such films as "Follow the Fleet" (1936), with Fred Astaire, "Stage Door" (1937), with Katherine Hepburn and Ginger Rogers, and "Room Service" (1938), with the Marx Brothers. She met Arnaz when the two were cast on the film "Too Many Girls" in 1940; they were married six months later. In 1947 Ball accepted a role that would become the precursor to Lucy; she played a hare-brained midwest housewife on the CBS radio show "My Favorite Husband."

When Ball and Arnaz came up with the idea of adapting "My Favorite Husband" for the new medium of television, with Arnaz in the lead male role, CBS executives at first balked because of skepticism at how well Arnaz's thick Cuban accent would play in middle America. The couple responded by forming their own production company, Desilu Productions, with $5,000 and taking their act on a nationwide tour to gauge audience response to the tandem. They then developed a 30-minute pilot for "I Love Lucy," which debuted on CBS television on October 15, 1951, and quickly became a Monday night institution for millions of viewers. The show featured Ball as the wife of the rumba band leader Ricky Ricardo. Also starring were William Frawley and Vivian Vance as Fred and Ethel Mertz, the Ricardos' landlords and neighbors. Most episodes found Lucy and Ethel over their heads in trouble, hatching one zany scheme after another to the obvious dismay of their husbands. Ball was a tremendous clown whose facial expressions and slapstick entanglements were endearing and hilarious. In the end she was always forgiven despite the momentous damages done. The show's most famous episode came on January 19, 1953, when Ball, pregnant in real life with Desi Arnaz Jr., gave birth to "Little Ricky" on a prerecorded episode. Forty-four million Americans watched that evening, more than watched the inauguration of President Dwight D. Eisenhower the following day.

Perhaps Ball's greatest triumph was her uncanny success in the traditionally male dominated circle of Hollywood producers. In 1957 Desilu purchased RKO Studios and began producing other programs, such as the highly successful series "Mission Impossible," "Star Trek," and "The Untouchables." That same year Desilu sold the rights to "I Love Lucy" to CBS for $6 million. As the first program pre-taped before a live audience, "I Love Lucy" was the pioneer in a long line of television series that enjoy a lucrative second-life in syndicated reruns. When Ball was divorced from Arnaz in 1960, she acquired his share of Desilu for $3 million; in 1967 she sold the company to Gulf and Western Industries for $17 million. After "Here's Lucy" ended in 1974, Ball was mostly through with television, appearing only sporadically on talk-shows and specials while her old shows thrived in reruns. She returned to star as a spirited bag lady in the 1985 television movie "Stone Pillow," and her 1986 attempt at reviving Lucy in the series "Life With Lucy" failed abruptly. Former President Ronald Reagan called Ball a "gifted comedienne.... Her antics on the screen, her timing and her zest for life made her an American institution. Just the mention of her name brings a smile." **Sources:** *New York Times*, April 27, 1989; *People*, May 8, 1989; *Washington Post*, April 27, 1989.

Mel Blanc

Full name, Melvin Jerome Blanc; born May 30, 1908, in San Francisco, Calif.; died of heart disease, July 10, 1989, in Los Angeles, Calif. Cartoon voice creator. Known in Hollywood as "The Man of a Thousand Voices," Blanc was the versatile cartoon voice creator of such unforgettable characters as Bugs Bunny, Porky Pig, and Daffy Duck. Blanc's voices have become standard-bearers for American popular culture throughout the world, heard, by some estimates, by more than 20 million people every day. Each of his characters is distinctive and many developed a trademark line that became famous, like "I tawt I taw a puddy tat!" (Tweety), "What's up, Doc?" (Bugs Bunny), "Thhhhufferin' Thhhhuccotash!" (Sylvester), and "Beep-beep!" (Road Runner). Blanc did the majority of his work for Warner Bros., performing in over 3,000 cartoons for that studio in a career that spanned more than 50 years, but he also worked for other animated film makers and as a memorable radio actor.

Growing up in Portland, Oregon, Blanc studied music, becoming proficient on the bass, violin and sousaphone. But he discovered a more amazing instrument in his own voice. "I used to look at animals and wonder, how would that kitten sound if it could talk," he said in the *New York Times.* "I'd tighten up my throat and make a very small voice, not realizing I was rehearsing." After marrying and working for a short time as a radio actor, Blanc moved to Los Angeles and joined Leon Schlesinger Productions, a cartoon workshop that eventually developed the Looney Tunes and Merry Melodies characters for Warner Bros. While playing the part of a drunken bull in "Porky Picador," Blanc relates in his autobiography *That's Not All Folks,* the actor who was then portraying Porky actually did stutter. When Blanc was later asked to play Porky, he left the stutter in the act, and his first major character was born. Blanc next developed the character who was to become his favorite, Happy Hare, in another Warner Bros. short. He lent a brash, Bronx accent to the wise-guy rabbit that eventually became Bugs Bunny. "He's a little stinker," Blanc told the *New York Times.* "That's why people love him. He does what most people would like to do but don't have the guts to do." More famous characters followed, including Pepe LePew, Wile E. Coyote, Elmer Fudd, Speedy Gonzales, and Yosemite Sam.

Despite his proficiency, Blanc did not own the rights to any of his characters and never earned more than $20,000 in a single year from Warner Bros., so he was forced to pursue other activities. In the 1960s he was co-producer and voice animator for ABC's "The Bugs Bunny Show," a Saturday morning series that featured Looney Tunes characters in new cartoons designed for television. He also provided the voices for Barney Rubble and Fred Flintstone's pet dinosaur, Dino, for the first prime-time cartoon series, "The Flintstones." Through the years, Blanc also kept up his work in radio, primarily as an actor and special effects creator for "The Jack Benny Show," on which he portrayed Benny's mexican gardener, Sy; his violin teacher, Mr. LeBlanc; his wise-cracking parrot; and his pet polar bear. Blanc also formed his own company to produce radio and television advertising. His last cartoon contribution came in the popular 1988 mixed-animation film "Who Framed Roger Rabbit," in which he performed the voices of Bugs Bunny, Daffy Duck, Tweety, and Porky Pig. In assessing why his characters have become so endearing to all age-groups, Blanc told the *New York Times:* "What we tried to do was amuse ourselves. We didn't make pictures for children. We didn't make pictures for adults. We made them for ourselves."
Sources: *Chicago Tribune,* July 11, 1989; *New York Times,* July 11, 1989.

John Carradine

Name originally Richmond Reed Carradine; adopted stage name, 1935; born February 5, 1906, in New York, N.Y.; died of heart and kidney failure, November 27, 1988, in Milan, Italy. American stage and film actor. A classic character actor who appeared in more than 475 films, Carradine, a gaunt, lanky man with a rich, baritone voice, was famous for his memorable portrayals of villains, mad scientists, and eccentrics. He was also the patriarch of an American acting family; of his five sons, four, David, Keith, Bruce and Robert, have all acted in movies or television. Only Christopher, an architect, did not follow in his father's footsteps. Because he was not a typical Hollywood leading man, and knew it, Carradine took almost any role that came along, and many of the films he appeared in were forgettable. But in a career which spanned five decades, the actor had excellent roles in such classics as "Stagecoach," (1939), "The Grapes of Wrath" (1940), "Around the World in 80 Days" (1956), and "The Man Who Shot Liberty Valance" (1962).

Born in the Greenwich Village section of New York, Carradine was the son of educated parents; his father was an attorney and writer and his mother was a surgeon. After high school he worked as a quick sketch artist and a scenery painter, which brought him into contact with the theater and eventually led him into acting. After playing a featured role in a New Orleans production of "Camille," he joined a Shakespearean touring company, which allowed him to cultivate his longtime fascination with the great English poet. The tour eventually brought him to Hollywood, where he earned a living in local stage productions and occasional small parts in B movies. At this time Carradine also began to gain fame as an eccentric and a ham. Dressed in an Edwardian cape and a wide-brimmed hat, he was often seen strolling along Hollywood Boulevard, reciting lines from Shakespeare in the booming voice that would become his trademark. He was also known to perform Shakespeare for himself, at midnight, in the darkness of the Hollywood Bowl. For this he became known in Hollywood as "The Bard of the Boulevard."

Carradine's first big break into the movies, he told the *New York Times* in 1944, came in the 1930s "when the great Cecil B. DeMille saw an apparition—me—pass him by, reciting the gravedigger's lines from 'Hamlet,' and he instructed me to report to him the following day." However, it was the actor's voice which really impressed DeMille; Carradine's role in DeMille's 1932 film "The Sign of the Cross" was cut so that only his voice made it into the movie—coming from another actor's mouth. Carradine's first important role came in John Ford's "The Grapes of Wrath," in which he played Preacher Casy. This began a long association between Ford and Carradine. He became a member of Ford's informal "stock company" of character actors, which included Ward Bond and Walter Brennan. Other Ford films in which Carradine appeared included "Drums Along the Mohawk" (1939), "The Last Hurrah" (1958), and "Cheyenne Autumn" (1964).

Carradine's reputation for versatility made him highly sought after in Hollywood, especialy in horror films. He starred in dozens of B movies as mad doctors and sadistic criminals; he also played the famous vampire Dracula three times. Carradine seemed to enjoy the oddball image these parts conveyed on him. "I never made the big money in Hollywood," he told the *New York Times.* "I was paid in hundreds, the stars got thousands. But I worked with some of the greatest directors in films, and some of the greatest writers. They gave me freedom to do what I can do best and that was gratifying." Some of the roles which Carradine most cherished included that of Lincoln in "Of Human Hearts" (1938), the writer Bret Hart in "The Adventures of Mark Twain" (1944), and Aaron in DeMille's "Ten Commandments" (1956). **Sources:** *Chicago Tribune*, November 29, 1988; *New York Times,* November 29, 1988; *Washington Post,* November 29, 1988.

Billy Carter

Full name, William Alton Carter, III; born March 29, 1937, in Plains, Ga.; died of pancreatic cancer, September 25, 1988, in Plains, Ga. Businessman. An irreverent, beer-drinking, self-described good ol' boy, Carter rocketed to fame in 1976 during his older brother Jimmy's successful run for the presidency. Billy was colorful and quotable and reporters often sought him out when looking for a fresh perspective on the long campaign. In that spirit, he once told the *Los Angeles Times:* "I've got a mother who joined the Peace Corps and went to India when she was 68. I've got a sister who races motorcycles and another sister who's a Holy Roller preacher. I've got a brother who says he wants to be President of the United States. I'm the only sane one in the family." But his antics at times embarrassed the Carter administration. In 1979, a federal grand jury investigated Carter's acceptance of a $220,000 loan from the government of Libya, a radical regime long suspected of promoting terrorism. Though nothing came of the charges, Carter was made known as a registered agent of the Libyan government. He had traveled to Libya in 1978 and 1979 trying to arrange a brokerage agreement for a U.S. company seeking an allotment of Libyan oil. The scandal was believed to contribute to Jimmy Carter's defeat in the 1980 elections.

The youngest of the four Carter children, Billy's problems in school were caused in part by his shyness and stuttering, as well as a need to distinguish himself in an overachieving family. When his father died in 1953, he continued to struggle at Emory University while his older brother ran the family peanut warehouse, but when Jimmy was elected Governor of Georgia in 1970, Billy took over the business's day-to-day operations. He proved a shrewd businessman; by 1976, he had turned the warehouse into a $5 million-a-year operation. When Jimmy became President, however, the younger Carter became embittered over arrangements made to protect Jimmy's 60 percent share of the business, which was placed in a blind trust managed by an Atlanta lawyer. When Billy's offer to buy his brother out was refused, he quit and went on to a series of public speaking appearances, self-promotional gimmicks, and wild business ventures. In 1977 he introduced the ill-fated "Billy Beer," which he promoted with his hard-drinking image (he was known to drink beer for breakfast). When Plains became beset with tourists, he was forced to move to the outskirts of town, and in the late 1970s the Libyan story began making headlines. By 1980 he was in debt to the IRS and under treatment for alcoholism.

To pay his debts, Carter was forced to sell much of the property he owned in Plains, including his beloved Amoco gas station, where he had spent long hours drinking beer and talking with his buddies. He moved to Alabama to take a job as a sales representative for a mobile home manufacturer and didn't return to Plains until 1986. Those who knew him said he was far more intelligent and sensitive than his public image conveyed. He once confided to the *Los Angeles Times* that he "may have created a monster" with his "redneck pose." But he was always his own man. According to a *New York Times* report, Carter, while appearing before a Senate committee over the Libyan charges said, "I refused to conform to an image that a lot of people thought a President's brother should adopt." In 1987 he was diagnosed as having inoperable pancreatic cancer, the same disease that killed his father and sister. **Sources:** *Los Angeles Times,* September 26, 1988; *New York Times,* September 26, 1988; *Time,* October 10, 1988.

Raymond Carver

Full name, Raymond Clevie Carver, Jr.; born May 25, 1938, in Clatskanie, Ore.; died of lung cancer, August 2, 1988, in Port Angeles, Wash. A poet and recognized master of the short story, Carver published 10 books in a career shadowed by alcoholism, poverty, despair and a fractured marriage. His stories chronicled the lives of America's working poor, and were effective—some critics contend—because that was a life Carver himself had known. By age 20 he was married and the father of two, wandering the West Coast in search of work to support his family while, at the same time, trying to get an education and find time to write. His best stories were borne out of these hardships and the characters he met along the way.

Most of Carver's stories are set in the Pacific Northwest, where he was born and raised by working-class parents. His father, Clevie Raymond Carver, a sawmill worker, taught the boy to fish and hunt, and entertained him by reading from Zane Grey novels. Shortly after graduating high school, Carver married 16-year-old Maryann Burk, who was pregnant with the first of their two children. The couple struggled for many years, working odd jobs, and in the daytime Carver attended college; he became serious about writing after taking a course taught by the late novelist John Gardner at Chico State College in California. Carver transferred to California's Humboldt State College and continued to write, publishing his first poems and short stories while still a student there. He received his degree in 1963, packed up his family, and moved to Iowa to attend the prestigious Iowa Writers Workshop, but the money ran out after a year and the Carvers returned to California, where Raymond took a job as a hospital janitor. In 1967, after latching on to his first white-collar job as a textbook editor, Carver's "Will You Please Be Quiet, Please?" was selected for the anthology *Best American Short Stories.*

Despite the growing recognition for his work, Carver's life began to crumble in the 1970s. His writing brought in little money and he eventually went bankrupt, turning increasingly to alcohol to ease the frustration. He lost his job and his marriage began to dissolve. By 1977 he was living alone and had been in and out of alcohol treatment centers, but he continued to write. His 1976 short story collection, *Will You Please Be Quiet, Please?* was nominated for a National Book Award. He taught at the University of California at Santa Cruz, the Iowa Writers Workshop, the University of Texas, the University of Vermont, and, from 1980–83, at Syracuse University, where he met his second wife, poet Tess Gallagher. In 1983, he quit teaching upon winning the Mildred and Harold Strauss Living Award, which provided a tax-free stipend of $35,000 a year for five years. That same year he published a fifth story collection, *Cathedral,* to almost universal acclaim. In 1988, dying of cancer, Carver collected what he considered the best of his stories, plus seven new ones, in the collection *Where I'm Calling From.* Shortly after that book's publication he was inducted into the American Academy and Institute of Arts and Letters. **Sources:** *Los Angeles Times,* August 4, 1988; *New York Times,* August 3, 1988; *Washington Post,* August 4, 1988.

John Cassavetes

Born December 9, 1929, in New York, N.Y.; died of complications resulting from cirrhosis of the liver, February 3, 1989, in Los Angeles, Calif. Film director, screenwriter, and actor. A fiercely independent screenwriter and film director who also acted to finance his own projects, Cassavetes defied the trappings of Hollywood and the lure of boxoffice dollars to produce unique, personal, improvisational films that have become classics of American alternative cinema. Despite his maverick image, he was one of only four people to be nominated for an Academy Award in three different categories. He was nominated as best director for his original film "A Woman Under the Influence" (1974), as best writer for his original screenplay for "Faces" (1968), and as best supporting actor for his role in "The Dirty Dozen" (1967). His films, often shot in grainy black-and-white and displaying Cassavetes's unmistakably quirky directorial stamp, were true to the nature of the man; ruggedly handsome, he preferred smoky barrooms and the company of good friends, including actor Peter Falk and Cassavettes's wife of more than 30 years, actress Gena Rowlands, both of whom appeared in many of his films.

A 1950 graduate of Manhattan's American Academy of Dramatic Arts, Cassavetes began his career as a television actor, appearing on such programs as "Omnibus," "Studio One," "Kraft Theater," and "Playhouse 90." While conducting a course in Method acting in 1956 Cassavetes had the idea for his first independent film project, which he shot over the next few years on a meager budget. Filmed with a hand-held, 16mm camera, in black-and-white, and without a script, "Shadows" made a daring statement on race relations by relating the story of a fair skinned black girl and her two brothers in New York City. The film won the 1960 Critics Award at the Venice Film Festival and is regarded by many film enthusiasts as a masterpiece of art.

"Faces" was Cassavetes's first financial success. A probing study of loneliness and marital breakdown, the film won five Venice Film Festival awards and received three Oscar nominations. "Faces" also made more than $10 million—a ten-fold return on its cost. "Husbands," which co-starred Cassavetes along with friends Falk and Ben Gazzara, studied the relationship of three men who must face their own mortality when they gather for the funeral of a friend. "A Woman Under the Influence" was Cassavetes's most commercial film, starring Falk and Rowlands and concerning the souring of a middle-class marriage. "Gloria," a 1980 film starring Rowlands, won the Golden Lion award at the Venice Film Festival.

American critics seem to be divided in their judgements of Cassavetes's films, which are so personal that they seem to draw a very strong response whether positive or negative. "You can never be sure," said *New York Times* critic Vincent Canby, "whether what you're seeing is artful or artless." Cassavetes had a much more devoted following among European cineastes, who considered him a major New Wave film director. Among the many films Cassavetes starred in to finance his films were "Rosemary's Baby," "Two Minute Warning," "The Fury," and a 1964 remake of "The Killers," which co-starred Ronald Reagan. Cassavetes's 1978 film "Opening Night" made its United States debut at the 1988 New York Film Festival. **Sources:** *Chicago Tribune,* February 5, 1989; *New York Times,* February 4, 1989; *People,* February 20, 1989.

Bruce Chatwin

Full name, Charles Bruce Chatwin; born May 13, 1940, in Sheffield, England; died of bone marrow disease, January 17, 1989, in Nice, France. British travel writer and novelist. In many ways a born wanderer, the multi-talented Chatwin, who had spent his life drifting from place to place and from one curiosity to another, eventually found a way to make a career of his travels by writing about them. Struck down tragically in his prime by a rare disease caused by a fungus that he contracted in China, Chatwin published only five books, three of them novels (an additional collection of his essays, *What Am I Doing Here?,* will be published posthumously). The first, *In Patagonia,* won him the Somerset Maugham and E.M. Forster literary awards and established him as a ranking member of a generation of writers that helped to revive travel writing as an art form. As *New York Times* critic Andrew Harvey noted in his review of Chatwin's last travel book, *The Songlines:* "Nearly every writer of my generation in England has wanted, at some point, to be Bruce Chatwin, wanted to be talked about, as he is, with raucous envy; wanted, above all, to have written his books."

The son of a naval officer who was often at sea, Chatwin spent his childhood in modest means, drifting throughout England with his mother, staying with friends and relatives. Having never attended college, Chatwin took a job in 1958 as a porter at the famous London auction house Sotheby's; he quickly established himself as an authority on Impressionist art and by 1965, at the age of 25, became the youngest director in the firm's history. That same eventful year Chatwin also married an American, Elizabeth Chanler, who shared his love of travel; he then turned down an excellent opportunity for a partnership at Sotheby's, and, "out of sheer boredom," quit the firm to study archeology at Edinburgh University.

At age 33 Chatwin took a job as travel writer for the magazine supplement of the *Sunday Times of London,* but during a trip to South America he left his magazine position with a terse cable ("Have gone to Patagonia") and declared himself an independent writer. *In Patagonia* was published in 1977 and drew on Chatwin's lonely travels through the desolate, southern third of Argentina and parts of Chile. Through a narrative technique he called "searches," Chatwin mixed anthropology, history, and fiction with local legends to relate in sparse style the story of people often overlooked in Western literature. True to his own experience, Chatwin's interest centered on nomadic peoples: "What interested me most," he told the *Los Angeles Times*, "were the people who had escaped the archeological record—the nomads who trod lightly on the earth and didn't build pyramids."

Chatwin followed *In Patagonia* with two novels, both based on historical research and information he had gathered in his own travels. *The Viceroy of Ouidah* concerned the true-life adventures of an early nineteenth-century Brazilian slave trader. *On the Black Hill* concentrated on the lives of twin brothers on a farm on the Welsh-English border. *The Songlines* is a travel-book study of Australia's nomadic aborigines; and *Utz*, a novel published in the United States just weeks before Chatwin's death, concerns the lonely life of a Prague art collector with an obsession for porcelain. As Michiko Kakutani pointed out in the *New York Times*, *Utz* "opens out to become an examination of art—its ability to confer immortality and its ability to become a substitute for life." *Utz* was nominated for the 1988 Booker Prize. Confined by his illness to a wheelchair for the last years of his life, Chatwin finished *What Am I Doing Here?* while living with his wife in Nice, France. In a 1987 *New York Times* interview he had dismissed his illness with the comment, "Hazards of travel—rather an alarming one." **Sources:** *New York Times*, January 19, 1989; *Times* (London), January 20, 1989; *Washington Post*, January 23, 1989.

Malcolm Cowley

Born August 24, 1898, in Belsano, Pa.; died of heart attack, March 28, 1989, in New Milford, Conn. American poet, critic, cultural and literary historian, and translator. A distinguished and influential literary critic for more than six decades, Cowley was perhaps best known for his chronicles of the so-called "Lost Generation" of expatriate American writers who rose to fame in the 1920s and 30s. He lived in Paris in the years following World War I and became acquainted with the works of blossoming young writers like Ernest Hemingway, F. Scott Fitzgerald, John Dos Passos, Hart Crane, E.E. Cummings, and William Faulkner. He also met, in his own words, "all the Dada crowd (later the Surrealist crowd), and helped to get out two expatriate magazines, *Secession* and *Broom*." He established his reputation with the 1934 publication of *Exile's Return*, an autobiographical literary history of his experiences in Paris. Now a cornerstone work to scholars trying to understand the period, *Exile's Return* is "the most vivacious of all accounts of literary life during the fabulous 1920s," according to Lloyd Morris in a *New York Herald Tribune Book Review* article. The book "offers an intimate, realistic portrait of the era that produced a renaissance in American fiction and poetry," Morris said. As literary editor for the liberal weekly *New Republic* (1929–44) and later as an editor for Viking Press, Cowley wielded a profound and lasting influence on the American literary scene for the rest of his life.

The son of a Pittsburgh physician, Cowley attended what he called "dreadfully snobbish" Harvard University for two years before leaving in 1917 to join the American Ambulance Service in France. After the war, he returned to graduate from Harvard in 1919 and lived for a time in Greenwich Village, where he met his first wife, Peggy Baird. He returned to France in 1921 to attend the University of Montpellier on an American Field Service Scholarship, and in Paris he encountered the lively expatriate literary scene he would later write about. During these years, with the encouragement of his friend Hart Crane (the hard drinking poet who later had an affair with Cowley's wife), Cowley also wrote poetry, and by 1929 his collection of 56 poems, called *Blue Juniata*, was published to favorable critical reviews. After returning to America in 1923, Cowley supported himself with work on the New York publication *Sweet's Architectural Catalogue*, and later as a free-lance writer and translator. In all he translated eight books from the French, including authors like Barrès and Gide, which are considered to be the best translations of those works available.

An early champion of William Faulkner, Cowley is widely credited with rescuing that great writer from literary oblivion. His introduction to *The Portable Faulkner*, a 1946 collection of Faulkner's stories and excerpts from his novels, is considered the best short essay ever on Faulkner. Faulkner was awarded the Nobel Prize for literature a few years later. Other influential Cowley works, many of them collections of his fine critical essays on authors like Walt Whitman, Fitzgerald and Hemingway, are *After the Genteel Tradition* (1937), *The Literary Situation* (1954), and the highly acclaimed 1973 collection *The Second Flowering*. Though he also encouraged more modern writers like Ken Kesey, Jack Kerouac, and John Cheever, Cowley most certainly concentrated his efforts on the post-World War I era. He told the critic Allen Geller that "there is a very interesting group of writers today" but added that the "great change from the 1930s is that nobody any longer believes in his duty or ability to any extent or in any manner whatever to reshape or alter conditions." **Sources:**

Los Angeles Times, March 29, 1989; *New York Times*, March 29, 1989; *Times* (London), March 30, 1989.

Salvador Dali

Born May 11, 1904, in Figueras, Spain; died of cardiac arrest, January 23, 1989, in Figueras, Spain. Spanish painter. Among the most influential and certainly most famous painters of the 20th Century, the eccentric and enigmatic Dali, in the words of John Russell of the *New York Times*, "made an inventive and enduring contribution to European Surrealism." Dali became equally famous on the sheer force of his personality; purposely outrageous in his conduct, he courted the press and loved to shock the public, and he was supremely confident of his own genius despite the consensus among art observers that he made little serious artistic contribution after his heyday in the 1930s. Indeed, the artist's later years were dedicated to his confessed "pure, vertical, mystical, gothic love of cash." He didn't hesitate to lend his name to advertisements for chewing gum, cars, and candy, and he was plagued throughout his career by hangers-on who duped him into unwise financial schemes. Throughout, however, he remained the irrepressible Dali—bent on reminding the world, in his life as in his pictures, of the dreamy, nonsensical landscape that lies just beyond reality.

Having displayed a precocious gift for drawing while a child, Dali was encouraged to be an artist and was eventually enrolled at the National School of Fine Arts in Madrid in 1921. He was a rebellious student who was expelled once for inciting students to riot, later readmitted, and then expelled for good for refusing to take an exam because he felt that his instructors were not fit to judge him. By this time Dali had already established a promising reputation as a painter in galleries in Barcelona and Madrid. His international reputation began to grow after his first trip to Paris in 1928, when he made contact with fellow Spanish painters Pablo Picasso and Joan Miro and the well-known Surrealist painter Andre Breton. Dali returned to Spain and began painting the pictures which would make him the annointed successor to the Surrealist movement, which stressed the liberation of suppressed images from the unconcious to create a new super-reality. An exhibition of these paintings at Paris's prestigious Galerie Goemans in 1929 was a resounding success. Dali's technique differed from that of other Surrealists in its exactitude. Aside from their content, his paintings were calculatedly realistic, to the point where no observer could doubt the validity of the whimsical images they portrayed. Dali's stated intention, through this method he called "critical paranoia," was to give order to chaos and to discredit everyday reality.

A self-described exhibitionist, Dali seemed to apply his artistic philosophy to his personal life. Already famous by the mid-1930s, Dali cultivated his image to the fullest, both for monetary gain and the pure fun of it. He was known to make appearances before the press in a full diving suit or to drive up in a limousine full of cauliflower. He once skipped an exhibition and sent his horse to stand in for him. All these stunts seemed to take attention away from his art, which, most critics agree, had degenerated by the 1940s, when Dali broke from the Surrealist movement, became a royalist and a Catholic, and started producing religious paingtings in a Daliesque fashion. He also cultivated a mutual love affair with America, where his outrageousness had won him a popular audience on Broadway and in Hollywood. He designed sets for opera, theatre and film, endorsed products, and rarely turned down an interview, which was his vehicle to the ear of the world. After one of his typical outbursts, he was known to wave off the press with the line: "Time's up now. You've got your money's worth."

Dali's later years saw the further decline of his artistic output, the abuse of his signature, and the fall of his fortune into the hands of reputedly unscrupulous business dealers. A notoriously poor businessman despite his love of money, Dali for years had left his finances to longtime manager Peter Moore. After a falling out in his relationship with Moore, Dali entrusted many of his copyright and reproduction rights privelages to people who then swindled him out of his share of the profits. In the mid-1970s Dali and his wife initiated a practice in which Dali spent hours each day signing his name to thousands of blank canvases, presumably for use in the printing of his lithographs. But when Dali discovered that many of the canvases had fallen into the hands of forgers, he scrambled to expose the scandal and establish another means of authenticity.

Dali went into seclusion after the 1982 death of his wife of 47 years, Gala, and in 1984, already confined to a wheelchair because of Parkinson's disease, he was badly burned in a fire at his home. The few bright moments in his last years came with the success of a major Dali retrospective at the Museum of Contemporary Art in Madrid in 1983 and the establishment, at the Salvador Dali museum in St.

Petersburg, Florida, of the largest collection of his works in the world. In addition to his painting, Dali collaborated on two Surrealist cinema classics with Luis Bunuel: "The Andulasian Dog" (1928) and "The Age of Gold" (1930). He also wrote three books: *The Secret Life of Salvador Dali* (1942), *The Diary of a Genius* (1965), and *The Unspeakable Confessions of Salvador Dali* (1976). **Sources:** *Chicago Tribune,* January 24, 1989; *New York Times,* January 24, 1989; *People,* February 6, 1989.

Antal Dorati

Born April 9, 1906, in Budapest, Hungary; died November 13, 1988, in Gerzensee, Switzerland. Conductor and composer. Internationally acclaimed as a great orchestra builder and interpreter of twentith-century music, Dorati led some of the great symphonies of the world to their peaks of notoriety and distinction. He also made more than 500 recordings, serving as one of the important liasons who helped usher the breadth of Western musical tradition into the age of electronic transcription.

Born in Budapest, Dorati studied music there at the Franz Liszt Academy under the tutelage of the great Hungarian composers Zoltan Kodaly and Bela Bartok, an experience which would later make Dorati one of the world's most highly respected Bartok scholars and interpreters. Dorati's early training came in dance; he conducted orchestras for ballet and opera theaters in Budapest, Dresden, and Monaco. From 1933 to 1941 he conducted the Ballet Russe de Monte Carlo and from 1941 to 1945 he was with the American Ballet Theater. Dorati became an American citizen in 1947, two years after he was named head of the Dallas Symphony and 10 years after his American debut with the National Symphony Orchestra.

It was during Dorati's 11-year stint as conductor of the Minneapolis Symphony, which began in 1949, that he began to establish himself as a knowledgeable and prolific leader in the burgeoning field of recorded music. As electronic transciption became more sophisticated, Dorati made best-selling recordings of works from Beethoven, Tchaikovsky, and Dvorak, as well as Bartok and the complete symphonies of Haydn. During this time he was also a frequent guest conductor in Europe, where he returned in the 1960s to serve as music director for the BBC Symphony (1963–66) and the Stockholm Philharmonic (1966–70).

Dorati's final decade on the conductor's stand, though filled with many great successes, was not without its disappointments. He was hired in 1970 to direct the National Symphony Orchestra, at the time beset by financial troubles and a strike by the orchestra personnel. Under Dorati the orchestra was viewed to have made great improvements and was well received when it performed the inaugural concert at the John F. Kennedy Center for the Performing Arts in Washington in 1971. David Lloyd Kreeger, then president of the National Symphony, told the *Washington Post* in 1977 that progess under Dorati had been "nothing short of spectacular." But financial problems continued to plague the symphony. A 1976 tour of Europe was cancelled and Dorati, who had been known to quarrel with the board of directors, was replaced in 1977 by Mstislav Rostropovich. Dorati followed this setback with another successful orchestra rebuilding, this time with the Detroit Symphony, which he led from 1977 to 1981. Unfortunately, orchestral financial troubles again brought about his resignation. Among Dorati's compositions were concertos, suites, chamber music, and a symphonic song cycle called "The Voices." Dorati's autobiography, *Notes of Seven Decades,* was published in 1979. **Sources:** *Los Angeles Times,* November 16, 1988; *New York Times,* November 15, 1988; *Washington Post,* November 15, 1988.

Roy Eldridge

Full name, David Roy Eldridge; born January 30, 1911, in Pittsburgh, Pa.; died February 26, 1989, in Valley Stream, N.Y. American jazz musician. A short, wiry man with boundless energy, Eldridge was known in the jazz world as "Little Jazz" for his fiery, crackling trumpet playing. He was often described as the link between the pioneering trumpeter Louis Armstrong and the great modern innovator Dizzy Gillespie, but fellow musician Jon Faddis, in the *Washington Post,* described Eldridge as "a giant in his own right" and "one of the most exciting" jazz trumpeters. Jazz historian Ross Russell told the *New York Times:* "Roy's trumpet went beyond Louis [Armstrong] in range and brilliance. It had greater agility. His style was more nervous. His drive was perhaps the most intense jazz has ever known." "God gives it to some and not to others," Ella Fitzgerald once told the *New York Times.* "He's got more soul in one note than a lot of people could get into the whole song."

Born in Pittsburgh, Eldridge began playing music at age six. He left home at 16 to play with traveling bands in various carnivals and finally reached New York in 1930. His first influences on trumpet were Rex Stewart and Red Nichols, but he began to base his style on the fluid solos of saxophonists like Coleman Hawkins and Benny Carter. The sound transferred to Eldridge's trumpet in a sleek, intense, staccato played at high speed; jazz lovers started taking notice when Eldridge performed with Fletcher Henderson's orchestra on tunes like "Stampede." Eldridge first saw Armstrong play in 1931. "I didn't think so much of him at first," he told the *New York Times.* "But I stayed for the second show and I suddenly realized he built his solos like a book—first, an introduction, then chapters, each one coming out of the one before and building to a climax."

Eldridge drew national attention in the 1940s when he became one of the first black members of Gene Krupa's and Artie Shaw's bands. With Krupa from 1941–43, he turned in fine performances with a trumpet solo in "Rockin' Chair" and as a vocalist with Anita O'Day on "Let Me Off Uptown" and "Knock Me a Kiss." But while touring with these bands Eldridge suffered racial humiliations, such as being denied entrance to hotels and restaurants with the rest of the musicians. He insisted that Krupa and Shaw and his fellow bandmates had been kind to him, but he swore that he would never again travel with a white band, though he later did. While touring the world with Norman Granz's Jazz at the Philharmonic in the 1950s, Eldridge, like many black jazz artists, found European audiences much more accepting of his race and appreciative of his music. He stayed in France for over a year.

Upon returning to the United States, where segregation had begun to lessen, Eldridge became a mainstay of the modern jazz scene, playing at New York clubs like the Metropole and Jimmy Ryan's. He helped usher in the bebop era and swing by influencing Gillespie and other up-and-coming stars. By the late 1950s he slowed down on the demanding trumpet and became an adequate performer on fluegelhorn, bass, piano, and drums, while maintaining his gruff-voiced vocal style. In the 1980s health problems forced him to stop playing, but he remained a fixture at jazz schools and major jazz events. His death came just three weeks after the death of his wife of 53 years. Friends of Eldridge said that after Viola's death the musician refused to eat and wished to die. **Sources:** *Chicago Tribune,* February 28, 1989; *Los Angeles Times,* February 27, 1989; *New York Times,* February 28, 1989.

"Lefty" Gomez

Full name, Vernon Louis Gomez; born November 26, 1909, in Rodeo, Calif.; died of congestive heart failure, February 17, 1989, in San Rafael, Calif. Former professional baseball player. In the mystical, man-child's world of professional baseball, known as much for its oddballs and eccentrics as for its heroes, Gomez was a rarity—a player whose prowess on the field equaled or surpassed his zany antics in the locker room. As a pitcher for the powerhouse New York Yankees teams of the 1930s, he compiled a perfect 6–0 record in World Series play, twice leading the American League in victories and earned-run average and three times totaling the most strikeouts. He was nicknamed "Goofy" by his teammates, who often endured his pranks right on the field. Gomez once stopped a game and, saying nothing, went and stood with his head bent over earnestly next to shortstop Phil Rizutto. When Rizutto finally asked him what he was doing, Gomez replied: "I heard your mother and father were in the stands and I wanted them to think the great Gomez was asking their son's advice." The game, to Gomez, often seemed to be a sideshow. He was even known to step off the mound in the middle of an inning to watch an airplane circle over the stadium.

A tall, slim, hard-throwing left-hander with a high-kick windup, Gomez signed with the Yankees for $35,000—at that time a large sum for a ballplayer—and went only 2–5 in 1930, his first season in the majors. But the next year he improved his record to 21–9 and was hailed as "another Lefty Grove." After compiling a 24–7 mark in 1932, Gomez took the Yankees' advice and put on 20 pounds before the 1933 season. That year his performance slipped noticeably; Gomez trimmed down to 160 pounds in 1934 and had his best season—a 26–5 record, 158 strikeouts, a 2.33 ERA, and 25 complete games. Overall, he had four seasons with 20 or more wins and a 189–102 career record, which places him 13th on the all-time winning percentage list. In his career with the Yankees, Gomez played with such baseball legends as Babe Ruth, Lou Gehrig, and Joe DiMaggio. He was the winning pitcher in four All-Star games, including the first ever played in 1933.

For all his pitching exploits, however, Gomez was a notoriously bad hitter, a fact he often made light of. Asked what was his only weakness at the plate, Gomez cracked, "A pitched ball." His sense of humor was often turned upon himself, particularly when the conversation came around to the subject of Jimmie Foxx, the great power-hitter who gave Gomez fits. Bill Dickey, who was Gomez's catcher for most of his career, told the *New York Times* that Gomez once shook off every sign Dickey flashed when Foxx came to bat. Finally, Dickey ran to the mound and asked Gomez, "What do you want to throw him?" "I don't want to throw him nothin'," Gomez said. "Maybe he'll just get tired of waitin' and leave." Gomez liked to tell the story about the time he and his wife were watching the Apollo astronauts walking on the moon on television in 1969. "They were walking back and forth picking up pieces of the moon's surface," Gomez told the *Los Angeles Times.* "Then they saw a strange white rock, something they couldn't identify. I said to my wife, 'I know what that is. It's a ball Jimmie Foxx hit off me.'" Gomez also coined a phrase that has become part of regular American speech. Asked about an inning in which three hard-hit balls were caught by his outfielders, Gomez quipped, "I'd rather be lucky than good." Gomez was married for over 50 years to the former June O'Dea, whom he fell in love with after watching her dance in a chorus line in a New York nightclub. After his baseball career ended in 1942, he made a living as a sporting goods representative and a popular speaker on the banquet circuit. Gomez was elected to baseball's Hall of Fame in 1972. **Sources:** *Chicago Tribune,* February 19, 1989; *Los Angeles Times,* February 18, 1989; *New York Times,* February 20, 1989.

George Hatem

Name originally Shafiek Hatem; born c. 1910 in Buffalo, N.Y.; died of cancer and diabetes, October 3, 1988, in Beijing, People's Republic of China. Physician. Known throughout China as the beloved Dr. Ma Hai-teh, or "virtue from overseas," Hatem, an American-born and educated physician, devoted more than fifty years of his life to eradicating venereal disease and leprosy in China. Hatem arrived in Shanghai in 1933 to find a city beset with pandemic venereal disease, rampant prostitution, and generally filthy, impoverished conditions. By 1970, largely due to his expertise and organizational efforts, both VD and prostitution were rarities in China, and Hatem had begun to concentrate on the country's leprosy problem.

Born of Lebanese parents, Hatem was raised in North Carolina, where he attended the University of North Carolina. Upon receiving his medical degree from the University of Geneva in Switzerland, he traveled with two classmates to study tropical diseases in Shanghai, where he discovered not only disease and poverty but also the seeds of revolutionary change. While practicing in Shanghai, he became acquainted with many members of the Communist underground, among them many Westerners, including Edgar Snow, the journalist who wrote *Red Star Over China.* When Mao Tse-tung became head of the Communist Party, he sent word to Shanghai that he needed a Western-trained doctor and a journalist, so Hatem and Snow, with the help of Madame Soong Ching Ling (widow of Sun Yat-sen), escaped through Nationalist Army lines and joined Mao's Red Army forces in Shaanxi. There, he supervised medical treatment of Mao's soldiers and trained thousands of "barefoot doctors," medical orderlies who provided treatment in the field.

A member of the Communist Party since 1937, Hatem was one of the first foreigners to be granted Chinese citizenship, in 1950, shortly after Mao took power. As a key adviser to the Ministry of Public Health, Hatem was given the project of treating the widespread venereal disease and stamping out its chief facilitator, prostitution. The task was enormous. In many areas, 10 percent of the population was syphylitic and young girls were routinely sold off to brothel owners by their parents. Illiteracy and mistrust of doctors made education difficult, and it took Hatem and his thousands of medical volunteers years to shut down the brothels, locate the transmitters of the disease, and treat the afflicted. Hatem also turned his attentions to leprosy, a disease which affected about 500,000 Chinese in 1949; by the time of his death that number had been cut to 100,000. **Sources:** *Los Angeles Times,* October 6, 1988; *Parade,* June 22, 1986; *Times* (London), October 13, 1988.

J.C. Heard

Full name, James Charles Heard; born 1917, in Dayton, Ohio; died of a heart attack, September 27, 1988, in Royal Oak, Mich. Jazz drummer and bandleader. Heard, a jazz leader and innovator during the height of the Big Band era of the 1930s and '40s, played drums for virtually every jazz giant, including Dizzy Gillespie, Cab Calloway, Count Basie, Duke Ellington and Woody Herman. Even in his later years, as he grew disillusioned with America's lukewarm response to jazz music, Heard, who had become a jazz legend, remained active as a drummer, bandleader, and teacher until the time of his death. Indeed, on the day he died Heard was scheduled to perform with Gillespie, who once grouped Heard with Kenny Clarke and Max Roach as the three men who wrote the rules for modern jazz drumming.

Raised in Detroit, Heard began his show business career there as a self-taught tap dancer in the 1920s. He was performing at the Coplin Theatre with a black vaudeville troupe when the pit band's drummer became ill and Heard was asked to fill in; "I never forgot that day," he told the *Detroit Free Press.* "I kept the drums. I really got hung up with the drums." One of Heard's early influences was the great Chick Webb, whom he met in 1937 and studied closely. By 1939, at the age of 22, Heard joined the Teddy Wilson Orchestra and later played with Benny Carter and Cab Calloway before forming his own sextet in 1946. His career peaked in the late 1940s and early '50s when he performed at concert halls throughout the world with Norman Granz's Jazz at the Philharmonic group, which featured such jazz greats as trumpeter Roy Eldridge, pianist Oscar Peterson, and vocalist Ella Fitzgerald.

But the popular international response to this tour only served to heighten Heard's notion that American audiences were underappreciative of jazz. "Jazz music today is nothing like it should be," he told the *Los Angeles Times.* "In fact it is at the bottom of the list as far as music is concerned throughout the country." The Jazz at the Philharmonic tour stopped in Japan in 1953, and Heard liked it so much he ended up staying for five years, touring China, the Phillipines, and Australia as well. In Japan he also met and married his wife Hiroko. After returning to the United States, Heard formed a quartet which performed in New Orleans, Dallas, Los Angeles, Las Vegas, and Detroit, where he settled permanently in 1968. Known to his family and friends as "Papa," Heard remained active with his own ensembles, as a sit-in performer in the bands of many of his friends, and as a highly coveted session musician for recordings. He appeared on an estimated 1,200 jazz records. **Sources:** *Detroit Free Press,* Sept. 28, 1988; *Los Angeles Times,* Sept. 29, 1988; *New York Times,* Sept. 30, 1988.

Hirohito, Emperor of Japan

Born April 29, 1901, in Tokyo, Japan; died of intestinal cancer, January 7, 1989, in Tokyo, Japan. Emperor of Japan. As the longest-reigning monarch in Japan's 2,500 years of recorded history, Hirohito presided over 62 years of dynamic social change. Though he was personally frail and soft-spoken, and his title, particularly after World War II, was mostly symbolic, Hirohito exuded profound influence on Japanese history and society; his death, after months of failing health, was grieved by all Japan. Because tradition dictates that the Chrysanthemum Throne cannot be empty, Hirohito's 55 year-old son, Crown Prince Akihito, was immediately declared Japan's 125th Emperor after an ancient ceremony in which he received the symbols of Japan's monarchy: the sacred sword, the imperial jewels, and the imperial seal. With his passing, Hirohito will henceforth be known by the name Showa, or Enlightened Peace, which was the title chosen for his reign when he succeeded his father, the Emperor Taisho, at the age of 25 on December 25, 1926.

Hirohito's era saw Japan attempting to embrace democracy, falling into authoritarian militarism, and finally emerging as a first-class economic power. The grandson of the great Emperor Meiji, who ushered Japan into the modern era by breaking with the feudal Shogun nobility and encouraging industrialization, Hirohito came to the throne at a time of political and economic optimism. When the world plunged into the depression of the 1930s, however, Japan gradually slipped into the control of a powerful fascist regime, which began a militaristic assault through China and the rest of Asia and ultimately led to the Japanese attack on the United States at Pearl Harbor in 1941. Though Hirohito had often stated that he opposed war with the United States, his signature appeared on Japan's declaration of war, and he ultimately bore the responsibility for the suffering of Japan during those years. In perhaps the most pivotal decision of his lifetime, Hirohito also made the decision to accept defeat in the waning days of World War II. Against the wishes of many hard-core militarists who favored a fight to the death, Hirohito—with Tokyo, Hiroshima, and Nagasaki in ruins—made a radio broadcast to the Japanese people and asked them to surrender. It was the first time the Japanese public had ever heard his voice.

With the end of the war, Japan found itself occupied by a foreign power for the first time. Hirohito was made to suffer the further embarrassment of confessing full responsibility for the war to General Douglas MacArthur, chief of the U.S. occupying army. Though he was not tried for any war crimes (the U.S. put primary blame on Prime Minister Hideki Tojo, who was hanged), Hirohito did renounce the divinity bestowed on him as emperor and, under a new European-style parliamentary government, declared that the people were sovereign. In the following years, as Japan's economy boomed and its technology rivalled that of its American conquerors, Hirohito became a symbol of the state, more visible to his people and even travelling abroad. He also put much time into his life's passion, the study of marine biology. Hirohito was a world renowned scholar on the subject of marine hydrozoa and published eight books on his specialty. **Sources:** *Chicago Tribune,* January 7, 1989; *Los Angeles Times,* January 7, 1989; *Newsweek,* January 16, 1989.

Abbie Hoffman

Full name, Abbott Hoffman; born November 30, 1936, in Worcester, Mass.; died of an apparent self-administered drug overdose, April 12, 1989, in New Hope, Pa. American writer and social activist. A deeply committed, if irreverent, protester with a flair for outrageous public theatrics, Hoffman burst onto the U.S. political scene in the turbulent 1960s and became a leader of the American left's movement for radical social change. As one of the famous Chicago Seven defendants who were tried in 1968 for conspiring to disrupt the Democratic National Convention, Hoffman held the national spotlight for 4½ months and made the most of the exposure, once entering the courtroom doing somersaults and another time wearing black judicial robes, which he threw on the floor to symbolize his feelings about the state of American justice at that moment. But behind the humor, which was usually the vehicle for his message, Hoffman was a man of serious convictions who grew despondent as the activism of the 1960s gave way to the languid 1970s and 1980s. Despite this, and despite his diagnosed manic-depressive condition, he continued to fight for his principles to the end. He defied being termed a "1960s protester." In a 1987 interview he told the *New York Times,* "You are talking to a leftist. I believe in the redistribution of wealth and power in the world. I believe in universal hospital care for everyone. I believe that we should not have a single homeless person in the richest country in the world."

A self-described troublemaker since childhood, Hoffman made it through high school with some difficulty and received his degree in psychology from Brandeis University, where he was influenced by the radical ideals of Herbert Marcuse. After receiving his master's degree from the University of California at Berkeley in 1960 he worked for a time as a pharmaceutical salesman before becoming involved in civil-rights protests in Mississippi. By 1967 his activism had become more intense. He moved to Manhattan's East Village, at that time a bastion for disaffected youth and flower children, and sought to organize them politically by forming, along with Jerry Rubin, the Youth International Party, whose members became known as Yippies. Demonstrative and ever-conscious of media exposure, the yippie pranksters set out on a series of adventures that delighted some and appalled others. In 1967 Hoffman spoofed Wall Street by sprinkling dollar bills over the floor of the New York Stock Exchange. In a Vietnam War protest he organized a group to circle the Pentagon in an attempt to make the building levitate 300 feet off the ground.

The Chicago Seven contended in their trial that they went to Chicago in 1968 merely to wage peaceful protest and have a rock concert, and that the riot that ensued was due to confrontational tactics used by the Chicago police. The largest political trial of the decade was often interrupted by emotional outbursts from the defendants and spectators. Bobby Seale, a California Black Panther leader and the eighth defendant in the case, was separated from the others when the judge had to order him bound and gagged because of his verbal explosions, including his calling the judge "a fascist pig." They were all acquitted of the conspiracy charges, but Hoffman, Rubin, David T. Dellinger, Rennie Davis and Tom Hayden were convicted of crossing state lines with intent to riot. The convictions were later overturned. Hoffman was arrested again in 1973 for selling cocaine to undercover officers, but he jumped bail and went into seclusion until 1980. During these years he maintained his activism on the part of ecological concerns in upstate New York, where he lived under the alias Barry Freed. He surfaced in 1980 to be interviewed by Barbara Walters on ABC television. The next day he turned himself in to police and pleaded guilty to a lesser charge. He served one month in jail before being freed to a work-release program.

In the 1980s Hoffman made his living primarily as a guest lecturer at universities throughout the country, where he spoke out against the South African government and U.S. involvement in Central America. He was arrested in 1987 along with Amy Carter [see index for *Newsmakers* entry], daughter of former president Jimmy Carter, for protesting the presence of CIA recruiters at the Massachusetts Institute of Technology. He could always find something to protest and never stopped fighting, but he was disturbed by the nostalgia for the 1960s he saw on college campuses. "We're reminiscing about our youth," he told the *New York Times.* "When you see young people nostalgic for a youth they didn't even experience, it's a little sad. They're supposed to be out making one for themselves." He was the author of several books, including *Steal This Book,* in which he advocated the use of marijuana and coined the phrase "Don't trust anyone over 30." Other titles were the autobiography *Soon To Be a Major Motion Picture* and *Steal This Urine Test. The Best of Abbie Hoffman* was scheduled for publication in 1989. Hoffman was eulogized by Timothy Leary as an "American legend, right up there in the hall of fame with rebel Huck Finn, rowdy Babe Ruth, and crazy Lenny Bruce." **Sources:** *New York Times,* April 14, 1989; *People,* May 1, 1989; *Washington Post,* April 14, 1989.

John Houseman

Name originally Jacques Haussmann; born September 22, 1902, in Bucharest, Romania; died of spinal cancer, October 31, 1988, in Malibu, Calif. Stage and film actor, director, producer and writer.

Though his extraordinary film and stage career dates back to his early collaborations with Orson Welles in the 1930s, Houseman did not achieve widespread notoriety until the age of 71, when his portrayal of the crusty, blueblood law professor Charles W. Kingsfield, Jr., in the 1973 film "The Paper Chase" won him an Oscar for Best Supporting Actor. In the years following, he reprised the role for a TV series of the same name, which ran from 1978 to 1986, and he managed to parlay his newfound reputation as a pompous curmudgeon into a series of lucrative commercial endorsements. In one memorable ad for the investment firm Smith, Barney, Houseman bellowed his trademark line: "They make money the old-fashioned way—they EARN it." But it was a little ironic that one advertising slogan should overshadow the career of one of the moving forces in American stage and film history. "I'll be 'the professor' into eternity," Houseman once grumbled to the *Washington Post.*

Born in Romania, Houseman was educated in England and came to the United States in 1924. For a time he worked in the grain business, holding a seat on the Chicago Board of Trade until the stock market crash of 1929 wiped him out, forcing him to move to New York, where he began working in the theater. In 1937, after spending two years in the government-funded Federal Theatre Project, Houseman met and began collaborating with the legendary and enigmatic Orson Welles. The two formed the Mercury Theater in New York and staged as their first production a controversial, modern-dress version of "Julius Caesar." As a producer and writer for the Mercury Theater of the Air, the radio division of the same troupe, Houseman was co-producer of the famous hoax "War of the Worlds," which created a nationwide panic with its realistic portrayal of radio coverage of aliens landing on earth. He also was instrumental in putting together Welles's landmark 1941 film "Citizen Kane," including collaborating on the script. Houseman split from the difficult Welles and, after serving as a director for Voice of America radio broadcasts during World War II, came to Hollywood to work as a vice-president at David O. Selznick Productions and later as a top producer for Metro-Goldwyn-Mayer. His feature credits included "The Bad and the Beautiful" (1952), starring Kirk Douglas, "Julius Caesar" (1953), with Marlon Brando, John Gielgud and James Mason, and "Lust for Life" (1956), the biography of Vincent Van Gogh.

Houseman's other acting credits include "Seven Days in May (1964), "Three Days of the Condor" (1975), "Rollerball" (1975), and roles in such television mini-series as "The Winds of War" and "Washington—Behind Closed Doors." In 1986, the John Houseman Theater Center in New York was named for him; it became home to the Acting Company, a touring repertory he co-founded in 1972, which boasts such alumni as Kevin Kline, Robin Williams, and Patti LuPone. Also in 1986 he was honored by the Congressional Arts Caucus. Houseman was the author of a critically-acclaimed, three-volume autobiography: *Run-Through, Front and Center,* and *Final Dress.* **Sources:** *Los Angeles Times,* November 1, 1988; *New York Times,* November 1, 1988; *Washington Post,* November 1, 1988.

Hu Yaobang

Born 1915 in Liuyang City, Hunan Province, China; died of heart attack, April 15, 1989, in Beijing, China. Chinese government official. As chairman of China's Communist Party for six crucial years during that country's liberalization, Hu became a champion of Chinese students and intellectuals for the same outspokenness and liberal theorizing that eventually got him removed from power in 1987. His "resignation" and public disgrace at that time touched off a series of tumultuous student demonstrations that caused top-level officials to re-think the direction of government policies aimed at increased Western-style democratization. However, those demonstrations were minor in comparison to the unrest that followed Hu's death in 1989. Indeed, the headline "Hu's Death Is Stirring Unrest" from the April 16, 1989 *New York Times* could not have been more prophetic. Within weeks of that date the Chinese capital of Beijing was paralyzed by massive demonstrations that carried on for nearly a month and ended only with a brutal, military crackdown that left, by most western news estimates, about 3,000 dead. The demonstrators, primarily students and intellectuals but consisting of more than a few ordinary citizens, were calling for greater freedoms in choosing their occupations, more liberalized economic policies, and a halt to corruption within the government—ideals which Hu had long espoused.

The son of peasant parents who received no formal education, Hu left his home in the remote Hunan Province at age 14 to join the Communist guerillas led by Mao Zedong. One of the youngest participants in the historic Long March, he became acquainted in the years of the revolution with Deng Xiaoping, a man who would serve as Hu's ally and mentor and who eventually became China's leader. As Deng's career rose, so did Hu's, and when Deng was purged twice during Mao's Cultural Revolution, Hu was likewise purged. After Mao's death in 1977, Hu played a crucial role in helping Deng consolidate power; by 1981 Hu himself had risen to General Secretary of the Communist Party, the Party's top position. For the next six years he played an increasing role in the day-to-day management of Deng's drive toward liberalization. Writing in the *New York Times,* Nicholas D. Kristof observed that "it was Mr. Hu as much as anyone who tugged China toward market economics and a more open political system. In some ways Mr. Hu seemed to resemble his mentor. Like Mr. Deng, Mr. Hu was barely five feet three inches tall, but fired with enormous energy and pragmatism."

But Hu's outspokenness and far-reaching plans for reform made him unpopular with many of the older party officials; eventually even Deng himself, whom it once appeared obvious that Hu would succeed, turned against him. He angered many of the Party's old ruling elite when he was one of the first to openly criticize Mao and the Cultural Revolution. He also embraced the ideas of intellectuals who were denounced by party traditionalists as "spiritual pollution," and he was despised by many bureaucrats for exposing the widespread corruption among high-ranking officials, actions which endeared him to the Chinese populace, which had grown frustrated with the favoritism granted toward the families and friends of government workers. Hu was daring enough to be seen on television in Western business suits, and he once even suggested that the Chinese might start using Western utensils and eating "each from his own plate," said the *New York Times.* "By doing so, we can avoid contagious diseases." He later publicly denounced the idea after being reproached by his colleagues, but it was obvious that Hu's mind was a little too practical in the face of 4,000 years of Chinese tradition. By 1986 pro-democracy student demonstrations were on the rise and the blame was placed on Hu. On January 16, 1987, he was forced to make a self-criticism before the Politburo, and his resignation was then announced. He was criticized by Deng and other leaders for promoting "bourgeois liberalization," or Western democratic influences. Hu lived his last years in seclusion. **Sources:** *Chicago Tribune,* April 16, 1989; *New York Times,* April 16, 1989; *Washington Post,* April 16, 1989.

Christine Jorgensen

Name originally, George Jorgensen, Jr.; born May 20, 1926, in New York, N.Y.; died of cancer, May 3, 1989, in San Clemente, Calif. Historic surgical patient. A former Army private, Jorgensen underwent hormone and surgical treatments in 1952 to change from a male to a female. Although the operation had successfully been accomplished on several previous patients, Jorgensen was the first person in the United States to public announce her change of sexual identity. The result was an international media barrage that caught Jorgensen by surprise. "At first I was very self-conscious and very awkward," she later told the *New York Times.* "But once the notoriety hit, it did not take long to adjust.... I decided if they wanted to see me, they would have to pay for it." Rather than shy away from publicity, Jorgensen basked in it, appearing for several years at public-speaking engagements, talk shows, and even a nightclub act, which featured the song "I Enjoy Being a Girl." Her 1967 autobiography, *Christine Jorgensen: A Personal Biography,* was made into a documentary film and released in Europe, though never in the United States. By the 1970s Jorgensen was able to retire in comfort; she owned a home in southern California, a condominium in Hawaii, and an extensive art collection.

Growing up, Jorgensen said in the *Los Angeles Times,* she was "a frail, tow-headed, introverted child" who was "not of the same sex, but the other sex." She said in her autobiography that the feeling that she was a woman trapped in a man's body stayed with her, even as she completed a tour of duty with the U.S. Army and returned to New York to work as a photographer. On hearing of sex conversion operations that were being performed successfully in

Denmark, Jorgensen began hormone treatment there under the direction of the Danish hormone expert Dr. Christian Hamburger in 1950. Her sex change was completed in 1952 with surgery at the Danish State Hospital in Copenhagen. She adopted her new first name in honor of her doctor and returned to the United States in 1955 as an instant celebrity. Though she did receive numerous offers to make films, Jorgensen vowed to turn them down and stuck to it. She also turned down strip show offers, deciding to concentrate on stage appearances in Los Angeles and Las Vegas.

Reflecting on her unique life in 1988, Jorgensen told the *Los Angeles Times* that for a time she could not understand the intense public reaction to her life-style. But history showed her that she had played a part in helping trigger the sexual revolution. "I am very proud now, looking back, that I was on that street corner 36 years ago when a movement started.... We may not have started it [the sexual revolution], but we gave it a good swift kick in the pants." **Sources:** *Chicago Tribune,* May 9, 1989; *Los Angeles Times,* May 4, 1989; *New York Times,* May 5, 1989.

Ayatollah Ruhollah Khomeini

Born c. May 27, 1900, in Khomein, Iran; died of internal bleeding following digestive surgery, June 4, 1989, in Tehran, Iran. Founder and leader of the Islamic Republic of Iran. Revered as a prophet by his followers and hated intensely in the West, particularly the United States, Khomeini led the revolution that rid Iran of 2,500 years of monarchy and established the new Islamic Republic in 1979. For ten years he was a commanding if not menacing presence on the world stage, denouncing the sprawling global influence of nations such as the "Great Satans", the Soviet Union and the United States, and at times promoting terrorism against those agents and nations he found threatening to his vision. At the same time he ruled over Iran with an iron fist, controlling its diverse political factions and zealously preaching to the citizenry his stern, fundamentalist Islamic doctrine, with which he sought to "purify" the Arab world and eventually the entire planet. He was a giant in his own country; his defiant, glaring gaze stared out from murals and banners everywhere, and his presence could be felt in every undertaking. But his success was certainly limited, for though Khomeini succeeded in tearing down a government, he was unable to provide a new one. At the time of his death, Iran was in a state of political and economic turmoil with no certain agenda for the future.

Raised by his mother and an aunt (his father had been killed, possibly by government agents, when the boy was 5), Khomeini received his early education in a Koranic school. After receiving his formal education in the holy city of Qom, he stayed on there as an instructor and became fascinated with the works of the Greek philosophers, particularly Plato, whose *Republic* provided a model for Khomeini's concept of the ideal state, with the philosopher-king replaced by an Islamic theocrat. As his stature rose in the clerical community, Khomeini became more active in his opposition to the Shah Reza Pahlavi, a dictator whose rush to modernize Iran outraged traditional Muslims. After leading several demonstrations against the government, Khomeini was imprisoned briefly and then exiled, first to Turkey and then to the Iraqi city of An Najaf, a shrine for Shiite Muslims. He stayed in Iraq for 14 years, writing and teaching, while the momentum for Islamic revolution continued to build in Iran under the leadership of Ayatollah Mahmoud Talaghani. Exiled from Iraq by President Saddam Hussein, Khomeini went to France in 1978 and continued to tape his sermons and speeches on audiocassette and relay them to his followers in Iran. Months later, after the death of Talaghani and the abdication of the Shah to Egypt, Khomeini returned triumphantly to Iran in February, 1979, to an ecstatic multitude, and the revolution was complete.

Finding himself suddenly with enormous power after years of exile, Khomeini moved swiftly to consolidate his government and destroy his opposition. His clergy-dominated security forces quickly engaged in a bloody purge of political opponents, criminals, prostitutes, and homosexuals in the first attempt at restoring the Islamic purity that would be Khomeini's obsession. The greatest threat to that purity, in his eyes, was the United States, a nation he provoked, taunted and, at times, successfully thwarted before the world. This was best illustrated in 1979, shortly after the revolution, when Iranian students, with the blessing of Khomeini, seized the American embassy in Tehran and held 52 Americans hostage there for 444 days. The depressing, frustrating vigil, played out nightly on American television, brought American self-esteem to its lowest point since Watergate and played a major role in crippling the presidency of Jimmy Carter. Carter, defeated by Ronald Reagan in the 1980 elections, suffered one final humiliation when Khomeini released the hostages on Reagan's inauguration day in January, 1981.

But the same unbending defiance that brought Khomeini to power also proved to be his major flaw in actually governing. He was an isolated dictator who turned on Iran's Parliamentary leaders when they became too pragmatic, and the one theme he had used to unify his country—the denouncement of the so-called moral and spiritual vacuity and imperialism of the West—also served to isolate world opinion against Iran. When a U.S. Navy frigate accidentally shot down an Iranian jetliner in 1988, killing 290 people, international response was notably reserved. Khomeini's religious fervor and rigidity were perhaps the chief facilitators of the protracted and devastating Iran-Iraq War of the 1980s. What had started as a border dispute in 1980 quickly escalated in Khomeini's eyes to a "holy war," in which he sought to overthrow Iraq and expand his dream of a pan-Arab Islamic Republic. Through religious sermons and propaganda he whipped his countrymen into a frenzied mindset of assault, despite the fact that the better-armed Iraqi's were losing a third as many soldiers. Indeed, manpower was Khomeini's arsenal. His speeches glorified martyrdom; every available male, many as young as 13, responded to the call, only to be sent badly armed into Iraqi gunfire as part of giant human-wave assaults. When he finally agreed to a cease-fire agreement in 1988, after a debilitating eight-year war that had cost the two countries more than $500 billion and over 1 million lives, Khomeini had seemingly not had enough. The decision, he said, as reported in *Time* magazine, was "more deadly than drinking poison."

In 1989 Khomeini further alienated international opinion when he placed a bounty of $1 million on the head of the British author Salman Rushdie, whose book *The Satanic Verses* blasphemed Khomeini's idea of the Islamic faith. Rushdie was forced into hiding, and the outraged British government broke off diplomatic relations with Iran. Though politically isolated, Khomeini, at the time of his death, was still an enormously powerful religious figure. He was mourned fervently by his followers as the world breathed a collective sigh of relief. **Sources:** *New York Times*, June 4, 1989; *Newsweek*, June 12, 1989; *Time*, June 12, 1989.

Sergio Leone

Born January 3, 1929, in Rome, Italy; died of heart attack, April 30, 1989, in Rome, Italy. Italian film director. An Italian who spoke little English, Leone was widely credited with reviving a unique American art form, the western film, which had declined noticeably by the 1960s. Stark, moody, and shot in a sparse, minimalist style, his films were darker and bloodier than traditional American westerns, and his heroes were violent, morally ambiguous loners. Three times, in the films "A Fistful of Dollars," "For a Few Dollars More," and "The Good, the Bad, and the Ugly," that hero was played by Clint Eastwood, who became an international star under Leone's direction. Leone's films came to be known as "spaghetti westerns," in part as a way for critics to dismiss what they felt was a cheap, blood-spattered imitation of a time-honored art form, and partly because the films were often shot in the Italian or Spanish countryside rather than the American west. In his own defense, Leone, who used as his inspiration the legendary American director John Ford, told the *New York Times* that "the killings in my films are exaggerated because I wanted to make a tongue-in-cheek satire on run-of-the-mill westerns.... The west was made by violent, uncomplicated men, and it is this strength and simplicity that I try to recapture in my pictures."

The son of the established Italian silent-film director Vincenzo Leone, young Sergio received his apprenticeship in Hollywood, as an assistant to several respected directors, including Mervyn LeRoy and William Wyler. Leone returned to Italy in the late 1950s as a screenwriter and assistant director on several of the low-budget, ancient Roman spectacles that had been popular at that time, including "Sign of the Gladiator" and "The Last Days of Pompeii." He made his directorial debut in 1961 with the forgettable "The Colossus of Rhodes." Leone's first distinctive mark as a filmmaker came with the 1964 film "A Fistful of Dollars," which starred Eastwood as the silent, sullen Man With No Name. Based on Japanese director Akira Kurosawa's classic film "Yojimbo," the movie stunned critics with its violence and seeming lack of moral content. Leone also co-wrote and directed two more films starring Eastwood in the mid-1960s, "For a Few Dollars More" and "The Good, the Bad, and the Ugly." Critics continued to express outrage at the violence in Leone's films, but some granted Leone his due as an artist. In *Cinema: A Critical Dictionary,* Richard Corliss called Leone's technique "a blend of seamless contradictions: labyrinthine plots and elemental themes, nihilistic heroes with romantic obsessions, microscopic close-ups and macrocosmic vistas, circular camera work and triangular shoot-outs, a sense of Americana and a European sensibility, playful parody and profound homage."

Leone's last two major projects were large, sweeping epics that opened to confused critics and audiences, forcing their panicked producers to make major editing changes that destroyed the work. The 1969 film "Once Upon a Time in the West" starred Henry Fonda as a brutal villain and Charles Bronson as The Man With No Name. Though the film had a miserable reception upon its release and was subsequently cut, a re-released 1985 version has been hailed as a masterpiece of the western genre. In 1984 Leone released the sprawling "Once Upon a Time in America," a complex, multiple time-frame epic about Jewish gangsters in New York City. The nearly four-hour long film received raves at the Cannes Film Festival, but American producers, fearing it would be too complex and exhaustive for audiences, cut the film drastically and rearranged the scenes into a chronological order. The result was a muddled film that flopped at the box-office. Later released in its restored version, however, "Once Upon a Time in America" was received with raves. The *New Yorker*'s Pauline Kael lauded Leone's "majestic, billowing sense of film movement" and "elegaic tone." The *Chicago Tribune*'s Gene Siskel declared the film a "rich tapestry of innocence and guilt." **Sources:** *Chicago Tribune,* May 1, 1989; *New York Times,* May 1, 1989; *Times* (London), May 1, 1989.

Konrad Lorenz

Full name, Konrad Zacharias Lorenz; born November 7, 1903, in Vienna, Austria; died of kidney failure, February 28, 1989, in Altenburg, Austria. Austrian scientist. A celebrated scientist known for his landmark studies of animal behavior, Lorenz sparked worldwide controversy after using his findings to explain certain human characteristics. For his lifelong efforts he was awarded, in 1973, the Nobel Prize for medicine, along with fellow Austrian Karl von Frisch and Nikolaas Tinbergen of the Netherlands. Lorenz's first important findings concerned the social life of birds, which he studied intently from childhood to old age on his parents' vast estate in Altenburg, Austria. Observing that the birds exhibited, from birth, a strong attachment to their biological mothers, a process he termed imprinting, Lorenz became convinced that many aspects of bird behavior were innate and instinctive, rather than learned. To demonstrate his conclusion Lorenz showed that, by substituting himself for a mother duck and making convincing quacking noises upon the birth of her ducklings, he could make the ducklings follow him around with the belief that he was their mother. In subsequent research, through a discipline known as comparative ethology—the comparative study of human and animal behavior through zoological methods—Lorenz argued that many human traits, such as aggressiveness, were likewise biologically innate. His ideas became linked to the long disputed theories of Charles Darwin, who held that characteristics of species and hereditary behavior were selected in response to a species' need to survive in a specific environment. Lorenz's critics attacked his conclusions as being sympathetic with the Aryan principles prevalent in Nazi Germany.

The son of successful physician parents, Lorenz grew up observing the abundant birds and "pets" that lived on the grounds of their family estate near Vienna. Urged by his father to become a doctor, he studied one year at New York's Columbia University but returned to the University of Vienna to receive his doctorate in zoology in 1933. As a lecturer in zoology and psychology at the Universities of Vienna and Konigsberg, he expounded the theories of biological imprinting he developed during what he called his "goose summers" at Altenburg. In a paper published during this period Lorenz argued that "socially inferior human material" could destroy the "healthy body of people," a position that critics later claimed was fuel to the rising racism of the German Nazi Party. After World War II, in which he served in the German Army as a field surgeon on the Russian Front, Lorenz admitted that "many highly decent scientists hoped, like I did, for a short time for good from National Socialism" but that "many quickly turned away from it with the same horror as I." After the war he was able to resume his studies with a grant from the Max Planck Institute for Behavioral Physiology, which he later served as director from 1961 until his retirement in 1973.

For his numerous books, many of which were widely read outside the scientific community, Lorenz was both praised for his wide-ranging understanding of mankind's role in nature and rebuked, as by Howard Gardner in the *New York Times,* for suspending "his scientific caution to give rein to speculation." In his *On Aggression,* Lorenz argued that human beings in nature had evolved "an excess of aggression" but that "in our day, with its changed ecological conditions, this excess has become a serious danger to mankind." He believed that inhibitions to aggression were removed with the advent of modern, impersonal weaponry, making the predicament even worse. Eliot Fremont-Smith, in the *New York Times,* said that *On Aggression* is "an epoch-making book. It is also a profoundly civilizing one." Other influential Lorenz titles include *Man Meets Dog, King Solomon's Ring,* and *Behind the Mirror: A Search for a Natural History of Human Knowledge.* **Sources:** *Los Angeles Times,* March 2, 1989; *New York Times,* March 1, 1989; *Washington Post,* March 1, 1989.

Robert Mapplethorpe

Born November 4, 1946, in Floral Park, N.Y.; died of complications from AIDS, March 9, 1989, in Boston, Mass. American photographer and sculptor. A talented photographer whose pictures presented a wide-ranging and often controversial subject matter in cool, detached perspective, Mapplethorpe was a versatile artist who did not wish to be recognized as merely a photographer. "I never wanted to be a photographer," he told *American Photographer* magazine. "It was sort of a mistake really. I only wanted to make a statement and photography ended up being the vehicle."

This sentiment is revealed in Mapplethorpe's work, in which his subjects are lighted and photographed to appear as sculpture, thus lending a classical elegance to the subjects themselves. And it was Mapplethorpe's choice of subject matter that undeniably brought much of the attention to his work. He first gained fame in the 1970s for the controversy surrounding his openly homoerotic and sadomasochistic photographs, which often hung in galleries next to ordinary floral still-lifes photographed in the same classic style. This juxtaposition caused *Los Angeles Times* critic Suzanne Muchnic to comment that Mapplethorpe's work "confuses expectation because it is a scattershop assortment of everything from delicate romance and good humor to brutal titillation. The artist who emerges seems to have an extraordinary talent and a dehumanizing sensibility."

Raised in New York state in a middle-class, Catholic household, Mapplethorpe studied at the prestigious Pratt Institute art school in New York City from 1963–70. He began his career as an independent filmmaker and artist who used photographs in his sculptural collages. During this time he began to associate with an eclectic group of artists, which included the poet and future New Wave rock star Patti Smith. At this time he also met Sam Wagstaff, who became Mapplethorpe's longtime patron and companion as well as a major collector of photography. Mapplethorpe's first exhibitions were included in larger showings of Wagstaff's collection. As his reputation grew, Mapplethorpe became much in demand as a commercial photographer, from fashion magazines to album covers to portraits of celebrities like Arnold Schwarzenegger, Susan Sontag, and C. Everett Koop. He was a well-heeled esthete who collected furniture, art objects, and photography. He also designed furniture.

Mapplethorpe learned in September, 1986, that he had AIDS, becoming the latest in a long line of promising young artists to be struck with the disease. To his credit he was candid about the progress of his struggle, thus drawing much needed focus to AIDS nationwide. His 1988 self-portraits graphically revealed his once handsome face in pale, emaciated starkness.

Over the last ten years of his life Mapplethorpe's pictures had become highly coveted and are now in the collections of New York's Metropolitan Museum of Art and Museum of Modern Art, the Chicago Institute of Art, the Pompidou Center in Paris, and the Institute for Contemporary Art in London as well as other major museums in the United States, Europe, and Japan. In 1988 he had his first American retrospective at the Whitney Museum of American Art. Before his death, Mapplethorpe established the Robert Mapplethorpe Foundation, which will jointly benefit medical research on AIDS and the visual arts, with an emphasis on photography. **Sources:** *Los Angeles Times,* March 11, 1989; *New York Times,* March 10, 1989; *Vanity Fair,* February, 1989.

John Matuszak

Full name, John Daniel Matuszak; born c. 1951, in Oak Creek, Wis.; died of apparent heart attack, June 17, 1989, in Burbank, Calif. Actor and former professional football player. Known in his football playing heyday as The Tooz', Matuszak helped embody the Oakland Raiders' legendary "evil" image with his imposing size and rough style of play. Standing 6-foot-9 and weighing 280 pounds, he was a black-bearded terror on the field who possessed great speed for a defensive end. When the game was over, Matuszak usually furthered his ruffian's image in the taverns and nightclubs. Indeed, his partying days continued long after his retirement from football, and there were frequent rumors that he was using drugs. When he died at age 38, apparently of a heart attack, it seemed apparent that drugs had contributed heavily to his condition. At the time, Matuszak was trying to piece together an acting career.

An all-state defensive end at his Wisconsin high school, Matuszak started his college career at the

University of Missouri before transferring to the University of Tampa. He was selected by the Houston Oilers as the number one pick in the 1973 NFL entry draft, but his first years in professional football were turbulent. After briefly playing with the Oilers, he abandoned the team to join the newly formed World Football League's Houston Texans, where he played briefly before a court injunction forced him to honor his original contract with the Oilers. Houston subsequently traded Matuszak to the Kansas City Chiefs for Curley Culp and a number one draft choice, but before the 1976 season he was again traded, this time to the Washington Redskins, who cut Matuszak after two weeks of training camp. Two games into the 1976 season, he joined the Oakland Raiders as a free agent, and his career blossomed. A crazy mix of oddballs, cast-offs, renegades and savvy veterans, the Raiders were the team America loved to hate, known for their taunting, intimidating style of play and an occasional cheap shot. It was a team perfectly suited to Matuszak, who helped lead them to several divisional titles and Super Bowl victories in 1976 and 1980.

While still a player, Matuszak began parlaying his new celebrity status into minor acting roles in commercials and television programs. After the Raiders moved to Los Angeles and Matuszak sat out the 1982 season with an injury, he decided to retire from football and pursue acting full-time. He landed several guest appearances, usually in tough-guy roles, in such feature films as "North Dallas Forty," "Caveman," and "Ice Pirates," and in the television shows "M*A*S*H," "Trapper John, M.D.," and "The Fall Guy." In 1985 he had a starring role in the short-lived ABC television series "Hollywood Beat," in which he played George Grinsky, a huge, gay, former football player whose nightclub is used as a cover by Hollywood cops. In 1987 he published his autobiography, *Cruisin' With The Tooz'*. Once heavily fined by the Raiders for partying past curfew the night before a Super Bowl, Matuszak didn't slow down when his playing days ended. In 1986 he made headlines when two persons, one a male stripper, brought a $1.5 million suit against him for allegedly beating up the stripper and trashing the Hollywood nightclub where he was performing; a jury ruled in favor of Matuszak. "The Tooz' wasn't one to stop the party at 8," said Tom Keating, Matuszak's friend and former teammate, in the *Detroit Free Press*. "He mixed pills and alcohol and generally lived each day as if it were the last one of his life." **Sources:** *Detroit Free Press*, June 19, 1989; *Los Angeles Times*, June 18, 1989; *Washington Post*, June 19, 1989.

John J. McCloy

Born March 31, 1895, in Philadelphia, Pa.; died March 11, 1989, in Stamford, Conn. American banker, lawyer, and diplomat. Little-known to the public but widely respected by business and political leaders throughout the United States and Europe, McCloy was at the forefront of the large, behind-the-scenes contingent that helped direct the American effort in World War II and the crucial years that followed. As assistant secretary of war to Henry L. Stimson from 1940–46, he served as a consultant to Allied war leaders at conferences in Casablanca, Cairo, and Potsdam. He was also a member of the State Department Commission on Atomic Energy and was one of the few who knew of U.S. plans to drop the atomic bomb on Japan; his proposal to warn the Japanese first was eventually overruled. After the war, he was made president of the World Bank and later served three years as U.S. high commissioner in Germany during the difficult post-war transition period. As a banker and lawyer in later years, McCloy sat on the boards of several large U.S. corporations and was often consulted by U.S. presidents, many of whom attempted to lure him back into public service. For all of this he was often referred to as the chairman of the American establishment.

As a student at Harvard Law School, McCloy's studies were interrupted by World War I, in which he served as an artillery officer in France. He returned to Harvard after the war and received his degree in 1921. In his first job with the New York firm Cadwalader Wickersham & Taft, McCloy was sent to head the firm's Paris office and became acquainted with Stimson, future head of the War Department, who said in his memoirs that McCloy's "energy was enormous and his optimism almost unquenchable" and questioned "whether anyone in the administration ever acted without having a word with McCloy." After the war, he rescued the fledgling World Bank in his brief stint as president by running it with conservative policies that gained the confidence of the international banking community. The World Bank was the chief source of funds at that time for the battered nations trying to recover from the war.

His next post, as the highest-ranking U.S. civilian in divided Germany, was an even greater challenge. He helped to integrate West Germany back into the European community of nations that had been its enemies in the war, even as West Berlin became the focal point of the developing East-West Cold War. "Germany ceased to be a stake in the game of power," said Jean Monnet in the *Washington Post.* "She became instead a full partner in the uniting of Europe." McCloy left government service in 1953 to become chairman of Chase National Bank. Before his retirement in 1960 he had engineered the bank's merger with the Bank of Manhattan; the new bank, Chase Manhattan, became the second largest in the country. He sat on the board of directors for Gulf Oil, AT&T, Westinghouse, Allied Chemical and United Fruit. Often sought out for advice by Presidents Eisenhower, Kennedy and Johnson, McCloy turned down key cabinet positions with all three but remained influential behind the scenes. He received the Distinguished Service Medal, the Medal of Freedom, and decorations from France, Italy, and Germany. **Sources:** *Chicago Tribune,* March 13, 1989; *Los Angeles Times,* March 12, 1989; *Washington Post,* March 12, 1989.

John Mitchell

Full name, John Newton Mitchell; born September 15, 1913, in Detroit, Mich.; died of a heart attack, November 9, 1988, in Washington, D.C. Former Attorney General of the United States. As a close friend, chief political adviser, and so-called "father figure" to President Richard M. Nixon, Mitchell, who served four years as Nixon's attorney general—the nation's highest law enforcement position—became a central figure in the Watergate scandal that forced Nixon to resign in disgrace in August 1974. Mitchell was the only attorney general in the history of the United States to serve a prison sentence. He spent 19 months in jail at Maxwell Air Force Base in Alabama, convicted, along with White House aides H.R. Haldeman, John Ehrlichman, and Robert C. Mardian, on charges of conspiracy, obstruction of justice, two counts of false testimony to a federal grand jury, and perjury. Throughout the controversy, however, Mitchell remained loyal to Nixon, refusing to implicate the president directly in relation to any of the Watergate crimes or the ensuing cover-up. Many observers believed that Mitchell's refusal to break with Nixon led directly to the bitter dissolution of Mitchell's marriage to his wife, Martha, who herself was a controversial—and oft-quoted—part of the whirlwind dissent which surrounded the downfall of the Nixon administration.

Mitchell first met Nixon in 1967, when the merger of two Manhattan law firms made the two men senior partners in the newly formed firm of Nixon, Mudge, Rose, Guthrie, Alexander & Mitchell. Later that year Nixon convinced Mitchell to become his campaign manager, and after the Nixon victory, he was asked to serve as attorney general, despite Mitchell's denial that he ever wanted a Cabinet position. As Attorney General, Mitchell pledged to suppress what many Americans saw as threats to their safety, such as black unrest, urban crime, and war resistance. He also began a series of activities to suppress individual rights—later found by the courts to be unconstitutional—designed to discredit those in outspoken opposition to Nixon. He prophetically told a *New York Times* reporter: "This country is going so far to the right you won't recognize it."

On January 27, 1972, a plot was unveiled in Mitchell's office which was designed to cripple foes of the Nixon administration by use of kidnapping, sabotage, blackmail, and burglary. On Memorial Day of that year, a team of burglars led by G. Gordon Liddy broke into the headquarters of the Democratic National Committee in the Watergate complex in Washington. Their aim was to photograph documents and plant microphones, but, according to testimony by Mitchell protege Jeb Stuart Magruder, Mitchell found the evidence insufficient and ordered another burglary. This second burglary was botched and the burglars were arrested, but Mitchell, who had recently resigned as attorney general to oversee the Nixon re-election campaign, then allegedly began the cover-up that would shield Nixon from any implication in the conspiracy. Nixon won the election that fall by a landslide victory over George McGovern.

Despite Nixon's victory, the Watergate story continued to unravel in the press and in congressional investigations. As evidence mounted against Nixon, the president's closest advisers allegedly agreed that Mitchell would have to take the blame. Mitchell, however, would not take his loyalty that far. He neither turned on Nixon nor admitted his own guilt. In the end, despite his resignation, Nixon continually blamed his aides, including Mitchell, for the crimes and cover-up. "He fell into the clutches of the King," Martha Mitchell said of her husband in the *New York Times.* Mitchell began serving his prison sentence of 30 months-to-8 years on June 22, 1977. After his release he worked for Global Research, Inc., a public policy institute in Washington, D.C. **Sources:** *Detroit Free Press,* November 10, 1988; *Los Angeles Times,* November 10, 1988; *New York Times,* November 10, 1988.

Laurence Olivier

Full name, Laurence Kerr Olivier; born May 22, 1907, in Dorking, Surrey, England; died of complications from dermatomyositis, July 11, 1989, in West Sussex, England. Film and stage actor, director. As king among actors of the twentieth century and literally the first lord of British theater (he was knighted in 1947 and raised to life peerage in 1970), Laurence Olivier mesmerized audiences for years with his versatility, boldness and charisma. Trained since childhood for a classical stage career, he might have been satisfied with his accomplishments there, but he went on to become a film star of great distinction, an ingenious stage and film director, and the founder and first artistic director of the National Theater of Britain. "He was the greatest actor of the century," Anthony Hopkins said in *People*—to which Peter Hall added, "He was perhaps the greatest man of the theater ever." Indeed, comments like those rung out from theater lovers everywhere and were not mere eulogizing. Olivier had become a living legend many years before his death, placed ahead of his great contemporaries Sir John Gielgud and Sir Ralph Richardson, and even mentioned along with the fabled names of British theater like Kean and Garrick. An admitted show-off (he dismissed the idea that his urge to act was anything more than that), Olivier believed he was simply born to act. "The only time I ever feel alive," he once said, "is when I'm acting. If I stopped acting, I'd cut my throat. I have to act to breathe."

Under the strict discipline of his father, an Anglican clergyman, the young Olivier showed early signs of a tendency to withdraw to his imagination; in fact, by age 9 he was already an actor, performing Brutus in "Julius Caesar" at his London school. In the audience for one performance of that play was Dame Sybil Thorndike and her husband, Lewis Casson. "He had been onstage for only five minutes," she recalled in the *New York Times*, "when we turned to each other and said: 'But this is an actor—absolutely an actor. Born to it.'" In time he was gaining recognition as one of England's leading young actors, which necessarily called for him to play Shakespeare. He delivered some of the most memorable performances of his career while playing Shakespearean roles, bringing to life such diverse characters as Hamlet, Macbeth, Othello, Richard III, Henry V, and Shylock with a stunning versatility. Preferring to think of himself as a character actor, he mastered the art of makeup to bring out the unique physical qualities of each of his characters with the belief, unlike that of many modern actors, that it was best to build a character from the outside and move inward. And his sheer physical presence was his greatest asset. Handsome, athletic, intense, he moved about the stage with great magnetism, to the point where some questioned whether he was not merely going for cheap, theatrical thrills. In one of his boldest and most famous staging displays, while portraying the Roman general in Shakespeare's "Coriolanus," he plunged headfirst from a 15-foot balcony, only to be caught by his ankles by two soldiers.

It was this quality of Olivier's to make the unthinkable leap that formed the other half of his genius. Not content to play it safe in established roles, he constantly sought out new challenges in the theater and in film acting and directing, often alternating from the stage to movies and back to keep things moving. In perhaps the most daring decision of his career, Olivier portrayed the second-rate vaudeville comedian Archie Rice in John Osborne's 1957 play "The Entertainer," a role that many people thought would ruin him; instead, the play was a resounding success. Another high point had occurred in 1945 when, in the same evening, Olivier delivered a sublime, gut-wrenching performance as the lead in "Oedipus," then returned in the double-bill to play the ridiculous Mr. Puff in Sheridan's "The Critic."

Olivier's work in film, also quite eclectic, was, like his stage career, grounded in the works of Shakespeare. He will be best remembered in the film genre for his trilogy of masterpieces—"Henry V," "Hamlet," and "Richard III"—all directed by and starring himself in the title role. His "Hamlet" won two Academy Awards in 1948, one for Olivier as best actor and one for best picture. In 1936 Olivier had acted in the otherwise ordinary film "Fire Over England," ordinary except for the fact that his co-star was the British actress Vivien Leigh. Though both were married to other people at the time, a romance blossomed, followed by a glamorous, but stormy, 20-year marriage that was hounded by international gossip and Leigh's eventual slide into schizophrenia and manic-depression. Those years included Leigh's great success and Academy Award for the classic film "Gone With the Wind" and Olivier's launching as a romantic, international leading man in the films "Wuthering Heights," "Rebecca," and "Pride and Prejudice."

The 1960s marked another period of change for Olivier as he parted with Leigh, married the actress Joan Plowright, and took on further responsibilities as the first artistic director of the newly-formed National Theater, where he had triumphs with "Othello" and Chekhov's "Uncle Vanya," as well as with several American plays, including Eugene

O'Neill's "Long Days Journey Into Night" and Tennessee Williams's "Cat on a Hot Tin Roof." In the 1970s, however, Olivier was stricken with the muscle-debilitating disease dermatomyositis, which severely limited his stage stamina. He was forced to give up the theater entirely in 1974 and concentrated exclusively on films after that. His later films included "Sleuth," "The 7 Percent Solution," "Marathon Man," "The Boys From Brazil," and "Clash of the Titans." He had performed in many television movies, most of them forgettable, but his harrowing performance in the British television production of "King Lear" in 1983 brought the brilliance of Shakespeare and, especially, of Olivier to a massive audience. Olivier wrote two books in his lifetime, *Confessions of an Actor,* his autobiography, in 1982, and *On Acting* in 1986. **Sources:** *New York Times,* July 12, 1989; *Newsweek,* July 24, 1989; *People,* July 24, 1989.

Roy Orbison

Full name, Roy Kelton Orbison; born April 23, 1936, in Vernon, Tex.; died of a heart attack, December 6, 1988, in Hendersonville, Tenn. Singer, songwriter, and musician. Rock and roll pioneer Orbison, a talented guitarist and songwriter, was best known for his surging, durable tenor voice, which often soared three octaves to a sweet falsetto in the songs of loneliness and isolation that made him a legend in his own time. A shy, untheatrical performer in his characteristic garb of black leather, dark sunglasses, and black pompadour, Orbison provided a counterpoint to the high-flying fun of rock's early days. His songs touched upon the bluesy, more sensitive side of life in a way that stars like Elvis Presley and Jerry Lee Lewis never approached. At Orbison's induction into rock's Hall of Fame in 1987, longtime Orbison devotee Bruce Springsteen explained how Orbison stretched the boundaries of the pop hit formula: "His arrangements were complex and operatic. They had rhythm and movement, and they addressed the underside of pop romance. They were scary. His voice was unearthly."

Orbison's unique style translated into a string of hit records in the late 1950s and early 1960s. During one stretch he had 27 consecutive songs on the charts, including "Only the Lonely" in 1960, "Crying," "I'm Hurting," and "Running Scared" in 1961, "Dream Baby" and "Leah" in 1962, and "In Dreams" and "Falling" in 1963. Orbison's 1964 song "Oh, Pretty Woman" was his biggest hit, selling more than 7 million copies. The son of an oilfield worker, Orbison learned to play the guitar at an early age while growing up in Wink, Texas. By age fourteen he was playing professionally in a country band called the Wink Westerners. He dropped out of North Texas State University after two years to form the rockabilly band Teen Kings and then, on the advice of country singer Johnny Cash, went to Memphis to record for Sun Records, the label that had launched the careers of Cash, Jerry Lee Lewis, Elvis and other stars. But Orbison had only mild success in the uptempo rockabilly strain and returned to songwriting. "Claudette," named for Orbison's wife, became a hit for the Everly Brothers, and in later years other Orbison songs became hit records for artists like Linda Ronstadt ("Blue Bayou"), Van Halen ("Oh, Pretty Woman"), and Don McLean ("Crying").

When Orbison returned to recording in his signature style the hits quickly followed, continuing until the mid-1960s when a series of tragedies set him back both personally and professionally. After his wife's death in a motorcycle accident in 1966 and the tragic 1968 fire at his Nashville home, which killed two of his three sons, Orbison quit writing songs for a number of years. He remarried in 1969 and performed through the 1970s without ever regaining his customary position at the top of the charts. Despite these setbacks, Orbison never wavered in the nature of his personality or his music. In the often cut-throat rock and roll world, he was considered one of the most loyal sincere personalities, and he refused to be exploited by the quick-money schemes of nostalgic "oldies" records, preferring instead to be recognized as a contemporary artist.

At the time of his death, however, Orbison's career was enjoying a major revival, thanks to the help of some fellow musicians. In 1987 he teamed with rock superstars Bob Dylan, Tom Petty, George Harrison, and Jeff Lynne to form the Traveling Wilburys and the group immediately produced a hit single, "Handle With Care"; their first album, *The Traveling Wilburys,* climbed to number one on the charts. "I've been rediscovered by young kids who had never heard of me before the Wilburys," Orbison happily told the *Chicago Tribune.* "They are getting into my original songs, and apparently the old stuff is selling at the rate of 20,000 copies a day." Indeed, a 1985 double album of rerecorded Orbison hits was selling well, and a 1988 Cinemax video honoring Orbison featured Bruce Springsteen, Elvis Costello, and Jackson Browne. With his new album, *Mystery Girl,* ready for release, Orbison, who had open heart surgery in 1979, seemed ready for a second try at fame.

Sources: *Chicago Tribune,* December 8, 1988; *Musician,* February, 1989; *People,* December 19, 1988.

Claude Pepper

Full name, Claude Denson Pepper; born September 8, 1900, near Dudleyville, Ala.; died of cancer, May 30, 1989, in Washington, D.C. Legislator, lawyer, educator, journalist, and author. Pepper represented Florida in the U.S. Congress as both senator and representative in a career spanning six decades. A Democrat whose integrity overrode all political considerations, Pepper became known as the champion of the elderly. He fought to protect Social Security and Medicare benefits and became instrumental in passing legislation eliminating the mandatory retirement age for government employees. For his public service Pepper was awarded the Medal of Freedom in May, 1989.

The son of a farmer, Pepper worked his way through college at the University of Alabama and then through Harvard law school, where he graduated sixth in his class in 1924. He taught law for a year at the University of Arkansas before establishing a private law practice in Florida. Pepper's political career began when he was elected to the state's house of representatives in 1929. A proponent of civil rights throughout his career, Pepper refused to support a racially biased resolution, became unpopular with his district, and was not reelected. He returned to his law practice, and after losing a 1934 bid for the U.S. Senate, was elected to that body unopposed in 1936 to complete the term of deceased Florida senator Duncan Fletcher. During his two terms as senator, the liberal Pepper became known as a staunch advocate of Roosevelt's foreign policy and New Deal programs for the ill and needy.

Pepper lost his senate seat in 1950 when his opponent launched a smear campaign against him, branding him a Communist sympathizer during the cold war mania sweeping the country at the time. He resumed private practice in Florida, remaining until 1962, when he won a newly created seat in the U.S. House of Representatives. As a representative, Pepper consistently supported civil rights legislation and worked for improvements to health care and social programs. During the next two decades Pepper chaired important Congressional committees on crime and aging; in 1983 he was nearly unanimously elected chairman of the powerful House Rules Committee, where he worked for passage of a reform bill restoring solvency to the Social Security system. Pepper was the recipient of numerous public service awards and honorary degrees, and he wrote a syndicated advice column, "Ask Claude Pepper," for the elderly. His autobiography, *Pepper, Eyewitness to a Century,* was published in 1987. **Sources:** *Chicago Tribune,* May 31, 1989; *Los Angeles Times,* May 31, 1989; *Washington Post,* May 31, 1989.

Gilda Radner

Born June 28, 1946, in Detroit, Mich.; died of cancer, May 20, 1989, in Los Angeles, Calif. Actress and comedian. As one of the now-legendary original cast members of the ground-breaking NBC variety television series "Saturday Night Live," Radner was the creator of some of that program's most memorable and endearing characters. Waifish, short, and unglamorous, she drew on memories of her father's sense of humor and her own childhood as an overweight, quirky little Jewish girl to compete with "SNL's" more established male stars for laughs and attention. Indeed, although the cast's other female players, Laraine Newman and Jane Curtin, often appeared as the straight foils to the wacky improvisations of John Belushi, Chevy Chase, Dan Aykroyd, Bill Murray and Garrett Morris, Radner more than held her own as a comic original.

She was perhaps best known for playing the crass, obnoxious Roseanne Rosannadanna, whose newsroom editorials often strayed into disgustingly detailed examinations of modern domestic life. Roseanne's catchphrase, "It's always something," became the title of Radner's autobiography. Like Belushi, who died of a drug overdose in 1982, Radner will be best remembered for the wacky spontaneity of the comedy she infused into her "SNL" characters. "There's a preciseness to her parody," Molly Haskell wrote in the *New York Times.* "Like Dickens, she's added people to the world who bear her stamp. And even when she's tasteless you don't wince. There's something very gentle and sweet in Gilda that comes through."

As a girl growing up comfortably in Detroit, Radner was enamored of her father's natural showmanship, humor and magic tricks, as well as with the show-biz celebrities who often stayed at the hotel he owned. After her father's death of a brain tumor when she was 14, she seemed even more drawn to perform, perhaps to please him by doing what he'd always loved. She spent six years in the theater department at the University of Michigan, occasionally dropping out and then returning, and eventually moving to

Toronto before graduating. In Toronto she worked on local stage productions before landing a job with the comedy troupe Second City, where she first worked with the likes of Dan Aykroyd and John Candy. Here she was also noticed by the producer Lorne Michaels, who was searching for talent for his "Saturday Night Live" program, the innovative, hip, ensemble variety that ran for 1 ½ hours at 11:30 P.M. each weekend. Radner was the first player cast by Michaels and the show, after suffering in the ratings the first year, became a classic. Among Radner's other characterizations were the nerdy, flat-chested Lisa Loopner, who was taunted by Bill Murray's noogie assaults; the dowdy commentator Emily Litella, whose news commentaries decried "violins" on television and urged the conservation of national "race horses"; and Baba Wawa, the speech-impeded parody of Barbara Walters. Yet her comedy was never bitter and seemed to provide a wholesome, Lucille Ball-like counterpoint to the sophomoric, albeit hilarious, work of Belushi and gang.

"Saturday Night Live" enjoyed its greatest success in the late 1970s, but as cast members left to escape the rigorous production schedules and to explore other opportunities, a new group of actors replaced them, and Radner left the show as well in 1980. In 1979 she had performed on Broadway in a show that featured several of her television characters; the show, "Gilda Live," was then filmed and made into a movie. In the 1980s she appeared in several feature films, including "First Family," "Hanky Panky," and "The Woman in Red," a 1984 hit written and directed by her co-star and future husband Gene Wilder. "They were constant honeymooners," said a friend of Wilder's in *People.* "It was fun and infectious to be around them, they were so in love. You were really happy for them. Both had been married before and they were very, very happy to have found one another."

Soon, however, Radner's life took a dramatic turn. In 1986 she was diagnosed as having ovarian cancer. Surgery was thought to have been successful, but it was soon learned that the cancer had spread, and Radner then underwent a 2½ year battle against the disease, which included chemotherapy, radiation treatments, and special diets. The cancer for a time went into remission, and Radner was able to make a 1988 appearance on the "Garry Shandling Show," for which she received an Emmy nomination. **Sources:** *Detroit Free Press,* May 21, 1989; *New York Times,* May 21, 1989; *People,* June 5, 1989.

Max Robinson

Born May 1, 1939, in Richmond, Va.; died of complications resulting from AIDS, December 20, 1988, in Washington, D.C. Television broadcast journalist. As the first black anchor of a nightly network news broadcast, Robinson experienced at once the highest achievement in his profession and the many frustrations and pressures brought on by his status as a role-model to black Americans. Possessing an eased, authoritative demeanor and penetrating screen presence, Robinson rose quickly through the ranks of broadcast journalism, first as a popular local newsman in Washington, D.C., and later as part of a unique three-anchor desk for ABC News. But his stay at the top was short-lived. Described by friends as moody and pressured, Robinson, who admitted to having problems with alcohol and depression, frequently spoke out on issues that concerned him as a leading black journalist. He was eventually phased out as anchor at ABC and, as his professional standing diminished in the middle 1980s, became plagued with chronic health problems. At the time of his death it was publicly revealed that Robinson had been stricken with AIDS.

Robinson left Ohio's Oberlin College to take a job as a booth announcer in Portsmouth, Virginia. In 1965 he moved to WTOP, the CBS affiliate in Washington, to work as a studio director and eventually a reporter. Four years later he was Washington's first black anchor, and his station dominated local ratings through the 1970s. Robinson came into national prominence in 1977 when he helped to negotiate the release of hostages held in three federal buildings by Hanafi Muslim leader Haamas Abdul Khaalis. In 1978 Robinson was hired by ABC News President Roone Arledge to join a three-anchor news desk that included Peter Jennings in London and Frank Reynolds in Washington. Robinson was assigned the domestic desk and was stationed in Chicago, a city which, he later told the *Chicago Tribune,* was "a city which has its racial problems. I think it shocked people when I came to town. They weren't ready for it."

Robinson's five years with ABC were marked by controversey. In a 1981 speech at Smith College in Massachussetts, he overtly critized ABC for failing to assign him to cover the Reagan inauguration and the simultaneous release of American hostages from Iran. He said that the network "wanted him to speak like any old white boy" and that "only by talking about racism, by taking a professional risk, will I take myself out of the mean, racist trap all black Americans find themselves in." Robinson's failure to appear at the funeral of fellow-anchor Reynolds in 1983, where he was to have sat with President and Nancy Reagan, also did not sit well with the network. Soon after, ABC changed its news format to a single-anchor desk chaired by Jennings, and Robinson was assigned to give weekend broadcasts and special reports. In 1984 Robinson returned to Chicago to serve as co-anchor of the NBC affiliate WMAQ, but he left the station 15 months later amid personality conflicts and unrest over his chronic absenteeism. He lived his last years in Chicago, painting and writing in the company of a few friends, while he battled his declining health. **Sources:** *Chicago Tribune,* December 21, 1988; *New York Times,* December 21, 1988; *Washington Post,* December 21, 1988.

Sugar Ray Robinson

Real name, Walker Smith, Jr.; born May 3, 1921, in Detroit, Mich.; died of Alzheimer's disease, diabetes, and hypertension, April 12, 1989, in Culver City, Calif. Former boxing champion. In a sport dominated by loose talk, bravado, sensationalism, and hype, Robinson was able to make all the experts agree on at least one thing: that he was, pound-for-pound, the greatest boxer who ever lived. He dominated the boxing world in the 1940s and 1950s with his explosive punching power in both hands, lightning-quick footwork, and a magnetic ring savvy. In a 25-year boxing career he compiled a 175-19-6 record with 110 knockouts, and many of the losses occurred when he continued to fight well past his prime. He was a man of great style, both in and out of the ring. A shrewd businessman who spent his money freely and vainly, he paved the way for outlandish, business-wise modern-day fighters like Muhammad Ali and Sugar Ray Leonard, who, with Robinson's permission, borrowed his idol's ring name.

Born Walker Smith, Jr. in Detroit, Robinson grew up idolizing his neighbor, Joe Louis, who was just rising to the top of the heavyweight ranks when Robinson moved with his mother to Harlem at age 12. He adopted the name Ray Robinson from an amateur fighter whose certificate he borrowed to qualify for a fight. He was dominant as an amateur, compiling an 89-0 record and winning a Golden Gloves championship.

Robinson continued his unbeaten streak as a professional as he rose through the welterweight ranks in the 1940s. He fought often, as much as 19 times a year, en route to his first championship, which came with a 15-round decision over Tommy Bell in 1946. He beat all welterweight challengers, including Jimmy Doyle, who died of injuries suffered in their 1947 bout. When asked at that time if he had intended to get Doyle "in trouble," Robinson responded, "Mister, it's my business to get him in trouble." He donated most of his $5,000 purse from that fight to Doyle's family.

Robinson's first professional defeat came at the hands of Jake LaMotta, the brawling New Yorker known as the "Raging Bull." LaMotta defeated Robinson by decision in Detroit in 1943, but in a rematch three weeks later at the same Olympia Stadium, Robinson won a close decision. In all, Robinson and LaMotta fought six times, with Robinson winning five. In their last altercation, Robinson stopped LaMotta with a 13th-round knockout to win the world middleweight title in Chicago in 1951. In the 1950s Robinson won and subsequently lost the middleweight title 5 times as the championship was contended by the likes of Randy Turpin, Gene Fullmer, and Carmen Basilio. Robinson also appeared to have the world light heavyweight title in his grasp in 1952, but, ahead on points in a fight with Joey Maxim in New York, Robinson collapsed in 100-degree heat and lost the bout. He continued to fight, despite his depreciating skills, until 1965, when he began losing more fights than he won to younger fighters.

A magnetic personality, Robinson refused to be exploited by promoters and handlers like many of the great champions before him. He negotiated many of his own purses and often said that he only boxed for the money. He was a sharp dresser who traveled with an entourage that included a hairdresser, tailor, butler, chauffeur, and scores of beautiful women. His pink cadillac was a hit in Europe, where he knocked out all the champions and won over the public. "I went through four million dollars," he told the *New York Times,* "but I don't regret it."

An adequate tap dancer, Robinson operated a Harlem nightclub and organized a dance troupe to tour the United States when his boxing days ended. Despite his vanity and love of the good life, he was generous and gregarious. In 1969 he organized the Sugar Ray Robinson Youth Foundation for inner city children in Los Angeles, where he lived his last years, comfortably but modestly, with his second wife, Millie. **Sources:** *Chicago Tribune,* April 13, 1989; *Detroit Free Press,* April 13, 1989; *New York Times,* April 13, 1989.

Art Rooney

Full name, Arthur Joseph Rooney; born Jan. 27, 1901, in Coultersville, Pa.; died of a stroke, August 25, 1988, in Pittsburgh, Pa. Sports franchise owner. As founder of the Pittsburgh Steelers and one of the last survivors of the generation of sportsmen who created the National Football League, Rooney was a dominant figure on the American sports scene and a beloved treasure of the city of Pittsburgh. After buying his franchise, then called the Pirates, in 1933 with $2,500 in race-track winnings, Rooney struggled through four decades of losing seasons before his patience paid off. The Steelers of the 1970s became one of the great sports dynasties of all time, winning Super Bowl championships in 1975, 1976, 1979, and 1980. Along the way, the cigar-chomping Rooney became a legendary citizen of Pittsburgh, genuinely loved by everyone from his players to stadium groundskeepers and the many recipients of his charity. Quoted in the *New York Times,* NFL commissioner Pete Rozelle said that Rooney "belonged to the entire world of sports. It is questionable whether any sports figure was more universally loved and respected."

In addition to football, Rooney had a passion for horse racing, and with good reason—during one glorious weekend of betting in 1936, he turned a $10 bet (some say it was $500) into $300,000. A shrewd businessman, he didn't let this fortune slip away. Rather, he and his five sons presided over a sports conglomerate which, in addition to the Steelers, included several race tracks and boxing promotions.

Rooney was one of nine children. His father, a saloon-keeper, moved the family to Pittsburgh in 1903, and Rooney spent the last 50 years of his life in an old Victorian house just across the street from where he grew up, and just five minutes walk from Three Rivers Stadium. "Why should I move?" he asked in the *Detroit Free Press.* "I'm a Pittsburgh guy."

A standout baseball player and amateur boxing champion as a youth, Rooney also starred as a halfback for the Duquesne University football team. He was clearly a winner, but for many years the Steelers weren't. Some believed that part of the problem was Rooney's loyalty to friends within the organization, so it wasn't until he turned over control of the team to his sons in the 1960s that the Steelers had success. Chuck Noll was hired as head coach in 1969, and over the next few years the club drafted legendary tackle "Mean" Joe Greene and quarterback Terry Bradshaw. The Steelers were soon the dominant team in the NFL, no longer the "Same Old Steelers," as they had been mockingly known for many years. Rooney remained active as chairman of the Steelers until his death at age 87. On August 17, 1988, he attended daily mass and then walked to his office at Three Rivers Stadium, where he suffered a stroke. His wife of 51 years, Kathleen Rooney, died in 1982. **Sources:** *New York Times,* August 26, 1988; *Sports Illustrated,* September 5, 1988; *Washington Post,* August 26, 1988; *Detroit Free Press,* August 26, 1988.

Franklin D. Roosevelt, Jr.

Full name, Franklin Delano Roosevelt, Jr.; born August 17, 1914, on Campobello Island, New Brunswick, Canada; died of lung cancer, August 17, 1988, in Poughkeepsie, N.Y. Businessman and former U.S. Congressman. The third son of the popular and powerful 32nd president of the United States, Franklin D. Roosevelt, Jr., was himself elected to serve three terms as a U.S. Congressman from New York. Roosevelt first won his seat in 1948 by defeating the Democratic candidate backed by Tammany Hall (a powerful Manhattan political machine) in a special election for the 20th Congressional District on the upper west side of Manhattan. In 1950 and 1952, with Liberal Party and Democratic support, he won re-election by successively wider margins, but after a failed bid for the state's Democratic gubernatorial nomination in 1954, Roosevelt retired from politics.

Roosevelt was born at the family's summer estate on Campobello Island, New Brunswick, off the coast of Maine. Though he came to resemble his father's looks and manner later in life, Roosevelt, who spent much of his youth away at boarding schools, told the *Chicago Tribune* that "you can't say I learned politics at my father's knee." Following a family tradition, he graduated from the Groton School in 1933 and Harvard University in 1937 before earning his law degree in 1940 from the University of Virginia. He fought with distinction as a Navy officer in World War II, serving as a destroyer gunnery officer and executive officer, and later as commander of the destroyer escort *Ulvert M. Moore.* He was decorated with the Navy Cross, the Purple Heart, and the Legion of Merit.

In the 1954 race for governor of New York, a position which had launched his father on his journey to the presidency, Roosevelt was considered the early favorite to capture the Democratic nomination. But Tammany Hall preferred W. Averell Harriman instead and Roosevelt was nominated to run for attorney general, only to be defeated by the popular Republican Jacob K. Javits. Roosevelt returned to the political scene to campaign for presidential hopeful John F. Kennedy in 1960. He worked in 45 states to help transfer the enormous popularity of his father into votes for the junior senator from Massachussetts, and his presence in the campaign served to ease the strained relations thought to exist between Eleanor Roosevelt and the Kennedy family. After Kennedy's victory, Roosevelt was made under secretary of commerce and was later the first director of the Equal Opportunity Employment Commission under President Lyndon B. Johnson. Married five times, Roosevelt had five children and eight grandchildren. A former New York lawyer, farmer, and car importer, Roosevelt, at the time of his death, was chairman of the Mickelberry Corporation, a holding company, and of the Park Avenue Bank in New York. **Sources:** *Chicago Tribune,* August 18, 1988; *New York Times,* August 18, 1988; *Washington Post,* August 18, 1988.

Herbert von Karajan

Born April 5, 1908, in Salzburg, Austria; died of a heart attack, July 16, 1989, in Anif, Austria. Austrian conductor. Probably the world's best known conductor and one of the most powerful figures in classical music in the twentieth century, von Karajan assumed directorship of the Berlin Philharmonic Orchestra in the mid-1950s and, with precision and an iron will, refined it into the most respected orchestra in the world. During the height of his powers, from the late 1950s to early '60s, he simultaneously directed the Berlin Philharmonic, La Scala Opera House, London Philharmonic Orchestra, Vienna Philharmonic, and Vienna State Opera House. His range of authority was so vast that envious conductors dubbed him the "general music director of Europe." A dashing, romantic figure whose arrogance created many enemies, von Karajan was often at the center of controversy, but as his friend Michel Glotz told the *Chicago Tribune:* "He is a bit of a tyrant, sure. You cannot achieve such perfection in music without being a tyrant." Surely, he will ultimately be judged on the quality of his music, which even his detractors admit is unsurpassed in technical precision and sonic breadth. Von Karajan was "the greatest, the last great one," said his underling, Gustav Kuhn, in Robert Vaughn's biography *Herbert von Karajan.* "He is the exception. No one can do it like he can. He is so egocentric, so clever; he uses all of his immense power to do the things he wants."

Born to a musical family in the birthplace of Mozart (Salzburg, Austria), von Karajan studied piano as a child. As a teenager he saw the great maestro Arturo Toscanini and from that day forward von Karajan pursued a conducting career, first studying under Clemens Krauss at Vienna's Academy for Music and the Performing Arts. Although the 1930s saw von Karajan's rapid rise in stature among young European conductors, it was a time in which he was forced to make several difficult choices if he was to continue making music in a region of the world increasingly dominated by the Nazi Party. At the time of his appointment to the Aachen Opera House in 1935, von Karajan proclaimed himself a Nazi, a move that haunted him for his entire career and the motivation for which has remained a mystery. It seems likely that von Karajan joined the Nazis for the obvious boost his career would receive in Berlin. Already popular in Germany for an acclaimed interpretation he had given of Wagner's *Tristan und Isolde,* he was appointed director of the Berlin State Opera when that post was vacated by Wilhelm Furtwangler, the famed German conductor who maintained his directorship of the Berlin Philharmonic. These years also saw a feud develop between von Karajan and Furtwangler; Furtwangler was so popular in Germany that he maintained his position despite his refusal to join the Nazis, and he made clear his contempt of von Karajan for having done so. But in the Vaughn biography, von Karajan attempted to explain himself: "Before me was this paper, which stood between me and almost limitless power and a budget to provide for an orchestra with which I could do however many concerts I liked.... So I said, what the hell, and signed. But afterwards people said, 'of course, you are a Nazi.'"

After the war von Karajan was excluded from the European musical scene for nearly two years because of his Nazi record, but in 1947, after a series of concerts with the Vienna Philharmonic, von Karajan achieved de-Nazification status and won back the hearts of musical society with his stupendous conducting. Despite being the rival of the older maestro Furtwangler, von Karajan also admired him and told the *New York Times* that his aim was a style that combined "Toscanini's precision with Furtwangler's fantasy." He was at his best in his interpretations of the late Romantic conductors, particularly Wagner, Bruckner, and Brahms, but his proficiency across a wide range of musical styles seemed limitless. After Furtwangler's death in 1954, von Karajan was named "conductor for life" of the Berlin Philharmonic and began his dominance, not only of that orchestra, but of the entire European music world. "The Karajan industry bears about the same relation to postwar European music that Krupp bore to prewar European steel production," wrote Martin Mayer in the *New York Times* in 1967. Indeed, a popular anecdote about von Karajan in those days had the conductor bounding into a taxi and, when asked his destination, replying, "No matter, I am in demand everywhere." His showpiece, however, remained the Berlin Philharmonic. A first-class orchestra when he inherited it, the Berlin Philharmonic became legendary under von Karajan, who refined the orchestra to exquisite precision and tonal polish. Of a Brahms symphony cycle the orchestra performed in Chicago, *Chicago Tribune* critic Howard Reich said the cycle was "nothing short of definitive. Here was Germanic music played with a nearly religious fervor, yet also with a clarity that more objective conductors would be hard-pressed to equal." Von Karajan so dominated the orchestra, however, that his players often resented him; there were several public feuds and, after a particularly bitter one, von Karajan abruptly resigned his post in 1989.

Conscious of his genius and possessing great vitality, von Karajan lived his life with a flair that drew attention to his ego and his music. His intense, expressive, eyes-closed podium style made him a natural for television, films, and record companies. In all, he made over 800 recordings for the Deutsche Grammaphon and EMI labels, which sold copies estimated to be in the hundreds of millions. His public image only enhanced those sales. "His name was seen in the gossip columns almost as often as it was on the music pages," wrote Joseph McLellan in the *Washington Post*. "A dashing figure who drove fast sports convertibles and vaulted into them without opening the door, he was known as a devotee of yoga and Zen Buddhism, an amateur pilot who owned his own plane, a daring skier and mountain-climber and above all a complete master of his own destiny." In failing health in his later years, von Karajan continued working at a hectic pace. At the time of his death, he was working eight-hour days to prepare for the upcoming Salzburg Festival, an annual event he had founded and controlled for twenty-five years. **Sources:** *Chicago Tribune*, July 17, 1989; *New York Times*, July 17, 1989; *Washington Post*, July 17, 1989.

—Obituaries by David Collins

Cumulative Nationality Index

This index lists all newsmakers alphabetically under their respective nationalities.

Index citations allow access to *Newsmakers* (entitled *Contemporary Newsmakers* prior to 1988, Issue 2) quarterly issues as well as the annual cumulations. For example, "Abbott, Jim **1988:3**" indicates that an entry on Abbott appears in both *Newsmakers* 1988, Issue 3, and the *Newsmakers* 1988 cumulation.

ANGOLAN

ARGENTINE

AUSTRALIAN

AUSTRIAN

BRITISH

Cumulative Nationality Index

Cumulative Occupation Index

This index lists all newsmakers by their occupations or fields of primary activity.

Index citations allow access to *Newsmakers* (entitled *Contemporary Newsmakers* prior to 1988, Issue 2) quarterly issues as well as the annual cumulations. For example, "Barbera, Joseph **1988:2**" indicates that an entry on Barbera appears in both *Newsmakers* 1988, Issue 2, and the *Newsmakers* 1988 cumulation.

EDUCATION

ENTERTAINMENT

Cumulative Occupation Index

LAW

POLITICS AND GOVERNMENT—FOREIGN

POLITICS AND GOVERNMENT—U.S.

RELIGION

SCIENCE

SOCIAL ISSUES

SPORTS

TECHNOLOGY

Cumulative Subject Index

This index lists key subjects, company names, products, organizations, issues, awards, and professional specialties.

Index citations allow access to *Newsmakers* (entitled *Contemporary Newsmakers* prior to 1988, Issue 2) quarterly issues as well as the annual cumulations. For example, "Barbera, Joseph **1988**:2" indicates that an entry on Barbera appears in both *Newsmakers* 1988, Issue 2, and the *Newsmakers* 1988 cumulation.

Cumulative Newsmaker Index

This index lists all entries included in the *Newsmakers* series (entitled *Contemporary Newsmakers* prior to 1988, Issue 2).

Index citations allow access to *Newsmakers* quarterly issues as well as the annual cumulations. For example, "**1988**:3" following "Abbott, Jim" indicates that an entry on Abbott appears in both *Newsmakers* 1988, Issue 3, and the *Newsmakers* 1988 cumulation.